The Victoria History of the Counties of England

EDITED BY WILLIAM PAGE, F.S.A.

A HISTORY OF

HAMPSHIRE

AND THE

ISLE OF WIGHT

VOLUME III

THE
VICTORIA HISTORY
OF THE COUNTIES OF ENGLAND

HAMPSHIRE
AND THE
ISLE OF WIGHT

PUBLISHED FOR
THE UNIVERSITY OF LONDON
INSTITUTE OF HISTORICAL RESEARCH
REPRINTED FROM THE ORIGINAL EDITION OF 1908
BY
DAWSONS OF PALL MALL
FOLKESTONE & LONDON
1973

Issued by
Archibald Constable and Company Limited
in 1908

Reprinted for the University of London
Institute of Historical Research
by
Dawsons of Pall Mall
Cannon House
Folkestone, Kent, England
1973

ISBN: 0 7129 0593 6

Originally printed in Great Britain by
Eyre & Spottiswoode, London
Reprinted in Belgium by Jos Adam, Brussels

INSCRIBED
TO THE MEMORY OF
HER LATE MAJESTY
QUEEN VICTORIA
WHO GRACIOUSLY GAVE
THE TITLE TO AND
ACCEPTED THE
DEDICATION OF
THIS HISTORY

Swan Electric Engraving Co.

The Hampshire Downs.

THE VICTORIA HISTORY OF HAMPSHIRE AND THE ISLE OF WIGHT

EDITED BY WILLIAM PAGE, F.S.A.

VOLUME THREE

PUBLISHED FOR
THE UNIVERSITY OF LONDON
INSTITUTE OF HISTORICAL RESEARCH
REPRINTED BY
DAWSONS OF PALL MALL
FOLKESTONE & LONDON

CONTENTS OF VOLUME THREE

b

CONTENTS OF VOLUME THREE

CONTENTS OF VOLUME THREE

CONTENTS OF VOLUME THREE

LIST OF ILLUSTRATIONS

★ *Reproduced in black and white in this edition.*

LIST OF ILLUSTRATIONS

LIST OF ILLUSTRATIONS

LIST OF MAPS

★ *Reproduced in black and white in this edition.*

EDITORIAL NOTE

The Editor wishes to express his thanks to all those who have assisted in the work of compiling the histories of the parishes dealt with in this volume, but particularly to the Earl of Northbrook, the Earl of Selborne, G.C.M.G., the Lord Hylton, the Lord Basing, the Lord Swaythling, the Lady Mary Shelley, the Lady Laura Ridding, Count Beaumont-Gurowski, Rev. H. Peto Betts, M.A., Rev. R. F. Bigg-Wither, M.A., Rev. Canon Braithwaite, M.A., Rev. E. Kenworthy Browne, M.A., Rev. F. J. Causton, M.A., Rev. J. W. S. Danbury, B.A., Rev. E. D. Heathcote, M.A., Rev. J. Jenkyns, M.A., Rev. W. H. Laverty, M.A., Rev. Campbell Lock, M.A., Rev. T. H. Masters, M.A., Rev. G. W. Minns, LL.B., F.S.A., Rev. Botry Pigott, Rev. Sumner Wilson, M.A., Mr. Arthur Arnold, Mrs. Pleydell Bouverie-Campbell-Wyndham, Mr. J. Ulick Burke, B.A., J.P., Mr. Tankerville Chamberlayne, B.A., Capt. Edw. Chawner, Mr. Spencer Clarke, Mr. W. Dale, F.S.A., F.G.S., Mr. William Deverell, M.A., D.L., J.P., Mr. H. J. Dutton, J.P., Mr. Edward Eames, Mr. Alfred T. Everitt, Mr. A. E. W. Fleming, Mr. Edgar Goble, Mr. C. R. Gunner, Mr. Charles Holme, F.L.S., Mr. F. H. T. Jervoise, F.S.A., Mr. Montagu G. Knight, D.L., Miss Lemprière, Mr. R. M. Lucas, Mr. A. R. Malden, M.A., F.S.A., Mr. Michael C. M'Creagh-Thornhill, Mr. H. B. Middleton, Col. Mildmay, Mrs. Barker Mill, Mr. H. Stuart Moore, F.S.A., Mr. N. C. H. Nisbett, A.R.I.B.A., Mr. George Parker, Mr. S. E. Pitter, Mr. H. F. Rawstorne, Mr. W. H. Saunders, Mr. A. E. Scott, J.P., Mr. John Silvester, Mrs. Vinn, Mr. J. C. Warner, Mrs. Harrison Wayne, and Mr. A. Ingham Whitaker, J.P., who, by the loan of manuscripts, supplying information, and otherwise have much lightened the work of the contributors.

The Editor is also indebted to the late Earl of Northbrook, the Rev. G. W. Minns, Mr. F. H. T. Jervoise, Mr. W. H. Barrell, and the Society of Antiquaries for illustrations.

Some discrepancies may occasionally be noticed between the amount of arable, pasture and woodland in each parish, which has been kindly supplied by the Board of Agriculture, and the total area of each parish taken from the Ordnance Survey maps. The former statistics are given as near as they can be obtained, but occasionally where holdings are in two parishes the owner has inadvertently returned the whole area of his holding under the parish in which he resides.

A HISTORY OF

HAMPSHIRE

AND THE

ISLE OF WIGHT

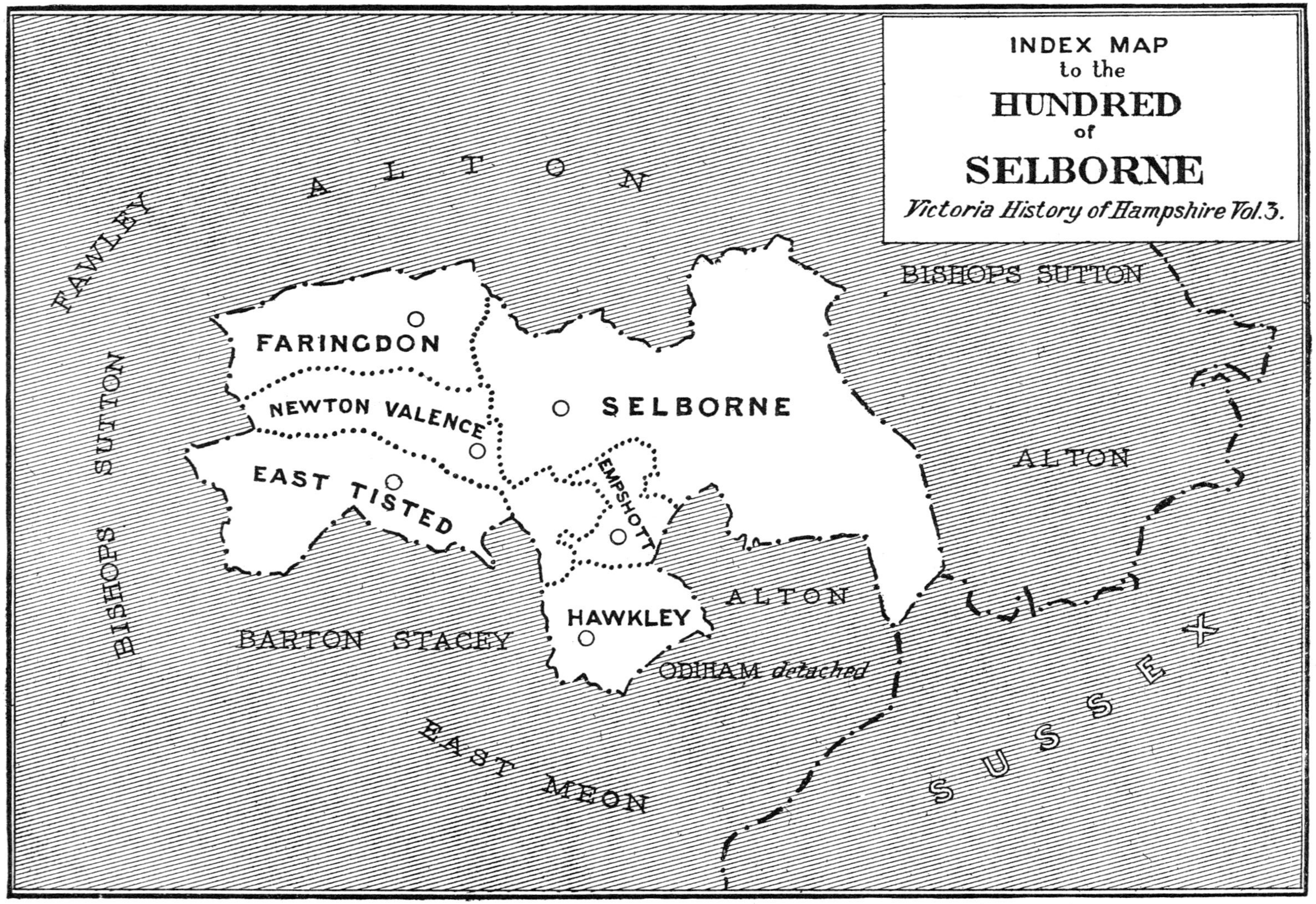
INDEX MAP
to the
HUNDRED
of
SELBORNE
Victoria History of Hampshire Vol. 3.
ALTON
FAWLEY
BISHOPS SUTTON
FARINGDON
NEWTON VALENCE
EAST TISTED
SELBORNE
EMPSHOTT
HAWKLEY
BISHOPS SUTTON
ALTON
ALTON
BARTON STACEY
ODIHAM detached
EAST MEON
SUSSEX

TOPOGRAPHY

THE HUNDRED OF SELBORNE

CONTAINING THE PARISHES OF

SELBORNE	FARINGDON	NEWTON VALENCE
EMPSHOTT	HAWKLEY	EAST TISTED

This list represents the extent of the hundred of Selborne at the time of the Population Abstract of 1831, and is identical with the hundred of the present day.

The hundreds of Alton and Selborne were both included in the hundred of Neatham at the time of the Domesday Survey,[1] and although no definite date can be given for the division it must have come before 1217, since Alton hundred was in existence at that date,[2] but whether the part that became Selborne hundred was immediately called Selborne or retained for a time the name of Neatham is unknown. The earliest mention of the hundred is in a hundred roll of 1275. In this it was stated that the hundred belonged to the king, who received from it one mark annually. The inquisition then taken showed that suit had been withdrawn from the hundred court by the prior of Selborne for the manor of Selborne, by William de Valence for the manors of Newton Valence and Empshott, by the bishop of Exeter for the manor of Faringdon, and by the master of the Templars for the manor of Sotherington.[3]

The divisions of the hundred seem to have changed very little from the fourteenth century onwards.[4] According to a map of 1788, on the west, the north-west part of the parish of Newton Valence and the west part of East Tisted, including Rotherfield Park, and on the east Oakhanger, Oakwood, Blackmoor, and Woolmer, are included in Alton hundred.[5] In another map of about the same date Faringdon was excluded from Selborne and included in Alton hundred.[6] This is however due to inaccuracy rather than to a change in the divisions.

[1] *V. C. H. Hants*, i, Dom. Surv.
[2] *Cal. Pat.* 1216–25, p. 41; *V.C.H. Hants*, ii, 471.
[3] *Rot. Hund.* (Rec. Com.), ii, 224.
[4] *Feud. Aids*, ii, 315.
[5] Map in possession of Miss Lempriere of Pelham.
[6] Map in possession of Mr. A. M. Downie of Alton.

SELBORNE

Salesbourne (xi cent.). Saleburne, Salebourne (xiii cent. et seq.).

The parish of Selborne, including the ecclesiastical parish of Blackmoor, formed in 1867, and the hamlet of Oakhanger, lies on the extreme north-east of the county almost midway between the towns of Alton and Petersfield. It covers about 7,915 acres,[7] of which 105 are land covered by water.[8] From west to east the soils are of chalk, upper greensand, gault, and lower greensand formation. The Selborne hops are grown on the upper greensand and gault, chiefly in the west and south-west of the parish, and also at Temple, on the edge of the lower greensand, where the soil is a wet, sandy loam 'remarkable for trees, but infamous for roads.' These hop-fields and hop-kilns, or 'oast-houses,' are characteristic features of the parish. Selborne Hill, west of the village, is on the 'two incongruous soils' blue clay and sand, called locally 'black malm,' which respectively mark gault and upper greensand formation. Between the chalk and the clay there is a layer of white stone very like chalk in appearance, but unlike it in properties, since it can endure intense heat, and is therefore used for hearth-stones and the lining of lime kilns.[9] The northern and eastern parts of the parish are wholly on soil of lower greensand, and beyond Temple the new formation is marked by a distinctly different vegetation—a change from hop-fields, beech trees and nut trees to furze, pine trees and heather. Thence the unfertile red-sand of the lower greensand continues on to Woolmer Forest, mingling here and there with the blue shelly clay which is also characteristic of this formation. Altogether there are only 1,485¼ acres of arable land in the parish as compared with 2,088½ acres of pasture land and 2,646¼ acres of woodland.[10]

The village of Selborne is on the west of the parish on high ground of an average of 400 ft. above the sea level, although the greater height of the Hanger and Noar Hill gives the impression that the village is in a secluded dell. As the road from Alton branches towards Selborne these two thickly wooded, long, sloping hills stand up in the distance the one behind the other. Approaching nearer the hills seem to grow higher as the road makes a sharp descent. Then before any glimpse of the village can be seen the road makes a sudden bend to the left, and rising abruptly to the middle of the village becomes the main street. On the left is the 'Plestor,' dating its name and existence back to 1271, when Adam Gurdon granted it to the prior and convent for a market-place. It is a green sloping oblong, one end formed by the high road and the other by the churchyard. In the centre stands a sycamore tree encircled by an old wooden seat; up in the left-hand corner is the little wicket-gate leading into the churchyard, and lower on the same side is the vicarage gate, while along the right-hand side stands a row of deep-roofed eighteenth-century cottages. At the end of this row, facing the village street, is Plestor House, lately repaired in the old style, and beyond it the quaint butcher's shop with its row of gnarled lime trees. On the other side of the street is 'The Wakes,' the once unobtrusive house, now greatly modernized and extended by the present owner, Mr. Andrew Pears, J.P., where Gilbert White wrote his *Natural History of Selborne*, in the little room about 5 ft. square leading out of his bedroom. The back of the house opens on an extensive lawn and well-wooded garden sloping up to the park and the Hanger, which, though teeming with animal and bird life and the drone of insects, has that peculiar peacefulness that seems to belong only to a beechwood. This same peacefulness seems to pervade the village street with its quaint thatched and timbered cottages nestling down at the foot of the Hanger. But here and there towards the upper or south end of the street, where the road rises and the Hanger becomes lower, brick or tiled cottages, and even suburban-like villas, give a touch of unrestful modernity. Then on the right-hand side stands a tiny Congregational chapel built of the local white stone. Just below this a turn to the right leads down to Well Head, where a spring rises from under Noar Hill. This spring, which has never been known to fail, was diverted by public subscription in memory of Gilbert White, in 1894, to form a water-supply for the village. The overflow discharges from a conventional lion-head fountain into an open trough, and then running underground for a few yards reappears and runs north-eastward through a narrow and extremely picturesque valley, with wooded slopes on either side, towards Oakhanger, where it becomes known as the Oakhanger stream. It then passes through the hamlet of Oakhanger, skirting the eastern side of Shortheath Common towards Kingsley. Another stream rises in the north-west of the parish and runs north-westwards, only appearing occasionally until it reaches Hartley Mauditt.

SELBORNE, THE MAIN STREET, LOOKING NORTH

[7] *Ord. Surv.* 1897.
[8] *Pop. Ret.* 1900.
[9] Gilbert White, *Nat. Hist. Selborne.*
[10] Statistics from the Board of Agriculture (1905).

Close by the Selborne Arms a path leads through the Punfle, a triangular field let out in allotments, to the foot of the Hanger. Here a path to the left called 'the Bostal' leads up through the wood to Selborne Hill and Common. As the path mounts higher and higher glimpses of the village and church are seen through the trees, and finally, at the point where the Bostal merges into the high wood, a full view of the village is seen through a cutting in the trees in a triangular frame of foliage. Besides the Bostal there is another pathway up the hill leading straight up from the Punfle through a cutting in the trees. This is the Zigzag, its name, so familiar to the general reader through Gilbert White, suggesting its formation. At the top of the Zigzag is a big round boulder known as the 'Wishing Stone.' Here at the top of the hill the wood changes its character and becomes a stretch of wild undergrowth, untrodden brambles, and avenues of tall bracken, with here and there grassy glades and yellow patches of rock roses in the early summer, or later in the season groups of foxgloves and briar roses and trails of honeysuckle. The pathways through the wood are many and bewildering, but one well-trodden way leads in almost a straight line through the wood to Selborne Common and across the common to the parish of Newton Valence, which lies south-east of Selborne. On the other side of Selborne village a steep lane called Hucker's Lane goes to Hucker's Cottages. Opposite is a stile leading across a meadow to a sloping and wooded hill and grassy valley known as the Short Lythe, and on again to a longer hill and valley known as the Long Lythe.

Norton Farm is almost directly north of Selborne on the right-hand side of the road from Alton at a corner where the road branches to the right to Faringdon. Further north-east of Norton are Lower and Upper Wick Hill Farms and Priory Farm on the site of Selborne Priory. Remains of the monastic house have been found here, and several stone coffins which have now been removed to Selborne church.

Further north and east of the parish is the hamlet of Oakhanger, including Oakhanger Farm and Chapel Farm. The houses of Oakhanger lie scattered for the most part over the sandy and barren common, though some are grouped along the road, which serves as a kind of village street. There is a small chapel of ease attached to Blackmoor church and a Congregational chapel.

Directly east of Selborne and south of Oakhanger are Sotherington Farm, backed by Fox Crag Meadow, and Upper Temple Farm. The latter is on the site of the manor of Temple Sotherington and commands a very beautiful view over Blackmoor to Weaver's Hill and Holywater Clump,[11] while beyond in the far distance is Hindhead, and to the left Crooksbury Hill. Temple Hanger and Plainbairn Copse are in the foreground to the north and west, and farther north are Shrub Copse and Ironpaddock Copse. To the south on high ground almost parallel with Temple is Bradshott Hall, owned by Lieut.-Colonel Thurlow, on the site of the original Bradshott Farm, dating at least in name back to the thirteenth century.[12] The house is modern and without special interest, except that it commands a splendid view. Looking directly north-east, Bradshott park and woods are in the immediate foreground, with Temple Hanger on the left and Blackmoor on the right, while beyond is Kingsley, and beyond Kingsley in the blue distance Farnham and the Surrey Hills.

Beyond Blackmoor, which lies due east of Temple, and south-west of Oakhanger, the whole parish is one long stretch of forest, since the three-fifths of Woolmer Forest that are in Selborne cover a tract of land about 7 miles in length by 2½ in breadth. There are three large ponds on the edge of the forest—two in Oakhanger, Oakhanger and Rookery, and one called Bin's or Bean's Pond, which is frequented by wild duck, teal, snipe, and other water fowl. Within the forest are the three ponds of Woolmer, Hogmoor, and Cranmer. The first is very shallow and generally fordable, varying in winter and summer from a broad sheet of water covering about 66 acres to a bed of sand almost entirely dry.

MANOR The manor of *SELBORNE* was the ancient demesne of the crown, and, according to the Domesday Survey, Queen Edith held it in the time of Edward the Confessor, and 'it never paid geld.' Then it was worth 12*s.* 6*d.*, but by the time of the survey only 8*s.* 4*d.* Half a hide of the manor, with the church, had been given by the king to Radfred the priest.[13] There is no evidence to show when the lands in Selborne, which afterwards became the manor of the prior and convent of Selborne, were granted to the family of de Lucy, but a patent of 1229 confirmed these lands to Stephen de Lucy for his life for an annual rent of £4 yearly.[14] In 1233 the land which Stephen de Lucy had held was granted by royal charter to Peter des Roches, bishop of Winchester, for the foundation of Selborne Priory.[15] In February of 1234 the king granted freedom from tallage 'on the land in the manor of Selborne which the king gave to Peter bishop of Winchester' to the prior and monks of Selborne.[16] In April of the same year he granted them further extensive rights and privileges, freedom from view of frankpledge and from any interference of the sheriff, while their lands which lay within the king's forest were to be free from view of regard.[17] The manor of Selborne remained in the possession of the prior and convent until the end of the fifteenth century, when the financial state of the priory was proved to be hopeless. Its possessions were then annexed by Bishop Waynflete in 1484 to his new foundation of Magdalen College, Oxford,[18] and belong to the college at the present time.

Priory Farm of modern days is on a site to the south of that of the priory buildings. The last mention of these buildings is in a rent roll of 1463, when, among the expenses of the convent, come repairs of the priory house, including 4,000 tiles for the roof of the 'frayter,' the stables, and the

11 Here a hermit is supposed to have lived, but nothing remains to prove the legend.

12 In 1250 Roger de Charlecote granted his messuage, mill, and 35 acres of land in 'Bradechete' to the prior and convent of Selborne. *Selborne Chart.* (Hants Rec. Soc.), i, 35. At a later date he confirmed his grant 'with a certain addition on the east side of his house between his old and new ditch,' and added also the land he had in 'Bradesate' 'by the gift of Laurence de Hayes of the tenure of Blakemer.' (Ibid. i, 44.)

13 *V.C.H. Hants*, ii, 451 *a*.

14 *Cal. Pat.* 1225–32, p. 235.

15 The charter runs thus: 'totam terram cum pertinentiis in manerio de Seleburne quam magister Stephanus de Lucy aliquando tenuit de concessione nostra.'

16 Close, 18 Hen. III, m. 29.

17 Exch. Trans. of Chart. No. 2.

18 *Selborne Chart.* (Hants Rec. Soc.), i, 119–35; *V.C.H. Hants*, ii, 179.

'dey-house.'[19] At the time of the impropriation to Magdalen the house was probably much out of repair, and disuse brought prompt decay, since the college seems to have made no use of any part of it except the chantry chapel and two rooms for the chantry priest, who was to reside at the priory and continue the masses for the benefactors of the priory,[20] not absenting himself for more than two months in a year and then finding a substitute. He was to have a stipend of £8 and the two chambers on the north side of the chapel, with a kitchen and a stable for three horses, and the orchard.[21] In 1534 this office was granted to Nicholas Langrish or Langerige to hold for forty years.[22] The said stipend was appointed for his salary not only for service at the chapel but also as superintendent of the woods and copses of Magdalen College in the parish.[23]

Magdalen College, Oxford. *Lozengy ermine and sable a chief sable with three garden lilies therein.*

Meanwhile apparently the priory lands had been leased at some time in the reign of Henry VII to Henry Newlyn,[24] who built a farmhouse and two barns on the south side of the priory, almost certainly out of some of the materials from the ruined house. A later lease for twenty years at an annual value of £6,[25] made in 1526 to John Sharp, mentions this house and barns and also a stable and a dovecote, which may have been that of the prior and convent.[26] The ravages of time, weather, and man have swept away every trace of the original building except one bit of wall hardly ten feet long, probably part of an outhouse. Part of the south side of the church was uncovered some years since, and a careful excavation of the site would probably reveal much of the original arrangements of the buildings. A few pieces of thirteenth-century detail lie on the site.[27]

Grange Farm at the corner of Gracious Street stands on the original site of Selborne Grange. In 1535 the farm of 'one tenement called Selborne Grange,' which had belonged to the Priory and Convent of Selborne, together with the rents from various tenancies belonging to the same, was entered at £15 4*s.*[28] The old grange existed until about the end of the seventeenth century, when it was replaced by the modern farm buildings. It was the manor-house of the convent possessions in Selborne, and at the present day the court-baron and court-leet are held by Magdalen College twice yearly in the wheat barn belonging to Grange Farm. A luncheon and dinner are given at the farm, and the usual presentments made as to trespass and surrender of estates are recorded.[29]

The prior and convent had a corn-mill at the priory to which they had the right of multure. Repairs for this mill were entered in the rent-roll of 1463,[30] and in 1535 the farm of the mill was entered at £1 3*s.* 4*d.*[31] The mill was in use during the seventeenth century, and in 1640 was leased with the other mills that had belonged to the prior and convent to John Hook.[32] The ruins of the mill house were standing within Gilbert White's memory, and when he wrote, the pond, the dam, and the miller's house also remained,[33] and at the present day remains of the sluices and ponds are still to be seen.

A mill also existed at Dorton, south of the priory, before 1233, in which year James de Norton made a grant of his water-course 'going down from his mill of Durton to the wood of Wm. Mauduit,' to Peter des Roches for the house of Austin Canons that he was about to found.[34] He also granted them a croft and several meadows, 'with power to make pools, erect mills, and do as they please on condition that the "refollum" of the water should not come from four perches to the mill of Durthone.'[35]

Besides the right of multure the prior and convent had all ordinary manorial rights, and rights of 'thurset' and 'pillory' and the more exceptional right of gallows. The gallows of the prior and convent were undoubtedly on the still unploughed field called Kite's Hill on the south side of the King's Field. The hill which this field tops still goes by the name of Galley Hill, and the road over it is called Galley Hill Lane. The prior and convent had a weekly market on Tuesdays at their manor by grant of Henry III,[36] who also gave them a yearly fair for three days on the vigil, the day, and the morrow of the Assumption of the B. V. Mary (14, 15 and 16 August).[37]

Apart from the manor of the prior and convent, Adam, the grandfather of the famous Adam Gurdon,[38] held lands in Selborne in chief as early as 1206,[39] but these are generally distinguished only as 'lands in Selborne' and were probably merged in the manor of East Tisted in the fourteenth century.[40]

After the death of Adam Gurdon the elder, before 12 August, 1231, his lands, while his heir was a minor, were granted to Ralph Marshall under burden of maintaining Ameria widow of Adam and her children.

[19] *Selborne Chart.* (Hants Rec. Soc.), i, 116.

[20] Chant. Cert. 52, No. 17.

[21] *Selborne Chart.* (Hants Rec. Soc.), i, 148.

[22] Ibid. The chantry certificate says for twenty-six years.

[23] Chant. Cert. 52, No. 17. *Selborne Chart.* (Hants Rec. Soc.), i, 150.

[24] Gilbert White, *Antiq. of Selborne*, Letter xxv.

[25] This tallies with the *Valor. Eccl.* (Rec. Com.), ii, 284.

[26] Gilbert White, *Antiq. of Selborne*, Letter xxv.

[27] In the hedges of the lane leading from Selborne to Priory are blocks of chalkstone which have evidently come from a building, presumably from the priory. In Gilbert White's time, when some labourers were digging at the foundations, they discovered what is termed 'a large Doric capital' and the base of a pillar on the traditional site of the south transept of the priory church, and at another time on the traditional site of the kitchen a thick stone vase, which may have been a standard measure for dry grain between the monastery and its tenants. Gilbert White, *Antiq. of Selborne*, Letter xxvi.

[28] *Valor Eccl.* (Rec. Com.), ii, 284.

[29] Information from Mr. A. M. Downie, steward of the manor.

[30] *Selborne Chart.* (Hants Rec. Soc.), i, 116.

[31] *Valor Eccl.* (Rec. Com.), ii, 284.

[32] Gilbert White, *Antiq. of Selborne*, Letter xxv, footnote.

[33] Ibid. The house was inhabited as late as 1717, when there is an entry on the parish register of the baptism of John son of Philip Walton, of Priory Hill.

[34] *Selborne Chart.*(Hants Rec. Soc.), i, 6.

[35] Ibid. ii, 64.

[36] Ibid. i, 64.

[37] Chart. R. 54 Hen. III; see *Geneal.* (New Ser.), iv, 4.

[38] See *V.C.H. Hants*, ii, 473.

[39] King John granted the first Adam 12 librates in Tisted and Selborne by serjeanty; Pipe R. 10 John; *Testa de Nevill* (Rec. Com.), 232*a*, 236*b*; *Geneal.* (New Ser.), iv, 2.

[40] They were probably the '100 acres of land and a rent in Selborne' granted with the manor of Tisted to James de Norton by Joan daughter of the third Adam, and her husband, Robert Achard, in 1308. See account of East Tisted Manor.

Within two years they were granted in dower to Ameria.[41] During her tenure she made several gifts of privileges and lands within those she held in Selborne to the prior and convent. In 1234 she released to them right in haybote and housebote and common in their wood at Selborne and 'in the common pasture of Durtone,[42] saving to all her men of Selborne common with all their animals in the said pasture as in times past.'[43] Adam Gurdon her son, who was of age and in possession of his lands by 1253,[44] also held lands in Selborne of the prior and convent by grant of Thomas Makerel, made probably soon after 1253 to Adam and Constance his wife, for the annual rent of a pair of white gloves of the value of 1*d.*[45] These lands were those comprised in the manor of *SELBORNE MAKEREL*, afterwards known as *GURDON*.[46] Walter son of Thomas Makerel confirmed the same to Adam and Constance probably about 1260.[47] In April, 1262, Adam de Gurdon granted to the prior and convent right of housebote and haybote in 'the wood of Norchere, saving to the said Adam and his wife Constance and their heirs and to the men of Selborne whom they have by the gift of Thomas Makerel that their pigs shall be free from pannage in the said wood of Norchore so many as pertain to the tenement of la Forde in Selborne.'[48] In return the prior and convent granted that Adam and Constance should hold of them all the land and tenement that they had in Selborne by gift of Thomas Makerel. In the June of the same year licence was given to Adam de Gurdon to build a domestic chapel in their court of Selborne 'quae fuit quondam Thomae Makerel.'[49] The next mention of the manor of Selborne Makerel comes in an inquisition *ad quod damnum* of 1307, when Joan the daughter of Adam de Gurdon was licensed to transfer the manor of East Tisted with 100 acres and a rent in Selborne to James de Norton, and was said to still hold the manor of Selborne Makerel, a manor worth £10, for life, of the prior and convent of Selborne.[50]

From this time the history of the manor apparently ceases. Whether, as Gilbert White supposes, Joan granted it to the Knights Templars, or whether after her death it merged in the manor proper of Selborne, must remain uncertain. (See under Temple.)

In 1271 Adam de Gurdon granted a place in Selborne called 'La Pleystowe' (the modern Plestor) to the prior and convent to hold there their market which they had by the gift of King Henry and to build houses and shops upon it, saving reasonable way for him and his heirs to a tenement and some crofts at the upper end of the Plestor near the churchyard.[51] Further, he granted that the prior and convent should peaceably hold the houses and curtilages which they had erected on their land in Selborne in which Adam had a right of common for himself and men, and made it lawful henceforth for the prior and convent or himself to build on their respective lands in Selborne which touched on the king's highway.[52]

The manor of *TEMPLE SOTHERINGTON* or *SOUTHINGTON* (Sudynton, Sydyngton, xiii cent.) is more generally known in later days as the manor of Temple, including the farm of Sotherington.

The Knights Templars had a preceptory at Sotherington and held the manor of Sotherington as early as 1240.[53] About 1250 Robert de Sanford, master of the order in England, granted all the tenements, lands, and meadows which the Templars had in Selborne by the gift of Almeric de Sacy[54] to the prior and convent of Selborne for £200 'to buy other lands in aid of the Holy Land.' About ten years later he granted 10*s.* 'from the chamber at the Templars' house of Sudington' to the prior and convent in lieu of 10*s.* worth of annual rent in lands and rents promised to the convent and to be settled on them as soon as possible, with power of distraint in case of failure, to be levied 'on the chattels found on the land which was Roger de Cherlecote's in Bradesate (Bradshott), which is in the hands of the Templars.'[55] About the same date also the Templars granted the prior and convent 'a sufficient way for leading cars and carts and driving cattle along the road which leads from Sotherington to Blackmoor.'[56] In 1275 the Master of the Templars was said to have withdrawn the suit owed to the hundred court of Selborne for the manor of Sotherington for the past thirty years, though by what warrant the jurors did not know. Also he had encroached on the king's land in the forest of Woolmer to the injury of the king, and again they knew not by what warrant.[57] One small farmhouse is the only building that preserves the name of Sotherington at the present day.

THE KNIGHTS TEMPLARS. *Argent a cross gules and a chief sable.*

According to Gilbert White the lands which Adam Gurdon held in Selborne by gift of Thomas Makerel were the lands surrounding and including the modern Temple Farm, while the Templars at a contemporary date held Sotherington. Then by a supposed grant by Joan, the heiress of Adam Gurdon the younger, Temple, not then known by that name, was united with Sotherington in the hands of the Templars. The tradition that Adam Gurdon lived at Temple has become firmly rooted, though as far as documentary evidence goes there is nothing to prove that his lands in Selborne were identical with Temple, and the few years that the Templars could have held it between the traditional grant after Adam's death in 1304 or 1305 and the suppression of their order in 1312

41 See account of East Tisted Manor.

42 The modern Dorton Woods, which lie between Selborne and the priory.

43 *Selborne Chart.* (Hants Rec. Soc.), i, 16.

44 By an inquisition 'ad quod damnum' made in that year he was allowed to hold his lands in Tisted and Selborne as half a knight's fee instead of by serjeanty. Inq. p.m. 38 Hen. III, No. 18.

45 *Selborne Chart.* (Hants Rec. Soc.), i, 52. Although here dated as *c.* 1260–70 it seems more likely to be previous to the confirmation made by Walter, and dated 1250–60, p. 41.

46 Ibid. 91. Here the court of 'Gordon' is evidently identical with the court of Selborne Mackerel.

47 Ibid. 41. 48 Ibid. 55. 49 Ibid. 56.

50 Inq. a. q. d. 1 Edw. II, No. 70.

51 *Selborne Chart.* i, 64. This tenement, according to Gilbert White, was the 'manorial house of the street manor.' By the eighteenth century it was only a poor cottage known by the name of Elliot's. White, *Antiq. of Selborne*, Letter x.

52 *Selborne Chart.* i, 64.

53 *Cal. Chart. R.* 1226–57, p. 251.

54 In the reign of Hen. III this Almeric held 60*s.* rent in Selborne with his manor of Barton, by gift of King John. *Testa de Nevill* (Rec. Com.), 235*b*, 236*b*.

55 *Selborne Chart.* (Hants Rec. Soc.), i, 49. 56 Ibid.

57 *Rot. Hund.* (Rec. Com.), ii, 224.

makes it seem unlikely that their name would have clung to the manor for centuries after. Having identified Adam Gurdon's lands with Temple, however, Gilbert White goes on to assume that the oratory built by Adam Gurdon by licence of the prior and convent 'in curia sua de Selburne' was at Temple. However, a charter of 1240 granting to the Templars six acres of land lying 'between their manor of Sudinton and the king's manor of Blakemore,' and found to belong to 'Blakemere,'[58] would seem to imply that Sotherington manor included the modern Temple, since Temple lies locally between Sotherington Farm and Blackmoor. Then when the manor in the fourteenth century began to be called the manor of Temple Sotherington, the manor-house, the Templars' preceptory, was called Temple, while the manor farm kept the old name of Sotherington. But this must for the present remain conjecture.

In 1317 the manor, by this time at any rate including Temple, but still called the manor of Sotherington, was in the hands of the earl of Hereford,[59] but in the next year Pope John issued a bull ordering the holders of the goods of the Templars in England to give them over to the Knights Hospitallers of St. John of Jerusalem,[60] and the manor evidently passed to the Hospitallers. By 1408 Thomas West was lord of the manor, which was held of him, as of his manor of Newton Valence, by the heirs of Nicholas Berenger.[61] Probably the Hospitallers, according to their general custom, had farmed out the manor to Thomas West, since it was in their possession in the sixteenth century, and was granted by the king at the dissolution to Sir Thomas Seymour of Sudeley.[62] Edward VI leased the manor to Edmund Clerk on the execution of Lord Sudeley in 1549, and in 1554 granted it in fee to Sir Henry Seymour,[63] brother of Sir Thomas, who died seised in 1578, leaving a son and heir John.[64] John Seymour conveyed the manor by fine made in 1588 to Sir Richard Norton,[65] who four years afterwards died leaving a son and heir Richard.[66] In 1599 Thomas West, as warden of Woolmer and Alice Holt Forests, brought an action against Richard Norton concerning a pound in Blackmoor which was stated to be a pound belonging to Woolmer Forest, not to the manor of Temple.[67] A special commission was issued in 1600 concerning 'the bounds, limits and circuit of the waste of soyle of the manor of Temple of which Richard Norton is seised.' In the depositions made on this occasion the bounds of the manor are said to begin at Owton's Lane, and 'on the further side of the right way leading to Farnham by a ditch and a bank directly and eastwards towards Cranmere Pond, then northward to a hill called Runneberry Hill, and from thence crosse a highway northwards to Henley corner, from thence to a stone lying by the pond side called Oakhanger pond, and towards the middle of the said pond and on the further side of the same pond, to the which the bounds of the said manor of Temple aforesaid doth extend.'[68] Like East Tisted, Rotherfield, and Noar (q.v.), the manor of Temple Sotherington passed through the Norton family and was held by the last baron, Sir John Norton, in 1672.[69] During the seventeenth and eighteenth centuries the manor passed through many hands. In the nineteenth century it was held by Sir A. K. Macdonald, bart., who sold it to the late Lord Selborne, father of the present earl, in 1865.

THE KNIGHTS HOSPITALLERS. *Gules a Maltese cross argent.*

SEYMOUR. *Gules a pair of wings or.*

Since it belonged to the Templars the manor is and always has been tithe free, 'for by virtue of their order the lands of the Knights Templars were privileged by the pope with a discharge from tithes.'[70]

The manor house had been used as a farmhouse 'from time immemorial' when Gilbert White wrote. All that then remained of the original house was the chapel or oratory and the hall, 27 ft. long and 19 broad, formerly open to the sky. The 'massive thick walls' of the chapel and the narrow windows made it, as Gilbert White remarked, 'more like a dungeon than a room fit for the reception of people of condition.'[71] He looked in vain for any trace of the lamb and flag, the arms of the Templars, in the hall of the farmhouse, and only found a fox with a goose on its back in one corner 'so coarsely executed that it required some attention to make out the device.'[72] No trace of this hall now remains, for the house has been greatly modernized and rebuilt; only in the kitchen apartments is there any trace of ancient workmanship. There is also an old well 90 ft. deep which is supposed to date back to the time when the Templars held the manor.

NORTON.—In 903, according to the Golden Charter of Edward the Elder to the abbey of Newminster near Winchester, three hides at Norton next Selborne were granted to the new foundation by the king.[73] The genuineness of this charter may well be doubted, since there is no mention of Norton in the manors of the abbey enumerated in the *Liber de Hyda*,[74] and since the Domesday Survey makes no reference to the fact that Hyde Abbey held any part of Norton. According to Domesday Norton was comprised of two manors both of royal demesne, both consisting of two hides. Two hides with land for one plough in demesne, and two villeins and three bordars with 7½ acres of meadow were held of the king as one manor by Earl Godwin as an alod. At the time of the survey this manor was held by Hugh

[58] *Cal. Chart. R.* 1226–57, p. 251.

[59] *Feud. Aids*, ii, 315.

[60] Delaville le Roulx, *Documents concernant les Templiers*, 50.

[61] Inq. p. m. 6 Ric. II, No. 17; ibid. 8 Hen. IV, No. 78; ibid. 8 Hen. V, No. 110.

[62] Deeds *penes* Mr. A. E. Scott.

[63] Deeds *penes* Mr. A. E. Scott.

[64] Inq. p. m. 20 Eliz. pt. 2 (Ser. 2), No. 64.

[65] Feet of F. Hants, East. 30 Eliz.

[66] Inq. p. m. 34 Eliz. pt. 2 (Ser. 2), No. 118.

[67] Exch. Dep. Trin. 41 Eliz. No. 13.

[68] Ibid. 42 Eliz. No. 2058.

[69] Add. R. 27991.

[70] See Gilbert White, *Antiq. of Selborne*, Letter xi, quoting Blackstone.

[71] Whether this chapel was the oratory built by Adam Gurdon in 1262, or a chapel attached to the Templars' preceptory, it is difficult to say. Some arches which are thought to be traces of the ancient chapel still remain at the beginning of what is supposed to have been a subterranean passage, now blocked up, connecting Temple and the priory.

[72] Gilbert White, *Antiq. of Selborne*, Letter ix.

[73] Kemble, *Cod. Dipl.* ii, 144. Birch, *Cartul. Sax.* ii, 256.

[74] See *Liber de Hyda* (Rolls Ser.).

de Port and held of him by Robert.[75] Although there is no mention of Hyde Abbey as overlord of Hugh de Port in 1275, his descendant John de St. John held half a knight's fee in Norton of the abbot of Hyde, who held the same in chief of the king.[76] This half knight's fee was undoubtedly the manor which Hugh de Port had held, for like the rest of the manors included in Hugh's extensive fief in Hampshire the manor of Norton remained in the hands of his heirs, and passed with the failure of his heirs male in the fourteenth century to the family of Poynings, by the marriage of Isabel, the only surviving child of Hugh de St. John,[77] to Luke de Poynings. The heirs male of the Poynings failed on the death of Hugh in 1426, and the manor of Norton passed to the Paulet family by the marriage of Constance, coheiress of Hugh de Poynings, with John Paulet. The latter died in 1437, but there is no inquisition on his lands in Hampshire.[78] Constance survived him until 1443, but evidently Norton was no part of her dower, as it is not again given in the inquisition taken at her death.[79] In 1460 John Paulet, son and heir of the former, no doubt to secure his tithe enfeoffed John Hilton, Edwin Brocas, and John Pole in the manor of Norton, then valued at 10 marks, who restored the same to John Paulet and Eleanor his wife jointly and their heirs and assigns.[80] John Paulet died in 1492 seised of the manor, leaving Eleanor his widow and John Paulet his son and heir.[81] In this inquisition the manor is said to be held of the bishop of Winchester, by what service the jurors do not know. The same overlord is given in the inquisition taken on Eleanor's death in 1507,[82] but on the death of John Paulet the younger in 1525 the manor is said to be held of Hyde Abbey.[83] However, between this year and 1540 the abbey lost all claim to the overlordship of the manor, for there is no trace of it in the list of the abbey possessions among the Ministers' Accounts for that year.[84] In 1471 William Paulet the first marquis of Winchester, son and heir of the John Paulet who died in 1525, sold the manor or farm of Norton to James Rythe and his wife Isabel.[85] In January, 1572, James Rythe settled the manor on Nicholas Tichborne and Marlion Rythe to be held by the said James and Isabel for term of life, and after their decease by George Rythe of Liss, who had married Isabel's daughter Elizabeth, and his heirs male.[86] James Rythe died in December of the same year, leaving his wife Isabel in possession of the manor of Norton.[87] In May, 1607, George Rythe, to whom the manor had reverted on the death of Isabel, died seised of the same, leaving a son and heir George.[88] In the same year Marlion Rythe and Nicholas Tichborne secured their right in the manor by fine and recovery dealing with the same.[89] Five years later George Rythe conveyed the manor by fine to Nicholas Steward,[90] who died seised of the same in 1633 leaving his grandson Nicholas his heir.[91] This Nicholas Steward, or Stuart, threw in his fortunes with the king during the Civil War, was fined £1,400 as a Royalist in 1647,[92] and was rewarded for his loyalty by being created baronet in 1660.[93] He died in 1710, and was succeeded in his estates by his grandson and heir, Sir Simeon Stuart, who held Norton until his death in 1761.[94] Thus in a perambulation of the parish of Selborne made in 1741, the bounds are said to 'take in Sir Simeon Stuart's land, rented by Edward Harrison, including the meadow called the Hose or Stocking, to pass thence on to Norton Farm, formerly rented by Farmer Matthews, lately by John Daborne, but now by Edward Wake,[95] as far as the gate that goes out of the Barrs into the stony lane.' A visit was to be paid to Norton Farm by the beaters of the bounds 'according to ancient usage.'[96] Sir Simeon was succeeded by his son and heir Sir Simeon Stuart, who died in 1779, leaving a son and heir, Sir Simeon, who died in 1816. The latter was succeeded by his son and heir, Sir Simeon Henry Stuart, who died at Haywards Heath in Sussex in 1868, leaving a son and heir, Sir Simeon Henry Stuart, who died in 1891 leaving a son and heir, the present baronet.[97]

Stuart of Hartley Mauditt. *Or a fesse checkered argent and azure and a scutcheon argent with a lion gules and a ragged bend or over all.*

The second manor of Norton consisting also of 2 hides was held of Edward the Confessor as one manor by Elwin.[98] At the time of the survey it was held by Ralph de Mortimer,[99] whose descendant, Roger de Mortimer, held half a knight's fee in Norton of the king in chief in 1275, while Walter de Raddene held the same of Roger.[100] In 1284 William de Brayboef died seised of half a knight's fee in Norton, which James de Norton held of him by the gift of Robert de Tisted,[101] rendering for the same 20*s.* for scutage and paying suit to William de Brayboef's court at Crambourne.[102] Hugh de Brayboef, son and heir of William, succeeded to his father's right in Norton, and in 1316 James de Norton was still holding the manor of him.[103] Thomas de Norton, son of James by his wife Elizabeth,[104] having in 1331 proved his right to the whole manor against a claim of dower made by his stepmother Margaret and her second husband Edmund

75 *V.C.H. Hants*, i, 485*b*.

76 *Rot. Hund.* (Rec. Com.), ii, 224. Yet in the taxation survey of 1291 the manor of Norton is not entered among the possessions of Hyde Abbey. *Pope Nich. Tax.* (Rec. Com.), 213.

77 The Ports assumed the name of St. John after the marriage of Adam de Port with Mabel, heir of Roger de St. John.

78 Inq. p.m. 16 Hen. VI, No. 49.

79 Ibid. 21 Hen. VI, No. 22.

80 Exch. Inq. p.m. (Ser. 2), bdle. 961, No. 9.

81 Inq. p.m. (Ser. 2), vol. 8, No. 74.

82 Exch. Inq. p.m. (Ser. 2), bdle. 961, No. 9.

83 Inq. p.m. (Ser. 2), vol. 44, No. 94.

84 Dugdale, *Mon.* ii, 448–50.

85 Feet of F. Hants, East. 14 Eliz.; Add. Chart. 16197.

86 Add. Chart. 16198; Inq. p.m. (Ser. 2), vol. 179. If the heirs of George Rythe failed the manor was to descend to Robert Rythe the brother of George, if his failed to Christopher Rythe, if his failed to Gilbert Tichborne, if his failed to Ambrose Tichborne, if his failed to Benjamin Tichborne.

87 Inq. p.m. (Ser. 2), vol. 179, No. 74.

88 Ibid. vol. 298, No. 73.

89 Feet of F. Hants, Mich. 5 Jas. I; Com. Pleas Recov. R. Mich. 5 Jas. I, m. 38.

90 Feet of F. Hants, Trin. 9 Jas. I.

91 Inq. p.m. (Ser. 2), vol. 473, No. 18.

92 *Cal. of Com. for Compounding*, 979–80. Here his estates are said to lie waste and untenanted through extremities suffered under the king's power.

93 G.E.C. *Complete Baronetage.*

94 Ibid.

95 Mr. Round suggests that the Wake family may have given their name to Gilbert White's house, 'The Wakes.'

96 From perambulation entered in the Selborne Parish Register.

97 G.E.C. *Complete Baronetage.*

98 *V.C.H. Hants*, i, 490*b*.

99 Ibid.

100 *Rot. Hund.* (Rec. Com.), ii, 224.

101 De Banco R. No. 286, m. 55.

102 Inq. p.m. 12 Edw. I, No. 13.

103 *Feud. Aids*, ii, 315.

104 *Cal. Pat.* 1313–17, p. 466.

de Kendal,[105] died seised of the same in 1346, held of Joan the widow of Hugh de Brayboef.[106] Margaret widow of Thomas had dower in the manor providing that she did not marry again without royal licence. Her dower was extended as part of the manor of Norton, namely a chamber at the east end of the hall with the adjacent kitchen, a third of the farmhouse, a third of the dovecote, one house called La S—w House, the house of the Westgate, and one third part of all the other houses, a court between the hall and Westgate with free entry and exit to a certain chapel, a small room attached to the chapel, a garden with free entry and exit at all gates, another plot of land, the third of a field called Brethfeld, and many other fields and pastures.[107] Ralph de Norton, son and heir of Thomas, was a minor on his father's death,[108] and hence the wardship of Thomas de Norton's lands was given to Peter de Brewes and the prior of Selborne.[109]

In 1368, on the marriage of Ralph de Norton with Margaret, the manor of Norton was settled on them with reversion, if they died without heirs, to Sir Bernard Brocas and his wife in fee, and if the latter should die, to the right heirs of Sir Bernard and his wife in fee.[110] In 1379 Bernard Brocas remitted the whole right in the manor to Ralph de Norton and Margaret.[111] In 1428 William Harlyngdon held the fourth part of one knight's fee in Norton which Peter de Brewes had held in custody in 1346, and the prior of Selborne held the twentieth part in fee alms, and 'they did not answer because it was divided between them.'[112] This unsatisfactory descent does not grow clearer in later centuries, but the probability seems to be that the second manor passed out of existence in the sixteenth century, when manorial rights were less clearly defined, and was merged in the other manor of Norton.

The ecclesiastical parish of Blackmoor (Blakemere, Blakemore, xiii cent. et seq.) was formed in 1865 by the late Lord Selborne, when he bought the estate from a lawyer named Blackmoor.[113] The modern village is on the northern and western part of the sandy ridges which inclose the basin of Woolmer Forest. Hogmoor, Whitehill, and Walldown rise to the north-east, and to the south-east across the forest is Hollywater or Holywater Clump. Blackmoor House, a modern house built by the late Lord Selborne, stands on the site of Blackmoor Farmhouse on the right-hand side of the road as it enters the village from Temple. A comparatively short drive from this side leads up to the house, but the grounds extend to the Petersfield Road, from which side there is another and a longer drive. The houses of the village are mostly modern, but opposite the lodge gates of Blackmoor House are two quaint half-timbered and thatched cottages certainly belonging to the seventeenth century.

BLACKMOOR MANOR was part of the ancient demesne of the crown as pertaining to the royal forest of Woolmer. Henry III, in 1240, granted six acres of land which pertained to his manor of 'Blackmore' to the Knights Templars, giving them permission to inclose the same with a dike and hedge so that the deer could not go in and out.[114] During the thirteenth century Roger de Cherlecote made a grant to the prior and convent of Selborne of land in Bradesate (Bradshott) which he had 'by the gift of Laurence de Heyes of the tenure of Blakemere.'[115] Hence it would seem that Laurence de Heyes or Heighes held Blackmoor probably in custody for the king, and that the manor included Bradshott. However, except frequent mention of Blackmoor in thirteenth and fourteenth century grants,[116] there seems to be nothing about the manor in ordinary sources of information.

Heighes. *Sable a cheveron argent between three boars' heads or.*

In the seventeenth century the family of Heighes held the manor of Blackmoor, together with those of South Heigh and Flood in Binsted. John de Heighes, who held 1 messuage and 12 acres in Binsted in 1268,[117] was the ancestor of this family, and was apparently either father or son of Laurence de Heighes, and probably held Blackmoor, although there is nothing to prove this. A later member of the family, Simon de Heighes, died seised of 1 messuage in Heyes in 1362, leaving a son and heir, Simon.[118] In 1399 Richard Heighes, who possibly was a son of the younger Simon, was holding the same.[119] Henry Heighes died seised of the same and of the manor of Flood in 1595, while in 1600 a certain Edmund Heighes paid rent for the same.[120] Nicholas Heighes, who held these two manors as well as that of Blackmoor in 1610, was evidently a descendant of Edmund; hence it seems just possible, although definite proof is wanting, that Blackmoor remained in the custody of the Heighes family from the time of Laurence de Heighes until the seventeenth century. Sir Nicholas settled Blackmoor with his other manors on his wife Martha in 1610, but being in debt, with the consent of his wife conveyed the manor of Flood to Richard Locke and Henry Wheeler in 1610 in trust for his debts. In 1620, after the death of Sir Nicholas and of Richard Locke, Martha, widow of Sir Nicholas, brought an action against Henry Wheeler, who had not only seized the manor of Flood, but had abused his trust and seized the residue of her estates for his own use.[121]

During the eighteenth and nineteenth centuries the manor evidently changed hands many times, until it was sold to the late Lord Selborne, father of the present earl, in 1865.

OAKHANGER (Acangre, x and xi cent.; Hohangra, xii cent.; Ochangra, Okhangre, Achangre, Hachangre, Halkangre, xii cent.).—The first mention of the land which became the manor of Oakhanger is in a charter of the early part of the tenth century, giving

[105] De Banco R. No. 286, m. 55.
[106] Inq. p.m. 20 Edw. III (1st Nos.), No. 23.
[107] Inq. p.m. 20 Edw. III (add.), 71.
[108] Inq. p.m. 20 Edw. III (1st Nos.), No. 23.
[109] *Feud. Aids*, ii, 334.
[110] Feet of F. 42 Edw. III, No. 100.
[111] Close, 2 Ric. II, m. 23 *d.*
[112] *Feud. Aids*, ii, 358.
[113] Information from Lord Selborne.
[114] *Cal. Chart R.* 1227–57, p. 251.
[115] *Selborne Chart.* (Hants Rec. Soc.), i, 44.
[116] In 1260 Robert de Sanford, master of the Templars, granted the prior and convent right of way for their carts and cattle along the road 'from Sudintone towards Blakemere'—the modern Sotherington Lane (*Selborne Chart.* i, 50). Within the next two years James de Oakhanger granted the prior and convent an annual rent of pepper and 2 pence from a garden lying at 'La Hunne' near the highway leading from Selborne Priory towards 'Blakemere' (ibid. i, 51). The road is still called locally Honey Lane.
[117] Curia Regis R. No. 184, m. 4.
[118] *V. C. H. Hants*, ii, 487–8.
[119] Ibid.
[120] Ibid.
[121] Chan. Proc. Jas. I, H. 37, 42.

the boundaries of lands granted by Edward of Wessex to Frithstan, bishop of Winchester.[122] In the reign of Edward the Confessor Oakhanger was assessed at one hide, and one virgate valued at 40*s.* was of royal demesne and held of the king by a certain Alwi.[123] At the time of the Domesday Survey Edwin held it by purchase of the king and Richard held it of Edwin.[124] Who this Edwin was is not clear, but during the twelfth century the manor was evidently held by a family that took the surname of Oakhanger. Thus William de Oakhanger was in possession in 1167,[125] and in the reign of Henry III, according to the *Testa de Nevill*, a certain Gilbert de Oakhanger, probably the son of William, held the manor of the king 'per veneriam.'[126] In 1250 James de Oakhanger, presumably the son of Gilbert, was lord of the manor,[127] and in 1279 his son William[128] was given licence to enfeoff Thomas Paynel of his manor of Oakhanger.[129] Thomas Paynel died in 1313 seised of the same,[130] and from him it passed to his son William, who died without issue in 1317, leaving his brother John[131] as his heir. John Paynel died in 1319, leaving his daughter Maud, the wife of Nicholas de Upton, heir to two parts of the manor, while Eva, the wife of Edward St. John, and late the wife of his brother William Paynel, held the third part in dower.[132] John Bernard and Ralph de Bocking, as trustees for Maud and Nicholas de Upton, received licence in 1320 to grant two parts of the manor to Aymer de Valence and John de Hastings and the heirs of the said John, and also to grant the reversion of the remaining third part then held in dower by Eva de St. John.[133] John de Hastings died in 1325 seised of the two parts of the manor, leaving his son Laurence as heir.[134] Fourteen years later Laurence de Hastings obtained licence to enfeoff Thomas West of the two parts of the manor, to hold the same in chief with knights' fees, advowson of churches, and all liberties pertaining.[135] Eva de St. John died in 1354 seised of the third part of the manor, which, instead of reverting to the heirs of John de Hastings, went to her kinsman and heir, Roger son of John de Shelvestrode.[136] Evidently Roger, if he ever entered into possession of the third part of Oakhanger, granted or sold it in 1355 to the Thomas West who already held the other two parts, since in 1355 Thomas paid 5 marks to the king for licence to acquire the third part.[137] Thomas West died in 1386 seised of the whole manor entailed by fine made in Hilary term 1381–2 on himself and his wife Alice and their heirs male.[138] In December of 1386 Alice, his widow, received pardon for having together with her husband alienated the manor for the purpose of entailment above referred to.[139] She died seised of the manor in August, 1395, leaving Thomas West her son and heir,[140] who died seised of the same in April, 1406, leaving a son and heir Thomas.[141] The latter died in September, 1416, leaving as heir his brother Reginald, who was created Lord De La Warr in 1426 as heir of his uncle Thomas.[142] In 1429 Reginald Lord De La Warr leased the site of his manor of Oakhanger for a term of twenty years at an annual rent of 100*s.* to the prior and convent of Selborne,[143] and in 1453 his son and heir, Richard Lord De La Warr, who succeeded his father in 1450,[144] made a similar lease for nine years at an annual rent of 113*s.* 4*d.*[145] Perhaps the most interesting point about these leases is that they give the boundaries of the whole site of the manor, viz., between the water of Tonford up to the chapel of Oakhanger, thence to 'le Courthacche,' thence by the close of the tenants of Oakhanger to the lane called 'Honnelane,' by the said lane to the west end of Wrikesgrove and the water of Tonford, thence between the close of Will Cook and 'le Broke' to 'la Redhacche,' thence by the close of the prior to the watercourse of Tonford. Besides the site of the manor the lord of Oakhanger also leased to the prior all common in the forest of Woolmer belonging to the manor, the fishery in the pool of Oakhanger, and the hares, rents, and services belonging to the manor.[146] In 1476 Richard Lord De La Warr died seised of the manor of Oakhanger, leaving a son and heir Thomas,[147] who died in 1525 leaving a son and heir, also Thomas.[148] The latter died without issue in 1554 seised of 'tenements in Oakhanger, late parcel of the manor of Oakhanger.'[149] Lady Jane Dudley, duchess of Northumberland, the daughter of his sister Eleanor, was his heir to these lands, which are described in the inquisition on her death in 1555 as 'one acre in Oakhanger held in chief for the hundredth part of a knight's fee.'[150] Similarly in a Chancery proceeding of the same date in which the will of Thomas Lord De La Warr is quoted, one acre in Oakhanger, parcel of the manor of Oakhanger, 'certainly divided and known from the rest of the said manor by evidences which is holden of the Queen's highness in chief,' is said to have descended to Lady Jane, duchess of Northumberland, to go to her children at her death.[151] This

PALMER, Earl of Selborne. *Argent two bars sable with three trefoils argent thereon and a running greyhound sable in the chief having a golden collar.*

WEST, Lord De La Warr. *Argent a fesse dancetty sable.*

[122] Kemble, *Cod. Dipl.* v, 178.
[123] *V.C.H. Hants*, i, 504*b*.
[124] *V.C.H. Hants*, i, 504*b*.
[125] *Pipe R.* 1167 (Pipe R. Soc.).
[126] *Testa de Nevill* (Rec. Com.), 235.
[127] *Selborne Chart.* (Hants Rec. Soc.), i, 36.
[128] Ibid. 63. In 1272–3 Adam Gurdon was giving to Selborne Priory land he held in Oakhanger of William de Oakhanger, and which William held by serjeanty. Ex inform. Mr. J. H. Round.
[129] *Cal. Pat.* 1292–1301, p. 303.
[130] Inq. p. m. 7 Edw. II, No. 34.
[131] Ibid. 10 Edw. II, No. 61.
[132] Inq. p.m. 12 Edw. II, No. 50.
[133] *Cal. Pat.* 1317–21, p. 415.
[134] Inq. p.m. 18 Edw. II, No. 83.
[135] *Cal. Pat.* 1338–40, p. 395.
[136] Inq. p.m. 28 Edw. III, No. 54. The inquisition on her land in Hants is almost impossible to read; nothing can be deciphered but the name of Eva, of Oakhanger, of Empshott, the other manor she held in Selborne, and of her heir Roger.
[137] *Rot. Orig.* (Rec. Com.), ii, 239.
[138] Inq. p.m. 10 Ric. II, No. 52.
[139] *Cal. Pat.* 1385–9, p. 249.
[140] Inq. p. m. Ric. II, No. 49.
[141] Ibid. 7 Hen. IV, No. 26.
[142] G.E.C. *Complete Peerage.*
[143] *Selborne Chart.* (Hants Rec. Soc.), i, 110.
[144] Inq. p.m. 29 Hen. VI, No. 21.
[145] *Selborne Chart.* (Hants Rec. Soc.), i, 114.
[146] Ibid. 110.
[147] Inq. p.m. 16 Edw. IV, No. 62.
[148] Ibid. 25 Hen. VIII, vol. 45, No. 100.
[149] Exch. Inq. p.m. 1 and 2 Phil. and Mary, file 995, No. 3.
[150] Ibid. No. 14.
[151] Chanc. Proc. (Ser. 2), bdle. 190, No. 27.

mysterious acre disappears as suddenly as it appeared. On her death, in 1554, it was settled on trustees[152] and evidently descended to Ambrose Dudley, but reverted probably to the crown with the rest of his property on his death without heirs in 1589. At any rate it evidently again became parcel of the manor and passed as part of the same to John Pescod of Newton Valence some time before 1558. In what year John Pescod acquired the rest of the manor it is difficult to say. It may have been that when Thomas Lord De La Warr was suffering under the royal displeasure in 1538 for his adherence to the old religion, and had to pay for his release from the Tower by the surrender of Halnaker (Sussex), he also surrendered the manor of Oakhanger all but the acre which was held as before described. This is borne out by a letter which he wrote to Cromwell in November, 1539, saying that if the lands in Hampshire which the king had promised him in exchange for Halnaker were worth more than the latter he would 'gladly part with other lands lying commodiously for His Grace.'[153] Possibly the grant was then made to John Pescod, who died seised of the manor in 1558, leaving his son Richard as his heir.[154] In 1564 Richard Pescod brought an action in Chancery against Richard Springham, citizen and mercer of London, who, knowing that Pescod was in debt and in great need of money, was 'greatly desirous to take lease' of the Oakhanger Ponds, promising to lend him £100 or £75 or more for a reasonable time, and a yearly rent of forty carps from the pond. The lease had therefore been made for forty years, but when one year of the time had elapsed the lessee refused to make the promised loan, or pay the yearly rent unless the plaintiff would mortgage to him the manor of Oakhanger and other premises as security for the repayment of the £100. Thereupon after Springham had promised that even if the said orator should break day with him by the space of one month or two or three he would not take any advantage of the mortgage, 'the said orator conceaved and had such trust and confidence in the said Richard' that he bargained and sold the manor on condition that if he should pay the £100 within the time agreed the bargain and sale should be void. Yet when he could not well pay the sum on the day fixed the defendant, in spite of his former promises not to take immediate advantage of the mortgage, 'being of covetous mind and intending subtily to get the manor and pond of Oakhanger,' tried to expel the plaintiff and seize the manor for debt. Defendant stated that he had acted according to the agreement, and when the plaintiff could not pay he offered him a further sum to make up the value of the manor, but Pescod 'obstinately and willfully refused to accept the offer.'[155] However the judgement eventually went for the plaintiff, who in 1568, evidently compelled by his debts and poverty, mortgaged the manor to a certain William Smith and others.[156] In August, 1571, Richard Pescod died leaving the manor to his son and heir Thomas,[157] who in June, 1578, granted the whole to his brother, John Pescod of Roxwell.[158] In 1587 John Pescod died seised of the manor, leaving his brother Nicholas as heir.[159] Nicholas Pescod had a son Nicholas baptized in Selborne church in 1594.[160] From the Pescods the manor passed to William Bishop of South Warnborough, who died at Swallowfield (Berks) in 1660, leaving the manor of Oakhanger with his freeholds in Swallowfield to his wife Flower (or Flora), daughter of William Backhouse, lord of Swallowfield. She married her second cousin, William Backhouse, two years later, and settled the manor on herself and her husband in that year.[161] In December, 1663, they mortgaged certain premises in Oakhanger, including a close called 'Chapple House,' to a certain George Ashton. Sir William Backhouse died in 1669, and in October, 1670, Flower was married a third time to Henry Hyde Viscount Cornbury, who became Lord Clarendon by his father's death in 1674. By 1685 the earl was in financial difficulties, and judgement was given against him to William Tallman for a debt of £800.[162] In July, 1694, Tallman, whose debt had evidently not been paid, assigned his judgement to Mr. Edward Wilcox of St. Martin's in the Fields, to whom in August, 1694, the earl and countess bargained and sold the manor subject to redemption on payment of £1,493 10*s.*[163] Edward Wilcox, by will dated 1724, left the manor in trust for his only daughter and heir Margaret, who in 1731, as Margaret Jeffries, bargained and sold the same to John Conduit.[164] By will of John Conduit, dated 1736, Oakhanger was settled on his only daughter and heir Catherine, who married Lord Viscount Lymington. By Act of Parliament of 1748–9 for selling the settled estates of Catherine Lady Lymington, Oakhanger was sold to Henry Bilson Legge. In 1750 Henry Bilson Legge married Mary, created Baroness Stawell in her own right in 1760. Their son, Henry Bilson Legge, Lord Stawell, married Mary daughter of Viscount Curzon, and died without heirs male in 1820. Their only daughter Mary married the Hon. John Dutton, only son and heir of James Lord Sherborne, from whom the manor of Oakhanger has passed by inheritance to Henry John Dutton, the present owner.[165]

PESCOD. *Sable ermined argent a chief or with three griffons sable therein.*

The modern Oakhanger Farm on the right-hand side of the road leading from Selborne through Honey Lane to Oakhanger is probably on the site of the

[152] Pat. 1 and 2 Phil. and Mary, pt. 6, m. 19.
[153] *L. and P. Hen. VIII*, xiv (2), p. 191.
[154] Exch. Inq. p.m. (Ser. 2), file 998, No. 7.
[155] Chan. Proc. (Ser. 2), bdle. 145, No. 2.
[156] Feet of F. Hants, Mich. 10 and 11 Eliz.
[157] Inq. p.m. 14 Eliz. vol. 162, No. 154.
[158] Ibid. 25 Eliz. vol. 234, No. 37. Confirmed by letters patent in 1589 (Pat. 31 Eliz. pt. 6).
[159] Inq. p.m. 29 Eliz. vol. 212, No. 51.
[160] Selborne Parish Register.
[161] Deeds *penes* Mr. H. F. Johnson, solicitor to Mr. Henry John Dutton.
[162] Ibid.
[163] Previous to this, the premises, which had been mortgaged to George Ashton, were transferred by his widow Elizabeth in May, 1670, to the bishop of Chester for the remainder of the term. On the death of the bishop, in 1687, these premises were mortgaged (his executor being party to the dealing), together with the manor, to Sir John Werdon for the residue of the 500 years. On the sale to Edward Wilcox, in 1694, Sir John was still holding as mortgagee, but by a poll deed of the same year he agreed, in consideration of £1,088 5*s.*, to assign the premises and manor to Wilcox. Deeds *penes* Mr. H. F. Johnson.
[164] Before the sale redemption was purchased from Elizabeth King, spinster, of Hampstead, cousin and heir of Lady Clarendon, and of the trustees of the late Lady Clarendon.
[165] Information from Mr. Henry John Dutton.

manor house of Oakhanger. On the opposite side of the road is Chapel Farm, marking, it is supposed, the site of the chapel of Oakhanger. This chapel, according to Gilbert White, was identical with the chapel of St. Mary of Waddon, or Whaddon, from which the vicar of Selborne received a moiety of all oblations.[166] Repairs to the chapel of St. Mary of Waddon, which had evidently been burnt down shortly before, were entered in the rent roll of the prior and convent in 1463. Here there is mention of a house for travellers attached to the chapel, which was evidently much repaired and reroofed in that year. There is also another entry, difficult to understand, of carriage paid for the conveyance of the image of the Blessed Mary of Waddon from Winchester to the chapel.[167] Besides this image three silver rings and one pyx belonged to the chapel.[168] There are no remains of the building existing, nor were there in Gilbert White's time. He tells, though, of a large hollow stone which, according to tradition, was the Waddon chapel baptismal font. Although Gilbert White so emphatically identifies this chapel of Waddon with that of Oakhanger, it is important to note that in the account of the endowment of the vicarage of Selborne in 1352, oblations from Waddon and oblations from Oakhanger chapel are given separately.[169]

CHURCHES

The church of *OUR LADY* at *SELBORNE* stands to the north of the village, at the north-east angle of the Plestor, and at the head of the narrow wooded valley through which runs the Oakhanger brook, the ground falling from it on all sides. On the left-hand side of the path leading to the church porch, and sheltering the church from view, is the famous yew tree. In Gilbert White's time it measured 23 ft. in girth and has increased since then by about four inches. Under the yew is a grave without any headstone, which tradition says is that of the village trumpeter. Tradition again explains his office, how he was the man who gathered the 'Selborne mob' during what seems to have been a period of famine or strike in the village in the early nineteenth century, and how he led them to an attack on the poor-house, where they broke in the doors and made a bonfire of the furniture. Then, as they marched on to the neighbouring village of Headley, soldiers who had been summoned from Winchester surrounded them and took them prisoners to Winchester, where many were tried and transported. The trumpeter, however, had escaped and was in hiding for some time on Selborne Hill, only coming down into the village at midnight. During one of these descents he was captured and taken to Winchester, but was pardoned, and returning to Selborne died some years after and was buried under the yew tree. The original churchyard was of small extent, but has been twice enlarged on the south side. The limestone rock lies near the surface of the ground, and on two occasions, in digging a grave in the new part of the churchyard, a large passage or chamber in the rock has been broken into, but not examined.

The church has a chancel 27 ft. 6 in. by 16 ft.; north vestry, north transept, nave 53 ft. by 18 ft., with a north aisle 6 ft. 7 in. wide, and large south aisle 17 ft. 2 in. wide, of the full length of the nave; south porch, and west tower about 11 ft. square. All measurements are internal.

The arcades of the nave are the oldest part of the building, dating from 1170 to 1180, and the north aisle, though rebuilt, probably retains its twelfth-century width. The width of the chancel is irregular, 15 ft. 10 in. at the chancel arch and 16 ft. 4 in. at the altar rails, and it is probable that part of the masonry of the walls is as old as the nave arcades, though no feature earlier than the thirteenth century is now to be seen. About 1220 the south aisle of the nave was replaced by a large south aisle or chapel, with entrances on south and west, and towards the end of the century a north transept was added. It is set out without reference to the nave arcade, and its internal dimensions are approximately a square of 19 ft. 6 in. At what date the west tower was added to the church is doubtful, owing to the many alterations it has suffered. The external masonry is covered with plaster, and the tower arch appears to be not older than the fifteenth century, but it is possible that part of the walling may be some centuries earlier. The west end of the south aisle was refaced in 1730, and the tower repaired and cemented in 1781. Practically the whole of the church has been refaced at various times in the last century with rubble of local white limestone and ironstone set at all angles with a most unpleasing effect. The chancel was 'restored' about 1840, the nave and north transept in 1877, the south aisle and tower in 1883, a new east window made in the chancel in 1887, and further work done in the chancel in 1889. The chancel has three modern lancets in the east wall, and in the north wall towards the east end an original lancet of *c.* 1220, and further west a second lancet which has been cut down to serve as a doorway to a modern vestry. In the south wall are two windows, each of two cinquefoiled lights, the stonework of that towards the east being modern, while in the other the head of one light and half that of the other are old, and belong to the end of the fourteenth century. Between the windows is a priest's door, the outer arch being of modern stonework, but the rear arch apparently of the thirteenth century. At the east end of the wall is a trefoiled thirteenth-century piscina. Over the altar is a painting of the Adoration of the Magi, with, on the north side, St. Andrew, and on the south St. George, and portraits of the donors behind each saint. It was given to the church in 1793 by Benjamin White, and is good Flemish work of *c.* 1500, attributed, but wrongly, to Mabuse. The chancel arch is a modern copy of the nave arcades, but the masonry of the responds is old, and in the north respond is a small niche or recess.

The nave is of four bays with pointed arches of one square order and scalloped capitals with circular shafts and bases, the latter having spurs in the north arcade, but not in the south.

The north transept has a large three-light north window with modern tracery, the head and jambs with engaged shafts dating from *c.* 1275. There is no window in the east wall, but four conical stone brackets, one at a higher level than the other three, point to the former position of two altars against the wall, and in the south wall is a piscina with geometrical tracery and a gabled head contemporary with the transept. The north aisle of the nave is entirely modern, but probably on the old lines.

166 *Selborne Chart.* (Hants Rec. Soc.), i, 92. 167 Ibid. i, 116. 168 Ibid. ii, 112. 169 Ibid. i, 92

The south aisle is nearly as wide as the nave, and a fine though much restored building. It is gabled at east and west, and has an east window of three lancets under a containing arch. In the south wall is a wide three-light window, an insertion of *c.* 1500 to give more light on the altar in the aisle ; its stonework is mostly modern. West of it are the built-up jambs of a second wide window, with a modern lancet set in the blocking, and beyond this a second modern lancet just east of the south doorway, which has a good moulded outer arch with jamb shafts.

Near the west end of the wall is an original lancet, and in the west wall an original window with two lancet lights under a segmental head. At the north end of the wall is a doorway of the same date, but, like the window, its external stonework is modern. The south porch is probably of the seventeenth century. The west wall of the aisle is faced in the small ironstone rubble with regular ashlar quoins, and has had a buttress, now destroyed, at its south end. In the gable is the date 1730 and initials G. W. for Gilbert White, grandfather of the naturalist. On the north side of the east window of the aisle is a fine niche, *c.* 1320, with an ogee head and a band of four-leaved flowers on the projecting sill. Near the south-east angle is a trefoiled piscina, and a roll-string goes round the aisle below the window sills, returned downward to pass underneath the piscina, but breaking up over the heads of the south and west doorways.

The tower opens to the nave by a pointed arch of two continuous chamfered orders, which may be fifteenth-century work. The quoins of the internal western angles of the tower look more like thirteenth-century work, and the jambs of the west doorway seem ancient, but its square head and the two-light square-headed window over it date from the repairs of 1781. The tower is covered with cement externally, including its parapet, and the belfry windows are single lights trefoiled, except that on the north, which has a plain round head. Within the tower is a solid timber framework resting on a set-back above the first stage and carrying the bell frame. It is strongly braced together and looks as if it had been intended to stand alone.

The roofs of the church are modern, except that of the chancel, which has coupled collars with arched braces below ; it has been plastered at one time, and the roughness of its timbers suggests that this was the original arrangement. In the south aisle the plate on the north side is old, carried on wooden corbels and strutted. There are a few old bench ends at the west of the nave, and one on each side of the south porch, with trefoiled arched panels of late fifteenth-century date. The south door of the nave is probably contemporary with the doorway, and is made of 1 in. oak planks set upright with rounded battens nailed horizontally to the back of the door. The original wrought-iron strap-hinges remain, and are beautiful specimens of their date. A few traces of wall-painting exist at the north-east of the south aisle, and the south doorway and north window of the north transept have traces of red paint.

At the east end of the south aisle are collected a number of glazed tiles with single patterns of griffins, lions, double-headed eagles, lis, &c., and several of finer work, with a quatrefoil inclosing a shield bearing a double-headed eagle between two birds. The quatrefoil is set in a lozenge and the corners of the tiles filled with palmettes. The tiles belong to the fifteenth or perhaps the end of the fourteenth century. The font stands at the west end of the south aisle and is plain, with a cup-shaped bowl on a thick round stem. Two stone coffins and several coffin lids of the thirteenth and fourteenth centuries are placed in the south aisle. On two specimens there are rings on the stem of the cross carved on the lid just below the head. A few pieces of twelfth-century masonry, with zigzag, earlier than any work now standing in the church, are also preserved here.

The plate consists of a silver cup and cover paten of 1638, quite plain.

There are five bells; the treble of 1735, given by Mary daughter of Sir Simeon Stuart, bears the Stuart arms in a lozenge on the waist, and is inscribed :—

Clara puella dedit dixitque michi esto Maria
Illius et laudes nomen ad astra sono.

The second, formerly of 1735, was recast by Mears & Stainbank in 1904. The fourth and tenor are also of 1735, all the bells of this date being cast by Samuel Knight, and the third is by Thomas Janaway, 1783.

There are no monuments of interest in the church except the mural tablet to Gilbert White, the naturalist, who died here in 1793.

The earliest parish register is a book with no cover, half paper and half parchment. It begins with the baptisms from 1562 to 1600. From 1578 the register seems to be copied from smaller books by Vicar White, since the previous handwriting ends in December, 1577, and the next 'Here I begin' is in his handwriting, with the heading 'Anno Dno' instead of 'Anno Dni.' The next section gives the burials from 1556 to 1594, with the same change in the writing in 1577. The writing changes in 1594, and then there is a gap filled up by a small register, roughly bound up with the big, covering the dates 1588–1631 for baptisms, marriages, and burials. There is also another small register bound up in part of this giving baptisms from 1577 to 1587, marriages from 1572 to 1586, and deaths from 1572 to 1587. Here the paper half of the book ends and the parchment begins, giving baptisms from 1632 to 1678, and burials from 1632 to 1641. The last few pages, written the wrong way of the book, give the marriages from 1632 to 1633, burials from 1654 to 1678, and three or four entries of marriage in 1637 and 1639. This is all the record that exists until after the period of the Civil War. The second book is of paper and leather bound, and contains a list of incumbents from 1673 to 1681 made by Vicar Gilbert White, who was inducted at the latter date, and the register of baptisms from 1679 to 1718. Under the year 1695 a mention is made of 'ye act of Parliament passed for granting to His Majesty certain rates and dues upon marriages, births, and burials and upon Batchelors and Widdowers for the term of five years, commencing from 1 May, 1695.' A stray entry under the year 1688 states that a certificate was given by the vicar for Mrs. Susanna Green on 8 October and for Stephen Green on 11 November, 'to be touched for the King's evil.' The third book, of paper and leather bound, registers the burials from 1718 to 1783 and the baptisms from 1719 to 1783.

Selborne Church : Nave looking East

Empshott Church : Nave looking West

Opposite the entries for 1728 comes a memorandum that Rebecca White, widow of vicar Gilbert White, granted the granary of the vicarage, a movable possession, built by her husband, to the vicar and his successors for ever. In 1730 it was certified that she had expended the £40 left by her husband for the repair of the church in building two large buttresses towards the east wall, 'being the parts of the church most decaying and dangerous.' Opposite the entries for 1766 is a note that the gallery at the west end of the church was built in that year at a cost of £31 4*s.*, of which £10 was given by the will of Dr. Bristow and the rest raised by public subscription.

The next register of burials begins in 1784 and ends in 1812, and that of baptisms in 1783, ending also in 1812. There is a gap in the register of marriages between 1717 and 1754, those after that date being entered in two books dating from 1754 to 1798 and from 1798 to 1812.

The churchwardens' accounts begin in 1687.

In 1720 an entry was made that no churchwarden was henceforth to give anything to travellers upon the parish account; if he did so he must refund it out of his own pocket. A quarrel which had evidently been brewing came to a head in 1832 over a question of church repair. The parish had refused to elect their churchwarden at Easter, and when a vestry meeting was called in November, 1832, to consider the repair of the church roof, which was in a very bad state, 'they refused to agree to any suggestion or adopt any plan until accounts were settled.' After several attempts at peace the vicar referred the question to the chancellor of the diocese, to whom the vicar's churchwarden, Henry Earle, wrote:—'It would give me the greatest pleasure to be on friendly terms with the rest of the farmers. I have striven hard, much harder than you have any notion, to be so. But all to no purpose—the more friendly I am the worse they behave to Mr. Cobbold.' Unfortunately the result of the dispute is not given, but probably the case was referred to the ecclesiastical court and the parishioners forced to yield.

Licence was granted to Adam de Gurdon and Constance his wife in 1262 to 'build an oratory in their court of Selborne which had formerly belonged to Thomas Makerel.' They were to attend the mother church on all solemn feast days, and the prior and convent of Selborne reserved to themselves right to suspend service in the oratory if it interfered with any of their privileges. They also stipulated that no heir of the said Adam should lay legal claim of this licence. And if in time to come a dispute should arise between the prior and convent and the vicar of Selborne concerning the licence, Adam and Constance were bound to defend the prior and convent.[170]

A chapel existed at *BLACKMOOR* as early as 1254, when the vicarage of Selborne was endowed with all small tithes and obventions belonging to the mother church and to the chapels of Oakhanger and Blackmoor.[171] The 'ecclesia de Seleburne cum capella' of the taxation return of 1291 evidently included the chapel of Blackmoor,[172] while in the agreement made between the prior and convent and the vicar of Selborne concerning the vicarial portion in 1352, the prior and convent are stated to be 'the impropriators of the parish church of Seleborne with the chapels of Oakhanger and Blakemere.'[173] Thus an estimate of the revenues and debts of the prior and convent made in 1462 includes repairs to the chancel of Blackmoor church in the expenditure of the priory.[174] Synodals from the chapel of Blackmoor were acknowledged by the dean of Alton in 1489 at 7½ pence,[175] and were grouped with those of Oakhanger, Selborne, and East Worldham in the *Valor* of 1535.[176] The modern church is at the north end of the village street just where the road bends to the left towards Oakhanger. A lych gate opens the way to the churchyard and to the church, with its square white stone tower roofed with red tiles built and dedicated in honour of St. Matthew by the late Lord Selborne and consecrated in Whitsun week, 18 May, 1869. On the north side of the church on the first pillar of the chancel is a white marble monument to Lord Selborne and his wife erected by the people of Blackmoor 'in gratitude for all the good that under God has come to this parish through their devotion to their Saviour and their love to their fellow men.'

ADVOWSON A church existed at Selborne at the time of Domesday, and it was held by Radfred the priest, to whom the king had given one yardland of the manor as endowment.[177] The advowson belonged to the abbey of Mont St. Michel at least as early as 1156, when it was confirmed to them by Pope Adrian IV. Godfrey de Lucy, bishop of Winchester, confirmed the church to the monks of St. Michel in 1194, as they had held it in the times of his predecessors in consideration of their labours and perils of the sea.[178] In 1197 Godfrey de Lucy, bishop of Winchester, granted the church, 'with the assent and at the wish of Abbot Jordan and the convent,' to Philip de Lucy, saving the annual pension of three marks to the abbey.[179] In 1233 the abbot and convent of Mont St. Michel granted the advowson of Selborne with whatever benefit they had received from the same to Peter des Roches,[180] who in the next year granted the same to the prior and convent of Selborne.[181] In 1291, in the Taxation of Pope Nicholas, the church of Selborne 'cum capella' is mentioned.[182] Probably this is an error for 'cum capellis,' since both the chapels of Oakhanger and Blackmoor were in existence in 1254, when the small tithes from the same were appropriated to the vicar of Selborne.[183] In 1353 the prior and convent, as the proprietors of the parish church of Selborne with the chapels of Oakhanger and Blackmoor, made a compact with Adam Sinclair (Seynclar), the perpetual vicar of the church, for the increase of his insufficient stipend. On account of 'the present pestilence and the scarcity of the times' he was to receive various rents and tithes in money and kind, and of wool and of all mills in Selborne except those of the convent, and of all hay except the hay of the

170 *Selborne Chart.* (Hants Rec. Soc.) i, 56.
171 Ibid. i, 46.
172 *Pope Nich. Tax.* (Rec. Com.) 210.
173 *Selborne Chart.* (Hants Rec. Soc.), i, 91.
174 Ibid. 117.
175 Ibid. 145.
176 *Valor Eccl.* (Rec. Com.), ii, 284.
177 *V.C.H. Hants*, i, 451*a*.
178 *Selborne Chart.* (Hants. Rec. Soc.), ii, 2.
179 The original charter with the bishop's seal is now in the Departmental Archives of La Manche (J. H. Round).
180 *Selborne Chart.* (Hants Rec. Soc., ii, 3.
181 Ibid. 4.
182 *Pope Nich. Tax.* (Rec. Com.). 210.
183 *Selborne Chart.* (Hants. Rec. Soc.), i, 46.

court (*De Cur*) of Gordon, Norton, and Oakhanger, and of the demesne lands of the convent 'originally assigned for the foundation of the conventual church.'[184] Later in the same year a further agreement was made. The vicar was to have in addition to other tithes one cartload of hay from the tithe hay of Norton and 'one cartload of straw at the courtyard of Gordon,' all tithes within Oakhanger and Blackmoor excepting corn and hay, the moiety of all oblations hereafter or newly arising in the parish beyond those at the church or the chapels of Oakhanger and Blackmoor, and a portion of the accustomed small tithes from the churches or chapels of Hartley and Empshott. From this time the vicar was bound to find a chaplain to celebrate in the chapels of Oakhanger and Blackmoor.[185]

In the fifteenth century the advowson of Selborne church passed in 1484, among the other possessions of Selborne priory, to Magdalen College, Oxford.[186] Thus the rectory is entered as appropriated to the college in the *Valor Ecclesiasticus* of 1535.[187] The chapel of Selborne is also mentioned as appropriated to Magdalen, but is bracketed with the vicarage of East Worldham.[188] Magdalen has held the church to the present day and endowed it in the eighteenth century with the great tithes of both Selborne and Oakhanger.[189]

CHARITIES (i) Richard Byfield, vicar of Selborne, by will, 1679, bequeathed £80 for the purchase of an annuity towards apprenticing poor children to good trades. The trust fund (with accumulations) is represented by £138 6*s*. 8*d*. consols held by the official trustees of charitable funds. By scheme, 1882, it is provided that in the absence of poor children eligible to be selected for apprenticeship the trustees may apply income in grants of clothing to children on going out to service, or in payments not exceeding £1 to deserving poor children to encourage the continuance of their attendance at school.[190]

(ii) Rev. Gilbert White, vicar, by will, 1719, gave £100 to be laid out in land, rent to be employed in teaching poor children to read and write, and say their prayers and catechism, and to sew and knit. In 1735 two closes called Collyer's in Hawkley were purchased and settled upon the trusts of the will. This property was exchanged in 1870 for 16a. 3r. 22p. in Selborne, producing £18 a year.[191]

(iii) The first earl of Selborne by will, 1895, bequeathed £56 7*s*. 3*d*. Bank of Ireland Stock (held by the official trustees) dividends for keeping the church of St. Matthew, Blackmoor, in proper repair and maintaining divine service therein.[192]

(iv) A site and buildings was by deed, 1885, settled in trust for a reading room at Oakhanger, and vested in the official trustee of charity lands.[193]

WOOLMER FOREST (Ulmere, Wolvemare, xiii cent.).

The history of the wardenship of Woolmer Forest is identical with that of Alice Holt in Binsted, following the descent of the manor of East Worldham (q.v.).[194]

Various notices throughout the Close and Patent Rolls show how carefully the kings guarded their rights in the forest, as in 1278 when Edward I ordered Adam Gurdon to take all indicted of trespass in the forest and cause them to be kept safely until otherwise ordered.[195] In 1286 Edward ordered Adam Gurdon to cause the prior and convent of Selborne to have from Woolmer Forest six good oaks fit for timber with all their strippings 'in recompense for the underwood and heather which the king caused to be taken from the priory for the expenses of his household when he was last there.'[196] A sharp winter probably brought the command of December, 1285, that the keepers of certain of the king's dogs in Woolmer Forest should have six oak stumps from the forest for fuel for the dogs aforesaid.[197] A similar command was given in 1315 for six leafless oaks to be delivered to the keeper of the king's horses at Odiham for fire for the king's horses.[198] In April, 1378, John Blake was appointed clerk of the works at the 'manor of Wolmer' with power to punish refractory workmen, and with 18*d*. daily wages.[199] William de Hannay, king's clerk, was in the same month appointed controller of the purveyances, purchases, and expenditure for the wages of workmen and carriage upon the works to be executed by the said John Blake on the manor of Woolmer.[200] The earliest mention of a lodge in the forest, probably the Waldron Lodge described by Gilbert White, is in 1386, when oaks to the value of 10 marks were to be felled, and the proceeds delivered 'for the repair of a lodge of the king within the said forest.'[201]

Until the eighteenth century, when deer-stealing had brought in its train such crime and atrocities that the 'Black Act' of 1722 had to be passed, Woolmer Forest was well stocked with the red deer whose disappearance Gilbert White so honestly bewailed.[202]

The forest was inclosed by the award of 10 July, 1857.[203]

184 *Selborne Chart.* (Hants Rec. Soc.), i, 91.
185 Ibid. 92.
186 Ibid. 119–33.
187 *Valor Eccl.* (Rec. Com.), ii, 12, 284.
188 Ibid. 12.
189 Gilbert White, *Antiq. of Selborne*, Letter vi.
190 *Char. Com. Rep.* xii, 531.
191 Ibid.
192 Ibid. lxxxvi, 434.
193 Ibid.
194 *V.C.H. Hants.* ii, 490, 518–20.
195 *Cal. of Close*, 1272–9, p. 437.
196 Ibid. 1279–88, p. 390.
197 Ibid. p. 381.
198 *Cal. of Close*, 1313–18, p. 140.
199 *Cal. of Pat.* 1377–81, p. 186.
200 Ibid. 210.
201 Ibid. 1385–9, p. 127.
202 See *V.C.H. Hants*, ii, 452–4. Here also an account is given of the report of commissioners of 1790 on Woolmer Forest. For further account of this report see Rev. J. Chas. Cox, *The Royal Forests of England*, 309–10.
203 Stat. 18 and 19 Vict. cap. 46.

EMPSHOTT

Hibesete, Imbesete, Yuleshate (xiii & xiv cent.); Impshott (xv cent. et seq.).

Empshott is a small parish of about 761 acres lying between Selborne and Hawkley. It is on exceptionally high ground, and is reached by a steep hill, both from Selborne on the north and Hawkley on the south. The village consists only of a few scattered farms and houses, a church, and vicarage.[1] Ellis's Farm is to the west, Reed's Farm and Butler's Farm to the east, Grange Farm to the north, and Brunstable and Burhunt to the far north near the border line between Selborne and Empshott. The road from Selborne enters the parish between the two farms and branches for a second time just below Grange Farm, which is probably on the site of the original manor house. The branch to the west leads to the vicarage and on to Ellis's Farm, while that to the east leads to Holy Rood Church. At the back of the church is the Grange, owned by Mr. A. E. Scott, standing in the midst of well-wooded country. A little further down on the eastern road is the old farmhouse, now almost in ruins, which, according to local tradition, was once a hiding place of Charles II. South-east of the Grange is Lithanger, now tenanted by Lord William Seymour, and still further east is Empshott Lodge, the residence of Mrs. Butler, backing on Empshott Terrace. The National school which was enlarged in 1872 and a few cottages are also in this remote corner. The parish lies on marl with a subsoil of rock, and consists of a series of corn and wheatfields with a few hopfields interspersed, nestling among small woods and hangers. The arable land of the whole parish only covers $362\frac{3}{4}$ acres, $244\frac{1}{4}$ acres are pasture land, and 38 woodland.[2] The River Rother rises in the south and flows along south of the village, otherwise with the exception of a fish-pond near Lithanger there is no water in the parish.

MANOR The manor of *EMPSHOTT* was held of the king in the reign of Edward the Confessor by Bundi and Saxi, and at the time of the Domesday Survey by Geoffrey Marescal,[3] otherwise Geoffrey de Venuz, the king's marshal.[4] From Geoffrey it descended to Robert de Venuz his son and heir, to Robert's son William,[5] to William's son Robert, and to Robert's son John who was holding in the reign of Henry III.[6] During the thirteenth century the manor remained in the hands of the Venuz family, but by the reign of Edward II it had come into the possession of Aymer de Valence, earl of Pembroke, who died seised of half a knight's fee in Empshott in 1323.[7] Like Newton Valence, Hawkley, and Oakhanger (q.v.) the manor then passed to Laurence de Hastings, grandson of Aymer's sister Isabel,[8] and seems to have been included, though not by name, in the grant made by Laurence to Thomas West in 1339[9] since in 1532 Empshott was said to be held of Thomas West, Lord De La Warr, as of his manor of Newton Valence.[10] From this date all trace of the overlordship seems to be lost, the tenure not being returned in later inquisitions.

William Dawtrey (de Alta Ripa) was holding the manor of Empshott in 1291, in which year he settled it on Peter de la Stane (or Stone)[11] for life, with reversion to John Dawtrey (possibly son of William) and Elizabeth his wife, who may have been a daughter of Peter,[12] with reversion to the heirs of Peter if John and Elizabeth died without issue. It is just possible that this Elizabeth survived her husband and became the wife of James de Norton who held the manor in the early fourteenth century.[13] By 1316, however, William Paynel was holding Empshott, evidently by the right of his wife Eva, who possibly was the direct heir of Peter de la Stane, and succeeded to the manor on the death of Elizabeth because Elizabeth had no children by her first husband.[14] William died without issue in 1317,[15] and Eva, who in 1321 was abducted and married by Edward de St. John, 'she being willing and consenting thereto,'[16] was holding the manor conjointly with her second husband in 1346.[17] She survived him also and lived until 1354, when the manor passed to her kinsman and heir Roger son of John de Shelvestrode.[18] Joan, the daughter and heir of John de Shelvestrode, and probably granddaughter of Roger, married John Aske of Yorkshire,[19] who in 1428 was holding the half fee in Empshott which Edward de St. John once held.[20] From this date the manor remained in the Aske family until it was confiscated in 1537 by reason of

[1] In the fifteenth century it was ascertained by an inquisition taken in 1428 that Empshott was one of the Hampshire parishes in which there were not ten inhabitants holding houses (*Feud. Aids*, ii, 342).

[2] Statistics from the Board of Agriculture (1905).

[3] *V.C.H. Hants*, i, 501*b*.

[4] Ibid. 430–1.

[5] This William de Venuz and Alice his wife granted two parts of half a virgate of land with appurtenances in Empshott to the abbots of Godstow (Cart. Antiq. G.G. 6), who in 1250 claimed the same against Thomas de la Dene, who stated that the lands he held had belonged to Adam de la Bretche father of Richard son of Adam who held them at the day of his death (Curia Regis R. No. 143, Mich. 34 & 35 Hen. III, m. 30*d.*) In 1253 Emma abbess of Godstow conveyed the same by fine to Richard de la Bretche (Feet of F. Hants, 37 Hen. III, No. 404).

[6] Curia Regis R. No. 143, Mich. 34 & 35 Hen. III, m. 30*d*.

[7] Inq. p.m. 17 Edw. II, No. 75, m. 118.

[8] *Cal. Close* 1323–7, p. 277. During the minority of Laurence the estates of John de Hastings were held of Thomas son and heir of William de Roos of Hamlake. *Rot. Orig.* (Rec. Com.), ii, 232.

[9] *Cal. Pat.* 1338–40, p. 395.

[10] Exch. Inq. p.m. 23 Hen. VIII, Ser. 2, file 983, No. 4.

[11] The family of de la Stane had held lands in Empshott as early as 1219, when John son of Gilbert granted half a virgate of land to Isabel de la Stane and her heirs (Feet of F. South. Trin. 3 Hen. III). In 1253 the abbess of Godstow at the petition of Richard de la Bretche granted Osbert de la Bretche and Eva his wife two parts of half a virgate in Empshott to hold for themselves and the heirs of Eva (Feet of F. Hants. Trin. 37 Hen. III). This Eva may have been Eva de la Stane before her marriage or else married a second time into the de la Stane family, since in 1275 Henry de Burhunt made claim against Eva de la Stane for two parts of half a virgate in Empshott (De Banco R. Mich. 4 Edw. I, No. 17, m. 88).

[12] Feet of F. South. 19 Edw. I, No. 184.

[13] *Feud. Aids*, ii, 334. James de Norton's first wife Elizabeth died before 1316, in which year he settled the manor of East Tisted (q.v.) on himself and his second wife Margaret.

[14] At present this can only be hypothesis, but it seems possible that if the Eva de la Stane of the De Banco Roll of 1275 was wife or daughter of Peter she may have had a daughter Eva who married Wm. Paynel, and who would be Peter's heir, and so succeed to Empshott if John Dawtrey and Elizabeth had no children.

[15] Inq. p.m. 10 Edw. II, No. 61.

[16] *Cal. Pat.* 1317–21, p. 559.

[17] *Feud. Aids*, ii, 334.

[18] Inq. p.m. 28 Edw. III, No. 54.

[19] *Harl. Soc.* xvi, 7.

[20] *Feud. Aids*, ii, 358.

'divers treasons made, perpetrated, and committed' by Robert Aske the leader of the Pilgrimage of Grace.[21] In May, 1537, Robert Aske wrote to Cromwell begging him to petition the king for the payment of his debts, among which came the 'board of my workmen at Imbishot about 30*s.* and workmen 30*s.* These may be paid out of my goods that my soul abide no pain for the satisfaction hereof, for at my coming to London I intended to have paid.' Moreover he asked that his lands in Hampshire might revert to the right heirs, 'for I only had them for life, and yielded £8 a year to my brother.'[22] However in 1537 Empshott was granted to Sir William Sandes, Lord Chamberlain of the Household,[23] who within the next few years conveyed the same to Sir William Fitzwilliam. Sir William Fitzwilliam conveyed Empshott by fine in 1548 to John Norton, the lord of East Tisted,[24] who in 1560 died seised of the manor, which from this time followed the same descent as that of East Tisted (q.v.) until sold by Norton Poulett to John Butler of Bramshott in 1750.[25] In 1762 John Butler by will devised the manor to his eldest son John, who died without issue, leaving the estate to be divided among his two brothers James and Thomas and his sister Ann.[26] In 1792 Ann and her husband, John Newland of Petworth, Sussex, conveyed their third in the manor to John Butler of Havant,[27] and in the same year Thomas Butler conveyed his third to the same, while in 1794 James Butler conveyed his third.[28] In 1805 Col. John Butler, who served in the Indian Mutiny, was still lord of the manor. After his death his widow Henrietta Butler and his brother Thomas Butler held the courts of the manor as trustees for his son Frederick John Butler, the present lord of the manor.[29]

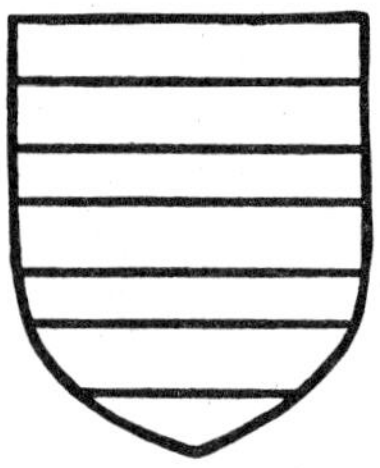

ASKE. *Or three bars azure.*

The courts of the manor have always been held in Grange Farm, which was originally the manor house, and in a conveyance of the farm made in 1792 a special provision was made that John Butler and his heirs and assigns, being lords of the manor of Empshott, should hold courts for the said manor 'in that part of the manor house where courts have usually been held.' The customs are for the most part quite ordinary, except that, according to the court book, all the tenants are supposed to purchase the timber on their estates.

CHURCH

The church of the *HOLY ROOD* has a chancel 24 ft. 6 in. by 14 ft. 9 in., with a modern south vestry, nave 43 ft. by 23 ft., and west porch, with a wooden bell-turret over the west end of the nave. A chapel at the north-west of the chancel, and north and south aisles to the nave, formerly existed. In 1860 the east wall of the chancel and its windows were repaired, and in 1868 the rest of the chancel, a new roof and south vestry being added. The bell-turret and walls of the nave were repaired in 1884.

The chancel is the oldest part of the building, and was begun soon after 1200, the north-west chapel being contemporary with it. The work was carried on slowly, the chancel arch and north arcade of the nave being next built, and then the south arcade. There is no evidence that a west tower was ever contemplated, and the east wall of the nave has been thickened on the west side, probably to carry a bell-turret on the gable above. By the beginning of the seventeenth century the church seems to have fallen into bad repair, and the date on the screen at the west end of the nave, 1624, is probably that of the alterations which have brought the building to its present shape. The north chapel has entirely disappeared, and the outer walls of the aisles have been rebuilt close to the nave arcades, leaving a space of barely two feet between them. A wide arched opening has been made in the west wall of the nave, and the screen before noticed set across it, with a porch forming the main entrance to the church at the west. The chancel has three lancets in the east wall, with keeled rolls on the inner heads and jambs, having bases at the level of the sills, and labels with dogtooth over the arches. Modern cinquefoiled heads have been inserted in the lights. The side walls of the chancel have been pushed outwards, whether by a roof or failure of foundation, and the gap between them and the east wall bonded with ashlar masonry. Each wall has two modern buttresses. In the north wall is a lancet window, in which at the glass-line have been inserted small half-shafts and capitals of twelfth-century style, with a round arch. East of the window is a modern recess with the Ten Commandments, and below it a shouldered locker. The arch formerly opening to a north-west chapel is of one square order, pointed, with a moulded string at the springing on the east side, and three moulded corbels at the west, the jamb on this side being set back six inches from the soffit of the arch. Over the arch is a label with dogtooth, partly overlapped at the west by the west wall of the chancel, which is cut back to expose it. The arch is blocked with a thin modern wall in which is a cinquefoiled light.

The south wall has at the east a modern recess like that in the north wall, and to the west of it a tall lancet, which seems to have been widened. Near the west end is a plain round arched opening 6 ft. 8 in. high, in which is a pointed arch, apparently modern, opening to a modern vestry. All the original masonry in the chancel has diagonal tooling.

The chancel arch is pointed, of two chamfered orders, with a label having a line of dogtooth and clustered responds, with foliate capitals and moulded abaci and bases. On its west face an arch of somewhat higher pitch has been built over it, projecting one foot, and overlapping the labels of the nave arcades; it is clearly an afterthought, and its jointing does not range with the responds of the arcades or chancel arch. The tooling on the chancel arch is vertical.

The nave arcades are of four bays, and though not far apart in date, differ considerably in detail. The north arcade has pointed arches of two chamfered

[21] Exch. Inq. p.m. 29 Hen. VIII (Ser. 2), file 988, No. 8.

[22] *L. and P. Hen. VIII*, xii (1), 563. On 16 Jan. 1531, Robert Aske, father of the rebel, had settled the manor on Robert his second son for life instead of on his elder son and right heir John (Exch. Inq. p.m. 23 Hen. VIII (Ser. 2), file 983, No. 4).

[23] *L. and P. Hen. VIII*, xii (2), 404.

[24] Feet of F. Mich. 2 Edw. VI.

[25] Deeds, *penes* Mr. A. E. Scott.

[26] Ibid.

[27] Ibid.

[28] Ibid.

[29] Ibid.

orders with dogtooth labels. All capitals have well-executed foliage, and square abaci moulded like those in the arch at the north-west of the chancel. The middle pillar of the arcade is octagonal and the other two round, while the responds have each had three shafts, which remain at the east, but the middle shaft of the west respond has been cut away and its capital replaced by a corbel. The tooling on the arches is diagonal, except on the soffits.

The south arcade differs from the north in having its arches worked with larger stones and rather coarser chamfers, and the tooling is vertical. The arrangement of the pillars is the same, but the responds have no shafts, and only a moulded corbel to take the inner order of the arch. The capitals have no foliage, like those on the north side, but that of the first pillar from the east has a late form of scallop, the middle pillar a plain hawksbill section, and the third is worked with hollow flutings. The side walls of the aisles, as has been said, have been rebuilt close to the arcades, and contain windows which may be, in part, of ancient date, but are mainly of the date of the rebuilding. The four on the north are all single pointed lights, the eastern window having a Jacobean quarter-round moulding, and on the south are three windows, two lancets and one two-light window. One of the lancets and the two-light window have the same Jacobean section, and the latter has a blank quatrefoil in the head. In the west bay on this side is a pointed archway with square jambs, blocked, with a single-light window set in the blocking. There is nothing to show whether a door has ever been hung here.

At the west end of the nave is a wide pointed arch of a single order, and in it a very good wooden screen with a cresting of pierced strapwork inclosing a shield. On the screen is the inscription, 'The gift of James Medecaulfe 1624,' and the arms on the shield are those of Metcalfe; vert, three calves gules, quartering four other coats.

The porch has small windows on the north and south, their heads being those of twelfth-century lights re-used, and a plain pointed west doorway with a panel over it inclosing a date of which the first numeral only is left.

Over the west end of the nave is a wooden bell-turret with a shingled spire. It is open to the church below, and the part immediately above the nave roof is glazed between the upright timbers, lighting the west end of the nave in a very satisfactory way. Its east side is carried on a seventeenth-century truss, probably part of the work done in 1624, and the turret is perhaps of the same date. The rest of the nave roof is modern, of fifteenth-century style, and the chancel roof is the same. Part of a Jacobean pulpit stands at the west end of the nave, and a panel from it is worked into the modern reading desk. The altar rails and table are of the seventeenth century, and in the nave are a good number of open benches with sunk trefoiled panels in the ends, of fifteenth or early sixteenth-century date.

The font is of Purbeck marble, with a square bowl ornamented with five shallow round-headed arches on each side, and carried on a central and four angle shafts. Its date is *c.* 1190. It has a wooden cover dated 1624. On either side of the east windows of the chancel are remains of late painting in black, a floral design apparently of seventeenth-century date.

The plate consists of a silver cup and paten of 1620, a paten of 1829, and a plated cup of old Sheffield make.

In the bell-turret are two bells, of 1627 and 1897. The earliest register dates from 1718 to 1795, and the second from 1754 to 1812. The churchwardens' accounts date from 1754.

ADVOWSON The chapel of Empshott was granted in free alms by Ralph son of Gilbert and Constance his wife to the priory of Southwick, probably soon after its foundation in 1133,[30] and was confirmed to them by Papal Bull between 1159 and 1181.[31] In 1242 a compact was made between the prior and convent of Southwick and the prior and convent of Selborne concerning the tithes of Empshott. The prior and convent of Southwick, by reason of their rights in the chapel of Empshott, were to have all the great and small tithes owed by the lord of the manor of Empshott, together with half the small tithes of the villeins of Empshott, while the prior and convent of Selborne were in the name of the parish church of Selborne by reason of parochial rights owned by them in the chapel of Empshott 'to have the other moiety of small tithes of villeins.'[32] In virtue of this agreement the prior of Selborne claimed the moiety from Gilbert vicar of Empshott in 1283, and by the judgement of the prior of Southwark, the papal delegate, the prior's right was established, and Gilbert was condemned to pay 20 marks for the tithes of which he had deprived them.[33] The vicarage was ordained in 1333.[34] The church remained in the hands of the house of Southwick as late as 1535, since it was entered in the *Valor Ecclesiasticus* as appropriated to the priory of Southwick.[35] Between 1535 and 1537 it was evidently granted away by the priory, and does not appear on the Ministers' Accounts.[36] In 1590 Elizabeth granted the free chapel or church of Empshott to William Tipper and others,[37] and confirmed the same in 1592.[38] In 1595 she granted the same to John Wells and Henry Best,[39] who conveyed to Richard Norton and George Leicester.[40] George Leicester sold to Richard Norton in 1596,[41] and in 1597 Richard Norton conveyed to William Brice.[42] The latter in 1601 conveyed back to Richard Norton,[43] and from that time the church and advowson followed the same descent as the manor of Empshott (q.v.) until 1803, when John Butler of Havant made release of it to his brother the late Rev. Thomas Butler, by whose representatives it is held at the present day.

30 Add. MS. 33282, fol. 202. This manuscript gives extracts made in 1831 from a chartulary in the possession of Thomas Thistlethwayte of Southwick Park. The charter giving Empshott Chapel to Southwick is not dated, but must have preceded the confirmation made by Pope Alexander (1159–81).

31 Ibid. fol. 61.

32 Ibid. fol. 200.

33 *Selborne Chart.* (Hants Rec. Soc.), i, 71.

34 Winton. Epis. Reg. Orlton.

35 *Valor Eccl.* (Rec. Com.), ii, 12.

36 Mins. Accts. 30–31 Hen. VIII, Ac. Roll.

37 Pat. 32 Eliz. pt. 4, m. 1.

38 Pat. 34 Eliz. pt. 4, m. 21.

39 Pat. 37 Eliz. pt. 11, m. 37.

40 Close, 39 Eliz. pt. 11, m. 15.

41 Ibid.

42 Ibid.

43 Close, 43 Eliz. pt. 14, m. 10.

FARINGDON

Faredone, Ferendon (xii cent.); Farndon (xiv cent.).

Faringdon parish covers about 2,358 acres which lie north of Newton Valence and north-west of Selborne. The village, divided into Upper and Lower Street, lies in the south of the parish near Newton Valence. From Selborne the Upper Street can be reached by Hall Lane. This narrow lane as it enters the parish rises steadily until below Plash Lane, a branch to the right, it slopes downhill and branches rather suddenly to the right into the village. A house lying back on the right is Deanyers, the residence of Mr. E. B. Kennedy, and along the road on the opposite side is Hall Farm. On the right and left again are picturesque cottages, those on the left lying back behind gay cottage gardens, those on the right fronting on the village street. Just before it reaches the village school the road bends sharply to the left and sends off a branch to the right which leads circuitously to the church, behind which is Manor Farm, and round by quaint thatched cottages and farm buildings along a shady lane past the rectory, uphill to meet the main road of the village again about a quarter of a mile from where it started. At the corner where the roads meet is West Cross House, an uninteresting-looking building with a slate roof, which tradition says was the manor house of the Pophams, and from which a bridle-way is said to have led to Popham. From here the road continues for about half a mile until it intersects the highway from Alton to Gosport. At the corner is the blacksmith's shop, and scattered along the high road on the right-hand side are the houses of the Lower Street. Street House Farm, Annett's Farm, and Ivy Farm lie along the high road towards Newton Valence.

To the north-west of the village is a group of well-wooded copses which make the county round this westerly part of Faringdon more beautiful though less fertile than that in the eastern part of the parish, where cornfield after cornfield and an occasional hopfield form the main features of the scenery. Of the whole parish 990¾ acres are arable land, 823¾ are pasture, and 257 woodland and plantation.[1] The soil is clay with a subsoil of chalk and gravel. With the exception of a few small ponds in the north-east and a pond near the rectory there is no water in the whole parish.

The manor of *FARINGDON* or *MANOR FARINGDON EPISCOPI* was held of King Edward the Confessor by Godwin the priest.[2] It was then assessed at 10 hides and was worth £15. In 1086 Osbern bishop of Exeter held the manor of the king as part of the honour pertaining to the church of Bosham in Sussex, and it was then assessed at 5 hides, and was worth £21.[3]

The church of Bosham itself belonged to the bishops of Exeter, who were visitors and patrons of the college of secular canons founded there by William Warelwast, Osbern's successor in the bishopric.[4] Henry III in 1243 confirmed the manor of Faringdon with all tithes, fees, services, liberties, and free customs thereto belonging to the bishop of Exeter and his heirs.[5] Thirty-two years afterwards in a hundred-roll return the manor was said to have been of ancient demesne, and to have been alienated by Henry II[6] to the bishop of Exeter, who by virtue of the same charter withdrew his suit for Faringdon from the hundred court of Selborne, and claimed view of frank-pledge and assize of bread and ale in his manor.[7] In 1291 the manor of Faringdon was returned among the lands of the bishop of Exeter, and was then valued at £10.[8] In 1546 the bishop made an exchange with the king of the manor of Faringdon for the manors of Pinhoe and Dramford in Devonshire,[9] and in the same year Henry VIII granted the same to Thomas Wriothesley.[10] The latter was created earl of Southampton in 1546,[11] and held the manor until his death in 1550, when it passed to his son Henry Wriothesley, earl of Southampton, who died seised of the same in 1582.[12] In 1596 his widow Mary and his son and heir Henry, earl of Southampton, conveyed the manor by fine and recovery to Robert Cage,[13] who died seised of it in 1624, leaving a son and heir William,[14] who was holding as late as 1663.[15] William Cage died in 1677 and was succeeded by his grandson William who died before 1689. His son William was married in the same year, and made his will in 1735. Lewis Cage, grandson of the last William, sold the manor, without advowson, in April, 1758, to Thomas Knight of Chawton,[16] from whom it has passed by inheritance to Montagu G. Knight of Chawton, the present lord of the manor (1905).

Knight of Chawton. *Vert a bend indented or with a cinquefoil argent in the foot and a canton gules* (for Knight); quartered with *Or a cheveron gules between three lions' paws razed sable* (for Austen).

A survey of the manor taken in 1595 gives its extent as 'the site of the manor with a pidgeon house, three barnes for corne, twoe barnes for hey and one gatehouse three stables a carthouse one orchard one back side and one garden —all which conteine iiii acres.' The demesne lands were said to contain 367 acres of land, 23 of wood and 85 'of cops and wood.' The 'farmer' of the manor had 'common for hogges' only in Faringdon Wood and the other tenants common for both 'hogges and sheepe.' Hewes Hill, a common wherein all the tenants

1 Statistics from the Board of Agriculture (1905).

2 On this Godwin see Mr. Round's notes in *Suss. Arch. Coll.* xliv, 142–3.

3 *V.C.H. Hants*, i, 469*a*.

4 The prebendaries were founded in the choir of the parish church, which was exempt from the ordinary jurisdiction of the bishop of Chichester and his archdeacon. Dugdale, *Mon.* vi, 1469.

5 *Cal. Chart. R.* 1226–57, 276.

6 This is hardly possible in the light of the Domesday statement.

7 *Rot. Hund.* (Rec. Com.), ii, 224.

8 *Pope Nich. Tax.* (Rec. Com.), 214*b*.

9 Pat. 27 Hen. VIII, pt. 2. Deeds of Purchase and Exchange, Box E, No. 33.

10 Pat. 37 Hen. VIII, pt. 1.

11 See *Dict. Nat. Biog.*

12 Inq. p.m. 24 Eliz. pt. 1 (Ser. 2), vol. 196, No. 46.

13 Feet of F. Hants, East. 38 Eliz. m. 15.

14 W. and L. Inq. p.m. (Ser. 2), bdle. 41, No. 46.

15 Lay Subs. R. Hants, 15 Chas. I, bdle. 247, No. 26.

16 Information from Mr. Montagu G. Knight of Chawton.

had common 'and a few trees growing therein,' contained 30 acres.[17]

The manor farm which stands behind the church in a quiet shady garden is undoubtedly on the site of the old manor house of Faringdon. The house itself probably dates back at least to the eighteenth century; it is of two stories with a tiled roof and a cemented front. At the back of the house the foundations of a chapel which formerly belonged to the bishops of Exeter can be traced.

The second manor of Faringdon held of the bishop's manor was that of *FARINGDON POPHAM*.

In the reign of Henry I Turstin, clerk to William de Pont de l'Arche, the king's chamberlain,[18] held the third part of a knight's fee in Faringdon 'of the bishop of Exeter, and of the honour of the church of Bosham . . . as William bishop of Exeter (1107–37) had granted in his charter.' [19] Matilda confirmed his lands in Faringdon to Turstin, who was sheriff of Hampshire by 1155, but in her charter they are said to have been held 'in fee of Henry the King.' [20] Henry II confirmed the same lands to Richard son of Turstin, sheriff of Hampshire,[21] and about the same time Arnulf, bishop of Lisieux,[22] addressed letters patent to all clerks and laymen pertaining to the church of Bosham, granting 'to Richard his clerk the land which Turstin the father of the latter held in Faringdon by the service of the third part of a knight.' [23] William son of Turstin succeeded his brother Richard as sheriff of Hampshire and heir to his estates before 1189,[24] and it is just possible that Agnes de Popham, who was holding at the time of the *Testa de Nevill* the lands that William had held, was his daughter and heir.[24a] Gilbert de Popham, son of Agnes, on his death in 1251 held the same lands,[25] and they passed to his son Robert.[26] By 1346 they had passed to John (more probably Robert) Popham,[27] who was evidently the grandson of the above Robert.[28] In 1378 and again in 1401 the lands were confirmed to Henry de Popham,[29] who in the latter year granted them as 'the manor of Faringdon' to John parson of Eastrop and others, that they might regrant it to himself and his heirs.[30] Stephen Popham, his son, held the manor in 1428,[31] but before his death in 1446 he alienated it to Sir John Lisle, evidently in trust for his daughters,[32] to the youngest of whom the manor passed before the death of Sir John Lisle in 1471,[33] probably on her marriage with Humphrey Forster. In 1476 Alice Forster died seised of the manor [34] which her husband held by courtesy until his death in 1500.[35] Their son and heir, George Forster, who inherited, conveyed the manor for purposes of trusteeship to Richard, bishop of Winchester, and others in 1513.[36] In 1574 William Forster, grandson of George, died seised of the manor, leaving Humphrey Forster his son and heir.[37] An extant court roll for 1585 and another for 1599 show Humphrey Forster as lord of the manor, and that at some time between the two dates he had been knighted.[38] He died in 1601, leaving a son and heir William,[39] who in 1608 conveyed or leased the manor by fine to Nicholas Steward.[40] By 1619 it had passed into the hands of Edward Knight,[41] who was still holding as lord of the manor in 1633.[42] William Knight as guardian of Richard Knight was holding in 1663.[43] From this date until 1770 there seems to be little possibility of tracing the history of the manor. In 1770 it belonged as to two-thirds to Richard Trimmer of Bramshott, yeoman, and as to one-third to Mr. Eames of Faringdon, yeoman. The two-thirds became vested in William Wilshere of Hitchin in 1821 by purchase from John Kersley and Olive his wife, was left by his will to his nephew William Wilshere, and was sold by the latter and his trustees in 1866.[44] All trace of the manor as such is now lost.

West Cross House in the Upper Street, Faringdon, is traditionally known as the manor house of Faringdon Popham. The manor itself must have been quite small, some fifty or so acres scattered about the parish. The most important part of it was about 40 acres of land called Pye's Plot.

CHURCH The church is dedicated in honour of *ALL SAINTS*, and stands at the north end of the village on a site with a fall from north to south, the soil having collected against the north wall of the north aisle to within a few feet of the eaves. The building consists of chancel with north vestry and organ chamber, nave with north aisle and south porch, and west tower with a short wooden spire. The chancel, which with the vestry and organ chamber is of modern date, is of fourteenth century style with an east window of three lights, and in the south wall two windows of a single light and two lights respectively. The chancel arch of two orders has continuous mouldings of fourteenth-century style, and is of the same date as the chancel.

The nave has a north arcade of three bays with semicircular arches of a single square order. The west bay is wider than the others, and the crown of its arch consequently higher. It dates from *c.* 1150 and is older than the rest of the arcade, its eastern column being formed by the addition of a half column to the east side of the east respond of the arch, and it is clear that at first the arch stood alone and did not form part of a continuous arcade. It has scalloped capitals with half-round shafts and moulded bases. The two eastern bays belong to the end of the twelfth century, and have plain bell capitals with round shafts and moulded bases. In the capitals of both

17 Survey *penes* Mr. Montagu G. Knight of Chawton.

18 For the position and importance of this Turstin, his appearance as sheriff of Hampshire in 1155 to 1159, and the appearance of his two sons Richard and William as heirs to the shrievalty as well as to his estates, and the possible descent of the Pophams from Agnes daughter of William son of Turstin, see *The Ancestor*, vii, 59–66.

19 According to the charter of Hen. I, quoted in *inspeximus Cal. Pat.* 1399–1401, p. 420.

20 *Cal. Pat.* 1377–81, p. 110.

21 Ibid.

22 It is difficult to discover how he gained his connexion with Bosham, but Mr. Round has shown that he actually held Bosham at this time (*The Ancestor*, vii, 62).

23 *Cal. Pat.* 1399–1401, p. 420.

24 *The Ancestor*, vii, 63.

24a Ibid. 64.

25 Inq. p.m. 35 Hen. III (Ser. 1), No. 211.

26 Ibid.

27 *Feud. Aids*, ii, 333.

28 See under Popham.

29 *Cal. Pat.* 1377–81, p. 110; 1399–1401, pp. 420, 421.

30 Recov. R. 3 Hen. IV.

31 *Feud. Aids*, i, 358.

32 Inq. p.m. 24 Hen. VI, No. 18.

33 Ibid. 11 Edw. IV, No. 59.

34 Ibid. 16 Edw. IV, No. 41.

35 Ibid. (Ser. 2), xiv, No. 136.

36 Feet of F. Hants, Mich. 4 Hen. VIII.

37 Exch. Inq. p. m. file 828, No. 9.

38 Add. R. 27950, 27951.

39 Inq. p. m. 44 Eliz. (Ser. 2), No. 108.

40 Feet of F. Hants, Hil. 5 Jas I.

41 Add. R. 27952.

42 Ibid. 27953.

43 Lay Subs. R. Hants, bdle. 175, No. 547.

44 Information from Mr. Montagu G. Knight of Chawton.

parts of the arcade the upper member of the abacus is of square section, but in plan the earlier abaci are rectangular and the latter circular. The arches in the eastern bays, being of square section, do not fit the rounded abaci, and their angles at the springing are cut away, as they would otherwise project beyond the line of the abaci. This feature generally implies that the wall over the arcades is older than the arcades, and such must be the case here. The nave must have had a north-west chapel, probably contemporary with a westward lengthening of the original nave, and a north aisle was afterwards added to the east of the chapel. A similar chapel, but of later date, occurs at Newton Valence.

It is to be noted that in neither respond of this arcade do the joints of the wall-quoins range with those of the half-round shafts, but this does not necessarily imply a difference in date. The north aisle is narrow, and had about midway in its wall a small blocked doorway with a square inner head and flattened outer arch, which may have been semicircular at first. Its date is doubtful. There are no windows in this wall, which is buried to two-thirds of its height by the accumulation of soil on the north, but in the east wall is a window of two lights with modern wooden tracery, while the masonry of its inner jambs is of the twelfth century, though possibly not in situ.

In the south wall of the nave is a doorway between two three-light windows, which have cinquefoiled lights and an early form of rectilinear tracery, *c.*1370, a quatrefoil between two trefoiled lights. The south porch is of plastered brickwork and stone rubble, much overgrown with ivy, and over its outer arch is a tablet with the date of its building, 1634.

The west tower is for the most part of the first half of the thirteenth century, having in the ground stage narrow and widely splayed lancets on the north, south, and west. There is no tower arch, but a doorway with a plain pointed head opens from the church, the door being towards the tower. The upper stage of the tower has been rebuilt or repaired, and has small quatrefoil openings, not earlier than the fourteenth century and probably later. It is covered with plaster externally and finished at the top with a short wooden spire, in the base of which the bells are hung.

All the wooden fittings of the church are modern, including stalls in the chancel and a screen across the chancel arch. The chancel roof is also modern, but at the east end of the nave on either side is a length of moulded wall-plate and above it an arched brace, which seem to be of the fifteenth century, and are perhaps the remains of a ceiling over the rood. The rest of the nave has a flat plaster ceiling at the plate level, the rough beams which carry the ceiling joists showing below the plaster. The font has a large cylindrical tapering bowl, standing on a low pedestal in the form of four hollow-fluted capitals of late twelfth-century date ; the base is square.

There are no traces of ritual arrangements, except the remains of a holy-water stone in the east inner jamb of the south doorway of the nave.

There are four bells, with the following inscriptions :—Treble, 'Henry Knight made mee 1666' ; 2nd, 'Henri Knight made mee 1622' ; 3rd, 1627 ; and Tenor, 'Henri Knight made mee 1615 I H . . .'

The church plate consists of a plain silver chalice, the cover forming a paten, a pewter plate, and one much worn plated cruet.

The parish registers begin in 1558. The first book contains mixed entries from that date to 1653 ; the second from 1653 to 1710 ; the third from 1710 to 1773 ; the fourth from 1773 to 1802, and the fifth from 1802 to 1812. The third book is the most interesting, since Gilbert White the naturalist was curate of Faringdon from 1760 to 1785, and his writing first occurs among the baptisms for 1760 and his last signature among those for 1785.

ADVOWSON From its earliest existence at some date between the Domesday Survey and the taxation return of 1291 [45] the church of Faringdon was held by the bishop of Exeter,[46] and followed the descent of Faringdon manor (q.v.) until 1797.[47] At the present day it is held by the rector of Faringdon, Thomas Hackett Massey.

In 1385 the bishop of Winchester directed a commission to the chancellor of Exeter bidding him absolve William Burgeys from the penalty of the greater excommunication incurred by administering the Sacrament to a parishioner of Faringdon without leave of the rector.[48]

In 1397 licence for non-residence was given to the rector of Faringdon in order that he might be in attendance on the bishop of Exeter.[49] Frequently the bishop held ordinations in Faringdon church. Thus in 1316 Walter de Stapledon bishop of Exeter ordained several subdeacons in Faringdon parish church, and among them a monk of Hyde,[50] and again in 1318 ordained Peter de Noreis de Edyndone, who on the same day had letters dimissory for the diaconate and priesthood.[51]

CHARITIES (i) Alice Fylder, by deed 37 Elizabeth, charged a certain tenement in Stedhams and lands in Iping, Sussex, with a yearly rent-charge of 40*s.*, to be applied in moieties for benefit of this parish and Binsted. The several properties were sold without notice of the charge, and the payments have ceased since 1801.[52]

(ii) Poor's Lands. In 1640 a parcel of arable containing an acre, and a parcel of wood ground adjoining called 'Post' containing an acre abutting on the highway and the common wood, were vested in the rector, churchwardens, and overseers, by whom the premises were demised to one John Applegarth for 1,000 years at the rent of 16*s.*

The annual sum of 16*s.* was received and applied in bread up to Michaelmas 1800, when Thomas Fielder, in whom the interest in the term of years was then vested, refused to continue the payment.[53]

(iii) Poor's Money. A sum of £10 given for the poor by an unknown donor was in or about the year 1819 in the hands of a Mr. William Eames on the security of a promissory note given to the overseers and churchwardens. No payment is now made in respect of this charity.[54]

[45] *Pope Nich. Tax.* (Rec. Com.), 210.

[46] *Winton. Epis. Reg.* Wykeham (Hants Rec. Soc.), i, 6, 203, 210, 226, 366.

[47] Inst. Bks. (P.R.O.), Ser. D.

[48] *Winton Epis. Reg.* Wykeham, ii, 365.

[49] Ibid. 476.

[50] Ibid. John de Sendale, 174 *n.*

[51] Ibid. 211 *n.*

[52] *Charity Com. Rep.* xii, 530.

[53] Ibid.

[54] Ibid.

HAWKLEY

Hauckle, Haveskle, Hauekleghe (xiii and xiv cent.)

The parish of Hawkley, covering an area of about 1,447 acres, lies on the slope of high ground stretching north and south between Noar Hill and Westham Hill. The houses of the village are very scattered, but lie for the most part on the west of the parish, near the church and vicarage. The main road through the parish starts at Lower Green, where roads from Newton Valence and Empshott meet, and stretches uphill for about a quarter of a mile.

About half-way up the hill is a small pond on the left and the postman's hut. At the cross roads at the top of the hill the branch to the right leads by a small pond, some farm buildings and small cottages, to the vicarage on the right and the church on the left. This part of the village, which is called Upper Green, includes the oldest group of cottages.

The National school, which is now being pulled down, stands at the churchyard gate.

On a small cottage at Lower Green, which was originally the mill house of Hawkley mill, is a tablet put up by the late J. J. Maberly of Hawkley Hurst, stating that this was the ancient mill of the bishops of Winchester, was taken from them by Adam Gurdon, given back by Edward I 1280,[1] burnt down and rebuilt in 1774,[2] and used as a cottage from 1882. In 1564 it was purchased by Thomas Stempe, warden of Winchester College,[3] and belonged to the college from that date. The stream at the back of the house, which is part of the River Rother, originally drove the overshot wheel of the mill.

Hawkley Hurst, the seat of Mr. Neale Black, stands on ground about 300 ft. high, looking out over a wide expanse of woodland country. Further southeast, below Lower Barn Copse, are Scotland's Farm and Farewell Farm, and further west, almost south of the village, are Combe Hanger and Cheesecombe Farm. Hawkley Hanger, although locally without the parish on the north-western border line, seems to be generally looked on as part of Hawkley. Gilbert White describes how in 1774 a great part of 'the great woody Hanger at Hawkley was torn from its place and fell down, leaving a high freestone cliff naked and bare, and resembling the steep cliff of a chalk pit.' From this cliff a splendid view of the range of the South Downs and much of the Wealden Valley can be obtained. The part of the Hanger nearest the village is known locally as Furry Hill.

The chief crops are ordinary cereals, and fields of oats and barley and wheat are only occasionally intercepted by hopfields. There are 389¼ acres of arable land in the parish, 460¼ of pasture land, and 124 of woodland.[4]

MANOR The manor of *HAWKLEY*, if it was ever a manor, seems to have no definite history until the thirteenth century. Probably it was originally part of the manor of Newton Valence, and passed with Newton among the lands of Robert de Pont de l'Arche to William de Valence in 1249.[5] It was definitely mentioned in the grant made by William de Pont de l'Arche, brother and heir of Robert, to William de Valence in 1252 as the hamlet of 'Haveksle,'[6] and in the royal grant confirmatory of the former made in the same year as the manor of 'Hauekel.'[7] In answer to a writ of *Quo Warranto*, brought against him in 1280, William de Valence pleaded for his tenants of the manor of Hawkley, as for his men of Newton Valence, that by the charter of Henry III they were quit of suit at shire and hundred court, and that no sheriff should enter the manor for view of frankpledge.[8] Aymer de Valence, the heir of William, died seised of 'one messuage and 2 carucates of land in Hawkley' in 1324,[9] and these passed as 'certain lands in Hawkley' to Laurence de Hastings,[10] son and heir of John de Hastings, and grandson of the John de Hastings who had married Isabel, sister and coheiress of Aymer de Valence (see Newton Valence and Oakhanger). During the minority of Laurence the so-called manor was in the king's hands, and in 1331 he granted the custody of 'certain lands and tenements with appurtenances in Hawkley' to the prior of Selborne and Richard de Bromley during the royal pleasure.[11] Before 1334 the custody had been granted to Hugh de St. John 'in part satisfaction of certain debts which the king owed him,' but in that year it was granted to the bishop of Winchester.[12] Henry de Eston, on his death in 1332,[13] held these lands in Hawkley, extended at one messuage, a dovecote, and 72 acres of land, with remainder to his heirs. He held them 'of the heir of Aymer de Valence as of the manor of Newton Valence in the king's hands by reason of the minority of Laurence,' and by service of the eighth part of a knight's fee, and by doing suit at the court of the manor from three weeks to three weeks and rendering 25*s.* 4*d.* yearly to the manor. The same Henry held in his demesne as of fee 'a virgate of land containing 30 acres of the heir, as of the said manor by the service of 10*s.* yearly for all service.'[14]

In 1339, when Laurence de Hastings was of age, he obtained licence to enfeoff Thomas West of his lands in Hawkley[15] (see also Oakhanger and Newton Valence). The latter died seised of the same in 1379, when Hawkley passed presumably to his heirs, for although there is no mention of it in any of the later inquisitions, it was undoubtedly included with Newton Valence as owing suit to the latter.

CHURCH The church of *ST. PETER* and *ST. PAUL*, standing back from the road at the westernmost part of the village, was entirely rebuilt in 1861 on the site of the old church, which was low-roofed and picturesque like that still existing at Priors Dean close by. It consists of chancel with north chapel and south vestry and organ chamber, nave of three bays with aisles, and west tower with gabled walls and a wooden spire. The style is an adaptation of Romanesque, and the church

1 *See* Gilbert White, *Antiq. of Selborne*, Letter x.
2 There is another tablet on the cottage W.R.M. 1774.
3 Kirby, *Annals of Win. Coll.* 280.
4 Statistics from the Board of Agriculture (1905).
5 *Cal. Chart. R.* 1226–57, p. 339.
6 Ibid. 402.
7 *Rot. Chart.* (Rec. Com.), 71. Unfortunately the membrane to which the calendar refers is missing from the charter roll itself, i.e. Chart. R. 36 Hen. III, m. 1.
8 *Plac. de Quo Warr.* (Rec. Com.), 765.
9 Inq. p. m. 17 Edw. II, No. 75.
10 *Cal. Close*, 1323–7, p. 360.
11 *Rot. Orig.* (Rec. Com.), ii, 51.
12 *Cal. Close.* 1333–7, p. 258.
13 Inq. p. m. 6 Edw. III(1st Nos.), No. 58.
14 *Cal. Close*, 1330–3, p. 446.
15 *Cal. Pat.* 1338–40, p. 395.

contains no ancient fittings but the font, of Purbeck marble with a square bowl on a round shaft, formerly surrounded by four angle shafts, the bases of which alone remain. It dates from *c.* 1190–1200.

In the south wall of the chancel is a fifteenth-century alabaster panel of English work, with the betrayal of Christ by Judas. It came from the old church, and was once doubtless part of the reredos of an altar; the background is gilt, with white spots.

The earliest parish register at Hawkley dates from 1797 to 1812. A mixed Hawkley register, dating from 1640 to 1797, is kept at Newton Valence, and before that date the entries were made in the Newton Valence registers.

The plate consists of two silver chalices (one 1861, the other undated), one silver ciborium dated 1903, one pewter paten cover, three patens (one silver, 1861, one pewter, and one electro-plated), and two glass flagons.

ADVOWSON The chapel of Hawkley was annexed to and subservient to the church of Newton Valence at least as early as 1291, when the entry 'Ecclesia de Niwenton cum capella' undoubtedly meant the church of Newton with the chapel of Hawkley.[16] In a composition made about 1364 between the rector and vicar of Newton Valence, the vicar was to have all obventions from the church of Newton and the chapel of Hawkley 'ab eadem ecclesia dependenti.'[17] Hence the advowson of Hawkley passed with that of Newton Valence to the monastery of Edington, thence to the lords of Newton Valence, until they sold it in the early nineteenth century.

Mr. James Maberly of Hawkley Hurst endowed Hawkley with a separate living, and it was finally severed from Newton Valence in 1860. The advowson then passed to the Maberly family and is held by them at the present day.

NEWTON VALENCE

Newenton, Niwenton, Nyweton (xii and xiii cent.)

The parish of Newton Valence, covering about 2,258 acres, lies to the south-east of Selborne. From Selborne the village can be reached by a hilly road leading from Gracious Street round Selborne Hill. Where the road branches at The Nap to left and right the uphill road to the left leads into the village, while the road to the right leads down to the main Alton road and to the Pelham estate, which with the 147 acres of the parish included in the Rotherfield estate covers the whole of that end of the parish. As the road branches upwards to the village the modern school[1] stands well back from the road on the left. Fronting on the street are several picturesque cottages, from the backs of which, over a foreground of field and meadow, can be seen Colemore and Priors Dean, while away in the distance on the left stretch the Sussex Downs. Further along the street broadens out, and in the left-hand corner is a pond almost hidden by overhanging trees. Beyond this is a gate opening up the path which leads both to the church of St. Mary and the manor house, for the manor house stands on the right almost behind the church. Beyond this gate on a green bank the village stocks were originally fixed between two ash trees in front of the back wall of the manor house farm stables, and remained there and in use within the memory of one of the oldest inhabitants of the village. Only one ash tree remains of the four that originally grew on this bank, and this is not one of those on which the stocks were fixed. Filling up the right-hand corner is the big pond, which is one of the most beautiful features of the village, with its wide circle of clear water, nearly dried up in summer, and its background of sturdy rushes. The vicarage stands on high ground where Selborne Common meets the border line of Newton Valence. Between the common and the house stands a splendid avenue of Scotch firs planted down among vegetation of very different character. In the old-world garden is another avenue of exceptionally tall yew trees. There are also traces of two fishponds, now filled up, and a sundial, the pedestal of which is supposed to be formed of a pillar of old London Bridge. On a window on the east side of the house is the date 1755, but the back of the house is much older, as is shown by the beams in some of the rooms and traces of an old archway in one. There is a fine oak staircase probably dating from the seventeenth century. Pelham, the residence of Miss Lempriere, at the other end of the parish, is a picturesque house of the Tudor style, built in 1782, when Admiral Thomas Dumaresq, who commanded the *Repulse* under Rodney in the 'Battle of the Saints,' bought the land called Pelham, or Pilgrim's Place, with his prize money and built the house. It is surrounded by an outer circle of well-wooded country —Mary Land Copse, Newton Common on the west, Kitcombe Wood on the north, Ina Wood Copse on the east, and Plash Wood in East Tisted parish on the south. In the grounds stands a beautiful tulip tree, one of the largest in England. Kitcombe House, which is part of the Pelham estate, lies to the north, while Headmoor,[2] including Potter's Land, Brewers and Hill Land, lies north-west beyond Newton Common. Close by Newton Wood Farm, south of the common, is a field in which was a messuage with two barns and two granaries and a wind grist or corn mill, called 'Cowdries Colpyn' in 1798,[3] now known as Golpyn. Windmill Field is west of Golpyn, and it was there probably in a big hollow still left in the ground[4] that the windmill stood. Close by is a copse called 'The Devil's Pleasure,' and a field called 'Dripping Pan Field.'

Noar Hill Farm, Hammond's Farm, and Lower House Farm are in Noar Manor. Noar Hill rises to a height of nearly 700 ft., and is almost surrounded by two thickly-wooded Hangers—Noar Hill Hanger and High Wood Hanger. Some of the most beautiful

16 *Pope Nich. Tax.* (Rec. Com.), 210.

17 Lansd. MS. 442, fol. 239.

1 Built in 1876. Before this the school was a small building consisting of two rooms in the vicarage garden.

2 Here in 1898 a broken pot containing the remains of human bones was turned up by the ploughs. Some very perfect flint axe-heads were also found near this spot.

3 Documents in the possession of Miss Lempriere of Pelham.

4 Information from Mr. A. E. Scott of Rotherfield Park.

Pelham

views in the whole district can be obtained from Noar Hill, especially towards the south-east. Empshott with its quaint church spire stretches in front; further away to the right is Hawkley, and to the left Greatham. Beyond Greatham to the left are Longmoor and Bordon Camps, and in the obscure distance over the group of intervening hills are Hindhead and Black Down.

Although there are no rivers in Newton Valence, Noar Hill is the watershed between the Rother, which after becoming part of the Avon flows into the English Channel, and the Oakhanger Stream, which becomes a branch of the Wey and flows into the Thames and on to the North Sea. The springs of the Rother are south of Noar Hill in the lower chalk, while the Oakhanger Stream has its source in the north at the outcrop of the upper greensand from beneath the chalk.

The parish lies entirely on chalk formation [5] with a subsoil of clay and gravel. The chief crops are wheat, oats, and barley, and hence the village population consists almost entirely of agriculturists. Of the whole parish 1,015$\frac{3}{4}$ acres are arable land, 495$\frac{1}{2}$ are pasture, and 264$\frac{1}{2}$ are woods and plantations.[6]

An Inclosure Act for the parish of Newton Valence was passed in May, 1848.[7]

MANORS

In the time of Edward the Confessor Bricteric held the manor of *NEWTON VALENCE* of the king, but at the time of the Domesday Survey it was held by Turstin son of Rolf.[8] The fief of Turstin was granted to the Ballons, from whom it passed through the Newmarches to Ralph Russell of Kingston Russell as co-heir.[9] Ralph Russell was holding in 1275,[10] but after this date the rights of overlordship seem to have lapsed.

In 1249 the manor was held by Robert de Pont de l'Arche, and was then of the annual value of £53 5*s.* 10$\frac{3}{4}$*d.*, including the dower which belonged to Constance widow of Robert. The demesne was worth £17 13*s.* 4*d.* yearly, the freemen paid £4 9*s.* 10$\frac{3}{4}$*d.* and 1 lb. of pepper, while their services were worth 2*s.* 2*d.* The villeins paid £8 5*s.* 3*d.* in rent, their services were worth £8 11*s.* 11$\frac{1}{2}$*d.*, their tallage 53*s.* 4*d.*, and for pannage they paid 23*s.* 4*d.* The issues of the meadow were worth 40*s.*, while the pasture of the whole meadow was worth 50*s.* The perquisites of the manor amounted to 36*s.* 8*d.*, and the issues of the garden of the manor to £4.[11] In the same year the manor of Newton Valence, among the other lands which had belonged to Robert de Pont de l'Arche, saving the dower of Constance, was granted by the king to William de Valence and his heirs 'to hold until the king restore them to the right heirs,' with a promise that if the restoration were made William and his heirs should not be disseised without an equivalent exchange.[12] In 1252 the king inspected and confirmed a charter given by William de Pont de l'Arche, brother and heir of the late Robert, by which he surrendered all his right in the inheritance of his brother to William de Valence.[13] In 1251 the king granted to William de Valence that his wood of Newton, of which he had made a park 'enclosed with ditch and hedge, within the metes of the king's forest of "Suthamptonsire,"' should be quit for ever of view of foresters, verderers, &c.[14] But in the next year an inquiry was made as to the encroachments made on the king in Hampshire by William de Valence. His bailiffs had withdrawn the suit due every three weeks from Newton manor to the hundred of Selborne and had refused ingress into the said manor to the foresters of the bailiwick of Woolmer and other bailiffs of the said county.[15] The same charge was brought against him in the hundred roll of 1275, where he is also said to have a gallows, assize of bread and ale, and all other liberties, and to hold view of frankpledge in Newton, though by what warrant is not known.[16] In 1280, in answer to a writ of *quo warranto*, William de Valence pleaded that Henry III granted that his men and tenants of Newton should be quit of suit at the shire and hundred court, and that no sheriff or bailiff should enter the manor of Newton for view of frankpledge.[17] In 1316 Aymer de Valence son of William seems to have held Newton in chief, since no overlord is mentioned,[18] and in 1324 the manor is said to have been held 'by the earl of Pembroke of the king in whose hands it now is on the death of the earl.'[19] On his death in 1323 Aymer de Valence left no issue, and his estates [20] were divided between the only two of his sisters, Isabel and Elizabeth, who had left any surviving heirs.[21] The manor of Newton fell to the son of his second sister Isabel, who had married John de Hastings, second Baron Abergavenny, and had herself died in 1305.[22] Her son John de Hastings died in 1324 before he could enter into his possessions, and the manor passed into the king's hands as guardian of the young Laurence de Hastings, son and heir of John.[23] An enrolment of the purparty of Laurence, made in 1325, states the value of the manor of Newton Valence at £24 1*s.* 1*d.*[24] The custody of the manor during the minority of Lawrence son and heir of John de Hastings was granted in 1331 to the bishop of Worcester. In 1339, when Laurence was of age,[25] he entered into the title and estates of his great-uncle,[26] and in the same year procured licence to enfeoff Thomas West of the manor of Newton, said to be held in chief with the knights' fees, advowsons of churches, liberties, warrens, and all other appurtenances.[27] From 1339 to the middle of the sixteenth century the manor of Newton

VALENCE. *Burelly argent and azure an orle of martlets gules.*

[5] *V. C. H. Hants*, i, map to face p. 16.

[6] Statistics from the Board of Agriculture (1905).

[7] Stat. 11–12 Vict. cap. 109.

[8] *V. C. H. Hants*, i, 494*a*.

[9] See J. H. Round, *Peerage Studies*, *The Family of Ballon*, and *The Origin of the Russells*.

[10] *Testa de Nevill* (Rec. Com.), 243*b*.

[11] Inq. p. m. 33 Hen. III, No. 45.

[12] *Cal. of Chart. R.* 1226–57, p. 339.

[13] Ibid. 402. Rudder in his *Hist. of Glouc.* p. 235, makes a misleading statement that the Newton included in this grant was Newton a tithing of Ashchurch (Glos.). It is undoubtedly Newton Valence.

[14] Pat. 35 Hen. III, m. 8.

[15] Inq. p. m. 36 Hen. III, No. 86.

[16] *Rot. Hund.* (Rec. Com.), ii, 224.

[17] *Plac. de Quo War.* (Rec. Com.), 765.

[18] *Feud. Aids*, ii, 315.

[19] Inq. p. m. 18 Edw. II, No. 68.

[20] Ibid. 17 Edw. II, No. 75.

[21] *Cal. Close*, 1323–7, pp. 272–8.

[22] G. E. C. *Complete Peerage*.

[23] *Cal. Close*, 1323–7, p. 275.

[24] Ibid. 360.

[25] He was five years old on the death of his father in 1324. Inq. p. m. 18 Edw. II, No. 83.

[26] *Cal. Pat.* 1338–40, p. 395.

[27] Ibid. The said Thomas was allowed after an inquisition a.q.d. to entail the manor on himself and his wife. Inq. p. m. 33 Edw. III (2nd Nos.), No. 36.

Valence, like those of Oakhanger and Hawkley, passed through the West family from father to son [28] until, in the reign of Henry VIII, the long chain of descent was broken. Thomas West, Lord De La Warr, conveyed the manor by fine in 1550 to Nicholas Dering, who had married Elizabeth daughter of his half-sister Dorothy.[29] Nicholas Dering died seised of the manor in 1557, leaving a son and heir Thomas Dering,[30] who within the next year evidently conveyed the manor of Newton to John Pescod, who died seised of it in 1558.[31] Thomas Pescod, who had succeeded his father Richard the son of John in 1571, granted the manor to his brother John Pescod of Roxwell,[32] who inherited at his brother's death in 1582.[33] In 1586 John Pescod leased the manor to Henry Campion,[34] and in 1590, on the death of John Pescod, Nicholas Pescod his brother and heir granted the reversion in fee to Campion, Thomas West, the eldest son of Leonard West, half-brother of Thomas Lord De La Warr,[35] who evidently had some residuary right in the manor, giving his consent.[36] Henry Campion conveyed the manor by fine in 1605 to Abraham Campion,[37] who in 1611 died seised of it, leaving a son and heir Henry.[38] In 1622 Henry Campion settled the manor on himself and his wife, the daughter of Thomas Edney. An indenture of 1653 shows that Henry's son Richard was then holding the manor, and was still holding it in 1698, when he and his grandson Richard [39] alienated it by fine and recovery to Dr. John Nicholas, warden of Winchester College.[40] On the marriage of Edward, son of Dr. John Nicholas, to 'Madame Anne Rachell Newsham' in 1711, the reversion of the manor was settled on him and his wife and their heirs male.[41] Their son William married Harriet, the daughter of Henry Boyle of Edgcott (Bucks.), in 1742, and settled the manor on himself and his wife in the same year.[42] Harriet died before her husband, leaving one son, Robert Boyle Nicholas, and two daughters, Harriet who died unmarried before her father, and Charlotte who afterwards married Dr. Joseph Warton in 1773.[43] William Nicholas died about 1762 or 1763, leaving the whole manor vested in his son Robert, with a legacy of £2,000 to Charlotte when she should come of age in 1764.[44] Robert Boyle Nicholas held the manor until his death in 1780. He was Captain of H.M.S. *Thunderer*, of 74 guns, 'in which he was, with the rest of his crew, unfortunately lost in a hurricane off the island of Hispania' [45] in the October of that year. By his will, dated 1776, he bequeathed the manor to his sister Charlotte, wife of Dr. Joseph Warton, with reversion to 'her second and third sons and every other son in tail male taking the surname of Nicholas.' In failure of such to her daughters and their heirs male, failing such to their daughters, and failing such to William Nicholas his eldest brother and his right heirs.[46] Harriet Warton, the only child and daughter of Charlotte, married Robert Newton Lee, and on her mother's death in 1809 inherited the manor. In the meantime, ever since the end of the seventeenth century, the various owners of the manor seem to have unscrupulously bargained away parcels of the demesne lands.[47] They seem to have seldom been resident at Newton Valence, and so manorial right gradually lapsed and became meaningless. Thus in 1826, after the Newton estate had been sold to Sir John Cope, Robert Newton Lee, in a letter to William Dumaresq of Pelham, stated that a Mr. Beaufoy had been in treaty for it, but 'declined the purchase when no copy of court rolls could be found or any other documents which had tended to prove it a manor by suit or service.' Hence it had not been sold to Sir John Cope as a manor.[48]

Henry Chawner, a London goldsmith, bought the manor property about the end of the eighteenth century of the trustees of Robert Boyle Nicholas,[49] converted the old house into kitchen apartments, and added a villa in the 'Grecian style.' On his death in 1851 his son Edward Chawner came into the property and held it until his death in 1868, when it fell to his son, the present owner, Captain Edward Chawner of the 77th Regiment, who served in part of the Crimean campaign of 1854 and 1855.

CHAWNER. *Sable a cheveron between three cherubs or.*

NOAR.—Whether the manor of Oures, Owres, Noare, or Nowers, known as Noar in modern days, was in existence before the thirteenth century is uncertain. In 1275 it is first mentioned in a hundred roll and said to be held by the abbot of Hyde in chief and in free alms, though from what time his tenure dated was unknown.[50] It continued in the possession of Hyde Abbey to the sixteenth century.[51] At the time of the dissolution Oures, as parcel of the possessions of Hyde, passed into the king's hand and is entered in the Ministers' Accounts from 1539 to 1542.[52] The king, in the latter year, granted the manor to Nicholas Dering,[53] and in the next year gave licence to Dering to alienate the same to John Pescod to hold by service of relief to the king.[54] John Pescod died seised of the manor held in chief for the hundredth part of a knight's fee in 1558, leaving his son Richard as his heir.[55] Richard Pescod, who seems to have had great

28 See Oakhanger in Selborne.

29 Feet of F. Hants, Mich. 4 Edw. VI.

30 Exch. Inq. p. m. (Ser. 2), File 997, No. 2.

31 Ibid. File 998, No. 7.

32 Pat. 31 Eliz. pt. 6, and 32 Eliz. pt. 5.

33 Inq. p. m. (Ser. 2), vol. 200, No. 37.

34 Feet of F. Hants, Mich. 28 and 29 Eliz. Confirmed by letters patent 32 Eliz. pt. 5.

35 Chan. Proc. (Ser. 2), bdle. 190, No. 27.

36 Feet of F. Hants, East. 32 Eliz.

37 Ibid. Trin. 3 Jas. I.

38 W. and L. Inq. p.m. (Ser. 2), bdle. 5, No. 93.

39 The son of his son Richard, who died before 1692.

40 Documents *penes* Miss Lempriere.

41 Ibid.

42 Ibid. This was evidently his second marriage, as he had an older son William as well as his children by Harriet. William inherited his Warwickshire property.

43 Ibid. *Dict. Nat. Biog.* Joseph Warton.

44 Documents *penes* Miss Lempriere.

45 So runs the inscription on his memorial in Newton Valence church.

46 Copy of will *penes* Miss Lempriere.

47 For instance, in 1687 Richard Campion had sold 'two closes of land called Pelhams adjoining the king's highway . . . part and parcel of the demesnes of the manor of Newton Valence, with rents, dues, and services reserved, due and payable' to William Knight of Faringdon. This was the nucleus of the Pelham estate which eventually swallowed up most of the demesne lands.

48 Letter *penes* Miss Lempriere.

49 Information from Captain Edward Chawner.

50 *Rot. Hund.* (Rec. Com.), ii, 224

51 *Pope Nich. Tax.* (Rec. Com.), 213*a*. *Feud. Aids*, ii, 315; Inq. p.m. 12 Ric. II, No. 150.

52 Mins. Accts. 30–1 Hen. VIII, R. 135; 32–3 Hen. VIII.

53 Pat. 33 Hen. VIII, pt. 8, m. 20.

54 Pat. 34 Hen. VIII, pt. 11, m. 21.

55 Exch. Inq. p. m. 4 and 5, 5 and 6 Phil. and Mary, File 998, No. 7.

debts and small means, sold it to Richard Norton in 1560.[56] The latter died in 1592 seised of the manor of Oures which formed part of the jointure of his wife Katherine,[57] who was holding the manor in 1602.[58] By 1610 Richard Norton, the son of Katherine, was holding the manor, and made a settlement by fine in that year entailing it on his heirs male by his wife Anne.[59] From this time the manor followed the same descent as the manor of East Tisted (q.v.), passing from the Nortons to the Paulets and from the Paulets to the Scotts. However, not all the manor of Oures passed from the Paulets to the Scotts in 1808. 'The farm and lands called the Manor farm part of the manor of Noar *alias* Temple Noar *alias* Ower *alias* Temple Sothington[60] held by copy of court roll of the said manor according to the custom of the manor,' remained in the hands of the marquis of Winchester until purchased by James Winter Scott in 1860.[61]

The customs of the manor still hold good, and a court baron is held by the steward for the admission of a copyhold tenant. The fine on entry is paid accordingly, and the heriot is commuted by a fine of about 15*s*.[62] However, most of the copyholds are being enfranchised. A perambulation of the bounds of the parish made in 1735 and entered on the court rolls gives many interesting place-names that still survive. The perambulation starts from Hatch Gate near Gallows Hill or Gallers Hill, turns down Bottom Lane, then also called Westcroft Lane, passing by 'Fatting Leaze Land Gate' to Selborne; thence skirting round to the south to Hale Coppice, to Tile Croft, and into Goley or Goleigh Hill Lane, then east to Empshott Common Field round by Noar Hill Farm again into Galley Lane.[63]

CHURCH The church of *ST. MARY* stands in the park in the south-east of the parish. A shady road branching to the left from the village street leads to the lych gate, which is the first sign of the church still hidden from view by the large yew tree on the left side of the path inside the churchyard. Under the tree a demarcation in the ground is all that remains to show the spot where once stood a tombstone to Colonel Phayre, one of Charles I's regicides. He is said to have lived at Cobden's farm-house at Empshott, but to have been buried at Newton Valence. Although many people remember the tombstone with the name clearly inscribed upon it, it has now curiously enough disappeared. Either it was accidentally removed during the restoration of the church in 1872, or a snowstorm caused it to fall and then it was carried away, but no one knows where or how. A pathway of old tombstones, with the inscriptions worn away and undecipherable, leads to the church porch. The church is a small building consisting of nave and chancel of equal width, and with no structural division, 19 ft. 2 in. wide by 48 ft. 6 in. long; a north chapel 9 ft. 4 in. by 16 ft. 9 in. at the west of the nave, a west tower, and a small vestry on the south of the chancel. Its plan, as first built *c.* 1220, was a simple rectangle, the present nave and chancel. The north chapel was added at the end of the same century, and the south vestry is modern. The tower is obscured with ivy and plastering, and its date not easy to determine, but it is probably an addition to the original plan. The material of the building is the local whitish limestone, used as ashlar for dressings and uncoursed rubble for the walling, and the roofs are tiled. The masonry details are plain but well designed.

The chancel has a triplet of lancets in the east wall, and two lancets in the north and south walls. A roll string runs at the level of the sills inside, and stops on the south side over the head of the priest's doorway, west of the second lancet on this side. On the north it continues westward, ending under the first window of the nave. All windows in the north and south walls have flat sills inside, with chamfered rear arches, and on the outside all have a chamfer and a reveal for a frame. The priest's doorway has a segmental inner arch, and pointed outer arch of two chamfered orders; it now opens to a vestry, but was at first external, and two sundials are cut on its east jamb. The nave has on the north side one original lancet, the rest of the north wall being occupied by the arch leading to the north chapel; while on the south side are three lancet windows with a doorway to the west of them, but of these only the first lancet from the east is ancient, the other two, with the doorway, being entirely modern. The west wall of the nave was rebuilt in 1812. The north chapel, 9 ft. 4 in. by 16 ft. 9 in. long, contains nothing ancient beyond a piscina in its east wall, of late thirteenth-century date, with engaged shafts and moulded capitals and arch, and a stone shelf in the recess over the drain. There are lancet windows in the east and west walls, and in the north wall a two-light window with a quatrefoil over, all of which are modern. The arch to the nave is of two chamfered orders, and though apparently modern springs at the east from a moulded half-octagonal corbel of the end of the thirteenth century, and at the west from a respond and moulded half capital of similar but not identical detail, which is either retooled or modern.

The west tower, 10 ft. 10 in. by 11 ft. 9 in., opens to the nave by a continuous arch of two chamfered orders, probably of fifteenth-century date. On the ground stage is a blocked west doorway, which has an outer arch with the fifteenth-century double ogee moulding, and in the north and south walls are small lancets. A few feet above them are other small lancets, narrower than those below, and at this level are similar windows in the east and west walls. These four windows point to the former existence of a floor or gallery in the tower about halfway between the present first floor and the ground level. At a higher level in the west wall is another lancet lighting the present floor, and in the belfry stage are four plain arched openings without mouldings or tracery, filled with wooden luffers. These, with a plain parapet at the top of the tower, are built with brick dressings, and date[64] from a reconstruction in 1812, when a 'cupola' of wood on the tower was taken down. Externally the tower is plastered with cement, and the lower part overgrown with ivy, and the date of this part is difficult to determine, the stonework of the small lancets being for the most part either modern or retooled.

56 Deeds in the possession of Mr. Archibald Edward Scott of Rotherfield Park.

57 Inq. p. m. 34 Eliz. pt. 2 (Ser. 2), No. 118.

58 Add. Chart. 27994.

59 Feet of F. Div. Cos. Mich. 8 Jas. I.

60 This must be an inaccuracy, since Temple Sotherington is absolutely distinct from Noar manor.

61 Documents *penes* Mr. A. E. Scott.

62 Information from Mr. A. M. Downie, steward of the manor.

63 Court Roll in possession of Mr. A. M. Downie, steward of the manor.

64 Faculty of 1 July, 1812, in the possession of the vicar, the Rev. A. C. Maclachlan.

All the woodwork of the roofs is modern, that of the chancel being of different design from that of the nave, and divided from it by an arched truss, resting on stone corbels with short shafts. The wood fittings are also modern. In the south wall of the chancel is a pretty trefoiled piscina with moulded arch and label, and a stone shelf. It is contemporary with the chancel, but its drain, in the form of a shaft with leaf capital, half buried in the wall, looks like an older pillar piscina of *c.* 1200 re-used. In 1812 a screen between nave and chancel was taken down. It was evidently in the nature of a framed partition, as its destroyers were in doubt whether it could be taken away without weakening the roof.

The font is modern, but in the churchyard, west of the south doorway, is an ancient circular bowl with lead lining, which may be of the thirteenth century; and outside the blocked west doorway of the tower is a dilapidated panelled shaft and bowl, the latter set upside down on the shaft, belonging to a second superseded font, not older than the end of the eighteenth century.

There is no ancient glass or wall painting. On the north wall of the chancel is a small brass plate in memory of Francis, son of Robert Johnson, who died in 1616 aged 2½ years. There are five bells, the treble being of the fourteenth century, and specially interesting from having an English inscription, as the use of English on bells was very rare at the time. It reads, 'Hal Mari ful of gras,' in Gothic capitals, with a round stop between each word on which is the figure of a cock. On the waist are the founder's initials, W. K. The second has 'Henri Knight made mee 1620,' and the third 'Let your hope be in the Lord, 1623, E. K.' The initials are those of Ellis Knight the founder. The fourth bell was cast by Taylor of Loughborough in 1871, and the tenor recast by John Warner & Sons of London, 1880.

The church plate consists of a chalice, paten, and alms-dish of plain silver, hall marked and dated 1725, and inscribed 'The gift of James Glyd gentleman, of the parish of Newton.'

The first book of the parish registers begins in 1538, and contains a rather irregular transcript of births, weddings, and burials to 1667. Then comes a transcript of the births, weddings, and burials between 1543 and 1548. Following this is a continuation of the registers from 1667 to 1740; then another transcript from 1627 to 1670, and from 1686 to 1695. The second book of burials and baptisms dates from 1740 to 1811, and that of weddings from 1754 to 1812. The Hawkley parish register of births, weddings, and burials entered in one book from 1640 to 1797 is also kept with those of Newton Valence, since the two parishes were originally united, and the vicar of Newton and his curate between them served the two churches.

There is also a diary of Richard Yalden, vicar of Newton Valence from 1761 to 1785. It is styled 'A journal of weather and other occurrences from February 10, 1775.' This book is a diverting mixture of parish accounts and private accounts, public events and personal experiences, vestry meetings and dinner parties.

ADVOWSON The church existed at the time of the Domesday Survey, and was held by Turstin son of Rolf who held the manor.[65] It then passed with the manor to Robert de Pont de l'Arche, and was granted by him to William de Valence.[66] In 1324 it was stated to be in the king's hands 'by reason of the lands late belonging to Aymer de Valence tenant in chief being in his hands.'[67] With the conveyance by Laurence de Hastings of the manor of Newton (q.v.) to Thomas West, the church as appendant to the manor went to him also, but in 1364 the king granted licence to William de Edington to obtain the church from Thomas West, and to grant the same to the newly-founded monastery of Edington.[68] Hence the church was appropriated to that house with reservation of a portion for one perpetual vicar and of an annual rent of 5*s.* to the bishop, to the prior and chapter of the cathedral church of Winchester, and 12*d.* to the archdeacon.[69] The monastery held the church until the dissolution.[70] In 1535 the king leased the advowson of the church of Newton Valence with the chapel annexed[71] 'to Henry Goldsmith for the term of 30 years,'[72] but the perquisites and tithes under the title of the 'rectory and church of Newton,' or 'the rectory and church within Newton Valence,' were held by the crown until 1544, when the king sold them to Edward Elkington and Humphrey Metcalf.[73] However, at the expiration of the lease of the advowson to Henry Goldsmith the rectory and advowson were evidently granted to the owner of the manor, since in 1578 Thomas Pescod was holding both, and granted the whole to his brother John,[74] whose heir Nicholas in 1588 granted the advowson to Henry Campion, to whom the manor passed at the same time,[75] and the rectorial tithes to William Wright of Kingsey (Oxon).[76] In 1602 the queen leased the rectory with the full complement of tithes and premises to John Duffield for a term of twenty-one years, with a special clause that John Duffield was to keep the chancel of Newton Valence church in repair, with all the houses and buildings adjoining.[77] In 1604, however, the rectorial tithes were confirmed again to William Wright, and later in the same year the advowson also was granted to him. Henry Fleetwood sold the advowson and rectory to Sir William Bowyer, who sold the same in 1614 to his second son Robert, who regranted the same to his mother, Lady Mary Bowyer, afterwards Lady Mary Ley, under indenture to be revoked if the said Robert returned safely from foreign parts.[78] Lady Mary Ley died seised in 1620, and the rectory and advowson evidently passed back to her son Robert, who was holding the same in 1624, and was forced in that year to make good his claim against Henry Fleetwood, from whom his father, Sir William, had bought the rectory.[79] In the depositions made on behalf of the defendant Sir William was said to have paid the plaintiff £700 for the same, and was liable for the repair of the chancel of the church of Newton, and the chapel of Hawkley, and the tithe

65 *V.C.H. Hants*, i, 494*a*.
66 See manor of Newton Valence.
67 *Cal. Pat.* 1324–7, p. 23.
68 Pat. 37 Edw. III, pt. ii, m. 32.
69 Lansd. MS. 442, fol. 237.
70 *Valor Eccl.* (Rec. Com.) ii, 2.
71 i.e. Hawkley.
72 Mins. Accts. 30–1 Hen. VIII, R.146.
73 Deeds of Purchase and Exchange, Box D, No. 23.
74 Pat. 31 Eliz. pt. 6, m. 29.
75 Ibid. 33 Eliz. pt. 50, m. 21.
76 Ibid.
77 Ibid. 44 Eliz. pt. 10, m. 23.
78 W. and L. Inq. p.m. 18 Jas. I (Ser. 2), bdle. 30, No. 157.
79 Exch. Depos. Southants, 22 Jas. I, No. 52.

barn of Hawkley.[80] From Sir William Bowyer the advowson seems to have passed to the Glyd family, one of whom, Michael Glyd, was vicar from 1628 to 1662, and his son Richard from 1662 to 1697.[81] James Glyd was patron from 1718 to 1761,[82] in which year he presented Richard Yalden to the vicarage. From 1785 to 1837 Edmund White was both patron and vicar.[83] In 1838 Edward Auriel was patron,[84] and presented his kinsman Edmund Auriel.[85] He sold it to Thomas Snow, who was vicar from 1842 to 1855.[86] From the Snow family the patronage passed by sale to the family of Mrs. A. N. C. Maclachlan, who is patron at the present day.

CHARITIES (i) Henry Knight of Faringdon, by will dated 1858, left £200 lands (held by the official trustees of charitable funds) for bread and fuel for the poor of Newton Valence.[87]

(ii) Michael Glyd, vicar of Newton Valence, according to his memorial inscription in Newton Valence church, by will dated 1735 left £50 to purchase land, the income of which should be distributed at the discretion of the vicar on St. Thomas's Day to the poor of the parish not receiving alms. The gift money was, however, evidently lost or squandered, since nothing but the memorial inscription remains to mark its existence.

EAST TISTED

Ostede (xii cent.); Esttystede, Estistede, Thistede (xiii and xiv cent.).

The parish of East Tisted, containing about 2,648 acres of land, lies immediately south-west of Newton Valence. The main part of the village is a group of half a dozen modernized cottages on the east of the high road leading from Alton to Gosport. They lie well back from the road with front gardens stretching up to a low stone wall which runs along in front of the group. They originally stood on the other side of the road, within Rotherfield Park, but were removed by Mr. James Scott when he bought the Rotherfield estate. One of the cottages does service as the village post-office, and another as the village inn. Near the church and vicarage, which are on the east side of the road north of the village, a road branches east to Home Farm past two blocks of almshouses built and endowed for the aged poor by Thomas and Septimus Scott in 1879 and 1893. Beyond Home Farm, where the road branches to the right to East Tisted station and on to Monkey's Lodge Farm, a small spring rises which supplies the meagre village pond. On the north side of the road are two or three old cottages and several modern ones which have sprung into existence since the building of the railway station, opened on Whit-Monday, 1903. Rotherfield Park estate lies west of the village and fills up the whole of that end of the parish. The park itself covers about 300 acres, and in it on high ground stands the manor house on the original site. Surrounding the park, especially on the north and west, is well-wooded country—Plash Wood on the north and Dogford Wood and Winchester Wood on the west—reaching away almost to the outer boundary of the parish.

The soil is entirely chalk, except here and there in the valleys where the subsoil is often gravel. Hence the chief crops are ordinary cereals, but the fertility of the ground is necessarily unfavourably affected by the remarkable lack of water in the parish. With the exception of the spring that rises west of Home Farm there is no river, not even a rivulet, to break the monotony of alternation of field and woodland. There are 745 acres of arable land in the parish, 767 of pasture, and 739 of woodland and plantations.[1]

MANOR The first mention of the manor of *EAST TISTED* does not come until the early part of the thirteenth century, when in 1206 King John ordered Geoffrey FitzPeter to inquire whether certain lands in 'Dokefert,'[2] held by William Peche, belonged to the demesne of Tisted which the king had granted to Adam de Gurdon.[3] However, a hundred roll of a later date states that half a knight's fee at Tisted and Selborne, meaning the manor of East Tisted, which was evidently comprised of lands in Tisted and Selborne, was held of Adam de Gurdon by the grant of King Richard to his father.[4] In 1218[5] a writ directed to the sheriff of Hampshire ordering him to seize the lands of Adam de Gurdon in Tisted and Selborne states that they were held by Adam of William de St. John.[6] This is difficult to explain, as in all other cases it is said to be held of the king in chief by grand serjeanty. On the death of the second Adam de Gurdon before 12 August, 1231, the manor reverted to the crown during the minority of his heir, and Henry III granted the whole to Ralph Marshall to hold during the royal pleasure, rendering 'what Ameria the wife of Adam had rendered while the lands were in her hands,' and saving to Ameria the corn which had been sown in the lands.[7] In 1233 the manor went as dower to Ameria until her eldest son should be of age.[8] Adam, her son, the famous supporter of Simon de Montfort, was of age and in possession of the manor by 1254, and by an inquisition *ad quod damnum* taken in that year he was allowed to hold his lands in Tisted and Selborne as half a knight's fee instead of by grand serjeanty.[9] On the hundred roll for 1275 Adam de Gurdon is said to hold half a knight's fee in 'Ostede' and Selborne of the king in chief and to have the right of free chase of wolves and hares both within and without the forest

80 Exch. Depos. Southants, 22 Jas. I, No. 52.
81 Parish Register.
82 Inst. Bks. P.R.O.
83 Warner, *Hist. of Hampshire*, ii, 237, and Parish Register.
84 Inst. Bks. P.R.O.
85 Parish Register.
86 Ibid.
87 *Parl. P.* 1873, vol. 51

1 Statistics from the Board of Agriculture (1905).
2 This name survives in the modern Dogford Wood.
3 *Rot. Litt. Claus.* (Rec. Com.), i, 73*b*, 'ad dominicum nostrum de Tisted quod dedimus Adamo de Gurdon servienti nostro.' King John had granted twelve librates in Tisted and Selborne to Adam. Pipe R. 10 John.
4 *Rot. Hund.* (Rec. Com.), ii, 224.
5 The first Adam de Gurdon was dead before this time, evidently before 7 August, 1214. Close R. 16 John. See *Geneal.* (New Ser.), iv, 2.
6 *Rot. Claus.* (Rec. Com.) i, 350*b*.
7 *Excerp. e Rot. Fin.* (Rec. Com.), i, 216.
8 Close, 18 Hen. III, m. 17; 19 Hen. III, m. 19.
9 Inq. p. m. 38 Hen. III, No. 18.

by charter of Henry III.[10] About 1305,[11] or earlier, Adam de Gurdon died seised of the manor of Tisted, leaving a daughter and heir Joan, who in 1308 settled the whole on herself for life with reversion to James de Norton and his heirs.[12] For licence to enter the manor James de Norton paid a fine of 5 marks to the crown during the next year.[13] In March, 1316, the manor was in his hands,[14] and in the May of that year he settled it upon himself and his second wife Margaret and their heirs; failing such it was to revert to Thomas the son of James by his first wife Elizabeth.[15] James and Margaret had a son John[16] who died before 1346, when the manor passed into the hands of Edmund de Kendale, Margaret's second husband,[17] in custody for John's son John, a minor,[18] who came of age in 1360.[19] This John only held the manor for ten years, dying abroad, probably on active service in the French wars in 1370, and leaving a son and heir John only three years old.[20] Before 1424 the latter conveyed the manor to trustees, who settled it in that year on his son John and Joan his wife and their heirs.[21] Richard Norton the son and heir of John and Joan died seised of East Tisted in 1503, leaving a son and heir Richard,[22] who married Elizabeth Rotherfield in 1495. He died in 1536, leaving a son and heir John[23] who died before 1564, in which year Anne his widow sought dower in East Tisted against her son Richard. She stated that she had been dispossessed by subtle practice between this her son and his uncle, who 'when the said orator was in great heaviness and sorrow for the death of her late husband came to her and brought a deed of release by which she should release unto the said Richard all right of dower in the said lands . . . while they swore to her that there was nothing in it but a note or remembrancer of such lands as her late husband held and nothing that would do her harm.' Trusting to them she signed the deed and her son seized the lands.[24] He died in 1592 while his mother Anne was still living, but the manor of East Tisted was settled on Katherine his wife.[25] Their son Richard, who was knighted in 1610,[26] succeeded to the manor on the death of his mother before that date, and held it until his death in 1612.[27] The manor then passed to his son Richard, who was several times sheriff of Hampshire, and who was created baronet in 1622.[28] The Norton family were staunch royalists and suffered heavily for their adherence to Charles. In July, 1644, Sir Richard was committed 'for maintaining the proceedings against the Parliament and for doing many disservices.' He was imprisoned in Lord Petre's house,[29] but was by order of the Committee for Prisoners discharged in August, 1644, on giving sufficient security. His estates were valued at £15,000 a year, and on admission to compound he was fined at £1,000.[30] This was reduced to £500 in March, 1645. He paid the fine, but died before August of that year, leaving his estate heavily charged, as his sons complained when they compounded for their own and their father's delinquency on his death. They stated that they had been in the king's army in Winchester garrison, and five days after its surrender had taken an oath administered by the county committee. They were now heavily burdened with their father's debts and the necessity of paying their mother's jointure, while Sir Richard the elder son had no other estate, and John the younger only a lease of £15 a year, now sequestered. In April, 1647, all proceedings against them were stayed, since they had paid £100, the sum to which their fine had been reduced in consideration of their poverty and their father's fine.[31]

NORTON. *Vert a lion or.*

The estate was not taken out until May, 1661, when, since Sir Richard had died in 1652 without male issue, it descended in tail male to his brother John as third baronet. In 1666 Sir John Norton settled the manor of East Tisted on himself and Dame Dorothy his wife and their heirs.[32] Sir John died in 1686 aged sixty-seven, and was buried in East Tisted church under an elaborate monument erected 'by the piety of his wife, Lady Dorothy.'[33] She, whom 'God blessed with a prosperous life and an easy death,'[34] survived

10 *Rot. Hund.* (Rec. Com.) ii, 224.

11 The last mention found of him so far is in 1292–3 in an Inq. a. q. d. 20 Edw. I, No. 130, by which it was found to be no damage to the king that Adam de Gurdon should give 8 acres of land and a rent of 6*s.* 8½*d.* in Oakhanger to the prior and convent of Selborne, for the weal of his own soul and that of his late wife Constance.

12 Inq. a.q.d. 1 Edw. II, No. 70; *Cal. Pat.* 1307–13, p. 133.

13 *Rot. Orig.* (Rec. Com.), i, 163.

14 *Feud. Aids*, ii, 315.

15 *Cal. of Pat.* 1313–17, p. 466.

16 In the proving of age of the John de Norton who inherited in 1360 he is called John son of John and kinsman and heir of James de Norton (Inq. p. m. 35 Edw. III pt. 1, No. 139), and in a later inquisition of Margaret's mother, reversion of certain lands in Surrey is made to John son of John son of John de Norton son of Margaret. [Inq. p. m. 45 Edw. III (wrongly calendared under 40 Edw. III.), 1st Nos. No. 4].

17 De Banc. R. No. 286, m. 55.

18 *Feud. Aids*, ii, 333; *Rot. Orig.* (Rec. Com.), ii, 84.

19 Inq. p. m. 35 Edw. III, pt. 1, No. 139.

20 Ibid. 44 Edw. III, No. 50.

21 *Cal. Pat.* 1422–9, p. 198.

22 Inq. p. m. 19 Hen. VII (Ser. 2), vol. 17, No. 49.

23 Exch. Inq. p. m. 28 Hen. VIII (Ser. 2), file 988, No. 8.

24 Chan. Proc. (Ser. 2), bdle. 132, No. 17.

25 Inq. p. m. 34 Eliz. pt. 2 (Ser. 2), No. 118.

26 *Hants N. and Q.* vi, 125.

27 W. & L. Inq. p. m.

28 *Dep. Keeper's Rep.* xlvii, App.; Pat. 130, 20 Jas. I, pt. 12, m. 19.

29 *Journ. of the House of Commons*, 15 July, 1644.

30 *Cal. of Com. for Compounding*, ii, 848.

31 Ibid.

32 Deed *penes* Archibald Edward Scott of Rotherfield Park.

33 No man's virtues have been better extolled than those of Sir John, both in his memorial inscription and in the sermon preached on his death by the rector of East Tisted. 'Loyal to his king and yet a studious preserver of the ancient privileges of his country. . . . firm and resolute always in upholding the established church of England and yet not factious against the right succession . . . no sufferings could terrify him, no public discontents could sour him, no private hardships could bias him . . . He spent his time and estate continually in the country and scarce ever went to London but to attend the Parliament. . . He preferred his habitation here before all the splendour and diversions of the city. . . . Cheerful and friendly in his large hospitality . . . and far from a hard landlord his land will never cry against him nor the furrows thereof complain. . . The only pomp in which he seemed to delight was in walking constantly to the house of God before a numerous and well-ordered family.' (Papers in possession of Miss Lempriere of Pelham.)

34 Ibid. Miss Lempriere has an interesting letter of 1662 to Lady Dorothy from her sister-in-law in London, telling her that she had made a required purchase for her of 2 lb. of holland costing 13*s.* 'I highly miss your good company here,' she goes on to say, 'and the want of the court and all the gallants make not the towne seem soe naked to me as your absence. . . .'

him until 1703, but as they had no issue the manor of East Tisted seems to have passed before this to Elizabeth, the daughter of the late Sir Richard, as heiress of her uncle. Elizabeth had married Francis Paulet of Amport in August, 1674,[35] and on his death in 1695 or 1696[36] their son Norton Paulet succeeded to the estate. The will of the latter is dated 1729, and by it Norton Paulet, his eldest son, was made sole heir and executor, and charged to pay his father's debts of £13,000.[37] Thus in 1756 he mortgaged the manors of East Tisted and Rotherfield to John Taylor, fellow of Winchester College,[38] but recovered the same before his death in 1758.[39] By his will Thomas Norton Paulet was made his sole heir after the death of his wife, Mrs. Anne Paulet, and was to have an annuity of £200 during the life of Anne.[40] Anne died about 1765, but before Thomas could enter into possession he had to prove his title against William Paulet, his father's eldest surviving brother, who denied the legitimacy of Thomas[41] and disputed the will. The depositions of the witnesses for the defendant were taken in 1766 at the 'White Swan,' New Alresford, and among the witnesses was the rector of East Tisted, who stated nothing more definitely than that the late Norton Paulet was the reputed father of the defendant.[42] The case evidently was decided in favour of Thomas, who was in possession in 1767,[43] but who sold the manor of East Tisted in 1787 to George Powlett or Paulet, the youngest but only surviving brother of Norton Paulet.[44] George Paulet as heir of Harry Paulet, his third cousin once removed, became twelfth marquis of Winchester in 1794, and on his death in 1800 the manor passed to his son Charles Ingoldsby Paulet,[45] who sold it with Rotherfield and Noar in October, 1808, to James Scott.[46] On the death of the latter in 1835 the estate passed to his son James Winter Scott, who died in 1873. Archibald Edward Scott, fourth but only surviving son of James Winter Scott, holds the estate at the present day.

SCOTT OF ROTHERFIELD. *Party palewise indented argent and sable a saltire countercoloured.*

It is thought that Old Place Farm may have been the old manor house of East Tisted, where the Norton family lived until Richard Norton wedded the heiress of Rotherfield in the end of the fifteenth century and went up to Rotherfield.

In the basement on the north side of the house is a row of stone-mullioned windows, *circa* 1600, the masonry and detail being very good, and evidently belonging to a house of some importance. At the west end of the north wall are traces of a wall running northwards, part of the old house, and near it is a shed covering a well with a large wooden wheel for drawing water.[47]

The house has been patched and altered at many dates, and contains nothing of interest beyond the windows described. On a chimney stack on the south side is the date 1742.

ROTHERFIELD (Rutherfield, Retheresfeld, xiii cent.). The history of the manor begins in the twelfth century when it was held by Adam de Rotherfield, who rendered account for the same on the Pipe Roll for 1166.[48] In the thirteenth century Adam de Rotherfield, son or grandson of the above, leased the manor for five years to E., archdeacon of Lewes, and the king confirmed the grant in 1226.[49] In 1234 Isabel de Rotherfield, widow of Adam, was given seisin of her dower in the lands of her late husband in Rotherfield, if they had been seized by the king with the lands of Adam her son, who had forfeited the manor of Rotherfield among his other possessions for felony.[50]

The king granted the manor to Roger de Wyavill for life 'for his support in the king's service,' but in 1257 the said Roger in the king's presence restored all the land for the use of Robert Walerond, to whom the king had formerly granted the reversion of the same.[51] In 1266 Robert Walerond leased the same to his nephew Alan Plugenet,[52] and before his death alienated it to William de Lyndhurst, who died seised of the same, leaving a son and heir William, a minor, called William de Rotherfield, because he was born there.[53] In 1274 Maud, late wife of Robert Walerond, demanded a third in dower from Rotherfield, against William de Rotherfield,[54] but a memorandum was made to the effect that she was not dowered from Rotherfield.[55] William de Rotherfield's son and heir John entered without homage done and died seised, leaving a son and heir John, a minor, who died in 1369 leaving a son and heir John who was sixteen in 1371.[56] The king granted out the manor to William de Lyndhurst during the minority of the latter John, and in 1373 in an inquisition made concerning Rotherfield it was stated that a rent of 36*s*. had always been paid from it to the lord of East Tisted.[57] In 1379

ROTHERFIELD. *Azure a fesse wavy between three crescents or.*

35 Document *penes* A. E. Scott, esq.

36 G.E.C. *Complete Peerage.*

37 Deed *penes* A. E. Scott, esq.

38 Ibid.

39 Document *penes* A. E. Scott, esq.

40 Ibid.

41 This seems probable, since otherwise a special clause in the will that Thomas should 'take and bear the same coat of arms' as Norton Paulet would seem unnecessary.

42 Documents *penes* A. E. Scott, esq.

43 Ct. R. *penes* A. E. Scott, esq.

44 The will of Norton Paulet the elder gives his sons as follows :—(1) Norton, (2) Henry, (3) John, (4) Charles, (5) William, (6) Herbert, (7) Francis, (8) George. The second, third, fourth, sixth, and seventh sons died unmarried before 1766 and William died unmarried in 1772, so that George was the rightful heir to his brother if Thomas was illegitimate. (From documents *penes* A. E. Scott, esq.)

45 Ibid.

46 The tale goes that the marquis had intended to bring his bride to live at Rotherfield, but the coach stuck in the mud, and the lady being of a hasty temper was much irritated and declared that he might sell 'dirty Rotherfield,' for she would never live there! Hence the marquis sold the estate.

47 This was worked until the last few years by two dogs, but is now falling into decay.

48 *Pipe R. 12 Hen. II* (Pipe Rec. Soc.), ix, 104.

49 *Cal. Pat.* 1225–32, p. 46.

50 Inq. p.m. 45 Edw. III (2nd Nos.), No. 84.

51 *Cal. of Chart. R.* 1226–57, p. 470.

52 Feet of F. Div. Cos. 50 Hen III, No. 3.

53 Inq. p.m. 45 Edw. III (2nd Nos.), No. 84.

54 Ibid. Edw. I, File 7, No. 89.

55 *Cal. Close*, 1272–9, p. 70.

56 Inq. p.m. 45 Edw. III (2nd Nos.), No. 84.

57 Ibid. 47 Edw. III (2nd Nos.), No. 37.

ROTHERFIELD PARK

John de Rotherfield entered into possession,[58] but as there is no inquisition on his death there is nothing to show how long he held the manor. William 'Rytherfield,' presumably his son, died in possession of Rotherfield in 1489, and on the inquisition then taken it was said to be held of Edward Lord de Duddeley, as of his manor of Alton Westbrook,[59] not, as before, in chief. William's heir Elizabeth married Richard Norton of East Tisted in 1495, and from that time the manor was vested in the same descent as that of East Tisted (q.v.). Thus in 1564 Anne Norton pleaded that her husband John Norton had left her the manor of Rotherfield as part of her dower. Within the manor was 'a great wood[60] adjoining the park pale of Rotherfield on the west side of the park containing threescore and seven acres or thereabouts . . . which hath been used time out of mind of man at the age of sixteen years growth to be lopped and sold.' Anne had therefore sent workmen to lop the trees, but her son Richard had hindered them and brought them before the King's Bench.'[61]

CHURCH The church of *ST. JAMES* has a chancel with north and south chapels, a nave with aisles, and a west tower, and was entirely rebuilt in 1846, with the exception of the lower part of the tower. The chancel arch of two chamfered orders appears to be old work re-used, and the south doorway of the tower is in part of the first half of the fourteenth century. The chief interest of the church at the present day centres in the monuments of the Norton family.

At the east end of the south aisle is the canopied altar-tomb of Richard, *ob.* 1556, and Elizabeth Norton, erected before the death of either, about 1530. The canopy is formed by a four-centred arch with a panelled soffit, under a cornice on which are three shields bearing respectively (1) the Norton coat, (2) the same impaling Rotherfield, and (3) Rotherfield. In the spandrels of the arch are shields with RN and EN. On the upright back of the tomb beneath the canopy are brasses representing the Resurrection of Christ, with Richard Norton and eight sons kneeling on the right hand, and Elizabeth and ten daughters on the left. Over both groups are scrolls, one illegible, the other, on the left, having JHU X̄PE FILI DEI MISERERE MEI. The base of the tomb is panelled and bears three shields with the same coats as those on the cornice, but set in early Renaissance ornament. An inscription in black letter is painted on the cornice and base of the tomb, as follows :—

Richardus Norton armiger et Elizabeth uxor ejus filia et heres Willī Retherfield ac cōsanguinea et una heredū Willī dawty . . . de f . . . ele qui quidem Ricūs obiit . . . die . . . Anno dni M CCCCC . . . et dicta Elizabeth obiit . . . die . . . Anno dni M CCCCC . . . Qiū aīaȝ ꝑpiciet' de' Amen.

Above the tomb is a panel with the Norton coat under a round arch with Renaissance detail, rather later in style than that on the tomb itself.

In front of the tomb lies an early fourteenth-century coffin lid, having a cross with a sunk quatrefoiled head in which is the bust of a woman holding a heart in her hands, and at the foot is a trefoiled arch beneath which appear the feet of the figure resting on a dog.

Against the north wall of the north aisle is a tall monument of the second half of the sixteenth century to John Norton, who died before 1564, and his wife Anne (Puttenham), with a pediment carried by two Ionic columns, resting on a panelled base. Beneath the pediment are two small figures of an armed man and a lady kneeling on either side of a prayer desk, with a strapwork panel behind them. On the base of the tomb are three shields in wreaths and strapwork borders, the first bearing the Norton coat, impaling Puttenham. The second has Norton impaling Rotherfield, and the third the Norton coat. The third shield also occurs in the pediment, with helm and mantling and the crest of a Saracen's head, and again above the pediment, held by a small figure.

At the east end of the north aisle is the recumbent armed effigy, in white marble, of Sir John Norton, 1686, resting on a white marble base with a large gadrooned cornice and a long inscription. Behind the effigy is a black marble frame, and above it a cornice on which is a shield with crest and supporters, bearing the Norton arms impaling March.

Two small brass plates are fixed in the north wall of the tower in memory of two vicars, Richard Burdon, 1615, and Thomas Emes, 1663, the date on the latter being given in a chronogram :

DeCeMbrIs 29to soLe non orto pIe eXpIrabat.

In the tower is a panel with the Royal Arms, dated 1706. The woodwork in the church is modern, but in the vestry is a seventeenth-century communion table. On the pulpit are figures of the evangelists, the work of a local carver and of modern date, but curiously like seventeenth-century work.

There are three bells, the treble by Ellis Knight, inscribed : 'Let your hope be in the Lord. E. K. 1623' ; the second, 'Prayse ye the Lorde 1590,' and the tenor, 'Honnor the King, 1635.'

The plate consists of a silver cup, paten, and alms-dish of 1702, the cup being inscribed D . N, and the paten and alms-dish L N, for Lady Dorothy Norton, widow of Sir John Norton, and Lucie, daughter of Sir Richard Norton ; a chalice, paten, and flagon of 1898, and a pewter flagon dated 1702 and inscribed 'Ye parish of East Tisted in ye County of Southampton.'

The earliest parish register is a parchment book beginning with the baptisms from 1561 to 1623. On the first page dated 1538 is an account of the proclamation by which the keeping of parish registers was made law. The next section gives the marriages between 1538 and 1594, and then from 1604 to 1654. After this come the baptisms between 1624 and 1679, then the marriages from 1657 to 1678. These are followed by the first entry of burials from 1670 to 1679, with one or two marriages in 1678 and 1680. Then the book ends with another entry of burials between 1562 and 1669. The second register, a parchment, leather-bound book, gives the baptisms and marriages ; the baptisms from 1680 to 1812, and the marriages from 1688 to 1758. Inside the cover is a notice of inductions to the rectory between 1680 and 1767. The third is a register of briefs and burials between 1683 and 1812. The fourth register is a paper book giving the marriages between 1761 and 1811.

The overseers of the poor accounts start in 1742. They call up the most graphic picture possible of the

[58] Close. 2 Ric. II, m. 17.

[59] Inq. p. m. 4 Hen. VII (Ser. 2), iv, No. 26.

[60] This is the modern Winchester Wood.

[61] Chan. Proc. (Ser. 2), bdle. 132, No. 17.

life of the parish in the years following. A sparrow club evidently existed quite early, since in the first year of the accounts there is an entry of 7*s.* 9*d.* paid for thirty-one dozen sparrows, and like entries follow in every year. For forty years or more a certain William Chitty, who seems to have been the village idiot, was clothed, and fed, and shaved. In one year (1763) they gave him 'skins for the pockets of his coat' besides his ordinary clothes, and in another year (1771) made him a 'hop surplice.' He died in 1781, for there comes an entry 'Paid Mr. Wilmott for 3 gals of beer when Chitty was bored and shaving Chitty 5*s.* o.'

In 1763, in spite of the triumph of Lord Bute's peace policy in the preceding year, is an entry 'Paid for Hirein a substitute in the Militia £4 14. 6,' and again in 1765 'Paid for substitute for Warren and expences £2. 13. 5.' The first idea of an organized system of housing the poor comes in 1771 with the entry 'Spent at Vestry about a poor house 1*s.* 6*d.*' In the next year is the 'Account of Arthur Kelsey and Thomas Eames, disbursments for Tisted poor house 1772.' The house was built for about £69, £10 was given by Winchester College, £15 by Magdalen College, Oxford, the timber by Thomas Norton Paulet, lord of the manor, £10 10*s.* was advanced out of the year's accounts, and Widow Eames lent £33 on note of hand. In 1780 the house had to be mended and thatched. These are but a few typical entries, but they serve perhaps to show something of the parish life in the eighteenth century.

ADVOWSON The advowson of the church was always held by the lords of the manor of Rotherfield[62] (q.v.), passing from the Rotherfield family to the Norton in 1495, and from the Nortons to the Paulets in 1687. From the Paulets it passed to the Scotts,[63] and is held at the present day by Archibald E. Scott, the lord of the manor.[64]

On the confiscation of Adam de Rotherfield's lands for felony about 1234, when the advowson of East Tisted was granted in reversion to Robert Walerond,[65] the latter evidently leased the same to the abbot of Hyde, since in 1263 the abbot had dealings concerning the advowson with Adam de Plugenet,[66] nephew of Robert, to whom Robert himself leased the advowson in 1266.[67] It was afterwards alienated to William de Lyndhurst,[68] and from that time was appendant to the manor of Rotherfield. John son of John de Rotherfield, while a minor, presented one Ralph Rande to the church,[69] and a presentation made by his son, John de Rotherfield, is recorded in 1387.[70]

CHARITIES (i) The Rev. Philip Valois, rector, who died in 1760, gave to the incumbents of East Tisted and five other parishes £300 secured on the tolls of the turnpike between Basingstoke and Winchester, the annual interest to be paid to a master and a mistress for teaching children of this parish, the boys to read and write, and the girls to read, write, and sew. The legacy is represented by £376 15*s.* 8*d.* consols held by the official trustees of charitable funds.[71]

(ii) The Rev. John Williams, rector, who died in 1822, gave £400 consols to the incumbents of East Tisted, Newton Valence, Colemore, Faringdon, and Chawton, in trust for the benefit of the charity school of East Tisted, subject to the condition that, in default of a regular school, the benefit might be claimed successively by each of the four other parishes. This trust fund consists of £354 12*s.* 9*d.* consols also held by the official trustees.[72]

The incomes of these charities are expended in the general maintenance of the national school.

62 See Inq. p. m. 45 Edw. III, No. 84.
63 Deeds *penes* Mr. A. E. Scott.
64 Ibid.
65 See manor of Rotherfield.
66 Feet of F. Hants, 47 Hen. III, Case 204, File 10, No. 57.
67 Feet of F. Div. Cos. 50 Hen. III, No. 3.
68 Inq. p. m. 45 Edw. III (2nd Nos.), No. 84.
69 Ibid.
70 *Winton. Epis. Reg.* Wykeham (Hants Rec. Soc.), i, 164.
71 *Charity Com. Rep.* xii, 529.
72 Ibid.

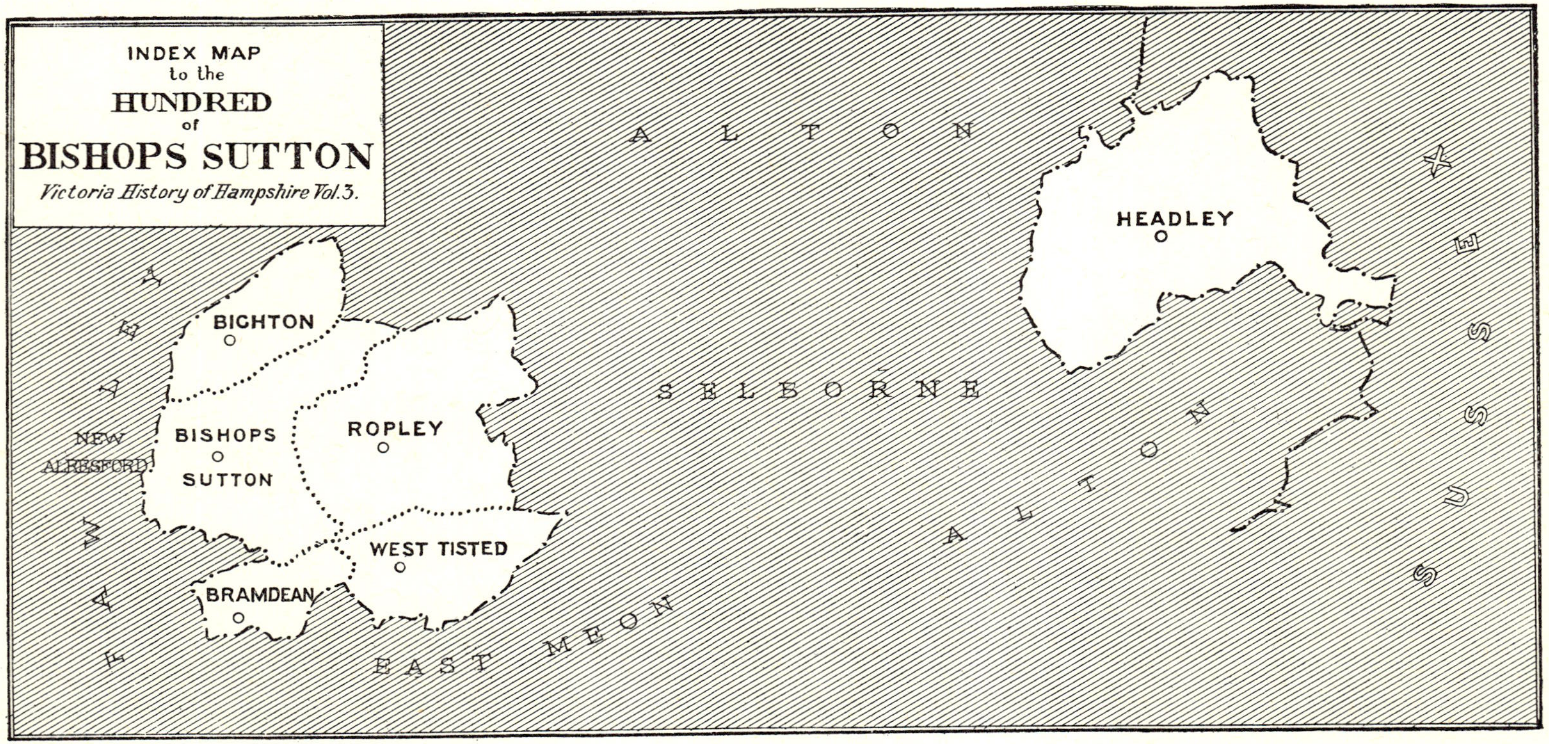
INDEX MAP
to the
HUNDRED
of
BISHOPS SUTTON
Victoria History of Hampshire Vol. 3.
ALTON
SELBORNE
ALTON
SUSSEX
FAWLEY
EAST MEON
HEADLEY
BIGHTON
BISHOPS SUTTON
ROPLEY
WEST TISTED
BRAMDEAN
NEW ALRESFORD

THE HUNDRED OF BISHOP'S SUTTON

CONTAINING THE PARISHES OF

BIGHTON
BISHOP'S SUTTON
BRAMDEAN
HEADLEY
ROPLEY
WEST TISTED[1]

At the time of the Domesday Survey the hundred of Bishop's Sutton was known as the hundred of Esselei, and comprised the following places :— West Tisted, Bishop's Sutton (which included Ropley), and Bramdean. The amount of the land assessed was 18 hides 1 virgate.[2] Headley, which was included in Bishop's Sutton hundred in 1831, and is now in Alton hundred, was entered under Neatham hundred, but was said to be reckoned as part of Esselei.[3] Bighton at the time of the survey was included in Chuteley hundred.[4] Ropley is not mentioned, but was most probably included in Bishop's Sutton. The land in Headley and Bighton was assessed at 12 hides, so that the total hidage of the land afterwards comprising Bishop's Sutton was about 30 hides. It is not possible to find out when the name of 'Esselei' disappeared and that of Bishop's Sutton was substituted. From 1207, the date of the earliest court-roll, the hundred was known as Sutton, and in 1316 included the vills of Ropley, Headley, West Tisted, Bramdean, and Bighton, and the borough of Alresford.[5] The last-named was a liberty in 1831, but at what date it became so is uncertain.[6] The court-rolls show that the bishops of Winchester were lords of the hundred from 1207 onwards, and held a tourn at Bishop's Sutton at Hock-tide and Martinmas. In a book of the customs of Sutton of the time of Henry III, there is a reference to a rather unusual service, apparently relating to the Alresford ponds. The text runs as follows :—'Item homines dicunt quod nihil debent cariare de instrumentis piscatoris quia vivarium non pertinet hundredo de Sutton immo hundredo de Alresford.'[7] At the time of John Poynet's accession to the see in 1551, when the episcopal manors were exchanged for a fixed rent,[8] the hundred of Bishop's Sutton, being in the king's hands, was granted to Sir John Gate.[9] It was, however, restored with the other episcopal property in 1558,[10] and continued to be held by the bishops of Winchester until 1869, when the lands of the bishop of Winchester were taken over by the Ecclesiastical Commissioners. The parish of Headley was removed from the hundred of Bishop's Sutton to that of Alton between 1831 and 1841.[11]

[1] The extent of the hundred as given in the Population Returns of 1831.
[2] *V.C.H. Hants*, i, 463, 477, 503–4.
[3] Ibid. 477.
[4] Ibid. 471.
[5] *Feud. Aids*, ii, 315.
[6] See hundred of Fawley.
[7] Duchy of Lanc. Rentals, bdle. 8, No. 26.
[8] *V.C.H. Hants*, ii, 66.
[9] Pat. 5 Edw. VI, pt. 5, m. 20.
[10] Pat. 4 and 5 Phil. and Mary, pt. 7, m. 24.
[11] Cf. Population Returns of 1831 and 1841.

BIGHTON

Bykingtune and Bicincgtun (x cent.), Bighetone (xi cent.), Byketon (xiii cent.), Biketon (xiv cent.), Bicketon (xvi cent.).

Bighton is a parish with an area of 2,095 acres, situated 2 miles north-east by east from New Alresford Station, on the London and South-Western Railway. The village is almost in the centre of the parish, and is reached from New Alresford by a road which runs east from the main Alresford and Basingstoke Road, between Old Alresford House on the north and Old Alresford Pond on the south. The village is set partly on the northern slope of a valley opening westward towards Alresford and partly along the road running down the middle of the valley. The church and manor house are at the highest point to the north, with the rectory immediately south of the church. From the church the road makes a steep descent, and turns sharply to the east towards the schools, the general shop, and the smithy, and then again southward with a second descent to the road in the valley. At the bottom of the hill stands the inn, with three horse-shoes nailed up as a sign, and there are many quaint thatched cottages on either side of the road. Higher up the valley, near to High Dell Farm, a substantial-looking building, the road forks north-east and south-east. To the north-east a shady lane runs to Bighton Wood House, the residence of Col. Heathcote, which is situated on the outskirts of Bighton Wood, in the north of the parish. The house was built in 1844, at a cost of £10,000, by the Rev. John Thomas Maine, and is surrounded by 280 acres of copse and woodland. The road to the south-east leads to Medsted. Woodlark Farm, which is situated south of the village, is mentioned as early as 1545.[12] The earliest mention of Breach Farm, the occasional residence of the duke of Buckingham, which lies a little to the east of Bighton Wood House, seems to be in 1734.[13]

The manor house, which has an early eighteenth-century south front with very good moulded brick details, is now occupied by the bailiff of Col. Hanning-Lee. In 1770 Haydell Farm is mentioned, which is represented by the modern High Dell Farm.[14] In the low-lying ground in the south of the parish near Drayton Farm, a stream rises which feeds Old Alresford Pond, and there are also numerous springs which afford an abundant supply of pure water.

Woods and plantations in the parish cover an area of 295 acres.[15] The following are found as names of copses in a patent roll of 1545 :—'Rosselwayes Coppe, Wike Coppies, Chorlewode Coppe, Rede Coppe, Pikedfelde Coppe, Wilkyns Coppe, Lordesdowne Coppe, and Jelyan Grove.'[16] 'Golberfield or Goblenfield Coppice or Goldberryfield Coppice or Groveryfield Coppice, Devil Acres Coppice, Spoyle Coppice, Gores Coppice, and Barnes Coppice' are found in a recovery-roll of 1734.[17]

The soil is for the most part a harsh flinty loam[18] resting on chalk, from which many flints are collected for the repair of the roads in this and the neighbouring parishes. Following the direction of the little brook which takes its rise in the parish the land is intermixed with gravel and is of a better quality. The chief crops grown in the neighbourhood are wheat, oats, barley, and turnips. Truffles are found in the beech woods, and in the autumn the wages of the labourers are considerably augmented from this source.

Arable land covers an area of 1,186 acres in the parish and permanent grass 572 acres.[19]

MANORS OF BIGHTON

As is shown under Bishop's Sutton, it seems probable that a large part of the manor and parish of Bighton, if not the whole of it, was included in a grant of land said to have been made by Ine to Winchester Cathedral in 701.[20] In 959 King Edwy granted 10 mansae in the parish of Bighton to Hyde Abbey (the monastery of St. Peter by Winchester, as it was then called), and shortly after this gift the monks, with the consent of the king, granted this land to a certain minister of the king, called Ælfric, for life, in return for a gift of 60 marks of gold.[21]

At the time of the Domesday Survey the manor of Bighton was held by Hyde Abbey, and was assessed at 7 hides. The monks, however, did not keep the whole of the manor in their own hands. They only retained 3 hides, the other 4 hides being divided equally between Fulchered and Borghill. What the abbey held was worth £8, while the tenants' holding in the manor was only worth £4.[22]

The manor continued to be held by the abbey or by tenants of the abbey until the dissolution.[23]

In 1256 Guy de Heydene granted a carucate of land in Bighton, which he probably held of the abbey, to Roger, abbot of Hyde, and his successors for ever. In return for this grant the abbot promised that he and his successors thenceforth would find a certain secular chaplain to celebrate divine service in the church of the abbey at the altar of St. Grimbald, and would pay this chaplain 5 marks a year. In addition the abbot and his successors were to pay an annuity of £10 to Guy, and on Guy's death an annuity of £6 to his brother Thomas. After the deaths of Guy and Thomas the annuities were to cease, but the convent was to receive yearly from the abbot and his successors 20*s.* for pittance on Guy's obit.[24] In 1329 the abbot and convent obtained a grant of free warren in their demesne lands of Bighton.[25] An inquisition was held in 1388 to ascertain what manors, lands, and tenements had been assigned as the portion of the abbot of Hyde, and what belonged to the convent as its portion. The manor of Bighton was returned as one of those which had belonged to the convent from time immemorial.[26] In the same year the king by letters patent granted to the abbot and convent and their successors that the premises assigned for the maintenance of the

[12] Pat. 37 Hen. VIII, pt. 3, m. 39.
[13] Recov. R. Trin. 6 and 7 Geo. II, m. 13–15.
[14] Close, 10 Geo. III, pt. 13, m. 24.
[15] Statistics from Board of Agriculture (1905).
[16] Pat. 37 Hen. VIII, pt. 3, m. 39.
[17] Recov. R. Trin. 6 and 7 Geo. II, m. 13, 14, and 15.
[18] Stonyland Copse is the name of a copse in the east of the parish.
[19] Statistics from Board of Agriculture (1905).
[20] Birch, *Cart. Sax.* i, 148.
[21] *Liber de Hyda* (Rolls Ser.), 174; Birch, *Cart. Sax.* iii, 251.
[22] *V. C. H. Hants*, i, 471.
[23] *Feud. Aids*, ii, 315, 334, 359.
[24] Feet of F. Hants Hil. 40 Hen. III.
[25] Chart. R. 3 Edw. III, m. 16.
[26] Inq. p.m. 12 Ric. II, No. 150.

convent, distinct from the abbot's portion as a prebend, should on voidances of the abbey be exempt from seizure.[27] The manor of Bighton was assessed at £14 16*s.* 1*d.* in 1291.[28] It was worth almost twice as much in the reign of Henry VIII.[29] After the dissolution of the abbey the king granted it to a Venetian, Dr. Augustine de Augustinis, physician to the king, Cardinal Wolsey, and Cardinal Campeggio, to hold for the term of his life,[30] but in July, 1545, Augustine received a grant of the reversion for a rent of £2 18*s.* 5½*d.*[31] Three months later Augustine and Agnes his wife by fine granted the manor to Thomas Wriothesley and his heirs.[32] On the death of Thomas, Bighton was one of the manors assigned to his widow Jane as dower. In 1581 Henry earl of Southampton died seised of the reversion of the manor of Bighton, which Jane was holding for the term of her life.[33] His heir was his son Henry, aged eight, who seventeen years later sold the manor to John Wither of Manydown (co. Hants).[34] The property was then settled for life upon the wife of John Wither's eldest son William as a marriage-portion.[35] Three years after her death in 1632 William Wither and his eldest son Paul sold the manor to Robert Eyre, Giles Eyre, and William Eyre.[36] William Eyre was still lord of the manor in 1665, for he then presented to the living which went with the manor.[37]

WRIOTHESLEY. *Azure a cross or between four falcons close argent.*

The descent of the manor has not been discovered from this date[38] till 1692, when Sir Robert Worsley, bart., purchased it from John Pathurst,[39] and presented to the living in 1701.[40] In 1726 Edward Stawell, George Pitt, and Sir John Cope, bart., bought the manor from Sir Robert Worsley and Frances his wife,[41] and they presented to the living in 1732.[42] They were probably trustees for Frederick Tilney of Tilney Hall in the parish of Rotherwick. Frederick's heir was his daughter Anne, who married William, Lord Craven. On the death of Anne in 1730,[43] her only daughter having predeceased her, the manor passed to Dorothy wife of Richard Child, Viscount Castlemaine, only daughter and heir of John Glynne and Dorothy his wife, the niece of Frederick Tilney. On his wife's succeeding to her inheritance Richard Child assumed the name of Tilney, and in 1731 was created Earl Tilney. The manor in 1734 was settled upon the Hon. John Tilney, Lord Castlemaine, the son and heir of Earl Tilney and Dorothy his wife, and his heirs and assigns.[44] From him it passed into the possession of Christopher Eyre, one of the prebendaries of Winchester Cathedral.[45] Christopher died in 1743, and was succeeded by his eldest son Philip Eyre,[46] who on his own petition presented himself to the living of Bighton in 1767.[47] On his death without issue the manor went to his brother Joseph Eyre, who in 1770 settled it on himself and his son and heir John and their heirs and assigns for ever.[48] From the Eyres it passed by purchase into the possession of James Brydges, duke of Chandos, whose only daughter and heir Anne Eliza married Richard, Earl Temple, in 1796. The latter being seised of the manor in right of his wife, dealt with it by fine in 1809,[49] and presented to the living in 1811, and again in 1827 under the title of duke of Buckingham.[50] It was in the latter year that the duchess built the schools at a cost of £100.[51] On the duke's death in 1839 the manor passed to his son and heir Richard Plantagenet, second duke of Buckingham and Chandos, who sold it in 1841 to the Rev. John Thomas Maine.[52] It remained in the latter's possession for over thirty years,[53] being sold on his death to Mr. Lee Lee of Dillington Park, Ilminster, Somerset, whose descendant, Col. Edward Hanning Hanning-Lee, is the present lord.

WITHER. *Argent a cheveron gules between three crescents sable.*

BRYDGES, Duke of Chandos. *Argent a cross sable with a leopard's head or thereon.*

A portion of the parish of Bighton, equal in value to the manor of Bighton held by the abbey of Hyde, still formed part of the bishop of Winchester's lands in the thirteenth and fourteenth centuries, and was held of the bishopric by the family of Gervays. In 1263 William Gervays granted the third part of a virgate of land to John de Bonehetone and Agnes his wife, to hold to them and their heirs of William and his heirs for the rent of a pound of cummin at Michaelmas.[54] William's heir was another William Gervays, who in 1332 obtained a grant of land in Bishop's Sutton and Ropley from Robert le Botiller.[55] On William's death his property in Bighton passed to his son Roger, who was holding it in 1346.[56] Roger's

[27] Pat. 12 Ric. II, pt. 1, m. 26.
[28] *Pope Nich. Tax.* (Rec. Com.), 213.
[29] Dugdale, *Mon.* ii, 449.
[30] *L. and P. Hen. VIII*, xvi, 718.
[31] Pat. 37 Hen. VIII, pt. 3, m. 39.
[32] Feet of F. Div. Cos. Mich. 37 Hen. VIII. Thomas was created earl of Southampton three days before the coronation of Edw. VI.
[33] Chan.Inq. p.m. (Ser. 2), cxcvi, No. 46.
[34] Feet of F. Hants, Hil. 40 Eliz.
[35] Chan. Inq. p.m. (Ser. 2), ccclxxxii, No. 25.
[36] Feet of F. Hants, Trin. 11 Chas. I.
[37] Inst. Bks. (P.R.O.).
[38] In 1687 Thomas Mompesson presented to the living (Inst. Bks. P.R.O.). He may have purchased the manor from William Eyre, but there seems to be no record of the sale. If he did, he must have sold it to John Pathurst before 1692.
[39] Recov. R. Trin. 6 and 7 Geo. II, m. 13, 14, and 15.
[40] Inst. Bks. (P.R.O.).
[41] Feet of F. Hants, Trin. 13 Geo. I.
[42] Inst. Bks. (P.R.O.).
[43] Warner, *Hist. of Hants*, i, 158.
[44] Recov. R. Trin. 6 and 7 Geo. II, m. 13, 14, and 15.
[45] Close R. 10 Geo. III, pt. 13, m. 24.
[46] Ibid.
[47] Inst. Bks. (P.R.O.).
[48] Recov. R. East. 10 Geo. III, m. 582. Joseph Eyre and John Eyre presented to the living in 1770 (Inst. Bks. P.R.O.), and Warner gives them as patrons in 1795; *Hist. of Hants*, ii, 236.
[49] Feet of F. Hants, Trin. 49 Geo. III.
[50] Inst. Bks. (P.R.O.).
[51] Sumner, *Conspectus Dioc. of Winchester*, 4.
[52] Close, 1841, pt. 86.
[53] His only sons, Henry Cracroft Maine and Arthur Francis Maine, predeceased him, dying respectively in 1864 and 1854. There are tablets to their memory in Bighton church.
[54] Feet of F. Hants, East. 47 Hen. III.
[55] Ibid. Mich. 5 Edw. III.
[56] *Feud. Aids*, ii, 334.

son Andrew in 1370 granted all his property in Bighton to William Wykeham, bishop of Winchester, for an annual payment of £20 for the term of his life.[57] The bishop granted the land to his college at Winchester,[58] and in 1428 it was stated that the warden of New College, Winchester, held in Bighton the fourth part of a fee in frankalmoign which Roger Gervays formerly held.[59]

CHURCH The church of *ALL SAINTS, BIGHTON*, consists of a nave and chancel without a structural division, 48 ft. long by 18 ft. wide, the chancel taking up 21 ft. of this length; north and south chapels and aisles, north-east vestry, south porch, and west tower. The exterior is uninteresting, all the windows except the east window of the chancel and a small cinquefoiled light west of the porch being single lancets of the plainest detail and modern appearance. The walls are plastered and the roofs red-tiled, that of the nave being carried without a break over the aisles.

The oldest feature in the church appears to be the north window of the chancel, a narrow round-headed light with inclined jambs on the inner splay, its outer face being hidden by the vestry roof. It may belong to the first quarter of the twelfth century, and, if in its original position, suggests a rebuilding and widening of the chancel at this date, the thickness of the wall in which it is set being 2 ft. 10 in. as against 2 ft. 5 in. in the nave. The dimensions of the present nave may be those of an earlier nave, 18 ft. by 27 ft., parts of whose walls may still exist above the arcades. In the last years of the twelfth century north and south aisles were added to this nave, with chapels to the east, a little wider than the aisles, and overlapping the chancel. The south chapel is 15 ft. long from east to west, while that on the north is only 7 ft., but the former may have been lengthened eastward at a later time, perhaps *c.* 1300, when work was evidently in progress here.

The chancel has an east window of three lights with modern tracery, but the rear arch and jambs, the latter with engaged angle shafts, date from *c.* 1300. Near the south-east angle of the church is a trefoiled piscina of the same date, with a projecting bowl for the drain, and close to it on the west a squint from the south chapel. The chapels open to the chancel with plain pointed arches of one square order, 6 ft. wide, with a chamfered string at the springing, of the same date as the nave arcades. The north chapel has an east window of two trefoiled lights, *c.* 1300, now blocked by the modern vestry, and in the east jamb of the arch opening to the chancel is a pretty trefoiled piscina of the same date as the window, with a shelf. The north window of the chapel is a plain lancet of the type already noted, with a semicircular rear arch. The south chapel has a south window of this type and a larger lancet at the east, on either side of which is a plain round corbel for an image. At the west ends of both chapels are thin walls carried by plain pointed arches, approximately on the line of the original chancel arch, which must have been destroyed at an early date.

The nave has arcades of two bays with pointed arches of a single square order, plain responds, and round central pillars with square capitals and moulded bases with angle spurs. The capital in the south arcade is scalloped, while that on the north has scrolled foliage, the date of the whole being about 1180–90. The aisles are lighted, very insufficiently, by lancets of the type already noted, and the ground stage of the tower, which is fitted with seats, is equally ill-lighted, though it has lancet windows on north, south, and west, as all are darkened with poor modern glass, and the absence of a clearstory in the nave is much felt. The south doorway has a pointed arch plastered over and showing no detail, and the south porch is plastered and of uncertain date. The tower, which is of masonry in the lower stage only, opens to the church with a modern pointed arch, and has a groined plaster ceiling. Its upper stages are of timber, the main beams being old, but covered with modern weatherboarding, and the tower is capped by a low slated roof. Of late years the church has been fitted with a good painted and gilt chancel screen, with a beam above it, and the roofs of nave and aisles have been panelled and coloured with very good effect.

The font, at the west end of the nave, is of a common late twelfth-century type, of Purbeck marble with a shallow square bowl having round-headed arcades on each face, and carried on a round central shaft. Four smaller angle shafts have disappeared, though their marble bases remain. Near the font, against the west respond of the south arcade, is set as a pedestal to a money-box a very good pillar piscina, with leaf-work on the bowl like that of the capital in the north arcade, but combined with leaves of normal thirteenth-century type. Its date is *c.* 1190.

In the tower are pits for three bells, but only one bell now remains, of early sixteenth-century date, with Roger Landon's lettering and stamps, the lion's head, groat, and cross, but not his founder's mark. The inscription, in black-letter capitals and smalls, is blundered, reading: SANCTA ANN OAR, for SANCTA ANNA ORA PRO NOBIS.

The plate comprises a large silver paten of 1696, and a communion cup, paten, and flagon of 1757.

The first book of the registers contains baptisms and burials from 1573 to 1805, and marriages 1573–1754; the second, baptisms and burials 1805–12, and the third, marriages 1754–1812. In the first book is a list of rectors from 1621.

ADVOWSON There was a church in Bighton at the time of the Domesday Survey.[60] The advowson has throughout followed the descent of the manor (q.v.).

CHARITIES In 1772 James, duke of Chandos, gave a bond to the rector and parish officers for £50 with interest at 5 per per cent., which is supposed to include a sum of £15 set aside to produce 15*s.* a year derived from the gift of John Pink in 1642. The fund is known as 'poor's money,' and with accumulations is now represented by £93 5*s.* consols with the official trustees.[61]

57 Feet of F. Hants, Hil. 43 Edw. III.
58 Pat. 15 Ric. II. pt. 2, m. 9.
59 *Feud. Aids*, ii, 359.
60 *V.C.H. Hants*, i, 471.
61 *Char. Com. Rep.* xii, 509.

BISHOP'S SUTTON

Sudtone (xi cent.) ; Sottone Bishop (xiii cent.) ; Sutton Bishops and Sutton episcopi (xiv cent.).

The parish of Bishop's Sutton, containing 3,739 acres of land and 9 acres of land covered with water,[1] is of irregular shape, the central part, in which the village stands, being in the comparatively low ground [250 ft. above sea level] by the head-waters of the River Alre, while a long strip runs north-east between the parishes of Bighton and Ropley, rising to a height of 500 ft. South of the river the boundary extends to the high ground above Cheriton Wood and Bramdean Common [450 ft.], its eastward limit being about a mile from West Tisted church. The village lies on the south side of the Alre, which takes its source about a mile to the east.[2] The main road from New Alresford to Alton runs through the parish from west to east, dividing it into two almost equal portions. The church stands a little back from the main road on the north, and is at the west end of the village, approached from a road which runs north from the village street. At the corner of this road is the Ship Inn, with its brightly-painted sign-board, a steamer on one side and a sailing-vessel on the other. Opposite is an ancient timber-built house, and eastward from this point the road is lined by cottages with narrow flower gardens in front. Beyond them is the Fox Inn, one of a group of little thatched cottages ; and past it on the outskirts of the village to the south of the road are several new villa residences and the large racing stables owned by Mr. A. Yates. As the road leaves the village and leads on to Ropley it passes through the low-lying country where the River Alre rises, running parallel with the railway, beyond which Sutton Beech Wood rises in the distance. About half a mile from Ropley Lodge a branch road runs southward to Bramdean, passing the fine beeches of Old Park Wood, which, extended at 95 acres and its timber valued at £60, was included in the sale of Bishop's Sutton manor to Sir John Evelyn in 1647.[3] Sutton Wood, Sutton Beech Wood, Hazel Wood, Barnett's Wood, Bower's Grove Wood, and Grant's Copse lie in the north-east of the parish.

There is a rifle-range in the south of the parish a little to the north of Old Park Wood. The soil round the village in every direction is a friable loam adapted to the growth of most crops, and particularly good for barley. Along the valley from the source of the river are rich meadow-lands, but on the outskirts of the parish, especially in the north-east and south-east, are tracts of land of an inferior quality. The subsoil is chalk, and hence the chief crops are wheat, oats, barley, and turnips. The parish contains 2,212½ acres of arable land, 1,028 acres of permanent grass, and 222½ acres of woods and plantations.[4] In 1685 Sutton Common or Windley Common, with the consent of the bishop of Winchester, was ordered to be inclosed and cultivated and divided among those copyhold and freehold tenements to which common of pasture there had always pertained.

At the same time twenty acres of the common were freed from tithes and annexed to the vicarage of Bishop's Sutton.[5] The remainder of the common lands were inclosed by Act of Parliament in 1796.

An interesting description of the manor as it was in the time of Edward VI exists at the Record Office[6] :—

'Sutton is distaunte from Alleresford a myle, and the mannor-howse being a verie olde howse, somtyme walled round abowte with stone, now decaied, well waterid with an olde ponde or moote adjoyning to it, and the ferme-howse being sett and within a stones cast of the said manner-howse, thowsing being but for a fermer, lying neer to Sutton churche. There is a xii score beneth the said manner-howse a corne-mill holden be copie, the ponde being the hed dam of the said mill, and a lyttell beneth that a faier great ferme-howse belonging to the Lorde Chief Justice and holden by copie of the manner of Sutten. The parke of Sutton being a lyttell myle from Sutton Towne, and all the ground betwixt bi the heighwaie side parcell of Sutton ferme, having allso a greate sheape pasture enclosed lyeing round abowte thone haulf of the parke, all plaine, callid the Parke Downe, bi estymacion 400 acres, parcell of the ferme, and the parke being abowte two myles good pasture, and muche wood lately fellid ther, the lodge standing faier upon a hill towards the northe end of the parke. A greate wood lying from the sowthewest corner of the parke, full west, a two myles in length, and being a quarter of a myle or more over in moost places set with beache and thicke upon the Lord's common, and a faier plaine comon belonging to the said Lordeshipp, lying all alongest the northe side of the said longe wood.'

The 'verie olde howse,' mentioned by the surveyor was no doubt the bishop of Winchester's palace, concerning which Mr. Duthy in his *Sketches of Hampshire* (1839) writes : 'Within the memory of many persons now living considerable vestiges of a strong and extensive building stood in the meadows to the north of the church, which were the dilapidated remains of an ancient palace of the bishops of Winchester. The walls were of great thickness and composed of flints and mortar, but it was impossible to trace the disposition of the apartments or the form of the edifice.' He conjectures that it was destroyed in the course of the Civil War. This conjecture seems a plausible one, for many skirmishes must have taken place in the neighbourhood both before and after the battle of Cheriton. In 1830 the remains of the palace were used as a malt-house, but only the site now remains. The bishops of Winchester kept a kennel from very early times in Bishop's Sutton.[7] In the

[1] *Pop. Ret.* 1901.

[2] Several springs close to the road mark the source of the river. After forming a series of ponds, in some of which watercress is cultivated, the river flows north-west towards Old Alresford Pond.

[3] Close, 23 Chas. I, pt. 10, No. 14.

[4] Statistics from Board of Agriculture (1905). In the reign of Edward VI the parish contained about 1,024 acres of wood: Park of Sutton 237 acres, New Park 89 acres, Wyneley 294 acres, Haylynge Grove 124 acres, and Ramscomble 280 acres (Eccl. Com. Ct. R. bdle. 136, No. 1).

[5] Eccl. Com. Ct. R. bdle. 152, No. 4.

[6] Duchy of Lanc. Rentals and Surv. 5 Edw. VI, bdle. 8, No. 22.

[7] Thus Mr. Duthy writes concerning it :—'A perennial pond in the midst of a group of trees on whose banks traces of old foundations used to be discoverable is pointed out by the traditional lore of the neighbourhood as marking the situation of the bishop's kennel' (Duthy, *Sketches of Hants*, 116).

early part of the thirteenth century mention is made of the expenses of keeping the king's hounds at Bishop's Sutton, which suggests that the king paid frequent visits to the bishop for hunting, and brought his hounds with him.[8] The bishops also had a park in Bishop's Sutton,[9] covering an area of 250 acres, which in 1649 was sold to Sir John Evelyn, together with 'all that warren of conies within it.'[10] A fair was held at Bishop's Sutton on the Feast of St. Giles and the following days from very early times. It seems to have been a popular one, for as long as it lasted seven men acted as constables (*custodinarii*),[11] and two others were employed to guard the woods, presumably against poachers.[12] As late as the middle of the last century two fairs were held—one on the Thursday after Holy Trinity and the other on 6 November,[13] but they seem soon afterwards to have died out. At the time of the Domesday Survey there were four mills,[14] but there is now only one, situated a little to the north-west of the site of the Bishop's palace, and probably occupying the site of the mill which in the reign of Henry VI was situated near the 'Court of Bishop's Sutton,'[15] and which in 1649 was described as 'all that messuage or tenement and mill commonly called Sutton mill, late parcel of the manor, consisting, as the same is now divided, of a dwelling house, two corn-mills, and a malt-mill, being now or late in the tenure of Jane Frost, widow.'[16] Among place-names mentioned in local records are 'Swetley, Pylk, Blayputtesthorne, Motynyard, Honeylynch, Windley, Verdelay, Brynkeworth, Mulcrofte, and La Holte.'[17]

William Howley, archbishop of Canterbury, 1828–48, was the only son of William Howley, vicar of Bishop's Sutton and Ropley, and was vicar of Bishop's Sutton from 1796 to 1813. He published several charges and sermons, and his library now forms part of the Howley-Harrison Library at Canterbury.

MANOR

It seems probable that part of the parish of *BISHOP'S SUTTON* was included in a grant made by King Ine to the church at Winchester in 701.[18] The lands are described as having been previously granted to the church by Ine's predecessor, Cynewalh. The northern boundary of the land thus granted started from Candover (Cendefer), thence to Bogmoor Hill (Bucgan oran), thence apparently along the northern boundary of Old Alresford parish, and into Medsted parish as far as Green Lane Farm (Grenmenes stigele). The eastern boundary started from Green Lane Farm, going south through Medsted parish, and entered Bishop's Sutton parish. The southern boundary started from Rampscomb Farm (Hremmescumbers geate), thence to Drayton Farm (Dregtune) in the parish of Bighton, and thence south-west as far as Tichborne (Ticceburnan). The western boundary passed north through Tichborne, Itchen Stoke, Swarraton, and Brown Candover. If the identifications of the place-names are correct, the land thus granted included the parishes of Godsfield, Bighton, Old and New Alresford, and Swarraton, and parts of the parishes of Brown Candover, Medsted, Bishop's Sutton, Tichborne, and Itchen Stoke. The part of the parish of Bishop's Sutton thus granted seems to have been the tongue of land which now separates the parishes of Bighton and Ropley. It seems probable that at the time of the grant this piece of land formed part of the parish of Bighton, from the fact that in the grant of Bighton by King Edwy to Hyde Abbey[19] there is mention of Brennescumbes Geat (probably for Hremmescumbes Geat), now probably represented by the modern Rampscomb Farm, which is situated in the north-east of the parish at the south of the tongue of land.

At the time of the Domesday Survey Bishop's Sutton was held by Count Eustace III of Boulogne.[20] In Edward the Confessor's reign it had been held by Earl Harold. Eustace IV, son of Eustace III, married Mary of Scotland, and had a daughter Maud, who became the wife of King Stephen. The manor thus came to the crown. In 1136 the king exchanged it with his brother Henry de Blois, bishop of Winchester, for the episcopal manor of 'Morden' (co. Surr.).[21] This exchange was confirmed by Henry II[22] and by Edward I.[23]

Edward II in 1324 confirmed a grant of a messuage and lands in Bishop's Sutton, afterwards called Western Court Farm (*q. v. infra*), made by Henry bishop of Winchester to William son of William de Overton.[24] The latter after the confirmation encroached upon the bishop's manor,[25] and in 1357 William de Edendon, bishop of Winchester, brought an assize of novel disseisin against William de Overton and Isabel his wife and Thomas the son of William and Isabel and others for unjustly disseising him of his 'free tenement in Bishop's Sutton.'[26] The case was decided in favour of the bishop, who recovered his seisin of the premises. The same year the bishop in the King's Court at Westminster recovered his seisin against William de Overton of three messuages, 3 virgates and 21½ acres of land, 10 acres of pasture, and 76 acres of wood, in Bishop's Sutton, Twyford, and Cheriton.[27]

Richard Fox, bishop of Winchester 1500–28, granted a lease of the manor in 1519 to Lewis Wingfield with the proviso that he should not let over the lease in his lifetime. Lewis on his death willed it to Henry Wingfield, who in his turn granted it in 1539 to Henry Norton,[28] who was still holding the site of the manor, in accordance with this indenture, in the reign of Edward VI.[29]

8 Eccl. Com. Ct. R. 159271 and 159280. King John was at Bishop's Sutton three times in 1205, once in 1208, and twice in 1212 (Itinerary of King John).

9 *Wykeham's Reg.* (Hants Rec. Soc.), ii, 413; Pat. 5 Edw. VI, pt. 5, m. 20.

10 Close, 1649, pt. 15, No. 2.

11 Eccl. Com. Ct. R. 159280.

12 Ibid. 159277.

13 Lewis, *Topog. Dict.* (1849).

14 *V.C.H. Hants*, i, 477.

15 Mins. Accts. 28 Hen. VI, bdle. 366, No. 6115.

16 Close, 1649, pt. 15, No. 2.

17 Mins. Accts. and Eccl. Com. Ct. R. *passim*.

18 Birch, *Cart. Sax.* i, 148.

19 *Liber de Hyda* (Rolls Ser.), 176.

20 *V. C. H. Hants*, i, 477.

21 *Hist. MSS. Com. Rep.* vi, App. 223.

22 *Pipe R. Soc.* x, 57 (Anct. Chart.).

23 Chart. R. 12 Edw. I, m. 5, No. 3.

24 Pat. 17 Edw. II, pt. 2, m. 23. William de Overton and Isabel his wife were already dealing with lands here in 1284 (Feet of F. Hants, 12 Edw. I), more than twenty years before they could have obtained the grant from Henry Woodlock, bishop of Winchester (1305–16).

25 Mins. Accts. 28 Hen. VI, bdle. 366, No. 6115.

26 Duchy of Lanc. Misc. bdle. 6, No. 14.

27 *Abbrev. Rot. Orig.* (Rec. Com.), ii, 246. William de Overton's encroachments seem to have made a deep impression, for as late as 1552 special mention is made of all messuages, lands, tenements, and hereditaments recovered from him (Pat. 5 Edw. VI, pt. 5, m. 20).

28 Duchy of Lanc. Rentals and Surv. bdle. 8, No. 22*b*.

29 Eccl. Com. Ct. R. bdle. 136, No. 1.

On 14 February, 1551, Stephen Gardiner, bishop of Winchester, was formally deprived of his bishopric, and the episcopal lands came into the king's hands.[30] With John Poynet's accession a month later Bishop's Sutton was included in the exchange of the episcopal lands for a fixed income of 2,000 marks,[31] and in 1551 was granted to Sir John Gate, together with the hundred and park.[32] Queen Mary, however, restored the manor to the bishopric in 1558.[33] In March, 1647, the manor of Bishop's Sutton was included in the sale of the bishop's lands, being purchased by Sir John Evelyn of West Dean (co. Wilts.), for £2,727 13*s.* 9*d.*[34] The manor and premises sold to him in this year, together with the royalties of hawking, hunting, fishing, and fowling, were stated to be of the annual value of £147 19*s.* 0½*d.*[35] Two years later the same John for £1,717 7*s.* 6*d.* purchased Sutton Park, which was then in the tenure of Sir Thomas Stewkley, an under-tenant, Sutton Mill, several parcels of meadow or pasture-ground commonly called Park Down and Brinkworths, and various other premises which were described as late parcels of the manor of Bishop's Sutton.[36] After the Restoration the manor was restored to the bishop, and at the present time the Ecclesiastical Commissioners as representing the bishops are lords of the manor.

SEE OF WINCHESTER. *Gules St. Peter's keys crossed with the sword of St. Paul.*

WESTERN COURT FARM (Westercourte xvi cent.; Westend Courte xvii cent.) is the farm described by the surveyor of Edward VI as 'the faier great ferme-house belonging to the Lorde Chief Justice and holden by copie of the manner of Sutten.'[37] No name is given to it in this survey, but in a perambulation of the parish made about the same time it was stated that Sir Richard Lyster was holding a capital messuage called 'Westercourte' with the lands belonging to it.[38] This farm was, as has been shown above, in origin the messuage and lands granted by Henry bishop of Winchester to William son of William de Overton. In 1346 William obtained a grant of free warren in his demesne lands of Bishop's Sutton,[39] which shows that by this time the property thus granted to him had developed into a manor. He died seised of the so-called manor of Bishop's Sutton in 1362, leaving a son and heir Thomas.[40] A Thomas de Overton, probably son or grandson of the latter, is described as 'of Sutton gentleman' in 1431.[41] From this date the history of the manor is uncertain until 1501, in which year John Wayte of Titchfield recovered seisin of the manors of Bishop's Sutton and Medsted against Eleanor Courte.[42] From John it passed with Medsted to Sir Richard Lyster, who died seised of it in 1553, his heir being his grandson Richard, aged twenty years nine months.[43] In the inquisition taken after his death it was called the manor of Bishop's Sutton, and was said to be held of the bishop of Winchester in socage for a money-rent. Some time after this Richard Lyster conveyed the manor to Sir John Leigh. The exact date is not known, but it was probably about 1557, for in that year there was a similar conveyance from Richard Lyster to Sir John Leigh of the manor of Coldrey in Froyle parish.[44] In 1567 Edward Fitzgarrett and Agnes his wife, daughter and heir of Sir John Leigh, and John Leigh conveyed the manor of Bishop's Sutton, as it was then called, to John More and Richard Bostock,[45] obviously in trust, as in 1575 John Leigh, nephew and heir-male of the same Sir John, died seised of it, leaving an infant son and heir John.[46] John's mother Margery married, as her third husband, William Killigrew, and in 1596 John Leigh, William Killigrew, and Margery his wife conveyed the manor in trust to William Onslowe and Walter Dickman.[47] John Leigh married Elizabeth West, daughter and heir of Sir Thomas West, and died in 1613, leaving a son and heir Thomas, aged six.[48] In the inquisition taken after his death he was said to be seised of the manor of Sutton. From Thomas West it seems to have passed to John Venables, who died in 1648 aged twenty-nine.[49] In 1685 it was called the manor of Westerne Court or Westend Court, and was in the possession of John Venables of Woodcote in the parish of Bramdean.[50]

LYSTER. *Ermine a fesse sable with three molets argent thereon.*

LEIGH. *Gules a cross engrailed and a border engrailed argent.*

The church of *ST. NICHOLAS, BISHOP'S SUTTON*, has a chancel 34 ft. 6 in. by 16 ft. 6 in. (at the west end 16 ft.), nave 55 ft. 4 in. by 19 ft. 8 in., north and south porches, and wooden bell-turret over the west end of the nave. The nave has been but little altered in its main features since its building about 1150, and preserves four original windows, plain round-headed lights set high in the walls, two on the north and two on the south, and north and south doorways set midway between the pairs of windows.[51] The west wall is 3 ft. 9 in. thick, and the east wall 3 ft. 5 in., the two side walls being only 3 ft. 3 in.: they are built of flint rubble

30 *V.C.H. Hants*, ii, 65. 31 Ibid. 66.

32 Pat. 5 Edw. VI, pt. 5, m. 20.

33 Pat. 4 and 5 Phil. and Mary, pt. 7, m. 24.

34 Close, 23 Chas. I, pt. 10, No. 14.

35 Various woods were included in the sale. Old Park Wood or Park Coppice, New Coppice, Ropley Wood and Charlwood Common. Messuages and lands other than customary lands or tenements held by copy of court roll were especially excepted from the sale.

36 Close, 1649, pt. 15, m. 2.

37 Duchy of Lanc. Rentals and Surv. 5 Edw. VI, bdle. 8, No. 22.

38 Eccl. Com. Ct. R. bdle. 136, No. 1.

39 Chart. R. 20 Edw. III, m. 4, No. 9.

40 Inq. p.m. 35 Edw. III, pt. 2, No. 18.

41 *Feud. Aids*, ii, 363.

42 De Banc. R. 17 Hen. VII, m. 249.

43 Chan. Inq. p.m. (Ser. 2), cxxiv, No. 22.

44 Feet of F. Hants, Hil. 3 and 4 Phil. and Mary.

45 Notes of F. Div. Cos. East. 9 Eliz.

46 Chan. Inq. p. m. (Ser. 2), clxxv, No. 82.

47 Feet of F. Hants, East. 38 Eliz.

48 Chan. Inq. p.m. (Ser. 2), cccxxxii, No. 162.

49 He is buried in Ropley Church.

50 Feet of F. Div. Cos. East. 1 Jas. II.

51 The east jambs of the doorways are exactly midway between the east and west walls of the nave.

with a few Roman bricks, brought to a face with a thick coating of brown mortar, which has been in great measure removed in the course of modern patching and pointing. Three of the four original external angles remain, with large ashlar quoins, the north-east angle having given way and been rebuilt in red brick with a heavy brick buttress. The north and south doorways have semicircular arches of two orders and a chamfered label, with nook-shafts with scalloped capitals to the outer order; the inner order being square and the outer moulded with a heavy roll, and in the case of the south doorway a line of beak-heads. The north doorway is as usual of plainer character, and has moulded wedge-shaped projections in place of the beak-heads. At the east end of the south wall a widely splayed lancet, *c.* 1220, has been added [52] to light the south nave altar, the plain circular piscina of which is in its sill. The original west window of the nave, if there was one, has given place to a two-light uncusped fourteenth-century window, and over it in the gable is a small narrow lancet, probably of the same date, and lighting the second stage of the wooden belfry. The belfry stands on four massive posts within the church, and from the absence of detail is difficult to date. It rises as a square above the nave roof, and its vertical sides are covered with oak shingles, with small wired openings near the eaves which admit air rather than light to the bell-chamber. It is finished with a pointed red-tiled roof. The chancel arch has evidently failed and been rebuilt with the old stones, and is now of two square orders of 13 ft. 9 in. span, bluntly pointed, and having nook-shafts on its western face with scalloped capitals which have lost their abaci.

BISHOP'S SUTTON CHURCH

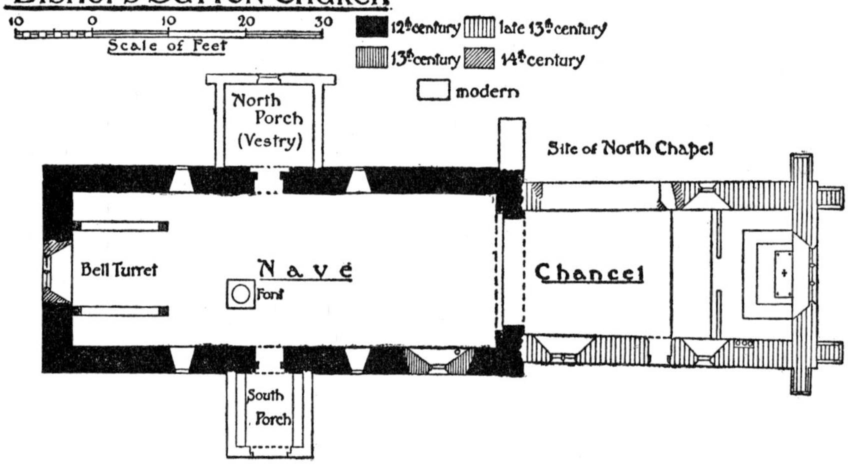

The chancel, though retaining at its west end the width of the twelfth-century chancel, has probably been entirely rebuilt in the last years of the thirteenth century, and no part of its masonry seems earlier than that date. It has an east window of three trefoiled lancets under an inclosing arch, the rear arch of which is moulded, and the arch having spread, the head of the central light has opened and been repaired by the insertion of an extra stone, so that the light is wider at the top than at the bottom. Externally pairs of modern buttresses are set at the angles of the east wall. In the north wall is a single trefoiled lancet, to the west of which was formerly a north chapel or vestry, now destroyed, a blocked squint from it, just west of the lancet, and commanding as usual the place of the high altar, being its only remaining feature. It is of the fourteenth century, as was probably the vestry, and the lower stones of the west jamb of the thirteenth-century lancet have been inserted when it was made. In the south wall is a trefoiled lancet corresponding to that on the north, and to the east of it a trefoiled piscina recess with three drains. It seems probable that the two outer drains are the original ones, the number being normal for the date, and the central drain a later addition, possibly superseding the other two at a time when the use of a pair of drains was abandoned. West of the window is a plain south doorway, and further west a two-light window widely splayed, with modern tracery of fourteenth-century style and a small quatrefoil in the head.

On either side of the east window are painted consecration crosses in red within a circular yellow border. None of the woodwork of the chancel is old except the roof, which has plain trussed rafters and was formerly ceiled, and the seventeenth-century altar rails, 2 ft. 9 in. high, with good turned balusters and a carved rail. On the floor are a number of marble slabs, on one of which are the mutilated brass figures of an armed man and his wife, *c.* 1500; while another retains the nails which once fixed another brass, and at the west of the chancel is a slab with indents of a shield and an inscription plate.

The south door of the nave is old, with its lock and strap hinges, and the roof is of the same type as that of the chancel, and probably of the same date. Both roofs, as well as that of the bell-turret, are covered with red tiles. The south porch of the nave is of eighteenth-century brickwork, with benches on east and west, and the north porch is modern and serves as a vestry, having no external door. On the south-east quoin of the nave are traces of two sundials. The font stands by the south door of the nave, large and baluster-shaped, with a moulded base, and inconveniently high. It is of eighteenth-century date. There are five bells, all re-cast by Warner of Cripplegate in 1893.

The plate includes a notable piece, a small silver paten of *c.* 1500, the centre being engraved with I H S on a gilt ground, in lettering of very good style and design. Besides this there is a communion cup of 1678, an alms dish of 1751, and a modern pewter flagon.

The registers are not preserved before 1711, the first book continuing till 1783, with marriages to 1754: the second has marriages 1754–1812, and the third baptisms and burials 1783–1812. There are also books of vestry minutes from 1842 to 1890.

[52] Its external stonework is all modern.

ADVOWSON At the time of the Domesday Survey there was a church in Bishop's Sutton with one hide attached, and it then belonged to Eustace count of Boulogne, lord of the manor of Bishop's Sutton.[53] Count Eustace granted the advowson of the church to the prior and convent of Merton (co. Surr.),[54] who continued to be patrons until the dissolution.[55] In 1539 Henry VIII granted the advowson to Charles Brandon, duke of Suffolk, in tail male.[56] He died in 1545, and his two sons Henry and Charles on 16 July, 1551, without male issue. In the latter year John Poynet succeeded to the see of Winchester and obtained a grant of the advowson of Bishop's Sutton.[57] Three months later, however, it was granted with the manor and hundred to Sir John Gate,[58] but was restored to the bishopric by Queen Mary in 1558.[59] However, in 1563 it was again taken from the bishop and granted to William Stanley, Lord Mounteagle, son and heir of Mary Mounteagle, who was one of the three daughters and co-heiresses of Charles duke of Suffolk.[60]

In 1604 James I granted the advowson to Anthony Crewe and William Starkey.[61] The following persons have since presented to the living: John Lowman in 1622; Thomas Jones in 1672; Mrs. London, widow, in 1711; Ann Alexander in 1724; James Brown Alexander in 1746; John Wood and George Jackson in 1757; the Rev. William Ralph and others in 1796; the Marquis of Abercorn in 1811; and the Marquis of Abercorn and wife in 1818[62]; Sir Thomas Baring, bart., and John Deacon are given as the patrons in 1831, and John Deacon as the patron in 1849.[63] The Misses Tanner were the patrons in 1878. The living is now a vicarage in the hands of the Peache trustees.

By an undated deed between the canons of the church of St. Mary of Merton, and Stephen, chaplain of Bishop's Sutton, it was agreed that Stephen should have all the tithes of the chapel of Ropley and all the land belonging to it by the rent of 3 marks, and that the canons should have all the tithes of the mother-church of Bishop's Sutton. In return for this convention Stephen gave up to the canons all the land which he held of them in Bishop's Sutton except his messuage in that vill.[64]

CHARITIES In 1796 under the provisions of a Private Act for the inclosure of the common fields in this parish and Crawley (34 Geo. III, cap. 81), an acre of arable land was awarded in respect of the right of the parish in a common field. The rent of £1 a year is applied by the churchwardens towards church expenses.[65]

BRAMDEAN

Brondene (xi cent.); Brundon, Brandun, and Brendon (xii cent.); Branden and Bromdene (xiii cent.).

Bramdean is a small parish, with an area of 1,237 acres, situated nine miles east from Winchester. The village, in the south-west of the parish, lies along the main road from Petersfield to Winchester, at an average height of 270 ft. above sea-level, the fall of the ground being westward, and close to the west boundary of the parish is the source of the little stream which runs through Cheriton and Tichborne to join the Alre below Alresford, a short distance above its junction with the Itchen. Bramdean Common in the north-east of the parish rises to 450 ft., and the view from the wooded ridge which forms its northern boundary is very striking. The open common slopes down, backed by woods on the south and east, and crossed by two roads, one running south-east towards West Meon, the other south-west to join the Winchester road in the middle of Bramdean village. At the south-west of the common is a group of thatched and timbered cottages, and beyond them the view opens out over the lower ground on which the village stands to the downs which form the western boundary of the Meon valley, Beacon Hill, five miles away, standing out against the skyline. The well-timbered park and grounds of Woodcote House, now occupied by Sir Francis Seymour Haden, are in the south-west angle of the parish, north of the Winchester road, and a short distance east of the village. The thatched and ivy-covered Manor Farm stands at the west of the village on the south side of the road, and beyond it is the Fox Inn with its large bay windows. On the higher ground to the south is a picturesque group of houses, to which a road strikes off at right angles. The rectory stands in the middle of the village, on the south of the road, at the point of junction with the road from Bramdean Common, and is in part of considerable antiquity, with some good early seventeenth-century panelling and beams. Further to the west is the church, standing half hidden by trees on the hillside to the south, and approached by a steep lane, at foot of which is a brick bridge over a dry water-course which runs all along the south side of the village street. To the east of the church is College Farm, an eighteenth-century red brick house of good style, with several well-designed chimney-pieces. The rectory meadow, planted with several fine trees, rises towards the church from the main road, and opposite to it on the north is Bramdean House. This house formed part of the property entailed by the Rev. Egerton Arden Bagot on his sister Honora, the wife of the Rev. the Hon. Augustus George Legge, about the middle of last century, and is at present the property of the Misses Legge, the heirs of the Rev. Augustus George Legge. The gravel valley in which the village lies was apparently in former times the bed of a river. At irregular intervals a spring bubbles up from what is called 'a pocket' in the chalk in Woodcote Park by the roadside, flows through the village and across the meadows to Hinton Ampner, and finally joins the Itchen at Cheriton. For years perhaps the brick arch of the church path and the channel by the roadside might be considered a needless precaution,

[53] *V.C.H. Hants*, i, 477.
[54] Dugdale, *Mon.* vi, 247.
[55] *Wykeham's Reg.* (Hants Rec. Soc.), i, 201; *Valor Eccl.* (Rec. Com.), ii, 49.
[56] Pat. 30 Hen. VIII, pt. 7, m. 23.
[57] Ibid. 5 Edw. VI, pt. 6, m. 26–29.
[58] Ibid. pt. 5, m. 20.
[59] Ibid. 5 and 6 Phil. and Mary, pt. 4, m. 6.
[60] Ibid. 5 Eliz. pt. 5, m. 18, 19.
[61] Ibid. 2 Jas. I, pt. 22.
[62] Inst. Bks. (P.R.O.).
[63] Samuel Lewis, *Topog. Dict.* (1831), iv, 248, and (1849), iv, 274.
[64] Cott. MS. Cleopatra C. vii, 73.
[65] *Char. Com. Rep.* xii, 509.

but as recently as the winter of 1903–4, after a very heavy rainfall during the summer and autumn, there was a swiftly-flowing stream covering the village street and flooding floors and cellars. Bramdean Lodge, the residence of Mr. Charles A. Linzee, lies to the north-west of the road from Bramdean Common, close to the schools. On the common is a small iron chapel of ease erected in 1883. Much of the land in Bramdean is a flinty loam on a subsoil of chalk well adapted for the growth of barley. Along the valley in which the village is situated the upper soil rests on a subsoil of gravel. The chief crops are wheat, oats, barley, and turnips. The parish contains 714¾ acres of arable land, 305½ acres of permanent grass, and 168 acres of woods and plantations.[1] Among place-names in Bramdean found in the thirteenth and fourteenth centuries are the following:—'Torte Acre, La Breche, Vineshawede, Sendrie londe, Setacres, Setesgrovesforlonge, Gritheth-horne, La Wogelonde, Hankeneweie, Eustrecumbe, and Schepehusezorne.'[2] A wood called 'Imbele' and a messuage and land called 'Jenettes lond' occur in inquisitions taken in the fifteenth century.

MANORS At the time of the Domesday Survey Miles the porter held *BRAMDEAN* of the king. Two freemen had held it, as three manors, in the time of King Edward.[3] The service by which Miles held must have been that of keeping the gate of the king's gaol of Winchester. This service and the personal character of the early owners seem to have determined the history of the manor.

In 1199 Henry de Bramdean, then owner of Bramdean, lodged his claim to the service of being porter of the gaol of Winchester, as his inheritance from his father, except one hundred shillingsworth of land which William de Hoe held of the grant of King Richard.[4] Documentary evidence between 1086 and 1198 is wanting, but the subsequent history would make it seem probable that the Bramdean family, being engrossed in pursuits which soon landed it in the grip of money-lenders,[5] neglected the service which they owed to the king of keeping his gaol in the city. As it was a matter of necessity that this service should be put in the hands of a responsible and local man, Richard I granted the one hundred shillingsworth of land before referred to to the less important personage who really performed the duty. The subsequent history of this land is shown under the heading of Woodcote (q.v.). For a time, however, there seems to have been some doubt as to the service, for in the *Testa de Nevill* it is said that Henry de Bramdean held Bramdean 'per custodiam gaole Winton quam dicit ad se pertinere.'[6]

From the year 1224 onwards Hugh de Bramdean was alienating his manorial lands piece by piece,[7] and finally in 1236 granted his capital messuage and 60 acres of land, together with 140 acres in Bramdean, 24*s.* quit-rent, Bramdean Wood, and the advowson of the church of Bramdean,[8] to the priory of Selborne in frankalmoign for the annual rent of 4*s.* and a covenant by the prior to give every year to Hugh and Maud his wife six loads of wheat and three of barley and 4 marks of silver, and to their son and heir Bartholomew 6 quarters of wheat and 1 of barley and 2 marks of silver.[9] The prior compounded with Alan Fitz-Warin,[10] John de Blakedown,[11] and Nicholas his brother, for their interests in the manor for £100,[12] but some fifteen or twenty years later Alan and John extorted 43 marks and £100 respectively for a final surrender of their claims.[13] Other premises in Bramdean which had been alienated by Hugh de Bramdean were bought up by the prior and convent as opportunity arose. Soon after 1260 Amice de la Cnolle released to the prior of Selborne all her right and claim in the wardship and marriage of John son and heir of Andrew de Caen, and in all his lands and tenements in Bramdean.[14] In 1289 Richard son and heir of Henry de la Putte granted lands in Bramdean to the priory.[15] Margery the widow of Walter Launcel in 1293 released to the priory the land which her father had given to her,[16] and some time afterwards her son Walter Launcel[17] made a further grant of 32 acres of land and 5 acres of wood. In 1302 the prior and convent of Selborne were pardoned for acquiring the lands in Bramdean from Richard de la Putte and Walter Launcel contrary to the statute of Mortmain.[18] By this time the priory was in possession of nearly, if not all, the lands in Bramdean formerly held by Hugh de Bramdean,[19] and the manor remained in its possession till the end of the fifteenth century. The affairs of the priory having become much involved, Bishop Waynflete, on 2 September, 1484, appointed Richard, prior of Newplace, and two others, to hold an inquiry as to annexing the priory to Magdalen College, Oxford, which the bishop had lately founded.[20] The decree of annexation was pronounced on 11 September, 1484, and in 1486 the manor of Bramdean was transferred with the other possessions of the priory to the college[21] and remains with them to the

[1] Statistics from the Board of Agriculture (1905).
[2] *Selborne Chart.* (Hants. Rec. Soc.), (Ser. 2), pp. 44–62.
[3] *V. C. H. Hants*, i, 503.
[4] Fine R. 1 John, m. 19.; Rot. Cur. Reg. 1 John, m. 16.
[5] *Selborne Chart.* (Hants. Rec. Soc.); (Ser. 2), 46, 47, and 51; Chart. R. 15 Hen. III.
[6] *Testa de Nevill* (Rec. Com.), 237.
[7] *Selborne Chart.* (Hants. Rec. Soc.), *passim.*
[8] Two years before Hugh de Bramdean had leased to Alan Fitz-Warin the 140 acres, 24*s.* rent, wood and advowson for the term of forty years to secure the sum of 40 marks advanced to pay off the Jew of Cambridge. *Selborne Chart.* (Hants. Rec. Soc.) (Ser. 2), 46.
[9] Feet of F. Hants. 20 Hen. III; *Selborne Chart.* (Hants. Rec. Soc.), (Ser. 2), 47 and 48. This grant was confirmed by Bartholomew in 1240; *Selborne Chart.* (Hants Rec. Soc.) (Ser. 2), 49.
[10] See footnote 8 above.
[11] John de Blakedown was the owner of 45 acres in Bramdean, which he had obtained by fine from Parnel, widow of William de Caen, in 1236 (Feet of F. Hants, East. 20 Hen. III). They formed her dowry from the free tenement in Bramdean, granted to her late husband by Matthew de Wallop, who had obtained it in his turn from Hugh de Bramdean early in the reign of Henry III; *Selborne Chart.* (Hants. Rec. Soc.), (Ser. 2), 44. The rest of William de Caen's property in Bramdean passed to Andrew de Caen.
[12] *Selborne Chart.* (Hants Rec. Soc.), (Ser. 2), 48.
[13] Ibid. 52 and 53.
[14] Ibid. 56. See footnote 11 above. These lands and tenements formed part of the premises originally granted by Hugh de Bramdean to Matthew de Wallop.
[15] Ibid. 60. These lands he had inherited from his father, to whom in 1254 Bartholomew de Bramdean had granted all the lands and tenements in Bramdean, which his sister Alice had once held; Ibid. 54.
[16] Ibid. She was the daughter of Henry de la Putte.
[17] He had inherited lands in Bramdean from his father, who between 1260 and 1270 had obtained a grant of a croft called La Breche and other premises from Andrew de Caen; Ibid. 57.
[18] Inq. a.q.d. 30 Edw. I, No. 124; Pat. 30 Edw. I, No. 22.
[19] *Pope Nich. Tax.* (Rec. Com.), 213.
[20] *V. C. H. Hants*, ii, 179.
[21] Ibid. ii, 55.

present day. The manor house was probably on the site of the modern 'Manor Place Farm,' which is at present occupied by Mr. George Anthony Dowling, to whom the college lets all its property in Bramdean except its woodland as one holding. The college has still certain manorial rights at Bramdean, particularly in regard to the common, but it no longer holds a court there as it does at Selborne.

Magdalen College, Oxford. *Lozengy ermine and sable a chief sable with three garden lilies therein.*

The manor of *WOODCOTE* (Wudecote, Wedecota, Wodecot, Wutecot, Woodecote, and Woodcot, xiii cent.; Wodekote, xiv cent.; Woodcott, xvi cent.), as has been shown, owed its origin to the neglect of the family of Bramdean to perform the service of keeping Winchester Gaol. King Richard I granted the manor to a certain William de Hoe to hold by this service.[22] As soon as King John came to the throne, Henry de Bramdean disputed William de Hoe's claim to the custody of the gaol, though not to the ownership of Woodcote.[23] John, however, disregarded the claims of both Henry and William, and in 1204 bestowed the custody of the gate of the castle and gaol of Winchester, together with the land of Woodcote, appertaining to the custody, upon Matthew de Wallop to hold to him and his heirs for ever.[24] In return, Matthew and his heirs were to mew the royal hawks within Winchester Castle, finding one servant at their own cost to mew them and to keep them throughout the whole mewing season. They were also to find the cost of three harehounds in the same castle throughout the same season. It is clear from the patent rolls that Matthew was still holding the office of warden of the gaol in 1207[25] and 1215.[26] In the latter year he evidently wished to resign, but the king ordered that, if he did so, Henry de Bramdean should receive the office with its appurtenances upon the payment of 20 marks.[27] Soon after the accession of Henry III, William de Hoe pressed his claim anew, this time against Matthew de Wallop.[28] He does not seem to have been successful, however, for Matthew was seised of the custody of the gaol with its appurtenances at the time of his death ten years later.[29] After his death the king committed the custody of the gaol to Warin Fitz-Geoffrey,[30] and ordered the sheriff of Hampshire to deliver over to Warin, without delay, the lands in Woodcote which appertained to the custody. Warin evidently neglected his duties as warden, and owing to the escape of prisoners he was at one time deprived of the custody of the prison and the lands appertaining to the service, but they were eventually restored to him,[31] though not for long. William de Hoe seems to have taken advantage of his adversary's inefficiency to press his claim, and eventually obtained restitution of his rights.[32] He was succeeded by Robert de Hoe, who granted the manor and service to Nigel Fitz-Robert and his heirs. This grant was confirmed by King Henry III in 1246.[33] In 1249 the same Nigel, described as 'son of Robert of Winchester,' re-granted the manor to Robert de Hoe to hold of Nigel and his heirs for the term of his life.[34] In 1270 Nigel, described as 'Nigel Beket, of Southampton,' died seised of the manor and service.[35]

His heir was his son Valentine, aged eighteen, who died seised of the manor in 1307, leaving a son and heir Richard, aged twenty-seven.[36] The latter died in the same year without issue, and was succeeded by his brother Valentine, aged twenty-four.[37] On Valentine's death in 1336 the manor passed to his son and heir Valentine, aged twenty-three.[38] In 1344 the latter obtained licence to convey the manor to trustees for purposes of settlement on himself and his heirs,[39] and this was done by fine in the following year.[40] The date of the inquisition taken after Valentine's death is 1354, but the manuscript is all but illegible, and it is impossible to decipher the date of his death and the name of his heir.[41] His widow Alice died in 1359,[42] and in the inquisition taken after her death it was stated that she was seised of the manor for the term of her life of the inheritance of William Beket, parson of the church of Colemore, the brother and heir of her deceased husband. In 1360, however, the escheator of Hampshire was ordered to take Woodcote into the king's hands on the grounds that certain prisoners had escaped from Winchester Gaol.[43] In the same document there is mention of the fees which the wardens of the gaol were accustomed to receive, viz.: for every prisoner in the gaol they received 4*d.* and for every prisoner brought up before the king's justices 5*d.* for irons.[44] The manor remained in the hands of the crown till 1363, when the escheator was ordered to give full seisin to William Beket upon receipt of a reasonable relief.[45] Two years later, however, the manor was in possession of John, who is described as son of Valentine Beket. It does not seem at all probable that he was the son of Valentine and Alice Beket, for there is no mention of him in the inquisition taken after Alice's death. He may perhaps be identified with John Beket, son and heir of a certain Valentine Beket who died in 1372 seised of the office of door-keeper of Winchester Castle by the service of finding two armed men within the tower of the king's castle of Winchester to guard it in time of war.[46] John may have

22 The original grant does not seem to be extant, but there are two references to it in later documents. Fine R. 1 John, m. 19; *Bracton's Note Book*, iii, 315.
23 Fine R. 1 John, m. 19; Rot. Cur. Reg. 1 John, m. 16.
24 Chart. R. 5 John, m. 7.
25 Pat. 9 John, m. 6.
26 Pat. 16 John, m. 6.
27 Close, 17 John, m. 23.
28 *Bracton's Note Book*, iii, 315.
29 *Testa de Nevill* (Rec. Com.), 237; Close, 11 Hen. III. ms. 17 and 20.
30 Close, 11 Hen. III, m. 20.; Pat. 11 Hen. III, m. 8.
31 Close, 11 Hen. III, m. 5; 15 Hen. III, m. 11; and 16 Hen. III, m. 1.
32 Close, 18 Hen. III, m. 33.
33 Chart. R. 30 Hen. III, m. 6.
34 Feet of F. Hants, Hil. 33 Hen. III.
35 Inq. p.m. 54 Hen. III, No. 3. Presumably Robert de Hoe predeceased him. Nigel's descendants were called Beck or Bekke. His surname is given as Beket, Beck, or Becch. The family was also sometimes called 'de Wodecote'; Assize R. Mich. 8 Edw. I.
36 Inq. p.m. 35 Edw. I, No. 12.
37 Ibid. 1 Edw. II, No. 39.
38 Ibid. 10 Edw. III, No. 30.
39 Pat. 18 Edw. III, pt. 1, m. 21.
40 Feet of F. Hants, Mich. 19 Edw. III.
41 Inq. p.m. 28 Edw. III, No. 13.
42 Ibid. 36 Edw. III, pt. 1, No. 14.
43 *Abbrev. Rot. Orig.* (Rec. Com.) ii, 257.
44 Custodes gaole predicte percipere consueverunt de quolibet prisone vivente ad dictam gaolam quatuor denarios, et de quolibet prisone coram justiciis regis deliberato pro ferris quinque denarios nomine feodi.
45 *Abbrev. Rot. Orig.* (Rec. Com.), ii, 276.
46 Inq. p.m. 46 Edw. III (1st Nos.), No. 7.

been a kinsman of William Beket, and it is possible that William, being an ecclesiastic, conveyed the office of warden of the gaol with all its appurtenances to him. In 1367 John son of Valentine Beket granted the manor of Woodcote to John Marshall and Agatha his wife, to hold to them and their issue by the same service.[47] In the inquisition *ad quod damnum* which was taken on this occasion, mention was made of the fact that holders of the manor were to repair the buildings of the gaol and get irons for the prisoners from the proceeds of Woodcote. John, however, neglected his duties and allowed the prison to fall into such bad repair that many prisoners escaped. Hence he was brought before the king's justices in 1372 and was fined 100*s.* for the escape of each prisoner and 7*s.* 6*d.* for the bad state of the gaol,[48] but was still allowed to keep the manor, of which he died seised in 1391, leaving a son and heir Edmund, aged thirty-four.[49] Edmund died seised of the manor in 1427, and on his death Woodcote passed to his daughter Joan, the wife of John Frampton.[50] Five years later John Frampton and Joan his wife settled the manor, 4*s.* 6*d.* rent and the rent of one pound of pepper and two pounds of wax, upon John Thornes and his heirs.[51] John Thornes conveyed the manor to trustees in 1453 for purpose of settlement on Elizabeth his daughter and her husband John Quydhampton.[52] The latter died seised of the manor in 1490, his heirs being his four daughters, Margaret wife of Edward Cowdrey, Anne wife of John Conewey, Elizabeth wife of Thomas Morley, and Iseult Quydhampton.[53] The manor was probably sold by the four co-heirs, as in 1505 it was settled upon William Tisted and Maud his wife and the heirs of William.[54] Six years later William died seised of the manor, his heir being his brother Thomas, aged forty and more.[55] On the death of Thomas Tisted without issue a few years later the manor was divided among his four sisters Amy, Christian, Thomazin, and Iseult, or their descendants.[56] In 1535 Henry VIII by letters patent granted the office of constable of Winchester Castle to Thomas Uvedale, but no mention is made of the manor of Woodcote in the grant.[57] It is possible that he had bought up the four moieties of the manor previous to this date, but there seems to be no record of the purchase.[57a] He was, however, seised of the manor in 1548, in which year it was settled on himself and his wife and their heirs on his marriage with Elizabeth Ringwood.[58] Their son Anthony Uvedale died seised of the manor in 1597, his heir being his daughter Eleanor, the wife of Richard Bruning.[59] Two years later the bishop of Winchester wrote to Secretary Cecil[60] that he had committed a certain priest, Edward Kenyon, to Winchester gaol 'in as strict manner as he could devise.' He had, however, 'been rather daily feasted as a guest than safely kept as a traitor, and had been suffered most wilfully to escape upon the very day that he had expected to be produced.'[61] An examination was held by order of the bishop, the results of which he sent to Cecil in 1599, adding that 'the manor of Woodcot in Hampshire was given to the ancestors of one Anthony Uvedale, a recusant lately dead, for the safe keeping of the gaol'; and that he 'fearing the danger of the law and loath that the prisoners for recusancy should come into any man's keeping but at his own appointing, conveyed the inheritance of the gaol with the aforesaid manor to Anthony Brewning his daughter's son, a child of seven years of age, his father and mother being both recusants'; and, therefore, 'no man has the keeping of the gaol but such as will favour recusants.' However, the child was a ward for the tenure, and hence both he and the manor were at Cecil's dispensation until he should come of age, 'if this and such other wilful escapes and releasing of prisoners do not endanger the inheritance and reduce it back into the queen's hands.' In 1608 Richard Bruning, father of Anthony, had forfeited the manor and the custody of the gaol because of recusancy.[62] On Richard's death the manor descended to Anthony, and there is a reference to his tenure of the manor in a fine of 1625.[63] The tenure of the manor was changed from socage in chief to knight's service in capite in 1628 in order to enable Anthony and his wife Mary to dispose of the manor more easily,[64] and in the same year Anthony held Winchester Gaol and the manor of Woodcote by the service of the fortieth part of a knight's fee.[65] In February, 1651, it was stated that until Anthony cleared himself before the committee for compounding his rents were to be stayed.[66] However, he was twice dealing with the manor in 1652,[67] and was succeeded by his son Charles Bruning who was holding Woodcote in 1663.[68] Before 1677 the manor passed by purchase into the family of Venables,[69] with whom it remained[70] until the death of Catharine Venables in 1789, when it descended to her kinsman, Edward Hooper of Hurn Court,

UVEDALE. *Argent a cross moline gules.*

[47] Inq. a.q.d. File 355, No. 2. *Abbrev. Rot. Orig.* (Rec. Com.), ii, 290. Feet of F. Hants, Mich. 41 Edw. III.

[48] Coram Rege R. Trin. 45 Edw. III.

[49] Inq. p.m. 15 Ric. II (1st Nos.), No. 42.

[50] Ibid. 6 Hen. VI, No. 16.

[51] Feet of F. Hants, East. 10 Hen. VI. In 1456, after Joan Frampton's death without issue, her cousins, the three daughters and coheirs of Walter Marshall, sued Nicholas Upton, William Husey, and John Thornes and Agnes his wife for the manor, but the case was dismissed owing to the death of William Husey (De Banc R. Hil. 34 Hen. VI, m. 311).

[52] Inq. p.m. 4 Edw. IV, 1st Nos. No. 36.

[53] Chan. Inq. p.m. (Ser. 2), vi, No. 33.

[54] De Banc. R. East. 21 Hen. VII, m. 430. Chan. Inq. p.m. (Ser. 2), xxvi, No. 13.

[55] Chan. Inq. p.m. (Ser. 2), xxvi, No. 13.

[56] Berry, *Hants Gen.* 29.

[57] Pat. 27 Hen. VIII, pt. 2, m. 8.

[57a] Nicholas Tichborne bought up the four moieties of the manor of West Tisted of which Thomas Tisted had also died seised. By a fine of 1519 Thomas Shalden and Margaret his wife, who was a descendant of one of the four Tisted sisters, dealt with the fourth part of the manors of Woodcote and West Tisted (Feet of F. Hants, Mich. 11 Hen. VIII).

[58] Memo. R. L.T.R. Hil. 1 Eliz. m. 81.

[59] Chan. Inq. p.m. (Ser. 2), cclviii, No. 41.

[60] S.P. Dom. Eliz. cclxxiii, 23.

[61] This was natural, since the Bruning family was always strictly recusant.

[62] Pat. 6 Jas. I, pt. 3, m. 19.

[63] Feet of F. Div. Cos. East. 1 Chas. I.

[64] S.P. Dom., Chas. I, civ, 20.

[65] Pat. 4 Chas. I, pt. 5.

[66] *Cal. of Committee for Compounding*, i, 380.

[67] Feet of F. Div. Cos. Trin. 1652.

[68] Subs. R. 15 Chas. II, bdle. 26, No. 247.

[69] In Woodcote House there is a rain-water head of 1677 with the Venables initials.

[70] Feet of F. Div. Cos. East. 1 Jas. II. In Bishop's Sutton Church are buried Jane wife of James Venables of Woodcote (1727), their youngest daughter Philippa (1776), their eldest daughter Jane, wife of Henry Collins (1779), and their second daughter Catharine (1789).

formerly M.P. for Christchurch, who only occasionally visited it, and bequeathed it on his death to the earl of Malmesbury. The latter in 1809 sold Woodcote to a speculator called Lipscombe, who, while Mr. Greenwood of Brookwood was deliberating on the purchase, bought the place and felled the timber. Mr. Greenwood, however, repented of his mistake, and eventually bought the manor without the timber at the price he had demurred to give for the estate. Woodcote remained in the Greenwood family until 29 September, 1900, when Mr. Ulick Burke, the present lord of the manor, purchased it.[71]

Woodcote House is a good example of a country house of the late sixteenth or early seventeenth century, to which time the oldest parts of it seem to belong. It is built of red brick of two stories with an attic, with four gables on its principal front, which faces the west, and two at the north end. All the windows were originally mullioned, but except in the gables the mullions have given place to sashes; those which remain are of brick, plastered, and the windows have lead latticed lights. The house formerly had wings running westward at the north and south, and inclosing a forecourt with a wall and gateway on the west; but nothing of this remains. The main entrance is by a porch on the west front, and the arrangement of the house is simple, there being four rooms on each floor in a line from north to south, opening into each other, the staircase being on the north-east. There are fine wooden chimney-pieces in three of the first-floor rooms and in the north room on the ground floor, the latter probably of somewhat later date than the others, which appear to be original. That in the second room from the north on the first floor has been freed from the paint which unfortunately covers the rest, and shows the remains of decoration in black and gold. In this room also is some tapestry, and some of the original panelling exists. On the ground floor, the south room, and that next to it, to which the porch opens, are fitted with good early eighteenth-century panelling. The staircase has solid turned balusters, and the doorways opening on to it have moulded oak frames with nail-studded doors hung by wrought-iron strap hinges. At the stair-head in the attics is a screen formed of two ranges of balusters like those of the staircase, and within it a room known as the 'priest's chamber,' from which a smaller room opens. Two of the rain-water heads on the west front are dated, one being of 1630, when Anthony and Mary Bruning were living at Woodcote, and the other of 1677, when it had passed to the Venables family.

BURKE. *Or a cross gules with a lion sable in the first and fourth quarters.*

At the present time the house contains a number of fine paintings and drawings, including many from the hand of its occupant, Sir Francis Seymour Haden.

At the back of the house is a charming walled garden, with picturesque red brick stables to the south, and at the south-east of the main block is the old brew-house, now used as a workroom.

CHURCH

The church of *ST. SIMON AND ST. JUDE, BRAMDEAN*, has a chancel 16 ft. 6 in. by 13 ft. 6 in., nave 36 ft. 8 in. by 16 ft. 8 in., with north porch, south vestry, and large south transept, and a wooden bell-turret over the west end of the nave. The oldest details are the north doorway of the nave and the chancel arch, which date from *circa* 1170, and if the walls of the nave are older than this there is nothing to show it, all the masonry being covered with plaster inside and out.

The chancel has undergone a good deal of restoration, and of the south wall of the nave only the west end is old, the rest having been destroyed by the addition of a large modern south transept 16 ft. 9 in. wide with a vestry to the east of it. An old drawing of the south side of the church, hanging in the vestry, shows in the south wall of the nave two curious windows, each of two round-headed lights, and a square-headed low-set window near the east end of the wall. The traces of one of these double windows may still be seen in the outer face of the wall just west of the transept, set rather high in the wall after the fashion of early windows, but there is nothing to fix their date, whether early or comparatively modern. The church is roofed with red tiles, and the west bell-turret is boarded and finished with a short octagonal shingled spire. The chancel was repaired and reroofed in 1863, and has a modern east window of three lancets under an inclosing arch. In both north and south walls are two plain and short lancet windows with modern rear arches, the external masonry being too much covered with plaster to show its character, but the windows are probably contemporary with the walls in which they are set and may belong to the end of the twelfth century.

The chancel arch is pointed, of two orders, with the springing line considerably below the level of the capitals and a small chamfer on the angles. The capitals have plain scrolled leafwork, and there are

WOODCOTE HOUSE, BRAMDEAN.

[71] Information given by Mr. Ulick Burke.

nook shafts on the west face and half-round shafts on the jambs with spreading moulded bases.

The nave has a square-headed fifteenth-century west window of three cinquefoiled lights, and above it in the gable a plain lancet of uncertain date. The north door has a round arch of one square order, with hollow chamfered abaci and a small chamfer on the jambs, but beyond this there are no old masonry details. East of the doorway are a large two-light window, with a quatrefoil in the head, and a single lancet high in the wall to light the pulpit, and west of the doorway a two-light window, all being modern. In the south wall is the door to the modern vestry and a wide arch to the south transept, which contains nothing of note. The north porch is of red brick, and modern.

The nave roof is old, with trussed rafters, and has been ceiled, and the chancel roof is a modern copy of it, dating from 1863. A west gallery in the nave was removed in 1877. The south door of the nave is old, made of two thicknesses of board, with old strap hinges and a wooden lock case, but otherwise all the fittings of the church are modern, except the altar table, which is of early seventeenth-century date, and on the south side of the chancel is a credence table made up from parts of the seventeenth-century altar rails, which were unfortunately taken away during 'restoration.'

The font, near the north door of the nave, is modern, of thirteenth-century style.

The bell-turret contains two small bells, and rests partly on the west wall of the nave and partly on a tiebeam, its angle posts not coming down to the floor of the church.

The plate consists of a chalice of 1842 with paten of 1852; a flagon given by Dame Frances Gould to the parish in 1731, the lid bearing the London date-letter for 1721 and the body that for 1706; and a silver-gilt alms dish of 1845, given in 1852.

The first book of the registers begins in 1573, containing baptisms and burials to 1773, and marriages to 1776. In the first pages is a list of benefactions from 1618 to 1675, recording among other things the gift of a silver chalice and paten in the latter year by Stephen and Catherine Green, and at the end are some paper leaves with a record of briefs from 1659 to 1663. The second book goes from 1774 to 1813, and there is a set of churchwardens' accounts from 1779 to 1852.

The small modern district church on Bramdean Common possesses a silver chalice and paten of 1838.

The advowson of the church followed the descent of the manor of Bramdean until 1234, when Hugh de Bramdean leased it for forty years to Alan Fitz-Warin.[72]

ADVOWSON

In 1236 Hugh de Bramdean granted it to the prior and convent of Selborne,[73] and this grant was confirmed by Hugh's son Bartholomew in 1240.[74] However, in 1250 John de Blakedown held the advowson, and granted it, together with the land he held in Bramdean by the gift of his brother Sir Nicholas, to the prior and canons of Selborne for £100.[75] The church was worth £5 per annum in 1291.[76] In 1395 the living was in the gift of the bishop of Winchester,[77] who continued to be patron till 1858,[78] when it was transferred to the crown, the bishop receiving in exchange the patronage of the rectory of All Saints, Southampton.[79] The living is at present a rectory in the gift of the Lord Chancellor.

CHARITIES

(1) In 1862 James Turner, by will proved this date, bequeathed to the rector and churchwardens £100 upon trust to invest the same and to pay the dividends on St. Thomas's Day equally among three of the most deserving poor families, members of the Church of England residing in the parish. Invested in £102 19*s*. Consols.

(2) In 1863 the Hon. Mrs. Honora Legge, by will proved this date, directed that £200 Consols should be transferred to the official trustees of charitable funds, the dividends to be remitted to the officiating minister of Bramdean, to be expended by him in purchasing candles and soap to be given to the wives and widows of labourers living in the parish.

(3) In 1893 Mrs. Louisa Frances Katharine Bishop, by will and codicil proved this date, directed her executors to purchase £170 Consols and to pay the dividends annually at Christmas among the mothers of children most regular in attendance at the Sunday school, with a provision for accumulations in case of unpunctual attendance. The legacy (less duty) is represented by £152 14*s*. £2 10*s*. per cent. annuities.

The same testatrix bequeathed £2,000 to be invested and income applied in providing divine service in the church on Bramdean Common, and other purposes. The legacy (less duty) was invested in £1,815 14*s*. 9*d*. £2 10*s*. per cent. annuities.

In 1898 Mrs. Honora Augusta Cowper-Coles, by codicil to her will proved this date, bequeathed £120 2½ per cent. annuities to the officiating minister of Bramdean, dividends to be applied in providing warm winter clothing for poor women. The several sums of stock are held by the official trustees of charitable funds, and the incomes of the charities are duly applied.

72 *Selborne Chart.* (Hants Rec. Soc.), (Ser. 2), 46.
73 Ibid. 47, 48.
74 Ibid. 49.
75 Ibid. 52.
76 *Pope Nich. Tax.* (Rec. Com.), 211.
77 *Wykeham's Reg.* (Hants Rec. Soc.), i, 199.
78 Ibid. i, 228, and Inst. Bks. (P.R.O.)
79 *Lond. Gaz.* 31 Aug. 1858, 3978.

HEADLEY

Hallege (xi cent.), Hertelegh (xiii cent.), Hedle and Hetlegh (xiv cent.), Hedley (xv cent.), Hethelie (xvi cent.), Hedleigh (xvii cent.), Heathley (xviii cent.).

Headley is a large parish near the borders of Surrey and Sussex containing 6,871 acres of land and 52 acres of land covered with water, of which 1,511½ acres are arable, 1,117½ permanent grass, and 852 woods and plantations.[1] The village lies about 4½ miles north of Liphook Station on the London and South-Western Railway, and is reached from it by narrow winding lanes. It extends north-west of Bramshott to the Surrey border, its high ground commanding a wide and picturesque view of the romantic scenery of the three counties, having Hindhead and its neighbours the Devil's Punch Bowl and the Devil's Jumps prominently outlined to the east. The village lies round a heath, for, as the name implies, Headley was in origin a settlement in a clearing. To the south-east of the village is Hilland, the residence of Mr. W. J. Phillips, J.P. The schools, with a recreation-ground adjoining, are on the heath itself. To the west of the heath is the rectory and the church of All Saints with its massive ivy-covered tower, and near by is the Holly Bush Inn, mentioned by Cobbett in his *Rural Rides*. The old pound still exists, and a chestnut tree marks the spot where the stocks once stood, though they themselves have disappeared. The road on the east of the heath makes a sharp descent past Arford House and Curtis's Hill, thence it turns by the Wheatsheaf Inn to the east, and climbs up steadily to Grayshott. The country through which it passes is most beautiful—dense pine-woods alternating with the wild stretches of heather which cover Headley Common, but there are signs that it will soon become as popular for a residential neighbourhood as Hindhead or Haslemere. Many roads are already marked out and many villas already built. Grayshott is a district which is fast becoming populous, owing to the growing appreciation in which the charming scenery of Wagner's Wells is held.

Thirty years ago there was only one primitive grocer's shop in the hamlet, then it became a receiving place for letters, and now the village has a whole street of shops and a fully equipped post and telegraph office. The late Lord Tennyson lived here for a short time, but finding the spot not sufficiently secluded removed to the house which he had built on the top of Blackdown. Grayshott Hall, near the village, is the residence of Mr. A. Ingham Whitaker. Other hamlets in the parish are Lindford with its inn, the 'Royal Exchange,' Hearn, Deadwater, Hollywater, Stanford, the property of Major-General W. Brownlow, C.B., of Eveley House, Wishanger, with its fish-pond in the north of the parish near Frensham Great Pond, Sleaford, and Barford. As most of these names imply, Headley is very well watered, this district being rich in shotts or natural springs, concerning which the late Mr. Shore wrote as follows :—'This is a county of springs, the most interesting of which are in the beautiful glen-scenery of Wagner's Wells at an elevation of from 400 to 500 ft. above the sea. The Wagner's Wells stream flows from Grayshott to Ludshott through a series of beautiful ponds at different elevations until it joins the Wey near Bramshott flour-mill. This southern Wey then flows past Bramshott paper-mill to Lindford, where it receives the streams from Woolmer Forest. One of these streams flows, except in dry seasons, from Woolmer Pond, and the other with which it unites has several branches, one of which flows from a pond on Weaver's Down, another from Forest Mere Pond and through Roody Pond, another from Wheatsheaf Pond and Bohunt Pond, and another from Fowley Pond. These streams unite and form the Holly-

Headley Mill

water at an elevation of about 245 ft. above the sea. . . Headley is one of the least known of our Hampshire villages, but is one of the most interesting. It has a character of its own, plenty of sand on a clay or loamy outcrop, and in one part of it, the part called Arford, plenty of water and springs at an elevation of about 255 ft.'[2]

In a perambulation of the parish taken in the reign of Edward VI five mills are mentioned: one built on Frensham Pond and held by Richard Drake for a rent of 13*s.* 4*d.*, another lying between the highway called 'Grevat Lane' on the west and a river bank and a meadow called 'Kyttsmede' on the east, a fulling-mill and a water-course held by Thomas Fygg, a mill held by Richard Gyll, and a messuage and fulling-mill abutting on Lacyes Marsh.[3] At the present day there

[1] Statistics from Board of Agriculture (1905).

[2] *P. and Proc. of the Hants Field Club,* ii (1), 52.

[3] Eccl. Com. Ct. R. bdle. 136, No. 1.

are the following six water-mills in the parish: Park Mill in Headley Park, formerly a corn-mill, used for electric light and pumping; Headley Mill to the west of the village, on the River Wey, used for corn; Lower Stanford Mill, formerly a corn-mill, but now disused; Upper Stanford Mill, used for electric light, formerly for paper-making; Barford Upper Mill, used for corn, and Barford Lower Mill, now disused, formerly used for flock, and previous to that for paper.

Broxhead Common, Headley Common, and Wishanger Common lie within the parish. The first of these originally formed part of Woolmer Forest, and is situated in the north-west of the parish. Wishanger and Headley Commons lie respectively in the north-east and south-east corners. It was an important day for Headley when Parliament sanctioned the inclosure of the forest land.[4] Some idea of the extent of the waste prior to that time may be gained from the fact that although large portions in this and adjoining parishes were disafforested and brought under cultivation by the Act no less than 8,000 acres are still held by the crown as a royal forest. There seems to be no doubt that Headley Park, the seat of Mr. C. W. McAndrew, was once part of the forest, and the same may be said of Eveley, the seat of Major-General W. V. Brownlow, C.B. The surveyor of the reign of Edward VI made the following return concerning the woods and wastes of 'Hethle': 'Wood of Hethle and waste being in the wood contain 240 acres, lying in length on the east of Graueshote, in length between Kyngswodd Bottom on the south and Graueshot and Shirley Dene on the north, and on the west abutting on Brokesbottom, and on the east abutting on Les Merke Okes, of which the wood contains 140 acres and the waste 100 acres. There is another waste containing 100 acres, lying on the east of Hetheleshyll and north-west even to Graueshott. There is also another waste called Eveley Marshe and Pryor's lose. There is another waste called Lacyes marshe lying on the west of Stanford. Another waste lies at the west of Erthpytlane.'[5]

A permanent military camp has been made at Bordon in the west of the parish. The soil and subsoil are sandy, the chief crops being barley and wheat. The manufacture of paper was once carried on in this parish,[6] Stanford Upper Mill and Barford Lower Mill being as before stated used for this purpose. In the time of the paper-tax, when paper had to be stored at a distance from the mill, the paper from Bramshott was stored and perhaps taxed in a building in Headley parish.

Amongst place-names may be mentioned 'Hearon (now Hearn), Bareland,[7] Wassellane, Wassheford (now Washford), Lynsted, Golland's Cross, Fulmore Oke, Bevelleshedge, and Oldsmith Corner'[8] (sixteenth century).

MANORS

In the time of the Confessor Earl Godwine held land at *HEADLEY* assessed at 3 hides. At the time of the Domesday Survey the same land, assessed at 5 hides, was held by Count Eustace of Boulogne.[9] It was reckoned a part of Bishop's Sutton, and consequently followed the descent of that manor (q.v.).

BROXHEAD (Brocheseve, xi cent.; Brockesheved, xii cent.; Brokkeshefd and Broxhed, xiv cent.; Brocas Head, xvii cent.) was held of Edward the Confessor by Spirites as an alod. At the time of the Domesday Survey it was placed under Neatham hundred, and was held of the Conqueror by Nigel the Physician.[10] In the latter part of the thirteenth century the manor was held of Baldwin de Calne by Hugh de Vaches and Margery his wife and Roger Launcelevy and Joan his wife by the annual payment of 40*s*.[11] In 1281 Roger and Joan granted lands in Broxhead to William son of Sampson to hold of them and the heirs of Joan at fee-farm by the annual payment of a mark of silver.[12] In 1295 Herbert de Calne died seised of 40*s*. rent in the vill of Broxhead which he held of Sir Hugh Despenser.[13] His heir was his son Herbert who it seems died young and was succeeded by his aunt Euphemia, sister of his father Herbert de Calne. Euphemia left a daughter and sole heir Margery who married John de Roches.[14] The latter was succeeded by his son and heir Sir John de Roches, who in 1333 settled the manor by fine on himself and Joan his wife and their heirs.[15] Five years later the manor was settled on John and Joan in tail-male with contingent remainder in fee-tail successively to their daughters Alice, the wife of Henry Romyn, and Mary, the wife of John de Borhunte.[16] Henry and Alice died without issue while Joan de Roches was holding the manor, and thus on her death in 1361[17] it passed to Mary the widow of John de Borhunte, who shortly after her mother's death became the wife of Sir Bernard Brocas.[18] Sir Bernard died in 1395, after Mary's death, having married Katharine relict of Sir Hugh Tyrrell, at whose death in 1398 the property is described as a tenement called 'Brokkesheved' in the parish of Headley. Sir Bernard Brocas, aged forty-three or more, was found to be the son and heir of her late husband Sir Bernard.[19] The younger Sir Bernard was executed for treason on the accession of Henry IV, but by means of settlements in trust[20] the greater part of his property, including Broxhead, escaped forfeiture and remained in the possession of the Brocas family till 1506,[21] when, on the death of William Brocas, his property was divided between his daughters Anne and Edith.[22] Anne married George Warham in 1514, but died without issue, leaving her sister Edith, wife of Ralph

Roches. *Sable two leopards argent.*

Brocas. *Sable a leopard rampant or.*

[4] Date of authorizing Act, 9 March, 1849; date of award, 24 Feb. 1859; (*Parl. Accts. and P.* lxxi, 485).
[5] Eccl. Com. Ct. R. bdle. 136, No. 1.
[6] Exch. Dep. 23 Geo. II, Mich. 3.
[7] Close, 43 Eliz. pt. 11.
[8] Eccl. Com. Ct. R. bdle. 136, No. 1.
[9] *V.C.H. Hants*, i, 477.
[10] Ibid. i, 501*b*.
[11] *Abbrev. Plac.* (Rec. Com.), 278.
[12] Feet of F. Hants, Hil. 9 Edw. I.
[13] Inq. p.m. 23 Edw. I, No. 15.
[14] Montagu Burrows, *The Family of Brocas of Beaurepaire*, 323–4.
[15] Feet of F. Hants, Trin. 7 Edw. III.
[16] Ibid. Trin. 12 Edw. III.
[17] Inq. p.m. 35 Edw. III, pt. 2, No. 49.
[18] *The Family of Brocas of Beaurepaire*, 323.
[19] Inq. p.m. 22 Ric. II, No. 8.
[20] Close, 1 Ric. II, m. 8.
[21] Inq. p.m. 1 Hen. IV, pt. 1, No. 17; 7 Hen. VI, No. 53, and 34 Hen. VI, No. 9.
[22] Exch. Inq. p.m. (Ser. 2), file 961, No. 9.

Pexall, her sole heir. Edith's son and heir Sir Richard Pexall died in 1571, leaving four daughters and heirs, Ellen, Margery, Anne, and Barbara. Ellen married John Jobson; Margery married firstly Oliver Beckett and secondly Francis Cotton; Anne married Bernard Brocas, who was descended from the Sir Bernard Brocas who was executed in the reign of Henry IV, and Barbara married Anthony Brydges. One-third of the manor of Broxhead was divided equally among the four sisters. The remaining two-thirds remained in the possession of Sir Richard's widow, Dame Elinor, to hold for the term of her life if she remained single, with remainder to Pexall Brocas the son and heir of Anne and Bernard Brocas.[23] Shortly after their father's death, Ellen Jobson and Barbara Brydges parted with their twelfths of the manor, the former to Dame Elinor and her second husband Sir John Savage, and the latter to Anne and Bernard Brocas.[24] Margery Cotton died in 1581, seised of one-twelfth of the manor, her heir being her son John Beckett, under age,[25] and her husband Francis died thirty years afterwards, also seised of a portion of the manor.[26] Anne Brocas, who only survived her husband Bernard two years, died seised of a portion of the manor in 1591, her heir being her son, Sir Pexall Brocas.[27] Sir Pexall died in 1630 possessed of ten-twelfths of the manor. His heir was his son Thomas, aged thirty-nine and more,[28] who in 1633 succeeded in securing the remaining twelfths of the manor.[29] Six years later he and his son Robert sold the manor of Broxhead and a free fishery and a free warren to Edward Knight,[30] of whom the site of the manor was purchased in 1641 by Stephen Lee.[31] Mr. Montagu Burrows, in *The Family of Brocas of Beaurepaire*, p. 341, states that after the Restoration the younger sons of the last-mentioned Thomas Brocas were possessed of an estate for life in the manor, but gives no authority for this statement, and it is difficult to ascertain the true history of Broxhead at this period. It is probable that the site of the manor remained in possession of the Lee family for over a hundred and fifty years, as Charles Lee and Mary his wife dealt with it by recovery in 1808.[32] In 1827 the manor of Broxhead, or Brocashead, Slayford Farm[33] (modern Sleaford Farm), and Groom's Farm, in the parishes of Headley and Kingsley, were the property of the Hon. Henry Legge,[34] who owned large estates in the neighbourhood. From him it passed into the Sherborne family, Lord Sherborne having married Mary Legge, the only daughter of Henry Lord Stawell, who was the son of Henry Bilson Legge. Lord Sherborne left the manor to his third son, Ralph Dutton, from whom it passed to his grandson Henry Dutton of Hinton House, Hinton Ampner. There is no longer a manor of Broxhead, the lordship having been divided a few years ago. The part on the east side of the road from Lindford to Sleaford was sold by Henry Dutton to the late judge, Sir R. S. Wright, and on his death in 1904 passed by purchase to Mr. C. W. McAndrew, of Headley Park. The remainder on the west side of the road was sold to Mr. Ulick Burke, lord of the manor of Woodcote, who sold it to Sir David Barbour, who in his turn sold it to the military authorities as an appendage to Bordon Camp.[35]

Dutton, Lord Sherborne. *Quarterly argent and gules, the gules fretty or, a crescent for difference.*

WISHANGER (Wissangra, Wishangla, Wishang, and Wishangra, xii cent.; Wisehanger and Westhangre, xiii cent; Wilhangre and Wychangre, xiv cent.; Wicchanger, xv cent.) was held in 1167 by Gerard.[36] The overlord seems to have been the bishop of Winchester, for Richard of Ilchester, bishop of Winchester, granted to the abbey of St. Mary of Waverley 1 hide of his land of Wishanger, which lay towards the forest, and the land of the monks themselves, which was called Dochenfield.[37] This grant was subsequently confirmed by Richard, John, Stephen, Edward II, and Edward III.[38]

Holt. *Argent a bend engrailed sable with three fleurs-de-lis argent thereon.*

In 1290 William de la Charité surrendered his right in a messuage and 2 carucates of land in Wishanger to Richard atte Rudde of Petersfield, and Margaret his wife.[39] A year later Richard and Margaret granted a messuage, 160 acres of land, 22 acres of meadow, 8 acres of wood, 180 acres of pasture, and rents in Wishanger to John of Pontoise, bishop of Winchester, to hold to him and his heirs.[40]

In 1346 John de Thudden was holding in Wishanger the fourth part of a fee which had belonged to John de Worstede.[41] It is probable that this John de Thudden left three daughters and heirs, one of whom married Richard Seman, another John Trop, and the third Richard Esteney.[42] In 1389 Richard Seman acquired one-third of the manor from John Trop and

Pounde of Drayton. *Argent a fesse gules between two dragons' heads sable cut off at the neck in the chief and a cross formy fitchy sable in the foot with three molets argent on the fesse.*

23 *The Family of Brocas of Beaurepaire*, 208–9.
24 Ibid. 212.
25 Chan. Inq. p.m. (Ser. 2), cc. No. 54.
26 W. and L. Inq. p.m. bdle. 55, No. 127.
27 Ibid. bdle. 56, Nos. 123 and 147.
28 Chan. Inq. p.m. (Ser. 2), ccccli xiii, No. 126.
29 *The Family of Brocas of Beaurepaire.*
30 Feet of F. Hants, East. 15 Chas. I.
31 Ibid. Trin. 17 Chas. I.
32 Recov. R. Hil. 48 Geo. III, rot. 286.
33 The Hon. Henry Legge purchased it from William Clear, yeoman, in 1757.
34 Close, 1827, pt. 27, m. 1–39.
35 From information supplied by the Rev. W. H. Laverty, rector of Headley, and Mr. Ulick Burke of Woodcote.
36 Pipe R. 13 Hen. II.
37 Dugdale, *Mon.* v, 242.
38 Cart. Antiq. S. 20; Chart. R. 7 John, m. 4; Pat 15 Edw. III, pt. 2, m. 6.
39 *Abbrev. Plac.* (Rec. Com.), 223.
40 Feet of F. Hants, Mich. 19 Edw. I.
41 *Feud. Aids*, ii, 325.
42 This theory is supported by the facts that in 1399 Richard Esteney paid rent for land in Thedden Grange to the lord of Alton (*V.C.H. Hants*, ii, 479), and that rent for lands appertaining to the manor of Thedden was paid by William Estone and Richard Esteney in 1454 and 1459 respectively (*Selborne Chart.* Ser. 2, 42). It is also worthy of note that the Semans were a family living in Thedden. The names Saeman de Theddene, Robert Seaman, Peter son of Seman de Theddene, John Seman, and Richard Seman all occur in the Selborne Charters as connected with that manor in the thirteenth century.

Joan his wife,[43] and in 1391 another third from Richard Esteney and Isabel his wife,[44] and probably by the latter date had the whole of the manor in his possession. From him it passed to Richard Holt, who was holding it in 1428.[45] Richard Holt's heir was his son Richard, who died seised of the manor held of William bishop of Winchester in 1458, leaving two daughters, Christine aged fourteen, and Elizabeth aged ten.[46] Wishanger was assigned to Elizabeth, who married Sir John Pounde, and had a son and heir William Pounde.[47] On William's death the manor passed to his son and heir Anthony Pounde. Anthony's son and heir Richard died without issue, and on his death his property was divided between his two sisters Honora and Mary,[48] Wishanger being assigned to the latter. She married her cousin Edward White, the son of John White and Katharine Pounde,[49] who was Anthony Pounde's sister. In 1580 Edward White died seised of the manor of Wishanger, which he held by courtesy after the death of his wife Mary.[50] His heir was his son John, aged eighteen, who some time afterwards was described as holding a capital messuage called 'Wysslehange,' and four tenements with appurtenances in 'Hetheley', abutting on 'Dokenfeld Water.'[51]

WHITE OF SOUTHWICK *Azure a cross quarterly ermine and or between four falcons close argent with a fret between four lozenges azure on the cross.*

In 1593 Jane Lambart acquired the manor from John White and Frances his wife.[52] She seems to have married subsequently Gerard Fleetwood, for Gerard was seised of it in right of Jane his wife in 1601,[53] when he sold it for £400 to Sir Hercules Paulet, who was still holding it in 1619.[54] From him it seems to have passed to a certain William Horne of Southampton, merchant, who by his will, dated 1668, provided for the payment of various annuities out of the proceeds of the sale of the estate. Wishanger appears to have been sold to or taken over by John Speed, his brother-in-law, and remained in the Speed family, also of Southampton, till 1797, about which date only it was released from the payment of the various annuities by which it was burdened. In that year John Silvester and Harriet his wife (née Speed) sold it to Sir Thomas Miller of Froyle.[55] The estate remained in the Miller family till 1868, when the executors of Sir Charles Hayes Miller sold it to John Rouse Phillips. On his death sixteen years later his executors sold it to Joseph Whitaker of Palermo, Sicily, on whose death a year later it passed to his son, Mr. A. Ingham Whitaker,[56] of Grayshott Hall, Haslemere, its present owner. Wishanger Manor, as shown in an old map in the possession of Mr. A. Ingham Whitaker, was apparently a very small manor, and in the deeds as far back as 1700, and for some time after, it is spoken of as 'My farm and manor or reputed manor of Wishanger.' The manorial rights have long since lapsed, and the manor is now represented by Wishanger Manor Farm, which stands on the southern boundary of Wishanger Common.

CHURCH

The church of *ALL SAINTS, HEADLEY*, is situated on the west side of the heath, the ground falling away to the east and west. The walls are of rubble composed of local sandstone and ironstone with ashlar dressings of sandstone, and the roofs are covered with red tiles. The church consists of a chancel with a north vestry, a nave with a south porch, and a north-west tower. The chancel and nave were rebuilt in 1859, and retain no ancient fittings. The west window of the nave is a three-light fifteenth-century window, reset, and in the south porch, which is of wood on a stone base, some of the old timbers remain. The nave roof is of the sixteenth century, of a wide span, 27 ft., with moulded wall plates, tie beams, king posts and struts, the rafters

HEADLEY CHURCH

[43] Feet of F. Hants, Trin. 12 Ric. II.
[44] Ibid. Mich. 14 Ric. II.
[45] *Feud. Aids*, ii, 348.
[46] Inq. p.m. 36 Hen. VI, No. 32.
[47] Stowe MS. 845, fol. 128.
[48] Berry, *Hants Gen.* 294.
[49] 'In the windows of Mr. Norton's Hall of Southwick are the arms of Whyte empaling Pounde with quarterings, as in the church, and under them this rhyme : "To thank God we be most bounde, John Whyte and Katharine Pounde" ' (Stowe MS. 845, fol. 128, dated 1703).
[50] Inq. p.m. 26 Eliz. (Ser. 2), No. 118.
[51] Eccl. Com. Ct. R. bdle. 136, No. 1.
[52] Feet of F. Hants, Hil. 35 Eliz.
[53] Ibid. Trin. 43 Eliz.
[54] Recov. R. East. 17 Jas. I, rot. 49.
[55] Cal. Feet of F. Hants, Mich. 38 Geo. III.
[56] Information received from Mr. A. Ingham Whitaker.

having collars and braces. The tower[57] is of the fifteenth century, of three stages, with modern pinnacles and battlements. Its internal measurements at the ground level are 9 ft. by 9½ ft., with walls 3 ft. 10 in. thick. There are no angle buttresses. In the ground stage is a two-light west window, and in the second stage a single-light window with trefoiled head in the same position; the belfry windows are of two lights with a quatrefoil in the head. The arch from the tower to the nave is of two orders with large hollow chamfers and semi-octagonal capitals, responds, and bases, of a local fifteenth-century type, which looks earlier than it really is. The font is modern. There are two bells by Thomas Mears of (Whitechapel) London, 1838. In the vestry are two large eighteenth-century paintings of Moses and Aaron, of more than the average merit of their class.

The plate consists of a silver communion cup and cover paten of 1567, a silver flagon given in 1734, and two pewter alms dishes.

The parish registers date from 1537.

ADVOWSON The rectory of Headley was appropriated to Merton Priory subsequent to 1317, when Walter de Brokesbourne, rector of the parish, was ordained priest by Bishop Sendale of Winchester.[58] The prior and convent presented to the vicarage until the dissolution of the priory,[59] when the advowson passed into the hands of the bishop of Winchester. It was included in the possessions of the bishop granted to Sir John Gate in 1551,[60] but remained the property of the crown after he was forced to surrender them until 1626, when at the intercession of the queen Charles I granted it to Queen's College, Oxford,[61] with whom the right of presentation has remained to the present day. There is a rectory house and 50 acres of glebe. The question of tithes was dealt with by the Court of Exchequer in 1749.[62]

The church at Grayshott, dedicated to the honour of St. Luke, was consecrated in 1900. This consolidated chapelry was formed, partly from Headley, and partly from adjoining Surrey parishes, by Order of Council of 30 January, 1901.[63]

There was in 1549 an obit kept in 'Hedleigh' church, supported by lands called 'Bedvelles,' then occupied by William Atmore, which yielded 36*s.* 6*d.* a year; 18*s.* 2*d.* of this sum was distributed to the poor.[64]

There are Congregational and Bible Christian chapels in the parish, and the Plymouth Brethren have an iron chapel at Standford.

CHARITY In 1755 a free school for twelve poor children was founded at Headley by the Rev. George Holme, D.D., who gave a master's residence and endowed the school with a house and 2½ acres of land in Whitmore Valley, and an annuity of £6 charged on an estate at Ash near Aldershot. The whole now yields about £13 a year. In 1872 the school-building was enlarged, and is now used as the National Schools for all the children of the parish. These schools were again enlarged in 1893–4, and now accommodate 300 children. There is a National School (mixed) at Grayshott, the property of Miss I'Anson.

ROPLEY

Ropeleia (xii cent.), Roppele, and Roppeleghe (xiv cent.), Ropeley (xv cent.).

Ropley is a large parish with an area of 4,684 acres, situated 4 miles east from New Alresford, with a station 1½ miles from the village on the Bentley, Alton, and Fareham branch of the London and South-Western railway, which passes through it on the north-west. Parallel to the railway runs the main road from New Alresford to Alton, which enters the parish at Ropley Dean,[1] close to Ropley Lodge, the residence of Mr. Bowdon, where it is joined by the main road from Petersfield. The village of Ropley is built on a ridge between these two roads, rising gradually from west to east, and approached by numerous narrow lanes running off north from the Petersfield road and east from the Alton road. Down the ridge runs a narrow road, entering the parish at the east and passing through the outlying hamlet of Lyeway. At the upper end of the village it divides, one branch going northwards to Gilbert Street, another continuing westward and forming the village street. The church stands in the north-east of the village, the street forming the southern boundary of the churchyard, while further down the hill on the south are the schools, the smithy, and the coffee and reading-rooms, which were built in 1884 by Miss Hagen of Ropley House for the use of the working men of the parish. From the west end of the village the road runs on to Ropley Dean, the vicarage and Ropley House, with its well-grown beech trees, being on the north, while to the south is Ropley Manor (formerly Ropley Cottage), at present in the hands of Captain Holroyd. There are several scattered hamlets in the parish. Lyeway in the east; Gilbert Street, north-east of the village, on the road leading up to Kitfield and the outlying farm of Kitwood, in the highest part of the parish; North Street, with its little inn 'The Shant,' and Ropley Soke, with a mission-room, both lying on the main road from Alresford to Alton; Charlwood and Monkwood, situated in the east and the south of the parish respectively; and Four Marks, with an inn called the 'Windmill,' on high ground within about five minutes' walk from Medsted railway station. The last is partly in Ropley and partly in Medsted.

The original schoolhouse is a whitewashed and thatched cottage on the Petersfield road, near the Anchor Inn, built in 1828 for the instruction of the children of Bishop's Sutton and Ropley. The present schools were built in 1869 and enlarged in 1888.

[57] The tower was apparently designed for a different form of nave roof from that at present existing. A few eighteenth-century monuments are now placed in the tower.

[58] *Winton. Epis. Reg.* (Hants Rec. Soc.), 199.

[59] Dugdale, *Mon.* vi, 248.

[60] Pat. 5 Edw. VI, pt. 5.

[61] Ibid. 2 Chas. I, pt. 7, No. 3; Ashm. MS. 828, F 28, fol. 95.

[62] Exch. Dep. 23 Geo. II, Mich. 3.

[63] *Lond. Gaz.* 8 Feb. 1901, p. 982.

[64] Chant. Cert. Hants.

[1] This section of the road is bordered by wide uninclosed grass margins, from the Chequers Inn at the east end of Ropley Dean, to the junction with the Bramdean road at the west. They have been encroached on in several places by cottages and gardens, on the south side near Dean Farm, and on the north side by the grounds of Ropley Lodge, further to the west.

An additional school was built in 1902 a little to the east of Ropley Soke with funds raised by the vicar, the Rev. W. H. Leak. There is a small Methodist chapel near Malthouse Farm and Gilbert Street.[2] The kennels of the Hampshire Hunt hounds are situated in the parish, and near them are new stables, which were erected in 1889.

There are no wide stretches of uninhabited country in Ropley; everywhere are scattered farms and houses, and the parish is intersected by a network of roads leading to them. Many bungalows and villas have already been built, and many more are being erected, especially in the north and east, where the average height above the sea level is about 550 ft. Ropley is not on the whole well wooded at the present day, the only wood of any size being old Down Wood near Swelling Hill, but there are numerous little copses and many scattered pine trees. A surveyor gives the following description of Ropley in 1551:—'Being a lyttell village a good myle from Sutton church, the lorde of Sutton being chief lorde ther, having sundry faier wodds lyeing four or five myles together in sundry places sett moost with beache, which woodds we came not in.[3] The following woods are named in a perambulation of the parish made about the same time:[4]—'Churlewood' containing 95 acres, 'East Byxtrydge' containing 148 acres, 'West Byxtrydge' containing 112 acres, 'Oysterslade' containing 150 acres, 'Rudgehomes' containing 78 acres, 'Highomes' containing 88 acres, 'Redhyll' containing 114 acres, 'Holthele' containing 136 acres, and 'Hamerdene' containing 116 acres.

Previous to July, 1882, Ropley was annexed to Bishop's Sutton for ecclesiastical purposes, but by an Order in Council dated August, 1882, it became a separate parish. It contains 2,277½ acres of arable land, 1,505½ acres of permanent grass, and 282½ of woods.[5] The soil is generally light, the subsoil chalk. The chief crops are wheat, oats, and green crops.

The following place-names occur in a court roll of 1628[6]:—'Kittiert, Lyshard, and Houndlose.' 'Grete Alberts and Threleggedcrosse' are found in the sixteenth century,[7] and in a patent roll of 1403 are the following[8]:—'Alfedoun, Wandelesworth, Pollardeswode, Hokereslane, Brechelond, Rykemannescroft, Pudelston, Kyteswode, Merelond, Couperescroft, Amkyncroft, Hokecroft, Sweolynge, Lytelreode, Gervaisdoun, La Stubbyng, Inhome by Buxterigge, Le Guletter, Le Colynge, Hamerden, and Solrugge.'

MANOR A large portion of the parish of Ropley and the vill of *ROPLEY* itself formed part of the demesne lands of the manor of Bishop's Sutton, and thus belonged to the bishop of Winchester, as forming part of his liberty.[9] In a survey taken in 1551 the lord of Bishop's Sutton was said to be chief lord of the vill of Ropley,[10] and the fact that Sutton-cum-Ropley[11] and Sutton Ropley[12] are sometimes mentioned shows a very close connexion between the two parishes. The descent of these demesne lands necessarily followed that of the manor of Bishop's Sutton (q. v.). The earliest evidence of the manor of Ropley, which was held of the bishopric, is between 1304 and 1316, when Henry, bishop of Winchester, granted licence to William Gervays of Ropley to hear service in a chapel in his manor of Ropley.[13] In 1332 Robert le Botiller of Brown Candover settled a messuage, 3 carucates of land, 20 acres of wood, and £10 rent in Bishop's Sutton and Ropley on William Gervays and Christine his wife, with remainder in fee-tail successively to their sons, William, Roger, and John, and their daughter Isabel.[14] William the son died without issue, and the manor passed in accordance with the above settlement to his brother Roger.[15] In 1369 Andrew, son of Roger Gervays, granted 2 messuages, 2 tofts, 4 carucates of land, 10 acres of meadow, 100 acres of pasture, 100 acres of wood, and £10 rent in Ropley, Bishop's Sutton, and other places to William de Wykeham, bishop of Winchester, in return for an annuity of £20.[16] The bishop in 1392 obtained royal licence to alienate a part of these premises[17] in frankalmoign to the warden and scholars of the college called 'Seynte Marie College of Wynchestre,' which he had lately founded.[18] Ten years later licence was granted him to alienate the rest of the premises[19] to Winchester College for an annual rent of £3 18*s.* 9½*d.* and 1*s.* 6*d.* tithing pence.[20] In this way the whole of the manor of Ropley came into the hands of Winchester College, to whom it belongs at the present day.[21] A court of the manor was held there as late as 1706.[22]

In 1399 William de Wykeham let out at farm for a hundred years to Winchester College for a fixed money rent various tenements in Ropley, and this lease was confirmed by the king in 1403.[23]

Divers free tenants also held lands in Ropley of the bishop at various times. In 1332 Thomas de Wandlesworth of Winchester granted a messuage, 2 virgates of land, and 60 acres of wood in Ropley to William de Wandlesworth of Winchester and Agnes his wife to hold for their lives of Thomas and his heirs by the annual rent of a rose.[24] The same Thomas in 1356 was seised of a messuage, 10*s.* rent, 80 acres of arable land, and 20 acres of wood in Ropley within the liberty of the bishop of Winchester.[25] In 1361 a certain Thomas de Alresford

[2] Probably so-named from the family of Gilbert, who lived in the parish for centuries. Here is an early eighteenth-century house with good brickwork details, known as the 'Alberts,' a name occurring in sixteenth-century court rolls; see below.

[3] Duchy of Lanc. Rentals and Surv. bdle. 8, No. 22.

[4] Eccl. Com. Ct. R. bdle. 136, No. 1.

[5] Statistics from Board of Agriculture (1905).

[6] Eccl. Com. Ct. R. bdle. 120, No. 1.

[7] Ibid. bdle. 136, No. 1.

[8] Pat. 4 Hen. IV, pt. 2, m. 15.

[9] *Feud. Aids*, ii, 315.

[10] Duchy of Lanc. Rentals and Surv. bdle. 8, No. 22.

[11] Chart. R. 12 Edw. I, m. 5.

[12] Early Chan. Proc. bdle. 10, No. 189.

[13] Egerton MS. 2031, fol. 122*b*.

[14] Feet of F. Hants, Mich. 5 Edw. III.

[15] De Banc. R. Hil. 7 Hen. V, m. 414.

[16] Feet of F. Hants, Hil. 43 Edw. III.

[17] Viz. 2 messuages, 1 toft, 3 carucates of land, 2 acres of meadow, 32 acres of pasture, 63 acres of wood, £10 rent, and the rent of a pound of cummin.

[18] Pat. 15 Ric. II, pt. 2, m. 9.

[19] Viz. 6 tofts, 4½ virgates, 40 acres of land, 16 acres of pourpresture, and 35 acres of wood.

[20] Inq. a.q.d. file 432, No. 4.

[21] In 1413 Nicholas Gervays, the brother of Andrew Gervays, released all the right he had in the manor to John Morys the warden of Winchester College (Feet of F. Hants, East. 1 Henry V). Six years later John Gervays, the son and heir of William Gervays, another of Andrew's brothers, made an attempt to regain possession of the manor on the ground of the settlement made by Robert le Botiller in 1332, but his attempt does not seem to have met with any success (De Banc. R. Hil. 7 Hen. V, m. 414).

[22] Stowe MS. 845, fol. 59.

[23] Pat. 4 Hen. IV, pt. 2, m. 15.

[24] Feet of F. Hants, Hil. 5 Edw. III.

[25] Inq. p.m. 30 Edw. III (1st Nos.), No. 61.

died seised of a messuage, a carucate of land and rents in Ropley which he held of the bishop of Winchester.[26]

SHETE FARM (La Syete, La Schyte, and La Shete xiii cent. ; Shete Ferme xvi cent.). Some time between 1250 and 1260 Ralph son of William de Wez granted to John Sanztere all his land of 'La Syete' which he had in the manor of 'Sultone, Roppele, La Syete, and Hedleghe' in exchange for all the land which John had in the vill of Overton, 30 marks, 4 quarters of wheat, 4 quarters of barley, 4 quarters of oats, 4 bacon pigs, and 2 robes for himself and his wife.[27] In 1266 John granted this tenement to the prior and canons of Selborne in frankalmoign to hold of the bishop of Winchester by the annual payment of a mark and suit at his court of Bishop's Sutton twice a year.[28] This grant was confirmed by the bishop the same year.[29] Towards the close of the thirteenth century, the question was raised as to whether the prior and convent were lawfully seised of this tenement. An inquiry was held and it was ascertained that the prior and his predecessors had been seised of it long before the Statute of Mortmain 'with just title and not by any fraud of parties or collusion.' A fine was accordingly levied whereby Richard de Wytheneye and Alice his wife quitclaimed from themselves and the heirs of Alice[30] a messuage and a carucate of land in Ropley to the priory.[31] This tenement remained the property of the priory till 1485, when it was transferred with the rest of its possessions to Magdalen College, Oxford. In a perambulation of the parish made in the reign of Edward VI the following is given as the property of the college :—A capital messuage called 'Shete Ferme,' a wood called Bromes and crofts called Rodebeche, Homefield, Hatchgatefield, and Pokefield, lying to the north of Lyeway.[32] There is still a Broom Copse near Lyeway, but the farm itself seems to have disappeared, although Magdalen College still owns property in the parish.

CHURCH The church of *ST. PETER, ROPLEY* consists of chancel 21 ft. by 14 ft. 3 in. with north and south chapels, and nave 44 ft. by 19 ft. with north aisle, south-east tower, and south porch. The oldest parts of the building belong approximately to the middle of the twelfth century, the church of that date having had an aisleless nave and chancel with a transept chapel at the south-east of the nave, and probably another like it at the north-east. The plan was very like that of Colemore church, but on a larger scale. The only architectural detail of this date is the small west doorway of the tower, but parts of the south and west walls of the nave and tower and of the east wall of the chancel are original work. The walling is of flint rubble with dressings of chalk and a brown sandstone. A south chapel was added to the chancel in the latter part of the thirteenth century, and probably about the same time (or perhaps somewhat earlier) the north transept chapel was lengthened westward, and made to open to the nave by an arcade of two bays with a round central column. It is not clear at what date the existing wooden south-east tower was built within the south-east transept chapel, but this may have been a fourteenth-century alteration. In the early part of the nineteenth century a north chapel was added to the chancel, and in 1896 the north transept chapel was lengthened westward and became a north aisle of equal length with the nave, its east and west walls being pulled down and a new north arcade of four bays built, the old arcade of two bays being destroyed. At the same time the west wall of the nave was heightened in gable form, having previously ended with a level top, the west end of the nave roof being hipped.

The chancel has an east window of three cinquefoiled lights with fifteenth-century tracery under a four-centred head, the jambs being perhaps older and cut back to suit the inserted tracery. On the north and south of the chancel are arcades of two bays with pointed arches of two chamfered orders and an octagonal central pillar with moulded capital and base, the arches dying into the walls without responds at east and west. The south arcade is of late thirteenth-century date, while the north is a modern copy of it. The twelfth-century chancel had quoins in its internal angles, as may still be seen in the east wall where the south wall has been cut away for the arcades.

The south chapel has a three-light east window with net tracery, the stonework being modern, and in the south wall a single trefoiled light, below which are a small piscina and a locker. West of the south window is a round-headed doorway, in modern stonework, and to the north of the east window are traces of two small thirteenth-century lights, one above the other. Under the east window are remains of two stone brackets for the images over the altar which once stood here.

The chancel arch is modern, and with the north arcade of four bays dates from 1896, and all the windows of the north chapel and aisle are likewise modern. On the south side of the nave is a pointed arch opening to a vestry under the south-east tower, and west of it a square-headed sixteenth-century window of two trefoiled lights. The south doorway of the nave is of the fifteenth century, with a four-centred arch under a square hood-mould with carved foliage in the spandrels. It doubtless replaces the original south doorway, and opposite it on the north side of the nave, before the building of the aisle, was a blocked north doorway. The west window of the nave is of three lights with modern tracery, but the jambs are old. The south porch is of timber and plaster, and in its north-east corner is an octagonal corbel for a holy-water stone.

The tower is a good specimen of timber framing, covered with weather-tiling in the upper part where it rises above the masonry and roof, and finished with a low-pitched pointed roof. Its lower stories are lighted by modern windows on the south, one above the other, but with a common round-headed rear-arch, the masonry of which seems to be old. The west doorway, near the south-west angle, has a plain round head and a chamfered string at the springing.

The roofs and fittings of the church are entirely modern, but in the vestry is a seventeenth-century communion table, and the font, at the west end of the north aisle, is of the fifteenth century, with a plain octagonal bowl and short panelled stem, and on the chamfer at the base of the bowl plain shields alternating with paterae of foliage.

[26] Inq. p.m. 34 Edw. III, pt. 1, No. 7.

[27] *Selborne Chart.* (Hants Rec. Soc.), (Ser. 1), 40.

[28] Ibid. 58.

[29] Ibid.

[30] Alice was probably the daughter and heir of John Sanztere.

[31] *Selborne Chart.* (Hants Rec. Soc.), (Ser. 1), 76 ; Feet of F. Hants, Trin. 19 Edw. I.

[32] Eccl. Com. Ct. R. bdle. 136, No. 11.

There are five bells, the ring having been recast from four old bells into five by Samuel Knight in 1701. The tenor bears the inscription:

John Gilberd did contrive
To cast from four this peale of fife.

John Gilberd was evidently the foreman in charge of the work. The fourth bell was recast by Robert Catlin in 1749, and the third is now cracked. The bell frame was made new at the general recasting, and is inscribed IG TO 1701.

The plate consists of a silver communion cup and cover paten of 1592, two flagons of 1714, and a paten of 1715.

The registers are complete from 1538, the first book running to 1675, the second to 1704, and the third to 1783, with marriages to 1753 only. The fourth contains the marriages 1755–1804, the fifth and sixth respectively the baptisms and burials, 1783–1812, and the seventh the marriages 1804–37.

ADVOWSON During the reign of Henry III there appears to have been some dispute in connexion with the chapel of Ropley.[33] In 1241 the sheriff of Southampton was ordered to remove the lay force by which the men of the prior of Merton were being obstructed, so that they might have free entry to the chapel. The sheriff was further commanded to attach Master Aubrey, the official of the archdeacon of Winchester, to answer for his action in collating and instituting to the chapel contrary to the claim of the king, in whose hands the right of presentation had devolved by reason of the voidance of the see of Winchester.

The chapel seems soon afterwards to have been annexed to the parish church of Bishop's Sutton, and from this time the descent of the advowson was identical with that of Bishop's Sutton till 1882, when by an Order in Council of August, 1882, Ropley became a separate civil parish. Since that date the advowson has been in private hands, the living, which is a vicarage of the net yearly value of £160, being at present in the gift of the Rev. E. J. Woodhouse.

The rectory, tithe-barn, and tithes of Ropley belonged to Merton Abbey until its dissolution, and were farmed out by the abbot for varying terms of years. John Pynke, who was the farmer early in the reign of Henry VIII, was succeeded by Robert Bulbecke, who gave up his right to William Wygmore.[34] On the dissolution of the abbey Henry VIII granted a lease of twenty-one years to William Wygmore, who sold his right to William Marten. Queen Elizabeth granted to the latter a lease of twenty-one years in return for £48 to hold by the annual payment of £12.[35] At the expiration of that term the queen leased the rectory, tithes, and tithe-barn to Humphrey Aplegarth for the term of the lives of the said Humphrey, Helen his wife, and their son William by the annual payment of £12, and on the deaths of Humphrey, Helen, and William, 20*s.* in name of a heriot.[36] They were to keep the chancel of the parish church of Ropley in good repair, but were to be allowed to take timber for that purpose, also 'housebote,' 'hedgebote,' 'firebote,' 'ploughbote,' and 'cartebote' from the premises thus let to them.[37] In 1606 William Aplegarth granted the reversion of the tithe-barn and rectory after the death of his mother, Helen, to Thomas Albery and Oliver Drawater,[38] but he still seems to have been holding them in 1629.[39] Sir Berkeley Lucy dealt with the grange and rectory by indenture in 1693,[40] and was the impropriator in 1706.[41] The tithe-barn is still standing.

CHARITIES In 1875 Henry Joyce Mulcock by will left £500 to be invested and the income applied in the distribution of meat and other gifts to the poor at Christmas and otherwise for the benefit of the poor, the charity to be called 'The Ropley Trust Fund.' The legacy is invested in £528 15*s.* consols, held by the official trustees of charitable funds, who also hold a sum of £51 11*s.* 11*d.* like stock, under the title of 'Charity for Poor,' arising from investment of the proceeds of the sale of cottages built on waste land granted by the lord of the manor in 1849, the dividends upon which are under a scheme of 31 January, 1890, applicable in augmentation of Henry Joyce Mulcock's Charity.[42]

In 1890 Mrs. Rosa Anna Onslow, by will proved this date, gave to the rector and churchwardens £300 to be invested in government securities and the income applied for the benefit of the parish in such way as they and their successors should consider most expedient. The legacy, less duty, was invested in the purchase of £273 1*s.* 6*d.* consols with the official trustees.[43]

WEST TISTED

Ticcestede (x cent.); Tistede (xi cent.); Westystude, Ticestede, Westistede, and West Stisted (xiii cent.).

West Tisted is a small triangular-shaped parish with an area of 2,356 acres lying on high ground between 500 and 600 ft. above the sea level, and comprises 944 acres of arable land, 935 acres of permanent grass, and 167 acres of wood and plantation.[1] The parish is but thinly populated, and the village, which lies in the centre of it, seems almost deserted. It is approached by four rough narrow roads or lanes between high banks of ferns and hedge growth. The schools are situated to the east of the road from Privett village, while the smithy stands at the junction of this road with that from Privett station on the Meon Valley Branch of the London and South-Western Railway, which lies about a mile off to the east. A steep road leads thence, through the pine-trees with which the whole parish is studded, to the church, vicarage, and manor house, standing close together a little way back from the road. The vicarage lies to the south-east of the church, and hard by is a field where stands the oak in which, according to tradition, Sir Benjamin Tichborne hid himself after

[33] *Abbrev. Plac.* (Rec. Com.), 113.
[34] Pat. 3 Eliz. pt. 11, m. 16.
[35] Ibid.
[36] Pat. 27 Eliz. pt. 11, m. 8.
[37] Ibid.
[38] Close, 4 Jas. I, pt. 14; Add. MS. 33278, fol. 176*b*.
[39] Eccl. Com. Ct. R.
[40] Recov. R. Hil. 5 and 6 Will. and Mary, m. 1 *d*.
[41] Stowe MS. 845, fol. 59.
[42] *Char. Com. Rep.* xlvii, 458.
[43] Ibid. lxv, 376.
[1] Statistics from Board of Agriculture (1905).

the battle of Cheriton.[2] North of the church on a moated site is the picturesque manor house of red brick and stone formerly belonging to the Tichbornes, but now a farm-house. It dates from *c.* 1600, and has a central hall with a large fireplace and a fine panelled room on the ground floor of the east wing with a tall chimney-piece of very good style. From the top of the hill wide views can be obtained of Privett and the neighbouring country. In the north-east of the parish is the wild expanse of West Tisted Common, north of which is the steep road lined with pine-trees leading to Ropley and Alresford.

The soil is clay and chalk, the subsoil chalk. The chief crops are wheat, barley, turnips, and oats. The population in 1901 was 239.

The following place-names are found in the 13th century : 'Trendelcrofte and Rykemannesdone.'[3]

MANOR *WEST TISTED.*—King Edmund granted 7 hides in *TISTED* to his faithful thegn Ethelgeard in 941, and confirmed this grant two years later. The boundaries are given in detail, and seem to prove that the land thus granted to Ethelgeard was situated in the parish of West Tisted.[4] At the time of the Domesday Survey West Tisted belonged to the bishopric of Winchester, and was held by Ranulf of the bishop.[5] The manor was held of the bishop of Winchester until the beginning of the thirteenth century, when Richard de Ilchester, bishop of Winchester, who had two illegitimate sons, Herbert le Poor, bishop of Salisbury 1194–1217, and Richard le Poor, bishop of Salisbury 1217–28 and bishop of Durham 1228–37, granted it to Herbert, treating it as though it was his personal property.[6] On Herbert's death it passed to his brother and heir Richard, who succeeded him as bishop of Salisbury. Peter des Roches, bishop of Winchester, however, realized that unless measures were taken West Tisted would be irretrievably lost to the bishopric, and accordingly he took proceedings against Richard, and between 1217 and 1228 recovered seisin of it.[7] The manor was held directly of the bishopric until the beginning of the fourteenth century.[8] In 1323, however, an inquisition was held on the petition of Femmota the widow of Robert de Tisted,[9] who complained that whereas her former husband had held the manor of West Tisted of John de St. John, the guardian of the bishopric of Winchester,[10] asserting that the manor was held of the bishopric by knight's service, had taken it into the king's hands by reason of the minority of the heir. By the inquisition it was ascertained that Robert de Tisted had held the manor of John de St. John, who held it of the bishopric by knight's service,[11] and the keepers of the bishopric were consequently ordered to intermeddle no further with the manor, but to restore the issues thereof.[12] After Edmund de St. John's death, without issue, in 1347,[13] the overlordship passed to his sister Isabel, the wife of Luke Poynings, and remained in the family of Poynings until Sir Thomas Poynings' death in 1428, when it was assigned to Alice the wife of Sir Thomas Kyngeston, one of his three granddaughters and heirs. The manor was held successively of their son Thomas Kyngeston and of his kinsman and heir John Kyngeston, as of the manor of Warnford.[14] John's brother and sister both died without issue,[15] and accordingly the manor of West Tisted, for want of an heir, escheated to the bishop. In an inquisition of 1555 it was stated that the manor was held of Stephen bishop of Winchester as of his bishopric of Winchester by the service of one and a half knight's fees.[16]

With regard to the actual holders of the manor, various members of the family of Limesi held lands in West Tisted in the twelfth and thirteenth centuries. Towards the end of the twelfth century Richard de Limesi died seised of one hide in West Tisted, leaving a son and a heir Henry.[17] As he was in debt to the king his lands were confiscated, but they were released to Henry on his petition in 1203, to hold from year to year as the farmer of the king, until the debt was paid in full.[18] Some thirty years later Roger de Limesi, who was also in debt to the king, was slain, and in 1234 the sheriff was ordered to deliver his chattels to any lawful man of the county who would be responsible to the king for part payment of the debts.[19] Roger's heir was a certain Adam de Limesi, who seems to have taken no steps in this direction, but alienated all his property to the priories of Newark and Selborne, apparently in order to shift the responsibility of payment from his own shoulders to theirs. Thus in 1242 he granted half a carucate in West Tisted[20] to the prior of Newark in frankalmoign in return for two corrodies in food and drink during his life : a canon's corrody and a groom's corrody at Newark.[21] About the same time he granted two messuages and lands in West Tisted to the prior and canons of Selborne to hold of him and his heirs by the annual payment of a pound of cummin.[22] As Adam had foreseen, King Henry III demanded the payment of Roger de Limesi's debts from the priory of Newark, and an

[2] There was a good deal of fighting in this district during the Civil War. A skirmish took place on West Tisted Heath, and the mound by the side of the road which cuts through West Tisted Common still marks the graves of those who fell in battle.

[3] *Selborne Chart.* (Hants Rec. Soc.), 23.

[4] Birch, *Cart. Sax.* ii, 495 and 529. For instance 'clincanleage' and 'Hatan hammas' are mentioned. The former is probably represented by the modern Clinkley Road, and the latter by the modern Hatman Wood, both of which are situated in the north-west of the parish of West Tisted.

[5] *V.C.H. Hants*, i, 463.

[6] Feet of F. Hants, Trin. 4 John ; Chart. R. 5 John, m. 19.

[7] *Selborne Chart.* (Hants Rec. Soc.), 2; Feet of F. Hants, East. 17 Hen. III.

[8] Inq. p.m. 43 Hen. III, No. 28.

[9] Ibid. 17 Edw. II, No. 112.

[10] Rigaud de Asser held this dignity but for a very short period ; and dying at Avignon, where the pope's court was, in 1323, John XXII, who was then pontiff, exercised his privilege of nominating as his successor, at the recommendation of Walter archbishop of Canterbury, John de Stratford, archdeacon of Lincoln and canon of York. As the king had endeavoured to get his chancellor, Robert Baldock, archdeacon of Middlesex, appointed bishop he ceased not to harass Stratford, outlawing him and seizing upon the temporalities of his see (Dugdale, *Mon.* i, 197). This explains why the manor had been taken into the king's hands.

[11] The manor was held by the service of 2*d.* a year and scutage for all services and demands, free from heriot, relief, wardship and marriage.

[12] Close, 17 Edw. II, m. 13.

[13] Inq. p.m. 21 Edw. III, No. 57.

[14] Chan. Inq. p.m. (Ser. 2), xxvi, No. 13.

[15] *Vide* manor of Warnford in hundred of Meon Stoke.

[16] Chan. Inq. p.m. (Ser. 2), cvi, No. 58.

[17] *Abbrev. Plac.* (Rec. Com.), 42.

[18] Ibid.

[19] *Excerpt. e rot. fin.* (Rec. Com.), i, 257.

[20] This was afterwards called the manor of Merryfield. See Merryfield below.

[21] Feet of F. Hants, Mich. 26 Hen. III.

[22] *Selborne Chart.* (Hants Rec. Soc.), 31.

arrangement was made that the prior should pay a mark every year into the royal exchequer until the debt of £276 14*s.* 3*d.* was paid in full. However, the prior of Newark pleaded that the prior of Selborne also was holding property in West Tisted which had belonged to Roger de Limesi and should also help in the payment of his debts. The possessions of both the priors in West Tisted were valued in 1266, and it was ascertained that those of the prior of Newark were worth £4 a year, while those of the prior of Selborne were only worth 8*s.* a year. It was accordingly arranged that the latter should pay 1*s.* 2½*d.* every year to the prior of Newark towards the payment of Roger de Limesi's debts.[23] It is clear, therefore, that all the lands which belonged to the Limesis in West Tisted were divided before 1250 between the priories of Selborne and Newark. Hence there is no mention of the family of Limesi in connexion with West Tisted after that date.

The Limesis, however, had held but a small portion of the vill of West Tisted. The main part of it was held by the Tisteds. Early in the twelfth century Hugh de Tisted held three knights' fees, and he was succeeded by his son Richard de Tisted, who was holding one and a half knight's fees in 1166.[24] The latter's son, Hugh de Tisted, was holding land in West Tisted in 1203.[25] The Tisteds probably held their property of the bishop of Winchester, and when Herbert bishop of Salisbury became overlord of West Tisted, he seems to have dispossessed them, and granted their lands to a certain Ralph de Winesham.[26] Shortly after confirming this grant, King John, knowing that Ralph's title was defective, confiscated his lands in West Tisted, and did not release them to him until he had paid 20 marks.[27] On the death of Ralph de Winesham, West Tisted passed to a certain Roger de Winesham. When, however, Peter des Roches recovered the overlordship of West Tisted against Richard, bishop of Salisbury, Joan le Hood, who was most probably the daughter and heir of the Hugh de Tisted who was holding West Tisted in 1203, pressed her claim against Roger de Winesham. In 1235 an assize of mort d'ancestor was summoned between Roger de Winesham and Robert le Hood and Joan his wife, and Roger was forced to give up West Tisted to Robert and Joan and the heirs of Joan.[28] In 1238 Joan, who was by this time a widow, granted to the prior and canons of Selborne in frankalmoign certain lands in the vill of West Tisted called Trendelcrofte and Rykemannesdone.[29] In 1240 she conveyed West Tisted to Ralph de Camois, possibly for purposes of settlement, and in return Ralph granted it to her to hold for the term of her life of himself and his heirs by the annual payment of a pair of gilt spurs or 6*d.* at Easter.[30] In the following year Joan surrendered her life-interest in West Tisted to Ralph in exchange for the manor of Wotton (co. Surr.).[31] Ralph de Camois died in 1259 seised of one and a half knight's fees in West Tisted which he held of the bishop elect of Winchester.[32] His heir was his son Ralph, aged forty and more. This latter Ralph in 1261 claimed the advowson of the church of West Tisted by virtue of his lordship of the manor.[33] He was not, however, seised of the manor at his death in 1276,[34] although he must have had some interest in it, since four years later John de Camois, son and heir of Sir Ralph de Camois, granted to Richard de Crofton, in return for his service, £10 annual rent paid by Geoffrey de la Flode and Alice his wife from the manor of West Tisted.[35] Geoffrey de la Flode is called 'lord of the vill' in 1281,[36] and his wife Alice le Hood, who was probably the daughter and heir of Robert le Hood and Joan his wife, and on whom West Tisted had probably been settled by the transactions of 1240 and 1241, is described as the 'lady of West Tisted' in 1284.[37] In the same year Richard de Crofton, who was called the son and heir of Robert de Crofton, released to the prior and canons of Selborne all his right in the advowson of the church of West Tisted,[38] and at some date between 1284 and 1293 he succeeded Alice le Hood in the lordship of West Tisted.[39] This Richard was probably the son and heir of Alice by her first husband Robert de Crofton, and the manor descended to him as his right and inheritance after his mother's death.[40] Shortly after succeeding to his inheritance he seems to have assumed the surname of Tisted, as after 1293 there is no further mention of Richard de Crofton, but a certain Richard de Tisted was witness to charters in 1301, 1305, 1307, 1308, and 1312.[41] Richard died about 1313,[42] and was succeeded by Robert de Tisted, probably his son.[43] Robert died before 1323, for in that year Femmota

[23] Harl. MS. 44, H. 42. *Selborne Chart.* (Hants Rec. Soc.), 59.

[24] *Red Bk. of Exch.* (Rolls Ser.), 206.

[25] *Abbrev. Plac.* (Rec. Com.), 42.

[26] Chart. R. 5 John, m. 19.

[27] *Rot. de oblatis et finibus*, 311. While Ralph was holding West Tisted he granted a virgate in the vill to Henry le Sauvage (*Selborne Chart.* 3). Henry released his right in it to Peter des Roches, who granted it in 1236 to the prior and canons of Selborne to hold by the service of giving every year a pound of cummin to Henry and his heirs (ibid. 16). Henry, however, gave up all right to this rent in 1238 (ibid. 24). Some time after, Henry's widow Cecilia granted the lands which she held in West Tisted as her dowry to the same priory (ibid. 33 and 48). In this way the priory acquired a part of the land in West Tisted which had once been held by Hugh de Tisted.

[28] Feet of F. Hants, Hil. 20 Hen. III. The fact that the manor was settled on the heirs of Joan seems to support the theory that Joan was the daughter and heir of Hugh de Tisted. This assize was no doubt held by order of the bishop, who two years before had acknowledged the manor to be the right of Robert and Joan, and had granted it to them to hold to them and the heirs of Joan of him and his successors and the church of Winchester (Feet of F. Hants, East. 17 Hen. III).

[29] *Selborne Chart.* (Hants Rec. Soc.), 23. This grant was confirmed by Peter, bishop of Winchester, in the same year. Later confirmations of this grant were made in 1261 and 1284 by lords of the manor of West Tisted (ibid. 54 and 71).

[30] Feet of F. Hants, Mich. 25 Hen. III.

[31] Feet of F. Div. Cos. Trin. 25 Hen. III.

[32] Inq. p.m. 43 Hen. III, No. 28. While Ralph was lord of West Tisted he confirmed the grant of land in West Tisted made by a certain Philip de Rammesye to the priory of Newark (Harl. MS. 47, G. 7). By this time both Selborne and Newark had considerable possessions in West Tisted. Selborne's property amounted to half a knight's fee, and comprised the gifts of Adam de Limesi, Henry le Sauvage and Cecilia his wife, and Joan le Hood (Inq. p.m. 11 Edw. III, No. 49), while Newark held 2 hides granted by Adam de Limesi and Philip de Rammesye (*Feud. Aids*, ii, 334 and 359). As Newark was a considerable distance from West Tisted, the prior probably let his property there to Selborne Priory. The fact that in 1463 the prior and canons of Newark were seised of a customary annual rent of 16*d.* from the prior and canons of Selborne lends support to this theory (*Selborne Chart.* 117).

[33] *Selborne Chart.* (Hants Rec. Soc.), 54.

[34] Inq. p.m. 5 Edw. I, No. 1.

[35] De Banc. R. East. 8 Edw. I.

[36] *Selborne Chart.* (Hants Rec. Soc.), 70.

[37] Ibid. 71. [38] Ibid. [39] Ibid. 76.

[40] The name of Robert de Crofton's wife was Alice (Feet of F. Hants, East. 47 Hen. III).

[41] *Selborne Chart.* (Hants Rec. Soc.), 79, 81, 82, 83, and 85.

[42] Cf. *Selborne Chart.* (Hants Rec. Soc.), 85, and *Abbrev. Rot. Orig.* (Rec. Com.), i, 222.

[43] *Feud Aids*, ii, 315, and *Selborne Chart.* (Hants Rec. Soc).

de Tisted is described as his widow.[44] Robert's heir was a minor in 1323, and apparently died before he came of age, for the manor of West Tisted had been divided before 1337 between Alice and Agatha,[45] who were the daughters and coheirs of John le Hood of West Tisted.[46] It is possible that this John le Hood was the younger brother of Robert de Tisted, for it seems to have been the rule for the heir to assume the surname of Tisted on succeeding to his property. Alice and Agatha, the daughters of John le Hood, and probably the nieces of Robert de Tisted, married respectively Richard de Tichborne and his brother Walter de Tichborne, the sons of Sir John Tichborne,[47] who in 1337 were seised of the manor in right of their wives.[48] In 1342 it was settled between them that if Walter and Agatha died without issue, the moiety of the manor which they held should revert on their deaths to the right heirs of Agatha.[49] Walter de Tichborne in 1345 acknowledged that he owed £100 to his elder brother Roger de Tichborne of Tichborne. As he had not paid the debt in 1346, Roger chose to hold half of Walter's land as a free tenement until he had recovered his £100. Walter's property at West Tisted was accordingly valued, and half of it was delivered over to Roger.[50] Walter de Tichborne and Agatha died without issue, evidently before 1364, for in that year Alice, as Agatha's right heir, was holding both moieties of the manor, and was described as the 'lady of West Tisted.'[51] On her death the manor descended to her son Richard Tisted,[52] by whose son Richard it was held in 1428.[53] On his death the manor descended to his son and heir William Tisted.[54] William's son William Tisted died in 1511 seised of the manor of West Tisted, leaving a brother and heir, Thomas Tisted, aged forty and more.[55] Thomas died without issue, and on his death the manor was divided among his four sisters and heirs, Amy, Christian, Thomazin, and Iseult.[56] Before the end of the reign of Henry VIII, Nicholas Tichborne[57] had bought up the different parts into which the manor had been divided from these sisters and their descendants.[58] On Nicholas's death the manor passed to his son and heir Nicholas Tichborne, who died seised of it in 1555.[59] From that date the manor has remained in the family of Tichborne,[60] the present lord of the manor being Sir Henry Alfred Joseph Doughty-Tichborne, bart.

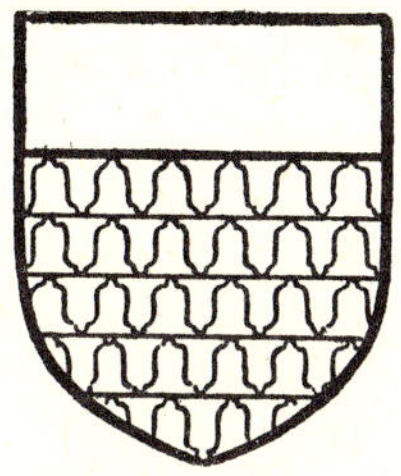

TICHBORNE. *Vair a chief or.*

MERRYFIELD (Mirefeld xiii cent.; Merifeld xvi cent.) was, as has been shown above, in origin half a carucate of land in West Tisted granted by Adam de Limesi in 1242 to the prior of Newark in frankalmoign. Shortly after this grant the prior and convent of Merton granted licence to the prior and convent of Newark to build a chapel in their territory of Merryfield, which was within the parish of Sutton and Ropley, and to hold service there as long as it was not to the prejudice of the mother church.[61] Merryfield continued the property of the prior and convent until the dissolution, the following entry being made in the Ministers' Accounts for 1545, under the heading of 'the lands and possessions of Newark':—Manor of 'Merifeld' with all lands and tenements in West Tisted and Ropley, and £9 from the rents both of free and customary tenants there.[62] Henry VIII granted the manor by letters patent in 1532 to John Wingfield,[63] who held it but for a short time, the king three years later granting it to Henry Tichborne, lord of the manor of West Tisted.[64] From this time it has remained in the family of Tichborne,[65] Merryfield Farm, situated in the north of the parish on the borders of Ropley, being still the property of Sir Henry Alfred Joseph Doughty-Tichborne, bart.

CHURCH

The church of *ST. MARY MAGDALENE, WEST TISTED*, is a small building with modern chancel and north vestry, and an aisleless nave with south porch and west bell-turret. The interior measurements of the original nave were 41 ft. by 15 ft., but it has been lengthened 10 ft. eastwards at the building of the chancel, and there is no structural division between the two. It probably dates from the early years of the twelfth century, the blocked north doorway and part of a small window west of the south doorway being of this time, the window being only 5 in. wide.

The north doorway has a plain round outer arch with a hollow-chamfered string at the springing, and the walls are 3 ft. thick, of flint rubble with sandstone ashlar dressings. The western angles have been rebuilt, and the south wall leans outward; its original masonry being much patched, and a large buttress added at the south-east angle. The main entrance to the church is by the south door, which has a plain pointed arch of one order with a continuous chamfer,

[44] Inq. p.m. 17 Edw. II, No. 112.
[45] Ibid. 11 Edw. III, No. 49.
[46] Berry, *Hants Gen.* 29.
[47] Ibid. The Richard de Tichborne who married Alice le Hood seems sometimes to have been called Richard de Tisted. For instance, in 1346 it was stated that Richard de Tisted and his coparceners were holding West Tisted (*Feud. Aids*, ii, 334). This Richard de Tisted cannot very well have been the son and heir of Richard de Tichborne and Alice, for Richard de Tichborne was living in 1357 and Alice in 1365 (*Selborne Chart.* 93–4).
[48] Inq. p.m. 11 Edw. III, No. 49.
[49] Feet of F. Hants, Trin. 16 Edw. III.
[50] Inq. p.m. 20 Edw. III (1st Nos.), No. 58.
[51] *Selborne Chart.* (Hants Rec. Soc.), 94.
[52] Ibid. Pat. 13 Ric. II, pt. 3, m. 29 *d.*
[53] *Feud. Aids*, ii, 359. In 1430 Richard son of Richard confirmed a grant of a right of way made to Selborne Priory by his grandmother Alice (*Selborne Chart.* 110).
[54] Berry, *Hants Gen.* 29.
[55] Chan. Inq. p.m. (Ser. 2), xxvi, No. 13.
[56] Berry, *Hants Gen.* 29.
[57] This Nicholas was the great-great-great-grandson of Roger Tichborne, the elder brother of the Richard and Walter Tichborne who had once owned the manor.
[58] Feet of F. Hants, Mich. 10 Hen. VIII; Mich. 11 Hen. VIII; East. 22 Hen. VIII; and Mich. 24 Hen. VIII.
[59] Chan. Inq. p.m. (Ser. 2), cvi, No. 58.
[60] Feet of F. Hants, Hil. 4 Eliz. Chan. Inq. p.m. (Ser. 2), cxli, No. 12. Feet of F. Hants, Mich. 11 Chas. I. Special Com. Double cos. 24 Chas. I, No. 6051. *Cal. of Com. for Comp.* iv, 2532. Recov. R. Mich. 11 Chas. I, rot. 85, and Mich. 18 Geo. III, rot. 467.
[61] Cott. xxi, 25. The Latin is 'Eustachius prior Mereton et eiusdem loci conventus salutem. Noveritis nos concessisse dilectis nobis in Christo domino Thome priori de Novo Loco et sacro eius conventui quod in territorio suo quod est in parochia nostra de Suttun et Roppelegh cappellam construant.' The prior and convent of Merton held the advowson of the church of Bishop's Sutton with the chapel of Ropley annexed. This fact seems to explain the 'nostra,' the parish being the ecclesiastical one in which the territory of Merryfield was included.
[62] Mins. Accts. Surrey, 36–7 Hen. VIII, No. 187, m. 46.
[63] Pat. 32 Hen. VIII, pt. 8, m. 36.
[64] Ibid. 35 Hen. VIII, pt. 1.
[65] Chan. Inq. p.m. (Ser. 2), pt. 1, No. 69. Recov. R. Mich. 1654, rot. 227; East. 4 Geo. I, rot. 203, and Hil. 46 Geo. III, rot. 330.

and is covered by a mean brick porch built by Magdalen College, Oxford, in 1750. In the north wall is a single window, a trefoiled fourteenth-century light close to the line of the former east wall of the nave, and opposite to it in the south wall is a trefoiled piscina of about the same date, with a stone shelf, marking the site of the south nave altar. Close to the piscina is a square-headed fifteenth-century window of three cinquefoiled lights, and the western part of the nave is lighted only by an early fourteenth-century window in the west wall, of two trefoiled lights with a quatrefoil over. The bell-turret is carried on four wooden posts, rising from the floor of the church at the west end of the nave, set close to the walls; they formerly carried a west gallery which is now taken down, the only access to the turret being by a trap door in the ceiling. The chancel is a poor specimen of modern fifteenth-century Gothic with a three-light east window and two two-light windows in the south wall. At its north-west angle is a door leading to a small modern vestry.

The timbers of the nave roof and bell-turret are old, but all other fittings are modern except the seventeenth-century altar table with its baluster legs, and the font, which stands in front of the blocked north door, and is perfectly plain with a round bowl on a roughly worked stem of uncertain date though ancient. In the face of the east jamb of the south doorway is a recess for holy water, the position being somewhat unusual.

There are a few mural monuments of the Tichborne family on the north wall of the nave, to Sir Benjamin Tichborne, 1665, Margaret his wife, 1671, and Margaret Tichborne, 1672, and a tablet to Richard Lacy, 1690. The plate consists of a cup and cover paten of 1568, with incised ornament round the top and base of the bowl, the paten being plain, and a second paten with a foot bearing the date-letter for 1723. There are two small bells in the bell-turret, said to be uninscribed.

The first book of the registers contains the baptisms from 1560 to 1747, the marriages from 1538 to 1740, and the burials from 1538 to 1755, and the second the remaining entries to 1812, but there are no entries of marriages between 1740 and 1754.

ADVOWSON

There was a church in West Tisted at the time of the Domesday Survey, but it is not stated whether the bishop held the advowson as well as the manor.[66] In all probability he did, for Peter des Roches in 1237 confirmed the grant of the advowson [67] made by Joan le Hood a year before to the prior and canons of Selborne.[68] Ralph de Camois claimed the advowson in virtue of his lordship of the manor of West Tisted, and presented Master John de Brideport, clerk, to the living. His claim was disputed by the prior and canons of Selborne, and Constantine de Mildehale, the official of Boniface archbishop of Canterbury in the diocese of Winchester, during the vacancy of the see, arbitrated between the disputants in 1261.[69] His decree assigned the patronage absolutely to the prior and canons as having been given to them by Peter des Roches; but inasmuch as Selborne was endowed with goods issuing from the manor, and in order that Ralph might be duly honoured by the prior and canons, he ordained that Ralph and his heirs should always have the right of presenting one fit clerk to be admitted as a canon into the convent, who should there celebrate for the souls of Ralph, his ancestors and successors. Constantine also decreed that the prior and convent should pay 100*s*. annually to Master John de Brideport until they procured his promotion to some better ecclesiastical benefice. In 1261 Ralph released all right in the advowson and patronage of the church of West Tisted.[70] Four years later the prior and convent of St. Swithun's, Winchester, confirmed Peter des Roches' charter confirming Joan le Hood's grant of the advowson to Selborne together with some lands, 'saving an honest and sufficient maintenance to the vicar.'[71] In 1282 John archbishop of Canterbury confirmed the appropriation of the church to the prior and canons in consequence of their request made to him when at their house in the course of his metropolitical visitation during the vacancy of the see of Winchester.[72] In 1284 Geoffrey de la Flode and Alice his wife and Richard de Crofton released all claim to the advowson,[73] which remained in the possession of Selborne Priory till 1484. In that year the priory was dissolved, and the advowson of West Tisted was among the possessions which were annexed to Magdalen College, Oxford,[74] the president and fellows of which still hold the advowson. Magdalen College often let out the rectory and tithes of West Tisted at farm. It was the rule to give the preference to a fellow of the college, and owing to this custom a dispute arose in the reign of Henry VIII.[75] Early in 1528 when the parsonage was unlet and in the hands of Master Thomas Knollys, the president of the college, Nicholas Tichborne, lord of the manor of West Tisted, asked him for a ten years' lease of the rectory and tithes. Thomas agreed to let them to him for that time, and it was arranged that on Lammas Day, 1528, either Nicholas or his messenger should go to Oxford to get the lease under the common seal of the president and scholars. Nicholas sent his brother Roger Tichborne, but when he arrived he found they were already let to Richard Cressweller, a fellow of the college. Nicholas was naturally annoyed when he heard the news, but nevertheless he suffered Richard to occupy the rectory for two years. On Michaelmas Day, 1531, however, they met at West Tisted and had a violent quarrel, and this quarrel culminated on 3 April, 1533, in a fight between the two parties at West Tisted parsonage, with what result, however, is unknown.

66 *V.C.H. Hants*, i, 463.
67 *Selborne Chart.* (Hants Rec. Soc.), 21.
68 Ibid. 20.
69 Ibid. 54.
70 Ibid.
71 Ibid. 58.
72 Ibid. 70.
73 Ibid. 71.
74 *V.C.H. Hants*, ii, 179. *Valor Eccl.* (Rec. Com.), ii, 284. *Selborne Chart.* (Hants Rec. Soc.), 147.
75 Star Chamb. Proc. bdle. 11, No. 36, and bdle. 22, No. 62.

THE HUNDRED OF EAST MEON

CONTAINING THE PARISHES OF

EAST MEON FROXFIELD AND STEEP WITH NORTH AMBERSHAM TITHING AND SOUTH AMBERSHAM TITHING[1]

In Domesday Book the hundred is represented by a single entry under 'Meon,' which no doubt, however, included the present parishes of Froxfield and Steep. The land within the hundred was assessed at 72 hides at the time of Edward the Confessor, and at 35 hides at the time of the Survey.[2] Westbury and perhaps Peak also were included in Meonstoke hundred in the Survey,[3] and the tithing of Westbury and Peak still formed part of it in 1841, Westbury being then situated partly in East Meon parish and partly in West Meon parish, and Peak wholly in the parish of Warnford.[4] It has, however, since been transferred to East Meon hundred. In 1316 the hundred appears to have comprised also the hundred of Hambledon, for the vills of Hambledon, Chidden, Glidden, and Denmead are included under it,[5] the three last-named being tithings of Hambledon at the present day. Hambledon, however, must soon afterwards have been detached, for it was a separate hundred in the reign of Edward III.[6] From that time onwards the hundred included the same parishes as are set out in the population returns of 1831. The parishes of Colemore, Privett, and Priors Dean were added to the hundred before 1841,[7] and the new parish of Langrish has been formed from the tithings of Langrish, Ramsdean, and Bordean. A further change was effected when the Ambershams, situated in Sussex, were detached from the parish of Steep under the Acts 2 & 3 Will. IV, cap. 64, and 7 & 8 Vic. cap. 61, and became part of Sussex.

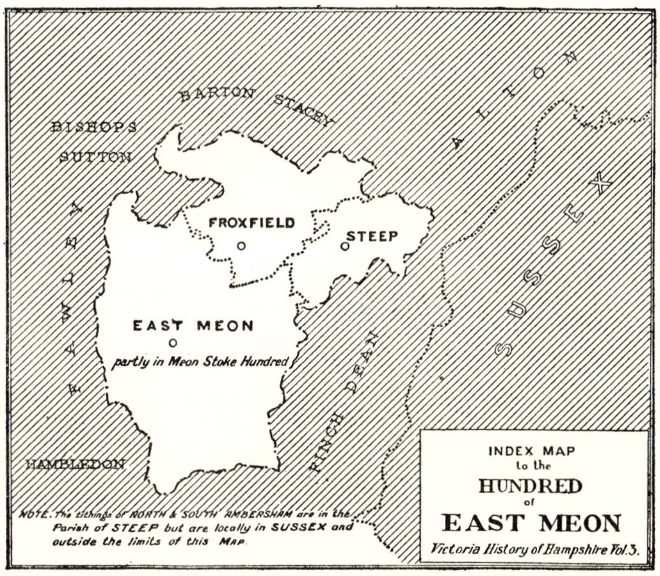

From the earliest date the hundred followed the descent of the manor of East Meon (q.v.), that is, it was in the hands of the bishop until it passed with the manor to the Ecclesiastical Commissioners on the resignation of the see by Bishop Sumner in 1869.

[1] The extent of the hundred as given in the Population Return of 1831.

[2] *V.C.H. Hants*, i, 452.

[3] Ibid. i, 481*a*.

[4] Population Return of 1841.

[5] *Feud. Aids*, ii, 319. 'Sunt in dicto hundredo ville subscripte—Estmune, Froxfeld, Rammesdon, Langeryshe, Stupe, Thorcope, Hameledon, Chidden, Gludden et Denemede.' This may of course have been a slip of the scribe.

[6] Lay Subs. R. Edw. III, Hants, bdle. 173, No. 33.

[7] Cf. Population Returns of 1831 and 1841.

EAST MEON

Menes (xi cent.) ; Meonis (xii cent.) ; East Menes (xiii cent.) ; Estmune, Estmunes, Moene and Estmeone (xiv cent.) ; Estmene (xv cent.) ; and Estmeane (xvi cent.).

Until 1894 the parish of East Meon included the tithings of Oxenbourn, Coomb, Riplington, Peak, Langrish, and Ramsdean, and contained 11,370 acres of land and 7 acres of land covered by water. In that year the tithings of Langrish, Ramsdean (including part of Stroud Common), and Bordean were formed into a separate parish of Langrish, and the area of East Meon was thus reduced to 8,818 acres of land and 5 acres of land covered by water. The parish falls naturally into two parts, namely, the rich pasture-land lying along the banks of the River Meon, and the lofty downs which hem the valley in on every side. The village is almost in the centre of the parish, and lies for the most part to the south of the road from Petersfield to West Meon, which here makes a sharp descent from Barrow Hill. Park Down, which rises to the north of the road and seems to dominate the whole village, has the schools, a row of cottages, the church, and vicarage standing on its lower slopes. On the south side of the road nearly opposite the church is Court Farm. Directly opposite the church Church Street runs southward to join the main village street, which follows the line of the Meon, here a small and shallow stream running westwards and spanned by several bridges. The almshouses, erected in 1863 by Mrs. Forbes of Bereleigh, in memory of her husband Mr. George Forbes, are at the corner of Church Street opposite the church, and at the other end is the George Inn. The main street, which runs on the south bank of the stream, is picturesque with its timber and plaster houses, and here and there a red brick building of more pretensions. Especially notable is a fine house on the north side, with heavy cornice and moulded brick door and window-heads, which dates from the beginning of the eighteenth century. In contrast to this comes a series of quaint thatched cottages, one of the prettiest of which, with a rose-covered porch and deep-eaved roof, serves as the butcher's shop. From the east end of the village a road runs south towards Clanfield, passing the smithy at the corner of a narrow lane which leads to Leythe House, the residence of Mr. Gerald Kingsbury. For about a mile the road passes through the low-lying fertile pasture-land bordering the stream, but after passing the source of the river it begins to ascend steadily, being confronted by the steep grassy slopes of Chidden Down, Hyden Hill, and Tegdown Hill, which separate the parish of East Meon from the parishes of Hambledon, Clanfield, and Catherington. As the road ascends the grass-grown banks, older disused tracks are seen on either side, and from the top of the ridge, where the way leads down to Clanfield through the copses which cover the southern slopes of the hills, a good view can be obtained of the village of East Meon, now more than two miles distant, with the church standing at the foot of Park Down, while the spire of Privett Church can be seen away in the distance.

Westbury House, the property of Colonel Le Roy-Lewis, stands in a park of 100 acres two miles west of the village on the borders of West Meon parish. A fine avenue of trees leads past the house, in front of which the River Meon is artificially widened into a lake. Bereleigh House, the seat of Mr. H. Curtis Gallup, stands in a park of 50 acres, about a mile and a half from the village to the east of a shady lane which leaves the main West Meon road near the vicarage, and joins the main road from Petersfield to Winchester. The following are tithings in the parish : Oxenbourn[1] on Oxenbourn Down about 2 miles south-east, Coomb about 2 miles south-west past Hockham and facing Teglease Down, which separates the parishes of East Meon and Meon Stoke, Riplington on the West Meon road near Westbury Park, and Peak about 3½ miles north-west. The soil varies ; the sub-soil is clay and chalk. The chief crops are wheat, barley, and beans. The parish contains 3,832¼ acres of arable land, 2,646¾ acres of permanent grass, and 764 acres of woods and plantations.[2] The common lands were inclosed in 1860.[3] The following place-names are found in East Meon in the sixteenth century : Selscombe, a grove called Estney, and Barnyparke in the tithing of Coomb, land called Maldles, a toft and land called Gentlemans, Fisherman's Mead, Bunny Bridge, Lake Bridge, Quarrey Lane, Peke Lane, Scutt's Close, an inn called the 'Angel' and the Litten in the tithing of East Meon ; Uscombes Dean, Glaselane, and Frexden in the tithing of Oxenbourn ; Bleyse Garden and Rookcomblane in the tithing of Ramsdean ; and a toft called Peppercombe and lands called Bevermon, Fernhills, and Shillingworth or Shillingore in the tithing of Bordean. The following place-names occur in a survey of the manor taken in the middle of the seventeenth century : Hyde Lane,[4] The Berry Garden,[5] Dove Garden, a meadow called Nuttsbury,[6] Gasson[7] Mead, two corn mills under one roof commonly called Shutt Mills, and Puddle Acre ; Killborow, Hackwermead, Mustardcomes, and Merrywethergate in the tithing of Ramsdean ; Fish Acres in Oxenbourn ; and Frogland, Abbeyland, and Cawseymead in the tithing of Meonchurch ; inclosed ground called Thisly Field and Partridge Furlong, and a lake called Weary Lake.

The modern parish of Langrish, covering an area of 2,552 acres of land and 2 acres of land covered by water, falls into two main portions—the comparatively low-lying land of Stroud Common, and the downs and hangers which form its northern, southern, and western boundaries. The village with its modern

[1] King John, when earl of Mortain, granted land in Oxenbourn to Fulk de Cantilupe to be held by service to the bishop of Winchester, and after John's accession Fulk gave him two palfries to obtain a confirmation of this grant (*Rot. de oblatis et finibus*, 317 ; Close, 7 John, m. 16 ; Chart. R. 7 John, m. 7).

[2] Statistics from Board of Agriculture (1905).

[3] *Parl. Accts. and Papers*, 1893–4, lxxi, 485.

[4] The piece of the main Petersfield road between the church and the schools is still called 'the Hyde' by the older inhabitants.

[5] The name is still in use and is applied to a piece of land let out in allotments on the south side of the Hyde to the east of Court House.

[6] The West Meon road where it makes a sudden bend to Drayton is still called Nuttsbury (pronounced Nuzbury) Arch.

[7] This name is still in use.

church, vicarage, and schools, is 2 miles north-east of the village of East Meon at the point where the road to Droxford breaks off south from the main road from Petersfield to Winchester. Langrish House, the seat of Mr. Charles William Talbot-Ponsonby, J.P., is about half a mile south from the village. At the base of Barrow Hill is the tithing of Ramsdean, a collection of farm-buildings and cottages with a small Congregational chapel, rebuilt and enlarged in 1887 by voluntary contributions at a cost of £200. In the tithing of Bordean, which is two miles north-west of Langrish, is a picturesque early seventeenth century thatched farm-house. Bordean House is on high ground about half a mile from Bordean and just to the south of the Petersfield road, which forms the north boundary of its grounds. This is the highest point on this section of the road (507 ft.), which runs eastward by a steep winding descent through the midst of the hangers to the village of Langrish and westward to Lower Bordean.

Hops are grown in this district. At Bordean there are lime-works which have existed at least from the seventeenth century.[8] At Stroud there is a brick, tile, and pipe manufactory, the latter industry dating from about the 16th century.[9] The parish of Langrish contains approximately 1,687 acres of arable land, 1,434¼ acres of permanent grass, and 431 acres of woods and plantations.[10]

MANORS

EAST MEON.—Since in early times no distinction was drawn between East and West Meon it is difficult to know whether the numerous pre-Conquest grants of land on and near the River Meon[11] refer at all to East Meon.[12] The first distinctive mention of East Meon comes in the middle of the eleventh century, when Alwin, bishop of Winchester, who died in 1047,[13] granted both the Meons[14] to the monks of Winchester,[15] retaining, however, the management of the lands. Thus Bishop Stigand held East Meon to the use of the monks[16] not only after he became primate but even after his deposition and to the day of his death, when it was seized by William I, who was holding it in 1086.[17] At the same time Walkelin, bishop of Winchester, was holding in East Meon 6 hides and 1 virgate with the church and a mill[18] probably the later tithing of Meonchurch.[19] The manor continued the property of the crown till some time between 1154 and 1161,[20] when Henry II granted it, together with all churches belonging to it, to the church of Winchester,[21] and this grant was confirmed by King John soon after his accession.[22] From this date the manor remained with the bishop[23] until it was sold with his other lands in 1648 and 1649 as a result of the Root and Branch Bill.[24] With the general restoration of bishops' lands in 1660 the manor once more came to the bishop, and is at present held by the Ecclesiastical Commissioners as his representatives. In the reign of Edward III there seems to have been a dispute between the bishop and the men of his manor of East Meon, for exemplifications of entries in Domesday Book relating to 'Menes' were made in 1342 and 1343 at the request of the men of the manor and of Adam Orlton, bishop of Winchester, respectively.[25] Again, in August, 1461, when Edward IV went on progress to Hampshire, the tenants of the manor of East Meon and elsewhere, 'in grete multitude and nombre,' petitioned the king for relief from certain services, customs, and dues which the bishop and his agents were attempting to exact.[26] According to one account the tenants had seized Bishop Waynflete. Edward, however, not only rescued him from the hands of those seeking his life, but arrested the ringleaders,[27] whose case was tried in the House of Lords on 14 December, 1461, when judgement was given for the bishop.[28] On 14 December, 1581, John Watson, bishop of Winchester, leased the manor to Queen Elizabeth for eighty-one years.[29]

There is an interesting survey of the manor taken on 31 July, 1647,[30] giving the name of every farm, field, tenant, and tenement, with the rent paid in each case.

'The manor-house called the Court House,' in which the courts-leet and the courts-baron of the manor were held, remains practically unchanged from that day. It was described then as 'being strongly built with stone, having a large hall, a large parlour, a dining-room, a kitchen, a buttery, a larder, a day-house, a kill, three lodging-chambers, a corn-

[8] At a court held 24 September, 1649, a certain William Musgrave was fined 6*d.* for emptying his lime-pits and throwing his skins into the water, whereby he had greatly offended his neighbours (Eccl. Com. Ct. R. bdle. 99, No. 9).

[9] In 1571 John Robynnet obtained a grant of a parcel of land of the lord's waste, lying in the north part of the Stroud, and with it licence to dig up mud and clay and make bricks and tiles on the said parcel, the custom of the manor notwithstanding (Eccl. Com. Ct. R. bdle. 111, No. 1).

[10] Statistics from Board of Agriculture (1905).

[11] The earliest mention of Meon seems to be A.D. 790, when King Beortric granted land in 'Hissaburn' to Prince Hemele in exchange for land on the River 'Meonea' which he had bought from King Kinewulf (Birch, *Cart. Sax.* i, 359). See also Birch, *Cart. Sax.* i, 514; ii, 378, and iii, 175, 477, and 654; and Kemble, *Codex Diplom.* 314, 553, 1031, 1067, 1107, and 1190.

[12] The probability is that they do not, since they are all royal grants, and as early as the reign of Edward the Confessor the manor was held by the bishop of Winchester.

[13] Dugdale, *Mon.* i, 195.

[14] East and West Meon.

[15] Dugdale, *Mon.* i, 210.

[16] *V.C.H. Hants*, i, 452*a*.

[17] Ibid.

[18] Ibid. i, 461*b*.

[19] Meonchurch was that part of the parish lying directly round the church as distinct from the tithing of Meon manor which lay more to the south.

[20] It could not have been later, because Theobald, archbishop of Canterbury, a witness to the charter, died in 1161.

[21] Add. Chart. 28658.

[22] Chart. R. 1 John, m. 29. In his confirmation John refers to a charter of his brother Richard, which seems to be no longer extant.

[23] Pat. 12 Edw. I, m. 11; *Red Bk. of Exch.* i, cxxix; *Rot. Orig.* (Rec. Soc.), i, 48; *Feud. Aids*, ii, 319; Close, 14 Hen. VI, m. 18.

[24] In 1648 the Court House and other premises in East Meon were sold to Nathaniel Hallowes (Close, 24 Chas. I, pt. 2, m. 24). In the same year Richard Dannald purchased South Farm with the lands appertaining to it in East Meon (Close, 24 Chas. I, pt. 8, m. 19). In the following year East Meon manor, East Meon park, Church farm, the Shutt mills, and other premises were sold to Francis Allein (Close, 1649, pt. 40, No. 24).

[25] Pat. 16 Edw. III, pt. 2, m. 35, and 17 Edw. III, pt. 1, m. 23.

[26] They petitioned for relief from the payment in hens and corn called 'churchetts,' tithing-pence, and pannage. They also complained that the court of the bishop was being held within the site of the parsonage of East Meon, and not within the site of the manor of East Meon, and asserted that the tenants within the ordship of East Meon were freeholders and not copyholders (*Parl. R.* (Rec. Com.), v, 476).

[27] *Three Fifteenth-Century Chron.* (Camd. Soc.), 174.

[28] *Parl. R.* (Rec. Com.), v, 475 and 476.

[29] Add. MS. 21497, fol. 390.

[30] This survey was formerly owned by the Bakers of Ashford, in the parish of Steep, and is at present in the possession of Mr. John Silvester of the Slade, Froxfield.

chamber, a cheese-chamber, with some other little rooms. Before the entrance of the house is a gate-house with three rooms thereunto belonging. The roof of the house is much out of repair. The site consisting of two little gardens, and a hopyard and two little courts west before the house, lying all together, between the street of East Meon on the west, and a field called the Berry Garden on the east. Near unto the same on the north-west is the church, and on the north is the highway called Hyde Lane, and on the south is a piece of ground called Dovegarden containing together one acre. This farm hath always been let tithe free.'[31]

The gate-house and the two little courts before the house have given way to a yard with farm-buildings of no architectural interest, but the 'large hall, strongly built with stone,' still stands, with a block of contemporary buildings on the north, and traces of a ruined south wing. Now, as in 1647, 'the roof of the house is much out of repair,' but unfortunately the lack of repair is not confined to the roof, and the house probably owes its survival to its massive flint and stone walls, 4 ft. thick. All the old work

THE COURT HOUSE, EAST MEON

seems to be of one date, and that probably the early part of the fifteenth century. The hall, which stands north and south, is lighted by two large two-light windows on the west, with cinquefoiled lights and transoms rebated for wooden shutters, and the passage through the screens is at the north, with arched doorways at either end, the framework of the screen, with a central and two side openings, being still in position. The south or upper end of the hall is partitioned off from the rest of the block, and in the west wall, south of the partition, is a blocked doorway leading to the first-floor rooms of the destroyed southern wing, the bonding of whose walls is still to be seen. The east and south sides of the hall have been more altered and pulled about than the north side, but an original two-light window remains in the southern part of the east wall, and this end of the block is divided into two stories and still used as living rooms, while the rest of the hall is gutted and serves for the storage of all manner of lumber. Its old roof has given place to rough timbers, though the original stone corbels remain, carved with heads of bishops and kings.

The northern block is of two stories, the upper being reached by a wooden stair, dilapidated but still practicable, in the south-west angle, opening to the courtyard close to the west entrance to the hall screens. The ground story is very scantily lighted by narrow single square-headed lights, and contains three rooms, two with doorways side by side opening from the screens, and a third to the north-west, reached only from the western of the other two rooms. These two occupy the normal position of pantry and buttery, and probably served as such; they are separated by a wooden partition, instead of being set, after the usual plan, on either side of a passage leading to the kitchen. The third room may have been a larder or dairy,[32] and the kitchen can have formed no part of the existing block, but probably stood to the east, where modern buildings now are, and in that case must have been approached through the eastern doorway of the hall passage. It may have been a wooden building, as in other instances, which would account for its disappearance. On the west side of the north-west room (the suggested larder or dairy) is a large block of masonry containing a shaft 10 ft. long by 3 ft. 2 in. wide, an opening into which has been broken from the north end at the ground level. It is probably the shoot of a latrine, but has been boarded over in the room above, and shows no evidence of this. The first-floor rooms of this block have been living-rooms or bedrooms, and in the south wall of that over the buttery (?) is a wide fireplace.

Nothing can be said of the arrangement of the south wing of the house, which must have contained the best living-rooms, the parlour and dining room of the Survey. The south-east angle of the central block seems to have stood clear of any buildings to the south, and has a diagonal angle buttress, which, however, is not part of the original work. The return of a plinth on the south wall 4 ft. to the west of the buttress gives the line of abutment of a wall running southwards from this point, forming the eastern limit of the south wing.

The hopyard of the Survey, with the two little gardens, seems to have been to the south-west of the house, and the 'kill' for drying the hops may have been near by, though the Survey reads as if it were part of the main buildings, and in the northern block.

Under the heading Hyden Woods there is a note to the effect that 'the "bacon" (beacons) on Butser Hill have usually been supplied out of their coppices both with timber and fuel.' Stroud Common belonged to the manor, and it is stated that 'this common is overgrown with bushes which the tenants claim a right unto for making and mend-

[31] It is tithe-free at the present time.

[32] Perhaps the three rooms are the buttery, larder, and day house (dairy) of the Survey, and the three rooms over them the three lodging chambers.

ing their fences, but the great wood belonging to the lord was of late destroyed except some very little and young oaks all at present not worth above 30*s*.'[33]

The boundaries of the manor are given in great detail and show well what a large area it covered[34]: 'This manor lieth part in Hampshire and part in Sussex and is bounded as follows, viz.: By a bound post standing in Basing Dean parting this manor and the manor of West Meon west . . . and by the parish of West Tisted upon the north-west to Hoar Thorns, and so by the manor of Colemeare and a wood called Colemearewood on the north . . . and from thence upon the manor of Prior's Dean upon the north-east to the rising of a little brook in Brooker's mead, and so by that little brook to the parish of Liss, and thence to Wheatham dell and the yew-tree at Wheatham Green, and by a little lake to the Prince's Bridge, and so by the river to Lord's mill and from thence by a little stream unto Kettler's brook and so by the highway to Polehill, then by a footpath to Tilmer gate . . . from thence to Beerland boundring upon the manor of Berriton, from thence to a great oak standing in the midst of Chescombe and so abutting upon the manor of Berriton and Mapledurham upon the south-east unto a great ash standing on the side of Butser Hill . . . and so to the lower gate of Hiden abutting upon the parish of Clanfield, on the south from the aforesaid gate to Broad Halfpenny abutting upon the parish of Katherington, thence to Pye Lane abutting upon the parish of Hambledon . . . from thence abutting upon the parish of West Meon, upon the south-west as far as Westbury, from thence towards the west upon certain lands belonging to Westbury, and so upon the land of Peak farm towards the north-west upon the parish of Privett . . . and so to Basing Post standing in Basing Dean aforesaid.' Certain payments were made from the manor to various officials of the bishopric—the measurer of the tithe-corn and wheat of the rectory, the surveyor and steward of the lordships belonging to the bishopric, the treasurer of 'Wolvesey,' the bailiff of the bailiwick of East Meon, the clerk of the bailiwick of East Meon and Meonchurch, and two reeves and a beadle, and the net annual value of the manor was estimated at £281 5*s*. 1½*d*.

PARK The park of East Meon belonged to the bishops, who were careful to maintain their right of free warren and free chase.[35] The following description is given of the park in the Survey of 1647: 'There is also belonging to this manor a park, situate and lying near the town of East Meon, known by the name of East Meon Park, lying between the way that leadeth from East Meon church and Petersfield called Hide Lane on the south, and another highway that leadeth from East Meon to Alton on the north-west; on the east are the grounds belonging to Magdalen College Oxford and the lands of Sir William Lewis kt. with the lands of other tenants; on the south-west is the church and churchyard of East Meon; on the north the grounds belonging to the manor of "Bearly."[36] The park has a lodge with five rooms, two little out-barns, a garden, a hop-yard all paled about and contains 1½ acres. This park is paled about, but hath not any deer therein. It is now stored with conies. It containeth by estimation 500 acres, and is worth per annum by improvement £70, and is now in possession of Sir William Lewis, bart. He claimeth to hold the office of keeper and the keeping of the park aforesaid and of the deer in the same park and all the herbage, pannage and agistment of it (competent and sufficient herbage and feeding for eight score deer in the same park always excepted), and also the office of measuring the tithe-corn and wheat of the rectory of East Meon with all the profits to the said offices belonging. There is not any tithe to be paid for this park.[37] . . . The grant was made to Queen Elizabeth by John Watson, bishop of Winchester, amongst other things, by indenture 14 December 24 Elizabeth. By her majesty assigned over to John Stockman by indenture 28 March 24 Elizabeth,[38] which said John assigned the same to William Neale . . . The right of this lease descended to his son Sir Thomas Neale,[39] and from him to his son Thomas Neale, who by indenture 13 Feb. 10 Charles granted the same to Sir William Lewis, for which he is to pay per annum two hundred conies worth per annum £5, as also herbage in the park for a hundred and sixty deer worth £40. The present profits of the park which may be made of beechen timber and firewood, now worth £900, all "bots"[40] being allowed.'

There is no longer a park in East Meon, although the name is preserved in the modern Park Farm and Park Down.

An annual fair held near South Farm in a field called Fair Field or Chapel Close[41] originally belonged to the lords of the manor of East Meon. It was kept on the Lady Day in harvest, and the annual profits therefrom were assessed at £1 10*s*.[42] in 1647. It existed until about ten years ago, by which time it had come to be a horse-fair held in the village itself.

At the time of the Domesday Survey there were six mills worth forty shillings in 'Menes,'[43] which was practically identical with the modern hundred of East Meon. The following mills are mentioned in a rent-roll of the manor of East Meon for 1567[44]: a mill called South Mill in the tithing of East Meon held

33 The rights of the tenants of the manor regarding this common were strictly enforced. On 4 April, 1651, a certain Giles Hall of Petersfield was fined 2*s*. for cutting and carrying away two loads of bushes out of the Stroud to Petersfield, being none of the customary tenants of the manor (Eccl. Com. Ct. R. bdle. 99, No. 9).

34 East Meon manor comprised the following tithings: Ambersham, Forcomb or Foxcomb, Aldersnapp, Froxfield, Longhurst, Ramsdean, Week, Oakshott, Langrish, Bordean, Rothercombe, Ashford, Oxenbourn, Meon Manor, Meonchurch, Coomb, and Riplington.

35 Thus in 1279 a commission of oyer and terminer was granted to Robert Fulconis and William de Brayboef touching the persons who broke the parks of Nicholas bishop of Winchester of East Meon &c., hunted therein and carried away deer (Pat. 7 Edw. I, m. 5 *d*.). Again in 1371 William bishop of Winchester brought a similar plea against certain malefactors, who, besides breaking into his parks and chases had also fished in his fisheries, and taken and carried away fish to the value of £200, and beasts from the said parks and chases, and also hares, pheasants, and partridges (Pat. 45 Edw. III, pt. 1, m. 27 *d*.).

36 The modern Bereleigh.

37 At the present day Park Farm and all the lands belonging to it, Park Down, &c., occupying the site of the Park, are tithe-free.

38 *Vide* also Pat. 24 Eliz. pt. 6.

39 Lord of the manor of Warnford.

40 House-bot, post-bot, pale-bot, and rail-bot.

41 So called because there was formerly a chapel of ease there called St. Mary's in the Field. This chapel is mentioned as early as 1318, but in 1703 is described as 'quite doun' (Stowe MS. 845, fol. 56).

42 MS. *penes* Mr. J. Silvester of Froxfield.

43 *V.C.H. Hants*, i, 452*a*.

44 MS. *penes* Mr. J. Silvester.

by Nicholas Write by the rent of 1*s.* 3*d.*, two mills in the tithing of Oakshott (which is now in the parish of Froxfield), viz. a fulling-mill held by John Pagelham by the annual rent of 10*s.*, and a water-mill called Sheet Mill held by Edward Roche by the annual rent of 10*s.* 4*d.*; and a water-mill in Ramsdean held by John Tribe by the annual rent of 15*s.* In the Survey of the manor taken in 1647 the following mills are mentioned: 'Two corn-mills under one roof commonly called or known by the name of Shutt Mill, which mills lie west from East Meon,' a mill called South Mill held by Thomas Searle, a mill held by William Heycroft in the tithing of Meonchurch, a water-mill held by John Tribe in the tithing of Ramsdean, and two fulling-mills in Foxcombe (now forming part of the parish of Steep) held respectively by Elizabeth Colebrooke and Jane the relict of Joseph Feilder.[45] In the measurement and valuation of the parish of East Meon made in May, 1820, by Mr. Vinn of Drayton [46] two mills are mentioned: Drayton Mill and Frogmore Mill, and they are still in existence.

WESTBURY (Wesberie xi cent.; Westburia xii cent.; Westbyrie xiii cent.) was held by Ulnod of King Edward the Confessor. At the time of the Domesday Survey it was held by Gozelin, not directly of the king, but of Hugh de Port as part of his barony which he held of the king.[47] It was assessed at 3 hides both in Edward the Confessor's reign and at the time of the Survey. Like the rest of the Port barony Westbury passed to the St. Johns,[48] from the St. Johns to the Poynings,[49] and possibly from the Poynings to the Paulets, although there is no mention of overlordship after the fourteenth century. There is no evidence to show to whom the manor descended after the death of Gozelin the son of Azor, who held it at the time of the Domesday Survey. In the reign of Henry II or even earlier it seems to have been granted to a family who took the surname of Westbury.[50] In the reign of Henry III John de Westbury held in Westbury one knight's fee of the ancient enfeoffment of Robert de St. John, and the same Robert of the king.[51] John de Westbury seems to have been succeeded by a certain William de Campania, who demised it for a term of five years to a certain Peter de Campania and Margery his wife.[52] Some time afterwards the same William quitclaimed for himself and his heirs all the right and claim which he had in the manor to the said Peter and Margery and their heirs.[53] In 1294 this Peter was in custody in Westminster gaol for the death of Adam Houel, but his lord, John de St. John, interceded for him, and obtained his pardon.[54] After the death of Peter his widow Margery married Robert le Ewer the king's yeoman,[55] evidently before 1316, since in that year he was holding the manor in right of his wife.[56]

In 1322 Robert obtained the king's permission to fortify his house at Westbury,[57] and about the same time the king granted to him and his heirs for ever free warren in all their demesne lands of Westbury.[58] Many details concerning the life of this Robert le Ewer can be gathered from a careful examination of the close and patent rolls of the reign of Edward II. The earliest mention of him is in 1306, in which year the king granted safe conduct to him and to certain others of his clerks and serjeants-at-arms while taking money to Scotland for the maintenance of the king's subjects on his service there.[59] For some time he rose steadily into favour with King Edward II. In 1308 he was farmer of the gaol of Somerton, and of the hundreds of Cattesashe and Stone.[60] In 1309 the reversion of the manor of Warblington was granted to him for his life,[61] and in 1311 Odiham Castle was committed to him to hold during the king's pleasure.[62] However, in 1320 he fell into disfavour with the king, and John de Felton and the king's serjeants-at-arms were commissioned to arrest him for certain trespasses, contempts, and disobediences.[63] He was arrested by them, but broke the attachment by armed force, publicly defied the serjeants, and in addition threatened some of the king's subjects with loss of life and limb, asserting that he would slay them and cut them up limb by limb, wherever he should find them, either in the presence or absence of the king, in contempt of the king's order and in rebellion.[64] By some means, however, he succeeded in making his peace with the king, and in 1321 the custody of Odiham Castle was re.tored to him.[65] In 1322 the king summoned him to join the English army in Scotland.[66] Robert disregarded the summons, however, and was accordingly deprived of the custody of Odiham Castle, John de St. John being appointed keeper in his stead.[67] Thereupon Robert rebelled. He placed himself at the head of an armed force, attempted to seize the castle, and entered the royal manor of Itchel and carried away the king's goods.[68] Edmund de Kendale, keeper of the peace in Hampshire, arrested him, and as a reward received a horse, a 'haketon,' and a dagger which were found with Robert when he was taken.[69] Robert, when charged with divers felonies before the king, refused to submit to the law of the realm, and being put to *peine forte et dure*, died in prison.[70] When her husband was taken, Margery fled, taking with her two coffers with jewels and other goods and chattels to the value of £200. She took sanctuary in the abbey of St. Mary's, Winchester, where two of her sisters were nuns,[71] but she was soon dragged from her hiding-place and thrown into prison. In the summer of 1324, however, she was released and delivered to Ralph Camois,[72] who in 1325 was appointed with others to inquire the names of those who had taken and concealed goods and chattels belonging to Robert.[73] In 1327 it was ascertained that Ralph Camois and Elizabeth his wife and Hugh their son had disseised Margery of the manor of Westbury long before the making of the charter whereby Edward II had granted it to them.[74]

[45] MS. *penes* Mr. J. Silvester.
[46] MS. *penes* Mrs. Vinn of Drayton.
[47] *V.C.H. Hants*, i, 481.
[48] *Testa de Nevill* (Rec. Com.), 230; Inq. p.m. 3 Edw. III, No. 67, and 11 Edw. III, No. 49.
[49] Inq. p.m. 47 Edw. III (1st Nos.) No. 10.
[50] Pipe R. 13 Hen. II.
[51] *Testa de Nevill*, 230.
[52] *Vide* Coram Rege R. Mich. 1 Edw. III, m. 117.
[53] Ibid.; *Feud. Aids*, ii, 336.
[54] Pat. 22 Edw. I, m. 16.
[55] *Vide* Coram Rege R. Mich. 1 Edw. III, m. 117.
[56] *Feud. Aids*, ii, 307.
[57] Pat. 15 Edw. II, pt. 1, m. 1.
[58] Chart. R. 15 Edw. II, m. 7.
[59] Pat. 34 Edw. I, m. 12.
[60] Close, 2 Edw. II, m. 20.
[61] Pat. 2 Edw. II, pt. 2, m. 5.
[62] Close, 5 Edw. II, m. 26.
[63] Pat. 14 Edw. II, pt. 1, m. 16.
[64] Close, 14 Edw. II, m. 21.
[65] Pat. 14 Edw. II, pt. 2, m. 4 and 5.
[66] Ibid. 16 Edw. II, pt. 1, m. 24.
[67] Ibid. m. 21.
[68] Ibid. m. 17.
[69] Close, 18 Edw. II, m. 6.
[70] Pat. 18 Edw. II, pt. 2, m. 14 *d.*
[71] Close, 17 Edw. II, m. 14.
[72] Ibid. 18 Edw. II, m. 39.
[73] Ibid. m. 6.
[74] Close, 1 Edw. III, pt. 1, m. 5.

The king accordingly laid the matter before Ralph de Bereford, John de Scures, and John de Tichborne, when it was decided that Robert le Ewer having only held the manor in right of his wife Margery, it should be restored to her, and in addition she should be awarded £160 damages.[75] It seems probable that shortly after this Margery married, as her third husband, a certain Nicholas de Overton, for in 1328 Nicholas de Overton and Margery his wife, and John de Thyngdene, chaplain, were parties to a fine whereby the manor of Westbury was settled upon Nicholas and Margery and the heirs of Margery.[76] Margery died before 1342, leaving as her heir a certain Margaret, described as 'Margaret who was the wife of James de Molyns,' who in 1342, in conjunction with Sir Aumary de Wykfort, granted the reversion of the manor after the death of Nicholas de Overton to Nicholas le Devenish of Winchester and his heirs male.[77] The latter died seised of the manor in 1350, leaving a son and heir Thomas, aged 17,[78] on whose death in 1373 it passed to his son and heir John, aged 10,[79] who died soon afterwards, and was succeeded by his brother Thomas. In 1382 Thomas died while still under age, and the manor passed to his sister and heir Nichola.[80] It is probable that Nichola married first Sir John Englefield of Warwickshire, and secondly John Golafre of Blakesley (Northants).[81] Certainly Sir John, who lived about the reigns of Richard II and Henry IV, married a certain Nichola,[82] and John Golafre married as his second wife a Lady Englefield.[83] Elizabeth, widow of Thomas Devenish, held the manor in dower and married a certain William Marshal before 1386, at which date the manor was dealt with by a fine, to which John Englefield and Nichola his wife were parties.[84] Nichola died before 1428, for in that year her second husband John Golafre was holding in Westbury half a fee which Nicholas Devenish formerly held.[85] Westbury passed with Greatham to the recusant family of Fawconer,[86] who held it for about two centuries,[87] Katherine Fawconer at length conveying it to John Holt and Katherine his wife, of Portsmouth.[88] In 1694 Richard Holt of Nursted (Hants), son and heir of John and Katherine, sold the manor for £4,000 to Richard Markes of Petersfield.[89] After the latter's death his widow Mary and his son and heir Richard became involved in financial difficulties, and in 1722 were forced to sell the manor to their tenant Philip Cavendish, obtaining a sum of £7,400 for it.[90] Philip dealt with the manor by fine in 1737,[91] no doubt on the occasion of his marriage with Anna Isabella Carteret, the daughter of Edward Carteret and Bridget his wife.[92]

FAWCONER. *Sable three falcons argent with bells and jesses or.*

Within the next ten years Westbury had been purchased by Admiral Sir Peter Warren, K.B.,[93] an Irishman by birth. He obtained his commission as a lieutenant in 1722, and from that time his promotion was rapid. He aided the New England colonies in the war with France, and in 1745, with General Pepperell, captured Louisbourg, as a reward for which he was made rear-admiral of the Blue. After the capitulation of Louisbourg Warren captured three French ships valued at £1,000,000, and from his share of the spoils of war realized a large fortune. In 1747 he won a great naval victory off Cape Finisterre, and for his gallantry on this occasion was made Knight of the Bath. On his retirement from active service in 1748 he received many civic honours, being elected M.P. for Westminster in 1750. He died of a violent fever in 1752 while at Dublin, whither he had gone to purchase estates. In 1735 he had married Susanna daughter of Stephen de Lancey, a wealthy citizen of New York, and by her he left three daughters and co-heirs—Anne, who married Lieut.-General Hon. Charles Fitzroy, first Lord Southampton, in 1758; Susanna, who married in 1767 Lieut.-General William Skinner; and Charlotte, who married Willoughby Bertie, fourth earl of Abingdon, in 1768.[94] The manor was at first divided among the three sisters, but in 1772 Charles Fitzroy and Anne and Willoughby, Earl of Abingdon, and Charlotte gave up their moieties to Lieut.-General Skinner and Susanna,[95] whose daughter and heir Susanna Maria married her first cousin Major-General Henry, third Viscount Gage, in 1789. Their son Henry, fourth Viscount Gage (1808–77), sold the manor to Mr. John Delawar Lewis, from whom it has descended to Colonel Le Roy-Lewis, the present owner.

The manor of *LANGRISH* (Langerisse xiii cent.; Langryshe, Langrissh, and Langeryssh xiv cent.; Langrishe xvii cent.) was a sub-manor dependent upon the manor of East Meon.[96] John Langrish, son of John, who had probably held the manor before him, was holding the manor in the early fifteenth century, and held his first court in 1419. At a court held in May, 1424, John granted certain premises in Langrish to his brother Thomas to hold for the term of his life. The first court of Thomas Langrish was held on 21 December, 1466, and in 1473 Robert the son of Thomas, probably on his

75 Coram Rege R. Mich. 1 Edw. III, m. 117.

76 Feet of F. Hants, Mich. 2 Edw. III.

77 Ibid. Hil. 16 Edw. III. About six months afterwards the manor was settled by fine upon Nicholas and Edith his wife, with remainder to Thomas son and heir of Nicholas and Matilda (who was probably the first wife of Nicholas) (Feet of F. Hants, Mich. 16 Edw. III).

78 Inq. p.m. 24 Edw. III (1st Nos.), No. 61.

79 Ibid. 47 Edw. III (1st Nos.), No. 10.

80 Ibid. 5 Ric. II, No. 19.

81 See under Sutton Scotney, Buddlesgate hundred.

82 *Harl. Soc.* xii, 123.

83 Lipscombe, *Bucks.* i, 394.

84 Feet of F. Hants, Hil. 9 Ric. II.

85 *Feud. Aids*, ii, 358.

86 *V.C.H. Hants*, ii, 506*b*.

87 Phillipps, *Hants Visitations*, 1575, 1623, and 1686, p. 26. During the reign of Elizabeth, William Fawconer recusant paid £72 4*s*. 4*d*. a year to the crown for two-thirds of the manor (Gasquet, *Hants Recusants*, 26).

88 Close, 6 Will. and Mary, pt. 9, No. 23.

89 Ibid.

90 Close, 9 Geo. I, pt. 14, m. 1, &c.; Recov. R. Mich. 9 Geo. I, rot. 35.

91 Feet of F. Hants. Mich. 11 Geo. II.

92 Edmondson, *Baronagium Geneal.* iii, 209.

93 It seems impossible to discover the exact date of the sale. It must have been before 1747, however, for in that year 'Sir Peter being attacked by illness was compelled to quit his command and retire to his country seat at Westbury in Hampshire' (*The Naval Chron.* xii, 271).

94 Rev. Thomas Warren, *Hist. of the Warren Family*, 187.

95 Feet of F. Hants, Trin. 12 Geo. III.

96 In an indenture of sale (*penes* Lord Hylton) the manor was said to be copyhold of inheritance and held under the bishop of Winchester. From the East Meon court-rolls it appears that the manor fell into the hands of the bishop on the death of the holder, whose successor paid a fine on taking up his inheritance. It was also always surrendered to the bishop prior to settlements and sales. Add. Chart. 27974–89

marriage, received a messuage and other premises in Langrish to hold to him and his wife and their male issue. In 1489 Nicholas Langrish, aged sixteen, described as kinsman and heir of John Langrish priest, held his first court. He had five sons, the eldest of whom, Edward by name, died without issue.[97] The manor accordingly passed to his brother William,[98] whose son and heir Nicholas was described as lord of Langrish in the visitation of 1634.[99] William son and heir of Nicholas sold the manor to Nathaniel Long and Mary his wife, upon whom it was settled in 1663 with remainder to Hugh Webb and Abigail Long, elder daughter of Nathaniel and Mary, and their issue.[100] In 1664 Nathaniel Long had a dispute with Edmund Bruning, lord of the neighbouring manor of Rothercombe, about his right of way through certain lands, parcel of the manor of Rothercombe, to certain woods called Beechenleith or Beechencliffe Woods, as also his right to timber in the woods. The matter was referred to the Court of Chancery, which gave its judgement in favour of Nathaniel, awarding him in addition £250 damages.[101] On the death of Nathaniel the manor descended to Hugh and Abigail Webb, in accordance with the settlement of 1663, and on their deaths to their son and heir Nathaniel, whose widow Lucy and son and heir Nathaniel sold it in 1719 to Thomas Ridge of Portsmouth for £2,850.[102] Thomas was succeeded by his son and heir Humphrey, who died without issue about 1730, when the manor passed to his brother Thomas, described as a brewer, distiller, and wine merchant of Portsmouth. Thomas, who was afterwards knighted, soon became involved in financial difficulties, and owed his mother Elizabeth £8,215 at the time of her death in 1750. He borrowed further sums from his younger brothers George and Richard after her death, and in 1764 was declared a bankrupt, John Ridge and Thomas Hampton being chosen assignees of his estate and effects.[103] The estate was put up for auction[104] and was sold in 1771 for £4,400 to William Jolliffe of Petersfield. It continued in the Jolliffe family till a few years ago, when it was sold by Lord Hylton to Mr. William Nicholson, D.L., J.P., of Basing Park, the present owner.

In the Langrish court-rolls from 1419 to 1523 there occur the following place-names: a wood called Musilcombe; crofts called Topelayns, Benepierks, and Yaldepierks; a common field called the Hampme, lanes called Bawfyshlane and Mustardcombeslane,[105] and crofts called Pycedcrofte and Thevelerscroft. From the court-rolls it is seen that most of the tenants held lands of the lord of Langrish by the service of finding men for the fishery in the River Meon. There is an interesting entry in the court-roll for 1479.[106] A certain John Baker received from the lord of Langrish a messuage and lands in Langrish to hold for the term of his life by the services of paying an annual rent of 13*s*., of finding two men for the great fishery of East Meon, and of paying 6*d*. per annum tithing-silver. John Baker and his successors were also to find two bushels of corn every Easter at their own expense. They were to make bread therefrom, and deliver over the loaves every year to Thomas Langrish and his heirs in the parish church of East Meon for distribution among the poor of the parish. In return for these bushels of corn Thomas reduced the rent of the premises from 16*s*. to 13*s*. a year.

In the East Meon court-rolls *ROTHERCOMBE* (Redecumbe xii cent.) is frequently mentioned as one of the tithings of East Meon, and now exists as a farm in the parish of Langrish. In the twelfth century Godfrey de Lucy, bishop of Winchester, granted in free alms to John, prior of Aldebiri in Sandes, afterwards known as the Priory of Newark, all the land of Rothercombe which appertained to his manor of East Meon, and which was worth 100*s*. a year.[107] On the dissolution of Newark Priory the king granted the manor of Rothercombe and woods called Cherry Copse, Beching Cliff, and Brokewode, situated in Rothercombe, to Thomas Knight,[108] who shortly afterwards sold the manor together with lands and rents in East Meon and Rothercombe to Thomas Uvedale for £126.[109] Anthony Uvedale, son and heir of Thomas, married Ursula Norton, and had an only daughter and heir, Ellen, by whose marriage to Richard Bruning the manor passed into the Bruning family.[110] In 1608 an inquiry was ordered to be held into the goods, chattels, lands, and tenements of Richard Bruning and Ursula Uvedale, since various sums of money were due to the crown on account of their recusancy. It was ascertained that Richard was seised of the manor of Rothercombe and of 30 acres of arable land and 20 acres of meadow and pasture in the parish of East Meon of the yearly value of £6 10*s*.[111] The manor, however, was evidently not sequestered, as Richard died seised of it in 1612, leaving a son and heir, Anthony, aged twenty-three.[112] The manor remained in the Bruning family until 1715,[113] in which year Richard Bruning sold it together with a messuage and lands in Steep and East Meon to John Clement of Steep for £1,730.[114]

On the death of John Clement the manor passed to his son William, whose only son and heir sold the manor or reputed manor of Rothercombe, the messuage or dwelling-house called Rothercombe Farm,

97 Berry, *Hants Gen.* 236.

98 Feet of F. Hants, Trin. 7 Jas. I.

99 Ibid.

100 Eccl. Com. Ct. R. bdle. 115, No. 2.

101 Chan. Enr. Decree, 1915, No. 2. The money was to be paid at East Meon at the sign of the 'George.'

102 Deeds *penes* Lord Hylton.

103 Thomas did not long survive his downfall, dying in October, 1766. By his will, dated October, 1765, he bequeathed the residue of his estate to his brothers George and Richard in fee-tail with contingent remainder to Mary Ridge daughter of John Ridge.

104 In the bill the property is described as follows:—'The manor, lordship, or royalty of Langrish, the Farm called Court Farm, £93 per annum; Stroode Farm, £35 per annum. There is payable to the bishop of Winchester out of these estates annually the sum of £3 6*s*. 6*d*. or thereabouts, viz. £2 10*s*. for the Manor and Court Farm, and 16*s*. 6*d*. for Stroode Farm. Langrish is situated in an exceeding fine sporting county, and there is great plenty of game on the manor. The house stands on the top of a beautiful hill at a convenient distance from the road, and commands an extensive and romantic prospect. The hill and inclosures between it and the road are now exceeding fine pasture and may be greatly improved. The whole estate is a very desirable object, being equally capable of improvements in husbandry and elegance.' It appears also from the East Meon court-rolls that a fine of £7 was due to the lord of the manor of East Meon from the heir when taking up his inheritance.

105 There is still a Mustercoombe Copse.

106 Add. Chart. 27985.

107 Dugdale, *Mon.* vi, 383.

108 Pat. 35 Hen. VIII, pt. 9, m. 33.

109 Feet of F. Hants, Mich. 35 Hen. VIII; Pat. 35 Hen. VIII, pt. 12.

110 Chan. Inq. p.m. (Ser. 2), cclviii, No. 41.

111 Pat. 6 Jas. I, pt. 3, No. 19.

112 Chan. Inq. p.m. 10 Jas. I (Ser. 2), pt. 2, No. 169.

113 Feet of F. Div. Cos. Trin. 1652.

114 Ibid. Hants, Mich. 2 Geo. I.

and 169 acres of land for £2,000 to George Clark, described sometimes as a carrier and sometimes as an inn-keeper of Petersfield, in 1763.[115] Whatever his profession he was a prosperous man, and during the fifteen years preceding his death bought up much landed property in the neighbourhood of Petersfield. Thus in 1755 he purchased Tilmore Farm from Richard Baker,[116] in 1763 he bought Bell Farm from John Rogers and Mary his wife,[117] while in 1764 Henry Smith conveyed to him the messuage or tenement and farm-house on a moor called Buckmoor.[118] On his death in 1768 it was found that by a will dated two years earlier he had left all his property to be divided equally among his three young grandsons, William, Richard, and George Clark Rout, the sons of Mary and James Rout, and had completely passed over the claims of his wife Elizabeth, his sons Richard, Thomas, and George, and his daughters Anne, Rose, and Elizabeth.[119] They appealed against it, but all to no purpose, for by a decree in the Court of Chancery it was ordered that the will should be established, and the trusts performed and carried into execution. The three grandchildren described as William Rout of Romsey, maltster, Richard Rout of East Wellow, yeoman, and George Clark Rout of Romsey, brewer, came of age in 1774, 1776, and 1777 respectively. Even while minors they had borrowed largely, and in 1778 were very deeply in debt. All the property which they had inherited from their grandfather—the manor of Rothercombe, the farms called Tankerdells, Tilmore and Buckmoor, Causeway Meads and Bell Farm—was put up for sale by public auction and was sold in 1778 to the highest bidder, William Jolliffe of Petersfield,[120] since which time it has followed the descent of the manor of Langrish (q.v.).

PEAK or *PEAK TYGALL* (Peek xiv cent.; Peke, Peake Tygoll, and Peeke Tigoll xvi cent.; Peake Tigall and Peake Farme xvii cent.). Three and a half miles north-west of the village of East Meon lies the tithing of Peak, and a little to the south of the tithing lies Tigwell Farm. The tithing and farm probably represent the site of the manor of Peak or Peak Tygall. It was in the possession of the family of Tygehall or Tygall for generations,[121] and was hence called the manor of Peak Tygall. In 1505 William Tygall and Joan his wife sold the manor and 3 messuages, 10 tofts, 400 acres of land, 20 acres of meadow, 120 acres of pasture, 60 acres of wood, and 20*s.* rent and the rent of a pound of pepper in Peak, East Meon, and Meonstoke to Sir William Warham, archbishop of Canterbury, for £200,[122] on whose death in 1532 the manor passed to his nephew William, being settled on him and his wife Elizabeth in tail-male in 1552.[123] In 1560 the manor was settled on William to hold for the term of his life, with remainder to Francis Morres and Anne his wife and their issue, with contingent remainder to the right heirs of William.[124] William had died before 1588, for in that year William Wright was seised of the reversion of the manor of Peak Tygall, immediately expectant and depending upon the estate for life of Dame Elizabeth Warham, widow, late the wife of Sir William Warham, knt. deceased, and sold it to William Neale of Warnford for £630.[125] For about a century the manor remained in the family of Neale,[126] passing from them in 1676, when it was purchased by Thomas Bonham, William Morgan, and Lawrence Cooke.[127] Three years afterwards it was settled upon Lawrence and his heirs. It descended to his grandson and heir Lawrence Cooke of Steep, yeoman, on whose bankruptcy in 1735 it was sold to John Bouverie the lord of the manor of Warnford.[128] Peak followed the descent of Warnford[129] until about the middle of the eighteenth century, when it seems to have again fallen into yeomen's hands.[130] It has changed hands at various times since then,[131] and is now owned by Colonel Le Roy-Lewis, forming part of the Westbury estate.

TYGALL. *Ermine a cheveron sable with three horse-shoes or thereon.*

BERELEIGH (Burley xiv cent.; Bereley xvi and xvii cent). The manor of Bereleigh was a sub-manor dependent upon the manor of East Meon, and in early times was held by a family called 'de Burlee.' In 1369 John de Burlee and Agatha his wife quitclaimed to William de Wykeham, bishop of Winchester, his heirs and assigns, the following tenements which they held of him as of his bishopric: 1 messuage, 1 mill, 205 acres of land, 10 acres of meadow, 60 acres of pasture, 50 acres of wood, and 40*s.* 6*d.* rent in East Meon and Drayton and the rents and services of Richard Tygenore, Richard Hethere, Reginald Tygall, John Southonore, and John Knollere for the tenements which they held of them.[133] The right of the bishop to these tenements was confirmed in 1382 when Clarice wife of William Fisher and sister of Agatha gave up all her claims to them.[133] There seems to be no record of the history of this estate until 1569, in which year the manor of

115 Deeds *penes* Lord Hylton.

116 In 1713 Richard Baker purchased it from John Heather.

117 Mary had inherited it from her cousin William Cox.

118 This farm had been in the Smith family for about two centuries.

119 Deeds *penes* Lord Hylton.

120 Deeds *penes* Lord Hylton; see also Feet of F. Hants, Mich. 17 Geo. III; Div. Cos. East. 18 Geo. III; and Div. Cos. Mich. 19 Geo. III.

121 See *The Gen.* (New Ser.), ii, 108, for a pedigree of the Tygalls. There is but scant documentary evidence as to the connexion of the Tygalls with the manor. In 1326 a messuage, a carucate of land, 20 acres of land and 26*s.* 8*d.* rent in 'La Stock' and 'Peek' were settled upon Thomas de Tygall and Maud his wife (Feet of F. Hants, Hil. 19 Edw. II). Again in 1333 Thomas de Tygall granted a messuage, 3 virgates of land and 4 acres of wood in Westbury and West Tisted to Thomas de la Stoke to hold for the term of his life by the rent of a rose, with reversion to Thomas de Tygall and his heirs (Feet of F. Hants, Mich. 6 Edw. III.)

122 De Banc. R. Trin. 20 Hen. VII, m. 437; and Mich. 21 Hen. VII, m. 2.

123 Com. Pleas. Com. R. 5 and 6 Edw. VI, m. 2.

124 Notes of F. Hants, East. 2 Eliz.

125 Close, 30 Eliz. pt. 5; Add. MS. 33278, fol. 122.

126 W. and L. Inq. p.m. (Ser. 2), bdle. 32, No. 129; Recov. R. Mich. 16 Chas II, rot. 102.

127 Feet of F. Div. Cos. Trin. 27 Chas. II; Close, 28 Geo. II, pt. 12, m. 10–12.

128 Close, 28 Geo. II, pt. 12, m. 10–12.

129 Ibid.

130 In 1764 John Waight and Mary his wife quitclaimed the manor to John Noss (Feet of F. Hants, Mich. 4 Geo. III).

131 In 1787 Richard Woolls and Anne his wife, Thomas Hall and Sarah his wife, and William Harris and Jenny his wife quitclaimed the manor to Thomas Bonham (Feet of F. Hants, Hil. 27 Geo. III). In 1820 it was owned by Mr. Michael Hoy (MS. *penes* Mrs. Vinn of Drayton).

132 Feet of F. Hants, Mich. 43 Edw. III. This grant was confirmed by Ric. II in 1390 (Pat. 13 Ric. II, pt. 3, m. 1).

133 Close, 6 Ric. II, pt. 1, m. 5 *d.*

'Burley' with appurtenances in East Meon and Burley was settled by fine upon Sir Thomas Sackville Lord Buckhurst and Cecilia his wife in fee-tail.[134] In 1582 Sir Thomas sold the manor for £200 to John Baker,[135] who died seised of it in 1606, leaving a son and heir, Sir Richard Baker, aged thirty and more.[136] Fourteen years later Sir Richard obtained a grant of free warren in his manor or lordship of Burley *alias* Beerley, as also licence to stock it with stags, does, hares, rabbits, pheasants, and partridges.[137] The manor passed by sale in 1631 from Sir Richard Baker and Margaret his wife to William Coldham of Stedham (co. Sussex).[138] It seems impossible to discover how long the manor remained in the Coldham family, but it was probably sold about the middle of the seventeenth century to Bartholomew Smith of Winchester, who left two sons James and Bartholomew. The former in 1685 joined a religious order, and all the property passed to Bartholomew, who left three sons and four daughters.[139] The three sons died unmarried of Winchester in 1728, and Frances who married Alexander Wells of Brambridge in 1733.[141] Elizabeth and Frances both died without issue, and consequently the whole manor became vested in Edward Sheldon [142] grandson of William and Anastasia, who mortgaged it in 1775 to Nicholas Baconneau.[143] The further history of the manor is uncertain, but it seems probable that Mr. R. Eyles of East Meon, who built the modern Bereleigh House at the beginning of the nineteenth century, bought up the whole estate, including the old manor-house, which by this time had probably fallen into decay.[144] The estate has been gradually added to during the last century, and has changed hands several times, the present owner being Mr. H. Curtis Gallup, who has recently purchased it from Col. Hudson.

CHURCHES

The church of *ALL SAINTS, EAST MEON*, consists of chancel with south chapel, central tower, north and south transepts, and nave with south aisle and south porch.

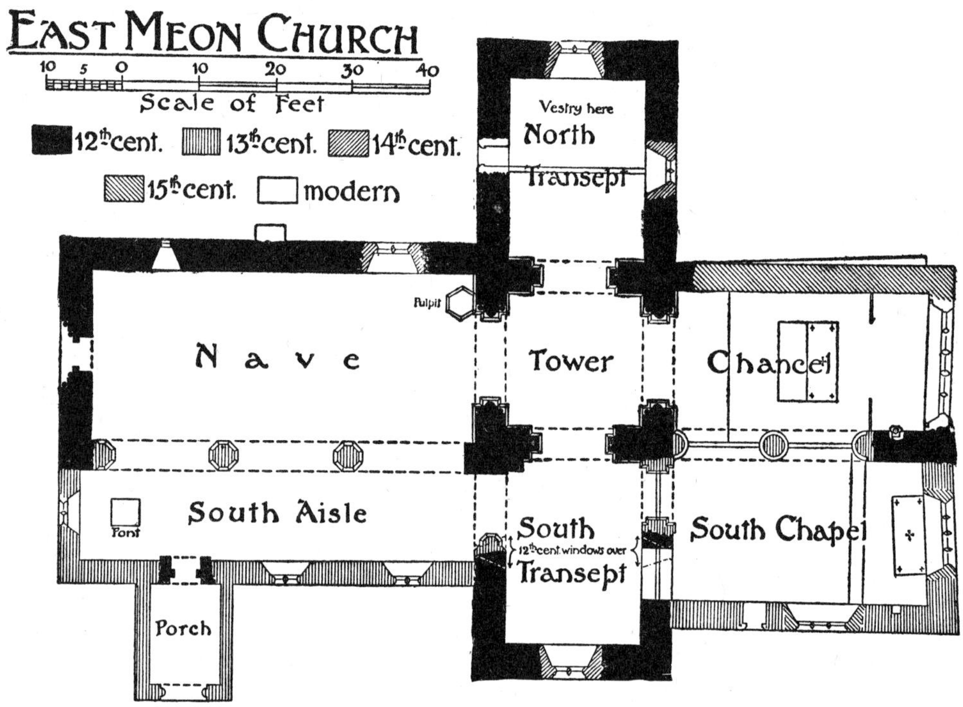

in the same year of small-pox, and one of the daughters became a nun. Consequently the manor was divided among the other three daughters, Elizabeth, Anastasia who married William Sheldon [140] The south chapel and aisle are thirteenth-century additions, and the north and east walls of the chancel have been rebuilt, but with these exceptions the church has preserved its twelfth-century plan and

134 Feet of F. Hants, Hil. 11 Eliz. It is just possible that the manor reverted to the bishopric after the death of William de Wykeham, that it fell into the hands of Sir Richard Sackville, who in the reign of Edward VI was patentee of the bishop of Winchester's lands, and that on his death in 1566 it descended to his son and heir Sir Thomas Sackville, but this is purely conjectural. Unfortunately the only document (Com. Pleas, Deeds Enrolled Recov. R. East. 24 Eliz.) which would cast any light on this subject is too decayed for production.

135 Feet of F. Hants, Trin. 24 Eliz.

136 Chan. Inq. p.m. (Ser. 2), ccxciv, No. 95.

137 Pat. 17 Jas. I, No. 22.

138 Feet of F. Hants, Mich. 6 Chas. I.

139 Duthy, *Sketches of Hants*, 228.

140 Edward Sheldon, third son of Edward Sheldon of Beoley (co. Worc.), was a recusant and was disturbed during the Civil Wars. He died in 1687, leaving several children who all distinguished themselves, viz. Lionel, O.S.B., D.D. and chaplain to the duchess of York; Dominic, general of horse in the service of France; Ralph, equerry to James II, who went privately with him from Rochester to France; Mary, dresser to Queen Catherine; and Frances, maid of honour to Queen Catherine. Ralph's only son and heir William married as his second wife Anastasia, and died in 1748, aged seventy-four. The family was strictly Roman Catholic, and many of its members entered the Society of Jesus (Foley, *Rec. of the Engl. Province*, v, 849, 850).

141 Close, 8 Geo. II, pt. 11, No. 19; and 8 Geo. II, pt. 16, No. 2. Recov. R. Trin. 30 & 31 Geo. II, rot. 222; Close, 31 Geo. II, pt. 11.

142 He was the son of Edward Sheldon of Winchester, whose will is dated 3 June, 1772 (Close, 15 Geo. III, pt. 7, No. 21).

143 Close, 15 Geo. III, pt. 12, No. 3.

144 In a survey of the parish taken in 1820 he is returned as holding 'Beerly House,' 'Beerly' Farm, and lands covering an area of 189 acres, 2 roods, 15 poles (MS. *penes* Mrs. Vinn of Drayton).

much contemporary detail. It seems to have been begun about 1130–40, and shows no evidence of any earlier work on the site, unless the excess of width of the nave over the chancel and transepts, unusual in a cruciform building, points to the former existence of a nave and chancel church, which was enlarged at the date above given by building a tower on the site of the chancel and adding transepts and a chancel on the north, south, and east. Even if this be so, the plan only of the former nave can be said to survive, as there seems no difference between the masonry here and in the other twelfth-century parts of the building.

The details are exceptionally good, both in design and workmanship; the walls are of a uniform thickness of 4 ft., built in flint rubble with ashlar dressings, while the central tower is ashlar-faced. The stone is of admirable quality, and has preserved its original surface to a remarkable degree, the upper stage of the tower showing hardly a trace of decay. The work was probably carried on slowly, after the usual fashion, and the details of the west doorway of the nave are more advanced than those of the tower, suggesting a date of 1150–60. The south chapel seems to have been added at much the same time as the south aisle, and their details point to the beginning of the thirteenth century, though the windows of the south aisle are of somewhat later date. There are noticeable irregularities in the setting out of the east walls of the chancel and south chapel, and the north wall of the chancel seems to have been rebuilt at a different angle, the base of an older wall with a more northerly inclination showing on the outside, and ending 3 ft. 6 in. from the north-east angle of the present chancel. Modern alterations have made it difficult to assign a date to this work, but the arms of Prior Hinton and the monastery of St. Swithun of Winchester, on the east wall of the chancel, point to the fact of a repair or rebuilding of this part of the church between 1470 and 1498. The chancel has a modern east window of five lights with geometrical tracery, and there are no openings in the north wall. In the remains of the former north wall may be seen the lower stones of what are probably the jambs of a doorway. On the south side of the chancel is an arcade of two bays, with circular central column and half-round responds, and circular moulded bases and capitals. The arches are pointed, of two moulded orders with labels, all the detail being very good. The south or Lady chapel has an east window of late fifteenth-century style, of four lights, and a south window of three lights of similar character but rather better design, and to the west of the latter a south doorway with modern stonework. These windows are probably part of the work done by Prior Hinton, and at the south-east is a modern piscina with a shelf. Part of a thirteenth-century piscina, with a projecting moulded bowl, has lately been found, and may have belonged to this chapel.

The transepts were originally lighted by single round-headed windows, one in the east wall and one in the west, and probably a third of the same kind in the gable walls. The east and west windows in the south transept survive, having escaped alteration because they are covered by the roofs of the south chapel and aisle, but the south window in the south transept and all three windows in the north transept have given place to later two-light insertions. The north window of the north transept is of two trefoiled lights with a quatrefoil in the head, and dates from the second quarter of the fourteenth century, as does the rear arch of the east window. The tracery of this window is modern, as is all the stonework of the west window, below which a doorway has just been inserted (1906). In the course of this work a carefully-plastered cavity was found in the wall containing a human bone, apparently placed there at the time of the building of the transept, and probably a relic. There was nothing to show that its position had been marked on the wall-face.

The south window of the south transept, *c.* 1320, has two trefoiled lights with tracery under a triangular head, with a moulded rear arch and label. Above it, in the gable, are three modern lancet windows. In the east wall of this transept, adjoining the south-east pier of the tower, is an early thirteenth-century pointed arch of two chamfered orders, with square-edged chamfered strings at the springing, opening to the south chapel, and contemporary with it, while further to the south is a fourteenth-century opening cut straight through the wall, 6 ft. 8 in. wide, with an arched head, the wall being solid from the springing of the arch downwards. It marks the site of the altar in the transept.

The central tower is of three stages, the ground stage open on all four sides, with slightly stilted round-headed arches, each of three slightly recessed square orders, with a deep string at the springing. The jambs of the north and south arches are simply recessed, the member which takes the inner order of the arches being corbelled off a little below the springing, while the east and west arches are emphasized by half-round shafts to the inner order and nook-shafts to the outer, with scalloped capitals and moulded bases. The walls are ashlar-faced below the string and plastered above, with wrought quoins to the internal angles, up to the under side of the roofs.

The second stage of the tower has plain round-headed openings on all four faces, and is reached by a wooden stair from the north-west angle of the south chapel, which leads to an opening in the east wall of the south transept, and thence by a landing to a narrow fifteenth-century doorway in the south-east of the tower.

Above the roofs the tower is faced with ashlar of excellent quality, and has bowtels at the angles. The third stage has a group of three windows in each face with round-headed arches of two orders, the outer plain and the inner with zigzag ornament. All have labels with billet ornament and jamb-shafts with scalloped capitals, and at their base a string with billet ornament runs round the tower. Above them is a second string with zigzag, and over that three circular openings on each face, with borders of zigzag, close to the eaves of the spire, which is a leaded octagonal broach of moderate height.

The nave had at first two north and two south windows, and probably one in the west wall, with west and south doorways, the steep rise of the ground to the north accounting for the absence of a north doorway. The west doorway remains in position, and the south doorway still exists, though reset in the wall of the south aisle, while the north-west window remains perfect, and traces of those on the north-east and south-east survive. The present north-east window is of the same type and date as that in the south wall of the south transept, while the west window is of three lights with modern tracery of fifteenth-century style, but early fourteenth-century window and rear arches of good detail. The original north-west window is a plain round-headed light, like those in the south transept.

The west doorway is of four orders, with a round-headed arch, and nook-shafts to the second and third orders. The outer order is shallow and of square section, while the second order has an edge-roll between square fillets, the third a double line of horizontal zigzag, and the inner order is plain, as is also the rear arch. Of the nook-shafts, those to the second order have leaf-capitals, and those to the third order scallops. The abacus, which has a square upper edge and a hollow chamfer below, does not project beyond the outer wall face. The south doorway is of similar character, but has only one pair of shafts, and being set in a wall thinner than that in which it originally stood, its rear arch projects from the inner face. Even so it must have lost some of its masonry, as it is now only 3 ft. 4 in. deep, and must have been 4 ft. deep at the first.

The south arcade is of three bays, with octagonal columns, moulded capitals and bases, and pointed arches of three orders, the inner and outer orders chamfered, while the second order has an edge-roll. The western respond of the arcade has a semi-octagonal shaft, and the eastern respond is plain and square. At the east end of the south aisle is a half-arch of the same detail and date as the south arcade, and close to its south respond a plastered recess with a low arched head of sixteenth-century date. In the south wall, east of the south porch, are two windows, each of two lancet lights, the eastern of the two having a quatrefoil above the lights and a flatter rear arch than the other. The masonry of the rear arch is also in larger stones, and it is possible that the quatrefoil is an addition, the arch being rebuilt when it was made. The west window of the aisle is of modern stonework, with a quatrefoil over a pair of lancets. The external south-west corner of the aisle is ashlar-faced, and has a bowtel on the angle.

The woodwork of the church is not ancient, and a great deal of new work has just been set up (1906), including new quire seats, and screens in the arcade between the chancel and south chapel. The altar has been brought forward from its former position against the east wall of the chancel, and a second altar fitted up in the south chapel.

A painting of the Doom over the west arch of the tower, discovered at a former repair of the church, has now entirely disappeared, and the only traces of ancient wall-decoration now existing, beyond remains of red colour in several places, are on the faces of the east responds of the north and south tower arches. They seem to be of thirteenth-century date, that on the north being a Crucifixion, while the other, which is very faint, shows nothing clearly except a crowned head.

The font, at the west end of the south aisle, is one of the best examples of a class of black marble fonts, almost certainly of foreign origin, which occur in three other Hampshire churches, Winchester Cathedral, St. Michael's Southampton, and St. Mary, Bourne. It is fully described in *V.C.H. Hants*, ii, 244. There are no monuments of importance in the church, but two wall tablets of rather unusual character are to be seen in the south wall of the chancel and the west wall of the south transept. Both are framed in a moulding of late Gothic section, and have inscriptions in somewhat heavy Roman lettering—the former in Latin to the wife of Richard Downes, 1659, and the latter in English :—

> Here lyeth the body of Richard Smyther,
> Who departed this life in hope of a better.
> March 16, 1633.

In the pavement of the south transept is set a small piece of stone, inscribed in eighteenth-century lettering 'Amens Plenty,' to explain which a local legend has arisen that it commemorates some soldiers killed in the Civil Wars, and buried here hurriedly, with no more funeral rites than the repetition of many Amens. There is a ring of eight bells, the treble, second, seventh, and tenor, by Taylor of Loughborough, 1890, the third by Chapman & Mears, 1782, the fourth and fifth by Thomas Mears, 1834 and 1819, and the sixth by William Tosier, 1722.

The plate consists of a silver-gilt communion cup of 1747, with a paten of the same date, both given by Ambrose Dickins; a silver paten of 1751, and a plated flagon and spoon, the latter having a bowl embossed and gilt.

The first book of the registers runs from 1560 to 1676, the second from 1677 to 1742, and the third from 1743 to 1812.

THE CHAPEL OF ST. NICHOLAS, WESTBURY, was annexed to the parish church of East Meon. In an account of the parish written in 1703 there is the following description of the chapel :—'There is also another chapel at Westbury, but there is no service in it. Upon a loose gravestone in this chapel, narrower at the feet than at the head, is an ancient portraiture of a priest or a woman deeply carved but much defaced, which if taken up shows it to have anciently been a place of sepulture.'[145] The ruined chapel still stands in the grounds of Westbury House, and can be seen from the road leading to West Meon.

It is in plan a simple rectangle,[146] 35 ft. by 16 ft. within, and appears to belong to the end of the thirteenth century. A curious variation in the thickness of the walls is noticeable, the north wall being thicker than the rest, and the east wall markedly thinner. The entrance is by a doorway in the south wall of which the outer arch is destroyed, but the semicircular rear-arch remains. East and west of it are two-light windows, uncusped, with an uncusped opening in the head, that to the east being well preserved,[147] while the other is blocked. In the east wall are the jambs of a wider window, said to have been formerly of three trefoiled lights, and in the north wall the lower part of a two-light window corresponding to the eastern of the two windows in the south wall. Near the west end of this wall is a square-headed opening low in the wall, with a wooden lintel, and evidently not in its original condition. The chapel is roofless and encumbered with destructive ivy, and preserves nothing of its ancient contents

145 Stowe MS. 845, fol. 56.

146 See a paper by Mr. N. C. H. Nisbett in the *Proc. Hants Field Club*, ii, 1.

147 What appears to be the east jamb of another window shows in the wall a little to the east of the existing window, with a recess below it.

East Meon Church : Western Arch of Central Tower

except a plain circular font at the west end, and near it part of a coffin slab, on which is the upper half of a figure in low relief under a gabled and crocketed canopy flanked by pinnacles, of early fourteenth-century date. This would seem to have been complete at the time of writing of the Stowe MS. above quoted.

THE CHAPEL OF ST. MARY'S-IN-THE-FIELDS in the tithing of East Meon was annexed to the parish church of East Meon. It was described in 1703 as 'quite down.'[148] The field called Fair Field or Chapel Close still marks its site.

In the various documents relating to Bereleigh there is usually mention of the advowson of the church of Bereleigh[149] which went with the manor. There is no church there now, nor was there one in early times. Possibly there was at one time a chapel here. During the seventeenth century and later, Bereleigh was the centre of a Jesuit community.

The modern church of *ST. JOHN THE EVANGELIST, LANGRISH,* a building of flint with stone dressings, in the Early English style, was erected in 1871, and a parish was assigned to it, as already mentioned, in 1894. The registers date from 1871.

There is a Congregational chapel at Ramsdean, which was rebuilt and enlarged in 1887.

ADVOWSONS

At the time of the Domesday Survey there was a church in East Meon which was held by the bishop of Winchester together with six hides and one virgate.[150] All churches which appertained to the manor of East Meon were included in the grant of the manor made by Henry II to the church of Winchester,[151] and this grant was confirmed by King John in 1200.[152] In 1331, on the petition of John Stratford, bishop of Winchester, it was decreed that, on any future voidance of the see, the custody of the parish church of East Meon should be held by the prior and convent of the church of St. Swithun, Winchester, as belonging to the spiritualities of the see, and that the keepers of the temporalities should not intermeddle with the same as Robert de Welle and his fellows had done during the voidance of the see in the reign of Edward II.[153] The bishop of Winchester was patron of the living until 1852,[154] in which year it was decreed by Order in Council that on the next voidance of the see of Winchester the patronage of East Meon vicarage, with the chapelry of Froxfield and Steep, should be transferred to the bishop of Lichfield.[155] The bishop of Lichfield, however, finding it better to have patronage in his own diocese, exchanged East Meon with the Lord Chancellor, who gave up certain advowsons in Lichfield. The living is still in the gift of the Lord Chancellor.

In the thirteenth century the vicarage of East Meon was endowed with :—Tithes great and small from the four tenements of the hamlet of Froxfield, tithes great and small from the chapelry of Westbury annexed to the church of East Meon, all offerings belonging to the church of East Meon with the chapels annexed to it, viz. Froxfield, Steep, and St. Mary's-in-the-Field, five eggs payable at Easter from every man holding land in the parish of the mother-church of East Meon and the hamlet and chapelry of Froxfield, all profits and fees arising from the punishment of offenders in the peculiar and exempt jurisdiction within the parish of East Meon and the chapelries adjacent to it, five quarters of corn from the granges of the bishop of Winchester, and ten acres of arable land. Henry de Woodlock, bishop of Winchester, had intended to augment the vicarage, but was prevented by death from doing so. Finally, in 1318, on the petition of Richard de Wardyngtone, perpetual vicar of the church of East Meon, it was augmented by John de Sendale, bishop of Winchester, who granted to the vicar and his successors for the bettering of the vicarage all small tithes of the parish of East Meon and chapelries annexed, viz. lambs, milk, cheese, calves, chickens, piglets, geese, eggs, mills, honey, hay, apples, pigeons, flax, and hemp. All other tithes he reserved to himself and his successors except tithes of wool from the chapelry of Westbury.[156]

The living of *ST. JOHN THE EVANGELIST, LANGRISH,* is a vicarage, value £256, with residence, in the gift of the bishop of Winchester.

CHARITIES

In 1851 a piece of land containing 6 acres on Oxenbourn Down was awarded under 2 and 3 Vic. cap. 1 (Private Act) as to 5 acres for the growth of furze and fuel to be cut and used by the occupiers of small cottages not exceeding the annual value of £4 in the tithing of Oxenbourn, and as to 1 acre for a recreation ground. These allotments being at a distance from the village were in 1894 under an order of the Charity Commissioners exchanged for 3 acres 3 roods 37 poles in East Meon, known as Pill Meadow, of the annual value of £7, to be used as a recreation ground. Under the scheme the managers let the grazing, and apply the annual sum of £5 in the distribution of fuel among the poor of the tithing, and the surplus in maintaining the recreation ground.

Under the same award 5 acres for the right of cutting furze was allotted to the poor of the tithing of Ramsdean and 1 acre for a recreation ground. The tithing of Ramsdean now forms part of the parish of Langrish.[157]

In 1863 Mrs. Joanna Agnes Forbes by deed conveyed to trustees a piece of land containing 19 perches with almshouse buildings thereon upon trust to be occupied by poor persons of good character of upwards of sixty-five years of age. In 1904 an additional site having a frontage to Church Street was purchased, upon which it is proposed to erect new almshouses. The endowment funds consist of certain securities held by the Official Trustees of Charitable Funds producing £197 a year, who also hold £1,979 18*s.* 7*d.* consols, which is being accumulated.[158]

148 Stowe MS. 845, fol. 56.

149 Feet of F. Hants, Mich. 6 Chas. I; Close, 31 Geo. II, pt. 11, and 15 Geo. III, pt. 12, No. 3.

150 *V.C.H. Hants*, i, 461.

151 Add. Chart. 28658.

152 Chart. R. 1 John, m. 29.

153 Pat. 5 Edw. III, pt. 1, m. 34.

154 Inst. Books (P.R.O.).

155 *Lond. Gaz.* 4 June, 1852, p. 1578.

156 *Winton. Epis. Reg.* (Hants Rec. Soc.), 103.

157 *Charity Com. Rep.* lxxxii, 1 and 4.

158 Ibid. xviii, 67.

FROXFIELD

Froxafeld (x cent.).

Froxfield is a parish of irregular shape containing several small groups of houses, the principal settlement being at Froxfield Green, where the old church formerly stood. Petersfield station on the London and South-Western Railway is about four miles from the Green, and reached from it by the road [1] which winds up the steep wooded slopes of Stoner Hill, reaching a height of over 750 ft. above sea level at the eastern boundary of the parish. This road runs north-west through the north of the parish, its highest point being 807 ft., and from it and the branch road leading to the Green fine views can be obtained over the valleys in which Petersfield, East Meon, West Meon, and the other villages lie. Beyond rise Teglease Down, Chidden Down, Wether Down, Oxenbourn Down, Butser Hill, and Ramsdean Down, and on a clear day the sea is distinctly visible. An earthwork or vallum which runs through the parish from south-east to north-west is supposed to have formed part of the boundary of the kingdoms of Wessex and Sussex, and a Roman encampment in the south of the parish in which several interesting remains have been discovered proves that there were settlers here at an early date. Froxfield Green, which is in the south of the parish at the junction of roads from High Cross, Stoner Hill, and Bordean, consists of a small triangular green round which are clustered several cottages and farms, a smithy, some old-fashioned houses of the better sort, one of them being the schoolhouse endowed by Mr. Robert Love in 1733, a post office and general shop, a reading-room, and the little church of St. Peter-on-the-Green. This was built in 1887 on the site of the chancel of the old church, which was pulled down, the expense being borne by Mr. William Nicholson, D.L., J.P., of Basing Park. At High Cross, about a mile north-east of the Green, stands the church of St. Peter-at-High-Cross, erected in 1862, Mr. John Silvester of The Slade presenting the site. Opposite to it are the schools which were built in 1876 and the vicarage, while a little to the east, on the north of the road leading to Week Green, is The Slade, the residence of Mr. John Silvester. The Trooper Inn, the police-station, and a general shop lie near each other in the east of the parish a little to the north of Week Green Farm, along the main road from Petersfield to Ropley. To the east, at the corner of Honeycritch Lane and Old Litten Lane, is a small Wesleyan chapel which was opened in September, 1851. A mission chapel with a reading-room attached has recently been erected by Mr. William Nicholson at Warren Corner in the north of the parish.

Basing Park, the seat of Mr. William Nicholson, lies in the north-western extremity of the parish, and extends into the neighbouring parishes of Colemore and Privett. The park is very richly wooded, and covers an area of 450 acres. The house, which is modern, is approached from the main road by an avenue of pines. Broadhanger, formerly the property of the Greenwood family and at present the residence of Mr. Reginald Montgomerie Caulfield, is on high ground between Stoner and Bordean Hills, and looks down upon the hanging woods of oak, ash, and chestnut which sweep down into the vale of Langrish. Oakshott, in the extreme north-east of the parish, was formerly a tithing of East Meon, as also was Week Green near Stoner Hill.

The area of the parish is 4,909 acres, including 2,847½ acres of arable land, 1,240¼ acres of permanent grass, and 471¾ acres of woods and plantations.[2] In 1680 there were the following common-lands in the parish of Froxfield—The Barnett, Ring's Green, Wheatham Hill, Staples Down, Old Litten, Stoner Hill, and Broadway—altogether covering an area of 723 acres 2 roods 6 poles.[3] Barnett Common was inclosed in 1805.[4] The principal landowners are Mr. William Nicholson and Mr. John Silvester, but much of the land is freehold. The soil varies from a stiff clay to a light vegetable loam, and the subsoil is chalk; the chief crops being wheat, barley, and oats. Among place-names occurring in a survey of the parish made in the seventeenth century are Pikes, Holehouse and Rutters in Froxfield tithing, Ruddlecombe, Hewet's Garden, Great and Little Hatchersnap and Hatchersnap Wood, Chesscombes and Old Lytten [5] in Oakshott tithing, Treddles, Mary Crosse and Burie Wood in Week tithing, and Basinges [6] in Longhurst tithing.

MANORS The first mention of *FROXFIELD* is in the tenth century, when the alderman Ælfeah left land at Froxfield to Ælfwine his sister's son.[7] It is not mentioned in Domesday Book by name, and it is probably included in the entry under 'Menes,' [8] as in after times most certainly it formed part of the great episcopal manor of East Meon.[9]

BASING PARK.—In a rent-roll of the manor of East Meon for the year 1567 John Love is mentioned as holding a messuage and lands called 'Basings' in the tithing of Longhurst by the yearly rent of 17*s.* 10*d.*, two churchetts and two harvest-days.[10] This seems to be one of the earliest mentions of the estate, which in later times came to be called Basing Park. It was held by the Loves of Froxfield for over two centuries,[11] and there are frequent mentions of them in connexion with their property in the court rolls of East Meon. For instance, in a court roll of 1675 occurs the entry that Richard Love came to the court and surrendered into the hands of his lord Basing Woods in the tithing of Longhurst.[12] On Richard's death in 1690 Basing passed to his son Robert, who by will left £1,000 for the founding of the free school which still stands by Froxfield Green with the

[1] This road was made at the beginning of the nineteenth century.

[2] Statistics from the Board of Agriculture (1905).

[3] MS. *penes* Mr. J. Silvester of The Slade.

[4] By authority of Local and Personal Act, 1803, cap. 59.

[5] Modern survivals are Happersnapper Hanger, Cheesecombe Farm, Old Litten Lane, and Old Litten Cottage.

[6] Represented by the modern Basing Park.

[7] Kemble, *Codex Diplom.* 593.

[8] *V.C.H. Hants*, i, 452 *a*.

[9] *Feud. Aids*, ii, 319. Froxfield, Week, Longhurst, and Oakshott are always mentioned as tithings in the court rolls of East Meon (Eccl. Com. Ct. R.).

[10] MS. *penes* Mr. John Silvester, of The Slade, Froxfield.

[11] A pedigree of the Loves of Basing Park is given in Berry, *Hants Gen.* 266.

[12] Eccl. Com. Ct. R. bdle. 155, No. 2.

inscription 'The gift of Robert Love 1733.' Robert was succeeded by his nephew Richard, whose daughter and sole heiress Susannah married Francis Beckford.[13] From the latter's son and heir Francis Love-Beckford Basing Park passed by sale to Joseph Martineau, on whose death in 1863 it was sold to Mr. William Nicholson, the present owner.

CHURCHES The church of *ST. PETER-AT-HIGH-CROSS* dates from 1862, three bays of the nave arcade of the old church which was at Froxfield Green being re-used in it. It has a chancel of two bays with an organ chamber on the north, a nave with north aisle and south-west tower, the ground story of which serves as an entrance porch. Three pillars in the north arcade are of late twelfth-century date, with round shafts and scalloped capitals, but their bases and all the rest of the arcade are modern. In the vestry at the west end of the north aisle is an eighteenth-century altar table, but no other fittings from the old church have been preserved.

In the tower are six bells, the treble and tenor of 1880, the others of 1890, by Mears & Stainbank. The little church of St. Peter on the Green, which stands on the site of the old church, was built in 1887, and contains no old work.

The plate consists of a silver communion cup and cover paten, a paten given by Robert Love of Basing, 1712, a cup and flagon given by Josephine Martineau in 1862, and a paten given by A. Z. Hosegood, 1893. There are also two pewter almsdishes and one of brass.

The registers begin in 1545, the first book ending in 1676, while the second contains baptisms 1693–1716, marriages 1677–1707, and burials 1677–1716. The third has baptisms 1717–87, marriages 1718–54, and burials 1694–1787. The fourth is the marriage register, 1754–93, the fifth has baptisms and burials 1788–1812, and the sixth marriages 1793–1812.

ADVOWSON The living of Froxfield was a vicarage annexed to the vicarage of East Meon[14] until 11 March, 1881, in which year by an Order in Council the patronage was transferred to Mr. William Nicholson, of Basing Park,[15] with whom it still remains.

STEEP

La Stuppe, La Stiepe, and Stupe xiv cent.; Steepe xvii cent.

The parish of Steep formerly included a strip of land called Ambersham in the county of Sussex situated near Midhurst and Petworth, but under the Acts 2 and 3 Will. IV, cap. 64, and 7 and 8 Vic. cap. 61, Ambersham was detached from Steep and became part of Sussex.[1] For ecclesiastical purposes it was divided into two portions, North Ambersham and South Ambersham, the former being annexed to Fernhurst and the latter to Easebourne. South Ambersham contains 1,497 acres of land and 7 acres of land covered by water, while North Ambersham has 1,169 acres. The parish of Steep contains over 700 inhabitants, and occupies the rising ground north-east of Petersfield, its western boundary running along the brow of the high table-land and including within it the steep wooded eastern slopes of Stoner Hill and Wheatham Hill. The parish is watered by a small stream which rises not far from Ashford Lodge and flows thence east to Steep Marsh, and a second stream rising at the foot of Wheatham Hill follows the north and east boundaries of the parish, joining the first stream close to the village of Sheet. Two main roads run through the parish, that from Petersfield to Farnham on the east and the Petersfield and Ropley road on the south-west, the latter winding up the steep slopes of Stoner Hill with a skilfully engineered gradient through beautiful hanging beechwoods. It was laid out by private enterprise early in the last century in the expectation of a grant of the tolls on it, but this being refused by the government the promoters lost heavily by their undertaking. There is no regular village, the houses being scattered here and there over the parish, but the principal group lies along the road from Sheet, which crosses the main Petersfield and Ropley road on the lower slopes of Stoner Hill. Here are several shops and some modern villas which are increasing in number, owing no doubt to the close proximity of Petersfield. All Saints' church stands on the south side of this road about half a mile east of its junction with the main road, on a site from which the ground falls steeply to the south and east, the vicarage lying below it on the east, while on the north are the voluntary schools built in 1875,[2] and the almshouses erected and endowed by Mr. William Eames in 1882. On the eastern boundary of the churchyard is an old red-brick house with a picturesque chimney-stack, dating in part from the latter half of the sixteenth century, and the churchyard contains two very fine yew-trees, that on the south of the church being specially notable, even in a district where nearly every parish can show a large tree of the kind, confidently claiming for it the conventional thousand years of growth. There are several good modern houses standing in their own grounds in the parish, the most important being Ashford Lodge on low ground near Stoner Hill, the property of Miss Hawker; Stonerwood, a large brick house in about the centre of the parish to the west of the Ropley road, built about thirty years ago by the Rev. J. Tasswell and sold at his death ten years ago to Mr. J. Waller; Coldhayes in the north of the parish, a large handsome stone house built about twenty-five years ago by the late Rev. George Horsley-Palmer, a brother of the late Lord Selborne, the architect being the late Mr. Waterhouse, R.A., and at present occupied by Mrs. Horsley-Palmer; Collyers, a large brick house built about twenty years since by the late Colonel Ughtred Shuttleworth, and now owned by his widow and occupied by Major Adam Bogle; Dunnanie, a modern stucco house owned by Mrs. Shuttleworth; Island, a large brick house built four years ago and owned and occupied by Mrs. Falconer;

[13] Berry, *Hants Gen.* 266.

[14] *Winton. Epis. Reg.* (Hants Rec. Soc.), 82, 83, 103, 104; Exch. Dep. 34 Chas. II, East. No. 2.

[15] *Lond. Gaz.* 11 Mar. 1881, p. 1138.

[1] There are men still living in Ambersham who remember the quit-rents being paid into the court of the bishop of Winchester. Up to 1842 the inhabitants of Ambersham brought their dead to Steep for burial, and also came to Steep as their parish church for marriages. The ratepayers of Ambersham maintained about a fifth part of the churchyard wall at Steep.

[2] The old schools were built in 1843 at a cost of £150.

Bedales, a large school built six years ago at a cost of about £60,000, with accommodation for 160 boys and girls; Little Stodham, a stucco house belonging to Mr. Money-Coutts, and occupied by Colonel Sir St. Vincent Hardwick, bart.; and Stoner House, built by the late Mr. Keeley Halswelle, a well-known artist, and now occupied by his widow. Bowyers Common lies in the east, and is intersected by the main road from Petersfield to Liss. Ashford, Forcombe or Foxcombe, and Aldersnapp were formerly tithings of East Meon, the two former being in the north-east of the parish,[3] while the latter is now represented by Aldersnapp Farm in the south. There was a water-mill a little to the south of Ashford Lodge, representing one of those formerly belonging to the manor of East Meon, and held of it by rent of 3*s.* It has been pulled down, however, during the past winter (1906), and the water-power is now used only to work a turbine and supply water to Coldhayes. Sheet Upper Mill is partly in Steep parish and partly in the parish of Sheet. The various fulling-mills in Steep, of which mention is made in connexion with the industries of Petersfield, have long ago fallen into decay.[4]

The soil is marl, clay, and sandy loam, the subsoil gravel and sand. The chief crops are wheat, barley, and oats, and a few hops are also grown. The area is 2,658 acres, including 443¾ acres of arable land, 1,222¼ acres of permanent grass, and 233½ acres of wood and plantations.[5] Steep Stroud, Steep Marsh, and Bowyer's Common were inclosed in 1866.

Among place-names occurring in the seventeenth century are 'Kettle House, Tankerdells, The Moore, Coleheye and Dundhill' in the tithing of Forcombe or Foxcombe, and 'Stoner Hill, Coaks, Coaks Great Wood and Ridge' in the tithing of Aldersnapp.[6]

MANORS

STEEP is not mentioned in Domesday Book by name, and it is most probably included in the entry under 'Menes,' as in after times most certainly it formed part of the great episcopal manor of East Meon.[7]

AMBERSHAM (Embresham x cent.; Ambrisham xiv cent.; Ambresham xvi cent.).

The first mention of Ambersham is in 963, when King Edgar granted land in Ambersham to the church of St. Andrew the Apostle at Meon.[8] It is not mentioned in Domesday, and the next mention of it seems to be in the reign of Henry II, when the king confirmed the agreement made between the brothers Robert and Andrew Taillard with reference to the land of Ambersham.[9] Andrew Taillard was to hold half of the manor of the king in chief for the service of 50*s.* a year. Robert was to hold the other half with soc and sac, toll and team, &c., just as his father Durant Taillard had held it in the reign of Henry I. In return for this agreement Robert gave Andrew 20 marks of silver. Shortly afterwards Ambersham was included in the grant made by Henry II of East Meon to the bishop of Winchester.[10] From this time onwards the manor of Ambersham was held of the bishopric, and its holders appear as free suitors at the courts of the manor of East Meon.[11]

The manor of Ambersham seems to have remained in the family of Taillard for about four hundred years, although there is not much documentary evidence of this, the only mention of a Taillard of Ambersham between the twelfth and sixteenth centuries being in 1327, when a certain Thomas son of Thomas Taillard of Ambersham is mentioned as owing 100*s.* to William la Zousche of Assheby.[12] In 1500 Nicholas Taillard and Alice his wife by fine granted messuages, lands, and rents in Ambersham to John Onley and his heirs.[13] It was no doubt the manor of Ambersham that was thus conveyed, since in 1537 Thomas Onley and Clemence his wife were seised of the manor of Ambersham, conveying it by fine in that year to Lady Katherine Arundel, one of the daughters of William, earl of Arundel,[14] who four years later sold it to William Yonge of Petworth, clothier, and Anthony his son.[15] The manor remained in the Yonge family for over a century, at length passing to Thomas Bonham of West Meon, by his marriage with Alice, sister of Anthony Yonge, from whom it was purchased in 1700 by Anthony Capron, of the parish of Easebourne (co. Sussex).[16] Anthony Capron, a descendant of the last-named, sold it towards the end of the eighteenth century to William Stephen Poyntz.[17] On his death it became vested in his three daughters, by whom it was sold in 1843 to George James, sixth earl of Egmont, whose nephew, Charles George Perceval, seventh earl of Egmont, is the present lord of the manor.

PERCEVAL. *Or a chief indented gules with three crosses formy or therein.*

MORE (Moore, xvii cent.) is a manor situated partly in Lodsworth and Easebourne (co. Sussex), and partly in Ambersham (co. Hants). Its descent has been identical with that of Ambersham (q.v.).

[3] As appears from the various place-names in the tithing. The name Forcombe or Foxcombe no longer survives.

[4] They were probably worked by the Ashford stream. In 1647 there were two fulling-mills in Steep—held respectively by Jane the widow of Joseph Fielder and Elizabeth Colebrooke (MS. *penes* Mr. J. Silvester).

[5] Statistics from Board of Agriculture (1905).

[6] MS. *penes* Mr. J. Silvester. These names are preserved in the modern Kettlesbrook Cottages, Tankerdale, The Moors, Coldhayes, Dunhill House and Dunhill Cottage, Stoner Hill, Cook's Farm, Ridge Farm, Ridge Copse, Ridge Hanger, and Ridge Common. In 1556 the common of pasture on Staveles Down was divided among the various tenants of land called Ridge land (Eccl. Com. Ct. R. bdle 79, No. 25).

[7] *Feud. Aids*, ii, 319. Ashford, Forcombe or Foxcombe, and Aldersnapp are always mentioned as tithings in the court rolls of East Meon (Eccl. Com. Ct. R.).

[8] Kemble, *Codex Diplom.* 1243; Birch, *Cart. Sax.* iii, 349.

[9] Cart Antiq. S. 23.

[10] Add. Ch. 28658. In this grant Ambersham is not mentioned by name, but in the charter of 1285 Edward I quitclaimed to John, bishop of Winchester, 'Estmenes manor with Ambresham' (Chart. 12 Edw. I, m. 5).

[11] Eccl. Com. Ct. R. *passim.*

[12] Pat. 1 Edw. III, pt. 1, m. 28 *d.*

[13] Feet of F. Div. Cos. Mich. 16 Hen. VII.

[14] Ibid. Hil. 29 Hen. VIII.

[15] Com. Pleas Deeds Enrolled, Trin. 33 Hen. VIII, m. 1 *d.*
In 1548, by fine between William Yonge, Anthony Yonge, and John Wassher and Joan his wife, the manor was settled on William and Anthony and the heirs of Anthony (Feet of F. Hants, Mich. 2 Edw. VI).

[16] Close, 12 Will. III, pt. 9. The Caprons were an ancient family, and appear to have resided for many generations in a moated house in Ambersham, adjoining Lodsworth.

[17] Elwes and Robinson, *Western Sussex*, 142. William Stephen Poyntz and Elizabeth Mary his wife, Robert Cotton St. John Lord Clinton and Frances Isabella Lady Clinton, Elizabeth Georgiana Poyntz, and Isabella Poyntz dealt with the manor by recovery in 1824 (Recov. R. East. 5 Geo. IV, rot. 225).

ASHFORD manor is a sub-manor dependent upon the great episcopal manor of East Meon,[18] and was held in the sixteenth, seventeenth, and eighteenth centuries by the Baker family.[19] In the beginning of the nineteenth century the then holder, who is said to have become bankrupt in making the Stoner Hill road, sold the property to Mr. Wentworth, who in his turn sold it to Lady Williams. Lady Williams married Admiral Edward Hawker, and left Ashford to his younger son, who was curate of Steep, and on the parish being separated from East Meon became the first vicar. It is now held by his grand-daughter, Miss Hawker, who comes of age October, 1907.[20]

CHURCH The church of *ALL SAINTS, STEEP*, has a chancel 16 ft. by 13 ft., nave 50 ft. 6 in. by 16 ft., north and south aisles 13 ft. and 5 ft. wide respectively, with north and south porches, and a tower at the west end of the north aisle. All measurements are internal.

The eastern bays of the south arcade of the nave, *c.* 1180, are the earliest pieces of detail in the building, but it seems probable that the oldest masonry on the site belongs to a church of the Colemore and Ropley type, and probably of the first half of the twelfth century, with aisleless nave and chancel, and a small transept chapel at the east of the nave on the north; perhaps also on the south. There may also have been a north-west tower, probably of wood, with a masonry base as at present, before the addition of the north aisle. This church was enlarged about 1180 by the addition of a narrow south aisle, and some twenty years later the north aisle was added, its width being determined by the projection of the north transept chapel, whose west wall, together with the east wall of the north-west tower, was taken down at the time and the area thrown into the aisle. The different wall-thicknesses in the arcade and aisles suggest that the wall for the length of the first three bays of the arcade was taken down and rebuilt of a less thickness when the aisle was added, the thicker wall being retained at the east and west. The rebuilding of the chancel, probably of a slightly greater width than the old chancel, followed in the first quarter of the thirteenth century, and no further structural additions took place. There is nothing to show at what time the wooden upper stages of the tower were made. The church has undergone 'restoration' in 1839, £370 being spent, and in 1875 at a cost of £2,377. A plan of the building, as it was before 1839, is in the library of the Society of Antiquaries, and shows the west bay of the south arcade blocked with a thick wall, and the east bay of the south aisle destroyed, a wall being built close to the east bay of the arcade. There is also no chancel arch. The destruction of the eastern bay of the aisle suggests that there may have been a transept chapel here which had fallen into decay and been pulled down.

The chancel has a modern triplet of lancets on the east, a single modern lancet on the north, and two widely splayed lancets on the south, which are ancient though patched with new stone in places. The chancel arch, of thirteenth-century style, dates from 1875, and is said to replace a plain round-headed arch, which, if the plan already referred to can be trusted, was not older than 1839.

The nave has arcades of four bays, the north arcade having semicircular arches of two orders with edge chamfers, and circular columns with circular moulded

All Saints' Church, Steep, from the West

capitals and bases. The third column, at the point where the wall thickens, is of larger diameter than those to the east of it, and the west respond has a plainer capital, with a square-edged abacus chamfered below, the other abaci in this arcade having a roll and hollow in place of the chamfer. The variation may be merely the result of repair, but the respond is thus given an earlier character, and may have belonged to an arch opening to the north-west tower from the original aisleless nave. The two east bays of the south arcade have semicircular arches of one chamfered order, and circular columns with scalloped capitals and abaci chamfered above and below. The arch in the third bay is of two orders with quarter-round

18 The tenants of the tithing of Ashford paid £10 per annum to the lord of the manor of East Meon. They likewise paid fines on the surrender of their lands, but all other fines and heriots they divided amongst themselves (from a survey of the manor of East Meon taken in 1647).

19 A manuscript formerly in the possession of the Bakers, and now owned by Mr. J. Silvester, of The Slade, Froxfield, contains an extract of all their copies taken in 1729. From this extract the following pedigree can be drawn up:—

William Baker = Elizabeth
(living 1615)

William Baker
(living 1615)

Richard Baker = Winifred
(died *c.* 1706)

Richard Baker (died *c.* 1717) — John Baker (died *c.* 1711)

Richard Baker
(living 1727)

There are several handsome monuments in the parish church to this family.

20 *Ex inform.* the Rev. H. Peto Betts, M.A., vicar of Steep.

mouldings, and it is evident from the claw-tooling of the inner order that it has been added in the thirteenth century to an arch of a single order like those to the east, but worked at the date of the addition with a moulding corresponding with the new order. The west bay is imitated from this, and with the west respond is modern. The north aisle is lighted on the east by a fourteenth-century window of two trefoiled lights, and has in its north wall three lancets of thirteenth-century style, of which only the eastern one and the west jamb of the next are ancient. The north door comes between the second and third windows, and has a pointed arch of two chamfered orders and a round-headed rear arch; it is probably thirteenth-century work, and over it is built a modern wooden porch. The west window of the aisle is modern, of two trefoiled lights. All windows in the south aisle are modern, but the south door is of thirteenth-century date with two moulded orders and a label with human heads for dripstones, which seem to be second-hand. The west window of the nave is of two trefoiled lights and fourteenth-century date, and over it is a modern round window, cinquefoiled.

The bell tower has a lower stage of masonry, but above the roof is of timber, hung with weather-tiles in the lower part, and finished with a shingled spire. Externally the church is entirely plastered, except over the brown sandstone quoins, and its roofs are red-tiled.

The chancel has an old timber roof with arched braces, and the nave roof is in the main old, with new tie beams. The north aisle also has an old roof; probably all are of the fifteenth century, but in the aisle the plates, ties, and king posts are new.

There are no old wood fittings in the church, the altar rails of seventeenth-century date having been lost in 1875; the north door, however, is of the fifteenth century, with applied tracery on its outer face.

The font at the west of the nave has a tapering round bowl, becoming hexagonal, with six projecting trefoiled arches on its sides, the capitals of which are shown in profile only. It stands on six modern dwarf columns and a central shaft, and is of early fourteenth-century date.

There are five bells, all of 1745, by Robert Catlin. The plate consists of a Communion cup and cover paten of 1568; a chalice, flagon, and paten of 1876; a seventeenth-century pewter dish, inscribed 'the church bason of the parish of Steep,' and three pewter plates and a flagon; also a plated paten.

The first book of the registers, copied in 1644 from an older book now lost, begins in 1610, the second running from 1633 to 1673. There are no baptisms from 1637 to 1651. The third book goes from 1695 to 1774 (baptisms), 1754 (marriages), and 1780 (burials); while the fourth contains baptisms 1780–1802, and burials to 1812, and the fifth baptisms 1803–12. The sixth and seventh are marriage books, 1754–1812. There are churchwardens' accounts from 1707 to 1735.

ADVOWSON Steep vicarage was from very early times annexed to the vicarage of East Meon. The advowson has consequently followed that of East Meon (q.v.). The living is at the present day a vicarage, net yearly value £170, with residence (erected in 1882), in the gift of the Lord Chancellor.

In 1678 there was a dispute as to the tithes belonging to the rectory of Steep, which Robert Mills and John Restall then held on lease from Dorothy Sessions, who held of the bishop of Winchester. The depositions of many of the inhabitants of the parish of Steep were taken, and the general opinion was that the tithes of wheat, barley, vetches, oats, rye, pease, field-beans, wool, lambs, apples, and pears [21] belonged to the proprietor or owner of the rectory of Steep, and not to the vicar of the parish church of East Meon, even though the parish church of Steep was a member of the vicarage of East Meon. It was also ascertained that owners and occupiers of land in the tithings of Langrish and Froxfield in the parish of East Meon paid tithes of apples and pears to the proprietors, tenants, or farmers of the rectories of Langrish and Froxfield, and not to the vicar of the parish church of East Meon, and that this was done in the whole hundred of East Meon, where parsonages were distinct from vicarages.[22]

Three years later occurred a dispute between Richard Downes, the vicar of East Meon and Steep, and John Clements, the lord of the manor of Rothercombe, as to whether the vicar of East Meon and Steep ought to have the tithes of 'all coppice, woodrise, or tytheable wood' cut down within the parishes of East Meon and Steep. The parishioners, on oath, with one accord, asserted that the tithes of copsewood were as due as any other tithes to the vicar of East Meon. It seemed to be the general opinion, however, that the parishioners had the right to compound for their tithes of copse-wood, since, although the former vicar had received tithe-wood in kind from several persons of the parish of East Meon, he had usually compounded with his parishioners for the vicarage tithes in which the tithes of copse-wood were included.[23]

In former times there was a great tithe-barn of two bays immediately adjoining the west end of Steep churchyard, but it was sold (presumably after the Commutation Act), and was included in Mr. Wentworth's sale of Ashford in 1842. The field adjoining the tithe-barn is known as Parson's field, but there seems to be no trace of the date at which it was alienated. A little house to the east of the churchyard is marked on some old maps as 'the old vicarage.' If so, it was alienated 150 years ago and made into cottages, and has recently been reconverted into one house. It was probably occupied by the parish priest, the vicar being vicar of East Meon. The present vicarage was built twenty-seven years ago on land bought for that purpose at a cost of about £2,300.[24]

The Primitive Methodists have two chapels in Steep.

CHARITIES In 1843 the bishop of Winchester, as lord of the manor, by statutory grant (duly enrolled) granted to the minister, churchwardens, and overseers of the chapelry of Steep, 10 roods, part of the common, as a site for a national school. On the inclosure in 1866 3 acres of

[21] It is interesting to note that at this time 'the parsons' and proprietors' servant went sometimes with a horse and a sack, and sometimes with a sack or wallet at his back to receive and take all tithes of apples and pears.'

[22] Exch. Dep. Mich. 30 Chas. II, No. 8.

[23] Ibid. Hil. 33 and 34 Chas. II, No. 11.

[24] *Ex inform.* the Rev. H. Peto Betts, M.A., vicar of Steep.

land on the common were awarded to the trustees for the benefit of the school, of which 2 r. 10 p. was in 1872 exchanged for 1 a. 2 r. 12 p. of land adjoining the recreation ground. A new school has been erected upon the land acquired by exchange, and the remainder of the allotment was sold in 1875, and one-half of the proceeds applied towards the cost of erecting the new schools, and the remaining half in the purchase of £210 16*s.* 1*d.* consols with the official trustees.

In 1872 the Rev. Henry Hawker by deed granted a piece of land to trustees to be used as a site for almshouses for poor people of the parish, or otherwise for the benefit of its inhabitants, or the inhabitants of any other parish at their discretion, and William Eames by his will, proved in 1879, bequeathed his residuary estate for the erection and endowment of the almshouses. In the result of proceedings in the High Court £1,000 was expended in the erection of the almshouses, and a sum of £2,321 4*s.* consols was transferred to the official trustees of charitable funds.[25]

[25] Since the foregoing account of Steep was in type, the Rev. H. P. Betts has kindly informed us that at the south end of the parish, on the Stroud Common, the remains of a Romano-British villa were discovered in the summer of 1906, and a systematic excavation, which is still in progress, was begun in the following June. This excavation has opened up two wings of a large courtyard type of house, one containing dwelling-rooms and the other baths. There is nothing remarkable in the former, the general arrangement and detail being typical of the period; but the bath chambers—by reason of their number and elaboration—are, for an isolated country villa, somewhat unusual. Of the many pavements only one—along the corridor of the north wing—has a patterned mosaic, and that is very badly damaged. But the excavators have reason to hope that foundations of more important chambers will be discovered in the south and east wings of the house next year.

THE HUNDRED OF FINCHDEAN

CONTAINING THE PARISHES OF

BLENDWORTH	CHALTON	PETERSFIELD BOROUGH
BURITON	Idsworth Chapelry	Sheet Tithing
CATHERINGTON	CLANFIELD	

The above list represents the extent of the hundred of Finchdean at the time of the population returns of 1831. The parishes of Bramshott, Greatham, and Liss were added to the hundred before 1841,[1] and Waterloo, constituted a parish in 1858, is also now included in the hundred.

At the time of the Domesday Survey this hundred was called 'Ceptune' Hundred, and included the parishes of Blendworth, Buriton, Catherington, Chalton, Clanfield, and Petersfield.[2] The land comprising the hundred was assessed in the time of Edward the Confessor at 83 hides, and in the time of the Survey at about half that amount. The hundred had assumed its modern name before the end of the twelfth century,[3] but seems sometimes to have been called 'Wlputta,' as in the *Testa de Nevill*, where Chalton, Idsworth, and Mapledurham are included in the hundred of that name.[4] The extent of the hundred has altered but little since the time of the Survey. Some of the parishes, however, of which it was composed had not exactly the same boundaries as they have at the present day. Thus the western part of the parish of Catherington was included in the hundred of Portsdown until the reign of Edward II, and in the reign of Edward I the manor of Hinton Daubnay is mentioned as being in the same

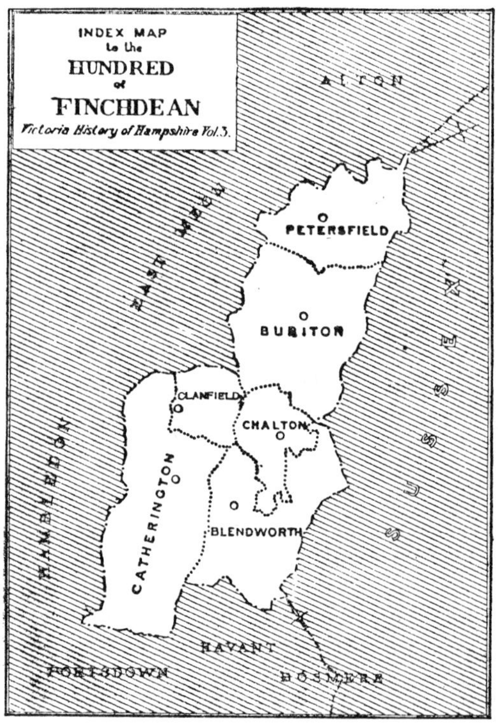

[1] Cf. the Population Returns of 1831 and 1841.

[2] *V. C. H. Hants*, i, 451 and 478. The parishes are not all mentioned by name, the only entries under 'Ceptune' Hundred being 'Malpedresham,' 'Ceptune,' and 'Seneorde,' but, as is shown under the parishes, 'Malpedresham' included the modern parishes of Buriton, Petersfield and Sheet, and 'Ceptune' those of Blendworth, Catherington, Chalton, Clanfield and Idsworth, while 'Seneorde' represents 'Sunwood' Farm in the parish of Buriton.

[3] *Pipe R.* (Pipe R. Soc.), 23 Hen. II, xxvi, 171.

[4] *Testa de Nevill* (Rec. Com.), 236*b*.

hundred,[5] while in 1316 it was included in Finchdean.[6] Wellsworth, which is situated in Idsworth chapelry, was also included in Portsdown Hundred in the reign of Edward I, when the abbot of Titchfield was forced to allow his villeins of Wellsworth to do suit at the hundred of the king at Portsdown,[7] and it was not until the beginning of the seventeenth century that it was transferred to Finchdean.[8] In 1431 the fourth part of a knight's fee in 'Oldestoke' was included in Finchdean,[9] but this place does not appear under the hundred in subsequent subsidy rolls.

The hundred originally belonged to the crown,[10] and was granted either in the twelfth or thirteenth century to William de Albini, earl of Arundel.[11] It was appendant to the earldom of Arundel for a considerable time,[12] finally passing to Henry V on the death of Thomas, earl of Arundel, in 1415.[13] The hundred then remained with the crown for nearly two hundred years, Elizabeth at length in 1600 granting it by letters patent to Henry Best and Robert Holland, who conveyed it the next day to Robert Paddon and his heirs.[14] In 1604 Robert sold it for £150 to Nicholas Hyde, lord of the manor of Hinton Daubnay,[15] since which date it has followed the descent of that manor (q.v.).[16] As late as 1651 a hundred court with view of frankpledge was held twice a year for the hundred at Hocktide and Martinmas.[17]

5 *Hundred R.* (Rec. Com.), ii, 223.
6 *Feud. Aids*, ii, 318.
7 *Plac. de Quo Warr.* (Rec. Com.), Edw. I, 765.
8 *Vide* Portsdown Hundred.
9 *Feud. Aids*, ii, 362.
10 *Hundred R.* (Rec. Com.), ii, 223; *Plac. de Quo Warr.* (Rec. Com.), 772.
11 The hundred roll is very illegible, the only words decipherable being 'Dicunt quod hundredum de F . . . . . . regis. Et ipse dominus rex dedit dictum hundredum Wilhelmo de . . .' Subsequent documents make it clear that it was William de Albini to whom the hundred was granted. There were three of that name, however—one who died *temp.* Hen. II, the second who died *circ.* 6 Hen. III, and the third who died 18 Hen. III—and it is not clear to which of the three it was granted.
12 Inq. p.m. 21 Ric. II, Nos. 8*a* and 8*b*; Assize R. Mich. 8 Edw. I. (The hundred is the hundred of John Fitz-Alan de Arundel by annual payment of 20*s.* to the king, and is worth 40*s.* per annum. Isabel de Mortimer holds the hundred *nomine dotis*, because John is under age and in the king's ward.)
13 *Vide* Close, 2 Jas. I, pt. 15.
14 Ibid.
15 Add. MS. 33278, fol. 146; Close, 2 Jas. I, pt. 15.
16 In a survey of 1651 (Parl. Surv. Hants, 1650–2, No. 11) the hundred is described as late parcel of the possessions of Charles Stuart, late king of England, but a mistake seems to have been made by the commissioners, for Sir Nicholas Hyde was seised of it at his death in 1633, and his descendant Arthur Hyde dealt with it by recovery in 1690 (Recov. R. East. 2 Will. and Mary, rot. 5).
17 Parl. Surv. Hants, 1650–2, No. 11.

BLENDWORTH

Bleneworth and Blonewrth (xiii cent.); Blednewyth and Blenelworth (xiv cent.).

Blendworth is a parish of scattered houses adjoining Bere Forest, and contains 2,333 acres of undulating land, including 1,376 acres of arable, 544 acres of permanent grass, and 629 acres of woods and plantations.[1] The parish is intersected by the main road to Havant, which runs south from Horndean, and by the road to Rowland's Castle, which, after skirting the grounds of Blendworth Lodge and Idsworth Park, turns due south, forming the eastern boundary of the parish.

The small group of houses which represents the old village of Blendworth stands on fairly high ground in the north of the parish close to the disused church of St. Giles, and from this point there is an extensive view over the thickly-wooded country to the south. The church of the Holy Trinity, erected in 1850–1, stands to the west of the old village, and nearer to the busy main road which passes through Horndean. To the north-west is Crookley, the residence of Mr. G. A. Gale, J.P.; while to the south are Cadlington House, the property of Lieut.-Colonel Sir Henry Clarke-Jervoise, and at present occupied by Mrs. Ashley Williams; and Blendworth Lodge, the residence of Mrs. Long, widow of the late Mr. Samuel Long.

At Padnell, a hamlet in the south-western extremity of the parish, bricks and tiles are manufactured. Woodhouse Lane and Woodhouse Ashes[2] are in the east of the parish. The elementary school for girls and infants was built about 1850. The boys attend Horndean School.

The soil is of a chalky nature, the subsoil chalk. The chief crops are wheat and oats. Blendworth Down was inclosed in 1816. The whole of the parish is within the manor of Chalton (q.v.).

CHURCHES Neither of the two churches has much architectural interest. *ST. GILES' CHURCH* is a little rectangular building with plastered walls and red-tiled roof, showing no features which can be older than the eighteenth century, though it may well be that the masonry of the walls is mediaeval. As has been already said, it is disused, and contains no old fittings. It is said to have had a small chancel, which was pulled down at the building of the new church, its material being used up in the new work.

The new church of the *HOLY TRINITY* consists of chancel with north vestry, nave with south aisle and south porch, and west turret with spire. It was built at a cost of nearly £3,000 in 1851, and stands in a well-kept churchyard, the rectory being near it to the north. The font is of alabaster, given to the church in 1893, and the oak quire seats date from the preceding year.

In the turret is one bell without inscription.

The plate consists of a silver cup and cover paten, a flagon given by Thomasina Francklyn in 1720, and an alms-dish given by William Francklyn, who died at Pembroke College, Oxford, 24 November, 1718, aged twenty-six. There is also a modern wine-strainer.

The first book of the registers contains baptisms 1586–1726, marriages 1587–1729, and burials 1586–1732, and is of parchment. The second, of paper, has a few burials in woollen 1678–95, but otherwise contains only the parish accounts from 1702 to 1827. The third book has baptisms 1726–91, marriages 1729–89, and burials 1733–90; and the fourth, baptisms and burials from 1791 and marriages from 1793 to 1812.[3]

ADVOWSON The prior, prioress, and convent of Nuneaton presented to the rectory of the church of *BLENDWORTH* until the dissolution,[4] when it passed to the crown like the rectories of the churches of Clanfield and Chalton. Queen Elizabeth presented Henry Hooper to the parsonage in 1579.[5] Some time later Edward, earl of Worcester, although possessing no legal right to the advowson, presented Richard Perkinson.[6] On the death of the latter, Toby Shaw was presented to the church by the Lord Chancellor, Sir Francis Bacon, whereupon the earl brought a plea of 'quare impedit' against the new rector, who relinquished his possession in the church to Launcelot Andrewes, bishop of Winchester, and accepted a presentation of the same from the earl,[7] to whom James I, by letters patent, granted the advowson in 1618.[8] The right of the crown to the advowson was re-established when Dr. Gillingham, by private agreement with Godfrey Price, rector of Chalton, regained the advowson of Chalton for Charles I.[9] The advowson of Blendworth then followed the advowson of Chalton until the end of the eighteenth century, when it passed out of the possession of Jervoise Clarke-Jervoise, the bishop presenting in 1794.[10] Since that time it has been in private hands,[11] Mr. M. Margesson being the present patron of the living.

CHARITIES The School (see article on 'Schools,' *V. C. H. Hants*, ii, 396, note 7).—William Appleford, by will proved at Winchester, 1696, left £200 to be laid out in land, the income to be applied in putting poor children to school. The legacy was in or about 1703 laid out in the purchase of a house and 17 acres. The property was sold in 1880 and the proceeds invested in Stock, which is now represented by £1,186 Consolidated 4 per cent. Preference Stock of the Great Eastern Railway Co. with the official trustees, producing £47 8*s.* a year, which is carried to the school account.

Church Lands Charity.—The parish was formerly in possession of a small piece of land known as the 'Church Acre.' Upon the inclosure of the common lands in 1816 an allotment was made in respect thereof. The land was sold in or about 1880, and the proceeds were invested in £54 8*s.* 5*d.* Consols with the official trustees. The annual dividends of £2 2*s.* 4*d.* are applied towards repairs of the church.

[1] Statistics from Board of Agriculture (1905).

[2] Woodhouse in the tithing of Blendworth is mentioned in 1656 (Exch. Dep. 1656, Trin. No. 4).

[3] Information from the Rev. E. J. Nelson, M.A., rector.

[4] Egerton MS. 2031, fol. 4; ibid. 2033, fol. 5; and ibid. 2034, fols. 4, 34, 72, and 160; *Wykeham's Register* (Hants Rec. Soc.), i, 183.

[5] *Rep. on the Salisbury MSS.* (Hist. MSS. Com.), ii, 248.

[6] Exch. Bills and Answs. Hants, Chas. I, No. 49.

[7] Ibid.

[8] Pat. 15 Jas. I, pt. 17.

[9] *Cal. of S. P. Dom.* 1668–9, p. 93. It was one of the two 'livings adjacent.'

[10] Inst. Bks. (P.R.O.)

[11] Ibid.

BURITON

Buyiton (xiv cent.) ; Buryton (xvi cent.) ; Beriton (xvii cent.).

The parish of Buriton lies on high ground, rising from north to south-east from a height of little more than 200 ft. above the sea-level to more than 680 ft. near the Sussex border. A fine view of the whole of the south-east can be obtained from the high ground at the back of Chalton church, while, away to the south-west, the main road from Petersfield to Portsmouth winds between high downs on the east and Butser Hill[1] and Oxenbourn Down on the west, in the midst of wild and impressive scenery.[2] Butser Hill, which here rises some 889 ft. above the sea-level, is thus referred to by Cobbett :—'This is as interesting a spot I think as the foot of man ever was placed upon. Here are two valleys, one to your right and the other to your left, very little less than half-a-mile down to the bottom of them, and much steeper than the roof of a house. These valleys may be, where they join the hill, three or four hundred yards broad. They get wider as they get farther from the hill. Of a clear day you see all the north of Hampshire ; nay, the whole county, together with a good part of Surrey and of Sussex. You see the whole of the South Downs to the east as far as your eye can carry you. Lastly, you see over Portsdown Hill, which lies before you to the south ; and there are spread open to your view the Isle of Portsea, Porchester, Wimmering, Fareham, Gosport, Portsmouth, the harbour, Spithead, the Isle of Wight, and the ocean.'[3]

The village of Buriton itself, surrounded by woods and downs, lies almost in the centre of the parish, and is approached by two roads running off south-east from the main road from Petersfield to Portsmouth, and by a narrow winding lane which turns off south-west from the road from Petersfield to South Harting by the grounds of Nursted House. This lane is very picturesque, being in places deeply sunk between high banks and completely over-arched by trees. It leads by a steep descent to the east end of the village street, the church standing immediately to the east of the junction of the two roads, with the manor-house close to it on the north. The two roads from the main Portsmouth road meet at the west end of the village, and near their junction are the Congregational church, the schools, and the Five Bells Inn with its blue sign. From this point the village street runs eastwards with a gentle downward slope to its junction with the South Harting Lane, bordered on either side with cottages and gardens. In front of the church is an open space with a broad pond on the south side of the road, fed from springs which rise in the steep wooded hillside immediately to the south of the village. From the east side of the pond the ground slopes up to the churchyard wall, shaded by a fine row of trees, and to the west of the pond is the rectory garden, the whole forming one of the most charming pieces of scenery in the district. Before the railway line was made between the village and the hillside on the south, it must have been still more beautiful. The manor house stands on the north side of a large yard, bounded on the south and west by farm buildings, and consists of a two-story range, the oldest part of the house, with a three-story eighteenth-century addition on the east. It is a pretty building with red brick quoins and window-frames, but its chief claim to distinction lies in its connexion with Gibbon the historian, who in his autobiography speaks of it thus :—'My father's residence in Hampshire, where I have passed many light and some heavy hours, was at Buriton near Petersfield, one mile from the Portsmouth road, and at the easy distance of 58 miles from London. An old mansion in a state of decay had been converted into the fashion and convenience of a modern house, of which I occupied the most agreeable apartment ; and if strangers had nothing to see, the inhabitants had little to desire. The spot was not happily chosen—at the end of the village and the bottom of the hill ; but the aspect of the adjacent grounds was various and cheerful : the Downs

CHURCH AND VILLAGE POND, BURITON

[1] There is now a rifle-range to the west of Butser Hill.

[2] A very good description of this road is given by Dickens in the chapter describing the journey of Nicholas Nickleby and Smike from London to Portsmouth : 'Onward they kept with steady progress, and entered at last upon a wide and spacious tract of downs with every variety of hill and plain to change their verdant surface. Here there shot up almost perpendicularly into the sky a height so steep as to be hardly accessible to any but the sheep and goats that fed upon its sides, and there stood a mound of green, sloping and tapering off so delicately and merging so gently into the level ground that you could scarcely define its limits. Hills swelling above each other, and undulations shapely and uncouth, smooth and rugged, graceful and grotesque, thrown negligently side by side—bounded the view.'

[3] Cobbett's *Rural Rides* (1885), ii, 262–3.

commanded the prospect of the sea, and the long hanging woods in sight of the house could not perhaps have been improved by art or expense. My father kept in his own hands the whole of his estate, and even rented some additional land, and whatsoever might be the balance of profit and loss the farm supplied him with amusement and plenty.'[4] The room occupied by Gibbon is still pointed out, the added portion of the house having fine rooms and a good staircase. In the older part is some late sixteenth or early seventeenth-century panelling, and some early eighteenth-century chimney-pieces and other details. The rectory house is of unusual interest. Though much altered, it is an H-shaped building, with a central hall and wings at the east and west. Part of the wooden partitions at the lower end of the hall—in which were the doors to buttery, pantry, and kitchen passage—is still to be seen, and appears to be of the fifteenth century, but at the south end of the east wing the arch and part of the jambs of an early fourteenth-century window in wrought stone witness to a considerably earlier date for the building. The window has been of two lights, with tracery in the head, but the tracery and central mullion have been cut away. The older roof timbers of the wing also exist below the present roof, and in the western gable of the rectory is a small arched opening high in the wall, which is of fourteenth-century date, and probably coeval with the window in the east wing.

Ditcham Park, about 100 acres in extent, is situated 2 miles south-east of the village. Nursted House, standing about midway between Petersfield and Buriton, the seat and residence of Mr. John Rowe Bennion, was purchased by him in 1863 from General Hugonin, whose family had long owned it. About a mile north-north-west of Buriton is West Mapledurham, known in modern days as Mapledurham only,[5] the property of the Legge family. In the north-western extremity of the parish is the little hamlet of Weston, marking the site of the reputed manor of Weston.

The soil varies; the subsoil is of the Upper Greensand formation. The chief crops are wheat, barley, beans, oats, and hops. There are lime works near the village.[6] The area of the parish is 5,625 acres, comprising 1,742½ acres of arable land, 988 acres of permanent grass, and 876 acres of woods and pasture. Buriton Holt and Head Down were inclosed by authority of an Act of Parliament dated 24 July, 1854.[7] The following are place-names in the parish:—Westcleye and Crowburghfeld,[8] Countesparke, Bellelond and Britteshore[9] (xv cent.); a tenement called Whekys and lands called Holwysashe, Goffys, Forengerys and Halpenny Londe,[10] a copse called Godlecombe,[11] lands called Medplatts and Stigant Brynche[12] (xvi cent.), and Gaston Purrocke and Alder's Crofte[13] (xvii cent.).

At the time of the Domesday Survey there were three mills worth 20*s*. in 'Malpedresham,'[14] but only one of them seems to have been situated in the modern parish of Buriton. This was a water-mill, and is included in the extents of the main manor of Mapledurham taken in 1296[15] and 1521,[16] but no trace of it now remains.

MANORS Malpedresham (xi cent.); Mapeldoreham (xii cent.); Mapeldereham, Mapledreham, Mapeldurham, Mapeldeham and Appeldoueham (xiii cent.); Mapuldrham (xiv cent.); Mapylderham (xv cent.); Mapel-Dereham (xvi cent.). Before the Conquest the extensive manor of *MAPLEDURHAM* was held by Wulfgifu ('Ulveva'), surnamed 'Beteslau,' who was the owner of wide estates in Hampshire and the neighbouring district. William the Conqueror deprived her of her lands, granting Mapledurham to his wife Maud,[17] on whose death in 1083 it reverted to King William, who was holding it at the time of the Domesday Survey.[18] Later, the manor formed 'parcel of the Honour of Gloucester,' and doubtless part of the original Honour which was bestowed upon Robert Fitzhamon by William Rufus for services rendered in suppressing the revolt of Odo of Bayeux. By his wife Sibyl of Montgomery Fitzhamon left no son, and his possessions passed with the hand of his daughter Mabel to Robert, a natural son of King Henry I, who was created Earl of Gloucester some time between April, 1121, and June, 1123.[19] William, second earl of Gloucester, the eldest son of Robert, died in 1183, leaving three daughters—Mabel, Amice, and Isabel, the youngest of whom Henry II gave in marriage to Prince John with the possessions of the earldom which he had himself retained for six years, and which John retained after his accession and divorce from Isabel. However, in 1205 he granted Mapledurham to Aumary count of Evreux, who had married Mabel, the eldest of the three daughters of William.[20] The count died before 1214, in which year the king ordered the sheriff of Hampshire to cause the executors of the count to have full seisin of all his chattels in Mapledurham.[21] The manor, however, reverted to the king, who in the same year granted it to Geoffrey de Mandeville, whom Isabel had married after her divorce from John,[22] but before the year was out Geoffrey was in rebellion against John and was deprived of his lands, the manor of Mapledurham being granted to Savary de Mauleon in May, 1215.[23] However, in October of the same year the king bestowed it on his faithful adherent Roger de la Zouche.[24] Henry III by letters patent dated 12 March, 1217, took the men of Mapledurham and all their lands and possessions under his

[4] *The Autobiographies of Edward Gibbon*, 246.

[5] The old manor house, a large gabled building approached by an avenue of elms, was pulled down during the last century, when the present farm-house was built on the site.

[6] Butser Hill lime-works are to the east of Butser Hill, and Buriton lime-works on the downs to the west of the village.

[7] *Parl. Accts. and Papers*, 1893–4, lxxi, 485.

[8] Add. R. 27656.

[9] Mins. Accts. bdle. 1117, No. 8.

[10] Ibid. Suss. 109, m. 17*d*.

[11] Add. Chart. 28026.

[12] Add. R. 28235.

[13] Ibid. 28178.

[14] *V.C.H. Hants*, i, 451*a*.

[15] Inq. p.m. 24 Edw. I, No. 107*a*.

[16] Chan. Inq. p.m. (Ser. 2), lxxx, No. 182.

[17] *V.C.H. Hants*, i, 429.

[18] Ibid. 451.

[19] *The Geneal.* (New Ser.), iv, 129–40.

[20] *Rot. Litt. Claus.* (Rec. Com.), i, 29.

[21] Ibid. 141.

[22] Ibid. 209.

[23] Ibid 213.

[24] Ibid. 231. The earldom and the honour of Gloucester had in reality descended, on the death of Geoffrey de Mandeville, to Aumary count of Evreux son and heir of Aumary count of Evreux and Mabel his wife who, as has been shown above, was the eldest daughter of William earl of Gloucester. Aumary had died before 15 Mar. 1217, for on that day the king ordered Roger to give a reasonable dowry from the manor of Mapledurham to William de Cantilupe the younger, who had married Millicent widow of Aumary (*Rot. Litt. Claus.* i, 300).

special protection,[25] and further in June, 1217, ordered the men of Mapledurham to be obedient in all things to Roger, to whom he had committed the manor to hold during his pleasure.[26] Four months later Randolph de Norewyz and Randolph . . . resham were appointed guardians of the manor.[27] After this date the manor again reverted to the Honour of Gloucester, which had devolved on Amice wife of Richard de Clare, earl of Hertford, as sole surviving heiress of William, earl of Gloucester. Richard de Clare, earl of Gloucester and Hertford, the grandson of Richard and Amice, granted the manor to his brother William de Clare and his right heirs for service of one knight's fee with reversion to the grantor and his heirs.[28] Henry III confirmed this grant in 1248, and granted free warren in his demesne lands in Mapledurham to William de Clare and his heirs.[29] William de Clare died of poison in 1258, leaving no issue. Consequently the manor reverted to Richard,[30] who died seised of it in 1262, leaving a son and heir Gilbert.[31] The descent of the manor of Mapledurham from this point is identical with that of Corhampton in the hundred of Meonstoke (q.v.), until the close of the seventeenth century. According to the *Hampshire Repository* for 1801 the family of Hanbury held the manor until 1691, when the sisters as co-heirs of the last male heir sold the estate to John Barkesdale, who shortly afterwards sold it to Ralph Bucknel, whose heirs-at-law conveyed it to Edward Gibbon,[32] to whom it was with other estates granted and confirmed by the Trustees of the South Sea Company in 1724.[33] The historian, Edward Gibbon, in his autobiography states that his grandfather, Edward Gibbon, having acquired a fortune of £60,000, was chosen a director of the South Sea Company in 1716, and became involved in the general ruin which fell on that company in 1720, but soon made a fresh fortune equal to that of which he had been despoiled, purchasing large landed estates in Buckinghamshire and Hampshire.[34] Edward Gibbon died in 1736, and the manor passed to his son Edward Gibbon, the father of the historian. He was early left a widower, 'and soon withdrew from the gay and busy scenes of the world, and his prudent retreat from London and Putney to his farm at Buriton in Hampshire was ennobled by the pious motive of conjugal affliction.'[35] He lived there for the remainder of his life, keeping the whole of the estate in his own hands, and even renting some additional land.[36] He died in 1770, and the manor then passed to his son Edward Gibbon the historian, who in April, 1789, sold it to Lord Stawell,[37] the only son of Henry Bilson-Legge, from whom it passed by purchase on 19 April, 1798, to Henry Bonham of Petersfield. Henry Bonham died in 1800; his brother and heir died in 1826, leaving his Buriton estates to his cousin John Carter, who assumed the name of Bonham, and was the first John Bonham-Carter. He died in 1838, leaving a son and heir John Bonham-Carter, who died in 1884, leaving a son and heir John Bonham-Carter. The last-named died December, 1905, leaving the Buriton estates to his brother Lothian George Bonham-Carter, the present owner.

While Richard de Clare earl of Gloucester and Hertford was lord of the manor of *MAPLEDURHAM* he granted away from it three carucates of land, in frankalmoign, to the prior and convent of St. Swithun, Winchester,[38] receiving in exchange the manors of Portland and Wyke, the vill of Weymouth and the land of Helewell.[39] This exchange was confirmed by Henry III in 1260.[40] The title of the prior and convent to these manors was defective,[41] and knowing this the earl caused a proviso to be inserted in the agreement to the effect that they would restore to him, his heirs or assigns all the land and tenements in the manor of Mapledurham which he had given to them in exchange for the Isle of Portland and its members in Weymouth, Wyke and Helewell in case the latter were recovered from him, his heirs or assigns in court of law.[42] John de Gervais bishop of Winchester 1260–8, and Nicholas of Ely bishop of Winchester 1268–80, in turn petitioned that the Isle of Portland should be restored to the bishopric,[43] but it was not until about 1280 that determined efforts were made to recover it from Gilbert de Clare earl of Gloucester and Hertford.[44] In the course of the proceedings the manor of Mapledurham, as the three carucates of land had come to be called, was taken into the king's hands by the justices in eyre, but was restored to the prior by the king's orders in 1281 so that he might till and sow the land until the next Parliament in order that there might then be done what the king should cause to be ordained by his council.[45] The lawsuit between the king and the earl extended over several years. Thus as late as 1284 John de Pontoise bishop of Winchester, while granting to the prior and convent all rights which he had in various manors and other lands, expressly excepted his rights in the Isle of Portland and its members in

CLARE. *Or three chevrons gules.*

[25] Pat. 1 Hen. III, m. 11.
[26] Ibid. m. 7.
[27] Ibid. m. 1.
[28] Chart. R. 32 Hen. III, m. 1.
[29] Ibid. m. 2.
[30] It must have been about this time that a portion of this manor was granted to the prior and convent of St. Swithun, Winchester, which in a short time developed into a separate manor with a distinct history of its own.
[31] Inq. p.m. 46 Hen. III, No. 34.
[32] It is probable that Edward Gibbon purchased the manor in 1719, for in that year he purchased the manor and borough of Petersfield from Bucknel Howard and Sarah Bucknel, grand-daughter and sole heiress of Ralph Bucknel (Close, 13 Geo. II, pt. 17, m. 36, &c.).
[33] *The Hampshire Repository*, ii, 205.
[34] Murray's *Autobiographies of Edward Gibbon*, 215.
[35] Ibid. 218.
[36] Ibid. 246.
[37] The purchase-money of £16,000 was not paid for a considerable time after the sale. The matter was referred to Chancery, and was not finally concluded till Apr. 1791. (Murray's *Private Letters of Edward Gibbon*, ii, 189, 222, 240 and 243).
[38] Assize R. Mich. 8 Edw. I.
[39] Coram Rege R. Mich. 7 & 8 Edw. I, rot. 20, 21.
[40] Ibid.
[41] Inasmuch as previous to this they had granted them to Ethelmar bishop-elect of Winchester, the grant being confirmed by Henry III in 1256. On the expulsion of Ethelmar from England in 1258 the manors fell into the king's hands, who granted them to Richard de Clare earl of Gloucester and Hertford to hold during his pleasure, shortly afterwards however re-granting them to the prior and convent (Coram Rege R. Mich. 7 & 8 Edw. I, rot. 20, 21).
[42] Coram Rege R. Mich. 7 & 8 Edw. I.
[43] Ibid.
[44] Ibid.
[45] Close, 9 Edw. I, m. 9.

exchange for which they held the manor of Mapledurham.[46] But it was ultimately decided in favour of the earl, as the manor of Mapledurham occurs in the list of the manors held by the prior of St. Swithun in 1290,[47] and the earl was seised of the Isle of Portland and its members at his death in 1295.[48] Evidently the manor of the prior and convent remained in a dependent position upon the chief manor of Mapledurham, and the tenants of the prior paid rent to the lord of the chief manor of Mapledurham. Thus for the year ending Michaelmas, 1448, the farmer of the chief manor accounted for 5*s.* 8*d.*, the price of 34 hens collected from divers tenants of the prior of St. Swithun, and 10*d.* the price of 200 eggs collected from the same tenants.[49] The manor remained the property of the prior and convent until the dissolution,[50] when Henry VIII granted it to Nicholas Dering of Liss,[51] who died seised of it in 1557 leaving it in dower to his wife Anne [52] with reversion to his son and heir Thomas aged twenty-one.[53] Anne Dering held a court at Mapledurham as late as April, 1591,[54] but she must have died shortly afterwards, for Thomas Hanbury, to whom Thomas Dering and Winifred his wife had given their reversionary interest in the manor in 1581,[55] held his first court there on 20 September, 1591.[56] Six years later Thomas purchased the chief manor of Mapledurham,[57] when the two manors were merged, and the subsequent history is given under the heading of the chief manor (q.v.)

The manor of *WEST MAPLEDURHAM* was parcel of the honour of Gloucester. It is mentioned in the *Testa de Nevill*, which states that Ralph de la Falaise and Robert 'Mercator' held three parts of a fee in Mapledurham of the old enfeoffment of the earl of Gloucester.[58] The one messuage and one carucate of land which Ralph de la Falaise had held was settled upon Peter de la Falaise (probably son of Ralph) and Alice his wife and their issue in 1271, no doubt on the occasion of their marriage.[59] Peter de la Falaise probably died before 1289, for in that year Alice quitclaimed to Richard Bruton and his heirs a messuage, 84 acres of land, 6 acres of wood, 5 acres of meadow and £1 7*s.* 5½*d.* rent in Mapledurham.[60] This part of the manor continued in the Bruton family until 1327,[61] when Alice Bruton quitclaimed it to Henry le Markaunt and Iseult his wife.[62] This Henry le Markaunt was the descendant of the Robert Mercator mentioned in the *Testa de Nevill*, and already probably held by right of inheritance a part of the manor.[63] The family of Markaunt continued in possession of the whole manor till the beginning of the fifteenth century,[64] when Joan the daughter and heir of Sir Robert Markaunt died, leaving as her heir her kinsman William Levechild of Sheet next Petersfield.[65] From William it passed to John Roger of Bryanston (co. Dorset),[66] and continued in the family of Roger until 1533, when Sir John Roger conveyed it by fine to trustees for purchase by Sir William Shelley, justice of the Common Pleas,[67] who died seised of the manor in 1548. By his will dated 6 November, 1548, he left the manor of Mapledurham and all lands in Hampshire which he had purchased of Sir John Roger to his son Thomas a recusant in tail male.[68] By an inquisition taken at Winchester 2 October, 1570, it was ascertained that Thomas Shelley, late of Mapledurham, had been a fugitive in foreign parts beyond the seas since 1 December, 1558, and was then living in Louvain, and that before his departure he had granted a twelve years' lease of all his lands and tenements in Mapledurham to Thomas Goldforde and John Jervys.[69] He died seised of the manor in 1577, his heir being his son Henry, aged thirty-eight,[70] whose name occurs five years later in a list of the prisoners for religion in the custody of Anthony Thorpe 'keeper of the Whyte Lyon in Southwarke.'[71] At this time the manor house was the refuge of numerous priests, who were always sure to find a welcome, a place to say their mass, and if necessary a secure hiding-place; and there are many references to it in the correspondence of the time. Thus Edward Jones, a recusant, writes as follows in June, 1586:—'At length old Mr. Titchborne, being then prisoner in the White Lion, in Southwark . . . sent for me and placed me with this Shelley's brother, being prisoner too, where I waited on him and his wife, and was reconciled there in my mistress' chamber by one Wrenche, who died in London two years agone; but being alive went down with my mistress unto her house named Mapledurham, near unto Petersfield, where he did say mass every day once, whither resorted certain priests more. . . . There I daily consociate withal and heard mass every day.'[72] Again, an informer, writing under the name of Ben Beard, gives the

SHELLEY. *Sable a fesse engrailed between three shells or.*

[46] Add. MS. 29436, fol. 53. 'Salvo nobis et successoribus jure nostro in insula de Portlande, et maneriis de Portlande, de Wyke et de Helewell et burgo de Waymue pro quibus dicti prior et conventus tenent manerium de Mapeldurham cum pertinentiis in escambium.'

[47] *Pope Nich. Tax.* (Rec. Com.), 213.

[48] Inq. p.m. 24 Edw. I, No. 107.

[49] Mins. Accts. bdle. 1117, No. 8.

[50] Chart. R. 29 Edw. I, m. 12; *Feud. Aids*, ii, 319; *Valor Eccl.* (Rec. Com.), vi, App. i, p. vii.

[51] Pat. 33 Hen. VIII, pt. 8, m. 20.

[52] Anne was summoned in 1560 to show by what title she held the manor, and stated that her husband had settled it upon her to hold for the term of her life (Memo. R. L.T.R. Mich. 3 Eliz. m. 18).

[53] Chan. Inq. p.m. (Ser. 2), cviii, No. 101.

[54] Add. R. 27663.

[55] Add. MS. 33278, fol. 161; Close, 23 Eliz. pt. 8; Notes of F. Hants, Hil. 23 Eliz.

[56] Add. R. 27663.

[57] Recov. R. Hil. 39 Eliz. m. 3.

[58] *Testa de Nevill* (Rec. Com.), 234*b*. Ralph had obtained his part from William de la Falaise in 1248 in exchange for lands in Rowner (Salzmann, *Suss. Fines*, 120).

[59] Feet of F. Hants, Hil. 55 Hen. III.

[60] Feet of F. Hants, Trin. 17 Edw. I.

[61] Inq. p.m. 30 Edw. I, No. 21; and 8 Edw. II, No. 68.

[62] Feet of F. Hants, Trin. 1 Edw. II.

[63] Inq. p.m. 8 Edw. II, No. 68. In subsequent lists of knights' fees Richard Bruton's name occurs as holding land in Mapledurham of the earls of Stafford, but his name was probably copied from an earlier return.

[64] Add. Chart. 28022, 28023; Inq. p.m. 10 Ric. II, No. 38; 16 Ric. II, pt. 1, No. 27, and 22 Ric. II, No. 46; Anct. D. (P.R.O.) B. 2543; Inq. p.m. 4 Hen. IV, No. 41.

[65] Close, 13 Hen. IV, m. 2.

[66] Close, 1 Hen. VI, m. 21; Feet of F. Hants, Hil. 4 Hen. VI.

[67] Feet of F. Hants, Trin. 25 Hen. VIII.

[68] P.C.C. 25 Populwell. In 1563 the manor was settled upon Thomas and Mary his wife for the term of their lives, with reversion to their son and heir Henry, with contingent remainder to the heirs of Sir William Shelley deceased (Recov. R. East. 5 Eliz. m. 119).

[69] Exch. Spec. Com. 12 Eliz. No. 2015.

[70] Inq. p.m. 20 Eliz. pt. 2, (Ser. 2), No. 51.

[71] *Hist. MSS. Com. Rep.* vii, 637*a*.

[72] Harl. M.S. 360, fol. 22.

following information in 1594 about the hiding-places in the manor house :—'At Mapledurham there is a hollow place in the parlour by the livery cupboard where two men may well lie together, which has many times deceived the searchers ;' [73] and again : 'In Mapledurham house under a little table is a vault, with a grate of iron for a light into the garden, as if it were the window of a cellar, and against the grate groweth rosemarye.' [74] Henry Shelley died in prison in 1585,[75] and in 1605 his widow and sons sold the manor to Thomas Bilson bishop of Winchester,[76] who held his first court there 25 April, 1606.[77] He died seised of the manor in 1616, leaving a son and heir Thomas, aged twenty-four and more.[78] The latter died without issue in 1649, and was succeeded by his brother Leonard, on whose son and heir Thomas the manor was settled in 1678 on his marriage with Susannah Legge [79] daughter of Colonel William Legge and sister of George Legge afterwards Baron Dartmouth.[80] Two sons were born of this marriage, both of whom died without issue, Thomas on 11 June, 1709, and Leonard on 6 October, 1715. Leonard left the remainder of his estate, after Thomas Bettesworth [81] and his heirs male, to Henry Legge son of the earl of Dartmouth, provided he took the name of Bilson. Thomas Bettesworth Bilson died without issue 25 March, 1754, and was buried at Rogate. Hence the manor passed to Henry Legge, a well-known politician who took the name of Bilson in accordance with the terms of Leonard Bilson's will. He died 23 August, 1764, in the fifty-seventh year of his age and was buried at Hinton Ampner (co. Hants). West Mapledurham still belongs to the Legge family, the present holder being the Rev. Augustus George Legge, vicar of North Elmham (co. Norfolk).

BILSON. *Gules a Tudor rose dimidiated with a pomegranate or, the stalk and leaves vert.*

LEGGE. *Azure a hart's head cabossed argent.*

WESTON (Westeton and Westreton xiii cent. ; Westynton xiv cent.) is a tithing in the parish of Buriton and seems to have been, to some extent, co-extensive with the manor of West Mapledurham. Thus in the assessment for an aid in 1316 the name of Henry Markaunt is given as a holder of land in the vill of Weston.[82] This land probably refers to the portion of a knight's fee which Henry was then holding of the chief manor of Mapledurham, as a parcel of the honour of Gloucester, and which in time, as has been shown, developed into the manor of West Mapledurham. That this is so seems to be supported by the fact that in the fine conveying West Mapledurham to the Shelleys in 1553, the property is described as 'the manor of Mapledurham and Weston.' [83]

There was also a free tenement in the tithing of Weston which in origin was of the lands of the Normans and not of the honour of Gloucester, as was ascertained by an inquisition taken in the reign of Henry III.[84] This tenement was held by Robert de St. Remy in the reign of Richard I.[85] King John granted it in 1204 to his groom Roald to hold during his pleasure,[86] and it was afterwards held by Roland de la Genwar.[87] In September, 1233, Henry III ordered the sheriff of Hampshire to cause his servant Geoffrey de Bathonia to have full seisin of the land which had belonged to Robert de St. Remy in Mapledurham, to hold during the king's pleasure, saving however to Earl Richard, the king's brother, the corn which he caused to be sown in that land, and the stock which he had in it.[88] Henry III some time afterwards bestowed it upon William de Radyng,[89] who, for the safety of King Henry III and the safety of his own soul and that of Margaret his wife, granted all the lands, rents, and possessions, which they held of his fee in the manor of Mapledurham, to the abbey and convent of Dureford.[90] His son John de Radyng is described as holding 100*s.* worth of land in Weston of the king in chief in 1280.[91] In 1294, by a fine between Adam Wygaunt and Maud daughter of John de Radyng, and John de Radyng, five messuages, 90 acres of land, 5 acres of meadow, 8*s.* rent, and rents of 4½ lb. of pepper, and 1½ lb. of cummin in Mapledurham and 'Westreton,' near Petersfield, were settled on John for the term of his life with reversion on his death to Adam and Maud, and the heirs of Maud.[92] This John probably left two daughters and coheirs, Margaret and Isabel, the latter of whom married Nicholas de Severyngton, who held land in the vill of Weston in 1316, no doubt in right of his wife.[93] In 1324 Margaret the daughter of John de Radyng and Nicholas de Severyngton and Isabel his wife quitclaimed lands in Mapledurham to Edelina de Ponte and John her son.[94] In the reign of Edward III Richard le Beel and Joan his wife acquired in fee from Margaret the daughter of John de Radyng the moiety of a messuage, 60 acres of land, 4 acres of meadow, and £1 17*s.* 10½*d.* rent in Weston without licence. On her husband's death Joan paid to the king a fine of £3, and obtained licence to retain

73 *Cal. of S.P. Dom.* 1591–4, p. 463.
74 Ibid. 510.
75 Ibid. 1581–90, p. 294.
76 Feet of F. Hants, Hil. 3 Jas. I ; Mich. 4 Jas. I ; Hil. 7 Jas. I.
77 Add. R. 28178.
78 W. and L. Inq. p.m. (Ser. 2), bdle. 55, No. 125. In this inquisition comes the latest mention of the dependence of the manor on the main manor of Mapledurham, since it is said to be held of Thomas Hanbury as of his manor of Mapledurham for money-rent and suit of court.
79 Feet of F. Div. Cos. East. 30 Chas. II ; deeds *penes* Lord Dartmouth ; Recov. R. East. 30 Chas. II, m. 8.
80 Phillipps' *Hants Visitations*, 1686.
81 Thomas Bettesworth was of Fyning Rogate (co. Sussex). His paternal grandmother was Susan daughter of Sir Thomas Bilson. He was also connected with the Bilsons by the marriage of Edith Bettesworth, a distant relation of his grandfather Thomas Bettesworth, with Thomas Bilson of Mapledurham (Dallaway, *Suss.* i, 212).
82 *Feud. Aids*, ii, 319.
83 Feet of F. Hants, Trin. 25 Hen. VIII.
84 Close, 17 Hen. III, m. 2.
85 Pipe R. 31 Hen. II, and 6 Ric. I.
86 Close, 6 John, m. 13.
87 Close, 17 Hen. III, m. 2. It is impossible, however, that Roald and Roland are the same man.
88 Close, 17 Hen. III, m. 2.
89 Assize R. Mich. 8 Edw. I.
90 Cott. MS. Vesp. E. xxiii, 7. His charter was confirmed by Hen. III.
91 Assize R. Mich. 8 Edw. I.
92 Feet of F. Hants, Trin. 22 Edw. I.
93 *Feud. Aids*, ii, 319.
94 Feet of F. Hants, Trin. 17 Edw. II.

the premises.[95] Richard le Beel died in 1346, seised of a messuage, 60 acres of arable land, 4 acres of meadow, £1 17*s.* 10*d.* rent from free men and villeins, and pleas and perquisites of court worth 6*d.* per annum in Weston in the manor of Mapledurham.[96] It has been shown that he had acquired a moiety of the premises from Margaret de Radyng. He probably held the other moiety in right of his wife Joan.[97] In the inquisition it was stated that Richard held the premises of the king in chief by the service of attending the view of frankpledge twice a year at Mapledurham. Before the year 1400 the manor had passed to the abbot and convent of Dureford who had gradually been acquiring lands in the tithing of Weston during the thirteenth and fourteenth centuries,[98] and in that year John the abbot of Dureford obtained an indult from Pope Boniface IX to retain for life and to convert to his own uses, even if he should resign or renounce the rule of the said monastery, the grange or manor of Weston, united to the monastery, and not valued at more than 20 marks.[99] The manor remained the property of the priory until its dissolution[100] when King Henry VIII granted it in tail male to Sir William Fitz-William[101] whom a day later he raised to the peerage as earl of Southampton. The earl was seised of the manor until his death without issue in 1542[102] when it reverted to the crown.[103] In 1545 Henry VIII, by letters patent, granted the manor to Frances Palmer, to hold for the term of her life with remainder on her decease to William Stone and his issue by Frances, with contingent remainder to the right heirs of William.[104] William Stone died seised of the manor in 1549 leaving a son and heir Henry aged one year and five months.[105] Both Henry and his younger brother William died without issue,[106] and consequently the manor was divided between their two sisters and coheirs Catherine and Mary, the former of whom married Christopher Willenhall of Willenhall, near Coventry, and the latter Stephen Vachell.[107] In 1571 Christopher and Catherine having obtained royal licence,[108] alienated half the manor of Weston to Stephen and Mary to hold to them and the heirs and assigns of Mary.[109] In a charter of 1579, settling a dispute between Stephen and Mary, and Henry Shelley of West Mapledurham concerning the bounds of a down, the two former are described as lords of Weston.[110] In September, 1600, Stephen forfeited two-thirds of his lands and possessions for recusancy, and in December of the same year the queen granted the capital messuage called Weston Farm and lands in the parish of Buriton to Arthur Hide, for a term of twenty-one years, if the premises should remain in the hands of the queen or her successors so long.[111] It is doubtful, however, whether Arthur Hide ever gained possession of the manor, for in 1598 Richard Willenhall, Stephen Vachell and Mary his wife had conveyed it to Nicholas Hunt and Mary his wife the owners of the manor of Anmore in the parish of Catherington.[112] Nine years later Thomas Bilson, bishop of Winchester, purchased Weston from Nicholas Hunt and Edmund Marsh,[113] to the last-named of whom Stephen Vachell and Mary his wife and Thomas Vachell had conveyed messuages and lands in Buriton and Petersfield,[114] and at the same time Sir George Cotton and Cassandra his wife quitclaimed to him rents of £50 issuing from the manors of Weston and Anmore.[115] After the purchase Weston formed part of the manor of West Mapledurham.[116] Weston Farm, as it is now called, still belongs to the Legge family, the present owner being the Rev. Augustus George Legge, vicar of North Elmham (co. Norfolk).

BOLINGEHILL FARM, situated about a mile north from the village of Buriton, and a little to the south-east of Weston Farm, seems from early times to have been a parcel of the manor of West Mapledurham. In the fine conveying West Mapledurham to the Rogers in 1426 'Bonelynche' is mentioned,[117] no doubt representing the modern Bolingehill. Again Bowlinch Farm is mentioned in a deed of 1678 between Leonard Bilson of West Mapledurham and Thomas his son, and George and William Legge.[118] Bolingehill Farm still belongs to the Legge family.

DITCHAM (Dicham, xiii cent.; Dycheham, xvi cent.) was probably included under the heading of Mapledurham in the Domesday Book, as in subsequent grants the land of 'Dicham' is described as being situated in the manor of Mapledurham.[119] In the reign of Henry III Henry Hoese or Hussey, lord of the neighbouring manor of Harting (co. Sussex), received from Richard de Ditcham a grant of all his land of Ditcham, and about the same time gained possession of a tenement in Ditcham formerly held by Richard le Bel. After acquiring this property he granted it in free alms to the abbot and convent of Dureford,[120] and his grant was confirmed by Richard le Bel himself in 1272.[121] The abbot of Dureford seems to have held one court for the two manors of Ditcham and Sunworth, and at the time of the dissolution the two manors had coalesced.[122] Henry VIII in 1537 granted Ditcham and Sunworth as the manor of 'Beriton' formerly belonging to the late monastery of Dureford, with appurtenances in Buriton, Petersfield, Winchester, Langrish and Liss', in tail male to Sir William Fitzwilliam.[123] On his death without issue the manor reverted to the crown, and on 16 April, 1544, the king granted the site of the manor of Ditcham and Sunworth and all messuages and lands belonging to the site to Edward Elrington and Humphrey Metcalf and the heirs of

95 Close, 20 Edw. III, pt. 2, m. 3; Pat. 20 Edw. III, pt. 3, m. 16; *Abbrev. Rot. Orig.* ii, 184.
96 Inq. p.m. 20 Edw. III (1st Nos.), No. 38.
97 Joan may possibly have been the daughter and heir of Nicholas de Severyngton and Isabel his wife.
98 Cott. MS. Vesp. E, *passim.*
99 *Cal. Pap. Let.* v, 327.
100 Mins. Accts. Sussex, 109, m. 17 *d.*
101 Pat. 29 Hen. VIII, pt. 1, m. 22.
102 Add. R. 28235. The earl died at Newcastle-upon-Tyne in October, 1542, while on his march into Scotland, leading the van of the English army commanded by the duke of Norfolk. He had married in 1513 Mabel, daughter of Henry Lord Clifford, but by this lady, who died in 1535, he left no issue.
103 Mins. Accts. Sussex, 188, m. 16
104 Pat. 37 Hen. VIII, pt. 11, m. 14, &c.
105 W. and L. Inq. pm. (Ser. 2), v, fol. 114.
106 *Harl. Soc.* xxi, 259.
107 Ibid. This Stephen Vachell was the son and heir of Oliver Vachell of Buriton who died in 1564, seised of the manor of North Marston, in Bucks (Lipscombe, *Bucks.* i, 336).
108 Pat. 13 Eliz. pt. 8, m. 38.
109 Feet of F. Hants, East. 13 Eliz.
110 Add. Chart. 28026.
111 Pat. 43 Eliz. pt. 4, m. 17, 18.
112 Feet of F. Hants, East. 40 Eliz.
113 Ibid. Mich. 4 Jas. I.
114 Ibid.
115 Ibid.
116 *Vide* deeds *penes* Lord Dartmouth.
117 Feet of F. Hants, Hil. 4 Hen. VI.
118 Deed *penes* Lord Dartmouth.
119 Cott. MS. Vesp. E. xxiii, 17 and 89.
120 Ibid. 17.
121 Ibid. 89.
122 Mins. Accts. Suss. 109, m. 17 *d.*
123 Pat 29 Hen. VIII, pt. 1, m. 22.

Edward to hold of the crown by annual payment of 30*s*.[124] The next year the king gave licence to Edward and Humphrey to alienate the site of the manor and the other premises to John Cowper and Margaret his wife to hold to them in fee tail.[125] The manor remained in the family of Cowper[126] till 1762, when it was devised by the will of the last Richard Cowper to his cousin John Coles.[127] Ditcham Park remained the seat and property of the Coles family until the middle of the nineteenth century. In 1868 it was purchased by Charles Cammel, by whom the mansion was much enlarged and improved. The estate was sold in 1885 to Lawrence Trent Cave. The mansion was burnt down in March, 1888, but has since been rebuilt. It is at present the residence of Mr. Charles John Philip Cave, J.P.

SUNWORTH (Seneorde, xi cent.; Sugnewrth, Suneworde and Sonneworthe, xiii cent.; Sandworthe and Sanworth, xvi cent.) was held at the time of the Domesday Survey by Walter of Earl Roger of Shrewsbury,[128] whose successors, the earls of Sussex and Arundel, were overlords of the manor until it finally passed into the possession of the prior and convent of Dureford (co. Sussex).[129] A family which took the surname of Sunworth held the manor 'de veteri feoffamento' of the earls of Sussex and Arundel by the service of one knight's fee.[130] It was in the time of William son of Otewy de Sunworth, who seems to have lived early in the thirteenth century, that a portion of the manor was detached from the whole and granted to the prior and convent of Dureford,[131] a portion which by 1252 had become a separate manor,[132] quite distinct from the manor of Sunworth, which continued for some time in the Sunworth family. In 1246 Ralph de Sunworth settled on his son and heir, Thomas de Sunworth, probably on his marriage, the third part of three carucates in Sunworth, and agreed henceforth not to alienate any of the lands and tenements which he was then holding in Sunworth, so that on his death they should wholly descend to Thomas and his heirs.[133] In 1256 the manor was in the possession of William Finamur and Joan[134] his wife, who granted it to William de Clare, brother of Richard de Clare, earl of Gloucester and Hertford, and his heirs, to hold of William and Joan and the heirs of Joan for ever by the service of a knight's fee, in return for 50 acres of land, 16 acres of wood, and 2 acres of meadow in Mapledurham.[135] A year later William de Clare received from Henry III a grant of free warren in his demesne lands in Sunworth.[136] He died without issue in 1258, leaving a brother and heir, Richard de Clare, earl of Gloucester and Hertford, on whose death four years later the manor passed to his son and heir Gilbert de Clare, earl of Gloucester and Hertford, who granted it to Roger Loveday, to hold to him and his heirs by the annual payment of a pair of gilt spurs at Easter.[137] In 1267 Roger released the manor of Sunworth to the abbot and convent of Dureford to hold at perpetual fee-farm for the annual payment of 24 marks to him, his heirs or assigns.[138] If Roger died leaving a minor it was agreed that the rent should be paid to Gilbert. A year later Roger released the fee-farm rent to the convent and granted them the manor in free alms,[139] and Gilbert de Clare shortly afterwards released to Dureford the annual payment of £16 from Sunworth, which was to be made to him in case Roger Loveday died leaving a minor.[140] With these final grants to Dureford the two manors of Sunworth naturally became one. The manor remained the property of the abbey[141] until its dissolution, by which time it had become attached to Ditcham, being known as the manor of 'Dycheham and Sandworth.'[142] Its subsequent history is given under the heading of Ditcham above. Sunworth is at the present day represented by several farm buildings called 'Sunwood.' Sunwood Farm still belongs to the Ditcham estate. The approach to it is by the private road leading to Ditcham House, and the farm is practically within the precincts of the park.

From a small memorandum book belonging to Mr. Bonham-Carter it appears there was also in the parish the manor of *MAPLEDURHAM RECTORY*. The entries appear to have been made about the year 1816, and were evidently extracted from a book which began in the year 1600. It also contains a copy of a presentment in 1761 of 'a true and perfect terrier of all the several messuages and lands held of

124 Pat. 35 Hen. VIII, pt. 15, m. 39, &c.

125 Pat. 36 Hen. VIII, pt. 25.

126 Memo. R. L.T.R. East. 37 Hen. VIII, rot. 81; Inq. p.m. (Ser. 2), cclxxviii, No. 126.

127 Dallaway, *Suss.* i, 193.

128 *V.C.H. Hants*, i, 478*a*. The manor had been claimed as part of the great manor of Chalton which before the Conquest had belonged to Earl Godwin, and it was this circumstance that led the jurors of the hundred to record that William Fitz-Osbern who gave Chalton to Earl Roger had not granted him Sunworth as well.

129 As late as 1280 Richard Fitz-Alan was said to be holding one knight's fee in chief of the king in Sunworth of the honour of Arundel (Assize R. Mich. 8 Edw. I). He was the great-grandson of John Fitz-Alan, and Isabel his wife one of the four sisters and co-heirs of Hugh de Albini, earl of Sussex and Arundel (G.E.C. *Complete Peerage*, i, 144).

130 *Testa de Nevill* (Rec. Com.), 231*b*.

131 William granted to the monastery of Dureford in free alms one virgate in his tenement of Sunworth, pasture for 100 sheep, 12 oxen, and 4 calves in his pasture, and sufficient fuel in his wood. Some time later he confirmed this gift, besides making an additional grant to the abbey. In return the canons gave him 'in his great need, to deliver him from the hands of the Jews,' 22 marks of silver, 1 palfrey, 50 ewes, 50 sheep, and 50 lambs, to Joan his wife a gold ring and 2*s*., to his son and heir Ralph 1*s*. and a gold ring, to his son Simon a silver buckle and 6*d*., and to his son Robert 6*d*. (Cott. MS. Vesp. E. xxiii, 78). William's grants were confirmed by his son Ralph some time afterwards (ibid. 81).

132 In that year Henry III granted to the abbot and convent of Dureford free warren in their demesne lands in the manor of Sunworth, provided that the said lands were not within the king's forest (Chart. R. 36 Hen. III, m. 11).

133 Feet of F. Hants, Trin. 30 Hen. III.

134 She was possibly the daughter and heiress of Thomas de Sunworth.

135 Feet of F. Hants, Hil. 40 Hen. III. While William was lord of the manor of Sunworth he granted to the abbot and convent of Dureford additional lands and rents in the manor of Sunworth, and all the services which the canons had been accustomed to pay and do for all their lands in the manor of 'Sonneworth and La Holte' to the lords of Sunworth, so that henceforth they should hold them of him and his heirs in frankalmoign (Cott. MS. Vesp. E. xxiii, 80).

136 Chart. R. 41 Hen. III, m. 1.

137 Cott. MS. Vesp. E. xxiii, 84.

138 Ibid. Feet of F. Hants, 52 Hen. III.

139 Cott. MS. Vesp. E. xxiii, 84. In spite of this quitclaim, various descendants of Roger Loveday at different times in the reign of Edward III claimed from the abbot of Dureford large arrears of rent from the manor of Sunworth, but their attempts met with no success (Coram Rege R. Hil. 6 Edw. III, Mich. 9 Edw. III, rot. 22, and 13 Edw. III, rot. 134).

140 Cott. MS. Vesp. E. xxiii, 84.

141 In 1280 the abbot of Dureford was constrained to pay rent of 12*d*. at the sheriff's tourn, and to do suit every three weeks at the hundred of Finchdean, by which services William de Clare had held the manor of Sunworth (Assize R. Mich. 8 Edw. I).

142 Mins. Accts. Suss. 109, m. 17 *d*.

this manor at the will of the lord according to the custom of the manor.'

CHURCH The church of *OUR LADY, BURITON*, is a good specimen of a village church of the larger kind, having a chancel 17 ft. 2 in. wide by 30 ft. long, with north vestry, a nave 58 ft. long, 17 ft. wide at the west and 9 in. less at the east, with north and south aisles and west tower.

Its history cannot now be taken back beyond the latter part of the twelfth century, to which date the nave arcades belong, but the irregularity in the width of the nave suggests that the eastern part preserves the width of an earlier nave, which was lengthened westwards at the time of building of the existing arcades or possibly before. The details of the arcades in the two western bays of the nave, which are very similar to each other, are different from those of the two eastern bays, and of slightly earlier type, but as the spacing is the same throughout, the whole arcades were probably set out at the same time, though the western bays may have been built first. The chancel was entirely rebuilt, and widened after the usual manner, towards the end of the thirteenth century, the north vestry being contemporary with it.

The aisles of the nave have undergone so much repair that their history is not clear, but the north aisle, now modern, probably retains the width (7 ft.) of its twelfth-century forerunner, its east wall being on the line of the chancel arch of that date, destroyed, as it seems, at the rebuilding of the chancel, and the south aisle, 2 ft. wider than the north, has preserved no features older than the beginning of the fourteenth century. At its west end is an extension of doubtful date, and the tower, which from its eastern arch seems to have had a thirteenth-century predecessor, was rebuilt in 1714 after a fire.

The chancel, which has a modern east window of three lights, is of fine proportions, and dates from *c.* 1280. In its north wall is a single trefoiled lancet towards the west, the eastern part being covered by the contemporary vestry mentioned above. At the level of the sill runs a roll-moulded string, continuing all round the interior of the chancel, and serving as a label to the vestry doorway, which has an arch with continuous mouldings, and to the east of it a large locker rebated for a door. There is a second locker in the vestry, west of the doorway. In the south wall of the chancel is a two-light window with a circle in the head, all uncusped, with a moulded rear-arch. Below it are the sedilia, three moulded trefoiled arches with circular shafts and moulded capitals and bases, both seats and arches being twice stepped downwards, and to the east is a trefoiled piscina recess with two drains and a shelf, the trefoiled arch and shelf being in modern stonework. To the west is a priest's door with a moulded rear-arch, and in the south-west of the chancel a second two-light window, like the first, but with its sill at a lower level, the bottom of the western light being cut off by a transom, while the corresponding part of the other is built up with masonry, an arrangement which appears to be original, from the traces of ancient painting on the blocking and east jamb of the window. The best-preserved part is a figure of our Lady and Child on the east jamb, under a trefoiled canopy with foliate capitals, the details of which go to show that the painting is nearly contemporary with the wall. Below are two lines of inscription too much worn to be legible, but apparently in black letter and of later date than the painting above. On the west jamb of the window is a masonry pattern of usual type, and the marks of the blocking up of the lower part of the window in the sixteenth century are still to be seen. It has been unblocked, and the paintings revealed, in modern times. The nave has arcades of four bays with semicircular arches of two square orders, square capitals recessed at the angles, and round columns with moulded bases. The capitals of the two eastern bays of the north arcade are carved with simple leaf-work, while the corresponding bays on the south have plain bells; the western bays on both sides have scalloped capitals of various designs. Parts of the north arcade fell during a late repair, when the north wall of the aisle was entirely renewed, and were rebuilt for the most part with the old stonework. The only old work in the north aisle is the west window, a single thirteenth-century light. The south aisle was probably rebuilt *c.* 1300, and contains a trefoiled light of that date at the east end of the south wall, with a piscina drain in its sill. The design of the east window of three trefoiled lights is of the same period, but the stonework is modern. The south doorway is plain work of *c.* 1330, of two moulded orders without a label, and to the east of it is a large three-light window with net tracery, of which only the jambs are old. The roof over the window is gabled north and south, breaking the line of the aisle roof, and the provision for extra lighting at this point suggests that there may have been a chapel here of some importance. West of the south door is a fourteenth-century window of two trefoiled lights under a square head, and beyond it another of the same description, but in modern stonework.

The tower has a fine thirteenth-century east arch, with half-round responds and moulded capitals and bases, set upon a low wall 3 ft. 2 in. thick, and projecting some feet in front of the bases, leaving an opening 4 ft. 9 in. wide in the middle. It is presumably part of the west wall of the church before the addition of the west tower, and the opening, which is not centrally set between the responds of the arch, may represent that of a former west doorway. The tower itself was burnt down in 1714 and rebuilt, and is a very plain structure, now for the most part hidden by ivy. It measures internally 10 ft. 10 in. from north to south by 11 ft. 7 in., and opens to the western extension of the south aisle by two low doorways. On this side also is a steep wooden stair leading to the first floor, which is the ringing chamber, and contains a set of rules for the ringers painted on the wall with the usual forfeits and warnings, apparently coeval with the tower.

On the chancel walls are several monuments to the Hugonin family, and a black marble slab engraved with the figures of Thomas Hanbury, 1595, and his last wife Elizabeth Grigge, together with six sons and two daughters. At the west of the south aisle is an altar tomb within an iron railing, to Thomas Bilson, 1692, and over it a white marble mural monument to Leonard Bilson, 1695. Near it, on the south wall, are several brass plates with inscriptions to members of the Hanbury family: Emma, 1595, Susannah, 1661, Thomas, 1668, Katharine, 1678, and Thomas, 1680.

The font stands at the west end of the south aisle, and is of late twelfth-century type, of Purbeck marble with a square bowl carried on a round central shaft and four shafts at the angles, the moulded bases of which are worked in one stone.

In the vestry is a seventeenth-century communion table with baluster legs and movable top, but with this exception there are no old wood fittings in the church, and there are no remains of ancient glass. There are five bells, the treble and tenor by Mears, 1864, and the other three by Richard Phelps of London, 1715, cast after the fire in the tower.

The church plate comprises a cup and cover paten of 1669, a standing paten of 1702 with the Hanbury arms in a lozenge, and a flagon given in 1740.

The first volume of the registers begins in 1678, and is continued to 1812.

ADVOWSON There was a church in *MAPLEDURHAM* (afterwards Buriton) at the time of the Domesday Survey;[143] by 1291 the church with a chapel, probably the chapel of Petersfield, was worth £46 13*s.* 4*d.* annually,[144] and by the reign of Henry VIII the rectory of Buriton was worth yearly £336 8*s.*[145]

William, earl of Gloucester, when lord of the manor of Mapledurham, granted the church with the chapel of Petersfield in free alms to the church of St. Mary of Nuneaton (co. Warwick),[146] and his gift was confirmed by Henry II[147] and Pope Alexander III.[148] The abbey seems to have conveyed the advowson to the bishop of Winchester, for in 1331 the chancellor, John, bishop of Winchester, obtained licence from the king to alienate in mortmain to the prior and convent of St. Swithun, Winchester, the advowson of the church of Mapledurham, with the chapel of Petersfield in his diocese.[149] The abbot and convent at the same time obtained licence from the king to appropriate the advowson, on the condition of paying over and above the sum which they already paid to the hospital of St. Mary Magdalen without Winchester, the yearly sum of £25 19*s.* 4*d.*, for the support of the sick poor there, which the bishop had been wont to pay at his exchequer at Wolvesey, out of his alms. The appropriation, however, never took place; the abbot and convent may have thought the annual payment too great. In 1337 the church of Mapledurham was described as of the bishop's patronage,[150] and the bishop has presented the rector up to the present day,[151] with but few exceptions.[152]

In 1265 Walter de Lichelad, rector of the church of Mapledurham, and the abbot and convent of Dureford, were parties to a deed concerning tithes in the parish of Mapledurham.[153] The rector of the church granted for himself that the abbot and convent should be quit for ever from the payment of tithes from the possessions which they had hitherto acquired, saving, however, to the rector and his successors the tithes of all gardens excepting the old garden, which was within the hey of the monastery of Dureford, from which the abbot and convent had not been accustomed to pay any tithes. Henceforward the abbot and convent were to pay every year to the rector and his successors, instead of tithes, in the nave of Petersfield Church (in majori ecclesia de Peteresfeld), 30*s.* a year, at Michaelmas and at Easter in equal portions. This deed was confirmed by John bishop of Winchester. Towards the end of the reign of Charles II, Richard Cowper, lord of the manor of Ditcham, had a long dispute with Dr. Barker, rector of Buriton, concerning the latter's right to tithes from the beech-woods of Ditcham Park, in the course of which controversy Richard 'used threatings, lampooned and made scandalous and reflecting verses which did very much disquiet and discompose Dr. Barker.'[154] The case was tried before Lord Chief Justice North, who decided in favour of Dr. Barker, but in spite of this judgement, some twelve years later, Richard Cowper, son and heir of Richard, to whom his father had conveyed Ditcham Park on his marriage, refused to pay tithes of beech-wood to Charles Layfield, rector of Buriton.[155]

At the time of the Domesday Survey there was a chapel in Sunworth,[156] but it must soon have fallen into decay, for there seems to be no mention of it in later documents. It is interesting to note, however, that 'Chapple Garden' and 'Chapple Furlong' are given as names of lands owned by John Cowper of Ditcham, in 1619.[157]

The Primitive Methodist chapel was erected in 1848, and restored in 1881.

CHARITIES *Bishop Laney's Gift.*—The Rev. Benjamin Laney, formerly rector of Buriton, and subsequently bishop of Ely, in his lifetime gave £130 to be placed out at interest, or in the purchase of land, the profits thereof to be applied in apprenticing of poor children of the parish of Buriton and the borough of Petersfield. In 1690 the gift was laid out in the purchase of 19 acres or thereabouts of land in the parish of Bramshott. The land is let at £20 a year for a term of twenty-one years. Two apprentices are selected yearly from Buriton and Petersfield.

Tithing of Weston.—Goodyer's Charity; see under Petersfield.

143 *V.C.H. Hants*, i, 451*a*.
144 *Pope Nich. Tax.* (Rec. Com.), 211*b*.
145 *Valor Eccl.* (Rec. Com.), ii, 22.
146 Dugdale, *Mon.* (2nd ed.), i, 519.
147 Ibid.
148 Ibid. 520. In Alexander's bull they are called the church of Petersfield and the chapel of Mapledurham.
149 Pat. 5 Edw. III, pt. 3, m. 22.
150 Pat. 10 Edw. III, pt. 2, m. 3.
151 *Wykeham's Register* (Hants. Rec. Soc.), i, 47, 58, 134, 152, 171, and 210; Inst. Bks. (P.R.O.).
152 Queen Elizabeth presented during the vacancy of the bishopric (Add. MS. 33284, fol. 447); Chas. II presented in 1660, St. John's College, Cambridge, in 1688, and the bishop of London in 1829 (Inst. Bks. P.R.O.).
153 Cott. MS. Vesp. E. xxiii, fol. 24 *d.*
154 *Vide* Exch. Dep. 5 Will. & Mary, Mich. No. 30.
155 Ibid.
156 *V.C.H. Hants*, i, 478*a*.
157 Chan. Inq. p. m. (Ser. 2), ccclxxviii, No. 126.

CATHERINGTON

Kateringeton (xii cent.); Katerinton (xiii cent.); Catrington (xv cent.); Katherington, Katteryngton, and Kethrington (xvi cent.).

Catherington is a large parish covering an area of 5,279 acres. The village lies almost in the centre of the parish, on the brow of the hill round the base of which runs the main road from Clanfield to Lovedean. The houses are almost entirely grouped on the east of the road, with fields opposite. In the middle of the village is a pretty rose-covered farmhouse, and beyond it the house known as St. Catherine's, for long the property of the Barnes family, and at present the residence of Mr. Albert William Still Barnes, J.P. Nearly opposite is the quaint Farmer Inn, and the smithy stands a little way further up the hill. Almost at the top is the vicarage, and opposite it to the east is the church of St. Katherine, standing well back at some little distance from the road. From the east end of the churchyard, where two fine yew trees stand, the ground falls quickly toward the valley in which the Portsmouth road runs, and there is a fine view of Windmill Hill and the country to the east and south. The road running northwards from the village makes a steep descent to join the road to Clanfield. Hinton Daubnay, the property of Mr. Hyde Salmon Whalley-Tooker, commands an extensive view, standing on high ground in a fine park about a mile west of the village. The house is modern, the old house of the Hydes having been pulled down in 1880. According to tradition it was here that the marriage between James duke of York (afterwards James II) and Anne Hyde took place. Also belonging to the Hinton Daubnay estate is a smaller house called Hinton Manor, which is at present let to Captain Bayly. After passing Hinton Daubnay the road degenerates into a mere zigzag track over the downs, and finally comes out on the main road from Clanfield to Hambledon by the Bat and Ball Inn, the home of the famous Hambledon Cricket Club. Shrover Hall, the residence of Sir William Pink, is in the west of the parish on the road to Barn Green. In the south of the village is Catherington House, the seat of Mr. Francis John Douglas. It was built by the first Viscount Hood towards the middle of the eighteenth century, and is several times mentioned in his correspondence.[1] Queen Caroline was entertained here previous to her trial. Yoells is a tithing situated a mile south of the village. Eastland Gate, Longwood, and Wecock, which is described as 'a place called Wycock' in 1591, are two miles further on.

The village of Horndean, the most populous and rapidly growing part of the parish, lies to the east where the main road from London to Portsmouth meets the road from Havant. The smithy and the national school for boys, built in 1860, are on the road which turns off north-west at the top of the hill towards Catherington. The workhouse for the district is in Horndean, and Messrs. George Gale & Co., Ltd., have a large brewery here. The Portsdown and Horndean Light Railway, opened in 1903, starts from Horndean and runs along the east side of the road through beautiful and well-wooded country. On the east there are woods and commons stretching to Waterlooville:—Hazleton Wood, Blendworth Common, and the Queen's Inclosure, and beyond them can be seen the well-wooded stretches of Havant Thicket and Stanstead Forest. Merchistoun Hall, formerly the residence of Admiral Napier,[2] is on the outskirts of Horndean, west of the road to Portsmouth. Beyond the hall a narrow road runs off west to the village of Catherington. About half a mile south is Keydell House, the residence of Lieut.-Gen. Sir Drury Curzon Drury-Lowe, the well-wooded grounds of which are skirted by a road which runs off west to Lovedean, a fair-sized hamlet about one and a quarter miles south-west of the village of Catherington. There is a smithy here, and at the corner of the road leading to Hinton Daubnay is a thatched cottage used as a general shop.

Cow Plain is a hamlet situated on the main road to Portsmouth about two miles south of Horndean. There is a general shop here, an inn called 'The Spotted Cow,' and many modern houses. South of Cow Plain and in the extreme south-west of the parish, Hart Plain House formerly stood in grounds extending to the Portsmouth road. The lodge still stands, but the estate called the Hart Plain Estate has been cut up into building-plots. Streets of new houses are already built, and many more roads are marked out. The Forest of Bere is partly within this parish. The soil varies from loam and chalk to stiff clay. The subsoil is chalk and clay. The chief crops are wheat, barley, and oats. The parish contains 2,287 acres of arable land, 1,478½ acres of permanent grass, and 554¼ acres of wood and pasture.[3] Catherington Common, Catherington Down, Wecock Common, and Horndean Down were inclosed in 1816. The following are place-names found in the sixteenth century:—Whyttames, Cockcrofte,[4] Lyewoods, a tree called Shambleayshe, a road called Millway, East Heath, a covert or bushy place called Hasell Deane,[5] Emerys, Little and Great Asheteedes, the Style Garden,[6] Durley Grove, Dencrofte, Shortridge, Stonridge, Tibs Purrocke, The Upper Crimpe, Lampitt's Close, and Handells.[7]

CATHERINGTON alias *FIVE MANORS HEADS*, (Fyfehydes in Kateryngton xv cent.; Kathrington *alias* Kathrington Fyfhed xvi cent.; Catherington *alias* Fiveheads xviii cent.) is probably included under the heading of 'Ceptune' in the Domesday Book. It seems to have formed part of the great manor of Chalton until the time of Robert de Belesme earl of Shrewsbury and Arundel, lord of Chalton from 1098 to 1102. Its subsequent history, however, for a short time after

[1] In a letter to the duke of Rutland in 1784 he calls it 'his little farm at Catherington, near Petersfield' (*Hist. MSS. Com. Rep.* xiv, App. pt. i, 134).

[2] He purchased it from Co' .el Conway towards the middle of the eighteenth century, and changed its name from The Grove to that of his birth-place, Merchistoun Hall, in Stirlingshire.

[3] Statistics from the Board of Agriculture (1905).

[4] Pat. 16 Eliz. pt. 8, m. 27.

[5] Special Com. 33 Eliz. No. 2039; Exch. Bills and Answs. Eliz. Hants, No. 81.

[6] Pat. 18 Eliz. pt. 7, m. 18–22.

[7] Close, 19 Jas. I, pt. 33, No. 36. There is still a Stoneridge Farm in the north of the parish near the Bat and Ball Inn.

this was determined by the fact that it was parcel of the honour of Arundel. It was therefore included in the settlement of the castle and honour of Arundel upon Adelicia the widow of Henry I by way of dower, and passed to William de Albini on her marriage with him in 1138.[8] It remained in the possession of the Albinis, earls of Sussex and Arundel, until 1243, in which year Hugh de Albini earl of Sussex and Arundel died in the 'flower of his youth,' leaving four sisters and co-heirs.[9] Thus at the time of the *Testa de Nevill* Catherington was held 'de veteri feoffamento' of the earl of Arundel by the service of one knight's fee.[10] It was allotted as portion of her inheritance to Nichola third sister of Hugh and wife of Roger de Somery,[11] and from her descended to her son and heir Roger de Somery, who in 1280 was holding one fee of the king in 'Katerington' of the honour of Arundel.[12] In the middle of the fourteenth century, however, Catherington, like Chalton, was held of the heir of the duke of Lancaster, as of the honour of Leicester.[13] It afterwards came to be looked upon as dependent on Chalton. Thus by an inquisition taken in 1442 it was stated to be held of Sir John Montgomery,[14] who was at that time lord of the manor of Chalton. Again in 1497 it was said to be held of Sir John Norbury,[15] who was one of those to whom Anne Montgomery had released all her interest in the manor of Chalton in 1496.[16] A certain Roger Tyrell granted a toft in Catherington to William de Arundel, son and heir of Juliana de Wade, in 1199, to hold of him and his heirs by the rent of a pair of gilt spurs.[17] Roger was succeeded by Thomas Tyrell, probably his son, who in the reign of Henry III was holding one knight's fee in Catherington of the earl of Arundel.[18] In 1280 a certain Olive Tyrell, possibly widow of Thomas, held half a knight's fee in Catherington of Roger de Somery.[19] Early in the fourteenth century Catherington seems to have been divided between two co-heiresses, Joan and Isabel, probably daughters or granddaughters of Thomas Tyrell. Thus in 1302 a messuage, a mill, 300 acres of land, 24 acres of wood, and 20*s.* rent in Catherington were settled upon Ralph de Hangleton and Joan his wife, and the heirs of Joan,[20] and in 1316 a messuage and half a carucate of land in Catherington were settled upon Nigel de Coombes in fee-tail with contingent remainder in fee-tail successively to John, Joan, Thomas, and Alice, the children of Isabel Haket,[21] probably sister of Joan. Ralph de Hangleton had by this time been succeeded by Richard de Hangleton, probably his son. Thus, in 1316, the vill of Catherington was held by Richard de Hangleton and Nicholas de Coombes.[22] In 1334 occurred a dispute between Sir John Le Strange and Richard de Hangleton, concerning the encroachments of the latter upon the manor of Chalton, an account of which is given under Chalton.[23]

ALBINI. *Gules a lion or.*

Nigel de Coombes died seised of the manor of Applesham in Coombes (co. Sussex) in 1336.[24] He left no issue, and his half of the manor of Catherington possibly passed to the Joan Haket mentioned in the fine of 1316. This Joan may have been the Joan who married William Bonet, lord of the manor of Wappingthorne in Steyning (co. Sussex),[25] or her mother. At any rate, William Bonet in 1346 was holding the land in Catherington which Nigel de Coombes had held in 1316,[26] and it is probable that he held it, as he did most of his property, of his wife's inheritance. Some time between 1346 and 1349 Richard de Hangleton seems to have parted with his moiety of the manor also to William Bonet, who at the time of his death was seised of a messuage, a carucate of land, 3 acres of wood, and 40*s.* rent in Catherington.[27] His heir was his son Nigel, aged twenty on 19 January, 1349. In the same year the king granted the custody of William Bonet's property in Catherington to William de Fifhide, to hold until the coming of age of the heir, by the rent of six marks.[28] Nigel died while still under age, and his widow Margaret shortly afterwards. By the inquisition taken after her death William Bonet, aged fourteen, was found to be Nigel's brother and heir.[29] William seems to have died shortly after coming of age.[30] There is no inquisition on his death, but the fact that his manor of Wappingthorne reverted to the over-lord, John Mowbray, duke of Norfolk, who died seised of it in 1362,[31] seems to support the theory that he died without heirs, probably about 1360. Hence William de Fifhide, to whom the custody of the manor of Catherington had been granted in 1349, probably entered into possession, and died seised in 1361, leaving a son and heir William aged eighteen.[32] The king, by letters patent, granted the custody of William de Fifhide's lands to Eustace Dabridgecourt, to hold during the minority of his heir William without money-rent.[33] The latter came of age on the Feast of St. Barnabas 1363, but was not possessed of Catherington until 1365, when the king ordered John de Evesham, escheator of Hampshire, to deliver to him seisin of all his lands in that county.[34] William died seised of the manor in 1387, his heir being his

[8] G. E. C. *Complete Peerage*, i, 140.
[9] Ibid. 144.
[10] *Testa de Nevill* (Rec. Com.), 231*b*.
[11] G. E. C. *Complete Peerage*, i, 142.
[12] Assize R. Mich. 8 Edw. I.
[13] Inq. p.m. 35 Edw. III, pt. 1, No. 88, and 10 Rich. II, No. 17.
[14] Inq. p.m. 20 Hen. VI, No. 35.
[15] Chan. Inq. p.m. (Ser. 2), xi, No. 110.
[16] Close, 11 Hen. VII, No. 20.
[17] Feet of F. Hants, 1 John, No. 10.
[18] *Testa de Nevill* (Rec. Com.), 231*b*.
[19] Assize R. Mich. 8 Edw. I.
[20] Feet of F. Hants, Trin. 30 Edw. I. Ralph probably owned land in Hangleton, which is a hamlet in the parish of Ferring (co. Sussex).
[21] Feet of F. Hants, Trin. 9 Edw. II.
[22] *Feud. Aids*, ii, 318. Five years later a messuage, a mill, 300 acres of land, 4 acres of meadow, 18 acres of wood, and 38*s.* rent in Catherington were settled by fine between Richard de Hangleton and Juliana de Putlegh on Richard and his heirs (Feet of F. Hants, Mich. 15 Edw. II).
[23] Anct. D. (P.R.O.), B, 3481.
[24] Dallaway, *Suss.* ii, pt. 2, p. 110.
[25] Elwes and Robinson, *Castles, Mansions, and Manors of Western Suss.* 70.
[26] *Feud. Aids*, ii, 335.
[27] *Abbrev. Rot. Orig.* (Rec. Com.), ii, 201.
[28] Ibid.
[29] Inq. p.m. 24 Edw. III, No. 105.
[30] Ibid. 32 Edw. III (1st Nos.), No. 57.
[31] Dallaway, *Suss.* ii, pt. 2, p. 161.
[32] Inq. p.m. 35 Edw. III, pt. 1, No. 88. The inquisition gives the following extent of the manor :—Two capital messuages, a dovecote, a windmill, 207 acres of arable land in severalty ; 150 acres of land in common, of which 12 acres can be sown, and the rest lie uncultivated and cannot be valued because they are common ; pasture in severalty containing 6 acres ; 8 acres of wood, the underwood and pasturage of which are worth 18*d.* ; a certain profit of 'housbote' and 'haibote' to be received from the wood of the lord of Chalton ; rents of eight free tenants ; rents of tenants at will, 45*s.* 6*d.* ; pleas and perquisites of court, 3*s.* 4*d.*
[33] Pat. 6 Ric. II, pt. 1, m. 5 and 4.
[34] Ibid.

cousin Joan, the wife of Sir John Sandys and daughter of Agnes, who was sister of Sir William Fifhide, father of William.[35] From this date the manor was sometimes called the manor of Fifhides or Catherington Fifhide, after the family who had held it.[36] Catherington remained in the possession of the Sandys family until 12 November, 1602,[37] when William, Lord Sandys, sold it for £750 to his principal tenant, Humphrey Brett.[38] The latter, in order apparently to put a stop to the dispute with the earl of Worcester concerning the common of pasture in East Heath, sold it to the earl nine years later.[39] The descent of the manor has from this time been identical with that of the manor of Chalton (q.v.). It is now represented by the farm of Five Heads, a short distance north of Horndean, on the road between Horndean and the village of Catherington.

In early times there was a windmill within the manor of Catherington Fifhide. It occurs in fines conveying the manor in the fourteenth century,[40] and in an extent of the manor taken in 1361,[41] but no trace of it now remains, and it seems to have early fallen into disuse, for there is no mention of a mill in the fine conveying the manor to the earl of Worcester in 1611.[42]

HINTON DAUBNAY (Henton xiii cent.; Henton Daubeneye and Henton Daubenay xiv cent.; Henton Dawebedney xv cent.; Henton Dawbney and Henton Dowbney xvi cent.) was in early times ten poundsworth of land in the parish of Catherington, held by a Norman, Ralph de Cumbray by name.[43] On his death it fell as escheat of the Normans to Henry III, who granted it to Juliana Daubnay, to hold to her and her husband William and their heirs by the service of half a knight's fee.[44] The manor remained with the family of Daubnay until on the death of Ellis Daubnay, in 1383,[45] it passed to his daughter and heir Elizabeth wife of Andrew Wauton,[46] to whom in the following year the escheator of Hampshire was ordered to deliver up the manor, together with all the profits therefrom since the death of Ellis.[47] Three years later Andrew was murdered by his servants Robert Blake, chaplain, and John Balle, at the instigation of Elizabeth. The latter was sentenced to be burned for the crime, and the manor, which was then worth twelve marks a year, was taken into the hands of the king,[48] who granted it in 1394 to his servants John Luffwyk, yeoman of the chamber, and William Gold.[49] In 1396, some ten years before his death, John conveyed the manor to trustees,[50] who finally disposed of it in 1415 to Henry Kesewyk,[51] on whose death a few years later William Wayte, the escheator of Hampshire, took it into the hands of the king, having ascertained by an inquisition taken in 1420 that it had been purchased without royal licence.[52] Henry's trustees, Robert Thurberne and William Park, denied this, and accordingly the manor was restored to them, William Wayte being fined 13*s.* 4*d.*[53] For some little time after this the manor was held as a free tenement by William Chamberlayn,[54] who was most probably the second husband of the widow of Henry Kesewyk, but by 1447 it had descended to Henry son and heir of Henry Kesewyk, who in that year released all right in it to William Port and Joan his wife.[55] The prior and convent of St. Swithun, Winchester, gained possession of the manor some years afterwards,[56] and continued seised of it until the dissolution,[57] when it became the property of the crown. In 1574 Elizabeth granted a messuage and lands called 'Whethames,' and two closes called 'Cockcrofts,' parcels of the manor, to Robert earl of Leicester,[58] who some time afterwards sold them to Robert Paddon and Arthur Swayne.[59] The rest of the manor was in 1590 granted to Robert Paddon and John Molesworth,[60] the latter of whom conveyed his moiety to Arthur Swayne.[61] While Robert Paddon and Arthur Swayne were lords of the manor of Hinton Daubnay, there occurred a dispute with Edward earl of Worcester concerning the right to common lands called Woodcrofts and a wood called The Lye Wood.[62] In 1604 Robert Paddon, William Pytt, and William Holcrofte *alias* Haycrofte,[63] of New Sarum, conveyed the manor to Sir Nicholas Hyde,[64] who had married Margaret the

35 Inq. p.m. 10 Ric. II, No. 17.

36 Thus in 1431 Walter Sandys was said to be holding half of one knight's fee called 'Fyfehydes in Kateryngton' (*Feud. Aids*, ii, 362). Again, in 1591, the name of the manor is given as 'Kathrington' *alias* 'Kathrington Fyfhed' (Exch. Bills and Answs. Eliz. Hants, No. 81, m. 2). It is described as the manor of Catherington *alias* Fiveheads in 1736 (Recov. R. Mich. 10 Geo. II, m. 1), and as the manor of Five Heads in 1774 (Recov. R. East. 14 Geo. III, m. 181).

37 *Feud. Aids*, ii, 358 and 362; Inq. p. m. 20 Hen. VI, No. 35, and 24 Hen. VI, No. 40; Feet of F. Hants, East. 9 Hen. VII; De Banc. R. East. 9 Hen. VII, m. 21; Chan. Inq. p.m. (ser. 2) xi, No. 110; Exch. Dep. 34 and 35 Eliz. Mich. No. 8.

38 Close, 45 Eliz. pt. 5.

39 Feet of F. Hants, Mich. 9 Jas. I.

40 Ibid. Trin. 30 Edw. I, and Mich. 15 Edw. II.

41 Inq. p. m. 35 Edw. III, pt. 1, No. 88.

42 Feet of F. Hants, Mich. 9 Jas. I.

43 Assize R. Mich. 8 Edw. I.

44 Ibid. *Hund. R.* (Rec. Com.), ii, 223.

45 *Feud. Aids*, ii, 318; Inq. p.m. 6 Edw. III (2nd Nos.) No. 3*a.*: *Abbrev. Rot. Orig.* (Rec. Com.), ii, 96; *Feud. Aids*, ii, 335; Inq. p.m. 26 Edw. III, (2nd Nos.), No. 43.

46 Inq. p.m. 7 Ric. II, No. 31. In 1373 the reversion of the manor, after the death of Ellis, was granted to Sir Gilbert Giffard and Elizabeth his wife and the heirs of Elizabeth. (Feet of F. Hants, Mich. 47 Edw. III; Inq. p.m. 47 Edw. III (2nd Nos.), No. 46). After Gilbert's death Elizabeth married as her second husband Andrew Wauton.

47 Close, 8 Ric. II, m. 50 *d.*

48 Coram Rege R. East. 11 Ric. II.

49 Pat. 18 Ric. II, pt. 1, m. 27.

50 Inq. p.m. 9 Hen. IV, No. 25.

51 Feet of F. Hants, Hil. 3 Hen. V.

52 Memo. R. L.T.R. Trin. 9 Hen. V, m. 13. It was also ascertained by this inquisition that the manor was held of the king in capite by the service of finding for him one hobbler (habellarius—a light horseman riding a hobby) whenever he crossed into Scotland in time of war. This statement was denied by Robert Thurberne and William Park.

53 Memo. R. L.T.R. Trin. 9 Hen. V, m. 13.

54 *Feud. Aids*, ii, 358 and 362.

55 Close, 25 Hen. VI, m. 22; Pat. 29 Hen. VI, m. 35 *d.*

56 It seems probable that they were already seised of it in 1474, as in that year Richard Smyth, late of 'Henton Dawebedney,' husbandman, was pardoned for not appearing to answer Robert Westgate, prior of the cathedral church of St. Swithun, Winchester, touching a debt of £40 (Pat. 14 Edw. IV, pt. 1, m. 25).

57 Mins. Accts. Hants, 32 and 33 Hen. VIII, No. 109, m. 49.

58 Pat. 16 Eliz. pt. 8, m. 27.

59 Exch. Bills and Answs. Eliz. Hants, No. 81, m. 3.

60 Pat. 32 Eliz. pt. 8, m. 9, 10, 11.

61 Exch. Bills and Answs. Eliz. Hants, No. 81, m. 3.

62 Special Com. 33 Eliz. No. 2039; Exch. Bills and Answs. Eliz. Hants, No. 81. Many witnesses declared that Woodcrofts was often called 'the king's purlieu of the manor of Henton Dawbney.' One witness, John Goodwyn by name, asserted that he had always maintained Woodcrofts as a purlieu, often coursing his greyhounds out of it and killing deer within the Forest of East Bere.

63 In 1603 Robert Paddon conveyed the manor to William Holcrofte and William Pytt (Close, 45 Eliz. pt. 6), and again in 1604 (Feet of F. Hants, East. 2 Jas. I).

64 Close, 2 Jas. I.

daughter of Arthur Swayne.[65] Sir Nicholas died seised of the manor, capital messuage, and demesne lands of Hinton Daubnay in 1631, leaving a son and heir Arthur, aged thirty-four and more.[66] Hinton Daubnay, however, passed to his second son Laurence, and continued in the family of Hyde until about the middle of the eighteenth century,[67] when on the death of — Hyde a minor it descended to his cousin Mr. Tooker, who was the owner in 1768.[68] His descendant, Mr. Hyde Salmon Whalley-Tooker, is the present lord of the manor.

HINTON MARKAUNT (Henton xiv cent.; Henton Markewaye *alias* Marchaunte *alias* Merchaunte xvi cent.; Hinton Merchant xviii cent.). The first mention of this manor seems to be in 1384 when Joan Meyres of Petersfield and her daughter Maud were pardoned for a trespass upon the grange of Sir Robert Markaunt at 'Henton' in the hundred of Finchdean.[69] Joan the daughter and heir of Sir Robert Markaunt died at the beginning of the fifteenth century, leaving as her heir her kinsman William Levechild of Sheet next Petersfield, from whom the manor of Hinton Markaunt passed, together with West Mapledurham, to John Roger of Bryanston

MARKAUNT. *Argent fretty sable with a chief gules.*

ROGER. *Argent a pierced molet sable and a chief or with a fleur-de-lis gules therein.*

(co. Dors.).[70] It was afterwards granted to the prior and convent of St. Swithun, Winchester, and remained with them until the dissolution.[71] Queen Elizabeth, in February, 1576, granted the capital messuage of 'Henton Marchaunte,' with its appurtenances[72] in the parish of Catherington, to Anthony Rotsey and William Fyssher, to hold of her and her successors by the annual payment of £7 3*s.* 10*d.*[73] A fortnight later Anthony and William sold the manor to Thomas Crompton and John Morley,[74] who in 1579 sold it to John Foster of Hinton Markaunt for £500.[75] On the death of the latter the manor descended to his son John Foster, from whom it passed by sale in 1621 to George Garth, of Morden (co. Surr.),[76] who died seised six years later.[77] Richard son of George Garth in 1633 sold the manor for £3,100 to George Vaughan and Margaret Caryll, widow of Sir Thomas Caryll,[78] from whom it was purchased a year later for £3,210 by George Brooke, of Beech, in the parish of Sonning (co. Berks), and Richard Bosson of Wootton Bassett (co. Wilts.).[79] The latter in 1635 conveyed Hinton Markaunt to Sir Edward Hungerford and William Moore, trustees for William Englefield, a younger son of Sir Francis Englefield, bart.[80] Mary Fetiplace, the granddaughter of William Englefield, brought the manor into the Caryll family by her marriage with Philip Caryll,[81] from whom it descended to their only surviving child Elizabeth, the wife of John Walker of Marylebone, who sold it in 1743 to Lieut.-Gen. Robert Dalzell.[82] The latter by will devised it to his grandson, Robert Dalzell, who sold it at the end of the eighteenth century,[83] since which time it has become merged with the rest of the Hinton property.

HINTON BURRANT (Henton, xiii cent.; Hienton, xiv cent.; Henton Bourhont, Henton Burhunt, xv cent.; Hinton Burrant and Henton Burrunt, xvii cent.) was a small manor dependent upon the manor of Hinton Daubnay. Thus, in an inquisition taken in 1358 it was stated to be held of Ellis Daubnay by the payment of a penny a year.[84] Again, in the inquisition taken after Elizabeth Uvedale's death in 1488, it was returned as held of the prior of St. Swithun, Winchester, who was at the time lord of the manor of Hinton Daubnay.[85] The first document relating to this manor seems to be a fine of 1283, whereby Rose de Henton quitclaimed to Roger de Molton a messuage and 80 acres of land in 'Hinton, near Catherington.'[86] Five years later Roger de Molton quitclaimed to Richard de Boarhunt and Maud his wife a messuage and 1½ carucates of land in Hinton and at the same time granted to them the reversion of half a carucate of land in the same place after the death of Anne, the wife of Aimery de Kaunvyle.[87] In the Patent Rolls there are several references to Richard de Boarhunt, in connexion with his property in Hinton.[88] On the death of Richard de Boarhunt the manor passed to Thomas de Boarhunt, whose son and

65 Hoare, *Wilts.* iv, 131.
66 Chan. Inq. p.m. (Ser. 2), Misc. dxxvi, No. 9.
67 Recov. R. East. 2 Will. and Mary, rot. 5.
68 *The Hampshire Repository* (1799), ii, 204; Add. MS. 9458, fol. 69 and 78.
69 Pat. 7 Ric. II, pt. 2, m. 11.
70 Close, 13 Hen. IV, m. 2, and 1 Hen. VI, m. 21.
71 Mins. Accts. Hants, 32 & 33 Hen. VIII, m. 49.
72 Lands called 'Emerys; crofts called 'Little Asheteddes' and 'Great Asheteddes'; lands called 'Les Leye,' in Hinton Daubnay, and a parcel of land called 'The Style Garden' in Hormer.
73 Pat. 18 Eliz. pt. 7, m. 18–22.
74 Close, 18 Eliz. pt. 5.
75 Ibid. 21 Eliz. pt. 6.
76 Ibid. 19 Jas. I, pt. 33, No. 36. The premises are thus described in the indenture:—The manor, grange, capital messuage and farm of Henton Marchant, lands called The Lees, Barlie Asted, Wheate Asted, Fetch Asted, Chawcrofte, the Barnefield, Durley Grove, Dencroft, Shortridge, Stonridge, Tibs Purrocke, Embres Meade, Oate Purrocke, Kingstoncrofte, The Upper and Lower Crumpe, Lampitts Close, The Homefield, The Gaston, The Outer Gaston, The Water Hill, The Outer Hill, Handells, Upper and Lower Breach, Breach garden meadow, and the Lawrences, a wood called Lee wood, the two Dencroft coppices, common in the Hurste and Lampitts coppice, fields in Henton Down, and common of pasture in the Forest of East Bere.
77 Chan. Inq. p.m. (Ser. 2) 3 Chas. I, pt. 1, No. 104.
78 Close, 9 Chas. I, pt. 4, No. 12.
79 Ibid. 10 Chas. I, pt. 9, No. 21.
80 *Vide* Recov. R. Hil. 1656, rot. 131. This William Englefield was a recusant (*Cal. of Com. for Compounding*, iii, 1793).
81 *Vide* Recov. R. Hil. 12 Anne, rot. 19, and Close, 17 Geo. II, pt. 8, No. 22. In a fine of 1691 the manor is called the manor of North Hinton (Feet of F. Div. Cos. Hil. 3 Will. and Mary).
82 Close, 17 Geo. II, pt. 8, No. 22.
83 Recov. R. East. Geo. III, rot. 216. It was then a farm worth £60 a year.
84 Inq. p.m. 33 Edw. III (2nd Nos.), No. 103.
85 Chan. Inq. p.m. (Ser. 2), iv, No. 16.
86 Feet of F. Hants, Trin. 11 Edw. I.
87 Ibid. East. 16 Edw. I.
88 Thus, for example, in 1303 a commission of oyer and terminer was granted to Philip de Hoyvill and Baldwin de Bellany, touching the persons who by night broke a dyke belonging to Richard de Boarhunt at 'Henton by Caterington,' cut down the trees in his wood there and carried them away (Pat. 31 Edw. I, m.

heir John de Boarhunt in 1342 granted 100*s.* yearly rent for life from the manor of Hinton, with right to distrain on the manor for any arrears of that rent, to his stepfather, William Danvers.[89] John died seised of the manor in 1358, leaving a son and heir John, aged fourteen.[90] The latter, however, must have died shortly afterwards, for in 1363 John the son of Herbert de Boarhunt granted the reversion of the manor after the death of Mary de Boarhunt, by that time the wife of Sir Bernard Brocas, to Valentine atte Mede of Bramdean.[91] From Valentine it seems to have passed to Sir Robert Markaunt,[92] lord of the neighbouring manors of West Mapledurham and Hinton Markaunt, and for some time followed the descent of those manors (q.v.), passing with them in 1422 to John Roger of Bryanston (co. Dorset).[93] The history of the manor for some time after this is somewhat obscure, and nothing definite can be learnt concerning it until 1488, in which year Elizabeth daughter of Sir Henry Norbury of Stoke d'Abernon (co. Surr.), and widow of Sir Thomas Uvedale, died seised of it, leaving a son and heir Robert, aged twenty and more.[94] The latter died without issue some twelve years later, leaving the manor in dower to his widow Elizabeth,[95] who subsequently married Thomas Leigh.[96] In 1529 Arthur Uvedale, who was either the son or grandson of Sir William Uvedale, half-brother of Robert,[97] granted the reversion of the manor of Hinton, after the death of Elizabeth Leigh, to Henry White and his heirs.[98] From Henry it passed to Giles White, who in 1572 granted the reversion, after the deaths of William Lawrence and Ellen his wife and Thomas Michelborne and Alice his wife, to Lawrence Michelborne, son of Thomas and Alice.[99] Twenty years later Lawrence sold Hinton to a yeoman of Catherington, William Chatfield,[100] who in 1603 joined with John Foster the elder, and John Foster the younger, of Hinton Markaunt, Nicholas Hunt, lord of the manor of Anmore, and others in a dispute with Robert Paddon of Hinton Daubnay, concerning a down or common called Hinton Down or Field.[101] On the death of William Chatfield the manor descended to his son and heir John, who sold it in 1626 to George Monnox, citizen and haberdasher of London, who in his turn conveyed it in 1629 to George Everlyn and William Christmas in trust for Thomas Keightley, a London merchant.[102] Thomas

BOARHUNT. *Argent a fesse between six martlets gules.*

must have sold the manor shortly afterwards, for Sir Nicholas Hyde died in 1631 seised of the manor of 'Henton Burrant,' described in the inquisition taken on his death as 'late Chatfield's lands.'[103] From this time the descent of the manor followed that of Hinton Daubnay[104] (q.v.).

ANMORE (Anedemere and Endemere, xiii cent.; Henton Enedemer and Andemere, xiv cent.; Andemer, Andever, Amner, and Anmer, xvi cent.; Aldemer, xvii cent.) in early times formed part of the manor of Hinton Daubnay. Ralph de Cumbray, when he was lord of the manor, granted 1 virgate of land on the west of the road leading from Anmore to Hinton, and 10 acres on the east of the road next Anmore to his brother William, to hold of him by the annual payment of a gilt spur at Easter.[105] Shortly afterwards William granted this land to the prior and convent of Southwick, on his admission to their brotherhood,[106] and his gift was confirmed by Ralph.[107] Ralph de Cumbray also gave to the same church in free alms 1 virgate of land on the east of Anmore, hard by the ½ hide which he gave to his brother William.[108] The gifts of Ralph and William were confirmed by their brother Geoffrey,[109] and by Ellis Daubnay, the latter of whom also in 1340 quitclaimed the services due: suit at his court of Hinton Daubnay and a rent of 2*s.*[110] In a deed of 1246, concerning the payment of tithes to the vicar of Catherington by the prior and canons of Southwick from their manor of Anmore, the messuage of the canons is described as situated on the south of the cultivated lands lying on the west of the road leading from the wood to Hinton.[111] Edward II in 1321 granted to the prior and convent free warren in their demesne lands of 'Andemere,' so long as those lands were not within the bounds of the royal forest.[112] The following extent of Anmore is given in an inquisition taken in 1381 after the death of Richard Bramdean, prior of Southwick:—20 acres of arable land, worth 3*s.* 4*d.* per annum; 20 acres of pasture, worth 20*s.* per annum; and underwood, worth 3*d.* per annum.[113] The manor remained the property of the prior and convent until the dissolution, when it fell into the hands of the king. It was then of the annual value of £3, which sum was made up as follows:—9*s.* 5*d.* rents of assize, 14*s.* 7*d.* rents of customary tenants, and £1 16*s.* farm of the site of the capital messuage.[114] It was granted at the same time as the manor of Weston to Frances Palmer and her issue by William Stone,[115] and, like Weston (q.v.), ultimately passed into the possession of Stephen Vachell and Mary his wife,[116] who sold it in 1593 to Nicholas Hunt.[117] Felix son of Nicholas Hunt died in 1638 seised of

17 *d.*). Again, in 1319, a commission of oyer and terminer was granted to Ralph de Camoys, William de Harden, and Ralph de Bereford, on complaint by Richard de Boarhunt that Richard de Hangleton with others had assaulted him at 'Henton by Kateryngton' (Pat. 13 Edw. III, m. 35 *d.*).

89 Close, 16 Edw. III, pt. 2, m. 30 *d.*

90 Inq. p.m. 33 Edw. III (2nd Nos.), No. 103. In 1344 the manor had been settled on John and Mary his wife and their issue (Feet of F. Hants, Mich. 18 Edw. III).

91 Feet of F. Hants, Mich. 37 Edw. III.

92 Anct. D. (P.R.O.), B 2543.

93 Close, 1 Hen. VI, m. 21.

94 Chan. Inq. p.m. (Ser. 2), iv, No. 16.

95 Ibid. xv, No. 7.

96 *Surr. Arch. Coll.* iii, 106.

97 Ibid. *Misc. Gen. et Her.* (2nd Ser.) vol. v.

98 Feet of F. Hants, Mich. 21 Hen. VIII.

99 Ibid. East. 14 Eliz.

100 Ibid. East. 34 Eliz.

101 Special Com. 1 Jas. I, No. 4469.

102 Recov. R. Mich. 2 Chas. I, rot. 70; Close, 4 Chas. I, pt. 10, No. 8, and pt. 17, No. 5.

103 Chan. Inq. p. m. (Ser. 2), Misc. dxxvi, No. 9.

104 Recov. R. East. 2 Will. and Mary, rot. 5.

105 Add. MS. 33284, fol. 442.

106 Ibid. fol. 444. 107 Ibid. fol. 443.

108 Ibid. Ralph also granted to the church of Southwick the service of his man Ernald, together with the whole land of 'Bekewode,' which he held of him, paying thence annually to him and his heirs 2*s.* sterling at the Feast of St. Giles (ibid. fol. 442).

109 Ibid. fol. 444.

110 Ibid. fol. 445. 111 Ibid.

112 Add. MS. 33280, fol. 103.

113 Ibid. fol. 275.

114 Ibid. Mins. Accts. Hants, 32 & 33 Hen. VIII, No. 109.

115 Pat. 37 Hen. VIII, pt. 11.

116 Pat. 13 Eliz. pt. 8, m. 38; Feet of F. Hants, East. 13 Eliz.

117 Feet of F. Hants, Hil. 35 Eliz.

the manor of Amner *alias* Andemer *alias* Aldemer, and common of pasture and free warren in Catherington, leaving a son and heir George, aged sixteen.[118] It seems probable that soon after this the manor was bought by the Hyde family, and became merged with the rest of the Hinton estates, of which it has formed a part for over two centuries. At the present day Anmore is the property of Mr. Hyde Salmon Whalley-Tooker.

HORMER (Horemare, Horemeare, Hormare Farm, Henton Hormere, and Henton Horner, xvi cent.) was a small manor dependent on the manor of Hinton Daubnay (q.v.), and followed the same descent. At the time of the dissolution the capital messuage was farmed out to William Padwick at a rent of £1 2*s*.[119] There are several references to it in the depositions of witnesses taken in the course of the lawsuit between Edward earl of Worcester and the lords of the manor of Hinton Daubnay in 1591.[120] Thus one witness declared that he knew John Goodwyn, surveyor to the Queen's Majesty's, dwelling in a 'farm called Hormer,' parcel of the manor of Hinton Daubnay, to fell and take certain timber trees within the ground called Woodcrofts for the building of that farm-house, and also take at divers times firewood there for his fuel to spend in the same farm-house. In the inquisition taken after the death of Sir Nicholas Hyde it is described as the farm called 'Hormer Farm' in Hormer.[121] Up to within twenty years ago the village was represented by three very old cottages. These have now been pulled down, but the piece of ground on which they stood is still called 'Harmer.'[122]

LOVEDEAN (Loveden xvii cent.). William Tisted, lord of the manors of West Tisted and Woodcote in Bramdean, died in 1511 seised of six messuages, 200 acres of arable land, 100 acres of pasture, 4 acres of meadow, and 2 acres of wood in the vills and parishes of Catherington and Blendworth, which were held of George earl of Shrewsbury as of his manor of Chalton.[123] On the death of his brother and heir Thomas without issue a few years later these tenements were divided among his four sisters and coheirs and their descendants.[124] Three of them sold their moieties to Richard Norton,[125] whose descendant Richard Norton died in 1584 seised of certain lands and tenements in Catherington, leaving a son and heir Anthony,[126] who ten years later granted three-fourths of the manor of Catherington to his sister Isabel Norton.[127] Isabel married Thomas Lovedean of East Meon, from which circumstance the manor in after years was called the manor of Lovedean. Thomas was a recusant, and in 1608 two-thirds of his lands and tenements lying in Blendworth and Catherington, of the yearly value of £3 12*s*., which he held in right of Isabel his wife, were granted to John Casewell, Christopher Stubbes, and Thomas Hutchinson, until the end of a term of forty-one years.[128] On the death of Thomas and Isabel the property in Catherington descended to Anthony Lovedean, on whose death in 1635 it was described as a cottage and 50 acres in Catherington, a messuage called Lovedean, and 5½ acres in Catherington held of the manor of Chalton by a rent of 1*s*. 4½*d*.[129] His heir was his son Sebastian, aged ten and a half years, who was a recusant like his grandfather.[130] John Hoare, whose family had been settled in Catherington as early as the reign of Henry VIII,[131] seems to have purchased the property shortly afterwards, but there seems to be no record of the sale. In 1639 his widow Anne purchased the remaining moiety of the manor of Lovedean from Thomas Hayes and Penelope his wife.[132] The history of this moiety after the death of Thomas Tisted is uncertain. It descended to William Tisted's granddaughter Mary, the wife of Sir Edward Rogers, and by fine of 1551 was settled on them for the term of their lives, with remainder to their son George Rogers and Joan his wife in fee-tail;[133] but it seems impossible to ascertain whether Thomas and Penelope were holding it by right of inheritance, or whether they had purchased it. John and Anne Hoare left two daughters and co-heirs. The manor of Lovedean passed to Anne, the wife of William Ellson of Barham and of Oving (co. Suss.),[134] and remained in the family of Ellson for about a century, William Ellson dealing with it by recovery in 1739.[135] The manor was subsequently purchased by the lord of the neighbouring manor of Hinton Daubnay, and still forms part of the Hinton Daubnay estates.

Ellson. *Argent a chief azure with an eagle gules over all.*

LUDMORE (Ledmere xiv cent.; Lidmer xvi cent.; Ludmere xvii cent.) formed part of the manor of Hinton Burrant, and was sold by John Chatfield in 1629[136] to Thomas Keightley, from whom it passed by sale to Sir Nicholas Hyde. It still forms part of the Hinton estate. In an indenture of 1629 the following description is given of the property:—A messuage called Ludmore *alias* Ludmere, sometime in the occupation of one Barnard, a close called the 'Home Close' containing 10 acres, a close called 'Cunstables' containing 26 acres, a close called 'Credies' containing 12 acres, a close lying to the north of the mansion house of Sir Nicholas Hyde in Hinton Daubnay, and a close of pasture and wood called 'Harecroft' containing 10 acres.[137]

In the fourteenth century Henry son of Herbert de Boarhunt granted to the prior and convent of Southwick the land of 'Aldelond' and 7 acres by 'Ledmere' at Hinton, which Robert de Henton had given him.[138] These lands subsequently formed part of the manor of Anmore, and passed with it to Nicholas Hunt, who in 1600 sold them to Arthur

[118] Chan. Inq. p.m. 14 Chas. I (Ser. 2), pt. 1, No. 75.
[119] Mins. Accts. Hants, 32 & 33 Hen. VIII, No. 109, m. 49.
[120] Exch. Spec. Com. 33 Eliz. No. 2039.
[121] Chan. Inq. p.m. (Ser. 2), Misc. dxxvi, No. 9.
[122] Information received from Mrs. H. Whalley-Tooker.
[123] Chan. Inq. p.m. (Ser. 2), xxvi, No. 13.
[124] Berry, *Hants Gen.* 29.
[125] *Vide* Feet of F. Hants, Mich. 11 Hen. VIII.
[126] Chan. Inq. p.m. (Ser. 2) ccli, No. 82.
[127] Close, 36 Eliz. pt. 3; Add. MS. 33278, fol. 131*b*.
[128] Pat. 6 Jas. I, pt. 3, No. 15.
[129] Add. MS. 33284, fol. 461.
[130] *Cal. of Com. for Compounding*, iii, 1788.
[131] Subs. R. Hants, bdle. 173, No. 218.
[132] Feet of F. Div. Cos. Mich. 15 Chas. I.
[133] Ibid. Mich. 5 Edw. VI.
[134] Elwes and Robinson, *Western Suss.* 161.
[135] Recov. R. Hil. 13 Geo. II, rot. 298.
[136] Close, 4 Chas. I, pt. 10, No. 5.
[137] Ibid. There is still a Constable's Copse to the north of Ludmore.
[138] Add. MS. 33280, fol. 150–2.

Swayne of Hinton Daubnay,[139] from whom they passed by sale, together with the manor of Hinton Daubnay, to Sir Nicholas Hyde.

CHURCH The church of *ST. KATHERINE* has a chancel 25 ft. in length, continuous with a nave of 52 ft., the width of both being 18 ft. 3 in. On the north side of the chancel is a chapel 27 ft. 3 in. by 16 ft. 3 in., its east wall being in a line with that of the chancel, and to the south-west of the chancel is a vestry and organ chamber 19 ft. deep by 13 ft. east to west. The nave has north and south aisles, and a south-west tower 10 ft. 4 in. square, all measurements being internal.

The greater part of the building belongs to the end of the twelfth century and the beginning of the thirteenth, and, though doubtless developed from an older church, gives but little evidence of its predecessor's size and arrangements. The south arcade of the nave and the south-west tower date probably from the last decade of the twelfth century, and from the evidence of the masonry seem to be contemporary with each other. The older nave, probably of the same width as the present, may at this time have been lengthened by 12 ft. The rebuilding of the north side of the church seems to have been undertaken with little if any interval after the completion of the tower and south arcade. If, as seems probable, the older church had a chancel narrower than its nave, it was now removed, the new work being built outside its lines after the usual fashion. The north arcade was set out to range with the south arcade, and continued eastward for two more bays, the eastern bay being only half the width of the others. The north aisle, which now runs as far west as the nave, may have been in the first instance one bay shorter, and equal in length to the south aisle. The north chapel appears to be contemporary with the arcade, but its length has not been determined by the spacing of the bays, or by any other obvious reason.

In 1883 the building was extensively repaired, £3,086 being spent on the work.

The chancel has an east window of three lights, the rear arch having engaged shafts in the jambs and a moulded head, *c.* 1300, while the tracery is of fifteenth-century style. In the south wall is a square-headed window of two cinquefoiled lights, of late fifteenth-century date, and west of it a wide modern arch to the organ chamber. In the south-east corner of the chancel is a trefoiled piscina recess with a stone shelf, of the same date as the rear arch of the east window, but with a modern label. The arcade on the north of the chancel is continuous with that of the nave, and forms one design, the pillars being alternately round and octagonal, the eastern respond and the second and fourth pillars from the east belonging to the octagonal type. The arches are semicircular of two moulded orders, the inner with an arris between two filleted rolls, and the outer having single rolls, also filleted. The capitals and bases are moulded, the section of the octagonal bases differing from that of the round as regards the upper member, which has a plain roll on the round bases, and a half-octagonal one on the octagonal bases. The capital of the western respond is unlike the rest, and has a late type of scallop. It seems possible that the first work, which, as already said, comprised the south arcade and tower, and lengthening of the nave, may have also included the western respond of the north arcade; in any case the pause between the two works can not have been a long one.

The north chapel has two lancet windows in the east wall, and between them on the site of the altar stands the large monument of Nicholas Hyde, 1631, described below. Above it in the gable is a circular window of the same date as the lancets, and the wall is covered with modern painted decoration. In the north wall are two windows, that to the east being of two square-headed lights of no great age, but having a moulded rear-arch and engaged jamb shafts like those of the east window of the chancel, *c.* 1300. Below its sill is a moulded string, with a carved head in the middle of its length. The second window has two modern uncusped lancet lights.

The south arcade of the nave is of three bays with round pillars, scalloped capitals, and moulded bases, and the arches are semicircular, of two moulded orders. The south aisle wall has no old features except the doorway at its west end, close to the tower; this has a semicircular head and rear-arch, and nook-shafts on the outer face with foliate capitals, and is probably contemporary with the aisle.[140] On the east face of the tower, against which the aisle abuts, is a raking weathering showing the line of the original roof, from which it appears that the walls over the south arcade and also the wall of the aisle were at first lower. The doorway must have been reset, as its rear-arch is now too high to go under the line of the late twelfth-century roof, and the position of the eastern arch of the tower makes it unlikely that the aisle was ever narrower than at present. At the east end of the south aisle is an opening to the south chapel; this has in its east wall a square-headed window of two trefoiled lights, perhaps *c.* 1340, and on the south a window of two cinquefoiled lights, also square-headed, of fifteenth-century date.

All windows in both aisles of the church are modern, and at the west end of the north arcade of the nave is a modern arch of the same general detail as the north arch of the tower, opening to the nave from the west end of the aisle. In the north wall a blocked doorway is to be seen, corresponding in position with that in the south aisle. The south-west tower is of three stages, the top stage being of eighteenth-century date in red brick and embattled, with a leaded cupola, while the lower stages, having shallow clasping buttresses at the angles, belong to the end of the twelfth century, and have small round-headed lights on the south and west on the ground and second stages. The tower opens to the nave by plain pointed arches of two orders on the north and east, 7 ft. and 4 ft. wide respectively, with chamfered strings at the springing. The weathering already noticed on its east face continues horizontally on the north face, and shows that the original roof of the nave was carried down in an unbroken line over the south aisle.

In the west wall of the nave is a plain pointed thirteenth-century doorway with a moulded label, and over it two lancets, with a circular window in the gable, all the stonework in the windows being modern. The church contains no ancient fittings, but the nave roof is a fine specimen, with tiebeams and collars, and curved struts and windbraces, and is probably of fourteenth-century date.

139 Add. MS. 33278, fol. 150*b*; Close, 42 Eliz. pt. 12.

140 On its outer face is an incised sun-dial.

On the north wall of the nave is a large early fourteenth-century painting of St. Michael weighing souls, the end of the balance being held down by our Lady.

The church contains many modern monuments of the Napiers, but the only tomb of any architectural interest is that of Nicholas Hyde and his wife, already mentioned, set against the east wall of the north chapel. It is an altar tomb on which lie the two effigies, with an arched panel containing the inscription on the wall above them. Above is a cornice and pediment carried on black marble columns with Corinthian capitals, surmounted by figures of Justice and Wisdom, while in the arched panel are other figures of Time and Death. On the base of the tomb are kneeling figures of six sons and four daughters, and in the pediment a shield bearing Hyde (az. a chevron between three lozenges or, differenced with a molet gules, impaling azure a chevron between three pheons or, and on a chief gules three maidens' heads, or (Swaine of Sarson).

Against the external north-west angle of the north chapel is set the shaft and part of the head of a stone cross. The shaft is 6 ft. high, with beaded edges, and the remains of the head 2 ft. 6 in. high are carved with a Crucifixion between our Lady and St. John, of fourteenth-century style. Near by in the churchyard is a fourteenth-century coffin slab.

In the tower are six bells, the treble and second by Mears and Stainbank, 1887, and the fourth by the same founders, 1888, while the third, fifth, and tenor, are by Wells of Aldbourne, 1751, having the inscription as usual with this founder, on the sound bow instead of the shoulder.

The church plate includes a silver communion cup given by Lawrence Hyde and Alice his wife in 1660, and engraved with a figure of Christ as the Good Shepherd, with the words: 'Ecce Agnus Dei,' and 'Congratulamini mihi'; a paten of 1663, given by Mrs. Hyde Whalley-Tooker, and a plated paten and flagon given in 1870.

The first book of the registers contains baptisms, marriages, and burials from 1602 to 1640, the second from 1640 to 1680, and the third from 1680 to 1701. There is another book in duplicate with baptisms and marriages 1681–1701, and the later books have (5) baptisms and marriages 1701–54, (6) burials for the same period, (7) baptisms and marriages 1754–1812, and (8) burials for the same period.

ADVOWSON The church of *ST. KATHERINE, CATHERINGTON*, was originally a rectory, but on 21 April, 1292, Bishop John of Pontoise decreed, on the petition of the prioress and convent of Nuneaton who held the patronage, that on the death or resignation of the existing rector it should be converted into a vicarage, and the rectorial or greater tithes be appropriated to the nuns.[141] The prioress and convent presented the vicars until the dissolution,[142] when the advowson passed to the crown. Edward VI and Mary granted the advowson to the bishop of Winchester in 1551 and 1558 respectively.[143] Elizabeth, however, by some means regained possession, presented Richard Roberts in 1561,[144] and in 1590 by letters patent granted it to Arthur Swayne and Henry Best.[145] The latter sold it the same year to Thomas Neale and Elizabeth his wife,[146] who dealt with it by fine in 1603.[147] The advowson remained for over eighty years in the Neale family,[148] in the course of which period Sir William Lewis, bart., presented in 1634 and 1660.[149] Thomas Neale sold it in 1674 to John Bugby, of the parish of Stepney, 'mariner,'[150] who presented to the vicarage in 1684 and 1690.[151] From him it seems to have passed to William Sutton and Hannah his wife, who dealt with it by recovery in 1733.[152] John Williams was presented in 1740 by John Brett,[153] who ten years later sold the advowson to the duke of Beaufort.[154] The advowson then followed that of Chalton until early in the nineteenth century,[155] when it was sold by Mr. Jervoise Clarke-Jervoise. Mr. George Pritchard presented in 1857, and Mr. John Pritchard in 1872.[156] Mr. John Pritchard sold the advowson to the Rev. Robert Fitzgerald Maynard, M.A., who has been vicar of Catherington since 1877, and is the present patron of the living.

There is a mission room at Lovedean in which service is held during the week, and school on Sundays.

CHARITIES For the educational charities of William Appleford, will 1696, Mrs. Margaret Lind Henville, will 1866, and of Miss Anne Harvey, will 1874, see article on 'Schools' (*V.C.H. Hants*, ii, 397).

In 1846 John Richards by will left £307 6*s.* consols (with the official trustees), dividends to be applied for the benefit of the poor at the discretion of the vicar for the time being. The annual dividends amounting to £7 13*s.* 8*d.* are duly applied.

Church Acre.—The parish had been in possession from time immemorial of 1 a. 3 r., known as the Church Acre, which in 1876 was sold with the sanction of the Charity Commissioners, and proceeds invested in £119 9*s.* 9*d.* Consols with the official trustees. The dividends, amounting to £2 18*s.* 4*d.*, are remitted to the churchwardens for church repairs.

Lovedean.—John Ring, by will proved 1834, left a legacy for education of poor labourers' children in this hamlet, now represented by £207 7*s.* 8*d.* Consols with the official trustees, regulated by scheme of the Charity Commissioners of 22 December, 1897.

141 Egerton MS. 2031, fol. 17.

142 *Winton. Epis. Reg.* (Hants. Rec. Soc.), 514. Egerton MS. 2032, fol. 134; 2033, fol. 20; 2034, fols. 35 and 80.

143 Pat. 5 Edw. VI, pt. 6, m. 26; and 5 & 6 Phil. and Mary, pt. 4, No. 7.

144 Catherington par. reg.

145 Pat. 32 Eliz. pt. 23, m. 9–15.

146 Close, 32 Eliz. pt. 14. By the indenture the advowson was settled in tail male on Thomas and Elizabeth with contingent remainder in tail male successively to Walter and Francis, brothers of Thomas.

147 Feet of F. Div. Cos. Hil. 1 Jas. I.

148 W. and L. Inq. p.m. (Ser. 2), bdle. 32, No. 129; Recov. R. Mich. 11 Chas. II, rot. 102, and Mich. 21 Chas. II, rot. 237.

149 Inst. Bks. (P.R.O.).

150 Close, 26 Chas. II, pt. 22, No. 20.

151 Inst. Bks. (P.R.O.).

152 Recov. R. Mich. 7 Geo. II, rot. 301.

153 Inst. Bks. (P.R.O.).

154 Feet. of F. Hants, Trin. 24 Geo. II.

155 Recov. R. East. 14 Geo. III, rot. 181, Inst. Bks. (P.R.O.). With one exception, viz. in 1790, when the vicar was presented by the dean and canons of Windsor (Inst. Bks.).

156 Catherington par. reg.

CHALTON

Ceptune (xi cent.); Chalghton and Chaulghton (xii cent.); Chaulton, Chauton, Chaueton, and Chawton (xiii cent.); Schalston, Charlton, Chalkton, and Chalughton (xiv cent.); Challeton (xv cent.).

Chalton is a small parish with an area of 1,749 acres,[1] shut in on nearly every side by lofty downs. Consequently the roads to the village are extremely rough, and it is probably owing to this that the parish seems so desolate and remote. The population in 1881 was 208, while in 1901 it was only 202, and from the general appearance it seems likely that it will probably decrease still more. Sir Frederick Madden, in his *Hampshire Collections*, especially mentions Chalton as being one of the least productive parishes of the county. The village is most easily approached by a little road called Chalton Lane, which runs off south-east from the main road from Petersfield to Portsmouth, and rapidly descends the northern slopes of Chalton Down. The village itself is situated on the western slopes of a down, and

THE RED LION INN, CHALTON

is seen in the distance nestling among trees with the church tower showing above. Old Farm stands at the outskirts of the village, and from it the road ascends steeply to a little green where it is met by roads from Ditcham and Rowland's Castle. It is round this little green that the village mostly lies. Here stands the old hostelry 'The Red Lion,' a picturesque half-timbered and thatched building, parts of which are said to be at least 500 years old. Opposite to it is the old grey church with its square ivy-covered tower, and next to the church is the rectory, which is a mediaeval building to which an eighteenth-century front has been added. A window, altered to a doorway in the sixteenth century, is to be seen on the ground floor. The schools are situated along South Lane, as the road is called which leads south to Finchdean and Rowland's Castle. Much of the timber used in the building of the cottages in the village is old oak ship timber, sometimes showing the form of the bows of a ship, acquired no doubt from wrecks on the south coast or brought from Portsmouth. There is a fine view at the back of the church from the Ditcham road, which looks out on the south towards the heights of Chalton Downs, on the north to the widely-stretching Ditcham Woods, and on the west towards Windmill Hill, while the road which joins the main Portsmouth road appears as a perpendicular white streak.

Chalton windmill, which stands on the summit of Windmill Hill, and has now fallen into decay, is mentioned as early as 1289, when it was worth 40*s.* per annum,[2] and is included in subsequent extents of the manor. Only a few place-names survive in Chalton. Netherley Farm Buildings, west of South Lane, mark the site of copyhold land called 'Netheley,' parcel of the manor of Chalton in the seventeenth century.[3] A certain William Trigge died in 1563 seised of a messuage called St. Andrew's Chapel in Chalton,[4] but there does not seem to be any trace of it now. The name John Wodecroft occurs in a dispute on the bishop's register in 1397. He probably lived at Woodcroft, which is at the present time a hamlet of Chalton at the foot of the Down near the railway on the way to Ditcham.

Windmill Down, the Peak and Chalton Down were inclosed by authority of an Act of 1812. The soil is light, the sub-soil chalk. The chief crops are wheat, barley, and oats.

Idsworth is a parochial chapelry on the borders of Sussex, in the midst of beautiful country, steep wooded hills alternating with rich park-land, where game of every description abounds. In shape it is long and narrow, being about five miles in length and not more than a mile broad at its widest point. Rowland's Castle, situated in the south, is the most populous part, and is rapidly growing, no doubt owing to the existence of its railway station, opened in 1859, on the Portsmouth branch of the London and South Western Railway. In the centre of the village is a wide green, around the north side of which are grouped various cottages, inns, and shops, constituting the older part of the village. On the west side is the Congregational chapel, originally erected in 1881. Along the south side runs a very tall old brick wall inclosing the grounds of Deerleap, the residence of Admiral George William Douglass O'Callaghan, C.B., J.P. In these grounds, between the house and the factory of the Rowland's Castle Brick and Tile Company,[5] there are the remains of a ruin covered with ivy, said to be all that is left of what was once 'Rowland's Castle.' There are but few references to this castle in documents preserved in the British Museum and the Record Office. It appears from Harleian

[1] The acreage of Chalton is divided as follows:—733 acres of arable land, 576 acres of permanent grass, and 146 acres of woods and plantations (Statistics from Board of Agriculture, 1905).

[2] Inq. p.m. 17 Edw. I, No. 17.

[3] Exch. Dep. 22 Jas. I, Mich. No. 29, and 8 Chas. I, Mich. No. 9.

[4] Exch. Inq. p.m. (Ser. 2), file 1004, No. 3.

[5] There are two brick and tile factories in the village.

MS. 6602 that the abbot and convent of Titchfield and their men of Wellsworth, in the time of Edward II, had common of pasture in the Forest of Bere, from a place called Meslyngforth, even to 'Rolokescastel.'[6] Another mention of it is in 1528, in which year John Byrcom was pardoned for having received certain cattle from John Yong, who on 10 September, 1523, broke into a place called 'Rowelands Castle at Warbelyngton,' and carried off the said cattle.[7] But neither of these entries throws any light on the history of the castle, which remains very obscure.

On the east side of the road going up the hill from the green to Havant is Stanstead College, which was built and endowed by Mr. Charles Dixon of Stanstead Park ('late a merchant of London'), as a house for six decayed merchants of the cities of London, Liverpool and Bristol. There is no Anglican church in Rowland's Castle itself, but the little church of St. John on Redhill, in the parish of Havant, is not much more than a mile from the green. The Castle Inn in the village has been kept for about two centuries by the Outen family. There were formerly two fairs held in Rowland's Castle—one for horned cattle on 12 May, and the other for horned cattle and hogs on 12 November—but they had become obsolete before the middle of the nineteenth century. Four good roads run in different directions from Rowland's Castle—one south-west to Havant, the second, along which several modern houses are being built, north-west uphill to Blendworth, the third south-east to Westbourne, and the fourth north-east to Dean Lane End. From Links Lane some of the finest views can be obtained of the surrounding country. Blendworth Common and the Holt lie to the west, on the east is Stanstead Forest, and on the south Havant Thicket and Emsworth Common.

The little village of Finchdean is almost in the centre of Idsworth, near the railway line, in the midst of very beautiful country. In the centre of the village is a small triangular green, near which are the smithy, the George Inn, and a small Congregational chapel. The manufacture of agricultural machines is carried on in Finchdean, and there is also a brass and iron foundry there. To the north is Idsworth House, the property of Lieut.-Colonel Sir Henry Clarke-Jervoise, bart., and at present the residence of Mr. John Bradley Firth. It stands in a fine park of 150 acres, commanding wide views over the surrounding country and the Isle of Wight. In the extreme north of Old Idsworth Park, a little to the east of the road from Dean Lane End to Compton, is the ancient church of Idsworth.

The soil varies, but consists principally of chalk. The subsoil is chalk. The chief crops are wheat, barley, and oats. The population in 1901 was 420, including Rowland's Castle. Idsworth contains 882 acres of arable land, 809 acres of permanent grass, and 291½ acres of woods and plantations.[8] Open fields and common lands in Idsworth were inclosed by authority of an Act of 1812.

MANORS The manor of *CHALTON*, which comprised the parishes of Blendworth, Catherington, Clanfield, and Chalton, a portion of the parish of Hambledon, and perhaps the parish of Idsworth, formed part of the possessions of Earl Godwin, and on his death in 1053 passed to his son Harold. It was seized in 1066 by William the Conqueror, who granted it to William Fitz-Osbern, whom he created earl of Hereford and lord of the Isle of Wight. At the time of the Domesday Survey Roger de Montgomery, earl of Shrewsbury, was holding the manor of the gift of William Fitz-Osbern.[9] On his death in 1094, Chalton, with his other English estates and dignities, passed to his second son Hugh, called 'Goch' (the red),[10] who being shot in the eye in the invasion of the Isle of Anglesey by Magnus, king of Norway, died unmarried[11] 27 July, 1098. On his death his estates passed to his elder brother, Robert de Belesme, earl of Shrewsbury and Arundel, who, in return for a payment of £3,000, was confirmed in his brother's earldoms in 1098 by William Rufus. He, however, fortified his castles in England against Henry I, and was accordingly expelled from the country, and deprived of all his honours and estates in 1102.[12] In this way Chalton fell into the hands of the king, who granted it, as parcel of the honour of Leicester, in 1107, to Robert de Beaumont, as a reward for establishing the English rule in Normandy.[13] The manor remained in the possession of the Beaumonts, earls of Leicester, till 1204,[14] when Robert de Beaumont, fourth earl of Leicester, died without issue, leaving a widow Lauretta, the daughter of William de Braose.[15] In 1214 King John ordered the sheriff of Hampshire to cause Lauretta, countess of Leicester, to have at her manor of Chalton as much in ploughs and stock as Henry Fitz-Count[16] received in the same manor when it was committed to him by the command of the king.[17] Lauretta probably held the manor for some time after her husband's death.[18] In 1207 Simon de Montfort, the younger son of Simon count of Evreux by Amice the sister and co-heir of Robert de Beaumont earl of Leicester, was confirmed by King John in his titles of earl of Leicester and steward of England, but later in the same year he was deprived of all his English possessions. However, eight years later he was restored, Randolph de Blondeville, earl of Chester, being made *custos* of the fief of the earldom of Leicester.[19] Randolph seems to have been looked upon as the lord of Chalton till 1232, when the earl's youngest son, the famous Simon de Montfort, earl of Leicester, was confirmed in all the land held by his father in England.[20] Thus in 1224 Henry III gave Randolph, earl of Chester, permission to hold at Chalton, until

MONTFORT. *Gules a lion argent with a forked tail.*

[6] Harl. MS. 6602, fol. 25.
[7] *L. and P. Hen. VIII*, iv (2), 5083 (15).
[8] Statistics from Board of Agriculture (1905).
[9] *V. C. H. Hants*, i, 478.
[10] G. E. C. *Complete Peerage*, vii, 133.
[11] Ibid.
[12] Ibid. 135.
[13] Ibid. v, 40.
[14] Pipe R. 13 Hen. II.
[15] G. E. C. *Complete Peerage*, v, 44.
[16] Afterwards (1217–20) earl of Cornwall.
[17] Close, 16 John, pt. 2, m. 13.
[18] In the *Testa de Nevill* she appears in the gift of the king, and her lands in Chalton are valued at £50 (*Testa de Nevill* [Rec. Com.], 236*b*).
[19] G. E. C. *Complete Peerage*, v, 44.
[20] Close, 15 Hen. III, m. 3.

his coming of age, a market every Thursday and a yearly fair on the eve and feast of St. Michael, unless such market and fair were to the damage of neighbouring markets and fairs.[21] Again in 1229 the king informed the verderers of his forest of Portchester that he had given orders to Robert de Waleton, the steward of the earl of Chester, to allow them to enter the wood of his lordship of Chalton which was in the forest, as they had been accustomed to do before the perambulation of the forest was made.[22] In 1246 Simon de Montfort granted the manor to Hereward Marsh and Rainetta his wife, to hold to them of himself and his heirs during the life of Rainetta, with immediate reversion to Simon if Rainetta died before her husband.[23] This evidently happened, as the earl was seised of the manor in 1265, when he was defeated and slain at Evesham. Hence Chalton escheated to Henry III, who gave it to his youngest son Edmund Plantagenet,[24] created earl of Leicester and steward of England 26 October, 1265, and earl of Lancaster 30 June, 1267.[25] Edmund in his turn gave the manor to Hamon le Strange[26] before 1272, in which year Hamon obtained a grant of free warren in Chalton.[27]

The manor was held of the earls of Lancaster and Leicester from the time of Edmund's grant to Hamon until in 1350[28] it became part of the duchy of Lancaster,[29] when Henry Plantagenet earl of Lancaster and Leicester was created duke of Lancaster,[30] and was merged in the crown[31] when Henry Plantagenet, duke of Lancaster, ascended the throne as Henry V.[32]

Le Strange. *Gules two lions passant argent.*

Hamon le Strange, while in the Holy Land, granted the manor to his brother Robert, who held a court there, and remained in possession till Hamon's death, when he was ejected by the sheriff of Hampshire,[33] Edmund the king's brother being appointed at will to the custody of the manor.[34] An inquisition was held early in 1275 to discover what right Robert had to the manor,[35] and in July of the same year the sheriff of Hampshire was ordered to cause Robert to have such seisin of the manor as he had before it was taken into the king's hands.[36] Robert was not seised of Chalton long, for in September, 1276, the king ordered the sheriff to cause Eleanor widow of Robert to have £30 yearly of land in the manor of Chalton, until dower should be assigned to her.[37] Robert's heir was still a minor in 1281, for in that year John de Aese, vicomte de Tartase, obtained a grant of the manor of Chalton, extended at £40,[38] to hold during the minority of Robert's heir.[39] John son of Robert died seised of the manor in 1289, his heir being his brother Fulk,[40] to whom Edward I in 1294 granted licence, since he was going on the king's service to Gascony, to sell, cut down, and carry away timber to the value of £40 out of his wood of Chalton, which was within the metes of the forest of Portchester, in those places where it would be to the least damage of the forest.[41] Fulk served his king well in Gascony, and obtained as a reward quittance from a debt of £24 which his uncle Hamon had owed at the time of his death for 'many defaults of the time when he was sheriff.'[42] He died seised of the manor in 1324, leaving a son and heir John.[43] While John was lord of the manor of Chalton, Richard de Hangleton, who was lord of the neighbouring manor of Catherington, encroached upon Chalton manor, and disseised him of 300 acres of wood in Chalton and two pieces of land in Catherington. By an indenture dated at Winchester on the Wednesday after the feast of St. James the Apostle, 1334, it was agreed that Richard should surrender the said wood and lands to John for ever, and should only claim reasonable 'housbote' and 'heybote' for the tenement which he inherited in Catherington, to be taken in the part of the wood called 'Estrenche' by view of John's bailiffs, together with common for his beasts in the said wood.[44] John held the manor until his death in 1349,[45] when it passed to his son and heir Fulk, aged nineteen,[46] who died the same year, leaving as his heir his brother John, aged seventeen.[47] The latter died before 1361, for in that year Ankarette wife of John le Strange died seised of the manor, held in dower, leaving a son and heir, John, aged seven,[48] whose wardship was granted to Richard earl of Arundel.[49] John died on 3 August, 1375, before he reached the age of twenty-one years,[50] and left the manor in dower to Isabel his wife, with reversion to his only daughter Elizabeth. The latter became the wife of Thomas Mowbray, earl of Nottingham, but died without issue in 1383. Isabel, who had married William Ufford, earl of Suffolk,

[21] Close, 8 Hen. III, m. 2.
[22] Ibid. 13 Hen. III, m. 13.
[23] Feet of F. Div. Cos. Trin. 40 Hen. III.
[24] Inq. p.m. 3 Edw. I, No. 52.
[25] G. E. C. *Complete Peerage*, v, 46.
[26] Inq. p.m. 3 Edw. I. No. 52.
[27] Chart. R. 56 Hen. III, m. 6.
[28] Inq. p.m. 17 Edw. I, No. 17; and 17 Edw. II, No. 73.
[29] Inq. p.m. 35 Edw. III, No. 122; Close, 35 Edw. III, m. 17; Inq. p.m. 49 Edw. III, pt. 2, No. 8.
[30] G. E. C. *Complete Peerage*, v, 7.
[31] Inq. p.m. 4 Hen. V, No. 48; 7 Hen. V, No. 68; 27 Hen. VI, No. 36; and 5 Edw. IV, No. 21.
[32] G. E. C. *Complete Peerage*, v, 10.
[33] Inq. p.m. 3 Edw. I, No. 52; Anct. Deeds (P.R.O.), B 3463.
[34] Pat. 3 Edw. I, m. 30.
[35] Inq. p.m. 3 Edw. I, No. 52.
[36] Close, 3 Edw. I, m. 7.
[37] Ibid. 4 Edw. I, m. 4.
[38] A year before it had been valued at £50 a year (Assize R. Mich. 8 Edw. I).
[39] Pat. 9 Edw. I, m. 15.
[40] Inq. p.m. 17 Edw. I, No. 17. In the inquisition the following extent was given of the manor:—A capital messuage, 250 acres of arable land, pasture for 300 sheep called 'Estdone,' a windmill, a wood the herbage of which is common containing 40 acres, a wood in the forest containing 200 acres worth 5*s.* per annum and not more 'propter dangerium forestariorum,' rents of freemen £3 3*s.* 3*d.*, with stallage and furze, fifty-two customary tenants who hold thirty-six virgates and pay £21 13*s.* 4½*d.*, rents of hens 1*s.* 6*d.*, rents of sheep at shearing 2*s.*, pannage of pigs 13*s.* 4*d.*, services of customary tenants £3 14*s.* 10½*d.*, and fines of lands and profits of courts with redemption of villeins £2. The total value of the manor per annum was £38 4*s.* 10*d.*, and it was held by the service of three fees.
[41] Pat. 22 Edw. I, m. 13.
[42] Close, 8 Edw. II, m. 12.
[43] Inq. p.m. 17 Edw. II, No. 73. In the inquisition the manor is said to be held of the earl of Leicester by the service of one knight's fee and the service of paying to the same earl every Easter a pair of gilt spurs.
[44] Anct. Deeds (P.R.O.), B 3481.
[45] Enrolled Accts. P. 2 Edw. III, No. 31; Chart R, 7 Edw. III, m. 41; *Feud. Aids*, ii, 335; Close, 21 Edw. III, pt. 1, m. 24*d.*; and Feet of F. Hants, Mich. 21 Edw. III.
[46] Inq. p.m. 23 Edw. III, pt. 1, No. 78.
[47] Ibid. 79.
[48] Ibid. 35 Edw. III, pt. 2, No. 66.
[49] Bankes, *Dormant and Extinct Peerage*, ii, 552.
[50] Inq. p.m. 49 Edw. III, pt. 2, No. 8.

as her second husband, died seised of the manor 29 September, 1416, when it passed to Sir Gilbert Talbot, son and heir of Ankarette, sister of John le Strange.[51] But shortly before Isabel's death Sir Gilbert had granted the reversion of the manor to trustees,[52] and died 17 November, 1418.[53] On 4 May, 1426, the executors of Sir Gilbert granted the manor to Sir John Montgomery of Faulkbourne (co. Essex) and Elizabeth his wife,[54] and on 12 October, 1448, the manor was settled upon Sir John and Elizabeth and their issue.[55] Nine months later Sir John died seised of the manor, his heir being his son John, aged twenty-three.[56] This John must have died before 1465, for in the inquisition taken after his mother's death in that year, it was stated that her heir was her son Sir Thomas Montgomery, aged thirty and more.[57] This Thomas was one of the most eminent men of his time, standing high in the favour of Edward IV, Richard III, and Henry VII. He made his will at Faulkbourne 28 July, 1489,[58] and died seised of the manor of Chalton in 1494, his heir being his sister Alice, the wife of Edmund Wiseman.[59] In 1496 Anne Montgomery, widow, probably the widow of Thomas, but possibly the widow of his brother John, released all her interest in the manor to Sir Reginald Bray, Sir John Norbury, and others for purposes of settlement on her sister-in-law Alice.[60] In 1505 Edmund Wiseman and Alice his wife, and John Fortescue and Philippa his wife, who was the granddaughter of Alice[61] by her first husband, Clement Spice, granted the manor to George earl of Shrewsbury,[62] whose title was confirmed in 1506 when Sir John Norbury and Joan his wife surrendered all their right to the manor,[63] and again in 1524, when Sir Edward Bray and Joan his wife renounced all their claim to it.[64] In 1532 the earl sold the manor to Margaret countess of Salisbury,[65] on whose attainder and execution in 1539 the king granted it to William Fitz-William, earl of Southampton, to hold for seventy-one years at a rent of £75 0*s.* 4½*d.*[66] In 1542 the manor was settled upon the earl in tail male with contingent remainder to William, Lord Herbert, son and heir apparent of Henry earl of Worcester, in tail male.[67] The earl of Southampton died without issue less than a year later,[68] and in accordance with the settlement the manor reverted to William, Lord Herbert, who succeeded to the peerage as earl of Worcester 26 November, 1549.[69] He died seised of the manor in 1588, his heir being his son Edward, Lord Herbert,[70] who, shortly after succeeding to his inheritance, engaged in fierce disputes with William, Lord Sandys, the lord of the adjoining manor of Catherington, concerning his right to the common called the East Heath, which he declared to be parcel of the manor of Chalton, and with Robert Paddon and Arthur Swayne, lords of the neighbouring manor of Hinton Daubnay, concerning their right to the parcel of waste called Woodcrofts.[71] The earl died seised of the manor in 1628, and was succeeded by his second but eldest surviving son Henry, Lord Herbert, aged forty and more.[72] Henry was a zealous supporter of the royal cause, raising and supporting two armies from 1642 to 1646, and being lieutenant-general of the forces in Monmouthshire. On 1 December, 1645, the Commons, in drawing up the peace propositions to be offered to the king, resolved that an estate of £2,500 a year should be conferred on Cromwell, and that the king should be requested to make him a baron. After the failure of the negotiations an ordinance of Parliament settled upon him lands to the value named, taken chiefly from the property of the marquis of Worcester,[73] and the king was forced by letters patent to grant to his 'beloved Oliver Cromwell,' his heirs and assigns, the manor of Chalton, 'which manor was lately the hereditament of Henry earl of Worcester, Edward, Lord Herbert, and Sir John Somerset, which earl, Edward and John, are *recusantes papistici*.'[74] Oliver Cromwell was seised of the manor till his death, when it passed to his eldest son Richard.[75] After the Restoration the manor was restored to Edward Somerset, marquis of Worcester, son and heir of Henry Somerset, earl of Worcester. He died seised of it in 1667,[76] and was succeeded by his son and heir Henry Somerset, marquis of Worcester, who petitioned Charles II for a grant of the reversions remaining in the crown of the manor of Chalton, in order to enable him to raise money to discharge the debts contracted by his father, which much encumbered his estate.[77] This petition was granted 26 December, 1667.[78] The marquis was created duke of Beaufort in 1682, and died seised of the manor in 1699.[79] Chalton continued to be the property of the duke of Beaufort[80] until about 1780,[81] when it was purchased by Jervoise

CROMWELL. *Sable a lion argent.*

[51] Inq. p.m. 4 Hen. V, No. 48.

[52] Feet of F. Hants. Mich. 4 Hen. V.

[53] Inq. p.m. 7 Hen. V, No. 68.

[54] Ibid. 27 Hen. VI, No. 38. This Elizabeth was the sister and co-heir of Sir Ralph Boteler, and married (1) Sir Henry Norbury, by whom she had issue a son and heir, Sir John Norbury; (2) Sir William Heron, Lord of Say, who died Oct. 1404, by whom she had no issue; and (3) Sir John Montgomery, by whom she had issue John, Thomas, Alice, who married first John Fortescue, and secondly Robert Langley, and another Alice who married first Clement Spice, and secondly Edmund Wiseman (vide Morant, *Hist. of Essex*, ii, 116).

[55] Inq. p.m. 27 Hen. VI, No. 36.

[56] Ibid.

[57] Ibid. 5 Edw. IV, No. 21.

[58] P.C.C. 22 Vox.

[59] Morant, *Hist. of Essex*, ii, 116.

[60] Close, 11 Hen. VII, No. 20.

[61] Close, 17 Hen. VII, No. 15.

[62] Anct. Deeds (P.R.O.), B 870 and B 2460; De Banc. R. East. 20 Hen. VII, m. 21; and Feet of F. Hants, East. 20 Hen. VII.

[63] De Banc. R. Mich. 22 Hen. VII, m. 21, and Deeds enrolled, m. 1 *d.*; Feet of F. Hants. Mich. 22 Hen. VII.

[64] Feet of F. Hants. East. 15 Hen. VIII.

[65] Ibid. 23 Hen. VIII.

[66] *L. and P. Hen. VIII*, xv, 291.

[67] Pat. 33 Hen. VIII, pt. 6.

[68] Inq. p.m. 36 Hen. VIII (Ser. 2), lxx, No. 56.

[69] G. E. C. *Complete Peerage*, viii, 201.

[70] Special Commissions, 11 Jas. I, No. 4502, and 14 Jas. I, No. 4506.

[71] Exch. Bills and Answs. Eliz. Hants. No. 81.

[72] Chan. Inq. p.m. ccccxlii, No. 26.

[73] *Thurloe Papers*, i, 75.

[74] Pat. 21 Chas. I, pt. 1, No. 74.

[75] Noble, *Memoirs of the Cromwell Family*, 334.

[76] G. E. C. *Complete Peerage*, viii, 203.

[77] *Cal. of S.P. Dom.* 1667, p. 369.

[78] Pat. 19 Chas. II, pt. 2; *Cal. of S.P. Dom.* 1667–8, pp. 77 and 101.

[79] G. E. C. *Complete Peerage*, viii, 203; and i, 281.

[80] Recov. R. Mich. 10 Geo. II, m. 1–6; and East. 14 Geo. III.

[81] It seems impossible to discover the exact date of the purchase, but it must have been some time between 1774 and 1787 (cf. Recov. R. East. 14 Geo. III, and Inst. Bks. P.R.O.).

Clarke-Jervoise, who in 1789 bought up the neighbouring manor of Idsworth (q.v.). His son, the Rev. Samuel Jervoise Clarke-Jervoise, was created a baronet 13 November, 1813.[82] Lieut.-Colonel Sir Henry Clarke-Jervoise, bart., grandson of the latter, is the present lord of the manor.

SOMERSET, Duke of Beaufort. *France quartered with England within a border gobony argent and azure.*

IDSWORTH is not mentioned in Domesday Book, and at the time of the Survey was probably included in the manor of Chalton, then held by Earl Roger of Shrewsbury.[83] It is probable that it was separated from Chalton when, on the rebellion of Robert de Belesme, third earl of Shrewsbury, in 1102, his lands were forfeited to the crown.[84] Then, when Henry I granted Chalton, as part of the honour of Leicester, to Robert de Beaumont, that part of Chalton which was afterwards known as Idsworth was evidently detached from the main manor, and was afterwards held by a certain Norman, William de Ferrers, directly of the king.[85] In 1204, King John ordered the sheriff of Hampshire to deliver up to Henry Hoese the land of Idsworth which had belonged to William de Ferrers, together with the stock of that land and seed to sow it. The corn, however, he was to retain to the king's use.[86] Henry held the manor for about eighteen years of the gift of King John.[87] In 1222, however, King Henry III granted it to one of his crossbowmen, Brito by name, to support him in the royal service, and Henry Hoese was ordered to surrender it to him.[88] This he did not do immediately, whereupon the sheriff of Hampshire was ordered to force Henry to give up the manor to Brito with all the profits therefrom since the king's grant to Brito.[89] Brito held it till 1226, when the king ordered the sheriff to cause Reynold de Bernevall to have full seisin of the land of Idsworth, saving, however, to Brito all his chattels found in that land.[90] Brito died less than a year afterwards, and the sheriff was commanded to give up to his widow Edelina all the corn, which he had caused to be sown in Idsworth, in order to support her and her sons.[91] The manor was next granted to the king's messenger William Blome, who held it for nearly thirty years.[92] On his death the king granted the reversion of the manor, valued at £16 a year, after the death of William's widow Alda, to his yeoman Herman de Budbergh, as a reward for his services. In the grant it was specially stipulated that Herman and his heirs should not alienate the land to any but the king without his special consent.[93] Herman, some time afterwards, granted the manor to Queen Eleanor, who, in her turn, with the consent of her husband, granted it in free alms to Tarrant Nunnery (co. Dors.),[94] a house to which she was so great a benefactress that it was sometimes styled in records 'Locus benedictus reginae' or 'Locus reginae super Tarent.'[95] Her gift was confirmed by Henry III in 1271,[96] and by Edward I in 1280.[97] In 1281 Iseult the abbess of Tarrant granted the manor of Idsworth to Henry de Bonynges and Isabel his wife to hold of the abbess and her successors for the rent of a penny at Christmas and by suit at the hundred court of Wollesthorn every three weeks.[98] From this time the abbess and her successors were overlords of the manor of Idsworth,[99] and as late as 1606 the manor was said to be held of Sir John Portman as of the site of his abbey of Tarrant.[100]

JERVOISE. *Sable a cheveron between three eagles close argent.*

From Henry de Bonynges and Isabel his wife the manor passed to John Romyn, who was holding it in 1316,[101] and remained in the family of Romyn until 1419,[102] when John Romyn died without issue, his heir being his distant kinsman Thomas de Wintershull,[103] lord of the manor of Wintershull in Bramley (co. Surr.).[104] He died without issue in October, 1420, leaving two sisters and co-heirs, Joan the wife of William Catton, and Agnes the wife of William Basset,[105] who, in 1431, released all right in the manor to Nicholas Banester and Isabel his wife,[106] the widow of the John Romyn who died in 1419.[107] The manor remained in the family of Banester for over two centuries,[108] passing at length into the family of Dormer by the marriage of Mary daughter of Edward Banester with Robert Dormer, third son of Sir Robert Dormer first Lord Dormer of Wyng.[109] Their grandson, Charles, fifth Lord Dormer of Wyng, was seised of it in 1723,[110] and it was held successively by the Rev. Charles Dormer, sixth Lord Dormer, who died in 1761,

DORMER OF WYNG. *Azure ten billets or and a chief or with three martlets azure therein.*

[82] Burke, *Peerage*, 881.
[83] *V.C.H. Hants*, i, 478*a*.
[84] G. E. C. *Complete Peerage*, vii, 135.
[85] *Rot. Litt. Claus.* (Rec. Com.), i, 7*b*; Assize R. Mich. 8 Edw. I. The land he held in Idsworth was of the annual value of £18.
[86] Ibid.
[87] *Testa de Nevill* (Rec. Com.), 236*b*.
[88] *Rot. Litt. Claus.* (Rec. Com.), i, 487*b*.
[89] Ibid. i, 488*b*.
[90] Ibid. ii, 95.
[91] Ibid. ii, 189.
[92] Ibid. ii, 174; Pat. 14 Hen. III, m. 2.
[93] Chart. R. 41 Hen. III, m. 6.
[94] Chart. R. 55 Hen. III, m. 10.
[95] Dugdale, *Mon.* v, 619.
[96] Chart. R. 55 Hen. III, m. 10.
[97] Chart. R. 8 Edw. I, m. 4.
[98] Feet of F. Hants, East. 9 Edw. I; Assize R. Mich. 8 Edw. I. This must really have been a confirmation of a preceding grant, for Henry was seised of the manor in 1275 (De Banc. R. No. 11, m. 22).
[99] Chan. Inq. p.m. (Ser. 2), viii, No. 69.
[100] Chan. Inq. p.m. (Ser. 2), ccxcii, No. 177.
[101] *Feud. Aids*, ii, 318.
[102] Close, 18 Edw. II, m. 1 *d.*; *Cal. of Close*, 1323–27, p. 520; Inq. p.m. 35 Edw. III, pt. 2, No. 82; Close, 2 Hen. IV, pt. 2, m. 2.
[103] Inq. p.m. 8 Hen. V, No. 92. This Thomas was the son of Thomas de Wintershull, son of Thomas de Wintershull, son of Walter de Wintershull and Juliana his wife, sister of John Romyn, father of John Romyn, father of John Romyn, father of Richard Romyn, father of John Romyn.
[104] Manning and Bray, *Surrey*, ii, 84.
[105] De Banc. R. Mich. 3 Hen. VI, m. 123.
[106] Feet of F. Div. Cos. Hil. 9 Hen. VI.
[107] Berry, *Hants Gen.*, 81.
[108] *Feud. Aids*, ii, 362; Chan. Inq. p.m. (Ser. 2), viii, No. 69; ccxcii, No. 177; Feet of F. Div. Cos. Trin. 14 Chas. II; Recov. R. Trin. 14 Chas. II, rot. 24.
[109] Burke, *Peerage*, 510.
[110] Recov. R. Trin. 9 Geo. I, rot. 53.

John, seventh Lord Dormer, who died in 1785, and Charles, eighth Lord Dormer.[111] The last named sold the manor in 1789 to Jervoise Clarke-Jervoise,[112] whose great-grandson, Lieut.-Colonel Sir Henry Clarke-Jervoise, bart.,[113] is the present lord of the manor.

At a short distance south-west of Idsworth church is the site of the old Idsworth House, but nothing remains of the building except some garden walls.

WELLSWORTH (Walesworthe, Welesworth, xiii cent.; Waleswith, xv cent.; Wallysworth, xvi cent.). In the reign of Henry II the manor was held by William de Say, and on his death passed to his daughter and co-heir Maud wife of William de Bocland, who was holding it by right of inheritance towards the end of the twelfth century.[114] On her death without issue it passed to her heir Geoffrey Fitz-Piers, the husband of her sister Beatrice,[115] who was created earl of Essex for his service to King John on the day of his coronation. On Geoffrey's death in 1213 the manor passed to his son and heir Geoffrey, who assumed the name of Mandeville.[116] He did not hold it long, however, for he was slain in a tournament in London, 23 February, 1216, and his estates passed to his brother William de Mandeville, earl of Essex, who gave it within a few years to Sir Geoffrey de Lucy for saving his life in a tournament at Lincoln.[117] Geoffrey de Lucy in his turn sold it to Peter des Roches, bishop of Winchester,[118] who soon afterwards granted it in free alms to the abbey of Titchfield which he had founded in 1233.[119] Henry III confirmed Wellsworth to Titchfield, and granted in addition that the abbot and the canons should have thol and theam, infangenthef and utfangenthef, and many other privileges in Wellsworth, and also that the lands of Wellsworth, which were within the bounds of the royal forest, should be for ever quit from waste, regard, view of foresters, etc.[120] In 1280 the abbot of Titchfield being summoned to show by what warrant he claimed to have pillory and the assize of bread and beer in Wellsworth, produced the charter of Henry III and the case was dismissed.[121] Again he produced the charter in the same year when he was summoned to show why he should not permit his villeins of Wellsworth to make suit at the king's hundred-court of Portsdown,[122] and the case was decided in his favour. In 1294 Edward I by charter granted to the abbot and convent free warren in Wellsworth,[123] and this grant was confirmed by Henry VI in 1424.[124] In the reign of Edward II, William de Cleydon, the deputy of Lord Hugh le Despenser, the justiciar of the forest 'citra Trentam' ordered the warden of the forest of Bere to allow the abbot and convent of Titchfield and their men of Wellsworth to have common of pasture in the said forest for all their animals except goats from a place called 'Meslyngforth' even to 'Rolokescastel,' according to charters of the kings of England.[125] The abbot and convent of Titchfield held Wellsworth until the dissolution,[126] when it was granted by the king to Thomas Wriothesley, earl of Southampton.[127] The manor remained the property of the earls of Southampton[128] until about the middle of the seventeenth century, when it was bought up by Richard Norton,[129] after which it followed the descent of the manor of Southwick,[130] in the hundred of Portsdown (q. v.).

The Romyns also had a tenement in *WELLSWORTH*, which followed the descent of the manor of Idsworth, passing with it to the Banesters. It was probably in origin the two messuages, 18 acres of land and 1 acre of wood in Chalton, granted to Henry Romyn and Joan his wife by Richard Baldwin of Wellsworth and Agnes his wife in 1345.[131] Henry Romyn died in 1349 seised of the following tenements in Wellsworth:—A messuage, 105 acres of land worth 26*s.* 3*d.* per annum, a dovecote worth 6*s.* 8*d.* per annum, and 17*s.* 5*d.* rents of free tenants and others—held of John Romyn by money-rent and suit of court.[132] His son and heir was Edmund, aged six, who probably died while under age, when the tenement reverted to John Romyn the overlord. It seems only to be called a manor in one document—the inquisition taken after the death of Edward Banester in 1606—when it is described as situated in the vill of Idsworth, and of the annual value of 10*s.*[133] It has continued to form part of the Idsworth estates, and is at the present day represented by the farm of Little Wellsworth.

CHURCHES

The church of *ST. MICHAEL, CHALTON*, has a chancel 32 ft. long by 18 ft. 3 in. wide, a nave 46 ft. by 21 ft. 8 in., with a north porch, a south transept 12 ft. 8 in. north to south by 12 ft. 2 in., and a west tower.

111 Recov. R. East. 23 Geo. III, rot. 262.

112 Feet of F. Hants, Trin. 29 Geo. III.

113 His grandfather, the Rev. Samuel Jervoise Clarke-Jervoise, was created a baronet 13 Nov. 1813 (*vide* Berry, *Hants Gen.* 341).

114 Harl. MS. 6602, fol. 26.

115 Ibid.

116 Ibid.

117 Ibid.

118 Ibid.

119 Ibid. 3. In 1239 a fine was levied between Richard de Lucy and Geoffrey de Lucy, the lord of the manor, whom Isaac, abbot of Titchfield, called to warrant and who warranted to him, whereby the following arrangement was made: (1) Richard quitclaimed from himself and his heirs to Geoffrey and his heirs and the abbot and his successors all right which he had in the manor. (2) Geoffrey warranted to the abbot and his successors the manor in free alms against all men. (3) The abbot granted for himself and his successors to Geoffrey and his heirs that he and his heirs should present to the abbot and his successors one fitting clerk 'in canonicum' to celebrate mass for the souls of Geoffrey, his ancestors, and successors. On the death of a canon another was to be appointed by Geoffrey and his heirs, and thus from clerk to clerk successively for ever. (4) The abbot received Geoffrey, Richard, and Geoffrey's son and heir John into all the orisons of the church. The concord was made in the presence of John, who agreed that his inheritance should be alienated to the abbot and his successors to hold in free alms (Feet of F. Hants, Hil. 23 Hen. III).

120 Dugdale, *Mon.* vi, 931. This charter was confirmed by Edw. I and Edw. II (Pat. 11 Edw. II, pt. 1, m. 15; Harl. MS. 6602, fol. 17).

121 *Plac. de Quo Warr.* (Rec. Com), 763.

122 Ibid. 765. The king's representative said that Henry III had been seised of the suit of the villeins even after the granting of the charter, but the case was finally decided by a jury of knights who swore that Henry III had never been seised of the suit of the villeins after the charter.

123 Chart. R. 22 Edw. I, No. 13.

124 Pat. 3 Hen. VI, pt. 1, m. 13.

125 Harl. MS. 6602, fol. 25.

126 *Testa de Nevill* (Rec Com.), 234; *Pope Nich. Tax.* (Rec. Com.), 213; *Feud. Aids*, ii, 320; Feet of F. Div. Cos. Mich. 29 Hen. VIII; Dugdale, *Mon.* vi, 935

127 Pat. 29 Hen. VIII, pt. 1, m. 4 and 5, and 38 Hen. VIII, pt. 4, m. 5.

128 Chan. Inq. p.m. (Ser. 2), xcii, No. 78, and cxcvi, No. 46; W. and L. Inq. p.m. (Ser. 2), bdle. 71, No. 120.

129 *Vide* Ct. of Wards. Misc. Bks. 656.

130 Recov. R. Hil. 20 Geo. II, rot. 265 and 16 Geo. III, Trin. rot. 164–5.

131 Feet of F. Hants, Trin. 19 Edw. III

132 Chan. Inq. p.m. 23 Edw. III, 1st pt. No. 19.

133 Chan. Inq. p.m. (Ser. 2), ccxcii, No. 177.

The chancel is the oldest part of the building, a fine and well-proportioned piece of mid-thirteenth-century work, with an east window unfortunately reset in a very clumsy manner at an early Victorian 'restoration.' It has four main lights uncusped, with two quatrefoils over them, and a cinquefoil in the head. In the north wall are three tall lancets, the first two set near each other, with a greater space between the second and third or western lancet, the sill of which is lower than those of the others. On the south side are three lancets similarly placed, with a blocked priest's door [134] between the second and third. The latter is only visible on the outer face of the wall, being blocked, and is much shorter than the others, having below it a wide low side window of two lights with shouldered heads, which seems to be part of the original work. It has lost its central mullion and, like the window over, is blocked, its iron grate remaining in the blocking, and the hooks for the shutters being still in position. At the south-east of the chancel is a double piscina with trefoiled arches, and under the east window in the north wall a locker. There is no chancel arch. In the nave the earliest feature is a two-light window in the south wall with a trefoiled circle in the head, of late thirteenth-century date; but with this exception everything appears to belong to the first quarter of the fourteenth century. The east window in the north wall is of this date, with two trefoiled lights and a quatrefoil in the head, and on either side of the plain north doorway is a tall trefoiled single light. In the south wall, west of the opening to the transept, is the two-light thirteenth-century window already noted, and west of it is a plain south doorway and a trefoiled light like that on the north. The transept, whose north arch is completely blocked by the organ, is of about the same date as the fourteenth-century work in the nave, and has a square-headed east window of two trefoiled lights, and a south window, also of two trefoiled lights, with a quatrefoil in the head. The nave roof preserves some old timbers, but the tie-beams are cased with modern boarding, and the chancel roof is modern. The north porch has been much repaired, but its main timbers are of fifteenth-century work. The tower, which is entered from the church by a plain chamfered doorway, has a plain blocked west doorway, and standing near the western boundary of the churchyard whence the ground falls rapidly, shows signs of failure, its upper stages being patched with brick and bound with iron tie-rods. The belfry windows have therefore lost their original detail, and the whole is very plain, but is of much the same date as the nave.

The font stands at the west end of the nave, and is octagonal, with quatrefoiled panels on the bowl inclosing alternately blank shields or paterae carved with heads or foliage. Its date is *c.* 1400, and it closely resembles the font at Idsworth a few miles away. Both fonts have also been broken at the base of the bowl, by tradition in the civil wars.

The most interesting monument in the church is that of Richard Ball, rector, who died in 1632. It is on the north wall of the chancel close to the east end, and shows a figure kneeling at a desk in the gown of a bachelor of divinity of Oxford, beneath a level cornice carried by Corinthian columns. On the underside of the cornice and in a frame above are the arms of Ball; argent a lion sable, on a chief sable three mullets argent. In the pavement at the south-east angle of the nave is part of a fifteenth-century slab with incised black letter inscription. In the south-east window of the chancel are a few fragments of late mediaeval glass, worked in with other pieces of eighteenth-century date, several other pieces of the latter occurring elsewhere in the church and the north porch, and in the cinquefoil in the head of the east window of the chancel.

The plate consists of a communion cup and paten of 1568, the cup having two bands of incised ornament, a circular saucer with embossed ornament of 1662, a cup of 1725, and a small paten of 1794. There is also a modern plated flagon. The Elizabethan paten and the saucer are not used, but kept for safety in a London bank. There are three bells—the treble of 1674, with the name of John Fleet, churchwarden, and the founder's initials W. E., the second blank, and the tenor a mediaeval bell by Roger Landon, inscribed Sancta Maria Ora Pro Nobis, with Landon's lion's face, founder's shield, groat, and cross.

The registers might serve as a model for many parishes. All are carefully and strongly bound up, with a transcript in the same cover, and an index of contents. The first book runs from 1538 to 1653, with a gap 1641–7, the second from 1684 to 1746, and the third, dealing with burials in woollen, from 1678 to 1746. The entries for the years between the first and second volumes, 1653–84, are in a separate book. The fourth and fifth books contain baptisms and burials from 1747 to 1807, and marriages to 1753, the sixth is the printed book of marriages 1754–1812, and a seventh has the baptisms and burials to 1812.

The small church of *ST. HUBERT, IDSWORTH*, stands in the middle of a field, at some distance from the nearest road, and separated from it by the shallow grass-grown channel of a periodical stream known as the Lavant.

It has a chancel 20 ft. 2 in. long and 16 ft. 2 in. wide, and a nave 33 ft. 8 in. by 20 ft., with a wooden bell-turret over the east end of the nave, and a west porch of brick and flint. The north and west walls of the nave are of twelfth-century date, and the chancel, whose north wall is continuous with that of the nave, is probably of the thirteenth century, having been built round the twelfth-century chancel. The width of the nave and chancel thus became equal, and remained so till the nave was widened southward in the sixteenth century, throwing the west doorway and chancel arch out of centre with it. A curious feature is the small twelfth-century arch, only 21 in. wide, at the east end of the north wall of the nave, and now blocked up. Its inner face is hidden by the pulpit, which stands in the north-east angle, and its original purpose can only be guessed at, though it must have opened to some small building, whether turret, porch, or chapel, set against the north wall of the church. (*See* Hamble for a similar feature.)

The east window of the chancel has lost its tracery and is filled with a wooden frame, but the jambs and rear arch are old, and are covered with fourteenth-century paintings, figures of St. Peter and St. Paul on the jambs, and two angels on the soffit of the arch. In the south wall is a square-headed door, of no great

[134] It has an incised sun-dial on its arch, the external jambs being modern.

age in its present shape, and on the outer face of the north wall a window of two uncusped lights is to be seen, anciently blocked, as on the inner face of the wall where it should show is a large late thirteenth-century wall painting in two tiers, the upper representing St. Hubert taming the Lycanthrope, a man-headed monster, and the lower the story of the death of St. John the Baptist. On the lower parts of the painting are a number of scratched inscriptions of the fifteenth and sixteenth centuries, among others the name of St. Hubert and a Latin inscription of several lines to our Lady. The chancel arch is pointed, of one order with a chamfer on the edge. The nave is lighted from the north by two 'churchwarden' windows with wooden frames, and from the south by two square-headed sixteenth-century windows, each of two four-centred lights without cusps. In the west wall, set centrally with the nave before its southward enlargement, is a pointed doorway, probably of the fourteenth century, and over it a small eighteenth-century porch of flint and brick. Externally there is little detail. The earliest walling on the north side of the church is of regularly-set flintwork, the sixteenth-century masonry on the south side being of coarser rubble with sandstone quoins, on one of which is an incised sun-dial. The roofs are red-tiled, and the bell-turret has a short spire finished with a copper ball. The church is ceiled on the underside of the rafters, the tie-beams being cased with eighteenth-century boarding. There is a west gallery to the nave, and the seating remains much as it was at the end of the eighteenth century, with high box-pews at the east end of the nave, and narrow upright benches of the most uncomfortable description towards the west. Below the bell-turret the nave is ceiled at the level of the tie-beams, access to the loft thus formed being by a trap-door at the south end, but whether this arrangement is as old as the widening of the nave is not clear.[135] The pulpit is of early seventeenth-century date, with arched panels and scrolled brackets to the book-board, but it has been repaired in the eighteenth century, and the tester above seems to be of this date, as well as other details. The font is octagonal with quatrefoiled panels on the bowl, exactly like that at Chalton, and doubtless of the same date. In the turret is one bell, uninscribed.

ADVOWSONS The advowson of the church of *CHALTON* probably belonged to the various lords of the manor of Chalton until 1102, when Robert de Belesme earl of Shrewsbury and Arundel was expelled from the country and deprived of all his honours and estates. As has been shown above, Henry I granted the manor as parcel of the honour of Leicester to Robert de Beaumont, but retained the advowson, which remained with the crown until the reign of Henry II, who granted it to the 'abbey which Robert earl of Leicester had made and founded at Eiton' (Nuneaton, co. Warw.).[136] From this time the prioress, prior, and convent of Nuneaton were patrons of the church,[137] and received from it an annual pension of 9 marks.[138] After the dissolution the advowson remained the property of the crown[139] until 1613, when, on the death of Thomas Nevill, Edward earl of Worcester presented Richard Ball, alleging that the advowson had been included in the grant of the manor made by Henry VIII in 1542 to William earl of Southampton in tail male with contingent remainder to William, Lord Herbert,[140] who succeeded to the peerage as earl of Worcester in 1549. The king presented William Todd the same year, and on the bishop's refusal to admit him brought a *quare impedit* against the bishop, the earl, and Richard Ball for preventing him from presenting to the church. The following year, however, he unaccountably stayed all proceedings, and by letters patent confirmed the estate which Richard had in the church.[141] The title of the earl was confirmed in 1618, when James I granted the advowson to him and his heirs and pardoned 'all intrusions, invasions, and ingresses of, in, or on it, made heretofore by him or William, Lord Herbert, without legal right or title.'[142] On the death of Richard Ball in 1632, Godfrey Price was presented by Charles Jones and William Morgan, to whom the earl had granted the next voidance of the church by a deed dated 1626.[143] Charles I, however, presented William Todd, and while the case was proceeding between him and the earl the living was served by two curates appointed by the bishop, whose wages were paid by the sequestrators out of the corn from the glebe-land.[144] Ultimately Dr. George Gillingham, the king's chaplain, made a private arrangement with Godfrey Price, and recovered the king's right to the rectory from 'the hands of a powerful adversary,' for which service he was promised the nomination of his successor.[145] In 1645 the advowson was granted to Oliver Cromwell,[146] who deprived Dr. Gillingham of the rectory and presented John Audley in his stead. Dr. Gillingham was persecuted from place to place and took shelter for some time at Southampton, but was at last driven thence likewise. However, he outlived his troubles, and at the Restoration was reappointed; 'John Audley, intruder, being turned out.'[147] On his resignation in 1668 Charles II presented Dr. Gillingham's son-in-law. Dr. Barker, in answer to his petition.[148] In the same year Henry marquis of Worcester petitioned for a regrant of the advowson,[149] but did not obtain it until 1670, in which year the king settled it on him and his heirs for ever after the death or removal of Dr. Barker.[150] The advowson then followed the descent of the manor until early in the nineteenth century,[151] when Jervoise Clarke-Jervoise sold it to King's College, Cambridge. The latter sold it towards the end of the last century, and it is at present in the gift of Mrs. Pearson Strange.

IDSWORTH was originally a chapelry dependent

135 On its west face are the royal arms of Geo. III.

136 Dugdale, *Mon.* (2nd ed.), i, p. 519. This gift was confirmed by Pope Alexander III (ibid. p. 520).

137 Egerton MS. 2033, fol. 9, and Egerton MS. 2034, fol. 36 and 73; *Wykeham's Reg.* (Hants Rec. Soc.), i, 183 and 199.

138 Egerton MS. 2032, fol. 46, and *Cal. of Pap. Pet.* i, 330.

139 In spite of the letters patent of 1558, granting it to John bishop of Winchester (Pat. 5 & 6 Phil. and Mary, pt. 4, m. 6 and 7), and the letters patent of concealment of 1576, granting it to John Farneham. Thus Queen Elizabeth presented John Constantine in 1583, and Thomas Nevill in 1584.

140 Exch. Bills and Answs. Hants, Chas. I, No. 49.

141 Ibid.

142 Ibid. Pat. 15 Jas. I, pt. 17, No. 3.

143 Exch. Bills and Answs. Hants, Chas. I, No. 49.

144 Exch. Dec. and Ord. Mich. 8 Chas. I, (Ser. 3), xii, fols. 211 and 212.

145 *Cal. of S.P. Dom.* 1668–9, pp. 93 and 113.

146 Pat. 21 Chas. I, pt. 1, m. 74.

147 Chalton parish registers.

148 *Cal. of S.P. Dom.* 1668–9, pp. 93 and 98.

149 Ibid. pp. 113 and 438.

150 Ibid. 1670, pp. 36 and 143.

151 Inst. Bks. (P.R.O.).

on the mother-church of Chalton. Hence a dispute concerning the advowson arose in 1275 between Henry de Bonynges, lord of the manor of Idsworth, who claimed it as an appurtenance of Idsworth manor, and the prioress of Nuneaton, who made good her right as patron of Chalton church, and therefore of the appendant chapel.[152] The rectors of Chalton were bound from very early times to find a chaplain at the chapel of St. Peter Idsworth[153] to say mass on Sundays, Wednesdays, and Fridays, and on double feasts throughout the year, and to administer the sacraments and other rites (except the burial of the dead) for the inhabitants of the hamlets of Idsworth and Dene (Horndean, or perhaps Finchdean).[154] Sir William Haughe, rector of the church of Chalton, discontinued this practice in 1394, and accordingly proceedings were taken against him in the Court of Arches by Richard Romyn, lord of Idsworth manor, and the rest of the inhabitants of the two villages before Thomas Stowe and Adam Uske, who decided that the rector was liable by custom to find a chaplain to minister in Idsworth Chapel. This sentence was published by the bishop of Winchester on 1 May, 1398, and confirmed by the prior and chapter of Winchester on 3 June following.[155]

In early times there was a chapel in Wellsworth. It is included in a list of churches and chapels in Hampshire made while Wykeham was bishop, was then not assessed *propter exilitatem*, but was burdened with a pension of 8*s.* 9½*d.* to Southwick Priory.[156]

CHARITIES Stanstead College, which was founded by Mr. Charles Dixon, of Stanstead Park (Suss.), by deed 1852, for the support and benefit of decayed merchants of London, Liverpool, or Bristol, being members of the Church of England, is situated in this parish. The college is regulated by schemes of the Charity Commissioners, dated 24 December, 1875, and 8 May, 1877. The official trustees hold the trust funds, which consist of £2,098 18*s.* 1*d.* bank stock, £9,000 colonial securities, and £4,000 Indian railway securities, producing an annual income of £588 16*s.* 10*d.*

CLANFIELD

Clenefeld and Clanefeud (xiii cent.); Clanefelde (xiv cent.), and Clanffield (xvii cent.).

Clanfield is a small parish with an area of 1,404 acres, shut in on the north and east by great chains of downs, being bounded on the north by Tegdown Hill, Oxenbourn Down, and Hilhampton Down, and on the east by Holt Down, Chalton Down, and Windmill Hill. The main road from Petersfield to Portsmouth runs through the east of the parish, keeping parallel with the line of downs which forms its eastern boundary. The village itself, dominated by Windmill Hill, which, capped by its windmill, towers to the east, is grouped round the cross-roads in the extreme west of the parish, and consists of a collection of half-timbered thatched farm-houses and cottages which, though somewhat out of repair, are of picturesque appearance. A little road which runs north past the New Inn has the thatched post office on one side and the village police-station on the other. The church of St. James, with a widely spreading yew in the churchyard, stands to the south of the cross-roads. Near it is the village well, with its dilapidated thatched roof. The schools stand to the south of the village at the junction of South Lane with the road leading to Hambledon. There is a small Wesleyan chapel in the parish.

The parish contains 989½ acres of arable land, and 248 acres of permanent grass.[1] The soil is light and dry, the subsoil chalk. The chief crops are wheat,

View in Clanfield Village

[152] De Banc. R. No. 11, m. 22.

[153] Its dedication has since been changed to that of St. Hubert.

[154] *Wykeham's Reg.* (Hants Rec. Soc.), ii, 481.

[155] Ibid.

[156] Ibid. i, 371.

[1] Statistics from Board of Agriculture (1905).

barley, and oats. Clanfield Down was inclosed in 1816. The population in 1901 was 213. The parish is wholly within the manor of Chalton (q.v.).

CHURCH

The church of *ST. JAMES, CLANFIELD*, was rebuilt in 1875 in brick with an external facing of flint and wrought stone, and consists of chancel with north vestry and organ chamber, and nave with south porch and west bell turret. It contains nothing ancient, but the two bells in the turret are both mediaeval, the work of Roger Landon. The treble has his founder's mark, his cross, and the lion's face, but no inscription, and the tenor is inscribed 'Ave Maria' in black letter capitals and smalls, with the three marks as on the treble.

The plate consists of a communion cup of 1672, with a band of ornament of Elizabethan type on the bowl, and a modern paten.

The registers, in two books bound together, begin in 1547, the first book ending in 1748, and the second in 1799.

There are burials in woollen from 1675 to 1735.

ADVOWSON

CLANFIELD seems in origin to have been a chapelry dependent on the mother church of Chalton. The first mention of it is in 1227, in which year Sybil, prioress of Nuneaton, arraigned an assize of darrein presentment to the chapel of Clanfield against Bartholomew, archdeacon of Winchester.[2] She proved her right to the advowson, but nevertheless had some difficulty in maintaining it, for a year later she summoned Alan, the official of the bishop of Winchester, for not having admitted a fit person at her presentation to the chapel.[3] By 1318 the chapelry had become a rectory, for in that year licence was granted to Walter de Mursele, rector of the church of Clanfield, to study at Oxford or elsewhere in England for a year.[4] Sybil evidently won her suit against Alan, for the prior, prioress, and convent of Nuneaton were patrons of the church until the dissolution,[5] from which time the advowson followed that of Chalton. In 1617 Giles Williams, incumbent of the church of Clanfield, by presentation of Queen Elizabeth, resigned the church by agreement with the earl of Worcester, during the vacancy of the see of Winchester, to George, archbishop of Canterbury.[6] The earl thereupon presented John Heathe, whose right to the church was confirmed by James I when he settled the advowson on the earl and his heirs.[7] The right of the crown to the rectory was re-established when Dr. Gillingham by private agreement with Godfrey Price, rector of Chalton, regained the advowson of Chalton for Charles I.[8] The advowson of Clanfield subsequently followed that of Chalton until 1787, in which year the rectory of Clanfield was united to that of Chalton with Idsworth chapelry by Brownlow North, bishop of Winchester.

CHARITIES

John Richards by will proved in 1846 left £200 to be invested, and income applied at the discretion of the rector for the benefit of the poor. The legacy was invested in £206 9*s.* 1*d.* Consols, with the official trustees. In 1905 the dividends, amounting to £5 3*s.*, were applied in the distribution of coals to six deserving persons.

PETERSFIELD

Petrefeld and Peterfeud, xiii cent.; Petresfeld, xiv cent.

The town of Petersfield is situated near the centre of the parish of Petersfield, in the midst of an extensive agricultural district, forming one of the most picturesque portions of Hampshire. Some two and a half miles to the south-west is Butser Hill (889 ft.), the highest point in the county, with the South Downs stretching away eastward in a long line, while on the north-west, at much closer range, the steep wooded slopes of Stoner Hill (770 ft.) and Wheatham Hill (813 ft.) look down on the town. To the east the ground is lower, the upper waters of the Rother running at no great distance, though the main stream is never actually within the parish boundaries. Three of its tributaries flow through the parish: the Tilmore Brook, which rises just beyond its eastern boundary at Stroud Common, passing through the town north of the High Street; a second stream running just to the south, and crossed by the Portsmouth road at Fore Bridge, in the south-east corner of the town; while a third is in the south of the parish, rising in Buriton, and skirting the grounds of Nursted House. The London and Portsmouth road passes through the east side of the town, and on the north side is the main road to Winchester, joined a little way west of the town by the road to Alresford. The importance of Petersfield as a market town is much increased by the existence of its railway station on the direct Portsmouth line of the London and South Western Railway, which is also the junction for a branch line from Midhurst and Rogate. Before the coming of the railway the town was a great posting-centre, as may be judged from the number of inns mentioned in the rent-rolls of the eighteenth century.[1] The plan of Petersfield is like that of most English boroughs of mediaeval origin—a central square with the principal streets radiating from it—High Street and St. Peter's Road to the east, Chapel Street to the north, and Sheep Street to the west. On the south side of the square stands St. Peter's church, until lately separated from it by the town hall erected in 1824, and adjoining buildings. In 1898 they were pulled down by Mr. William Nicholson and Lord Hylton, and although the spot has lost something of its old-time quaintness, the church stands out as it never did before. On the east, at the corner of the High Street, is the Corn Exchange, a white brick building erected in 1866. In the centre of the square is a fine equestrian statue of William III, the money for which

[2] Pat. 11 Hen. III, m. 2 *d.*

[3] *Bracton's Note Bk.* ii, 229.

[4] *Winton. Epis. Reg.* (Hants Rec. Soc.), 203.

[5] Ibid. 523 ?, 16; Egerton MS. 2032, fol. 47 and 134; Egerton MS. 2033, fol. 9; Egerton MS. 2034, fol. 36; *Wykeham's Reg.* (Hants Rec. Soc.), 201, 222 and 226.

[6] Exch. Bills and Answs. Hants, Chas. I, No. 49.

[7] Pat. 15 Jas. I, pt. 17, No. 3.

[8] *Cal. of S.P. Dom.* 1668–9, p. 93. It was one of the two 'livings adjacent.'

[1] Nine inns are mentioned in a rent-roll of 1696–7: the White Hart, the Anchor, the Lion, the Half Moon, the Crown, the Swan, the Dragon, the Ship, and the George (Add. R. 19779).

was left in March, 1750, by Sir William Jolliffe, M.P. for Petersfield, a great admirer of that monarch as the 'avenger of liberty.' The statue stood first in the courtyard of Petersfield House, which was for over sixty years the seat of the Jolliffe family in Petersfield,[2] and it was not until its demolition in 1793 that it was removed to its present position. At one time both the horse and the rider were gilded, and the Golden Horse Inn, on the east side of the square, owes its name to the fact. At the south-west angle of the square is Castle House, architecturally the most interesting domestic building in the town. It dates from the early years of the seventeenth century, retaining the mediaeval arrangement of a central block representing the hall, with wings at right angles to it at each end, but for the rest the old disposition of rooms is abandoned. The entrance is in the middle of the central block, and on either side are projecting rooms filling the angles between it and the wings, and representing the bay window and entrance porch of the mediaeval hall. Here the hall has become a mere central lobby, and the chief living-rooms are in the north wing, on the ground and first floors. Fortunately a great deal of the original panelling and several fine chimney-pieces are preserved, though under a coat of white paint. The house is of two stories with an attic, with a kitchen yard and offices on the north, and a long garden on the west. The front of the house is much overgrown with ivy, and plastered, and the replacement of the mullioned windows by sashes detracts from the general effect; but the hipped roofs and recessed front, and the wrought-iron entrance gateway to the little forecourt, are enough to make it the chief architectural feature of the square. On the jambs of the entrance doorway are the initials E M and W M, which are doubtless those of the first owner. The house was purchased about the middle of the seventeenth century by the Bilson family, and in a deed of 1678 is described as a capital messuage and dwelling-house in Petersfield, in the occupation of Sir John Biggs.[3] In 1713 Dame Susanna Bilson of Mapledurham, widow, and Leonard Bilson of Mapledurham sold it for £300 to Robert Love of Basing in the parish of Froxfield.[4] In the deed of sale it is described as 'all that capital messuage with another messuage adjoining, lately in the tenure or occupation of John Corps and Robert Brett, situated in the borough of Petersfield, bounded by the Market-place and High Street on the east, by Parsonage Lane on the north, and on the south by the messuages and gardens of William Heather, Richard Cowper, Thomas Westbrook, William Layfield, John Woolgar, Nicholas Page, senior, Nicholas Page, junior, and others.' Seven years later Robert sold it to Edmund Miller of Serjeants Inn, serjeant-at-law, together with the pews or seats in the church of Petersfield, formerly used or enjoyed by the inhabitants of the messuage. The price he obtained was £620, a considerable advance on the sum for which he had purchased it.[5] Baron Miller, by his will dated 30 October, 1729, left all his estates in Norfolk, Hampshire, Middlesex, and London to his nephew Richard Hassell of Lincoln's Inn in tail-male, with contingent remainder to his nephew John Hassell. Eleven years later Richard and John sold the messuage described as being in the tenure of Browne Langrish, doctor of physic,[6] together with a great deal of other property in Petersfield, to John Jolliffe.[7] Castle House remained in the possession of the Jolliffe family for over fifty years, being finally let on a 999 years' lease [8] about the end of the eighteenth century to Mr. Carter, lord of the manor of Mapledurham. Eventually it became a boys' school, and was used for this purpose until about eight years ago. It next became the residence of the Right Rev. the Hon. Arthur Temple Lyttelton, D.D., bishop of Southampton, who died 19 February, 1903. It is at the present time occupied by the Rev. E. M. Tomlinson, M.A., formerly vicar of East Meon.

Sheep Street leads from the Square to the Spain,

THE MARKET PLACE, PETERSFIELD

[2] Mr. John Jolliffe built Petersfield House in the Lawn where was previously the residence of his father-in-law, Mr. Robert Michell. It was a fine red-brick mansion with stone facings of the style of Queen Anne. It occupied the site of the schools and the police-station between St. Peter's Road and Hylton Road, and traces of artificial canals can still be seen. When the house was pulled down in 1793, owing to parish disputes, the entrance-gates of Sussex iron were removed to Merstham House, Redhill, where they are at the present day.

[3] Deeds *penes* Lord Dartmouth.

[4] Ibid. Lord Hylton.

[5] Ibid.

[6] Browne Langrish was a celebrated physician of the eighteenth century. He was elected a fellow of the Royal Society, 1734. He delivered the Cromian Lectures on Muscular Motion before the Royal Society in 1747, and published them 1748. He died at Basingstoke in 1759. His works include: *A New Essay on Muscular Motion, The Modern Theory and Practice of Physic, Physical Experiments on Brutes*, and *Plain Directions in regard to the Small-pox.*

[7] Deeds *penes* Lord Hylton.

[8] Lord Hylton still receives a quit-rent for it.

a tranquil old-fashioned thoroughfare said to be so-called from the Spanish merchants who resorted there for wool-dealing.[9] Hylton Road[10] runs eastwards from the Spain, and crossing the Portsmouth road at Fore Bridge, becomes Sussex Road, skirting the south side of the Heath Pond. The last house in the town to the north of the road is the vicarage. From the north-west corner of the Spain a road leads to the Borough and Borough Hill, close to which runs the railway.

There is no lack of good eighteenth-century brick-work in the town, especially on the north side of the market square; and on the south side of High Street is a timber front (No. 19) with a moulded beam beneath the gables having pendants below, on one of which is the date 1613. This house has some good seventeenth-century panelling and a chimney-piece in the ground-floor room to the right of the entrance.

In the east of the town are several picturesque groups of houses, along Dragon Street[11] and College Street—in the latter the fine red-brick buildings of Churcher's College, 1722,[12] and the blocked stone-arched doorways of Antrobus's Almshouses, 1622—now part of a brewery—are the chief attractions.

The Heath, a large public recreation ground in the east of the town, was formed from wet swampy ground in 1867, and comprises 35 acres in the parish of Sheet, 4 acres in the parish of Buriton, and 5 acres in the parish of Petersfield. The formation of the large lake within it, which covers an area of 22 acres, and lies half in Petersfield manor and half in Mapledurham manor, was the result of certain drainage operations in 1750. The Heath House, the residence of Captain the Hon. William Sydney Hylton-Jolliffe, D.L., J.P., is about half a mile south-east.

Petersfield parish covers an area of 1,609 acres of land and 23 acres of water.[13] Sheet, which was a tithing in the parish, is now a separate parish containing 1,350 acres of land and 8 of water.[14] Adhurst St. Mary, the seat of Mr. George Lothian Bonham-Carter, a mansion in the Elizabethan style, erected in 1858 and enlarged in 1902–3, stands in well-wooded grounds to the north of the road from Godalming to Petersfield. The river Rother intersects Sheet, and on it are two mills called Sheetbridge Mill and Sheet Mill, the latter of which certainly represents one of the mills entered under 'Malpedresham' in Domesday Book.[15] The common fields in Petersfield and Sheet were inclosed by authority of an Act of Parliament, 18 & 19 Vic. cap. 61. Among place-names mentioned in the sixteenth century are Bullockes Leses,[16] Whit-redden,[17] Chappelfields,[18] Berelands, and Polehill.[19]

PETERSFIELD BOROUGH is a mesne borough, its descent being identical with that of the manor of Petersfield. In the reign of Henry II, William earl of Gloucester granted to the burgesses of Petersfield all the liberties and free customs enjoyed by the citizens of Winchester, and to have a merchant gild. These privileges were confirmed by the charter of his widow Hawise. The charter of the earl is lost, but that of the countess is still preserved.[20] King John, when count of Mortain, confirmed the same liberties and free customs to the burgesses in 1198,[21] and in 1415 Henry V granted them freedom from toll, stallage, picage, pannage, murage, and pontage throughout the realm of England.[22] While Maud countess of Buckingham was lady of the borough,[23] a sum of two marks was exacted every year from the burgesses under colour of a payment *pro certo lete*, but in 1440 Humphrey earl of Buckingham by letters patent granted to the burgesses of his lordship of Petersfield release for ever from that payment.[24] That the burgesses were afterwards quit from this payment is supported by entries in the accounts of successive reeves of Petersfield.[25] It has not been ascertained by what authority the burgesses of Petersfield assumed the corporate name

9 A sheep-market was formerly held in Sheep Street, and a horse-market in the Spain; see *A History of Petersfield*, by Rev. J. Williams, p. 34.

10 The following description from the Rev. J. Williams's *History* is interesting:—'What is now Hylton Road was a street 150 years ago, with small houses on each side, and by the little stream were tan-pits. These houses were pulled down to make the grounds for the house that Mr. John Jolliffe built' (Petersfield House).

11 So called from the Green Dragon Inn, now gone.

12 No longer in use for their original purpose; the new college buildings lie to the north-east on Ramshill.

13 The parish contains 340 acres of arable land and 1,210 acres of permanent grass (Statistics from Board of Agriculture, 1905).

14 The parish contains 476¾ acres of arable land, 317¼ acres of permanent grass, and 192 acres of woods and plantations (Statistics from Board of Agriculture, 1905).

15 *Vide* manor of Sheet below.

16 Pat. 18 Eliz. pt. 13.

17 Chant. Cert. 30, No. 17. This name is still preserved as White Readins.

18 Chan. Inq. p.m. Misc. dxxxvii, No. 13.

19 Pat. 37 Hen. VIII, pt. 1, m. 8.

20 The charter is preserved in the offices of the Petersfield Urban District Council, and runs as follows:—'Ego Hawisia comitissa Gloecestrie concessi et confirmavi burgensibus meis de Peteresfeld, qui in burgo de Peteresfeld edificaverunt et manent, que qui in illo edificabunt, omnes libertates et liberas consuetudines in eodem burgo quas homines Wintonie habent in civitate sua qui sunt in gilda mercatorum et easdem habeant in gilda mercatorum de Petrisfeld . . . meus Willelmus comes Gloecestrie eis per cartam suam concessit.'

21 His charter, which is also preserved in the offices of the Petersfield Urban District Council, is in exactly similar terms.

22 Close, 3 Hen. V, m. 20.

23 This lady's name is usually given as Anne. She was the wife of Edmund Stafford, earl of Stafford, who died in 1403, and had by him a son and heir Humphrey, aged one year at his father's death. She was probably called the lady of the borough of Petersfield during the minority of Humphrey. She died in 1438 (G. E. C. *Complete Peerage*, vii, 211).

24 The letters patent are also preserved in the offices of the Urban District Council; they are as follows:—'Humfridus comes Bukyngham, Hereford, Stafford, etc., omnibus, etc., cum quedam pensio duarum marcarum de burgensibus dominii de Peteresfeld in comitatu Southton per quandam Matildam dudum dominam ibidem tempore ipsius comitisse tantum et non antea neque postea, ut per evidencias duorum burgensium inde nobis et consilio nostro ostensas evidenter apparet, minus juste levata et ad duos dies legales nomine cuiusdam certi capta extitisset, nos, nolentes quod aliqua injuria burgensibus nostris de Petresfeld predictis seu quibuscunque aliis ex parte nostra fieret, concessimus et concedimus pro nobis et heredibus nostris prefatis burgensibus nostris de Petresfeld, quod ipsi et heredes eorum de huiusmodi annua pensione sive certo, ut profertur, tempore dicte nuper comitisse minus juste capta et levata, erga nos et heredes ac officiarios nostros omnino sint quieti et penitus exonerati in perpetuum per presentes, salvis semper et reservatis nobis et heredibus nostris omnibus aliis redditibus et serviciis quibuscunque per ipsos nostros burgenses et eorum heredes ac antecessores suos dicto dominio nostro antiquitus debitis et consuetis, et omnibus aliis juribus nostris prout ab antiquo ibidem ante hec tempora juste fieri, levari, et reddi consueverunt, volentes quod receptores et auditores compotorum nostrorum ibidem qui sunt vel qui pro tempore erunt dictos burgenses nostros et eorum heredes de supradicta pensione sive certo duarum marcarum solvenda ad duos dies legales supradictos quietos et exoneratos faciant, ipsos contra tenorem harum brevium patentium ea de causa non molestantes.'

25 Add. R. 27679 and 27680.

and style of 'the mayor and burgesses' or 'the mayor and commonalty,' but most probably their right was prescriptive. Mr. Illingworth, deputy-keeper of the records in the Tower, made a careful search in the various depositories of public records in the early part of the eighteenth century, but failed to find any royal charter of incorporation, although the draft of a charter from James I incorporating the inhabitants was for many years in the possession of the Gibbon family, and is possibly still extant. It is probable that Thomas Hanbury, lord of the borough at that date, to whose advantage it was that the burgesses should receive no charter of incorporation, exerted his influence as an auditor of the Exchequer to prevent the completion of the grant. From the Petersfield court rolls of the latter part of the sixteenth century it appears that the various officers of the borough were elected in the court leet of the manor, and at that time included a mayor, a constable, a bailiff, two aldermen or tithing men, ale-tasters, and sometimes two leather sealers.[26] The burgesses of Petersfield undoubtedly enjoyed many privileges and, besides exercising the elective franchise, acted in a corporate capacity by taking and making grants of lands and of rents charged on lands.[27] Under the Tudors, especially, the borough seems to have grown steadily in importance, its increase in prosperity no doubt being due to the development of its cloth and leather manufactures, to both of which industries its cattle market gave rise. A significant entry occurs in the account of the reeve of Petersfield for 1428 to the effect that he had received nothing from the miller of 'Wadeleshall,' near Petersfield, for licence to carry corn from the borough to his mill, because the mill had recently been turned into a fulling-mill.[28]

Most of the court rolls give evidence of the industries of the burgesses, particularly with regard to the trade of tanning,[29] and in nearly every roll occurs a list of tanners fined 'for using fraud in their trade.' The manufacture of cloth, however, was the principal industry of the inhabitants, and by the reign of James I had grown to such dimensions that it maintained 1,000 poor people in work without begging.[30] The general prosperity of the place at this time may be judged from the fact that 'forty men for the service of the realm in the wars were maintained at the public charge, besides every man's private charge.'[31] With this increase in prosperity came a desire for greater independence on the part of the burgesses. During the fifteenth and sixteenth centuries it seems to have become the rule for the lords of the borough to accept from the mayor and burgesses £7 1*s.* 2*d.* for the rent of the borough, 16*s.* for fairs and markets, and diverse sums of money, sometimes more and sometimes less, for profits and perquisites of court.[32] These sums came to be looked upon by the burgesses as a fee-farm rent.[33] Further, the mayor and burgesses caused houses to be erected on fit and convenient places in the borough, which they let for money-rents, and held the three weeks' courts themselves. They also sometimes seized felons' goods to their own use.[34] The mayor and burgesses moreover came to be accounted owners of the fairs and markets, and collected toll, picage, and stallage from those resorting to them. In short, they seem to have acted very much as they pleased while Sir Henry Weston and Sir Richard Weston, who were members of a Surrey family, and never seem to have lived near Petersfield, were lords of the borough. However, everything was changed when Thomas Hanbury, who lived in the neighbouring parish of Buriton, purchased the borough in 1597. He determined to maintain his rights,[35] and appointed William Yalden steward for the keeping of courts and leets within the borough, and Anthony Rouse and Lawrence Patrick collectors of picage and stallage.[36] Naturally the burgesses resisted, and on 20 October, 1601, when William Yalden went to the town hall to keep the three weeks' court in the name of the lord of the borough, 'he was prevented from doing so by Robert Tolderton *alias* Pynner, the mayor, who commanded Francis Clement to thrust him out of the room, which he did with great violence once or twice.[37] The collectors of picage and stallage were moreover hindered in the execution of their duties by the burgesses, who, in addition, refused to pay any rents for the borough save as a fee-farm rent. At length, in Easter, 1608, Thomas Hanbury filed his bill in the Court of Exchequer, setting forth that Roger Tirrell, John Colebrooke, William Pagglesham, Gregory Triggs, James Mills, John Salter, Gregory Page, and William Ford, who 'unjustly pretended themselves to be burgesses of the borough of Petersfield,' having got into their possession sundry documents belonging to him, had unlawfully entered upon waste grounds in the borough

[26] Add. R. 28010 and 28017. No earlier court rolls of Petersfield seem to have been preserved.

[27] The rents and profits of these estates were appropriated to the general use of the inhabitants of the borough. In the offices of the Urban District Council is still preserved a deed of 1373 whereby Robert la Vowel of Langrish and Alice his wife granted in fee to the burgesses of Petersfield a rent of 12*d.* issuing out of a tenement held by Nicholas Colebrooke at Stoneham. Several other deeds also are preserved whereby the mayor and burgesses leased out lands to various persons.

[28] Add. R. 26871.

[29] On a court roll of 1603 occurs a presentment against certain persons for polluting the river and throwing their sheepskins into it (Add. R. 28012). A similar entry occurs on a court roll of the same year. Again in 1605 John Mylls, Roger Terrell, and others were warned not to wash their inwards and Lawrence Gudge his dossers, 'to the great annoyance of a great many poor men,' in the brook in the Brook Lane under penalty for each offence 3*s.* 4*d.* (Add. R. 28015).

[30] Exch. Bills and Answs. Hants, Jas. I, No. 220, m. 2.

[31] Ibid.

[32] Add. R. 27679.

[33] They asserted that the borough and markets, &c., had been granted to them at fee-farm by charter. The statement on an inquisition of 1307, that the burgesses of Petersfield rendered every year £7 1*s.* 6*d.* rents of assize, £2 10*s.* toll, and 5*s.* pleas and perquisites of court, rather supports this (Inq. p.m. 35 Edw. I, pt. 2, No. 47). On the other hand, in other documents of the thirteenth, fourteenth, and fifteenth centuries, the value of the borough varies between £7 and £19.

[34] Once it came to Sir Henry Weston's knowledge that Thomas Westbrooke, while mayor of Petersfield, had seized a mare as felon's goods. He thereupon wrote a letter to Thomas demanding the mare as his property, and Thomas was forced to surrender it to him (Exch. Dep. Hants, 6 Jas. I, Mich. No. 1). After this the mayor seems, as a matter of course, to have delivered all felons' goods to the lord of the borough. Thus on a court roll of 1607, occurs an entry to the effect that, William Fyske, having killed himself feloniously within the jurisdiction of the court, his goods and chattels to the value of £18 4*s.* 9*d.* had been seized by Thomas Osborne, late reeve or mayor of the borough, to the use of Thomas Hanbury, lord of the borough, and afterwards delivered over by him to Thomas Hanbury at his dwelling-house in Buriton (Add. R. 28016).

[35] Probably the burgesses were petitioning for their incorporation charter at this date.

[36] Exch. Dep. Hants, 6 Jas. I, Mich. No. 1.

[37] Ibid.

and built upon them, 'of purpose to defraud and disinherit him of the same,' that they prevented him from keeping his courts in the borough, refused to pay him his rents and services, and lastly, that although the tolls and other profits of the fairs and markets belonged to him, yet they refused to allow those who came to the fairs and markets to have picage and stallage unless they paid toll, picage, and stallage to them; 'and that the same fairs and markets by their occasion, were like in time utterly to decay, which tended not only to his disinheritance, but was like also to turn to the prejudice and hurt of the country near adjoining the borough.' [38] On 3 May following, the defendants answered that Petersfield had time out of mind been an ancient borough, and had sent two burgesses to Parliament, that the mayor and burgesses were seised in fee simple of the borough, and had paid the fee-farm of £7 1*s.* 2*d.* to Sir Richard Weston and his ancestors for a long time, and that as owners of the borough they had built on the waste grounds within it, and had taken picage, toll, and stallage, at the fairs and markets. They, however, expressed themselves willing to pay him the fee-farm rents with the arrears, 'if he would accept thereof.' [39] Thomas Hanbury filed his replication in Trinity Term, 1608, alleging, 'That it did not appear in the defendants' answer that the mayor and burgesses of Petersfield were a body corporate, and that he was seised in fee of the borough, the rent of £7 1*s.* 2*d.* not being a fee-farm rent.' [40] In their rejoinder the defendants asserted that the mayor and burgesses had for a long time been a body corporate, 'and had used to implead and be impleaded, and to take and purchase lands by the said name.' [41] The depositions of various witnesses for both sides were taken at Petersfield on 22 September, 1608.[42] The witnesses nearly all agreed that Petersfield was an ancient borough and mayor-town, but when called upon to adduce any evidence, charter, or grant, whereby privileges or liberties had been granted to the mayor and burgesses, all of them except one declared that they had never seen or heard of any such document. The exception was William Yalden, who said that twenty-five years ago he had seen an ancient charter or parchment in the custody of the mayor and burgesses, wherein 'one Earle Marrett [43] did grant certain privileges for merchandizing to the inhabitants of the said borough.' The decree of the court was pronounced in Michaelmas Term, 1610,[44] and was completely in Hanbury's favour. It was ordered that he and his heirs should from henceforth peaceably and quietly have, hold, and enjoy the waste grounds of the borough whereon no houses were built, as also the rents of assize, the burgage-rents, duties, services, and customs, and all profits and perquisites of the courts of the borough, and the profits of the fairs and markets, and toll, picage, and stallage, without interruption or disturbance. The court, however, forbore to make any decree touching the houses built upon the waste ground of the borough, although it was of opinion that they belonged to Hanbury, but advised him to take his course for the recovery of them at the common law.[45] From the loss of this suit dates the gradual decline of the borough.

In 1652 cloth was still manufactured in Petersfield, for in that year the clothworkers and the other inhabitants of the town presented a petition to the lord of the manor of East Meon, complaining that two fulling-mills in the parish of Steep being copyholds of the manor had been suffered to fall into decay for want of repairs 'and tended to their great charge and hindrance,' [46] but the very fact that they had been thus allowed to fall into ruins shows that the industry even then was a waning one. The leather industry also probably declined at the same time, and no manufactures are carried on in Petersfield at the present day. The constitution of the borough for centuries underwent but little change. In the Herald's Visitation of Hampshire and the Isle of Wight in 1686, there is the following account of Petersfield, no doubt furnished by Thomas Hanbury the lord of the borough: 'The burrough of Petersfield is an ancient burrough, the lord whereof is Thomas Hanbury, esq., who by his steward keepeth yearly a court-leet on the Monday after St. Hillary, at which leet the jury elect a mayor and a bailiff to attend him, both out of the freeholders of the said borough, and two other officers called *Aldermanni sive "testatores panis et cervisiae,"* which execute the office of tithing-men within the said borrough, and are also chosen (*ratione tenurae*) out of the freeholders of the said borrough. At the same court is chosen a constable out of the most substantiall inhabitants, which constable is for that year one of the constables for the Hundred of Finchdean. The present mayor is John Heather, mercer, the bailiff, John Warne, the constable, Robert Betsworth. This burrough hath no charter.' The mayor and the other officers continued to be elected at the court-leet of the manor held on the first Monday in Epiphany [47] until 1885. In that year, by the Redistribution of Seats Act, the representation of the borough was merged in that of the county, and consequently the mayor, who had been the returning officer for the parliamentary borough,[48] was deprived of his sole duty. Naturally the court leet was discontinued, the sole function of which had been to elect the mayor and the other officers, whose duties had long been merely nominal. Under the provisions of the Local Government Act, 1894 (56 & 57 Vic. ch. 73), the town is now governed by an Urban District Council of nine members, which takes the place of a Local Board, established 1893.

Petersfield first sent members to Parliament in 1306–7, when two burgesses were returned,[49] but from this period it was unrepresented until 1552–3, when Sir Antony Browne and John Vaughan were returned.[50] The right of election, as established by a committee of the House of Commons in 1727, was in the freeholders of lands or ancient dwelling-houses, or shambles or dwelling-houses, or shambles built upon ancient foundations in the borough.[51] Until 1831 the number of electors was only about 140. By the Reform Act of 2 Will. IV, cap. 45, it was deprived of

38 Exch. Bills and Answs. Hants, Jas. I, No. 220, m. 1.
39 Ibid. m. 2.
40 Ibid. m. 3.
41 Ibid. m. 4.
42 Exch. Dep. 6 Jas. I, Mich. No. 1.
43 By 'Earle Marrett' he probably meant John, count of Mortain, whose charter to the burgesses of Petersfield has been given above.
44 Exch. Dec. and Ord. (Ser. 2), ix, fols. 206–10.
45 Ibid.
46 Eccl. Com. Ct. R. bdle. 99, No. 9, p. 30.
47 *Parl. Papers*, 1835, xxiv, 138, and 1880, xxxi, 102 and 251.
48 Ibid.
49 *Return of Members of Parl.* pt. 1, 26.
50 Ibid. 379.
51 Carew, *Rights of Elections*, ii, 46.

one member, and by the same Act, to save it from total disfranchisement, the parliamentary borough was extended so as to include Sheet Tithing, the whole of Buriton, Froxfield, and Liss parishes, the Hampshire part of Steep parish and the tithings of Langrish, Ramsdean, and Oxenbourn in East Meon parish. The town continued to return one member until 1885, when the representation was merged in that of the county. It is interesting to note the rather remarkable Parliamentary connexion between the Jolliffes and Petersfield, members of the family sitting for the borough with but few gaps from 1734 until 1880.

As has been shown above, William de Clare in 1255 received a grant of two yearly fairs at his manor of Petersfield, viz. on the eve, the feast, and the morrow of St. Peter and St. Paul (28, 29, and 30 June), and on the eve, the feast, and the morrow of St. Andrew (29 and 30 November and 1 December).[52] They were both held until 1902, when the summer fair, which was then held on 10 July, was abolished. The autumn fair, which is now held on 6 October (on the Heath), is for both business and pleasure, a large amount of stock of every description being brought to it. The market, which was formerly held every Saturday,[53] is now held on alternate Wednesdays in the market square, and is well attended, a good trade being done in corn, live stock, and farm produce. The market rights were purchased by the Urban District Council from Lord Hylton in 1902 for £1,000.

MANORS *PETERSFIELD* is not mentioned in the Domesday Survey by name, but it is most probably included in the entry under Mapledurham in Finchdean hundred.[54] Hence the history of the manor of Petersfield is identical with that of Mapledurham (q.v.) until 1484, when Henry second duke of Buckingham, having entered into a conspiracy to dethrone Richard III, was beheaded at Shrewsbury. His possessions thereupon passed into the hands of the king, who, on 23 May, 1484, granted the manor of Petersfield to trustees to hold for seven years for the payment of the duke's debts.[55] On 28 February, 1485, the king granted the reversion of the manor, on the expiration of this term of seven years, to his kinsman John duke of Norfolk and the heirs male of his body.[56] The duke did not live to enjoy this gift, however, for on 22 August, 1485, he was slain at Bosworth while leading the van of Richard's army.[57] On 7 November, 1485, he was attainted by Act of Parliament and all his honours were forfeited to Henry VII, who restored Petersfield to Edward son and heir of Henry duke of Buckingham, whom he had reinstated in 1486.[58] The descent of Petersfield is identical with that of Mapledurham from this date until the time of Edward Gibbon, the father of the historian, who sold it in 1739 to John Jolliffe, M.P. for Petersfield.[59] William George Hylton Jolliffe, great-grandson of the latter, was raised to the peerage as Lord Hylton in

JOLLIFFE. *Argent a pile vert with three right hands or thereon.*

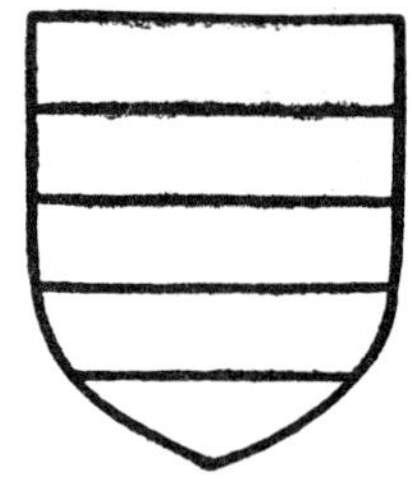

HYLTON. *Argent two bars azure.*

1866. His grandson, Hylton George, Lord Hylton, is the present lord of the manor.

SHEET (Sithe, Shite, and Schyte, xiii cent.; Shete, xv cent.; Shett, xvi cent.) formerly formed part of the great manor of Mapledurham, and was granted by Aumary, earl of Gloucester, son of Aumary, count of Evreux, to Eustace de Greinville, to hold to him and his heirs of the grantor and his heirs by the service of the third part of a knight's fee. The tenement of Richard the miller with the mill and the suit and multure of the men of the manor of Mapledurham and Petersfield was included in the grant, as also the annual payment of two cart-loads of brushwood and one sufficient tree at the Feast of St. John the Baptist from the wood for the maintenance of the mill.[60] The overlordship was changed in 1210, in which year Aumary conveyed to Peter des Roches, bishop of Winchester, all the fee which Eustace held of his gift in Mapledurham, to hold to the bishop and his successors in free alms.[61] In 1237 Eustace granted to the prior and canons of Selborne in free alms all the land which he had by the gift of his lord Aumary, earl of Gloucester, in the manor of Mapledurham with the mill, saving to the bishop the service of the third part of the knight's fee,[62] and his gift was confirmed by Peter des Roches in the same year.[63] After the death of Eustace, his widow Joan received as her dowry the third part of fourteen marks' rent from the tenement in Sheet, but this rent she quitclaimed to John prior of Selborne and his successors in 1251 on her marriage with Stephen Symeon.[64] In 1281 Prior Richard and the convent of Selborne farmed out to Abbot John and the convent of Dureford all their lands and tenements at Sheet for a rent of fourteen marks.[65] From this

52 Chart. R. 39 Hen. III, m. 3.

53 Inq. p.m. 16 Ric. II, pt. 1, No. 27; 22 Ric. II, No. 46; 4 Hen. IV, No. 41. The weekly market of Saturday was changed to the fortnightly Wednesday, *c.* 1850.

54 *V.C.H. Hants*, i, 451. Evidently from the entry the name of Mapledurham was applied to a much larger extent of land in 1086 than in later times. For instance, it was assessed at 13 hides, there were no fewer than three mills in the place, the woodland alone could support thirty swine from the pannage, and the whole was valued at £25 a year.

55 Pat. 2 Ric. II, pt. 2, m. 22.

56 Ibid.

57 G.E.C. *Complete Peerage*, vi, 46.

58 Ibid. ii, 64.

59 *The Hampshire Repository*, ii, 205; Close, 13 Geo. II, pt. 17, m. 36, &c. The Jolliffe family came originally from Leek (co. Staffs.). John Jolliffe settled in Petersfield in 1730, on his marriage with Catherine, only daughter and eventually heiress of Robert Michell, whose second wife, Jane, was the only daughter and heiress of Arthur Bold (Deeds *penes* Lord Hylton), whose family had owned property in Petersfield since the sixteenth century or even earlier. (William Bold died in 1582 seised of a messuage called The Gate House, and many other messuages and lands in Buriton, Petersfield, and Nursted, which he had purchased from Thomas Dering and others. His heir was his son William, aged seventeen, Chan. Inq. p.m. [Ser. 2], ccii, No. 186.)

60 *Selborne Chart.* (Hants Rec. Soc.), (Ser. ii), 63.

61 Ibid. In 1226 Peter confirmed to Eustace all the lands and tenements which Aumary gave him in his manor of Mapledurham (ibid. 64).

62 Ibid. 65.

63 Ibid.

64 Feet of F. Hants, Mich. 35 Hen. III.

65 *Selborne Chart.* (Hants Rec. Soc.), (Ser. ii), 67. This grant was confirmed by the king in the same year (Pat. 9 Edw. I, m. 7).

time onwards until the dissolution the abbot and convent of the Blessed Mary of Dureford continued to hold these lands and tenements, which developed into a small manor, for this fixed annual payment, and their connexion with this parish can still be traced in the names Adhurst St. Mary and St. Mary's Well. The prior and convent of Selborne sometimes had some difficulty in securing the payment of the rent, and in 1425 brought an assize of novel disseisin against Thomas abbot of Dureford and John Atte Wode about a tenement in Sheet,[66] the result of which was that the latter were forced to enter into a bond for £40 for securing the punctual payment of the fourteen marks.[67] In spite of this, however, they owed Selborne Priory over £50 fee-farm rent in 1462.[68] The abbot and convent of Dureford in their turn leased out their property in the parish at various times. Thus in 1466 they granted all their lands and tenements in Sheet, which they held at fee-farm of the prior and convent of Selborne, to Nicholas Huse and others to hold for twenty years at a rent of £9 6*s.* 8*d.*[69] Again in 1532 they leased out to Launcelot Sympson of Petersfield the site of their manor of South Sheet and all the houses built there, with all the meads, leasures, &c., as wholly as Martin Frayll held them, except one moor let to Magdalen College, to hold for the term of sixty years at a rent of 40*s.*,[70] while in the following year Richard Massam of Henley, who was probably acting for Magdalen College, obtained a ninety-nine years' lease of a moor in Sheet for a rent of 8*d.*[71] Thus at the dissolution most of the property which Dureford had held at fee-farm of Selborne[72] was let on lease. Like most of the Dureford property the manor of Sheet was granted to Sir William Fitzwilliam, afterwards earl of Southampton, in tail male,[73] and on his death without issue reverted to the king, who in 1546, in return for £1,569 15*s.* 2*d.*, granted to George Rithe and Thomas Grantham 60 acres called Martyns in Petersfield now or late in the occupation of Launcelot Sympson, together with other lands, tenements, rents, and services formerly belonging to Dureford Abbey.[74] In the same year George and Thomas sold Martyns, 10 acres of moorland in the occupation of Magdalen College, and a cottage, to Roger Childe of Sheet, described sometimes as a yeoman, and sometimes as a miller, who two years later sold the property for £42 to William Standish of Oxford and others. William was an Oxford notary who was regularly employed by the college, and no doubt he was the college agent in the purchase; but it was not until 1556 that he conveyed the property to the college,[75] the delay in conveying being probably due to the uncertainty of the time; when it was doubtful, first whether the colleges would not go the way of the monasteries, and then whether the monastic possessions might not be reclaimed. Magdalen College still owns Sheet Mill and a great deal of landed property in the parishes of Petersfield and Sheet.

HEATH HOUSE (Hethehouse, xvi cent.). In the reign of Henry III a certain Henry de Chalvers granted 'Holemed' with an aqueduct and a croft to the abbot and convent of Dureford.[76] In the same reign Aumary, earl of Gloucester, granted to Richard Talbot and his heirs his mill at 'Chalfversh,' the tenement which Warren de Chalfversh held of him, and the tenement which Sigar de Chalfversh held of him,[77] and shortly afterwards William Talbot made grants to the abbey of Dureford of lands which are not specified, but which were probably identical with those which Aumary had bestowed upon Richard.[78] In 1292 the abbot and convent were seised of 108 acres of land, 4 acres of meadow, and a mill at the Heath.[79] Hence it seems clear that these lands comprised those of Chalfversh, possibly indeed being identical with them. There is no mention of any messuage at the Heath in the survey of the lands of the monastery in 1292, but at the time of the dissolution of the monasteries the abbot and convent of Dureford were seised of the farm of Heath House[80] and lands called 'The Est Chalverishe,' parcel of the grange of Heath House.[81] At the dissolution Henry VIII granted the messuage called Heath House to Sir William Fitz-William in tail male.[82] On his death without issue in 1542 it reverted to the king, who, on 30 May, 1545, granted it to Sir Edmund Mervyn to hold to him and his heirs for ever.[83] On Edmund's death Heath House passed to his son and heir Henry Mervyn,[84] upon whom it was settled in 1555.[85] In 1613 Henry Mervyn, senior, and Henry Mervyn, junior, and others released all right which they had in the capital messuage called Heath House and closes called 'Chalveries' and 'Hollwaies' to Thomas Bilson, bishop of Winchester,[86] the owner of the manor of West Mapledurham, who died seised of them in 1616.[87] Its subsequent history is obscure, but it is perhaps identical with Heath House Farm, which Edward Rookes left by will in 1694 to his son Edward, with contingent remainder to his brother-in-law, Edward Hunt.[88]

MERVYN. *Sable three leopards parted palewise or and argent.*

[66] *Selborne Chart.* (Hants Rec. Soc.), ser. ii. 71.
[67] Ibid.
[68] Ibid. (Ser. 1), 115.
[69] Ibid. (Ser. 2), 71.
[70] Ibid. 72.
[71] Ibid.
[72] The fee-farm rent ought to have passed to Magdalen College with the other property of Selborne, but it is uncertain whether the college ever established its claim to the rent under the deed of 1281.
[73] Pat. 29 Hen. VIII, pt. 1, m. 22. The manor is not mentioned by name in the grant, but it must have been included in it, as the earl held courts at Sheet in 1538 and 1539 (Add. R. 28228).
[74] Pat. 37 Hen. VIII, pt. 1, m. 38. In the ministers' accounts the manor of Sheet is not mentioned by name, but it is probably represented by the entry :—rents of assize in Petersfield coming from tenements called Berelonds, Athurst, Sandhurst, Bonneyslonde, Knyghts, Marteyns, &c. (Mins. Accts. Suss. 29 Hen. VIII, 109, m. 17 *d.*). It has been shown that in 1532 Dureford leased out to Lancelot Sympson the site of the manor of South Sheet formerly held by Martin Frayll. This site was afterwards called Martyns, and was probably identical with the land let out to Dureford in 1281. Probably the right to the manor depended on the possession of Martyns. The rest of the property was granted to other people, and thus the manor was broken up.
[75] Ex inform. the librarian and the estates bursar of Magdalen College, Oxford.
[76] Cott. MS. Vesp. E. xxiii, 96.
[77] Ibid. 101.
[78] Ibid. 102.
[79] Ibid.
[80] Mins. Accts. Sussex, 188, m. 16; and 109, m. 17 *d.*
[81] Pat. 35 Hen. VIII, pt. 15, m. 39, &c.
[82] Pat. 29 Hen. VIII, pt. 1.
[83] Pat. 36 Hen. VIII, pt. 19.
[84] Memo. R. L.T.R. East. 1 & 2 Phil. and Mary, rot. 47.
[85] Pat. 1 & 2 Phil. and Mary, m. 16; Add. Chart. 27709.
[86] Memo. R. L.T.R. Trin. 14 Jas. I, rot. 8.
[87] W. and L. Inq. p. m. (Ser. 2), bdle. 55, No. 125.
[88] Deeds *penes* Lord Hylton.

In the sixteenth and seventeenth centuries there seems to have existed side by side with this Heath House another messuage called Heath House, which was held by copy of court-roll of the manor of Mapledurham. Edmund Marshe of Preston Candover, who had purchased it from Stephen Vachell and Mary his wife,[89] the owners of the manor of Weston, in the parish of Buriton, sold it in 1608 to Thomas Antrobus of Lincoln's Inn,[90] who died seised of it in 1622.[91] In the latter part of the seventeenth and the beginning of the eighteenth century it was the residence of the Jacobite family of Matthews.[92] It seems impossible to discover when they parted with it, but it was before 1800, for in that year it was occupied by Captain Kidson. Colonel Hylton Jolliffe purchased it about 1829,[93] since when it has remained in the possession of the Jolliffe family. It is at the present day the residence of Captain the Hon. William Sydney Hylton Jolliffe, great-nephew of Colonel Hylton Jolliffe, who purchased it from his nephew, Lord Hylton, in 1904.[94]

CHURCHES The church of *ST. PETER, PETERSFIELD*, consists of chancel 32 ft. by 14 ft., with modern vestry and organ chamber on the north, nave 61 ft. 3 in. by 16 ft. 6 in., with north and south aisles, 16 and 17 ft. wide respectively, north porch, and engaged west tower 16 ft. 6 in. by 17 ft. All measurements are internal. It is a fine building, of great interest for several reasons, and its earliest parts are not later than the beginning of the twelfth century. The church to which they belong was cruciform, with an aisleless nave 41 ft. by 16 ft. 6 in., central tower 16 ft. 3 in. square, north transept of practically the same dimensions, south transept somewhat longer from north to south, and a chancel whose length and eastern termination are uncertain. This church also had a second tower at the west, a very interesting fact which brings it into relation with the normal English type of the larger eleventh-century churches. Its details are not so early as those of the central tower and transepts, and the building was doubtless spread over a number of years as funds could be obtained for the work, but the church must have stood complete with its two towers for some considerable time before the enlargements next to be noticed.

About 1170–80 the church was enlarged by the addition to the nave of north and south aisles of the full width of the transepts, and carried up to the west face of the west tower, the nave walls being pierced with arcades of three bays. The west walls of the transepts must have been pierced, or perhaps removed, at this time. No structural change seems to have been made, beyond the insertion of windows, in the thirteenth and fourteenth centuries, but in the fifteenth century the upper stage of the west tower was either added or rebuilt, and as many of the stones used in this work have worked details like those in the chancel arch and the arcade above, it is possible that at this time the west wall of the central tower was taken down and its area thrown into the nave. The north and south walls of the tower were left standing, though probably lowered, and the north wall at any rate so remained till 1731, when it was destroyed, and the arcade continued up to the east respond of the north arch of the tower. The same thing happened to the south wall, but whether at this date or not is not recorded. The north arcade of the nave was also altered, perhaps at this time,[95] by the moving of its pillars, probably in the interests of galleries, so that it had two narrow arches at the west and two wide ones at the east. In modern times they have been reset and more evenly spaced.

The chancel has at the east a modern triplet of windows in twelfth-century style, replacing a five-light fifteenth-century window. In the north wall is a late twelfth-century round-headed light, now blocked by the vestry roof, with inner jamb-shafts continued as a roll round the head of the window, unbroken except for a fillet on the springing-line of the arch. Opposite to it in the south wall is a pair of modern round-headed lights, and below them modern sedilia and a piscina. West of the north window is a doorway with a four-centred head, opening to the vestry, and there seems to have been a late twelfth-century doorway opposite to it on the south, set in a wide pilaster buttress. In the west bay of the chancel are arched recesses on either side, perhaps for quire seats; the arrangement is old, a single-light fourteenth-century window being set in the southern recess. On the north the recess is pierced with a modern arch opening to the organ chamber.

The chancel arch, formerly the east arch of the central tower, is a fine and rich example of early work, with a slightly stilted semicircular arch of two orders, the outer of which has a large roll and hollow and a double line of zigzag, while the inner is a modern restoration, with a plain edge-roll. A wide label with two rows of billets runs round the arch. The jambs have engaged shafts to the outer order on the west, with early bases and volute capitals, and larger shafts to the inner order, projecting for more than half their diameter from the responds, as in the eleventh-century work at Winchester Cathedral. The capitals have cabled neckings, and are carved with flat early leaf-work and volutes at the angles, and the abaci are hollow-chamfered below, with an enriched vertical face above. The inner shafts of the chancel arch are corbelled off a little below the capitals, and are modern copies of old work. Over the chancel arch is a very fine piece of early detail; three tall round-headed openings, the central one looking only into the chancel roof, and the other two inclosing windows. Each has tall jamb-shafts with volute capitals barely projecting beyond the line of the shafts,

[89] Add. MS. 33278, fol. 172 *b*. The date is cut off. In a recusant roll of 1590 Stephen Vachell, 'gentleman and recusant,' is described as of Heath House near Petersfield (Gasquet, *Hampshire Recusants*, 26), and in 1597 'The fardest parte of the lane next Petersfield Heath' was in the tenure and occupation of Stephen Vachell (Add. Chart. 27947).

[90] Close, 5 Jas. I, pt. 11, m. 6. Thomas Antrobus was descended from William Antrobus of Antrobus (co. Ches.). His pedigree is given in *Harl. Soc.* xxii, pp. 123–4. He married Elizabeth, daughter of Sir Richard Norton of Rotherfield (co. Hants).

[91] By his will dated 1622 he left money for the foundation of the almshouses which still bear his name.

[92] *A History of Petersfield*, by the Rev. J. Williams, p. 24.

This family was probably descended from the Glamorganshire family of that name. A certain Richard Matthews was seated at Stanstead (co. Sussex) in the early part of the seventeenth century. His son George and his grandson Richard also lived at Stanstead. All his descendants remained Roman Catholics, and migrated to Cadiz about 1700 (Berry's *Suss. Gen.* 9).

[93] Information supplied by Captain the Hon. William Sydney Hylton Jolliffe.

[94] Information supplied by Lord Hylton.

[95] The Churchwardens' Accounts show that a gallery was erected on the north side of the church in 1760.

Petersfield Church : The Nave looking East

and arched heads with a roll and two rows of zigzag. Between the openings are groups of three shafts, the central shaft in each group worked with a spiral fluting, having volute capitals like the rest, moulded bases, and common plinths and abaci. From these spring round-headed arches with edge rolls and a deeply cut radiating ornament, having labels worked with a band of circles inclosing lozenges. Above is a horizontal string with billet on the under side, and the spandrels between the arches are filled with a deeply cut diaper pattern. All four sides of the tower were evidently treated in this manner, and the whole effect must have been exceedingly fine. Above the string in the east gable of the nave is a blocked round-headed window with jamb-shafts and scalloped capitals, and a roll in the head, with a little old masonry on either side of it. The bases look early, but the capitals and arch are modern, and of a later type, probably the result of restoration. The gable has been lowered and again raised, but must in the first instance have formed part of the east wall of the tower, being the only remaining piece of its third stage.

The east responds of the north and south arches of the tower, with part of their labels, remain in position, and are of the same detail as the east arch, except in having nook-shafts on both sides.

The nave arcades are of four bays, the east arches on both sides being wider than the west, for the reasons given above. All are round-headed, of two square orders, but only the two western arches of the south arcade are old. The columns are circular, as are the capitals of the north arcade, but those of the south are square, with recessed angles, being of somewhat earlier type than the others. They have small scallops and a deep vertical face above them, while in the north arcade the capitals have convex flutes.

As already noted, the pillars of the north arcade have been altered and reset, but the two western pillars and the western respond of the south arcade are in their original positions, the capitals being at a higher level than those of the third pillar and eastern respond. The reason is that the arcade, being set out before the destruction of the central tower, was not continuous with the arch opening to the south transept, and did not need to correspond in height with its springing; but when the arcade was made continuous after the final removal of the tower the discrepancy between the capitals had to be adjusted, and this was done by lowering the capital of the third pillar to the level of that of the eastern respond. The clearstory of the nave is a modern addition, with pairs of round-headed lights.

The north and east walls of the early north transept, now forming part of the north aisle, are easily distinguished from the later masonry by their herring-bone walling, and the remains of similar work are to be seen in the south wall of the chancel. The quoins are of fairly large size, but not in any way remarkable. No original windows are left, the north transept having a north window of two cinquefoiled lights, fifteenth-century work renewed, and the south a wide lancet in modern stonework in its south wall, and three round-headed windows on the east, 'restored' from part of a jamb which still exists, with billet string-courses at sill level within and without. There was formerly a three-light early fourteenth-century window here.

The remaining windows in the north aisle are a plain square-headed two-light window, of no great age, and to the west of it two fifteenth-century windows each of three cinquefoiled lights with tracery. The north doorway is of late twelfth-century date, round-headed of two square orders, with nook-shafts having foliate capitals, renewed. Over it is a modern stone porch, and to the west of the porch a round-headed window with an outer rebate which looks earlier than anything else in the aisle, and may be a re-used detail from the nave walls. The remains of a blocked doorway are also to be seen here, which seems to have been in use when this end of the aisle was used as a schoolroom. There is here a tall modern window of twelfth-century style, and another like it in the west wall.

In the south aisle are four large round-headed windows, of which only the third from the east is ancient, of the date of the aisle wall. West of them is a doorway in late twelfth-century style, with two shafts in each jamb, all the stonework being modern. In the west bay of the aisle is a late twelfth-century south window, part of the jambs being original, and in the west wall two similar windows, which preserve old masonry only on the inner face. There is a late thirteenth-century piscina with a shelf at the south-east of this aisle, and a fourteenth-century piscina with a shelf on a line just west of that of the west wall of the early transept, showing that there was an altar here, and therefore some screen or division at this point—possibly part of the old wall left standing. Below the windows of the aisle is a moulded string which also stops here, just east of the piscina, and doubtless on the line of the division.

The west tower is of four stages, the top stage being of fifteenth-century date, embattled, with belfry windows of two cinquefoiled lights, and the lower three stages are of the twelfth century. At the south-west angle is a stair entered from without the church. The side walls on the ground stage are solid, but in the east wall is a wide semicircular arch of two square orders, *c.* 1120–30, with hollow-chamfered abaci like those of the chancel arch, and over it a plain round-headed opening from the second stage of the tower, which must have given access to the roof of the early nave, as just above it is a gabled weathering. This latter is not quite central with the opening, its apex being to the south.

In the west wall is a round-headed doorway, with an outer order of zigzag, the stonework being entirely modern, except for two voussoirs of the arch. Above it are two round-headed windows, replacing a two-light fourteenth-century window.

The roofs and fittings of the church are entirely modern, including the font at the west end of the nave; but an older font, octagonal with panelled sides, of early fifteenth-century date, stands in the churchyard west of the tower. A few mediaeval coffin lids are preserved in the church, and in the west bay of the north aisle are two brass plates, one with an inscription to Anne Holt, 1655, the other to Dr. Thomas Aylwin, 1704, and his wife Mary, 1693. Other monuments formerly on the nave walls are now fixed in the tower.

There are eight bells, the treble and second by Warner, 1889; the third and seventh by Taylor, 1895; the fourth and fifth by Robert Catlin, 1750; the sixth by Thomas Lester, 1746, and the tenor by Pack and Chapman, 1771.

The plate comprises a silver communion cup and cover paten of 1568; a second cup and cover paten of 1612, given by Thomas Antrobus, senior, of Heath House; a flagon of 1707; a standing paten of 1721, given in 1830 by Thomas Chitty; an alms dish of 1757, given 1758, and a second dish of 1812, given 1813.

The first book of the registers runs from 1558 to 1667, and contains entries of deaths from plague in 1563 and 1666; the second from 1669 to 1757, the marriages ending at 1754; the third has baptisms and burials, 1758–1807; the fourth marriages, 1754–84—this is a MS. book, and not the printed book ordered by the Act of 1753; the fifth and sixth continue the marriage entries to 1804 and 1812; the seventh contains baptisms 1808–13, and the eighth burials for the same period. There are churchwardens' accounts in six books from 1751 to 1815, and poor-rate accounts from 1697.

The churchyard lies chiefly on the south, having a gate at the east. The churchwardens' accounts mention the making of steps, a wall, and a gate on the east side of the churchyard opposite New Street (now St. Peter's Road) in 1754.

The church of *ST. MARY, SHEET*, built and consecrated in 1869, is of stone in the thirteenth-century style, consisting of chancel, nave, south porch, and south-east tower with spire. The register dates from year of erection.

ADVOWSON

The chapel of Petersfield was dependent on the church of Buriton till 13 August, 1886,[96] when by an Order in Council it was separated, and with the district of Sheet and the tithings of Lower Weston and Lower Nursted constituted a separate benefice in the gift of the bishop of Winchester.

Among lands forfeited in 1547 for superstitious uses were a close called Whitredden of the yearly value of 16*d*., which had been left for the maintenance of a lamp-light, and lands then in the tenure of John Myll, and of the yearly value of 12*d*., the issues of which maintained a morrow-mass priest.[97]

The Roman Catholic church of St. Lawrence, situated in Station Road, was commenced in 1890 at the expense of Mr. Laurence Cave of Ditcham Park, and completed in 1901 by his widow Lucy Cave and his two sons Charles and Adrian Cave. Attached is a residence for the rector, also presented by Mr. Cave. The church is served by monks of the English Benedictine Order. The Congregational church, erected in 1882, is in College Street.[98] The Wesleyan church, erected in 1903 at a cost of £5,000, is in Station Road. The Primitive Methodist church, with Sunday school and vestry, was erected in Station Road in 1900. The Salvation Army Barracks are in Swan Street. The Union church was built by voluntary subscription, and opened by the bishop of Southampton on Easter Sunday, 1900.

Churcher's College stands on high ground outside the town of Petersfield, and has extensive grounds.

The Elementary School (St. Peter's Road) was built in 1894 at a cost of £2,764; the infants' school has been enlarged at a cost of £866. Sheet Elementary School was erected at a cost of £2,400, and opened September, 1898.

The Cottage Hospital in the Spain was built in 1871 at an expense of £1,400.

CHARITIES

The almshouses founded in 1622 by will of Thomas Antrobus were sold in 1882, and the proceeds invested in £197 6*s*. 3*d*. Consols. The annual dividends, amounting to £4 18*s*. 6*d*., are given in pensions.

Church Estate.—In 1869, 3 r. 9 p., formerly constituting part of endowment, was sold, and proceeds invested in £181 16*s*. 7*d*. Consols. The annual dividends of £4 11*s*. are remitted to the churchwardens.

Churcher's College.—See article on schools, *V.C.H. Hants*, ii, 387-92.

Bishop Laney's Apprenticing Charity.—See parish of Buriton.

In 1827 Miss Ann Phillips by her will left £200 Consols, the income (subject to the repair of vault, &c.) to be applied in the distribution of bread to poor men and women of 52 years of age and upwards.

In 1837 John Meere by will left £5 a year for Sunday school—a sum of £166 13*s*. 4*d*. Consols was set aside in satisfaction of the legacy.

In 1847 John Holland by will left £5 a year for distribution in bread on St. Thomas's Day, represented by a sum of £166 13*s*. 4*d*. The several sums of stock above-mentioned are held by the official trustees.

In 1861 the Reverend Thomas Robert Jolliffe by will left £135 Consols, two-thirds of the dividends to be applied towards the maintenance of certain monuments in the church, and one-third for poor at Christmas in coals or other necessaries. The stock is held by the official trustees and the dividends are duly applied.

In 1863 Mrs. Mary Anne Kennett by deed founded the almshouses known as the Willow Almshouses for the poor of this parish and of Sheet, and endowed the same with £2,000, now represented by £2,036 12*s*. 3*d*. New Zealand £3 per cent. Stock with the official trustees.

In 1882 Mrs. Mary Anne Kennett by her will also bequeathed £2,000 to be invested; the income to be applied in the distribution of coals, blankets, sheets, bread, or clothing on 1 December and 14 February in each year. The charity is administered under a scheme of the High Court of 2 December, 1890. The trust fund is now represented by £2,001 14*s*. 5*d*. Queensland £3 per cent. Inscribed Stock with the official trustees.

The Town Trust.—By a scheme made by the Charity Commissioners under the Municipal Corporations Act, 1853, for the application of the property of the late corporation of 'The Mayor of Petersfield,' the mace, bearing date 1596, and the charters, one by John count of Mortain (afterwards King John), bearing date 1198, were entrusted to the custody of the lord of the manor of Petersfield, and the churchwardens and overseers of the poor.[99]

Tithing of Sheet.—In 1674 John Lock by his will charged certain lands with the yearly payment of 50*s*.

[96] By an Order in Council of 1657–8 the chapelry of Petersfield, Sheet tithing, and parts of Weston and Nursted, were detached from the parish of Buriton and made a separate parish (*Cal. of S.P. Dom.* 1657–8, p. 270), but it is doubtful whether this order was carried into effect.

[97] Chant. Cert. 30, No. 17.

[98] Chapel Street was the site of a Nonconformist place of worship, succeeded by a chapel built in College Street in 1801.

[99] They have since entrusted them to the custody of the Urban District Council.

for maintenance of a sufficient person to teach poor children of the tithing to read the English tongue. The rent-charge, which is payable out of a farm in Sheet, called Westmark, was at various times in arrear, which arrears on recovery were invested in £130 10*s.* 4*d.* consols. The income was applied for educational purposes.

Poor's Allotment.—By an award dated 1859 two acres were appropriated as allotments for the use of the poor, the profits of which, averaging £2 a year (subject to a yearly rent-charge of 15*s.*), are applied with assistance from the rates in improving the allotments; 4 a. 0 r. 27 p. of land was also awarded as a recreation ground and village green.

Miss Frances Cobb by will proved in 1905 bequeathed £448 2*s.* 5*d.* Consols with the official trustees, dividends to be applied at Christmas in providing coals and blankets, and in such other way as trustees may think proper for the benefit of the poor of Sheet.

The Willow Almshouses.—See parish of Petersfield.

Tithing of Weston.—John Goodyer, by his will dated in 1664, and proved in the bishop's court, Winchester, devised to trustees tenements and lands in Weston in this parish and Buriton containing 17 a. 3 r. 28 p., in trust that the rents and profits should be employed for ever thereafter for the putting forth and placing abroad of poor children in the tithing of Weston, and that the overplus thereof should be distributed to the poorest inhabitants of the said Tithing.

The official trustees also hold £1,052 2*s.* 5*d.* Consols arising from sale in 1876 of a house and two cottages and gardens. The land is let at £52 a year, which with £26 6*s.* dividends was in 1905 applied, after payment of expenses of management, in the distribution of £35 in money and clothing to seventy-five persons, clothing allowance at £1 to each of eight servant girls, £5 to the schoolmistress, and £26 in connexion with apprentices. By an order of the Charity Commissioners of 2 July, 1897, trustees were appointed, and the legal estate vested in the official trustee of charity lands.

HAVANT PARISH AND LIBERTY

Hamanfunta and Hafunt, x cent.; Havehunt, xi–xiii cent.; Havonte, xiv–xv cent.; Havant, xvi cent.

The market town of Havant is situated on the approximate line of the Roman road from Clausentum to Regnum, now the main road from Chichester to Southampton, and is built very regularly round the intersection of this road with that running north and south from Hayling Island to Rowland's Castle. In the south-west angle of the cross roads stands the church of St. Faith, with a low central tower which is nevertheless seen above all the houses near it, the most interesting of which is the late sixteenth-century

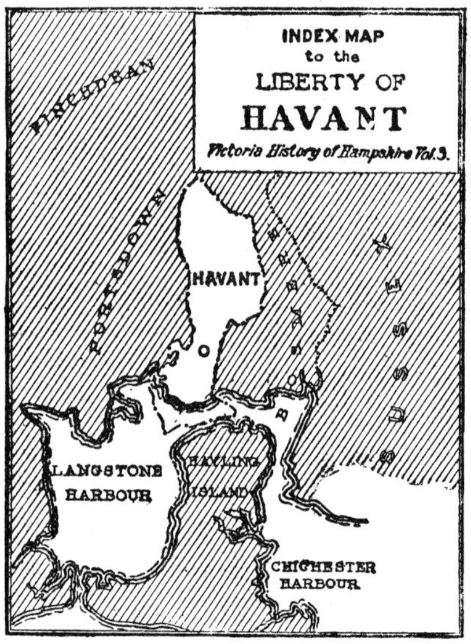

half-timbered 'Old House at Home.' At a short distance to the south-west of the church rises the copious spring of Homewell, which never fails in summer nor freezes in winter. West Street leads past the church, by large parchment works and tanneries. The fellmonger's trade, indeed, has prospered in Havant since the seventeenth century.[1] A still older industry, now extinct, was the manufacture of cloth. In 1571 William Simpson, of Rye, cloth-merchant, travelled to Havant in pursuit of 'some gainful bargain,' and was detained there as a suspicious character until the bailiff and constable[2] of the town were advertised of his honesty.[3] This trade was also centred in West Street,[4] which leads through Brockhampton tithing towards Bedhampton, past the Roman Catholic church of St. Joseph, and the Wesleyan chapel built in 1888. On the borders of the two parishes stands the Primitive Methodist chapel, and by a high-walled garden Brockhampton Road takes the traveller past the Portsmouth Waterworks through green fields watered by a small stream and across a bridge past more tanneries back into the town. Brockhampton Mill, on the right of this road, probably stands on the site of a mill valued at 15*s.* in the Domesday Book.[5] In the same Survey two mills are mentioned under Havant; these seem to have been represented later by South Mill and Asshewell Mill.[6] Amongst other mills in the town the most picturesque is the disused one at Langstone. It stands on the harbour of that name, near the causeway which connects Hayling Island with the main-land, and is surrounded by a few houses, some thatched and some roofed with red tiles, which, together with a coastguard station, form the hamlet of Langstone. There were also salterns here, one of which dated from the eleventh century,[7] and close by across the meadows are the grounds of Wade Court. The greater part of the parish is used for pasture, 1,150 acres being permanent grass, while only 557½ acres are employed as arable land, this lying chiefly around the town, and in the north of the parish there are over 750 acres of wood.[8] The soil differs considerably, the subsoil near Langstone being chalk while the town itself is built on a bed of clay, and the northern part of the parish is also of Eocene formation. This northern portion has been formed for civil purposes into a separate parish, known as North Havant. The road northwards skirts Leigh Park, in a well-wooded and well-watered country. Green slopes studded with fine old trees stretch up to the house which is now the residence of the lord of Havant manor. Beyond it, in the distance, are the trees of the 'Thicket,' the old 'Havant Chace' of the bishop of Winchester, which form the southern extremity of the forest of Bere. Here at the Thicket was obtained, in 1436, potters' earth.[9] When the park is passed the road curves downhill, and in the hollow lie a few houses, each with its garden abounding in

[1] Early in the seventeenth century William Hayter and William Bayly were the chief fellmongers of the town. Add. Chart. 9454.

[2] Probably the bailiff and constable appointed in the manorial court.

[3] *Hist. MSS. Com. Rep.* xiii, App. 4, p. 15.

[4] In 1614 Roger Novell, *clothworker*, of Havant purchased land here. Add. Chart. 9430.

[5] *V.C.H. Hants*, i, 468*a*. In the fifteenth and sixteenth centuries it consisted of two mills under one roof. Close, 23 Chas. I, pt. xi, 16; Egerton MS. 2034, fol. 139*b*.

[6] Mins. Accts. bdle. 1142, No. 15; bdle. 1141, No. 14.

[7] *V.C.H. Hants*, i, 468*b*. One of these, Longcroft (*Hund. of Bosmere*, p. 3), locates to the south of Wade Court.

[8] Board of Agric. Returns (Hants).

[9] Eccl. Com. (var.), bdle. 86 (159486). No. 3.

fruit trees. This hamlet is known as Durrants; still further north on another slope of the road lies Redhill, which was formed into an ecclesiastical district in 1840, when the little church of St. John was built half-way up the hill.

Havant has a station on the direct Portsmouth branch of the London, Brighton, and South Coast Railway. It is also connected with Hayling by the Hayling Island Railway, laid down in 1851,[10] which crosses Langstone Harbour. The shore along the harbour is in most places shingly. The fishery, which was once of considerable importance, has decreased materially during the last two centuries, though the oyster trade still flourishes.

The name Billy which survives in Billy Lawn and Billy Copse dates from early in the seventeenth century, when pastures called 'Billyes' were conveyed with Havant manor to William Wolgar:[11] half an acre in 'Conquerauntescrouch' was owned by Jordan the Hayward in 1289,[12] and 'Boyes Buttes' in Leigh tithing was sold by Richard Softley in 1692.[13] In the same tithing lies Stockheath Common, known in the fifteenth century as Stoke Heath.[14] It was inclosed in 1870 together with Havant Thicket, Leigh Green, and South Moor,[15] the award being in the custody of the Deputy Clerk of the Peace.

MANORS

In 935 A.D. King Athelstan granted seven 'mansae' at *HAVANT* to his thegn Witgar for three lives.[16] The third in succession after Witgar was a certain widow who gave the land to the monks of St. Peter and St. Paul, Winchester, to whom King Ethelred confirmed the gift in 980 and again in 984.[17] At the latter date it was extended at 10 hides, its assessment before the Conquest according to the Domesday Survey in 1086, at which time it was still held by the monks of St. Swithun.[18] The monks were given a weekly market there on Tuesdays in 1200, and the sheep and cattle market is still held on that day.[19] In July, 1284, the monks exchanged Havant manor with the bishop of Winchester for certain privileges.[20] In January, 1450–1, the bishop was granted a market, probably for corn, on Saturdays, and an annual fair to be held on the eve and feast of St. Faith (6 October).[21] This fair was held till 1871, when it was abolished together with another formerly held in June.[22] From 1553 onwards the bishop leased the manor from time to time. Under the Act of the Commonwealth for the sale of bishops' lands it was purchased by William Wolgar of Havant,[23] who obtained a lease of it after the bishop's restoration in 1660.[24] Finally Sir George Thomas Staunton, then lessee of the manor, purchased the fee in 1827.[25] It ultimately passed to W. H. Stone, from whom Sir F. W. FitzWygram purchased it in 1875. He was succeeded by his son Sir F. L. FitzWygram, the present owner.[26]

HAVANT LIBERTY

Under the terms of Ethelred's grant to the priory Havant was free from all service except the *trinoda necessitas*, and before the exchange with the bishop the monks had return of all writs there. This privilege was confirmed to the bishop in 1284.[27] The profits of court leet, formerly held twice yearly,[28] were very valuable, since it seems to have been considered an advantage to be under the bishop's jurisdiction. Thus in 1337 Henry le Bold gave the lord 4*d*. to be allowed to remain in his liberty and to come to two lawdays yearly. Tithingmen of Hayling, Leigh, Brockhampton, and Havant attended the tourns, and as late as 1817 two constables for the liberty, a coroner of the market, leather-sealer, ale-taster, and haywards besides the tithingmen were appointed at the court leet.[29] After the exchange between the prior and the bishop the men of Havant still owed suit at the prior's hundred-court of Fawley, for Havant was included in Fawley hundred in 1316,[30] and in May, 1465, the tithingman of Havant paid a fine at the hundred-court of Fawley to have release from suit of court of four men till Michaelmas.[31] The lord of Havant also had wreck of sea.[32] He was responsible for the repair of the market house, and in 1645 was amerced £5, to be paid to the poor of the town failing its repair before a fixed date.[33]

BROCKHAMPTON (Brochemtune, xi cent.; Brokhampton, xiv cent.), on the western borders of the parish, was held of Earl Harold by Sired, who also held Newtimber in Warblington. After the Conquest the overlordship with that of the neighbouring manor of Bedhampton was vested in Hugh de Port, Herbert the Chamberlain being the actual tenant.[34] It was subsequently known as a hamlet of Bedhampton, and was held in dower with that manor by Joan widow of Reginald FitzPeter,[35] and the histories of the two are coincident till 1428, after which Brockhampton seems to have been merged in Bedhampton manor[36] (q. v.).

There was also at Brockhampton at the time of the Domesday Survey land with a mill, part of the possessions of the monks of St. Swithun.[37] It was apparently amalgamated with the manor of Havant, with which it was conveyed to the bishop of

[10] Local and Pers. Act, 14 & 15 Vict. cap. 68.
[11] Close, 23 Chas. I, pt. xi, 16.
[12] Mins. Accts. bdle. 1141, No. 14.
[13] Add. Chart. 9446.
[14] Eccl. Com. Ct. R. bdle. 81, No. 9.
[15] *Return of Commons* (*Inclosure Awards*), 1904, p. 157.
[16] Birch, *Cart. Sax.* ii, 411.
[17] Kemble, *Codex Dipl.* 624, 642.
[18] *V.C.H. Hants*, i, 468*b*.
[19] *Rot. Chart.* i, 78. The treasurer of the priory paid 20 marks and a palfrey worth 5 marks for this privilege. Pipe R. 2 John.
[20] Add. MS. 29436, fols. 49, 85; Chart. R. 12 Edw. I, m. 5.
[21] Ibid. 27–39 Hen. VI, m. 34. The corn-market is still held on Saturdays.
[22] *Lond. Gaz.* 7 Oct. 1873.
[23] Close, 23 Chas. I, pt. xi, 16.
[24] Longcroft, *Hund. of Bosmere*, 12.
[25] Ibid. 18 et seq. where a detailed account of the lessees is given.
[26] Ex inform. Rev. Canon S. G. Scott, rector of Havant.
[27] Chart. R. 12 Edw. I, m. 5.
[28] Ct. R. Eccl. Com. bdle. 80. The tourns were held at Hocktide and Michaelmas until the eighteenth century. In 1817 it was said to be held yearly in Oct.
[29] *Topographical Acct. of Bosmere Hund.* L.P. 1817.
[30] *Feud. Aids*, ii, 320.
[31] Eccl. Com. Ct. R. bdle. 80, No. 1. The fine was 10*d*. Perhaps the suit of four men was due from the four tithings of Havant, Leigh, Brockhampton, and Hayling.
[32] Ibid. bdle. 82, No. 7.
[33] Ct. R. quoted by Longcroft, *Hund. of Bosmere*, 43.
[34] *V.C.H. Hants*, i, 483*a*.
[35] *Cal. Close*, 1279–88, p. 399.
[36] See *Feud. Aids*, ii, 356. The duchess of York held a knight's fee and a half in 1428. There are, however, certain conveyances of 'the manor of Brockhampton,' viz. by James Engler to Robert Woods in 1589, by John Woods to Arthur Baylie in 1635–6, and by Arthur Baylie to Richard Stones in 1636, from which it might be inferred that Brockhampton was separate from Bedhampton at those dates, unless they refer to the tenancy of the bishop's lands at Brockhampton mentioned below. Feet of F. Hants, Mich. 31–2 Eliz.; East. 12 Chas. I; Mich. 12 Chas. I.
[37] *V.C.H. Hants*, i, 468*a*.

Winchester. The farm of the mill there formed an important item in the profits of Havant manor.[38] According to an account dated 1319 this land consisted of rather more than 60 acres, and the jurors then stated that six oaks had been felled in 'the Newgrove.'[39] It is doubtful whether separate courts were ever held for the bishop's tenants at Brockhampton. In an account tendered by the bailiff of Brockhampton perquisites of court are mentioned, but from other items on the same roll it would appear that the bailiff was including also the profits of Havant manor.[40]

The manor of *FLOOD*[41] (Flode, xiii–xv cent.; Fludd, xvii cent.) was held of Havant manor by a certain 'Geoffrey de la Flode,' who was succeeded late in the thirteenth century by Ralph de Swanewych, the bishop's servant.[42] In 1483 Joan, wife of William Vernon, joined John Goring the elder and John Goring the younger in releasing the 'manor of Flood' to Reginald Bray and others.[43] Sir Reginald Bray bequeathed a large part of his estates, and apparently Flood with them, to his niece Margery wife of Sir William Sandys, knt.[44] afterwards Lord Sandys of the Vyne, whose son and heir, Thomas, Lord Sandys, died seised of Flood.[45] In 1612 William Sandys conveyed the manor to John Dean with warranty against the heirs of William, Lord Sandys, and others.[46] Probably this conveyance was in trust to sell, for Flood came with Hall Place[47] to Francis Wooder,[48] who bequeathed it to his half-sister Dorothy Evans,[49] whose sister and legatee, Elizabeth wife of Ascanius Christopher Lockman, conveyed it in 1725 to Isaac Moody.[50] Under the will of his son John it passed to Richard Bingham Newland, who conveyed it in 1812 to William Garrett,[51] who sold it again in 1820.[52]

SANDYS OF THE VYNE. *Argent a ragged cross sable.*

The manor of *LIMBORNE*, which includes Wade Court, was probably parcel of Warblington manor, for the lands of Wade were amongst the 'terrae Normannorum,' and as such were granted in 1204[53] to the earl of Arundel, with whose successors the overlordship remained. Rominus Hospinel, who succeeded Juliane de Wade as actual tenant, gave 1 carucate in Wade in marriage with his daughter Agnes to Richard Falconer in 1205.[54] William Falconer, probably a descendant, was enfeoffed of a messuage at Wade by Hilary wife of Adam de Wanstead in 1250;[55] and John Falconer, to whom Isabel de Merlay in 1256 granted a messuage and land in 'La Wade and Nytimbre,'[56] died seised of Limborne c. 1305, leaving a daughter and heir, Joan wife of John Butler.[57] In 1352 John Butler was holding Limborne of the earl of Arundel,[58] and twelve years later settlement was made upon John Butler, probably son of the former John and his wife Katherine.[59] It was possibly the same Katherine who, as wife of William Upton, was imprisoned there and almost starved to death in 1389,[60] and whose husband, William Upton, had been outlawed for felony in the previous year, while his estates, including Limborne, fell to the mortgagees, John Brinkebon, Gilbert Bannebury, and Hugh Tildesleghe.[61] Nevertheless, Isabel wife of Geoffrey Roukele and sister and heir of John Butler, died seised of Limborne,[62] which was inherited by her grandson William Wayte of Wymering (q.v.), who apparently conveyed it to Richard Dalingrigge and his wife Sybil, for it was released to them in 1441 by Margaret wife of William Wayte.[63] Richard Dalingrigge died in 1470–1, having settled Limborne upon Thomas Pound and his wife Mercy in payment of a debt of 200 marks.[64] This Thomas died 23 November, 1476, leaving a son and heir John,[65] afterwards Sir John, Pound, who was succeeded by a son William,[66] whose son Anthony inherited Limborne on his father's death in 1525.[67] Anthony Pound entailed his estates on his son and heir Richard Pound and Elizabeth daughter of William Wayte of Wymering in 1542, with remainder in tail-male to his own daughters Honor and Mary.[68] The latter evidently married Edward White, for in November, 1580, Edward White died holding Limborne by courtesy after the death of his wife Mary. He was succeeded by his son John White,[69] who conveyed

38 Eccl. Com. (var.) bdle. 86 (159486).

39 *Reg. of Bp. Sandale* (Hants Rec. Soc.), 241. The stock included two cart-horses, four oxen, one mule, three asses, one mill-stone.

40 Eccl. Com. (var.), bdle. 86 (159486), No. 1. It is evidently of the tenants of the bishop's lands in Brockhampton that Longcroft states that Thomas Shepherd was 'lord' in 1748, being succeeded in 1764 by Thomas Laud who bequeathed to Francis Foster.

41 There seems no conclusive evidence of separate courts being held for Flood. Longcroft (*Hund. of Bosmere*, 26) states that William Wolgar held courts there in 1646, but it seems probable that he held them as tenant of Havant manor under the bishop.

42 Egerton MS. 2031, fol. 15.

43 Feet of F. Hants, Trin. 1 Edw. V. No. 1.

44 Sir N. H. Nicolas, *Testamenta Vetusta*, 447.

45 Chan. Inq. p.m. 2 Eliz. pt. i, No. 143.

46 Feet of F. Hants, Mich. 10 Jas. I.

47 In 1443 a messuage and court called Hall Place, which had been held by John Barbar, were granted with a water-mill to John Tauke and his heirs (Eccl. Com. var. bdle. 86, 159486). John Barbar had had a grant of all John Halle's lands (ibid.). Mr. C. J. Longcroft, owner of Hall Place in 1857, states that a John Tauke died seised of the property in 1541 and that it was held later by Francis Wooder, with whose lands it passed to Elizabeth Lockman, whose grand-daughter, Elizabeth Halsey, sold it in 1777 to Thomas Jeudwine of Havant, and that it was ultimately purchased by John Crasweller, who bequeathed it in 1825 to Jane Longcroft, mother of the writer (Longcroft, *Hund. of Bosmere*, 21).

48 Com. Pleas. D. Enr. Hil. 8 & 9 Will. and Mary, m. 3.

49 Will quoted by Longcroft, *Hund. of Bosmere*, 21.

50 Feet of F. Hants, Hil. 11 Geo. I.

51 Ibid. Hil. 55 Geo. III.

52 Longcroft, *Hund. of Bosmere*, 26.

53 Close, 6 John, m. 21.

54 Feet of F. Hants, 7 John, No. 63.

55 Ibid. Hil. 34 Hen. III, No. 1.

56 Ibid. 40 Hen. III, No. 84.

57 Chan. Inq. p.m. 33 Edw. I, No. 44.

58 Ibid. 26 Edw. III (2nd Nos.), No. 23.

59 Feet of F. Hants, 38 Edw. III, No. 70.

60 *Cal. Pat.* 1388–92, p. 266. The offenders were Richard Wayte, Gilbert Estene, Simon Jordan, and Robert Jugeler. It is significant also that one of the mainpernors for the accused was a John Butler.

61 Chan. Inq. p.m. 12 Ric. II, No. 136.

62 Ibid. No. 46.

63 Feet of F. Hants, Trin. 19 Hen. VI. Apparently some of the lands were retained, for Thomas Wayte sold East Wade to Robert Long and his wife Margaret in 1444; ibid. Div. Cos. Hil. 22 Hen. VI, No. 20.

64 Chan. Inq. p.m. 9–10 Edw. IV, No. 48; Early Chan. Proc. lxvi, 44. Thomas Pound's right was unsuccessfully disputed by Sir Roger Lewkenor, nephew and heir of Richard Dalingrigge.

65 Chan. Inq. p.m. 17 Edw. IV, No. 72.

66 Ibid. (Ser. 2), vol. 25, No. 19.

67 Exch. Inq. p.m. (Ser. 2), file 978, No. 23.

68 Chan. Inq. p.m. (Ser. 2), vol. 85, No. 45.

69 Ibid. 26 Eliz. pt. 1, No. 118.

the manor in 1594 to Robert Paddon,[70] from whom it was purchased in 1604 by Henry Best,[71] who immediately conveyed it to Arthur Swayne of Anne Savage.[72] In 1615 Edward Swayne of Anne Savage died seised of Limborne, leaving a brother and heir Robert,[73] who conveyed the estate in 1619 to William Dunches and Thomas Southe,[74] perhaps in trust for sale, for Arthur Hyde was in possession in 1646,[75] and was succeeded in 1654 by Lawrence Hyde.[76] Late in the same century it seems to have become the property of Sir John Stonehouse, with whose daughter Elizabeth it passed in marriage to Thomas Jervoise of Herriard,[77] who conveyed it to trustees, from whom it was purchased in 1752 by Robert Bold.[78] His son James died without issue, and his coheiresses sold the manor to John Knight,[79] who bequeathed it to his two sons John and William.[80] John Knight, having purchased his brother's moiety, in his will dated 6 March, 1824, directed that the whole manor should be sold. It was purchased by Messrs. Knight and Moore, who sold it in 1846 to Charles John Longcroft, author of a history of the hundred of Bosmere,[81] in whose family it still remains.

Longcroft. *Party fessewise nebuly gules and sable a lion argent between six crosslets fitchy or.*

The *CHURCH OF ST. FAITH, CHURCHES HAVANT*, is an interesting cruciform building, with a vaulted chancel, 30 ft. 6 in. by 19 ft. 3 in.; north vestry and south organ chamber; central tower, 18 ft. 7 in. square; north transept, 21 ft. 9 in. by 19 ft. 6 in. with north porch and west aisle, 13 ft. wide; south transept of practically the same dimensions; and nave 55 ft. long by 19 ft. 3 in., with north and south aisles 7 ft. 6 in. wide.[82]

The oldest architectural details date from the end of the twelfth century, and are to be seen in the tower, transepts, and nave. The chancel belongs to the first quarter of the thirteenth century, the north vestry to the fourteenth, while the stair-turret at the north-east angle of the tower is a fifteenth-century addition. There was no doubt an earlier church on the site. From a note on the destruction of the nave in 1832,[83] it appears that a concrete foundation of Roman brick and cement underlay the pillars, and several Roman coins were found during the work. The only feature in the present building which suggests the incorporation of work older than the end of the twelfth century is the fact that the west wall of the tower is 6 in. thinner than the others, and may therefore represent the east wall of an earlier nave. The unusual western aisles to the transepts (if indeed they are contemporary with the transepts) may owe their existence to some previous arrangement. The whole building has been much repaired; in 1832 the nave arcades were taken down, apparently to give more room for galleries, and the nave practically rebuilt. In 1874 the central tower was found to be unsafe, perhaps by reason of the loss of abutment brought about by the destruction of the nave arcades, and it was taken down, except the north-east stair-turret, and rebuilt with the old materials. A plaster ceiling which hid the vaulted roof of the chancel was taken away, an organ-chamber added at the south-west of the chancel, and the nave was entirely rebuilt on the old lines, the capitals being copied from a late twelfth-century capital belonging to the nave destroyed in 1832, and now reset on the first pillar from the east in the south arcade. The chancel is of two bays with a quadripartite stone vault with moulded ribs springing from Purbeck marble corbels, the rubble filling of the vault being set in courses parallel to the ridge. The east window is a modern triplet of lancets, but in the north wall the original lancet window remains in the east bay, blocked on the outside by the fourteenth-century vestry. In the west bay on this side is a fifteenth-century window of three cinquefoiled lights with tracery in the head, set somewhat to the west in the bay in order to clear the west wall of the vestry.

In the south wall is a fifteenth-century window of two cinquefoiled lights with tracery in the head, and below it modern sedilia and piscina, with a small south doorway to the west of them, also of modern stonework. In the west bay on this side is a modern arch opening to the organ-chamber. The vestry on the north of the chancel opens to it by a plain fourteenth-century doorway, and has also a modern external doorway at the north-west. It is lighted on the east by a fourteenth-century window of two trefoiled lights, and in the north gable is a second window, much restored, set at a height which suggests that the vestry once had an upper floor.

The four arches carrying the central tower are pointed, of two orders with edge-chamfers, the outer orders on the west side of the east and west arches having a keeled roll between hollows, as being those which are most conspicuous from the nave. Their capitals are scalloped and of late twelfth-century type, and the jambs have half-round shafts to the inner orders, flanked by fine Purbeck marble nook-shafts, while the responds of the north and south arches are of plain half-round section, and have modern foliate capitals. The rood-loft was set against the east arch, and the fifteenth-century stair leading to it still exists at the north-east angle of the tower, and is continued upwards to the battlements. The upper stage of the tower has in each face a belfry window of two pointed lights divided by a shaft with base and capital of late twelfth-century style, and the level of the eaves or parapet of this date is shown by a row of corbels projecting from the wall. The tower has been heightened, and now ends with an embattled parapet, the turret being carried up above it and having a like finish.

The north transept has an early sixteenth-century east window of three cinquefoiled lights, and a north

70 Feet of F. Hants, Trin. 36 Eliz.
71 Close, 2 Jas. I, pt. iv.
72 Ibid. pt. v.
73 Chan. Inq. p.m. (Ser. 2), vol. 518, No. 12.
74 Feet of F. Mich. 17 Jas. I.
75 Ibid. Mich. 22 Chas. I.
76 Ct. R. quoted by Longcroft, *Hund. of Bosmere*, 152.
77 Close, 5 Geo. II, pt. 9, m. 16; the entail on the heirs of Elizabeth Stonehouse having been barred in 1731. Recov. R. East. 4 Geo. II, 213.
78 Longcroft, *Hund. of Bosmere*, 152.
79 Feet of F. Hants, East. 22 Geo. III. Trin. 27 Geo. III; East. 28 Geo. III; Hil. 31 Geo. III.
80 Longcroft, *Hund. of Bosmere*, 152.
81 Ibid.
82 All measurements are internal.
83 Longcroft, *Hund. of Bosmere*.

window with modern stonework of three cinquefoiled lights and tracery of fifteenth-century style. Both transepts have the unusual addition of a western aisle, that in the north transept having an arcade of two bays in late fifteenth-century style with moulded arches and octagonal columns. It is lighted by a west window of two uncusped lights, perhaps fifteenth-century work with the cusps cut away, and is entered at the north end through a modern porch and doorway, over which is a window, also modern.

The south transept has no window on the east, its place being taken by an arch opening to the modern organ-chamber.

Its south window is of three lights and modern, and in the west aisle, which is separated from the transept by a modern arcade of like detail with that in the north transept, is a fifteenth-century south window of three cinquefoiled lights with tracery over, and a round-headed west window of late twelfth-century date. This if in position shows that the west aisles are contemporary with the rest of the transepts. In the nave the eastern responds of the late twelfth-century arcades remain in position, and as before noted the capital of the first column of the south arcade is in part original work re-used. The rest of the arcades are modern, but old material is worked into the west respond of the south arcade. The clearstory has round windows enclosing quatrefoils or cinquefoils. The height of the original nave roof may be recovered from openings on the west face of the tower below the present roof, one in the centre being a round-headed doorway formerly opening on to the nave roof, while on either side of it at a higher level are two blocked pointed windows which looked over the roof.

Into the west wall of the nave is built a Purbeck marble slab with a curved lower edge, on which is carved in twelfth-century style a lion between two rosettes. It is perhaps part of a font. The existing font, which stands near the west door of the nave, was made in 1847.

AILEWARD. *Sable a cheveron between three sheaves or.*

None of the wood fittings of the church are old, and the only monument of interest is the fine brass of Thomas Aileward, rector, who died 6 April, 1413. His effigy is shown in a cope, fastened with a morse, bearing his initials T. A., while on the orphreys are sheaves, roses, and fleurs-de-lis. The sheaves are taken from his arms, which are shown on the only remaining one of the four shields which formerly surrounded the effigy and inscription. The inscription ends with the couplet:

Sis testis Christe quod non jacet hic lapis iste
Corpus ut ornetur sed mors ut permedicetur.

Thomas Aileward was rector 1397–1413, and was chaplain to William of Wykeham, becoming his executor and biographer.

In the central tower is a ring of eight bells, the treble and second given by Sir F. W. Fitzwygram in 1876, the third, fourth, fifth, and tenor being cast in 1714, the seventh in 1723, and the sixth recast in 1896.

The plate is modern, comprising a communion cup of 1825, and a cup, flagon, two plates, and glass flagon with silver stopper of more recent date.

The registers begin in 1653, the first book containing baptisms to 1703, marriages to 1726, and burials to 1731. The second contains the burials in woollen, 1678–1730, and the third the burials from 1730–1812. The fourth contains baptisms 1713–1812, and marriages 1730–54, and there is also a list of inductions of the rectors from 1618 to 1892. The fifth book is the printed marriage register 1754–93, and the sixth continues the marriages to 1812.

The oldest book of accounts runs from 1719 to 1748 and the vestry minutes from 1834 onwards are preserved.

There is no mention of a church in the Domesday Survey of Havant, though one of the two churches included in the survey of Warblington may have been at Havant.

The *CHURCH OF ST. JOHN* is of flint in the Norman style, consisting of small chancel, nave, transepts, and aisles. The register of baptisms dates from 1841, and of burials from 1842.

ADVOWSONS The advowson of the church of St. Faith was, like the manor, a possession of the monks of St. Swithun, and was transferred with the manor to the bishop, in whose gift it has been ever since.[84] Under Bishop Stratford inquisition was made for the ordination of Havant vicarage,[85] but no appropriation seems to have taken place, for the living was and is still a rectory.[86] The rector had peculiar jurisdiction in the parish,[87] but these rights were virtually abolished early in the last century.[88] There was also a rectory manor the lands of which are now practically enfranchised.[89] Special privileges had been attached to the church before the reign of Henry I, who confirmed to it exemption from pleas as in the time of William II and Bishop Walkelin.[90]

A parish was assigned to the chapelry of St. John Redhill in 1840,[91] the chapel having been built there two years before.[92] The living, which is a rectory, is in the alternate gift of the rectors of Havant and Warblington.

Under the will of Richard Dalingrigge of Wade, a chantry was founded in the church about 1471, and maintained for a time from the profits of his manor of Iford in Sussex. Two priests were provided to sing continually in Havant church for the souls of Richard Dalingrigge, his wife Sibyl and their ancestors, but four years after his death, Roger Lewkenor, his nephew and heir-at-law, entered upon the manor of Iford, declaring that Richard had made no such will, and that Iford had descended from Sir Roger Lewkenor to Thomas Lewkenor, his father.[93] The chantry evidently fell into disuse, for no mention of it occurs in the certificates of chantries returned in 1547;

[84] In 1660, however, before the restoration of the bishops' lands, the crown presented to Havant; Inst. Bks. (P.R.O.).

[85] Egerton MS. 2032, fol. 57*b*.

[86] *Cal. Pap. Pet.* i, 319.

[87] *Return of Causes . . . in Peculiars, Parl. Papers*, 1831-2, xxiv, 556.

[88] Under 1 & 2 Vic. cap. 106, s. 108; 5 & 6 Vic. cap. 27, s. 6.

[89] Ex inform. Rev. Canon S. G. Scott, rector of Havant.

[90] Add. MS. 29436, fol. 17.

[91] *Lond. Gaz.* 18 Aug. 1840, p. 1904.

[92] Sumner, *Conspectus of the Dioc. of Winton.* 1854.

[93] Early Chan. Proc. bdle. 168, No. 37.

mention is made, however, of a stipendiary priest maintained in Havant church for the ministration of a brotherhood there, founded 'of the devotion of the inhabitants,' and endowed with land and money.[94]

A chapel in connexion with the church was built at Langstone in 1869. There is also a Roman Catholic church (St. Joseph's) in West Street, founded in 1874–5.

The elementary school was built in 1895, and another in connexion with St. Joseph's was opened in 1875, while of the two Nonconformist schools, that at Redhill was opened in 1860 and the Havant and Bedhampton school in 1871.

CHARITIES The Congregational Chapel trust property and charities consist of the chapel, schoolroom, and other buildings erected on a site conveyed by deed of 13 January, 1891, with the proceeds of sale of the old chapel (1791), and of a piece of land on the south side of the vestry thereto; the Lecture Hall erected on part of the same site with the proceeds of sale in 1893 of the British School formerly in Market Road; the Parsonage House, let at £18 a year; £252 2*s.* 8*d.* Consols given by Thomas Bayly Silver, two-thirds of dividends for the pastor and one-third for the chapel alms fund; £203 13*s.* 1*d.* Consols given by Isaac Clements, by deed of 1880, for the benefit of the pastor; and £46 17*s.* 2*d.* Consols left by will of Miss Elizabeth Moore, proved 1886, dividends for the poor of the chapel. The sums of stock are held by the official trustees, and the trusts are administered under a Scheme of the Charity Commissioners, dated 11 December, 1891.

In 1876 William Henry Stone by deed gave 5 acres, 5 poles adjoining the cemetery on the east side, to let in allotments for the poor, the rents to be applied in prizes to the cultivators. In 1894 1 acre, 3 roods, 8 poles were taken for the enlargement of the cemetery, and a like quantity of land to the north of the allotment was acquired by exchange.

94 Chant. Cert. (Edw. VI).

THE HUNDRED OF BOSMERE

CONTAINING THE PARISHES OF

HAYLING ISLAND, INCLUDING NORTH AND SOUTH HAYLING

WARBLINGTON WITH EMSWORTH CHAPELRY [1]

In the Domesday Survey the hundred of Bosmere, or Boseburg as it is there called,[2] included Hayling, as yet undivided, Brockhampton, a tithing of Havant, Havant itself, which does not appear to have been quit of suit at the hundred court till later, and Newtimber, a tithing of Warblington. Warblington is assessed under Westbourne in Sussex, but was most probably included in Bosmere Hundred. The total assessment before the Conquest was fifty-seven hides and a half, which by 1086 had decreased to thirty-four. Havant had become a separate liberty before the thirteenth century,[3] and the manor of Hayling in South Hayling became quit of suit at the hundred court under a grant from Queen Mary to Henry earl of Arundel, in 1553.[4] The hundred was thus diminished to one parish, viz. Warblington, and it seems probable that, owing to its small extent, the sheriff held one tourn for the hundreds of Portsdown and Bosmere.[5] This assumption is strengthened by the fact that in 1465 the tithingman of Farlington 'in the hundreds of Portsdown and Bosmere' made presentment at the sheriff's tourn at 'Grenefeld' of the obstruction of a footpath from Hambledon to Havant.[6] Bosmere Hundred was in the hands of the king, and appears to have been farmed occasionally.[7]

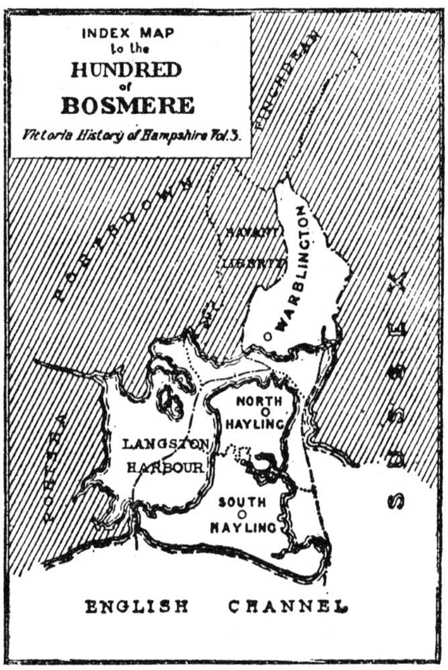

[1] The extent of the hundred as given in the *Population Return* of 1831.

[2] Boseburgh is the usual form of the name before the fifteenth century.

[3] Chart. R. 12 Edw. I, m. 5; *Plac. de Quo Warr.* (Rec. Com.), 771.

[4] Pat. 1 Mary, pt. ii, m. 5. Hence, in 1587, separate certificates of musters were returned for 'the hundreds of Havant, Bosmere, and Hayling.' *Cal. S.P. Dom.* 1581–90, p. 438.

[5] On the other hand the sheriff accounted separately for the two hundreds (Mem. R. Exchеq. L.T.R. Mich. 47 Edw. III, 'Recorda,' m. 16). It is also worthy of notice that the profits of Bosmere at one time exceeded those of Portsdown, the one being 59*s.* 8*d.* and the other 30*s.* 3*d.*

[6] Anct. D. (P.R.O.), A 6568.

[7] Inq. a.q.d. file 2, No. 31, where the jurors decide that it would not be to the king's damage to farm the hundreds of Titchfield, Portsdown, and Bosmere.

HAYLING ISLAND

Heglingaig (x cent.); Heilinciga or Halingei (xi cent.); Hailinges or Haringey[8] (xii cent.); Heyland or Heling (xiii cent.).

Hayling Island is only separated from the mainland by a narrow channel known as Sweare Deep. Nevertheless it was inaccessible in heavy weather before 1823, when an Act was passed for building a bridge across Langstone Harbour from Havant up to the Ferry House in North Hayling.[9] The single line of railway to Langstone from Havant has since been extended across the harbour and two stations built, one in North Hayling and the other in South Hayling.[10] The sea has encroached on the island very considerably. In the fourteenth century more especially the inhabitants suffered through this and other calamities. In 1324–5 the losses of Hayling Priory through the ravages of the sea were at least £42, for the priory buildings and the whole hamlet of East Stoke had been submerged.[11] Shortly afterwards the islanders were called upon to defend themselves against the incursions of hostile galleys during the French wars, and again in 1340 a great part of the island was entirely drowned by the sea.[12] In 1346 it was said to be laid waste daily,[13] and subsequently nearly half of the inhabitants died of the Black Death.[14] The sea again encroached to a large extent during the seventeenth century.[15] A considerable part of the east coast is now defended by sea-walls, built when the manor was in the possession of the dukes of Norfolk.

The island is divided into two parishes of almost equal extent, the northernmost being known as North Hayling or Northwood.[16] Along the channel which divides it from the mainland the country is flat and for the most part barren, though some profits are yielded by the oyster beds off Creek Point to the west. The road along the coast leads eastwards past large salterns and then curving to the south passes through the hamlets of Northney, Eastney, and Westney, with their low thatched houses and well-stocked orchards. North Hayling church is in Eastney, standing close to the road in a small churchyard. The soil from this point onwards is more fertile, stretches of arable land alternating with oakwoods in which there is a dense undergrowth of brushwood and brambles. Tracts of waste-land are, however, frequent, though many commons were inclosed during the last century,[17] and the island though lowlying is bleak and much exposed, so that when a fire broke out in North Hayling on 23 March, 1757, the violence of the wind increased it to such an extent that the unfortunate villagers were practically burnt out in a few hours.[18] West of the village, in Towncil Field, a Roman building has been discovered, and excavations are still being continued there. The same road leads on past the hamlet of Northney to South Hayling. To the west of Northney is the hamlet of Stoke, which is divided into East and West Stoke, and consists of a few farm-houses and cottages, old and new, with a Congregational chapel. The western coast is again more barren, the soil being very light and producing but scanty crops of wheat, while its marshy wastes can only be used for pasture, and that not of the best. The sub-soil is for the most part chalk, which is succeeded in the south by Woolwich and Reading Beds. The arable land, which predominates, covers 734 acres; there are 219 acres of pasture and 15 acres of wood.[19] The whole area of the parish is nearly 2,626 acres.

The greater part of the parish is held by tenants of Havant manor, the land being evidently identical with four hides in Hayling held by the monks of St. Swithun in 1086.[20] They annexed it to their neighbouring liberty, the tourns of which the tithingman of Hayling has always since attended.

South Hayling, or Southwood, includes the more prosperous portion of the island. The soil is richer than that of North Hayling, the subsoil being London clay, and stretches of flat pasture-land and flourishing wheatfields betoken its fertility. On the east and west coasts, however, there are marshy wastes such as Mill Pond, which, together with Mill Cottage, probably marks the site of the old manorial mill mentioned in a thirteenth-century assessment of South Hayling.[21] The arable land extends over 1,165 acres, the pasture covers 427 acres, and there are 43 acres of wood.[22] The total area of the parish is 4,803 acres. Near the Mill Pond is a thickly wooded inclosure surrounded by a moat, and known as Tourner Bury. In 'My Lord's Pond,' close by, oyster beds have been laid down, which with other beds near the island were the source of a dispute that arose in 1850 between the local fishermen and the lord of the manor, who based his claim on the mention of two fisheries in the Domesday Survey of Hayling.[23]

Mengham salterns are also relics of an ancient industry dating from the Conquest, for in 1086 the lord of Hayling had a saltpan in the island.[24] Mengham is a hamlet at the neck of the most eastern peninsula, and is made up of one or two weather-stained farm-houses, with thickly thatched outbuildings and a Congregational chapel built in 1888.

East Stoke Common, which forms a peninsula to the south-east of the island, was inclosed in 1867,[25] and is partially submerged at high tide; it was the men of this hamlet who suffered most from the encroachment of the sea during the fourteenth century. About halfway across the promontory a wall of cement was built some years back, but it is now cracked and broken.

8 This form occurs in the documents relating to East Stoke.

9 4 Geo. IV, cap. ix. The first pile was driven 30 Sept. 1822; *Hants Telegraph*, 13 Sept. 1824. The bridge was acquired by the London, Brighton and South Coast Railway Company in 1878. The tolls are still collected under the original Act.

10 Under 23 & 24 Vic. cap. 166.

11 See *V.C.H. Hants*, ii, 216.

12 *Cal. Close*, 1339–41, p. 392.

13 *Cal. Pat.* 1345–8, p. 131.

14 Orig. R. 29 Edw. III, m. 8.

15 Exch. Spec. Com. 5629 and 6848.

16 *Epis. Reg. Winton.* (Hants Rec. Soc.), i, 37.

17 Of these Eastney Common Fields and Salterns Duckard Hill were inclosed in 1840, Stoke Common Field in 1874 and Verner Common in 1876.

18 Church Brief (B.M.), A. iv, 1.

19 Board of Agriculture Returns (1905).

20 *V.C.H. Hants*, i, 468*a*. These four hides were quite distinct from the land in dispute between the monks of St. Swithun and of Jumièges.

21 *Pope Nich. Tax.* 214.

22 Board of Agriculture Returns (1905).

23 *Hants Advertiser*, Sat. 9 Mar. 1850.

24 *V.C.H. Hants*, i, 473.

25 *Commons Inclosure Rep.* 1904.

From East Stoke westwards firm white sands stretch to Sinah Common, whence a steam ferry carries the traveller to Portsea. The common, on which golf links have been laid out, is a mass of golden gorse in spring, and affords a fine view both of the Hampshire coast and the distant hills of the Isle of Wight. The magnificent sands and the outlook over the English Channel have caused the hamlet of West Town to grow into a seaside resort with a parade along the south beach. The church stands to the north of the West Town, and at some distance north of the church is the manor house, a pretty red brick building of eighteenth-century date in well wooded grounds, in the occupation of the vicar, the Rev. C. H. Clarke. This part of the parish is the most picturesque in the island, and from the abundance of trees has the great additional advantage of being sheltered from the gales which sweep across the island in winter.

MANOR

At the time of the Domesday Survey the abbey of Jumièges near Caen held about half the island of *HAYLING* in demesne with the overlordship of the rest by the gift of William I, but their possession was disputed by the monks of St. Swithun, who based their claim on a grant of Queen Emma.[26] She is said to have given this manor to the Priory in 1043 with eight others as a thank-offering for having passed safely through the ordeal of fire,[27] and the monks stated that she gave them one-half of the manor and the reversion of the other half at the death of Ulward White to whom she gave it for life and that Ulward died in the time of William I, who thereupon granted the manor to the abbey of Jumièges.[28] In a cartulary of St. Swithun there occurs a charter purporting to be a bequest of the Lady Elgifu[29] of five hides at Hayling to the Old Minster together with the reversion of five hides, which she had bequeathed to one Wulfward the White, evidently identical with Ulward White, for life, and stating that the Priory, at Wulfward's request, had farmed their moiety to him.[30] Hayling was evidently part of the queen's dower, as Ulward himself held it of Queen Edith before the Conquest.[31] The abbey of Jumièges, however, having once obtained a grant of so rich a manor, refused to give it up, and though William I himself confirmed Queen Emma's gift to the priory,[32] Henry I regranted Hayling to Jumièges.[33] Early in the twelfth century Bishop Henry de Blois and the monks of Winchester renounced their right to the manor in favour of Jumièges Abbey at the prayer of Pope Innocent and in consideration of the poverty of that church, and in 1150 Theobald, archbishop of Canterbury, bore witness to this concession.[34] During the whole of Stephen's reign the abbey seems to have lost power over its English possessions, to judge from the mandate of Henry II to the officers throughout England to restore to the abbot and monks all their fugitives who escaped after the death of Henry I[35] and from his confirmatory charters to them.[36] He confirmed to the abbot and monks free warren in Hayling as they had had it under Henry I,[37] and allowed them to carry all things from the demesne of the church freely to all the ports of England and Normandy;[38] hence it seems that the produce of the island was exported to the Norman abbey, and, from the accounts of the manor rendered when the priory of Hayling, founded in the island by the abbey of Jumièges, was in the hands of Edward I by reason of the war with France, it appears that the profits of the manor at that date were considerable. They included 3*s.* for 100 doves, 49*s.* for 114 cheeses, and 15*s.* 9*d.* for 21 gallons of butter.[39] In 1414, after the general dissolution of the alien priories in England, Henry V granted Hayling to the priory of Sheen in Surrey.[40] The prior seems, thenceforward, to have leased the site of the manor reserving all jurisdiction.[41] Sheen Priory surrendered in 1539 and Henry VIII granted Hayling manor and the site of Hayling Priory in 1541 to Holy Trinity College, Arundel, in exchange for the manor of Bury.[42] In 1548 the lands of the college were bestowed on Henry, earl of Arundel,[43] who settled them on his daughter Joan wife of John Lord Lumley. She died without issue and her husband, who survived her, conveyed all the Arundel estates to his nephew Philip, duke of Norfolk, in February, 1579–80. He was attainted in 1589, but the Arundel estates, and Hayling with them, were restored to his son Thomas in 1604.[44] It remained part of the property of the successive dukes of Norfolk till 1825 when William Padwick, a distinguished lawyer, purchased it under an Act of Parliament from Bernard Edward the then duke.[45] The new lord brought several suits relating to the liberties of the manor against his tenants, the most important being one concerning the oyster fisheries.[46] After his death the greater part of the manor was enfranchised, the remainder being purchased in 1871 by Mr. J. C. Park, whose son, Mr. C. J. Park, the present owner, inherited it in 1887.[47]

FITZALAN, Earl of Arundel. *Gules a lion or.*

Besides a court baron the lord of Hayling held view of frankpledge twice yearly, which was attended by tithingmen from Northney, Mengham, and West Town.[48] In 1553 Queen Mary granted the earl of Arundel return of writs and pleas of the crown in this manor as in Alton hundred.[49] Wreck of sea

[26] *V.C.H. Hants*, i, 473*a*.
[27] *Historia Major Winton.* (*Anglia Sacra*, i, 235). But the authenticity of this account is questionable.
[28] *Cal. Doc. France*, i, 526.
[29] Queen Emma was also known as Elgifu.
[30] Add. MS. 15350; see Kemble, *Codex Dipl.* No. 1337.
[31] *V.C.H. Hants*, i, 473*a*.
[32] According to the Priory's cartulary; Add. MS. 29436, fol. 11*b*.
[33] Cartae Antiq. EE. 8. One clause in the charter, evidently directed against the Priory, forbids anyone to take away or diminish anything of it.
[34] *Cal. Doc. France*, i, 55, 56.
[35] Ibid. 55.
[36] Cartae Antiq. EE. 8.
[37] *Cal. Doc. France*, i, 55.
[38] Cartae Antiq. EE. 9.
[39] The account is given in full in Longcroft, *Bosmere Hundred*, 208.
[40] See foundation charter of Sheen. Dugdale, *Mon.* vi, 31.
[41] Mins. Accts. 31–2 Hen. VIII, Surr. bdle. 146, m. 45.
[42] *L. and P. Hen. VIII*, xvi, 1056 (69).
[43] Ibid. xix (2), 800 (35).
[44] Pat. 2 Jas. I, pt. 17, m. 37.
[45] Local and Pers. Acts, 6 Geo. IV, cap. 57.
[46] *Southampton County Paper*, Sat. 9 Mar. 1850. For full details of these suits see Add. MS. 24788.
[47] Ex inform. Mr. C. J. Park, lord of the manor.
[48] Court R. (P.R.O.), bdle. 205, No. 56.
[49] Pat. 1 Mary, pt. 2, m. 5.

was granted to Henry, earl of Arundel, in 1548, but the tenants of East Stoke had already had that privilege throughout the island under the charter of Henry III to William Falconer.[50] Hence in 1634 when a butt and a hogshead of wine were cast up by the sea the earl of Arundel's tenant claimed the one and the tenant of East Stoke the other.[51]

Howard, Duke of Norfolk. *Gules a bend between six crosslets fitchy argent with a scutcheon or upon the bend charged with a demi-lion in a tressure of Scotland pierced through the mouth with an arrow all gules.*

EAST STOKE, the land including the south-eastern corner of the island, was given by Edwy to his faithful servant Ethelsig and his heirs in 956.[52] It appears to have been identical with the 5 hides in Hayling, held by Ulward before the Conquest. They were granted by William I to Earl Roger of Shrewsbury, who bestowed them on the abbey of St. Martin, Troarn.[53] The gift was confirmed by Henry I and Henry II.[54] The Norman monks reserved their land in Hayling in 1260 when exchanging their English possessions for the Norman property of Bruton Abbey in Somerset,[55] probably owing to the convenience of the situation of the island, for it appears from a licence granted by King John that 'cheeses and bacons' were exported from their English demesnes for their own consumption.[56] In the following year, however, the abbot of Troarn conveyed the land to John Falconer of Wade to hold at the yearly rent of 1*d*.[57] William Falconer, John's predecessor in Wade (q.v.), had already obtained a few acres in Hayling,[58] and was granted wreck of sea in the whole hundred of Bosmere, both within and without Hayling Island.[59] For some time the successive lords of Limborne and Wade retained lands and rents in East Stoke, North Stoke, and Westney in Hayling. In 1316 the tenants of John and Joan Botiler of Limborne, in the island of Hayling, accused them of exacting excessive services, at the same time stating that their land was ancient demesne of the crown, producing in evidence an extract from the Domesday Survey of 2½ hides held by Earl Harold before the Conquest. Joan proved that the land was that which was held by the abbot of Troarn, and therefore was not ancient demesne.[60] The descent of East Stoke is coincident with that of Limborne (q.v.) until the death of Anthony Pound, when East Stoke evidently became the portion of his daughter Honor, who married Henry, earl of Sussex.[61] In 1596 Sir Robert Ratcliffe, earl of Sussex, and son and heir of Earl Henry, conveyed East Stoke to Jonah Latelais, whose son Harison Latelais sold the 'manor or lordship of Northstocke, Eastocke, and Westhaye (evidently Westney),[62] with a house called Kent in Westhay,' to Thomas Peckham of London.[63] From Thomas Peckham it ultimately descended to Peckham Williams,[64] who bequeathed it to John Williams, and he vested it in trustees for sale.[65] It was purchased by Elizabeth Poole Penfold, at whose death in 1842[66] the estates passed to her great-nephew, John Leigh Hollest, who took the name of Williams.[67] In 1845 he conveyed East Stoke to Thomas Harris of Donnington,[68] from whom it was purchased by Mr. Lynch White of Streatham in 1870. From 1890 onwards he sold the estate in building plots, the largest portion being bought in 1902 by Mr. Frank Pearce of Portsmouth.[69]

Ratcliffe, Earl of Sussex. *Argent a bend engrailed sable.*

In 1086, 2½ hides in Hayling, which had been held by Edward the Confessor by a certain Leman, and later seized by Earl Harold, were held by the king himself.[70] They seem to have been annexed to the honour of Gloucester, for towards the end of the thirteenth century Ralph de Anvers held 2 hides of land in Hayling of that honour.[71] The later history of this fee is uncertain, it seems probable, from the claim by Joan Botiler's tenants to hold in ancient demesne, that at any rate a portion of it was at some time alienated to the owners of East Stoke.

CHURCHES

The church of *OUR LADY, SOUTH HAYLING*, lies to the west of the road from the manor house to West Town. It has a chancel 41 ft. by 19 ft., with a north vestry, central tower 18 ft. 7 in. square (24 ft. 3 in. square over all), with nave and aisles 54 ft. 10 in. long by 41 ft. 6 in. wide, the aisles being prolonged to overlap the tower on the north and south. Over the south door of the nave is a wooden porch.

The whole building is set out as one design, and was probably in course of construction from the second quarter of the thirteenth century to the end of the third quarter, the chancel being the earliest part. The treatment of the tower is a very interesting modification of the cruciform plan, its walls being only 2 ft. 10 in. thick, and its western supports reduced to a minimum, so that the space it covers is treated as the east bay of the nave rather than the base of a central tower, and the transepts to which it opens on north and south are merely eastern chapels of the same width as the aisles. The arches opening from the aisles to these eastern chapels die into the walls, so that there is no loss of width in the aisle, their existence being only due to the constructional

50 Chart. R. 51 Hen. III, m. 11.

51 *Cal. S.P. Dom.* 1634–5, p. 581.

52 Kemble, *Codex Dipl.* 1193. The boundaries of the five 'mansae' given to Ethelsig were as follows: First out to the old inclosure for horses, thence to the lea, from the lea on to 'Ceanninga Mœre,' from 'Ceanninga Mœre' out on sea.

53 *V.C.H. Hants*, i, 478*a*.

54 *Cal. Doc. France*, i, 67.

55 *Bruton Cartul.* (Somers. Rec. Soc.), 310.

56 Ibid. 326.

57 Feet of F. Hants, 46 Hen. III, No. 36.

58 Ibid. 34 Hen. III, No. 2.

59 *Rot. Chart.* (Rec. Com.), 95.

60 *Plac. Abbrev.* (Rec. Com.), 325.

61 Feet of F. Div. Cos. Hil. 3 Eliz.

62 Cf. *Parl. Writs* (Rec. Com.), ii (2), 344, where the hamlets of Northstratton and Westney are given as under the lordship of John Botiler in 1315.

63 Close, 6 Chas. I, pt. ii, m. 12.

64 For an account of the family see Dallaway's *Suss.* i, viii.

65 Act of Parl. 42 Geo. III, cap. 53.

66 *Gent. Mag.* (New Ser.), xvii, 675.

67 Ibid. xviii, 196.

68 Longcroft, *Bosmere Hund.* 193.

69 Information kindly supplied by Mr. H. F. Trigg of Hayling.

70 *V.C.H. Hants*, i, 451*b*.

71 *Testa de Nevill* (Rec. Com.), 234.

necessity of giving abutment to the west arch of the tower.

The chancel has five tall lancet lights under an inclosing arch in the east wall, four tall lancets on the north, and four on the south, the lower part of the westernmost window on the south being cut off by a square-headed low side window of two lights; the stonework of this window is modern. The lancets have a keeled roll on the rear arches and jambs, and a roll-string at the sill level. Between the third and fourth windows on the south is a plain pointed doorway, part of the original arrangement, and at the south-east of the chancel is a double piscina with trefoiled arches, and round shafts with moulded bases and capitals. East of it is a square-headed cupboard in the wall, 15 in. deep and 2 ft. 7 in. wide, with a rebated opening 1 ft. wide by 1 ft. 10 in. high, and in the east jambs of the north-east and south-east lancets are thirteenth-century corbels with recesses above to take the ends of a beam which crossed the chancel at this point, showing that the high altar was set forward with a space behind it for a vestry. It is to be noted that these corbels are worked from the same template, instead of being right and left handed, as their positions require.

The tower stands on four wide pointed arches of two chamfered orders, with half-octagonal responds to the inner orders. These have moulded capitals on the eastern piers, while those on the western piers are foliate, and of interesting and rather unusual detail. The walls of the tower only rise to about a foot above the ridge of the nave roof, and have two small lancet windows in each face of the upper stage, with single lancets of a like character at a lower level on the north and south, showing that the eastern chapels of the aisles were from the first designed to have lean-to roofs like the aisles instead of being gabled north and south like transepts. The tower is finished with a low-pitched hipped roof from which springs a short octagonal wooden spire, both being covered with oak shingles.

The nave is of three bays, with widely spaced arcades like those under the tower, their chamfered orders dying on to octagonal dies. The octagonal capitals are unusually shallow in the bell, but are most effectively treated with carved foliage, while shafts beneath are markedly slender in comparison with the dies above. The effect of lightness and space thus obtained is most satisfactory. The clearstory has two circular windows on each side, set over the columns instead of the arches, and inclosing quatrefoils with pierced spandrels.

The east bay of the north aisle has a modern east window of two lights with a trefoiled circle in the head, and in its north wall two lancet lights with modern heads and a quatrefoil over, the same arrangement occurring in the east bay of the south aisle. Under the south window in the south aisle is a trefoiled thirteenth-century piscina. At the west of these bays are sharply-pointed drop-arches of two chamfered orders, the outer order dying into the side walls, while the inner rests on half octagonal corbels, those on the tower piers having curious foliate carving.

The remaining three bays of the aisles have small lancet windows in the first and third bays, and wide pointed north and south doorways in the middle bays, with plain chamfered arches. The west windows of the aisles are of two lights with quatrefoils over, and the nave has a plain thirteenth-century west doorway and over it a large four-light window with fifteenth-century tracery, the main lights having a transom at half height. The south porch is a very pretty fifteenth-century construction, with moulded plates, tie-beams, and outer arch; it is in rather shaky condition, and a good deal patched with later work.

All the church except the tower has tiled roofs, the timbers of the nave roof, which has trussed rafters and moulded tie-beams with king posts, being perhaps contemporary with the nave walls, and a rare specimen of their kind.

In the chancel is an eighteenth-century wooden reredos, but all other wood fittings are modern. In the second stage of the tower, below the bell frames, are some seventeenth-century timbers which seem to have been intended to be seen from below, and the tower was probably meant to be open to the nave as high as the floor of the bell-chamber.

At the west end of the north aisle is the font, with a square Purbeck marble bowl, *c.* 1200, on a central column and four modern angle shafts with stone capitals and bases. At the east end of the same aisle is a very interesting and early rectangular stone bowl, the sides curving outwards at the top, and ornamented with interlacing patterns. There appears to be no drain in the bottom, and its original purpose is not certain. On the external south-east angle of the south aisle and the south-east buttress of the chancel are incised sun-dials.

There are pits for three bells in the tower, but only one bell remains, inscribed 'In God is my hope,' 1634, with the founder's initials I. H.

The church plate is modern, and consists of two chalices, two patens, a flagon, a cruet and an alms-dish.

The registers of North and South Hayling churches are kept together, and the first book, the parchment copy of 1598, contains baptisms to 1653, and marriages and burials to 1649, and belongs to North Hayling. The second, with entries 1672–1801, belongs to South Hayling. The third has North Hayling entries 1653–1724, and the sixth continues the list to 1801. The fourth book has South Hayling marriages 1754–88, and the fifth continues the same to 1812. The seventh has North Hayling marriages 1754–1804, and the eighth the same to 1812. The ninth has North Hayling baptisms and burials 1802–12, and the tenth the corresponding entries for South Hayling.

To the south of the church, near the south porch, is a very fine yew tree, which though somewhat past its prime is still full of leaf, and adds greatly to the beauty of the churchyard.

The church of *ST. PETER, NORTH HAYLING,* consists of chancel 20 ft. 2 in. by 13 ft. 2 in., nave 45 ft. 2 in. by 19 ft. 8 in., with aisles and north transept chapel, north and south porches, and a wooden bell turret over the east bay of the nave. Nothing in the building seems to be older than the end of the twelfth century, the north arcade of the nave being probably of this date, while nearly every other detail in the church belongs to the early part of the thirteenth century. The walls of the nave are only 2 ft. 1 in. thick, but this in a building of small scale does not necessarily imply an early date, and the north wall of the north aisle, which is not likely to be older than

South Hayling Church : South Arcade of Nave

South Hayling Church from the South-west

the existing arcade, is of the same thickness. The probable growth of the plan has been that a former chancel, whose west wall was a little to the east of the responds of what is now the second bay of the nave arcades, was prolonged eastward early in the thirteenth century, the line of the chancel arch being moved eastwards to its present line, and a north transept chapel (and probably also a like chapel on the south, now destroyed) added. Openings were made into both these chapels from the new east bay of the nave, which was probably occupied from the first by a wooden belfry as now, representing the central tower of a more ambitious design, as at South Hayling. There have been no later additions to the plan, except the north porch. The chancel has three tall lancet windows on the east, and two smaller windows on north and south, with a priest's door at the south-west angle. The heads of the lights are bluntly pointed or round, but the rear arches are in all cases pointed, and a moulded string runs round the inner face of the walls at their sill level. Near the north-east angle is a recess rebated for a wooden door, and opposite to it on the south a pointed piscina recess with a projecting bowl, both features being of the date of the chancel. The east wall leans outward dangerously, and is supported by three large raking buttresses. The chancel arch is pointed, of two chamfered orders, of the full width of the chancel, save for small half-round shafts on the responds with moulded capitals.

The north transept, which is approximately 13 ft. square, a dimension found elsewhere in the county in transepts of this kind, has two tall lancets on the east like those in the chancel, and between them a large trefoiled recess, having a small image bracket over it, marking the site of a former altar. The north window of the transept is like those on the east, and the west window, also a single lancet, is lower, with a pointed head.

The nave arcades are of four bays, the three western being continuous, but the east bay on each side seemsto be an addition, as suggested above. The arches here are quite plain, pointed, with a square-edged string at the springing, chamfered below; the north arch is not central with the transept, probably because a transept set centrally with it would have been inconveniently small.

The other three bays of the north arcade have pointed arches of one order with edge chamfers, square abaci, with simple leaves at the angles of the capitals, circular columns, and moulded bases with spurs on a square plinth. The east respond has a capital with a row of plain heart-shaped leaves on the bell. In the south arcade the arches are like those of the north, but the capitals, columns, and bases are circular. The abaci are of square section, and the bases are moulded, the capitals being quite plain, without any ornament. There are two small lancet lights in the north aisle, and between them a plain pointed thirteenth-century doorway under a wooden porch, which may be in part of the fifteenth century. The south aisle, the east end of which is used as a vestry, contains no old features except the south doorway, which has a low four-centred head, and may be of the sixteenth century. In the west wall of the nave is a fifteenth-century doorway, and over it a window of three cinquefoiled lights, with modern tracery.

The roofs of the nave, transept, and north aisle are old, and of plain character with trussed rafters, while the east bay of the nave is ceiled at the level of the tie-beam, and boarded in above, access to the belfry being by a stair at the south-east, which may represent an old stair to the rood loft. In the spandrel between the tie-beam and the nave roof is a fifteenth-century beam with cusped and pierced hanging tracery, like a barge-board. The other woodwork in the church, beyond a seventeenth-century chest, has no archaeological interest.

The font stands in the third bay of the south arcade, and has a round tapering bowl without a stem. The top edge of the bowl is scalloped, but this seems to be a modern adornment, though the font itself may be of the thirteenth century. On the capital of the pillar against which it stands is a fifteenth-century stone bracket.

St. Peter's Church, North Hayling

There are three bells, fitted with half wheels, in frames which are probably mediaeval. Two of the bells are blank, but seem to be contemporary with the tenor, which is inscribed in good Gothic capitals Sancta [M]aria ora pro nobis; it is a late fourteenth or early fifteenth-century bell.

The plate consists of a cup of 1569, with a cover paten of the same date, and a second cup and cover paten a little larger, and of slightly different outline, but probably made locally as a copy of the other, and bearing no hall-marks. There is also a modern paten, 1858.

For the registers see South Hayling.

ADVOWSONS

The church of *SOUTH HAYLING* was held by the abbey of Jumièges, and was appropriated to that monastery in 1253–4,[72] and the advowson was

[72] Harl. Chart. 83 C. 32.

vested in the successive lords of the manor until Mr. William Padwick gave it to his daughter, the present Mrs. R. F. Clarke.

The church of *NORTH HAYLING* is a chapelry attached to South Hayling, but no chapel was assessed with the church in the *Taxatio* of 1291. In 1304, however, and during the next ten years, there were several petitions from the inhabitants to the bishop praying that the vicar should celebrate in the chapel of St. Peter, Northwood. The dispute between the vicar and his parishioners was settled in 1317, when the vicar agreed to hold full and complete service there every Sunday and on certain festivals, and to provide the necessary books.[73] Under Bishop Edendon (1346–66) the chancel was repaired, Bishop Waynflete (1447–87) issued a commission for the dedication of Northwood chapel,[74] and shortly afterwards another agreement was made between the vicar of Southwood and his parishioners at Northwood chapel as to the services to be held there.[75] The living is still a perpetual curacy attached to South Hayling.

A Congregational chapel was built in 1888 at Mengham and a Free Church mission house at Elm Grove in 1894. The South Hayling elementary school was opened in 1875–6.

CHARITIES There are no endowed charities within the parish of North Hayling, but in South Hayling a small piece of land in the Church Road, called 'The Surplice Piece' has been in the possession of the vicar and churchwardens for many years, and according to tradition was given to provide a fund for washing the vicar's surplice. A church room was erected on part of the land in 1904. By an order of the Charity Commissioners, dated 5 September, 1905, the real estate was vested in 'the Official Trustee of Charity Lands' and a scheme established directing that the church room should be used for the benefit of members of the Church of England in the parish of St. Mary, and that the income of the charity, subject to the up-keep of the church room, should be applied towards defraying the expenses in connexion with the parish church.

WARBLINGTON

Warbliteton (xi cent.); Warblinton (xiii cent.).

The civil parish of Warblington, governed by Warblington Urban District Council, extends over 3,254 acres and includes the ecclesiastical parishes of Warblington and Emsworth and a part of Rowland's Castle. The village, which lies on the main road from Southampton to Chichester, consists of a few houses clustered about the cross-roads, where one way curving round by the village pond leads northwards towards Eastleigh, and another, known as Pook Lane,[1] winds its way through the meadows to Langstone Harbour. Most of the southern part of the parish is well-watered pasture-land. Of the whole parish 663 acres are arable land, about 808 acres pasture-land, and 425 acres are covered with wood.[2] The streams served to work water-mills, one of which is mentioned as appurtenant to the manor in 1086,[3] while another stood in the tithing of 'Neutibrige.' At the east end of the village a lane leads southwards past the avenue leading to the rectory house, to the 'Castle,' a comparatively modern house with farm buildings, conspicuous only for the ruins of a tall sixteenth-century gateway. At the end of the lane stands the church with several fine yew trees in the churchyard, one to the south-east being a notable specimen, and across the graveyard there are glimpses of the channel between Hayling Island and the mainland. The soil here is chalky, but further north the subsoil is clay, the surface being a rich loam used mostly for pasture land, though some wheat is grown. The whole of the northern part of the parish is thickly wooded. Leigh Park, the residence of Sir Frederick FitzWygram, bart., is surrounded by oaks, larch and firs, and the woods stretch eastwards to Emsworth Common. It was probably from them that Herbert son of Matthew, then lord of Emsworth, sent forty oaks to provide pales for the bishop of Chichester's park in 1231.[4] Warblington Park was frequently mentioned with the manor towards the end of the fifteenth century, and was granted to Sir Richard Cotton with it in 1551.[5] It may have originated in the grant of free warren to Herbert son of Matthew in 1231,[6] and if, as was presumably the case, it surrounded the castle, it may possibly have been destroyed during the civil wars. The tithe-map of the parish is in the custody of the rector.

MANORS *WARBLINGTON MANOR* was originally parcel of Westbourne in Sussex, which formed part of the possessions of Earl Godwin,[7] at whose death Warblington was probably inherited with its tithing of Newtimber by Earl Harold.[8] After the Conquest the manor was granted to Roger earl of Shrewsbury, who died in 1094. His English lands were inherited by his second son, Hugh, who was succeeded in 1098 by his elder brother, Robert of Bellême, on payment of a heavy fine. The latter forfeited them by his rebellion against Henry I, and Warblington was evidently granted to a member of the de Courci family, for William de Courci, dapifer to Henry II, was in possession of it in 1186.[9] His son Robert, preferring to retain his Norman lands, forfeited his claim to Warblington,[10] which thus became an escheat to King John, of whom it was held by his ardent supporter Matthew son of Herbert, sheriff of Sussex under John and Henry III, in exchange for lands which he had lost

73 Winton. Epis. Reg. Sendale, fol. 21.
74 Egerton MS. 2033, fol. 44.
75 Ibid. fol. 89.
1 The name seems connected with a certain Roger 'Pouke' associated with Robert Le Ewer in a writ concerning Emsworth in 1312; *Cal. Pat.* 1307–13, p. 430.
2 Board of Agriculture Returns (1905).
3 *V.C.H. Hants*, i, 526.
4 *Cal. Close*, 1227–31, p. 431.
5 *Cal. Pat.* 1476–85, pp. 117, 495.
6 *Cal. Chart. R.* i, 133. The grant was confirmed eight years later; ibid. p. 242.
7 *V.C.H. Hants*, i, 526*b*.
8 Ibid. 478.
9 Pipe R. 32 Hen. II. Its seems probable that Hen. I granted Warblington to his dapifer Robert de Courci father of William de Courci, who died in 1177, leaving a son, the William de Courci of the text, *see Magni Rot. Scacc. Norman.* (Soc. of Antiq.), xcv.
10 *Hist. of Noble Brit. Families*, by Hen. Drummond; *Testa de Nevill* (Rec. Com.), 237.

in Normandy. In February, 1230–1, Matthew's son Herbert was granted the manor for maintenance so long as he should remain in the king's service across the seas,[11] and in the following June the king entailed it on him and his heirs failing the restoration of the heirs of Robert de Courci, at the same time granting him free warren there.[12] Herbert son of Matthew evidently died without issue, for his brother, Peter son of Matthew, did homage for his lands in 1245, and was succeeded by a third brother, John son of Matthew, who paid relief for his inheritance in 1255. Presumably he was dead before July, 1269, at which date the tenants of various lands were summoned to answer to the custodian, Nicholas son of Martin, for 600 marks owing to William de Valence.[13] John's widow Margaret was holding Warblington in dower in October, 1287[14] with remainder to Matthew son of John Ude, who quitclaimed his right to Henry III and Queen Eleanor, receiving in return a grant of the manor for life.[15] He died before 1309,[16] the reversion of the manor having already been granted for life to the king's yeoman, Robert Le Ewer,[17] who, after having steadily risen in the royal favour for some years, forfeited his estates by rebellion, and died in prison in 1324–5.[18]

In 1309 the reversion of the manor at Robert's death was granted to Ralph Monthermer, who had married Joan of Acres, sister of Edward II, and to Ralph's two sons Thomas and Edward,[19] the younger of whom, Edward, succeeded to Warblington according to an agreement made after Robert Le Ewer's death.[20] His lands were seized by the king upon suspicion of his adherence to the earl of Kent, but were restored to him in December, 1330,[21] and his brother Thomas seems to have succeeded to them as his heir.[22] Margaret widow of Thomas Monthermer held Warblington in dower till her death in May, 1349,[23] when it was inherited by her daughter Margaret wife of Sir John Montagu, kt., who died in March, 1394–5, leaving a son and heir John, afterwards earl of Salisbury.[24] The latter forfeited his lands by reason of his resistance to Henry IV,[25] but Warblington was granted in March, 1400–1, to his young son Thomas,[26] who was restored to his father's honours in 1409.[27] His daughter Alice took the manor in marriage to Richard Nevill, father of the 'Kingmaker,'[28] after whose death in February, 1477–8, it was held by the latter's daughter Isabel, wife of George, duke of Clarence.[29] In June, 1478, the custody of the manor during her son's minority was given to Edmund Mille, groom of the king's chamber.[30] This son was the unfortunate Edward earl of Warwick, executed in November, 1499. In 1509 Sir Francis Cheyne was appointed steward of the manor, William and Stephen Cope being bailiff and parker,[31] and, in spite of a previous grant in tail male to William Arundel, lord of Maltravers and his wife Anne,[32] it was restored in 1514 to Margaret, countess of Salisbury, sister and heir of Edward earl of Warwick, with other lands.[33] She was living at the castle in 1526.[34] She was a staunch papist, and from her house her son-in-law, Lord Montagu, and others sent frequent messages to their friends on the continent, especially to Cardinal Pole,[35] using as an agent a certain Hugh Holland of Warblington, who had already been convicted of piracy.[36] After her attainder in consequence of her share in these conspiracies Warblington was granted temporarily to William earl of Southampton, and to Sir Thomas Wriothesley, the king's secretary.[37] In 1551 it was finally entailed on Sir Richard Cotton, kt.,[38] whose son George succeeded to it at his death in 1556.[39] George Cotton was living at Warblington in 1596,[40] and died there in 1609–10, leaving a son and heir Sir Richard Cotton.[41] In 1635 a Richard Cotton died seised of the manor leaving a young grandson and heir of the same name who was a staunch Royalist.[42] In January, 1643–4, 'the strong house at Warblington' was captured by sixty soldiers and a hundred muskets,[43] and Richard Cotton was obliged to compound for his lands.[44] He is said to

MONTAGU. *Argent a fesse indented of three points gules.*

NEVILL, Earl of Salisbury. *Gules a saltire argent and a label gobony argent and azure.*

11 *Cal. Close*, 1227–31, p. 477.
12 *Cal. of Chart. R.* i, 133.
13 Misc. Inq. (Hen. III), file 15, No. 13; *Excerpt. e Rot. Fin.* ii, 205; i, 432.
14 *Cal. Pat.* 1281–92, p. 280.
15 Feet of F. Div. Cos. 15–16 Edw. I, 52; *Cal. Close*, 1279–88, p. 480. In these agreements he is variously called Matthew son of John, Sir Matthew son of John, and Matthew son of John Ude. In 1308 he obtained licence to grant his life interest in land in Westbrook, parcel of the manor, to his father and his wife Christina, so it appears that he was not a son of that John son of Matthew whose widow held Warblington in dower in 1287. *Cal. Pat.* 1307–13, p. 71.
16 Chan. Inq. p.m. 3 Edw. II, No. 49.
17 *Cal. Pat.* 1307–13, p. 160.
18 Ibid. 1224–7, p. 142. For an account of Robert Le Ewer see under Westbury.
19 Chart. R. 3 Edw. II, m. 8. They were given the manor of Westendale to hold until the reversion fell due. Pat. 4 Edw. II, pt. 2, m. 27.
20 *Cal. Close* 1323–7, p. 492.
21 Ibid. 1330–3, p. 74.
22 Chan. Inq. p.m. 14 Edw. III (1st Nos.), No. 34.
23 Ibid. 23 Edw. III (1st. Nos.), pt. 2, No. 90.
24 Ibid. 18 Ric. II, No. 31.
25 Ibid. 10 Hen. IV, No. 54.
26 *Cal. Pat.* 1399–1401, p. 466.
27 *R. of Parl.* (Rec. Com.), iv, 141.
28 De Banc. R. 674 (Trin. 7 Hen. VI.), m. 331 *d.*; Chan. Inq. p.m. 7 Hen. VI. No. 57.
29 Ibid. 18 Edw. IV, No. 47.
30 *Cal. Pat.* 1476–85, p. 117. He was succeeded in the office of bailiff by Edward Berkeley, John Bulle and others.
31 *L. and P. Hen. VIII*, i, 567, 1239
32 Pat. 2 Hen. VIII, pt. 3, m. 4.
33 *L. and P. Hen. VIII*, i, 4848.
34 Ibid. i, 2343.
35 Ibid. xiii (2), 702, 772, 797.
36 Ibid. vi, 316.
37 Ibid. xiv (2), 113 (18); xvii, 1154 (2).
38 Pat. 5 Edw. VI, m. 5.
39 Chan. Inq. p.m. (Ser. 2), file 997, No. 1.
40 *Cal. of MSS. of Marquis of Salisbury* (Hist. MSS. Com.), vii, 25.
41 W. and L. Inq. p.m. 7–8 Jas. I (Ser. 2), bdle. 3, No. 232.
42 Chan. Inq. p.m. 11 Chas. I (Ser. 2), iii, No. 158.
43 *Cat. Codicum MSS. Bibl. Bodl.* D. 395, 46. According to a letter from Wilmot, lord-lieutenant of the Royalist forces, in which he states that 'he has not yet had a reply to the message sent to Arundel Castle' (then besieged by Sir William Waller), and that 'they have taken the strong house at Warblington . . . which commands a pretty port, and will be of good advantage.' Thus leaving it ambiguous as to which party actually captured Warblington.
44 *Cal. Com. for Compounding* (Rec. Com.), 2088.

have bequeathed them to his only surviving son William,[45] who died in 1736. Under his will the manor passed to Thomas Panton,[46] who sold his life interest to Richard Barwell of Stansted. The latter also bought the reversion from Baroness Willoughby de Eresby,[47] and bequeathed the manor to trustees for sale.[48] It was purchased in 1825 by Messrs. Brown & Fenwick, and in 1875 was held by the trustees of John Fenwick.[49] In 1885 the manor was acquired by Messrs. H. G. Paine and Richard Brettell of Chertsey.

Cotton. *Azure a cheveron between three hanks of cotton argent.*

The lords of Warblington had both a court baron and a court leet, but have ceased to hold either.[50]

It was probably at George Cotton's manor-house, i.e. at Warblington Castle, that Queen Elizabeth stayed for two days during her progress through the southern counties in 1586.[51]

The 'Castle,' Warblington

The 'strong house of Warblington' of Civil War days exists no longer, though whether by reason of damages then sustained does not appear. The only relic of its former importance is a tall octagonal turret of red brick and stone, once forming the angle of an entrance gateway, which must have been a fine building, dating from the early part of the sixteenth century. It was of four stories, and enough remains to show that it had square-headed mullioned windows, with arched heads to the lights. The present house, standing to the east of the gateway, is of no architectural interest.

The tithing of *NEUTIBRIGE* or *NEWTIMBER* is mentioned in the Domesday Survey. Land was held there before the Conquest by Earl Harold, and his tenant Sired continued to hold it of Earl Roger of Shrewsbury after 1066.[52] John Dake, parson of Warblington, made an unsuccessful attempt to claim land and rent in Newtimber and Hayling in 1249, when William of Newtimber was said to be holding the premises in villeinage of Adam de la More.[53] Subsequently William Falconer of Wade released land and rents there to John, parson of Warblington.[54] The successive lords of Wade were possessed of a moiety of Newtimber,[55] while in 1316 another moiety was held by Henry Romyn,[56] probably a descendant and successor of John son of John Romyn, who in 1272 conveyed a messuage, a mill, 2 virgates of land and 2 acres of wood to Adam de la More for life.[57]

EMSWORTH (Emeleworth and Emelesworth, xiii cent.; Empnesworth and Emmesworth, xiv cent.), situated at the head of the harbour to the east of Warblington, where the River Ems flows into the sea, is a small town of some importance, and has lately become a popular yachting station. It is a member of the port of Portsmouth, and as such, exports timber and flour and imports coal. In the fourteenth century the trade in foreign wines was considerable, and smuggling was rife.[58] The fisheries are prosperous, chiefly owing to the success of the oyster-beds in the harbour. In 1340 the fishing and profits of the shore at Emsworth formed a valuable item in the revenues of Warblington Manor.[59] The lord of Warblington also had a weekly market and an annual fair in Emsworth, under a grant of Henry III in 1239.[60] The fair was held on the morrow of the Translation of St. Thomas (4 July). The town is a growing one, its prosperity being chiefly due to its situation at the head of the harbour and on the road from Portsmouth to Chichester. It has a station on the Portsmouth line of the London Brighton and South Coast Railway. The High Street is a wide open space from which the smaller streets run irregularly down to the various quays or to the 'Foreshore,' where men are always busy lading and unlading ships.

Emsworth was originally a tithing and hamlet of Warblington, and is not mentioned in the Domesday

45 Add. MSS. 33284; Recov. R. Trin. 1 Anne, No. 42.

46 Longcroft, *Bosmere Hund.* 98.

47 Sister and heiress of Robert, duke of Ancaster and Kesteven. The reversion had been settled on Mary duchess of Ancaster, *née* Panton, in 1767.

48 P.C.C. Will proved 12 Oct. 1804; quoted by Longcroft, 99.

49 Kelly, *County Topographies, Hants*, 1875.

50 Court R. (P.R.O.), bdle. 201, No. 68.

51 *Cal. MSS. of Marquis of Salisbury* (Hist. MSS. Com.), iii, 178.

52 *V.C.H. Hants*, i, 478.

53 Assize R. 777, m. 23 *d.*

54 Feet of F. Hants, 35 Hen. III, 12.

55 Ibid. 40 Edw. III, 84; Chan. Inq. p.m. 9–10 Edw. IV, No. 84.

56 *Feud. Aids*, ii, 319.

57 Feet of F. Hants. 56 Hen. III, No. 42. It is difficult to locate these lands. Possibly they were near Wade Court, in Havant; from the fact that a fishery was attached to them in 1086, it may be concluded that they were near the sea.

58 *Cal. Pat.* 1345–8, pp. 163, 167.

59 Chan. Inq. p.m. 14 Edw. III (1st Nos.), No. 34. The lords of Emsworth claimed fishing rights in 1314, when the lords of Warblington had dispossessed them, but they do not seem to have made good their right to this privilege, nor is it mentioned in the restoration of Emsworth to Thomas Bardolf.

60 *Cal. Chart. R.* i, 242. The grant was confirmed to Thomas, earl of Salisbury, *c.* 1403; Chart. R. 4 Hen. IV, pt. 2, No. 26.

View of Emsworth

(From an old print)

Survey, but when the manor of Warblington was in King John's hands as an escheat of Robert de Courci he granted 100*s.* rent from it to William Aguillon, and in 1230 Henry III confirmed to him the land late of Robert de Courci in Emsworth and Warblington for the yearly rent of a pair of gilt spurs,[61] the land being extended at four hides.[62] In 1280 Robert Aguillon, son and heir of William,[63] when summoned to show why he took amendment of the assize of bread and ale in Warblington, pleaded the custom of its former Norman tenants.[64] His widow Margaret received seisin of 100*s.* rent in 'the manor of Emsworth' in April, 1286,[65] and died before 29 July, 1292, leaving a daughter and heir Isabel wife of Hugh Bardolf,[66] who held the rents in Emsworth by right of his wife.[67] In 1304 she surrendered the 'manor of Emsworth' to the crown and obtained a fresh grant of it with remainder to her younger son William,[68] but in 1312 she sued Robert le Ewer, then lord of Warblington, and another for trespass,[69] and in the following year sought restitution of her lands in Emsworth and Warblington,[70] which had been seized into the king's hands on an inquisition as to her rights. It was then stated that the original grant to William Aguillon only referred to 100*s.* rent to be received from the reeve of Warblington manor, that when Peter son of Matthew was lord of the manor he assigned 100*s.* rent from certain villeins in Emsworth to Robert Aguillon, but Matthew son of John had through negligence allowed Robert Aguillon to usurp the lordship of the villeins and a fishery in Emsworth.[71] The suit dragged on for some years while Robert le Ewer received all the profits of the lands according to a grant of 1317,[72] and was only ended after his forfeiture of Warblington. In 1325 the king's bailiff held a court there[73] and in December of the same year the 'manor of Emsworth' was released to Thomas elder brother and heir of William Bardolf according to the grant of Edward I.[74] Thomas Bardolf's son John sold Emsworth with Greatham to Nicholas le Devenish in 1342.[75] It descended with that manor to the Faukoners who evidently retained it when they sold Greatham to John Freeland,[76] for a William Faukoner conveyed it to Anthony Browning, and Elizabeth Cotton, widow, in 1635.[77] Thus, apparently, it became the property of the Cottons, for it was included in the lands for which Richard Cotton compounded, and has since remained in the possession of the successive lords of Warblington.

Aguillon. *Gules a fleur-de-lis argent.*

Devenish. *Vert a saltire engrailed argent between four crosslets fitchy or.*

CHURCH

The church of *ST. THOMAS OF CANTERBURY*,[78] *WARBLINGTON*, consists of chancel 45 ft. by 15 ft. 6 in., with north vestry and organ chamber, nave 41 ft. by 18 ft. 3 in., with north and south aisles and north porch, and a small tower between the nave and chancel. It is a building of unusual interest, not only on account of the beautiful Purbeck marble detail of the south arcade, but also because part of the tower is of pre-Conquest date. This latter is only 9 ft. square over all, and 4 ft. 6 in. square within the walls, and can hardly have been other than western. Only one stage of it now exists, the second; the ground stage having disappeared in the course of alterations noted below. It is not clear whether there was formerly a third stage, or whether it was rather a two-story porch than a tower. Nothing remains of the nave and chancel which stood to the east of it, but the width between the chancel arches may perhaps preserve that of the former nave, 13 ft. 6 in. In the early years of the thirteenth century a new nave with aisles was built to the west of the tower, the lower part of the tower being removed, to open up the old nave east of the tower, which now became the chancel of the enlarged church, but in the latter half of the same century, with its original chancel, was entirely pulled down, and its site occupied by a large new chancel with a north-east vestry. The aisles of the nave were either remodelled or rebuilt at this time, and perhaps lengthened eastward to the line of the east wall of the old tower. The tower, which probably had open archways on all four sides on the lower stage, has small arched doorways on the north, south, and west in the second stage, and these may have opened to the roof or upper floors of buildings set against the tower. The question is one which arises in connexion with many of the existing western towers of pre-Conquest date, and may in this instance have had some effect on the later alterations. The blocks of masonry abutting the arches under the tower may perhaps contain parts of the walling of such buildings, and the east responds of the thirteenth-century arcades may have been built against them, the eastern limit of the aisles being on this line. At the rebuilding of the whole of the work east of the tower, the aisles were lengthened to the line of the east wall of the tower, and perhaps widened, as there seems to be nothing in either as early as the arcades of the nave. The chancel, whose unusual length for a church of this scale may be accounted for by the fact of its having been built round the whole of the nave and chancel of the Saxon church, has an east window of three lights with modern tracery, but the rear arch is original. On the north-east of the chancel is the apparently contemporary vestry, formerly of two stories, and entered from the chancel by a plain chamfered door at the south-west. Immediately to the east of the door is a small squint, wide towards

[61] *Cal. Chart. R.* (Rec. Com.), i, 134.
[62] *Testa de Nevill*, 234*b*.
[63] Pat. 7 Edw. II, pt. 2, m. 21 *d.*
[64] *Plac. de Quo Warr.* (Rec. Com.), 771. The plea is unfinished.
[65] *Cal. Close*, 1279–88, p. 389.
[66] Ibid. 1288–96, p. 239.
[67] Chan. Inq. p.m. 32 Edw. I, No. 64.
[68] Chart. R. 33 Edw. I, No. 77.
[69] *Cal. Pat.* 1307–13, p. 430.
[70] *Cal. Close*, 1313–18, p. 72.
[71] Pat. 17 Edw. II, pt. 2, m. 21 *d.*
[72] *Cal. Pat.* 1313–17, p. 638.
[73] Mins. Accts. bdle. 1148, No. 19.
[74] *Cal. Close*, 1323–7, p. 436.
[75] Feet of F. Hants, East. 16 Edw. III, 23.
[76] *V.C.H. Hants*, ii, 506*b*.
[77] Feet of F. Hants, Hil. 11 Chas. I. Later in the same year John Faukoner suffered recovery of the manors of Emsworth and Middleton.
[78] From the architectural evidence, this cannot be the original dedication.

the chancel, and narrow towards the vestry, with a groove for a sliding panel, by which it could be closed, on the vestry side. The vestry has a two-light east window with modern tracery, but old rear arch, and an original lancet in the north wall. In the south jamb of the east window is a small trefoiled recess with a fourteenth-century canopy and pinnacles over it; the recess is rebated for a wooden door, and has holes for the fastening of bolts. Its original use can only be conjectured, and it is not certain that it is in situ, but it may be compared with other small and carefully secured recesses which may have held the church plate, or even the Host, as it seems that suspension, though the characteristic English method, was not exclusively practised.[79] West of the vestry is a modern organ chamber, and beyond it a length of original walling containing a window of two uncusped lights, with remains of tracery over the lights, indicating re-used material. In the south wall the first window from the east has two fifteenth-century cinquefoiled lights under a square head, but the rear arch is like the others in the chancel, with a wave-mould.

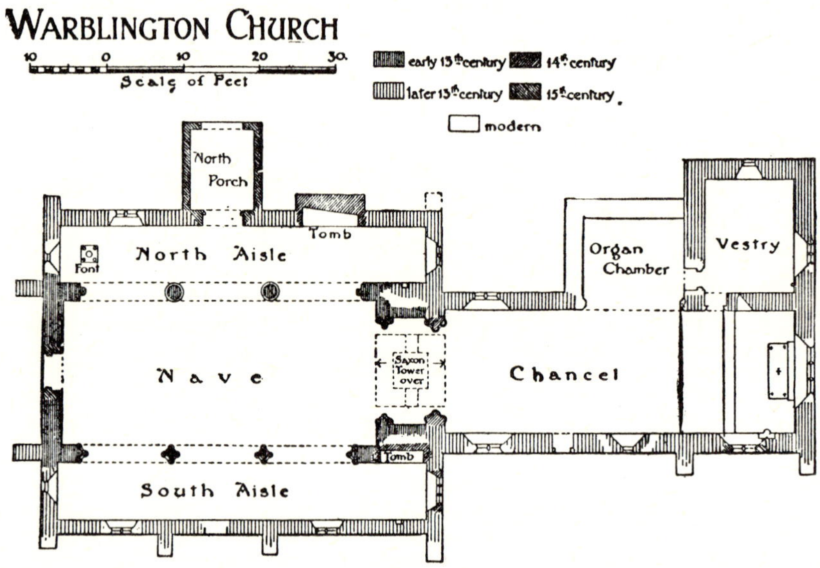

Below it is a trefoiled piscina with a Purbeck marble bowl, and in the next bay to the west a lancet window with wave-mould rear arch, of the date of the chancel, but not in situ, having been moved here from a place in the north wall when the organ chamber was built.[80] West of it is a plain segmental-headed doorway with modern stonework in the head, and a window with a modern square head and two trefoiled lights, under an old rear arch. Under the tower are two arches, the space between them being covered by a pointed barrel vault. The eastern arch, which dates from the beginning of the fourteenth century, is of two chamfered orders with three engaged shafts in the jambs, having moulded capitals and bases; the springing of an earlier arch, wider, and of a different radius, and probably contemporary with the western arch, is to be seen on its eastern face.

The tower carried on these arches and the vault is now of three stages, its original ground stage having been cleared away in the early thirteenth-century alterations. The first stage now in existence has plain round-headed doorways on north and south of rough rubble with no wrought stone dressings, and on the west side a blocked doorway with thirteenth-century stonework, but round-headed, and probably representing a third pre-Conquest opening; the east wall is not pierced. This stage is the only remaining piece of pre-Conquest work, and its walls are 2 ft. 3 in. thick. On the west face of this stage, over the head of the west opening, is the line of a former roof, and the quoins of the western angles of the thirteenth-century work in the tower also appear, showing that the roof was that existing in the thirteenth century. The stage above is a thirteenth-century addition, with thinner walls and small lancet windows on north and south, their rear arches being semicircular, while the top stage, in which is the single bell, is an addition of *c.* 1830, replacing a wooden turret. It has double openings on each face, divided by a shaft of thirteenth-century style, and is crowned with a short shingled spire. The nave is of three bays, its eastern arch and south arcade being of the same detail, while the north arcade is of plainer work. Both have pointed arches of two chamfered orders, but while the north arcade has round stone columns and moulded capitals, the south has beautiful clustered columns of Purbeck marble, four round shafts with an octagonal central shaft, the moulded bases and foliate capitals being also of the same material. In the east respond the capitals are of stone and the outer shafts have stone bands, and in the chancel arch the same thing occurs. The responds in the north arcade are planned as for triple shafts, but have never had them. There is probably no great difference in date between the two arcades, a marked difference in design between practically contemporary works being very common in such cases; the south arcade and chancel arch may have been built first in this instance, the funds not sufficing to build the north arcade in the same elaborate and beautiful style.

The north aisle has a late thirteenth-century east window of two uncusped lights with a trefoiled circle in the head, and in the north wall two modern two-light windows. The west window is a single uncusped light, but its head is a piece of early fourteenth-century tracery—the lower part of a trefoiled opening, re-used here at some uncertain date. In the south-east of the aisle is a large late thirteenth-century trefoiled piscina with a projecting bowl, and below the first window on the north wall a tomb-recess probably of the fourteenth century, the back of which projects beyond the outer face of the wall. It contains the Purbeck marble effigy of a lady in a long gown and wimple, of very poor workmanship, and perhaps of late thirteenth-century date; and at the

[79] The object of reservation being viaticum, not adoration.

[80] There was, however, an original window in this position at an earlier date.

back of the recess is carved a soul carried by angels, probably contemporary with the recess, and later than the effigy. The north door of the aisle is of plain fifteenth-century work, under a very picturesque wooden porch of the same date, much patched with later work, but retaining a very good barge-board and framed wooden arch of entrance. In the south aisle the east window has three-light tracery *c.* 1370, but the rear arch is late thirteenth-century work, like that in the north aisle. Of the same date is the first window on the south side, of two uncusped lights with a pierced spandrel over, the other two windows in this wall being modern copies of it. Traces of the south doorway are visible in the middle bay of the aisle, below the modern window which has taken its place. The west window here is a plain lancet, perhaps of the date of the aisle. At the south-east of the aisle is a plain trefoiled piscina of late thirteenth-century date, and at the north-east a cinquefoiled fourteenth-century tomb-recess with corbels for images above it, and containing the very beautiful fourteenth-

Church of St. Thomas of Canterbury, Warblington (from the East)

century effigy of a lady lying with her arms at her sides, the treatment of the hands and drapery being of quite unusual excellence.

The west window of the nave is of three uncusped lights of early fourteenth-century date, and above it is a modern cinquefoiled circle, while below is a late fifteenth-century doorway.

The nave roof runs unbroken over the aisles, and is covered with red tiles, and has a brick coping at the west. The eaves of the aisles are low, and the side windows are set in gablets rising above their level.

The chancel roof is modern, and there are no ancient wood fittings. In the floor of the chancel are some fifteenth-century glazed tiles, showing among other devices two beasts back to back, eagles holding a shield of France, two embattled towers, fleurs-de-lis, &c. There are also two Purbeck marble coffin-lids with crosses in the chancel floor, and the matrix of a brass. At the east end of both aisles of the nave a large coffin-lid with a cross is set on the floor, but there are no monuments of interest beyond the tomb-recesses already described.

The font at the west end of the north aisle is modern, with a central and four angle shafts and a square bowl.

On the south-east window of the south aisle is an incised sundial. There is one bell, probably of early sixteenth-century date, inscribed in black-letter capitals and smalls :—

Sancte Pale ora pro nob.

The plate comprises a cup of 1709, with a modern foot, a small paten of 1825, and a jug-shaped flagon of 1823.

The first book of the registers contains baptisms 1631–1735, marriages 1644–1736, and burials 1647–1736. Up to 1660 it is a copy of older entries, whose originals are now lost. The second book runs from 1736 to 1760, the marriages stopping at 1754. The third has baptisms and burials 1760–87, and the fourth is the printed marriage register, 1754–92. The fifth has baptisms and burials 1787–1808, the sixth marriages 1793–1812, and the seventh baptisms and burials 1809–12.

ADVOWSON This was orginally vested in the lords of the manor. It was granted in dower to Eleanor, widow of Matthew son of John in 1309.[81] John Helyar, rector in the time of Henry VIII, having forfeited his goods as a traitor, the crown presented for one turn.[82] Edward VI granted the advowson with the manor to Sir Richard Cotton, but apparently he parted with it soon afterwards, for in 1619 George Oglander presented.[83] In 1780 Anne Norris, widow, was patron, and the advowson still remains in her family, the present owner being the Rev. William Burrell Norris.

A part of the parish was assigned to the chapelry of Redhill in 1840.[84] The elementary school was built in 1865, and is of Nonconformist endowment.[85]

In 1841 Emsworth was formed into an ecclesiastical parish separate from Warblington,[86] and declared a rectory in 1866.[87]

The church of St. James was built in 1840,[88] with a chancel, and nave with aisles and two octagonal west turrets. The chancel has since been rebuilt (1892). There is one bell.

The plate consists of a set given in 1840 by R. J. Harrison, two communion cups, a paten, and a flagon ; a silver-gilt cup and paten given in 1892, and a plated paten. The registers begin in 1841.

Before the building of this church the district was served by the chapel of St. Peter, built in 1790.[89]

There is a Baptist chapel built in 1848, a Primitive Methodist chapel in 1876, and a Congregational chapel founded in 1891.

The elementary school was opened in 1865.

CHARITY The following is the sole endowed charity of the parish :—Mrs. Jane Bellamy, by a codicil to her will, proved in 1892, left a legacy, invested in £102 0*s.* 10*d.* Consols, with the official trustees, income to be applied —subject to the repair of the donor's grave—in keeping the churchyard in order.

81 *Cal. Close*, 1307–13, p. 176.
82 Egerton MS. 2034, fol. 174.
83 Longcroft (*Hund. of Bosmere*, 126), states that the lord of Warblington retained the advowson till 1764, when Thomas Panton sold it to John Unwin. In this case George Oglander and the Breretons must have purchased the right of presentation for one or more turns.
84 *Lond. Gaz.* 18 Aug. 1840, p. 1904.
85 *V.C.H. Hants*, ii, 406.
86 *Lond. Gaz.* 6 Aug. 1841, p. 2022.
87 Ibid. 5 June, 1866, p. 3313.
88 Sumner, *Conspectus of the Dioc. of Winton.* 1859.
89 Ibid.

THE HUNDRED OF PORTSDOWN

WITH THE

LIBERTIES OF PORTSMOUTH AND ALVERSTOKE

CONTAINING THE PARISHES OF

BEDHAMPTON
BOARHUNT
FARLINGTON WITH DRAYTON
PORTCHESTER
SOUTHWICK
WYMERING WITH COSHAM AND HILSEA
WIDLEY [1]

THE LIBERTY OF PORTSMOUTH AND PORTSEA ISLAND
THE LIBERTY OF ALVERSTOKE

At the time of the Domesday Survey the hundred of Portsdown included Bedhampton, Wymering, Cosham, Boarhunt, Portchester, Buckland, Copnor, and Fratton. It is impossible to give the total assessment in 1086, as Wymering and part of Portchester were not assessed in hides; the amount

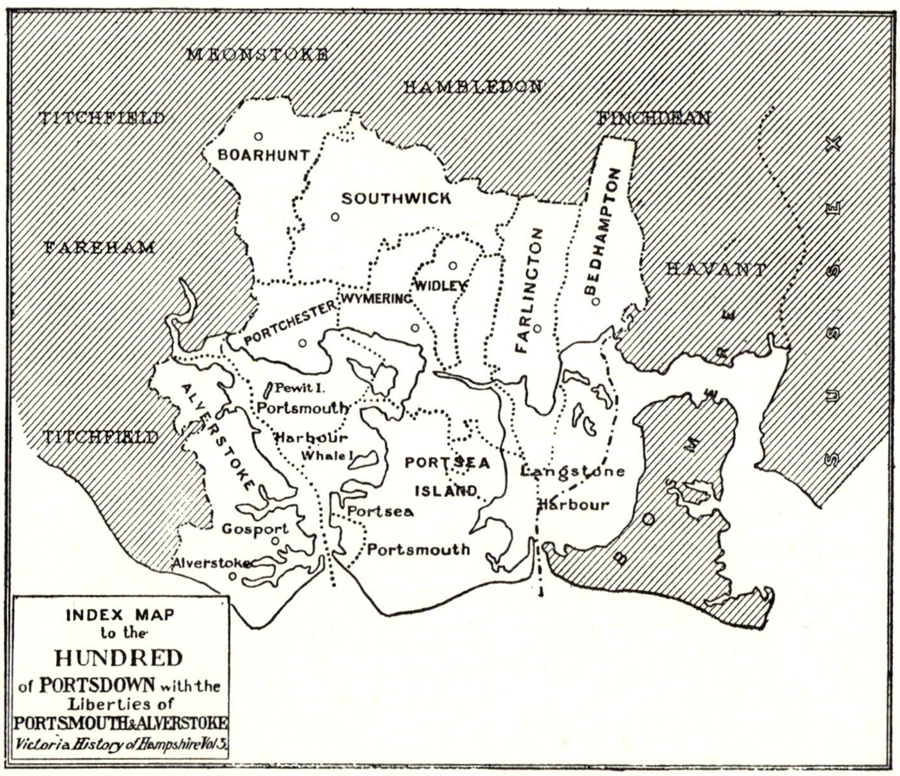

of the land assessed was 39½ hides, so the hundred probably contained about 45 hides.

By the fourteenth century the hundred had undergone considerable alteration ; Portchester had become a separate liberty ; and Southwick, Farlington, Walesworth, Portsea, Eastney, and Milton had been added.

[1] The extent of the hundred as given in the Population Returns of 1831.

Portsea, Eastney, and Milton, with Buckland, Copnor, and Fratton, comprised practically the whole of modern Portsmouth, which was therefore in all probability included in Portsdown.

The part of Portsea called Portsea gildable was still included in Portsdown Hundred in 1637, for in that year the inhabitants of Portsea, under the command of the governor of Portsmouth, petitioned against the commands of the constables of Portsdown Hundred; but the suit terminated in favour of the constables.[2]

A small portion of Brockhampton parish was originally part of the parish of Bedhampton, and consequently formed part of this hundred; the remainder being in Havant parish and Bosmere Hundred.[3]

Walesworth must have been included in Portsdown Hundred by the reign of Edward I, for in this reign the abbot of Titchfield was forced to allow the villeins of Walesworth to pay suit 'at the hundred of the lord king at Portsdown.'[4]

Owing evidently to the small extent of Bosmere Hundred, which is so often mentioned with that of Portsdown, the sheriff held only one tourn for the two hundreds. Thus in 1465 the tithing men of Farlington made presentment at the sheriff's tourn for the two hundreds at Grenefeld, at which place the sheriff's tourn seems usually to have been held.[5] On the other hand the sheriff's returns were sometimes made separately for the two hundreds[6]; and it is remarkable that the profits of Bosmere Hundred at this time were 59*s.* 8*d.* and those of Portsdown, which was a far larger hundred, were only 30*s.* 3*d.*[7]

In 1549 a levy of a tenth produced £74 9*s.* from the hundreds of Bosmere and Portsdown.[8] A similar tax in 1570 produced £123 19*s.* 8*d.* from the two hundreds.[9]

By 1605 there was a change in the arrangement of the hundred; Portchester, which in 1316 had been a liberty by itself, was included, though it was still assessed separately; Portsmouth, on the other hand, which had formerly been included in the general assessment, was rated separately.[10]

Probably about this time, though the exact date is not certain, Walesworth was removed from Portsdown Hundred and included in that of Finchdean. In 1835 the borough boundaries of Portsmouth include Portsea.[11] The hundred of Portsdown therefore assumed its modern proportions, consisting of seven parishes with numerous tithings, the most important of which are Waterloo, Drayton, Hilsea and Cosham.

The hundred of Portsdown has always been in the hands of the king. In an inquisition taken in 1267 the jurors said that it would be no damage to the king if he farmed the hundred of Portsdown.[12] In 1160 40*s.* was returned for a murder fine,[13] and in 1168 20*s.* for false judgement.[14] The liberty of Portchester in 1316 was also 'of the lord king but in the hands of Margaret the Queen.'[15]

[2] *Cal. of S.P. Dom.* 1637–8, p. 566.
[3] *Feud. Aids*, ii, 319–20.
[4] *Plac. de Quo Warr.* (Rec. Com.), Edw. I, rot. 36.
[5] Anct. D. (P.R.O.), A. 6568. In the sixteenth and seventeenth centuries courts leet for the hundred of Portsdown were held at an inn at Cosham (Parl. Surv. Hants, No. 9).
[6] Mem. R. Exch. L.T.R. Mich. 47 Edw. III, Recorda. m. 16.
[7] Ibid.
[8] Lay Subs. R. 2–3 Edw. VI, Hants, $\frac{174}{300}$.
[9] Ibid. 13 Eliz. $\frac{174}{387}$ (a).
[10] Ibid. 3 Jas. I, Hants, $\frac{175}{467}$.
[11] Municipal Corp. Act, 1835, 5 & 6 Will. IV, cap. 76, Sched. A.
[12] Pipe R. 7 Hen. II, rot. 8, m. 2.
[13] Inq. a.q.d. 51 Hen. III, file 2, No. 31.
[14] Pipe R. 14 Hen. II, rot. 12, m. 1.
[15] *Parl. Writs*, vol. ii, div. iii, 345.

BEDHAMPTON

Betametone (xi cent.) ; Bodehampton (xv cent.) ; Bedhampton (xvi cent.).

The parish of Bedhampton is very long and narrow, being about $1\frac{1}{2}$ miles in breadth at the widest part and $6\frac{1}{2}$ miles in length ; its southern part extending down Langstone Harbour nearly as far as the South Hayling farm, and including the four islands, Baker's Island, Long Island, and North and South Binness. A small part of the town of Havant lies within its boundaries. The London Brighton and South Coast Railway passes through the village, which is about a mile west from Havant Station and 6 miles north-east of Portsmouth. A cluster of low houses near the church forms the older part of the village, while a group of inns, shops, and houses lying along both sides of the high road from Portsmouth to Havant, and separated from the church by a wide meadow called Bedbury Mead, marks the modern outgrowth. Here are the schools which were built in 1868, enlarged in 1873, and again in 1895, for about 180 children ; and also a Primitive Methodist chapel erected in 1875. From the schools a footpath over Bedbury Mead leads south-west to Lower Bedhampton, as the part near the church is called. Opposite the church are the rectory, a large white house, and Bedbury House, which is at present unoccupied. Directly north-west of the church the manor house stands on rising ground overlooking Bedbury Mead. Other houses are The Elms, at the corner of the road to the west of the church, occupied by Mr. Lionel Fawkes, and The Towers, occupied by Miss Meiklam, on the main road from Portsmouth to Havant, west of the village.

There are numerous springs in the village, which have become quite famous for their properties ; St. Chad's Well, near the manor house, being supposed to possess the most health-giving virtues. A stream rising near the post office runs parallel with the village street. The hamlet of Belmont lies on high ground north of the church, and is almost a continuation of the village.

Belmont Park, the seat of Mr. W. H. Snell, lies to the north and covers an area of some 20 acres. The north-west part of the parish of Bedhampton is thickly wooded, once forming part of the Forest of Bere, which in early times extended as far south as the range of the Portsdown Hills.

The road which leads northward from Belmont to Waterlooville goes through the heart of this beautifully wooded country, Little Parkwood, Neville's Park, and Beech Wood being the names of the largest stretches of woodland. The area of the parish is about 2,401 acres of land, and 4 acres of land covered by water ; 228 acres covered by tidal water and 1,166 acres of foreshore.[1] The proportion of land in the parish is $542\frac{3}{4}$ acres of arable land, 1,125 acres of permanent grass, and $413\frac{1}{2}$ acres of woodland.[2] The soil is loam ; subsoil chalk ; and varies in quality. The chief crops are wheat, barley, and oats.

MANORS Early in the ninth century King Egbert granted the manor of Bedhampton to the cathedral church of Winchester.[3] By the reign of Edward the Confessor it had passed to the abbey of Hyde, of whom it was held by a certain Alsi. However, at the time of the Domesday Survey Hugh de Port held it of the abbey as he held so many other Hampshire manors.[4]

By 1086 the manor had decreased in value, probably owing to the incursions of the Norsemen, who sailed into Portsmouth Harbour and devastated the surrounding abbeys and lands. The St. Johns continued to hold the manor from the abbey of Hyde, and eventually obtained the over-lordship.[5]

Bedhampton was held by Herbert in 1167, the son of Herbert the Chamberlain, ancestor of the baronial Fitz Herberts, who held the manor until the beginning of the fourteenth century.[6]

Herbert Fitz Peter, a descendant of the above, held Bedhampton in 1236, and was forced in that year to acknowledge the right of Walter abbot of Hyde to exact scutage and relief from two knights' fees there.[7] Reginald his brother died seised of the manor in 1281, leaving a son John, a minor, and a widow Joan,[8] who received dower in the manor in 1286.[9] Eight years later Bedhampton, which had been taken into the king's hands by reason of default made by Joan against the master of the Hospital of St. John and St. Nicholas at Portsmouth,[10] was evidently recovered by her, and in 1314 she died seised of the manor which she held of the abbot of Hyde.[11] Hugh le Despenser the elder held Bedhampton in 1316[12] by enfeoffment from John son of Reginald and Joan in 1305.[13] Upon his attainder and forfeiture in 1326 the manor passed to Edmund earl of Arundel, who held it for a short time before his attainder at the end of the year 1326.[14] In 1327 the manor was granted to Edmund of Woodstock earl of Kent,[15] youngest son of Edward I. After the deposition of Edward II the earl of Kent was soon engaged with the earl of Lancaster against Isabel and Mortimer, who therefore plotted to inveigle him into an attempt to release Edward II by inventing stories that he was still imprisoned abroad or at Corfe Castle. The earl at once began to take measures for his release, and was thereupon arrested for treason on 13 March, 1329 ; and having been hastily and unjustly condemned, he was beheaded outside the walls of Winchester on 19 March.[16] Upon his forfeiture Bedhampton was granted for life to John Maltravers,

EDMUND OF WOODSTOCK, Earl of Kent. *The arms of England with a silver border.*

[1] Ordnance Survey.

[2] Statistics from Board of Agriculture (1905).

[3] Dugdale, *Mon.* i, 210 ; Leland, *Coll.* i, 613.

[4] *V.C.H. Hants*, i, 471.

[5] Inq. p.m. 20 Edw. II, No. 49.

[6] *Pipe R.* (Pipe R. Soc.), 14 Hen. II.

[7] Feet of F. Hants, Hil. 21 Hen. III ; *Testa de Nevill* (Rec. Com.), 232.

[8] Inq. p.m. 14 Edw. I, No. 142.

[9] *Cal. of Close*, 1279–88, p. 399.

[10] Ibid. 1288–96, p. 439.

[11] Inq. p.m. 8 Edw. II, No. 42.

[12] *Feud. Aids*, ii, 320.

[13] Feet of F. Hants, Hil. 34 Edw. I.

[14] Inq. p.m. 20 Edw. II, No. 49.

[15] Chart. R. 1 Edw. III, No. 82, m. 43.

[16] *Dict. Nat. Biog.* xvi, 410–12.

steward of the household, in consideration of his agreement to stay always with the king.[17] However, the attainder of the earl of Kent was reversed in favour of his son Edmund in 1330.[18] In 1346 Margaret countess of Kent, widow of Edmund of Woodstock, held one-and-a-half fees in Bedhampton by right of wardship, since her son Edmund had died in 1333 and his brother and heir John was a minor.[19]

In 1352 John died without issue seised of Bedhampton manor, which therefore passed to his sister Joan, the Fair Maid of Kent, wife of Thomas lord Holland, who became earl of Kent in right of his wife.[20] The manor remained with the Hollands as earls of Kent until the extinction of the male line of that house, when it descended through Margaret, one of the co-heirs of the last earl, to her son John Beaufort first duke of Somerset,[21] whose daughter Margaret became the countess of Richmond and mother of Henry VII; and it was hence merged in the crown on her death in 1509.[22]

Henry VIII leased the manor in 1522 to Stephen Copes for a term of 21 years.[23] Before this term had expired the king again granted it in 1537 to William Fitz William earl of Southampton,[24] on whose death without issue in 1542 the estate again reverted to the crown.[25]

Edward VI on his accession granted the manor to Richard Cotton 'in consideration of long and faithful service'; and it remained with the Cotton family for a considerable period.[26] On the death of Richard Cotton in 1556[27] his lands passed to his son George, who died in 1609 and was succeeded by his son Richard.[28] Richard conveyed Bedhampton manor to the king in 1610 by fine,[29] probably for assurance of title, as it was re-granted to him in the same year,[30] and he died possessed of it in 1635, Richard his grandson, son of his son George, being his heir.[31]

COTTON. *Azure a cheveron between three hanks of cotton argent.*

The manor was still in the hands of the Cottons in 1714, and was sold by them to Adam Cardonnell, who gave it to his daughter Mary on her marriage with the Rt. Hon. William Talbot.[32]

Mr. Legge, afterwards Lord Stawell, purchased Bedhampton from Lord Talbot in 1778, and was in possession of it in 1790.[33] Lord Stawell left Bedhampton to his daughter and heir, Mary Legge, who was married to Lord Sherborne as her second husband. By his will Lord Sherborne left the manor to his third son, Ralph Dutton, from whom it passed to his grandson, Henry Dutton, in whose hands it remains at the present day.[34]

The old manor house, pulled down in 1881, was an L-shaped building of red brick and timber framing, which for some time before its destruction had fallen into disrepair, and was divided into six tenements. It was a picturesque building of two stories, the upper overhanging, and the roof was thatched, but contained nothing of architectural interest, and was probably only a fragment of a more important building. A view of it drawn by Mr. M. Snape in 1876 is published in the *Proceedings of the Hants Field Club*, ii, 253.

At the time of the Domesday Survey there were two mills in Bedhampton parish, and also two salt pans worth 37*s.* 8*d.*[35] The mills are mentioned as a water-mill and a fulling-mill in 1338,[36] and again in 1352.[37] In 1537,[38] and again in 1547, two mills 'built under one roof'[39] are mentioned among the appurtenances of the manor.

CHURCH

The church of *ST. THOMAS* consists of chancel 28 ft. by 18 ft. 6 in. (18 ft. at the west end), with north vestry, and nave 46 ft. by 19 ft. 3 in., with north aisle and south porch.

The chancel arch, *c.* 1140, is the oldest piece of architectural detail remaining, and the south and west walls of the nave may be in part of the same date. The chancel, the south wall of which is in line with that of the nave, seems to have been rebuilt in the thirteenth century, and probably lengthened about 1360–70, the south wall being set outside the line of the former south wall. The line of the north wall, however, has probably not been altered, and the wall may contain older masonry in its western portion. The north arcade and aisle were added to the nave in 1878, and the chancel was repaired and the north vestry added in 1869. The old walls are of flint and freestone rubble with ashlar quoins, and in the upper part of the wall at the south-west of the nave a piece of twelfth-century zigzag ornament is used up.

The chancel has an east window of three trefoiled lights, with two quatrefoils in the head, *c.* 1370, and north and south windows of the same date, with square heads, two-light trefoiled tracery, and segmental rear-arches. In the south-east angle is a contemporary cinquefoiled piscina, with a stone shelf. The western part of the north wall is taken up by the organ, opposite to which in the south wall is a square-headed window of two shouldered lights, probably of thirteenth-century date, and in the south-west angle a square-headed low side window 16 in. wide at the glass line by 3 ft. high, splayed internally with a segmental head, its sill being 2 ft. from the present floor, which is slightly above the old level. In the north vestry a trefoiled fourteenth-century light is re-used.

The chancel arch is semicircular, of one order and 11 ft. wide, having a roll and lozenge pattern on the western side, a label with a double line of hatched ornament, and small angle shafts with scalloped capitals and moulded bases with spurs. The abacus has a

17 Pat. 4 Edw. III, pt. 1, m. 25.
18 *Dict. Nat. Biog.* xvi, 412.
19 *Feud. Aids*, ii, 335.
20 Inq. p.m. 26 Edw. III, No. 54.
21 Ibid. 22 Hen. VI, No. 19.
22 Ibid. 2 Hen. VIII (Ser. 2), No. 17.
23 Pat. 14 Hen. VIII, pt. 2, m. 28.
24 Ibid. 29 Hen. VIII, pt. 1, m. 21.
25 *Dict. Nat. Biog.* xiv, 230–2.
26 Pat. 1 Edw. VI, pt. 4, m. 36.
27 Esch. Inq. p.m. 3 & 4 Phil. and Mary, file 997, No. 1.
28 Chan. Inq. p.m. 8 Jas. I, vol. 318, No. 168.
29 Feet of F. Hants, Hil. 8 Jas. I.
30 Pat. 8 Jas. I, pt. 51, m. 32.
31 Chan. Inq. p.m. 11 Chas. I, vol. 477, No. 158.
32 Add. MS. 33282, fol. 216. Lord and Lady Talbot sold the park of Bedhampton to a Mr. Moody in 1774. (ibid.)
33 Ibid. fol. 217.
34 Information supplied by Mr. Dutton.
35 *V.C.H. Hants*, i, 471.
36 Inq. p.m. 4 Edw. III, No. 38.
37 Ibid. 26 Edw. III, No. 54.
38 Pat. 29 Hen. VIII, pt. 1, m. 21.
39 Inq. p.m. 1 Edw. VI, pt. 4, m. 36.

hollow chamfer below, and is continued as a string on the west face, and on the east face of the south respond are parts of a string of different section, perhaps not in situ.

The nave has a modern north arcade of three bays and a north aisle, the west window of which is a late fourteenth-century two-light window re-used, with trefoiled lights and tracery. In the south wall of the nave is a similar window, and to the east of it two single-light windows one over the other. The upper, which has a square head, has been inserted to light the rood-loft, and the lower, which is pointed, with a segmental rear-arch, lighted the south nave altar. There are no other traces of this altar, but the remains of a fifteenth-century niche on the north of the chancel arch mark the site of the corresponding north altar of the nave.

The south doorway of the nave has a plain late fourteenth-century arch with continuous mouldings, and to the west of it is a contemporary window of two trefoiled lights with a trefoiled opening in the head. In the wall above its west jamb is a stone corbel, which may have carried a beam supporting a western gallery.

The west window is of early fourteenth-century style, with three acute cinquefoiled lights; the tracery looks like old work re-used. On the west gable is a modern bell-turret containing one bell by Clement Tosier, 1688, but its corbelled base on the east face of the wall seems to be ancient.

The roofs are red tiled, the timbers of the chancel roof being modern, while those of the nave are old, with plain tie-beams and trussed rafters. Otherwise all woodwork is modern, but within the chancel rails are a seventeenth-century chair and bench. The font, near the south door, is modern, with a square bowl and a central and four angle pillars of twelfth-century style, the angle pillars being of yellow marble.

The first book of the registers contains all entries from 1690 to 1813. There is a book of parish accounts, 1692-1783. The plate consists of a silver almsdish, paten, chalice and flagon.

ADVOWSON In 1086 there was a church in Bedhampton.[40] At the time of Pope Nicholas's taxation (about 1291) the rectory of Bedhampton was assessed at £10 16*s.* 8*d.*; and the tithes at £1 1*s.* 8*d.*[41] In the reign of Henry VIII the rectory was valued at £10 14*s.* 10*d.*[42]

The advowson followed the descent of the manor until the year 1634, when it was granted by Richard Cotton, the holder of the manor, to Thomas Greene for a turn.[43] The crown held it for a turn in 1660, and in 1688 William Heycroft so held it; but in 1713 it was again in the hands of the Cotton family, who were still holding the manor. It continued to follow the descent of the manor till 1801, when the duke of Beaufort held it; and in 1817 the marquis of Downshire.[44] The Rev. C. B. Henville bought the advowson for his own use in 1818 and remained the incumbent until 1836.[45] Andrew Reid held the advowson from 1836 until 1844, when it was bought by St. John Alder for his own use.[46] From 1866 until 1888 both the living and the advowson were held by Rev. E. Daubeny. The Andersons held the advowson from 1888 until 1897, when it passed into the hands of Mrs. Poyntz-Sanderson, who holds it at the present time.[47] The living is a rectory of the net yearly value of £285 with residence and 26 acres of glebe.

CHARITIES In 1875 Henry Snook by deed gave £500 consols, dividends to be applied as to £10 for encouraging further education of girls, the remainder for clothing to boys or girls as prizes. The stock is in the name of the Bedhampton School Board, for the benefit of whose schools the dividends are applied.

BOARHUNT

Boorhunt, Burghunt (xiii cent.), Bourhunt Herberd (xv cent.), Burrant Harbard (xvi cent.), Boarhunt (xvi cent.).

Boarhunt is a small parish 3 miles north-east from Fareham station and 8 miles north from Gosport. The River Wallington flows westward through the parish, dividing it into two parts, of which the northern is larger than the southern. South Boarhunt is a tiny secluded hamlet lying in the midst of fertile country on the lower slopes of Portsdown, and consists of a few cottages, the little church of St. Nicholas standing picturesquely on the edge of a disused chalk-pit, overgrown with trees, and the old manor house, now used as a farm. The principal road in the parish is that running from Wickham to Southwick, through beautiful wooded country. Boarhunt Mill, with its back-ground of copses, stands at a little distance to the west of the bridge by which the lane running south from the Wickham road crosses the river, and probably occupies the site of one of the two mills mentioned in Domesday Book.[1] Near the southern boundary of the parish, on the heights of Portsdown, is a monument to Nelson erected about 1814—a stone column about 120 ft. high supporting a bust—while at the base are inscriptions recording the results of the battle of Trafalgar. From the Portsdown heights fine views can be obtained of the surrounding country. To the north stretches the Forest of Bere, while to the south there are spread open to the view Portsmouth Harbour with its shipping, Portsmouth Town, Fareham, Gosport, the Isle of Wight, and the English Channel. The more populous part of the parish is North Boarhunt, which lies north of the river about a mile and a half from the church, and consists of a straggling street running northwards to the Forest of Bere. Nearly all the buildings lie on the west side of the street, and opposite them are allotments, for market gardening is the chief occupation of the inhabitants. In the village is a small Wesleyan chapel, and an elementary school which was built in 1873 for about fifty children and is supported by Mr. Alexander Thistlethwayte, who owns most of the land in the parish. To the north is the pound. The West Walk extends as far as Wickham on the west, while to the north and east as far as the eye can reach stretches the Forest of Bere.

[40] *V.C.H. Hants*, i, 471.
[41] *Pope Nich. Tax.* (Rec. Com.), 211*b*.
[42] *Valor Eccl.* (Rec. Com.), ii, 22.
[43] Inst. Bks. (P.R.O.).
[44] *Clerical Guide*, 1817.
[45] Ibid. 1822-36.
[46] Ibid. 1836; *Clergy List*, 1841-66.
[47] *Clergy List*, 1866-1904.
[1] *V.C.H. Hants*, i, 477.

The soil of the parish is clay and loam, subsoil chalk and clay; the area is 2,538 acres, of which 1,033 acres are arable land, 377½ permanent grass, and 457 woodland.[2]

The following place-names occur in 1538: Crageland, Aishe Land, and Langislond;[3] and in 1775 Mitchell Land.[4]

MANORS

Boarhunt had at least three manors, all of which can be traced in Domesday with a fourth holding in addition. These were subsequently known as Boarhunt, East Boarhunt, and West Boarhunt. Domesday assigns in addition to the monks of St. Swithun's, Winchester, a holding of half a hide.

The principal manor was *WEST BOARHUNT*, which Earl Roger held at the time of the Domesday Survey; three freemen had held it of King Edward as an alod. A knight held one hide of this manor where he had one plough.[5]

The over-lordship of Boarhunt passed from Earl Roger to his son Robert de Belesme, earl of Shrewsbury and Arundel;[6] and after his forfeiture to the earls of Arundel, for in 1273 one-third of the manor of Boarhunt was held in dower by Maud de Verdun, late the wife of John Fitz Alan, senior; and two thirds were held by John de Mareschall as guardian of the heirs of John Fitz Alan, junior.[7]

In the reign of Henry III Westburhunte[8] appears among the fees of the earl of Arundel, being then held of him by the prior of Southwick as half a fee of the old feoffment;[9] it remained in the hands of this priory until the Dissolution.[10] After the Dissolution the manor of West Boarhunt was granted to Thomas Wriothesley, earl of Southampton,[11] in order that he might alienate it to Ralph Henslowe. Thomas Henslowe, Ralph's grandson, died seised of the manor in 1617, leaving a son Thomas aged eleven.[12] After this date, however, there seems to be no mention of West Boarhunt until 1691, when Henry Lacy and his wife Catherine were holding half the manor and advowson, though whether by right of inheritance or by purchase it seems impossible to discover, and conveyed them in that year to Richard Caryll, evidently for the purpose of a settlement.[13]

Three years later Richard Caryll, Henry Lacy, and Catherine sold the manor to Richard Norton for £660;[14] and from this time it evidently follows the descent of the manor of Boarhunt (q. v.).

The manor of *BOARHUNT* was held by Hugh de Port in 1086; at the time of the Survey he held one hide in Boarhunt and Tezelin held it of him; Lefsi and Merman had held it of King Edward as an alod. In the time of King Edward the Confessor, as well as in 1086, it paid geld for one hide. There was enough demesne land for one plough and a mill worth 5*s.*; the whole manor being worth 20*s.*[15] In the reign of Henry III it was held of his heir Robert de St. John as 'Borhunte' by Herbert de Boarhunt, who owed him the service of two knights' fees.[16] These were held by Thomas de Boarhunt at his death in 1262.[17]

The family which took the name of Boarhunt were holding lands in the parish early in the thirteenth century,[18] and by the beginning of the fourteenth century were in possession of the manor, which on the murder of Sir Herbert Boarhunt in 1312 was divided between his two sons Richard and Henry. One part, known as the manor of Boarhunt, the manor proper, remained with Richard the elder, and the other part, subsequently known as Boarhunt Herbelyn (q.v.), passed to Henry the younger.[19] Sir Richard de Boarhunt settled the manor on his son Thomas for the term of his own life in 1305,[20] and in 1314 on him jointly with Margaret his wife in fee.[21] Thomas held the manor in 1316,[22] and died seised of it in 1339.[23]

Boarhunt. *Argent a fesse between six martlets gules.*

His widow, Margaret, married William Danvers as her second husband,[24] and held the manor until her death, which took place before 1359, when the manor passed to her son John de Boarhunt and his wife Mary des Roches.[25]

John died seised of it in 1359, leaving an only son John, aged fourteen,[26] who probably died soon afterwards, since in 1363 the reversion of the manor after the death of Mary, widow of John, now wife of Bernard de Brocas, is said to have belonged to John son of Herbert de Boarhunt, a cousin of her former husband, and to have been made over by him to Valentine atte Mede of Bramdean.[27] Bernard Brocas and Mary conveyed their estate in Boarhunt to William of Wykeham, then archdeacon of Lincoln, in 1365[28]; and two years later Valentine atte Mede also granted to William of Wykeham, bishop of Winchester, all his right in the manor of Boarhunt, now sometimes known as Boarhunt Herberd.[29]

Finally in 1369 the king confirmed the manor of Boarhunt Herberd to William of Wykeham, together

[2] Statistics of the Board of Agriculture, 1905.

[3] Mins. Accts. 29–30 Hen. VIII, R.113. m. 37.

[4] Recov. R. Trin. 16 Geo. III, m. 84–90.

[5] *V.C.H. Hants*, i, 477 (*a*).

[6] G. E. C. *Complete Peerage*, i, 138–9; vii, 135.

[7] Inq. p.m. 47 Hen. III, No. 29.

[8] In 1262 Basilla the wife of Hugh Loe quitclaimed her dowry of West Boarhunt to her sons Clement and Siward Boarhunt (Feet of F. Hants, Trin. 4 John).

[9] *Testa de Nevill* (Rec. Com.), 231.

[10] *Feud. Aids*, ii, 319. The Sandfords must have held land for a short time from the convent of Southwick, for licence was granted to Richard de Sandford in 1327 to grant to Lawrence de Pageham the reversion of a messuage and land in West Boarhunt after the death of the tenant for life. Joan, wife of Thomas de Sandford (*Cal. of Pat.* 1327–30, p. 132) and Lawrence de Pageham paid Richard de Sandford 20*s.* for acquiring the same. (*Abbrev. Rot. Orig.* [Rec. Com.], ii, 14).

[11] Pat. 37 Hen. VIII, pt. 8, m. 28.

[12] Chan. Inq. p.m. 15 Jas. I, vol. 361. No. 138.

[13] Feet of F. Div. Cos. Hil. 3 Will. and Mary. [14] Ibid. Hants, Hil. 6 Will. III.

[15] *V.C.H. Hants*, i, 483.

[16] *Testa de Nevill* (Rec. Com.), 230.

[17] Burrows, *Brocas Family of Beaurepaire*, 336.

[18] Thus in 1250 Adam de Lammere and Alice his wife granted a messuage and land in Boarhunt to Thomas de Boarhunt and his heirs. (Feet of F. Hants, East. 35 Hen. III).

[19] Montagu Burrows, *The Brocas Family*, 336.

[20] Feet of F. Hants, Mich. 33 Edw. I.

[21] Ibid. 7 Edw. II.

[22] *Feud. Aids*, ii, 319.

[23] Inq. p.m. 14 Edw. III (1st Nos.), No. 22.

[24] Feet of F. Hants, Mich. 18 Edw. III; *Feud. Aids*, ii, 335.

[25] Burrows, *Brocas Family*, 336.

[26] Inq. p.m. 33 Edw. III (2nd Nos.), No. 103.

[27] Feet of F. Hants, Mich. 37 Edw. III.

[28] Ibid. Hil. 39 Edw. III.

[29] Close, 41 Edw. III. m. 3.

with all the lands which had belonged to John de Boarhunt, in order that he might give them to the prior and convent of Southwick.[30]

The manor remained in the hands of the prior and convent until the Dissolution, when it was granted in 1543 to Thomas Wriothesley, earl of Southampton.[31] In the next year licence was granted to the earl to alienate the manor to John White of Southwick,[32] and from this time onwards the manorial descent follows that of Southwick (q.v.).

WILLIAM OF WYKEHAM. *Argent two cheverons sable between three roses gules.*

There were two mills in Boarhunt at the time of the Domesday Survey, one worth 42*d.* and one for the use of the hall ; there were also two salt-pans which were valued at 22*s.* 4*d.*[33]

In 1365 there was a mill among the appurtenances of the manor, which Bernard Brocas and his wife Mary conveyed to William of Wykeham.[34]

A grant of free warren in his demesne lands of Boarhunt was made to Richard de Boarhunt in 1358,[35] also the right of holding a market every week on Saturday and a fair every year to last three days, namely, the eve, day, and morrow of St. Thomas the Apostle.[36] There are no traces of these remaining at the present day.

The manor of *BOARHUNT HERBELYN* (Burrant Harbelyn, xiv cent.) evidently takes its name in the reign of Henry III from Herbelin who held it by serjeanty.[37] Earlier in the reign it was held by William de Boarhunt as one carucate, elsewhere described as worth 40*s.* a year, by the serjeanty of serving in Portchester Castle, with a 'habergellum' in time of war for twenty (or forty) days.[38] At this date the manor of Boarhunt Herbelyn passed to Henry de Boarhunt, who held it until his death in 1320, when it passed to his son Gilbert.[39] Thomas son and heir of Gilbert died unmarried, but before his death he granted his estate to Richard Danvers, who resettled it on himself and his brother William, who had married Margaret de Boarhunt ; Thomas[40] cousin of William Danvers died in 1361 and Richard in 1362.[41] On the death of William, Richard made over this estate to trustees in order that they might convey it to the prior and convent of Southwick.[42]

The manor remained with the prior and convent until the Dissolution, when it was granted in 1543 to Thomas Wriothesley, earl of Southampton.[43] From this time the descent of this manor follows that of Boarhunt Herberd (q.v.).

The manor of *EAST BOARHUNT* is identical, in Mr. Round's opinion, with one of the two unnamed holdings of William Mauduit in Portsdown Hundred, recorded in Domesday Book. For in the reign of Henry III it was held of his descendant and namesake as 'Estburhunt' by Robert de Bello Alneto, and is there entered as half a hide of land.[44] In 1262 it was found to be held of William Mauduit by William de Bello Alneto as half a knight's fee. The same tenant was holding a quarter of a fee of Thomas de Boarhunt, the St. John's tenant in the manor of Boarhunt[45]

The tithing of *HIPLEY* (Huppeley, Hippeleye, Ipley, xiv and xvi cent.) lies to the north-west of the parish of Boarhunt. The earliest mention seems to be in the year 1248, when Basil de Hipley granted half a carucate of land in Hipley to Robert le Burgeys after an assize of mort d'ancestor.[46]

Philip de Benstede and his wife Imania granted the fourth part of half a carucate of land, 25 acres of meadow and 6*s.* 11*d.* rent in Hipley, to the prior and convent of Southwick in 1270.[47]

From this time the prior and convent were gradually acquiring lands in Hipley, from Geoffrey de Wanstede in 1335,[48] from John, son of Robert le Porter, and William Rushmere in 1336,[49] from Hugh Beneyt in 1343.[50]

After the dissolution in 1537 the lands in Hipley belonging to the prior and convent were granted to John White of Southwick,[51] and as there is no further separate record of Hipley, the lands evidently followed the descent of the manor of Southwick (q. v.).

CHURCH The church of *ST. NICHOLAS* has a chancel 15 ft. 3 in. east to west by 14 ft. 9 in., and a nave 41 ft. by 19 ft., with a bell-turret on the west gable. It is a very valuable specimen of a small pre-Conquest building, preserving its main dimensions unchanged. The walls are 2 ft. 6 in. thick, built of flint rubble, originally covered with a thick coat of yellow plastering, of which a certain amount remains intact, and the angles have Binstead stone dressings of excellent quality, preserving in places short diagonal tool-marks. The stones are not set after the common pre-Conquest fashion of long and short work, and though in some cases of good size are not remarkable in any way.

All internal angles, whether salient or re-entering, are built with ashlar quoins.

The only original window is on the north side of the chancel, and is a round-headed light 2 ft. wide at the outer opening, and double splayed, the pierced midwall slab having an opening 1 ft. 10 in. high, surrounded by a double line of cable-moulding. The head and jambs within and without are of good fine-jointed ashlar work, the sills being of plastered rubble. Internally this window is blocked by a sixteenth-century monument.

The east and south windows of the chancel are inserted thirteenth-century lancets, and at the west end of the south wall is a plain segmental-headed doorway, now blocked.

On either side of the east window are image

30 *Abbrev. Rot. Orig.* (Rec. Com.), ii, 304.

31 Pat. 35 Hen. VIII, pt. 10, m. 21.

32 Ibid. 36 Hen. VIII, pt. 25, m. 47.

33 *V.C.H. Hants*, i, 477.

34 Feet of F. Hants, Hil. 39 Edw. III.

35 Chart R. 32 Edw. I, No. 97.

36 Ibid. 4.

37 'Herbellinus de Burhunt tenet terram suam per serjantiam ibidem' (*Testa de Nevill*, 242).

38 *Testa de Nevill* (Rec. Com.), 235, 237 ; *Liber Rubeus*, 459.

39 Burrows, *The Family of Brocas*, 335–7.

40 Inq. p.m. 17 Edw. III (2nd Nos.), No. 40.

41 Ibid. 36 Edw. III (1st Nos.), No. 56.

42 Ibid.

43 Pat. 35 Hen. VIII, pt. 10, m. 21.

44 *Testa de Nevill* (Rec. Com.), 235.

45 Inq. p.m. 47 Hen. III, file 28, No. 15.

46 Feet of F. Hants, Hil. 33 Hen. III.

47 Ibid. Hil. 55 Hen. III.

48 Inq. a.q.d. 9 Edw. III, No. 28*a*.

49 *Cal. of Pat.* 1334–8, p. 232.

50 Ibid. 1343–5, p. 137. Richard earl of Arundel held 1 messuage and 60 acres of land in Hipley in 1397 (Inq. p.m. 21 Ric. II, bdle. 7 *a*, No. 8 *a* and *b*), probably a lease from the convent of Southwick.

51 Mins. Accts. 29–30 Hen. VIII, R. 113, m. 21.

Boarhunt Church : The Chancel Arch

brackets, that on the north side being the larger, while that on the south has a carved human head beneath it. Close to the latter is a small piscina with a groove for a shelf and a projecting bowl, and near it in the south wall, in the jamb of the south window, is a second recess which has been fitted with a shelf.

The chancel has had a flat ceiling, perhaps representing the original arrangement, but is now covered with a canted plastered ceiling. The chancel arch, 6 ft. 8 in. wide, is semicircular, of a single plain order, with a square-edged rib-mould, and a deep moulded abacus chamfered below, and setting out to take the rib, which was originally continued down the jambs, though now cut back. The masonry here, as in the external quoins, shows no tendency to 'long and short' work.

The west face of the wall on either side of the chancel arch is occupied by segmental-headed recesses 20 in. deep, the side walls of the nave being also cut back at the east end and carried on half arches; the object being to make convenient room for the nave altars. The northern recess is lighted on the north by a small lancet, but the southern recess has lost its south half-arch by the insertion of a square-headed two-light sixteenth-century window. The recesses are of thirteenth-century date, as shown by the moulded strings at the west of the lateral recesses, and the corbel which is set beneath the abacus of the rib-mould on the north jamb of the chancel arch is of the same date. Below the south window is a small piscina.

The present nave was originally divided into a nave and a western chamber by a wall 2 ft. 6 in. thick, which crossed it at right angles 26 ft. from the chancel arch. In it was probably an archway, and the western chamber may have been of two floors, but nothing beyond the bonding of the cross wall now remains.

The original north and south doorways of the nave, of which traces only remain, were further to the east than those which now exist. These are blocked with masonry, but show pointed archways of thirteenth-century date, their eastern jambs just overlapping the western limits of the doorways they replace. The cross-wall was probably in existence when they were built, or they would have been set further to the west. At the same time lancet windows were inserted in the north and south walls of the western chamber at a height which tells against any division into two floors at the time. Both lancets are widely splayed, with sloping sills, and in the west wall is a third lancet in modern stonework with a modern west doorway below it. The west wall with its buttresses and bell-cot above is all modern or refaced.

The nave has a canted plaster ceiling with deal-cased tie-beams, and the fittings of the church are of plain deal, with a west gallery. In the chancel are considerable remains of wall paintings, with indistinct subjects under a trefoiled arcade and painted drapery below.

The font, at the south-west of the nave, has a plain round tapering bowl without a shaft or any detail to suggest its approximate date.

Against the north wall of the chancel is set a monument dated 1577, with no inscription except the initials C P, R H, and K P of the persons commemorated.

The upper part has three panels surmounted by a flat cornice on which are three pediments, one of rounded form between two which are angular; on these stand three headless figures, apparently Charity between Faith and Hope. Under the soffit of the cornice are angels holding shields inscribed with I H S, and the panels below are divided from each other by Corinthian columns carrying an architrave, on which over the columns is the date 1577, one figure over each column, and over the panels the initials already noted. In the panels are shields, as follows:—Under C P, the arms of Pound, Argent a fesse gules between two dragons' heads and a cross formy fitchy sable with three molets argent on the fesse; under R H, the arms of Henslow, Argent a cross gules with five lions' heads erased or on the cross; and under K P, the arms of Poole, Party or and sable a saltire engrailed counterchanged. The central shield is that of Ralph Henslow, who married a sister of John White, the grantee of Southwick Priory.

In the bell-cot is one modern bell.

The plate comprises a silver communion cup of Elizabethan type, *c.* 1570, with a wide engraved band on the bowl, a standing paten of 1691, and a plated flagon and almsdish.

BOARHUNT CHURCH

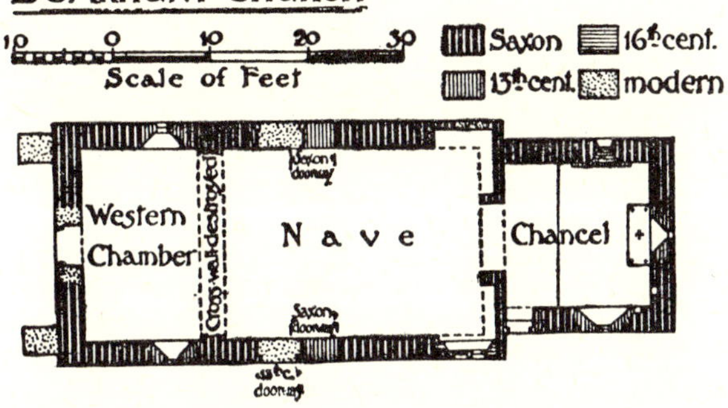

The earliest book of registers contains baptisms from 1578 to 1628, and burials from 1588, and the next contains all entries from 1653 to 1805. The remaining entries to 1812 are in three small books.

ADVOWSON At the time of the Domesday Survey there was a church in Boarhunt,[52] which probably became at a later date the parish church of West Boarhunt as it was called. The church and the advowson of the rectory of West Boarhunt evidently passed into the hands of the prior and convent of Southwick between 1262 and 1316, together with the manor of West Boarhunt (q.v.), and remained in their possession until the time of the Dissolution.[53] The value of the rectory was given in 1291 as £7 6*s.* 8*d.*, tithes 14*s.* 8*d.*[54] After the Dissolution the advowson followed the descent of the manor (q.v.). The living is now consolidated with that of Southwick, and is in the gift of Mr. Alexander Thistlethwayte, who is lord of the manor.

[52] *V.C.H. Hants*, i, 477.

[53] *Wykeham's Register* (Hants Rec. Soc.), i, 25, 122, 137, 191.

[54] *Pope Nich. Tax.* (Rec. Com.), 211*b*.

FARLINGTON

Ferlingeton (xi cent.) ; Farlington (xviii cent.)

Farlington is a parish running northwards from Langstone Harbour with a nearly uniform width of about a mile and a quarter, its extreme length being a little over four miles. The parish included in 1831 the villages of Purbrook, Portsdown, Stakes Hill or Frendstaple, and part of Waterlooville called 'Wait Lane End' on the north side of Portsdown Hill, and the hamlet of Drayton, a mile west on the south.

In the south of the parish is the low-lying expanse of Farlington Marshes, from which the ground rises gradually to the foot of the range of Portsdown, beyond which to the north is the well-wooded country of Purbrook, Stakes Hill, and Waterloo, which once formed part of the Forest of Bere. The parish is crossed about midway by a road which runs along the downs between the villages of Portsdown and Bedhampton at a height of 300 ft. above the sea-level. Parallel to it at the base of Portsdown runs the main road from Portsmouth to Havant, along which lie the hamlets of Drayton and Farlington, the former at the western extremity of the parish and the latter about half a mile to the east.

The church and rectory, with Farlington House, the residence of Mr. Robert Edgcumbe Hellyer, and one or two houses to the south of the road, make up the whole of Farlington village.

To the south of the road between Drayton and Farlington are the Borough of Portsmouth Waterworks, while to the north on the slopes of Portsdown are large reservoirs belonging to the waterworks company. These are used in conjunction with Havant for supplying the forts on Portsdown and the towns of Portsmouth, Portsea, and Southsea. There is a race - course south of the waterworks between Drayton and Farlington Marshes, and meetings are held there under the National Hunt Rules. There is a station near it which is a junction for the London and South-Western and the London Brighton and South Coast railways. Fort Purbrook and Farlington Redoubt are situated in this parish on Portsdown.

The hamlet of Drayton is now gradually developing into a residential locality. To the north of the road immediately past the New Inn is the Drayton building estate, on which new villas are rising steadily. South of the road is Drayton Manor, the residence of Lieut.-Col. Alfred Robert William Thistlethwayte, approached from the main road by Drayton Lane.

The village of Purbrook in the north-west of the parish lies on the London and Portsmouth road, and is surrounded by small copses and woods which once formed part of the Forest of Bere. Along the main street of the village, which is composed of a few houses and inns, among them the 'White Hart,' the 'Leopard,' and the 'Woodman,' runs the Cosham and Horndean light railway. The church of St. John the Baptist, built in the last century, stands opposite the junction of Chalky Road with the High Street. On one side of it are the schools, and on the other the Primitive Methodist Chapel erected in 1875. Purbrook Heath House, the residence of Mr. Thomas William Harvey, stands to the west of the village on the borders of the parish of Cosham. Purbrook Park, the property of Mr. William Deverell, and the residence of Major Henry Gundry, is about eighty acres in extent, and through it runs the stream which gives the village its name. The Portsmouth and South Hants Industrial School, a rather gloomy-looking building, stands to the south of Stakes on the Stakes Hill road. To the east of Purbrook is Morelands, the residence of General Sir John William Collman Williams, K.C.B., J.P., and near it a lane leads to Crookhorn farm, probably the remains of the small manor of Creuquer in Farlington.

The village of Portsdown, also in this parish, lies on the main road from London to Portsmouth, one and a half miles north by east from Cosham Station and four miles north by east from Portsmouth. On the northern slope of Portsdown to the east of the road is Christ Church, built in 1874, and opposite to it is Portsdown Lodge, at present unoccupied. To the south on the summit of Portsdown are the George Inn and the Bellevue Tea Gardens.

Stakes Hill or Frendstaple, as it was formerly called, once the site of a small manor, is now a hamlet in the northern part of the parish, about a mile south-east of Waterlooville, and is surrounded by woods known as Stakes Hill Coppice. Stakes Hill Lodge, with 400 acres of well-wooded land attached, is the residence of Mr. John Henville Hulbert, while Oaklands, a fine house half a mile to the south, is at present unoccupied.

Waterlooville, a modern settlement, as its name implies, lies on the London and Portsmouth road about three miles north of Cosham, traversed by the Cosham and Horndean light railway, and provided with numerous inns, including one with the appropriate name of the 'Heroes of Waterloo.' The church of St. George, built in the early part of the nineteenth century, stands to the north of the road to Barn Green on the borders of the parishes of Cosham and Farlington, and in the main street is the Baptist Chapel, erected in 1884–5.

The soil varies a good deal ; there is a mixture of clay, sand, and loam along the southern part of the downs ; the subsoil is flint and chalk. The area of the parish is 2,389 acres of land, 10 acres of water, 56 of tidal water, and 535 of foreshore. Of the land 878½ acres are arable, 1,205¼ acres permanent grass, and 206¾ acres woodland.[1] In Waterloo there are 32 acres of arable land, 125½ acres of permanent grass, and 206¾ acres of woodland. The soil around Waterloo is clay, with a clay subsoil.

MANORS

FARLINGTON seems originally to have been a royal manor, lands in which were leased out by the king to various tenants. On his death in 1312 John de Berewyk is said to have held the manor of Robert le Ewer,[2] who was probably the tenant-in-chief.

William de Curci was holding land in Farlington in 1187[3] ; and in 1200 a suit concerning the presentation to the church was in progress between Robert de Curci and Roger de Scures, the latter claiming that Robert, uncle of Robert de Curci, had

[1] Statistics of Bd. of Agric. (1905).

[2] Inq. p.m. 6 Edw. II, No. 43.

[3] *Pipe R.* (Pipe R. Soc.), 33 Hen. II.

given one moiety of Farlington to his father William, and the other to his uncle Roger, sons of Walter de Scures, and that he, Roger, ought therefore to have the whole manor, as heir of his father and uncle.[4] Unfortunately it seems impossible to find the termination to this suit.

In 1248 Roger de Merlay granted one and a half carucates of land and 7*s.* rent in Farlington to William son of Alan Stake and his wife Ellen, for which and for another tenement[5] William rendered yearly a pair of gilt spurs or 6*d.* at the feast of St. Michael.[6]

Roger de Merlay also gave £20 worth of land in Farlington as a dower to his daughter Alice or Agnes on her marriage with Nicholas son of Thomas de Gimises in 1250,[7] and by 1286 she was evidently in possession of the manorial lands, which she sought to regain from the king's hands for her default against Hugh de Turbevill.[8] Agnes evidently gained her suit, and the lands passed from her to her son John, who alienated them to John de Berewyk in 1290.[9] John de Berewyk died seised of the manor in 1312. His heir was Roger Husee, his great-nephew ; but Roger de Upton, servant of John de Berewyk, claimed to possess a charter granting the manor to him and his wife and their son John, and since Roger Husee made no claim after his uncle's death, he took possession of the manor, which he held in 1316.[10] John son of Roger de Upton succeeded his father, and conveyed the manor to Hugh le Despenser in 1320.[11]

After the death of Hugh le Despenser in 1327, and the forfeiture of his lands, the king granted the manor of Farlington, worth £20 a year,[12] to Alice late wife of Edmund earl of Arundel, for the support of herself and her children until other provision was made for her.[13] Alice only held the manor for a short time, for by 1330 it had come into the king's hands, and was granted to John Montgomerie and his wife Rose for life.[14] On the death of John Montgomerie in 1347,[15] the manor passed, in the next year, to the prior and convent of Southwick[16] in accordance with a grant made to them in 1346 in consideration of the losses which they had sustained through the invasion of the king's enemies.[17] The manor remained in the possession of the prior and convent until the Dissolution,[18] when it was granted, in 1540, to William Pound of Beaumonds,[19] whose father William, son of Sir John Pound and Elizabeth Holt, had held lands in Farlington of the prior and convent of Southwick, and had left the same to his younger son on his death in 1525.[20] William died seised of the manor in 1558, and was succeeded by his son Thomas, then aged twenty.[21]

In 1663 the Pounds were still holding the manor, for in that year Henry Pound conveyed it to John Wolfe,[22] and again in 1684 to Nathaniel Hunt,[23] evidently as settlements. Henry Pound must have sold the manor about 1684 to Thomas Smith, and it remained in his family until 1769, when it was sold by the trustees to Peter Taylor.[24] In 1815 the manor was sold by the trustees of the Taylors' estates to Lord Keith by a private Act of Parliament.[25] Lord Keith sold the estate to Mr. John Walker in 1818, from whose trustees it was purchased by Mr. John Deverell in 1857.[26] At Mr. John Deverell's death in 1880 the manor passed to his son, Mr. William Deverell, the present owner.[27] At the time of the Dissolution 10*s.* was returned for the farm of a fishing in the manor of Farlington.[28]

In 1316 Thomas de Sandford and John Beaumond were holding lands in Drayton in Farlington[29] ; and the lands of the latter may possibly have been the tithing of *BEAUMONDS* (Bemonds, Bermonds) reputed a manor in the sixteenth century.

There seems to be no separate record, however, of the property until the year 1511, when Elizabeth Pound died seised of part of the manor of Beaumonds in 1511, being sacceeded by her son and heir William, then aged thirty-seven.[30] From this date the descent of Beaumonds follows that of the manor of Farlington (q.v.).

4 *Abbrev. Plac.* (Rec. Com.), 29. Geoffrey Puleyn was holding one carucate of land in Farlington in 1244, and conveyed it in that year to William son of Alan Stake and his wife Elena (Feet of F. 29 Hen. III, No. 297). This land was probably Stakes or Frendstaple in Farlington.

5 Also possibly Stakes or Frendstaple.

6 Feet of F. Hants, 33 Hen. III, No. 344.

7 Inq. p.m. 35 Hen. III, No. 53. Thomas de Gimises, with the consent of his son Nicholas and his wife, granted to Richard son of Andrew Stake and Richard son of Alan Stake all common belonging to the free tenement which they held of him in Farlington in 1255 (Anct. D. P.R.O. A. 8635).

8 *Cal. of Close*, 1279–88, p. 435.

9 Feet of F. Hants, 19 Edw. I, No. 181. The prior of the Hospital of St. John of Jerusalem evidently held some land in Farlington from the king at this time, for in 1290 a commission was issued touching John of Gimises and others who had intruded on the prior's lands in Farlington, expelled his servants and driven away his oxen. *Cal. of Pat.* 1281–92, p. 403.

10 Inq. p.m. 6 Edw. II, No. 43 ; *Feud. Aids*, ii, 320.

11 Feet of F. Hants, Mich. 14 Edw. II.

12 Note that this amount corresponds to the value of the dower given by Roger de Merlay to Agnes his daughter in 1250.

13 *Cal. of Pat.* 1327–30, p. 30. A certain William de Stotevill held a messuage and some land in Farlington ; and in 1328 an order was issued to Alice countess of Arundel not to meddle with this estate, which the king had lately granted to her with the manor of Farlington for the maintenance of herself and her boys, as the king learnt by inquisition that Hugh le Despenser unjustly disseised William de Stotevill of these possessions, and William never remitted his right to Hugh ; *Cal. of Close*, 1327–30, p. 254.

14 *Cal. of Pat.* 1330–4, p. 240.

15 Inq. p.m. 2 Edw. III, No. 21.

16 *Cal. of Close*, 1346–9, p. 348.

17 Ibid. 1345–8, p. 153.

18 Mins. Accts. 29–30 Hen. VIII, R. 113, m. 28. The Husees were holding lands in Farlington in the beginning of the 15th century, evidently as tenants of the prior and convent ; for in 1403 John Husee enfeoffed Richard Stake and his wife Mary of lands in Farlington (Anct. D. P.R.O. A. 8938), and they in their turn granted the lands to Thomas Snokeshulle (ibid. A. 8682). The lands of Thomas Snokeshulle, who was the son and heir of Alice daughter of the late John Stake of Frendstaple, descended by right to his son Henry, and were by him granted to Robert Snokeshulle his brother, Agnes the wife of Robert, and Alice their daughter (ibid. A. 6245). Robert Snokeshulle's lands seem to have passed to his daughter and heir, Alice the wife of William Johnson (ibid. A. 9486, 9100), who conveyed them by fine to John Gunter and John Holt (Feet of F. Hants, Hil. 31 Hen. VI). From John Holt the lands descended to his heirs the Pounds, his granddaughter Elizabeth having married Sir John Pound ; Berry, *Hants Genealogies*, 194.

19 Pat. 32 Hen. VIII, pt. 5, m. 36.

20 Exch. Inq. p.m. 16–17 Hen. VIII, file 978, No. 23.

21 Chan. Inq. p.m. 1–2 Eliz. vol. 119, No. 146. Thomas Pound granted the reversion of part of the manor of Farlington to his niece Ann, daughter of his sister Catherine and wife of George Britten, in 1579 ; Berry, *Hants Genealogies*, 194; Add. MS. 33278, fol. 121.

22 Feet of F. Div. Cos. Mich. 15 Chas. II.

23 Ibid. Trin. 36 Chas. II.

24 Add. MS. 32282, fol. 158–9.

25 Information supplied by Mr. Deverell.

26 Ibid.

27 Ibid.

28 Mins. Accts. 29–30 Hen. VIII, R. 113, m. 28.

29 *Feud. Aids*, ii, 320.

30 Esch. Inq. p.m. 3 Hen. VIII, file 963, No. 4.

Until the beginning of the fourteenth century the descent of the manor of *CREUQUER* (Creuker xiv cent.) is the same as that of the manor of Farlington (q.v.). Upon the death of John de Berewyk in 1312, and the failure of Roger Husee to claim his inheritance,[31] the manor returned to John de Gimises, and being forfeited for his felony [32] was granted in 1217 to Hugh le Despenser for life,[33] and after this date it again followed the descent of the manor of Farlington (q.v.).

The earliest mention of *DRAYTON* (Dreton xiv cent.) in Farlington seems to be in the year 1250, when Henry III gave a moiety of the land there to Roger de Merlay [34]; and between 1250 and 1271 he seems to have given the remaining lands to Richard de Sandford.[35] Roger de Merlay apparently gave his share in the lands which only amounted to four acres to Ralph atte Brigge from whom they passed to Henry Wade by fine.[36]

Richard de Sandford died seised of twelve acres of land in Drayton in 1289 of the gift of the king, and the lands passed to his son and heir Thomas.[37] Henry Wade [37a] granted his share in Drayton also to Thomas de Sandford in 1303 by fine [38]; so that Thomas became possessed of the whole estate. Thomas de Sandford still held Drayton in 1316 [39]; and died seised of lands and rent there in 1327.[40]

Licence was granted to Richard de Sandford, son of Thomas, in 1327 to enfeoff Laurence de Pageham of two messuages, lands, and rent in Drayton; and in the same year Richard died in possession of lands in Drayton.[41] Laurence de Pageham held the eighth part of a knight's fee in Drayton in 1346,[42] and died in 1361 seised of Drayton, for the first time described as a manor, which he held by the service of finding a man in time of war to guard the east gate of the castle of Portchester for fifteen days. Drayton passed to his grandson and heir John, then aged only six months.[43] John Pageham died in possession in 1389 and was succeeded by his son John who was only two years old.[44] This John died in 1399 a minor in the king's wardship; his heir was his brother William who was twenty-one in 1411.[45]

William Pageham held Drayton at the time of his death in 1322, when he left a son Philip aged six,[46] who died seised of the manor held of the king in 1442. His heir was Geoffrey Borrard his cousin, son of Parnel daughter of Laurence Pageham.[47]

Between 1442 and 1476 Geoffrey Borrard or his heirs must have conveyed the manor of Drayton to the Pounds, for Thomas Pound died seised of it in 1476, leaving a son and heir John, aged thirty.[48] Drayton was still in the hands of the Pounds in 1542, for in that year Anthony Pound the grandson of John Pound [49] conveyed it to William Wayte.[50] Anthony evidently gave the manor to his daughter Honora on her marriage with Henry earl of Sussex [51]; and in 1593 Henry Radcliffe died seised of the manor, which he held jointly with his wife, leaving a son Robert, aged twenty.[52] Robert earl of Sussex conveyed it to Richard Garth in 1592, in whose family it remained for about forty years.[53] Robert Garth, Richard's son, died seised of it in 1613, his brother George being his heir.[54] Richard, probably the son of George Garth, was in possession of Drayton in 1629 [55]; and died seised of the manor leaving a son George by his wife Dorothy; and by his wife Beatrice, who survived him, two sons, Thomas and William.[56] The later descent of Drayton seems to be the same as that of the manor of Farlington (q.v.).

POUND OF DRAYTON. *Argent a fesse gules with three molets argent thereon between two dragons' heads sable cut off at the neck in the chief and a cross formy fitchy sable in the foot.*

The descent of *FRENDSTAPLE* or *STAKES* follows that of Farlington manor down to the year 1480, but after that date it passed into the hands of the Gunters. William Gunter, brother and heir of John Gunter of Rakton, Sussex, released his rights in Frendstaple to Thomas Lovell and others in 1480, probably for a settlement,[57] for we find Arthur Gunter holding Frendstaple in 1575.[58] George Gunter and Mary Lady Gunter his wife were in possession of it in 1624 [59]; and from them it passed to their son Arthur who died seised in 1637.[60] Arthur was succeeded by his sister Mary Drewry his heir, who died two years later; her heirs were her cousins Thomas Bickley, Constance Brigham, and Elizabeth Lewes.[61]

After this date no further mention of Frendstaple or Stakes has been found until 1820, when Stakes Farm was purchased by Mr. William Taylor for £5,020; and the hamlet of Stakes Hill by Mr. John Hulbert for £1,200.[62] Stakes Hill is now a hamlet in the parish of Farlington about a mile south-east of Waterloo, and is still owned by the Hulbert family, Mr. J. H. Hulbert of Stakes Hill Lodge being the present owner.

The church of *ST. ANDREW, CHURCHES FARLINGTON*, consists of chancel with north vestry, and nave with north aisle and west bell-cot. It is almost entirely modern, the chancel having been rebuilt by Street in 1872, and the nave in 1875. The lower part of the

31 Inq. p.m. 6 Edw. II, No. 43.
32 Feet of F. Hants, 19 Edw. I, No. 181.
33 *Cal. of Pat.* 1317–21, p. 45.
34 Inq. p.m. 35 Hen. III, No. 53.
35 Feet of F. Hants, 56 Hen. III, No. 614.
36 Ibid. 5 Edw. I, No. 37.
37 Inq. p.m. 18 Edw. I, No. 8.
37a Henry Wade was *of Drayton* in 1269.
38 Feet of F. Hants, 32 Edw. I, No. 259.
39 *Feud. Aids*, ii, 320.
40 Inq. p.m. 1 Edw. III, No. 25.
41 Ibid. 1 Edw. III (2nd Nos.), No. 41.
42 *Feud. Aids*, ii, 336.
43 Inq. p.m. 35 Edw. III, No. 31.
44 Ibid. 13 Ric. II, No. 88.
45 Ibid. 13 Hen. IV, No. 22.
46 Ibid. 10 Hen. V, No. 260.
47 Ibid. 21 Hen. VI, No. 35.
48 Inq. p.m. 16 Edw. IV, No. 37 & 17 Edw. IV, No. 72.
49 Berry, *Hants Genealogies*, 194.
50 Feet of F. Hants, Trin. 34 Hen. VIII.
51 In 1560 Henry Radcliffe and Honora conveyed Drayton to Humphrey and John Radcliffe evidently as a settlement; Feet of F. Div. Cos. Hil. 3 Eliz.
52 Chan. Inq. p.m. 36 Eliz. No. 241. In 1592 Robert, earl of Sussex, mortgaged the manor to Alice and Benedict Barneham for the sum of £1,054, but three months later the enrolment was cancelled and the earl redeemed the manor for £1,024; Close, 36 Eliz. pt. 18, m. 11.
53 Feet of F. Hants, Mich. 36–37 Eliz.
54 Chan. Inq. p.m. 11 Jas. I, vol. 333, No. 40.
55 Feet of F. Hants, Hil. 5 Chas. I.
56 Chan. Inq. p.m. Chas. I, vol. 492, No. 137.
57 Anct. D. (P.R.O.), A. 2420.
58 Chan. Inq. p.m. 17–18 Eliz. vol. 175, No. 79.
59 Ibid. 21–22 Jas. I, vol. 404, No. 112.
60 Ibid. 12–13 Chas. I (Ser. 2), vol. 28, No. 44.
61 Ibid.
62 Add. MS. 33282, fol. 201.

west wall of the nave retains some old masonry, the jambs of the west window, a single lancet, being probably of thirteenth-century date, with a dwarf buttress below its sill.

The chancel is a good example of Street's work, of thirteenth-century style, with a stone-ribbed vault and elaborate details and fittings. In the north vestry is an old piscina, a seventeenth-century altar table, and a small fourteenth-century coffin lid, with a cross flory having a ring on the stem. It probably covered the burial of a heart or some other part of a body rather than that of a child.

The font, at the west of the nave, has an old octagonal base, of the fourteenth or fifteenth century.

There is a brass plate in memory of Anthony Pound, 1547, bearing the arms of Pound; or on a fesse gules three molets argent; in chief two boars' heads and in base a cross paty fitchy sable. There are two bells by Thomas Bartlett of Portsmouth, 1767.

The plate consists of a silver-gilt and jewelled chalice, paten, and flagon of 1853.

The first book of the registers, of parchment, contains baptisms and burials 1538–1656, and marriages to 1647, and the second has baptisms and marriages from 1654, burials from 1656 to 1718, and entries on paper beginning in 1721 of marriages to 1750 and burials to 1792. The third book is the printed marriage register, 1754–1812, and the fourth begins with copies of the entries of baptisms from 1766 to 1792, the originals having been damaged by damp, and combines the baptisms and burials to 1812. The tithe map of 1839 is preserved at the rectory.

The church of *ST. JOHN THE BAPTIST, PURBROOK*, is of flint with stone dressings in the Decorated style, consisting of chancel, nave, south aisle, vestry, south porch, and western tower. The register dates from 1858.

The church of *ST. GEORGE, WATERLOOVILLE*, is of brick, faced with rough-cast, consisting of apsidal chancel, nave, aisle, and small embattled western tower containing one bell. The register dates from 1836.

ADVOWSON

The earliest mention of a church at Farlington seems to be in the year 1200, when there was a suit between Robert de Curci and Roger de Scures concerning the presentation to the church of St. Andrew at Farlington.[63] In 1231 the church was served by a chaplain of Philip de Albini and was in need of repairs.[64]

The rectory of Farlington was valued in 1291 at £13 6*s.* 8*d.*,[65] and in 1535 it was worth £10 4*s.*[66]

The advowson follows the descent of the manor until the end of the eighteenth century.[67] From 1789 until 1803 Charles Williams was the holder,[68] and in 1817 Mr. C. W. Taylor presented.[69] About 1837 the advowson was bought from the trustees of the Taylor estates by Mr. E. T. Richards, in whose family it has remained until the present day.[70] The living is a rectory, net yearly value £300, with residence and four acres of glebe.

The advowson of Purbrook church in this parish is a vicarage in the gift of the rector of Farlington.

The advowson of the church of St. George at Waterlooville is a vicarage in the hands of the bishop of Winchester.

PORTCHESTER

Rich as Hampshire is in antiquities, the county possesses but one or two villages that can compete with Portchester in archaeological and historical interest. Portchester is situated on the tongue of land which juts out into Portsmouth Harbour from the north. South, east, and west its shores are washed by the tide, while the sides of Portsdown form its northern boundary. The London and South-Western Railway has a station a short distance north of the village, which lies low—scarcely 10 ft. above the sea level—and consists of two principal streets:—West Street on the Fareham road, and the long and straggling Castle Street, which runs southwards and leads to the castle and the harbour.

In the south-east corner of the castle inclosure is the priory church of St. Mary, still used as the parish church. The village pound is still to be seen. The schools were built in 1873 and enlarged in 1893 to accommodate 164 children. There is a brewery near the junction of Castle Street and West Street, and the manufacture of tobacco-pipes and whiting is carried on in the village, which also contains many market gardens. There is a Methodist chapel situated in the centre of the village, and Portchester Farm lies to the north-east, close to the railway. Wyker Farm, formerly a small manor, is in the west of the parish, north of Fareham Lake, and is surrounded by a marsh and lake of the same name. Further north-east is the smaller farm of Little Wyke. Wyke mill-house and a disused windmill is reached by Wyke Path.

The soil of the parish is loam, with a clay subsoil, and chalk on the hills, on which crops of wheat and other cereals are grown. The area is 1,379 acres of land, of which 874¼ are arable and 156¾ permanent grass[1]; there are 141 acres of land covered by water, 330 acres of tidal water, and 1,471 acres of foreshore.[2] The common lands in Portchester were inclosed in 1807.[3]

The following place names occur in 1538:—'Whettecrofte, Berestronde, Sawyer's Land, Hall Ground, Purwels, and Ossyldeane.'[4]

CASTLE

The history of the Roman fortress of Portchester has been already given, so far as it can be ascertained. In Domesday there is mention of a 'halla,' but nothing to suggest that the place was of particular importance. Although the mediaeval castle was commenced early in the twelfth century, there is no reference to it until 1153, when

63 *Abbrev. Plac.* (Rec. Com.), 29.
64 *Cal. of Close*, 1227–31, p. 551.
65 *Pope Nich. Tax.* (Rec. Com.), 211.
66 *Valor Eccl.* (Rec. Com.), ii, 22.
67 *Wykeham's Register* (Hants Rec. Soc.), i, 60, 182, 222; Egerton MS. 2034, fol. 13 and 42. There are three exceptions to this statement. In 1619 William Fowle held the advowson for a turn, in 1662 a certain Richard Colson, and in 1869 Thomas Brereton (Inst. Bks. P.R.O.).
68 Inst. Bks. (P.R.O.).
69 *Clerical Guide*, 1817.
70 Add. MSS. 33, 282, fol. 158–9; *Clerical Guide*, 1837; *Clergy List*, 1841–1904.

1 Statistics from Bd. of Agric. (1905).
2 Ordnance Survey.
3 Local and Pers. Acts of Parl. 48 Geo. III, cap. 63.
4 Mins. Accts. 29–30 Hen. III, m. 30.

it was granted by charter of Henry II with the manor (q.v.) to William Mauduit's second son Henry. In 1163 the king's treasure was carried from Winchester to Portchester,[5] presumably to the castle. Perhaps treasure was sent here in connexion with a visit of the king, as he crossed to Normandy frequently at that time,[6] and was staying at Portchester in 1164, when Rotrou, bishop of Evreux, came to the king to try to mediate between him and Becket in their dispute over the Constitutions of Clarendon.[6a] This place was used by the English kings as the port of embarkation during the long struggle to retain their French possessions. In 1172 Henry II passed through Portchester on his way to France,[7] where he declared his innocence of Becket's murder before the papal legates, and hoped to come to terms with his rebellious son. During his absence an insurrection was raised in favour of Prince Henry, but the rebels were defeated and the earl of Leicester and his wife the countess Parnel captured and sent to Henry in France. On his return to England the king brought these prisoners back with him and placed them with many others in Portchester Castle in 1174, when there is a record of £16 paid for their keep.[8] In the same year sums amounting to £158 were paid for knights and serjeants in garrison in the castle, and over £20 for victualling it.[9] In 1176 Prince Henry, as a pretext to escape to the Continent, professed a desire to make a pilgrimage to the famous shrine of St. James of Compostella. With his wife and retinue he reached Portchester,[10] but was delayed there for many days by contrary winds. King Henry was celebrating Easter with great pomp at Winchester, whither he summoned young Henry and extracted a promise from him to defer his pilgrimage until his brother Richard had made peace with his barons in Aquitaine. The prince then returned to Portchester, where he had left his wife, and on 20 April they started, reaching Barfleur the next day.[11] On the accession of Richard I the charge of the castles of Winchester and Portchester was among the things purchased by the bishop of Winchester from the king. The Pipe Rolls of 1177 and 1181 record treasure being sent to Portchester, and that of 1185 proves that Queen Eleanor and her son-in-law, the duke of Saxony, stayed there.[11a]

King John was frequently at the castle. In 1200, after his return from Scotland, he went to France to marry Isabel of Angoulême, staying at Portchester and in its vicinity from 21 to 28 April.[12] It was to Portchester that he summoned the barons of England in the following May[13] to set out on an expedition against Philip of France, who had taken up the cause of Prince Arthur and of the young count of La Marche. In 1204 the king transacted business here while making a prolonged visit to Hampshire in April and May,[14] and here the news of the loss of almost all his French possessions probably reached him. In the following spring he made vast preparations for reconquering them, and went down to Portchester[15] to meet his troops. Ralph of Coggeshall gives a graphic description of the anger and disappointment of the king when he was obliged to abandon the expedition owing to the opposition of the archbishop of Canterbury and the earl marshal. He left Portchester on 9 June *cum magna tristitia*,[16] and went as far as Winchester, only to return to Portsmouth immediately in the hope of carrying out his plans, but the barons remained firm and refused to leave England. A year later his time seems to have been more pleasantly spent, when he wrote to the barons of the Exchequer that 'we lent our brother, the earl of Salisbury, at Portchester, ten shillings to play.'[17] He was at Portchester on 26 March, 1208,[18] when the pope's interdict fell on England. The king visited the castle again in 1209[19] and 1211.[20] In June, 1213, he mustered his force at Southampton, intending to invade France, but the barons would not follow him.[20a] While waiting at Portchester in January, 1214,[21] he appears to have hunted in the park attached to the castle, as he afterwards sent an order to William de Harcourt to send his hunting dogs to Portsmouth from Portchester.[22] The castle surrendered to Louis of France at the end of June, 1216.[22a]

Eustace the Monk, a well-known freebooter of the Channel, was detained in the castle with other prisoners in 1214.[23] John's methods were economical, and they were obliged to provide themselves with food and other necessaries. In 1217 an order was sent to Oliver d'Aubigny to destroy the castle, or if he was unable to level it, to burn it completely.[24] That this order has a connexion with the troubles at the end of John's reign is to be assumed, but its precise connexion is more difficult to fix. In the same year there is a similar order about Chichester,[25] in pursuance of a command given by John some years before, and this appears to have been carried out. But perhaps in consequence of the expulsion of Louis and his invading army, the circumstances which made the destruction of Portchester expedient ceased to exist, and the next year the king ordered that the castle should be repaired.[26] It had been perhaps in preparation for the expedition to Poitou that Henry III had his armour brought to Portchester in 1224, paying four knights 20*s.* each for carrying it there,[27] and four 'doles' of wine taken as booty were hurriedly ordered to be sent there against the king's arrival on 13 July.[28] Henry summoned his vassals to meet him at Ports-

[5] *Pipe R.*(Pipe R. Soc.), 10 Hen. II, p.26.
[6] Nich. Trevet, *Ann.* (Engl. Hist. Soc.), 53, 54, &c.
[6a] *Materials for Hist. of Thos. Becket* (Rolls Ser.), iv, 37.
[7] Matt. Paris, *Hist. Angl.* (Rolls Ser.), i, 371.
[8] *Pipe R.* (Pipe R. Soc.), 20 Hen. II, xxi, 125, 136.
[9] *Pipe R.*(Pipe R. Soc.), 20 Hen. III, xxi, 125, 138.
[10] Benedict of Peterborough, *Gesta Hen. II et Ric. I* (Rolls Ser.), i, 114.
[11] Ibid. 115.
[11a] Richard of Devizes, *Chron.* (Rolls Ser.), 338.
[12] *Rot. Chart.* (Rec. Com.), i, pt. i, 49, 50, &c.
[13] *Rot. Lit. Pat.* (Rec. Com.), i, Itinerary of King John, *sub anno.*
[14] *Rot. Chart.* (Rec. Com.), i, pt. i, 125, 128, &c.
[15] Ralph of Coggeshall, *Chron. Angl.* (Rolls Ser.), 152.
[16] Ibid. 154.
[17] *Rot. Lit. Pat.* (Rec. Com.), i, Introd. p. xxxiii.
[18] *Rot. Chart.* (Rec. Com.), i, pt. i, 176.
[19] *Rot. Lit. Pat.* (Rec. Com.), i, Itin. of King John, *sub anno.*
[20] Ibid.
[20a] Roger of Wendover, *Flor. Hist.* (Rolls Ser.), ii, 82; Walter of Coventry, *Memoriale* (Rolls Ser.), ii, 212.
[21] *Rot. Lit. Pat.* (Rec. Com.), i, Itin. of King John, *sub anno.*
[22] *Rot. de Oblatis et Finibus* (Rec. Com.), 545.
[22a] Histoire des Ducs de Normandie, 174; Histoire de Guillaume le Marechal, ll. 15, 101.
[23] *Rot. Lit. Claus.* (Rec. Com.), 177.
[24] Pat. 1 Hen. III, m. 8.
[25] Ibid.
[26] Close, 2 Hen. III, m. 3.
[27] *Rot. Lit. Claus.* (Rec. Com.), 5.
[28] Ibid. 50.

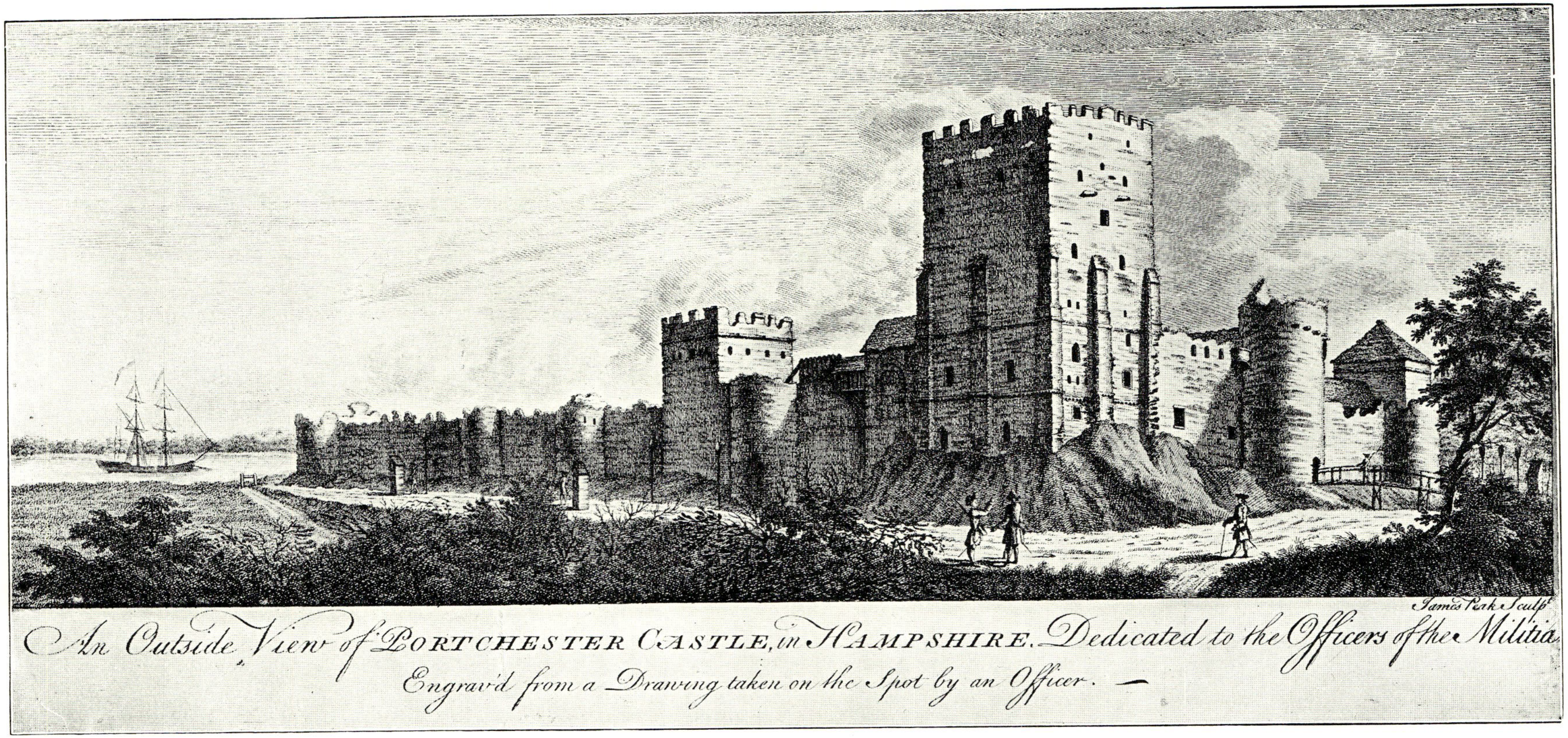

Outside view of Portchester Castle in the Eighteenth Century

mouth in October, 1229, for another French campaign, but his ships being insufficient he spent a few days at Portchester and Portsmouth and returned to London.[29] He appears to have landed here when returning from France in 1243,[30] after the battles of Taillebourg and Saintes, where he barely escaped capture. During the French wars the constables were responsible for keeping the castle supplied with arms and provisions, ready to be shipped abroad. The neighbouring forest supplied oaks, from which as many as eighty bridges and 600 good hurdles were ordered to be made at one time for the castle.[31] The sheriff of London was required to provide carts to carry tents to Portchester,[32] and there are many records of large quantities of provisions being stored there. In 1320, when the younger Despenser was constable, he found so much wine that it had become 'corrupt and putrid.' With characteristic tyranny he detained certain citizens of Winchester and Salisbury until they agreed to buy the wine at £3 per tun.[33]

Edward I does not appear to have visited Portchester, although he issued orders for its repair, and in 1306 Robert Wychard, bishop of Glasgow, and other Scotch prisoners,[34] were kept in chains in the castle. The king made a grant of part of the revenues of the castle, as well as of the manor (q.v.), to Queen Eleanor,[35] in dower, and a similar grant was made by Edward II to Queen Margaret.[36]

During the reign of Edward II there were many rumours of an invasion, and the castle was kept fully equipped and in constant repair. In 1325 Robert de Hausted was appointed to the custody of the tower, with its 'armour, springalds, engines and other munition,' so that if need be he should apply all the force that he was able to the custody of the outer bailey.[37] On any appearance of danger from a foreign fleet or otherwise the castle was to be garrisoned with men-at-arms, horses, and footmen of the parts adjoining, and all spies within the precincts of the castle were to be arrested.[38] Edward II visited the castle for the first time in October, 1321,[39] after a visit to Sheen. Three years later, when the Queen went to France with her son and there was talk of war between the two countries, Edward spoke of leading an expedition in person. With this intention, probably, he spent many weeks at Portchester in July, September, and October, 1324,[40] and again in the following May.[41] In August, 1326,[42] he issued writs of array from the castle and took other precautions.[43] On 2 September following, while there, he was informed where the queen was likely to land, and directed the march of his forces to the Orwell.[44] He had, however, great difficulty in collecting troops. Some footmen, archers, and others in Sussex were ordered to join him at Portchester to set out upon the sea in his service, but the men refused and were imprisoned.[45] The king, being unable to prevent the queen's advance, retreated and shortly afterwards was taken prisoner. Queen Isabel received a much larger grant for life of the revenues of the castle than the previous queens had had, 'in furtherance of a resolution of parliament, for her services in the matter of the treaty with France and in suppressing the rebellion of the Despensers and others.'[46]

Edward III usually stayed at Southwick Priory on his passages to France,[47] but he was at Portchester for several weeks in 1346[48] when preparing for the expedition in which he was to win Crecy and successfully besiege Calais. For more than sixty years after this, no interesting events centre round Portchester, although the post of constable was coveted by such men as Roger Walden, archbishop of Canterbury,[49] and John Tiptoft, earl of Worcester, who was made constable of England and of Portchester in the same year, 1462.[50] His ancestor, Robert de Tiptoft, had been governor of the castle 200 years before.[51] The custody of Portsmouth was joined to that of Portchester in the fifteenth century,[52] and so continued, although separated for a time by Charles I.[53] In 1415 the castle was filled with soldiers assembled by Henry V for his invasion of France to recover his 'ancient rights.' Among them were Richard, earl of Cambridge, Henry, Lord Scrope of Masham, and Sir Thomas Grey of Heton, whose plot to place the earl of March on the throne during the king's absence was discovered while they were at Portchester.[54] Upon their confession they were taken to Southampton and there beheaded.

Henry VIII and Anne Boleyn were at Portchester in October, 1535. 'The king and queen were very merry in Hampshire,'[55] and hawked daily. The last royal visitor was Elizabeth, who held her court at the castle.[56] From this time the story of Portchester Castle is that of a military prison and hospital. In the sixteenth century it was bought by Lord Sussex for £180,[57] and Charles I granted the castle and vill of Portchester to Sir William Uvedale and his heirs.[58] Though frequently leased by the crown afterwards it remained in private hands, Uvedale Corbett holding it in 1691,[59] and Francis Whitehead in 1747.[60] In 1563 Sir F. Knollys wrote to Sir William Cecil, pointing out the advantages of the castle as a place for a muster, there being space for lodging 2,000 men.[61] In the autumn it was used as a hospital for the

[29] Close, 13 Hen. III, m. 1 *d.*; Pat. 13 Hen. III, m. 3 *d.*
[30] Pat. 27 Hen. III, m. 2.
[31] *Rot. Lit. Claus.* (Rec. Com.), 19.
[32] Ibid. 119.
[33] Close, 1 Edw. III, pt. 2, m. 27.
[34] *Syllabus of Rymer's Foedera*, 141.
[35] Pat. 1 Edw. I, m. 5.
[36] Ibid. 3 Edw. II, m. 15, 14.
[37] Ibid. 19 Edw. II, pt. 1, m. 12.
[38] Close, 19 Edw. II, m. 11 *d.*
[39] Pat. 15 Edw. II, pt. 1, m. 15.
[40] Ibid. 18 Edw. II, pt 1, m. 37.
[41] Ibid. 18 Edw. II, pt. 2, m. 4.
[42] Ibid. 20 Edw. II, m. 23.
[43] *Chronicles Edw. I and II* (Rolls Ser.), ii, Introd. p. xciii.
[44] Ibid.
[45] Close, 20 Edw. II, m. 8 *d.*
[46] Pat. 1 Edw. III, pt. 1, m. 2.
[47] Pat. 20 Edw. III, pt. 2, m. 29.
[48] Ibid.
[49] Pat. 18 Ric. II, pt. 2, m. 11.
[50] Pat. 1 Edw. IV, pt. 4, m. 12.
[51] *Dict. Nat. Biog.* lvi, 414.
[52] Pat. 7 Edw. IV, pt. 2, m. 13.
[53] *Cal. S.P. Dom.* 1629–31, p. 333.
[54] *Letters from Northern Registers* (Rolls Ser.), 432. Shakespeare makes Southampton the scene of the discovery of the plot, but it is here recorded to have taken place 'apud castrum de Porchestre juxta Southampton.' Portsmouth or Southampton with their larger harbours were the ports to which the troops for foreign expeditions were summoned, but the kings appear to have preferred to stay at Portchester during the preparations. This was probably done on this occasion.
[55] *L. and P. Hen. VIII*, viii, 190.
[56] J. Mackenzie, *Castles of Engl.* i, 210. In 1601 'the Queene in her Progresse entered into Hampshire' and said she was never so honourably received in any shire. It 'is full of delights for princes of this land, who often make their progresses thither,' being 'well inhabited by auncient gentlemen, civilly educated, and who live in great amitie together' (T. Nichols, *Progresses and Public Processions of Queen Elizabeth*, ii, *sub anno*).
[57] *Rep. on MSS. of Marquis of Salisbury* (Hist. MSS. Com.), pt. iv, 438.
[58] Pat. 8 Chas. I, pt. 5, m. 24.
[59] Recov. R. 3 Wm. and Mary, rot. 273.
[60] Recov. R. 20 Geo. II, rot. 265.
[61] *Rep. on MSS. of Marquis of Salisbury* (Hist. MSS. Com.), pt. i, 275.

sick and wounded from the French war, of whom Sir A. Ponyngs gave a list, with the charges amounting to £4 4*s.* 10*d.* daily.[62] In 1628 a suggestion was made to use it as a storehouse for the Navy,[63] but the idea was abandoned, and twenty-five years afterwards, when Blake's victories in the Channel brought many prisoners to England, the Navy Commissioners recommended the castle as a naval hospital, the situation, air, and water being good, but it 'may cost as much to repair as a new house.'[64] During the Civil War some of Sir W. Balfour's 4,000 horse and dragoons were quartered at Portchester, 21 March, 1644. They were probably Sir Arthur Haslerig's cuirassiers, known to fame as The Lobsters from their iron shells, as six days later, 27 March, Sir W. Balfour was leading these against the cavaliers under Lord Hopton at Cheriton.[65] In 1665, during the war of Charles II, 500 Dutch prisoners were detained in the castle. Thomas Middleton writing to Samuel Pepys complained that the Dutchmen refused to work on the plea that they were servants of the states of Holland and their wives would get no relief from their masters if they worked for the King of England.[66] The commissioners for victualling proposed to erect a brew-house in the castle in 1712,[67] but as it was difficult of access to vessels and would be costly in other ways the project was abandoned. Four thousand French prisoners captured during the Seven Years' War were kept here in 1761,[68] and others during the Napoleonic wars of 1799.[69] Paterson describes the castle in 1821 as a 'noble pile in form quadrangular and surrounding an area of near 5 acres . . . and it is in sufficient preservation to be appropriated to the purposes of a military prison, for which use it was rented by the government of the proprietors, and during the last war 5,000 persons were secured here at one time.'[70] In 1855 the castle was 'examined by Dr. Mapleton and Sir Frederic Smith with a view to ascertain its fitness for conversion into a military hospital. They agreed in returning that it was as unfit for the purpose as could well be. A building ruinous and falling to pieces, badly ventilated, badly drained, without out-houses, its seven rooms 39 ft. by 18 ft. badly lighted, the site low, bleak, with miles of exposed mud lying before it, difficult of access, and containing within its limits the parish church and churchyard, there could scarcely be chosen a less desirable site for the proposed hospital.'[71] By the end of the eighteenth century the castle had passed with the manor (q.v.) into the hands of the Thistlethwayte family,[72] and the ruins still remain in their possession.

The Roman walls of Portchester Castle, which stand in an excellent state of preservation, due allowance being made for the patching and repair which their use in the Middle Ages has caused, inclose an area of some nine acres. They have already been described,[73] and it is unnecessary here to do more than point out that they belong to the latest type of Roman fortress met with in Britain, namely, that in which the defences consist of a wall with towers projecting on the outer face, with no trace of the earthen bank which occurs in the earlier types. On the north and west sides it is still protected by a ditch, and there may have been the like defences on south and east, where now is a sea beach, as it is evident from mediaeval records that the sea has encroached on the land to some extent. To the west, outside the first line of ditch, is a much larger bank and ditch, possibly a pre-Roman earthwork.

The original arrangement of the projecting towers was that there was one set diagonally at each angle of the fortress, and four on each side, except perhaps on the east where there may have been two only, making eighteen towers in all. Of these, two of the angle towers and twelve of the others still stand, and a thirteenth was destroyed as lately as 1790. That the loss of the others was of ancient date is clear from a record of 1369,[74] when 'all the fifteen turrets' were ordered to be fitted with wooden tops, and a round turret opposite the church otherwise repaired. The angle turret at the north-west must have been destroyed when the mount on which the keep stands was made, early in the twelfth century or late in the eleventh century. The entrances to the fortress were in the middle of the east and west walls, both probably protected by inner rectangular gatehouses, the eastern of which still exists in part. Whether they were covered by external defences is not clear, but there are no traces of drum towers like those flanking the probably coeval west gate of Pevensey.

The position of the mediaeval castle is very like that of Pevensey, set in the north-west corner of the inclosure,[75] a small piece being walled off to serve as the inner bailey, while the rest of the area within the Roman walls serves as the outer bailey. The Roman wall forms the north and west curtain of the inner bailey, but has been broken through at the north-west angle, and the great keep projects some feet beyond it in both directions. The inner bailey measures 189 ft. east to west by 120 ft. north to south, and is surrounded by a wall 6 ft. thick with a projecting tower at the south-east angle, and a gateway towards the east end of the south wall. There are ranges of buildings, all roofless and in ruin, on the west, south, and east, and a tower within the north-east angle, the buildings formerly on the north side of the bailey, except those belonging to the keep, being entirely destroyed.

The earliest masonry on the site, not reckoning the Roman walls, belongs to the middle of the twelfth century, or perhaps a little later. The first reference to the castle buildings occurs in 1172–4,[76] 40*s.* being assigned to the *reparacio* of the gates and tower of the castle, and £9 for work on the bridge, gates, and wall. The word *reparacio*, it must be noted, does not generally mean 'repair' in the modern sense, but rather the fitting up of a building, which may be entirely new, so that the entry does not necessarily imply a much earlier date than 1172 for the building of the castle. The lower part of the keep is probably the oldest work, and the east and south curtain walls of the bailey, with the south-east tower and the first 23 ft. of the south gateway, are probably of the time of Henry II. There is also some twelfth-century

[62] *Rep. on MSS. of Marquis of Salisbury* (Hist. MSS. Com.), pt. i, 282.
[63] *Cal. S.P. Dom.* 1625–49, p. 311.
[64] Ibid. 1652–3, p. 224.
[65] Godwin, *Civil War in Hampshire*, 127, 128.
[66] *Cal. S.P. Dom.* 1664–5, p. 519. *Cal. of Treas. Papers*, vol. 147, p. 388.
[68] *Cal. of Home Off. Papers*, 29.
[69] *Rep. on MSS. of T. B. Fortescue* (Hist. MSS. Com.), pt. iv, 2?0.
[70] Paterson, *Descr. of Roads*, 1821.
[71] B. Woodward, T. Wilkes, and C. Lockhart, *Hist. of Hampshire*, iii, 332.
[72] Recov. R. Trin. 16 Geo. III, m. 84–89.
[73] *V.C.H. Hants*, i, 329.
[74] Exch. K.R. 479, No. 21.
[75] At Pevensey the south-east corner is occupied by the castle.
[76] Pipe R. 20 Hen. II.

INSIDE VIEW OF PORTCHESTER CASTLE IN THE EIGHTEENTH CENTURY

work in the buildings at the south-west corner of the bailey, and the king's houses in the castle are mentioned in 1192. In the same year £10 was paid to Eyas de Oxeneford for carpenters and workmen at the castle, and in the next year work and repairs to walls and ditches cost a like sum. In 1200 there were further repairs, and in the Close Rolls for 1204–6 the king's chamber at Portchester is mentioned, and the king's houses there in 1208. By this date the *magna turris* or keep must have assumed its present form, its upper part being an addition of the last years of the twelfth century. The battlements now to be seen on the east and west sides are a late addition, but the tower is now about 100 ft. high. It is divided internally by a central wall running east and west for the full height of the building, and originally contained four floors, the present arrangement of its interior dating from 1793, when it was fitted up to hold French prisoners, many of whom have left their names painted or cut on its walls. The basement has been vaulted in two spans with pointed barrel vaults resting on cross-springers, of which the skew-backs only are now left; the vault was set up in 1398, as appears from the accounts,[77] and cost £20. The two chambers here were lighted by narrow round-headed windows with double splays, the walls being 8 ft. thick; there are six of these windows in all, two in each of the north, south, and west sides, and the original entrance to the basement was by a newel stair in the south-west angle, the present entrance from the basement of the chapel being probably modern. Access to the basement must therefore have been from the first floor of the keep only. From the existence of windows on the south side, against which a range of buildings now abuts, it seems that the keep was originally free on this side, the twelfth-century 'king's houses' not covering the full length of the west curtain wall.

Against the east face of the tower was set the fore-building, which seems to have contained three divisions, that to the south being the chapel, with a basement beneath it; that to the north, which projected beyond the Roman wall to the same extent as the north wall of the keep, a room of uncertain use, perhaps a guard-room; while between them was a passage or lobby leading to the round-headed entrance door of the keep. These rooms were all on the first-floor level, and must have been reached from the court-yard by an outer stair occupying much the same position as that which now serves the purpose. Of the chapel only the west end, with a large round-headed recess, and part of the south wall remain. In the latter is a late fourteenth-century doorway leading to a building at the south-east angle of the keep, which overlaps the south wall of the chapel for 8 ft., and to the east of it the jamb of a sixteenth-century window, beneath which is a doorway to the basement, of like date, and the royal arms of Henry VII. Part of a small blocked twelfth-century window is to be seen near the jamb of the sixteenth-century window. The room corresponding to the chapel on the north has had a wide sixteenth-century bay window in its north or outer wall. Over the entrance to the keep, or perhaps to the lobby leading to it, was a tower, called the East Tower in a roll of accounts of 1385.[77a] The first floor of the keep contained the two principal rooms, and was lighted by large round-headed windows, now blocked up. In the south-west angle of the south room is a doorway, now also blocked, to the newel stair which leads from the basement to the battlements, and the entrance to the north room is by a door at the west end of the dividing wall. In the south-east angle of the keep is the circular shaft of a well, which is continued upwards to the upper stories.

In the second floor of the keep are small round-headed lights on the south and west sides, and the weatherings of the original roof are here to be seen, showing two parallel gables running east and west.

The added upper part of the tower has narrow square-headed openings on the north and west, but towards the interior of the castle, on east and south, there are coupled square-headed lights under round-headed inclosing arches. The walls in this upper stage are 4 ft. 6 in. thick, as against 8 ft. in the basement.

There are no traces of original openings in the twelfth-century curtain walls, but the south-east angle tower, which has been divided into two, or perhaps three, stories, and is of irregular plan, narrower at the gorge than at the outer end, has a small blocked round-headed light in its south-east face on the first-floor level. The twelfth-century gatehouse on the south has likewise been of two or three stories lighted by narrow windows on the three projecting sides, and must have been closed in on its north or inner face by a masonry wall carried on an arch, now destroyed, or by a wooden partition. All the twelfth-century work is faced with excellent Binstead stone, and where the facing has not been picked off it remains in very good preservation.

There is no evidence of building in the thirteenth century as far as the actual remains are concerned. In 1220 100*s.* was paid for the strengthening of the castle, and in the same year the roof of the keep was being covered with lead.

The work next in point of date to be seen at the present time is the vaulted gateway added to the twelfth-century south gateway. This belongs to the first quarter of the fourteenth century, and building accounts[78] of this time, 1320–1, are extant. They show that work on the north wall of the castle was going on, and a small doorway of this date is to be seen just east of the forebuildings of the keep in this wall, and was doubtless part of the work.

The king's chamber was being roofed, and in the keep some mason's and carpenter's work was being done. Much timber was also cut in the neighbourhood for use in the castle, and the mention of work on the middle gate of the castle and stones for foundation of a bridge within the castle probably refers to the building under notice. It has a pretty ribbed vault, a segmental inner arch, and an outer arch with portcullis grooves, flanked by two massive buttresses. In its east and west walls are small doorways, which must have opened to a berm between the walls and the moat which defended the inner bailey on east and south, and at the outer southern angles of the gate are narrow walls starting diagonally and flanking the bridge head which must have existed at the time. The gate has received two additions since then, one of late fourteenth-century date, 18 ft. long, with an

77 Exch. K.R. 479, No. 23. Bonchurch stone was used for the springers and ribs.

77a Ibid. No. 22.

78 Ibid. No. 17.

outer archway and portcullis groove, and a seventeenth-century lengthening, making up the total projection from the curtain wall to 67 ft. This latter consists merely of two parallel walls, in the western of which is a recess for the porter's seat. There were apparently two towers over the gate, one over the twelfth-century part, and one probably over the late fourteenth-century addition, known as the Portcullis Tower.

In 1338 a further set of accounts[79] deals with reroofing the queen's chamber and the knights' chamber and for repairs to the keep, a big crack (*crevesce*) having formed in the latter, perhaps a predecessor of the present crack at the south-west angle. The barbican is mentioned in this account, and was evidently not new at the time, as an old doorway was now walled up in it; a further mention of the two barbicans goes to show that they were connected with the east and west gates in the outer bailey, otherwise the Roman fort. The 'Brokene Tour' at which a stockade was made was probably one of the Roman turrets which have now disappeared; perhaps that at the south-east angle. There are also provisions for a 'false wall' against a sudden attack from seaward, *contra insidias Galiarum*. Twelve of the Roman turrets were fitted with wattled boards, and a weak part of the wall was similarly defended. This must mean that a part of the masonry breastwork which ran round the tops of the Roman walls had been destroyed and was now replaced by wattled defences. The roof of the king's hall in the inner bailey having been damaged by a great wind was now repaired.

In 1362 is another list of repairs,[80] mostly to roofs, the hall, kitchen, larder, &c., being mentioned. A second tower besides the keep is mentioned, probably the south-east tower, and there is an entry about a new water channel between the larder and the kitchen. A number of payments are made, exclusively to carpenters, about the making of a hall, a *camera*, and a chapel, but there is nothing to show that the hall and chapel were other than timber buildings, and they are not to be confused with the great hall and chapel then in existence. In the Pipe Roll for the same year,[81] however, the size of the new *camera* is given as 104 ft. by 25 ft., and it evidently had masonry walls; its length is rather too great for a position on the north or east of the inner ward as at present arranged, but as the north-east tower was not built at this time the difficulty is not insuperable. The rooms mentioned as repaired are: three king's chambers, the queen's chamber, the chamber next the hall, the kitchen, bake-house, and lead-house.

The sea-gate, or east gate of the fort, now received a portcullis; the existing gate seems to have been rebuilt about 1397.[82] It projects beyond the line of the Roman walls and has diagonal angle buttresses and a rather narrow entrance, but has lost much of its wrought stonework. It is set in front of a rectangular gatehouse built within the walls, the lower parts of which, with its eastern arch, are apparently of Roman date, the arch being semicircular, of one square order, with ironstone and Binstead voussoirs and jambs.

In 1384–6[83] a great deal of work was going on. 'Ashtonestour,' at the north-east of the inner bailey, was being fitted with hinges, bolts, &c., and its roof leaded; Sir Robert Assheton was constable in 1376, and this probably gives the year when it was begun. It contains the latrines, its lower part being divided into several wide shoots, the general arrangement of which is still clear, though much of the masonry has been removed. It has an entrance on the west from the now destroyed vaulted ground story of the northern range, and the rampart walk is continued through it at a higher level.

The great quantities of materials accounted for by the returns of 1396–9 show the large extent of work then being carried out. The *camera* between the keep and Ashton's Tower, although called new in the account, and probably being that built in 1362, was in a ruinous state, and was repaired, or rather rebuilt, the masons working on it through practically the whole of 1396. It is now again completely ruined and destroyed to the foundations.

A list of the stone used is interesting; freestone from Bonchurch, and ragstone or ragplatener stone from Bembridge for the walling, and Beer stone from Devonshire for the details of doors and windows and fire-places. A thousand cart-loads of flints were used, and 1,000 white tiles of Flanders were brought for the fire-backs—*les reredoses caminorum*—being shipped at Billingsgate in London and taken to the Pool and thence by sea to Portchester. Hearth-tiles were also bought for the fire-places, and a great lime kiln was made at the foot of Portsdown, 14 ft. wide and 11 ft. deep, and filled and burnt six times, producing 800 quarters or 87 cartloads of lime. Chalk was also quarried at Portsdown for the fillings of vaulting and walls. 'Plastureston de Purbik' was used for the plastered partitions between the various rooms.

There was much renewing of leaden roofs, and a lead downpipe was made to carry the water from the roof of the keep. Lead from the dismantled Mere Castle in Wiltshire was brought to be used at Portchester.

The most important entry is that mentioning the setting out and beginning of the present south-west range, containing the hall, kitchen with buttery and pantry, and the rooms adjoining. In the western range most of what exists dates also from this time or a little earlier, as it seems that the fitting up of the chapel east of the keep, and the king's apartments in the west range, preceded the rebuilding of the hall and offices. The south gateway and its vault were repaired at this time, and the second addition to the original gate, already mentioned, probably dates from this repair. The vault here is called 'duplex,' and as the same term is used in speaking of the great outer gate on the west, where both the ground and first story were vaulted, this may have been the case in the south gate also. The vault of the basement in the keep is said to be *cum duplici pendente;* in this case it may mean 'in two spans.'

In 1398 the hall was far advanced, as oaks for its rafters and for the kitchen are mentioned. An item of oil for preserving its timbers against sun and wind points to the existence of a wooden louvre on the roof, and a later entry shows that there was one over the kitchen. They are called *femoralli*, fumerels, and were covered with lead, like the roofs. In 1399 glass was being made and painted with shields,

79 Exch. K.R. 479, No. 18.
80 Ibid. Nos 19, 20.
81 Pipe, 36 Edw. III, 41.
82 Exch. K.R. 479, No. 23.
83 Ibid. No. 22.

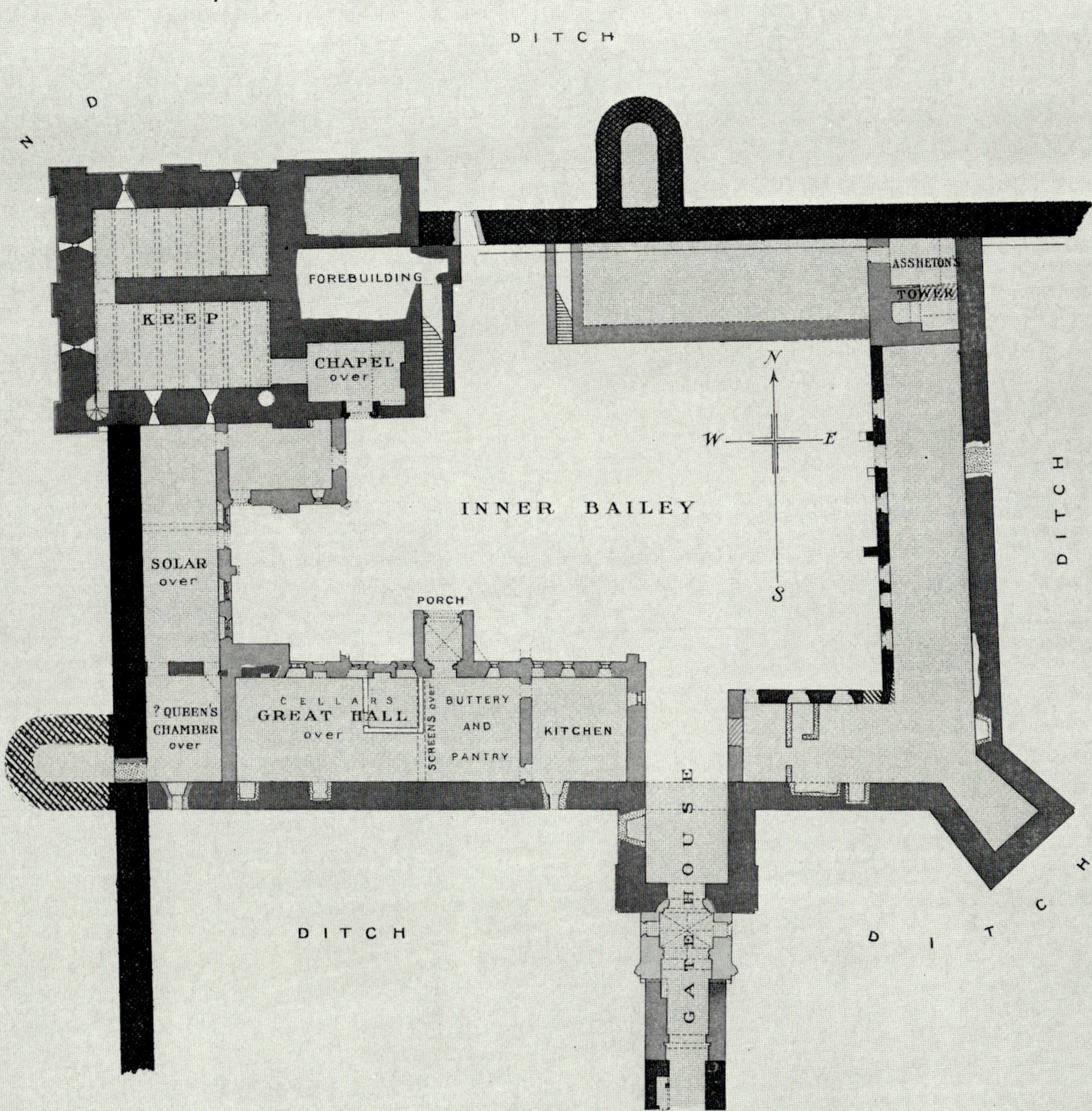

PORTCHESTER CASTLE

Ground Plan.

C.R.PEERS, F.S.A.
Mens et del. 1902

badges, and borders, for the windows of the hall, the great chamber, the chapel, the exchequer or treasury room, and the high chamber adjoining it, and also for the windows of the *tresancia* or passage, the kitchen, and the basement beneath the great chamber ; and it is perhaps a sign of Richard's anxiety, amid the dangers and difficulties of the last year of his reign, to see his work finished, that between the feasts of All Saints and the Purification of our Lady the workmen used 26 lb. of candles by working at night.

His buildings still stand, but roofless and floorless, and are the most picturesque part of the castle. The hall was on the first floor, with cellars beneath, and was entered by a flight of steps under a projecting vaulted porch. On either side of the entrance are brackets for lanterns. The square building east of the hall was clearly the kitchen, and there are traces of a large fireplace in its east wall ; it was on the ground floor, and there was a stair at the south-west leading from it to the hall. The arrangements of buttery and pantry are not clear, but they may have been below the hall screens. A passage contrived in the north-west angle of the hall[83a] led to the great chamber and private apartments, the queen's chamber being probably at the west end of the hall, and the king's chamber next to the south face of the keep. The Roman bastion west of the queen's chamber, now completely pulled down, seems to have been fitted up as living rooms, and part of a garderobe is still to be seen in the wall. From the king's chamber a passage ran eastwards through the exchequer chamber (if this identification of the building at the south-west angle of the keep is correct) to the chapel. A little older work is incorporated with Richard's buildings, as at the north-west angle of the hall, where part of a late twelfth-century arcade is to be seen, but the greater part of the work seems to have been built from the ground at this time, as the accounts would imply.

There is nothing to show whether anything of importance was done to the building in the next few reigns, but in 1488 a writ[83b] was issued under the privy seal for the delivery of sufficient sums of money to Sir Reginald Bray for the repairing of the castle. Very little work now remains which can be attributed to this time beyond the royal arms on the south wall of the chapel, a doorway and part of a window near by, and the wide window in the north curtain wall near the keep.

The last document of importance which need be quoted here is Norden's survey of the castle in 1609.[83c] It is accompanied by a bird's-eye sketch of the buildings from the south-east, which, though very distorted, shows a good many interesting details. At this time the castle was ruinous, Norden reports, 'by reason the leade hathe beene cutt and imbezeled.' He recommends that the remains of the lead should be removed and a lighter roof-covering substituted, with new roof-timbers. In the great hall, 'verye fayer and spacious,' 'to which was an assent by 4 fayer stone stepps,' the leaded roof was ready to fall. The adjoining rooms were 'maine spacious though darke and malincolie.' Three towers are mentioned, the keep being described as the 'mayne towre,' of four stories 'dowble raunged.' Norden suggests that it should be lowered to half its height, because it 'annoyeth the reste of the howse by raflexe of the chimneye smoake,' but fortunately this was never done.

The range of buildings on the north side of the inner bailey, now entirely ruined, was then standing, but in bad repair. It is described as a building not long since in part newly erected, containing four fair lodgings above and as many below ; its windows were unglazed, and its roof had lost its slating. From this it would appear that the 'camera between the keep and Ashton's tower,' repaired or rebuilt in 1396, had been again rebuilt for the most part in the latter years of Elizabeth's reign. On the Roman bastion to the north a chamber was built, as on the south-west bastion. This latter is shown rectangular in Norden's drawing, but this is probably mere convention.

The south gate of the castle was approached by a drawbridge over the ditch in 1609, and flanked by walls running at an obtuse angle towards the main curtain ; it seems that the latest or southern extension of the gateway was not at this time in existence. On the annexed plan it is shown, together with the eastern range of the inner bailey, as of sixteenth-century date, but both actually belong to the early years of the seventeenth century.

The eastern range, the walls of which still stand, was built by Sir Thomas Cornwallis, as Norden reports, at a cost of £300 and more, in place of older work of which nothing has been preserved. It was probably quite new at the time of the survey, as in 1608 sixty timber trees were delivered to Cornwallis from the forest of East Bere, evidently for work at the castle.[83d] The design is very simple : of the latest Gothic type with no renaissance detail, with four-centred doorways and three-light mullioned windows with square heads. Norden's drawing shows windows of this kind, with transoms, in the curtain wall at this point. The range is returned along the south curtain wall as far as the gateway, and it is probable that the whole was built to provide suitable accommodation for the officials in charge of the castle, the royal apartments built by Richard II being by now too much out of repair to be fit for use.

There is nothing to show whether there were any buildings in the outer ward of the castle in mediaeval times ; in any case, they are not likely to have been of much importance. In the accounts of Sir John Daunce, 1521–27, printed in *Archaeologia*, xlvii, 335, is an item of £400 paid to Lord Lisle 'upon the buldyng of a stores house at the castell of Porchester, and other causes,' and the foundations of a long buttressed building, 240 ft. by 30 ft., near the south-west angle of the ward,[83e] may be those of the store-house in question. The barracks built for the French prisoners in the eighteenth century stood along the north side of the ward, between the buildings of the inner ward and the east wall of the Roman fortress.

The great west gate of the castle, now as always the chief entrance to the outer ward, is in a very fair state of preservation, and dates for the most part from the last years of Richard II's reign, though the lower parts of its walls may be older. In the first story are

83a In Norden's drawing, 1609, a rounded bay window is shown on the north side of the hall to the west of the porch.

83b *Materials illust. of Reign of Hen. VII* (Rolls Ser.), ii, 438.

83c S.P. Dom. Jas. I, xlviii, No. 46.

83d Ibid. xxxi, No. 78.

83e 170 ft. from the west wall.

traces of the arrangements of a drawbridge and portcullis, the castle ditch having been doubtless continued from one end of the west side of the fortress to the other. This gate is now the only inhabited part of the castle, being occupied by a caretaker.

FOREST The southern ward of the royal forest of Bere, which extended northwards from the Portsdown Hills, was known in early times as Portchester Forest. There are frequent records of gifts of oak timber from the forest, chiefly for the purpose of repairs. In 1232 an order was issued for repairs to two of the king's galleys with timber from 350 oaks in the forest of Portchester.[84]

In 1269 Master Henry Wade was licensed for the term of his life to hunt with his own dogs the fox, hare, cat, and badger through the forest of Portchester;[85] and in 1297 a similar grant was made to Thomas Paygnel.[86] The wood of 'Chalghton' within the forest of Portchester is mentioned in 1307.[87]

In 1341 the forest of Portchester was worth nothing because 'the oaks were old and short, and for the most part rotten and bear nothing.'[88] Therefore, in 1347, an order was issued for the re-afforestation of Portchester, with a proviso saving the rights of commoners,[89] the proviso being confirmed in 1466.[90]

Portchester Forest was under the control of the warden of the castle till the fifteenth century, when it was attached to the forest of Bere.

BOROUGH It seems possible that Portchester was a royal borough growing up round the castle, and granted with the castle and manor. Nevertheless, evidence of any borough is very scanty; there is no charter of incorporation, and no members were ever returned to Parliament. As early, however, as 1177, Portchester rendered an aid of 10 marks, which was about as much as Andover or Basingstoke,[90a] and in 1258 Hugh de Camoys was holding land in chief in Portchester for annual rent and for such serjeanty as he and 'all the other burgesses of the town of Porchester were bound to pay'; namely, to find twelve men to serve for fifteen days in time of war at Portchester Castle.[91]

In 1233 a command was issued to the constable of Portchester Castle that the 'men of Porchester' should be allowed to have the same common of pasture for beasts in the wood of Kingesden which they had had before the king took the wood into his custody.[92]

The 'men of Porchester' were granted free turbary in Southmore in 1260;[93] and in 1273 an order was issued to the bailiffs and men of Portchester to pay their rents to Eleanor, the king's mother.[94] The town of Portchester was assigned in dower to Margaret, sister of Philip, king of France, in 1299,[95] and in 1316 the liberty[96] of Portchester was 'Domini regis sed in manu Margarete regine.'[97]

The king granted the custody of Portchester town to Hugh le Despenser in 1320;[98] but after the rebellion of the Despensers in 1327 and the consequent forfeiture of their lands, Portchester was granted to Queen Isabella for life in furtherance of a resolution of Parliament that for her services in the matter of the treaty with France, and in suppressing the rebellion of the Despensers, the lands assigned to her by way of dower should be increased in value to £2,000 a year.[99] Richard earl of Arundel was holding the custody of Portchester town in 1341,[100] but he afterwards granted it to John de Edynton, which grant the king confirmed in 1361.[101]

Robert de Assheton was granted the custody of the town in 1376.[102] He was followed by Robert Bardolph, and Robert by Roger Walden.[103]

Ralph de Camoys was holding the town of Portchester at the time of his death in 1421.[104]

After Edward IV's marriage with Elizabeth Woodville, he granted titles and lands to many of her relations. Among other grants the custody of Portchester town was entrusted to Anthony Woodville, the queen's brother, for life;[105] and afterwards to Edward Woodville.[106]

From this time onwards the descent of Portchester town seems to follow that of the manor (q.v.).

MANORS In the reign of Edward the Confessor there were three manors in *PORTCHESTER*, held by three freemen of the king, but at the time of the Domesday Survey William Mauduit held them as one manor.[107] Mr. Round has thrown fresh light on its early history and connexion with the chamberlainship of the treasury and exchequer[107a] by showing that it passed to William's son and heir Robert, after whose death it was promised to his younger brother William by a remarkable charter of Henry II, issued in 1153, before his accession, in which Portchester Castle and its appurtenant lands are definitely mentioned; but evidently Henry did not fulfil his promise,[107b] as in 1230 the king granted two-thirds of the manor to Peter des Roches, bishop of Winchester, who gave them to the abbey of Titchfield.[108] The remaining third part was granted by Edward I to his mother Eleanor in dower in 1272.[109]

John Randulf was granted the custody of the king's manor and castle of Portchester in 1330 for the payment of a rent to the king of 25 marks.[110]

The abbey of Titchfield[111] continued to hold their part of the manor of Portchester until the Dissolution,

[84] *Cal. of Close*, 1231–4, p. 206.
[85] Pat. R. 53 Hen. III, m. 5.
[86] *Cal. of Pat.* 1292–1301, p. 290.
[87] Inq. a.q.d. 1 Edw. II, No. 102.
[88] *Cal. of Close*, 1341–3, pp. 178–9.
[89] *Cal. of Pat.* 1345–8, p. 264.
[90] Ibid. 1461–7, p. 495.
[90a] *Pipe R.* (Pipe R. Soc.), 23 Hen. II, 174.
[91] *Plac. Abbrev.* (Rec. Com.), 146. The defence of the castle was further provided for by granting small estates in the neighbourhood to be held by the serjeanty of providing an armed man there in time of war.
[92] *Cal. of Close*, 1231–4, p. 215.
[93] Inq. p.m. 53 Hen. III, No. 31
[94] *Cal. of Close*, 1272–9, p. 31
[95] *Cal. of Pat.* 1292–1301, p. 452.
[96] Apparently the only time that Portchester is called a liberty.
[97] *Feud. Aids*, ii, 323.
[98] *Abbrev. Rot. Orig.* (Rec. Com.), i, 254.
[99] *Cal. of Pat.* 1327–30, p. 69.
[100] Inq. p.m. 15 Edw. III, No. 70.
[101] *Abbrev. Rot. Orig.* (Rec. Com.), ii, 266.
[102] Ibid. ii, 345.
[103] *Cal. of Pat.* 1391–6, p. 572.
[104] Inq. p.m. 9 Hen. V, No. 29.
[105] *Cal. of Pat.* 1467–77, p. 41.
[106] Ibid. 1476–85, p. 180.
[107] *V.C.H. Hants*, i, 492.
[107a] Round, *The Commune of Lond.* 82–3; 'Mauduit of Hartley Mauduit,' *Ancestor*, v, 207–10.
[107b] 'Reddidi eidem camerariam meam thesauri . . . cum omnibus pertinentibus castellum scilicet de Porcestra . . . et omnes terras ad predictam camerariam et ad predictum castellum pertinentes sive sint in Anglia sive Normannia sicut frater suus.'
[108] Chart. R. 15 Hen. III. pt. 1, m. 2; *Plac. de Quo Warr.* (Rec. Com.), rot. 37. A perambulation of the boundaries was ordered to be made by jury in 1233. (*Cal. of Close*, 1231–4, p. 186.)
[109] *Cal. of Pat.* 1272–81, p. 27.
[110] *Abbrev. Rot. Orig.* (Rec. Com.), ii, 41.
[111] The abbey and convent were granted protection with clause nolumus in their manor of Portchester in 1324 (*Cal. of Pat.* 1324–7, p. 24).

Portchester Castle : The Keep from the South-west

when it passed, by grant of Henry VIII in 1537, to Thomas Wriothesley earl of Southampton,[112] who, however, in the following year reconveyed it to the king, who thus held the whole manor.[113]

The manor remained in the possession of the crown until 1632, when it was granted to Sir William Uvedale,[114] son of Sir William Uvedale, who was sheriff of Hampshire in 1594, and Mary daughter of Sir Richard Norton.[115] On his death the manor of Portchester was divided between his two daughters and co-heirs Victoria, who married Sir Richard Corbett in 1663, and Elizabeth, first the wife of Sir William Berkeley, and afterwards of Edward Howard earl of Carlisle.[116]

One-half of the manor passed, on the death of Elizabeth countess of Carlisle, to her son Charles earl of Carlisle, by whom it was conveyed to Mr. Norton of Portchester Castle,[117] the ancestor of the Thistlethwaytes of Southwick, who still own the manor.[118]

The other half of the manor was purchased from the Corbetts by Jonathan Rashleigh in 1724,[119] and from him it passed to his son Philip, who was holding it in 1771.[120]

In 1775 this half was evidently sold by the trustees of the Rashleighs to Robert Thistlethwayte,[121] and the two halves of the manor were united in the hands of the Thistlethwaytes, whose descendant Mr. Alexander Thistlethwayte, of Southwick Park, is the present lord of the manor.

At the time of the Domesday Survey there was a mill in Portchester worth 30 pence,[122] and at the present day Wyker Mill still exists in the tithing of Wyker.

In 1086 there was a fishery in the manor for the use of the hall,[123] and in 1198 Walter de Boarhunt conveyed a salt-pit and 3 acres of land in Portchester to Thomas de Hoo.[124]

In 1294 an order was issued that a market should be held in the king's manor of Portchester on Saturday in every week, and that a fair lasting three days was to be held there on the eve, day, and morrow of the Assumption yearly, but these have long since been discontinued.

WYKER or *WICCOR* in Portchester was probably among the lands in Portchester granted to the abbey of Titchfield in 1230,[125] though not mentioned by name in the charter of Henry III. Described as the manor of Wykes in Portchester, it was included among the possessions of the abbey at the time of the Dissolution,[126] and was afterwards granted to Thomas earl of Southampton for life.[127] At his death in 1550 it reverted to the crown.[128] It was granted in 1556 to John White of Southwick,[129] after which it followed the descent of the manor of Southwick (q.v.).

MORALLS in Portchester seems to have been among the possessions of the priory of Southwick until the time of the Dissolution, but it is not known how that house obtained it. At the suppression of Southwick Priory it was granted, in 1559, to John White, when it was described as lately belonging to the priory of Southwick.[130] From this date the descent follows that of the manor of Southwick (q.v.)

CHURCH

The church of *OUR LADY, PORTCHESTER*, was given by Henry I in 1133 to his new house of Austin Canons, as their priory church, and from its scale and arrangements the present building must have been built for the royal foundation. The site for some reason or other was soon found to be inconvenient, and between 1145 and 1153 the priory was removed to Southwick.[131] So that the date of the building can be set within narrow limits; and as there is nothing to suggest a pause in the work, it is probable that the whole church was completed about the time of Henry's grant.

It is cruciform, faced with wrought stone throughout, with presbytery 19 ft. long by 21 ft. wide, central tower 21 ft. 6 in. by 18 ft. 3 in. (28 ft. by 25 ft. external measurement), north transept 23 ft. 2 in. by 18 ft. 3 in., with eastern chapel, and nave 84 ft. 9 in. by 23 ft. (23 ft. 6 in. at the west). The south transept is destroyed, but probably had an eastern chapel like that of the north transept. On the south side lay the cloister and its surrounding buildings, but nothing of these is now to be seen above ground except the traces of abutment against the church, and some arches of a twelfth-century arcade on the upper floor, at the south end of the eastern range, where it joined the Roman wall of the fortress. They evidently formed part of the reredorter, and shoots through the wall are to be seen below them. The Roman wall was cut away to some depth for their insertion, and it has been argued from this that the monastic buildings must have been left standing after the removal of the priory, as otherwise the weakening of the wall thus caused would have been made good during the time that the walls were used as the outer defences of the mediaeval castle.

The church itself seems to have suffered but little from its abandonment by the canons. The doorways to the cloisters are walled up, as is a large doorway on the north of the nave, and the south transept, as before noted, is pulled down. For the rest, the structure can never have been badly neglected, but the presbytery has lost its vault and has been in part rebuilt in Elizabethan days, and it is recorded in a petition of 1705 to Queen Anne that the church, having been used for the keeping of prisoners of war in Charles II's time, 'was by their means set on fire and for the greatest part ruined.' This, however, can only apply to the roofs and fittings. The church was repaired in 1888.

The chancel—more accurately the presbytery—was vaulted in one square bay, the eastern vaulting shafts remaining intact. The east wall was probably entirely rebuilt, and the north wall refaced externally in the end of the sixteenth century, the three-light east window being of this date. On the north and south walls are plain round-headed arcades which have lost their springers and shafts, and to the west of them are

112 Pat. 29 Hen. VIII, pt. 1, m. 31–2.
113 Feet of F. Hants, Trin. 30 Hen. VIII.
114 Pat. 8 Chas. I, pt. 5, m. 24.
115 Berry, *Hants Pedigrees*, 75.
116 Ibid. 117 Add. MS. 19056, fol. 2.
118 The Thistlethwayte pedigree appears in the account of the parish of Southwick (q.v.).
119 Recov. R. Trin. 12 Geo. III, rot. 339.
120 Ibid. 121 Ibid.
122 *V.C.H. Hants*, i, 492.
123 Ibid.
124 Feet of F. Hants, Hil. 10 Ric. I.
125 Chart. R. 15 Hen. III, pt. 1, m. 2.
126 Dugdale, *Mon.* vi, 935.
127 Pat. 29 Hen. VIII, pt. 1, m. 31–2.
128 W. & L. Inq. p.m. 4 Edw. VI (Ser. 2), vol. 5, No. 103.
129 Pat. 3 & 4 Phil. and Mary, pt. 9, m. 10.
130 Ibid. 2 Eliz. pt. 5, m. 23.
131 This is proved by two bulls of Eugenius III (1145–53); one addressed to the prior and convent of Portchester, the other to the same at Southwick.

doorways, that on the north now leading to the eastern chapel of the north transept, and that on the south side being blocked; they must have served as the *ostia presbyterii*, the upper entrances to the quire, while the church was used by the canons.

The tower, which is of two stages, the upper stage rising but little above the ridges of the nave and transept roofs, stands on four semicircular arches, having a roll between two square orders, and a label ornamented with billets. Over them at the level of the belfry floor is a projecting course of masonry with the same ornament. The jambs have central half-round shafts and engaged shafts in the outer order, and the capitals are chiefly of the volute type, others being scalloped. The southern arch is blocked up, and the loss of the south transept has weakened the tower so that the east and west arches have cracked slightly, but in the main the work is in very good preservation. The north transept was designed for a vault of a single bay, the vaulting-shafts remaining at the angles, but there is nothing to show that it was ever completed, the north window of the transept indeed proving the contrary, if it is in its original position, as its head is too high to be cleared by the vault.

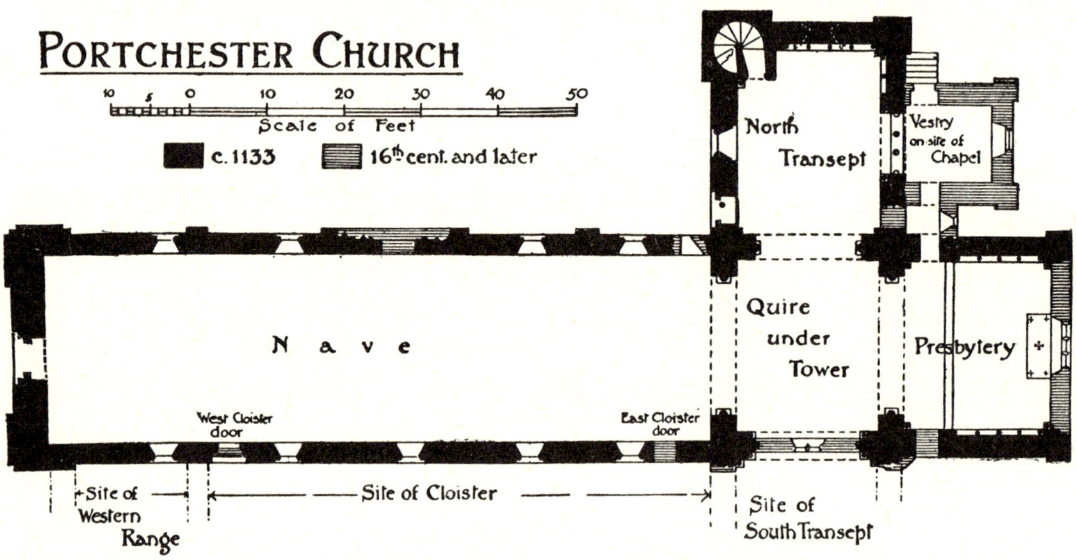

On the east of the transept is a rectangular chapel rebuilt in 1864 on the old foundations, and used as a vestry, and entered through a doorway on the south, its west arch towards the transept being blocked by a modern stone screen. This arch is ornamented on the west side with a hatched label and zigzag on the outer order. Near the south-east angle of the transept are traces of the passage from the upper entrance to the quire, which led through a doorway to the transept at the back of the north-eastern pier of the tower.

On the lower part of the north wall of the transept is a plain wall arcade of which only the arches are old, and in the north and west walls are single round-headed windows with jamb shafts, labels with lozenge ornament, and a radiating pattern on the arches, much like that in the earlier work at Petersfield. At the north-west angle is a circular stair in a projecting square turret, leading by a passage over the ceiling of the transept to the upper stage of the tower, and at the south-west angle of the transept is a modern doorway.

The nave is of the plainest character, with four round-headed windows on the north and a central doorway, of which only the inner arch now remains. It was set in a gabled projection 19 ft. long, and must have been a conspicuous feature, but has been entirely effaced on the outside. In the south wall are five round-headed windows, the lower parts of the first four having been partly blocked by the cloister roof, while the fifth is completely blocked, and from its position within the lines of the western range of claustral buildings must always have been so. The eastern and western procession doors to the cloister are also blocked up, and there is evidence of a slight change of position in the eastern door, two round-headed arches remaining in the wall. The monastic quire must clearly have been to the east of these doors, and therefore under the tower, whose side arches it probably completely filled. Marks of a rood screen and loft are to be seen at the east of the nave, and low in the north wall at the east end is a small window which must have lighted the altar here under the loft. The nave is wider than the presbytery or tower, though the church is accurately cruciform, the extra width being obtained by thinning the north and south walls in the nave, while keeping their outer faces on the same plane as those of the tower.

The west wall of the nave, on the other hand, is 5 ft. thick without the wide buttresses, and has a central doorway of three orders with twisted shafts, and above it a wall arcade of three bays, the central bay pierced with a window. Both doorway and arcade are very richly ornamented, and the whole is a valuable example of a twelfth-century west front almost unaltered.

The fittings of the church are mostly modern, but the nave roof is old, of trussed rafter form. In 1888 a number of fifteenth-century oak bench-ends were found serving as footings for the pews in the nave, and one of them is now in the chancel. On the south wall of the nave is a board with the arms of Queen Elizabeth, dated 1577, and on the north another with those of Queen Anne, 1710.

The font at the west of the nave is an unusually fine

Portchester Church : Crossing Arches

Southwick Church : The White Tomb

twelfth-century specimen,[132] circular, with a band of interlacing foliage over an arcade of interesting round-headed arches. The top only is old, the lower part dating from 1888, and replacing a brick and plaster imitation of the original work. In 1845 the original base was in existence, and is described as having the baptism of Christ sculptured on it.

The only monument of interest is that to Sir Thomas Cornwallis, groom porter to Queen Elizabeth, 1618, with an alabaster half-effigy in armour, and heraldry over.

There are three bells, the treble of 1633, with the initials R.V. I.H. W.W.; the second, inscribed 'In God is my hope,' 1632, with the founder's initials I.H.; and the tenor of 1589, inscribed 'Obey God and the prince,' by John Wallis of Salisbury.

The plate consists of a communion cup, *c.* 1850, with paten and flagon of 1854, and a spoon of foreign make.

The first book of the registers goes from 1607 to 1640, and the second from 1654 to 1683. The third, a paper book, contains the entries for 1684–93, and the fourth for 1694–1803, the marriages ceasing in 1751. The fifth is the printed marriage register 1755–1812, and the sixth and seventh contain respectively the baptisms, 1805–12, and the burials 1804–12.

ADVOWSON There is no mention of a church at Portchester at the time of the Domesday Survey. One must have existed here, however, early in the twelfth century, for in 1133 Henry I founded in the church of St. Mary, Portchester, a priory of Austin canons, afterwards known as the priory of Southwick. Its foundation charter assigned to the canons the appropriation of the church at Portchester.[133]

The advowson and rectorial tithes remained with the prior and convent of Southwick until the Dissolution.[134] Tithes of wheat and barley in Portchester parish were granted to Peter Tichborne in 1553.[135] In 1558 they were given to the bishop of Winchester,[136] who held them until 1587, when the tithes were granted to the earl of Sussex for the term of twenty-one years.[137] The earl died in 1593,[138] and in 1595 they were granted to John Wingfield,[139] in whose family they remained until 1635, when Sir Richard Wingfield, Lord Powerscourt, died seised of the tithes.[140]

The advowson was held by the king[141] until 1865,[142] when it was bought by Thomas Thistlethwayte, the lord of the manor,[143] and passed with the manor (q.v.) to his descendant Mr. Alexander Thistlethwayte, of Southwick Park.

The vicarage of Portchester was valued in 1291 at £9 6*s.* 8*d.*,[144] and in 1535 at £6 6*s.* 11*d.*[145]

CHARITIES In 1807, under the provisions of the Inclosure Act, 48 George III, cap. 63, an allotment of 6 acres 3 roods 36 poles was awarded to the churchwardens in respect of certain lands known as the Church Lands formerly existing in the parish, described in a terrier dated 1728. The rent of about £20 a year is carried to the churchwardens' general account.

In 1826 a site and building thereon were conveyed for the purposes of a Methodist chapel. By an order of the Charity Commissioners, 2 October, 1867, trustees were appointed, and the property vested in them upon the trusts of 'The Wesleyan Chapel Model Deed.'

SOUTHWICK

Seuewic (xiii cent.); Suwic, Suthwyk (xiv cent.); Southwike (xvi cent.).

The parish of Southwick consists of well-wooded and undulating country and contains 725¼ acres of wood. A part of the Forest of Bere lies to the north, and there are many detached woods and copses. Southwick Park also covers a wide area. The road which skirts the north-west of the park passes through the midst of the Forest of Bere, and in its progress north to the hamlet of Denmead traverses some beautiful wooded country. The parish is well watered by the River Wallington and its tributaries, and contains seventeen acres of water. The south boundary follows the east of Portsdown for about a mile and a half, and one of the forts on the ridge is named after the parish. The village lies almost in the centre of the parish, to the east of the junction of the Wallington with one of its tributaries, the main village street running parallel with the south-western boundary of the park and containing many picturesque half-timbered houses. The church of St. James stands just outside the park to the west, facing a second street which runs westward to join the Wickham road, the vicarage being near the junction of the roads. Bridge House, below Newman's Bridge, is very prettily situated, and there are many other delightful views of river-scenery in the parish.

The remains of Southwick Priory, a house of Black or Austin canons, founded by Henry I in 1133, and in which, in 1445, Henry VI was married to Margaret of Anjou, lie in the extreme south-west corner of Southwick Park, and would doubtless repay a careful investigation. The buildings were not entirely destroyed at the suppression, but converted into a house, like those of Titchfield and Mottisfont. There is a record that in Richard Norton's time Dryden's play 'The Spanish Friar' was performed in the frater. In course of time parts of the old work became ruinous, and in the beginning of the nineteenth century the house was rebuilt, and much of the monastic building finally disappeared in the process. Till this date a great chapel with fourteen windows on each side, attributed to William of Wykeham, is said to have remained standing. The new house was burnt in 1838, and the present building was begun shortly afterwards. Southwick House, the residence of Mr. Alexander Thistlethwayte, is pleasantly situated in the centre of the park, which is

132 Illustrated in *V.C.H. Hants*, i, 248.
133 Cited in the inspection and confirmation charter of Edw. III (Chart. R. 27 Edw. III, m. 9, No. 19).
134 Egerton MSS. 2031–4, vol. 4, fol. 22, 56, 86, 102, 141, 170.
135 Pat. 1 Mary, pt. 12, m. 2.
136 Ibid. 5 and 6 Phil. & Mary, pt. 14, m. 6.
137 Ibid. 29 Eliz. pt. 3. m. 11.
138 *Dict. Nat. Biog.* xlvii, 144.
139 Pat. 37 Eliz. pt. 2, m. 10.
140 Inq. p.m. 11 Chas. I (Ser. 2), No. 93
141 Inst. Bks. (P.R.O.).
142 *Clergy List*, 1865.
143 Ibid.
144 *Pope Nich. Tax.* (Rec. Com.), 211*b*.
145 *Valor Eccl.* (Rec. Com.) ii, 23.

finely timbered. The great room of the house is called the Old Playhouse. The stream running through the south of the park is artificially widened for the greater part of its course.

Wanstead Farm, which represents what is left of the so-called manor of Wanstead, lies to the north-east of the park, Lye Heath and Lye Heath Farm to the east.[1] Belney Farm, Great Belney Copse, and Little Belney Copse mark the site of the manor of Belanney, and Newlands Farm in the east represents the manor of Newlands. In the south-eastern extremity of the parish is a part of Purbrook Heath. The schools, which stand immediately opposite the church, were built about 1845, and are supported by Mr. Alexander Thistlethwayte.

The soil is clay and loam; the subsoil chalk. The chief crops are wheat and other cereals. The area is 3,866 acres of land and 17 acres of water, the proportions of land in the parish being as follows: 1,502½ acres of arable land, 1,790 acres of permanent grass, and 724¼ acres of woodland.[2]

The following place-names occur in 1538: "Steynynge, Drawlegges, Pontein Lee, Amery Croft, Cockesdell, Stapull Crosse,[3] Offwell (which still survives in Offwell Farm), Little Russhams, Halecroft, Beeters, Plashet and Astele Mead,[4] and in 1775 Shorts Meads and Edwards Meads.[5]

MANORS

The earliest mention of *SOUTHWICK* seems to be in the year 1133, when Henry I founded a priory of Austin canons at Portchester,[6] assigning to them by the foundation charter the manor of Candover, a hide of land in Applestead, and a hide of land in Southwick.[7]

Southwick Priory. *Argent a chief sable with two roses argent therein.*

The priory was removed from Portchester to Southwick between 1145 and 1153, and this land with the addition of other lands acquired by grant of Richard de Boarhunt and Gilbert de Boarhunt during the thirteenth and fourteenth centuries evidently became the manor of Southwick,[8] which remained in the hands of the prior and convent until the time of the Dissolution.[9]

After the Dissolution the site of the priory church of Southwick was granted to John White,[10] servant to Sir Thomas Wriothesley,[11] in 1538, and eight years later the manor and church of Southwick were granted to Sir Thomas Wriothesley that he might alienate them to John White.[12] On the death of John White

Southwick, the Church from the South

[1] There was evidently a church in Wanstead as early as the fifteenth century (vide Advowson).

[2] Statistics from Bd. of Agric. (1905).

[3] Mins. Accts. 29–30 Hen. VIII, R. 113, m. 21.

[4] Pat. 30 Hen. VIII, pt. 6, m. 17.

[5] Rec. R. Trin. 16 Geo. III, m. 84–90.

[6] *V.C.H. Hants*, ii, 164.

[7] Cited in the inspection and confirmation charter of Edw. III (Chart. R. 27 Edw. III, m. 9, No. 19).

[8] In 1381 the priory manor of Southwick consisted of 193 acres of land, 41 of pasture, and 22 of meadow; Add. MS. 32280, fol. 506.

[9] *Feud. Aids*, ii, 319; Chart. R. 14 Edw. II, m. 8, No. 32; Dugdale, *Mon.* vi, 244. Among the various tenants who held land in the manor of the prior and convent was Richard de Boarhunt in 1285 (Inq. p.m. 14 Edw. I, No. 59), and four years later he granted fifty acres of land and the site of a mill in Southwick to the prior and convent in exchange for a mill and fifteen acres of land (Pat. 18 Edw. I, m. 45). In 1323 Gilbert de Boarhunt was granted licence to alienate fifteen acres of land in mortmain to Southwick Priory (Pat. 17 Edw. II, pt. 1, m. 6). John le Hunte and his wife Juliana held two mills and an acre of land in Southwick in 1343 (Inq. p.m. 17 Edw. III (2nd Nos.), No. 27), and Bernard Brocas held five acres of land in Southwick from the convent in 1383 (ibid. 7 Ric. II, No. 137). In 1388 and again in 1395 Michael Spencer, a grocer of London, and his wife Margaret conveyed half the lands, tenements, and rent which they held in Southwick to William Weston of London and Alice his wife (Feet of F. Hants, East. 12 Ric. II). Thomas Turner held thirty acres of land in Southwick in 1467; from him they passed to William Smith (ibid. Trin. 7 Edw. IV).

[10] Pat. 30 Hen. VIII, pt. 6, m. 17.

[11] *V.C.H. Hants*, ii, 168.

[12] Pat. 38 Hen. VIII, pt. 4, m. 17. In this grant common of pasture for 200 sheep annually is granted on the commons of Portsdown in Southwick.

in 1567 the manor passed to his son and heir Edward.[13] In 1580 Edward died, leaving a son and heir, John,[14] who, in 1606, settled the manor on his daughter and co-heir Honor on her marriage with Sir Daniel Norton,[15] and they came into possession of the manor on the death of John White in the following year.[16]

White of Southwick. *Azure a cross quarterly ermine and or between four falcons argent with a fret between four lozenges azure on the cross.*

Sir Daniel Norton died seised of the manor in 1636, leaving a son and heir, Richard, who had married Anne daughter of Sir William Earle.[17] Richard died 10 December, 1732,[17a] and his daughter and heir Sarah married Henry Whitehead; they had two children Richard and Mary. Richard died young, 25 December, 1733, leaving all his estates to his nephew Francis Thistlethwayte, son of his sister Mary, who had married Alexander Thistlethwayte in 1717 and died before 1728.[18] Francis Thistlethwayte of Southwick took the name of Whitehead, and died 30 March, 1751, leaving his estates to his elder brother with remainder to his younger brother, Robert Thistlethwayte. From that time the manor has remained in the hands of the Thistlethwayte family; Mr. Alexander Thistlethwayte of Southwick Park being lord of the manor at the present day.

Thistlethwaite. *Or a bend azure with three pheons or thereon.*

Numerous liberties and immunities, together with free warren in their demesne lands of Southwick, were granted to the prior and convent in 1320 and 1445.[19] A fair, together with a weekly market, was granted to the priory by charter of 18 April, 1235. It was changed in 1513 from the vigil of the Assumption of the Blessed Mary to the feast of St. Philip and St. James the Apostles and the two following days; because the date of the original fair was damaging to the neighbouring fairs.[20] In 1343 John le Hunte and his wife Juliana were holding two mills in Southwick. In 1381 it was stated that the priory water-mills and dovecote in Southwick were of no value.[21]

At the time of the Domesday Survey William Mauduit held two hides less one virgate of land, which Alvric had held as one manor from King Edward, and also one hide of land which Fulcold held from him.[22] It seems possible that either of these two parcels of land may have become later the manor of *BELANNEY* (Belamy, Belney) in Southwick, which was held of William Mauduit in the thirteenth century.

The overlordship of the manor probably passed from the Mauduits, with the extinction of the male line of the family at the end of the fourteenth century, to the prior of Southwick, from whom the manor was held in the fifteenth century.[23]

William de Belanney died seised of half a fee in Belanney in 1263, which he held of William Mauduit, and in consequence of this tenure William Mauduit claimed the custody of the lands and heir of William de Belanney.[24]

Baldwin de Belanney held one fee in Belanney in 1346: and in 1350[25] and in 1359[26] the same Baldwin granted the manor of Belanney to Henry Sturmy of Elvetham and Margaret.[27] The manor remained in the hands of the Sturmys for more than fifty years, and was then granted by Sir William Sturmy in 1416 to Sir William Hankford and Robert Hall, probably as trustees.[28]

In 1428 Richard Holt held one fee in Belanney which Baldwin de Belanney had formerly held[29]; and died seised of the manor in 1457[30]; but it is not known how it passed to the Holts. Joan, widow of Richard Holt, who afterwards married Constantine Darrell, held the manor in dower after the death of her late husband, until her death in 1495, when on the partition of the property between her granddaughter Lora, wife of Thomas, earl of Ormond, and her daughter Elizabeth, wife of John Pound, the manor of Belanney passed to the latter,[31] who died seised of it in 1511.[32] Elizabeth was succeeded by her son and heir William, who died in 1525, leaving the manor to his second son, another William[33]; and on the marriage of his granddaughter Mary with Edward White of Southwick[34] it passed into the hands of the Whites, and subsequently followed the descent of the manor of Southwick (q.v.).

A grant of free warren in his demesne lands of Belanney was made to Henry Sturmy and his heirs in 1359.[35]

Courts leet for the manor are mentioned as late as 1803.[36]

The so-called manor of *NEWLANDS* in Southwick was part of the possessions of Southwick Priory at the time of the Dissolution.[37] It was then granted to John White of Southwick in 1546,[38] and from this date follows the descent of Southwick manor (q.v.). It is now represented by Newlands Farm in Southwick. It must originally have formed part of Peter de Cosham's serjeanty in Cosham, for in the thirteenth century the prior of Southwick held by serjeanty a

13 Chan. Inq. p.m. 9 Eliz. (Ser. 2), vol. 145, No. 8.
14 Ibid. 23 Eliz. (Ser. 2), vol. 195, No. 120. This John conveyed the manor in 1599 to Giles Kent (Feet of F. Hants, Mich. 42–43 Eliz.), evidently the settlement of a jointure from the manor on Frances wife of John White, quoted in the Inq. p.m. on Daniel Norton (q.v.).
15 Feet of F. Hants, Mich. 4 Jas. I.
16 Chan. Inq. p.m. 7 Jas. I, vol. 312, No. 138.
17 Ibid. 12 Chas. II (Ser. 2), vol. 478, Nos. 101, 129.
17a *Gent. Mag.* 1125, iii, 57.
18 Berry, *Hants Genealogies*, 194.
19 Chart. R. 14 Edw. II, m. 8; ibid. 21–24 Hen. VI, No. 7.
20 Pat. 5 Hen. VIII, pt. 2, m. 30.
21 Add. MS. 32280, fol. 506.
22 *V.C.H. Hants*, i, 493; entered under Portchester.
23 *Herald and Genealogist*, vii, 386.
24 But this is probably East Boarhunt (q.v.).
25 Feet of F. Hants, Trin. 24 Edw. III.
26 This was probably only a confirmation of title.
27 Feet of F. Hants, East. 33 Edw. III.
28 Close, 4 Hen. V, m. 1–2.
29 *Feud. Aids*, ii, 356.
30 Chan. Inq. p. m. 36 Hen. VI, No. 32.
31 Ibid. 12 Hen. VII (Ser. 2), vol. ii, No. 121.
32 Ibid. 3 Hen. VIII, File 963, No. 4.
33 Ibid. Esch. Inq. p.m. 16–17 Hen. VIII, file 978, No. 23.
34 Berry, *Hants Genealogies*, 194.
35 Chart. R. 33 Edw. III, m. 3.
36 Feet of F. Hants, Trin. 44 Geo. III.
37 Dugdale, *Monasticon*, vi, 244.
38 Pat. 38 Hen. VIII, pt. 4, m. 17.

virgate and a half at Newland, out of the land which the abbot of Titchfield had obtained from Peter de Cosham (see under Cosham).[38a]

As early as the middle of the thirteenth century the family of Wanstead held land at *WANSTEAD*,[39] in Southwick, of the king by the service of finding a man to serve for eight days in time of war at Portchester Castle.[40] They continued to hold this land until 1453, when John Wanstead died seised of lands, tenements, and rent in Wanstead, his heirs being his two sisters, Agnes, the wife of John Joye, and Joan, the wife of John Kentyshe.[41] The estate, however, does not appear to have been described as a manor until the year 1495, when Sir John Dawtry died seised of it, held by the same service, leaving a son and heir, Francis, under age.[42] It is possible that the lands may have passed to the Dawtrys by the second marriage of the surviving co-heir of John Wanstead with Sir John Dawtry. However this may be, Sir Francis Dawtry sold the manor in February, 1541–2, to Richard Bennett of Portchester, and Agnes his wife.[43] Agnes survived her husband, and in 1548 settled the manor on her married daughter, Margaret Tichborne, from whom it passed ten years later to Agnes's son, John Maryner,[44] and thence in 1593 to Peter son of this John.[45]

Peter Maryner died in March, 1614, leaving the manor to his only daughter Mabel, wife of Edmund Plowden.[46] In the following spring Dorothy Maryner and Edmund Plowden and his wife Mabel conveyed the manor to John Waller and Francis Plowden evidently as a settlement.[47]

From the beginning of the seventeenth century the Whites were holding the rectory, advowson, and lands in Wanstead,[48] which passed with the marriage of Honor White to the Nortons[49]; and from the Nortons to the Thistlethwaytes. The Thistlethwaytes evidently bought up the whole manor from the heirs of the Plowdens, for Alexander Thistlethwayte and his wife Mary were seised of it in 1768[50]; and it has remained in their family until the present day.

CHURCH The church of *ST. JAMES* has a chancel with north chapel, nave with north aisle and south porch, and a west tower over the last bay of the nave. Its oldest details are evidently re-used material from the ruins of Southwick Priory, but the eastern angles of the chancel seem to be of thirteenth-century date, and the south and west walls of the nave have fourteenth-century features.

The chancel was remodelled by John White in 1566, as an inscription above the east window records:

IOHANNES WHYTE ARMIGER PATRONUS HUIUS ECCLESIE
ET DNS MANERII
HANC FENESTRAM ET OPUS FIERI FECIT ANNO
DNI 1566.

The window in question is of three trefoiled lights with tracery which might be taken for fifteenth-century work, but the two contemporary windows on the south, the eastern of which has the date 1566 on the dripstones of its label, are of three square-headed lights with ovolo mullions of Renaissance detail. Over the eastern of these two windows is a panel of early seventeenth-century character, with three divisions enclosing heraldry, in the first a Moor's head, in the second a quartered coat with sable, a lion or in the first quarter, and in the third sable a lion or.

At the north side of the chancel is the tomb of John White and his second wife, and west of it a four-centred sixteenth-century arch to the north chapel.

There is no chancel arch, and the north jamb of the opening to the nave is cut back. A beam spans the chancel at the west, with a plastered partition above it, on which is the Creed.

The nave has a north arcade of two wide bays and one narrow eastern bay, of the same detail and date as that on the north of the chancel, and the north aisle and chapel seem to be coeval with it, being lighted by square-headed windows with uncusped four-centred lights. The east window is of four lights, and the three on the north and one on the west of two lights.

The external north-east angle of the old aisleless nave, projecting into the north chapel, has been cut back, and the upper part carried on the fine thirteenth-century capital of a clustered column of Purbeck marble, doubtless from the priory church.

At the east end of the south wall of the nave is a recess spanned by a late twelfth-century moulded and pointed arch, obviously re-used, and in the back of the recess is a window of two cinquefoiled lights, perhaps eighteenth-century work, with a later mullion. To the west of it is a tall window, *c.* 1330, of two trefoiled ogee lights, and beyond it a plain south doorway opening into a long and narrow vestry, which has developed from a porch, and has in the southern half thirteenth-century wall arcades of three bays, on east and west, with Purbeck marble capitals on the west, and in one instance on the east also, doubtless more relics of the priory.

The west end of the nave is occupied by a gallery carried on twisted wooden columns, and at the west by four big wooden posts, which may once have supported a wooden bell-turret, replaced apparently in the sixteenth century by the existing plain masonry tower. The east wall of this tower is built on a round arch spanning the gallery, with narrow side arches, the southern of which contains the stair to the gallery, and the other its continuation to the belfry. The west wall of the nave is of the first half of the fourteenth century, with a central west doorway of two continuous orders with a moulded label, and a three-light window over it with net tracery. The lower part of the wall is faced with chequers of stone and flint, and there are heavy angle buttresses. The church is full of tall deal pews, with a large 'squire's pew' on the north side of the chancel. The pulpit is, however, of oak, a half octagon in plan, at the south-east of the nave, with a good cornice and fluted upper panels. The

38a *Testa de Nevill* (Rec. Com.), 242.

39 Adam de Wanstead held half a carucate of land in 1254 (Feet of F. Hants, Hil. 39 Hen. III). Henry de Wanstead was holding a little later, and William de Wanstead owned land there in 1362, and died about 1376 (*Abbrev. Rot. Orig.* (Rec. Com.), ii, 342). Adam de Wanstead and Robert de la Hurst held one virgate in La Lye, now represented by Lye Heath Farm (*Testa de Nevill*, 242).

40 *Testa de Nevill* (Rec. Com.), 235–237; Chan. Inq. p.m. 36 Edw. III (1st Nos.), No. 80.

41 Ibid. 32 Hen. VI, No. 6.

42 Ibid. 11 Hen. VII (Ser. 2), vol. 34, No. 12.

43 Ibid. 1 Edw. VI (Ser. 2), vol. 85, No. 40.

44 Ibid. 1 Eliz. (Ser. 2), vol. 124, No. 159.

45 Ibid. 36 Eliz. (Ser. 2), No. 80.

46 Ibid. 12 Jas. I (Ser. 2), vol. 345, No. 120.

47 Feet of F. Hants, Hil. 12 Jas. I.

48 W. and L. Inq. p.m. 7 Jas. I (Ser. 2), bdle. 12, No. 108.

49 Chan. Inq. p.m. 12 Chas. I (Ser. 2), pt. 1, Nos. 101–29.

50 Feet of F. Hants, Mich. 9 Geo. III.

THE GARRISON CHURCH, PORTSMOUTH, FROM THE SOUTH-WEST

[W. H. Barrell, photo.

THE GARRISON CHURCH, PORTSMOUTH : INTERIOR OF CHANCEL

altar-rails have eighteenth-century twisted balusters, and the east end of the chancel is panelled, with a large eighteenth-century painted altar-piece in the middle.

The font at the south-west of the nave, *c.* 1200, is octagonal, of Purbeck marble, with two shallow round-headed arcades on each face. It stands on a modern octagonal base.

John White's tomb, already mentioned, is a Purbeck marble altar-tomb with panelled sides, with the brass figures of himself and his second wife, Katherine Pound, on the upper slab, with their arms and figures of six sons and four daughters. The tomb dates from 1548 or soon after, when his wife died, the date of his own death (1567) being filled in afterwards. The inscription which runs round the edge of the slab is in English, and of very beautiful lettering. There have been brass shields in each panel of the sides of the tomb, but only those on the south remain, bearing respectively White,[50a] White impaling Pound, and Pound. The stone canopy of the tomb is dated 1566, having evidently been set up by White when he was altering the chancel, and is of Renaissance character, with a central pediment and columns on either side, surmounted by smaller pediments. A small figure holding a shield stands on each pediment, and the arms of White and Pound, with the White crest, a horse's head, are repeated in the spandrils and on the shields. With the Pound arms are quartered (2) Argent three fleurs-de-lis azure, for Holt, (3) Argent a cheveron between three eagles' legs razed sable, for Braye, and (4) Argent a cross engrailed gules, for Tiptoft.

On the north wall of the north chapel is a brass plate to Anne, first wife of John White, and widow of John Pound of Drayton, the date of her death being lost.

There are four bells, said to have been brought from the old church of St. Lawrence, Portsmouth. The treble, by John Wallis of Salisbury, is inscribed 'Praise God, 1600,' and the tenor, inscribed 'Searve the Lord,' is of the same date and by the same founder. The second is a mediaeval bell, *c.* 1440, by a London foundress, Joanna Sturdy, and is inscribed 'Sancte Paule Ora Pro Nobis.' The third, bearing 'In God is my hope, 1623,' is by an uncertain founder I.H., whose bells are common in the district.

The plate is silver-gilt, given in 1691 by Richard Norton, and consists of a communion cup, a standing paten, two flagons, an almsdish and a rat-tail spoon.

The registers begin in 1628, the entries up to 1812 being contained in six books.

ADVOWSON Southwick Church was assessed in 1291 at £10, tithes £1.[51] At the time of the Dissolution the rectory of Southwick was in the hands of the prior and convent,[52] and was granted, with the site of the priory, to John White in 1538, when he immediately pulled down the conventual church.[53]

The advowson followed the descent of the manor (q.v.), and, with the manor, is now in the hands of Mr. Alexander Thistlethwayte. The living is a vicarage consolidated with Boarhunt.

There was evidently a church at Wanstead in Southwick in the beginning of the fifteenth century, the advowson of which was in the hands of the prior and convent.[54]

The rectory was in the possession of the priory at the time of the Dissolution,[55] and from this date the advowson of the rectory has followed the descent of the manor of Southwick (q.v.).

CHARITIES In 1599 Honor Wayte, by will, gave to the poor of this parish 20*s.* yearly, to be paid out of the manor of Denmead, to be distributed amongst the aged sick and needy poor people.

The annual sum of 20*s.* is duly paid and distributed in money among ten parishioners.

In 1837 John Soaper, surgeon, by will, proved this date, bequeathed £400 new three per cents., and directed the interest thereof to be laid out in bread for distribution to the poor on 25 January each year for ever. The Trust Fund now consists of £390 8*s.* 1*d.* consols, with the official trustees, the dividends of which are given away in bread.

WYMERING

Wimeringe (xii cent.); Wemering; Wymerynnge (xiv cent.); Wymering (xv cent.).

In 1831 Wymering was a parish about four miles north from Portsmouth, containing the villages of Wymering and Cosham, and the tithing of Hilsea, about one mile south of Cosham. It was about three miles in length and three miles in breadth, and contained 3,079 acres of land. It was, however, amalgamated with Widley in 1894,[1] and formed into the present parish of Cosham. The combined area of the two parishes is 4,035 acres of land, 33 of water, 83 of tidal water, and 621 acres of foreshore.[2]

The village of Wymering, which is very small, lies about half a mile west of Cosham, on the main road between Cosham and Fareham. The church and vicarage are on the north side of the road, with the new churchyard opposite to them, and the manor house close by on the east. Both vicarage and manor house are old buildings, but much alteration has deprived the former of any features by which the date of its oldest parts can be determined; and the latter, though retaining more evident traces of age, owes its interest at the present day rather to its contents than its structure. It is H-shaped in plan, with a panelled entrance hall in the centre, the kitchen and offices being attached to the south side of the south wing. The beams in this part of the building witness to its antiquity, and foundations are said to exist to the north of the house belonging to buildings connected with the still-existing north wing.

A large room of comparatively modern date, built out into the garden at the back of the south wing,

50a Mr. Percy G. Langdon, in a valuable paper on 'The Brasses of the White family at Southwick' (*Hampshire Field Club*, vol. iii, pt. 1), gives these arms as Argent on a cross quarterly ermine and or between four falcons azure a fret gules between four lozenges counterchanged gules and or; a different blazon from that given above, which is taken from Berry's *Hampshire Genealogies*.

51 *Pope Nich. Tax.* (Rec. Com.), 211*b*.

52 Dugdale, *Monasticon*, vi, 244.

53 *V.C.H. Hants*, ii, 168.

54 Egerton MSS. 2031-4, iv, 26.

55 Dugdale, *Monasticon*, vi, 244.

1 Loc. Govt. Bd. Order.

2 Ordnance Survey.

contains a number of good pictures and a fine stone chimney-piece from Bold Hall, in Lancashire, and there are other relics of this destroyed house in other rooms.

At the back of the house is a pretty walled garden.

East Wymering Farm is a substantial building, a little further to the east, on the south of the road, with a large pond before the house; and Upper Farm and Lower Farm lie respectively north and south of the side road which runs northward along the west boundary of the churchyard, dividing it from the grounds of the manor house. To the north of the village runs the ridge of Portsdown, crowned by the new buildings of the Alexandra Hospital, while to the south are the low-lying lands and mud-flats of Horsea Island.

Cosham village is in the east of the parish, at the foot of Portsdown, where the road from Havant to Fareham crosses the high-road between London and Portsmouth after its sharp descent from Portsdown Hill. To the south, east and west stretch tracts of low-lying land commanded by the long range of Portsdown and its impressive but obsolete array of forts. The village is of considerable size, falling naturally into two parts:—East Cosham, which lies along the road to Havant, and Cosham, which is situated along the main road to Portsmouth. The former consists chiefly of residential houses surrounded by pleasant gardens, while Cosham is the commercial quarter. Situated as it is on the high-road to Portsmouth, a considerable amount of traffic passes through it, and it contains an unusually large number of inns and restaurants. 'The Swan,' 'The Ship,' 'The King and Queen,' 'The Red Lion,' 'Uncle Tom's Cabin' and 'The Pure Drop' are the names of some of the former, but there are others too numerous to mention. The Portsmouth corporation electric tramway has a terminus here to the north of the railway station, worked in connexion with the Portsdown and Horndean Light Railway, which runs through Cosham a little to the west of the High Street. Cosham Park, at present unoccupied, is of considerable extent; it lies to the north of the railway. In the centre of the village is the cattle-market, where a market is held every Monday for the sale of live-stock. East Cosham contains a small Baptist chapel erected in 1871. Divine service is held in Cosham elementary school, which is licensed for the purpose, and has a portion screened off to serve as a chancel. There is a brewery in Cosham High Street, and also a seed, coal, corn, and artificial manure manufactory; and in East Cosham the manufacture of sieves and baskets is carried on. Cosham almshouses were erected and endowed by Mistress Honor Wayte in 1608, for four poor, honest women.

Hilsea lies to the south of Cosham on the main Portsmouth road, about three miles north of Portsmouth, and is practically a suburb of Portsmouth. In the centre of the village are the Royal Artillery Barracks, the fortifications of which have been strengthened, and are now very extensive. There is also a garrison school for the children of soldiers and a military hospital.

Two lines of railway pass through the parish, the London and South-Western and the London Brighton and South Coast, the junction being at Farlington Station; a branch line at Cosham unites the two railways.

The soil of the parish is loamy; and the subsoil is chalk, the chief crops being wheat, oats, and barley.

According to the latest returns of the Board of Agriculture, the proportions of land in Cosham parish are as follows: 1,409½ acres of arable land, 1,029¾ acres of permanent grass, and 144¾ acres of woodland.

The common lands in Wymering, Widley, Cosham and Hilsea were inclosed in 1811–12.[3]

The following place-name occurs in a fine of 1318, 'Palegrove';[4] it still survives in Paulsgrove Lake and Paulsgrove Quay, and is the basis of a tradition that St. Paul landed here on a visit to England.

MANORS At the time of the Domesday Survey *WYMERING* was ancient demesne of the crown. Land in Cosham and Portchester belonged to this manor.[5]

The king possibly granted Wymering to the Albemarles before 1167, for at that date the Vidame of Picquigny held land in Wymering,[6] in right of his wife, who was the eldest daughter of Stephen, second earl of Albemarle.[7] In the reign of Henry III William de Fortibus earl of Albemarle held the manor,[8] of which he died seised in 1260.[9] On the extinction of the family the manor reverted to the crown, and in July, 1280, it was assigned by Edward I, with several other manors in Hampshire, to his mother Eleanor in part satisfaction of £1,065 16*s.* 7*d.*, which she formerly received from the exchequer.[10] But this assignment was superseded in the following year by a grant in fee simple of the manors of Wymering and Blandford (co. Dorset) to John le Botiller by Ralph de Sandwich, the king's steward, in exchange for the manor of Ringwood.[11]

De Fortibus, Earl of Albemarle. *Gules a cross paty vair.*

In 1285 a grant was made to John le Botiller and his heirs of 15*s.* yearly at the exchequer until provided with lands to that amount, because when he accepted Wymering manor for Ringwood manor no mention was made in the extent of Wymering of a rent-charge of three quarters of corn worth 15*s.*, which the master and brethren of the Domus Dei at Portsmouth received from the tenants of Wymering by the gift of William de Fortibus earl of Albemarle.[12]

In 1309 John le Botiller died seised of Wymering manor,[13] which was assigned to his widow Joan in dower, Joan taking oath not to marry without royal

[3] Local and Pers. Acts of Parl. 52 Geo. III, cap. 40.

[4] Feet of F. Hants, Mich. 12 Edw. II.

[5] *V.C.H. Hants*, i, 451.

[6] Pipe R. (Pipe R. Soc.), xi, 188.

[7] Banks, *Dormant and Extinct Baronetage*, iii, 35.

[8] *Testa de Nevill* (Rec. Com.), 232.

[9] Inq. p.m. 44 Hen. III, No. 26. The property is described as the manor of Wymering held of the king in chief, and it included the township Hethangavell. All through the middle ages this manor continued to be held of the king in chief.

[10] *Cal. of Pat.* 1272–81, p. 386. Possibly Eleanor received other lands in the next year in exchange for Wymering, for it is stated in the Patent Rolls that the annual value of the manor was £33 4*s.* 8¾*d.*

[11] Ibid. 426. Ringwood was valued at £60, Wymering and Blandford at £40 and £7 9*s.* 11½*d.* respectively, and the deficit was to be made up to John from some of the king's lands elsewhere.

[12] *Cal. of Pat.* 1281–92, p. 175.

[13] Inq. p.m. 3 Edw. II, No. 53.

licence.[14] Her son, John le Botiller, was seised of Wymering in 1316, and married a certain Joan as his first wife before 1320.[15] In 1330 John le Botiller settled the manor on himself and his wife Joan and their heirs;[16] but on his death in 1350 Wymering passed under a later settlement[17] to his second wife, Margery, for life,[18] who married a certain Richard Chike as her second husband.[19] She died in 1387, when Wymering reverted to her stepson John Botiller of Limbourne, son of John le Botiller and his first wife Joan.[20]

John of Limbourne[21] died in the same year, and Wymering passed to his daughter and heir Isabel wife of Geoffrey de Roucle.[22]

Geoffrey survived his wife and held the manor until his death in 1390, when it passed to Richard Wayte son of Isabel by her first husband Richard Wayte of Denmead.[23] On his death in 1423 Wymering passed to his son William, who had married Margaret daughter of Robert Barbot of Ernelles.[24]

In 1448 William died leaving it to his son Edward, then aged five,[25] from whom it passed to Simon Wayte, who died in 1518, leaving a brother and heir William.[26] The latter died in 1561, leaving Wymering and other lands in Hampshire and the Isle of Wight to be divided among his six daughters and coheirs, Eleanor the wife of Richard Bruning, Mary the wife of William Cresswell, Honor who had married her cousin William Wayte, Margaret the wife of Henry Perkins, Elizabeth who had married Richard Norton, and Susan married to William Wollascot.[27]

Wayte. *Argent a cheveron gules between three hunting horns sable.*

In 1582 Honor Wayte ceded her portion of the manor of Wymering and of the other lands to William Cresweller senior and her sister Mary his wife,[28] whose son William Cresweller in 1595 granted his reversion of these two shares to Thomas Grene[29]; and accordingly, thirteen years later, on the death of William Cresweller senior the reversion of these two shares in Wymering passed to Thomas Grene.[30]

The Wollascots conveyed their portion of the manor of Wymering in 1587 and 1613 to Thomas Farmer and Edmund Plowden together with their other lands and rents in Hampshire,[31] evidently as a settlement, and in 1613 they again conveyed it to Otho Gayer and George Parker, probably trustees.[32]

Eleanor Bruning died in 1593 leaving one-sixth of the manor to her son and heir Francis, charged with an annuity to her son William and with a jointure settled on Ellen, wife of her son Richard, the daughter and heir of Anthony Uvedale.[33] Christina Bruning, most probably the widow of Francis Bruning, conveyed this sixth part of the manor to Humphrey Sandford and Thomas Wollascot in 1604.[34] But in 1610 the manor was again in the possession of the Brunings.[35] Richard Bruning died in 1612, leaving Wymering to his son Anthony with a jointure settled upon Mary, Anthony's wife.[36] Conveyances of the manor were made by Anthony Bruning in 1625,[37] in 1636,[38] and in 1646,[39] after which date there is no record of this part of the manor.

The part of Wymering which passed into the hands of the Perkins family by the marriage of Margaret Wayte and Henry Perkins remained to them nearly 150 years, for in 1703 Anne Perkins, one of the Perkins of Beenham (co. Berks), who had married her cousin Francis Perkins of Ufton, the great-great-grandson of Henry Perkins[40] and Margaret, together with Frances and Margaret her sisters-in-law, conveyed her share in the manor to her cousin Thomas Perkins, who belonged to a younger branch of the family.[41] This is the latest date at which there is a record of the divided manor; and some time before 1730 the separate shares must have been acquired by one family, since at that date the whole manor was in the hands of George Kelly in right of his wife Sarah,[42] and we have evidence of their ownership three years later, when they apparently conveyed it to Sir John Huffield, kt.[43] Thomas Gosling was holding the manor in right of his wife Elizabeth[44] in 1821, and sold it in that year to Thomas Thistlethwayte,[45] in whose family the manor has remained until the present day.

Perkins. *Or a fesse dancetty between six billets sable ermined argent.*

14 *Cal. of Pat.* 1317–13, p. 195.

15 *Abbrev. Plac.* (Rec. Com.), 325. The men of Hayling asserted that they were tenants of land which was ancient demesne of the crown; and that John and Joan exacted other services than those due and accustomed.

16 *Cal. of Pat.* 1330–4, p. 22.

17 In 1348 he apparently wished to settle the manor of Wymering upon his children by Margery; but it was considered prejudicial to the royal right of wardship, and the reversion remained therefore to the son of his first wife (Inq. p.m. 22 Edw. III (2nd Nos.), No. 54).

18 Inq. p.m. 23 Edw. III (1st Nos.), No. 61.

19 Ibid. 50 Edw. III (2nd Nos.), No. 45.

20 Ibid. 10 Ric. II, No. 8.

21 John had previously made a settlement of the reversion of the manor of Wymering on himself and his wife Katherine in tail. Katherine survived until 1439 (Inq. p.m. 18 Hen. VI, No. 48).

22 Inq. p.m. 10 Ric. II, No. 8. In 1387 Geoffrey and Isabel received pardon on payment of 20 marks for having entered the manor without licence (*Cal. of Pat.* 1385–9, p. 353).

23 Inq. p.m. 13 Ric. II, No. 42. In this year an inquiry was made into the alleged forcible entry of this Richard into the manor after it had been taken into the king's hands on the death of Geoffrey Roncle. Richard's title, however, was allowed (*Cal. of Pat.* 1388–92, p. 270).

24 Inq. p.m. 2 Hen. VI, No. 17; *Cal. of Pat.* 1422–9, p. 168; *Feud. Aids*, ii, 361.

25 Inq. p.m. 26 Hen. VI, No. 9.

26 Ibid. 10 Hen. VIII (Ser. 2), vol. 33, No. 83.

27 Ibid. 3 Eliz. (Ser. 2), No. 181.

28 Feet of F. Hants, Trin. 24 Eliz.

29 Ibid. Hil. 37 Eliz.

30 Chan. Inq. p.m. 6 Jas. I (Ser. 2), pt. 1, No. 70.

31 Feet of F. Div. Cos. Hil. 29 Eliz.; Pat. 30 Eliz. pt. 11, m. 26.

32 Feet of F. Div. Cos. Trin. 11 Jas. I.

33 Chan. Inq. p.m. 35 Eliz. pt. 1, No. 25.

34 Feet of F. Hants, Trin. 2 Jas. I.

35 Ibid. East. 8 Jas. I.

36 Chan. Inq. p.m. 10 Jas. I, vol. 332, No. 169.

37 Feet of F. Div. Cos. East. 1 Chas. I.

38 Ibid. Div. Cos. Trin. 12 Chas. I.

39 Ibid. Hants, East. 22 Chas. I.

40 A. M. Sharp, *Hist. of Ufton Court.*

41 Feet of F. Hants, Hil. 1 Anne.

42 Ibid. Div. Cos. Mich. 4 Geo. II.

43 Ibid. Hants, Mich. 7 Geo. II.

44 Elizabeth may possibly have been either the daughter or granddaughter of George Kelly and Sarah, though no record of such a relationship can be found (Feet of F. Hants, Trin. 2 Geo. IV).

45 Ibid.

At the time of the Domesday Survey the king held four hides in *COSHAM*,[46] which were part of the royal manor of Wymering.

William de Cosham held land worth 60*s.* in Cosham by serjeanty, providing one armed man for the defence of Portchester Castle in time of war.[47] He was succeeded by his son Peter de Cosham, who held his lands in Cosham by the same tenure.[48] This Peter de Cosham seems to have had several daughters, the two eldest of whom divided the land in Cosham.[49] Peter, son of Agnes the eldest daughter, conveyed his land in Cosham to Henry Wade in 1269.[50] From Henry Wade it passed to his son John, who in 1288 came before the king and tried to replevy his lands in Bray and Cosham, which were taken into the king's hands for his default against Margery, his father's widow.[51] In 1303 John son of Henry Wade obtained licence to enfeoff Thomas de Sandford with his land in Cosham which was held in chief,[52] and on his death in the same year the property passed to Thomas de Sandford.[53] William de Erle died seised of Cosham Manor in 1307,[54] which he held of the castle of Portchester, part of which he had acquired by inheritance, being a descendant of the second daughter of Peter Cosham, and part probably in right of his wife Maud who was the daughter of John Wade.[55]

Two years later the grange opposite the wall at Cosham was assigned in dower to Maud widow of William de Erlee.[56]

In 1321 [57] John son of William de Erlee granted his land in Cosham to Thomas de Sandford and Joan his wife,[58] who thus became seised of the whole estate.

Thomas died seised of lands in Cosham held of Portchester Castle in 1327;[59] part of his lands were held by his widow Joan in dower, the rest descended to his son Richard, who shortly before his death in the same year sold his own share and the reversion of his mother's dowry to Laurence de Pageham.[60] Laurence de Pageham still held land in Cosham in 1375.[61] It would seem possible that Laurence's name was Darrell, for in 1486 John Wallop held lands and tenements in Cosham of his successor in title, Constantine Darrell of Pageham.[62]

In 1604 this part of Cosham was in the hands of the Brunings, who were also holding the manor of Wymering; and from this time onwards Cosham evidently became merged in the manor of Wymering and followed its descent (q. v.).[63]

At the time of the Domesday Survey Anschitel son of Osmund held Cosham of the king, Bricsmar had held it of King Edward as an alod; the same Anschitel also held half a hide of the king which Norman had held of King Edward as an alod.[64] This entry in Domesday probably refers to *EAST COSHAM*, which was held by Maud de Bokland in the twelfth century.[65] It is never called a manor, but merely land in East Cosham. From Maud it passed to Roger de Maundeville, then to his son Geoffrey and his grandson Geoffrey, who held East Cosham in 1241.[66] This Geoffrey had two sons, Geoffrey and William; William held East Cosham after his brother Geoffrey and gave it to Geoffrey de Lucy,[67] who sold it to Peter des Roches, bishop of Winchester. The bishop assigned it in free alms towards the foundation of the abbey of Titchfield.[68]

An order was issued in 1281 to cause the lands of East Cosham which were held of the king in chief to be replevied to the abbot of Titchfield, since the abbot had entered on them without licence.[69] Licence was granted to the abbot of Titchfield and Thomas de Sandford to exchange their lands in East Cosham in 1310.[70]

A confirmation of the grant by Peter bishop of Winchester to the abbey of Titchfield of land in East Cosham and Cosham, of the release by Peter de Cosham of all service due to him from the abbot and convent from their land in East Cosham, was made in 1318.[71] After the dissolution of the monasteries the land in East Cosham which had belonged to the abbey of Titchfield was granted to Henry Wriothesley in 1607, together with toll and theam, infangtheof and utfangtheof.[72]

After this no record of the descent of East Cosham has been found until 1779, when it was in the hands of Thomas Joliffe and his wife Elizabeth, who conveyed it to Thomas Wrenford.[73] Sixteen years later Thomas Wrenford and his wife Mary Shapleigh conveyed the manor to Young Meller.[74] From Young Meller it seems to have passed to Thomas Gosling and his wife Elizabeth. They in their turn sold it to Thomas Thistlethwayte, lord of the manor of Wymering, in 1821, in whose family it still remains.[75]

The hamlet of *HILSEA* or *HULSEA* (Hulseye, xiv cent.; Hulsea, xvii cent.) seems to have no separate recorded history until the fourteenth century, when in 1316 John le Botiller was holding Wymering and Hilsea;[76] it is therefore probable that up to this time Hilsea was included in Wymering manor, and followed the descent of the manor till 1730 (q.v.). In 1813 it was in the possession of Richard Cater, and was sold by him to William Padwicke.[77] A court baron was held at Hilsea until about this date,[78] but after 1813 the manorial rights seem to have lapsed, and Hilsea was once more included in Wymering, Mr. Thomas Thistlethwayte being lord of the manor.

In the thirteenth century the family of Esturs, lords of the manors of Gatcombe (Calborne and Whit-

[46] *V.C.H. Hants*, i, 451.
[47] *Testa de Nevill* (Rec. Com.), 237.
[48] Ibid. 232.
[49] Add. MS. 33282, fol. 285.
[50] Feet of F. Hants, Trin. 53 Hen. III.
[51] *Cal. of Close*, 1279–88, p. 540.
[52] *Cal. of Pat.* 1301–7, p. 157.
[53] Inq. p.m. 31 Edw. I, No. 151. John Wade's holding in Cosham consisted of one messuage, half a carucate of land and rent of 8*s.* 3*d.* and 1½ lb. of pepper.
[54] This seems to be the only time that the land held by the Coshams is called a manor.
[55] Add. MSS. 33282, fol. 285–6.
[56] Close, 2 Edw. II, m. 8 *d.*
[57] About this time the king made a grant of the royal manor to Piers Gaveston and his wife Margaret and their heirs (Chart. R. 5 Edw. II, m. 10 *n.* 17).
[58] Inq. a.q.d. 15 Edw. II, 49.
[59] Inq. p.m. 1 Edw. III (1st Nos.), No. 75.
[60] *Cal of Pat.* 1327–30, p. 42; Inq. p.m. 1 Edw. III (2nd Nos.), No. 41. In 1328 the king granted the royal manor to his sister Mary, a nun at Fontevrault, for life; *Cal. of Close*, 1327–30, p. 347.
[61] Inq. p.m. 49 Edw. III (2nd Nos.), No. 24. For the next century no records of the manor have been found.
[62] Ibid. 2 Hen. VII (Ser. 2), vol. 2, No. 31.
[63] Feet of F. Hants, Trin. 2 Jas. I; ibid. Trin. 2 Geo. IV.
[64] *V.C.H. Hants*, i, 503*a*.
[65] Add. MSS. 33282, fol. 113.
[66] Ibid.
[67] Ibid.
[68] Cart. Antiq. 11.
[69] *Cal. of Close*, 1279–88, p. 78.
[70] Inq. a.q.d. 4 Edw. II, No. 102.
[71] *Cal. of Pat.* 1317–21, p. 143.
[72] Pat. 5 Jas. I. pt. 15, m. 1.
[73] Feet of F. Hants, Trin. 20 Geo. III.
[74] Ibid. Mich. 36 Geo. III.
[75] Ibid. Trin. 2 Geo. IV.
[76] *Feud. Aids*, ii, 320.
[77] Feet of F. Hants, Hil. 53 Geo. III.
[78] Add. MSS. 33282, fol. 114.

well) in the Isle of Wight, also held a small portion of land at Hilsea, in Wymering, and in Portsea, which was known later as the manor of *LITTLE GATCOMBE*, to distinguish it from the larger manor in the Isle of Wight. The origin of Hilsea manor appears to have been one of the Portchester serjeanties, for under Henry III Fulk 'de Wymeringes' held his land by service there for eight days in time of war.[78a] In 1291 Sir William de Esturs died seised of 20 acres of land in Hilsea, held by the service of suit at the court of Portchester Castle every three weeks, and of providing for eight days in time of war one man armed with a lance, helmet, and shield; he also held 20 acres of land from the lord of Warblington, and 20 acres of land from Richard de Portsea for the rent of a pound of pepper and one rose.[79]

Sir William was succeeded by his brother Geoffrey Lisle, who died two years later, leaving a son and heir Baldwin, then aged twenty-three.[80] Baldwin died in 1307, and was succeeded by his son John, who was only four years old, and a minor in the king's wardship.[81]

John de Lisle of Gatcombe, as he was called, died in 1337 seised of the manor of Hilsea,[82] which was still held from the king in chief by grand serjeanty, for the service of arming a man in time of war for the defence of Portchester Castle.[83] He left a son John, aged thirteen, the custody of whose lands was granted to his mother Joan during his minority.[84] On his death in 1349 he was holding 40 acres of land in Portsea at Hilsea,[85] also a messuage, garden, dove-house, 60 acres of arable land, and 2 acres of Wood in Portsea, held of the manor of Warblington for an annual rent, and for doing service at the court of Warblington. His heir was his son John, aged six,[86] who died in 1369, his land passing to his sister Elizabeth, the wife of John Bramshott, of Bramshott, in Hants.[87]

In 1432 William Bramshott, lord of the manor of Gatcombe, granted his lands in Hilsea and Copnor to his son Baldwin,[88] who before his death in 1468 granted the so-called manor of Little Gatcombe to his brother John,[89] and at his death in 1479 the lands passed to Elizabeth and Margaret, the daughters and co-heirs of John Bramshott, Elizabeth being the wife of Sir John Dudley, and Margaret of Sir John Pakenham.[90]

Sir John Pakenham and his wife Margaret both died in 1485, and they seem to have left two children, Edmund who inherited their estates in Bramshott,[91] and Constance who inherited their lands in the Isle of Wight, and who married Sir Geoffrey Poole of Lordington in Sussex.[92] The manor of Little Gatcombe is not mentioned in any of the inquisitions on Sir John Pakenham or Sir John Dudley, but it seems probable that it was included in the share of Sir John Dudley and his wife Elizabeth Bramshott. Elizabeth died in 1498 and her husband in 1501; they left a son and heir Edmund who was thirty-six at the time of his mother's death,[93] and who married Elizabeth daughter of Edward Viscount Lisle.[94] This Edmund was attainted for high treason and beheaded on Tower Hill in 1510; the attainder was reversed, however, in the following year and his lands restored to his son John[95]; but it seems probable that Little Gatcombe was not restored, but was granted to William Erneley, who died seised of it in 1445, though no record of such a grant can be found.[96]

At his death William Erneley was holding two messuages, 100 acres of land, 10 acres of meadow, 20 acres of pasture, and 10 acres of wood in Little Gatcombe and Little Bramshott, called the manor of Little Gatcombe, with lands in Bramshott, which he left by will to his eldest son Francis, with reversion to his second son Richard.[97] Francis died a few years later and the lands passed to Richard, who held them until his death in 1607, when they passed to his son Richard,[98] who sold Little Gatcombe and 120 acres of land in Portsea and Wymering to William Marshe in 1613[99]; the latter died seised of the estate in 1622, leaving the manor by will to his eldest daughter Lucy.[100]

In 1691 Little Gatcombe was in the hands of William Chafin and his wife Mary in right of the latter, who was possibly a granddaughter of Lucy Marshe, and was sold by them to Thomas Brounker,[101] who kept it until 1714, and then sold it to Captain Matthew Teate.[102]

Captain Teate apparently had a daughter, who married Matthew Brady, the possessor of Little Gatcombe in 1744.[103] They had two daughters, one of whom, Sarah,[104] married Admiral Sir Roger Curtis,[105] who was obliged to sell his lands to the government, as the estate was required for military purposes. Barracks were commenced in 1780, and in 1794 a camp was formed for several thousand men.[106]

CHURCH The church of *ST. PETER AND ST. PAUL* is a small building with chancel, north vestry, nave and aisles, and south porch. At the west end of the nave is a wooden bell-turret replacing a small embattled west tower pulled down in 1860. Most of the modern work in this church dates from this time.

The north arcade of the nave belongs to the last quarter of the twelfth century, and is the earliest part of the church to which a date can be assigned. The south arcade was added about 1220, and the chancel was probably rebuilt about the same time. There are no traces of later enlargements of the plan, but

78a *Testa de Nevill* (Rec. Com.), 232.
79 Inq. p.m. 20 Edw. I, No. 16.
80 Ibid. 22 Edw. I, No. 32.
81 Ibid. 1 Edw. II, No. 60.
82 This is the only time that this land is called the manor of Hilsea.
83 Inq. p.m. 11 Edw. III (1st Nos.), No. 55.
84 *Abbrev. Rot. Orig.* (Rec. Com.), ii, 237.
85 This land was still held by serjeanty, one armed man being provided for defence of Portchester Castle for forty days in time of war.
86 Inq. p.m. 23 Edw. III (2nd Nos.), No. 155.
87 Ibid. 43 Edw. III (1st Nos.), No. 68.
88 *Cal. of Anct. D.* 11 Hen. VI, C. 2658.
89 Ibid. 8 Edw. IV, C. 307.
90 Inq. p.m. 19 Edw. IV, No. 24.
91 Ibid. (Ser. 2), vol. 22, No. 12.
92 Betham, *Baronetage*, i, App. 22; and Lodge, *Peerage*, iii, 368.
93 Chan. Inq. p.m. (Ser. 2), vol. 22, No. 12.
94 Esch. Inq. p.m. file 962, No. 13.
95 Dugdale, *Baronage*, ii, 217.
96 Esch. Inq. p.m. Ser. 2, file 993, No. 7.
97 Ibid.
98 Chan. Inq. p.m. (Ser. 2), vol. 300, No. 184.
99 Feet of F. Hants, Mich. II, Jas. I.
100 W. and L. Inq. p.m. (Ser. 2), bdle. 66, No. 101.
101 Feet of F. Hants, Hil. 3 & 4 Will. and Mary.
102 Ibid. Trin. 13 Anne.
103 Recov. R. Trin. 179. 18 Geo. II, m. 222.
104 According to Betham Sarah was a daughter of Captain Matthew Teate, but as Captain Teate was holding the manor in 1714, and Sir Roger's marriage did not take place until about 1780, it seems far more likely that she was a granddaughter, and this would explain the fact that the Bradys were holding the manor in 1744.
105 Betham, *Baronetage*, iv, 259.
106 Local information.

the restoration of 1860 was drastic, and part of the history of the church doubtless disappeared at the time.

The chancel has a modern east window of three lights, replacing a three-light fifteenth-century window. In the north wall is a recess with shafts in the jambs, a door to the vestry, and an arch to the organ-chamber, all being modern, and in the south wall a lancet window, the stonework of which has been renewed, and a modern window of two lights replacing a single-light opening. At the east end of this wall is a square recess, and to the west of it a cinquefoiled fifteenth-century piscina and two thirteenth-century sedilia, with arched heads, and shafts with moulded capitals and bases.

The chancel arch is modern, of two chamfered orders, the inner of which springs from corbels.

The nave is of four bays, the north arcade having pointed arches of a single order with a label of half-round section, square scalloped capitals with the angles chamfered off, and circular columns with moulded bases. The eastern arch of this arcade has an added inner order.

The south arcade has pointed arches of two hollow-chamfered orders with moulded labels, and circular moulded capitals with octagonal abaci, resting on very slender round columns, only 11 in. in diameter. This arcade is very well designed, though rather a daring piece of building, the springers of the arches being no less than 12½ in. wider than the columns. No old details remain in the north aisle, and the windows of the south aisle replace square-headed windows with transoms, while the south porch is also the modern successor of a former porch. In the south aisle is, however, a late thirteenth-century piscina with a shelf, and to the west of the first window in the south wall a recess with an arched and moulded head.

All the wooden fittings of the church and the roofs are modern, the latter being covered with red tiles and carried in one span over nave and aisles. The font is modern, a round Purbeck marble bowl standing near the south doorway of the nave.

A painting of St. Christopher was found over the north arcade of the nave in 1860.

In the bell-turret are two bells by John Warner, 1861.

The plate is modern, consisting of a chalice and paten of 1855, a flagon of 1861, and a pair of cruets. The registers of both Wymering and Widley are kept here. The two earliest books run from 1655 to 1699, and 1700 to 1744. The third book, with Wymering entries only, goes from 1745 to 1748, and the fourth, which is for Widley only, from 1738 to 1812. The fifth has Wymering entries 1738–90, the marriages stopping at 1754, and the sixth is the marriage book for Widley, 1754–1813. The seventh and eighth books both belong to Wymering, and contain respectively the baptisms and burials 1791–1813, and the marriages 1755–1812.

The vestry book for 1744 to 1834 is preserved, and contains a list of church goods in 1744.

ADVOWSON

Wymering church[107] was assessed in 1291 at £8.[108] In 1535 the vicarage was worth £8 2*s*.[109] The advowson of the vicarage was held by the prior and convent of Southwick until the Dissolution,[110] after which it followed the descent of the manor of Southwick until 1817. From this date until 1847 it was held alternately by Thomas Thistlethwayte, the lord of the manor of Wymering, and by Winchester College.[111]

Wymering vicarage was consolidated with the rectory of Widley at the beginning of the nineteenth century[112]; and the right of presentation to the consolidated benefice was bought by F. T. Nugée from Thomas Thistlethwayte in 1847,[113] and has remained in his family until the present day.

CHARITIES

The Cosham Almshouses.—In 1600 Honor Wayte, by deed, granted to trustees her interest in a lease for 5,000 years acquired by her in 1594 of a messuage, orchard, and garden in Cosham, upon which she had settled a poorhouse for four poor, honest women, and a yearly rent of 6*s*. 8*d*. to be paid out of 'Stakes Garden,' and a yearly rent of £6 to be paid out of her manor of Denmead to the intent that the said messuage and premises should for ever remain a dwelling-house for four poor sole women of Wymering, or failing such out of the parish of Wickham; the said yearly rent of 6*s*. 8*d*. to be employed about the repairing of the said house, and such uses in charity as the trustees should think most meet, and the said annuity of £6 to be divided equally among the four occupants.

The rent-charge of 6*s*. 8*d*. is duly paid by Mr. Thomas Thistlethwayte, and the annuity of £6 is paid by Mr. John Kennett and equally divided among the four occupants, who also receive the benefit in fuel of the interest of £100 consols bequeathed in 1818 by the will of John Soaper and of £100 consols given in 1839 by the Rev. James Henville. The income of another sum of £100 consols belonging to the charity of the Rev. John Taylor is also received by the occupants. (See parish of Widley.)

The said Honor Wayte by her will, proved in December, 1600, also charged her manor of Denmead with a further yearly rent of 20*s*. for sick and aged poor. The annual sum of 20*s*. is duly received and applied.

107 *V.C.H. Hants*, i, 451.
108 *Pope Nich. Tax.* (Rec. Com.), 211*b*.
109 *Valor Eccl.* (Rec. Com.), ii, 23.
110 *Epis. Reg.* (Hants Rec. Soc.), 50; *Wykeham's Register* (Hants Rec. Soc.), i, 109, 197, 200; Egerton MSS. 2031-4, iv, 13.
111 *Clerical Guide*, 1817–36; *Clergy List*, 1841–47.
112 *Clerical Guide*, 1817.
113 *Clergy List*, 1847–1904.

WIDLEY

Wydelig (xii-xiii cent.); Wydele (xiv cent.); Widley (xvi cent.).

In 1881 Widley was a small parish about five miles north of Portsmouth. It was about two miles in breadth and a mile in length, and contained 1,109 acres of land. In 1894, however, it was amalgamated with Wymering and formed into the present parish of Cosham.[1]

Widley is now a small secluded hamlet to which the most direct approach from Cosham and Wymering is by a track down the northern slope of Portsdown, at the back of the Alexandra Hospital. Its only buildings, beyond a few cottages, are the little church of St. Mary Magdalen and a farmhouse close to it on the west, called the Mill Farm. A little to the north of the church a tributary of the Wallington, which rises in Purbrook Park, runs north-west towards Southwick, Purbrook Heath House and Broomfield House lying to the north of its course.

The soil is loamy, the subsoil chalk; the chief crops are wheat, oats, and barley. The common lands in Widley were inclosed in 1811–12.[2]

MANOR

At the time of the Domesday Survey Geoffrey held Cosham under Hugh de Port; Bricsmar had held it from King Edward as an alod; it was assessed at two hides.[3] These two hides evidently became later the *MANOR OF WIDLEY*, which was held in the fourteenth century of the St. Johns, the descendants of the Ports, and was closely connected with Cosham and Wymering.

The earls of Albemarle held Widley in the thirteenth century as under-tenants; William de Fortibus, earl of Albemarle, died seised of the manor in 1260,[4] leaving five children, four of whom died young. The youngest and only surviving child Avelina married Edmund earl of Lancaster,[5] and on her death without issue in 1274 the manor passed to Isabel countess of Albemarle, widow of William de Fortibus.[6] She died without children in 1293, and the manor reverted to the St. Johns as overlords.[7]

The Scures family evidently succeeded the Albemarles in Widley, and in the reign of Henry III Lord William de Clynton and Eva his wife, the daughter and heir of Roger de Scures, gave five acres of land to the chapel of Widley.[8]

John de Scures, probably the nephew of Eva de Clynton née Scures, held Widley in 1316,[9] and was probably the same John de Scures who was holding one fourth of a knight's fee in the manor in 1346;[10] between this date and 1428 Widley must have passed from John de Scures to the Uvedale family. In 1428 and 1431 John Uvedale held the fourth part of one knight's fee in Widley, which had formerly been held by John de Scures,[11] and the family must have continued to hold Widley; for Dorothy, widow of William Uvedale, great-grandson of John Uvedale, died seised of the manor in 1531, and from her it passed to Arthur her son and heir.[12] Arthur Uvedale was succeeded by his son William, who died in 1569,[13] and was followed by his son William, who married Mary daughter of Sir Richard Norton.[14] The Uvedales were deprived of two-thirds of their lands for recusancy in 1605, and Widley was granted among other manors to Henry Wriothesley.[15] By 1607,[16] however, they had recovered their lands, and in 1616 Sir William Uvedale senior died, and Widley passed to his son William.[17] This William conveyed the manor to Sir Francis Neale and Edward Woodward in 1618 evidently for the purpose of a settlement.[18] After this date, however, there seems to be no record of the manor of Widley until the year 1766, when it was in the possession of John Suffeild Brown and Roger Griffith and was conveyed by them to William Woodrow.[19] The manor was still in the hands of the Woodrow family and their connexions by marriage, the Maidments, in 1823; but after that date the manor was sold to Mr. Thistlethwayte, in whose family it remains at the present day.[20]

UVEDALE. *Argent a cross moline gules.*

A fair, for three days from 15th July, with a court of pie powder, in the manor of Widley, was granted to Richard Turner in 1715.[21] This fair was still among the appurtenances of the manor in 1823,[22] but in 1862 an order was issued that the fair called Portsdown Fair, held under charter in the manor of Widley, was to cease henceforward.[23] There was a windmill in Widley in 1823,[24] but there is no trace of it at the present day except in the name Mill Farm.

CHURCH

The church of *ST. MARY MAGDALEN* was entirely rebuilt in 1849, in an imitation of twelfth-century style, and has an apsidal chancel and a nave with north aisle and south porch, and a bell-cot for one bell on the west gable of the nave

Nothing of the old church has been preserved except a small font with a slender bowl on which is IS 1690. It is built into the north wall of the chancel to serve as a credence, three faces of the bowl being exposed, on one of which is the date

1 Local Govt. Bd. Order.

2 Local and Personal Acts of Parl. 52 Geo. III, 1811–12, cap. 40.

3 *V.C.H. Hants*, i, 486.

4 Inq. p.m. 44 Hen. III, No. 26.

5 *Coll. Top. et Gen.* vi, 264; Poulson's *Holderness*, i, 35.

6 Ibid. 7 Ibid.

8 Add. MSS. 33282, fol. 33. About the middle of the thirteenth century Emeric de Savoy held 'Wydelig' for one knight's fee from Lady Eva de Clynton (*Testa de Nevill* [Rec. Com.], 230).

9 *Feud. Aids*, ii, 320.

10 Ibid. ii, 335.

11 Ibid. ii, 356.

12 Chan. Inq. p.m. 23 Hen. VIII (Ser. 2), No. 3.

13 Ibid. 12 Eliz. (Ser. ii), No. 103.

14 Berry, *Hants Genealogies*, 75.

15 Pat. 1 Jas. I, pt. 3, m. 3.

16 In this year Sir William Uvedale senior and Mary his wife, William Uvedale, James and Richard Uvedale, conveyed Widley to Sir Robert Carye and Sir Richard Norton, Mary's father, evidently as a settlement; Feet of F. Div. Cos. Hil. 5 Jas. I.

17 W. & L. Inq. p.m. 14 Jas. I, bdle. 55, No. 123.

18 Feet of F. Div. Cos. Trin. 15 Jas. I.

19 Ibid. Hants, Hil. 7 Geo. III.

20 Ibid. Hil. 7 Geo. III; ibid. Trin. 44 Geo. III; ibid. Hil. 1 Geo. IV; ibid. Trin. 4 Geo. IV.

21 Pat. 2 Geo. I, pt. 5, m. 29.

22 Feet of F. Hants, Trin. 4 Geo. IV.

23 *Lond. Gaz.* 11th July, 1862, p. 3480.

24 Feet of F. Hants, Trin. 4 Geo. IV.

already noted, and on the others an acanthus leaf and a crowned rose respectively.

The plate consists of a modern chalice and paten.

For the registers see Wymering.

ADVOWSON The earliest mention of a church at Widley seems to be in the year 1291, when the rectory of Widley was assessed at £4 6*s.* 8*d.*[25]; by 1535 the value had increased to £7 4*s.*[26] The advowson of Widley was granted to the prior and convent of Southwick by Matthew de Scures, and was held by them until the time of the Dissolution.[27] From 1538 down to the year 1817 it followed the descent of the manor of Southwick (q.v.). From 1817 to 1847 the advowson was held alternately by Thomas Thistlethwayte, the lord of the manor, and Winchester College.[28] In 1847 the advowson was bought by F. J. Nugée, and has remained in his family until the present day.[29]

Since the beginning of the nineteenth century the living has been a consolidated benefice, consisting of the rectory of Widley and the vicarage of Wymering; joint net yearly value, £280.[30]

CHARITIES In 1771 John Taylor, rector of Widley and vicar of Wymering, by deed gave £100 consols for the benefit of the said two parishes, and declared that out of the annual outcome £2 should be applied in purchasing Bibles, Prayer Books, and other pious books, to be distributed amongst the poor of the two parishes. When that end had been fully answered, the £2 should be applied in instructing poor children of the two parishes to read and write, and the residue of the income towards repairing the almshouses at Wymering founded by Honor Wayte. The income of the charity has for some years, at the discretion of the trustees, been applied for the benefit of the Cosham almshouses. See parish of Wymering.

THE LIBERTY OF PORTSMOUTH AND PORTSEA ISLAND

The island of Portsea is separated from the mainland by a narrow channel known as the Port Creek, crossed by means of an iron bridge which replaces one of stone. North of the island rise the grassy slopes of Portsdown, while the Portsea side is fringed with the loopholes of half-hidden fortifications. In 1831 part of the island, viz. Hilsea, which is now included in Cosham parish (q.v.), and a portion of Portsea parish known as the Gildable, lay in the hundred of Portsdown, while the rest of the island was within the borough of Portsmouth. Now (i.e. since 1835) the whole of Portsea is contained in the borough, which includes that part of the island south of an irregular line crossing from Langstone Harbour at a point north of Great Salterns to Portsmouth Harbour, midway between Great Horsea Island and Tipner.

Borough of Portsmouth. *Azure a star between the horns of a crescent or.*

The district which is now Portsmouth borough was sparsely inhabited in the eleventh century, for in 1086 there were only a few villeins, bordars, and serfs on the demesne lands of the manors of Buckland, Copnor, and Fratton, while the town of Portsmouth did not then exist.[1] The island is, for the most part, unproductive. The soil is either sand or gravel upon Bagshot and Bracklesham beds in the south, and London clay farther north. Vegetables only are grown in any quantity, and all wheat is imported. In the seventeenth century the inhabitants depended almost entirely on the Isle of Wight for their supplies of wheat and flour.[2] This fact doubtless accounts for the scarcity of mills in the island. At present a windmill stands in Fratton. It may have been built on the site of the windmill which belonged to the Domus Dei at the time of its dissolution.[3] There used also to be a water-mill, known as Beeston's Mill, or the King's Mill, since it was used for grinding wheat for the garrison of the town. It stood on the Old Gun Wharf, but has not been rebuilt since it was burnt down about 1891. The mill-stream entered through the Gun Wharf and reached as far as the site of the Mill-Dam Barracks, where it terminated in the Mill Pond.[4] The mill took its name from the Beeston family, its former tenants.[5] In a map of the town dated 1668 two fresh-water mills are marked near each other at the head of the mill-pond.[6] They appear to have been those granted to the abbey of Fontevrault in 1189.[6a] It appears, from a papal confirmation in 1201, that one of these mills was granted to the abbey by Richard I.[7] A mill called 'le Brendemulne' at Portsmouth was in the custody of Maud countess of Ulster in 1340, and was granted for life to Stephen Lambyn of Winchelsea for his good service to the king at sea.[8]

Late in the twelfth century the town of Portsmouth grew up in the south-western corner of the island, doubtless owing its origin to the increasing difficulty of reaching Portchester by sea. When the docks, which had been built on the peninsula to the north of the town, came into importance in the seventeenth and eighteenth centuries, the town of Portsea arose round the dockyard to accommodate the workers there; and during the nineteenth century it has grown until, at the present day, Portsmouth and Portsea, with their members of Landport, Southsea, Milton, and Eastney, form practically one town almost co-extensive with the island.

25 *Pope Nich. Tax.* (Rec. Com.), 24.
26 *Valor Eccl.* (Rec. Com.), ii, 23.
27 *Wykeham's Register* (Hants Rec. Soc.), i, 76, 98, 109, 179, 238. Egerton MSS. 2031–4, iv, 69.
28 *Clerical Guide*, 1817–36; *Clergy List*, 1841–7.
29 *Clergy List*, 1847–1904.
30 *Clerical Guide*, 1817.
1 In Buckland there were 6 villeins, 2 bordars, and 2 serfs; in Copnor 5 villeins, 2 bordars, and 2 serfs; in Fratton 4 villeins, 4 bordars and 4 serfs.
2 *Cal. S.P. Dom.* 1629–31, p. 391.
3 Mins. Accts. 31–2 Hen. VIII (Hants), R. 139, m. 77. A windmill in Portsmouth was granted to Edward Ferrers and Francis Phelipps by James I. Pat. 7 Jas. I, pt. 16.
4 Information kindly supplied by Mr. W. H. Saunders. The position of the mill is clearly shown on the plan of Portsmouth in 1762.
5 East, *Extracts from the Portsmouth Rec.* (ed. 1891), 37.
6 Add. MS. 16371; *Cal. Doc. France*, 385.
6a *Cal. Rot. Chart.* (Rec. Com.), 72*b*.
7 Add. Chart. 17861.
8 Pat. 14 Edw. III, pt. 3, 48.

The town of Portsmouth (Portesmue xii–xiii cent.; Portesmuth xiv cent.) proper is a wedge-shaped district, separated from the larger inhabited parts of the island by the Civil Service Recreation Grounds and Southsea Common. The High Street, or main thoroughfare, runs north-east and south-west, and contains several buildings of interest. At the north end of the street stand the red-brick gabled buildings of the Portsmouth Grammar School. Opposite are the Cambridge Barracks, named after the late Duke of Cambridge, and occupying the site of the old theatre once under the management of Charles Kemble. Further down the street is the house formerly known as the "Spotted Dog," where the murder of the duke of Buckingham took place in 1628. Facing it, but lower down, is the church of St. Thomas, the old parish church of Portsmouth, while opposite, at the corner of Pembroke Road, is the old Guildhall, now used as the Borough Museum. This building took the place of a former hall, built in 1738,[9] which stood across the High Street. In a house in the High Street, George Meredith was born in 1828.

Across the south end of the High Street stands a strong stone fort, which forms the corner of the Point Barracks, and overlooks the old Victoria Pier, from which can be obtained a fine view of the narrow entrance to Portsmouth Harbour, and of the distant hills of the Isle of Wight. The King's Stairs lead down to a shingle beach, whence in former times a strong chain could be drawn across to the Gosport side as an additional defence to the harbour mouth. Nothing of this is visible from the High Street, the view thence being bounded by the grey stone wall of the fort, in which is set a niche containing a bust of Charles I as Prince of Wales, with an inscription recording his safe arrival at Portsmouth in October, 1623, after his travels in France and Spain. Soon after the bust had been set up, the Governor, Viscount Wimbledon, recommended that the signs of the inns in the High Street should be set in to the houses 'as they are in all civil towns,' since they not only obscured but outfaced the figure, and ordered that all officers and soldiers should doff their hats in passing it.[10] A series of narrow streets running at right angles to High Street contains some of the oldest houses in the town, for the most part two-storied buildings interspersed with warehouses, and it is noticeable that in this district the population has decreased of late years, while in other parts of the island it has more than doubled itself. At the back of these narrow streets, which form the old town of Portsmouth, are the Colewort Barracks, which take their name from the Colewort Garden, which was still in use as a burying ground in 1817.[11] It is said to have belonged to the chapel of St. Mary, which existed in this part of the town in the time of Queen Elizabeth,[12] and from which, doubtless, St. Mary Street took its name. The present church of St. Mary, which stands at the back of the barracks, was not built till 1839.[13]

At the back of the Point Barracks, and parallel with the coast line, Broad Street leads from the High Street to the Point, a small peninsula washed by the waters of the harbour and the Inner and Outer Camber. In the latter are the docks which accommodate the few trading vessels, chiefly coasting ships, that visit the town. Between the Point and Gosport plies a steam ferry capable of transporting thirty carriages as well as passengers. This 'floating bridge,' which was established under an Act of 1838,[14] and the ferry are the chief means of communication with Gosport. The ferry had been maintained by the inhabitants of Gosport, and in 1600 it had fallen into decay as the sailors had been pressed in great numbers. Consequently a decree was issued forbidding the lease of the ferry to private individuals, and commanding the maintenance of twenty boats and a skilful man in each.[15] Subsequently it was leased to certain decayed seamen,[16] but after their lease had lapsed no grant of the ferry was made for nearly a century, during which time the men-of-war and merchantmen took advantage of the opportunity of smuggling when carrying people across the harbour.[17]

Near the Camber is a dry dock for trading vessels, and still farther north is the Gun Wharf, the arsenal where is stored ordnance both for the fleet and for the garrison of the town. It consists of the old and the new Gun Wharf, separated by a small basin where barges enter to carry the naval guns from the wharf to the battleships in the dockyard, or to unlade stores of rifles and bayonets, which are kept in the Armoury. The latter is ingeniously decorated with obsolete weapons and armour of all descriptions and from all countries. The main entrance of the wharf is near the United Service Recreation Grounds, which form a fine open space between Portsea and Portsmouth, and are entered through one of the old town-gates, the Landport Gate, which formerly stood at the entrance of Warblington Street.

It is evident that Portsmouth did not exist as a town before the twelfth century, though the favourable position of its present site, more especially as a landing place, was recognized some time before any settlement was made there. The story runs that in 501 Port landed with his two sons Bieda and Mægla, 'at a certain place which is called Portes Mutha,' and there slew a very noble young Briton.[18] It is evident that the chroniclers in reciting this story were merely trying to account for the name of the place,[19] another form of which is preserved in the *Chronicle of Abingdon Monastery*.[20] To that abbey King Edgar granted the catch of fish from one vessel at 'Portmonna hyth,' besides a certain rent from Southampton, in 962. No mention of Portsmouth occurs in Domesday Book, but with the Norman Conquest and the consequent closer relations between England and the continent such a harbour could not fail to become of importance.[21] Henry II took advantage of the harbour, and many times crossed thence to his continental possessions, and in 1189 Richard I landed at Portsmouth.[22] At that date there

[9] *Extracts from the Portsmouth Records*, 230.

[10] *Cal. S.P. Dom.* 1635, p. 443.

[11] Lake Allen, *Hist. of Portsmouth* (1817), p. 145.

[12] It is marked on a map of that date, and is said to have been demolished in the seventeenth century, the material being used to repair the church of St. Thomas.

[13] Sumner, *Conspectus of the Diocese of Winchester* (1854), p. 20.

[14] 1 & 2 Vict. cap. 11, and 3 & 4 Vict. cap. 54.

[15] Exch. Dep. Mich. 42–3 Eliz. No. 22; Exch. Spec. Com. 44 Eliz. No. 2168.

[16] Pat. 12 Jas. I, pt. 15.

[17] *Cal. S.P. Dom. Treas. Papers*, 1702–7, p. 490.

[18] *Angl.-Sax. Chron.* (Rolls Ser.), i, 24.

[19] Cf. *Richard of Cirencester* (Rolls Ser.), i, 26.

[20] Rolls Ser. i, 321.

[21] Robert of Normandy is said to have chosen it as a landing-place when he crossed to England to claim the crown in 1101 (*Angl.-Sax. Chron.* (Rolls Ser.), ii, 205), and Henry himself embarked there for Normandy in 1114 (ibid. 213).

[22] Matt. Paris, *Hist. Anglorum* (Rolls Ser.), ii, 5.

appears to have been no town there, but merely a few sea-faring people, while the town of Southampton had control of the harbour.[23] It was doubtless the strategical advantages of the island that induced Richard I to build a town there.[24] He let out the land to various men to build thereon, and granted a charter to the inhabitants in 1194.[25] It is dated 2 May, from Portsmouth, where he had been staying since the preceding 24 April, just before leaving England for the last time.

The king himself had houses built there, for in 1197–8 £2 18*s.* 3*d.* was spent on the improvement of his houses and hall (curia) at Portsmouth, and in the same year 4*s.* was accounted for as the rent of building sites.[26] From these accounts, and from the sums spent in the following year on tables and benches for the king's house, it would appear that the latter at least was new.[27] In 1298 it was in such bad repair that it threatened to collapse, and an inquisition being taken as to its value, the hall, with certain other houses, was assessed at £40, the chapel at £20, and the site at 2*s.*[28] The position of this building may be marked by the name Kingshall Green, which was given to the site of the former Clarence Barracks in Penny Street.[29]

It was only fitting that the early history of a town founded by Richard Cœur-de-Lion should be filled with war and preparations of war. During the thirteenth and fourteenth centuries the town was used as a rendezvous for expeditions to Normandy,[30] Poitou,[31] and more especially to Gascony,[32] while ships from most of the maritime towns of England were sent thither to transport men and horses, provisions, and arms gathered from all the country,[33] and in 1254 the Great Council of the realm itself met there.[34] Besides the trade thus brought into the town, it carried on considerable traffic with the western and northern countries of Europe. Large quantities of wheat were exported to France and Spain,[35] in addition to that conveyed from Portsmouth for the provision of troops during the French wars. The wool-trade also was so considerable that Portsmouth was among the fifty-seven towns summoned to send wool-merchants to consult with the king at York in 1327–8,[36] and the townsmen joined in a petition that the wool-staple for South England should be at Southampton and not at Winchester, as had been appointed.[37] In 1449 three pockets of wool and eighty-nine sheepskins called 'Moreyns' were arrested on board a boat of Harfleur at Portsmouth.[38] The chief import was wine, most of which was brought from Bayonne and Bordeaux.[39] Woad also was imported from Normandy in considerable quantities,[40] and wax and iron from France.[41] Nevertheless the vessels belonging to the port were neither many nor large, for when summoned in 1336 to send to the king's aid all their vessels capable of carrying over forty *dolia* of wine, they could only provide two, one of which was out of repair.[42]

Judging by the number of conveyances of houses in the town, even early in the thirteenth century, it would seem that it was of fair size. Some of the buildings had an upper room or solar.[43] The majority were probably made of wood, for in 1338 only the Domus Dei and the parish church escaped the fire when the French burnt the town. The inhabitants were all but ruined by the four hostile assaults which they suffered during the fourteenth century, and until the building of the docks by Henry VII the prosperity of the town was at a low ebb, though the wool and wine trades were still carried on.[44] The building of the docks brought new life to the town; brew-houses were built and leased to private individuals on condition that the king should have the use of them in time of war,[45] and in 1525 there were also five royal brew-houses, the 'Rose,' the 'Lion,' the 'Dragon,' the 'White Hart,' and the 'Anchor,'[46] and foreign trade increased. Leather was brought from Spain,[47] and Portsmouth vessels traded largely with Holland,[48] and the import of woad was still continued.[49] An effort was also made to encourage weaving in the town, a petition being addressed to the queen in 1585 to allow clothiers residing within the liberties freedom from custom for twenty years on condition that they should each keep two corselets and able men to wear them, and to fix the wool-staple for the adjoining counties at Portsmouth.[50] Nevertheless, in 1579 the townspeople were obliged to seek relief throughout the realm for the losses which they had sustained by sea and by fire.[51] Camden described the town as 'populous in time of war, but not so in time of peace.'

The presence of the fleet at Portsmouth during the sixteenth century obliged the laying of posts to London, first through Bagshot and later by way of Petersfield and Guildford.[52] The port at this time was infested with smugglers and pirates, even the mayor being accused of dealing with them,[53] while it was frequently used by priests and recusants in escaping from the country.[54] In 1554 precautions were taken to prevent merchants from bringing in goods duty-free under pretence that they belonged to the king,[55] and during the seventeenth century merchant vessels made a

23 Since the ferm of Southampton was reduced when the men of Portsmouth were allowed to hold their town in ferm separately. Pipe R. 6 Ric. I.

24 *Plac. Abbrev.* (Rec. Com.), 85. Juratores dicunt quod quando placuit Domino Regi Ricardo edificare villam de Portesmue ipse commisit placeas ejusdem ville pluribus hominibus et placeam illam (the site in dispute) commisit Gervasio de Suthantonia edificandam. These 'placeæ' were definite areas similar to burgages: an arrangement of the same kind existed at Newport, see P. G. Stone, F.S.A. *Archit. Antiq. of the Isle of Wight*, 115.

25 *Liber Custumarium* (Rolls Ser.), ii, 655.

26 Pipe R. 9 Ric. I.

27 Ibid. 10 Ric. I.

28 Misc. Inq. file 36, No. 13.

29 East, *Extracts from the Portsmouth Records*, 753.

30 Matt. Paris, *Hist. Anglorum* (Rolls Ser.), ii, 90.

31 *Chron. of Grey Friars* (Rolls Ser.), ii, 145.

32 *Rot. Lit. Claus.* (Rec. Com.), ii, 28 *passim*.

33 Ibid. i, 134 *b*.

34 *Annales Mon. Tewkesbury*, i, 155.

35 There exists at the Public Record Office an interesting letter from Alphonso King of Castile to the Commonalty of Portsmouth concerning sureties left by a merchant who carried wheat from Portsmouth to Castile. Anct. Corresp. xlii, 7.

36 *Cal. of Close*, 1327–30, p. 237.

37 Anct. Pet. file 160, No. 7979.

38 Pipe R. 27 Hen. VI, 'Rutland et res Suth.'

39 *Rot. Lit. Claus.* (Rec. Com.), i, 579, 604; ii, 98; *Parl. R.* (Rec. Com.), i, 413.

40 *Abbrev. Plac.* (Rec. Com.), 157.

41 Anct. Pet. Exch. 49–50.

42 Anct. Corresp. xxxviii, 125.

43 Anct. D. (P.R.O.), B. 2946.

44 Pipe R. 27 Hen. VI. "Rutland et res Suth."

45 *L. and P. Hen. VIII*, iii, 3376 (1).

46 Ibid. iv, 1020. The first four of these stood on the site of the present Clarence Barracks, while the 'Anchor' was in St. Thomas Street near the corner of St. Mary Street. Cf. plan of the town, *temp.* Eliz.

47 *Acts of P.C.* (New Ser.), v, 60.

48 Exch. Dep. Mich. 8 Jas. I, 30.

49 *Acts of P.C.* (New Ser.), ix, 321.

50 *Cal. S.P. Dom.* 1580–1625, p. 142.

51 *Acts of P.C.* (New Ser.), xi, 307.

52 Ibid. vi, 248.

53 Ibid. xi, 431.

54 *Cal. of S.P. Dom.* 1591–4, p. 389.

55 *Acts of P.C.* (New Ser.), v, 54.

practice of sinking hogsheads and casks in the harbour till an opportunity should arise for landing them.[56]

From the sixteenth century till the middle of the nineteenth Portsmouth was essentially a garrison town, and, more especially during the sixteenth and seventeenth centuries, the inhabitants found the consequent restrictions somewhat irksome.[57] During the seventeenth century, also, the quartering of soldiers upon the already overcrowded inhabitants became a serious grievance.[58] In 1665 Commissioner Thomas Middleton complained that nine people were packed in a room 16 ft. by 12 ft., while in the house of the mayor himself there were twenty-six in family.[59] The number of poor in the town also became so alarming to the garrison that the Council of State sent an urgent command to the mayor in 1651 to provide for their employment and relief.[60] Poverty had doubtless been increased by the siege of 1642, and for many years vain attempts had been made to secure the more effectual paving and cleansing of the town.[61] The inhabitants suffered severely from small-pox and the plague during the seventeenth century, the latter being rife in the town both in 1625[62] and 1665,[63] and even when the plague had left the town there were more deaths from fever and ague than there had been in its time.[64] The overcrowding was relieved during the next century by the growth of Portsea, while the paving and watching of the town were improved under a series of Acts of Parliament, the first of which was passed in 1763–4.[65] The commissioners for the paving and cleansing of the town first met in 1768, and under them its general condition was rapidly improved.[66] Their work is now ably carried on by the Urban Sanitary Authorities.

The discovery of New England had opened a fresh field of commerce to the merchants of Portsmouth. They were especially anxious to obtain the monopoly of the tobacco trade, and petitioned in 1625 that all tobacco should be unladen in their port, and that all ships bound for New England should be obliged to set forth thence, but without apparent result.[67] A proposal made in 1632 for a joint-stock company to monopolize all trade in the port and ten miles out to sea also seems to have come to nothing.[68] Nevertheless, by the end of the seventeenth century the customs paid there had increased from £800 to £6,000,[69] the chief import still being French wine.[70]

Early in the last century the import of coal had increased,[71] while cattle were brought from the west of England and cows from Ireland. The coasting trade is now alone considerable, and it has been gradually diminished by the ever-increasing facilities for transport overland. The watermen were loud in their protestations against stage-coaches, and proposed in 1673 that, as the latter had of late strangely increased to the great prejudice of watermen and seamen, the coach-owners should be obliged to contribute towards the building of hospitals in several ports.[72] Both the coasting and foreign trade are limited by the restrictions imposed upon Portsmouth as a naval harbour, and the use of the greater part of the neighbouring coast-line for Government purposes. The Portsmouth and Arundel Canal was intended to facilitate the coasting-trade by allowing barges to enter from the Langstone Harbour and unlade near the site of the present town station. It was opened on 28 May, 1823,[73] but was never a success owing to the slowness of transport. The London & South Western Railway, a branch of which was laid down to Portsmouth under an Act of 1839,[74] and the Portsmouth Railway from Godalming to Havant, extended to Portsmouth in 1853,[75] superseded the canal, which was ultimately filled in, since it had been found that the salt water percolated to the fresh springs in the town. Its former course is marked by such names as Arundel Street.[76]

During the American and Napoleonic wars the town increased rapidly in size and importance, and with the establishment of peace its prosperity did not fail.[77] In 1544 there were not more than a hundred able-bodied persons besides the garrison in the town,[78] while three centuries later the population of Portsmouth was over nine thousand, and that of Portsea was nearly forty-four thousand.

Previous to 1194 all customs from the port of Portsmouth had evidently been assessed with those of Southampton. Immediately after Richard I had given the town its charter, £7 was deducted from the ferm of Southampton for the portage and customs of Portsmouth, and for these William of Ste. Mère-Église, afterwards bishop of London, was to account separately.[79] In 1196 £8 was similarly deducted,[80] but no separate account for Portsmouth is to be found on the Pipe Roll of the following year. In 1198, however, the receipts of the sheriff included £10 6*s.* 6*d.* for the year's pontage and small customary dues apart from the ferm (*census*) of Portsmouth and Kingston, which amounted to £14 2*s.* 7*d.*[81] It appears, therefore, that it was only the pontage and petty customs of Portsmouth that had been separated from those of Southampton. The port itself remained a member of the latter, and the greater customs were still collected and accounted for with those of Southampton, an arrangement which gave rise to several disputes between the two towns. Portsmouth did not become a separate port until late in the eighteenth century.

The petty customs together with the pontage were all the rent paid by the men of Portsmouth for their town before 1197, and even in the following reign the bailiffs declared that the dues arising from custom and pontage were all that they owed to the king by way of ferm,[82] yet in 1198 the sheriff had accounted for £14 odd as the 'census' or ferm of Portsmouth and Kingston,[83] while the receipts from the town amounted

56 *Cal. S.P. Dom.* (*Treas. Papers*), 1702–7, p. 490.
57 Add. MS. 33283, fol. 85; *Hist. MSS. Com. Rep.* vii, 420.
58 Ibid. xi, App. v, 242.
59 *Cal. S.P. Dom.* 1664–5, p. 512.
60 Ibid. 1651, p. 298.
61 Ibid. 1652–3, p. 236; *Acts of P.C.* (New Ser.), xv, 279.
62 *Cal. S.P. Dom.* 1625–6, p. 112.
63 Ibid. 1664–5, *passim.*
64 Ibid. 1666–7, pp. 573, &c.
65 4 Geo. III, cap. 92; 8 Geo. III, cap. 62; 16 Geo. III, cap. 59.
66 East, *Extracts from the Portsmouth Records*, 281.
67 *Cal. S.P. Dom.* 1625–6, p. 94.
68 *Hist. MSS. Com. Rep.* xii, App. i, 474.
69 *Cal. of Treas. Papers*, 1696–7, p. 554.
70 See *Cal. S.P. Dom.* 1629–31, p. 48.
71 *Parl. Accts. and Papers*, 1835, xxiv, 819.
72 *Cal. S.P. Dom.* 1672–3, p. 625.
73 Pigot, *Hants Directory*, 1823–4.
74 Stat. 2 & 3 Vict. cap. 28.
75 Ibid. 16 & 17 Vict. cap. 99; 22 & 23 Vict. cap. 31.
76 Information kindly supplied by Mr. W. H. Saunders.
77 *Pop. Return*, 1851; *Parl. Accts. and Papers*, 1835, xxiv, 799.
78 *L. and P. Hen. VIII*, xx (2), 719.
79 Pipe R. 6 Ric. I.
80 Ibid. 7 Ric. I.
81 Ibid. 9 Ric. I.
82 Cur. Reg. R. 36, m. 2 *d.*
83 Pipe R. 9 Ric. I.

to over £15 in the following year.[84] The next Pipe Roll gives no details of the sheriff's account for Portsmouth, and in May 1201 only £5 is given as the amount of ferm paid.[85] In the year ending May, 1202, the ferm was £18,[86] and so continued until November, 1229, when it was raised to £20.[87] This ferm, which had been previously received by the sheriff for the crown, was granted by Edward I to his mother, Queen Eleanor, for life, in May, 1281,[88] and confirmed to her five years later.[89] Later it formed part of the dowers assigned successively to the queens of Edward II and Edward III.[90] In 1403 Henry IV granted it for life to Eleanor widow of Nicholas Dagworth, but the gift was almost immediately cancelled.[91] Henry VI gave the ferm of Portsmouth to his uncle Humphrey duke of Gloucester for life in 1442.[92] In 1450, three years after the duke's death, this ferm with many others was definitely assigned to the use of the royal honsehold,[93] and was partly employed on repairs in the Palace of Westminster and the Tower of London.[94] The former settlement was confirmed in 1485,[95] but Henry VIII granted £10 from the petty customs of Portsmouth to Alice Davy in November, 1519, in reward for her services as gentlewoman to Katharine of Aragon and nurse to Margaret queen of Scotland.[96] £12 odd rent from the town was granted to Queen Anne by James I and to Queen Catherine by Charles II,[97] and finally under an Act of Parliament dated 1670 it was conveyed to the trustees for the sale of fee-farm rents.[98] No record of its sale has been found, and in 1835 the farm to the crown was still included among the expenses of the corporations,[99] but it has since ceased to be paid.

Portsmouth, therefore, has existed as a borough since 1194.[100] The charter then granted to it by Richard I recites that the king had retained in his own hands the 'borough' of Portsmouth, and that he had established a fair to be held there annually to last fifteen days, commencing on the feast of St. Peter ad Vincula (1 August), while all men who should come to it from places within his kingdom should enjoy the same liberties as those who attended the fairs at Winchester and Hoyland. At the same time he granted that his burgesses there should have a weekly market to be held on Thursdays, with all such privileges as were enjoyed by the citizens of Winchester and Oxford; that all the burgesses in the town, and holding of the town, wherever they should go within his realms, should be quit from toll, pontage, passage and pavage, stallage and tallage, and from shires and hundreds, and from summons and aids of the sheriff, and from all pleas, including pleas of the forest; and that his burgesses having houses and tenements within the town should hold them with toll and theam infangtheof and utfangtheof as freely as the citizens of Winchester and Oxford held theirs. Finally, he forbad their being impleaded touching any tenement in the town save before himself.[101] In October, 1200, soon after his accession, King John confirmed his brother's charter, at the same time extending the clause as to pleas about tenements in the town so that they might be heard either before him or the chief justice.[102] For this confirmation the men of Portsmouth paid ten marks and a palfrey.[103] Henry III also in a charter dated 18 November, 1229, renewed the former grant of his father and uncle, but omitted entirely the phrase as to pleas before the king or his justice; on the previous day the ferm of the town had been increased from £18 to £20.[104] On 5 April, 1255, the same king confirmed to the burgesses of Portsmouth all their liberties included in his own charter and those of Richard I and John,[105] and in July 1256 he granted a gild merchant to the good men of Portsmouth and freed them from caption of person or goods for debt save where they were principal debtors or securities or where the principal debtor belonged to their community and was able to satisfy the debt while the men of the gild had failed to do justice; at the same time he confirmed to them the freedom from cheminage throughout the king's forest, and other privileges which they had been wont to enjoy.[106] Edward II, in February 1312–13, inspected and confirmed the charters of 1194, 1200, 18 November, 1229, and 5 April, 1255,[107] and this confirmation was itself confirmed in 1358 by Edward III.[108] In 1384 Richard II confirmed the charter of Edward III, and also the grant of a gild merchant.[109] There followed successive confirmations of the same charters in 1401, 1423, 1461, 1484, 1489, 1511, 1550, and 1561.[110] The town was thus practically governed by the charters of Richard and John until the end of the sixteenth century; then, in February 1599–1600, Queen Elizabeth reorganized the corporation of the town.[111] In this its first definite charter of incorporation, after reciting the ancient constitution and privileges of the borough, and referring to the ambiguities in its former charters and to its important position as a port and frontier town, she declared that, at the petition of Lord Mountjoy, then captain there, the borough of Portsmouth should henceforth be a free borough, and its inhabitants a body corporate under the name of the Mayor and Burgesses of Portsmouth, with the usual ability to acquire lands and privileges, to plead and be impleaded, and to possess a common seal. The charter then recounts the details of the

84 Pipe R. 10 Ric. I.
85 Ibid. 2 John.
86 Ibid. 3 John.
87 Charter R. 14 Hen. III, pt. 1, m. 4. Less an allowance of 35*s*. 4*d*. which had been deducted for the rent of Kingston. In *Testa de Nevill* (Rec. Com.), 237, Portsmouth is referred to as an escheat of the king valued at £20. Probably the ferm had already been granted out and had escheated to the crown, by whom it had been given to Gilbert de Kaunpiun.
88 *Cal. Pat.* 1272–81, p. 439.
89 Ibid. 1281–92, p. 218.
90 Ibid. 1307–13, p. 216; 1327–30, p. 69; Mins. Accts. bdle. 1092, No. 3.
91 *Cal. Pat.* 1401–5, p. 266.
92 Mins. Accts. bdle. 1280, No. 6.
93 *Parl. R.* (Rec. Com.), v, 174*b*.
94 *Cal. Pat.* 1476–85, p. 365.
95 *Parl. R.* (Rec. Com.), vi, 302.
96 *L. and P. Hen. VIII*, iii, 524.
97 Pat. 11 Jas. I, pt. 13; ibid. 17 Chas. II, pt. 9, m. 1.
98 Ibid. 22 Chas. II, pt. 2 (*a*), m. 1.
99 *Parl. Accts. and Papers*, 1835, xxiv. 817.
100 The tradition that it was founded by Henry I in the sixth year of his reign is obviously mythical. It is based on a statement signed by the mayor of Portsmouth in a heraldic visitation of Hampshire, dated 1686; cf. *Parl. Accts. and Papers*, 1835, xxiv, 799.
101 *Liber Custumarium* (Rolls Ser.), ii, 655.
102 *Cal. Rot. Chart.* (Rec. Com.), 77.
103 *Rot. Cancell.* 3 *John* (Rec. Com.), 255.
104 *Cal. Chart. R.* i, 106.
105 Pat. 39 Hen. III, m. 9.
106 Ibid. 8 Ric. II, pt. 1, m. 22.
107 Chart. R. 6 Edw. II, 28.
108 See Pat. 8 Ric. II, pt. 1, m. 22.
109 Ibid.
110 *Cal. Pat.* 1399–1401, p. 473; 1422–9, p. 121; 1461–7, p. 145; Confirm. R. 2 Ric. III, iii, 2; 4 Hen. VII, ii, 17; 3 Hen. VIII, ii, 3; 4 Edw. VI, i, 4; 3 Eliz. i, 11.
111 Orig. R. 42 Eliz. v, 43. A full translation of this and other charters is given in East's *Extracts from the Portsmouth Records* (ed. 1891), p. 578.

corporation and the functions of its various officers. In spite of the new life inspired by Elizabeth's charter of incorporation the town had fallen into great decay by 1625, and the mayor and inhabitants petitioned for a renewal of their privileges with a grant of certain trading advantages.[112] In November, 1627, a new charter of incorporation was granted to the town, enlarging considerably the privileges bestowed by Elizabeth, making some changes in the constitution of the body corporate, and giving the inhabitants licence to weave, make, and sell all kinds of kersies and broadcloths.[113] In April, 1666, the king threatened to take the town into his own hands and proposed giving the care of it to the Lieutenant-Governor, Sir Philip Honeywood, owing to the remissness of the mayor and aldermen in not providing for the removal of the plague-stricken soldiers and inhabitants to the pest-house.[114] In 1682 Charles II invited all corporate towns and boroughs to show their loyalty to the crown by surrendering their charters. This Portsmouth did in the same year, and, though the surrender was not formally enrolled, the king granted the town a new charter in August, 1682.[115] It recited the surrender of the charter of Charles I and re-incorporated the borough, adding to it the town of Gosport. The corporation, according to this charter, was similar to that organized under that of Charles I, save that its jurisdiction extended over Gosport. One clause alone sufficed to give the crown almost absolute power over the borough : mayor, aldermen, and burgesses were all to be removable by the king's sign manual. By this charter the town was governed till October, 1688, when James II issued a proclamation revoking all charters granted after the surrender of the boroughs to Charles II, since in almost every case the deeds of surrender had not been enrolled ;[116] accordingly, the men of Portsmouth applied for the return of their former charter to Lord Dartmouth, among whose papers it had been found.[117] They were evidently successful, for the charter is still among the corporation records, and the town is still governed by it, subject to such modifications as were provided by the Municipal Reform Acts of the last century.

The town of Portsmouth had a corporate existence soon after its foundation. Richard I in his charter granted definite privileges to the burgesses, and before 1214 they possessed lands in common, for the burgesses of Portsmouth had alienated a messuage and land in Portsmouth called Westwood to the Domus Dei there.[118]

This corporate body had no definite name till the sixteenth century. King John's charter was addressed to 'the burgesses of Portsmouth,' but the men of Portsmouth paid for its enrolment.[119] The bailiffs of Portsmouth acted for the town in the time of King John,[120] and a royal writ was addressed to them in 1224,[121] and subsequent writs were sent to the bailiffs and men or to the men of Portsmouth.[122] The 'customs and usages' of the town, which may be assigned to the latter part of the thirteenth century, were drawn up by the mayor, bailiff, constables, serjeants, and jurats,[123] but it is doubtful whether the word here translated 'mayor' may not have been 'prepositus' in the original document, which, unfortunately, is not in the possession of the corporation. The office of mayor certainly existed in 1323, when a writ was addressed to the mayor and bailiffs of Portsmouth ordering them to search for and arrest all letters coming into the realm.[124] The bailiffs continued in existence long after the introduction of the offices of 'prepositus' and mayor, and in Elizabeth's charter of incorporation it is stated that the town had formerly been governed by a mayor, two bailiffs, two constables, and other public officers, and the name of the reorganized corporation is given as 'the Mayor and Burgesses of the Borough of Portsmouth.' Under the charter of Charles I the name of the corporation was 'the Mayor, Aldermen, and Burgesses of Portsmouth,' but the government of the town was practically vested in the mayor and aldermen only. This charter also mentions a recorder, justices of the peace, common clerk, and two serjeants at mace. Under the charter of Charles II (1682), the recorder was included in the governing body ; but since this grant was cancelled under the proclamation of October, 1688, the corporation of the town remained unaltered till the Municipal Reform Act of 1835, under which its nature was entirely changed. It now consists of forty-two councillors, one-third of whom retire in rotation every three years, and fourteen aldermen, from among whom the mayor is chosen.[125] The councillors are chosen by the burgesses, and serve for a term of three years. In 1888, under the Local Government Act, Portsmouth became a 'county borough' for administrative purposes.[126]

The number of burgesses varied considerably from time to time. The privileges granted by Richard I were to be enjoyed only by those who held land or property in or of the town.[127] In the earliest recorded list of burgesses (*c.* 1575) there are fifty-four names, including that of the mayor, but of these six are marked as deceased ;[128] twenty-five burgesses besides the mayor and twelve aldermen are named in the charter of Charles I, and Charles II appointed the same number in 1662 when no fewer than eighty-eight burgesses

112 *Cal. S.P. Dom.* 1525–6, p. 94.

113 Pat. 4 Chas. I, pt. 24, m. 5.

114 *Cal. S.P. Dom.* 1665–6, p. 355. It seems probable that this was one more step in the struggle between the garrison and the town ; see *infra.*

115 Pat. 34 Chas. II, pt. 5, m. 13.

116 *Lond. Gaz.* No. 2391, Oct. 1688.

117 *Hist. MSS. Com. Rep.* xi, App. pt. v, 202.

118 *Rot. Chart.* (Rec. Com.), 202.

119 *Rot. Cancell.* 3 John (Rec. Com.), 255.

120 Curia Regis R. 36, m. 2 *d.*

121 *Rot. Lit. Claus.* (Rec. Com.), i, 599.

122 *Cal. of Close*, 1272–9, p. 270 ; 1231–4, p. 377.

123 For a transcript of these 'customs' see *Extracts from the Portsmouth Records*, 1. The only existing copy is evidently both inaccurate and imperfect, but from the names of the officers the original would seem to have been drawn up late in the thirteenth century. These included the mayor, Harry le Pesener, bailiff John Phelyp, constables Nicholas Raggi and Richard Cooptor, and sergeants Robert le Molender and Robert Clerk. Of these Nicholas Raggi, Richard Cooptor, Robert le Molender, and Robert Clerk, with Peter Copas, witnessed a grant of land by Stephen Justice to Southwick Priory, 'with all the court of Portsmouth,' of which Herbert Manniet was then serjeant (serviens), and a Stephen Justice and Peter Coperas witnessed another charter to the priory in 1278 (Add. MS. 8153, fol. 63 *et passim*). Stephen Justice was one of the two burgesses returned by Portsmouth to the Parliament of 1295.

124 *Cal. Close*, 1323–7, p. 138.

125 5 and 6 Will. IV, cap. 76, schedule A.

126 Stat. 51 and 52 Vict. cap. 41, schedule 3.

127 *Extracts from the Portsmouth Records*, 141.

128 Ibid. 133. In 1835 a calculation based on the returns of members to Parliament was made, showing that in the fifteenth and sixteenth centuries the number of burgesses was never greater than thirteen (*Parl. Accts. and Papers*, 1835, xxiv, 799). It remains, however, to be proved that all the burgesses exercised the privilege of voting.

were disfranchised.[129] There was evidently no limit to the number of burgesses elected each year, for within five months of the year 1773 no fewer than forty-three were admitted to the freedom of the borough,[130] and in 1834 seventy-eight burgesses were sworn besides nine aldermen.[131] There was apparently no qualification necessary for a burgess. It was not even needful for him to be a resident, for the following names occur on the list of burgesses :—John White of Southwick, 1553 ; William Gage of Havant, 1557 ; William Bennet of Fareham, 1634 ; and so on throughout the list.[132] It was possible also for the soldiers in the garrison and officers in the dockyard to become burgesses ; thus in 1531 Richard Palshyd, a captain of the garrison ; in 1594, Joshua Savour, master gunner ; in 1575, Richard Popinjay, government surveyor ; and in 1576, William Davison, admiralty-serjeant, were burgesses.[133] Early in the seventeenth century, however, when the relations between the town and the garrison were somewhat strained, it was considered contrary to the customs of the town for a soldier of the garrison to be given the freedom of the borough, and in 1618 Thomas Mondaie, one of the burgesses, was disfranchised because he had bought a soldier's place, and was under the command of the governor.[134] On the other hand an ordinance had been made in 1545–6, forbidding the captain of the town from receiving any inhabitant as a soldier there.[135] Before the charter of Charles I (1627), burgesses were elected with the common consent of the mayor and burgesses in the borough court. After 1627 till the Municipal Reform Act of 1835 they were chosen by the mayor and aldermen whenever they thought fit.[136] In 1682 an ordinance was made providing against the proposal of any new burgess save in the council in the Council-house.[137] Since 1835 every ratepayer has been accounted a burgess.

The fine paid for the freedom of the borough varied considerably, while in many cases no fine at all is recorded. In 1546 Francis Botkyn gave 10*s.* at his election,[138] while Richard Jenens paid 26*s.* 8*d.* on a similar occasion in 1593,[139] and in 1531 John Playfoote of Copnor agreed upon his admission as burgess 'of his mere mind and good will' to repair the prison house.[140] William Heaton, gentleman, paid 10*s.* fine and 10*s.* upon a breakfast for the burgesses at his election in 1597. These conditions were determined by two arbiters, one representing the town and one the burgess-elect, evidently the customary mode of agreement as to the fine to be paid.[141] On the election of honorary burgesses at the request of the mayor and aldermen, the town paid certain fees to the town clerk and other officers.[142] Many famous men have thus been burgesses of Portsmouth : the list includes Sir Christopher Hatton, Sir Julius Cæsar, Thomas Pride, George Monk, Samuel Pepys, Admirals George and John Byng, Lord Chancellor Erskine, and many other well-known men. Burgesses were disfranchised before 1662 by the common consent of the mayor and burgesses.[143] In that year many members of the corporation were disfranchised by the Royal Commissioners on grounds of disaffection,[144] and in the charter of Charles II it was definitely stated that the burgesses and other members of the corporation were removable by the king's sign manual, but this clause was only in force till the proclamation of 1688 annulled the charter of Charles II.

Once elected the burgesses formerly enjoyed many privileges, which have now fallen into insignificance. Their share in the government of the town was probably considerable until the rise of the twelve assistants and afterwards of the aldermen, and at all times these last have been chosen from their number. Under the charter of Richard I they were free from toll and passage and the many other dues paid by ordinary travellers in the king's realms. They were quit of suit at the shire and hundred courts and from pleas of forest ; in fact, they had all the liberties granted to the citizens of Winchester and Oxford.[145] The burgesses who brought pleas to the borough courts paid a smaller fee than the ordinary inhabitant or 'stranger.'[146] Besides this they had various trading advantages. They could buy and sell within the town without a licence from the mayor,[147] while the non-burgess who did so was amerced in the court leet.[148] Early in the seventeenth century the townsmen struggled to maintain this right against the soldiers of the garrison, who persisted in keeping ale-houses and victualling-houses in the town.[149] In 1630, in answer to a petition from the soldiers stating that, if not allowed to trade, they would not be able to live, since they only had 8*d.* a day, and that not paid, it was ordered that they should be allowed to trade in the town till they received their full pay, or the matter should be debated in the presence of both parties.[150] Two years later it was again ordered that no soldier should trade or keep an ale-house in the town, but the regulation seems to have been broken very soon.[151] The borough also regulated trade in the harbour, for Robert Reeve was heavily fined in 1594 for having bought a ship in the harbour while not a burgess.[152] Under Elizabeth's charter of incorporation neither the burgesses nor inhabitants of the town were to be impanelled on any jury save in causes affecting property within the borough ; and to the present day they are free from serving on county juries. They were for many years exempt from wharfage dues, but this privilege was disputed early in the last century.[153] Perhaps the most important privilege enjoyed exclusively by the burgesses was their right to vote for the two members returned by the town to Parliament. This they retained till the Reform Act of 1832. Their functions primarily included all the responsibility of the government of

[129] *Extracts from the Portsmouth Records*, 169.
[130] Ibid. 234. [131] Ibid. 264.
[132] Ibid. 343, et seq.
[133] Ibid. [134] Ibid. 155.
[135] *Acts of P.C.* (New Ser.), i, 322.
[136] Pat. 4 Chas. I, pt. 24, m. 5.
[137] *Extracts from Portsmouth Rec.* 10.
[138] Ibid. 126.
[139] Ibid. 141.
[140] Ibid. 116.
[141] Ibid. 142 and 147.
[142] Ibid. 277.
[143] Ibid. 153, 155, &c.
[144] Ibid. 169 and 157. Robert Bold was discharged from being a burgess in 1625, in respect of his many infirmities, and since he did not inhabit in the town.
[145] It seems probable, however, that these liberties were extended to all inhabitants of the town, for the charter gives them to 'the town of Portsmouth and all our burgesses in it and holding of it.'
[146] See 'Customs and Usages of Portsmouth,' East, *Extracts from the Portsmouth Rec.* 2. [147] Ibid. 4.
[148] Ibid. 77, a list of more than thirty-five classes of tradesmen (non-burgesses) amerced for exercising their trades in the town.
[149] Add. MS. 33283, fol. 85.
[150] *Cal. S.P. Dom.* 1625–49, p. 375.
[151] Ibid. 1635, p. 574.
[152] *Extracts from the Portsmouth Rec.* 142.
[153] *Parl. Accts. and Papers*, 1835, xxiv, 799.

THE NEW MAGAZINE ON THE CAMBER, 1716

(*Brit. Mus.* K, xiv, 42, o)

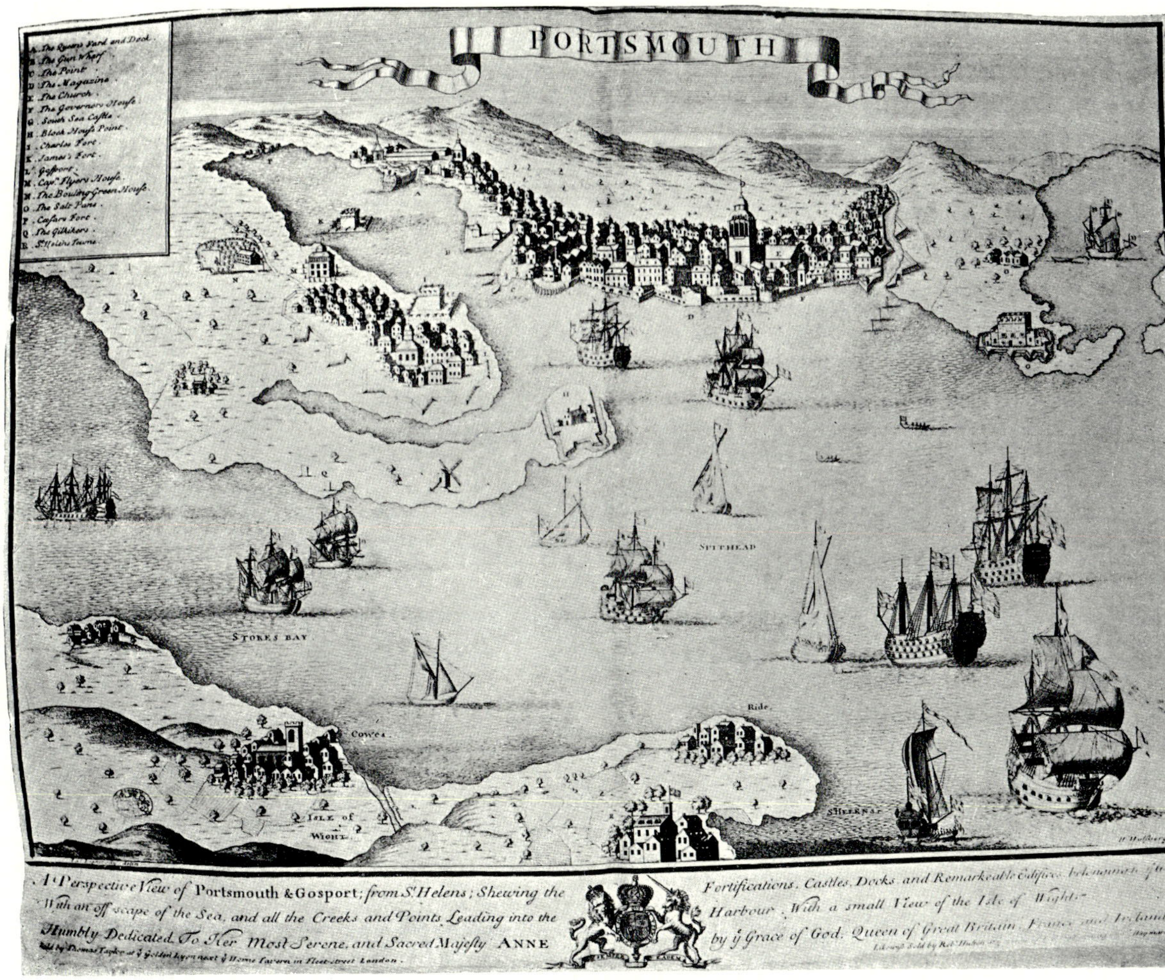

PORTSMOUTH AND GOSPORT, *temp.* QUEEN ANNE

(*From Nouveau Théâtre de la Grande Bretagne*, 1724)

the town, until the growth of the office of alderman. Then their duties became more formal; they were obliged to attend the mayor in their gowns when summoned, and their presence at the election of a new mayor was also enforced.[154] In 1605 their gowns were known as cloaks in contradistinction to the gowns of the assistants.[155] In 1700 it was agreed that since many burgesses, in spite of their oath, had absented themselves from the mayor's courts and assemblies, all inhabitants when admitted as burgesses should either pay a fine of £5 or take a special oath to attend the mayor's courts and assemblies.[156]

A method of government which placed supreme control in the hands of an indefinite number of burgesses must have proved somewhat clumsy in the working. It is not surprising, therefore, to find a more limited number of the burgesses gradually forming a council to aid the mayor or bailiffs in the executive branches of their business. Owing to the absence of early records it is difficult to discover at what date such a council first existed, but in the list of usages and customs of the town which was probably drawn up late in the twelfth or early in the thirteenth century, mention is made of twelve jurats, who were apparently identical with the mayor's council of twelve men which he himself chose yearly upon his election.[157] In 1537 it was the twelve jurats who made certain regulations concerning trade in the town.[158] Probably these twelve men were those 'senior and principal better and more honest burgesses' from whom the mayor was to be chosen according to the terms of Queen Elizabeth's charter of incorporation, and represented the mayor's assistants. The latter term occurs about the middle of the sixteenth century. There were evidently eight assistants, two of whom attended the mayor in rotation at the weekly courts of the borough.[159] In 1585 the mayor, aldermen, and inhabitants of Portsmouth petitioned the queen with regard to the decay of trade in the town,[160] hence it seems probable that the terms 'alderman' and 'assistant' were interchangeable before the charter of 1627, in which it is definitely stated that there should be twelve aldermen to form the council of the borough, and aid and assist the mayor. They were to be chosen for life from the burgesses, and vacancies were to be filled up by the remaining aldermen and mayor or the majority of them. On at least one occasion a newly elected burgess was immediately chosen as alderman.[161] This occurred in 1656. In 1662 the Royal Commission appointed four new aldermen in place of four removed for alleged disloyalty.[161a] Under the charter of Charles II the aldermen were removable, like the burgesses, by the royal sign manual. Towards the end of the seventeenth century there were continual discords among the aldermen. In the words of a contemporary tract, 'the beginning of our divisions and distractions may be dated from the time Mr. Ward, our vicar, made choice of Mr. Ely Stamyford for churchwarden at Easter, 1703.[162] These divisions continued with increasing acrimony between the Whig and Tory parties. Both parties chose numerous burgesses for political purposes, and the struggle continued till 1711, when the two leading Whigs, Henry Seagar and Thomas White, were ousted from among the aldermen by a mandamus from the Queen's Bench. A similar conflict arose in the latter part of the eighteenth century.[163] From 1782 onwards the Whig party was supreme in the town, and until the Reform Act of 1832, their selection of burgesses was openly based on political considerations, while the aldermen were almost all of the Carter family.[164] Under the Municipal Reform Act of 1835, the number of aldermen was altered to fourteen, half of their number retiring every three years, an arrangement which is still in force.

There appear to have been no privileges attached to the office of alderman beyond its political and social power. The former rested chiefly in the ability of the aldermen to choose burgesses and hence to influence both the parliamentary and municipal elections. Their duties included all the government of the town and the management of the corporation estates. They were bound to attend the common council when summoned by the mayor.[165] In 1678 a rule was made that they should attend him to church every Sunday, and in 1682 it was agreed that they should wear their scarlet gowns on election day, certain feast days, the first Sunday in the month, and any other day appointed by the council.[166]

The earliest government of the town appears to have been by a reeve and bailiffs. Possibly William de Ste.-Mère Eglise, who accounted for the petty customs of the town when they were first separated from those of Southampton, acted as the first reeve.[167] Theobald, the reeve of Portsmouth, witnessed a conveyance of land in Portsmouth in 1201,[168] and in 1216 a royal writ was addressed to the reeve and men of Portsmouth,[169] while the reeve and whole court of Portsmouth witnessed a conveyance of the thirteenth century.[170] In 1270 Peter Coperas was reeve.[171] The number of bailiffs is so far unknown. Probably, as at Winchester, there were two; Elizabeth's charter states that the town had been governed by a mayor and two bailiffs. It was the bailiffs who collected the rents and customs and were responsible to the crown for the farm of the borough during the reign of King John.[172] Pleas were also held before them and writs addressed to them[173]; they acted as the king's escheators in the town.[174] Their duties also included the hearing of recognizances of debt,[175] and the sealing of conveyances of lands within the borough, since the seals of the parties to the deeds were unknown to most men.[176] Towards the end of the thirteenth

154 *Extracts from the Portsmouth Rec.* 8 and 127.
155 Ibid. 153.
156 Ibid. 19.
157 Ibid. 1.
158 Ibid. 119. It is curious to note that on the same day in the same court the twelve jurats presented that Henry Byckeley was heir of John Byckeley—a function of the grand jury.
159 Ibid. 136.
160 *Cal. S.P. Dom.* 1580–1625, p. 142.
161 *Extracts from the Portsmouth Rec.* 167.
161a Ibid. 169.
162 *A Plain and True Account of the Divisions in Portsmouth*, 1711, p. 1. This tract gives an account of the discords from the Whigs' point of view. The proceedings of the Tories, who included Charles Bissell, the town clerk, are contained in Book 13 of the Corp. Rec. See also Add. MS. 33278, fol. 85.
163 See *Extracts from the Portsmouth Rec.* 244 et seq.
164 *Parl. Accts. and Papers*, 1835, xxiv, 799.
165 *Extracts from the Portsmouth Rec.* 8.
166 Ibid. 11.
167 Pipe R. 6 Ric. I.
168 *Cal. Doc. France*, 304.
169 *Rot. Lit. Claus.* (Rec. Com.), i, 302.
170 Anct. D. (P.R.O.), B. 2950.
171 Ibid. B. 2946.
172 Curia Regis R. 36, m. 2 *d.*
173 *Rot. Lit. Claus.* (Rec. Com.), ii, 606; i, 599.
174 Misc. Inq. (Hen. III), ii, 3.
175 Anct. D. (P.R.O.), B. 2935.
176 Add. Chart. 15857, 15858.

century the government seems to have been modified in form. The ancient usages of the town, which apparently belong to the latter end of the century, were drawn up by the mayor and one bailiff.[177] The mayor evidently succeeded the reeve, and in 1323 definite mention is made of the mayor and bailiffs.[178] Subsequently the importance of the mayor's office increased, while the bailiffs gradually lost their authority. In a deed of sale of a stall or shop in the market dated 1450 the rent was said to be paid to the king by the hands of the bailiffs, but only one bailiff witnessed the deed,[179] and only one is recorded as accounting for the farm of the town in 1443.[180] In 1521 the bailiff of Portsmouth gave a detailed account of a suspicious character lately seen near Havant,[181] and on 28 April, 1538, when Thomas Carpenter was mayor, Thomas Yonge, bailiff of the town, evidently had full authority over the watchmen and constables there.[182] Unfortunately, owing to the loss or destruction of the corporation records for the sixteenth century, there is no clue to the time when the bailiff's office lapsed,[183] but apparently it was in disuse before 1600, the date of Queen Elizabeth's charter to the town. The ancient usages of the town state that the bailiff received one-half of the surplus of any fine which exceeded 24*s.* and 12*d.* in every pound recovered in the borough court, besides 6*s.* 8*d.* fine for drawing a weapon, and 6*d.* for bloodshed in the case of any frays in the town. From the first the mayor seems to have been chosen by the burgesses from among themselves.[184] The election took place on the Monday preceding Michaelmas Day,[185] a custom which continued till 1627, when, under the charter of Charles I, it was altered to the Monday week before that feast. In 1835 the day of election was again changed to 9 November. Before this time the mayor had been sworn into office on the Michaelmas Day after his election. Under Elizabeth's charter he was to be chosen from among the senior and better burgesses, and by the charter of 1627 it was ordained that he should be chosen by the majority of the aldermen and burgesses from the aldermen. By the Municipal Corporations Act of 1835 the election was vested in the borough council, i.e. the mayor, aldermen, and councillors. His duties necessitate residence within the borough limits.[186] Under the charter of Charles I the mayor was removable at the will of the aldermen, and so continued till 1835, except during the few years that the charter of Charles II was in force, when he might have been removed by the royal sign manual, as has been before pointed out. During the bitter political struggle between the Whig and Tory aldermen Henry Seagar, who had been chosen mayor by one party, was ousted under a mandamus from the Queen's Bench in 1711, as having been unduly elected.[187] Again, at the latter end of the same century party feeling was so strong that for three years the mayoralty was in dispute.[188] In October, 1779, John Carter was elected by the Whig party, Edward Linzee, who had been chosen in the preceding September, not having appeared to be sworn. Carter was ousted in the following January, and John Godwin, who took his place, resigned in May, so that from that time till Michaelmas, 1780, there was no mayor at all in the town, and during a whole year no justices nor minor officials were sworn.[189] Early in the seventeenth century there were evidently objections raised to the choice of members of the garrison as mayor, for William Winter at his election in 1635 renounced his position in the garrison and promised 'hereafter to be none of their company.'[190] In the case of Benjamin Johnson, a storekeeper who was chosen mayor in 1665, a deputy fulfilled the greater part of his functions, though he attended the more important councils, e.g. to consult as to the prevention of the plague.[191] He refused to relinquish office, saying that only the king and council could remove him,[192] and in spite of definite orders to the contrary several officers in the docks were chosen mayor, for in the words of a letter addressed to Samuel Pepys, 'the king had as good as taken away the charter from the town as prohibit his officers from being magistrates.'[193]

The appointment of a deputy mayor in case of the mayor's sickness or any other reasonable cause of absence was provided for in the charter of Charles I. The deputy was to be one of the aldermen and was chosen by the mayor himself.

As the office of bailiff became extinct, it devolved upon the mayor to preside over the court leet and view of frankpledge in the town. In the charter of Charles I it is stated that either the mayor or the recorder must be present at these and at the court of record. The charter of Elizabeth provided that he should be *ex officio* a justice of the peace, and, with the common clerk, should hear and seal recognizances of debt.

The mayor's hospitality consisted mainly in great banquets on special occasions. At first he was bound to provide two grand feasts at the time of the sessions and one on the Friday following, together with other banquets on election days and Michaelmas Day, and a piece of roast beef on Christmas Day, Easter Day, and Whitsunday. Late in the seventeenth century the mayor's salary having been reduced by £10 to increase the fund for paving the town, one of these feasts was abolished; and in 1681, when the town was burdened with the costs of a suit concerning the elections, the two grand feasts of the session were excused.[194]

At first there was no definite allowance due to the mayor from the corporation funds, but he had certain perquisites, e.g. two bushels of wheat from every boat-load brought into port,[195] and certain amercements at law days and courts,[196] the latter privilege being evidently a survival of the old custom which allowed the bailiff 12*d.* in every pound recovered in the court.[197] In 1543 these amercements were commuted for an annual payment to be settled at the election of the mayor.[198] Latterly the amount assigned to him yearly was £30, but late in the seventeenth century this was reduced to £20, and in 1671 this was changed for the use of the butchers' shambles and the loft above

177 *Extracts from the Portsmouth Rec.* 1.
178 *Cal. Close*, 1323–7, p. 138.
179 Add. Chart. 15855.
180 Mins. Accts. bdle. 1280, No. 6.
181 *L. and P. Hen. VIII*, iii, 1256.
182 Ibid. xiii (1), 859.
183 In those election books for this period which have been printed in *Extracts from the Portsmouth Rec.*, no mention is made of the election of a bailiff.
184 *Extracts from the Portsmouth Rec.* 150. In 1598 the majority of the burgesses elected the new mayor.
185 *Extracts from the Portsmouth Rec.* 1.
186 Ibid. 241.
187 Ibid. 207, 210.
188 Ibid. 255.
189 Ibid. 244 et seq.
190 Ibid. 160.
191 *Cal. S. P. Dom.* 1665–6, p. 316.
192 Ibid. 308.
193 Ibid. 547.
194 *Extracts from the Portsmouth Rec.* 6, 9.
195 *Cal. of S. P. Dom.* 1651–2, p. 153.
196 *Extracts from the Portsmouth Rec.* 122.
197 Ibid. 3.
198 Ibid. 122.

them, the corporation keeping them in repair,[199] while, in 1693, it was arranged that the mayor himself should pay the cost of repairs.[200] Finally, in 1785, it was arranged that all the former perquisites of the mayor should be added to the common fund, from which the expenses of the mayoralty up to £300 yearly were to be paid by the chamberlain.[201] It was a privilege of the mayor to elect a burgess on retiring from office.[202] At an election of aldermen in 1690 a discussion arose as to whether the mayor had a casting vote in the matter, and the decision was in the negative,[203] but by 1835 it was customary for him to have a casting vote.[204] At that date also he had the appointment of certain minor officers such as the serjeants-at-mace. In 1682 it was ordained that when not wearing his robe he should carry a white staff 6 ft. to 7 ft. in length.[205]

By Elizabeth's charter the powers of justices of the peace were first definitely conferred on the mayor and three of the senior or better burgesses of the town,[206] though some at least of their functions, e.g. the suppression of riot and the prevention of forestalling, must have been previously exercised by officials of the corporation. Under the charter of 1627 the mayor, ex-mayor of the previous year, the recorder, and three other aldermen were justices of the peace for one year, being chosen Monday week before Michaelmas by the mayor, aldermen, and burgesses for the time being. The three aldermen then appointed by the king had all previously acted as mayor, and it evidently became the custom later for the office only to be given to ex-mayors, for Hugh Salisbury, an officer of the dockyard who had been elected justice in 1666, excused himself for taking such an office since there were only three aldermen besides himself who had been mayors.[207] The charter of Charles II extended the jurisdiction of the justices of Portsmouth to Gosport, but otherwise no change was made, except that it definitely stated that only aldermen who had been mayors could become justices of the peace. Owing to the party struggles of the eighteenth century no new justices were sworn into office in 1779.[208] The number of magistrates has since increased.

The recorder, or presiding officer in the court of record, and more recently the quarter sessions of the borough, is definitely mentioned in the charter of Charles I. It is evident, however, that the office was in existence previous to that time, for in 1601 John Moore, 'recorder of Portsmouth,' was returned as member of Parliament for the town.[209] He had been under-steward of Portsmouth during the high-stewardship of Henry, earl of Sussex, who was appointed in 1590.[210] Again, in 1615, Moore was entered in the list of officers as serjeant-at-law and recorder.[211] According to the charter of 1627 the recorder was to be a man learned in the laws of England, to be elected by the mayor and aldermen and to continue in office during good behaviour, but before 1833 his term of office had been changed to one for life.[212] The charter of Charles II included the recorder among those who had power to make by-laws for the government of the town. His fee, which was paid from the rent-roll by the mayor, amounted to £10 in 1682.[213] By the Municipal Reform Act of 1835 the choice of a recorder was vested in the crown. Among those who have held this office was Judge Jeffreys, appointed in 1685, presumably on the nomination of the earl of Dartmouth.[214] His duties were fulfilled by a deputy.

The stewards have been said to be predecessors of the recorders, but little is known of their office. In the ancient usages and customs of the town, the steward is named among the officers to be elected with the mayor,[215] and record is kept of the appointment of seneschals or stewards in the sixteenth century, John Moore, the recorder of 1600, being deputy-steward under the earl of Sussex, as stated above.

The chamberlain or treasurer of the corporation was of considerable importance in the sixteenth and following centuries. In 1531 there were two chamberlains,[216] and again in 1561 the 'chamberlains' had charge of the town muniments,[217] but in 1620 there was only one.[218] In addition to his ordinary duties as treasurer he was responsible for the repair of the town property, e.g. the pound. He was elected annually by the mayor and a majority of the aldermen, but as a rule the chamberlain of the previous year was re-elected.[219] His place is now taken by a treasurer and accountant.

The coroner's office is prescriptive. The 'Customs' of the fifteenth century state that he was elected yearly with the mayor.[220] During the eighteenth century it was customary for the town clerk to be chosen as coroner each year.[221] Controversies arose in the eighteenth century between the admiralty coroner and the coroner of Portsmouth as to the extent of their jurisdictions, and in 1738, the matter having been laid before the King's Bench, it was decided that they held concurrent jurisdiction on board the men-of-war in the harbour.[222]

The charter of 1627 provided that there should be a town clerk of the borough who should also be a clerk of the peace, but the two offices are now held separately and the town clerk himself is assisted by a deputy.

In attendance on the mayor were the serjeants-at-mace, their duties including the care of the town-

199 *Extracts from the Portsmouth Rec.* 6.
200 Ibid. 16.
201 Ibid. 20. The common fund included the seal money, clerk of the market's dues, reliefs, fines for opening of shop windows, groundage and anchorage, capon rents, court fees and fines at sessions (ibid. 11).
202 Ibid. 19.
203 Ibid. 14.
204 *Parl. Accts. and Papers*, 1835, xxiv, 799.
205 *Extracts from the Portsmouth Rec.* 11.
206 The charter is somewhat ambiguous as to whether the three justices included the mayor or not. It states that three burgesses should be elected at Michaelmas; then that the said mayor and three burgesses should exercise the jurisdiction pertaining to justices of the peace, and finally appoints three justices for the ensuing year, one of them being Owen Tottie, who was also appointed mayor by the same charter; cf. Orig. R. 42 Eliz. v, 43.
207 *Cal. S.P. Dom.* 1666-7, p. 136.
208 *Extracts from the Portsmouth Rec.* 250.
209 *Ret. of Mem. P.* i, 439.
210 *Extracts from the Portsmouth Rec.* 137.
211 Ibid. 420.
212 *Parl. Accts. and Papers*, 1833, xiii, 110.
213 *Extracts from the Portsmouth Rec.* 12, 19.
214 *Hist. MSS. Com. Rep.* xi, App. pt. v, 123. The mayor and aldermen requested Lord Dartmouth to accept the office himself or to appoint whom he thought fit.
215 *Extracts from the Portsmouth Rec.* 1.
216 Ibid. 116.
217 Ibid. 129.
218 Ibid. 36.
219 *Parl. Accts. and Papers*, 1835, xxiv, 799.
220 *Extracts from the Portsmouth Rec.* 1.
221 *Parl. Accts. and Papers*, 1833, xiii, 110.
222 *Extracts from the Portsmouth Rec.* 206.

hall,[223] the summoning of members of the council,[224] and the preservation of the peace.[225] From the fourteenth century onwards there were apparently two serjeants.[226] At first certain fees from burgesses and strangers pleading in the borough court were due to them,[227] but in 1682 their salary was a fixed one.[228] By 1835 there was only one serjeant, and he was appointed annually by the mayor, the choice generally falling on the officer of the previous year.[229]

Other officers were the beadle, whose duties in 1685 included the cleaning of all gutters;[230] the hayward, who had care of the cattle in the common fields, and impounded strays; the constables, whose numbers increased from three in 1531[231] to twenty-two in 1833,[232] but whose influence in the government of the town decreased after the thirteenth century, when they had a voice in the formation of by-laws;[233] and the ale-tasters and searchers of market, who sought offenders against the assize of bread and ale. There were also four cofferers, who in the thirteenth century had charge of the borough muniments,[234] an office which was filled in 1531 by the mayor and two other burgesses,[235] and seems, later on, to have been exercised by the justices of the peace, while the cofferers' duties were those of auditors.[236] In connexion with the port there were also water-bailiffs, a wharfinger, and a measurer.[237]

Richard I exempted the town of Portsmouth and the burgesses holding in it and of it from pleas of the shire and hundred, and from all other pleas, including forest pleas;[238] moreover, he gave them the right of infangtheof and utfangtheof, so that from the first foundation of the town the burgesses had criminal jurisdiction therein. The early 'Customs' recite the punishments awarded in various cases: the pillory for minor thefts, death by burning or drowning at Catcliff (the site of the older portion of the royal dockyard) for murder, the cucking-stool for scolds, and fixed fines and the forfeiture of the weapon drawn in breaking the peace for assault.[239]

Under the Municipal Corporation Act of 1835 Portsmouth was allowed to retain quarter sessions of the peace.[240] The business of these courts had also included the lighting and cleansing of the town until special trustees were appointed for that purpose in the eighteenth century.[241] It is curious that burgesses were occasionally disfranchised at the sessions of the peace, although their removal was dependent on the votes of the mayor and aldermen, and not only on those of the magistrates.[242] For more than a century the sessions have been held three times a week, while the court of record, instituted by Charles I to deal with civil cases in the town, has been held every Tuesday. In 1819 a Bill was introduced for the more easy recovery of small debts in Portsmouth, but the attempt was unsuccessful,[243] and as yet the borough has no separate court of requests.

Court-leet and view of frankpledge were probably the oldest of the borough courts. It was doubtless the perquisites of these courts for which £8 10*s.* 3*d.* were accounted in 1198.[244] Their business included the supervision of weights and measures, the making of presentments concerning such misdemeanours as encroachments, frays, and bloodshed, breach of the pound, and all offences affecting trade in the town, such as breaking the assize and using false weights. It appears also that the court-leet dealt with such matters as would elsewhere have been heard in the court-baron of the lord of the manor; for instance, tenants were there admitted to the town lands, at the same time taking an oath to be true tenant to the mayor, aldermen, and burgesses.[245] During the seventeenth and eighteenth centuries the criminal work of the court-leet was gradually assumed by the justices of the peace, and its local duties, such as the supervision of the repair and lighting of the streets, were executed by the commissioners for that purpose. Thus, early in the nineteenth century, though the court was nominally held every Tuesday, the presentments were invariably postponed till the court day next before the Easter or Michaelmas sessions,[246] and it is doubtful if they performed any real business even then, for no leet presentments later than those for 1778 are to be found among the corporation records.[247]

A court of piepowder was formerly kept during fair-time.[248] The same court was held for burgesses as well as strangers during a month which commenced a fortnight before Michaelmas Day.[249] A memorandum made on the cover of a seventeenth-century book of sessions of the peace and view of frankpledge notes that 6*s.* was due to the mayor and 4*s.* to the town clerk for every court of piepowder held;[250] but the court fell out of use as the fair deteriorated.

The fair itself was granted to the burgesses by Richard I. It was to be held on the feast of St. Peter ad Vincula (1 August) and during the following fortnight, and the charter extended to those who attended it all the privileges enjoyed by visitors to the fairs at Winchester.[251] The grant of this fair was confirmed in the subsequent charters, and doubtless it brought much trade to the town and profit to the corporation, who took the tolls. In 1585, when the prosperity of Portsmouth was at a low ebb, the mayor and corporation, in petitioning for various trading advantages, begged that they might be allowed to hold two free fairs yearly, each to last for twenty days, and that during fair-time all men might discharge merchandise there for half the usual custom;[252] but apparently no grant of a second fair was made, nor is the original one definitely mentioned in the charter of 1600. Charles I, in 1627, confirmed the fair or feast to be held on the feast of St. Peter ad Vincula and the fourteen days following according to the grant of Richard I, but abolished 'a certain other fair'

[223] *Extracts from the Portsmouth Rec.* 12, 51.
[224] Ibid. 7, 21.
[225] Early Chan. Proc. bdle. 45, No. 53.
[226] Ibid.
[227] *Extracts from the Portsmouth Rec.* 3.
[228] Ibid. 12.
[229] *Parl. Accts. and Papers*, 1835, xxiv, 799.
[230] *Extracts from the Portsmouth Rec.* 81.
[231] Ibid. 116.
[232] *Parl. Accts. and Papers*, 1833, xiii, 110.
[233] *Extracts from the Portsmouth Rec.* 1.
[234] Ibid. 2.
[235] Ibid. 116.
[236] *Parl. Accts. and Papers*, 1835, xxiv, 799.
[237] Ibid.
[238] *Liber Custumarium* (Rolls Ser.), ii, 655.
[239] *Extracts from the Portsmouth Rec.* 1 et seq.
[240] Stat. 5 & 6 Will. IV, cap. 76.
[241] *Extracts from the Portsmouth Rec.* 205.
[242] Ibid. 176 et seq.
[243] *Lords Journ.* lii, 716, 725, 997.
[244] Pipe R. 10 Ric. I.
[245] *Extracts from the Portsmouth Rec.* 55. In 1638 the mayor was presented for failing to cause the common fields of the town to be driven according to custom.
[246] *Parl. Accts. and Papers*, 1835, xxiv, 811.
[247] *Extracts from the Portsmouth Rec.* 23.
[248] Ibid. 14.
[249] Ibid. 4.
[250] Ibid. 163.
[251] *Liber Custumarium* (Rolls Ser.), ii, 655.
[252] *Cal. S.P. Dom.* 1580–1625, p. 142.

which the burgesses had been wont to hold for fifteen days from the first day of August. It seems probable that, as the fair was subsequently held on 29 June and the fortnight following, it was under this charter that the date of the fair was altered from its original date to the only feast of St. Peter observed in the English calendar. With the change of style in 1752, the first day of the fair was again altered to 11 July. It was a trading fair of some importance, held in the open street, and was resorted to not only by the people of the neighbourhood, but by traders from Normandy and Holland. The chief articles sold were cutlery and earthenware from the Midlands, cloth from the west of England, baskets from Normandy, and Dutch metal and delftware. The fair opened with the display of an open hand or glove, which was placed at the end of a pole and exhibited from the window of the old gaol in the High Street, and latterly from the old town-hall. The glove is now kept in the borough museum: it replaced an older one which had been stolen and sold in America.[253] Towards the end of the eighteenth century the fair began to deteriorate, becoming a mere gathering of shows and gingerbread stalls, and a great inconvenience and nuisance to the inhabitants. Several attempts were made to put an end to it, but they were ineffectual, until in 1846 a clause inserted in a Local Improvement Act finally abolished it after an existence of more than six centuries.[254]

The markets also instituted by the charter of 1194 are held on Tuesdays, Thursdays, and Saturdays, though the original grant only mentions Thursday as market-day. The charter gave to the burgesses all the liberties enjoyed by the citizens of Winchester and Oxford at their markets. During the seventeenth century 'standings' were let out in the market-house,[255] which was presumably under the gildhall, which stood across the High Street. Later, the ground floor of the old town-hall, at the corner of Pembroke Road, was known as the market, but was let to a yearly tenant as a shop.[256] It is now held in the Commercial Road, the main thoroughfare northwards from the present town-hall. Vegetables, fruit, and dairy produce are sold wholesale and retail. The market begins in the early hours of the morning, when cars are driven in from all the country round, and even from over the Sussex borders. The carts themselves are drawn up in the road and used as stalls, or the fruit and vegetables are exposed for sale in baskets placed along the curb, while the salesman stands in the gutter. The corporation still takes 2*d.* toll for each standing.

On 4 July, 1256, Henry III granted to the 'good men' of Portsmouth that they and their heirs might have a gild merchant in the town, with all the liberties thereto belonging. A clause in the charter was evidently intended to free the community from liability for the debts of its individual members,[257] and the grant ends with a confirmation of exemption from cheminage and the other privileges enjoyed by the men of the town during the reigns of Richard I and John. It is curious to note that, though the burgesses obtained several confirmations of their other charters, it was not till 1384 that this grant of a gild-merchant was exemplified.[257a] Owing to the unfortunate loss of the earlier town records, the relations between the gild and the corporation remain unknown; nevertheless, it may be inferred that they were closely allied, from the fact that it was the mayor and burgesses who regulated the trade in the sixteenth and following centuries, and that the borough courts were held in the Gildhall.[258]

The earliest known common seal of the town is in the possession of the Society of Antiquaries, and is said to date from the thirteenth century. It shows a single-masted vessel on the waves, with furled mainsail. Above the vessel are a crescent and star.

The common seal at present in use bears on the obverse a similar vessel, with an anchor at the bow and an indented flag at the mast-head. Before the mast are two figures rowing; two others in a tower at the stem are blowing long trumpets. The legend is 'Sigillum Commune de Portemutha.' On the reverse are three canopied niches. In the centre niche are the Virgin and Child; in the right-hand niche St. Nicholas with hand raised in benediction; and in the left-hand niche St. Thomas of Canterbury, holding his archiepiscopal cross. The legend is 'Portum Virgo Juva Nicholae Fove Roge[259] Thoma.'

The seal of the mayoralty is circular, and bears the crescent and star of the borough arms, and the legend 'S. Prepositi de Portesmuth.'

A seal affixed to warrants authorizing flogging during the eighteenth century bears the Tudor rose surmounted by a crown, and the legend 'Prepositus Portesmouth.'

The corporation insignia include:—

(1) A small silver mace with cup-shaped head, on one side of which is the Tudor rose and on the other the fleur-de-lis crowned; no hall-mark.

(2) A silver parcel-gilt mace with semi-globular head engraved with the star, a five-bladed shaft, and the arms of Charles II on a boss on the head, so fixed that it may be reversed to show the arms of the Commonwealth; no hall-mark.

(3) A silver-gilt mace 'converted' at the Restoration. The head is surmounted by a crown, of which the arches are of unusual character. The maker's mark is W. H.

(4) The mayor's chain of office, purchased in 1859, is of gold. Attached is a pendant bearing the borough arms.

Among the fine collection of corporation plate are:—

(1) A silver-gilt cup with the hall-mark of 1525–6 and the inscription 'Si Deus Nobiscum quis contra nos.' On the inside of the foot the initials F. B.

(2) Three silver spoons of Elizabethan pattern marked with the hall-mark of 1558–9 and bearing the letters F. B. pounced on the stems; and three silver spoons marked respectively with the hall-marks of 1588, 1601, and 1618, the earliest having the initials I. S. A. engraved on the knob.

(3) A standing silver-gilt cup with cover. On the edge of the bowl the legends 'Multa cadunt inter calicem supremum labra' (*sic*) and 'Vivite ad

253 Information kindly given by Mr. W. H. Saunders.

254 *Extracts from the Portsmouth Rec.* 303.

255 Ibid. 37.

256 *Reports on Markets*, 1889, iii, 370.

257 '. . . non arestentur pro aliquo debito de quo fideiussores aut principales debitores non extiterunt nisi forte ipsi debitores de eorum fuit communia et potestatem habentes unde de debitis suis in toto vel in parte satisfacere possint et dicti homines creditoribus eorundem debitorum in iusticia defuerint et de hoc rationabiliter constari possit.'

257a Pat. 8 Ric. II, pt. 1, m. 22.

258 *Extracts from the Portsmouth Rec.* 230.

259 For 'rege.'

extremum C.C.' The following inscription referring to the donor, Sir Benjamin Berry, is pounced round the lip of the cup : 'This sweete berry from benjamin did falle then goode sir benjamin berry it call.'

(4) Silver tazza pounced with the initials I. S. A, and marked with the hall-mark of 1582.

(5) A silver-gilt covered cup surmounted by a female figure. On the bowl is an inscription stating the cup to be the gift of Robert Lee of London, merchant-taylor, and on the cover the legend 'Amieorum beneficia non peribunt.' The hall-mark is of the year 1590–1.

(6) A silver-gilt standing cup and cover bearing the arms of Portsmouth and of the three donors, John Watts, William Bryan, and John Riddlesden, and the legend 'Tres prohibet supra rixarum metuens gratia.'[260] The hall-mark is of 1606.

(7) Silver-gilt standing cup and cover inscribed 'The gift of Thomas Bonner, 1609.'

(8) Silver double salt-cellar, with cover bearing the hall-mark of 1615.

(9) Two small silver wine-cups pounced with the name of the donor, William Haberley, and marked with the hall-mark of 1617. A third somewhat similar cup has the hall-mark of 1618. A modern facsimile of the last was given to the corporation in 1875.

(10) A plain silver cup, having the hall-mark of 1619, and inscribed 'The gift of Elizabeth Ridg, widow, 1629.'

(11) A plain silver cup, 'the gift of James Moray,' marked with the hall-mark of 1625.

(12) A plain silver rose-water salver and ewer, both marked with the hall-mark of 1637, and inscribed 'The gift of John Herman, Esq, deceased, to ye mayor and aldermen. of ye towne of Porstmouth.'

(13) A plain silver salt-cellar marked with the hall-mark of 1665. On the foot is inscribed the name of Edward Silvester.

(14) A plain tankard marked with the hall-mark of 1679, and inscribed 'The gift of Thomas Hancock, alderman, to the corporation of Portsmouth, 1679.'

(15) A plain flagon, with the hall-mark of 1681. Engraved on the front is the inscription 'The gift of Captain Thos. Allin, commander of His Majts ship ye Rubie, to ye corporation of Portsmouth, Anno Domini, 1682.'

(16) A pair of silver-gilt flagons, the gift of Louise, duchess of Portsmouth, in 1683. They bear her arms with the motto 'Abeb. Ent. Lealdet.'

(17) A silver-gilt loving-cup, presented to the corporation by Robert East in 1890.

(18) A silver rose-water dish and ewer, the gift of Alderman Ridoutt to the corporation in the same year.[261]

According to the thirteenth-century custumal of the town, the jurisdiction of the borough extended 'from the Est side of Hambroke[262] to Hasilhorde,[263] and ynward as far as it ebbith an Floweth into the Byrg of Faram ande to Palsgrove as strong as we have hit in Lond yn owre Fraunchise.' Thus the borough claimed jurisdiction over the whole harbour. Proceedings were taken in Chancery in 1435 by John Matthew, deputy to the lord admiral, against the bailiff and burgesses of Portsmouth for assaulting him and preventing him from holding a court in the borough.[264] It appears that on the first attempt to hold an admiralty court there in February, 1434–5, the bailiff showed the deputy a copy of the town charter, which did not satisfy him that the borough was without the jurisdiction of the admiralty, whereupon the bailiff pleaded the town's customs, and begged for respite until the Lord Chancellor's decision as to the meaning of the charter should be known. The deputy agreed, but nevertheless held a court at the water-side some time later, and was interrupted by the bailiff, serjeant, and constables. A struggle ensuing, it was reported that the bailiff was killed, and the whole town came out against the deputy, who had to be escorted to his house by the bailiff's officers. He pathetically complained that in the confusion the king's books were cast to the ground, and that he had 'never yet found a purse of black leather, in which was £13 of gold . . . . and a seal of office.' The same question arose from time to time. In the corporation books of the eighteenth century is an entry recording a request from the vice-admiral of Hampshire for permission to hold a court of admiralty in the town. In acceding to this request, the corporation added a saving clause for their privileges, and asserted the non-precedential nature of the occasion.

In 1822 the question of the right of the corporation to the foreshore and soil of the harbour was raised,[265] but the case was not proceeded with until 1869. In 1877 the cause was heard, but the corporation failed to establish its right, except to that part of the harbour adjacent to the old town.[266]

From a perambulation of the borough and its liberties in 1566,[267] it appears that its jurisdiction extended as far north as a line from Tipner to the Green Post on the London Road, and as far east as the bounds of Copnor, Kingston, and Fratton, while the sea formed the southern boundary. The borough proper was co-extensive with Portsmouth parish, the liberties were part of Portsea parish, the east of Portsea being known as the Gildable.[268] Under the Reform Act of 1832 the Gildable was included in the borough for parliamentary purposes,[269] and three years later the parliamentary boundaries were adopted for municipal purposes,[270] the town being divided at first into six, and later into fourteen wards.[271] Under this arrangement the borough included all the old parishes of Portsmouth and Portsea. In 1895 the small extra-parochial district of Great Salterns was added to it.[272]

In 1295 Portsmouth returned two burgesses to Parliament, viz. Richard de Reynold and Stephen

[260] Horace, Ode III, 19.

[261] A fuller description of the plate and insignia is given in Jewitt and Hope's *Corporation Plate and Insignia*, i, 274.

[262] This has been identified as the morass which formerly existed to the west of Southsea Common.

[263] Haslar, near Gosport.

[264] Early Chan. Proc. bdle. 45, No. 53. The suit must have been brought in 1435 since the date of the chancellorship limits it to 1467–72 or 1433–43. John duke of Bedford, mentioned therein as lord admiral, held that office from 1426 till his death in September, 1435, and the first warrant made out by Matthew was dated February in the thirteenth year of the then king, i.e, 1434–5.

[265] Stuart A. Moore, *Hist. of the Foreshore* (ed. 1888), 450.

[266] Ibid. 555–6.

[267] East, *Extracts from the Portsmouth Rec.* 720.

[268] *Parl. Accts. and Papers*, 1833, xiii, 110.

[269] Stat. 2 & 3 Will. IV, cap. 64.

[270] 5 & 6 Will. IV, cap. 76, schedule A.

[271] *Lond. Gaz.* 10 Dec. 1835; 20 Dec. 1881.

[272] *Pop. Ret. (Hants.)*, 1901, p. 15, note *c*.

Justice,[273] and from that date until the present day it has sent two burgesses to every Parliament with some few exceptions. These occurred chiefly in the fourteenth century, when the bailiffs failed to return burgesses to six several Parliaments.[274] This failure was probably due to the burden of their expenses, which fell upon all the burgesses, for as late as 1597 one representative was paid *2s.* a day during the session of Parliament.[275] The lord of Portsea manor was bound to contribute towards these expenses, since divers of his lands lay within the liberty of the town.[276] It might therefore be concluded that the vote was vested in landholders within the borough; but, so far as can be drawn from the existing returns, the bailiff and burgesses alone had a voice in parliamentary elections. This was the case in 1477–8; in 1572 the mayor, chamberlains, and commonalty of the town elected two burgesses, and in 1584 the election was by the burgesses and freeholders, but with these exceptions the returns were always made by the bailiff, or mayor, and burgesses, until the charter of incorporation granted by Elizabeth, after which they were made by the mayor, aldermen, and burgesses, except in 1688, when the commonalty also voted. In 1695–6, the election of Colonel Gibson and Admiral Aylmer having been contested on the grounds that non-burgesses had been allowed to vote, decision was given in favour of the mayor, aldermen, and burgesses.[277] At a former election the inhabitants of Portsea who paid scot and lot endeavoured to vote, but the gates of the town were shut upon them.[278] During the eighteenth and early nineteenth centuries further difficulties arose respecting non-resident burgesses. The question was finally brought before a committee of the Commons in 1820, and a decision given in favour of the non-residents,[279] but the Reform Act of 1832 gave the vote to householders both in the old borough of Portsmouth and in the parish of Portsea, an arrangement which has not since been altered.[280]

The jurisdiction of the town over the harbour has been the subject of much dispute owing to the early relations between Southampton and Portsmouth. Evidently before the foundation of the town by Richard I the customary dues from ships lading and unlading in what is now known as Portsmouth Harbour were accounted for by the men of Southampton; then, after Richard's charter to Portsmouth, £7 was deducted from the ferm of the former for the pontage and petty customs of Portsmouth.[281] The greater customs were still collected by the men of Southampton, and the customer there accounted for them until the end of the eighteenth century.[282] The port of Portsmouth was named in King John's charter to Southampton. Perhaps from this grant arose a plea between the men of the two towns as to what right the bailiffs of Portsmouth had to take the ferm of their town, which was alleged to belong to Southampton. They asserted that they collected the pontage and other water-dues, of which their ferm consisted, under the sheriff's writ, and denied that the bailiffs of Southampton had any right in their town.[283] Unfortunately no account of the termination of this plea has been found, but in 1239 an agreement was made by which the burgesses of Southampton retained only their rights over the water.[284] Thenceforward the customer of that town collected the greater customs, while the petty customs were retained by the men of Portsmouth, who also had jurisdiction over the whole of the harbour from the western portion of Southsea Common to Haslar and northwards to Fareham Bridge and Paulsgrove.[285] In 1279 a commission was issued to inquire into the alleged exaction of undue customs at Portsmouth, by which the trade of the town had been greatly prejudiced,[286] and again, in 1344, merchants began to abandon the town owing to the double customs exacted, first by the men of Southampton in the port, and then by the bailiffs of Portsmouth in the town, in accordance with letters patent granting them the dues on goods bought and sold there towards building the town walls.[287] In 1432 the men of Newport complained that no deputy customers were appointed in the various havens of Hampshire, and the customers at Southampton were commanded to place deputies at Portsmouth and other harbours for one year.[288] In the fifteenth century the water-toll of Portsmouth was farmed out by the steward of Southampton,[289] and again in 1571 the township petitioned that a deputy-customer might be appointed there 'as in former time,'[290] and in 1602 Portsmouth was named as a member of Southampton,[291] and was still so in 1696, at which date the customer of Southampton reported that it had formerly paid to the king £800 yearly in customs, but had so grown in recent years as to produce £6,000.[292] Nevertheless Portsmouth remained a member of Southampton port till late in the eighteenth or early in the nineteenth century, when it was separated and became itself a port.[293] Its extent, set out in 1852, includes the whole coast-line from the limits of the port of Arundel at Bosham Creek westwards as far as Hill Head, the limit of Southampton port.[294]

It is as a naval station rather than a trading centre that Portsmouth has gained its importance. Before the building of the town the harbour was used as a starting-point for Normandy; the royal treasure was sent there from Winchester for transport,[295] and in 1177 almost all the ships of England were gathered at Portsmouth and Southampton.[296] For two centuries after the town had been founded it was used as a rendezvous for expeditions to Normandy and

[273] *Ret. of M.P.* (1878), i, 5. Owing to the incompleteness of the records between 1265 and 1295 it is impossible at present to state whether the town sent burgesses to Parliament before 1295.

[274] i.e. to those of 1318, 1319, 1322, 1327–8, 1337, 1379–80 and 1384; in some cases also no returns have been found.

[275] *Extracts from the Portsmouth Rec.* 149.

[276] Ibid. 669.

[277] *Commons Journ.* xi, 411.

[278] W. Bohun, *Coll. of Debates touching the Right of Electing Members to Parl.* (ed. 1702), 244.

[279] *Commons Journ.* lxxv, 118, 232, 235, 275.

[280] Stat. 2 & 3 Will. IV, cap. 64.

[281] Pipe R. 6 Ric. I.

[282] Customs Accts. 137/15, 138/1, 138/7.

[283] Cur. Reg. R. 36, m. 2 *d.*

[284] Oak Bk. of Southampton, fol. 28.

[285] *Extracts from the Portsmouth Rec.* 5.

[286] Pat. 7 Edw. I, m. 21 *d.*

[287] *Cal. Pat.* 1343–5, p. 322.

[288] *R. of Parl.* (Rec. Com.), iv, 417.

[289] *Hist. MSS Com. Rep.* xi, App. pt. iii, 135.

[290] *Cal. S.P. Dom.* 1566–99, p. 351. The customer of Southampton was to be consulted as to such an appointment.

[291] Customs Accts. bdle. 146, No. 26.

[292] *Cal. of Treas. Papers,* 1556–1696, p. 554.

[293] Warrants for Customers' Pat. (P.B.), bdles. 1–6. Under the Municipal Reform Act of 1835 all jurisdiction of Southampton within the port of Portsmouth was abolished. See Rev. J. S. Davies, *Hist. of Southampton,* 242.

[294] *Lond. Gaz.* 26 Nov. 1852, p. 3301.

[295] *Pipe R.* (Pipe R. Soc.), xv, 34; xxi, 133; xxvi, 177.

[296] *Gesta Henrici II* (Rolls Ser.), i, 167.

Gascony.[297] King John gathered a fleet of unprecedented size there in 1205. Under Edward III men-at-arms took ship there for Brittany,[298] and in 1416 the French blockaded the English fleet then lying at anchor in the harbour.[299]

King John caused some kind of protection to be made for his ships there during the winter months, for in 1212 he commanded the sheriff of Hampshire to cause the royal basin or dock (*exclusa*) at Portsmouth to be inclosed with a strong wall for the safe-keeping of his ships during the following winter.[300] It appears that the 'basin' here referred to was a pond belonging to the abbey of Fontevrault, probably attached to the mills granted to the abbey by Richard I, in which case it was situated near the present Gun Wharf. Sixteen years after the building of the walls, at the petition of the abbess, Henry III commanded the constable of Rochester to provide wood to fill up the basin and to make another causeway there, notwithstanding that King John had caused walls to be built close by for the protection of his vessels from storms.[301] There was still a royal ship at Portsmouth in 1232 under the custody of Vincent de Hastings,[302] to whom a grant of the 'water of Portsmouth' by King John had been confirmed in March, 1216–17.[303] Probably, therefore, the king's ships continued to have their winter quarters at Portsmouth, though no definite mention of a dock is found before 1495, when Henry VII ordered the construction of a dry dock there.[304] It is said to have been situated near the King's Stairs, i.e. in Portsmouth itself. Throughout the reign of Henry VIII large sums were expended on this dockyard and the storehouses attached, and in 1523 a new dock was rebuilt for the *Henri Grâce à Dieu*.[305] Towards the end of the reign special efforts were made to maintain the importance of the harbour. Sir Anthony Knyvet, governor of the town in 1544, set forth its convenience, since the greatest ships could get in and out at all tides, and it was only one night's sailing from Newhaven, Dieppe, Harfleur, and the Seine.[306] In 1545 a new chain was stretched across the harbour, and the whole fleet concentrated to defend the town;[307] but after the succession of Edward VI Portsmouth fell into comparative insignificance as a naval station, owing to its distance from London.[308] The old dry dock had been filled in before 1627, when Buckingham was earnest in his endeavours to build a new double dock in its place.[309] Unfortunately his death deferred its construction, and, though ships were stationed in the harbour and estimates made for a new dock, the latter was not commenced till 1656.[310] The yard was partly fortified in 1667.[311] Subsequently the docks were extended northwards, many acres being reclaimed from the harbour for this purpose, and their importance increased during the eighteenth and nineteenth centuries with that of the Channel Fleet. Portsmouth from this time has been intimately connected with naval history, notably with the execution of Admiral Byng in 1757, the loss of the *Royal George* in 1782, and the mutiny at Spithead in 1797. The Naval College was established within the dockyard in 1733, and in 1798 a new dock was built to receive ten sail of the line.[312] With the introduction of steam vessels more accommodation was needed, and for this purpose a new steam-basin was opened in 1848.[313] Between that date and 1876 the area of the yard was more than doubled, a large extension including fitting-out, rigging, and repairing basins being opened in 1876.[314] Small additions have been more recently made. The yard now occupies the greater part of the peninsula to the north of Portsmouth, and gives employment to many thousands of men, since it is used for the building and repairing of all kinds of vessels, from the torpedo-destroyer to the largest of our men-of-war.

The position of Portsmouth, favourable as it is for a trading port and naval station, lays the town open to foreign invasion. It was here that Robert of Normandy is said to have landed in 1101, when he sought to wrest the kingdom from his brother Henry,[315] though it is probable that the chroniclers refer to the whole harbour as Portsmouth, and that the actual landing was effected at Portchester.[316] The fortification of such a town was, therefore, of the utmost importance, yet little effort was made to protect it before the fourteenth century. There is, indeed, record of the serjeanty due from William of Cosham in the thirteenth century of providing one man in the 'castle of Portsmouth' in time of war,[317] but the name seems to be either an error of the scribe for Portchester, or to have been given to that castle owing to its position at the head of Portsmouth Harbour. When the town was first founded a house was built there for the king, and ditches were made about its court,[318] but there is no evidence of a royal castle there previous to the fifteenth century. The first assault on the town came, however, not from the Continent, but from the barons of the Cinque Ports. In 1216 they had served as allies with the men of Portsmouth in aiding the Dauphin against King John,[319] but in the succeeding reign both the men of Portsmouth and Southampton suffered grievously from the violence of the barons, who seized cargoes on their way to Portsmouth and transferred them to their own ships, and refused to allow the bailiffs to enter their vessels to buy wine.[320] In 1265 the barons of the Cinque Ports, joining in the political struggles of that date, and doubtless inspired with no good feeling against a prosperous port in their immediate neighbourhood, landed in force at Portsmouth, slew some of the men who had gathered

[297] On the Patent and Close Rolls of Hen. III, Edw. I, Edw. II, and Edw. III, are numerous commands to the men of various ports to send vessels to Portsmouth.

[298] *Cal. Close*, 1343–6, p. 570.

[299] Capgrave, *Hist. of the Henries* (Rolls Ser.), i, 119.

[300] *Rot. Lit. Claus.* i, 117.

[301] *Cal. Close*, 1227–31, p. 32.

[302] Ibid. 1231–4, p. 28.

[303] *Rot. Lit. Claus.* i, 302*b*.

[304] For a full description of this dock see M. Oppenheim, *Accts. and Invent. of Hen. VII*, 143–60.

[305] *L. and P. Hen. VIII*, iii (2), 2935.

[306] Ibid. xx (2), 719.

[307] *Acts of P.C.* (New Ser.), i, 253.

[308] See M. Oppenheim, *Administration of the Royal Navy*, i, 297 et seq.

[309] *Cal. S.P. Dom.* 1627–8, p. 210.

[310] Ibid. 1634–5, p. 449; *Hist. MSS. Com. Rep.* xii, App. i, 388; *Administration of the Royal Navy*, i, 299.

[311] *Cal. S.P. Dom.* 1666–7, p. 590.

[312] *Gent. Mag.* lxviii, 620.

[313] Ibid. (New Ser.), xxx, 32.

[314] Ibid. xxx, 82.

[315] *Anglo-Saxon Chron.* (Rolls Ser.), i, 365; Capgrave, *Hist. of the Henries* (Rolls Ser.), i, 54.

[316] Cf. Freeman, *Reign of William Rufus*, ed. 1882, ii, 405.

[317] *Testa de Nevill* (Rec. Com.), 417; *Red Book of the Exch.* (Rolls Ser.), 459.

[318] See above.

[319] *Rot. Lit. Pat.* i, 196.

[320] *Hist. MSS. Com. Rep.* xi, App. iii, 40. Consequently the bailiffs and men were for five years released from payment of ferm on account of the damages and losses sustained by them for the king during the late disturbances (*Cal. Close*, 1272–9, p. 270).

together in defence of the port, put the rest to flight, and finally burnt the town.[321] Some years later an affray in the Isle of Wight, though it did not closely affect the town, must have caused no little excitement there. In 1293 some English sailors set upon certain men of Bayonne and slew them, mistaking them for Spaniards. It was in Portsmouth Church that they swore to their mistake, and bound themselves to provide three chaplains at Portsmouth and three at Bayonne to pray for the souls of the slain.[322] The defenceless state of the town is well shown by its fate during the Hundred Years' War. Early in 1338 some ships and galleys which were reported to have come from Normandy landed on the south coast and plundered and burnt the towns and villages near Southampton and Portsmouth, all the latter town save only the parish church and the Domus Dei being destroyed by fire.[323] The king, having compassion on the misery of the townspeople, pardoned them the triennial tenth and fifteenth then due,[324] and in the following year gave them respite from the exaction of wool.[325] These concessions were extended from time to time;[326] in 1339 efforts were made to strengthen the defences of the town, and the commissioners of array for the guard of the sea in Oxfordshire were charged to increase their payment for this purpose in order to provide a man-at-arms and two archers to do guard at Portsmouth.[327] In 1342 further steps were taken to protect the town, which had offered no resistance to the first French attack.[328] In that year townsmen were released from payment of all tallages and contributions to the king on condition that they applied the contingent due from them in walling and fortifying the town, this work being under the sheriff's supervision.[329] An order was also sent to the sheriff to cause the king's grant to be proclaimed, and to permit the men of Portsmouth to levy customs in their town for the purpose of walling and paving it.[330] This last grant, however, proved more hindrance than help, for when merchants discovered that they must pay dues to the burgesses of Portsmouth on selling their goods in the town, as well as custom to the men of Southampton on entering the port, they took their merchandise elsewhere, so that two years after the grant of this doubtful privilege the townsmen petitioned for its reversal.[331]

After the renewal of hostilities with France in 1369 the town was again burned by the enemy, whereupon the impoverished inhabitants petitioned for respite from the payment of ferm,[332] and after inquisition had been made on the subject they were released from payment for ten years.[333] The town is said to have been again assaulted and plundered by the French expedition which, under Jean de Vien, ravaged the south coast in 1377.[334] There is a tradition that it was again attacked in 1380.

The necessity for strong fortifications having been thus forcibly proved, Thomas earl of Kent, Nicholas Sharnesfield, knight of the chamber, and Robert Cholmelegh, king's esquire, were appointed to survey Portsmouth and take order for its defence in 1386,[335] and in 1421 Robert Barbot was clerk of the king's works there.[336] Within the three following years he received over £690 for works about the town. These included the erection of a new tower 'for the safe custody of the king's ships,' and the construction of a wharf at 'Chiderodd' as a foundation for another new tower.[337] No record of any former tower is at present forthcoming, but from the wording of Robert Barbot's account it might be inferred that the tower built by him took the place of an older one, perhaps built after the survey of 1386.[338] Robert Thorpe accounted for repairs about the 'castles' of Portchester and Portsmouth from 1441 to 1443.[339] One of these towers was still standing in 1483, when it was mentioned in the grant of the government of the town to John le Moyne.[340] It was doubtless identical with the round tower which is shown at the mouth of the harbour on a plan of the time of Henry VIII.[341]

In 1513 special instructions were given to the earl of Arundel for the keeping of the tower and block-houses at Portsmouth,[342] and at about this date a large storehouse was built and the old brew-houses were repaired.[343] Nevertheless in 1518 Fox, then bishop of Winchester, wrote to Wolsey: 'If war be intended against England the Isle of Wight and Portsmouth are too feeble for defence. Our manner is never to prepare for war to our enemies be light at our doors.'[344] A few years later, in accordance with further advice from the bishop urging that Portsmouth and the Isle of Wight should be provided with artillery, 'for if they be lords of the sea Calais will never be lost,'[345] ten ships were engaged in carrying ordnance to Portsmouth.[346] Still, in 1526 the town was 'in sore ruin and decay,'[347] and when in 1538 a vessel from Southampton, pursued by four French ships, ran aground beside Palshyds Bulwarks, the ordnance of the town was out of order and the Frenchmen boarded and carried off their prize unresisted.[348] In the following year new ramparts and fortifications were well advanced owing to fear of a French war,[349] but two years later the hastily-built ramparts were 'clean fallen down' and the king so annoyed that he went in person to direct how they should be rebuilt.[350] In 1544 Sir Anthony Knyvet, then governor of the town, petitioned for more men to defend it, stating that whereas there had formerly been a hundred gunners there, there were latterly only fifty, besides four or five hundred bakers and brewers and also labourers repairing the wall, and reinforcement would be difficult in time of war owing to the single approach to the island over Portsea Bridge.[351] In 1545 arose

321 *Ann. Mon. Worcester* (Rolls Ser.), iv, 456.
322 *Cal. Close*, 1288–96, p. 324.
323 Thos. Walsingham, *Hist. Angl.* (Rolls Ser.), i, 200.
324 *Cal. Close*, 1337–9, p. 406.
325 Ibid. 1339–41, p. 102.
326 Ibid. 1339–41, p. 476; 1341–3, p. 699.
327 *Parl. R.* ii, 111*b*. These men should have been supplied by the prior and canons of Bicester.
328 *Cal. Pat.* 1338–40, p. 180.
329 Ibid. 1340–3, p. 563.
330 *Cal. Close*, 1341–3, p. 603.
331 *Cal. Pat.* 1343–5, p. 322.
332 Pat. 43 Edw. III, pt. 2, m. 22 *d.*
333 *Cal. Pat.* 1377–81, p. 313.
334 Froissart, *Chron.* translated by Thomas Johnes, ii, 181; Pipe R. 2 Ric. II, m. 2*a*.
335 *Cal. Pat.* 1385–9, p. 214.
336 Ibid. 1422–9, p. 68.
337 Foreign Accts. 10 Hen. VI, H.
338 Barbot accounts for £50 'pro constructione cuiusdam Nove Turris de avisamento eiusdem nuper Regis (Henry V), apud Portsmouth *de novo* construende.'
339 Foreign Accts. 21 Hen. VI, A.
340 *Cal. Pat.* 1476–85, p. 339.
341 Printed in *Extracts from Portsmouth Rec.*
342 *L. and P. Hen. VIII*, i, p. 973.
343 Ibid. p. 960.
344 Ibid. ii (2), 3952.
345 Ibid. iii, 2207.
346 Ibid. 2916.
347 Ibid. iv, 2123.
348 Ibid. xiii (1), 485.
349 Ibid. xiv (1), 1091.
350 Ibid. xv, 533.
351 Ibid. xx (2), 719.

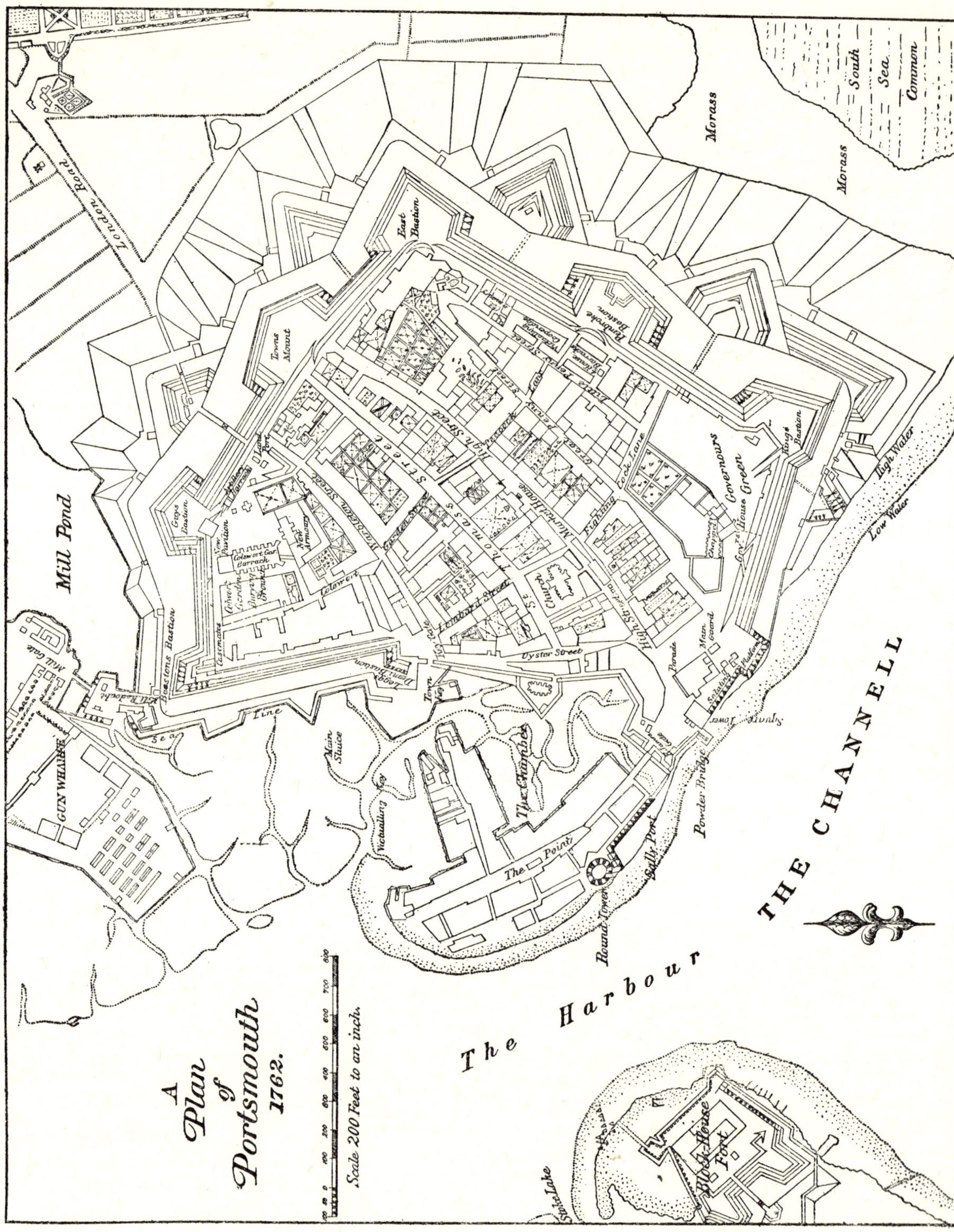

Reproduced by Henry Lewis, 114 High Street, Portsmouth—1890—from a copy in the possession of R. East Esq.

another alarm of attack; the council met there to consider its defence, artillery from the Tower of London was sent thither, the whole navy gathered for its defence, and four of the inhabitants were appointed to watch nightly with the soldiers.[352] In the following year plans were made for the partial inclosure of the town with ramparts of turf and a ditch, and for the protection of the wharves with mounds of earth,[353] but in 1559 Portsmouth was reported to be 'nothing strong' and a man could gallop his horse up the ditch,[354] and this in spite of many plans for its defence in the preceding years.[355] In June, 1557, a terrible fire broke out and destroyed the royal storehouse known as the Broomehouse.[356] During the latter part of Queen Elizabeth's reign the work of fortification went on apace under the direction of Sir Henry Radcliffe, then governor of the town. A commission was issued to assemble and train the townsmen and islanders,[357] and an estimate made for the building of a 'new great bridge' and gates to the town,[358] the work being done by labourers levied from the country round.[359] In 1587 the inhabitants were ordered to cut down all hedges within forty or fifty yards of the town walls.[360] At this date it was considered that a thousand men could hold the town until the navy could come to their aid,[361] but in 1590 able men to the number of 2,000 were appointed in fourteen neighbouring hundreds to be ready to repair thither in case of assault.[362] Again in 1596 special preparations were made to resist a threatened attack from Spain.[363] In 1624 the ramparts were severely damaged in a great storm.[364] A few years later the town was filled with the men levied for the duke of Buckingham's expedition,[365] yet the fort itself was in ruins.[366] In 1634 it was proposed to remove the old town wall,[367] and three years later the townsmen were commanded to cover all houses near the king's buildings with tiles instead of thatch as a precaution against fire.[368] The chain which had been laid across the harbour in 1621, was by this time destroyed.[369] It has since been replaced, for it can still be seen at low tide.

The strength of the town was tried during the civil wars. It being the policy of the Parliamentarians to secure for themselves the chief maritime towns, they were necessarily anxious to make sure of Portsmouth, and the more so that it was reported in May, 1641, that the queen was besieged there, while the king himself was said to be on his way thither with the army.[370] Colonel George Goring, then governor of Portsmouth, was suspected of complicity in a plot to possess the Papists of the town, and was sent to London to be examined before Parliament, where he succeeded in justifying his conduct. The soldiers themselves not being trusted, trained bands from the county, which was for the most part inclined to favour the Parliamentarians, were sent into the town.[371] The townspeople were very ill-disposed towards the governor owing to his royalist principles. There had also been a growing feeling of dissension between the garrison and the townsfolk for many years past. As early as January, 1546–7, Edward Vaughan, then captain of Portsmouth, had brought a complaint against the mayor touching the gauge of beer,[372] and in 1564 a quarrel arose between the corporation and the governor as to houses which the latter had built on waste land.[373] Irritation increased under the government of the earl of Sussex, captain of Portsmouth from 1571 to 1593, who caused the townsmen to cut down the hedges near the walls. They welcomed his successor, 'thinking his coming amongst them to be their year of jubilee, and having now some hope to grow rich, which heretofore was impossible by reason of the great dislike between them and the dead earl.'[374] Again in 1609 the mayor and his brethren petitioned the governor, the earl of Pembroke, for more liberty of ingress and egress, for equal benefits of the law with the soldiers, for special provisions for the relief of poor soldiers and their families, and that members of the garrison should not be allowed to trade in the town.[375] The governor acceded to most of these requests, but the soldiers again raised the question of the trading privilege in 1627 (*vide supra*), while in 1632 the mayor and aldermen objected to the removal of the wall between the Quay Gate and the Square Tower,[376] and further difficulties arose with regard to the mayor's having assessed the garrison as well as the town for ship-money. The sergeant-major then in command complained at this time that the townspeople had always shown themselves 'like most splenetive men' to the garrison.[377] In 1635 the townsmen recited the concessions made by the earl of Pembroke, and stated that they had been confirmed by the king in 1632, but complained that they had since been broken, their chief grievance being that the soldiers traded within the town.[378] The dislike of the townsfolk to Colonel Goring was increased by political considerations.[379] He stood by the Parliament until they had paid him over £5,000 for fortifications and other sums for arrears due to the garrison,[380] and these having been received, declared for the king on 2 August, 1642,[381] whereupon the gentry of Hampshire surrounded the town to prevent aid reaching him from the king, while Parliament appointed the earl of Pembroke governor in his stead.[382] Having built a wooden fort to protect Portsbridge and commandeered provisions from the whole island, Colonel Goring administered an oath of loyalty to the king to his soldiers, and ejected those who refused to take it.[383]

352 *Acts of P.C.* (New Ser.), i, 215, 253, 322.
353 *Hist. MSS. Com. Rep. on Salisbury MSS.* i, E. 49.
354 Ibid. 159.
355 *Cal. S.P. Dom.* 1547–80, pp. 2, 82, 100–2.
356 Add. MS. 5752, fol. 62.
357 *Cal. S.P. Dom.* 1566–7, p. 350.
358 Ibid. 1581–90, p. 186.
359 Add. MS. 5702, fol. 85.
360 *Acts of P.C.* (New Ser.), xv, 279.
361 Ibid. xvi, 174.
362 Ibid. xix, 255.
363 *Cal. S.P. Dom.* 1595–7, pp. 303–4.
364 Ibid. 1623–5, p. 352.
365 Ibid. 1627–8, pp. 157, 162, 181, &c.
366 Ibid. 95.
367 Ibid. 1634–5, p. 449.
368 Ibid. 1637, p. 226.
369 *L. and P. Hen. VIII*, iii (2), 2073; *Cal. S.P. Dom.* 1640, p. 188.
370 Ibid. 1640–1, p. 585.
371 Ibid. 1641–3, p. 179; *Hist. MSS. Com. Rep.* iv, App. 295.
372 *Acts of P.C.* (New Ser.), i, 568.
373 Ibid. vii, 190, 207, and 234. The matter was determined in favour of the corporation, the governor paying them rent for the houses built on their waste lands. East, *Extracts from the Portsmouth Rec.* 432, &c.
374 *Hist. MSS. Com. Rep. on Salisbury MSS.* iv, 440.
375 Add. MS. 33283, fol. 85. A copy of the townspeople's petition and the earl's answer lent to Sir F. Madden.
376 *Cal. S.P. Dom.* 1631–3, p. 366.
377 Ibid. 1634–5, p. 487; 1635–6, p. 12.
378 Ibid. 1635, p. 574.
379 Ibid. 1641–3, p. 179.
380 *Hist. MSS. Com. Rep.* v, App. 34.
381 Ibid. 161.
382 B.M. Pamphlets, E. 112 (2), *The King's Resolution Concerning Portsmouth.*
383 B.M. Pamphlets, E. 117 (10), *A Declaration of all the Passages at the taking of Portsmouth.*

Before 16 August he was forced to abandon the wooden fort at the bridge, which was at once seized by the Parliamentary adherents of the neighbourhood.[384] The king's ships, which had declared for Parliament, prevented stores being brought in, and early in September the batteries from Gosport opened fire upon the town [385] and Southsea Castle surrendered without a blow. The majority of the soldiers, finding that no help came from the king, took part with the town in opposing all further resistance, and the officers were obliged to surrender on 4 September.[386]

The work of fortification was subsequently continued by Parliament.[387] In 1648 the garrison petitioned for the trial of the king,[388] but their pay was still in arrears, and £6,000 was needed for the repair of the fortifications to prevent the tower at the harbour mouth from falling into the sea.[389] In 1660 the town stood for Parliament against the army.[390] In 1665 a new plan for the fortifications of the town made by Sir Bernard de Gomme was carried out by Dutch prisoners of war.[391] The king himself visited these new works in September 1668,[392] and the lands acquired for this purpose were vested in him and his successors two years later.[393]

New barracks were built in 1688 at a time when they were most grievously needed, for the inhabitants were overburdened with the number of soldiers quartered upon them.[394] Nevertheless the townspeople remained loyal, and in 1690 prepared to raise five companies of foot should they be needed.[395] Early in the eighteenth century more land was purchased for the fortifications of Portsea,[396] and in 1748 the town was secured from attack by land by the raising of works round the dockyards and gun-wharf. At this time the ancient town of Portsmouth, i.e. that part which lies entirely within the south-western corner of Portsea Island, was completely surrounded by earthworks, the ramparts being strengthened at the angles by King's Bastion, Pembroke Bastion, and East Bastion, all looking over what was then a morass between the town and Southsea Common, Town's Mount, and Guy's Bastion facing inland, and Beeston's Bastion at the corner of what is now the new gun wharf, but was then below water. The Point, protected by its round tower, was without the town, access to it being gained through King James's Gate. This with King William's Gate, Quay Gate, and Lion Gate, the last being the entrance to Portsea, has been destroyed, but the Landport or St. George's Gate has been removed to form the entrance to the recreation ground, while the old Unicorn Gate is one of the entrances to the Dockyard.[397]

The town walls were demolished between the years 1871 and 1878.[398] The present line of fortifications extends along the coast, a part of the old ramparts remaining near Governor's Green. The most southerly point of the island is guarded by Southsea Castle, a formidable building within a strong high wall partly surrounded by a deep fosse, and flanked by two batteries. The first castle was built before 1547, in which year a stone platform was raised, and the neighbouring bulwarks of earth strengthened.[399] It was possibly identical with the Southampton Castle of Portsmouth to which John Chalderton was appointed captain in 1555.[400] A plan of the castle of this date shows it to have been a square fort within diamond-shaped walls, flanked by two platforms.[401] In 1627 this building was burnt to the ground, the woodwork of the chimney having first caught fire.[402] At the time of the fire there were neither guns, men, nor powder in the castle,[403] and two years later the captain of Southsea complained that it was 'a castle where is neither house nor lodging, to guard a fort that is unprovided for defence or offence.' [404] It was rebuilt in 1634,[405] but the lodgings and storerooms were again burnt down in March 1639–40.[406] Its surprise and capture by the Parliamentarians during the siege of Portsmouth in 1642 rendered the town untenable.[407] Towards the end of the century it was used as a state prison,[408] and was under the control of the governor of Portsmouth.[409] Beyond the castle are the Eastney Batteries overlooking the Channel, and behind them a well-kept road leads past the military church, known on account of its shape as the 'Crinoline Church,' towards the Eastney Barracks. The church has recently been replaced by a large red-brick building on the Henderson Road farther inland.

The military governor of Portsmouth at first held also the office of governor of Portchester Castle.[410] It appears that in early times the latter was *ex officio* governor of Portsmouth, but during the troubled years when the town was burnt by the French, separate captains were appointed to the two places with full power to rule and punish all the men of the towns and their neighbourhoods as well as men-at-arms, hobelers and archers, and to hold an array there in order to resist the enemy.[411] A saving clause for the jurisdiction of the governor was inserted in the later charters of the town. After the reign of Henry VIII the office was not always granted with the constableship of Portchester, though the two were occasionally held together.[412] Since 1834 a lieutenant-governor has ruled the town. Governor's Green, an open turfed space forming the south-east corner of Portsmouth town and protected towards the sea by part of the old town ramparts, is the site of the old governor's house, which has been

384 B.M. Pamphlets, E. 112 (34), *An exact Relation of Fourteen Days' Passages at Portsmouth.*

385 *Hist. MSS. Com. Rep.* xiii, App. i, 55.

386 Ibid. *Rep.* x, App. vi, 149.

387 Ibid. *Rep.* xiii, App. i, 184; *Cal. S.P. Dom.* 1644, p. 357; 1644–5, pp. 244, 290, 321.

388 B. M. Pamphlets, 669, fol. 13 (71). *To the . . . Commons House of Engl. the humble Petition of the Officers and Soldiers of Portsmouth.*

389 *Cal. S.P. Dom.* 1652–3, p. 171.

390 Ibid. 1659–60, p. 281; Sloane MS. 970, fol. 6.

391 *Cal. S.P. Dom.* 1664–5, pp. 510, 515.

392 Ibid. 1667–8, p. 582.

393 Portsmouth Fortification Bill. See *Hist. MSS. Com. Rep.* ix, App. ii, 5.

394 Ibid. *Rep.* xi, App. 5, p. 242; *Rep.* vii, 420.

395 *Cal. S.P. Dom.* 1690–1, pp. 41, 56, and 58.

396 Petty Bag. Spec. Com. bdle. 18; Pat. 8 Anne, i, 4; 1 Geo. I, i, 6.

397 Information kindly given by Mr. W. H. Saunders; cf. the plan of the town in 1762.

398 Information kindly supplied by Mr. W. H. Saunders.

399 *Hist. MSS. Com. Rep. on Salisbury MSS.* i, E. 49.

400 Memo. R. (Exch. L. T. R.), East. 1 Mary, 'Recorda,' m. 42.

401 S.P. Dom. Eliz. cxv, 39.

402 *Hist. MSS. Com. Rep.* xii, App. i, 299 and 301.

403 *Cal. S.P. Dom.* 1627–8, p. 122.

404 Ibid. 1628–9, p. 411.

405 Ibid. 1634–5, p. 454.

406 Ibid. 1640, p. 173.

407 *Hist. MSS. Com. Rep.* x, App. vi, 149.

408 Ibid. *Rep.* iv, App. i, 279; *Cal. S.P. Dom.* 1663–4, pp. 532 and 546.

409 *Hist. MSS. Com. Rep.* xi, App. v, 281.

410 Cf. the list of governors printed in *Extracts from the Portsmouth Records*, 635.

411 Pat. 43 Edw. III, pt. 2, m. 22.

412 For instance Viscount Wimbledon held both offices in 1630 (*Cal. S.P. Dom.* 1629–31, p. 336), and Colonel Tollemache in 1690 (ibid. 1690–1, p. 180).

replaced by a modern building standing in its own grounds near Cambridge Road. On the green stands the *GARRISON CHURCH*, a building of very great historical and architectural interest, which after a somewhat chequered career is now most efficiently cared for and maintained. It has a vaulted chancel of three bays with north vestries, and a nave with aisles of five bays, the chancel having been the chapel, and the nave the living-rooms of the hospital of St. John Baptist and St Nicholas,[413] otherwise known as *Domus Dei*, or God's House, founded by Bishop Peter des Roches of Winchester (1205–1238) shortly before 1214. It was brought to its present condition, after various repairs mentioned below, by a thorough renovation and refitting in 1866 under Street. The chancel is lighted by triplets of lancets on north and south, and three trefoiled lancets on the east, and is covered with a quadripartite ribbed vault springing from clustered wall shafts which stop on the moulded string running at the level of the window-sills. In the south-west angle of the chancel is a small doorway leading to an octagonal stair turret which gives access to the roof over the vault, and the middle bay on the north of the chancel is taken up by a modern organ chamber, with a vestry added to the east. The nave arcades, the western bay of which is entirely modern, are very finely proportioned, with lofty pointed arches of two chamfered orders on octagonal pillars with moulded capitals and bases. The roof originally stretched in one span over nave and aisles, the outer walls of the latter having been heightened in modern times and two-light windows of fourteenth-century style inserted, but parts of the older and thicker walls are still to be seen, being best preserved at the south-east angle. The south doorway is in the west bay of the south aisle, and with the south porch and west front of the nave is entirely modern. Attached to the pillars in the nave are the colours of the 7th Royal Fusiliers, of the Scinde Camel Corps placed in the church in memory of General Sir Charles Napier, and of the 67th (South Hampshire) Regiment.

After the surrender of the hospital in 1540 it was handed over to the military authorities, and for a time the church was used for the storing of armour, while the rest of the building was used as the governor's house.[414] In 1582 plans were made for its repair, two of the arches being in ruin, while there was a breach 50 ft. long in the wall of the house.[415] The latter was again repaired in 1644;[416] in it took place the marriage of Charles II and Catherine of Portugal, and the allied sovereigns lodged there in 1814. The whole building except the church was demolished in 1826.[417]

Without the town, i.e. outside what was once the walled town of Portsmouth, lies the extensive parish of *PORTSEA*, which includes Kingston, Buckland, Stubbington, Stamshaw, Fratton, Copnor, Milton, Eastney, and Southsea. All these are now within the municipal borough of Portsmouth, but before the Reform Act of 1835 only a part of Portsea was within the liberty of Portsmouth, while the remainder of the parish, known as the Gildable, was included in the hundred of Portsdown.[418] The men of the Gildable were accustomed to do watch and ward without the town,[419] and had a separate constable.[420] Buckland, Copnor, and Fratton are assigned to Portsdown Hundred in the Domesday Book, but this was before the existence of Portsmouth borough. Stamshaw was certainly within the liberty of Portsmouth,[421] while Kingston, which was apparently included in the borough in 1194, is mentioned separately on the Pipe Roll of 1198.[422] In 1606 Richard Earnley of Gatcombe, whose hall lay in Hilsea, while his parlour was in Portsea parish, had to do service for the Portsea half of his house at Southsea Castle.[423]

The town of Portsea stands on the former site of Portsmouth Common, and took its present name in 1792.[424] The streets are narrow, and the houses for the most part low, with tiled roofs and doors approached by two steps from the street. Some of the lowest houses are still known as 'garrison houses,' because, it is said, the inhabitants were not allowed to build them higher lest they should interfere with the outlook from the old fortifications. Still narrower, ill-paved alleys intersect the town in its poorest parts. The high walls of the dockyard bound it on two sides, while along the third runs the Hard, a roadway leading by the harbour-side to the main gates of the yard. The Portsea Extension Railway connects the town station with the harbour, where a new station was built on a pier in 1876. Facing the harbour is a row of houses, chiefly taverns, where the sailors used to be paid off, while on the wooden seats opposite watermen wait to take visitors to Nelson's flagship, the *Victory*, or round the harbour. Following the dockyard wall Queen Street is reached. It is the main thoroughfare of Portsea, and is lined with single-windowed shops stocked with goods to suit the needs of sailors and dockyard men. Indeed, it is to the docks that Portsea owes its origin, and this appears most clearly in the names of the streets, which date from the beginning of the eighteenth century. Queen Street itself was named after Queen Anne, as appears from a legend on one of the houses there, and the names Marlborough Road and Orange Street are significant of the date of the town. Defoe described it as a suburb, or rather a new town, which promised to outdo Portsmouth as to the number of inhabitants and the beauty of the buildings, especially as it was unencumbered by the laws of the garrison and the town duties and services.[424a] Complaints of encroachments on the town common were frequent after about 1690,[425] when it is said to have been an open field with one hovel upon it; but by 1775 it was closely built with houses for the dockyard-men,[426] and the population increased with great rapidity as the dockyard rose in importance. In 1764 an Act was passed for the better paving and cleansing of the common,[427] and under a new Act for the same purpose, passed in 1792, the town was first named Portsea.[428] The lighting and paving have since been transferred to the Portsmouth authorities.

413 *Cal. of Close*, 1288–96, p. 439.
414 *Hist. MSS. Com. Rep.* iv, App. 207.
415 Lansd. MS. 31, fol. 178. Mention is here made of the hall, kitchen, and dining-chamber.
416 *Cal. S.P. Dom.* 1644, p. 179.
417 *Story of the Domus Dei*, by Archdeacon Wright.
418 *Parl. Accts. and Papers*, 1835, xxiv, 811.
419 *Acts of P. C.* (New Ser.), i, 322.
420 *L. and P. Hen. VIII*, xiii (1), 859.
421 Chan. Inq. p.m. 20 Edw. I, 15.
422 Pipe R. 9 Ric. I.
423 Exch. Dep. Mich. 4 Jas. I, 24.
424 Stat. 32 Geo. III, cap. 103.
424a Defoe, *Journ* (ed. 1778).
425 *Extracts from the Portsmouth Rec.* 85 et seq.
426 *The Portsmouth Guide*, 1775, p. 39.
427 Stat. 4 Geo. III, cap. 92.
428 Ibid. 32 Geo. III, cap. 103.

The fortifications of Portsmouth were extended in the eighteenth century to surround Portsea, but were so formed that the borough and its suburb were two walled towns adjacent to each other. The Portsea lines were complete in 1809.[429]

Long before the town of Portsea had come into existence there was a manor of that name in the island, a large portion of which was demesne land of the manor. The manor or court-house has long since disappeared.[430]

PORTSEA MANOR is not distinctly mentioned in the Domesday survey of Hampshire. From the fact that it was held by later tenants of the fee of the successors of Hugh de Port it may be concluded that in 1086 it was then considered as part of Hugh's possessions in Buckland (q.v.). The actual tenants in the twelfth century took their name from the manor. Baldwin of Portsea gave a virgate of land in Porteswald (Portswood) to the abbey of Quarr in the Isle of Wight.[431] This Baldwin in 1166 was holding two knights' fees of John de Port and forfeited half a mark in 1167–8 on the non-appearance of an alleged murderer for whom he had become bail.[432] It was he who in 1170 granted the church of Portsea to Southwick. He had also granted a virgate in Fratton with his two tenants William and Ernulf and their children, and firebote and hedgebote in Portswood, to the monks of Sherborne for the welfare of the souls of Henry de Port and his wife Hawise, and of his own soul and those of his wife Adelis and his parents. To this gift the overlord, John de Port, son of Henry, gave his consent.[433] Baldwin of Portsea evidently died childless, for he was succeeded by his brother Payne before 1189. The latter confirmed his brother's gift to Quarr Abbey, and exchanged his demesne lands at 'Leuchestoche' with the monks for half a virgate at Copnor.[434] Payne of Portsea had a son Adam, who may possibly have been identical with the Adam of Portsea who was justice in assize for Hampshire in 1218,[435] and accounted for the fifteenth levied in the county in 1226.[436] In 1230 Adam of Portsea witnessed a charter in conjunction with his eldest son Andrew and the whole borough-moot of Portsmouth[437]; Andrew was still living six years later,[438] and was probably the father or grandfather of Richard of Portsea, who came into prominence at the latter end of the thirteenth century. In March, 1302–3, he obtained a grant of free warren in his demesne lands of Portsea.[439] In 1310 he was one of those appointed to arrange a loan of victuals to the king for his expedition to Scotland,[440] and in 1315 was a commissioner of array.[441]

De Port. *Barry azure and argent a saltire gules.*

At his death, which took place before 21 December, 1318, he was said to hold the manor of Portsea of Sir John de St. John (a descendant of Hugh de Port), by service of a knight's fee.[442] His sister and heir, Alice Loveraz, was then aged 50. In 1322 she conveyed the manor, together with the reversion of the dower in it held by Scolastica, her brother's widow, to Robert Halsted in exchange for an annuity of 100 marks for life.[443] Halsted immediately obtained a renewal of the grant of free warren in the demesne lands,[444] but apparently failed to pay the annuity.[445] Consequently the manor reverted to Alice Loveraz, who nevertheless settled the remainder of it at her death on Robert Halsted and his wife Nichola in tail male, with contingent remainders to Nicholas son of Ralph de Crophull and his wife Margery, and to the right heirs of Robert.[446] Evidently Robert and Nichola died without male issue, for in 1346 Nicholas Crophull was in possession of the manor.[447] From him and his wife it passed, presumably by deed of gift,[448] to Sir Richard Willoughby,[449] who conveyed it first to William Willoughby, clerk, and other trustees,[450] and later to John Edindon, to whom Nicholas and Margery de Crophull made quitclaim.[451] Edindon's trustees granted it in June, 1373, to the abbey of Titchfield to find a lamp to burn every day before the high altar at high mass.[452] During the abbot's possession a dispute arose between him and the lord of Chalton manor as to the bounds of Portsea Sewood; it was, therefore, agreed that trenches should be made between the woods of the two lords, i.e. from the way called 'Strogetway' to a certain pasture called Stubbs.[453]

In 1537 the manor was surrendered to the crown together with the other possessions of Titchfield Abbey,[454] and with them was immediately granted to Thomas Wriothesley, afterwards earl of Southampton,[455] whose political influence was thus strengthened in Portsmouth, for two years later he wrote to Cromwell, 'For Portsmouth I intend John Chadreton to be one (burgess), and for his fellow and for the burgess of Midhurst I will furnish honest men.'[456] The earl was succeeded at Portsea by his son Henry,[457] whose eldest son Henry sold it in 1598 to Robert Bold of Idsworth,[458] who was mayor of Portsmouth in 1613.[459] He died in December, 1626,[460] having settled Portsea on his son William in tail male with contingent remainder to William's brother Henry.

[429] *The New Portsmouth Guide*, 1865.

[430] *Extracts from the Portsmouth Rec.* 665.

[431] Add. Chart. 15687. The abbot paid 2*s.* rent to the town of Portsmouth in 1469; East, *Portsmouth Records*, 493.

[432] *Red Bk. of Exch.* (Rolls Ser.), 208; *Pipe R.* 14 *Hen. II* (Pipe R. Soc.), xiv, 183.

[433] *Hist. MSS. Com. Rep.* iv. App. 453.

[434] Add. Chart. 15687. For this charter the abbey gave him 20*s.* and a fowl, and another fowl to his son Adam.

[435] *Cal. Pat.* 1216–25, p. 147.

[436] *Rot. Lit. Claus.* (Rec. Com.), i, 147.

[437] Chart. R. 14 Hen. III, pt. 2, m. 5.

[438] Feet of F. Hants, 20 Hen. III, 189.

[439] Chart. R. 31 Edw. I, m. 96.

[440] *Cal. Close*, 1307–13, p. 264.

[441] *Cal. Pat.* 1313–17, p. 350.

[442] Chan. Inq. p. m. 12 Edw. II, 44.

[443] Feet of F. Hants, 16 Edw. II, 32.

[444] Chart. R. 15 Edw. II, m. 5.

[445] Orig. R. 1 Edw. III, 36.

[446] Feet of F. Hants, 2 Edw. III, 10.

[447] *Feud. Aids*, ii, 335.

[448] In East's *Extracts from the Portsmouth Rec.* p. 663, is quoted a memorandum from a Court Book of Portsea stating that Nicholas and Margery gave the manor to 'Richard Willey.' It appears that the whole transaction was a gift to Titchfield Abbey, not by Willoughby or Edindon, but by the Crophulls.

[449] Chan. Inq. p.m. 26 Edw. III (2nd nos.), 28.

[450] Feet of F. Hants, 29 Edw. III, 4.

[451] Ibid. 30 Edw. III, 8, 9.

[452] Chan. Inq. p.m. 47 Edw. III (2nd nos.), 36. The abbot and convent paid £80 for licence to receive the grant; *Abbrev. Rot. Orig.* (Rec. Com.) ii, 328.

[453] *Extracts from the Portsmouth Rec.* 665.

[454] Feet of F. Hants, Mich. 29 Hen. VIII.

[455] *L. and P. Hen. VIII*, xii, 1311 (40).

[456] Ibid. xiv (1), 520.

[457] Chan. Inq. p.m. (Ser. 2), vol. 92, No. 78.

[458] Close, 40 Eliz. pts. 14 and 15 (no membranes marked).

[459] *Extracts from Portsmouth Rec.* 157, 313.

[460] Chan. Inq. p.m. (Ser. 2), vol. 426, No. 90.

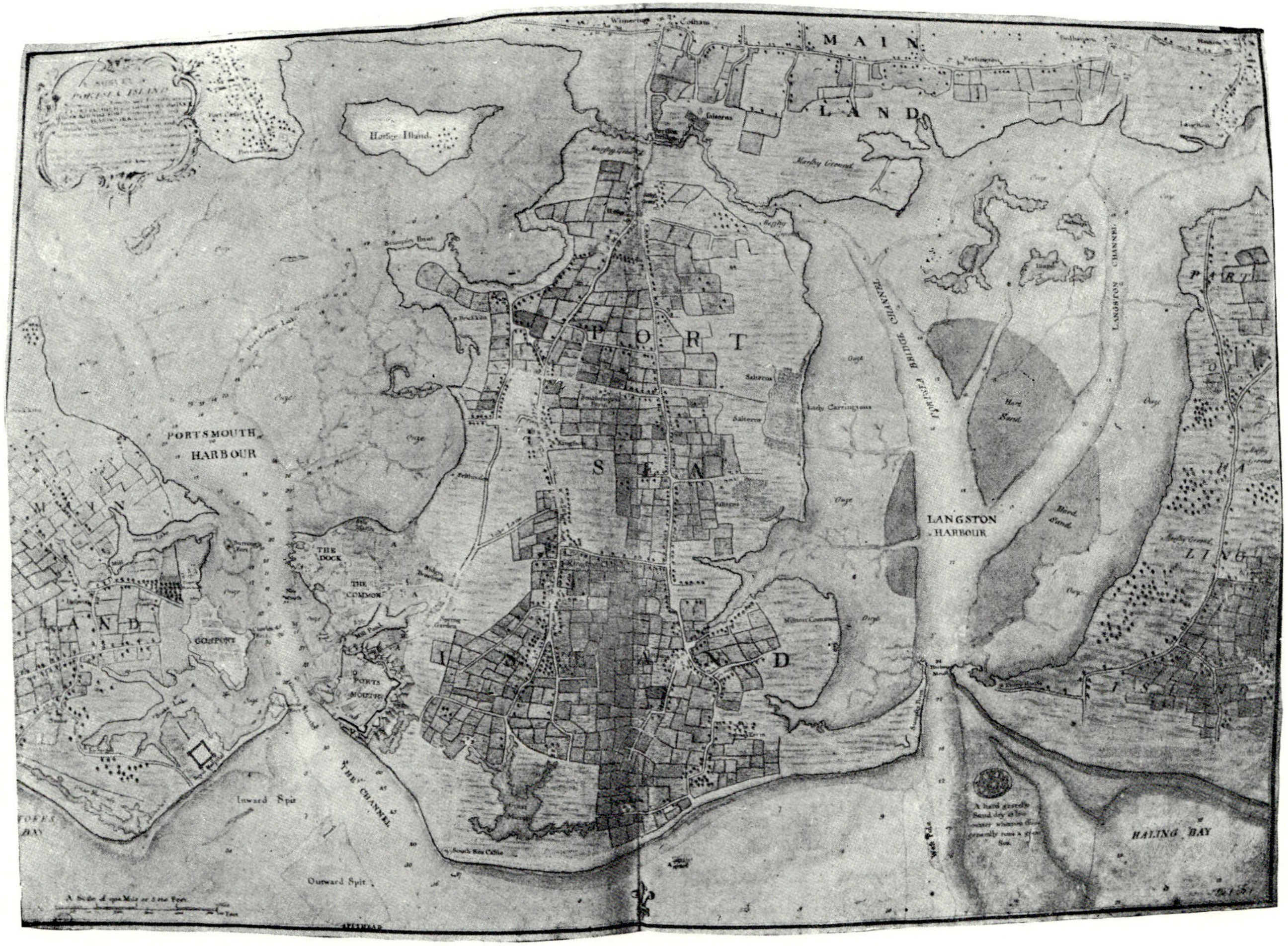

Survey of Portsea Island, 1716

(*Brit. Mus.* K, xiv, 11, 1)

William died without issue male in 1631,[461] and John and Henry Bold were in possession of his lands in 1638.[462] Subsequently it passed into the possession of Anne Mason who in 1669 bequeathed it to her son Robert Mason with contingent remainder to her kinsman William Bold.[463] Robert Mason was in possession of the manors of Portsea and Copnor with free warren and view of frankpledge in Portsea in 1704,[464] and in 1725 Hannah Mason, single woman, probably his daughter, obtained a settlement of the estate,[465] which passed by her marriage to Isaac Moody, whose son John Moody bequeathed it to a kinsman, Samuel Leeke, in whose family it still remains.[466]

Court baron only was attached to the manor of Portsea.[467] The lord had common of pasture over a large part of the island, in the liberty of Portsmouth and in the Forest of Bere.[468] His rights of common pasture also extended to Fratton, and an apportionment of the common appurtenant to the two lordships was effected in 1600.[469] Right of wreck was also attached to the manor. In 1383 three hundred tuns of wine came ashore upon the land of the lords of Portsea and Fratton. It was immediately seized by the two lords, but certain citizens of London and merchants to whom it belonged prayed that it might be released to them because two of the men from the wreck had been saved alive. The wine was therefore restored to its owners on payment of a fine.[470]

LANDPORT is still more modern than Portsea. It is a suburb of Portsmouth and consists of numerous small streets of two-storied houses and cottages leading east and west out of the main thoroughfare, the Commercial Road, which may well be called the most busy street of the town. Near its base, where it curves slightly, is the centre of the borough. On one side stands the town-hall, a magnificent building opened in 1890; it contains a spacious assembly hall, council chamber, and court rooms, and has ample accommodation for the numerous officials of the borough in addition to the police station and public library. Behind it an imposing erection is being built as a technical institute, while opposite the hall stands a statue of the late Queen Victoria. The tramways pass before the main entrance of the town-hall, this being the centre of a complete system of tram service by which any part of the borough may be reached. Tramways were first laid down in 1870,[471] and rapidly extended to Landport, Southsea, and Portsea. In 1883 the various companies were amalgamated.[472]

Leaving the town-hall on his left the traveller passes up Commercial Road by the most important shops in the town, on his right is the joint station of the London and South Western and London Brighton and South Coast Railways, built before 1859. Still further up the road, where the shops give place to villas interspersed with timber-yards and inns, is the house where Dickens was born. It has recently been bought by the corporation and converted into a Dickens Museum. On the same side of the road is the Portsea Island cemetery which overlooks the harbour. This district took its name from the Landport Gate in the middle of the last century. It was previously called the Halfway House, from an inn known as the Halfway House to Kingston. Within the last century this inn and a few scattered houses were the only buildings along what was then a country road, and where streets of cottages are now crowded together a footpath led across the fields to Kingston Church.[473] Twyford Avenue, a continuation of the Commercial Road, brings the traveller to *STAMSHAW* (Stampeshaw, xiii cent.; Stanneshowe, xv cent.). This district has always been included within the liberty of Portsmouth.[474] Late in the thirteenth century it was in the possession of Nicholas Malmains, who held it of the king by the service of rendering a sparrow-hawk yearly and paying 35*s.* 4*d.* to the bailiffs of Portsmouth towards the ferm of the town. He died before 1292, leaving a son of the same name aged seventeen. The latter was seised of a house and lands in Stamshaw at his death in May, 1349,[475] when his possessions were divided among the heirs of his three daughters.[476]

Henry Kesewyke held a toft and lands called Stamshaw, in the parish of Portsea, 'within the bridge called Portesbrygge' at his death in 1420,[477] and his son Henry conveyed the 'manor' of Stamshaw in February, 1437–8, to William Chamberlayn,[478] who had, however, parted with it before his death.[479] It is said to have been sold by a certain Constantine Derrell to Henry White, whose son Robert conveyed it to Richard Playfote in 1548.[480] In 1553 Richard Playfote died, leaving a daughter and heir Grace,[481] who was probably the same Grace, wife of John Wateryng, who joined with her husband in a sale of the manor of Stamshaw to Henry Bickley in 1659.[482] The later descent is unknown.

A branch road from Stamshaw leads to *STUBBINGTON*, which was for many years in the possession of the priory of Southwick. It is situated to the right of the road from London to Portsmouth, the centre of the prior's possessions being doubtless marked by Stubbington Lodge and Stubbington Farm, the residences respectively of Mrs. E. H. and Mr. A. L. Kent. The land around is laid out in building plots, while near at hand bricks are burnt for the new houses. The priory of Southwick had lands in or near Portsmouth at the beginning of the thirteenth century, for in 1201 the prior and convent granted to the abbeys of Savigny and Aunay a certain place which they

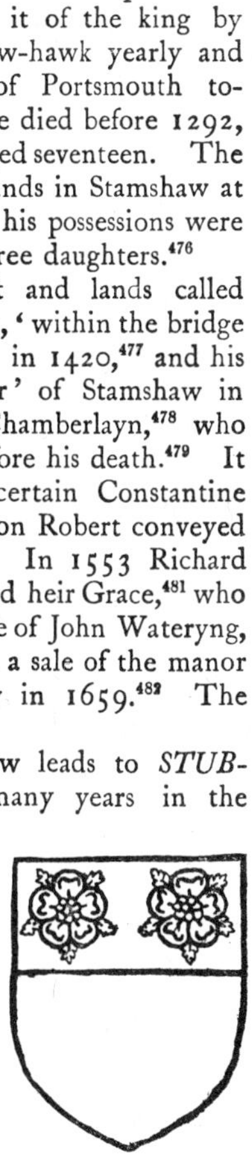

SOUTHWICK PRIORY. *Argent a chief sable with two roses argent therein.*

[461] Chan. Inq. p.m. (Ser. 2), vol. 463, No. 111.
[462] Recov. R. Trin. 14 Chas. I, 15.
[463] MS. Notes of the late Daniel Howard, town clerk of Portsmouth.
[464] Recov. R. East. 3 Anne, m. 153.
[465] Ibid. East. 11 Geo. I, m. 222.
[466] Information kindly supplied by Mr. A. T. Everitt.
[467] *Extracts from the Portsmouth Rec.* 665.
[468] Ibid. 666.
[469] Exch. Spec. Com. 42 Eliz. No. 2059.
[470] Harl. MS. 6602, fol. 204.
[471] Stat. 33 & 34 Vic. cap. 170.
[472] Ibid. 46 & 47 Vic. cap. 112, and cap. 187.
[473] *The New Portsmouth Guide* (1865).
[474] Chan. Inq. p.m. 20 Edw. I, 15.
[475] Ibid. 23 Edw. III, pt. 2, No. 160.
[476] Fine R. 24 Edw. III, m. 44.
[477] Mem. R. (Exch. L.T.R.) Trin. 9 Hen. V, 'Recorda,' m. 6*d.*
[478] Close, 16 Hen. VI, m. 14*d.*
[479] Chan. Inq. p.m. 23 Hen. VI, 43.
[480] Feet of F. Hants, East. 2 Edw. VI.
[481] Information kindly supplied by Mr. A. T. Everitt.
[482] Feet of F. Hants, Trin. 2 Eliz.

held of William de Ste. Mère-Église, and which extended from 'the east road leading to the mill of the town of Portsmouth, to the sea.[483] In 1320 the prior and convent received a grant of free warren in their demesne lands of Stubbington next Portsea,[484] a privilege which was confirmed to them by Richard II and Henry VI.[485] It appears that the prior had manorial rights over Stubbington, together with reliefs, heriots, fisheries, and fowling, and these rights were reserved while the demesne lands were leased out from time to time. Thus Thomas Carpenter had a lease of the lands in January, 1525–6.[486] The manor was surrendered with the other possessions of the priory in April, 1538.[487] In January, 1539–40, the manor was settled on Anne of Cleves in part satisfaction of her dower, and in the following January it was granted to her successor, Catherine Howard, who was beheaded in February, 1541–2.[488] In July, 1543, the king granted the manor to the warden, scholars, and clerks of St. Mary's College, Winchester,[489] a foundation to which it still belongs, while under them, as under the priory of Southwick, the demesne lands have been leased to various tenants from time to time.[490]

WINCHESTER COLLEGE. *Argent two cheverons sable between three roses gules.*

A cross road leads from the highway to London past Stubbington House to *COPNOR* (Copenore, xi–xii cent.; Copenhever and Coppenore, xiii cent.; Cupenore, xiv cent.; Copenore, xv cent.). Here there is a small hamlet still known as 'Copnor Village,' though it is now practically a part of Landport, for a broad road lined on either side with modern red-brick houses leads from New Road East, the terminus of the tramway, through Copnor to Little Gatcombe, and new roads are being laid out in all directions. To the west of the road Copnor Manor Farm stands surrounded by thatched barns, and facing it is Manor House, the residence of Miss Russell. To the north, further from Landport, are large brick-kilns surrounded by waste land, with here and there a scanty crop of vegetables; and to the east are flat marsh-lands, stretching out towards Great Salterns. The saltings, which are on the north side of a creek known as Great Salterns Lake, represent a very ancient industry in the island, for in 1086 the saltings of Copnor were assessed at 8*d.*[491] By the seventeenth century, however, the salt-works had been separated from the manor, for in November, 1629, the king granted the land known as Copnor or the Salt Pit in Portsea to Sir Edward Sidenham, with power to make salt there.[492] Nevertheless he appears only to have had a moiety of the profits.[493] In 1662 a dispute arose between the owners of the salt-works and the lord of Copnor manor as to a fish-pond which the former claimed as part of the salt-works, but the latter considered as waste belonging to the manor.[494]

The manor of Copnor was among the possessions of Earl Godwin, and was held of him by Tovi. After the Conquest it was held by Robert son of Gerold, the tenant under him being a certain Heldred. Of the successors of Heldred nothing is known until the thirteenth century, when the lords of Portsea (q.v.) also held the manor of Copnor.[495] Andrew of Portsea then held both the manors, and from that time the two manors have been held by the same lords. The manorial rights attached to Copnor were more extensive than those pertaining to Portsea, for the lord held view of frankpledge as well as court-baron for his tenants there.[496] In addition to this privilege he had rights of fishery at Milton Fleet and Burfield Fleet, besides the whole of the fishing at 'Mileresde Fleet' and 'Midomstonores Fleet,' and fowling at 'Setore' and other places within the lordship.[497]

South of Copnor lie *KINGSTON* and *BUCKLAND*, two adjacent suburbs of Portsmouth. Buckland was held of Earl Godwin by Alward before the Conquest, and in 1086 was among the lands held of Hugh de Port by Heldred.[498] Kingston contains the church of St. Mary, Portsea. It was evidently a hamlet of some importance at the time of the settlement of Portsmouth, probably owing to its proximity to the church, and was at first included in the liberty of the borough, for in 1198 the farm of Portsmouth and Kingston was accounted for as £14 2*s.* 7*d.*,[499] and in 1201–2 the rents of assize of Portsmouth and Kingston together amounted to 41*s.* 7½*d.*[500] The chief tenant there was Richard de Landa, who in 1225 held a carucate of land in Kingston under a charter of King John.[501] Apparently it was separated from the borough at this date, for 35*s.* 4*d.* was deducted from the farm of the town for the lands in Kingston which Richard de Landa held in farm.[502] This carucate formed a part of the portion which Richard gave his daughter Joan on her marriage with Robert de Audley.[503] The road from Copnor to Milton crosses the railway line near Kingston cemetery. From the level-crossing a rough roadway leads almost due east to a picturesque farm-house which lies beyond a broad willow-fringed sheet of water known as Baffin's Pond, while a wide curving road leads past the grim stone walls of the borough gaol, which has recently replaced a much smaller building in the High Street. On the same side of the road are the warmer-toned brick walls of the union workhouse, facing which stands the hospital for infectious diseases, while beyond, over stretches of flat waste land, the gabled roofs of the borough asylum appear among the trees, and in the far distance the woods of Hayling Island can be seen across the blue waters of Langstone Harbour. The road leads on to the picturesque village of Milton, which consists of one street. On either side are old weather-beaten

[483] *Cal. Doc. France*, 304. Another reference to lands held by the prior of Southwick in Stubbington in 1276 is difficult to identify owing to the fact that the prior also had lands at Stubbington in Crofton, then a part of Titchfield; *Cal. Close*, 1272–9, p. 355; *Cal. Pat.* 1377–81, p. 78.

[484] Chart. R. 14 Edw. III, No. 32.

[485] Ibid. 15–17 Ric. II, 34; 21–4 Hen. VI, 17.

[486] Mins. Accts. (Hants), 29–30 Hen. VIII, R. 113, m. 32.

[487] See *V.C.H. Hants*, ii, 168.

[488] *L. and P. Hen. VIII*, xv, 20 (2); ibid. 716.

[489] Ibid. xviii (1), 981 (46).

[490] Exch. Dep. Mich. 4 Jas. I, 24.

[491] *V.C.H. Hants*, i, 488.

[492] Pat. 5 Chas. I, pt. 4, m. 5.

[493] Exch. Dep. Hil. 13–14 Chas. II, 14.

[494] Ibid.

[495] *Testa de Nevill* (Rec. Com.), 231.

[496] Close, 40 Eliz. pt. 15; *Extracts from Portsmouth Rec.* 667.

[497] Ibid.

[498] *V.C.H. Hants*, i, 482.

[499] Pipe R. 9 Ric. I.

[500] *Rot. Cancell.* 3 *John* (Rec. Com.), 243.

[501] *Rot. Lit. Claus.* (Rec. Com.), ii, 606.

[502] Chart. R. 14 Hen. III, pt. 1, m. 14.

[503] Ibid. 14 Hen. III, pt. 2, m. 15.

cottages, and, half-hidden by the trees of overgrown gardens, dilapidated plastered and thatched farm-buildings. On the left of the road stands the stone church of St. James, built as a district chapel to Portsea in 1841,[504] and facing it is the Baptist church. The village still retains its rural character, though the streets of Fratton and Eastney are fast extending to it.

MILTON manor was granted with Warblington, of which it was a member,[505] to Matthew son of Herbert by King John.[506] Peter son of Matthew alienated Milton, where he apparently had three tenants in villeinage, together with the tenants and pasture land there to William Falconer of Hurstbourne Priory to hold by the service of rendering a pair of gloves yearly at Easter.[507] The overlordship of Milton thus remained with the lords of Warblington, but the descendants of William Falconer and his wife Emma were the actual tenants for more than three centuries. In 1388 John Falconer obtained a confirmation of the original grant by Peter son of Matthew,[508] while in 1635 John Falconer was in possession of it together with the manor of Emsworth, another member of Warblington.[509] Both Emsworth and Milton were purchased by Richard Cotton of Warblington, with the history of which manor theirs is thenceforward coincident. It appears that Peter son of Matthew did not grant all his lands at Milton to William Falconer with the manor, for in 1494 the lord of Warblington held, in addition to the rent due from John Falconer, certain rents from tenants-at-will and the profits of the woods, besides fishing and fowling.[510] The common lands belonging to Milton and the neighbouring hamlet of Eastney were inclosed under an Act of 1810, at which time also the common field known as the Velder or Welder was inclosed.[511]

EASTNEY is a fast-growing suburb of Southsea lying to the south of Milton. The farm at the head of Eastney creek or fleet probably represents Eastney manor-house. Like Milton, Eastney was originally a member of Warblington manor.[512] Herbert son of Matthew, who received a royal grant of Warblington, with its hamlet of Eastney, in 1231, had free warren granted to him in Portsea in 1239.[513] Some years later he was returned as holding four hides in Eastney.[513a] His brother and heir, Peter son of Matthew, was said to have permitted his tenant at Eastney to exercise manorial rights in the hamlet.[514] This tenant, Philip son of Peter of Eastney, added to his holding there an acre of land which he purchased from Ralph Lumpe and his wife Cecily.[515] The land was doubtless a part of the farm known latterly as Lumpstead.[516] The manor of Eastney was settled on Philip, evidently son and heir of Philip of Eastney, and his wife Alice in 1308.[517] Four years later, Eleanor widow of Matthew son of John, late lord of Warblington, sued Philip and Alice for dower from Eastney, and it having been found that Philip of Eastney had usurped the lordship there[518] the lands were seized by the king's escheator.[519] Philip then came into Chancery and proved that he and his ancestors had held the hamlet in demesne, and that Matthew son of John had had no right therein save the wardship of himself during his minority, and the lands were restored to him in 1314.[520] Two years later Alice of Eastney was holding the manor in accordance with the settlement of 1308;[521] she married as her second husband Sir Robert Norton, to whom Gilbert son and heir of Philip of Eastney quitclaimed the manor for life, receiving in return during the life of Alice a robe of an esquire's suit at Christmas, 40*s.* yearly, and maintenance for himself, his horse, and his groom so often as he was entitled to stay with his step-father. After the death of Alice the yearly allowance was to be increased to £10.[522] Eastney suffered with Portsmouth from French attacks during the Hundred Years' War.[523] In 1339, Sir Robert Norton evidently being dead, the manor was settled on Gilbert of Eastney and his wife Joan.[524] At about this date Gilbert obtained licence for the celebration of divine service within his house in Portsea parish.[525] The right of his grandson, Gilbert son of Philip, to a certain messuage and lands in Milton was disputed by John Beek and his wife Maud in 1391, but unsuccessfully, as the premises had been included in the settlement of Eastney manor on Philip and Alice of Eastney in 1308.[526] Between 1391 and 1458 Eastney appears to have escheated to the overlords, for in 1458 Alice wife of Richard earl of Salisbury, then lady of Warblington, bestowed it on her son John Neville and his wife Isabel and their heirs.[527] During the minority of George Neville, duke of Bedford, the young son and heir of John and Isabel, the latter's second husband, Sir William Norrys, knight, had the custody of the manor.[528] Upon the death of George Neville in 1461 his lands were divided among his five sisters or their heirs, Eastney evidently being assigned to his third sister, Lucy, then wife of Sir Thomas Fitzwilliam,[529] whose son, Sir Anthony Browne, was in possession of the manor at his death in 1548.[530] His son, Anthony Viscount Montagu, sold it to George Cotton of Warblington in 1567;[531] thus the manor was again united to Warblington, from which it has not since been separated.

Browne, Viscount Montagu. *Sable three lions passant bendwise between double cotises argent.*

FRATTON (Frodintone or Froditon xi-xiii cent.; Frodington xiv-xvii cent.) is a considerable district to the east of Landport and the north of Southsea. Its main thoroughfare, the Fratton Road, is the route of the electric trams from North End to

504 Sumner, *Conspectus of the Dioc. of Winchester* (1854), 20.
505 Chan. Inq. p.m. 3 Edw. II, 49.
506 *Testa de Nevill* (Rec. Com.), 237.
507 *Cal. Pat.* 1334–8, p. 565.
508 Ibid.
509 Recov. R. Mich. 11 Chas. I, m. 46.
510 Exch. T.R. Misc. Bks. 150, fol. 83–99.
511 The award is dated 13 Aug. 1813.
512 *Cal. Pat.* 1313–17, p. 139.
513 *Cal. Chart. R.* i, 242.
513a *Testa de Nevill* (Rec. Com.), 234.
514 Chan. Inq. p.m. 6 Edw. II, 124.
515 Feet of F. Hants, 9 Edw. I, 22.
516 Ralph and Cecily Lumpe acquired for life in 1284 a messuage and eighty acres of land, together with a water-mill, in Eastney; Feet of F. Hants, 12 Edw. I, 56.
517 Ibid. 2 Edw. II, 17; he is called Philip son of Philip of Eastney in 1314.
518 Chan. Inq. p.m. 6 Edw. II, 124.
519 *Abbrev. Rot. Orig.*(Rec.Com.), i, 201.
520 *Cal. Close*, 1313–18, p. 52.
521 *Feud. Aids*, ii, 320.
522 *Cal. Close*, 1323–7, p. 354.
523 Ibid. 1337–9, p. 528; 1339–41, pp. 108 and 267.
524 Feet of F. Hants, 13 Edw. III, 60.
525 Egerton MS. 2033, fol. 61.
526 De Banco R. East. 14 Ric. II, m. 75.
527 Feet of F. Div. Cos. 36 Hen. VI, 90.
528 *Cal. Pat.* 1476–83, p. 63.
529 Chan. Inq. p.m. (Ser. 2), vol. 2, No. 84.
530 Ibid. vol. 89, No. 132.
531 Feet of F. Hants, Trin. 9 Eliz.

Southsea, while the London and South Western and London Brighton and South Coast railways have a joint station near the junction of Fratton Road with the main road from Portsmouth Town Hall to Milton.

Before the Conquest there was a little settlement at Fratton. The manor was held of Edward the Confessor by Chetel, and was among the lands obtained by William de Warenne under William I. The actual tenant under him was Orsmelin, who had one plough in demesne, while there were four villeins and four bordars with two ploughs.[532] The overlordship belonged to Earl Warenne in the thirteenth century, while Hugh de Plaiz, a successor of Orsmelin, had granted half a knight's fee in Fratton to the Domus Dei of Portsmouth.[533] Hugh de Plaiz had other lands in Portsea by virtue of a royal grant, but these were given in 1215 to Walter Rufus,[534] and afterwards to William Briwer.[535] The master of the Domus Dei obtained a grant of free warren in his demesne lands at Fratton in 1306,[536] and this privilege was confirmed to the house in 1321–2.[537] In 1346 the master's holding at Fratton was described as one fee.[538] Though there is now no trace of a manor house, the hospital appears to have had a house of some kind within the vill, for in 1470 William Cocke and his wife Joan sold a cottage in Fratton 'opposite the door of the warden of the Domus Dei.'[539] At the surrender of the lands of the hospital to the crown in 1540, its possessions included rents of assize at Fratton and rents from various fields in the neighbourhood, and from Henry Bickley, who farmed the demesne lands, while the perquisites of court, together with the hall, parlour, rooms, stables, and dove-cote, were reserved to the master of the hospital and his successors.[540] Some of the lands, such as the field called Feldersche or Feldryche, were granted out separately,[541] while the demesne lands were leased from time to time to various tenants,[542] the manorial rights being reserved by the crown.[543] In 1599–1600 an apportionment of the common land belonging to the two manors of Fratton and Portsea took place,[544] but the common of Fratton was not inclosed till 1786. The manor was granted to Henry Prince of Wales, eldest son of James I, in 1610,[545] but excepted from the grant to Prince Charles (afterwards Charles I) in 1623.[546] The demesne lands finally passed in moieties to Anne wife of George St. Loe Beeston, and Elizabeth wife of William Dugard.[547] Thomas Beeston conveyed a moiety to Jude Storer in 1743,[548] while Mary wife of John Clempson and Margaret Charlotte wife of John Thompson were in possession of a moiety in 1783.[549] The estate has long since been divided into building plots. The manorial lands originally extended over the greater part of Southsea northwards as far as Lake Road.[550]

SOUTHSEA is a well-known seaside resort, which, though it lies within the boundary of Portsmouth borough, and is contiguous to Portsea and Landport, differs from them considerably in style. The north-western district, being the nearest to Portsmouth and Landport, resembles them in that its streets are narrow and its buildings chiefly in use as small shops. This district is divided from the rest of the town by a broad street known as Somers Road, to the east of which the wide roads of detached villas, hotels, and private residences which form the town of Southsea proper extend over a flat country celebrated for the amount of sunshine which it enjoys. Southwards from the centre of the town, Palmerston Road, lined with the best shops of the neighbourhood, leads on to Southsea Common directly opposite the castle. The common, which is the property of the War Office, is a flat, turf-covered expanse extending from Portsmouth town beyond Southsea Castle. It is traversed by asphalt paths which lead across it to the Clarence Esplanade, the favourite walk of visitors, which stretches from the Clarence Esplanade Pier, whence a fine view of the harbour and Spithead is obtained, along the coast to Southsea Castle, where it is continued in a paved walk past the Canoe Lake, surrounded by well-laid-out public gardens. At intervals along the esplanade there are monuments to commemorate naval victories, including the anchor of the *Victory*.

The whole town is of very recent growth. Southsea Common, which lay within the manor of Fratton, was inclosed in 1785. During the Peninsular War Southsea first came into favour as a seaside resort, and hotels were built along the parade facing the sea; but the common, which was originally a stretch of morass and marsh land, was not completely drained till the middle of the last century.[551] The western portion of the town was then already built, its central and most compact district being temporarily called Croxton Town.[552] About 1865 large districts now known as Havelock Park and Nelsonville were laid out in building sites.[553] This part of the town was then known as New Southsea, and is still being extended eastwards towards Eastney and Milton. The London and South Western, and London Brighton and South Coast railways have a branch line to Fratton from East Southsea, where a station was opened in 1885.

CHURCHES No church is mentioned in the Domesday Survey of the manors of Buckland, Copnor, and Fratton. The earliest foundation was probably the parish church of Portsea, now represented by *ST. MARY, KINGSTON*, one of the finest modern churches in the country, begun in 1887 while the present bishop of St. Albans was vicar, and built at an enormous cost from the designs of Sir A. W. Blomfield. It has a shallow chancel and transepts of two bays with side chapels, a nave of five bays with aisles and porches, and a lofty west tower embattled and pinnacled, which in spite of its low-lying site is a landmark for miles around. The churchyard contains a monument to Admiral Kempenfeldt and the crew of the *Royal George*.

The registers date from 1753, except the marriage register, which begins in 1754. There is also a register of marriages for the chapel of St. Peter from

532 *V.C.H. Hants*, i, 492.
533 *Testa de Nevill* (Rec. Com.), 234.
534 *Rot. Lit. Claus.* (Rec. Com.), i, 236*b*.
535 Ibid. i, 242*b*.
536 Chart. R. 35 Edw. I, m. 8.
537 Ibid. 15 Edw. II, m. 15.
538 *Feud. Aids*, ii, 336.
539 Anct. D. (P.R.O.) D. 1110.
540 Mins. Accts. 31 & 32 Hen. VIII (Hants), R. 139, m. 77.
541 Pat. 24 Eliz. pt. 3, m. 6.
542 Ibid. 8 Jas. I, pt. 36.
543 Exch. Spec. Com. (Eliz.), 2059.
544 Ibid. 545 Pat. 8 Jas. I, pt. 41, No. 3.
546 Ibid. 14 Jas. I, pt. 20, m. 29.
547 Feet of F. Hants, East. 1 Geo. I, Hil. 1 Geo. II.
548 Ibid. Trin. 17 Geo. II.
549 Ibid. Hil. 23 Geo. III.
550 Information kindly supplied by Mr. W. H. Saunders.
551 *Post Office Directory, Hants*, 1848.
552 Pigot's *Commercial Directory for Hants*, 1823–4.
553 *The New Portsmouth Guide*, 1865, p. 14.

[W. H. Barrell, photo.

THE PARISH CHURCH, PORTSMOUTH: INTERIOR LOOKING EAST

[W. H. Barrell, photo.

THE PARISH CHURCH, PORTSMOUTH: INTERIOR LOOKING WEST

1788 to 1794. Extracts from the interesting book of churchwardens' accounts for Portsmouth from 1560 onwards have been printed in *Extracts from the Portsmouth Records*.[554]

Portsea church was appropriated at an early date to Southwick Priory. In 1291 the value of the church with its chapel was £30 and of the vicarage £10.[555] The chapel here mentioned may possibly have been the chapel of St. Andrew, Fratton, which was granted to Edward Wymarke in 1588.[556]

In 1339 Stephen, vicar of Portsea, craved respite from the triennial tenth granted by the clergy, as his vicarage, houses, goods, and chattels had been burnt by the French, and a similar petition had been made by Walter, vicar of Portsmouth, in the preceding year.[557] After the surrender of the priory of Southwick to the Crown in 1538 the rectory and advowson of the vicarage were granted to the college of St. Mary, Winchester, in whose possession they still remain.[558]

There was a devotional brotherhood attached to Portsea church for the purpose of maintaining lights there. At the time of its abolition by Edward VI it had lands in Portsmouth liberty.[559]

The parish church of *ST. THOMAS OF CANTERBURY*, which stands in the High Street, was also a possession of Southwick Priory, to which it had been appropriated before 1291.[560] The rectory and advowson were granted with those of Portsea to the college of St. Mary, Winchester, in 1544,[561] and are still retained by the college.

The church has a chancel of two double bays 54 ft. by 25 ft. with vaulted aisles, modern north porch and south vestry, north and south transepts 25 ft. wide, the north transept being 39 ft. long and the south 29 ft., and nave of four bays, including the site of the former central tower, 86 ft. by 27 ft. 6 in., with north and south aisles 18 ft. 6 in. wide, and west tower 23 ft. square, flanked by north and south porches. All measurements given are internal. A grant of land by John de Gisors in 1180 'for the erection of a chapel in honour of the glorious martyr Thomas, formerly archbishop of Canterbury,' gives the earliest limit of date for the building, and the details of the eastern part show that work must have been begun soon after the grant was made. The church was probably completed according to the first design, but the evidence of the finishing of the work is lost, as the central tower was taken down, and all west of the crossing rebuilt between 1683 and 1693, the date 1691 over the west door of the tower showing the progress of the work. The chancel has been lately repaired and made structurally sound, the arcades having been in a dangerous state for some time.

The internal effect has been injured by the removal of the plaster in 1844, leaving the rubble masonry exposed.

In spite of the decay of the Caen stone-work which is much used in its construction—the Binstead stone as usual standing well—the external effect of the church is imposing from its scale and the massive clasping buttresses at the salient angles. The nave stone-work is in better condition, the ashlar facing of the tower being very sound and good. The chancel is lighted from the east by three wide lancet windows on the upper or clearstory level, at the sills of which a wall passage runs round the chancel, communicating with a passage in the south transept, which is reached from a vice in the south-west angle of the transept.

The arches of these windows are carried on Purbeck marble shafts with moulded capitals and bases, and rings at half height, the half-shafts at either side being of stone, with similar details. The clearstory windows on the north and south of the chancel are of the same description, but the Purbeck shafts have no rings. Below the east window is an ill-designed reredos of 1844, masking a pointed recess, in the back of which is a small lancet, still to be seen on the outer face of the wall. In the gable above the clearstory is a large blocked circular window. The north and south arcades of the ground story of the chancel are of two bays, with clustered responds at either end, and an octagonal column in the middle. Each bay has two pointed sub-arches of two moulded orders with a central column of Purbeck marble, included under a round-headed arch of a single moulded order. Before 1904 two of the Purbeck marble columns, those in the western bays, were ancient, the two in the eastern bays having been replaced by iron columns in 1842. All four are now of marble, and date from 1904, but the old circular moulded marble capital of the south-west bay has been preserved, the other three capitals being of stone and modern.

The chancel was designed for and probably once covered with a quadripartite stone-ribbed vault. The old vaulting shafts with foliated capitals, and stopping on corbels in the spandrels of the main arcades, are still in position. At the present time there is a plastered wooden vault, set up in 1844 in place of a flat wooden ceiling, the chancel arch being poor work of the same date. The aisles of the chancel are vaulted in four bays with ribbed vaults, springing from triple vaulting shafts in the outer walls, and from single shafts in the eastern angles. The capitals, which in the main arcades are moulded, are here foliate of various designs, and square abaci and plain leaf-work show the Romanesque feeling which still lingers. The west arches of the aisles are pointed, of three moulded orders, that to the north having foliate capitals in the north respond, and moulded in the south. The aisles were originally lighted by single lancets in each bay, but only those in the east bay on the north, and the two east bays on the south, are ancient. The east windows of the aisles, each of two uncusped lights, are in modern stone-work. The transepts, like the chancel, have been vaulted in stone, the north transept in two bays, the south in one wide bay, but both now have flat plastered ceilings. The north transept has two trefoiled lancet windows in the clearstory stage on the east, and a third light to the north, while in the north wall are three trefoiled lancets with a sexfoiled opening in the gable above. The west wall has a single trefoiled lancet in the clearstory. In the lower stage is a north window

554 Extracts from a register beginning in 1556 are given in Additional MS. 8153, with a memorandum to the effect that the original was missing in 1830.

555 *Pope Nich. Tax.* (Rec. Com.), 211 *b*.

556 Pat. 30 Eliz. pt. 7.

557 *Cal. Close*, 1337–9, pp. 546 and 632.

558 *L. and P. Hen. VIII*, xviii (1), 981 (46).

559 Chant. Cert. (Edw. VI), Hants, 33.

560 *Pope Nich. Tax.* (Rec. Com.), 211 *b*.

561 *L. and P. Hen. VIII*, xviii (1), 981 (46).

of three uncusped lancets, set considerably to the east of the centre-line of the gable, and in the east wall are two recesses, that to the north having a wide and tall pointed arch, continuing down to the floor level, and lighted from the back by two lancets with a quatrefoiled circle over, while the second recess, whose sill is some four feet from the floor, has a trefoiled head, and fortunately retains most of its original plastering, with remains of painting on it; traces of a Majesty in a vesica are to be seen. In the south jamb of the large recess is a piscina and a small locker, and it is probable that there were two altars in the transept. In the north wall near the north-west angle is a large square-headed locker, rebated for a door; the reason for the irregular setting of the three-light window to the east of it may be connected with some former arrangement of a vestry or cupboards in the west angle of the transept.

The south transept, which, perhaps because of the nearness of the High Street on the south, has been built of less projection than the north transept, has a single lancet on the east, and below it an arched recess like that in the north transept, and formerly lighted by a single lancet. To the north is a second recess corresponding to that in the north transept, but much narrower, with a trefoiled head, and preserving traces of paintings on the back. In the south wall are two lancets, and over them a single lancet in the clearstory, while in the west wall is part of a similar lancet, destroyed in the seventeenth-century alterations, and in the south-west angle a small doorway leading to the vice already mentioned.

The only remaining part of the central tower is the east wall, on which show the internal quoins of the eastern angles, and the eastern piers of the crossing, which have lost their old capitals and are fitted with clumsy substitutes.

The nave is of four bays, the eastern bay, representing the crossing, being wider than the others, and has round-arched arcades springing from tall Tuscan columns which support large curving north and south galleries with panelled fronts. At the west is an organ gallery containing a fine organ, said to be by Father Smith, set up here in 1718. At the crown of the east arch of the north arcade is the date 1691, and in the corresponding position on the south T.B.M^r^, for Thomas Brouncker, mayor.

The nave has a coved plaster ceiling, and a canted ceiling over the galleries, both pierced with sky-lights which appear as a double row of dormers on the external elevation. The aisles beneath the galleries are lighted by square-headed three-light windows. The west tower is very plain and massive, having small belfry windows which are nearly hidden by large clock dials in the upper stage, below a plain parapet with embattled angles, and at half height a moulded string-course, below which, on the west, is the west window and doorway. The tower is capped by a large wooden domed cupola set up in 1702, with a lantern above, from which rises a spirelet adorned with a fine gilded vane in the form of a three-masted ship with flags on the bowsprit, fore, main, and mizen masts, and a large flag on the gaff. This was set up in 1710, the flag on the fore-top being inscribed MCES 1710.

The fittings of the chancel are almost entirely new, but the pulpit dates from 1695, and has a new sounding board copied from a former one, surmounted by the gilt figure of an angel. The soffit of the sounding board is covered with wooden stars made from famous old ships, the *Tremendous*, *Queen Charlotte*, *Actaeon*, and *Chesapeake*, and the central star is of wood from the *Victory*. The poor-box under the western gallery and the mayor's seat and desk were also made in 1904 from the wood of the *Tremendous*. The carved wooden head of the west door of the nave is dated 1674. On the pulpit is a red velvet hanging with a silver fringe and the date 1694, and the altar table has a similar frontal of 1695. There is a good modern mace-stand in the mayor's pew. The font, at the west end of the south aisle, is of the fifteenth century, with a panelled octagonal bowl, ornamented with blank shields in the panels and on the chamfered lower edge of the bowl, the shaft and moulded base being also octagonal.

The monuments in the church are of no great interest, except that of the duke of Buckingham, assassinated here in 1628. It was formerly at the east of the chancel, and is now in the west bay of the south aisle of the chancel. The upper part consists of a phoenix on an urn, under a pediment bearing the duke's arms, and flanked by warlike trophies, while on the base is a marble slab with an inscription between two allegorical female figures. In the tower are eight bells, five of which are said to have been brought from the Roman pharos in Dover Castle in 1702, and recast at the expense of Prince George of Denmark. They are the present treble, second, third, fifth, and sixth, and are by Abraham Rudhall, of Gloucester, 1703; the fourth is by Joshua Kipling, of Portsmouth, 1737; the seventh by Thomas Lester, of Whitechapel, 1749; and the tenor by Richard Phelps, of Whitechapel, 1730. There is also a fire-bell, bearing on the waist the arms of Leon and Castile, the work of Matthias Solano, at the beginning of the eighteenth century. It is possible that it was brought here as loot after the taking of Gibraltar.

VILLIERS, Duke of Buckingham. *Argent a cross gules with five scallops or thereon.*

The plate is of very great interest, consisting of two communion cups with domed covers, two flagons, two patens, ten plates, and a strainer. On 12 November, 1687, James II gave to the church a set of plate comprising a chalice and small paten, two flagons and two standing patens, weighing 119 oz.; the record of this gift being preserved in the registers on the back of Charles II's marriage certificate. The small paten has been lost, but the five pieces which remain and are older than 1687 together weigh 113 oz. 8 dwt., leaving the very probable weight of 5 oz. 12 dwt. for the lost paten.

It so happened that in 1683 the garrison of Tangier was brought home by Lord Dartmouth, landing at Portsmouth, and among other things the plate of the church of St. Charles the Martyr was brought with them. Lord Dartmouth in a letter of 5 November asked that the plate might be given to Godshouse chapel,[562] and a list of the plate,[563] exactly

[562] *Hist. MSS. Com. Rep.* xv, App. i, 34. [563] Ibid.

[W. H. Barrell, photo.

THE PARISH CHURCH, PORTSMOUTH : WEST ARCH OF SOUTH AISLE OF CHANCEL

[W. H. Barrell, photo.

THE PARISH CHURCH, PORTSMOUTH : ONE BAY OF NORTH ARCADE

agreeing with that in the register, was drawn up on 16 January, 1683–4, doubtless just before its departure for England. Of the two flagons which the church has, one is of 1639, and the second apparently a locally made copy of it, without hall-marks, and inscribed 'Alder^n John McMath his Gist (*sic*) to the Chirrch of Tangier November the 10 1672.' These are a pair, the second made to match the first, and obviously formed part of the Tangier plate. The other pieces, which, as seems possible, also belonged to Tangier, are a cup, with no mark but that of Anthony Nelme, a London goldsmith of the latter part of the seventeenth century, and two standing patens of 1677. The inference is that James II handed over the set of Tangier plate to Portsmouth church, and not, as it seems, to Godshouse chapel.

The remaining pieces of plate are (1) a cup made to match that already noted in 1764, and fitted with a domed cover of 1803; the other cup has a like cover of 1858; (2) nine silver plates, two of 1708 given 1725, two of 1804, two of 1809 given 1810, two of 1812 given 1812, and one of 1900; (3) a strainer of 1805 given 1806. There is also one plated plate, modern, and a silver verger's rod of 1812 given 1812. The earliest register runs from 1653 to 1662, the second being a finely-bound book beginning with the record of Charles II's marriage, 22 May, 1662—now cut out and framed—and containing baptisms and marriages to 1694, and burials to 1678, with a few of 1683–6. The third book goes from 1695 to 1710, the fourth 1710 to 1727, the fifth 1727 to 1748, and the sixth 1748 to 1769, with marriages to 1758 only. The seventh, eighth, and ninth contain marriages 1754 to 1758, 1758 to 1763, and 1763 to 1778. The tenth has baptisms and burials 1770 to 1787, the eleventh and twelfth marriages 1778 to 1785, and 1785 to 1795, the thirteenth baptisms and burials 1787 to 1800, the fourteenth and sixteenth marriages 1795 to 1806, and 1806 to 1813, and the fifteenth baptisms and burials 1801 to 1812.

In addition to these and to the Garrison Church described above, numerous churches have been built during the last two centuries to meet the needs of an ever-increasing population. St. Mary's in Highbury Street was built as a chapel of ease to Portsmouth parish church in 1839,[564] but the greater number of the more modern churches are attached to St. Mary, Portsea. Of these daughter churches St. George's in St. George's Square, Portsea, was built in 1754 for the benefit of the town which was then fast rising in the neighbourhood of the Dockyard,[565] but the district was not erected into a separate parish till 1875, the church being still in the gift of the vicar of Portsea.[566] In 1822 the church of St. Paul, Southsea, was erected,[567] and a part of Portsea parish assigned to it to form a district chapelry in 1835.[568] All Saints' in the Commercial Road was built in 1828, a part of Portsea parish being assigned to it in 1835.[569] Holy Trinity, Portsea, was built in 1841[570] on ground belonging to the Government, by which it has recently been resumed for the purpose of extending the Dockyard, while the district which had been assigned to it has been divided between the churches of St. George and St. John. In 1841 also a church under the invocation of St. James was built in the outlying district of Milton,[571] which was formed into a district chapelry three years later.[572] St. Mark's church, North End, was built in 1874, a portion of Portsea parish being assigned to it in the following year.[573] In 1898 was erected the mission church of St. Agatha, Conway Street, well known as the scene of the labours of the late Father Dolling. These are all in the gift of the vicar of Portsea. The church of St. John in Prince George's Street, Portsea, was built in 1788[574] and is in the gift of five trustees. A district was assigned to it in 1835.[575] St. Jude's, Southsea, also in the gift of five trustees, was built in 1851,[576] and erected into a parish in 1879.[577] In 1862 three new churches were built: St. Luke's, Marylebone, of which the bishop of Winchester is patron, was endowed as a separate parish church in 1865;[578] St. Bartholomew's, Southsea, originally built as a chapel of ease to St. James, Milton, is also in the gift of the bishop; St. Simon's, Southsea, in the gift of the Church Patronage Trust, was built as a chapel of ease to St. Jude's. A part of the parish of St. Paul's, Southsea, was assigned to the church of St. Michael and All Angels in Park Road in 1882.[579] In the following year a part of the parish of St. Jude and the chapelry of St. Paul was assigned to St. Peter's, Southsea.[580] The churches of St. Stephen, Portsea, and St. Matthew, Southsea, of more recent date, are in the gift of the bishop, as also is St. Margaret's, Eastney, to which a district was assigned from that of St. James, Milton. The Circus church in Surrey Street is in the gift of the trustees of the Rev. J. C. Martin.

The Roman Catholic diocese of Portsmouth includes Hampshire, Berkshire, and the Channel Isles. It was formed in 1882, in which year was opened the Cathedral of St. John in Edinburgh Road.

There is a Roman Catholic church in Gladys Avenue, and the church of St. Swithun in Saxe-Weimar Road was opened in 1901 to replace a smaller church, which has since been converted into a school.

There is a Presbyterian church in Commercial Road, and another in St. Michael's Road, built in 1878.

In the seventeenth century there were many Nonconformists in Portsmouth. Among those fined for preaching at conventicles was John Hickes, well-known for his share in Monmouth's Rebellion.[581] Conventicles were frequently held at a house called the Golden Ball, which belonged to a baker, Robert Reynolds,[582] while the bitter animosity between Dissenters and members of the Church of England in the town is shown by the disputes between them in 1710.[583] In 1865 there were more than sixteen

564 Sumner, *Conspectus of the Dioc. of Winton*, 1854, p. 20.
565 Register book of the church.
566 *Lond. Gaz.* 3 Dec. 1875, p. 6203.
567 *Conspectus of the Dioc. of Winton*, 1854, p. 20.
568 *Lond. Gaz.* 5 May, 1835, p. 881.
569 Ibid.
570 *Conspectus of the Dioc. of Winton*, 20.
571 Ibid.
572 *Lond. Gaz.* 15 Nov. 1844, p. 4057.
573 Ibid. 19 Mar. 1875, p. 1705.
574 *Conspectus of the Dioc. of Winton*, 1854, p. 20.
575 *Lond. Gaz.* 5 May, 1835, p. 881.
576 *Conspectus of the Dioc. of Winton*, 1854, p. 20.
577 *Lond. Gaz.* 14 Feb. 1879, p. 731.
578 Ibid. 4 Apr. 1865, p. 1869.
579 Ibid. 21 July, 1882, p. 3414.
580 Ibid. 28 Aug. 1883, p. 4215.
581 The warrant against him is exhibited in the Borough Museum.
582 *Extracts from the Portsmouth Rec.* 179.
583 Ibid. 207, et seq.

Nonconformist places of worship in the neighbourhood; of these five were Baptist chapels, four Wesleyan, and three Independent. The number of meeting-houses of all denominations has increased rapidly to meet the needs of a large population. There are now nine Baptist chapels; one in Kent Street is said to occupy the site of a meeting-house founded in 1698. The Bible Christians have three places of worship; the Plymouth Brethren meet at the Assembly Room, Bush Street, Southsea, and at St. James's Hall, Commercial Road. The Congregationalists have seven chapels, chiefly at Landport and Southsea. The Unitarians have a meeting-house in the High Street. The Primitive Methodists have four places of worship, two at Southsea, one at Stamshaw, and one on the Eastney Road; and the Wesleyans have fourteen.[584] There are also numerous mission halls.

CHARITIES The following is an account of the principal charities in Portsmouth:—

In 1679 Thomas Winter by his will gave £200 for the benefit of the poor. At a subsequent date Thomas Mills gave the lease of a house to the poor with power of sale. The house was sold for £100. In respect of these sums, and probably of other small legacies, the Corporation pays £15 a year, which is distributed on St. Thomas's Day among the poor in sums varying from 1*s.* to 2*s.* 6*d.*

In 1765 Charles West by will left £100 Old South Sea Annuities, one moiety of the income towards the relief of the poor at Christmas, and the other moiety to be given to thirty poor housekeepers. The fund is represented by £113 15*s.* 4*d.* consols, the dividends of which are duly applied.

John Bass Eltham, by will proved 1880, left a legacy invested in £2,927 0*s.* 8*d.* consols, income amounting to £73 5*s.* 6*d.*, distributable between the months of October and April to the poor of Portsmouth and Southsea, in money or in articles of kind. In 1905 disbursements were made to 152 aged persons.

Alderman Joseph George Whitcombe, by his will proved with four codicils 23 November, 1892 (*inter alia*) bequeathed £6,000, to be known as 'The Whitcombe Charitable Trust Fund,' for providing pensions of £10 per annum to poor persons of sixty years of age or upwards, resident in the borough of Portsmouth. The trust fund consists of £5,339 17*s.* 6*d.* India £3 per cent. stock. In 1905 annuities of £10 each were given to fifteen poor persons. On the determination of certain life interests the trust fund will be considerably augmented. The same donor founded scholarships in connexion with the grammar school and other schools.

The above three charities are administered by the Corporation.

In 1774 William Pike by his will left £300 on trust for the interest to be paid on St. Thomas's Day to the poor. The legacy was invested in Old South Sea Annuities, which are now represented by £440, £2 10*s.* per cent. annuities, with the official trustees, the dividends on which, amounting to £11 a year, are duly applied. The vicar and churchwardens were appointed trustees by an order of the Charity Commissioners of 12 March, 1869.

The Highbury Street Almshouses.—There was formerly an almshouse in Penny Street which, being required for the enlargement of the county gaol, was sold in 1831 for £650. With this sum and voluntary subscriptions a site was acquired in St. Mary's Street, afterwards called Highbury Street, and almshouses containing ten rooms for ten aged women were erected, and a schoolroom used for infants. Mrs. Caroline Jones, by her will proved in 1883, left £1,000 to be invested and income to be paid to the inmates, 5*s.* each on Lady Day and Michaelmas Day, and £1 each on Midsummer Day and Christmas Day, any surplus for such charitable purposes as the vicar should think fit. The investment was made in the purchase of £980 7*s.* 10*d.* consols with the official trustees, and the dividends are duly applied.

Miss Anne Marie Williams, by her will, 1843, bequeathed to the vicar of Portsmouth an immediate legacy of £600 consols, and a further legacy of £600 consols after the determination of a life interest therein, and directed that the income thereof should be applied for the use of the most deserving poor, including poor women in the almshouse, at Christmas and Easter in each year, in such articles as the vicar should think proper. The two legacies are represented by £1,071 3*s.* 8*d.* consols with the official trustees. In 1905 the dividends, amounting to £26 15*s.* 4*d.*, were applied in grocery and coal tickets to seventy-four persons.

By deed, dated 31 March, 1865, Mrs. Anna Victoria Little, widow of Major Robert John Little, settled a sum of £100 consols (held by the official trustees) upon trust that the dividends should be applied in the distribution of bread and coals among the wives and families of corporals, gunners, and drummers in H.M. corps of Royal Marine Artillery resident at Portsmouth. The income is distributed among necessitous families of non-commissioned officers and men through the agency of the Royal Marine Artillery Benevolent Fund.

In connexion with the General Baptist Chapel, St. Thomas's Street, is Bowes's Charity, which is supposed to have originated in a gift of a Dr. Bowes, the earliest deed in existence being dated 20 January, 1792, whereby the appointment of trustees is regulated. Its endowment formerly consisted of £2,000 new 3 per cents., but now of £1,467 North Eastern Railway 4 per cent. debenture stock, producing £58 12*s.* 4*d.* yearly, which together with £15 9*s.* 3*d.* the rent of a dwelling-house, 19, St. Thomas's Street, belonging to the chapel, was in 1905 applied in providing pulpit supplies, &c., £40, expenses of the chapel £24, and the balance in repairs.

The High Street Meeting House Charity Fund now consists of £1,320, £2 10*s.* per cent. annuities held by the official trustees, arising from gifts of various donors, producing £33 a year, of which $\frac{7}{12}$ are paid to the minister of the chapel (now known as the Unitarian Chapel), and $\frac{4}{12}$ to the poor of the congregation. Last appointment of trustees 23 May, 1901.

[584] The site of the Wesleyan Chapel in Daniel Street was conveyed in trust by a deed of 1875, together with the adjoining property, the rent of which is applied towards the expenses of the chapel. By a scheme of the Charity Commissioners of 10 May, 1867, the property was vested in trustees in trusts of 'The Wesleyan Chapel Model Deed.' New trustees were appointed 18 April, 1889. The site of the Wesleyan Chapel in Victoria Road South was conveyed by deed of 1865, and vested in trustees by the Charity Commissioners 23 July, 1886.

Jacob Nathan, by will, proved 1867, left £63 0*s.* 9*d.* consols, dividends to be applied for benefit of poor Jews, through the agency of the Jewish Mendicity Society.

By will, proved 12 May, 1884, the Rev. Edward Sheridan bequeathed his residuary estate to the Roman Catholic bishop of Portsmouth and his successors upon trust to apply income in support of charitable objects in his diocese. The trust fund at present consists of £547 8*s.* 4*d.* consols, the dividends of which are applied towards the pension of one ecclesiastical student. The charity is further entitled to £562 on the determination of a life interest.

The Royal Portsmouth, Portsea, and Gosport Hospital, Fitzherbert Street, Landport, which was founded in 1849, was possessed in 1904, in addition to its general funds, of various securities valued at £29,598, producing an annual income of £939, arising from legacies and gifts of various donors, including legacies by will of John Bass Eltham (1880) and of Miss E. M. Scale (1884).

Henry Wood, by will and codicil, proved 1887, bequeathed contingently his residuary trust funds for investment, and, subject to certain existing life interests, directed income to be applied in gifts of £15 to poor persons born and resident in the borough of Portsmouth, with a further trust for the above mentioned hospital.

Mrs. Caroline Jones, by will, proved in 1883, left £1,000 in augmentation of the endowment of the existing church of St. Mary's parish. The legacy was invested in £973 3*s.* 5*d.* consols with the official trustees.

Mrs. Hannah Stokes, by will, proved in 1883, directed her trustees to invest in consols such a sum as would produce £3 a year to be applied in keeping in order a tomb in the Portsmouth Cemetery, the unapplied surplus thereof to be paid to the porter residing at the lodge of the said cemetery. The official trustees hold a sum of £100 consols in respect of this charity.

The following charities apply to Portsea :—

Edward Crafts, by his will, 1780, directed his trustees to lay out certain securities in paying for the schooling of as many poor boys as the interest would allow to learn to read and write and arithmetic to fit them for trades, subject as therein mentioned. In 1782 the minister and commissioners of St. George's Chapel agreed to accept the charity, which became attached to the schools in Kent Street, established by the Portsea Beneficial Society. The endowment, including a legacy of £50 consols given in augmentation by will of John Ring, proved in 1839, consists of £1,000 consols held by the official trustees.

By a scheme of the Board of Education, dated 21 September, 1905, trustees were appointed, and a sum of £10 a year was directed to be paid to the said school so long as it continued to be conducted as a public elementary school, the residue of the income in the maintenance of exhibitions equivalent to the tuition fees, with £5 added at the discretion of the trustees, tenable at secondary or technical schools in Portsea, with a view to training the exhibitioners for pupil teachers.

Richard Wilmot, by will, proved in the P.C.C., on 27 April, 1805, left certain securities as a perpetual fund for educating boys in the knowledge of the English language, writing, accounts, and navigation, with a preference for the sons of widows. The endowment now consists of a messuage on the north side of Trafalgar Buildings, Portsea, let at £13 a year ; a messuage in Bow Street, let at £11 14*s.* and £388 4*s.* 1*d.* consols with the official trustees. By a scheme of the Charity Commissioners of 20 March, 1894, the yearly income—subject to the payment of all outgoings—is directed to be applied in the advancement of the education of the sons of widows *bonâ fide* resident in the parish of Portsea, who are scholars in the schools of the Portsea Beneficial Society, with a preference to those who have shown aptitude for the study of navigation, in granting prizes of from £1 to £5, and in the maintenance of exhibitions of £10 at the Portsmouth Grammar School, or any place of higher education.

Major Ebenezer Vavasour, by will, 1808, also left to the said schools £100, represented by £92 8*s.* 2*d.* consols, with the official trustees.

The charity of Thomas Brewer, will 1666, consists of 20*s.* a year charged on land in Buckland, 10*s.* to be applied on St. Thomas's Day, and 10*s.* on Good Friday.

Eleanor Brewer's charity was instituted by her will, dated 1667, bequeathing 40*s.* a year out of a close called Bird's Close.

William Sheppard, by will, proved in the P.C.C., 1798, left £100, interest to be applied on Whit Monday in distribution of bread among four widows resident in the parish, invested in £102 6*s.* consols with the official trustees. — Claypitt, by will, 1848, left £265 13*s.* 6*d.* consols upon the like trusts. These charities are administered together by the vicar and churchwardens. In 1904 an allowance of 2*s.* each was made to eighty-six widows.

Thomas Fitzherbert, by a codicil to his will, 1821, directed that £10,000 stock should, after the determination of certain life interests, be applied in annuities for five poor men and ten poor widows, and five poor single women of the parish of Portsea of fifty years and upwards. The Trust Fund, consisting of £10,350 consols, was transferred to the official trustees, and was sold out on the 15 August, 1906, and re-invested in the following colonial securities, namely, £2,576 9*s.* New South Wales 3 per cent. stock ; £2,512 9*s.* 7*d.* New Zealand 3 per cents. ; £2,569 3*s.* 7*d.* Victoria Government 3 per cent. consolidated stock ; and £2,613 8*s.* 3*d.* South Australia 3 per cent. consolidated stock. The dividends are applied in annuities of £15, payable quarterly, to persons qualified under the trusts.

Henry Moody, by will, proved 14 November, 1889, left £10,000 to the trustees of Thomas Fitzherbert's charity, income to be applied by them upon similar trusts. The estate was administered in the High Court (Chancery Division), and proved to be insufficient to pay the legacies in full. By an order of the court of 11 April, 1906, a sum of £3,691 1*s.* 7*d.* consols was transferred to the official trustees, in satisfaction of the legacy. The stock was subsequently sold out and re-invested in £1,858 13*s.* 1*d.* Queensland Government 3 per cent. stock, and £1,819 12*s.* 2*d.* Western Australia Government 3 per cents. The two charities will be administered together.

Aria College is an institution founded and endowed by the will of the late Mr. Lewis Aria, for the training and maintaining therein of young men, natives of Hampshire, as Jewish divines, up to twenty-one years of age, but with an extension of not more than three years in the discretion of the trustees. The benefits may also include residence and maintenancy in London to attend the Jews' College and University College; each student to receive a yearly stipend of from £20 to £30. The endowment fund is estimated to be about £20,000. The institution was regulated by a scheme of the Court of Chancery, dated 30 May, 1873 (amended in 1876), but its operation has recently been suspended.

By will of Miss Emily Catherine Scale, proved in 1884, a sum of £199 10*s*. consols (with the official trustees) was bequeathed upon trust that the dividends be distributed among poor persons of the parish of All Saints on St. Thomas's Day.

The Albert Cottages Institution, situated in Canal Walk, Fratton, was founded in 1866 by members of the registered friendly societies of Portsmouth, and was discontinued in 1891. It was purchased by Sir John Baker, knt., who by deed dated 8 March, 1897, conveyed the property to trustees for the benefit of necessitous members of registered friendly societies of the borough, their wives and children. The inmates receive the dividends on £210 0*s*. 8*d*. consols (with the official trustees) left by will of Miss Emily Catherine Scale above mentioned.

The following charities relate to Southsea:—

The poor of Southsea are entitled to share in the charity of John Bass Eltham (see above).

The School and Home for the Blind, St. Edward's Road, was established in 1864 by Miss I. Henn-Gennys for the purpose of educating and giving industrial instruction to the blind of both sexes. By an indenture dated 11 March, 1867, William Thorngate, among other annual payments to various charitable institutions, provided that £5 a year should be paid to this institution. By an order of the Charity Commissioners made under the Board of Education Act, 1899, it was provided that a sum of £200 consols should be set aside in the books of the official trustees under the title of the Educational Foundation of William Thorngate in connexion with this institution.

By will proved 24 November, 1894, William Pelham Winter left £350 to be invested and income applied by vicar and churchwardens of St. Luke, Southsea, in such manner as they should think most advisable for the education at the Portsmouth Grammar School of one or more boys who should have attended the day school in connexion with the church. The legacy was invested in the purchase of £326 14*s*. 5*d*. India 3 per cent. stock.

William Pelham Winter likewise bequeathed £221 4*s*. 9*d*. consols, dividends to be applied in support of a soup kitchen. The two sums of stock are held by the official trustees.

William James Patterson, by will proved 1884, left £1,000 to be invested and income distributed to the poor of the parish of St. Paul, Southsea. The legacy was invested in £902 5*s*. 1*d*. consols which is held by the official trustees. The dividends, amounting to £22 11*s*., are applied by the vicar and churchwardens in giving tickets for groceries and coals and clothing.

There are more than forty elementary schools within the borough limits, the oldest foundation being that of the Portsea Beneficial Society's School, established under a deed of 1754.[585] They include also the Royal Marine Artillery School, opened in 1872, and the Royal Seamen and Marines Orphan School, built in 1874.[586]

The Portsmouth Grammar School was founded by Dr. William Smith, who endowed it with land by his will proved in 1733.[587]

In Highbury Street stands the house of John Pounds, a local cobbler, who held a ragged school there.

THE LIBERTY OF ALVERSTOKE WITH GOSPORT

Alverstoke (Alwarestoch and Halwarestoke, xi to xiii cent.; Alvardestoke, xiv cent.; Aillewardstoke, xv cent.; Alverstoke, xvi cent.).

The liberty of *ALVERSTOKE*, including *GOSPORT*, is bounded on the east by the waters of Portsmouth Harbour, and on the south by Spithead. In the south-east of the district, between the inlets called Forton Lake and Haslar Lake, stands the populous town of Gosport, from which the lines of houses extend northward along the Fareham Road and westward to Alverstoke. To the north are the hamlets of Bridgemary, Elson, Hardway, and Brockhurst, and to the east Forton, now rapidly becoming indistinguishable from Gosport itself. The land lies low, and where not built over is well-wooded and picturesque, especially on the south-west towards Stokes Bay. The South Western Railway line from Fareham runs through the parishes to Gosport, with two branches, one to Stokes Bay, and the other on the western boundary to Privett, and along the coast to Lee-on-Solent. In the extreme south angle of the parish is Gilkicker Point with its fort, and close to it on the east is Fort Monkton. Haslar Hospital lies further to the north, close to the mouth of Portsmouth Harbour, where Blockhouse Fort defends the entrance, and the chain which in former days closed the passage yet lies, it is said, in the mud at the bottom of the channel. Inland, and in the west of the parish are Forts Gomer and Grange, and Brown Down Battery; and Fort Rowner is partly in the parish. From the shore of Stokes Bay Henry II crossed to France on more than one occasion. East of the village of Alverstoke is Bay House, built in 1838, and now the residence of Mr. Francis Sloane-Stanley. Haslar Hospital dates from the reign of George II, and though of no particular architectural merit, is a good building of its kind, set round a courtyard, with open colonnades and a chapel. It takes its name from a farmhouse once on the site. There is a ferry from Portsmouth to the end of the High Street of Gosport, a floating bridge capable of taking great weights running every ten minutes to and fro, and the town is intersected with electric tramways. The buildings are in no way remarkable; in High Street, which is the principal road, is a market hall built in 1812, and other public buildings are the free public library,

[585] *V.C.H. Hants*, ii, 402.

[586] Ibid. 403.

[587] Ibid. 387 and 391.

opened 1901, and the Thorngate Memorial Hall, 1885, while in South Street is the Connaught Drill Hall, built in 1902.

MANORS *ALVERSTOKE* was among the possessions of the Old Minster or priory of St. Swithun, Winchester, in Saxon times. It is said to have been bestowed on the minster by a noble Saxon lady, Alwara, for the soul of her husband Leowin.[1] In 1086 the bishop of Winchester held it for the support of the monks of St. Swithun,[2] to whom it was confirmed by the pope in 1205, and again in 1243;[3] but in 1284, a critical year in the continuous dispute which had been maintained for some centuries between the bishop and the monastery, the manor of Alverstoke with Gosport was transferred to the bishop with two other manors in return for certain important concessions relating to the appointment of obedientiaries and secular servants.[4] In June, 1284, the king confirmed to the bishop the manors which he had thus acquired from the priory,[5] and a second confirmation of the agreement was issued in the following May.[6] The successive bishops of Winchester retained the manor until, under the Act of 1641 confiscating all episcopal lands, it was seized by the state and sold in 1648 to George Wither,[7] who was noted early in his life for his lyrics, and later for pamphlets in support of Cromwell's government. At the Restoration the bishops regained their lands, and Alverstoke remained a possession of the see of Winchester until it was taken over by the Ecclesiastical Commissioners.

The tenure of the manor under the monastery and bishops was of a somewhat extraordinary nature, in that the villeins themselves were 'farming' the land in 1086.[8] Early in the thirteenth century an agreement was made between the monks and their men of Alverstoke by which the latter promised to pay 4*d.* an acre yearly for their lands at Alverstoke with the exception of the land lying between the two watercourses, one where the almoner's mill was situated, and one below the garden of the parson of Alverstoke, for which land 6*d.* an acre was to be paid by the men of Stokes, Forton, Brockhurst, and Bury. The land for which the extra farm was to be paid was evidently that on which Gosport is now situated, for to the north of Gosport is Forton Lake or Creek, which formerly extended further inland as a mill-pond; and to the south is Stoke Lake, which terminates a little to the south of the church and rectory of Alverstoke. The same charter recited the privileges allowed to the men of Alverstoke by the prior and monastery: they were to be quit of tallages, pannage, and salt-rent; they were to be free to make wills and dispose of their goods; they were to be quit of wards and suit of hundred courts without the manor. At the same time the prior granted that they should hold their lands hereditarily with power to alienate them, and that all pleas save pleas of the crown should be heard without delay in the presence of the prior or his steward at the court of Alverstoke. The charter also regulated the election of the bailiff of the manor.[9] Thus the men of the manor were practically free tenants. They had a common seal which represented

Common Seal of Alverstoke

St. Swithun as bishop of Winchester seated on a throne holding the pastoral staff in his right hand and in his left a book. The legend is as follows:—

SIGILL' COMUNE HOMINUM PRIORIS SCI SWITHUNI DE ALWARESTOKE.[10]

In 1284, after the priory had transferred Alverstoke to the bishop, the king granted him return of writs in his manor there,[11] and at the same time free warren and freedom from pleas of forest in all his lands.[12] Disputes between the bishop and his tenants as to their privileges seem to have arisen in 1461 and again in 1606.[13] The bishop or his steward held court-baron and hundred court every three weeks for the tenants of the manor, while twice a year they also held the tourn, the tenants being quit of the sheriff's tourn.[14] The courts were occasionally held at the 'Red Lion' in Gosport.[15] The bishop also had rights of wreck as lord of the manor,[16] though his claim seems to have been disputed by the lord admiral in 1613.[17] The bishop's bailiff or reeve for the manor was always elected in court at the Michaelmas tourn,[18] his chief duty apparently being that of collecting the rents of the tenants.[19] A constable or beadle was also elected at the same time.[20]

BEDENHAM (Bedeham, xiii cent.; Badeham, xiv cent.; Bednam, xvi cent.) gives its name to three farms which lie on a broad peninsula to the north of Gosport, at the head of Portsmouth Harbour, where it is joined by the estuary of the Wallington River.

1 Winton Epis. Reg. Pontoise, fol. 160*b*; see *Proc. of the Royal Arch. Inst. at Winchester* (1846), p. 112.
2 *V.C.H. Hants*, i, 466*b*.
3 *Cal. Papal Letters*, i, 21 and 201.
4 Chartul. of St. Swithun; Add. MS. 29436, fol. 55.
5 Ibid. fol. 65.
6 *Cal. Chart. R.* ii, 289.
7 Close, 24 Chas. I, iv, 33.
8 *V.C.H. Hants*, i, 466*b*; see also i, 442.
9 *Proc. of the Royal Arch. Inst. at Winchester* (1846), 113. The charter was given by Prior Andrew, whose term of office lasted from 1239 to 1243.
10 There is a sulphur impression of this seal at the British Museum, xxxvi, 185.
11 *Cal. Chart. R.* ii, 273.
12 Ibid. 274.
13 *Proc. of the Royal Arch. Inst. at Winchester* (1846), p. 113.
14 There is a large number of court-rolls of Alverstoke, ranging from 1378 to 1713, among the Ecclesiastical Commissioners' Court Rolls at the Public Record Office.
15 Eccl. Com. Ct. R. bdle. 180, No. 5; bdle. 174, No. 1.
16 Ibid. bdle. 81, No. 13.
17 Ibid. bdle. 88, No. 2.
18 On most occasions the jurors appear to have nominated three men to the office, but only one was sworn in each year.
19 Ibid. bdle. 163, No. 1.
20 Ibid. bdle. 81, Nos. 9 and 31; bdle. 180, No. 5.

Here as elsewhere in the parish the land is level and the chief feature is the wide expanse of the harbour, with Portchester Castle as its most conspicuous landmark. Beyond Bedenham Farm are the Foxbury Brick and Tile Works.

Bedenham was evidently originally parcel of the manor of Alverstoke, but was held in 1303 by John de Drokensford, Keeper of the Wardrobe, who was consecrated bishop of Bath and Wells in 1308. The manor of Bedenham was held of the bishop of Winchester,[21] and is possibly identical with the half hide at Alverstoke held before the Conquest by Sawin and in 1086 by a certain knight.[22] In 1303 John de Drokensford granted the manor together with the advowson of Bedenham church to Roger Lanceleue 'for life with reversion to John and his heirs.[23] By 1316 it had reverted to John, who died 9 May, 1329,[24] leaving a brother and heir, Philip de Drokensford, then aged forty.[25] He twice obtained licence for the celebration of divine service in the oratory of his house at Bedenham in Alverstoke,[26] a fact which favours the possibility that the 'church' granted with the manor to Roger Lanceleue was no more than a private chapel attached to the manor-house. Philip de Drokensford died in 1356 and is said to have been succeeded by a son and heir John.[27] In 1370 Margaret, then wife of Maurice le Brun, was holding the manor of Bedenham in dower, perhaps as widow of Philip of Drokensford, of the inheritance of Margaret, then wife of Walter Mildecombe. Walter and Margaret then granted it for life to Maurice le Brun.[28] Later a moiety of the manor was in the possession of Margaret, granddaughter of Philip de Drokensford.[29] Her husband, Peter Courtenay, held a moiety of the manor in her right at his death in 1404,[30] but she survived him and her lands descended to her daughter Elizabeth by a former husband, Sir John de St. Lo.[31] Elizabeth married Sir William Botreux, on whom the moiety of Bedenham was settled in 1417.[32] Their son and heir Sir William Botreux, knight, held the whole manor jointly with his wife Margaret at the time of his death in 1462.[33] The latter, with her second husband Thomas Burgh, conveyed it in 1464 to certain feoffees,[34] probably in trust, for a moiety was purchased from Margaret Hungerford, daughter and heir of Sir William Botreux, by Robert White of Farnham.[35] After the death of his son John the possession of this moiety was disputed by Robert and Richard White, sons of John, since Richard, the younger son, claimed that it should descend to him according to the terms of the will of his grandfather Robert.[36] The termination of this quarrel is unknown, but in 1535 Henry White died seised of a moiety of the manor, leaving a son and heir Robert,[37] who settled it in 1546 on Agnes wife of Richard Bennett.[38] She conveyed it to her daughter Margaret Tichborne, at whose death it reverted to John Marriner, son and heir of Agnes.[39] John died in 1593,[40] and his son and heir Peter Marriner together with his wife Dorothy purchased the other moiety from Robert White.[41] The whole manor thus reunited was bequeathed by Peter Marriner to his only daughter and heir, Mabel wife of Edmund Plowden, who was aged seventeen at her father's death in March, 1613–14.[42] Within a few years she had parted with it, for in 1624 Robert Bold of Portsea was in possession of it.[43] In 1628 his son William Bold conveyed the manor to his kinsman John Mason,[44] in whose family it remained until 1654, when Robert Tufton otherwise Mason and Anne Gibbon widow were dealing with it,[45] probably for purposes of sale. Before 1683 it was devided into the two farms of Upper and Lower Bedenham. The 'manor' was settled by Thomas Beverley on his son Thomas and the latter's wife Anne in 1713.[46] This Anne survived her husband and was in possession in 1729,[47] after which it appears to have been inherited by coheiresses, Anne wife of John Bonham Smith and Susannah wife of John Carter.[48] Fanny wife of Daniel Carter Hobbs quitclaimed a third of the manor to Anne Bonham in 1782.[48a] Upper Bedenham was bequeathed by Owen Bird to James White of Portsmouth in 1766. In 1774 he bequeathed it to Sir John Carter, who in 1808 held one-sixth, while his son John Bonham Carter had the remaining five-sixths. Lower Bedenham had been mortgaged by Andrew Wall in 1683

JOHN DE DROKENSFORD, Bishop of Bath and Wells. *Quarterly azure and or with four (?) heads of croziers counterchanged.*

WHITE OF FARNHAM. *Six pieces azure and or, in the chief a lion's head razed gules between two roundels argent, each having two bars wavy vert upon it, and in the foot a like roundel between two of the like lions' heads.*

21 Chan. Inq. p.m. 6 Hen. IV, 38. But in 1349 the overlordship was accounted a possession of Hugh de St. John and as such assigned to one of his coheiresses, Margaret wife of John de St. Philbert; *Cal. Close*, 1349–54, p. 68.

22 *V.C.H. Hants*, i, 466*b*.

23 Feet of F. Hants, 32 Edw. I, file 15, No. 36.

24 *Reg. of John de Drokensford* (Somerset Rec. Soc.), 303.

25 Chan. Inq. p.m. 3 Edw. III (1st Nos.), 41.

26 Egerton MS. 2032, fol. 91; 2033, fol. 46.

27 Exch. Inq. p.m. (Ser. 1), file 14, No. 27. According to which John was son of Philip; but in a later pleading John is said to be grandson of Philip, i.e. son of Philip's daughter Mary. De Banc. R. No. 514 (Trin. 12 & 13 Ric. II), m. 95.

28 Feet of F. Hants, 44 Edw. III, file 27, No. 32.

29 De Banc. R. 514, m. 95. She was daughter of John son or grandson of Philip. If it may be assumed that Margaret wife of Maurice le Brun was widow of Philip of Drokensford (he is said to have left a widow Margaret), it would appear that Margaret wife of Walter Mildecombe was daughter of Philip, possibly identical with the daughter 'Mary' named in the plea. The possibility that Margaret Mildecombe was identical with Margaret Courtenay is lessened by the fact that her former husband Sir John de St. Lo died in 1375.

30 Chan. Inq. p.m. 6 Hen. IV, 38.

31 Feet of F. Somerset, 14 Ric. II, 20.

32 Close, 5 Hen. V, m. 14 *d.*

33 Chan. Inq. p.m. 2 Edw. IV, 15.

34 Feet of F. Div. Cos. 4 Edw. IV, file 74, No. 25.

35 Chan. Inq. p.m. 9 & 10 Edw. IV, 25.

36 Early Chan. Proc. lii, 43, &c.

37 Chan. Inq. p.m. 27 Hen. VIII.

38 Feet of F. Hants, Trin. 38 Hen. VIII.

39 Chan. Inq. p.m. Eliz. (Ser. 2), vol. 124, No. 159.

40 Ibid. 36 Eliz.

41 Feet of F. Hants, Hil. 44 Eliz.

42 Chan. Inq. p.m. Jas. I (Ser. 2), vol. 345, No. 120.

43 Ibid. 2 Chas. I (Ser. 2), ii, 90.

44 Feet of F. Hants, Trin. 4 Chas. I.

45 Recov. R. Hil. 1654, m. 109.

46 Ibid. Hil. 12 Anne, m. 146.

47 Feet of F. Hants, East. 2 Geo. II.

48 Ibid. East. 7 Geo. III.

48a Ibid. Trin. 23 Geo. III.

and in 1779 was conveyed by James Stares to Sir John Carter. His heirs sold both farms to Mr. Henry Stares in 1868. He conveyed them to Mr. Woodman Hill, from whom they were purchased in 1904 by Mr. Montague Foster of Stubbington House.[49]

GOSPORT (Goseport xiii cent.)[50] covers the district between Forton Lake and Haslar Lake, i.e. the land for which the villeins of St. Swithun paid twopence more the acre than they paid for the rest of the manor.[51] It is not mentioned in the Domesday Book, nor is there any trace of it in the records relating to Alverstoke before the thirteenth century. In 1284 it was 'the manor of Alverstoke with Gosport,' which the monks transferred to the bishop of Winchester,[52] and doubtless before that time Gosport had only existed as a member of Alverstoke, being perhaps the more important on account of its situation at the mouth of Portsmouth Harbour. In the following century Gosport rather than Alverstoke was the centre of the shipping on the west side of the harbour, for in 1302 Portsmouth and Gosport together were ordered to provide a vessel for the Scotch expedition.[53] The bishop held separate courts for Alverstoke and Gosport in the thirteenth century, but the profits of both were accounted for by the same two men.[54] During the fourteenth and fifteenth centuries the bishop or his officers held the two yearly tourns at Gosport and at Alverstoke on the same day,[55] but in 1507 and the following 150 years the tourns for both places seem to have been held together, although there were different jurors for each.[56] It is a significant fact that in the court-rolls of Alverstoke and Gosport previous to 1461, the date when the bishop's tenants obtained an exemplification of the entry relating to Alverstoke in Domesday Book, no record occurs of the election of separate officers for Gosport, although a bailiff and a beadle were chosen at the tourns at Alverstoke in 1459 and 1461,[57] but that in April, 1462, John Bonsergaunte was chosen to the office of bailiff of Gosport, and did homage to the bishop in the same court for two burgages and eight acres of arable land which he had acquired in the borough of Gosport.[58] This is the earliest record yet obtained of Gosport as a borough, though under the thirteenth-century charter granted to the men of Alverstoke it enjoyed exceptional privileges. In 1463 the bailiff of Gosport accounted for £6 2*s.* 8½*d.* as rent of assize, besides the profits of various vacant sites and the perquisites of the two yearly tourns.[59] In 1648 these rents of assizes or borough rents were of the yearly value of £6 4*s.* 8¾*d.*[60] No charter of incorporation has been found, nor does the bishop appear to have granted any special privileges to Gosport. Early in the sixteenth century Leland described it as a little village of fishermen approached (from Titchfield) by much heathy and fern ground.[61] It was then beginning to rise in importance owing to its proximity to Portsmouth. A block-house and bulwark were raised about the year 1540 for the defence of the harbour,[62] and later in the same century the increased value of the ferry or passage between Portsmouth and Gosport is shown by disputes which arose as to its ownership. It appears to have been held and maintained by the tenants and inhabitants of the borough and town of Gosport.[63] In 1597, however, an attempt was made to prevent its being so casually maintained. It was found to be insufficiently provided with boats, and was taken into the queen's hands and leased to Stephen Riddlesden and John Jeffries.[64] The inhabitants struggled to retain what appears to have been their only common property of any importance, and in 1602 the lessees were commanded to surrender the ferry to them, and arrangements were made for the provision of twenty boats with a skilful man in each, and the nomination of two supervisors of the passage at each law-day.[65] Nevertheless James I granted the ferry to Edmund Duffield and John Babington in 1614,[66] but they evidently failed to make good their right to it, for the two supervisors continued to be chosen in the borough courts during the seventeenth century.[67]

In 1627 a survey was made of Portsmouth Dock with a view to deciding whether it would not be better to make a new one on the Gosport side.[68] This plan, however, was not carried out, though the town became an important victualling station, and considerable store-houses, timber-yards, and rope-walks were established there in connexion with Portsmouth.[69] During the Civil War Gosport was held by the Parliamentarians, who set up batteries there which were of great use in the reduction of Portsmouth.[70] The borough had been taken over by the state with Alverstoke Manor, and sold to George and Elizabeth Withers,[71] under whom it appears that no courts were held.[72] After the restoration of the bishops' lands only the two yearly tourns were resumed, so that the tenants and inhabitants of Alverstoke and Gosport were obliged to seek justice at Portsmouth.[73] From 1462 onwards a bailiff had been chosen annually at the Michaelmas tourn, together with a constable, and, after 1537, a sergeant.[74] As a rule two men were chosen for each office, but only one was sworn.[75] In 1691 the constable was removed from office by the same court, on grounds of incapacity.[76] No election of a bailiff is recorded on the court rolls after the Restoration ; the office had apparently ceased to exist, at least as an elective one.[77] Finally, in 1682, the corporation of Portsmouth obtained the extension of their borough limits in order to include Gosport.[78]

49 Feet of F. Hants, East. 7 Geo. III. Information kindly supplied by Mr. A. T. Everitt.

50 The name was sometimes spelt Gosper or Gosberg in the seventeenth century.

51 *Proc. of the Royal Arch. Soc. at Winchester* (1845), p. 113.

52 Add. MS. 29436, fol. 55.

53 *Cal. Pat.* 1301–7, p. 75.

54 Mins. Accts. (Gen. Ser.), bdle. 1142, No. 15.

55 Eccl. Com. Ct. R. bdle. 80, Nos. 9 and 10, &c.

56 Ibid. bdle. 82, No. 17 ; bdle. 88, No. 3, &c.

57 Ibid. bdle. 81, No. 9.

58 Ibid.

59 Eccl. Com. (Various), bdle. 83, No. 159482.

60 Close, 24 Chas. I, pt. 4, No. 33.

61 Leland, *Itin.* (ed. Thomas Hearne) 96.

62 *L. and P. Hen. VIII*, xv, 323.

63 Exch. Dep. Mich. 42 & 43 Eliz. 22.

64 Exch. Spec. Com. 40 Eliz. 2054.

65 Ibid. 44 Eliz. 2068.

66 Pat. 12 Jas. I, xv.

67 Eccl. Com. Ct. R. bdle. 165, No. 3 ; bdle. 174, No. 1 ; bdle. 99, No. 1, &c.

68 *Cal. S.P. Dom.* 1627–8, p. 812.

69 Ibid. 1634–5, p. 352 ; 1651–2, p. 479 ; 1658–9, p. 401.

70 *Hist. MSS. Com. Rep.* x, App. vi, 149 ; *Rep. on Portland MSS.* i, 61.

71 Close, 24 Chas. I, pt. 4, No. 33.

72 Add. 33278, fol. 54.

73 Eccl. Com. Ct. R. bdle. 100. Nos. 2 to 4, &c.

74 Ibid. bdle. 81, No. 9 ; bdle. 83, No. 9.

75 Ibid. bdle. 88, No. 3, &c.

76 Ibid. bdle. 174, No. 3.

77 The 'bailiff' is mentioned on a court roll of 1705 (bdle. 180, No. 3), and Richard Burgis, bailiff, signed a roll of the borough court in 1706 (bdle. 180, No. 5), but it is quite possible that both these references are to the bishop's bailiff of Alverstoke.

78 Pat. 34 Chas. II, pt. 5, 13.

Upon this the freeholders and inhabitants of the manor of Alverstoke and the borough of Gosport petitioned George Morley, then bishop of Winchester, to resume his three-weekly courts, complaining that the mayor and corporation of Portsmouth had encroached upon their privileges by arresting tenants and inhabitants of the borough under warrants from Portsmouth, by forcing several of the inhabitants to serve as jurors there, by sending their officers to survey the weights and measures at Gosport, by taking away the profits of the ferry, by forewarning the freeholders from allowing cattle to graze on the common or from fishing in Oyster Pool Lake, by collecting anchorage in the harbour (an ancient right of the bishop), and by commanding the overseers of the poor to serve a second time.[79] One of the bishop's tenants, Albinas Knapton, was fined for protesting against these acts and saying that 'although the mayor of Portsmouth be mayor of the borough of Gosport, yet he was not mayor of the whole parish of Alverstoke.'[80] Gosport was again separated from Portsmouth in 1688, when the charter of Charles II to the latter was annulled,[81] but the election of a bailiff in the borough court was not revived, though for a time the constable, coal-meter, ale-taster, and supervisors of the ferry continued to be appointed at the Michaelmas tourn.[82] The two yearly tourns were held as late as 1749, although the business done in them gradually decreased, their work consisting chiefly in the cleansing of the town and the prevention of encroachments.[83] All traces of burgage tenure had by this time disappeared, and before 1749 the courts were known as the courts baron of the manor of Gosport, whereas in 1706 they had been termed the borough courts of Gosport.[84]

In the seventeenth century important ironworks were established in the town, and employed chiefly in connexion with the Portsmouth Docks.[85] Shipbuilding also increased,[86] and the town afforded accommodation for many of the workmen in Portsmouth Docks. These suffered severely in the outbreak of plague which raged in Gosport early in 1666,[87] when numbers of the townspeople left their homes there.[88] For the benefit of the increasing population the bishop of Winchester obtained a grant of two yearly fairs to be held at Gosport on the feasts of St. George and St. Michael, and three weekly markets on Tuesdays, Thursdays, and Saturdays. This grant to the bishop is dated 1717.[89] The fairs had much deteriorated in the nineteenth century, when toys were the only articles sold in any quantity. The dates were also changed to 4 May and 10 October.[90] They were finally abolished under an order in council in 1900. The old market-house stood in the High Street, but in 1812 the present market-hall was built near the beach, and the markets were held outside. No market has been held during the last fifty years.[91]

In 1763 a board of trustees for paving Gosport was appointed,[92] and in 1814 a more effectual Act was passed for the watching, lighting, and paving of the town.[93] Both Acts were partially repealed in 1874, when Gosport was included in the urban sanitary district of Alverstoke,[94] which adopted the Public Health Act of 1875 in 1887,[95] and since 1894 has been formed into the Gosport and Alverstoke Urban District Council.

During the wars of the eighteenth century the population increased rapidly, but the prosperity of the town diminished after the restoration of peace,[96] until the transfer of the victualling establishment to the Royal Clarence Yards again revived it.

CHURCHES

The church of *OUR LADY, ALVERSTOKE*, has been gradually rebuilt, and it is now entirely modern, with a chancel erected in 1865, a nave of five bays built in 1885, and a west tower. The old church, of which a plan is preserved in the library of the Society of Antiquaries, was of the same general plan, with north and south chapels added to the nave in the early part of the nineteenth century. The present church contains a number of monuments from the former building, and stands well in a large churchyard, but is of no antiquarian interest. In the west tower are two bells from the old church, dated 1699 and 1766, and the church possesses a silver paten of 1702, and cup of 1783, the rest of the plate being quite modern—a silver chalice of 1901, a silver-gilt chalice of 1875, and paten of 1880, and a silver paten of 1838, besides a glass flagon with plated mounts.

The registers begin in 1559, the first book running to 1686, and the second to 1737 for baptisms, 1714 for burials, and 1710 for marriages. The third volume continues the baptisms and burials to 1801, and the marriages to 1763, and the fourth takes the baptisms and burials to 1812. The marriages from 1763 to 1812 are contained in no less than seven books, beginning in the years 1763, 1765, 1777, 1784, 1791, 1799, and 1809.

No church is mentioned in the Domesday Survey. In 1122 William Giffard, then bishop of Winchester, disputed with the prior of St. Swithun the possession of nine churches attached to the manors held by the monks.[97] Among these was Alverstoke church, which the bishop restored to the monks in 1124.[98] Thenceforward the history of the rectory was coincident with that of the manor until the latter was transferred to the Ecclesiastical Commissioners while the bishop retained the rectory and advowson. Apparently they were not appropriated to the prior or the bishop.[99] A pension from the church was assigned to the hospital of St. Cross at Winchester, and is still paid.[100] The bishop had within the parish a peculiar court, the records of which commence in 1612, and are deposited at Winchester.

There are now two chapels-of-ease attached to St. Mary, Alverstoke—one, under the invocation of St. Mark at Anglesey, was built in 1844[101]; the other,

79 Add. MS. 33278, fol. 55.

80 Ibid.

81 *Lond. Gaz.* (No. 2391), 15–18 Oct. 1688.

82 Eccl. Com. Ct. R. bdle. 180, No. 5, &c.

83 Ibid. bdle. 180, Nos. 3 and 4, &c.

84 Ibid.

85 *Cal. S.P. Dom.* 1665–6, p. 356; 1666–7, p. 159.

86 Ibid. 1660–70, p. 70.

87 Ibid. 1665–6, pp. 268, 285.

88 Ibid. 369.

89 Pat. 3 Geo. I, pt. 3, No. 1.

90 Pigot's *Directory*, 1823–4, p. 324.

91 Information kindly supplied by Mr. A. T. Everitt.

92 Stat. 3 Geo. III, cap. 56.

93 Ibid. 54 Geo. III, cap. 20.

94 Ibid. 37 & 38 Vic. cap. 89.

95 Ibid. 50 & 51 Vic. cap. 99.

96 *Pop. Returns* (1851), p. 51.

97 *Ann. Mon.* (Rolls Ser.); *Ann. de Wintonia*, 46, 47.

98 Add. MS. 29436, fol. 16.

99 The entries in the Episcopal Register all refer to the 'rectory' or the rector, although in the *Taxatio* of 1291 the following entry occurs: 'Ecclesia de Alwardestok cum Vicaria £36 13*s.* 4*d.*'

100 Harl. MS. 1616, fol. 6*b*.

101 Sumner, *Conspectus of the Dioc. of Winton*, 1864.

Christ Church at Newton, is a modern building enlarged in 1862, and has a chancel with nave of four bays.

There was a chapel at Gosport attached to the parish church in 1284.[102] Leland states that there stood, before his time, a 'prophanid' chapel near the shore of Portsmouth Haven, 'scant half a mile from the very mouth of the haven.'[103] The present church of the Holy Trinity was built in 1696; for some years it was a chapelry of St. Mary, Alverstoke, but it was assigned a separate parish in 1860.[104] St. Matthew, Gosport, was formed into a parish out of Alverstoke in 1845,[105] the church being built in the same year.[106] Holy Trinity Church is a brick building stuccoed, consisting of chancel, nave with aisles of eight bays, west porch, and detached north-west tower. It was entirely remodelled in 1887, and the west end rebuilt, the tower being added in 1889. It contains a great deal of good modern woodwork and other fittings, and the organ came from the chapel at Canons, Stanmore, the famous house of the dukes of Chandos, having been purchased by the parishioners when the house was dismantled. St. Matthew's, built in 1846, has a chancel, nave with aisles of five bays, and south porch, of thirteenth-century style.

The church of St. John, Forton, was built in 1831, to serve as a district chapel.[107] In 1841 a distinct parish was assigned to it.[108] A new church is partially built, though the old one still exists.

At Elson the church of St. Thomas was built in 1845, and assigned a portion of Alverstoke parish in December of that year.[109] It has a chancel, nave, and west turret, and is designed in thirteenth-century style.

The Baptists, Congregationalists, and Wesleyans all have chapels in Gosport, and the Roman Catholics have a chapel in High Street.

CHARITIES The following charities exist within the liberty:—

Captain John Mann, by his will 1660, gave £5 yearly for the poor out of certain messuages in George Alley, in the parish of St. George, Southwark, vested in the governors of St. Thomas's Hospital, from whom the sum of £4 is received annually—£1 being deducted for land tax.

In 1671 Abraham Hewlett by will gave 20*s.* yearly to the poor out of his dwelling-house in Gosport. The annuity is secured on a house in High Street, Gosport, and is regularly paid by the owner.

In 1711 Jane Holmes by will charged a house and garden with 40*s.* yearly, for the benefit of two poor widows. The annuity is regularly received from Mrs. Seward, the owner of the house in the village. Two cottages adjoining the property charged are occupied by two widows, who in addition to the annuity of 40*s.* receive £36 8*s.* from the Thorngate Charity No. 4 (see below).

William Allen, by will 1719, charged his estates in Gosport and Alverstoke with £4 a year for the poor. It is secured on the King's Arms public-house, High Street, Gosport, and is received from Messrs. L. N. Blake & Co., solicitors for the owner.

In 1773 William Poore, by his will, charged his house in Gosport with £5 yearly for ever, payable to the churchwardens of the liberty part of the parish of Alverstoke for bread, to be given after every Sunday morning's service to poor persons therein, widows in preference. The devise was confirmed by deed enrolled in Chancery, dated 2 October, 1775. The rent-charge fell into arrear, but, owing to the intervention of the Charity Commissioners, the payment was resumed (with arrears) by the owner of No. 30, Clarence Square, Gosport, which represents the property charged.

In 1828 James Spaycock by his will left £78 11*s.* consols (with the official trustees), dividends to be given to two of the poorest and most respectable watermen residing in the parish.

The above-mentioned charities are administered together by the rector and churchwardens. Bread is given weekly to aged widows, fourteen old widows receive 5*s.* each, and the dividends on the stock are divided between two poor old watermen.

In 1880 Thomas Paul by will left £3,000 consols to the rector and churchwardens of Alverstoke, the dividends to be applied in the distribution of coals at Christmas-time to poor residents in the parish without regard to age, sex, or religious profession, in quantities of one-fourth of a ton to each person. In 1905, 78 tons of coal were distributed among 312 recipients at a cost of £73.

In 1887 Frederick John Lowes, M.D., bequeathed £1,000 consols to the rector and churchwardens upon trust, that the dividends thereof should be applied in the distribution of money at Christmas among fifty poor inhabitants residing in the parish as constituted in the year 1887, when the charity came into operation. The sum of 10*s.* is given to each recipient.

The two sums of stock are held by the official trustees.

The above apply to the whole parish of Alverstoke. In connexion with the town of Gosport there are the following charities:—

By deed dated 27 September, 1693, Lambert Peachey conveyed a piece of land for the erection thereon of almshouses. Augmentations were made to the charity by members of the Peachey family, and in 1786 a sum of £360 arising under the will of Richard Pilfold (1760) was laid out in the purchase of 3 acres 2 roods in the parish of Wickham, the rents to provide weekly bread for the inmates.

The endowments of the Almshouse Charity now consist of a messuage in North Cross Street, let at £40 a year; an annuity of £2 10*s.* paid by the Urban District Council out of New Short Road, Gosport; and £78 0*s.* 4*d.*, £2 15*s.* per cent. annuities, arising from investment of balances in hand.

The endowments of Richard Pilfold's augmentation consist of 2 acres 20 poles of land at Wickham, £196 19*s.* 4*d.*, £2 15*s.* per cent. annuities, arising from investment of proceeds of sale in 1899 of part of the land at Wickham to the London and South Western Railway Co., and £96 10*s.* 4*d.* consols from investment of surplus income. The sums of stock are held by the official, and the charities are administered under a scheme of the Charity Commissioners, dated 15 May, 1900.

In 1838 Mrs. Ann Paul, by will proved in the P.C.C., left £200 to be invested and income applied (subject to an invalid trust for repair of certain tombs in the chapel-yard of Holy Trinity), to be divided on 1 February and 1 August in every year among indi-

[102] *Cal. Chart. R.* ii, 273.
[103] *Itin.* (ed. Thos. Hearne), p. 96.
[104] *Lond. Gaz.* 25 Jan. 1860, p. 298.
[105] Ibid. 3 Sept. 1845, p. 2695.
[106] *Conspectus of the Dioc. of Winton*, 1864.
[107] Ibid.
[108] *Lond. Gaz.* 7 Sept. 1841, p. 2250.
[109] Ibid. 23 Dec. 1845, p. 7281; *Conspectus of the Dioc. of Winton*, 1864.

gent widows. The legacy was invested in £20 10*s.* 6*d.* consols with the official trustees.

The Thorngate Almshouses at Brockhurst :—

Thorngate Charity No. 1—

By deed dated 6 March, 1866, John Batty Thorngate and William Thorngate conveyed to trustees a piece of land at Brockhurst, upon which ten almshouses had been erected for the occupation of ten females (spinsters or widows), and endowed the same. The present endowment consists of £2,409 18*s.* 8*d.* consols. In 1905, £52 was expended out of the dividends of the stock in weekly payments to the inmates. (See also Thorngate Charities, Nos. 3 and 5.)

Thorngate Charity No. 2—

By deed dated 11 March, 1867, the said William Thorngate conveyed to trustees a piece of land at Camden Town, Forton, upon which fifteen almshouses had been erected, and endowed the same with £7,500 consols. In 1905 the sum of £155 12*s.* out of the dividends of this sum of stock was expended in weekly payments to the inmates. (See also Thorngate Charities, Nos. 3 and 5.)

Thorngate Charity No. 3—

By another deed, also dated 11 March, 1867, William Thorngate settled a sum of £42,000 consols upon trust to provide certain fixed payments to certain institutions and schools and poor persons within the parish of Alverstoke, and certain institutions not within the parish. The stock, which is held by the official trustees, has, as regards the educational charities, been apportioned by an order dated 10 April, 1906, made by the Charity Commissioners under the Board of Education Act, 1899.

For Cook's Ragged School and Home in South Street, established in 1853 (now known as 'The Henry Cook Institute and Boys' Home'), a sum of £1,200 consols has been set aside to produce £30 a year. To produce £10 a year for each of the following institutions, viz. :—The Sunday School at Alverstoke ; the Sunday School at Elson ; the Ragged School, Haslar Street, Gosport ; Holy Trinity Sunday School ; St. Matthew's Sunday School ; and Forton St. John Sunday School, six sums of £400 consols have been set aside as educational foundations in connexion with each of these objects.

In 1905 the sum of £78 was paid to the inmates of the ten almshouses at Brockhurst (Charity No. 1) ; and £64 15*s*, to the fifteen almshouses at Gosport (Charity No. 2).

Thorngate Charity No. 4—

By deed dated 24 August, 1867, William Thorngate and Emmanuel Churcher conveyed to trustees land at Camden Town, Forton, for the erection of forty or more three-roomed almshouses for married couples or females above fifty years of age, for the endowment of which certain securities were assigned by deed 4 February, 1868. (Thorngate Charity, No. 5).

In 1905 the endowment fund consisted of £71,940 13*s.* 7*d.* consols (with the official trustees), the income of which is applicable by the trustees in annual specified subscriptions to numerous existing educational and charitable societies and institutions, with power for the trustees to retain £120 per annum for their expenses in executing the trusts. In 1905 the payments for local objects included Gosport and Alverstoke Victoria Nursing Institution, £10 ; to inmates of two almshouses (Jane Holmes), Alverstoke, £36 8*s.* ; to inmates of ten almshouses at Brockhurst, £52 (Charity No. 1) ; to inmates of almshouses at Gosport, £51 16*s.* (Charity No. 4) ; to inmates of fifteen almshouses, Camden Town, £116 14*s.* (Charity No. 2) ; sixty poor people also received £10 each, twenty-one received £15 each, and ten received £5 each ; £20 were paid to four poor old watermen, and £20 to four poor old fishermen.

Thorngate Charity, No. 6—

By deed dated 22 January, 1868, William Thorngate conveyed to trustees certain messuages, tenements, and lands, and assigned certain bonds and securities upon the charitable trusts therein mentioned, namely, for the benefit of poor persons resident in the town of Gosport and elsewhere in Great Britain and Ireland. Under the authority of an order of the Charity Commissioners, dated 4 July, 1890, several pieces of land (part of the trust property), containing together 96 acres 2 roods 20 poles, situated at Hoe Gate, in the parish of Soberton, were sold, and the net proceeds, amounting to £1,908 1*s.* 2*d.*, were invested in New South Wales 4 per cent. stock. The endowment (1905) consists of four freehold tenements in Gosport, producing about £50 a year ; a rent-charge of £20 on land known as the Gurnard Estate, in the Isle of Wight (about to be redeemed) ; £3,072 4*s.* 2*d.* Queensland 4 per cent. stock ; £4,692 11*s.* 7*d.* New South Wales 4 per cent. stock ; £5,561 3*s.* 4*d.* New Zealand 4 per cent. stock ; and £644 7*s.* 6*d.* Canada 3½ per cent. stock, producing £550 a year. In 1905, £300 was expended in donations of £20 each, and £200 was distributed in fuel, meat, and other necessaries to 500 people ; and £100 was, as directed by the deed, retained by the trustees.

The several sums of stock belonging to the above-mentioned Thorngate Charities are held by the official trustees.

Thorngate Charity No. 7 was founded by deed dated 4 January, 1868, whereby certain freehold and leasehold property in Ireland (including a fee-farm rent of £89 10*s.* 9*d.* issuing out of the lands of Bredagh, in the barony of Kilconnell, in the county of Galway), were settled upon trust to apply the rents in sums of £20 to decayed and unfortunate tradespeople or other persons of Gosport and elsewhere. By an order of the Charity Commissioners dated 26 June, 1906, the trustees were authorized to sell the said fee-farm rent for £2,300, the price fixed in accordance with the provisions of the Irish Land Act, 1903. The particulars of the trust estate have not yet been supplied to the Charity Commissioners.

In 1885 a memorial hall was erected in the High Street, Gosport, at a cost of about £9,000, as a memorial to the late William Thorngate, esquire, merchant of this town, who died in the year 1868, the founder of the several Thorngate Charities.

The Gosport Royal Marine School dates from 1850. An elementary school was opened at Forton in 1830, and another at Gosport in connexion with Holy Trinity Church in 1831. In 1842 a school was founded at Alverstoke, and about two years later St. Matthew's School, Gosport, and Elson School, were opened. In 1853 an elementary school was founded at Newton, and another in connexion with the Roman Catholic Church of St. Mary was established in 1811. Leesland School was opened in 1850.[110]

[110] See *V.C.H. Hants*, ii, 395.

THE HUNDRED OF FAREHAM

CONTAINING THE PARISH OF[1]

FAREHAM

At the time of the Domesday Survey the hundred of Fareham consisted of Fareham only, and it had probably been included in the grant of the latter to the see of Winchester about the ninth century. In 1284 the king, probably as the result of a suit of which, however, no record can be found, gave up to John bishop of Winchester, and his successors, all his right in the hundred of Fareham.[2] In the thirteenth century Peter des Roches withdrew the suit of Bromwich from the hundred of Titchfield to his court of Fareham, and by 1279 the tithings of North Fareham, Catisfield, Dean, Pokesole, Cams, and Bedenham had been added and are mentioned as having neglected to do

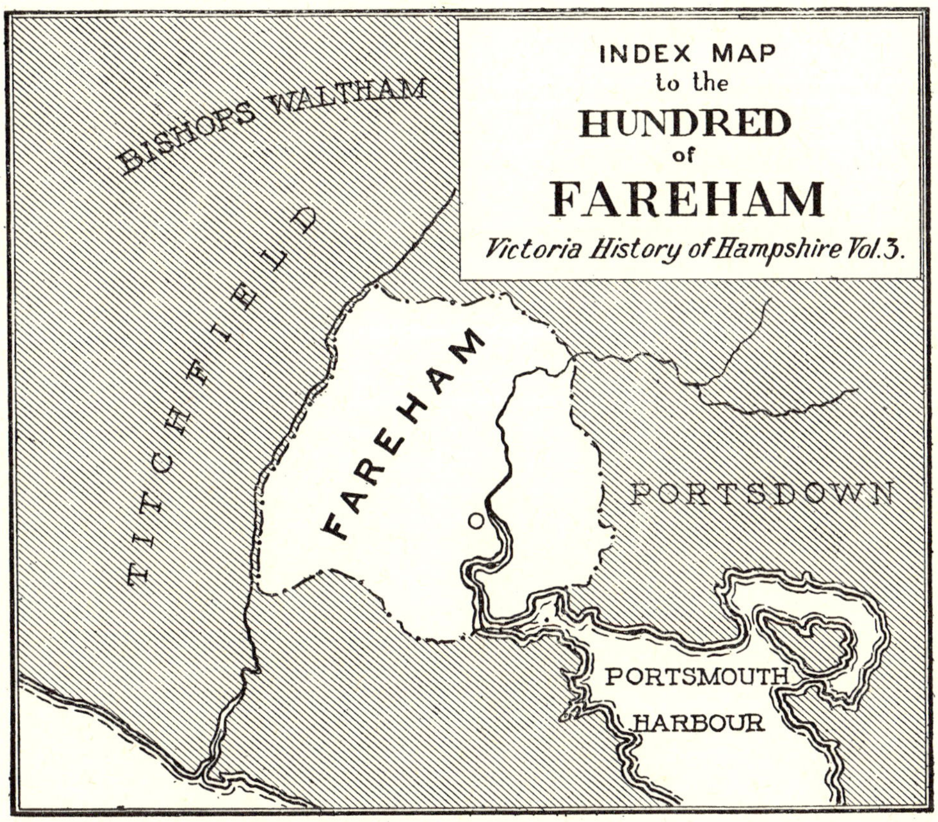

suit at Fareham.[3] By 1346 Fareham had been still further enlarged by the addition of Crockerhill, Camsbishop, and Prallingworth, the latter having been transferred from Titchfield Hundred, while some time during the next century Abshot was added.[4] Of these places Camsbishop has probably been merged in Camsoysell, Dean is in Bishop's Waltham, Bromwich and Abshot in Titchfield; Crockerhill and Catisfield are small hamlets in Fareham, while Prallingworth, Bedenham, and Pokesole have ceased to exist.

[1] According to the *Pop. Ret.* 1831.
[2] *Cal. of Chart. R.* 1257–1300, p. 274.
[3] Assize R. No. 784, m. 51.
[4] Eccl. Com. Ct. R. bdle. 80, No. 8; ibid. bdle. 81, No. 12. *Feud. Aids*, ii, 335.

FAREHAM

Ferneham (xi cent.) ; Ferham (xiii cent.) ; Fareham (xiv cent.).

The parish of Fareham consisting of 6,736 acres, of which eleven are covered by water, is situated on the shore of a deep inlet of the sea forming the north-western branch of Portsmouth Harbour. The two main streets of the town are West Street, on the Portsmouth road, the houses extending from the railway station on the east to the tidal mill on the west, and High Street, which runs northward from the west end of the former street. From the middle of West Street another road runs southward to the harbour, skirting the quays on the west. In its western part West Street is bordered by small red-brick villas, and then broadens out into what is really an elongated market-place, with shops, inns, and public buildings. The modern church of the Holy Trinity is on the south side of West Street. The High Street, though broad at first, narrows down quickly as it ascends a rise on the crest of which stands the old church, well back from the road in a large churchyard. There are many specimens of good eighteenth-century brick fronts in the town. The most picturesque part is at the east, where the river is held up by the sluices of a tidal mill, and forms a wide sheet of water with wooded banks. The mill is an old tarred wooden building at the head of the harbour, on the eastern side of which are the wooded grounds of Cams Hall. There are 2,768 acres of arable land, 2,299 of permanent grass, and 415 of woods and plantations.[5] The road from Southampton to Havant crosses the parish from west to east ; a second road enters the town from Bishop's Waltham, while a third runs southwards to Gosport. The London and South Western Railway has a station at Fareham, at which is also the junction of a branch line to Gosport and Stokes Bay. Fareham Harbour, formed by a long broad inlet called the Cams, lies to the south-east of the parish, and though unimportant to-day, in the seventeenth century it had a considerable reputation, as may be seen from the following letter written from Portsmouth in 1630 to Sir John Coke, Principal Secretary of State. 'The river leading to Fareham within a mile of the town is an absolute good and safe place to moor ships and in all respects as convenient and safe a harbour as Chatham. £2,000 may be saved to the king in moorings and men.'[6] The Portsmouth road cuts across the head of this inlet, on a causeway with swinging water-gates opening inwards, through which the tide flows into a big natural reservoir, the water being used to work the old mill already mentioned, probably formerly known as the 'Tyde or Sea Mill.'[7] There is a small house in West Street, now used as a lending library, where Thackeray is supposed to have written several of his novels. A little out of the town on the Wickham road is Roche Court, now occupied by Mr. H. F. Rawstorne, who acquired it through his wife—a member of the Gardiner family whose ancestors have possessed the estate since 1661. It is of some antiquity, the original house being said to have been built by Peter des Roches. The oldest part now existing is a block standing east and west, with thick walls of flint masonry, but, unfortunately, no architectural features of very ancient date. It is doubtless mediaeval, but its original windows, &c., have long been replaced by later work. At its east end is a large chimney breast, and against it on the north-east is built a wing standing north and south, of timber construction, with two pretty half-timbered gables on the east side. The first floor room contains some good early seventeenth-century panelling, and the wing is probably an addition of this date. It has been lengthened northward in the eighteenth century, and the panelling is made out in the detail of the time. The main entrance is on the west side of this wing, and with the entrance passage, is a comparatively modern addition. In front of it is a fine cedar, which is, unfortunately, rather too near the house. The stables and offices stand to the south-west, and the

Roche Court, Fareham

[5] Statistics from the Bd. of Agric.(1905).

[6] *Hist. MSS. Com. Rep.* xii, App. iii, 406.

[7] Exch. Dep. Hil. 6 & 7 Chas. I, No. 6. There were two mills in the 17th century—the Tyde or Sea Mill and Wallington Mill rented at £4 in money and 5 quarters of wheat ; Close, 24 Chas. I, No. 41.

garden is mainly to the east, with a pretty garden house. The approach to the court is through the park from the Fareham road, by a gate and lodge in Strawberry Hill Gothic. There are some very fine trees in the park, and a thick belt of trees shuts off the road on the north boundary. Cams Hall, a large house on the east bank of the Cams, standing back in a large park is now occupied by Captain Ramsey, J.P. The house was built in 1781 of materials taken from Place House, Titchfield, and contains some woodwork brought thence and now in the stables. Blackbrook Grove, a large thatched house on the Titchfield road, belongs to Mr. J. H. Harvey, and on the opposite side is Blackbrook House, the residence of Lady Parker. Uplands House, formerly owned by Mr. Sidney Waterlow, and Wallington House, owned by the War Department, are now empty. In mediaeval times Fareham was a free port, and in 1346 the mayor of Southampton was pardoned for having taken 'divers distresses under the name of customs to the great damage of Fareham.'[8] It was famous too as a wine port in the fourteenth century, while in the sixteenth and seventeenth centuries it was largely used as a shipping port for timber, especially that supplied from Titchfield Park, though subject to some competition from Warsash, the charge for wood bought at Titchfield being 38*s.* the load if shipped from Warsash and 40*s.* from Fareham.[9] In 1637 Robert Rigge, 'undertaker on the part of the county of Hants' for the carriage of 1,000 loads of timber to the waterside of Fareham at 3*s.* 4*d.* per load, was accused of having detained from the carters 4*d.* on every load. He was also charged with not repairing the bridge at Fareham Quay 'which he is bound to do taking quayage.'[10] At this time the charge for timber conveyed from Titchfield Park to Fareham Quay was 5*d.* per mile.[11] In 1636 a sum of £50 was levied on the parish of Fareham for ship-money, while two years later 'the good men of Fareham' were asked to supply the king with a ship of 400 tons, with 160 men, to be ready at Portsmouth within four months.[12] To-day a few fishermen find occupation round the Cams but the shipping is quite unimportant, the chief article imported being coal. Brick-making, which has been carried on in Fareham for at least two and a half centuries,[13] is still a flourishing industry—'Fareham Reds' being well-known throughout the south of England. There is also a large tanyard. Agriculture is in a good condition, there being no unoccupied land in the parish. The soil is loam on chalk in some parts; gravel on chalk in others, while in the north there is a good deal of loose flint. The corn crops are good. Sheep-rearing, once an important industry at Fareham, has died out. A weekly cattle market is held, but the annual fair, formerly of great importance, was abolished in 1871.[14]

Among other names there are:—Witelcroft,[15] Christonman's Land, Bletchinors, Brookfurlong, Clapgate, Grubbwood, Gunnersclose, Brithfrithheath, Toppett, Horgaston,[16] and Broadcroft.[17]

BOROUGH Fareham was a mesne borough owned by the bishops of Winchester,[18] and, except for a short period in the seventeenth century, always retained by them.[19] In 1648, after the ordinance for the sale of bishops' lands the borough, including rents, fairs, markets, courts, &c., of the yearly value of £4 14*s.* 8*d.*, was bought by Peter Wilkins for £909 14*s.* 8*d.*,[20] but it was probably restored to the see of Winchester with the other episcopal estates at the Restoration. There is no evidence to show when the borough originated, and the first definite proof of its existence is to be found in 1261 when Elias of Rochester obtained a grant under letters patent of a burgage, and a stall in the borough of Fareham, which was in the king's hands by reason of the vacancy of the see of Winchester.[21]

In the reign of Edward I two members were returned to the Parliament of 1306,[22] and this is the only occasion that Fareham was represented in Parliament. The first record of a borough court is in 1337, and from that date the courts were held almost continuously until 1729, but it is possible that during the next century the privileges of the burgesses were allowed to lapse, as Fareham is omitted from the Hampshire boroughs in the Report of 1835. The town was governed by a bailiff, who was elected in the borough court; the accounts were always noted separately from those of the manor, and a detailed account is given of the proceeds of the court, the assize rent being 64*s.* The Public Health Act was adopted in Fareham in 1849, and the government of the town vested in a Board of Health of nine members, but under the provisions of the Local Government Act (1894) the Urban District Council became the local authority.

MANORS At the time of the Domesday Survey Fareham was held by the bishop of Winchester, and it appears to have formed part of the original endowment of the bishopric. Though it actually contained 30 hides it had always been assessed at 20 because of its exposed position and its liability to attacks from the Danes. In King Edward's time it was worth £18, its value after falling to £10 rose to £16 before the date of the Survey, when it was farmed at £20; 'it cannot however bear it.'[23] In 1284 the king granted all right and claim in the manor of Fareham to John bishop of Winchester and his successors.[24] Land in the manor or rents from the manor were granted to various tenants from time to time.[25] In 1455 John archbishop of York was granted rents from the manor of Fareham,[26] while about 1541 Sir Thomas Wriothesley, who

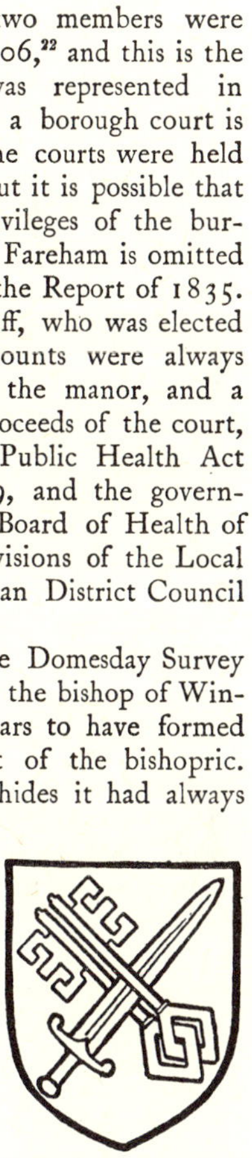

SEE OF WINCHESTER. *Gules St. Peter's keys crossed with St. Paul's sword.*

[8] *Cal. of Pat.* 1377–81, p. 81; ibid. 1345–8, pp. 163, 167.
[9] *Cal. of S.P. Dom.* 1668–9, p. 28.
[10] Ibid. 1637, p. 298.
[11] Ibid. p. 426.
[12] Ibid. 1638–9, p. 88.
[13] Eccl. Com. Ct. R. bdle. 102, No. 2.
[14] *Lond. Gaz.* 12 Sept. 1871.
[15] *Cal. of Pat.* 1348–50, p. 110.
[16] Eccl. Papers, var.
[17] Mins. Accts. Exch. Dep. Mich. 5 Will. and Mary, No. 10.
[18] In 1284 the king agreed to give up to the bishop any right he possessed in the borough; *Cal. of Chart. R.* 1257–1300, p. 274.
[19] Eccl. Com. Ct. R. bdle. 80, No. 7 et seq.
[20] Add. MS. 9049, fol. 9; Close, 24 Chas. I, pt. 6, m. 41.
[21] Pat. 46 Hen. III, m. 10.
[22] *Parl. Writs* (Rec. Com.), i, 57.
[23] *V.C.H. Hants*, i, 462*a*.
[24] *Cal. of Chart. R.* 1257–1300, p. 274.
[25] Anct. D. (P.R.O.), A. 8938, 8682, 8676.
[26] Close, 14 Hen. VI, m. 18.

already held 100*s.* rent in Fareham,[27] was granted a lease of the park.[28] In 1641 a lease of the manor was granted to Ralph Riggs for three lives, and in 1647 Margery his widow petitioned the Commons to confirm to her and her sons this lease, otherwise they would be reduced to great extremity, because on its security she had lent her husband £1,000 in 1645, which lease was void by the ordinance of October, 1646, for taking away bishops' lands, and annulling all estates taken of the bishops since December, 1641.[29] Once only the manor passed out of the bishop's hands. After the ordinances of 1646 for the sale of bishops' lands, it was sold in 1648 to Nicholas Bond for £1,632 12*s.* 7¼*d.*,[30] but was restored in 1660 to the see of Winchester, and retained until the estates of the see were taken over by the Ecclesiastical Commissioners in 1869.[31]

PARK Fareham Park has existed from a very early date. In 1279 complaint was made that certain persons had broken into the bishop's park at Fareham and carried away the deer,[32] while on the Pipe Roll for the year 1323 the wage of the park keeper is noted among the expenses of the manor.[33] Various references to the park are made in the Court Rolls from time to time. In 1477 there was a payment of 3*s.* 4*d.* for a hedge round the park, while during the seventeenth and eighteenth centuries 50*s.* for the farm of the park is a yearly entry among the receipts.[34] A lease of the park was granted to Sir Thomas Wriothesley about 1541, when he acquired 100*s.* of rent in Fareham from the bishop, and this lease was devised to his wife Jane during the minority of her son, and was held successively by the second and third earls of Southampton.[35] The timber, like that of Titchfield Park, appears to have been in great demand for shipbuilding, and there are various records of sales of the wood made to the Admiralty.

A letter written on this subject by Sir Antony Windsor to Lord Lisle, deputy of Calais and sheriff of Hampshire in 1538 is interesting, and it also throws some light on the political intrigues of the time. 'As to your great wood you wrote for there is a thousand ready tallied in Farahame Park and a thousand more shall be ready shortly and then your warrant is expired. I would advise you to make suit to my lord of Winchester to have a quantity of wood every year for there is a new woodward a servant of Sir William Paulet's. As to game there is no great plenty of male deer but there is a pretty score of rascal as all the borders, gentlemen, and others, report . . .[36] Your lordship will understand that by sudden changes of officers there will be secret enemies and when the wrongdoers are tried it will be well to have a friend about the King. You should write a loving letter to my Lord Admiral to assist your officers. I doubt not the forest will increase in spite of all your enemies, and this will be a good means to stay warrants which are like to come thick and threefold if some persons can help it.' The 'bishop's meadow' containing 15 acres, is mentioned in the sale of the Fareham estate in 1648.[37]

It is probable that the 7½ hides in Fareham held by Ralph in 1086[38] developed later into the manor of *NORTH FAREHAM* (Norfarham, xiii cent.), which always belonged to the bishops of Winchester.[39] At the beginning of the thirteenth century this manor was held by William Fitz Roger, though there is no evidence to show how it came into his possession. On his death about 1225, Peter des Roches, in right of his see, held the wardship of William's daughter Emma Fitz Roger, whom he gave in marriage to his nephew Geoffrey des Roches.[40]

Des Roches. *Sable two leopards argent.*

North Fareham, which about this time became known by the alternative name of Roche Court, descended to Martin their son, but as he left no child on his death in 1277, the property passed to his brother Hugh subject to the life interest of Lucy widow of Martin.[41] On the death of Lucy, who survived her husband certainly ten years, John des Roches son of Hugh came into possession of the manor, which he held for half a knight's fee, for which he did suit at the bishop's court of La Soke, and at his view of frankpledge at South Fareham. On his death in 1312 his widow held the estate in dower,[42] it being then worth yearly £7 17*s.* She died in 1361, and was succeeded by her daughter Mary des Roches, widow of Sir John Boarhunt, and the property passed on Mary's marriage, about 1381, to Sir Bernard Brocas,[43] one of a family of great importance at this period. Sir Bernard Brocas represented Hampshire in most of the Parliaments of the reign of Richard II, and he obtained, first by right of his wife and afterwards by purchase, the mastership of the Royal Buckhounds,[44] an office which remained in the Brocas family for three centuries. In 1363 he received a grant of free warren in his demesne lands of North Fareham.[45] After his death in 1395 the manor was held in dower by his third wife Katherine,[46] from whom it descended to her step-son Sir Bernard Brocas, who was beheaded in 1400 for his share of the conspiracy in favour of Richard II.[47] Much of Bernard's property being in trust escaped forfeiture, but North Fareham, together with other manors in Surrey and Dorset,

Boarhunt. *Argent a fesse between six martlets gules.*

[27] Feet of F. Mich. Hants, 33 Hen. VIII.
[28] *Cal. S.P. Dom.* 1598–1601, p. 601.
[29] *Hist. MSS. Com. Rep.* vii, App. pt. i, 6*a*.
[30] Add. MS. 9049, fol. 21. At a survey taken in the previous year the rents and profits of the manor were valued at £243 12*s.* 5*d.* while the timber was said to be worth £164 12*s.* 10*d.*
[31] *Lond. Gaz.* 1 Ap. 1870.
[32] *Cal. of Pat.* 1272–81, p. 349.
[33] Pipe R. 17 Edw. II.
[34] Eccl. Papers, var. No. 6; Eccl. Com. Ct. R. bdle. 81, No. 9.
[35] *Cal. of S.P. Dom.* 1598–1601, p. 601.
[36] *L. and P. Hen. VIII*, xiii (1), 382.
[37] *Coll. Top. et Gen.* i, 123.
[38] *V.C.H. Hants*, i, 462*a*.
[39] *Feud. Aids*, ii, 307; Chan. Inq. p.m. 22 Ric. II, No. 8; ibid. 1 Ric. III, No. 23.
[40] Burrows, *Family of Brocas*, 321.
[41] Close, 14 Edw. I, m. 2 *d.*
[42] Chan. Inq. p.m. 5 Edw. II, No. 44.
[43] Ibid. 35 Edw. III, pt. 2, No. 49; ibid. (2nd Nos.), No. 19.
[44] Chan. Inq. p.m. 41 Edw. III (2nd Nos.), No. 40*b*.
[45] Chart. R. 37 Edw. III, pt. 1, No. 9, m. 11.
[46] Chan. Inq. p.m. 22 Ric. II, No. 8.
[47] *Dict. Nat. Biog.* vi, 366.

escheated to the crown.[48] Bernard's widow shortly after his execution was granted dower in all the forfeited lands,[49] and her son William obtained restitution of his father's estates in November, 1400.[50]

William was succeeded by a second William Brocas in 1456, whose son John also had a son William, on whose death in 1506 without heirs male North Fareham passed to one of his two daughters, Edith, afterwards wife of Ralph Pexall,[51] from whom it descended to their son Richard about 1540. On his death in 1571 he demised the whole of the property to his second wife Eleanor Cotgrave for thirteen years until his grandson Pexall Brocas, son of his eldest daughter Anne, should be of age, and left a legacy of £500 each to three of his daughters by his first wife Eleanor Paulet, the eldest, Anne, who had married Bernard Brocas, being passed over. The will was declared void as regarded one-third of the property, and this was divided amongst four daughters :—Anne, who married Bernard Brocas ; Margery, wife of (1) O. Beckett, (2) F. Cotton ; Elizabeth, wife of J. Jobson ; and Barbara, who married A. Brydges, as co-heiresses. In 1572 Lady Eleanor bought the one-twelfth belonging to Elizabeth Jobson for £1,800.[52] Pexall Brocas came of age in 1584, when Lady Eleanor's legal claim was reduced to the one-twelfth she had purchased from the Jobsons. In the following year Pexall settled his two-thirds of the property in North Fareham on his wife Margaret, daughter of Sir Thomas Sherley.[53] The descent will be more easily seen from the following pedigree :—

Brocas. *Sable a leopard rampant or.*

Pexall. *Argent a flowered cross engrailed sable between four birds azure having beaks and legs gules and collars argent with a scallop argent on the cross.*

Sir Bernard Brocas = (1) . . . .
= (2) Mary daughter of Sir John de Roches, widow of Sir J. Boarhunt, *ob. circa* 1331
(3) Katherine

Bernard Brocas = Joan, *ob.* 1429
ob. 1400

William Brocas = Sybil
ob. 1456

William Brocas = Agnes

John Brocas = Anne

William Brocas = Mary Griffin

Anne | Edith = Ralph Pexall, *ob. circa* 1540

Richard Pexall = (1) Lady Eleanor Paulet
(2) Eleanor Cotgrave, who = (2) Sir John Savage

Anne = Bernard Brocas | Margery = (1) O. Beckett (2) F. Cotton | Eliz. = J. Jobson | Barbara = A. Brydges

Pexall = Margaret Shirley

Thomas = ...

Robert = Jane Bodley

Jane = Sir Wm. Gardiner

In spite of Sir Pexall's extravagance much of his property was saved by the efficiency of his trustees, and on his death in 1630 he was possessed of ten-twelfths of the Des Roches property, and his son Thomas secured the remainder by purchasing the Jobson and Beckett twelfths.[54] In order to escape his creditors, Thomas handed over the estate to his mother's trustees, and it thus remained in the family until 1661, when the marriage of his granddaughter Jane Brocas with Sir William Gardiner brought the manor of Roche Court

48 Burrows, *Family of Brocas*, 137.
49 Chan. Inq. p.m. 1 Hen. IV, pt. 1, No. 17.
50 *Cal. of Pat.* 1399–1401, p. 386.
51 Feet of F. Hants, East. 4 Hen. VIII.
52 Burrows, *Family of Brocas*, 208–10. This was later settled on Edward Savage, son of her second husband, Sir John Savage.
53 Burrows, *Family of Brocas*, 214–15.
54 Ibid. 212, 223.

into a family of great political distinction at this time. On the death of Sir William Gardiner, grandson of the above, in 1779, without children, the baronetcy became extinct, but was revived in the person of Sir John Whalley Smythe Gardiner, representative of a younger branch of the family in 1783, and from his brother Sir James W. S. Gardiner it descended in direct succession to Sir John Brocas W. S. Gardiner, who died in 1868, and in whom the baronetcy became extinct for the second time.[55] The property passed to his only daughter Mabel, who died in 1892, and who in 1887 had married Mr. H. F. Rawstorne, the present lord of the manor.

GARDINER. *Argent a cheveron gules between three griffons' heads razed azure with two lions azure counter passant on the cheveron.*

The Court Rolls of the manor of North Fareham from the years 1632 to 1749 are in existence, and an interesting entry under the latter date is to the effect that 'this manor is out of the jurisdiction of the Court of the lord bishop of Winchester called the Cheney Court,' and 'that no tenant or inhabitant of the manor ought to take the office of tithing man of the tithing of North Fareham by the authority of the Court of the lord bishop of his manor of South Fareham, but ought to take the said office and be sworn into the same at the Court of this manor, and by the order thereof as have from time immemorial (been) usual and accustomed.'[56]

The second holding in Fareham belonging to the see of Winchester consisted of 4 hides, mentioned in Domesday as held by William, formerly held by Earl Godwin,[57] and probably became the manor of *CAMS* (Cammes, xiii cent.; Cammes Oysell, xiv cent.; Camoyse Oysell, xvi cent.). The early history is obscure, but by the twelfth century it seems to have passed to the Oysell family, for in 1166 Robert Oysell was holding one knight's fee of the bishop of Winchester in Hampshire.[58] This was probably Cams, which seems to have been held subsequently by that service. In 1306, in the only Parliament in which Fareham was represented, John Oysell, probably a member of the same family, sat as one of the representatives of the borough.[59] In 1316 the vill of Cams was held by Nicholas Oysell, who appears to have been the last member of the family connected with the place.[60] In 1346 Nicholas Stake, a man evidently of some importance in Hampshire, who witnessed various deeds relating to the Brocas property, held one knight's fee in Cams.[61] There are no records to show how the manor came into the hands of the Audley family, but in 1397–8 it was conveyed by William Audley and Julia his wife to trustees, one of whom was Sir William Scrope, for the use of the heirs of Henry Maupas,[62] while in 1417–18 John Kingsmill and Cecily his wife conveyed it to trustees for the use of the heirs of Reginald Curteys.[63] Robert Barbot, one of the trustees, was holding in 1428,[64] and in 1451 Nicholas Wymbish, another trustee, conveyed the manor to Matilda, wife of Thomas Radford, kinswoman and heiress of Reginald Curteys.[65] The Ludlow family, probably a branch of the important Wiltshire family of that name, appears to have had some interest in Cams early in this century, for in 1437 William and Richard Ludlow were granted £10 from the manor.[66] A hundred years later John Ludlow held the manor as one knight's fee,[67] and it remained in his family until the beginning of the seventeenth century, when it passed into the hands of Emmanuel Badd,[68] who died in 1632, and whose son Thomas, created a baronet in 1642, succeeded to the estate. Thomas died without male heirs in 1683,[69] having previously conveyed his manor worth £500 a year to trustees for the use of himself and his wife Joan, with the direction that after his death the estate should be sold and the proceeds divided among his five daughters.[70] Before 1701–2 Richard Chandler had purchased the manor from two of the daughters,[71] possibly the only two then surviving, and later in the century it passed probably by purchase to the Carnac family.[72] In 1781 it was bought by Mr. John Delmé, in whose family it remained until 1895, when it was acquired by Mr. Montagu Foster, who is the present lord of the manor.[73]

CHURCH The church of *ST. PETER* and *ST. PAUL* preserves of its mediaeval building only the chancel. To the north of it is the large modern chancel and vestry, and the nave of the church is a great rectangular room with a coved plaster ceiling and large round-headed windows of the plainest description. Externally it is of red brick, and though it has the merit of being exceedingly spacious and well adapted for preaching, it is a distinctly unattractive building. Local tradition goes so far as to say that the designs from which it was built were originally intended for a silk factory. The tower at the north-east, built in 1742, is also of red brick, but has its merits, and is rather attractive than otherwise.

The general appearance of the old chancel is that of a thirteenth-century building with later windows inserted, but its south-west angle has at its lower part ashlar quoins of distinctly pre-Conquest character in long and short work, and the lower courses of the walls are of larger and coarser flint rubble than the rest.

In the east wall are three thirteenth-century lancets, and in the north wall five windows altogether, blocked or open. The first is a thirteenth-century lancet, the second a square-headed window of two cinquefoiled lights, *c.* 1500, and the third a round-headed trefoiled light, probably *c.* 1320. Of the fourth window, which was like the third, only a jamb remains, and

55 Recov. R. Hants, Mich. 20 Geo. II, rot. 375; Com. Pleas Recov. R. Hants, Hil. 47 Geo. III, m. 100; Burrows, *Family of Brocas*, 471.
56 Ct. R. in possession of the lord of the manor.
57 *V.C.H. Hants*, i, 462.
58 *Red Bk. of Exch.* (Rolls Ser.), i, 205. In 1235–6 William Oisel was holding one messuage with appurtenances in Fareham, and in 1263 Sybil Oyssel, probably his daughter, was holding the same; Feet of F. Hants, Hil. 20 Hen. III; ibid. Hants, East. 47 Hen. III.
59 *Parl. R.* (Rec. Com.), i, 765.
60 *Feud. Aids*, ii, 307.
61 Burrows, *Family of Brocas*, 349; *Feud. Aids*, ii, 335.
62 Feet of F. Hants, Mich. 21 Ric. II.
63 Feet of F. Hants, Hil. 5 Hen. V.
64 *Feud. Aids*, ii, 357.
65 Feet of F. Hants, Hil. 27 Hen. VI; Close, 32 Hen. VI, m. 23.
66 Feet of F. Hants, Mich. 16 Hen. VI.
67 Chan. Inq. p.m. (Ser. 2), xxv, 20.
68 Feet of F. Hants, Trin. 14 Jas. I; ibid. 22 Jas. I.
69 Burke, *Extinct Baron.* 32.
70 *Hist. MSS. Com. Rep.* xiii, 285–7.
71 Feet of F. Hants, Hil. 13 Wm. III.
72 Feet of F. Hants, East. 13 Geo. III.
73 Private information.

the westernmost window is of three trefoiled lights under a square head, *c.* 1500. Between the third and fourth windows is a fifteenth-century doorway.

On the south of the chancel the windows correspond to the first three windows on the north, and the third has at the west angle of its sill on the outside a small square-headed opening rebated for a frame, and splayed inwards, but not showing on the inner face of the wall. The chancel arch is of late twelfth-century date, with half-round responds and a pointed arch of two chamfered orders. There are a number of seventeenth and eighteenth-century wall tablets in the chancel, and at the south-west an old stone coffin has been placed.

The fittings of the rest of the church are of no particular interest ; there is a large west gallery running right across the nave, but the eighteenth-century arrangements are destined to give way to modern Gothic work in continuation of the chancel. At present only the foundations of the nave arcades serve to show the form of the future building.

There are eight bells, of which the treble and second, by Warner, were added in 1883, and the rest are by Joshua Kipling of Portsmouth, the tenor being dated 1745, and the other 1742. On the tenor are a set of verses referring to the rising of 1745, which witness rather to their writer's loyalty than his poetic skill.

> In vain the rebls strive to gain renown
> Over our Church, the laws, the King and
> Crowne ;
> In vain the bold ingratfull rebls aim
> To overturn when you support the same.
> Then may great George our King live for to see
> The rebllious crew hang on the gallows tree.

The plate consists of two Communion cups of 1830, given in 1831 ; a standing paten of 1718, given by Edward Jenkins, vicar ; a flagon of 1720, towards which Mrs. Susanna Hobbs gave £10 ; an alms dish of 1723, and another of 1734, and a spoon of 1852. There is also a very beautiful secular standing covered cup, parcel gilt, of English work, undated, but its approximate date must be *c.* 1500.

The register books are as follows ; i, 1558–1634 ; ii, 1634–90, with at the end a list of briefs, 1663–7 ; iii, 1690–1743 ; iv, 1743–92, the marriages ceasing at 1753 ; v, baptisms and burials 1792–1812 ; vi–ix, marriages, 1754–1812.

The church of *HOLY TRINITY*, erected by funds bequeathed by the late Lady Thompson, is a brick building with stone dressings, and consists of small chancel, nave, aisles, north and south porches, and an embattled western tower and spire. A district was assigned to it in 1835, and the registers date from 1836. The living is a vicarage in private gift.

ADVOWSON There was a church at Fareham in 1086[74] and it is probable that it was included in the grant of the manor to the bishopric of Winchester. As there is no mention of the advowson being held by the feoffees of the manor it may be assumed that the bishop kept the right of presentation in his own hands. In 1157 Henry de Blois, bishop of Winchester, appropriated the church of Fareham with all its appurtenances to the hospital of St. Cross, and in the valuation of Henry VIII it appears among the revenues of that house as yielding a sum of 60 marks yearly.[75] In 1544 the parsonage was leased to Thomas Wriothesley for fifty years,[76] and in the middle of the seventeenth century a lease of the rectory was granted to the family of Benett for a term of three lives. In 1693 the tithes were worth £180 per annum but by 1697–8 they had risen to £300. In the reign of William III, and again in that of Anne, several disputes arose between the master and brethren of St. Cross and the vicar of Fareham as to the payment of certain tithes, and evidence was brought to show that the former had no interest in any lands that had hitherto paid tithes to the vicar.[77] The tithes were retained by the Benett family until 1840 when the lease was sold to Sir John Whalley-Smythe Gardiner and on its expiration it reverted to the hospital of St. Cross.[78] In 1879 Fareham and the parochial chapelry of Holy Trinity were included in the rural deanery of Alverstoke and in 1881 the chapelry was endowed with £17 10*s.* out of the common fund.[79]

The lords of the manor of North Fareham had a free chapel at Whipstrode St. James, first mentioned at the beginning of the thirteenth century, when it belonged to Emma des Roches.[80] It followed the descent of the manor until the sixteenth century,[81] when the chapel passed to the crown by the surrender of the incumbent, and was pulled down. The tithes and glebe lands were impropriated by the Pexalls, the heirs of the original donors, and passed to successive owners of the manor.[82] The tithes have, however, gradually diminished in value, and now are quite unimportant.

The rectory of Whipstrode was granted to Thomas Wriothesley some time before 1550,[83] and followed the descent of Titchfield until 1762.

The Roman Catholic church of the Sacred Heart was founded in 1873 and rebuilt in 1878. There are also Congregational, Wesleyan and Baptist chapels in the town.

CHARITIES Miss Elizabeth Barnard by will dated 1819 left consols to the amount of £494 4*s.* 8*d.* the dividends of which, producing £12 7*s.* yearly, are to be applied for educational purposes.

Mrs. Harriet Lawson by will dated 1852 left £1,000 invested in consols to the amount of £904 10*s.* 3*d.*, the income from which, amounting to £22 12*s.* to be applied in the discretion of the vicar and churchwardens in the support of the Sunday school, the church house, and the provident funds for the poor.

Mary O'Bryen by will dated 1838 left consols to the amount of £270 13*s.* 6*d.*, producing an income of £6 15*s.* 4*d.*, to be applied to the distribution of fuel among the poor of the hamlet of Catisfield.

The Paddon Memorial Almshouses were erected in 1850 by Joseph Paddon for two almspeople in memory

74 *V.C.H. Hants.* i, 462*a*.
75 Harl. MS. 1616, fol. 7.
76 Egerton MS. 2031, fol. 74.
77 Exch. Dep. Mich. 5 Will. and Mary, No. 10; Hil. 8 & 9 Will. and Mary, No. 10 ; Mich. 2 Anne, No. 13 ; Hil. 7 Geo. I, No. 4.
78 Information supplied by the lord of the manor of North Fareham.
79 *Lond. Gaz.* 14 Feb. 1879.
80 Add. Chart. 15692.
81 Chan. Inq. p.m. 35 Edw. III, pt. 2, No. 49 ; ibid. 34 Hen. VI, No. 9.
82 Burrows, *Family of Brocas*, 331.
83 W. and L. Inq. p.m. 4 Edw. VI (Ser. 2), v. 103.

of his wife, and by his will they were endowed with £41 0*s.* 8*d.* Bank of England land stock. This was increased, in 1878, by the will of Miss Mary Ann Paddon, who left a sum amounting to £206 19*s.* 8*d.* consols; by the gift of £63 16*s.* 7*d.* Bank of England stock by John Edward Paddon in 1884; and by £167 14*s.* 7*d.* India three per cent. stock left by Miss Anne Agnes Follet. The income amounts to about £18 regulated by the scheme of 21 November, 1879.

Mrs. Isabella Watts by will dated 1875 left £500 which, invested in £476 15*s.* 1*d.* consols, produces an income of £11 18*s.* 4*d.* to be given to twelve poor widows. She also left a legacy of £100 for the repair of her tomb in the churchyard and her monument in the church. The official trustees hold the sum of £476 15*s.* 1*d.* consols and a sum of £10 2*s.* consols, producing 5*s.* a year in respect of the last-mentioned legacy, the court having declared that the trust for the repair of the tomb in the churchyard was void.

Mrs. Louisa Ayling by her will dated 1883 left a legacy represented by £195 7*s.* 4*d.* consols, the income from which, amounting to £4 17*s.* 8*d.*, is distributed in coals to the poor.

Frederick Bradley by his will dated 1890 left a legacy to be invested, and the income to be applied in pensions to five aged poor persons to be elected by the minister and deacons of the Congregational church. The legacy, invested in £925 18*s.* 2*d.* India three per cent. and producing an income of £32 8*s.* was in 1905 given in weekly payments of 2*s.* 6*d.* each to five persons.

In 1886 about four acres of land was acquired as a recreation ground by means of the 'Assembly Room Fund' under an Order of the Chancery Division of the High Court, and in 1891 an additional piece of land consisting of 3 acres, 1 rood, 24 poles was secured for the same purpose.

The Rev. Sir H. Thompson by deed of trust dated 1835 gave £1,089 18*s.* 4*d.* consols in augmentation of the salary of the minister of Holy Trinity, subject to the payment of £10 to the clerk and £242 15*s.* 2*d.* consols for the church repair fund.

Mrs. Elizabeth Harriet le Blanc by deed dated 1850 gave £6,312 4*s.* consols, the income from which amounting to £157 16*s.* is applicable as to one moiety for the curate, and as to the other moiety for church expenses, salary of the organist, &c., in connexion with the church of Holy Trinity.

Seymour Robert Delmé by will dated 1894 left a legacy represented by £460 6*s.* consols, producing an income of £11 10*s.* to be distributed among the poor of Holy Trinity. He also left the same amount for the poor of the church of St. Peter and St. Paul.

For the school, founded by the will of William Price, see article on 'Schools,' *V.C.H. Hants.* ii, 387, 398.

THE HUNDRED OF TITCHFIELD

CONTAINING THE PARISHES OF

ROWNER TITCHFIELD WICKHAM[1]

The hundred at the time of Domesday included Titchfield, Faccombe, Meon, Bromwich, Bentley, Crofton, Funtley, Wickham, Segenworth, Hook, Stubbington, and Rowner, and it was assessed at 46 hides.[2] It belonged to the crown and appears to have been farmed occasionally, its value in 1266 being 58*s.* 4*d.*,[3] though by the reign of Richard II it was reduced to 30*s.*[4] By the beginning of the fourteenth century the area of the hundred had been materially reduced. First the abbot of Titchfield withdrew his suit in respect of his manor of Swanwick in Titchfield parish, and being called upon in 1279 to show by what warrant he claimed to do so, pleaded successfully the charter of Henry III, granting to Titchfield Abbey freedom from service at the courts of the shires and hundreds.[5] Earlier in the same century Peter des Roches transferred the suit of Bromwich manor to Fareham; in 1279 William de Valence, being summoned for neglecting to pay the suit due from his manor of Hook, pleaded that Hook was a member of his manor of Newton Valence, which was exempted from suit at the courts of the shire and hundred, and his claim was allowed.[6] In the same year John of Brittany withdrew his suit in respect of his manors of Crofton, Lee Markes, and Funtley, and as he did not appear the sheriff was ordered to distrain upon his land.[7] These withdrawals had reduced the hundred in the time of Edward I to Wickham, Rowner, Stubbington, and Segenworth. By 1316 Prallingworth and Bonewood had been added and Faccombe and Bentley had been transferred to the hundreds of Pastrow and Thorngate respectively, while the king had recovered his suits of Funtley and Crofton.[8] In 1651 the hundred consisted of the tithings of Rowner, West Hook, Chark, Wickham, Great Funtley, Little Funtley, and Stubbington,[9] all of which are in the hundred of Titchfield to-day, with the exception of Prallingworth.

[1] According to the *Pop. Ret.* 1831. [2] *V.C.H. Hants*, i, 456*b*. [3] Chan. Inq. a.q.d. file 2, No. 31.
[4] Add. MS. 33284, fol. 106. [5] *Cal. of Close*, 1227–31, p. 179; *Plac. de Quo Warr.* (Rec. Com.), 765.
[6] Ibid. 765; Assize R. 788. [7] *Plac. de Quo Warr.* (Rec. Com.), 772; Coram Rege R. No. 70.
[8] *Feud. Aids*, ii, 308, 309, 311. [9] Parl. Surv. 1651.

ROWNER

Ruenore (xi cent.) ; Rowenor, Revenore, Rugenhore (xiii cent.) ; Rouwenore (xiv cent.) ; Roughner (xvii cent.).

The parish of Rowner, containing 1,245 acres, of which two are covered by water, is situated in the exteme south of the county, the most southern point of the parish being about half a mile from the Solent. In this connexion it is interesting to note that Henry I was detained in 'the town that is called Rowner' in 1115 while waiting for a fair wind to carry him across to France.[9a] There is no actual village, only a number of old cottages scattered over a long narrow strip of land, the southern and eastern portions of which have been bought by the War Office for the land defences of Portsmouth, and the forts of Rowner, Brockhurst, and Grange, now obsolete and turned into barracks, lie to the east and south of the parish. Most of the cottages are very old and still bear the names of former occupants, although in many cases the families have been extinct for generations. The soil is loam on clay. In the south-east of the parish there are several disused gravel pits and also the site of an old windmill, probably the one belonging to the Grange Farm of Chark, at which the monks of Quarr were permitted to grind their corn in the twelfth or thirteenth centuries. The Grange Farm in the south of the parish is an old house of some interest. There are 506 acres of arable land, 653 of grass, and only three of wood.[10] The sole industry is agriculture, the crops being chiefly grain. There is a recreation ground in the centre of the Government land, but no parish land or commons. An offshoot of the main road from London to Gosport divides the parish into two nearly equal parts. The River Alver enters Rowner to the east of Chark Common in the neighbouring parish of Crofton, and after forming for a short time its south-western boundary passes out of the parish in a south-easterly direction. The land skirting the river is low and subject to floods. The church is in the centre of the parish, and near it on the south-west are the very scanty ruins of a building supposed to have been the old manor house of the Brune family. The nearest station is Brockhurst, where the London and South Western line joins the Lee-on-the-Solent Railway. Some field-names are :—Hangmans Coppice, Great Whores, and Conygar.[10a]

MANOR At the time of Domesday the manor of *ROWNER* was held by William Mauduit.[11] The family of Mauduit seems to have been of considerable importance at this time as the possessor of large estates in Hampshire, and its members were among the chamberlains of Henry I and II, William Mauduit, who died in 1171, being made Chamberlain of the Exchequer by grant of the king.[12] In what way the manor passed from the Mauduit family does not appear, but in 1240-1 Elias de la Falaise held 3½ virgates and 63 acres of land in Rowner which he had exchanged with the prior of St. Swithun's for 30 acres of land in the same parish, and which may probably be identified as part of the knight's fee which William de la Falaise was holding as early as 1187.[13] Seven years later Elias made a grant of 5½ virgates of land from the manor of Rowner to the abbot of Quarr, which grant was confirmed by Henry III in 1266. At his death in 1254 Elias was holding the residue of the manor of the king in chief by serjeanty, providing one armed man for forty days every year in time of war, for the defence of Winchester Castle.[14] In the same year William de la Falaise, his brother, died seised of land in Rowner which he held by the same service, though by a fine made by his brother Elias he rendered 40*s.* yearly to the exchequer for alienation of the serjeanty, his brother's widow, Lady Ida, holding dower in the estate.[15] Before 1277 the property had escheated to the crown by the felony of William de la Falaise, grandson of William, and was granted in that year to Sir William le Brune, chamberlain to the king, to hold jointly with his wife Isolde, a lady of the household of Queen Eleanor, by the yearly payment of 40*s.* to the king's exchequer in lieu of service,[16] and seven years later William le Brune was granted free warren in his demesne lands.[17] William died in 1301,[18] and the estate was then held by Isolde until her death in 1307, when it passed to Maurice her son and heir.[19] William son of Maurice succeeded to the property in 1355,[20] and in 1358 obtained a licence to convey the manor to his daughter Joan and her husband, Thomas de Overton, in tail.[21] William died between 1360 and 1370, and in 1371 Joan released all her right in the manor to her mother and her husband, Sir Robert de Marny, and to her brothers Ingram and Richard.[22] Sir Robert de Marny and his wife transferred the manor to Ingram Brune between 1390 and 1392,[23] and he died seised of the same in 1400, when the property passed, under a settlement made in 1392,[24] to his wife Elizabeth, in tail male with remainder to William de Marny, son and heir of Robert de Marny.[25] Elizabeth held the manor in dower during the minority of her son till her death in 1403. Her son Maurice came of age in

[9a] *Angl.-Sax. Chron.* 335.

[10] Statistics from Board of Agriculture (1905).

[10a] Ordnance Map.

[11] *V.C.H. Hants*, i, 492*a*.

[12] Add. MS. 33284, fol. 198.

[13] Feet of F. 25 Hen. III, No. 252 ; *Red Bk. of the Exch.* (Rolls Ser.), i, 68.

[14] Chan. Inq. p.m. 39 Hen. III, No. 3. The land is here described as 'one hide of land in Rowner.' A later inquisition, taken at the instance of the abbot of Quarr, who complained that the land granted to him in free alms had been taken into the king's hands, states that the manor consisted of a messuage and garden 2*s.* ; meadow 2*s.* ; wood 2*s.* ; 110 acres : total value with advowson of chapel £5 12*s.* 8*d.*

[15] Ibid. No. 34.

[16] Chart. R. 5 Edw. I, No. 70 ; Pat. 5 Edw. I, m. 22 ; Cart. Antiq. R. G. 3.

[17] Chart. R. 11 Edw. I, No. 76.

[18] Chan. Inq. p.m. 29 Edw. I, No. 44.

[19] Ibid. 1 Edw. II, No. 64.

[20] Ibid. 29 Edw. III (1st nos.) No. 38.

[21] Ibid. 32 Edw. III (2nd nos.), No. 53. The manor then consisted of a capital messuage with garden, yearly value 3*s.* ; rent of five tenants with the work of the same £4 8*s.* 7*d.* ; 160 acres of arable land at 4*d.* an acre ; 30 acres of pasture 5*s.* ; 3 acres of meadow 6*s.* ; 10 acres of wood 2*s.* 6*d.* Pleas and perquisites of court 5*s.* brought the annual value up to £8 3*s.* 11*d.* The liberty of Crofton also belonged to the manor.

[22] Close, 45 Edw. III, m. 36.

[23] Feet of F. (Div. Cos.), 12, Ric. II ; Close, 16 Ric. II, m. 15 *d.*

[24] Close, 16 Ric. II, m. 15 *d.*

[25] Chan. Inq. p.m. 1 Hen. IV, No. 39.

1407,[26] and from him the estate passed to his son Henry, who held it till his death in 1461,[27] when it reverted to a Maurice Brune, probably his brother, who, dying in 1468, was succeeded by his son Thomas.[28] The manor passed on the death of Thomas in 1497 to his son William Brune,[29] who was succeeded in 1512 by his nephew, Sir John Brune, who died in 1559 leaving a son Henry.[30] The latter bequeathed a 'manor or farm called the Grange' in the parishes of Rowner and Stoke, to trustees, to provide portions for five unmarried daughters, and on his death in 1594 the manor and advowson of Rowner passed to his son John,[31] who died in 1639, his heir being his nephew John, son of his brother Charles.[32] On the death of John, who died without heirs male in 1645, his brother Charles succeeded to the estate. He died in 1703, and by the death of his grandson Charles Brune in 1769 the family became extinct in the male line. By his will his estates, including the manor and advowson of Rowner, eventually devolved on his grand-nephew the Rev. Charles Prideaux-Brune of Padstow, Cornwall, who died in 1833, and whose grandson Mr. Charles Glynn Prideaux-Brune is the present owner.[33]

BRUNE. *Azure a cross moline or.*

CHURCH

The church of *ST. MARY THE VIRGIN, ROWNER*, is a small building, consisting originally of a chancel 14 ft. 2 in. by 11 ft. 5 in., and nave 25 ft. by 15 ft., being apparently work of the first half of the twelfth century, to which in the thirteenth century were added a wide north aisle and north chapel, which have become the nave and chancel, the older chancel being used as organ chamber and vestry. The church was extensively repaired in 1874, and shows little old work outside, none of the windows having preserved their old stonework.

At the south-east of the old chancel a modern doorway in twelfth-century style has been inserted, with a ring of reused twelfth-century sunk star ornament over the outer arch. The old chancel arch is pointed, of two chamfered orders, with voussoirs alternately of Binstead stone and clunch, the same arrangement occurring in the responds, which have keeled shafts to the inner order and round shafts in the outer, with moulded capitals and bases. The angles of the north arcade of two bays are like the chancel arch, but of Bembridge stone. The south doorway of the nave is modern.

In the north wall of the present chancel is a thirteenth-century piscina, and opposite to it on the south a single recessed sedile, to the west of which is a wide round-headed thirteenth-century arch, springing from moulded corbels, and opening to the old chancel. The font at the west end of the nave has an octagonal bowl and shaft. The woodwork is all new, but a panel of the royal arms, dated 1705, is hung on the east face of the old chancel arch.

On the north of the chancel is a fine tomb dated 1559, with no inscription recording the name of the person whom it commemorates, but the heraldry shows that he was a member of the Brune family, and the date makes it evident that he was Sir John Brune. The tomb is in the form of a panelled base, on which is a semicircular arch, over which are three pedestals supporting putti, who hold shields with the Brune arms. Beneath the arch are the arms of Brune with helm and mantling, and on the base four shields with the arms of Brune, Brune impaling Tichborne, Brune impaling Knowles, and Brune impaling Bamfilde, the names being written above the shields. Above the tomb are a helm and breastplate, placed here within recent years. All the details are exceedingly good and well executed, in the delicate early Renaissance style, which ten years later had lost much of its purity.

Externally the church shows little signs of age; the roofs are red-tiled, with a shingled bell-turret at the west containing one bell of 1709. In the churchyard are some specimens of eighteenth-century tombstones, with beautiful lettering, some being carefully repainted and set up against the church wall, and church and churchyard are models of neatness.

Copies of several wall paintings found during the repairs of 1874 are preserved at the rectory.

The plate consists of an alms dish of 1677, a standing paten of 1728, and a communion-cup probably of the same date, a flagon of 1726, and a pewter plate.

The first book of the registers is on parchment, and goes from 1590 to 1683, with one baptism of 1583, and at the end are paper leaves with entries for 1673–81. The second book has births and deaths 1669–1775, and marriages 1669–1754. The number of marriages for so small a parish is abnormal, and is explained by the fact that Rowner was a favourite place for marriages among the naval men from Gosport and Portsmouth. The third book contains marriages 1754–1810, and the fourth baptisms and burials 1775–1812.

ADVOWSON

The history of the advowson of Rowner is identical with that of the manor.[34] From the time of the grant of Edward I the family of Brune with few exceptions have exercised the right of presentation.[35] Very few members of the family have actually held the living. In 1292 Philip le Brune was presented to the living by Sir William le Brune, and he was succeeded in 1306 by Nicholas le Brune. The family was not again represented until 1884, when the present rector, the Rev. Edward Stapland Prideaux-Brune, was instituted.[36]

There are apparently no endowed charities in this parish.

[26] Chan. Inq. p.m. 8 Hen. IV, No. 18.

[27] Ibid. 1 Edw. IV, No. 27.

[28] Ibid. 8 Edw. IV, file 28, No. 24.

[29] The manor was still held by the ancient service of providing one armed man for forty days every year for the defence of Winchester Castle.

[30] Exch. Inq. p.m. 2 & 3 Eliz. (Ser. 2), file 1000, No. 9.

[31] Chan. Inq. p.m. 36 Eliz. No. 112.

[32] Ibid. 15 Chas. I, No. 106.

[33] Maclean, *Hist. of Trigg Minor*, ii, 216, 217; *Papers and Proc. Hants Field Club*, ii (3), 345.

[34] Chan. Inq. p.m. 1 Hen. IV, No. 39; ibid. 4 Hen. VIII (Ser. 2), vol. 27, No. 79; ibid. 15 Chas. I, No. 106.

[35] In 1403–6 Hen. IV, in 1566 Queen Eliz., and in 1593–4 Thomas Wade presented during the minority of the heir to the manor.

[36] *Papers and Proc. Hants Field Club*, ii (3), 349–52.

TITCHFIELD

Ticefelle (xi cent.); Tichefelde (xiii and xiv cent.).

The parish of Titchfield, containing 4,826 acres, of which 45 are covered by water, is situated to the south-west of the county, about 2 miles from the Solent. There are 1,491 acres of arable land, 1,239 of pasture, and 811 of woodland.[1] The ancient parish was of wide extent, its foreshore stretching 7 miles from the River Hamble to Stokes Bay, while it included Swanwick, Crofton, Lee, Stubbington, Hook, Funtley, Chark, Posbrook, Bromwich, Segenworth, and Meon. Of these, Crofton, with Stubbington and Lee-on-the-Solent, Hook with Warsash, and Sarisbury with Swanwick were formed into civil parishes under the Local Government Act of 1894; Sarisbury with Swanwick, Crofton, and Hook with Warsash having been previously constituted ecclesiastical parishes in 1837, 1871, and 1872, respectively.

The parish stretches about seven miles up the Meon valley, and has one mile of foreshore called Titchfield Haven on the Solent. The town itself is grouped round a central market-place, with streets leading from it on the north, south, and east. There are no buildings of any particular architectural merit, but the square is picturesque, and the Bugle Inn, with its bay windows, gives character to it. The stocks once stood here in front of the inn, and the market-house and cage, once in the square, are now set up in Barry's Charity Yard to the north-west. The market-house is a wooden building with an open lower story, part of which, inclosed with brickwork and lined with oak, was the cage. The fire engine used to be kept behind it. The church stands a short distance to the south-west of the square, and the rectory is close to it on the south. To the north the town extends along the Fareham road, and at the north-west the houses follow the road which runs northward to the ruins of Place House. The River Meon forms the eastern limit of the town, and though now a small stream, was formerly a tidal harbour, for in the beginning of the seventeenth century Titchfield was a port, and the site of the wharves can still be traced in the tan-yard close to the church. The third earl of Southampton, however, wished to reclaim the large stretch of sea-marsh lying between the town and the haven, and for that purpose built a sea-wall across the river mouth, which was completed in June, 1611. In the parish registers this is noted as the 'shutting out of Titchfield haven by one Richard Talbottes industrie under God's permissione.' The main road from Southampton to Fareham passes through the town, and the London and South-Western Railway crosses the parish from east to west, the nearest station being Fareham, about two miles distant. To the north are the ruins of Place House, being the buildings of the Premonstratensian Abbey converted into a mansion by Thomas Wriothesley, first earl of Southampton, and where his son Henry entertained both Edward VI and Elizabeth. In 1625 Charles I brought his bride to Titchfield immediately after their marriage,[1a] while the State Papers for 1675 contain many allusions to the king's visit to Titchfield in that year, where he dined with Edward Noel, afterwards lord-lieutenant of Hampshire.[2] In November, 1688, when the Dutch invasion was imminent, 'Lord Gainsborough's

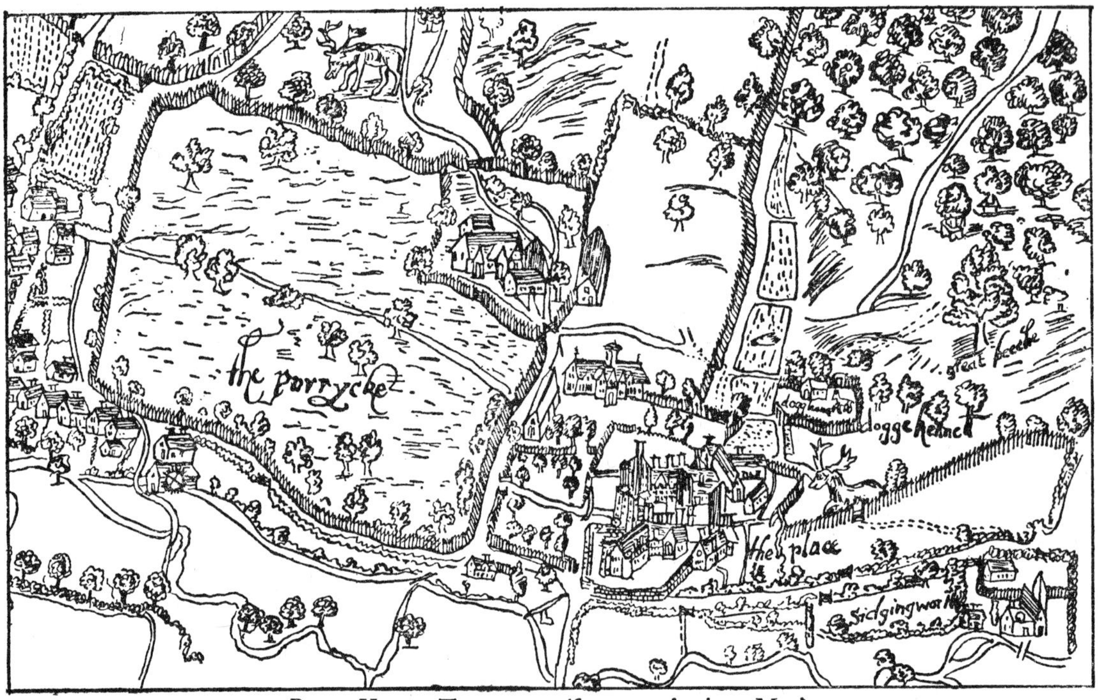

Place House, Titchfield (from an Ancient Map)

[1] Statistics from Bd. of Agric. 1905.

[1a] *Dict. Nat. Biog.* xxv, 429.

[2] *Cal. S.P. Dom.* 1675–6, pp. 195–8.

Titchfield : South Front of Place House

house Titchfield' was taken for the queen presumably as a convenient point from which to escape to France.[2a]

A bridge over the Meon close to Place House bears the date 1625. West Hill, a large house on rising ground west of the town, belongs to the executors of James Dredge, C.M.S., late owner of *Engineering*. St. Margaret's is a large red-brick house on high ground to the west of the town: a long range of building with picturesque chimneys and a tower at the south end. It appears to be entirely of early seventeenth-century date, with much of its original wooden framings, and stands in a pretty garden surrounded by a belt of trees. Several industries formerly of importance have now almost entirely disappeared, amongst them brick-making, of which the only remaining trace is a field called 'Clay-pits.' A garden called Skin House Piece marks the site of a building where parchment-dressing was formerly carried on. Gravel was worked at Meon in former days, and salt was obtained by evaporation from Hook and Warsash, where the name 'salterns' still survives. At Funtley in the north of the parish are the ruins of an old mill —the iron mill where ore was smelted, local ironstone being used. Early in the seventeenth century the third earl of Southampton, alarmed at the decay of trade caused by the suppression of the monastery, started a woollen industry, and men were brought from Alton 'to teach the poor the art of weaving.' The experiment was not altogether successful, although the older inhabitants can still remember the time when blankets were manufactured in the parish. The chief local industry to-day is strawberry growing; Titchfield Common, formerly called Swanwick Heath, and until comparatively recent times a stretch of waste heather land, being now cut up into small allotments generally consisting of a few acres of strawberry fields round a cottage. In the strawberry season every available person is employed in picking the fruit, the schools are closed, and all the children go to work in the strawberry fields. Swanwick is the chief station for this trade, a special staff and special trains being provided by the railway company during the busy season. Market gardening on a large scale is carried on in the parish, Titchfield supplying most of the cabbages for the Royal Navy, while turnip greens are largely grown for the London market, 'green cutting' being a recognized industry among the girls of the locality. There is a large tannery in the town on the site of the old wharves, and a jam factory on the common belonging to the Army and Navy Stores. Titchfield mill, probably the one mentioned in Domesday and later as being worth 20*s*.,[3] is in the town on the Meon, and there is a windmill on Peel Common at Crofton. Though no traces of any dovecots remain, there is a field called the 'Dovecot' near Place House.

Crofton and Stubbington consist of a few dozen cottages and farms scattered over a tract of flat country, and only round the green in Crofton is there anything in the nature of a village. Crofton House, south-east of Titchfield, belongs to Col. Boyd, and Stubbington House, which stands at the corner of the green, is used as a naval school. Its bell is said to have come from Place House at Titchfield. Whiteleys, in the north of the parish, is an interesting old house formerly standing within the park of Place House, and now, from its isolated position, used as a smallpox hospital. In late years old land drains have been discovered near the house filled in with deer's horns. Lee-on-the-Solent is a modern watering place, there being very little more than the site to mark its ancient history.

Sarisbury, Locks Heath, Swanwick and Lower Swanwick form a modern parish on the east bank of the River

St. Margaret's, Titchfield

[2a] *Cal. S.P. Dom.* 1641, p. 250; *Hist. MSS. Com. Rep.* xliv, 123.

[3] *V.C.H. Hants*, i, 456; *Cal. of Pat.* 1307–13, p. 20.

Hamble. At Sarisbury there are two or three inns, a church, a schoolhouse, and a few cottages standing round a stretch of village green, along the north side of which runs the Southampton road. Swanwick is merely a collection of modern red-brick cottages straggling up the stretch of hill which leads from the railway station to the Southampton road. Lower Swanwick is a picturesque village lying on low ground along the east bank of the Hamble. Brooklands, a large house on the Hamble River, is the residence of Lt.-Col. Babington, J.P., and Cold East, south of the main road, belongs to Mr. Claude Montefiore. Sarisbury Court is the residence of Mr. W. Sarton. Curbridge is a tiny hamlet in the north of the parish.

Hill Head consisted, till lately, of a few cottages and fishermen's sheds at Titchfield Haven, but is now developing into a seaside resort with rows of houses along the shore. Chillinge is a desolate-looking house of Elizabethan date, now cut up into two cottages, standing alone by the seashore a little to the east of Hook. Hook House Park, east of the parish of Hook with Warsash, is well wooded, but a large tract of bare heather land stretches from there to Warsash. A great part of it is now being brought under cultivation as strawberry ground. Hook House, built by Mr. William Hornby, governor of Bombay, at the end of the eighteenth century, which was a reproduction of Government House, Bombay, was burnt down a few years ago. From Warsash House, the property of G. A. Shinley, the road descends a sharp hill to the shore where, by the Crab and Lobster inn, the crab tank of the well-known local industry is built. The village of Warsash is small, and its inhabitants are chiefly employed in the crab and lobster trade, which occupies them through the late autumn, winter, and spring, many of them in the summer working as sailors on the many yachts which make their head quarters in the Solent and Southampton Water.

The remains of the buildings of the Premonstratensian abbey of St. Mary, Titchfield, stand at a little distance to the north of the town. Founded in 1222 for a colony of White Canons from Halesowen, the ruins show that the church and claustral buildings were completed within a few years of the foundation, and, as far as can be judged, survived without material alteration till the suppression. The note in the register of the abbey (Harl. 6602, fol. 140–3) mentioning that John bishop of Elphin, eighteenth abbot, *c.* 1535, rebuilt the ruinous church, may refer to work done in the now destroyed east end. The church had an aisleless nave, a central tower, transepts with eastern chapels, and a presbytery, the whole being vaulted in stone. The cloister lay on the north of the church, the parlour, chapter-house, and warming house being on the east, and the dorter over them, extending with its subvault a considerable distance northwards; the frater with its subvault on the north, having the kitchen at its west end, and the cellarer's building and great guest hall on the west. The site of the infirmary is uncertain. The only parts of the church now standing are the nave walls and the lower part of the west wall of the south transept. The nave was vaulted in six bays, each bay being lighted by a pair of tall lancets, below the sills of which ran a moulded string at which the vaulting shafts stopped. The pulpitum seems to have stood in the west arch of the tower, with the east doorway from the cloister immediately to the west of it. Part of the west cloister door is also preserved, and in the western bay of the nave on the south is a third doorway, built up, but retaining a consecration cross on its east jamb. There was also a west doorway, and in the western angles of the nave were vices entered from within the church, their blocked doorways being yet to be seen. The church was entirely faced with wrought stone, and had a battering plinth, the bays being marked off by projecting buttresses. In the west wall were probably three tall lancets, the outer jambs of the northern and southern of which still remain. The arrangement of the eastern part of the church as shown on the separate plate was deduced from excavations undertaken by the Rev. G. W. Minns, with the help of Mr. W. H. St. J. Hope. The chapter-house, which was separated from the north transept by the inner parlour, was vaulted in two bays, with a vestibule of two bays opening to the cloister by a central doorway with clustered Purbeck marble shafts, and flanked by double openings with marble shafts and sills, parts of which yet remain blocked up in the wall. The doorway to a passage east of the frater remains, with a little of the frater wall, but beyond this nothing is left to show the details of the monastic buildings, except the traces of a barrel vault which covered the outer parlour in the western range against the north wall of the church.

The abbey was granted at the suppression to Thomas Wriothesley, who converted the buildings into a house for himself, a good deal of which still remains. The process of conversion is illustrated by a very interesting series of letters among the State Papers, which have been printed by Mr. Hope in the *Archaeological Journal* for Dec. 1906. After several schemes of adaptation had been proposed and abandoned, the monastic frater became the hall, and the chapter-house the chapel; the cloister being treated as the courtyard of a four-square house. The south side of the church became the main front, and a large gateway with octagonal angle turrets was planted

THE GATEWAY, PLACE HOUSE, TITCHFIELD

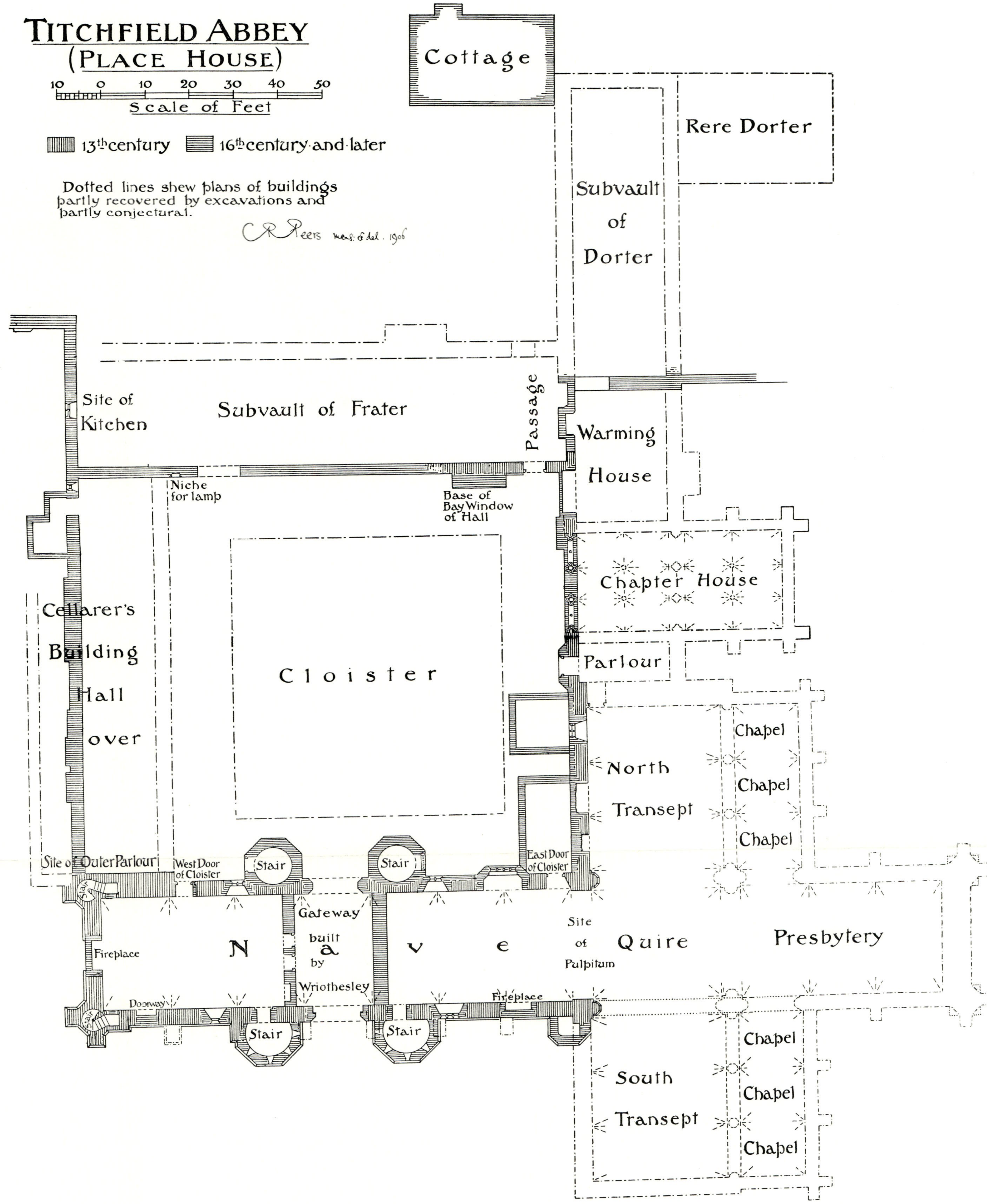

TITCHFIELD ABBEY
(PLACE HOUSE)
10 0 10 20 30 40 50
Scale of Feet
13th century
16th century and later
Dotted lines shew plans of buildings partly recovered by excavations and partly conjectural.
C R Peers mens. & del. 1906
Cottage
Rere Dorter
Subvault of Dorter
Site of Kitchen
Subvault of Frater
Passage
Warming House
Niche for lamp
Base of Bay Window of Hall
Chapter House
Cellarer's Building Hall over
Cloister
Parlour
North Transept
Chapel
Chapel
Chapel
Site of Outer Parlour
West Door of Cloister
Stair
Stair
East Door of Cloister
Gateway built by Wriothesley
Fireplace
N a v e
Site of Pulpitum
Quire
Presbytery
Doorway
Fireplace
Stair
Stair
Stair
Stair
South Transept
Chapel
Chapel
Chapel

across the nave, while the central tower was taken down to the roof level and the south transept destroyed, for the sake of symmetry. The remaining parts of the church lost their vaults and were divided into two stories, the porter's lodge being on the ground floor to the west of the gateway, its door, window, and fireplace being still to be seen. The thirteenth-century windows were blocked up and square-headed mullioned windows cut through the wall, while large brick arched fireplaces were set in the west wall of the nave, the south wall near the crossing, the gatehouse walls, and elsewhere, some of the cut brick chimney shafts still remaining. Wriothesley's work, where not made of the old material reused, is of Caen stone, and of excellent workmanship, without a trace of Renaissance feeling. His kitchen occupied the site of the monastic kitchen, and parts of walls of his date stand here, with two windows on the west, and part of a lamp niche in the north-west angle of the cloister. Till the latter part of the eighteenth century the whole house stood with little alteration, but it was then dismantled, part of its materials going to Cams Hall near Fareham, and has since then gradually decayed under the influences of weather, ivy, and general neglect. A still inhabited cottage on the north, adjoining the north-west angle of the monastic dorter, is probably in part of a copy published in the *Hants Field Club Proceedings*, by permission of the Rev. G. W. Minns. A projecting chimney breast on the north of the frater is doubtless an addition of Wriothesley's time, and a rectangular block of masonry still existing on the south side of the frater seems to be the substructure of the bay window of the hall. A doorway with the arms of Southampton in the head, masking the western entrance to the inner parlour, may also have had a projecting window over it, lighting a stair which Wriothesley seems to have put here to lead to the first-floor rooms in the north transept and dorter range. The whole of Wriothesley's alterations were probably completed by 1542, in which year he received pardon for having fortified his manor house of Titchfield without licence, and in the same year, or a little earlier, Leland visited the house, and remarked on the fine conduit-house or fountain in the middle of the cloister, of which no trace now remains.

Old place-names are :—Byttenfeld,[4] Newe Court, Parva Mirabyll, Warishassefield,[4a] and Chilling.[5] The parish was inclosed in 1859. The subsoil is gravel and clay and the surface loam.

MANORS In Domesday Book, *TITCHFIELD* is described as a berewick belonging to Meonstoke, and held by the king as it had been held by Edward the Confessor.[5a] It is possi-

North Aspect of Titchfield House

From a drawing by Grose, 1782, in the possession of J. R. Fielder, Esq.

Wriothesley's time, and has a good four-centred stone fireplace in one of the ground-story rooms. A large walled garden incloses the church and monastic buildings, extending beyond them to east and west, and at some distance further to the west are the remains of a sixteenth-century building of Wriothesley's date, whose original use cannot be determined. On the north-west are the banks of large fish-ponds, and on them till lately stood a very large oak tree, now fallen. In a letter to Wriothesley reference is made to these ponds. The writer reports that he has viewed the fish-ponds, four of them being a mile in length—and that the bailiff will give Wriothesley 500 carp to stock them, so that in three or four years' time he may sell £20 or £30 worth of fish every year.[3a] A general view by Grose of the buildings from the north-west, showing the north side of the frater and the west side of the dorter range, is preserved in Titchfield, and is here reproduced from ble that part of the manor was in the hundred of Meonstoke and part in that of Titchfield, as it is certain that the hundred of Titchfield was in existence at the time of the Domesday Survey.[6] An account of the descent of the manor given by the abbot of Titchfield, in a dispute in the reign of Henry III, shows that William I held it by conquest, that it was given by his son William Rufus to Payn, ancestor of John de Gisors,[7] and that the latter forfeited it by his adherence to the king of France.[8] King John then granted from it £15 of rent to his supporter Robert de Vipont, and £5 worth to Oliver de Beauchamp,[8a] but Robert died in 1227. Henry III in 1228 granted the manor to Hubert de Burgh, earl of Kent and justiciar, 'to hold as freely as John de Gisors held it until the king shall restore it to the heirs of John of his free will or by a peace.'[9] However, during the next year, Hubert de Burgh gave back Titchfield to Henry in exchange for the manors of Eylesham

[3a] *L. and P. Hen. VIII*, xiii (1), 19.
[4] Chan. Inq. p.m. (Ser. 2), No 7.
[4a] Pat. 29 Hen. VIII, pt. 1, m. 4.
[5] W. & L. Inq. p.m. 4 Edw. VI (Ser. 2), No. 103.
[5a] *V.C.H. Hants*, i, 456*b*.
[6] Add. MS. 33284, fol. 1.
[7] John de Gisors was holding before 1195, in which year the sheriff accounted for £14 from Titchfield 'which had belonged to John de Gisory.'
[8] Add. MS. 33284, fol. 4.
[8a] *Testa de Nevill* (Rec. Com.), 237.
[9] *Cal. of Chart. R.* i, 71.

(Norfolk), and Westhall (Suffolk),[10] and the sheriff of Southampton was ordered to free the men holding in that part of Titchfield formerly granted to Hubert de Burgh, but now retained in the king's hands, from suit at shire and hundred courts.[11] In 1232 Henry granted the manor to Peter des Roches, bishop of Winchester, for the part endowment of the Premonstratensian abbey which he was about to found there,[12] and from this date until the Dissolution the manor remained with the abbot and convent of Titchfield. Free warren in their demesne lands of Titchfield was granted to the abbey by Edward I in 1294[13] and afterwards confirmed by Henry VI,[14] who also granted many liberties and immunities to the abbey and convent in consideration of the many services rendered by them to himself and his queen on the occasion of their marriage in the abbey of St. Mary, Titchfield. One of the most important of these liberties was the right to hold an annual fair to last for five days.[15] John Sampson, bishop of Thetford, the last abbot of Titchfield, surrendered the possessions of the abbey to the king in 1537,[16] and in the same year the estates were granted to Thomas Wriothesley[17] (created earl of Southampton in 1547), for the services which he had rendered at the dissolution of the monasteries, subject to a pension of £20 to the late abbot.[18] Shortly afterwards he was knighted by the king, and on his death in 1550 he was succeeded by his son Henry,[19] who during his lifetime entertained both Edward VI and Elizabeth at Titchfield. Henry his son, third earl of Southampton, attainted in 1601 for his complicity in the plots of the earl of Essex, was condemned to imprisonment for life[20] and the confiscation of his estates; but on the accession of James I he was released, restored to his possessions and the earldom of Southampton.[21] He died abroad in 1624, and the property passed to his son Thomas, who, leaving no heirs male, was succeeded by his eldest daughter Elizabeth, who married Edward Noel, first earl of Gainsborough.[22] Their only son died without issue, and the Titchfield estate ultimately passed to their two granddaughters and co-heiresses Elizabeth, who married William Henry Bentinck first duke of Portland, and Rachel wife of the second duke of Beaufort. The third duke of Beaufort acquired both moieties of the property in 1711,[23] and the fifth duke sold the manor to Peter Delmé in 1741.[24] On the failure of male heirs to the Delmé family in 1894 the estate passed to the descendants of two co-heiresses: Elizabeth wife of the Rev. C. Delmé Radcliffe, and Julia married to Captain James Arthur Murray, R.N., the present joint-owners being their respective sons, Colonel Emilius Charles Delmé Radcliffe, and George Delmé Murray.[25]

Wriothesley, Earl of Southampton. *Azure a cross or between four falcons close argent.*

Mention is made in Domesday of one mill in Titchfield worth 20*s.*,[26] but it does not appear to have been

Radcliffe. *Argent a crosslet gules between three bends engrailed sable a label and a quarter sable with a crosslet or in the quarter.*

Delme. *Or an anchor sable between two lions passant gules.*

included in the grant of Titchfield to the abbot, as in 1307 Simon and John Whorstede received licence to alienate in mortmain to the chapel of St. Elizabeth, Winchester, a rent of 20*s.* issuing out of the mill of Titchfield.[27] In 1272 two mills and certain lands in Titchfield were granted to Henry, abbot of Titchfield, by Philip de Molyns for a rent of 33*s.* 4*d.*[28] However, before 1330, John de Molyns released this rent, since his release was confirmed by letters patent in that year.[29]

There was a market at Titchfield in 1086, and though it was said to be injurious to a neighbouring market it was still existing in 1535, when Richard Towris reports to Lord Lisle that the clerk of the market was keeping his court at Titchfield and had commanded that no man should sell wheat above 8*s.* a quarter on pain of imprisonment and forfeiture. There is no record of its history after this date.[30] In 1424 the abbot received permission by charter to inclose and make a park of 60 acres of land, 10 acres of pasture, and 50 acres of wood in Titchfield. There is an interesting reference to this park in the State Papers for the year 1635, when notification was made to the Lords of the Admiralty that the officers of the Navy had contracted for timber from the wood of the earl of Southampton at the rate of 22*s.* the load, and that 'they had had assurance the whole kingdom could not better 1,000 trees agreed for there.' They also added that the ministers of the earl 'had acquainted them with the prejudice sustained by the Earl in having his timber so long restrained from sale, since ready money for the disengagement of his debts was the principle motive occasioning his felling thereof.' That the timber grown in this park was highly

[10] *Cal. of Close*, 1227–31, p. 132.
[11] Ibid. 179.
[12] *Cal. of Chart. R.* i, 168. Evidently the manor was at this time farmed out for a term of years to Geoffrey de Lucy, warden of Portchester Castle and Forest, and in the charter he was acquitted of £16 due from the farm of the manor.
[13] Chart. R. 22 Edw. I, No. 87.
[14] *Cal. of Pat.* 1422–9, p. 260.
[15] Chart. R. 25 & 26 Hen. VI, No. 27.
[16] Feet of F. Hants and Berks. Mich. 29 Hen. VIII.
[17] Pat. 29 Hen. VIII, pt. 1, m. 4.
[18] There is a letter from Sir Humphrey Forster to Wriothesley asking his favour for John Sampson, late abbot of Titchfield, and stating that if he would obtain for him the benefice of Horsted, Sussex, valued at £13 6*s.* 8*d.* and pay the firstfruits he thought the abbot would release him from the pension; *L. and P. Hen. VIII*, xiii, (1), 381.
[19] W. & L. Inq. 4 Edw. VI (Ser. 2), v, No. 103.
[20] *Dict. Nat. Biog.* liii, 143.
[21] Pat. 1 Jas. I, pt. 2.
[22] *Papers and Proc. Hants Field Club*, iii (3), 331.
[23] Feet of F. Southants, Trin. 10 Anne.
[24] Ibid. Hil. 15 Geo. II.
[25] *Papers and Proc. Hants Field Club*, iii (3), 331.
[26] *V.C.H. Hants*, i, 456*b*.
[27] *Cal. of Pat.* 1307–13, p. 20.
[28] Feet of F. Hants, Hil. 56 Hen. III.
[29] Pat. 4 Edw. III, pt. 1, m. 38.
[30] *Hund. R.* (Rec. Com.), ii, 24; *L. and P. Hen. VIII*, ix, 467.

valued is shown by a letter of Capt. Anthony Deane to the Naval Commissioners in 1668, in which he writes: 'Mr. Eastwood gave you notice of the timber felled in Titchfield Park and bought by private men, and all the best trees docked for buckets, which would grieve anyone to behold such strange destruction to such rare goods and indeed jewels.' He adds that he had treated about 500 loads at 38*s.* the load. He knew of no timber like it except in the New Forest.[31]

Apart from the manor of Titchfield proper, there appears to have been an estate in Titchfield called the manor of Titchfield in the sixteenth century, probably owing its origin to the purchase by Thomas de Overton from John de Masseworth of 1 carucate and 6 acres of land in Chark and Titchfield in the fourteenth century.[32] The estate subsequently passed to his daughter Isabel and her husband Thomas le Warrener,[33] who held it until 1407.[34] From them it appears to have descended in a direct line through five generations to Joan Tawke, who married firstly Robert Ryman and secondly Edmund Bartlett, who both predeceased her.[35] She held the manor at her death in 1561,[36] when it passed to her son William Ryman for life with reversion to his brother Humphrey. The latter appears to have died during his brother's lifetime,[37] and from this date all assumed status of manor was lost, and the estate evidently merged in Titchfield proper.

At the time of the Domesday Survey *BROMWICH* (Burnewick xi cent.; Bromwych, Brunewych, xiv cent.; Bromwiche, xviii cent.) was held by Walkelin bishop of Winchester of the king, though not as a part of his bishopric. Angot held it under him, and it had been held by Edric in the time of Edward the Confessor.[38] At what date it came into the possession of the Bromwich family does not appear, but in the fourteenth century it was held by Lucas Bromwich and John Bromwich successively.[39] By 1428 it had passed to the Uvedale family, John Uvedale, son of Sybil de Scures, having acquired the property probably by purchase from Thomas Bromwych.[40]

In 1434 it was granted or sublet to Reginald West, Lord De La Warr, who was probably connected with the Uvedale family, for in the time of Henry III a certain Thomas Uvedale married Margaret daughter of Roger De La Warr.[41] On the death of Lord De La Warr in 1451 the manor again reverted to the Uvedales, and was held for a time by William son of John Uvedale.[42] By a deed dated 1480–1 it was granted by Thomas son of William Uvedale to his father's brother Sir Thomas, to hold jointly with Agnes Paulet his wife,[43] and shortly afterwards it was leased to a certain John Estuy for twelve years at a rent of 16 marks and 2 pence. The lessor granted to the tenant annually one robe of the suit of a groom, and the latter was to pay the fifteenth to the king when payable and all the church dues.[44] Before his death, in 1513, Henry Uvedale settled the manor on his wife Mary,[45] but in 1530–1 the presumptive heirs to the manor all sold their interest in the reversion to Sir Henry Wyatt.[46] Mary Uvedale survived him, however, and his son, Sir Thomas Wyatt, sold the reversion in 1538 to Sir Thomas Wriothesley.[47] Two years previously Mary Uvedale had given up her life interest,[48] and later Sir Thomas Wyatt made a fresh conveyance in confirmation of the Wriothesley title.[49] The same year the manor was granted to Sir Thomas Wriothesley's sister Anne Knight and her husband for their lives and that of the survivor at a rent of 6*d.* a year, but it was regranted to the donor almost immediately 'in consideration of the many benefits received from him.'[50] Ten years later the manor was granted to Roger Polstin and his wife, servants of Thomas Wriothesley (now earl of Southampton), with the explanation that it was for services to be rendered as well as for those already received. They were to hold it for three lives at a rent of £10, but the grant did not include the right of fishing in the pond by the manor house.[51] Henry Wriothesley succeeded to his father's estates in 1550, and thence they passed to his son Henry, who in 1617 leased the 'messuage and farm called Bromwich Farm' to Philip Gifford at a rent of £10 16*s.*—the tenant was to make all payments and duties 'for the King's Majesty, the Church, the Parish and the poore of the same.' Also twice in every year he was to provide for the officers of the earl when they came to hold courts there 'sufficient meat and drink and other provision befitting their officers and servants, and sufficient room hay litter and provender for their beasts.'[52] On the expiration of this lease another for twenty-one years at a rent of £10 16*s.* was granted to Sir Henry Wallop,[53] who had married the sister of the third earl of Southampton. Bromwich followed the descent of Titchfield until 1734, when on the sale shortly afterwards of a considerable part of the Titchfield property to the duke of Beaufort it was retained by the duke of Portland, in whose possession it was in 1762. From him it was purchased by Mr. William Hornby, governor of Bombay at the end of the eighteenth century, in whose family the property remained until the death of Mrs. Hood, the last survivor of the family, whose husband, the Hon. Albert Hood, is the present owner.[54]

There is no mention of the manor of *CHARK* in the Domesday Survey, but it is probable that it was included at this date in that part of Titchfield which was held by the king. Some time in the twelfth century the overlordship was granted to John de Gisors, who was certainly holding lands in Hampshire as early as 1161.[55] He never held Chark, however, in demesne, but received a rent of 50*s.* from the sub-tenants, 40*s.* of which he granted in alms to the priory of Hamble. On the forfeiture of the estates of de Gisors the remaining 10*s.* rent escheated to the crown, and King John granted it to Oliver de Beauchamp as part of 100*s.* of land and rent which he had

[31] Chart. R. 9 Edw. III, No. 72; *Cal. S.P. Dom.* 1635, pp. 121, 278; ibid. 1668–9, pp. 26–8.

[32] Chan. Inq. p.m. 30 Edw. III (2nd Nos.), No. 10.

[33] Feet of F. Hants, East. 37 Edw. III.

[34] Chan. Inq. p.m. 9 Hen. IV, No. 27.

[35] Feet of F. Southants, Trin. 34 Hen. VIII.

[36] Chan. Inq. p. m. 5 Eliz. pt. i (Ser. 2), No. 15.

[37] Ibid. 11 Eliz. (Ser. 2), No. 141.

[38] *V.C.H. Hants*, i, 463*b*.

[39] *Feud. Aids*, ii, 307, 335.

[40] Ibid. ii, 357; *Surrey Arch. Coll.* iii, 89.

[41] Berry, *Hants Geneal.* 198; Add. MS. 34655, fol. 4.

[42] Ibid.

[43] Ibid. fol. 5.

[44] Ibid.

[45] Deeds relating to the manor of Bromwich, fol. 5.

[46] Ibid. fol. 6; Add. MS. 34655, fol. 7.

[47] Deeds relating to the manor of Bromwich, fol. 10.

[48] Ibid.

[49] Anct. D. (P.R.O.), A. 3235.

[50] Add. MS. 34655, fol. 10.

[51] Ibid. fol. 8.

[52] Ibid.

[53] Ibid. fol. 9.

[54] Private information.

[55] *Red Bk. of the Exch.* (Rolls Ser.), i, 28.

licence to acquire in Chark and Titchfield in exchange for the manor of Melbourne in Derbyshire [56]

The rent was still paid to the De Beauchamp family in 1302, but eight years later Richard de Beauchamp granted it, together with a messuage and a carucate of land in Titchfield and Chark, to William son of John de Masseworth.[57] From John de Masseworth (son of John) it passed in 1356 to Thomas de Overton,[58] who died in 1361, and two years later it was conveyed to his niece Isabel and her husband, Thomas de Warrener.[59]

The under-tenants of this manor in the twelfth century were members of the family of Bruton—probably the Hamo Brito and Gilbertus le Bret who alienated lands in Chark to Quarr Abbey.[60] In 1292 William Bruton died seised of nine virgates of land in Chark held in socage paying 10*s.* rent to Richard de Beauchamp.[61] About the middle of the thirteenth century Richard Bruton was holding a moiety of Chark, while in 1316 William Bruton was returned as holding the vill of Chark,[62] which, however, from this date disappears from the assessments of the Feudal Aids. It was probably included in the one-third of a knight's fee in Warde held by him in 1346,[63] and mentioned below in the descent of Lee Bruton, and it may be suggested, therefore, that it passed at some time before the year 1428 to Thomas Wayte.[64] It was certainly settled on John Wayte and his heirs in 1453.[65] The subsequent history of the manor is the same as that of Lee (q.v.).

At the time of the Dissolution the abbey of Quarr held a farm in Chark valued at £12 2*s.* 6*d.*,[66] which was probably part of the grant made to the abbey by the Bruton family about the thirteenth century, when the monks received permission to have their boat free of toll along the seaboard of Chark or Lee, and to send their men to grind their corn at Chark.[67]

At the time of the Domesday Survey *CROFTON* was held by Count Alan of Brittany as it had been by Ulward, 'who could betake himself where he would with this land.' [68] It is probable that Crofton formed part of the possessions of Edwin earl of Mercia, the whole of which were granted to Alan of Brittany for his services at the Conquest, and afterwards formed the honor of Richmond, of which Crofton was held certainly as late as 1355.[69] Some time during the twelfth century the manor seems to have been granted to the Furneaux family, with whom it remained until 1331,[70] but shortly after that date it apparently passed, probably through some family connexion, to Maurice le Brune, who died seised of the manor then termed 'a liberty called Crofton,' belonging to the manor of Rowner, in 1355–6, leaving a son and heir William, who was holding the same in 1358–9.[71]

Of the subtenants of the Furneaux Geoffrey Talbot was seised of the manor in the reign of John,[72] and was succeeded by his son Lawrence,[73] who married a certain Benedicta, and their daughter Alice became the wife of Henry of Glastonbury, who was in possession of the property in 1316.[74] After the death of Henry the manor was settled on Alice with reversion to her son Henry, on whose death without heirs it passed to John son of John le Venour, as son and heir of Eva sister of Geoffrey Talbot. He released his right to Benedicta widow of Lawrence and Elias de Cherleton, her second husband.[75] In May, 1331, licence was granted to Elias and Benedicta to alienate the manor in mortmain to the abbot and convent of Titchfield on condition that they should find a chaplain to celebrate divine service daily in the chapel of St. Edmund, Crofton, for the soul of Edward II and for the souls of Elias and Benedicta after their deaths; the abbot undertook to regrant the manor to the grantors for life.[76] By a charter given four years later the abbot received a grant of free warren in his demesne lands in Crofton.[77] In 1537 the last abbot of Titchfield surrendered the manor with his other possessions to the king, and it was granted the same year to Thomas Wriothesley.[78] From this date Crofton follows the descent of the manor of Titchfield (q.v.).

Mention is made in Domesday of a mill at Crofton worth 12*s.* 6*d.*, but there is no further trace of its history.

There were two manors in *FUNTLEY* (Funtelei, xi cent.; Funceley, xiii cent.; Funtelegh, xiv cent.) at the time of the Domesday Survey. Of these, one[79] held before the Conquest by Ulward under Earl Godwin had passed in 1086 into the hands of Count Alan of Brittany,[80] whose descendants, except for one short period, held the overlordship until 1279, when the honor of Richmond was in the hands of Peter of Savoy.[81] The history of the overlordship for the next two centuries is obscure, but in 1305 a dispute arose between the king and Henry of Glastonbury as to the custody of the heir.[82] The matter was settled in favour of the king, who granted the lordship to his daughter Mary, nun of Ambresbury.[83] On her death the overlordship was possibly granted or restored to Henry of Glastonbury, and given by him with the manor of Crofton to the abbot and convent of Titchfield, as in 1338 the manor of Funtley was granted to the latter to be held as of their manor of Crofton.[84]

The first undertenant of the manor of Funtley Parva of whom there is record was Nicholas Fostebire, who held one messuage and half a hide of land there[85] in 1269–70. The manor appears to have been granted to the family of St. Martin later in the century, as in 1303–4 William de Pageham was

[56] Chan. Inq. p.m. 30 Edw. I, No. 21.
[57] Pat. 4 Edw. II, pt. 1, m. 9.
[58] Chan. Inq. p.m. 30 Edw. III (2nd Nos.), No. 10.
[59] Chan. Inq. p.m. 37 Edw. III (2nd Nos.), No. 16.
[60] *Papers and Proc. Hants Field Club*, iii (1), 3.
[61] Chan. Inq. p.m. 21 Edw. I, No. 14.
[62] *Testa de Nevill* (Rec. Com.), 235; *Feud. Aids*, ii, 308.
[63] Ibid. 336.
[64] Ibid. 356.
[65] Feet of F. Southants, Mich. 32 Hen. VI, file 33, No. 38.
[66] Dugdale, *Mon.* v, 320.
[67] *Papers and Proc. Hants Field Club*, ii (3), 242.
[68] *V.C.H. Hants*, i, 476*a*, 476*b*.
[69] Chan. Inq. p.m. 29 Edw. III (1st Nos.), No. 38.
[70] Add. MS. 33284, fol. 59; *Testa de Nevill* (Rec. Com.), 233; Chan. Inq. a.q.d. 5 Edw. III (2nd Nos.), No. 123.
[71] Ibid. 32 Edw. III (2nd Nos.), No. 53.
[72] Add. MS. 33284, fol. 59.
[73] *Testa de Nevill* (Rec. Com.), 233.
[74] *Feud. Aids*, ii, 308.
[75] Add. MS. 33284, fol. 17*b*; Feet of F. Hants, Trin. 1 Edw. III.
[76] Pat. 5 Edw. III, pt. 1, m. 5.
[77] Ibid. 3 Hen. VI, pt. 1, m. 13.
[78] Ibid. 29 Hen. VIII, pt. 1, m. 4.
[79] Afterwards known as the manor of Funtley Parva, and after the thirteenth century as the manor of Funtley Pageham.
[80] *V.C.H. Hants*, i, 476.
[81] *Plac. de Quo Warr.* (Rec. Com.), 772; Pat. 33 Hen. III, m. 2.
[82] Chan. Inq. p.m. 33 Edw. I, No. 268.
[83] *Cal. of Pat.* 1301–7, p. 325.
[84] Chan. Inq. p.m. 12 Edw. III (2nd Nos.), No. 35.
[85] Feet of F. Hants, 54 Hen. III, No. 592.

holding it by gift of his father-in-law, Hugh de St. Martin.[86] It then consisted 'of a hall built with tiles, a grange and ox-house built with straw . . . 90 acres of arable land . . . 20 acres of pasture worth an acre per annum 2*d.*, 4 acres of meadow worth an acre per annum 2*s.*, one water mill worth per annum 10*s.*, 3 acres of large wood and 3 acres of underwood worth an acre per annum 6*d.*, and eight customary tenants who paid rent per annum 21*s.* 9*d.*'[87] From William it passed to his son John, whose daughter Mary granted it in 1338 to the abbot and convent of Titchfield,[88] in whose possession it remained until the Dissolution, when it passed with the other Titchfield property to Thomas Wriothesley, earl of Southampton, and followed the descent of Titchfield (q.v.).

The second manor in Funtley was held at the time of Edward the Confessor by a certain Turi under Earl Godwin. In 1086 it was in the possession of Ranulf Flamme,[89] and being confiscated with the rest of his estates in 1100, passed into the king's hands,[90] and was granted some time prior to the year 1241 to the Arundel family,[91] in whose possession it remained until 1615,[92] after which the rights of overlordship probably lapsed.

Of the subtenants Hugh de Hoyvill was holding one-fourth of a fee in Funtley in 1241, which he had inherited from Richard de Hoyvill his father, which passed to Philip de Hoyvill, probably his son, who in 1294 was granted free warren in his demesne lands there.[93] Seventy years later William de Hoyvill, probably a grandson, was assessed in the Feudal Aids as part owner of the vill.[94] In 1346 it was held by William de Hoyvill,[95] probably son of the former one, but before 1428 it had passed to the Uvedale family, John Uvedale being then in possession.[96] It then followed the descent of Wickham until 1721, when it was held by Sir Richard Corbett, from whom it was purchased by Jonathan Rashleigh, M.P. for Fowey, Cornwall, in 1724.[97] It apparently passed out of the hands of the Rashleigh family at the end of the eighteenth century, and since then the property appears to have been broken up.[98]

At the time of the Domesday Survey *HOOK* (Houch, xi cent.; Hoke, xiii cent.; Houke, xiv cent.; Hooke, xv cent. onwards) was held by Hugh de Port,[99] and the overlordship probably followed the descent of the St. John barony (see Wickham), though it is difficult to be certain of this after the fourteenth century.[100] In 1086 one German was holding Hook of Hugh de Port, but for the next two centuries its history is unknown. At the beginning of the fourteenth century the vill of Hook was held jointly by Aymer de Valence, Roger Mortimer, John Pageham, and Richard of Winchester,[101] but of these holdings the two former only appear to have had any manorial history. On the death of Aymer de Valence without issue in 1324,[102] his property in Hook, afterwards known as Hook Valence, probably passed to John de Hastings, one of his heirs, and through him in a direct line to John earl of Pembroke, whose widow Philippa, daughter of Edward Mortimer, was holding it in 1389.[103] She married as her third husband, between 1393 and 1400, Thomas Poynings lord St. John of Basing[104]—a connexion which, assuming that the St. Johns were still the overlords of Hook, might explain the possession of Hook by the Wests, also connexions of the Mortimers in the sixteenth century. In 1488 Elizabeth Uvedale was holding 16 messuages and 132 acres of land in Hook of Thomas West, Lord De La Warr,[105] and this property was held until his death in 1501 by her son Robert.[106] Sixty years later Thomas West sold the manor of Hook Valence to Sir Richard Lyster, son-in-law of Thomas Wriothesley,[107] and as the latter died possessed of the manor in 1550,[108] it probably passed to him by some family settlement. From this date until 1762 it follows the descent of Swanwick (q.v.).

The manor of *HOOK MORTIMER* held by Robert Mortimer in 1316 probably escheated to the king on his attainder in 1330, but apparently was restored with the earldom to Roger his grandson in 1355, as Roger's son Edmund was holding rents in Hook Mortimer in 1381, 'from divers tenants there who hold according to the custom of the manor, as of the ancient demesne of the crown.'[109] Edmund Mortimer died without issue in 1425, and the Mortimer estates went to his nephew Richard duke of York,[110] whose eldest son Edward afterwards became Edward IV, and in this way the estate again came into the king's hands. In 1540 Henry VIII granted Hook Mortimer to Anne of Cleves,[111] and in the following year to Queen Catherine as her jointure;[112] in 1543 it was leased for thirty years to Edmund Clerke,[113] and if, as seems probable,[114] the manor of East Hook can be identified with Hook Mortimer, it passed before 1550 to Thomas Wriothesley earl of Southampton, who also possessed the manor of Hook Valence.[115] From this date the descent of both is identical with that of Titchfield until

MORTIMER. *Barry azure and or a chief or with two pales azure between two gyrons azure therein and a scutcheon argent over all.*

86 De Banc. R. Mich. 10 Edw. III, m. 404 *d.*
87 Chan. Inq. p.m. 33 Edw. I, No. 43.
88 Close, 3 Edw. III, m. 12.
89 *V.C.H. Hants*, i, 502*a*.
90 *Dict. Nat. Biog.* xix, 237.
91 *Testa de Nevill* (Rec. Com.), 231.
92 W. and L. Inq. p.m. 14 Jas. I (Ser. 2), bdle. 24, No. 123.
93 Chan. Inq. p.m. (Ser. 1), 35 Hen. III, No. 54; Chart. R. 1257–1310, p. 436.
94 *Feud. Aids*, ii, 308.
95 Ibid. 336.
96 Ibid. 356.
97 Recov. R. Trin. 12 Geo. III, No. 339.
98 Private information.
99 *V.C.H. Hants*, i, 480*b*.
100 Chan. Inq. p.m. 21 Edw. III, No. 57; *V.C.H. Hants*, i, 480*b*. At the end of the thirteenth century the prior of Boxgrove was holding ⅛ of one knight's fee of ancient feoffment of Robert de St. John. *Testa de Nevill* (Rec. Com.), 230.
101 *Feud. Aids*, ii, 308.
102 Chan. Inq. p.m. 17 Edw. III, No. 75.
103 Ibid. 2 Hen. IV, No. 54.
104 Dugdale, *Baronage*, ii, 137.
105 Chan. Inq. p.m. (Ser. 2), iv, No. 16.
106 Ibid. xv (2nd Nos.), No. 7.
107 Feet of F. Southants, Mich. 1 Edw. VI.
108 W. and L. Inq. 4 Edw. VI (Ser. 2), bdle. 5, No. 103.
109 Chan. Inq. p.m. 5 Ric. II, No. 43.
110 *Rot. Parl.* iv, 397; Close, 11 Hen. VI, m. 19.
111 *L and P. Hen. VIII*, xv, 144 (2).
112 Ibid. xvi, 503 (25).
113 Pat. 5 & 6 Phil. and Mary, pt. 3, m. 40.
114 Thomas Wriothesley died seised of East Hook and Hook Valence in 1550, while his widow Jane countess of Southampton possessed Hook Mortimer and Hook Valence in 1553, no mention being made of East Hook.
115 W. and L. Inq. p.m. 4 Edw. VI (Ser. 2), bdle. 5, No. 103.

1734, after which it is the same as that of Bromwich (q.v.).[116]

A chapel appears to have been opened in Hook in the fourteenth century, without the authority of the bishop, and the archdeacon was therefore sent to admonish those responsible. As, however, services continued to be held, the offenders were summoned to appear before the bishop in Winchester Cathedral. They did not appear, and sentence of excommunication was passed upon them in 1379.[117] In what way the dispute was finally settled does not appear, but the chapel was still existing at West Hook in 1570–1.[118]

LEE-ON-THE-SOLENT (Ly, La Lige, xiii cent.; Lye xv cent.) is not mentioned by name in the Domesday Survey, but was probably included at that date in the fee held by Count Alan of Brittany in Funtley and Crofton, which subsequently became part of the honour of Richmond.[119] In 1302 Richard Bruton died seised of land in Lee held of Isolda le Brun as of the honour of Richmond 'in manu ipsius Isolde existent ibidem.'[120] The overlordship had probably passed to her husband William with the liberty of Crofton, 'by commission' of John of Brittany.[121] There seems to be no further documentary evidence as to the descent of the overlordship, but it was probably for some time at least included in Crofton liberty.

Of the subtenants Roger Markes seems to have held one carucate of land, subsequently known as the manor of *LEE MARKES*, about the middle of the thirteenth century,[122] and in 1327 Edmund Markes, probably son of Roger, paid 2*s.* subsidy, presumably assessed on the same estate.[123] Thirty years later William Markes was holding land in Lee of Thomas Warrener, which was to pass to the abbot and convent of Titchfield on the death of William, and in this way it came into the hands of Thomas Wriothesley at the Dissolution.

In 1236 Gilbert de Bret (*alias* Brut) died seised of the manor of 'Ly' (which subsequently became known as Lee Britten or Bruton), being 1 carucate, by the service of a third of a knight's fee of the honour of Richmond, and some years later this was held by the guardian of the heir of John le Bret from Peter of Savoy as of the honour of Richmond.[124] The manor seems to have passed from John to Richard Bruton, who held a moiety of Lee and Chark as one-third of a knight's fee by the serjeanty of crossing the sea with the king, and who was succeeded by his son Richard. The latter died in 1302, leaving a son William, a minor, who was holding in 1327 and probably in 1346 if, as seems likely, Warde was a local name for the Bruton estates in Lee and Chark.[125] From William the manor passed to his son John, and from Alice daughter of John to her son Thomas, who died without heirs at the end of the fourteenth century. He appears to have alienated it to Thomas Wayte, as in 1310 the latter was sued by John Wallop, who claimed the manor as descendant of Alice sister of William Bruton. John's claim was allowed,[126] but the reversion was apparently granted to Thomas Wayte, as in 1428 he was holding one-third of a knight's fee in Warde jointly with the abbot of Titchfield.[127] The history of the manor for the next hundred years is obscure, but in 1528 John Wayte, a descendant of Thomas, leased the manor of Lee to Arthur Plantagenet.[127a] In 1530 John Wayte conveyed the manor to Sir Richard Lyster, from whom it probably passed to his father-in-law, Sir Thomas Wriothesley, some time within the next ten years, for in 1540 a dispute was tried before the Privy Council between Wriothesley and one Walter Chandler, Walter having complained that Sir Thomas had withheld the manor of Lee from him without paying for it. The council, however, decided that the charge was wholly unfounded, and Chandler was ordered to make apology and restitution.[128] From this date the descent of both manors is the same as that of Titchfield (q.v.).

At the time of Domesday *MEON* belonged to the bishop of Winchester, having been held previously by a certain Toui who rented one-half of the king and held the other by grant from the earl of Hereford,[129] on whose death the whole appears to have been granted by the king to the bishop. No further mention of Meon is found until 1510, when Thomas Uvedale granted to Henry Uvedale his heir lands and rent in Meon.[130] The property then follows the history of Bromwich (q.v.) until 1550, when Thomas Wriothesley earl of Southampton died seised of the same, then for the first time called the manor of Meon.[131] After this date there is no further reference to the so-called manor, which probably became merged in that of Bromwich.

POSBROOK (Passebroc or Postbrook xiii cent.) is not mentioned in Domesday Book, and very little is known of its early history. It appears to have been held by members of the Passebroc family in the early part of the thirteenth century,[132] and in 1243–4 it was acquired either by purchase or grant from a certain William de Setteville by Isaac abbot of Titchfield.[133] A grant of free warren in Posbrook was made to the abbey in the reign of Edward I,[134] and the manor remained in the possession of the monastery until the Dissolution in 1538,[135] when it was granted to Thomas Wriothesley as part of the abbey estates, and from this date the descent of the manor is the same as that of Titchfield (q.v.).

116 Private information.

117 *Wykeham's Reg.* (Hants Rec. Soc.), ii, 281.

118 Pat. 3 Eliz. pt. 3, m. 26.

119 Lee was held of the honour in the thirteenth century. *Testa de Nevill* (Rec. Com.), 241, 233*b*, 235; Inq. p.m. 21 Edw. I, No. 14; *Plac. de Quo Warr.* (Rec. Com.), 772, 811, &c.

120 Chan. Inq. p.m. 30 Edw. I, No. 21.

121 *Cal. of Close*, 1279–88, p. 81.

122 It was held by the serjeanty of crossing the Channel with the king or as elsewhere expressed (*Red Bk. of the Exch.* 460) crossing to Brittany; *Testa de Nevill* (Rec. Com.), 233, 235, 241*b*. This is of interest, as Henry II crossed from Stokes Bay (see Alverstoke).

123 Lay Subs. R. $\frac{173}{4}$.

124 *Cal. of Inq. Hen. III*, p. 1; *Testa de Nevill* (Rec. Com.), 233*b*. Peter died in 1268. The Brito or Bruton family had probably been here for some time. There are two undated deeds in the possession of the lord of the manor of Rowner, one being a grant by Hamo Brito de Leya to St. Mary's Abbey of Quarr (founded 1133) and the other a similar deed by Gilbertas le Bret. Both are probably of an early date. *Papers and Proc. Hants Field Club*, iii (1), 3.

125 *Testa de Nevill* (Rec. Com.), 235; Chan. Inq. p.m. 21 Edw. I, No. 14; ibid. 30 Edw. I, No. 21; Lay Subs. R. $\frac{173}{4}$; *Feud. Aids*, ii, 336.

126 Wrottesley, *Pedigrees from the Plea Rolls*, 269.

127 *Feud. Aids*, ii, 356.

127a Close, 20 Hen. VIII, No. 397, m. 35.

128 *Acts of the P.C.* vii, 101–2.

129 *V.C.H. Hants*, i, 462*b*.

130 Feet of F. Southants, Trin. 2 Hen. VIII.

131 Chan. Inq. p.m. 4 Edw. VI (Ser. 2), No. 103.

132 Feet of F. Hants, 4 John, No. 32.

133 Ibid. 28 Hen. III, No. 292.

134 *Cal. of Pat.* 1422–9, p. 260.

135 Feet of F. Div. Cos. Mich. 29 Hen. VIII.

Though the name of *QUOB* (Quabbe, xiii–xvii cents.) now survives only in Quob Farm and Copse, there were formerly two separate estates of that name, one of which belonged to the lords of the manor of North Fareham in the thirteenth century, and of which the following mention is made. In the reign of Edward I Emma de Roches granted her son Hugh 'the land of Quabbe in the parish of Titchfield.'[136] In 1571 Sir Richard Pexall, descendant of Hugh, died seised of land and tenements in 'Quabbe'[137] and his grandson Sir Pexall Brocas was holding the same in 1610.[138] In 1635 the property, then called for the first time a manor, was in the possession of Thomas Brocas,[139] and certainly as late as 1762 the lords of North Fareham received £1 yearly as lords' rent from 'Quabbe' Farm,[140] which had evidently become merged in the manor of North Fareham.

The second holding that bore the name was first mentioned in 1311, when Richard de Beauchamp held one tenement called 'La Quabbe' with two gardens, 6 acres of arable land, 5 acres of meadow, 3 acres of wood, 20 acres of pasture, and an assize rent of 39*s.* 2*d.*—property which Oliver de Beauchamp his ancestor had licence to acquire in Titchfield in exchange for the manor of Melbourne in Derby, granted to King John. It was held by the service of doing suit at the court of the king at Titchfield and by a rent of 16*d.* yearly. Richard apparently held it only for the life of William de Masseworth, but his co-heiresses put in a claim for the property, which was disallowed, and the escheator was ordered to deliver up the land to William,[141] and on his death, in 1335, the estate passed to his brother Walter, who held it by the service of doing guard at Portchester for 30 days.[142] In 1361 Thomas de Overton died seised of the manor of 'Quabbe,'[143] which had probably (like the second Titchfield manor) been included in the carucate of land, 6 acres of meadow, 12 acres of wood and rent in Titchfield and Chark acquired by him in 1356 by purchase from John de Masseworth.[144] William, brother and heir of Thomas, appears to have died shortly after his brother, and the estate passed in 1363 to his daughter Isabel and her husband Thomas le Warrener,[145] who three years later acquired the one-third part of the manor which Agnes, widow of William, was holding in dower.[146] During the next seventy years the estate appears to have been broken up, since there is no further mention of the manor as such, while in 1426 Thomas Warrener was possessed of only one toft and 2 virgates of land called Quabland in the vill of Titchfield—'which he held jointly with Isabel Overton, formerly his wife.'[147] It is probable that this property as well as the rest of the Overton estate gradually became merged in Titchfield proper.

SEGENWORTH (Sugion, xi cent.; Suggenwerch, xiii cent.; Sokyngworth, xiv cent.; Sechingworth, Siginworth, xvi cent.) was one of the lordships granted to Hugh de Port by William I, and at the time of Domesday Herebald held it from him as Ulric had held it under King Edward.[148] At the end of the thirteenth century William de Stratton was holding one knight's fee of Robert de St. John,[149] descendant of the De Ports; but by the middle of the fourteenth century it had passed to the family of Wayte, and was then in the hands of William Wayte.[150] In the fifteenth century it was held by Margaret Wayte, wife of another William Wayte,[151] and through her it descended to John Wayte, probably a grandson, who leased the manor in 1528–9 to Arthur Plantagenet Viscount Lisle, his kinsman.[152] From this date the descent of the manor is the same as that of Lee Britten (q.v.).

Wayte. *Argent a cheveron gules between three hunting horns sable.*

At the time of Domesday *STUBBINGTON* (Stulbinton, Stubynton, Stobington, xiii cent.), which under King Edward formed part of the possessions of Earl Godwin, was held by the De Port family,[153] from whom it passed to the St. Johns, descendants of the De Ports, early in the thirteenth century, and in whose possession the overlordship remained until 1309, when it was granted by John de St. John, lord of Basing, to the abbot and convent of Titchfield.[154]

From an early date Stubbington was held under the St. Johns by Reginald de Mohun and his successors, who before the end of the thirteenth century had granted it to John de Rayny,[155] whose grandson, William de Rayny, about 1293 granted all his lands in Stubbington to the abbey of Titchfield,[156] which, during the following century, acquired other lands in Stubbington by various grants.[157] This grant was confirmed by royal charter in 1320, and mention is made in the same deed that the abbot was freed from all suits and services due to him from such land.[158] A grant of free warren was made to the abbot in 1293.[159] It continued to be noted separately among the possessions of the abbey until 1428,[160] from which date it disappears from the Titchfield records, and was probably included in Titchfield itself.

136 Add. Chart. 15692.
137 Chan. Inq. p.m. 14 Eliz. No. 137
138 Feet of F. Southants (Div. Cos.), Hil. 8 Jas. I.
139 Feet of F. Hants, Mich. 11 Chas. I.
140 From documents in the possession of the lord of the manor.
141 Close, 5 Edw. II, m. 25; Chan. Inq. p.m. 5 Edw. II, No. 47.
142 Chan. Inq. p.m. 9 Edw. II, No. 28.
143 Chan. Inq. p.m. 35 Edw. III, pt. 2, No. 17. The vill and manor of 'Quabbe' was held at this date of the king in chief by the serjeanty of finding one man for 40 days in time of war in Scotland. The profits of the court were worth 6*d.* per annum.
144 Chan. Inq. p.m. 31 Edw. III (2nd Nos.), No. 10.
145 Feet of F. Hants, East. 37 Edw. III, file 26, No. 60.
146 Feet of F. Hants, Trin. 40 Edw. III.
147 Chan. Inq. p.m. 4 Hen. VI, No. 41. Possibly the Overtons made gifts to the abbey and convent of Titchfield, as the latter held tenements and rent in 'Qwobe' at the Dissolution. Mins. Accts. 30 & 31 Hen. VIII, m. 135.
148 *V.C.H. Hants*, i, 480 *a* and *b*.
149 *Testa de Nevill* (Rec. Com.), 230.
150 Feet of F. Hants, Mich. 13 Edw. III; *Feud. Aids*, ii, 336.
151 Ibid. 356.
152 Close, 20 Hen. VIII, No. 397, m. 20 and 25.
153 *V.C.H. Hants*, i, 480*b*. In 1202 Wales de Possebroc granted to Wiburga his wife 50 virgates of land in Stubbington from the fee of the bishop of Avranches; Feet of F. 4 John, No. 32.
154 Dugdale, *Mon.* vii, 934–5.
155 *Testa de Nevill* (Rec. Com.), 230.
156 Dugdale, *Mon.* vii, 934.
157 In 1285 John de Fareham was granted licence to alienate 10 acres in Stubbington to the abbot and convent of Titchfield, and five years later 30 acres in addition; *Cal. of Pat.* 1281–92, pp. 157, 336.
In 1346 the abbot acquired 2 acres of land in Chark from John de Chark and Alice his wife; Chan. Inq. p.m. 20 Edw. III (2nd Nos.), No. 57.
158 Dugdale, *Mon.* vii, 934–5.
159 Ibid. 931.
160 *Feud. Aids*, ii, 308, 336, 356.

There is no mention of *SWANWICK* (Swanewik, xv cent.) in Domesday Book, and the first record relating to it is in 1231, when Henry III confirmed to Peter des Roches, bishop of Winchester, the gift made to him by Humphrey de Millers of all the land and rent in Swanwick, which Humphrey had acquired by grant of William, bishop of Avranches.[161] This land became part of the possessions of the newly founded abbey of Titchfield, and was held of the bishop of Avranches.[162] A grant of free warren was made to the abbot by Edward I in 1294.[163] Swanwick was held by the abbey[164] until surrendered to the king with the other possessions of Titchfield Abbey in 1537, and in the same year it was granted to Thomas Wriothesley,[165] and from this date follows the descent of Titchfield until the first half of the eighteenth century, when it was retained by the duke of Portland on the sale of a considerable part of the Titchfield estate to the duke of Beaufort between 1734 and 1741.[166] Its descent is then the same as that of Bromwich (q.v.).

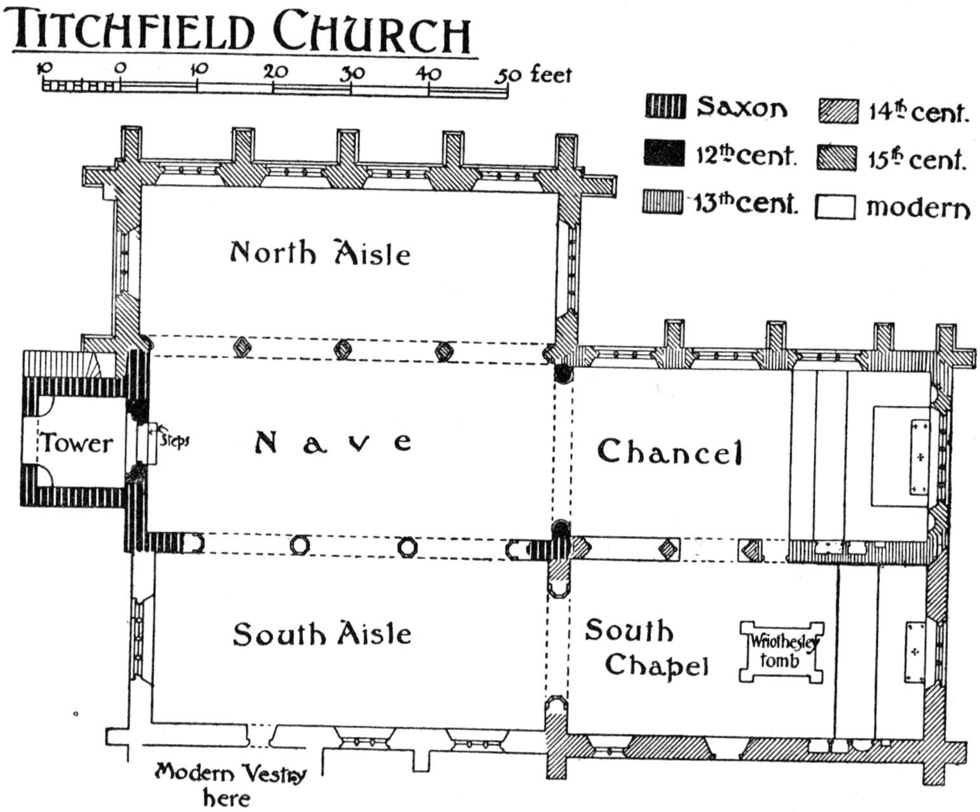

CHURCHES

The church of *ST. PETER, TITCHFIELD*, has a chancel with south chapel, nave with aisles and south-west vestry, and west tower, and is a fine and interesting building, with a long architectural history, the lower part of its tower and the west end of the nave being probably the oldest piece of ecclesiastical architecture now standing in Hampshire. The church to which they belonged had an aisleless nave probably of the same dimensions as the present, a chancel and a western porch, the latter probably of two stories. The feature is an early one, and as there are none of the characteristics of the latest style of pre-Conquest architecture to be seen, it is possible that this building may have its origin in the ninth century, or even earlier. Its subsequent history was that a south aisle was added to the nave in the twelfth century, a new west doorway made, and probably towards the end of the century a new chancel arch. The tower seems to have been raised to its present height about the same time, and about 1220 the chancel was rebuilt round the older one, becoming of the full width of the nave, and the chancel arch was now, or perhaps later, widened, the old responds being reused. About 1320 the south chapel was built, and in the fifteenth century the present north aisle of the nave was built, probably superseding an older one, of which nothing remains, the south and east walls of the chancel being remodelled to harmonize with the new work. In 1867 the twelfth-century south arcade of the nave gave place to a modern one, the whole of the south aisle being rebuilt, and a few years since a vestry was added at its south-west angle.

The chancel has a fifteenth-century east window of five lights, and three three-light windows of the same date on the north. On either side of the east window are two tall canopied niches for images of the patron and other saints, one over the other, also of the fifteenth century. At the south-east are three thirteenth-century sedilia under moulded arches, the eastern seat being higher than the other two; to the east is a

[161] *Cal. of Chart. R.* i, 140. There is no evidence of the date of Humphrey's acquisition of the property.

[162] *Testa de Nevill* (Rec. Com.), 233*b*; *Plac. de Quo Warr.* (Rec. Com.), 765.

[163] Chart. R. 22 Edw. I, No. 87.

[164] Pat. 3 Hen. VI, m. 13; ibid. 1 Edw. IV, pt. v, m. 25.

[165] Feet of F. Southants, Mich. 29 Hen. VIII; Pat. 29 Hen. VIII, pt. 1, m. 4; being called the manor of Swanwick for the first time.

[166] Recov. R. Southants, Trin. 2 Geo. III, No. 59.

Titchfield Church from the West

Titchfield Church : The Wriothesley Tomb

trefoiled piscina with a modern projecting bowl, and at the west a thirteenth-century priest's door. The rest of the south wall is taken up by an arcade of two bays, *c.* 1320, with clustered shafts and foliate capitals, that of the central shaft having four winged beasts among the foliage. The arches are of two orders with wave-moulds, and the bases rest on a dwarf wall, not coming down to the floor level.

The chancel arch is pointed, of one order with chamfered angles, springing from half-round responds, the southern capital having plain foliage, while that on the north has been mutilated and repaired without ornament. The chancel has a fifteenth-century roof with arched principals and trussed rafters, its other woodwork being entirely modern.

The south chapel, which is of the same length as the chancel, and slightly wider, has an original east window of three trefoiled ogee lights, and three two-light south windows of a similar type, a later four-centred doorway having been inserted under the second window from the east. At the south-east are three trefoiled sedilia, also original, the eastern of which is higher than the rest, and has a rounded back, and to the east is a trefoiled piscina of the same date. At a little distance from the east wall are large corbels in the north and south wall, 7 ft. from the floor, to carry a beam at the back of the altar; a moulded string over the piscina stops at this line, and this space at the east was evidently screened off to serve as a vestry. The centre of the chapel is occupied by the splendid Wriothesley monument described below.

The south arcade of the nave, of three bays, and the south aisle, are modern, in fourteenth-century style; but the north arcade, of four bays, with tall and slender clustered piers, moulded arches, and octagonal moulded capitals and bases, is a pretty piece of fifteenth-century detail. The east window of the north aisle, of five lights under a segmental head, is flanked by elaborate contemporary canopied niches, and there is a third niche set against the north face of the east respond of the arcade. There are in this aisle four three-light windows on the north and one on the west, all contemporary with the arcade, and the roof is probably plain work of the same date. The nave roof is old, with trussed rafters, but the tie-beams are modern, and at the east end is a rood beam set up in 1889 with a wall painting of the Crucifixion over it. On the west wall of the nave is a large wall painting of the miraculous draught of fishes, and above it, high in the wall, a blocked round-headed window, now opening to the top stage of the tower, but, before its building, to the open air, above the roof of the early porch.

The west doorway is a fine specimen of the latter part of the twelfth century, of three ornamented orders with nook shafts. It opens to the west porch or ground story of the tower, whose walls are only 2 ft. 3 in. thick. The western arch of the tower is plain and roundheaded, in large blocks of Binstead and iron stone, like those used in the Roman east gate of Portchester Castle. The angle quoins are of the same character, the walls being of rubble, and above the arch a bonding course of Roman bricks, three deep, runs round the tower, and is continued across the west end of the nave. At a late repair it was found to go right through the wall. The belfry stage of the tower has single lights, probably *c.* 1200, and the tower is finished with a rather heavy wooden spire. Its upper stages are reached by an external stair on the north, leading to a doorway in its north-east angle.

The font at the north-west of the nave is modern, and the only monument of much interest, except that of the Wriothesleys, is a small tablet on the north wall of the chancel to William Chamberlaine of Beaulieu, 1608, showing a man and his wife kneeling under a cornice with heraldry, and two sons and two daughters below.

The Wriothesley monument, commemorating the first earl and countess of Southampton, and their son the second earl, was set up in accordance with the will of the latter, proved 7 February, 1582, by which the enormous sum of £1,000 was left for the making of 'two faire monuments' in the 'chapel of the parish church of Tichell, co. Southampton.' The directions for two monuments were however ignored, and one only was made, on which the three alabaster effigies rest. It is a raised rectangular tomb, with projecting pilasters at the angles, which carry tall obelisks; the central part of the tomb is raised some feet above the rest, and on it lies the effigy of Jane countess of Southampton, 1574, that of her husband the first earl, 1551, lying at a lower level on the north, and that of her son the second earl, 1582, in like manner on the south. The whole is of alabaster and marble most elaborately and beautifully worked, carved, and panelled, the inscriptions being on black marble panels at the feet of the three effigies. In the vault beneath are also buried Henry third earl of Southampton and his son James Wriothesley, 1624, and the fourth and last earl, Thomas, 1667.

In the north-east angle of the south aisle is an inlaid wood panel with the Wriothesley arms, with a pediment supported by caryatides, and below it the motto VNG PARTOUT. It was formerly in the Bugle Inn.

There are six bells, the first two of which were added and the rest recast in 1866. The fifth was a Salisbury bell, *c.* 1400, inscribed AVE MARIA PLENA; the fourth of 1628, inscribed IN GOD IS MY HOPE I. I.; the third by Francis Foster of Salisbury, 1675, and the tenor by Wells of Aldbourne, 1769. There is also a small bell uninscribed of some antiquity

The plate is a very fine silver-gilt set, consisting of two cups with cover patens, inscribed THE GIFT OF THO CORDEROY GENT AÑO DOM̃ 1673, with the arms of Corderoy—a cheveron between two molets and in base a lion, all with a border—the crest being a crowned heart (*cœur de roi*); in spite of the inscription, the date letter on the cups is that of 1675; two flagons of the same date and gift; two alms dishes of 1670 of the same gift; and a standing salver of 1679, given by William Orton.

The first book of the registers contains entries from 1589 to 1634, and is of paper; the second covers the years 1634–78, and the third 1678–1762. The fourth, fifth, seventh, and eighth books contain the marriages from 1754 to 1812, and the sixth the baptisms and burials, 1762–1812. In these registers there are twelve entries of burials of soldiers between 27 November and 16 December, 1627, probably men wounded in the disastrous expedition to La Rochelle. In August, 1628, the duke of Buckingham's murder is very fully chronicled: 'The Lorde Duke of Buckinghame was slayne at Portesmouth the 23 day of

August being Satterday, Generall of all ye fleete by sea and land, whose name was George Villers Ryght Honorable.'

The church of the *HOLY ROOD, CROFTON*, has a chancel with south chapel, a north transept with north vestry, a large south transept, and a nave with south porch and west bell-turret.

The plan is irregular, the chancel not being on the same axis as the nave, and owing to modern alterations there is little guide to the earlier history of the building. The chancel and north transept seem to be early fourteenth-century work, their walls being unusually thin, nowhere more than 2 ft.

The south transept is a modern addition in poor Gothic style, of much larger area than the north transept, and contains nothing of note beyond the large white marble monument of Thomas Missing, 1733, with his arms, gules a cheveron between three molets argent and a chief or.

The chancel, 15 ft. 8 in. by 13 ft., has a modern two-light east window, on the north a repaired square-headed window of two trefoiled lights, *c.* 1320, and on the south a single uncusped light. To the west of this a pointed arch of two orders opens to the south chapel, which has a two-light east window cinquefoiled, and a modern south doorway. To the north of the window is a plain corbel for an image. The chancel arch, which seems to be of fourteenth-century work, dies out at the springing, and on the same line at the west of the south chapel is a half arch with a moulded string at the springing, which looks like early thirteenth-century detail.

The north transept, 12 ft. 9 in. by 8 ft. 6 in., which opens to the nave by an arch like the chancel arch, has a three-light north window with net tracery, and a square-headed east window of two lights, both *c.* 1320–30. In the north wall is a narrow doorway, and west of it a blocked low side window with an internal rebate for a wooden frame. The doorway now opens to a modern vestry built against the north wall of the transept. In the west wall of the transept is a single trefoiled fourteenth-century light.

The nave, 51 ft. 3 in. by 19 ft., has three square-headed north windows, each of two trefoiled lights, one south window of the same type, and a four-centred south doorway, all of fifteenth-century style, but mostly of modern masonry. There is a three-light west window with a circular window over it, both modern.

The roofs of the chancel, nave, and north transept are old, but without detail by which their approximate date may be deduced; all other woodwork in the church is modern, except the pulpit, which is of eighteenth-century date.

Externally the roofs are red-tiled, and at the west end of the nave is a boarded turret containing one bell by Clement Tosier, 1710.

The church of *ST. MARY, HOOK*, built in 1871, is of stone in Early English style, and consists of chancel, nave of four bays, aisles, transepts, north and south porches, and a western turret containing one bell. The register dates from 1871.

The church of *ST. PAUL, SARISBURY*, built in 1836, and partly rebuilt and enlarged in 1888, is of brick and stone in Early English style, and consists of chancel, with organ chamber and vestry, nave, transepts, and western tower containing a clock and one bell. The register dates from 1837.

The font, near the south door, has an octagonal bowl on a short stem, and may be of fifteenth-century date. This church is now used only as a mortuary chapel, a new building of the same name having been erected in 1871 to serve as the parish church.

ADVOWSONS The first mention of the advowson of Titchfield appears to be in 1231, when the right of presentation was granted with the manor to the abbot and convent of Titchfield.[168] The abbey presented from 1302 to 1539, and from that time the descent of both the manor and advowson are identical till 1856, when the patronage passed to the dean and chapter of Winchester.[169]

There was a church at Crofton in 1086 which is probably identical with the chapel of St. Edmund mentioned in the fourteenth century in connexion with the grant of the manor to the abbot and convent of Titchfield.[170] As it was never assessed separately in any ecclesiastical valuation, and there is no evidence to show that it has ever been a separate ecclesiastical unit, it was probably a chapel of ease to Titchfield and was served by the same incumbent. The ecclesiastical parish of Crofton was formed from Titchfield in 1871.

The living of St. Mary's, Hook, is a vicarage in the gift of the bishop of Winchester, and that of St. Paul's Sarisbury, also a vicarage, is in the gift of the vicar of Titchfield. There is an iron church at Lee-on-the-Solent, Congregational chapels at Sarisbury and Warsash, a Baptist chapel at Sarisbury, and a Wesleyan chapel at Lee-on-the-Solent.

CHARITIES The charities of Robert Godfrey, of Henry earl of Southampton, and Richard Godwin, are now dispensed under a scheme issued by the Charity Commissioners, dated 17 December, 1897, and 9 December, 1902, under the title of 'The Charities of the Earl of Southampton and Others.' Robert Godfrey's charity founded by deed 1597, consists of land, cottages, and stable, let at £28 a year. Richard Godwin's charity is a rent-charge of £4 issuing out of Pressmoore's estate at Glastonbury, Somerset. The trust estates of the earl of Southampton's charity consist of about twenty-seven acres of land, tenements, and garden-grounds, producing a gross income of £115 a year. By the schemes above referred to the annuity of £4 is directed to be applied in the advancement of the education of children in a public elementary school, by way of prizes, together with a further sum of £10 out of the general income, and subject thereto the residue of the yearly income for the benefit of poor persons resident in the civil parish, and in default in the ancient parish of Titchfield. In 1905 £24 was paid to pensioners, £5 in tools for apprentices, and subscriptions were made to provident clubs.

Mrs. Charlotte Hornby, by her will proved 1890, bequeathed a legacy represented by £1,865 5*s.* 8*d.* consols, the income from which, amounting to £46, is applied equally in subscriptions to clothing clubs and in the distribution of blankets at Christmas.

Seymour Robert Delmé in 1894 bequeathed £1,000 to the vicar and churchwardens of Titchfield church, which is invested in consols to the amount of

168 *Cal. of Chart. R.* i, 168; Pat. 3 Hen. VI, pt. 1, m. 13.

169 Inst. Bks. (P.R.O.).

170 Pat. 5 Edw. III, pt. 1, m. 5.

£910 12*s.*, the income from which, amounting to £22 15*s.*, to be distributed among the poor. He also left £500 invested in consols to the amount of £455 5*s.* 8*d.*, producing an income of £11 7*s.* for the repair of the church.

A recreation ground, 4 acres in extent, was by an award in 1866 dedicated to the use of the parishioners, to which an additional 5 acres was given by deed in 1897.

Seymour Robert Delmé, by his will proved in 1894, left £1,383 7*s.* 5*d.* India stock, producing an income of £41 10*s.*, one-third of which is to be applied in the advancement of the children of Crofton, and two-thirds for the benefit of the poor. In 1867 4 acres and 22 poles of land were awarded to Crofton as a recreation ground, any profits from the pasturage, averaging £3 a year, to be applied for public uses.

In 1885 E. J. Sartoris gave a site, and building thereon, to be used as a reading room for Hook with Warsash.

In 1866 a recreation ground of 6 acres and 22 poles was awarded for the use of the inhabitants of Sarisbury, and by deed dated 1892 Mrs. L. Seymour gave a parish room, which was vested in 'The Official Trustee of Charity Lands,' by an order of the Charity Commissioners, dated 5 July, 1892.

WICKHAM

Wykham (xiii cent.).

The parish of Wickham, containing 2,446 acres, of which 18 are covered by water, is situated in the south of the county west from Portsmouth. In the east the soil is light, black, and somewhat stony; in the west it is heavy, with a certain amount of clay. There are 796½ acres of arable land, 931½ of grass, and 332 of wood.[1] The chief crops are wheat and other cereals. Wickham Common, about 20 acres in extent, is a mile from the village on the Southwick Road, and there are golf links on a smaller common on the Bishop's Waltham Road. The main road from Alton, entering the parish from the north-east, runs past the village on the east, whence it takes a direct course south towards Fareham. Another road from Bishop's Waltham joins it a little to the south of the village. The land is undulating, and slopes from a height of 200 ft. above the ordnance datum at Shervill Copse in the north of the parish to Wickham Common in the south-east, which only rises to a height of 154 ft. The River Meon, after forming the north-east boundary of the parish for about a mile, flows across it in a south-easterly direction to the neighbouring parish of Titchfield, passing along the east side of the village. The land on either bank of the river is low, and liable to floods at certain times of the year. The church, schools, and rectory are on the west side of the river, and the village proper stands on rising ground to the east. The houses are built round a large market place, from the north-east corner of which a street runs down to the north mill and bridge. In this street are several old timber-built houses, and a good specimen of eighteenth-century cut and moulded brickwork. In the market place are several good eighteenth-century houses, and the general effect of the wide open space, surrounded by an irregular line of buildings, is very attractive. The rectory, which is some little distance south-east of the church, has in its garden a plane tree planted between 1798 and 1801 by Dr. Wharton, who was the rector at that time. There are two bridges over the Meon, with a water-mill attached to each, the upper one of which was built from the timbers of the *Chesapeake*. Just below this mill, on the opposite side of the bridge, is a brewery. There is also an old foundry; the edged tools made in Wickham having been formerly very celebrated, but their manufacture has long died out. Market gardening is the chief industry, fruit especially being cultivated—a ready market having been found for it in Portsmouth and Gosport since the opening of the Meon Valley Railway. A fair is held in the market place on 20 May. The lord of the manor owns the tolls on booths and vehicles at fair-time, but at present these dues are sublet. A court leet and court baron are still held in the manor house, and those summoned to the former are sworn in the cellar of the manor house, while before the opening of the court baron all those attending walk in procession across the northern bridge to a low wall opposite the churchyard, and look at the spot where the house of the Uvedales stood. At the court leet tithingmen are still appointed, as also a borough constable, who is sworn for the purpose of driving gipsies off the parish land. The stocks have stood in the public square within the memory of the older inhabitants. Two commons are in the manor—Wickham Common and Shedfield Common. 'Place House,' the old manor house of the Uvedales, which stood as already noted in a field nearly opposite the church, was pulled down about 1780. Some of the old garden wall remains, and in a dry season the traces of the foundations are still to be seen.

A station on the Meon Valley Railway was opened in 1903, and near it there is a small group of cottages built by squatters, who encroached on the crown lands of the Forest of Bere. Rookesbury, a large house on the Droxford road, is the seat of the Garnier family, though now occupied by Mr. Arthur H. Lee, M.P. for South Hants. Little Park, a short distance out of the village on the Botley road, belongs to Col. Radcliffe. Crocker Hill, a small hamlet, is partly in Wickham and partly in Fareham parish.

William of Wykeham, bishop of Winchester, who was born here in 1324, took his name from the place.

BOROUGH The first mention of the borough of Wickham is in 1607, when Sir William Uvedale, who then held it, settled it by fine upon Mary daughter of Sir Richard Norton for life.[2] It passed to her on her husband's death in 1616,[3] but in 1626 it was in the hands of her son

[1] Returns of Board of Agriculture (1905).

[2] Feet of F. Southants, Div. Cos. Hil. 5 Jas. I.

[3] W. & L. Inq. p.m. 14 Jas. I. (Ser. 2), bdle. 24, No. 123.

Sir William Uvedale,[4] who probably held it till his death in 1652. It then follows the descent of the manor (q.v.). A court of the borough is held every year, at which a constable, town crier, tithing-man, and hayward are appointed, the constable being provided with a truncheon and handcuffs. The bounds of the borough are beaten from time to time, and all people selling goods are liable to market tolls within the borough.

MANOR At the time of the Domesday Book *WICKHAM*, which had been held under Edward the Confessor as two manors by four brothers, was held by Hugh de Port,[5] being one of the many lordships granted to the De Port family by William I. The overlordship, following the descent of the rest of the De Port barony, passed in succession to the families of St. John, Philibert, and Paulet; William Paulet, marquis of Winchester, holding it in 1616, after which the rights of the overlord probably lapsed.[6] It was held under the De Ports by the family of Scures. In 1268 Roger de Scures received a grant of free warren, a market and fair in his manor of Wickham,[7] and in 1287 Matthew de Scures was lord of Wickham.[8] Later in the same century Eva de Scures, granddaughter and heir of Matthew, held this manor as one knight's fee,[9] and, having no children, was succeeded by Sir John de Scures, probably a cousin, warden of the castle of Winchester, who died in 1353.[10] His son John held the manor until his death in 1381, when his sister Sybil, who had married John Uvedale, became his heir, and thus brought Wickham to a family with whom it remained for 350 years.[11] John and Sybil Uvedale had two sons, William and John, each of whom succeeded to the family property in turn. From John Uvedale the estates passed, some time between 1445 and 1461, to his son Sir Thomas, a man of considerable importance in the fifteenth century, who died in 1484, leaving Wickham, then worth £44, to his son William, whose estates escheated to the crown on his attainder in 1484 for his hostility to the government of Richard III. He received a free pardon in 1485,[12] and was succeeded in 1524 by a son William, who, before his death in 1528, conveyed the estate to trustees for the use of his wife Dorothy for life,[13] and directed that a small annual allowance should be made to his son and heir Arthur, who appears to have been of weak intellect. The duty of keeping the estate in repair was entrusted to his uncle Thomas and his brother John.[14] Arthur succeeded on his mother's death in 1530,[15] and his son and heir William died in 1569, leaving a son aged nine years, afterwards Sir William Uvedale. He died in 1616, and the borough, manor, and advowson of Wickham, worth £40 per annum, passed, under a settlement made by fine in 1607, to his wife Mary, daughter of Sir Richard Norton, for life.[16] She survived him many years, and on her death, before 1634, the estates passed to her son William.[17] During his life, possibly owing to his adherence to the royal cause, his property became much reduced, some estates being sold and others vested in trustees for the payment of his debts. By his will he left the manor to his second wife, Victoria, daughter of Henry Cary Viscount Falkland, for life, whose son William, dying before 1663, left two sisters co-heirs of the estates.[18] The elder, Victoria, married Sir Richard Corbett, and on her death, before 1683, her interest in the manor passed to her son Sir Uvedale Corbett.[19] The younger sister, Elizabeth, married secondly Edward earl of Carlisle. She was the last representative of the elder branch of the family of Uvedale, and shortly after her death, in 1696, her property was divided between her son Charles earl of Carlisle and Sir Uvedale Corbett her nephew.[20] The Wickham property apparently went to the Corbetts, and in 1721[21] Sir Richard Corbett was holding Wickham, but in 1724 it was purchased by Jonathan Rashleigh, M.P. for Fowey, Cornwall,[22] and in 1764 sold by Philip Rashleigh to George Garnier, sheriff of Hampshire in 1766,[23] from whom it passed to his son William Garnier, whose nephew Mr. John Carpenter-Garnier, of Rookesbury Park, is the present lord of the manor.

UVEDALE. *Argent a cross moline gules.*

GARNIER. *Azure a sword bendwise point downwards between a fleur de lis or and a branch of oak or all within a border battled or.*

CARPENTER. *Party indented or and azure an eagle and in the chief two roundels countercoloured.*

CHURCH The church of *ST. NICHOLAS* has a chancel 22 ft. 8 in. by 16 ft., with south chapel and organ chamber, north transept 23 ft. by 18 ft., south transept 34 ft. by 18 ft. 4 in., nave 59 ft. by 20 ft., and west tower. In spite of a severe 'restoration' in 1862–3, the church retains some ancient features, the north-east angle of the nave and the north doorway of the chancel showing twelfth-century masonry, and the west doorway of the tower is also re-used twelfth-century work.

4 Feet of F. Southants, Hil. 2 Chas. I (Div. Cos.).

5 *V.C.H. Hants*, i, 480*a*.

6 *Testa de Nevill* (Rec. Com.), 230; Chan. Inq. p.m. 27 Edw. III. (1st Nos.), No. 12; ibid. (Ser. 2), vol. 18, No. 24; Exch. Inq. p.m. 23 Hen. VIII. (Ser. 2), file 983, No. 3; W. & L. Inq. p.m. 14 Jas. I (Ser. 2), bdle. 24, No. 123.

7 Chart. R. 1257–1300, p. 124.

8 Feet of F. Hants, Mich. 16 Edw. I, No. 160.

9 *Testa de Nevill* (Rec. Com.), 230.

10 Chan. Inq. p.m. 27 Edw. III. (1st Nos.), No. 12.

11 *Surrey Arch. Coll.* iii, 83.

12 *Cal. of Pat.* 1476–85, pp. 504, 523.

13 *Surrey Arch. Coll.* iii, 99, 171.

14 Ibid. 110.

15 Exch. Inq. p.m. 23 Hen. VIII (Ser. 2), file 983, No. 3.

16 Feet of F. Southants (Div. Cos.), Hil. 5 Jas. I.; W. & L. Inq. p.m. 14 Jas. I (Ser. 2), bdle. 24, No. 123.

17 *Surrey Arch. Coll.* iii, 122.

18 Ibid. 130, 131.

19 Ibid. 132.

20 Ibid.

21 Recov. R. Mich. 8 Geo. I, rot. 198.

22 Ibid. Trin. 12 Geo. III, rot. 339.

23 *Surrey Arch. Coll.* iii, 133.

The chancel has a three-light east window with net tracery, and two square-headed north windows, each of two cinquefoiled lights, all the stonework being modern. Between the two latter windows is a doorway which appears to be of late date on the inside, but externally, as already noted, shows twelfth-century masonry. Over the east window is a vertical rib of stone, springing from a horizontal band at the level of the eaves of the roof, after the manner of pre-Conquest work, but in this instance its date is doubtful.

The south chapel opens to the chancel by a pointed arch of two chamfered orders, with a moulded half-round capital and half-octagonal abacus to its western respond, *c.* 1300, probably giving the date of the chapel, which has no other ancient features, but contains parts of two fine Uvedale monuments, moved here in 1863. The chancel arch is modern, as are all the details of the transepts and nave, both of masonry and woodwork. The south transept was built in 1803, the tomb of John Swan, 1781, and his son John, who died in the same year, being moved to make place for it, and built into its south wall as it now appears.

Before 1862 the church had a wooden bell-turret, the present three-story masonry tower then taking its place. Its re-used west doorway is a good piece of mid-twelfth-century work, with a lozenge ornament on its label, and zigzag on its arch. The jambs have nook-shafts, and on the capital of the northern shaft is carved a centaur shooting at a lion (as on the tympanum at Stoke sub Hamdon, Somerset), the southern capital having a foliate ornament.

There is old stonework also used up in the two lancet windows in the south wall of the tower.

The font is modern, with an octagonal panelled bowl.

Of the two Uvedale monuments in the south chapel, the older is part of a large monument to William Uvedale, 1569, mutilated in 1863. It had a panelled base, and a cornice carried by female figures, the scrolled panel bearing the inscription being at the back of the recess beneath the cornice. The second monument, which is better preserved but badly put together and in rather shaky condition, is that of Sir William Uvedale, 1615, and has recumbent effigies of Sir William and his wife, the lady being on a lower level, under a semicircular panelled arch flanked by obelisks and surmounted by a coat-of-arms with crest and supporters, the open scroll-work on either side of the heraldry ending in clumsily treated lions' heads. On the base of the tomb are kneeling figures of four sons and five daughters, and the whole monument is very elaborately worked and worthy of study, though the detail is not quite first-rate.

In the chancel floor are two fourteenth-century coffin-lids with crosses in relief, and two blue marble slabs, dated 1692 and 1696, the latter in memory of Elizabeth countess of Carlisle, the heiress of the Uvedales.[24]

There are six bells, the second, third, and fifth by Wells of Aldbourne, 1767, and the tenor by the same founder, 1772, all having inscriptions on the sound-bow; the fourth was also by Wells, 1767, but was recast by Taylor of Loughborough, 1897; and the treble, of 1890, is also by Taylor.

The plate consists of a large, plain communion cup, a standing paten, a flagon and an alms dish, all of 1639, and there is also a modern plated dish.

The registers begin in 1556, the first book being a copy made in 1606, with a fine title-page. The births, marriages, and deaths are entered together till 1609, and then separately in the following order: baptisms, 1611–29; marriages, 1612–26; burials, 1612–24; baptisms, 1635–54 (some pages are here missing); marriages, 1631–54; burials, 1629–54. The second book begins in 1695 and runs to 1783, the marriages stopping in 1761. The third and fifth books continue the marriages to 1812, and the fourth does the same for the other two headings. In the third book is a list of briefs for 1706–51, and in the second book a note of the population of the parish in 1695. There were 413 parishioners, 300 of whom were communicants, 'two papists, dissenters not one.' There were 97 families, and 50 seats in the church.

The churchwardens' accounts from 1777 are preserved.

ADVOWSON The advowson of the church at Wickham followed the descent of the manor until 1764.[25] It was a rectory, and in the Taxatio of Pope Nicholas it is valued at £12,[26] out of which a pension of 20*s.* was paid to the abbey and convent of Titchfield,[27] while in the valuation of Henry VIII it is returned as worth £9 11*s.* 5*d.*[28] On the sale of the manor to George Garnier in 1764 the advowson was retained by the Rashleigh family, the present patron being Mr. Jonathan Rashleigh of Menabilly, Cornwall.

Sir William Uvedale granted land in Wickham to found an obit, the yearly rent of which amounted to £3.[29]

The Wesleyans have a chapel in the parish.

CHARITIES By an order of the Charity Commissioners of 24 May, 1867, the charities existing in this parish were consolidated:—

Honor Waite's Charity: by will dated 1599, consisting of 20*s.* yearly, issuing out of her manor of Denmead in the parish of Hambledon, now paid by Mr. G. B. Gale of Denmead Mill.

John Pierson's Charity: by will dated 1702, consisting of a rent-charge of 20*s.* a year out of his copyhold lands in the parish.

Elizabeth countess of Carlisle, by will dated 1696, gave £100 for the use of the poor of Wickham. In 1758 George Garnier, by deed in respect of this sum which had come into his hands, charged a farm known as Pye's Farms with £10 10*s.* annually for the benefit of the poor. These two annuities are now paid by John Carpenter-Garnier, Esq., of Rookesbury Park, Wickham.

John Swann, by will dated 1778, gave £100 consols—increased by accumulations to £153 1*s.* 7*d.* consols—for the poor, or for the instruction of the children of the poor.

Poor's Money: Subscriptions raised in 1801 for the relief of the poor during the then severe winter,

[24] For the Uvedale family see *Surrey Arch. Coll.* 1865, p. 63.

[25] Egerton MS. 2032, fol. 17; Chan. Inq. p.m. 27 Edw. III (1st Nos.), No. 12; Feet of F. Southants, Hil. 5 Jas. I.

[26] *Pope Nich. Tax.* (Rec. Com.), 211.

[27] Egerton MS. 2034, fol. 69.

[28] *Valor Eccl.* (Rec. Com.), ii, 23.

[29] Chant. Cert. 52, No. 28.

together with the surplus of a church repair fund, was laid out in the purchase of £100 stock.

The Rev. George Andrew Thomas, D.D., rector, by will dated 1804, left £5 a year for five poor widows—regular attendants at the church—represented by £166 13*s.* 4*d.* consols.

By the order above referred to, the clear annual income, after reserving £5 a year in respect of John Swann's charity towards the support of a school, was directed to be applied for the benefit of necessitous inhabitants with a preference to poor widowers or widows, by providing clothes, food, or other articles in kind, or by aiding the funds of any provident society. In 1905 £5 was given to five widows, £5 expended in boots to nineteen children, and thirty-three poor persons received articles in kind. By an order made in 1903 under the Board of Education Act, 1899, the sum of £419 14*s.* 11*d.* consols, comprising the several sums of stock above mentioned, was apportioned in the following way: £200 for providing the £5 a year for education, and £219*s.* 14*s.* 11*d.* consols for eleemosynary purposes.[80]

[80] Information supplied by the Charity Commissioners.

THE HUNDRED OF HAMBLEDON

CONTAINING THE PARISH OF

HAMBLEDON, with the tithings of DENMEAD, CHIDDEN, GLIDDEN, and ERVILL'S EXTON [1]

At the time of the Domesday Survey Hambledon was not entered as a hundred. It was assessed at two hides, which were included in Meonstoke Hundred; one hide being among the lands of William de Perci,[2] and the other among those of Earl Roger.[3]

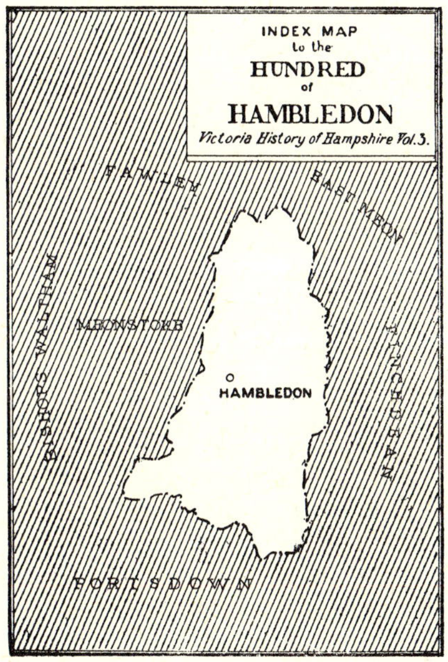

In 1316 Hambledon, with Chidden, Glidden, and Denmead, was included in East Meon Hundred, which was held by the bishop of Winchester.[4]

Hambledon seems first to have been formed into a separate hundred in the reign of Edward III,[5] when it contained the tithings of Chidden, Glidden, and Denmead, and was owned by the bishop of Winchester.[6]

In this reign a tax of a fifteenth and a tenth levied on the country produced £5 6*s.* 8*d.* from the hundred of Hambledon,[7] and similar taxes levied in the reigns of Henry VIII,[8] Elizabeth,[9] and James[10] produced exactly the same amount.

In 1422 the whole of the modern tithings, Chidden, Glidden, Denmead, and Ervill's Exton or Leigh, were included in the hundred.[11] The hundred of Hambledon has always been in the hands of the bishop.[12]

[1] The extent of the hundred as given in the Population Returns of 1831.
[2] *V.C.H. Hants*, i, 487.
[3] Ibid. i, 478.
[4] *Feud. Aids*, ii, 319.
[5] Lay Subs. R. Hants, Edw. III, $\frac{173}{88}$.
[6] Ibid.
[7] Ibid.
[8] Ibid. 32 Hen. VIII, $\frac{173}{204}$.
[9] Ibid. 1 Eliz. $\frac{174}{366}$.
[10] Ibid. 21 Jas. I, $\frac{175}{499}$.
[11] Eccl. Com. Ct. R. 159, 483 $\frac{1}{3}$ (3) $\frac{80}{28}$.
[12] Ibid. 3 & 4 Phil. and Mary, 159, 475 $\frac{2}{2}$ (7) $\frac{79}{25}$; ibid. 18 & 19 Chas. I, 155, 748, $\frac{98}{10}$.

HAMBLEDON

Ambledune (xi cent.). Hamuldon (xiv cent.).

Hambledon is eight miles north of Cosham station, and twelve miles north of Portsmouth. The parish is about six miles in length, and three and a half miles in breadth at the widest part. The area is 9,446 acres, including the tithings of Denmead or Barn Green, Chidden, Glidden, Rushmere, and Ervill's Exton.

The village of Hambledon lies in the west of the parish, and is thus described by Cobbett in his *Rural Rides* (1853):—'Hambledon is a long straggling village lying in a little valley formed by some very pretty but not lofty hills. The environs are much prettier than the village itself, which is not far from the north side of Portsdown Hill. This must have once been a considerable place, for here is a church pretty nearly as large as that at Farnham in Surrey, which is quite sufficient for a large town.' The entrance to the village from the south by the road from Portsmouth is extremely picturesque. Bury Lodge, the residence of Captain Butler, is situated to the east of the road, while to the west a little nearer the village are green meadows sloping upwards from the road to one or two houses, which stand well back with a back-ground of trees. Cams Cottage, one of these, is the residence of Captain Francis H. Harvey. The church of St. Peter and St. Paul stands on high ground to the north of the village street, and is approached from it by a short and steep road bordered by old-fashioned timber cottages. There are several large houses in the village, the most important being Hambledon House, the residence of Captain Bernhard Liebert; Fairfield House, at present occupied by Captain Edward Adderley, J.P.; and Whitedale House, at the outskirts of the village on the north, the residence of Mrs. Charnock. The main street, after leaving the village, runs north-east, entering the down country near Park House, and gradually ascending till it enters the parish of Catherington by the Bat and Ball Inn, the home of the famous Hambledon Cricket Club, which occupies a lonely position, some 400 ft. above the level of the sea. In the north of the parish are the tithings of Glidden and Chidden, the former of which lies two miles east of the village on the southern slopes of Broadhalfpenny Down,[13] and the latter some two miles north-east.

Opposite Hambledon church a steep shady lane leads southwards to Hambledon windmill, which has now fallen into picturesque decay, and thence past Rushmere Farm, with its large sheet of water, to Denmead, which is an ecclesiastical parish formed in 1881 from Denmead tithing, a part of Ervill's Exton tithing, the East or Creech Walk of the Forest of Bere, until then extra-parochial, which is now inclosed and planted chiefly with Scotch and other firs, and a part of the parish of Catherington. The village of Denmead, or Barn Green as it is usually called from its small triangular green, lies to the north-east of the Creech Walk, and its church, dedicated in honour of All Saints, was built in 1880 at a cost of £2,000. Ashling House in the village is the residence of Mr. George Chadwick Booth, who is a large landowner in the parish. The window-arches and general appearance of one of the farm-houses near the village suggest that it contains the structure of a chapel which

HAMBLEDON VILLAGE

[13] This down was long the cricketing centre for Hampshire, Surrey, and Sussex, and many celebrated matches have been played here.

was dependent upon the parish church of Hambledon until the Reformation, but tradition also points to a spot on the downs near Denmead Mill as the site of this chapel, and it is stated that in the last century a number of graves were found there. Other places in this parish are Anmore,[14] half a mile east, once in Catherington parish; Apless, 1½ miles west; Broadway, 1½ miles east; Bunker's Hill, ½ a mile south-west; Bunn's Lane, 2½ miles west; Crabbick, 1 mile west; Eastland Gate, 2 miles east; Ervill's, 1½ miles west; Furze Hill, 1 mile south-east; Piper's Hill, 1½ miles south-east; Soake, 1 mile east; and World's End, 1½ miles west.

The soil of the parish varies from a light clay in the north and north-east to a stiff clay in the south. The chief crops are wheat, barley, and oats.

The land is divided as follows: 4,392 acres of arable land, 2,993 of permanent grass, and 1,101 of woods and plantations.[15] The following place-names occur in Hambledon parish: Bullpyrke Meadow;[16] in 1452, 'Scutescroft';[17] in 1556, 'Appullons' in Denmead;[18] in 1702, 'Furze Field' and 'Brithlands' in the tithing of Chidden;[19] in 1712, 'Westhookes' near Anthill Heath, 'Keepmore' and 'Inholmes' in the tithing of Denmead.[20]

West End Down in Hambledon parish was inclosed on 24 January, 1861;[21] Anthill Common on 7 September, 1870,[22] and Chidden Down 14 December, 1871.[23]

John Nyren (1764–1837), a writer on cricket, was born at Hambledon. He was the son of Richard Nyren, founder of the famous Hambledon Cricket Club.

Charles II on his way from Somerset to Shoreham, whence he escaped to Fécamp, passed the night of 13 October, 1651, at Hambledon, at the house of a brother-in-law of Colonel Gunter (at that time the king's guide). 'The master of the house, who had been all day long playing the good fellow at an ale-house in the town, came in at supper, and declared that the king looked like "some round-headed rogue's son," but was soon appeased. Afterwards, in the time of entertaining his guests, he did by chance let fall an oath; for which Mr. Jackson (the name by which the king went) took occasion modestly to reprove him.'[24] The house at that time belonged to one of the Symonds family; it is now used as a gardener's cottage.

MANORS The main manor of *HAMBLEDON*, which must have escheated to the crown under Henry I, was granted to the bishop of Winchester by King John in 1199[25]; and remained in his hands until 1650, at which date the manor, together with the manor farm, view of frankpledge, court leet and court baron, was sold to George Wither for £3,796 18*s.* 11*d.*[26] Hambledon was restored to the bishopric at the Restoration, and remained in its possession until 1869, when the lands of the see of Winchester were taken over by the Ecclesiastical Commissioners, who are lords of the manor of Hambledon at the present time.

At the time of the Domesday Survey there was a mill in Hambledon,[27] and in the reign of Edward I there was a mill in the bishop's manor.[28]

CAMOYS. *Argent a chief gules with three bezants.*

In 1612 a market was granted to Thomas bishop of Winchester, to be held on Tuesday in each week; and two fairs, one at the feast of the Purification of the Blessed Virgin Mary, and the other at the feast of St. Matthew.[29] There is no trace of these, however, at the present day.

Besides the bishop's manor of Hambledon there were evidently some lands in the parish which were held under the overlordship of the De Ports and St. Johns successively. At the time of the Domesday Survey William de Perci was holding this land in right of his wife,[30] Emma de Port,[31] who probably obtained it by grant of Hugh de Port.[32]

ST. PHILIBERT. *Bendy argent and azure.*

His heir, Alan de Perci, held a knight's fee in Hambledon of John de Port in 1166, and William de Perci held the same of Robert de St. John under Henry III.[33] Ralph de Punda was holding this knight's fee in Hambledon of William de Perci under Robert de St. John in the thirteenth century.[34] In 1259 Ralph de Camoys was holding half a knight's fee in Hambledon as the under-tenant of Robert de St. John[35]; and in 1329 Ralph de Camoys, his grandson, was holding a whole fee there worth 40*s.* of John de St. John.[36] In 1349 an order was issued that the knight's fee in Hambledon which Ralph de Camoys was holding should be delivered up to John de St. Philibert and Margaret his wife, eldest sister and heir of Edmund de St. John, tenant in chief, who had died a minor in the king's wardship.[37]

ST. JOHN. *Argent a chief gules with two molets or.*

Maurice de Brun, Aymer de Valence, and John de Boarhunt were also holding lands in Hambledon in 1347 from Edmund de St. John,[38] and in 1349 an order was issued to deliver this land to Elizabeth late the wife of Edmund de St. John as her dower, with reversion to Luke de Poynings and his wife Isabel, sister and heir of Edmund de St. John.[39]

14 For its history see Catherington parish.

15 Statistics from the Bd. of Agric. (1905).

16 Eccl. Com. Ct. R. 159, 493 $\frac{3}{7}$ (3) $\frac{82}{5}$.

17 Ibid. 31 Hen. VI, 159, 483 $\frac{1}{3}$.

18 Ibid. 3 & 4 Phil. & Mary, $\frac{79}{25}$.

19 Ibid. 1 Anne, 155, 811 $\frac{106}{1}$.

20 Ibid. 11 Anne, $\frac{183}{3}$.

21 *Parl. Accts. and Paps.* vol. 71, 485–523.

22 Ibid.

23 Ibid.

24 *Boscobel Tracts.*

25 Chart. R. 1 John, m. 29.

26 Close, 1650, pt. 3, m. 19.

27 *V.C.H. Hants*, i, 487.

28 Mins. Accts. $\frac{1142}{15}$, $\frac{978}{27}$ and $\frac{1141}{21}$

29 Pat. 11 Jas. I, pt. 6, m. 17, No. 29.

30 *V.C.H. Hants*, i, 487.

31 *Red Bk. of Exch.* 206.

32 Ibid.

33 Ibid.

34 *Testa de Nevill* (Rec. Com.), 230.

35 Inq. p.m. 43 Hen. III, No. 28.

36 Ibid. 3 Edw. III (1st Nos.), No. 67.

37 *Cal. of Close*, 1349–54, p. 20.

38 Inq. p.m. 21 Edw. III (1st Nos.) No. 57.

39 *Cal. of Close*, 1349–54, p. 16.

After this date there is apparently no further mention of these lands in Hambledon. The only explanation of this seems to be that they may have become amalgamated with some other manor in the hands of the St. Johns, possibly Warnford.

DENMEAD in Hambledon was in the hands of the bishop of Winchester in 1316,[40] and it is always mentioned under Hambledon on the Ecclesiastical Commission Court Rolls as paying suit at the bishop's court of Hambledon. It was evidently leased by the bishops to various tenants during the thirteenth century.[41]

It is first called a manor in 1449 when William Wayte[42] died seised of it, and held it of the bishop of Winchester, leaving a son and heir Edward, then aged five.[43] From Edward it passed to his son Simon, who died in 1518, leaving a brother and heir William.[44]

WAYTE. *Argent a cheveron gules between three hunting horns sable.*

On the death of the latter in 1561 his extensive lands in Hampshire and the Isle of Wight were divided among his six daughters, Eleanor the wife of Richard Bruning, Mary the wife of William Cresweller, Honor who had married her cousin William Wayte, Margaret the wife of Henry Perkins, Elizabeth who had married Richard Norton, and Susan who had married William Wollascot.[45]

Eleanor Bruning died in 1593, leaving one-sixth of the manor to her son and heir Francis, charged with an annuity to her son, William Bruning, and with a jointure settled on Ellen wife of her son Richard, the daughter and heiress of Anthony Uvedale.[46]

BRUNING. *Gules two bends wavy the upper argent the lower or.*

Christine Bruning, most probably the widow of Francis Bruning, gave this sixth part to Humphrey Sandford and Thomas Wollascot in 1604.[47] In 1610 their share of the manor came back into the possession of the Brunings,[48] and though presumably only a sixth part it is subsequently described as the manor of Denmead; and in 1612 Richard Bruning died seised of it, leaving it to his son Anthony with a jointure settled on Mary, Anthony's wife.[49]

Anthony was still holding the manor in 1652, and conveyed it in that year to Richard Love and John Bold, probably trustees.[50] Richard Bruning was in possession of the manor in 1718 and settled it at that date on George Parker.[51]

The Wollascots were still holding their share of the manor of Denmead in 1613, for in that year William Wollascot junior and his wife Anne and their son William conveyed property described as the manor to Otho Gayer and George Parker,[52] evidently as a settlement, for in 1618 William Wollascot senior died seised of lands and tenements in Denmead in right of his wife Susan, daughter and co-heiress of William Wayte, and the lands descended to his son and heir William Wollascot junior.[53] William Wollascot and Anne settled their share of the manor of Denmead and the so-called manor of Glidden on their son Edward in 1621,[54] his brother William apparently having died;[55] and in 1656 Edward Wollascot and his wife Anne conveyed them to Thomas Battlesworth.[56] The parts of Denmead and Glidden which passed into the hands of the Perkins family with the marriage of Margaret Wayte and Henry Perkins evidently remained to them for some time; for in 1671 Richard Perkins and Francis Perkins made a settlement of the so-called manors of Denmead and Glidden.[57]

In 1703 Anne Perkins (one of the Perkins of Beenham, Berkshire, who had married her cousin, Francis Perkins of Ufton, the great-grandson of Henry Perkins and Margaret)[58] together with Frances and Margaret, her sisters-in-law, granted her share in the manors to her cousin Thomas Perkins.[59] A few months later Thomas Perkins and his wife Sarah conveyed the manors to George Norris and Richard Heverden, probably as a settlement.[60]

PERKINS. *Or a fesse dancetty between six billets sable ermined argent.*

William du Gard and his wife Elizabeth, possibly a daughter of Thomas Perkins, and Sarah were holding Denmead and Glidden in right of Elizabeth in 1713, and conveyed them in that year to Robert Heart.[61]

William Smith and his wife Jane were holding the manor of Denmead[62] in right of Jane in 1744[63] and conveyed it in that year to Thomas d'Oyley, probably as a settlement.[64] Twenty-five years later William and Jane sold the manor to Thomas Bernard,[65] who in his turn conveyed it to Thomas Martin and William Hatch.[66]

In 1831 Henry Kennett and his wife Fanny were holding the manors of Denmead and Glidden with courts leet, courts baron, and view of frankpledge, and settled them in that year on William Higgins.[67] After this date there seems to be no further mention of the manors. Denmead is now a tithing in the parish of Hambledon, the whole of which is in the hands of the Ecclesiastical Commissioners, who are apparently lords of the manor. The tithing is now called Barn Green.

40 *Feud. Aids*, ii, 319.
41 Feet of F. Hants, Hil. 56 Hen. III.
42 His father, Richard, had held tenements in Denmead in 1397 (Chan. Inq. p.m. 21 Ric. II No. 8*a* and *b*).
43 Chan. Inq. p.m. 26 Hen. VI, No. 9.
44 Ibid. 10 Hen. VIII (Ser. 2), vol. 33, No. 83.
45 Ibid. 3 Eliz. (Ser. 2), No. 181; ibid. W. and L. 3 Eliz. vol. 8, No. 9.
46 Ibid. 35 Eliz. pt. 1, No. 25.
47 Feet of F. Hants, Trin. 2 Jas. I.
48 Ibid. East. 8 Jas. I.
49 Inq. p. m. 10 Jas. I, vol. 332, No. 169.
50 Feet of F. Div. Cos. Trin. 4 Commonwealth.
51 Ibid. Hants, Mich. 5 Geo. I.
52 Ibid. Div. Cos. Trin. 11 Jas. I.
53 Inq. p. m. 16 Jas. I, vol. 372, No. 154.
54 Feet of F. Hants, East. 19 Jas. I.
55 Blore, *Rutland*, 61.
56 Feet of F. Hants, Hil. 8 Chas. I.
57 Ibid. Div. Cos. Hil. 23–4 Chas. II.
58 A. M. Sharp, *Hist. of Ufton Court.*
59 Feet of F. Hants, Hil. 1 Anne.
60 Ibid. Trin. 2 Anne.
61 Ibid. East. 12 Anne.
62 Denmead seems to have become one manor again by this date, as the extent given is larger than in any previous fine.
63 Perhaps a daughter of William du Gard and Elizabeth, as the manor evidently descended in the female line.
64 Feet of F. Div. Cos. Trin. 18 & 19 Geo. II.
65 Ibid. Hants, Mich. 12 Geo. III.
66 Ibid. 16 Geo. III.
67 Ibid. East. 2 & 3 Will. IV.

Besides the manor of Denmead there seems to have been a holding in the parish known by the name of *DENMEAD MOLYNS*, from the family who held it in the thirteenth and fourteenth centuries. In 1272 Richard de Lys and Florence his wife granted a third part of a messuage and a carucate of land in Denmead to Philip de Molyns and Joan his wife.[68] Again in 1299 William de Raunville granted a messuage and carucate of land in Hambledon to Simon de Fareham ;[69] which may possibly have been Denmead Molyns, as in 1346 John de Molyns of Fareham was holding 5 messuages and 50 acres of land in demesne at Denmead from the bishop of Winchester.[70] At the time of the dissolution of the monasteries Denmead Molyns was held by the prior and convent of Southwick,[71] though how and when it came into their possession is unknown. In 1543 the so-called manor was granted with all its appurtenances to Thomas Wriothesley.[72] Lord Chancellor Wriothesley granted this manor to Anthony Cope and his heirs in June, 1544,[73] and in 1593 licence was granted to John Cope and Jane his wife, Anne Cope, widow, and others to alienate the manor of Denmead Molyns, held of the queen in chief, to John Knight and his heirs.[73a] There seem to be no later records concerning Denmead Molyns.

The earliest mention of the manor of *ERVILL'S EXTON* (Ernelles, xiv cent. ; Ervelys, Ervills Exton, xv cent.) seems to be in the year 1397, when William Audeley and his wife Julia conveyed the reversion to Sir William Lescrope, Henry Maupas, and others, evidently for a settlement.[74] From this fine it appears that the manor was held by William Haket Julia in right of Julia, who was apparently the daughter of William and Julia Audeley.[75] In 1417 the manor was in the hands of John Kyngesmill in right of his wife Cecily, who may possibly have been the daughter of Julia Haket.[76] Eight years later William Heverfield and his wife Cecily, probably the above Cecily or her daughter, were holding lands in Exton near Hambledon and conveyed them to Henry Merston and others as trustees.[77] Thomas Radford and his wife Matilda in 1448 conveyed the manor of Ervill's Exton in Matilda's right to William Warburton and Robert Dynelly and the heirs of Robert.[78] Robert Dynelly married a daughter of William Ludlow of co. Wilts. ;[79] who, together with John Ludlow, was seised in 1473 of the manor of Ervill's Exton held of the bishop of Winchester. They conveyed it to Thomas Jurdew and William Coltyng, who settled it on 20 October, 1473, on William Kirkeby and his wife Margery. The former died in 1476, his heir being his son John.[80] Ervill's Exton remained in the possession of the Kirkeby family until 1597, when Thomas Kirkeby and his wife Sarah sold it to William Stockman for £500.[81] Five years later William Stockman in his turn sold it for the same amount to Christopher Perrin,[82] who died seised of the manor in 1612.[83] He was followed by his son Henry who in 1662, conveyed the capital messuage, farm, and demesnes of Ervill's Exton, called Ervill's Farm, to Bartholomew Smith of the Soak, near Winchester.[84]

The Perrins were still holding the manor in 1705, for in that year Christopher Perrin and his wife Sarah conveyed it to Elizabeth Perrin.[85] Thomas Futcher and William Pistell were holding the manor in 1767 in right of their wives Mary and Sarah, possibly the granddaughters of Sarah Perrin, and conveyed it in that year to Henry Whitear.[86] Nine years later William Pistell and Sarah and others quitclaimed the manor to Edward Bradley.[87] After this date there seems to be no further mention of Ervill's Exton. Ervill's Exton is now a tithing in the parish of Hambledon, the whole of which is in the hands of the Ecclesiastical Commissioners, who are apparently lords of the manor.

The tithing of *BURWELL* in Hambledon, part of which seems to have developed later into the manor of *BUTVILLENS* (Botevyleyns, xv cent. ; Butvillens, xvi cent. ; Bittles, xix cent.), is first mentioned in 1316, when it was held by Ralph de Camoys.[88] But before this date it must have been held by William Butvillens, who gave his name to the manor, for in 1346 Ralph de Camoys and Robert de Popham were holding one fee in Burwell which had formerly been held by William Butvillens or his assignees.[89]

In 1428 New College, Winchester, was holding half the fee in Burwell, which had been granted to it by the crown, and the college still holds lands in the parish.[90] The other half-fee which formerly belonged to William Butvillens was in the possession of Elizabeth Wayte in 1428,[91] and evidently continued as the so-called manor of Butvillens, which followed the descent of the manor of Wymering (q.v.) until 1561. At William Wayte's death in 1561 his lands were divided among his six daughters and co-heiresses.[92] Butvillens evidently fell to the share of Mary Wayte who had married William Cresweller, for in 1597 William Cresweller conveyed it to John Kent.[93] After this there seems to be no record of Butvillens until the year 1733, when Thomas Lintott and his wife Mary and John Angell conveyed it to Benjamin Martin.[94] The manor was then evidently divided among four co-heiresses, for in 1771 William Slader and his wife Frances conveyed a fourth part of the manor of Butvillens which was held in right of Frances to Thomas Cooke.[95] In 1790 John Richards and his wife Maria and William Haverkam and his wife Anna Catherine sold the whole manor to Hugh Seymour Conway for £400 ;[96] but whether they held it by right of inheritance or by purchase has not been ascertained. Hugh Seymour Conway was the fifth son of Francis second Lord Conway and earl of Hertford and the Lady Isabella Fitzroy, daughter of the duke of Grafton ;[97] and in 1801 Hugh Seymour and

68 Feet of F. Hants, Hil. 56 Hen. III.
69 Ibid. 28 Edw. I, No. 232.
70 Inq. p. m. 20 Edw. III (1st Nos.), No. 14.
71 Dugdale, *Monasticon*, vi, 245.
72 Pat. 35 Hen. VIII, pt. 10, m. 21.
73 *L. and P. Hen. VIII*, xix, 114.
73a Pat. 36 Eliz. pt. 7, m. 12.
74 Feet. of F. Hants, Mich. 21 Ric. II.
75 Ibid.
76 Ibid. Hil. 5 Hen. V.
77 Ibid. Mich. 4 Hen. VI.
78 Ibid. Hil. 27 Hen. VI.
79 *Harl. Soc.* xix, 548.
80 Inq. p.m. 16 Edw. IV, No. 31.
81 Feet of F. Hants, Mich. 39 & 40 Eliz.
82 Ibid. Mich. 44 & 45 Eliz.
83 Chan. Inq. p.m. 10 Jas. I (Ser. 2), pt. 11, No. 8.
84 Close, 14 Chas. II, pt. 13, No. 24.
85 Feet of F. Hants, East. 4 Anne.
86 Ibid. Mich. 8 Geo. III.
87 Ibid. East. 16 Geo. III.
88 *Feud. Aids*, ii, 308.
89 Ibid. ii, 336.
90 Ibid. ii, 358.
91 Ibid.
92 Inq. p.m. 3 Eliz. (Ser. 2), No 181.
93 Feet of F. Div. Cos. Mich. 39 & 40 Eliz.
94 Ibid. Hants, East. 7 Geo. II.
95 Ibid. Mich. 12 Geo. III.
96 Ibid. 31 Geo. III.
97 Archdall, *Lodge's Peerage*, vii, 36–7.

Ann Horatia his wife conveyed the manor to George Henry earl of Euston, his cousin and George Seymour his brother, evidently as a settlement.

After this date there seems to be no further record concerning Butvillens, which probably became merged in the main manor of Hambledon. Butvillens or Bittles is now a tithing in Hambledon parish.

GLIDDEN (Gluddon, xv cent.) is a tithing in Hambledon parish lying about two miles east of the village. It is mentioned with Hambledon as paying suit at the bishop's court.[98] A messuage, land, and tenements in Glidden were granted to Thomas Wriothesley earl of Southampton in 1543,[99] and from this date the descent of Glidden becomes the same as that of the manor of Denmead in the parish of Hambledon (q.v.). The whole of Hambledon parish, inclusive of the tithing of Glidden, is in the possession of the Ecclesiastical Commissioners at the present day.

The tithing of *CHIDDEN* lies about two miles north-east of Hambledon ; it owed suit at the bishop's court of Hambledon.

As early as 956 King Eadwig granted land in Chidden in the parish of Hambledon to Ethelgeard a thegn.[100] After this date there is no mention of Chidden until the year 1284, when William de Colriche and Eleanor his wife granted 20 acres of land and 12*s.* 6*d.* rent in Chidden to Thomas de Colemore.[101]

Henry VIII granted lands, tenements, and rent in Chidden in 1543 to Thomas Wriothesley, earl of Southampton,[102] together with numerous lands and manors in Hampshire.

RUSHMERE is a tithing in the parish. The earliest mention of it seems to be in 1510, when Sir John Pounde died seised of the so-called manor of Rushmere held of the bishop of Winchester ;[103] his widow Elizabeth died soon afterwards and the manor passed to their son and heir William.[104] Anthony Pound, William's son,[105] died in possession of Rushmere in 1547, when it was entailed on his son Richard and his wife Elizabeth daughter of William Wayte of Wymering and their heirs.[106] It then passed to Honor, Richard Pounde's sister and the wife of Henry earl of Sussex,[107] who died seised of it in 1593,[108] leaving a son and heir Robert. This Robert, earl of Sussex, sold it to Jonas Latelays in 1601,[109] who in 1609 sold it to Nicholas Foster.[110] After this there seems to be no further mention of Rushmere until the year 1765, when it was in the hands of Thomas Godwin.[111]

At the present day Rushmere as a tithing in Hambledon is in the hands of the Ecclesiastical Commissioners.

The manor of *PUTTE*, which is possibly represented at the present day by the tithing of Pithills in Hambledon, follows the descent of Wymering manor (q.v.) from 1448 until 1561 ; after which date it is lost sight of.

CHURCHES

The church of *ST. PETER AND ST. PAUL, HAMBLEDON*, is a fine and very interesting building, which has developed its rather complicated plan from a small pre-Conquest nave and chancel, of which a good part still remains. The nave measured 37 ft. by 18 ft. 6 in. internally, and the chancel was 14 ft. 3 in. wide, and probably about 16 ft. long, the walls being 2 ft. 7 in. thick. In the latter part of the twelfth century north and south aisles were added to the nave, and in the thirteenth century the church was greatly enlarged eastwards, out of all proportion to the old nave, the plan of which, however, was retained, so that it has now become little more than a vestibule to the present nave, which occupies the site of the old chancel. The thirteenth-century enlargements are evidently of several dates, and their development is rather difficult to follow, obscured as they are by later work. The pre-Conquest chancel was apparently not altered in the twelfth century, but the first part of the thirteenth-century enlargements continued its lines eastwards as far as the west end of the present chancel, a total length of 41 ft. from the old chancel arch. Later in the century an entirely new chancel was built to the east, 38 ft. by 19 ft., and transept chapels flanking the east bays of the prolongation of the old chancel seem to have formed part of this scheme. Whether the first enlargement of the chancel included aisles or not, it probably developed them before the building of the second chancel and transept chapels, and the difference in the arcades suggests that the work was not continuous. The arches at the east end of the old nave and aisles are also of late thirteenth-century date, and show that the aisles must have attained their present width by that time, unless the arches have been widened at a later time, a fact difficult to verify. A twelfth-century light at the west end of the south aisle appears to be in its original position, and suggests a width some 2 ft. 6 in. less than at present for the twelfth-century aisle ; that in the north aisle is central with the present width, but may have been moved outwards when the tower stair was built, to escape blocking. A west tower was added to the nave in the thirteenth century, as a window in the south wall on the ground stage shows ; its upper part was rebuilt in 1794, and the axis of the tower is to the south of that of the nave and of the thirteenth-century arch which opens from nave to tower, so that its present plan seems to be the result of a rebuilding. The south wall of the south aisle of the old nave seems to have been entirely rebuilt, on the old lines, in the fifteenth century, and a south porch and south-west chamber, both of two stories, added. The chancel has an east window of three lancet lights under a pointed arch, the tracery being modern, and there are three pairs of lancet lights in the north and south walls, of the same character, with a plain south doorway between the second and third on the south side. The western pair of windows are at a lower level than the rest. At the south-east of the chancel is a trefoiled piscina with a projecting drain, but all other fittings are modern, and the walls have been heightened and a new roof put on. The chancel arch is of two chamfered orders, with a small half-octagonal shaft and capital to the inner order, and on either side of it are squints from the aisles.

98 Eccl. Com. Ct. R.
99 Pat. 35 Hen. VIII, pt. 10, m. 21.
100 Birch, *Cart. Sax.* iii, 166.
101 Feet of F. Hants, 13 Edw. I, No. 122.
102 Pat. 35 Hen. VIII, pt. 10, m. 21.
103 Chan. Inq. p.m. 2 Hen. VIII (Ser. 2), vol. 25, No. 19.
104 Ibid. (Ser. 2), vol. 26, No. 35.
105 Berry, *Hants Gen.* 194.
106 Chan. Inq. p.m. 1 Edw. VI (Ser. 2), vol. 3, No. 55.
107 Berry, *Hants Gen.* 194.
108 Chan. Inq. p.m. (Ser. 2), vol. 241, No. 109.
109 Feet of F. Hants, Trin. 44 Eliz.
110 Ibid. Mich. 7 Jas. I.
111 Recov. R. Hil. 5 Geo. III, rot. 59.

Hambledon Church : The Nave looking East

The eastern division of the nave has arcades of three bays, the two east bays of that on the north having round columns with moulded capitals and bases of clunch, except the capital of the western respond, which is in green sandstone, while the third bay is of later date, a plain pointed opening with Binstead stone strings at the springing and green sandstone dressings in its east respond; it dies into the wall on the west, and is cut through the pre-Conquest masonry, the stone eaves course of which shows above it, running eastward as far as the centre of the middle bay of the arcade. The south arcade is continuous, and has octagonal columns and capitals, the two eastern capitals being modern; its western arch dies into the east wall of the pre-Conquest nave without a respond.

The north aisle has an east window of three lancets with a foiled circle above and engaged jamb-shafts; in its north wall are two small lancet lights, and between them a three-light fifteenth-century window. The south aisle has an east window of the same date and description as that in the north aisle, but the central lancet is higher than the others, its head taking the place of the foiled circle. Its three south windows are: a pair of lancets with a trefoil over, a three-light fifteenth-century window with uncusped tracery, and a pair of lancets. The first of these three windows is set in a thicker piece of wall than the others, and at the junction of the thicker and thinner walls a change in direction is noticeable; the latter is clearly later than the former, and points to a widening of this part of the aisle as already suggested. At the south-east of the aisle is a locker. The roofs over this part of the church are old, but have no details from which a precise date might be assigned to them; they have tie-beams with arched collars, and the trusses of the middle span probably had king-posts at one time.

The western division of the nave has arcades of two bays, *c.* 1180, with round pillars and pointed arches of different detail, those in the north arcade having one square order and chamfered labels with hatched ornament on the vertical face and rosettes alternating with dogtooth on the chamfer, while in the south arcade the arches are of two chamfered orders, with dogtooth on the labels. The capitals are scalloped in both instances, but the bases of the north arcade are square, with angle spurs, and those of the south arcade round. Above the arches on the outer faces of the walls the upper parts of pre-Conquest pilaster strips remain, two on each side, in Binstead stone, and the walls are characteristically high. In the south wall near the west angle is a wide round-headed opening, splayed inwards, apparently a window opening of the pre-Conquest church, which was probably filled with pierced wooden boarding, but its width makes it an altogether unusual feature. The arch which takes the place of the original chancel arch is a fine piece of thirteenth-century detail, of two-moulded orders, more elaborate on the west face than on the east, with three shafts in each respond and moulded capitals; it is abutted by arches of late thirteenth-century date at the east ends of the old aisles, that on the north having three engaged octagonal shafts in the jambs, while the southern arch is plainer, with half-octagonal responds. In the north aisle is an early fourteenth-century doorway between two three-light windows, one of the fifteenth century and the other an ornamental modern copy of it, and at the west end a twelfth-century round-headed light, which, as already noted, may have been further to the south at first. The south doorway of the nave is of good fifteenth-century detail, and opens to a contemporary porch which formerly had an upper floor, reached by a short passage or gallery from the upper floor of the south-west vestry. There are fifteenth-century windows in the aisle wall, on either side of the porch, both square-headed, that to the east having arched tracery under the square head, with pierced spandrels. In the west wall of the aisle is an original twelfth-century light, and to the north of it a fifteenth-century door to the vestry, while at the first-floor level, near the south-west angle, is a doorway which formerly led by a gallery to the parvise over the porch. The vestry, which is now of one story only, was probably used as a living room in former times, and has a south window in the upper stage with a stone shoot through the wall below it. The upper part of the tower is of flint with red-brick dressings, dating from 1794, and the west door and window are modern. In the south wall is a blocked thirteenth-century light, already referred to, and the tower arch, whose north jamb is overlapped by the north wall of the tower, is also of the thirteenth century, with half-octagonal responds, moulded capitals and bases, and a pointed arch of two chamfered orders. The tower stair is at the north-east. In the south wall is a recess used as a cupboard, and on either side of the west window is hung a regimental colour.

The roof of the western part of the nave is good fifteenth-century work in four bays, with moulded tie-beams, collars, and braces, but the fittings of the church generally are modern. The altar table is of the seventeenth century with baluster legs, and the font, at the west end of the south aisle, is octagonal and modern.

There are six bells, the treble by Taylor of Loughborough, 1882, and the others by Robert Catlin of London, 1749, the fifth recording that the old bells were cast into a ring of six in that year.

The plate is modern, a fine set consisting of two chalices, three patens, a flagon, two alms dishes, and two candlesticks, made in 1876 and weighing in all 200 oz. There are also two patens, a cup, and flagon of pewter.

The first book of registers runs from 1601 to 1662, but one leaf of the paper register for 1596 is preserved. The succeeding books date from 1662–1706, 1708–1778, and 1778–1812, and there is a printed marriage register for 1754–1798.

Near the south door of the church is a fine yew tree.

The church of *ALL SAINTS, DENMEAD*, built in 1880, is of flint in the thirteenth-century style, and consists of chancel, nave, south porch, and bell-turret. The register dates from 1881.

ADVOWSON The earliest mention of a church at Hambledon seems to be about the year 1155, when Hambledon church and Meonstoke manor were granted to St. Swithun's Priory.[112] In 1327, on the petition of John bishop of Winchester, the king ordered that the keeper of the temporalities of the see was not to interfere

[112] Add. Chart. 28,658

with the church of Hambledon, which was a parish church and annexed to the bishopric as a spirituality, by accounting for the fruits at the exchequer among the temporalities of the see.[113] Four years later the bishop obtained letters patent ordering that in any future vacancy of the see the custody of the church of Hambledon was to belong to the prior and convent of St. Swithun at Winchester.[114]

The advowson of Hambledon was in the hands of the bishop of Winchester until 1870;[115] the bishop of Lichfield then held it for about fifteen years, at the end of which it passed to the Lord Chancellor, in whose gift the living still remains.[116]

The living of Denmead is a vicarage in the gift of the Lord Chancellor.

In the thirteenth century Hambledon vicarage was assessed at only £13 6*s.* 8*d.*;[117] but in the sixteenth century the value had increased to £27 8*s.* 9*d.*[118]

The living is now a vicarage, net yearly value £378, with 101 acres of glebe.

Tradition points to the fact that there must originally have been a chapel in Denmead attached to Hambledon church (*vide ante*), but no record of the existence of such a chapel can now be found.

There is a Methodist chapel in Denmead.

CHARITIES

In 1626 Thomas Bettsworth, in consideration of £80 received from the executors of Richard Binsted, conveyed to trustees 16 acres of land in Rogate, Sussex, upon trust to employ the rents for the relief of four poor, needy, and impotent single or sole persons of Hambledon. The land has been sold and proceeds invested with the official trustees of charitable funds, who now hold £999 2*s.* 2*d.* consols in trust for the charity.

In 1895 a scheme was established limiting the number of future pensioners to two, who are to be residents of Hambledon.

This parish was formerly possessed of 3½ acres known as the Church Lands. In 1874 the land was sold, and net proceeds invested in £377 15*s.* 11*d.* consols with the official trustees, the dividends of which are applied for church purposes.

The poor's allotments, consisting of 7 acres, bring in a rental of about £10 a year, which is applied for the benefit of the poor of the parish.

In 1878 John Foster bequeathed £200 in aid of a blanket fund for the poor. The legacy—less duty—was invested in £183 18*s.* 9*d.* consols, transferred to the official trustees.

In 1892 Mrs. Arabella Louisa Moody by deed of trust (enrolled with the Charity Commissioners) settled a sum of £100 for keeping the paths, &c., of the churchyard in good order, represented by £102 16*s.* 7*d.* India 3 per cent. stock, with the official trustees.

In 1894 John Boulderson Barkworth by will left £500 to the rector and churchwardens, income to be applied for benefit of sick and infirm poor of the parish at their discretion. The legacy was invested in the purchase of £523 10*s.* 2*d.* Metropolitan Consolidated 2½ per cent. stock, with the official trustees.

In 1834 John Ring by will gave a fund, income to be applied for educational purposes, and also a fund for the distribution of wood and fuel; the former fund is represented by £619 1*s.* 4*d.* consols, and the latter by £183 15*s.* 8*d.* like stock, both held by the official trustees. By scheme of 4 February, 1896, the dividends are applied respectively in prizes, &c., and in the distribution of fuel to the poor, or in subscription to provident societies, &c.

[113] *Cal. of Pat.* 1327–30, p. 65.
[114] Ibid. 1330–34, p. 73.
[115] *Clergy List*, 1870.
[116] Ibid. 1870–85.
[117] *Pope Nich. Tax.* (Rec. Com.), 211.
[118] *Valor Eccl.* (Rec. Com.), ii, 21.

THE HUNDRED OF MEONSTOKE

CONTAINING THE PARISHES OF

CORHAMPTON MEONSTOKE SOBERTON WARNFORD

The above list represents the extent of the hundred at the time of the Population Returns of 1831. The parishes of West Meon, Exton, and Bramdean, and part of the parish of Upham, were added to the hundred before 1841, and probably at the same time the tithing of Burwell in Hambledon parish was transferred to the hundred of Hambledon, and the tithing of Liss Abbas in the parish of Liss to the hundred of Finchdean.[1] The tithing of Westbury and Peak in the parish of East Meon was removed to the hundred of East Meon at some later date.

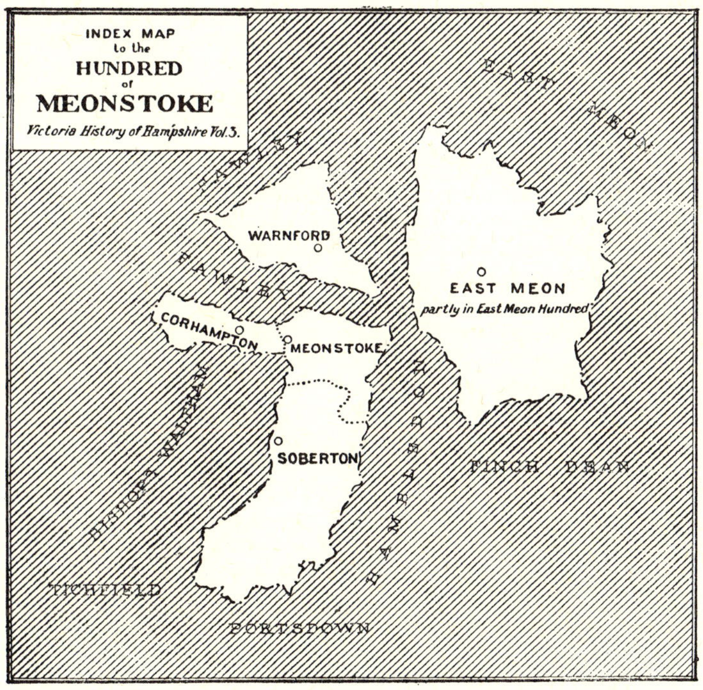

At the time of the Domesday Survey the hundred included the parishes of Abbott's Worthy,[2] Alverstoke,[3] Corhampton,[4] Exton,[5] Hambledon,[6] Liss,[7] Meonstoke,[8] Soberton,[9] Warnford,[10] and West Meon[11] and the tithing of Westbury,[12] in the parish of East Meon.

The land comprising the hundred was assessed in the reign of Edward the Confessor at 89 hides, and at the time of the survey at about 56 hides. By the beginning of the fourteenth century the area of the hundred had much decreased. West Meon, Exton, Alverstoke, Abbott's Worthy, a large part of the parish of Hambledon, and the tithing of Liss Turney in the parish of Liss had been removed, and in 1316 the hundred comprised the

[1] Cf. the Population Returns of 1831 and 1841.
[2] *V.C.H. Hants*, i, 466*b*.
[3] Ibid.
[4] Ibid. 471*a*, 481*a*.
[5] Ibid. 466*b*.
[6] Ibid. 487*b*.
[7] Ibid. 473*b*.
[8] Ibid. 452*a*.
[9] Ibid. 451*b*, 452*a*, 459*b*, 481*a*, 500*a*.
[10] Ibid. 471*a*, 481*a*.
[11] Ibid. 461*b*.
[12] Ibid. 481*a*.

parishes of Meonstoke, Soberton, Warnford, and Corhampton, the tithing of Liss Abbas in the parish of Liss, the tithing of Westbury in the parish of East Meon, and the tithing of Burwell in the parish of Hambledon.[13] From this date the extent of the hundred remained practically unchanged until after 1831.[14]

This hundred has always belonged to the crown. In a survey of the hundred taken in the Commonwealth period it was stated that the courts-leet and law-days of the hundred were still then held at Easter and Michaelmas and that the three-weeks' courts or sheriff's tourns were also regularly held.[15]

CORHAMPTON

Quedementune (xi cent.) ; Cornhampton (xiii cent.) ; Corhamtone, Cornhamtone and Cornehampton (xiv cent.) ; Corehampton (xvi cent.).

The parish of Corhampton on its western side consists of wide stretches of wooded common and down land, standing about 300 ft. above the ordnance datum, and falls to a little under 200 ft. towards the River Meon and the village on its eastern border. On 24 March, 1894, part of Corhampton parish, with a population of forty-seven, was transferred to the parish of Exton.[1] This portion lay to the north-west, and included the whole of the wooded downs of Preshaw Park, and also the little farm of Lomer, which no doubt marks the site of the manors of Lomer and Lomer Turville. The small village of Corhampton lies in the valley of the Meon River, in the extreme east of the parish, the river forming the boundary. The nearest station is in the adjoining parish of Droxford. The main road from West Meon to Droxford runs through the village from the north-east, crosing the rivers just below the mill and close to the church and vicarage. A little further on it divides, one road going westward to Bishop's Waltham, and the other eastward to the village of Meonstoke, and so to Droxford. The church stands on a little mound on the right-hand bank of the stream, the churchyard lying to the south, and containing a yew-tree 26 ft. in circumference. To the north of the church and at the back of the mill is a group of half-timber cottages, probably of early seventeenth-century date. The old-fashioned vicarage in its shady grounds stands opposite the church on the east side of the road, the stream forming the eastern boundary, while the wooded grounds of Corhampton House, the residence of Mrs. Pleydell Bouverie-Campbell-Wyndham, occupy the angle between the Droxford and Bishop's Waltham roads. The area of the parish is 1,246 acres.[2] The soil is chalk and loam, the subsoil chalk, stone, and flint. The chief crops are oats and barley.

As early as the fifteenth century there is mention of 'the tenement called Seynclers,'[3] no doubt representing the modern St. Clair's Farm, which is situated in the north of the parish. It seems generally to have been leased to the farmer of the chief manor of Corhampton, who was entitled to have reasonable housebote, hedgebote, and firebote in St. Clair's Wood.[4] The following place-names in Corhampton are found in a fine levied in the reign of Henry III[5] : 'Lide, Frilande, Norlehe, and Freecroft.' In the fourteenth and fifteenth centuries the following place-names occur : 'La Hethen Street and Butmesfeld,[6] Stanbury, La Gores, Abbotesheuedacre, Baroneshurne, Haselholte, and Hackedwode'[7] ; a wood called 'Stene'[8] ; 'Pulter's Pasture[9] ; Deneyslonde and Wakelens.'[10]

MANORS

In the reign of Edward the Confessor *CORHAMPTON* was assessed at three hides, and was held by Alwin, but by the time of the Domesday Survey it was assessed at only one hide, and formed part of the possessions of Hugh de Port.[11] If the statements made on the occasion of levying of subsidies in 1346 and 1428 are to be relied on, the manor was at one period in the hands of a Geoffrey the Marshal.[12] It is possible that this Geoffrey was Geoffrey the Marshal of the twelfth century, although there is no definite evidence of this ; and, if so, he must have succeeded Alwin in the tenancy of the manor, the overlordship continuing with the St. Johns, the descendants of Hugh de Port, as late at least as the fifteenth century.[13] In 1228 two carucates of land in Corhampton, probably representing the manor, were settled on Adam de Corhampton by Gilbert de Hattingley.[14] Adam had died before 1233, for in that year Basile, the widow of Adam de

ST. JOHN. *Argent a chief gules with two molets or.*

[13] *Feud. Aids*, ii, 307.

[14] Ibid. 336 and 358. Exch. Lay Subs. R. Hants, bdle. 173, No. 218 ; bdle. 174, No. 404 ; bdle. 175, No. 499 ; and bdle. 176, Nos. 559 and 565.

[15] Parl. Surv. Hants, No. 8.

[1] Loc. Gov. Bd. Ord. No. 16412.

[2] Containing 722 acres of arable land, 141 acres of permanent grass, and 24 acres of woods and plantations. (Information from Bd. of Agric. 1905.)

[3] Add. Chart. 28003.

[4] Ibid. 27679.

[5] Feet of F. Hants, Mich. 17 Hen. III.

[6] MS. *penes* the lady of the manor.

[7] Add. MS. 33285, fol. 187; Hazelholt Park and Hazelholt Copse are now in the extreme north of the parish of Droxford.

[8] Add. MS. 33285, fol. 186 ; there is still a Stain's Cottage in the parish.

[9] Add. Chart. 27679.

[10] Ibid. 28008.

[11] *V.C.H. Hants*, i, 481*a*.

[12] *Feud. Aids*, ii, 336 and 358.

[13] Inq. p.m. 35 Edw. I, pt. 2, No. 47.

[14] Feet of F. Hants, East. 12 Hen. III.

Corhampton, was holding tenements in Corhampton in dower.[15] His heir was Nicholas de Corhampton,[16] who in the same year granted the third part of the two knights' fees which he was then holding in Corhampton to his nephew, Adam de Corhampton, the son of his brother Richard.[17] From Nicholas the remaining two-thirds must have passed soon afterwards to William de Clare,[18] brother of Richard de Clare, earl of Gloucester and Hertford, who in addition in 1256 acquired from William de Moleyns and Sarah his wife a messuage, lands, rents and a mill in Corhampton in exchange for tenements in Mapledurham.[19] On the death of William de Clare without issue in 1258, his property passed to his brother Richard, who was seised of the manor of Corhampton at the time of his death four years later.[20] He was succeeded by his son and heir Gilbert de Clare, earl of Gloucester and Hertford, who in 1289 married Joan de Acres, the king's daughter.[21] Gilbert died in 1295 seised of certain lands and tenements, including probably the manor of Corhampton.[22] Two years afterwards Joan de Acres married clandestinely Ralph de Monthermer, a plain squire,[23] which incensed the king, who imprisoned his new son-in-law in Bristol Castle. In 1305, however, he granted him the custody of the late earl's lands in Corhampton during the minority of Gilbert the son and heir.[23a] Joan de Acres died in 1307 seised of the manor of Corhampton, held of John de St. John by the service of two knights' fees.[24] In 1313 Gilbert de Clare, earl of Gloucester and Hertford, granted to Gilbert de St. Owen and Joan his wife the manor of Corhampton, with reversion in default of heirs to Earl Gilbert.[25] However, the young earl was slain at Bannockburn, 24 June, 1314,[26] and since he died without issue his property was divided between his sisters and co-heirs Eleanor and Margaret.[27] Corhampton, however, remained with the widow of Gilbert de St. Owen, who was holding in 1316,[28] and it was not until her death without issue that the manor was assigned to Margaret. The latter was married to Hugh de Audley, who assumed the title of earl of Gloucester in right of his wife.[29] Their only daughter and heir Margaret married Ralph second Lord Stafford,[30] and brought him the manor of Corhampton among other possessions. The manor remained with the Staffords till 1521,[31] when Edward Stafford, third and last duke of Buckingham, was attainted of treason and beheaded and his estates were forfeited.[32] In March of the following year Henry VIII granted Corhampton to Sir Richard Weston in tail-male.[33] Francis Weston, son and heir of Richard, one of the alleged accomplices of Anne Boleyn, was attainted and executed in his father's lifetime. His father died seised of the manor in 1541, his heir being his grandson Henry Weston, son of Francis.[34] Richard son of Henry conveyed Corhampton in 1595 to Hugh Sexey,[35] who a year later sold it to Thomas Hanbury, lord of the manor of Mapledurham, in the parish of Buriton.[36] In 1599 Queen Elizabeth granted the reversion of the manor remaining in the crown to Thomas in consideration of a payment of £266 17*s.* 6*d.*[37] Thomas died seised of the manor in 1611, his heir being his son Thomas, aged forty,[38] who died seven years later, leaving a son and heir Thomas, aged eleven.[39] The manor remained in the family of Hanbury until 1655, in which year Thomas Taylor and Elizabeth his wife and John Hanbury conveyed it by fine to Henry Chroucher,[40] from whom it passed into the possession of the family of Henslow.[41] Mrs. Henslow, the widow of Thomas Henslow, was the lady of the manor in 1703.[42] Stapleton, daughter and heir of Thomas Henslow, married Henry Williamson and brought the manor to her husband.[43] Their son and heir Edmund Thomas Williamson[44] sold it to Henry Wyndham, who was lord of the manor in 1750.[45] Henry married Arundel Penruddocke and had a son Henry Penruddocke Wyndham, who died in 1819, being then in his eighty-third year. In the course of his life he published *A Tour through Monmouthshire and Wales,*

DE CLARE. *Or three cheverons gules.*

MONTHERMER. *Or an eagle vert.*

STAFFORD. *Or a cheveron gules.*

HANBURY. *Or a bend engrailed vert vith plain cotises sable.*

WYNDHAM. *Azure a cheveron between three lions' heads razed or.*

15 Feet of F. Hants, Mich. 17 Hen. III.
16 He is returned as holding one fee of Robert de St. John (*Testa de Nevill*, 230).
17 Feet of F. Hants, Mich. 17 Hen. III; MS. *penes* the lady of the manor.
18 While lord of the manor he subtracted the suit formerly paid by Nicholas de Corhampton at the hundred court of Meonstoke (Assize R. Mich. 8 Edw. I).
19 Feet of F. Hants, 40 Hen. III.
20 Inq. p.m. 47 Hen. III, No. 34.
21 G.E.C. *Complete Peerage*, iv, 41.
22 Inq. p.m. 24 Edw. I, No. 107*a*.
23 G.E.C. *Complete Peerage*, iv, 41.
23a *Cal. of Pat.* 1301–7, p. 388.
24 Inq. p.m. 35 Edw. I, pt. 2, No. 47.
25 Feet of F. Div. Cos. East. 6 Edw. II.
26 G.E.C. *Complete Peerage*, iv, 42.
27 Inq. p.m. 8 Edw. II, No. 68.
28 *Feud. Aids*, ii, 307.
29 G.E.C. *Complete Peerage*, iv, 42.
30 Ibid. vii, 209.
31 *Feud. Aids*, ii, 336, 358, 372; Inq. p.m. 46 Edw. III (1st Nos.), No. 62; 10 Ric. II, No. 38; 16 Ric. II, pt. 1, No. 27; 22 Ric. II, No. 46; 4 Hen. IV, No. 41.
32 Chan. Inq. p.m. (Ser. 2), vol. 80, No. 182; Add. Chart. 28181.
33 Com. Pleas Recov. R. Mich. 37 and 38 Eliz. m. 13.
34 Exch. Inq. p.m. (Ser. 2), file 991, No. 11.
35 Feet of F. Hants, Mich. 37 Eliz.; Recov. R. 37 & 38 Eliz. m. 13.
36 Recov. R. Hil. 39 Eliz. m. 3.
37 Pat. 41 Eliz. pt. 6, m. 30.
38 W. and L. Inq. p.m. (Ser. 2), bdle. 14, No. 104.
39 Chan. Inq. p.m. (Ser. 2), vol. 368, No. 122.
40 MS. *penes* the present lady of the manor of Corhampton.
41 Ibid.
42 Stowe MS. 845, fol. 96.
43 Chan. Enr. Decree, 1842, No. 2.
44 Ibid.
45 MS. *penes* the present lady of the manor.

The Diary of the Late George Bubb Doddington, Baron of Melcombe Regis, and other works, and is described as an 'ornament of Wadham College, Oxford.'[46] His son and heir Wadham Wyndham died without issue in 1843, and on his death Corhampton passed to his sister and heir Caroline Frances, who had married John Campbell. Their son John Henry assumed the surname and arms of Wyndham on succeeding to the estates of his maternal ancestors. On his death without issue in 1868 Corhampton passed to his second sister[47] Mrs. Thornton-Wyndham, and on her death a year later, to his third sister Mrs. King-Wyndham, who died without male issue in 1890. The manor then passed to the present holder, Mrs. Caroline Mary Pleydell Bouverie-Campbell-Wyndham the daughter of Mr. Richard Hetley of the Close, Salisbury, by Caroline Letitia, the eldest sister of John Henry Campbell-Wyndham, who succeeded under the will of Wadham Wyndham because neither Mrs. Thornton-Wyndham nor Mrs. King-Wyndham left a son.

The sub-manor of *CORHAMPTON* was in origin the third part of the two knight's fees granted to Adam de Corhampton by his uncle Nicholas de Corhampton.[48] The grant is given in great detail, and special mention is made of the third part of the mill and the third part of the fishery there. Adam gave his uncle thirty marks, and moreover granted for himself and his heirs that they would give nothing of the said tenements *in religionem*, nor alienate them in any way whereby Nicholas and his heirs should lose their service from the tenements. Shortly afterwards Adam sold this third part to Peter des Roches, bishop of Winchester, for sixty marks of silver.[49] The latter soon afterwards granted this land in free alms to the abbey of Titchfield, which he had founded in 1231, together with his wood called 'Cherlewood,' which he had purchased from Jordan de Walterville.[50] William de Clare in his confirmation of the grant calls the land 'the third part of the manor of Corhampton.'[51] In return for this confirmation he received £10 and the third part of the mill of Corhampton, which henceforward belonged to the chief manor.[52] The abbey continued to hold this third part, which developed into a separate manor,[53] until its dissolution in 1537,[54] when the king granted it to Thomas Wriothesley,[55] who was created earl of Southampton three days before the coronation of King Edward VI. During his lifetime a certain Isabel *alias* Alice Collen *alias* Collins held the manor at farm for the annual payment of £4.[56] The earl died seised of the manor in 1550, leaving a son and heir Henry, aged three,[57] and under his will the manor of Corhampton was left to King Edward VI to hold during the minority of his son, 'for a remembrance of my duty towards my sovereign lord, and for the great benefits that I have received of his most noble father of famous memory, the late King Henry VIII.'[58] Henry, second earl of Southampton, died seised of the manor in 1581, his heir being his son Henry, aged eight,[59] who, seventeen years later, conveyed it to William Fisher, William Petty, and Henry Collins in trust for Nicholas Collins and Clara his wife during their lives, with remainder to their eldest son William and his issue and their second son Henry successively.[60] Nicholas Collins died seised of the manor in 1601, his heir being his son William, who was aged twenty-two in 1611.[61] Some time between 1655 and 1669, in a dispute between this William and Henry Chroucher, lord of the main manor of Corhampton, concerning 'the long meadow near the vicarage-house,'[62] the following statement was made concerning the manor of Corhampton: 'The manor after it was divided lay all in common fields, and about a hundred years since was by joint consent divided equally and many exchanges made of each other's lands for convenience to each parties, and was then inclosed with quick-set hedges and hath so continued to this time.'[63] William Collins died without issue in 1669, aged eighty years, and the manor passed to 'his brother's daughter who was married to one Mr. Collins of Sussex.'[64] The manor continued in this family of Collins for about a hundred years. In 1750 there was a dispute between Henry Collins and Henry Wyndham, lord of the chief manor of Corhampton, as to who was really lord of the manor of Corhampton.[65] In October of that year, to end disputes, they agreed that 'they and their heirs, tenants, and assigns should futurely hold and enjoy the same lands, woods, commons, rights, and privileges as their ancestors or predecessors respectively had formerly done. And 'twas furthermore particularly agreed that all timber-trees and other trees growing and to be growing on the commons or waste-grounds should be the joint property of them the said Henry Collins and Henry Wyndham and their respective heirs and assigns, and should not be cut, sold, or converted without each party's consent, and also that all estrays should be equally shared and divided between them.' As a confirmation of this agreement the two lords

COLLINS. *Gules a bend or in a border ermine with three martlets azure on the bend.*

[46] *Gent. Mag.* 1819, i, 485.

[47] His eldest sister, Mrs. Hetley, died in 1829.

[48] Feet of F. Hants, Mich. 17 Hen. III; MS. *penes* the lady of the manor.

[49] MS. *penes* the lady of the manor.

[50] Ibid.

[51] MS. *penes* the lady of the manor.

[52] Ibid.

[53] *Pope Nich. Tax.* (Rec. Com.), 213; Chart. R. 22 Edw. I, No. 13. Pat. 18 Edw. II, pt. 1, m. 23 and 24; *Feud. Aids*, ii, 336 and 358; Add. MS. 33285, fol. 187; Pat. 3 Hen. VI, m. 13.

[54] Feet of F. Div. Cos. Mich. 29 Hen. VIII.

[55] Pat. 29 Hen. VIII, pt. 1, m. 32.

[56] MS. *penes* the lady of the manor (being the roll of the second court of Thomas Wriothesley, 15 June, 30 Hen. VIII). This indenture does not seem to be extant, but another indenture whereby Wriothesley farmed out the parsonage of Corhampton for fifty-six years to 'Isabel Collen of Cornehampton, widow, and Robert Collen her son, of Exton, husbandman, by the annual payment of £7 6*s.* 8*d.*, is in possession of the lady of the manor. It is also interesting to note that as far back as 1372 a certain John 'Collan' was holder of the rectory of Corhampton.

[57] W. and L. Inq. p.m. (Ser. 2), vol. 5, No. 103.

[58] Ibid.

[59] Chan. Inq. p.m. (Ser. 2), vol. 196, No. 46.

[60] MS. *penes* the lady of the manor. Feet of F. Hants, Trin. 40 Eliz. and Hil. 41 Eliz.

[61] Chan. Misc. Inq. p.m. 9 Jas. I (Ser. 2), pt. 11, No. 6.

[62] MS. *penes* the lady of the manor.

[63] Ibid.

[64] Stowe MS. 845, fol. 96.

[65] MS. *penes* the lady of the manor.

then sold some beech-trees standing on waste-land in Corhampton to farmer Richard Matthews of Corhampton for six guineas, which they divided equally between them. Henry Collins by will left the manor and rectory to Edward Horner and William Horner. The latter, who survived his brother, in his turn devised them to Richard Richards[66] some time before 1768.[67] Richard by will directed that the manor and rectory should be sold, and the purchase money divided among his three sons, Henry Richards of Burton (co. Dorset), Richard Richards of Bishop's Waltham, and William Richards of Winchester College, and his daughter Elizabeth, wife of Thomas Jonas of Bishop's Waltham.[68] The property was sold in 1777, the purchaser being Henry Wyndham, lord of the chief manor of Corhampton.[69] From this time the two manors have merged.

CLEVERLY (Claverlegh, xiii cent.; Claverley and Claverle, xiv cent.; Cleverlys, xviii cent.). Franklin Farm in the extreme west of the parish and Cleverly Wood on the borders of the parishes of Bishop's Waltham and Corhampton mark the site of the tenement, consisting of a messuage and a carucate of land, which the family of Cleverly held of the abbot and convent of Titchfield, as of their manor of Corhampton, by the rent of half a pound of cummin at Michaelmas, and suit of court every three weeks.[70] A Thurstan Cleverly is mentioned as early as 1233.[71] and the name of Cleverly frequently occurs in the court rolls of Corhampton. In a court roll of 1372 it appears that at the court held at Michaelmas of that year Philip Cleverly did homage for lands held of the abbey in Cleverly, and claimed right of way to the pasture of Cleverdown.[72] In 1413 John the son of Philip had a dispute with the abbot of Titchfield, concerning the relief.[73] John Cleverly in 1538 was holding a free tenement of Thomas Wriothesley as of his manor of Corhampton by the rent of a pound of cummin.[74] He was succeeded by his son and heir Thomas, who in the reign of Elizabeth petitioned Sir Nicholas Bacon to force his stepmother Elizabeth to restore a messuage at Cleverly and 112 acres of arable land and 10 acres of wood in Lomer, Corhampton, and Bishop's Waltham, which she had held since his father's death.[75] Towards the end of Elizabeth's reign this holding seems to have passed into the hands of William Fisher.[76] It remained in the Fisher family until 1741, in which year Forbes Fisher sold it to Henry Collins, lord of the sub-manor of Corhampton.[77] It was included in the sale of the sub-manor to Henry Wyndham in 1777, under the description of a 'messuage and tenement called Cleverleys *alias* Franklins and fifteen closes of arable land and pasture land containing 160 acres belonging to it situated in Corhampton,'[78] since which time it has formed part of the manor of Corhampton.

In 1294 the abbot and convent of Titchfield obtained a grant of free warren in their demesne lands of Corhampton,[79] and this grant was confirmed in 1424.[80] A free warren and park are also mentioned in the grant of the chief manor to Thomas Hanbury in 1611.[81]

There were two mills worth twenty-two shillings in Corhampton at the time of the Domesday Survey,[82] one of which seems to have soon fallen into decay, and after the reign of Henry III only one is mentioned. One-third of the mill 'which is before the church of the vill' was included in the grant of the third part of the manor of Corhampton to Titchfield Abbey,[83] but was given up to William de Clare in return for his confirmation of the grant of the third part of the manor to the abbey.[84] The mill was usually farmed out at forty shillings a year, but it was very often out of repair, and there are frequent references to expenses incurred in repairing it.[85] The present water-mill of Corhampton probably marks the site of this mill, for it certainly stands 'before the church of the vill.' There was also a several fishery in Corhampton which is mentioned as early as the reign of Henry III.[86] The River Meon still affords good trout-fishing.

King Ethelred the son of King Edgar and Queen Estrilda granted *LOMER* (Lammere, xi cent.; Lomere, xiv cent.; Lowmer, xvi cent.), with three hides and a church, to Hyde Abbey.[87] In the reign of Edward the Confessor the abbot granted it to a certain Alward to hold for the term of his life in return for an annual payment of six sestiers of wine,[88] and at the time of the Survey it was held by Ruald of the abbey, no doubt for a like payment.[89] The manor continued to be held until the end of the fourteenth century by various tenants of the abbey by an annual payment in wine.[90] In the reign of Henry III Geoffrey de Lomer held the manor of the abbey.[91] Geoffrey was succeeded by his son and heir Robert de Lomer.[92] John de Lomer was holding in 1316,[93] while Ellis de Lomer was at one time lord of Lomer[94]—most probably at the end of the thirteenth century. In 1317 a messuage, one carucate of land

66 *Vide* Close, 18 Geo. III, pt. 16, No. 16.

67 In that year Richard mortgaged them to Henry Shales of Stonydean (Feet of F. Hants, Trin. 8 Geo. III).

68 Close, 18 Geo. III, pt. 16, No. 16.

69 Ibid. Feet of F. Hants, Mich. 18 Geo. III. The price paid was £12,500. In the deed of sale the property was described as follows: 'The manor of Corhampton, a farmhouse built upon Blackland Field and 150 acres, a farm called Steens and 107 acres, a messuage called Bittoms and eighty acres, Common Down and Cow Common called Little Dean, the rectory and parsonage of Corhampton, and a messuage called Cleverleys *alias* Franklins, and fifteen closes of arable and pasture land containing 160 acres belonging to it.' From this description it would appear that the manor lay in the west of the parish. At the present day there is a Staines Cottage in about the centre of the parish, a little to the north of the road to Bishop's Waltham. Franklin Lane and Franklin Farm are in the extreme west of the parish, while a little to the south is Cleverly Wood, partly in Bishop's Waltham parish and partly in Corhampton parish. Dean and Dean Lane are now in Bishop's Waltham parish.

70 MS. *penes* the lady of the manor.

71 Feet of F. Hants, Mich. 17 Hen. III.

72 MS. *penes* the lady of the manor.

73 Ibid.

74 Ibid.

75 Chan. Proc. (Ser. 2), vol. 37, No. 19.

76 MS. *penes* the lady of the manor.

77 Close, 18 Geo. III, pt. 16, No. 16.

78 Ibid.

79 Chart. R. 22 Edw. I, m. 3.

80 Pat. 3 Hen. VI, m. 13.

81 Ibid. 9 Jas. I, pt. 18, No. 11.

82 *V.C.H. Hants*, i, 481*a*.

83 Feet of F. Hants, Mich. 17 Hen. III.

84 MS. *penes* the lady of the manor.

85 Add. Chart. 27679, 28000, and 28003.

86 Feet of F. Hants, Mich. 17 Hen. III; Add. Chart. 28003.

87 Dugdale, *Mon.* ii, 428.

88 *V.C.H. Hants*, i, 471.

89 Ibid.

90 Pat. 12 Ric. I, pt. 1, m. 26. By an inquisition taken in 1392 it was ascertained that a messuage and lands in Lomer, Preshaw, Exton, and Warnford were held of the abbot and convent for the service of one pipe of Gascon wine, 2*s*. rent, and suit every three weeks at the hundred courts of 'Grenefeld' and Meonstoke (Inq. p.m. 16 Ric. II, pt. 1, No. 143).

91 Feet of F. Hants, East. 6 Hen. III.

92 Add. MS. 33284, fol. 165.

93 *Feud. Aids*, ii, 308.

94 Add. MS. 33284, fol. 160.

and 5 acres of wood in Preshaw and Lomer were settled on Thomas de Mareis[95] and Florence his wife.[96] Thomas died between 1346 and 1359, for in the latter year by fine between Walter de Haywode and Joan his wife and Laurence de Mareis a messuage, 2 carucates of land, 200 acres of pasture, 5 acres of wood, and 50*s.* rent in Lomer, Lomer Turville, Preshaw, Exton, and Warnford[97] were settled on Laurence for life to be held of Walter and Joan and the heirs of Walter for the rent of a rose.[98] In 1392 the same lands were held by Joan de Haywode and Margaret de Mareis for life of the inheritance of Thomas le Warenner and John Hampton, who in that year obtained licence from the king to grant the reversion of them after the death of Joan and Margaret to Hyde Abbey.[99] The manor of Lomer remained the property of the abbey until the Dissolution, when it was farmed out at £4 8*s.* 10*d.* to John Croppe and Thomasina his wife.[100] In 1542 Henry VIII granted it to Sir William Paulet Lord St. John and Elizabeth his wife,[101] who three years later sold it to John Lorimer and Agnes his wife.[102] John died seised of the manor in 1546 leaving a son and heir John aged two,[103] who was followed on his death in 1578 by his son and heir Roger aged three,[104] who dealt with the manor by fine in 1605.[105] Lomer next became vested in Lady Anne Sandys widow of William Lord Sandys, who in 1634 settled it upon her grandson John Stewkley, the younger son of Sir Thomas Stewkley by her only daughter and heir Elizabeth.[106] It remained in his possession until 1677, in which year he joined with his sons William and John in selling it to his nephew Sir Hugh Stewkley, bart.,[107] who in 1707 sold it to David Bone, timber merchant.[108] David, who died a year later, by will left the manor to his wife Mary to hold as long as she should remain single, with remainder on her death or marriage to his daughter Mary. His widow married —— Lacey as her second husband, and consequently Lomer passed to David's daughter Mary, who died unmarried in 1732. By her will (proved 8 April, 1732) she left the manor to her mother Mary Lacey for life, with remainder to William Moore and his issue, with contingent remainder to her half-sisters Mary and Catherine Lacey and their issue, with contingent remainder to her cousins John, William, Robert, and Hawkesworth Cleverley and her cousins John, Mary, Sarah, Joan, and Anne Wilkes.[109] Mary Lacey died in 1735, and the manor then passed to William Moore, who died without issue about 1750. In his lifetime Mary and Catherine Lacey, John, Robert, and Hawkesworth Cleverley, and Mary, Sarah, Joan, and Anne Wilkes had all died without issue, and consequently the manor was divided between William Cleverley and John Wilkes.[110] William Cleverley died intestate, and his moiety of the manor passed to his daughter and heir Sarah the wife of John Clewer before September, 1766, who by will proved 3 May, 1777, left it to her son John. Four years later he sold it to John Griffin younger son of Sarah Griffin, who had inherited the other moiety from his uncle John Wilkes in 1766.[111] John Griffin sold the whole manor in 1782 to Admiral Mark Robinson,[112] who sold it ten years later to Henry Penruddock Wyndham,[113] since when its descent has been identical with that of the manor of Corhampton.

The manor of *LOMER TURVILLE* (Lammer Turvill, Launver Turvill, and Lamere Turvyle, xiv cent.; Lomers Turvill, xvi cent.) was held partly of the abbot and convent of Hyde as of their manor of Lomer, and partly of the St. John family as of their manor of Warnford. The part which was held of the St. Johns was valued sometimes at 20*s.*[114] and sometimes at 10*s.*,[115] and comprised 12 acres of land in 1392, when it was held of Isabel de St. John as of her manor of Warnford for 1*d.* rent, and by her of the abbot and convent.[116]

TURVILLE. *Gules three cheverons vair.*

The manor was in the possession of the Turville family in the thirteenth century, and perhaps earlier. At about this time David Turville was lord,[117] and at the beginning of the thirteenth century the manor belonged to William Turville, passing on his death to Maurice Turville, who in 1222 granted to Thomas de Chancumbe and Amice his wife a reasonable dowry for Amice from the free tenement which belonged to William her former husband in Lomer.[118] Maurice seems to have been succeeded by Peter Turville, whose tenants in 1274 withdrew the suit which they owed at the hundred court of Meonstoke.[119]

95 He was also a holder in Lomer Turville (q.v. *infra*).

96 Feet of F. Hants, Hil. 10 Edw. II.

97 Comprising the three manors of Lomer, Preshaw, and Lomer Turville (q.v.).

98 Feet of F. Hants, Hil. 33 Edw. III.

99 Chan. Inq. p.m. 16 Ric. II, pt. 1, No. 143.

100 Mins. Accts. Hants, 30 & 31 Hen. VIII, m. 37.

101 Pat. 33 Hen. VIII, pt. 4, m. 48. In an inquisition taken in 1546 it is stated that Lord St. John and Elizabeth his wife were seised of the manor of Lomer in right of Elizabeth (Exch. Inq. p.m. (Ser. 2), file 993, No. 9). As the king most certainly did not grant it to Lady Elizabeth alone, it is possible that her husband subsequently settled the manor upon her.

102 Exch. Inq. p.m. (Ser. 2), file 993, No. 9; Memo. R. L.T.R. Hil. 4 Eliz. rot. 80. They do not seem to have paid for it in full, for in 1554 John Lorimer (son and heir of John) and Lawrence Kydwelly and Agnes his wife (widow of John) paid William marquis of Winchester and Elizabeth his wife £240 for the manors of Preshaw and Lomer (Feet of F. Hants, Trin. 1 Mary).

The manors were subject to a quit-rent of 25*s.* (Chan. Inq. p.m. (Ser. 2), vol. 262, No. 125), which seems to have been paid to the marquis and his heirs until the nineteenth century (*vide* Recov. R. Mich. 28 Geo. II, rot. 383, and Mich. 44 Geo. III, rot. 47).

103 Exch. Inq. p.m. (Ser. 2), file 993, No. 9.

104 Chan. Inq. p.m. (Ser. 2), vol. 187, No. 94. By his will dated 2 August, 1578, he granted an annuity of £6 13*s.* 4*d.* to his younger son John to be paid out of the rents and issues of the manors of Preshaw and Lomer.

105 Feet of F. Hants, Hil. 3 Jas. I. In that year he conveyed it to John Catcher and Philip Morgan.

106 Deeds *penes* Mr. A. R. Malden, The Close, Salisbury.

107 Ibid.

108 Ibid.

109 Ibid. By her will she burdened the manor with an annuity of £20 to the master of the Free School at Bishop's Waltham for teaching reading, writing, Latin, arithmetic, and the Church Catechism to ten poor boys of the parish of Bishop's Waltham between the ages of eight and fifteen.

110 Ibid.

111 Ibid.

112 Feet of F. Hants, Mich. 23 Geo. III.

113 *Ex inform.* Mr. A. R. Malden.

114 Inq. p.m. 3 Edw. III, No. 67; and 11 Edw. III, No. 49.

115 Ibid. 21 Edw. III, No. 57.

116 Ibid. 16 Ric. II, pt. 1, No. 143.

117 *Feud. Aids*, ii, 336.

118 Feet of F. Hants, East. 6 Hen. III.

119 Assize R. Mich. 8 Edw. I; in 1280 they were forced to resume their suit, and were in addition amerced 2*s.*

In the early part of the fourteenth century the Turville family seem to have parted with their property, which fell into two moieties. In 1326, by fine, two messuages, 24 acres of land, and 18*s.* rent in Lomer and Lomer Turville were settled on Thomas Mareis and Florence his wife,[120] who already held Lomer and Preshaw (q. v. *supra*), and as late as 1346 Thomas Mareis was holding in Lomer a portion of the tenth part of a knight's fee which had belonged to David Turville.[121] The other moiety passed to John de Basing, who in 1329 was holding one fee in Lomer of John de St. John.[122] He died before 1343, in which year John de Basing, son and heir of Sir John de Basing, renounced his claim to all the lands which his mother Joan was holding in Lomer Turville.[123] In 1346 Joan, widow of Sir John de Basing, was still holding the remainder of the tenth part of the knight's fee which had belonged to David Turville in Lomer.[124] By 1392, however, the whole of Lomer Turville had become merged in the manors of Lomer and Preshaw, forming part of the property which was then held by Joan de Haywode and Margaret de Mareis for life, of the inheritance of Thomas le Warenner and John Hampton.[125] Although it no longer had any existence as a separate manor, the name was for some time preserved. Thus in the Ministers' Accounts for 1539 mention is made of a rent of 10*s.* from one toft and 22 acres called 'Lomers Turvill,' lately in the tenure of John Papworth and William atte Noke, and now held by Alexander Seward by copy of court roll.[126]

By 1381 the abbot and convent of Titchfield had a considerable amount of property in *LOMER* belonging to their church of Lomer which had been granted to them by successive lords of Lomer.[127] At the Dissolution this property was most probably included in the grant of the sub-manor of Corhampton and the advowson of the church of Lomer to Thomas Wriothesley.

PRESHAW (Presshawe, Presthawe, and Preishawe, xiv cent.) was probably included in the entry under Lomer in Domesday Book,[128] and seems to have been held of Hyde Abbey for the same service and by the same tenants as Lomer.[129] At the time of the dissolution of the abbey it was worth £8 8*s.* 8*d.* by the year, which sum was made up as follows:—£1 4*s.* rents of assize,[130] £1 18*s.* rents of customary tenants,[131] and £5 6*s.* 8*d.* farm of the site of the manor.[132] Preshaw was granted with Lomer to Sir William Paulet, Lord St. John, in 1542, and followed the descent of Lomer until 1707, in which year Sir Hugh Stewkley, bart., sold it to Robert Kirby.[133] The latter, by will dated 23 August, 1721, left it to his cousins, John Waight, John Binsted, and Peter Newlyn, in trust, to dispose of it for the payment of his debts and various legacies to his brother-in-law Augustin Fisher, his nephews Henry and John Fisher, and his nieces Mary the wife of George Graham, Frances the wife of Joseph Freeman, and Katherine the wife of John Smith.[134] John Long purchased the manor from them in 1728 for £7,600.[135] He died unmarried on 23 November, 1742, having by will devised Preshaw to his brother Walter for life, with remainder to John the eldest son of Walter by his second wife Philippa Blackall.[136] The manor remained in the Long family until 1898,[137] when Mr. Walter Long sold it to Baron de Bush, who sold it on 1 March, 1901, to Captain Reginald Harry Cholmondeley, the present lord of the manor.[138]

Long of Preshaw. *Sable a lion argent between four crosslets or and two flaunches or with three crosslets sable in each.*

Preshaw House, set in a beautifully-timbered park on the southern slope of Millbarrow Down, is a picturesque gabled house of at least three dates, though owing to careful copying of the older work by the later builders, this is not very noticeable at first sight. Tradition points to an early occupation of the site, but there are no architectural features in the existing building which can claim a more remote date than 1630–40. The principal front is to the north, and has five gables, the two towards the east being early eighteenth-century additions, following the design of the other three. These latter formed the north front of the seventeenth-century house, which had a central block between projecting wings, after the mediaeval fashion, with a gabled porch over the main entrance at the north end of the central block, and is so shown in a coloured drawing of 1720, a copy of which is preserved in the house. It is of two stories with an attic, built of flint masonry with red-brick dressings, and having Ionic pilasters at the angles and centres of the projecting wings, while the central block is divided into three divisions by the same means, and the stories are marked by moulded brick strings with dentil courses beneath them. The windows in the gables have cut brick labels, and the gable copings, also of brick, are plainly recessed, and less effective than the other details of the building. The roofs are red-tiled and the chimney-stacks simply treated, adding little to the architectural effect. The windows have

120 Feet of F. Hants, Mich. 20 Edw. II.

121 *Feud. Aids*, ii, 336.

122 Inq. p.m. 3 Edw. III, No. 67; Close, 3 Edw. III, m. 4; a settlement of this property was made on the occasion of his marriage two years later (Feet of F. Hants, 5 Edw. III). John de Salesbury, parson of the church of Warnford, was summoned some time between 1333 and 1345 to answer John de Basing '*de parco fracto*' (Egerton MS. 2032, fol. 124).

123 Close, 17 Edw. III, pt. 1, m. 23 *d.*

124 *Feud. Aids*, ii, 336.

125 Inq. p.m. 16 Ric. II, pt. 1, No. 143.

126 Mins. Accts. Hants, 30 & 31 Hen. VIII, m. 36.

127 Add. MS. 33284, fol. 160.

128 *V.C.H. Hants*, i, 471.

129 Pat. 12 Ric. II, pt. 1, m. 26; Inq. p.m. 16 Ric. II, pt. 1, No. 143.

130 Viz. 2*s.* from the 'Eight Acres' in the tenure of the college of St. Elizabeth by Winchester; 5*s.* from a toft, a messuage, and 30 acres in the tenure of Corpus Christi College, Oxford; 2*s.* from a toft and 4 acres in the tenure of the same; 8*s.* from a messuage, 40 acres, and a copse of 4 acres in the tenure of Thomas Cleverly; 2*s.* and a red rose from a capital messuage and 30 acres in the tenure of William Lomer; 5*s.* from a messuage and 11 acres formerly in the tenure of Nicholas Parson and Joan his wife, daughter of John Lomer, lately in the tenure of Richard Osborne and Rose his wife, daughter of John Lomer, and now in the tenure of Richard Purdewe and Margaret his wife, daughter of John Lomer.

131 Viz. 12*s.* from 4 tofts and 28 acres called Pilates, Webbes, Martens, and Florens, held by copy of court roll; 10*s.* from a toft and 22 acres called Lomers Turvill held by copy of court roll; 16*s.* from lands and tenements in Warnford and Bere, held by copy of court roll.

132 Mins. Accts. Hants, 30 & 31 Hen. VIII, m. 36.

133 Deeds *penes* Mr. A. R. Malden.

134 Chan. Enr. Decree, rot. 1936, No. 2.

135 Close, 2 Geo. II, pt. 9, No. 12.

136 Burke, *Commoners*, iv, 73.

137 Berry, *Hants Gen.* 23; Recov. R. Hants, East. 9 Geo. III, rot. 55.

138 Information furnished by Captain Reginald Harry Cholmondeley.

had wooden casements from the first, but the old woodwork and the latticed panes have given place to modern frames. There is a second porch on the west side of the house, the masonry of which seems to belong to the seventeenth-century work, but the position is unusual, and the doorway itself of comparatively modern date. Probably the building was not a porch in the first instance. The eighteenth-century additions, in the form of a block added to the east of the older house, follow it in all details except in being entirely faced with brick and showing no flint work. In the early years of the nineteenth century a set of rooms was added to the south side of the house, doubling its thickness from north to south. Here also the details follow the older work for the most part, but are worked in cement instead of brick, and the south front is faced with cement marked with false masonry joints. The whole of the interior of the house seems to have been remodelled at this time, with finely-worked plaster cornices and ceilings far superior to the unattractive exterior of this date. The hall occupies the traditional position, with the entrance doorway at its lower end, but is merely a one-story vestibule, and a good example of the nearly completed transition from the mediaeval to the modern treatment.

CHURCH The church of *CORHAMPTON*, which has no known dedication, is a small building with chancel and north vestry, nave and south porch, and a wooden bell-turret on the west gable of the nave.

Except the vestry and porch, and the east half of the chancel, it dates from pre-Conquest times, and perhaps belongs to the first half of the eleventh century. The features of this date which still exist are the chancel arch, the north doorway of the nave and part of the south, the external pilaster strips on the nave and chancel, the angle quoins of the nave, the sun-dial east of the south porch, and perhaps the openings for bells high in the west wall. The upper part of the west gable has been rebuilt, the roof renewed, the north door blocked, and the south nearly entirely removed to make way for a later doorway, while the east half of the chancel has given way at some time and been rebuilt in brick, and is probably a little shorter than at first. The chancel measures 10 ft. 6 in. east to west by 14 ft. within the walls, and has a modern east window of three lights, and a narrow thirteenth-century lancet at the south-west, while at the south-east is a stone seat with arms, perhaps of thirteenth-century date, and formerly serving as a sedile. Externally a length of original walling remains at the south-west, of flint rubble with a pilaster strip of Binstead stone set in it. The chancel arch, 7 ft. 9 in. wide by 13 ft. high to the crown, is semicircular, of one square order, with plain imposts, and has on the west face a projecting rib framing the arch, and formerly running down the jamb. At its apex is a small projecting keystone. The nave, 36 ft. by 17 ft. 3 in. (17 ft. 9 in. at the west), is 16 ft. high to the plate level, not having the excessive proportion of height to breadth so often found in early churches. It has no traces of original windows, being lighted towards the east by single lancet windows on the north and south, while a third is inserted in the blocking of the north doorway. This doorway is the most interesting architectural feature of the church, and has a plain semicircular head and jamb cut straight through the wall without a reveal. A plain rib frames head and jambs on the outside, having imposts at the springing with characteristic horizontal mouldings, and stepped bases. The doorway is disproportionately high to the wall in which it is set, and from the highest point of the rib which frames it a pilaster strip runs to the eaves. The south doorway was of the same description, but nothing but the rib framing its arch is now to be seen, with the pilaster strip over it. In the north and south walls of the nave are pilaster strips, two in each, symmetrically set at an average distance of 9 ft. from the east and west angles, and in the middle of the west wall is another. All rise from a projecting base course, and at the eaves were stopped by a horizontal course of wrought stone, which is continued across the west gable, having above it the two square-headed openings which seem to have held bells in the first instance. The angles of the nave have quoins of long and short work, all these details being worked in Binstead stone, except the openings in the western gable. The heads of these latter have lately been rebuilt in flint and tiles. The grooves made in their jambs by the bells can now be clearly seen from the west gallery in the nave. An unusual feature is the treatment of the bases of the pilaster strips; they spring from a group of three simply-treated scrolled leaves or brackets, resting on the base-course, the best preserved example being that to the west of the south doorway of the nave. To the east of the doorway is a square stone set in the wall carved with a circular dial, the angles of the stone being filled in with groups of three-pointed leaves; it is probably contemporary with the wall in which it is set.

The south doorway has a pointed arch with a wide hollow chamfer, and is probably of thirteenth-century date; a modern masonry porch is built over it, in which is now preserved an altar slab of irregular shape, 5 ft. long by 1 ft. 10½ in. wide at the north end, and 1 ft. 7 in. wide at the south. Till lately it served as a seat under the yew tree south of the church, but in the earlier part of the last century was in the floor of the church. It is notable for having, besides the five usual crosses, a sixth on the front edge, in the middle of its length.

The nave walls have gone over southwards, the greatest lean being of 10 inches in the middle of the south wall, and near the west angle of the same wall a large raking buttress of brick has been built. The nave roof retains some old timbers, perhaps of fifteenth-century date, and the wooden bell-turret has lately been renewed, with details copied from some early seventeenth-century woodwork found in it at a late repair. A good deal of the internal plastering is ancient, and on the north, south, and west walls of the nave are a number of incised lines, done when the plaster was fresh, chiefly in the form of circles containing crosses formed by intersecting arcs of similar circles, a detail commonly used in consecration crosses. Here there seem to be too many of them to be thus identified—there are three side by side on the north wall—and they are probably decorative. Some very interesting remains of decorative painting have been lately uncovered on the west face of the chancel arch, and on the north, south, and west walls of the chancel. The latter show a band of figure subjects high on the wall, and painted drapery below, in which are set square panels inclosing circles, which

Corhampton: Preshaw House from the North-west

contain pairs of birds set back to back. The figure subjects are unfortunately very faint, but enough remains to show that they are of considerable merit; the best preserved are at the east of the south wall, a female figure standing before a seated bishop.

The altar-rails in the chancel are of the eighteenth century, but most of the woodwork in the church, including the west gallery, is modern. A new set of pews is recorded to have been made in 1636, and a little carved work of this date is preserved.

The font at the west end under the gallery has a curious small round bowl, with a line of cable moulding round the middle; the detail suggests a twelfth-century date, but the small size and general reworking of the surface make its attribution to so early a period doubtful.

There are two bells, the treble inscribed 'In God is my hope, 1619, I.H.,' and the second dated 1828.

The church possesses a communion cup, unmarked, but of *c.* 1570, with conical bowl and expanding lip, and a saucer-shaped cover paten. Both are very roughly engraved with scrollwork and dotted ornament, and are probably of local make. There is also a standing paten of 1791, given in 1792 by Dr. John Chelsum, rector of Droxford, a plated flagon of old Sheffield ware, and an alms dish of 1874.

The earliest preserved book of registers is a copy, made about 1760, the baptisms beginning in 1665, the marriages 1667, and the burials 1695. Marriages end at 1750, but the other entries continue to 1812. The second book is the printed marriage register, 1754–1812.

ADVOWSON There was a church in Corhampton at the time of the Domesday Survey,[139] the advowson of which followed the descent of the manor until about the middle of the thirteenth century, when Robert de St. John, overlord of Corhampton, granted it in free alms to the abbey of Titchfield.[140] In the reign of Edward I John de St. John, son and heir of Robert de St. John, attempted to recover the advowson, granting the presentation for one turn only to the abbey of Titchfield in 1288.[141] The abbot, however, produced the charter of Robert de St. John, which John was ultimately forced to confirm.[142] The advowson thenceforward followed the descent of the sub-manor of Corhampton (q.v.).

The living is at the present day a vicarage, net yearly value £42, including 70 acres of glebe situated in the parish of Clanfield, in the gift of Mrs. Pleydell Bouverie-Campbell-Wyndham.

The annual value of the church was £6 13*s.* 4*d.* in the thirteenth century,[143] and the rector, Henry de Guildford, resigned the living in 1291 'on the account of the poverty of the same because it is hardly sufficient to the support of one chaplain.'[144]

In 1271 by deed between the abbot of Titchfield and John de Petersfield, rector of the church of Corhampton, it was agreed that the canons should be for ever free from the payment of all tithes coming from the lands they already possessed in the parish, paying instead to the rector half a mark every year, but that they should pay tithes from all lands subsequently acquired.[145]

There was also a church in Lomer at the time of the Domesday Survey[146] which Geoffrey de Lomer, lord of the manor of Lomer, granted to the abbot and canons of Titchfield in the reign of Henry III.[147] The church was appropriated to the abbey some time between 1282 and 1304.[148] Its annual value is given as £4 0*s.* 7*d.* in 1381.[149] The advowson remained in the hands of the abbot and convent until the Dissolution, when it passed to the king,[150] who granted it, together with the manor and advowson of Corhampton, to Thomas Wriothesley,[151] from whom it passed to Henry Wriothesley, earl of Southampton.[152] In the inquisition taken on the death of Thomas in 1550, it is stated that the rectories and churches of Corhampton and Lomer had been united, annexed, consolidated, and reduced to one by the king.[153] They must have been separated again, however, in the seventeenth century, for in 1635 Lady Anne Sandys settled the rectory and the advowson of the vicarage of Lomer upon her grandson John Stewkley.[154] The advowson subsequently followed the descent of the manor.[155] It was dealt with by fine as late as 1783,[156] but only the site of the church now remains. Bishop Stratford (1323–33) ordered the church to be re-consecrated because it had been polluted by the shedding of blood.[157]

Close to Preshaw House is a chapel built by the late Mr. Walter Jervis Long, and opened at Christmas, 1864. Divine service is held here twice a day on Sundays.

CHARITIES In 1669 William Collins by will proved in the P.C.C. gave to trustees a messuage, then newly erected as a schoolhouse, and garden containing one acre, for the use of a schoolmaster performing the office of minister. The testator also directed that a sum of £450 should be expended in the purchase of freehold lands of the clear yearly value of £22 to be paid to such schoolmaster, for the teaching of three poor boys of Corhampton, two of Meonstoke, one of the parish of Exton, and two of Droxford. By deed dated 29 September, 1677, in consideration of £450 (with £10 added by Dorothy Collins the testator's widow), a rent-charge of £22 per annum issuing out of land known as Chalfryth, otherwise the Chalverys, at Nursted, in the parish of Buriton, was purchased and settled upon the trusts of the will.

By a scheme of the Charity Commissioners of 27 July, 1900, the old school buildings and gardens may be occupied by the vicar at a yearly rent of £10, and the yearly income of the charity is directed to be applied in the advancement of education by way of

139 *V.C.H. Hants*, i, 481.

140 Add. MS. 33284, fol. 166. This grant was confirmed by William de Clare.

141 De Banc. R. Trin. 16 Edw. I.

142 MS. *penes* the lady of the manor.

143 *Pope Nich. Tax.* (Rec. Com.), 211*b*.

144 MS. *penes* the lady of the manor.

145 Ibid.

146 *V.C.H. Hants*, i, 471.

147 Add. MS. 33284, fol. 165. His grant was confirmed by his son and heir Robert de Lomer, and by William bishop of Winchester. (Ibid.)

148 Egerton MS. 2031, fol. 29.

149 Add. MS. 33284, fol. 162.

150 Feet of F. Div. Cos. Mich. 29 Hen. VIII.

151 Pat. 29 Hen. VIII, pt. 1, m. 32.

152 Chan. Inq. p.m. (Ser. 2), 24 Eliz. pt. 1, No. 46.

153 W. and L. Inq. p.m. (Ser. 2), vol. 5, No. 103.

154 Deeds *penes* Mr. A. R. Malden.

155 Ibid.; Recov. R. Hil. 4 Geo. II, rot. 139; Feet of F. Hants, Mich. 7 Geo. III.

156 Feet of F. Hants, Mich. 23 Geo. III.

157 Egerton MS. 2032, fol. 63.

prizes or rewards to boys resident in the four interested parishes qualified as therein mentioned, or in payments to encourage continuance at school of such boys, or in exhibitions, evening classes, or technical instruction. The official trustees hold a sum of £40 Local Loans 3 per cent. stock, which under the provisions of the scheme is to be maintained as a repair fund.

By deed 1872 a national school was founded for this parish and Exton.[158]

MEONSTOKE

Menestoche (xi cent.); Mienestoch, Mionstoke (xii cent.); Manestoke, Menestoke (xiii cent.); Munestoke, Munestokes, Maonestoke, Moenestoke (xiv cent.).

Meonstoke parish, covering an area of 2,055 acres, lies five miles north-east of Bishop's Waltham, and about one and a half miles north of Droxford. The village is situated in the extreme west of the parish, close to the river, the church being on the left bank of the stream, while the village lies to the south and east, on the lower slopes of the east side of the valley. The houses are built along two streets which meet at right angles, the one running eastward from Corhampton, and the other following the line of the river and going southwards to Soberton. A swiftly-flowing mill-race near the bridge at the west end of the village probably marks the site of the mill which is mentioned in Domesday Book,[1] and is included in the extent of the manor of Meonstoke Waleraund taken in the reign of Edward II.[2] The smithy stands close by, to the north of the road, and by the Buck's Head Inn a little path runs off north to the church of St. Andrew. The rectory, which stands on the higher ground east of the church, was built in 1895, replacing the old rectory-house, which, with the glebe, was sold in that year. There are few old cottages, since the greater part of the village was burnt down at the beginning of the eighteenth century, and in place of the older houses were built rows of houses fronting on the street and entered by tall flights of steps. The manor house lying to the east is the residence of Dr. George William Butler. To the east of the village runs the Meon Valley branch of the South Western Railway, and beyond it rise the downs, Old Winchester Hill, in the north-east corner of the parish, reaching a height of 650 ft. The only houses in the eastern part of the parish are a few scattered farms reached by rough roads which in some cases are merely tracks across the downs. The south-eastern corner of the parish is well wooded, containing Little Sheardley Wood, Great Sheardley Wood, Stoke Wood, and Stockram Copse. There are 987 acres of arable land in the parish, 134¼ acres of permanent grass, and 31½ acres of woods and plantations.[3] Meonstoke Down was inclosed in 1863.

The soil is chalk and loam, the subsoil chalk and flint. The chief crops are wheat, oats, and barley. The following field-names are found in the fourteenth century: 'Jamesland, Crouchland, and Martinsland.'[4]

MANORS *MEONSTOKE* formed part of the lands of King Edward the Confessor, being then assessed at one and a half hides. At the time of the Domesday Survey it was part of the ancient demesne of the crown, and was therefore not assessed.[5] In 1180 Meonstoke was the land of Henry de Bulleis.[6] He was succeeded by Hamon de Bulleis, who died in 1187, when it passed to the crown.[7] Until the reign of Henry III Meonstoke formed part of the sources of the royal ferm. Thus in 1189 Richard de la Bere accounted for £20 farm of Meonstoke, paying thence 10 marks for her dowry to Joan widow of Hamon.[8] Again in 1202 Thomas de Hoe paid 40 marks for two years' farm of Meonstoke. In the reign of Henry III Meonstoke was divided into three portions worth respectively £10, £5, and £2 a year,[9] and from this time there were three manors of Meonstoke—each with a distinct history—until the later consolidation in the time of William of Wykeham.

MEONSTOKE WALERAUND, afterwards *MEONSTOKE PERRERS*. The first mention of the largest of these portions as a separate manor seems to be in 1224, when the sheriff was ordered to give seisin to Pain de Chaworth of his land in Meonstoke.[10] This land was afterwards granted to William de Percy, who, however, cannot have held it long, as in 1239 Henry III granted it to Fulk de Montgomery, with the proviso, however, that if the property were restored by the crown to the heirs of William de Percy, Fulk should receive £30 yearly from the exchequer, until he received an equivalent grant of escheated lands.[11] In 1231 Fulk sold the manor to Sir John Maunsel, chancellor of St. Paul's,[12] who in the same year obtained a grant of a weekly market on Monday at Meonstoke and of a yearly fair there on the vigil, the feast, and the morrow of St. Margaret,[13] and two years later a grant of free warren in all his lands in Hampshire.[14] Sir John stood high in favour with Henry III, who heaped preferments on him with so lavish a hand that at one period he was holding no fewer than seventy benefices of different kinds. When Simon de Montfort became supreme the king was forced, though much against his will, to deprive his favourite of his possessions, granting them by letters patent in 1263 to Simon de Montfort the younger.[15] After the battle of Evesham, Meonstoke escheated to the king, who granted it to Geoffrey de Percy, probably the heir of William de Percy, who in 1268 sold

[158] *V.C.H. Hants*, ii, 398.
[1] Ibid. i, 452*a*.
[2] Inq. p.m. 2 Edw. II, No. 80.
[3] Statistics from Bd. of Agric. (1905).
[4] Inq. p.m. 26 Edw. III (2nd Nos.), No. 56.
[5] *V.C.H. Hants*, i, 452*a*.
[6] Pipe R. 26 Hen. II. While Henry was lord of Meonstoke, he granted in free alms to the church of St. Mary of Southwick and the canons of that place 2*s*. in his manor of Meonstoke, payable every year on the Feast of the Assumption of the Blessed Virgin Mary (Add. MS. 33285, fol. 176).
[7] Pipe R. 33 Hen. II.
[8] Ibid. 1 Ric. I.
[9] *Vide* Assize R. Mich. 8 Edw. I.
[10] Close, 8 Hen. III, pt. 1, m. 8.
[11] Chart. R. 23 Hen. III, m. 3.
[12] Ibid. 31 Hen. III, m. 12.
[13] Ibid. m. 11.
[14] Ibid. 33 Hen. III, m. 3.
[15] Pat. 47 Hen. III, m. 5.

it to Robert Waleraund.[16] The latter died seised of the manor in 1272, his heir being his nephew, Robert Waleraund, son of his younger brother William.[17] Meonstoke, however, was for some time held in dower by Maud widow of Robert Waleraund, the uncle,[18] and never seems to have been delivered over to Robert Waleraund, the nephew, who died without issue about the end of the thirteenth century. His heir was his brother John, who died seised of the manor at the beginning of the reign of Edward II.[19] By an inquisition taken after his death the following were returned as his heirs: (1) His cousin, John de Eddeworth, second son of his aunt Alice, who was the eldest surviving sister of his father William; (2) his cousin Alice de Everingham, second daughter of his aunt Cecily, who was his father's second surviving sister; (3) his cousin's son Bevis de Knoville, son of Joan, who was the eldest daughter of his aunt Cecily; (4) his cousin's son Alan de Plunkenet, son of Alan de Plunkenet, who was the eldest son of his aunt Alice; (5) his cousin's daughter Maud de Croupes *alias* Bret, eldest daughter of Cecily, who was the third daughter of his aunt Cecily; and (6) her younger sister Cecily wife of Peter de Hulyon. The question as to the succession was finally decided in favour of Alan de Plunkenet,[20] who died before 1325, in which year the king assigned to his widow Sybil the third part of the manor of Meonstoke of the yearly value of £10 10*s*.[21] Joan de Bohun of Kilpeck, sister and heir of Alan, without licence, quitclaimed the manor to Nicholas de Useflete, who had obtained a lease of it some years before,[22] and the manor escheated to the king, who, however, in 1328 pardoned Nicholas, and restored the manor to him.[23] Joan de Bohun died without issue in 1327, her heir being her cousin's son Richard de la Bere, grandson of Richard de la Bere, brother and heir of her father, Alan de Plunkenet,[24] to whom Thomas de Useflete, parson of the church of Meonstoke, some four years later, quitclaimed two-thirds of the manor and the reversion of the remaining third after the death of Sybil, wife of Henry de Pembrigge.[25] Richard de la Bere, while lord of the manor, alienated parts of it at various times without licence,[26] finally granting a life-interest in the whole manor to Robert de Hoe and Lucy his wife, who in 1347 obtained licence to retain it for that term in return for the payment of 1 mark.[27] Robert and Lucy were still living in 1353, in which year they acquired other premises in Meonstoke,[28] and while still in possession obtained licence from William de Edendon, bishop of Winchester, to celebrate mass in the oratory of their dwelling-house in the parish of Meonstoke.[28a] Some time afterwards the manor seems to have escheated to the king, who granted it to trustees to the use of the celebrated Alice Perrers,[29] from which circumstance it was commonly called the manor of Meonstoke Perrers. In 1376 the Good Parliament sentenced Alice to banishment and forfeiture, but in the following year the Bad Parliament reversed this sentence,[30] and she regained her possessions. However, in the first Parliament of Richard II she was brought before the lords at the request of the commons, and the sentence against her was confirmed.[31] Meonstoke accordingly escheated to the crown, and for two years was in the hands of stewards, Thomas Illeston being appointed in 1378,[32] and John Barell the following year.[33] On 14 December, 1379, the sentence against Alice was revoked, and on 15 March, 1380, the manor was granted in fee-simple to her husband, William de Windsor,[34] who in the following June obtained licence from the king to sell it to William of Wykeham, bishop of Winchester,[35] by whom it was granted to Winchester College in 1385.[36] The manor still forms part of the possessions of the college.

Winchester College. *Argent two cheverons sable between three roses gules.*

MEONSTOKE FERRAND was in origin the land worth 100*s*. granted by Henry III from his manor of Meonstoke to his Gascon cross-bowman Ferrand.[37] He was seised of it as late as 1233, when he obtained licence to lease it for six years.[38] His successor is unknown, but in 1280 Sir Peter Ferrand, most probably his grandson, was holding 100*s*. worth of land in Meonstoke.[39] He continued seised of it until 1305, in which year he sold it to John de Drokensford, bishop of Bath and Wells (1309–29),[40] who died in 1329 seised of 100*s*. rents coming from certain free tenants in the vill of Meonstoke, his heir being his brother Philip, aged forty and more.[41] The date of the death of the latter is uncertain,[42] but his son and heir Philip[43] died in 1355, leaving a son and heir

16 Chart. R. 52 Hen. III, m. 12.

17 Inq. p.m. 1 Edw. I, No. 6.

18 In 1280 Maud was summoned to show by what warrant she took the fines of the assize of bread and beer in Meonstoke (*Plac. de Quo Warr.* (Rec. Com.), 771). In the same year she proved her right to pillory, tumbril, and a free market every Monday in the manor which she was holding in dower of the inheritance of Robert Waleraund, who was still in the king's ward (Assize R. Mich. 8 Edw. I).

19 Inq. p.m. 2 Edw. II, No. 80.

20 Ibid. In 1362 Sir Lawrence de St. Martin and Miles son of Sir Miles de Stapleton brought an action to recover the manor of Meonstoke Waleraund from its owner, Thomas de la Bere, basing their claim on their descent from Walter Waleraund, uncle and heir of John Waleraund, no mention of whom was made in the various inquisitions taken after John's death, but failed to make good their claim (De Banc. R. Mich. 36 Edw. III, m. 81).

21 Close, 19 Edw. II, m. 27.

22 Inq. p.m. 2 Edw. III (2nd Nos.), No. 95.

23 Pat. 2 Edw. III, pt. 2, m. 17.

24 Inq. p.m. 1 Edw. III (1st Nos.), No. 81; Pat. 2 Edw. III, m. 19.

25 Pat. 5 Edw. III, pt. 1, m. 12; Inq. p.m. 5 Edw. III (2nd Nos.), No. 20. Sybil was widow of Alan de Plunkenet.

26 Pat. 21 Edw. III, pt. 3, m. 32.

27 Inq. p.m. 21 Edw. III (2nd Nos.), No. 62*b*; Pat. 21 Edw. III, pt. 3, m. 25.

28 Inq. a.q.d. file 307, No. 6.

28a Egerton MS. 2033, fol. 57.

29 Pat. 46 Edw. III, pt. 2, m. 23; Close, 47 Edw. III, m. 38.

30 *Parl. R.* (Rec. Com.), ii, 374.

31 Ibid. iii, 12*b*.

32 Pat. 1 Ric. II, pt. 3, m. 9.

33 Close, 2 Ric. II, m. 30.

34 Pat. 3 Ric. II, pt. 3, m. 5.

35 Ibid.; Feet of F. Hants, Trin. 4 Ric. II.

36 Pat. 8 Ric. II, pt. 2, m. 4.

37 Ibid. 9 Hen. III, m. 7; 11 Hen. III, m. 1; *Testa de Nevill* (Rec. Com.), 232.

38 Pat. 17 Hen. III, m. 6.

39 Assize R. Mich. 8 Edw. I.

40 Kirby, *Annals of Winchester Coll.* 20. In the same year he purchased one toft, 17 acres of land, and the third part of one mill in Meonstoke from Simon de Bolyngton and Maud his wife (Feet of F. Hants, Mich. 34 Edw. I).

41 Inq. p.m. 3 Edw. III (1st Nos.), No. 41.

42 It must have been after 1337, however, for in that year he obtained licence from the king to enfeoff Philip his son and heir of a moiety of a carucate of land in Meonstoke (Pat. 11 Edw. III, pt. 3, m. 26).

43 While he was lord of Meonstoke Ferrand he alienated 16 messuages, 5 cottages, 14 virgates, 15½ acres, and 18*s*. rents in Meonstoke to Henry Sturmy of Elvetham without the royal licence (Inq. a.q.d. file 301, No. 13).

John,[44] who seems to have died without issue before 1357, in which year Maurice le Bruyn and Margaret his wife sold twenty-two messuages, one mill, lands, rents, and the third part of a mill in Meonstoke and Droxford to William de Edendon, bishop of Winchester.[45] William of Wykeham purchased Meonstoke Ferrand from the executors of his predecessor,[46] and granted it to Winchester College,[47] since which time it has become merged in Meonstoke Perrers.

MEONSTOKE TOUR was in origin the 40*s.* worth of land granted by Henry III from his manor of Meonstoke to Geoffrey Peverel.[48] In 1240, however, it was again in the hands of the king, who in that year granted it to his serjeant Henry de la Tour.[49] On the death of Henry it passed to his brother and heir Hugh,[50] who died seised of a free tenement in Meonstoke in 1283, leaving a son and heir Thomas aged twenty-six.[51] The latter died ten years later leaving a son and heir Thomas, aged five,[52] who died without issue, his heir being a minor, Hugh de la Tour, son of William de la Tour.[53] It is doubtful, however, whether Hugh succeeded to his inheritance, for in 1316 a certain Thomas de la Tour was holding lands in Meonstoke.[54] He was succeeded by William de la Tour, who died in 1350 seised of six messuages and six virgates of land in Meonstoke, leaving as his heir a daughter Alice, wife of John de Roches, aged forty and more.[55] From them Meonstoke Tour passed by sale to William de Edendon, bishop of Winchester, who was seised of it in 1353.[56] Its subsequent history is identical with that of Meonstoke Ferrand (q.v.).

Other lands in the parish known as *COSTARDS*[57] and *WESTONS*[58] were bought up by the agents of William of Wykeham in 1388,[59] and granted by them to Winchester College three years later.[60]

In an assize roll of 1280 it is stated that Walter de Cumbe, parson of Meonstoke, had the fines of the assize of bread and beer from his tenements in the vill of Meonstoke and did not permit his men to be on the king's assize.[61] This points to the existence of a *MANOR OF THE RECTORY* which still survives.

The lord of the manor of Meonstoke Waleraund had free warren, assize of bread and beer, pillory, tumbril, a market every Monday, and an annual fair in Meonstoke.

At the time of the Domesday Survey there was one mill in Meonstoke worth 10*s.*[62] In later times there were two, one appurtenant to the manor of Meonstoke Waleraund[63] and the other to Meonstoke Ferrand.[64] The last mention of the latter is in 1357, and it seems to have fallen into decay before 1385, for there is no mention of it in the grant of Meonstoke Ferrand to Winchester College in that year.[65] The mill-race west of the village still marks the site of the other mill, which gradually fell into disuse, no doubt, owing to the close proximity of Corhampton Mill.

CHURCH The church of *ST. ANDREW, MEONSTOKE*, has a chancel 31 ft. 10 in. by 16 ft. (16 ft. 3 in. at the west end), nave 52 ft. 9 in. by 18 ft. 7 in. with north aisle 8 ft. 2 in. wide and south aisle 8 ft. 4 in., north and south porches, and west tower 11 ft. 2 in. square, all measurements being internal.

The main fabric of the church dates from the thirteenth century, with no trace of earlier work, but the tower is a later addition. The details of the clearstory windows in the nave point to *c.* 1260, and the chancel may be some thirty years older than this. It has an early fifteenth-century east window of three cinquefoiled lights with tracery, flanked by tall niches for images, with cinquefoiled crocketed canopies and embattled cornices over; below the southern niche is a trefoiled recess fitted with a modern drain. The chancel was originally lighted on the north and south by three lancets, but the middle window on either side has been built up. Between the second and third windows on both sides is a fourteenth-century tomb-recess under a segmental arch, in each of which a marble coffin lid, also of fourteenth-century date, has been placed. A thirteenth-century string runs at the level of the window sills within the chancel. The wooden fittings are modern, and there is a coved plaster ceiling with a moulded eighteenth-century cornice.

The chancel arch is, in spite of considerable repairs, a very pretty piece of thirteenth-century detail, of two moulded orders, with a label and three shafts in each respond with moulded capitals and bases. The arch is semicircular with a good deal of modern stonework at the crown, and the capitals and upper parts of the shafts are new. The outer order of the arch towards the chancel is of plainer detail than that towards the nave, and has a rather unusual section.

The nave is of four bays, the arcades having pointed arches of two chamfered orders, with columns alternately round and octagonal, the responds in each case being half-octagonal, and moulded capitals and bases. Over the arches are circular clearstory windows inclosing quatrefoils, with an outer rebate for the glazing; they are now unglazed, as the roof runs in one span over nave and aisles. Marks of a former steep-pitched nave roof are to be seen on the east wall of the tower, and below the roof-line is part of a circular window in the former west gable of the nave as it was before the addition of the tower. Its lower half has been destroyed by the head of a small arched opening to the second stage of the tower, now glazed, but originally open to the nave.

44 Exch. Inq. p.m. (Ser. 1), file 14, No. 2.

45 Feet of F. Hants, East. 31 Edw. III. In the fine the premises were quitclaimed from Maurice and Margaret and the heirs of Margaret. It is therefore probable that Margaret was the sister and heir of John.

46 Kirby, *Ann. of Winchester Coll.* 20.

47 Pat. 4 Ric. II, pt. 2, m. 30; 8 Ric. II, pt. 2, m. 4.

48 Chart. R. 24 Hen. III, m. 2.

49 Ibid.

50 *Testa de Nevill* (Rec. Com.), 232.

51 Inq. p.m. 11 Edw. I, No. 23.

52 Ibid. 21 Edw. II, No. 11.

53 Pat. 31 Edw. I, m. 29. The king granted the custody of lands in Meonstoke during the minority of Hugh to Thomas de Columbrigg.

54 *Feud. Aids*, ii, 307.

55 Inq. p.m. 24 Edw. III, No. 18.

56 Inq. a.q.d. file 307, No. 6.

57 Costards was purchased from William Costard and Agnes his wife, and consisted of 2*s.* rent, the moiety of three messuages, 80½ acres of land and pasture for two horses, ten bulls, fifteen pigs, 140 sheep, and a moiety of a moiety of a virgate of land (Feet of F. Trin. 12 Ric. II).

58 Westons was in 1387 granted to William Weston, citizen and grocer of London, and Alice his wife by Nicholas Spencer, citizen and grocer of London, and Margaret his wife (Pat. 10 Ric. II, m. 10), and consisted of the moiety of a messuage, a virgate of land, and pasture for two horses, ten bulls, fifteen pigs, and 140 sheep, and a moiety of a moiety of a virgate of land (Feet of F. Hants, Hil. 11 Ric. II).

59 Feet of F. Hants, Hil. 11 Ric. II and Trin. 12 Ric. II.

60 Pat. 15 Ric. II, pt. 2, m. 9.

61 Assize R. Mich. 8 Edw. I.

62 *V.C.H. Hants*, i, 452*a*.

63 Inq. p.m. 2 Edw. II, No. 80.

64 Feet of F. Hants, East. 31 Edw. III.

65 Pat. 8 Ric. II, pt. 2, m. 4.

The north aisle has a fifteenth-century east window of two cinquefoiled lights with a quatrefoil over, and three similar windows in the north wall, between the second and third of which is a thirteenth-century north doorway, now opening into a vestry, and having a single moulded order and a label. The west window is a lancet, but has been inserted within the lines of a wider window of uncertain date. At the north-east of the aisle is a plain square locker, and parts of two fourteenth-century coffin lids are placed in the aisle. The windows in the south aisle are like those in the north except that there is no west window. The aisle has been refaced [66] except the east wall, and all the window tracery of the south windows is modern. The south doorway has a pointed arch of two continuous hollow-chamfered orders, and is probably late thirteenth-century work while the south porch is modern.

The tower is finished with a wooden stage open on all sides, and covered with a low red-tiled roof. This is a recent addition, the rest of the tower being of flint rubble with angle buttresses, probably of fifteenth-century date. The west window is a tall lancet, which seems to be of the thirteenth century, and may have been moved here from the west wall of the nave. The tower arch is modern.

The tower was repaired and the present red-tiled roof put on the nave in 1900. The corbels of the former aisle roofs are still to be seen. The pulpit belongs to the latter part of the seventeenth century, and is hexagonal, with modern carved panels but old twisted columns standing free at the angles and carrying an arcade under a projecting moulded cornice. In the north aisle are the arms of one of the Georges, and a wood-carving of Jacob wrestling with the angel, German work of the seventeenth century, and inscribed 'Du solt nicht mer Jacob sondern Iserael heisen.'

On the north-east side of the first pillar of the north arcade is a deeply-cut cross, as if to take a metal inlay.

The font at the west end of the south aisle is of a late twelfth-century type, with a square bowl on a central shaft, formerly flanked by four shafts at the angles. Its material is probably Purbeck marble, but it is covered by a coat of dark grey paint mottled with white spots in imitation of such a marble, and its real surface cannot be seen. The bowl has arcades on the east and north faces, and zigzag patterns and what seem to be trefoiled leaves on the west.

There are pits for six bells, but only three remain, the treble and second by Robert Catlin, 1749; and the tenor by Pack & Chapman, 1773.

The plate consists of a cup of 1682, with a cover paten by the same maker and doubtless of the same date, though without the date letter; a modern box for bread, two small flagons (1899), and a brass alms dish.

The first book of the registers begins in 1599, the entries down to 1678 being copied from an older book not now in existence, and ends in 1812; the second book contains the marriages from 1754 to 1812.

ADVOWSON There is no reference to a church in Meonstoke at the time of the Domesday Survey,[67] and the earliest mention of one seems to be in 1284, when Edward I quitclaimed to John bishop of Winchester the advowson of the church of Meonstoke with a chapel annexed,[68] whereof he had recently impleaded the bishop.[69] The advowson has remained in the hands of the bishop up to the present day.[70]

In 1291 the church of Meonstoke, with a chapel annexed,[71] was assessed at £33 6*s.* 8*d.*[72] In the reign of Henry VIII the annual value of the rectory was £46 13*s.* 4*d.*[73]

William of Wykeham, on 7 March, 1401–2, deputed Thomas bishop of Chrysopolis to dedicate two portable altars for Thomas Lavington, rector of Meonstoke.[74]

There is a Primitive Methodist chapel in the parish, built in 1864. The elementary school was built in 1842 for seventy children.

CHARITIES This parish is entitled to benefit from Collins School at Corhampton (q.v.).

SOBERTON

Sudbertune (xi cent.); Subertune and Sobertona (xiii cent.); Subberton (xv cent.); Supporton and Soperton (xvi cent.); Sauberton (xviii cent.).

Soberton is a large parish with an area of 5,873 acres of land and twelve acres of land covered by water, with a station at Brockbridge in the parish of Droxford on the Meon Valley branch of the London and South-Western Railway. Two good roads run through the parish, one on the east side to Hambledon, and the other on the west to Newtown and thence south to Southwick, through the West Walk of the Forest of Bere. The River Meon forms the western boundary of the parish, which is, on the whole, low-lying, containing much marsh and heath, and many scattered copses, probably detached portions of the Forest of Bere. The general rise of the ground is from south to north, the highest ground being in the north-east, where some outlying spurs of the Downs come within the parish boundaries.

The village is in the north-west of the parish, and lies along the road from Brockbridge to Southwick, which here makes a sharp descent, meeting at right angles a road from Grenville Hall at the bottom of the hill. Soberton Towers, the residence of Mrs. Bashford, which is surrounded by extensive lawns and shrubberies, occupies a site on the outskirts of the village to the west of the road. At the top of the hill, by the White Lion Inn, a path runs off west from the village street to St. Peter's church, which stands some way back from the road overlooking the river valley. Further down the hill are the schools, built in 1875, and opposite them a row of villas.

66 The west wall has an external facing of brick.

67 *V.C.H. Hants*, i, 452*a*.

68 i.e. the chapel of Soberton.

69 Chart. R. 12 Edw. I, m. 5; Pat. 12 Edw. I, m. 11.

70 *Winton Epis. Reg.* (Hants Rec. Soc.), 454 and 455; *Wykeham's Reg.* (Hants Rec. Soc.), i, 220; Egerton MS. 2032, fol. 64; Inst. Bks. (P.R.O.).

71 i.e. the chapel of Soberton.

72 *Pope Nich. Tax.* (Rec. Com.), 211.

73 *Valor Eccl.* (Rec. Com.), ii, 22.

74 *Wykeham's Reg.* (Hants Rec. Soc.), ii, 537.

There are many scattered groups of houses throughout the parish, which on the whole is well populated. To the south of Brockbridge, near the railway station, are a number of new villas already built, and many more in the course of erection. East Hoe is a tithing one and a half miles south-east, near the source of a small stream which works Rudley Mill. Newtown, in the south, is an ecclesiastical parish formed in 1851 from the parishes of Soberton and Hambledon, and consisting of a large part of the West Walk of the Forest of Bere. The church of the Holy Trinity was built in 1850. The schools near by were built in 1851, and have since been enlarged. There is also a reading and recreation room, with a small library. Southend is a hamlet situated one mile north of Newtown church. The parish contains 2,526¾ acres of arable land, 1,104½ acres of permanent grass, and 1,668½ acres of woods and plantations.[1] Soberton Heath, Southend Plain, Great Down and Little Down were inclosed in 1867. The soil is chalk, clay, and loam, the sub-soil gravel, chalk, and flint. The chief crops are wheat and oats.

Among place names mentioned in records are a pourpresture called La Breche,[2] a road called Hameleway, a ford called Maslyngford[3] (fourteenth century), a messuage and lands called Awbreys, and a messuage and lands called Kyrkebrygge[4] (fifteenth century).

MANORS

At the time of the Domesday Survey there were three large estates in *SOBERTON*—one formerly part of Godwin's estates and added to the crown lands by King Harold,[5] the second formerly held by Alnod and then in the possession of Herbert the Chamberlain,[6] and the third which had belonged to Andrac and then formed part of the possessions of Henry the Treasurer.[7] Owing to later subinfeudation it is difficult to trace the subsequent history of these three estates.

The family of Clere from early times owned a manor of *SOBERTON* which was probably in origin part of the royal manor of Soberton. Ralph de Clere granted it to Jordan de Walterville, who in his turn granted it to the abbot and convent of Beaulieu to hold of him and his heirs for a rent of £12 10*s*.[8] In 1230 in the course of a dispute concerning the customs and services which Jordan owed to Ralph for his tenement in Soberton, the sheriff was commanded to take into the king's hands the rent which the abbot and convent paid to Jordan.[9] Some time later Jordan gave up to the abbot and convent all claim to this rent,[10] and his charter was confirmed by Henry III,[11] Ralph de Clere, and Roger de Clere son of Ralph.[12] The rent of £12 10*s*. shows the manor to have been a considerable one, and in course of time the property of the abbot and convent in the parish was augmented. John de Windsor in the reign of Henry III granted them 100*s*. worth of land in Soberton.[13] Again in the reign of Edward III the abbot of Beaulieu purchased a so-called manor of Soberton from Richard Bulgy who had inherited it from his grandfather Roger.[14] As early as 1229 the woods of the abbot and convent in Soberton were extensive enough to warrant the king's order to them to supply the royal navy with five hundred wickerwork baskets (*cleias*) and two hundred bridges,[15] and in 1291 their grange at Soberton was assessed at £15.[16] In 1359 the abbot and convent obtained a grant of free warren in Soberton,[17] and in 1393 the king confirmed the right of common of pasture within the Forest of Bere for the animals of their men and tenants, free and bondmen, of the town of Soberton.[18] About this time the abbot and convent formed the custom of farming out the manor. Thus in 1398 they let it out at farm to Thomas Tauk for thirty years for a rent of 24 marks. Thomas, however, allowed the buildings to fall into bad repair, and fell behindhand with his payments, owing the abbot £40 in 1404.[19] The abbot and convent thereupon re-entered the manor, and in 1411 obtained licence to lease the manor to Richard Newport and his heirs for two hundred years.[20] This lease was equivalent to a sale, as no annual payment is mentioned in the indenture. As the lease was in being at the Dissolution Soberton is not included in the possessions of Beaulieu at that date,[21] and in an inquisition on the death of Richard Newport in 1477 the manor is said to be held of the duke of Buckingham, as of his honour of Clare.[22] A John Newport of Soberton is mentioned in 1451 as owing 600 marks to John Tichborne.[23] Richard Newport, probably his son, died in 1477, leaving a son and heir John, aged twenty-three. Before his death he had conveyed the manor and other premises in Soberton to John Dale and Richard Kingsmill, probably as trustees.[24] John Newport, described as serjeant-at-law, died seised of

BEAULIEU ABBEY. *Gules a crosier enfiled with a royal crown or within a border sable billetty or.*

[1] Statistics from Bd. of Agric. (1905).

[2] Inq. p.m. 36 Edw. III, pt. 1, No. 65.

[3] Add. MS. 33284, fol. 196. Maslyngford still survives as Meslingford, a ford over the River Meon.

[4] Inq. p.m. 17 Edw. IV, No. 35.

[5] *V.C.H. Hants*, i, 451 and 452. In the time of Edward the Confessor this had been held as two manors by Godwin of the king in parage and by Leman of Godwin respectively.

[6] *V.C.H. Hants*, i, 500.

[7] Ibid.

[8] *Vide* Assize R. Mich. 8 Edw. I. Walterville is also spelt Walkyville (*Rot. Lit. Claus.* i, 180).

[9] Close, 13 Hen. III, m. 5 *d.*; *Bracton's Note Bk.* 468.

[10] Harl. MS. 6603, fol. 277.

[11] Ibid. fol. 266.

[12] Ibid. fol. 278 and 279. Ralph de Clere was one of the barons who opposed King John. He forfeited his lands in Hampshire, including Lasham and Greatham, and in 1216 Henry Belet was commanded not to receive him into the king's peace until further orders (*Rot. Lit. Claus.* i, 42, 235, 242 and 250). He was restored to favour by Henry III, who in 1217 ordered Fulk de Breauté to give him full seisin of all the lands he possessed when he withdrew from allegiance to King John (ibid. 310). He is probably identical with the Ralph de Clere who was a benfactor to the nunnery of Geddingham (co. Yorks), for this Ralph likewise had a son and heir Roger (Dugdale, *Mon.* iv. 273).

[13] *Vide* Assize R. Mich. 8 Edw. I.

[14] Inq. p.m. 11 Ric. II, No. 6. He may have been the Richard Bulgy who was excommunicated in 1369 at the instance of John the abbot of Beaulieu (*Wykeham's Reg.* ii, 102).

[15] Close, 13 Hen. III, m. 5 *d.*

[16] *Pope Nich. Tax.* (Rec. Com.), 214.

[17] Chart. R. 33 Edw. III, m. 3.

[18] Ibid. 17 Ric. II, m. 19.

[19] De Banc. R. Trin. 4 Hen. IV, m. 181, and Hil. 5 Hen. IV, m. 107.

[20] Pat. 12 Hen. IV, m. 29.

[21] Mins. Accts. Hants, 29 & 30 Hen. VIII, rot. 113.

[22] Chan. Inq. p.m. 17 Edw. IV, No. 35.

[23] Close, 29 Hen. VI, m. 15 *d.*

[24] Chan. Inq. p.m. 17 Edw. IV, No. 35.

the manor in 1521 leaving no issue.[25] His widow Elizabeth, who died six years later, directed that her body should be buried in the chapel of Our Lady in Soberton church beside that of her husband. She left half a hundred sheep and two kine and ten marks in money to the parish church of Soberton, and 3*s.* 4*d.* to each of her tenants in Soberton, and ordered her executors to dispose of the rest of her property at their discretion.[26] In 1544 William Dale,[27] probably a trustee, conveyed the manor of Soberton together with the manors of Longspiers, Flexland, and Englefield, also in the parish, to Walter Bonham and Alice his wife,[28] who five years later sold them to Thomas Wriothesley, earl of Southampton.[29] The earl died seised a year later, leaving a son and heir Henry, aged three,[30] who died in 1581, his heir being his son Henry, aged eight.[31] The latter towards the end of Elizabeth's reign was drawn into the conspiracy of the earl of Essex, on the failure of which he was sent to the Tower. On 19 February, 1600–1, he was with Essex convicted of treason. Cecil, however, secured the commutation of his sentence to imprisonment for life, pleading that 'the poor young Earl merely for love of Essex had been drawn into this action.' He was sent to the Tower, but was released by James I on 10 April, 1603. On 16 May following the king restored to him the manor of Soberton,[32] four years later granting to him free warren, view of frankpledge, assize of bread and beer, waifs and estrays, and various other privileges within it.[33] The earl died on the king's service abroad in 1624,[34] leaving as his heir his son Thomas, aged sixteen,[35] who dealt with the manor by fine in 1641.[36] Within the next few years Soberton passed by sale to Dr. Walter Curll, bishop of Winchester, who retired thither after the surrender of Winchester to Cromwell on 5 October, 1645. 'He led a retired life there in a sort of obscurity for a year and a half or thereabouts in a declining state of health. He was brought up to London for advice, but died 1647 about seventy-two.'[37] After his death the manor was sequestered, and in 1651 Elizabeth Curll his widow and William Curll his son and heir petitioned for its discharge.[38] It was subsequently restored to them and descended to Sir Walter Curll, bart., son and heir of William, who dealt with it by fine and recovery in 1674.[39] He died in 1678, aged twenty-seven. His daughter and heir Anna Maria married Thomas Lewis son of Richard Lewis and grandson of Sir Edward Lewis of an ancient family of The Van in Glamorganshire, and brought the manor to her husband,[40] who retained it after her death without issue in 1709,[41] until his own death in 1736. The history of the manor for some time after this is uncertain, but it ultimately passed into the possession of Humphrey Minchin of Ballinakill (co. Tipperary) and Clarinda his wife, who dealt with it by fine and recovery in 1791.[42] It has remained in the Minchin family ever since, the present lord of the manor being Mr. Falkiner John Minchin of Annagh (co. Tipperary) and Holywell in Hampshire.

CURLL. *Vert a cheveron engrailed or.*

LEWIS of The Van. *Sable a lion argent.*

MINCHIN. *Ermine a cheveron with couple-closes gules between three fleurs de lis azure.*

A large part of the manor of *SOBERTON*, which had been held by Herbert the Chamberlain in 1086, was in the time of Henry III held by Thomas de Windsor by the serjeanty of weighing the money at the Exchequer.[43] He was succeeded by his son John, who alienated his property at Soberton, granting 100*s.* worth of land to the abbot and convent of Beaulieu and the remainder which was worth £10 a year to Geoffrey de Chaworth.[44] Geoffrey in his turn alienated to Richard son of Simon de Winton,[45] who died seised of a capital messuage, 120 acres of

25 P.C.C. Wills, 22, Maynwaryng.
26 Ibid. 19 Porch.
27 He may have been a son of the John Dale mentioned above.
28 Feet of F. Hants, East. 36 Hen. VIII.
29 Ibid. Trin. 3 Edw. VI; Close, 3 Edw. VI, pt. 2, m. 13.
30 W. and L. Inq. p.m. (Ser. 2), vol. 5, No. 103. The earl died in debt to Henry VIII. Consequently some of his possessions, including Soberton, were taken into the hands of the crown and in 1555 were let out at farm to Jane, countess of Southampton, to hold by the annual payment of £40 until the debts were paid in full (Pat. 2 & 3 Mary, pt. 4, m. 35; Memo. R. L.T.R. Hil. 4 Eliz. rot. 74).
31 Chan. Inq. p.m. (Ser. 2), vol. 196, No. 46. Elizabeth granted Soberton to the notorious 'fishing grantees' William Typper and Robert Dawe to hold during the minority of the heir (Pat. 30 Eliz. pt. 16, m. 17; 34 Eliz. pt. 7, m. 1).
32 Pat. 1 Jas. I, pt. 2, last m.
33 Ibid. 5 Jas. I, pt. 15, last m.
34 W. and L. Inq. p.m. (Ser. 2), bdle. 41, No. 120.
35 In 1625 the king granted the manor to Elizabeth, countess of Southampton, to hold during the minority of the heir (Rymer, *Foed.* xviii, 199, 200).
36 In that year he conveyed it to William Carter and Robert Crues.
37 Edmund Curll, *Life of Dr. Walter Curll* (1712), 8.
38 *Cal. of Committee for Compounding*, iv, 2883 and 2884. The county committee in 1655 reported that the manor was sequestered as the estate of Dr. Curll, that he contracted for it on 14 January, 1647, at £60 rent and died the following April, and that it had never been compounded for. Elizabeth and William denied this, declared that it was not sequestered until 1651, and begged their discharge anew under the act of pardon.
39 Recov. R. Hil. 26 & 27 Chas. II, m. 4.
40 Stowe MS. 845, fol. 71.
41 On a tablet to her memory in Soberton church are the words 'reverendo edita proavo (Carolo primo imperante) Wintoniensi episcopo et ad proavi exemplum ecclesiae Anglicanae et monarchiae fidelis et amantissima, que omnibus pietatis et charitatis officiis perfuncta morti nunquam magis invidendae succubuit.'
42 Feet of F. Hants, Trin. 31 Geo. III; Recov. R. Hil. 31 Geo. III, rot. 57. Humphrey was the son of Paul Minchin of Bogh (co. Carlow).
43 *V.C.H. Hants*, i, 431; *Testa de Nevill* (Rec. Com.), 233, 235.
44 Assize R. Mich. 8 Edw. I.
45 Ibid. Simon, usually called Simon the draper of Winchester, possessed 28½ acres in Soberton, consisting of all the land of Richard Ulfus and all the land of John Colesuen. This property had been held by the abbot and convent of Dureford (co. Suss.) of the abbot and convent of Beaulieu by suit of court, and was granted to Simon by John, abbot of Dureford, for a rent of a pound of frankincense in exchange for his tenement in 'St. Giles's Fair,' Winchester, free from suit of court and all other services and demands. The abbot and convent of Beaulieu, however, claimed suit of court, and Simon accordingly agreed to pay them 1*s.* 2*d.* a year in lieu thereof. He naturally claimed compensation from the abbot and convent of Dureford, and was successful in obtaining a promise from them to pay him 2*s.* a year (Cott. MS. Vesp. E, fol. 1, 2, 3).

arable land, 6 acres of meadow, wood worth 5*s.* a year, pasture worth £1 a year, £2 8*s.* 7½*d.* rents of assize and 2*s.* pleas and perquisites of court in Soberton in 1296, leaving a son and heir Richard, aged fourteen.[46] Richard de Winton was holding the manor in 1316.[47] He was succeeded by Sir John de Winton, probably his son, who died seised of the manor of Soberton in 1361, his heir being his brother Richard, aged forty.[48] Richard became involved in financial difficulties, owing Hugh Craan, citizen and merchant of Winchester, no less than £100 in 1377.[49] In 1383 he raised £200 on the manors of Soberton and Lainston,[50] but apparently this was not enough to satisfy his creditors, and nine months later he was ordered to be imprisoned and his property valued in order that his debts might be paid.[51] He died, however, the same year and immediately afterwards his widow Agnes married Nicholas Brus.[52] Nicholas and Agnes dealt with the manor by fine in 1384.[53] The history of this manor cannot be traced further, unless it is identical with that called the manor of Longspiers in later times or that held by the Fawconer family in the fifteenth, sixteenth, and seventeenth centuries (q.v. *infra*).

Herbert the Chamberlain seems to have granted a portion of his manor of Soberton to his daughter on the occasion of her marriage with Robert de Venuz.[54] At the beginning of the thirteenth century this portion, which was then called the manor of *FLEXLAND* (Flexland Cobham xiv cent. ; Englefield *alias* Inglefield xvi cent.), was held by Robert de Venuz grandson of Robert de Venuz by the service of acting as marshal in the king's household.[55] Robert the grandson must have died before 1219, for in that year his widow Constance quitclaimed to her son John the third part of 100*s.* rents in Soberton, which she was holding in dower, in exchange for 60*s.* rents in Worldham and Draycote.[56] John de Venuz died without issue and was succeeded by his brother Thomas,[56a] whose daughter Agnes in 1249 granted one carucate of land in Flexland and Soberton to William de Cobham,[57] to be held by the rent of a pair of white gloves or 1*d.* at Easter.[58] In the same year William purchased 5 acres of land and 12*d.* rent in Flexland from William le Waleys and Beatrice his wife.[59] In 1281 his daughter Joan de Heigham[60] quitclaimed the manor of Flexland to Agnes de Cobham to hold for life by the rent of a chaplet of roses.[61] Philip de Hoyville and Mary his wife, who was probably Joan's sister, at the same time brought forward their claim to the manor,[62] and seem to have been successful in establishing their right, for Mary de Hoyville, who was by this time a widow, was holding land in the parish in 1316.[63] Nine years later she granted the reversion of two-thirds of a messuage, 2½ carucates of land, and a pound of pepper in Flexland and Soberton, after the death of Thomas de Hoyville, to Roger son of Roger de Englefield,[64] who some twenty years afterwards obtained licence from William de Edendon, bishop of Winchester, to celebrate mass in the oratory of his dwelling-house of Flexland.[65] He died in 1361 seised of 20 acres in Flexland held of the king, a messuage, a carucate of land, rents of assize and pleas and perquisites of court in Flexland Cobham, held of Sir Maurice le Bruyn[66] as of his manor of Russell Flexland for 2*s.* a year, and a cottage and an acre of land in Flexland Cobham held of the abbot of Beaulieu by the rent of a quarter of a pound of pepper.[67] Sir Maurice le Bruyn granted the custody of his lands in Flexland Cobham by the name of 'the third part of the manor of Flexland Cobham'[68] to Geoffrey Dene of Chidden to hold during the minority of the son and heir Roger. Constance widow of Roger, notwithstanding this grant, forcibly ejected Geoffrey and was prosecuted by him for so doing in 1364.[69] This seems to be the last mention of the manor of Flexland Cobham, its name being afterwards changed to Englefield *alias* Inglefield. Its history for some time after this is obscure,[70] the next mention of it being in 1544, when it was purchased by Walter Bonham and Alice his wife from William Dale.[71] Its subsequent history is identical with that of the manor of Soberton originally belonging to the abbot and convent of Beaulieu (q.v. *supra*). It is represented at the present day by Ingoldfield Farm in the centre of the parish.

[46] Inq. p.m. 24 Edw. I. No. 21 ; in the inquisition it was stated that the lands were held of Simon de Winton by the service of one clove annually at the feast of St. Michael and one pair of gauntlets or 1*d.* annually at Easter to the heirs of John de Windsor.

[47] *Feud. Aids*, ii, 307.

[48] Inq. p.m. 36 Edw. III, pt. 2, (1st Nos.), No. 78.

[49] Ibid. 7 Ric. II, No. 107.

[50] Feet of F. Hants, Hil. 6 Ric. II.

[51] Inq. p.m. 7 Ric. II, No. 107 ; the property in Soberton was valued as follows: capital messuage 6*d.* ; rents of freemen and villeins £3 6*s.* 8*d.*; water-mill 13*s.* 4*d.*; 6 acres of meadow 6*s.*; 4 acres of arable land 1*s.* ; pasture for sheep 10*s.*; 10 acres of underwood, 2 acres of which can be sold yearly for 2*s.*

[52] In the same year the manor was settled on them for life with reversion to Richard, son and heir of Richard de Winton and Agnes for life, with remainder to Agnes and her heirs and assigns (Close, 7 Ric. II, m. 31 *d.*).

[53] They conveyed it to Thomas Wolvele and John King, chaplain (Feet of F. Hants, Hil. 7 Ric. II.)

[54] *V.C.H. Hants*, i, 425.

[55] *Testa de Nevill* (Rec. Com.), 235.

[56] Feet of F. Hants, 3 Hen. III.

[56a] *The Herald and Genealogist*, v, 321.

[57] William de Cobham already at the beginning of the thirteenth century was holding the fourth part of a knight's fee in Flexland *de veteri feoffamento* of Robert de Pont de l'Arche, who in his turn held of John de Venuz (*Testa de Nevill*, 233), but this portion afterwards fell into the hands of the abbot and convent of Titchfield (Harl. MS. 6602, fol. 59).

[58] Feet of F. Hants, Hil. 33 Hen. III.

[59] Ibid.

[60] *Coll. Top. et Gen.* vii, 336.

[61] Feet of F. Hants, Hil. 9 Edw. I.

[62] Ibid. 'Philippus de Hoyvile pro se et Maria uxore eius apponit clamum suum.'

[63] *Feud. Aids*, ii, 307.

[64] Feet of F. Hants, Mich. 19 Edw. II. The family of Hoyville was probably so named from a small place in Normandy, and had a permanent footing at St. Swithun's, Winchester, from early times (*Obedientiary Rolls of St. Swithun's*, 248). Roger son of Roger de Englefield was probably a kinsman of Mary de Hoyville, for in an almoner's roll of St. Swithun's of 1352 Philip de Englefield is called brother of Thomas de Hoyville. On the same roll there is also mention of a Roger de Englefield (ibid. 253). Philip de Hoyville, probably identical with Philip de Englefield, rented three tenements in Kingsgate Street, Winchester, from St. Swithun's (ibid. 408, 410), to this day called Hoyvil's Garden. The site is on the west side of the street, not far from Culver's Close.

[65] Egerton MS. 2033 (Register of Edendon, bishop of Winchester, 1346–66), fol. 57.

[66] Sir Maurice le Bruyn was at this time lord of the manor of Russell Flexland in right of his wife Margaret (q.v. *infra*).

[67] Inq. p.m. 36 Edw. III, pt. 1, No. 65.

[68] It was roughly the third part of the premises owned by Mary de Hoyville, which are described in 1325 as one messuage, 2½ carucates of land, and a pound of pepper (Feet of F. Hants, Mich. 19 Edw. II).

[69] De Banc. R. East. 37 Edw. III, m. 228.

[70] It may have become merged with the manor of Russell Flexland (q.v. *infra*), or it may possibly be identical with the manor of Soberton purchased by the abbot of Beaulieu from Richard Bulgy towards the end of the reign of Edw. III.

[71] Feet of F. Hants, East. 36 Hen. VIII.

The Wallop family, from very early times, had a manor in this parish, later known as *WALLOP'S MANOR*, probably in origin the manor which Henry the Treasurer held at the time of the Domesday Survey.[72] In the reign of Henry III it was held *de veteri feoffamento* of Herbert Fitz Peter, who held it of the abbot of Hyde,[73] but in later times it was held of the bishop of Winchester,[74] and it is most probable that the overlordship changed hands in 1332, when a certain William de Hattingley gave up all his right in the manor to John de Stratford, bishop of Winchester.[75] Richard de Wallop, who held the manor in the reign of Henry III,[76] recovered 40*s.* from the abbot and convent of Beaulieu for the damage done to the manor during the time they held it at farm of him, his father John, and his mother Mabel.[77] He died without issue, and was succeeded by his brother Sir Robert Wallop, who also died childless, when the manor passed to his nephew William Burton *alias* Wallop.[78] Richard Wallop son of the latter is mentioned in 1346 as holding the fourth part of a knight's fee in Soberton formerly belonging to Euphemia de Wallop.[79] Thomas Wallop son of Richard died in 1362 seised of a messuage, a carucate of land, 20*s.* rents of assize, and 12*d.* pleas and perquisites of court in Soberton held of Edward de St. John as of his manor of Wolverton by the service of the fourth part of one knight's fee, of 25 acres in Soberton held of the king by the rent of 8*s.* 4*d.* to the sheriff at Winchester Castle, and of meadow-lands in Soberton held of Isabel Wayte by the rent of 2*s.*[80] His heir was his son John, aged eight, but Soberton for a considerable time seems to have been held in dower by Margaret widow of Thomas, who probably married, as her second husband, William Vachell.[81] However, it ultimately reverted to the Wallop family, John grandson of John Wallop dying seised of it in 1486.[82] His heir was his son Richard, aged thirty and more, who died seised of Soberton manor, held by the bishop of Winchester, in 1503, leaving a brother and heir Robert.[83] On the death of the latter without issue in 1535 the manor passed to his brother Stephen. Henry, Stephen's grandson, dealt with Soberton by recovery in 1566,[84] but does not seem to have been seised of it at his death in 1599.[85] However, in 1616 his son Sir Henry Wallop obtained a grant of free warren, court-leet, and view of frankpledge within his manor of Soberton.[86] On Henry's death, in 1642, Soberton passed to his son Robert, who, as one of the judges at the trial of King Charles I, was excepted by Parliament at the Restoration from receiving any benefit from his estates, and was sentenced to be drawn upon a sledge to and under the gallows of Tyburn with a halter round his neck, and to be imprisoned for life.[87] This sentence was carried out on 30 January, 1662. In 1661 the king had granted Robert Wallop's property in Soberton to Thomas earl of Southampton, Anthony Ashley Lord Ashley, Sir Orlando Bridgeman, and Sir Henry Vernon, and had empowered them to sell the whole or part of the premises for the advantage and preferment of Lady Anne, sister of the earl of Southampton and wife of Robert Wallop, and Henry Wallop their son and heir.[88] The manor of Soberton was sold, and was probably purchased by the lord of the main manor of Soberton, who was adding to his property in the parish at the beginning of the eighteenth century.[89] The site of the manor is marked by Wallopswood Farm in the extreme east of the parish.

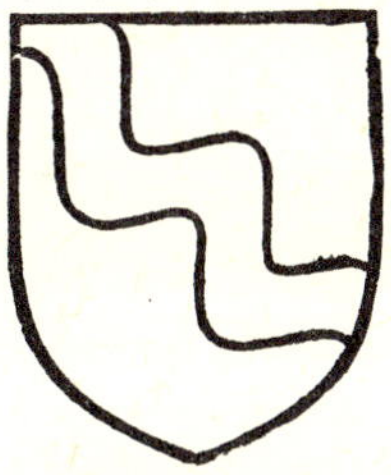

WALLOP. *Argent a bend wavy sable.*

The abbot and convent of Titchfield also had a manor in *FLEXLAND* and *SOBERTON* consisting of lands granted to them at various times. Thus John de Windsor in the reign of Henry III gave them 10*s.* rents in Soberton.[90] Again, Peter des Roches bishop of Winchester granted them various lands in Flexland in free alms,[91] and they also acquired the fourth part of a knight's fee which William de Cobham was holding in the reign of Henry III 'of the old enfeoffment' of Robert de Pont de l'Arche, who held it of John Venuz.[92] The abbot and convent entered on some of these lands without licence, and in the reign of Edward I their property in Flexland escheated to the crown,[93] but was ultimately restored. In 1381 it consisted of a messuage, 12 acres of pasture in severalty, 70 acres of pasture in common, 1 acre of wood in severalty, and 100 acres of wood in common, and was worth 10*s.* 6½*d.* by the year.[94] John Wayte of Titchfield seems to have purchased the manor in the reign of Henry VIII or even earlier, for the abbot and convent were certainly not seised of any property in the parish at the time of the Dissolution.[95] He granted a lease of it by the name of the manor of Soberton to Arthur Plantagenet, Viscount Lisle, in 1528,[96] and there are many references to it in Lisle's correspondence.[97] It was finally bought by Walter Bonham,[98] and passed from him to

72 Both Soberton and Eastleigh in South Stoneham were held by Henry the Treasurer at the time of the Domesday Survey, and of Herbert Fitz Peter in the reign of Hen. III, seemingly following the same descent. The Henry de Soberton son of Henry mentioned in 1166 as holding one knight's fee, whereas his father had held five, may have been a descendant of Henry the Treasurer (*Red Bk. of Exch.* i, 206.)

73 *Testa de Nevill* (Rec. Com.), 232.

74 Chan. Inq. p.m. (Ser. 2), vol. 2, No. 31; and vol. 17, No. 31.

75 Feet of F. Hants, Hil. 5 Edw. III. In 1363 the manor is described as held of Edward de St. John as of his manor of Wolverton by the service of a fourth part of a knight's fee (Inq. p.m. 36 Edw. III, pt. 2 [1st Nos.], No. 76), but this may be an error.

76 *Testa de Nevill*, 232.

77 Harl. MSS. 6603, fol. 292.

78 Berry, *Hants Gen.* 41. The sister and heir of Sir Robert Wallop married Peter Burton of West Burton (co. Hants).

79 *Feud. Aids*, ii, 336.

80 Inq. p.m. 36 Edw. III, pt. 2 (1st Nos.), No. 76.

81 In 1428 William Vachell and Margaret his wife were holding in Soberton the fourth part of a knight's fee which Richard Wallop formerly held (*Feud. Aids*, ii, 358). The name of Thomas Wallop's wife was Margaret (Edmondson, *Baronagium Genealogicum*, iii, 247).

82 Chan. Inq. p.m. (Ser. 2), vol. 2, No. 31. 83 Ibid. vol. 17, No. 31.

84 Com. Pleas, Hil. 9 Eliz. m. 113.

85 Chan. Inq. p.m. (Ser. 2), vol. 256, No. 6.

86 Pat. 14 Jas. I, pt. 25, m. 24.

87 *Statutes of the Realm*, v, 317, 318.

88 Pat. 13 Chas. II, pt. 20, No. 10.

89 Feet of F. Hants, Hil. Anne; and Mich. 1 Geo. I.

90 Assize R. Mich. 8 Edw. I.

91 Harl. MS. 6602, fol. 3.

92 Ibid. fol. 59.

93 Close, 9 Edw. I, m. 8 and 9.

94 Add. MS. 33284, fol. 196.

95 Mins. Accts. Hants, 30 & 31 Hen. VIII, m. 135.

96 Close, 20 Hen. VIII, m. 20 and 35; Feet of F. Hants, Mich. 20 Hen. VIII; Trin. 22 Hen. VIII.

97 *L. and P. Hen. VIII passim.*

98 He demurred much over the price. *L. and P. Hen. VIII*, xiii (1), 158, 299, 332, 338, and 343 (2), 165, 188, 256 and 370; xiv (1), 453 and 456.

Thomas Wriothesley earl of Southampton in 1549.[99] It has since followed the same descent as the manor of Soberton originally owned by the abbot and convent of Beaulieu (q.v.).

The manor of *FLEXLAND* or *RUSSELL FLEXLAND* was in origin a sub-manor dependent on the manor of Soberton belonging to the abbot and convent of Beaulieu, and as late as 1462 was said to be held of the abbot and convent by the rent of a pound of pepper.[100] At the close of the thirteenth century the manor was held by Ralph Russell, who, with the consent of Martha his wife, granted to the abbey six acres of land which he held of it in Soberton.[101] He seems to have been succeeded by Geoffrey Russell, whose lands in Flexland of the annual value of four marks three shillings were forfeited for his rebellion towards the close of the reign of Henry III.[102] The Russells, however, must have ultimately regained possession of their property in Flexland, for in 1308 John Russell, son and heir of Sir William Russell, released to Sir John de Drokensford, bishop of Bath and Wells (1309–29), all his right in a messuageand lands in Flexland and in all other lands in Hampshire that his mother Alice was holding in dower of his inheritance.[103] On the death of Sir John de Drokensford, Russell Flexland passed to his brother Philip.[104] Philip de Drokensford, son and heir of the latter, died in 1355, leaving a son and heir John, who seems to have died a year or two afterwards without issue.[105]

In 1371 Walter de Mildecombe and Margaret his wife dealt by fine with half the manor which Sir Maurice le Bruyn and Margaret his wife were then holding for the life of Margaret.[106] It is possible that Margaret wife of Sir Maurice le Bruyn was the widow of John de Drokensford, as she held the moiety for life only, but it is more probable that she was sister and heir of John,[107] and that the moieties of the manor were entailed upon her daughters and co-heirs by a former husband, John de Clyvedon,[108] viz. (1) Margaret wife of Walter de Mildecombe, and (2) Margaret who married first John St. Loe and second Sir Peter Courtenay, seventh son of Hugh de Courtenay, earl of Devon.[109] If such was the case, Margaret wife of Walter de Mildecombe probably died without issue, for Sir Peter Courtenay at his death, in 1405, was seised of the whole manor in right of his wife Margaret.[110] On her death some years later, Flexland passed to her grandson William, Lord Botreaux,[111] son and heir of William, Lord Botreaux, and her daughter Elizabeth.[112] He died in 1462 seised of the manor of Flexland, together with the hamlet of Soberton, parcel of the manor.[113] His heir was his daughter Margaret, widow of Sir Robert Hungerford, who after her father's death usually styled herself Margaret, Lady Botreaux. She afterwards married Sir Thomas Burgh, and joined with him in 1464 in granting the manor of Flexland to John Mervyn,[114] who was one of her confidential friends, trustees, and general managers,[115] while the next year she conveyed a messuage, 100 acres of land, 8 acres of meadow, 80 acres of pasture, 20 acres of wood, and 40*s.* rent in Flexland Russell and Soberton to other trustees.[116] Soon afterwards the manor was settled on William Warbleton and Margery his wife in fee-tail, with contingent remainder to Elizabeth Syfrewast, aunt of William, for life, with remainder in fee-tail to Agnes wife of Miles Skulle and daughter of Elizabeth, with contingent remainder to Margaret Breknok wife of David Breknok, and Sybil widow of Thomas Rykys, sisters of Agnes.[117] William died seised of the manor in 1469, the following being returned as his heirs—(1) his cousin Henry Puttenham son and heir of his aunt Margaret Puttenham, aged sixty and more, (2) his cousins Margaret Breknok and Sybil Rykys, aged forty and more, and thirty-six and more, respectively, and (3) his second cousin William Skulle son and heir of his cousin Agnes Skulle, aged thirty and more.[118] In accordance with the settlement Flexland descended to William Skulle, who was seised of it in 1484.[119] The history of the manor for some time after this is obscure, but it eventually fell into the hands of William Dale, who conveyed it with the other Soberton manors to Walter Bonham and Alice his wife,[120] who in their turn sold it to Thomas Wriothesley, earl of Southampton, in 1549.[121] Since this date its descent has been identical with that of the chief manor of Soberton (q.v. *supra*). The site of the manor is marked by Russell's Farm and Russell's Wood in the east of the parish.

The early history of the manor of *LONGSPIERS* or *LONGSPERYS* is obscure, unless it is identical with the manor of Soberton owned by the De Winton family in the thirteenth and fourteenth centuries. The first mention of it, though under a different name, is in 1474, when John Horewood was said to have held four marks rent in Candover of Thomas Langford as of his manor of Soberton by the service of 1*d.* a year.[122] Thomas died seised of the manor in 1494, leaving a son and heir John,[123] who nine years later sold it by the name of the manor of Longsperys, with

[99] Feet of F. Hants, Trin. 3 Edw. VI.
[100] Inq. p.m. 2 Edw. IV, No. 15.
[101] Harl. MS. 6603, fol. 284.
[102] Chan. Inq. Misc. file 21, No. 12.
[103] Close, 2 Edw. II, m. 18*d.*
[104] *Vide* Meonstoke Ferrand. [105] Ibid.
[106] Feet of F. Hants, Hil. 45 Edw. III.
[107] Most authorities state that William le Bruyn and his son and heir Maurice le Bruyn married respectively Iseult daughter and heir of Philip Rokesle, and Maud daughter and heir of Philip Rokesle. This seems unlikely, and 'Margaret daughter and heir of Philip de Drokensford' seems a plausible emendation for 'Maud daughter and heir of Philip Rokesle,' especially as Drokensford is sometimes spelt Throkkelsford.
[108] The manor of Meonstoke Ferrand cannot have been thus entailed, for, as has been shown above, Maurice le Bruyn and Margaret his wife sold it in 1357.
[109] Jewer, *Wells Cathedral*, 293; *Misc. Gen. et Heraldica* (2nd Ser.), ii, 314.
[110] Inq. p.m. 6 Hen. IV, No. 38.
[111] In 1417 Richard Kayton released to William, Lord Botreaux, all right in half the manor of Flexland, which he had lately held, in conjunction with Nicholas bishop of Bath and Wells and others, of the gift and enfeoffment of William (Close, 5 Hen. V, m. 14).
[112] Jewer, *Wells Cathedral*, 293. Elizabeth was her daughter and heir by her first husband John St. Loe.
[113] Inq. p.m. 2 Edw. IV, No. 15; the manor in 1431 comprised 7 messuages and 2 carucates of land (*Feud. Aids*, ii, 372).
[114] Feet of F. Div. Cos. Mich. 4 Edw. IV.
[115] According to Vincent's pedigree, John Mervyn was the husband of Joan, either daughter or granddaughter of Margaret (*Misc. Gen. et Heraldica* [New Ser.], i, 358), but this statement cannot be relied on implicitly (Sir William Drake, *Fasciculus Merviniensis*, 4).
[116] Feet of F. Hants, Trin. 5 Edw. IV.
[117] Of the gift and enfeoffment of William Brocas, jun., and John Brawe, rector of St. Leonards, Sherfield.
[118] Inq. p.m. 8 Edw. IV, No. 44; by his will he left 3*s.* 4*d.* to the church of Soberton (P.C.C. will 19 Godyn).
[119] De Banc. R. Mich. 2 Ric. III, m. 328.
[120] Feet of F. Hants, East. 36 Hen. VIII.
[121] Ibid. Trin. 3 Edw. VI.
[122] Inq. p.m. 14 Edw. IV, No. 28; Thomas had inherited it from his father Edward (Chan. Inq. p.m. (Ser. 2), vol. 9, No. 66).
[123] Chan. Inq. p.m. (Ser. 2), vol. 9, No. 66; he was a member of a Hertfordshire family (Clutterbuck, *Herts.* iii, 33).

lands in Soberton and Flexland, to John Newport of Soberton.[124] From this time its history has been identical with that of the chief manor of Soberton (q.v. *supra*).

The Fawconers also in the fifteenth, sixteenth, and seventeenth centuries, possessed a manor of *SOBERTON*,[125] the early history of which is uncertain unless it is identical with that owned by the de Wintons in the thirteenth and fourteenth centuries. It seems to have been finally purchased by Thomas Lewis, lord of the chief manor of Soberton, probably in 1714, since in that year Anne Goldsmith, widow, and William Goldsmith sold him a manor of Soberton for £400.[126] In a recovery roll of 1791, by which Humphrey Minchin dealt with his property in Soberton, it appears as the manor of Faulkner's Pleck or Pluk,[127] but this name seems to have now disappeared.

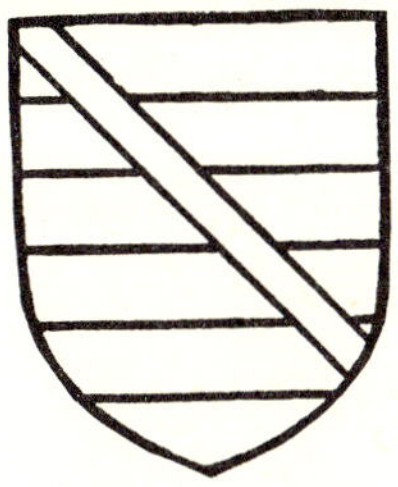

Poynings. *Barry or and vert with a baston gules.*

In the reign of Edward the Confessor the manor of *EAST HOE* (Hou, xi cent.; Hoo, xiii cent.; Hooe, xvi cent.) was held by Ulward of King Edward, but at the time of the Domesday Survey it was one of the possessions of Hugh de Port, who did not, however, keep it in his own hands, but farmed it out.[128] The manor continued with the heirs of the Ports, passing by inheritance to the Poynings family,[129] until Thomas de Poynings confirmed the grant made by Bernard Brocas to Southwick Priory in 1385.[130] It was held of the Ports and the Poynings by the Mohuns,[131] and of the Mohuns in the twelfth and thirteenth centuries by a family who took the surname of Hoe. In 1167 the manor was held of the Mohuns by Robert de Hoe.[132] Some time later William de Hoe was lord of the manor,[133] and his son and heir, Roger, in 1280 was holding half a knight's fee in East Hoe of John de Mohun.[134] Roger's daughter and heir married Sir Hugh des Roches, and brought the manor into the family of des Roches.[135] Sir Hugh des Roches was succeeded by his son and heir John, who in 1300 granted half the manor for life to Roger Launcelevee and Joan his wife in exchange for those tenements in Broxhead which Roger de Hoe, grandfather of John, once held.[136] Two years afterwards John confirmed that half of the manor to Roger and Joan for a rent of one rose annually at the feast of St. John the Baptist.[137] Evidently Roger and Joan both died before John, since at the time of his death in 1311 he was seised of the whole manor, which he held, according to the inquisition, of Richard de Boarhunt for half a knight's fee.[138] His son and heir John settled the manor a few years later upon himself and his wife Joan, in tail-male.[139] John died before 1346, in which year his widow Joan was in possession.[140] On the death of Joan in 1361 it passed to her daughter and heir Mary widow of John de Boarhunt.[141] Mary married, as her second husband, Sir Bernard Brocas, and hence, in the autumn of 1361, the manor was settled on Mary and Bernard and their issue, with contingent remainder to the right heirs of Bernard.[142] In 1363 Bernard obtained a grant of free warren in the demesne lands of his manor of East Hoe.[143] Twenty-two years later he granted the manor to the prior and convent of Southwick for celebrating divine service daily for the good estate of the king, the said Bernard, and Katherine his wife while living, and for their souls after death, and for the souls of the late king, Mary the late wife of Bernard, and the parents and ancestors of Bernard and Mary.[144] The manor continued to be the property of the prior and convent until the Dissolution,[145] when it was granted by Henry VIII to Thomas Knight.[146] It continued in the family of Knight until 1619,[147] when Andrew Knight and his mother, Joan Knight, widow, sold it to William Browne, senior, of Hoe, and William

Roches. *Sable two leopards or.*

Boarhunt. *Argent a fesse between six martlets gules.*

Brocas. *Sable a leopard rampant or.*

[124] Feet of F. Hants, East. 18 Hen. VII.

[125] In 1477 Richard Newport held a messuage and a virgate of land called Kyrkebrygge in the parish of Soberton of William Fawconer by the rent of 6*d.* (Inq. p.m. 17 Edw. IV, No. 35). In 1564 and 1567 William Fawconer dealt with the manor of Soberton by fine (Feet of F. Hants, Trin. 6 Eliz. and Div. Cos. Hil. 9 Eliz.); again, in 1635 William Fawconer conveyed it to John Trahearn (Feet of F. Hants, East. 11 Chas. I).

[126] Feet of F. Hants, Mich. 1 Geo. I.

[127] Recov. R. Hil. 31 Geo. III, rot. 57.

[128] *V.C.H. Hants*, i, 481*a*.

[129] *Testa de Nevill* (Rec. Com.), 230; Inq. p.m. 3 Edw. III, No. 67.

[130] Add. MS. 33280, fol. 280.

[131] At the beginning of the thirteenth century Reginald de Mohun held the manor of Robert de St. John (*Testa de Nevill*, 230); it occurs in a list of knights' fees belonging to John de Mohun, who died in 1279 (Inq. p.m. 7 Edw. I, No. 13); Joan de Mohun granted licence to alienate the manor 'which is held of us' to Southwick Priory in 1385 (Add. MS. 33280, fol. 280).

[132] Pipe R. 13 Hen. II.

[133] Add. MS. 33285, fol. 175.

[134] Inq. p.m. 7 Edw. I, No. 13.

[135] Montagu Burrows, *The Family of Brocas of Beaurepaire*, 323.

[136] Ibid. 339 (being a transcript of No. 212 of the Brocas deeds).

[137] Feet of F. Hants, 30 Edw. I, No. 238.

[138] Inq. a.q.d. file 92, No. 3; Inq. p.m. 5 Edw. II, No. 44. In the inquisition on his death, the manor was said to owe suit to the king's hundred-court of Meonstoke every three weeks.

[139] Add. MS. 33280, fol. 286; contingent remainders were to John de Boarhunt and Mary his wife in fee-tail, to Henry Bouyn and Alice his wife in fee-tail, and finally to the right heirs of John des Roches.

[140] *Feud. Aids*, ii, 336.

[141] Inq. p.m. 35 Edw. III, pt. 2, No. 49.

[142] Feet of F. Hants, Mich. 35 Edw. III.

[143] Chart. R. 37 Edw. III, m. 11.

[144] Inq. a.q.d. 7 Ric. II, No. 137; Feet of F. Div. Cos. Hil. 7 Ric. II; Pat. 8 Ric. II, pt. 1, m. 36; Add. MS. 33280, fol. 280. Some time after this the prior and convent granted the manor to Bernard for life by the annual payment of £2 10*s.* 4*d.* (Add. MS. 33280, fol. 280).

[145] *Feud. Aids*, ii, 358; Chart. R. 24 Hen. VI, No. 17.

[146] Pat. 35 Hen. VIII, pt. 9, m. 33.

[147] Exch. Inq. p.m. (Ser. 2), file 994, No. 3; Chan. Inq. p.m. 2 Eliz. pt. 2 (Ser. 2), No. 74; Memo. R. L.T.R. Hil. 5 Eliz. rot. 19; Chan. Inq. p.m. (Ser. 2), vol. 165, No. 170; Feet of F. Hants, Hil. 10 Jas. I; W. and L. Inq. p.m. (Ser. 2), bdle. 57, No. 38.

Browne, junior, his son and heir.[148] The descent of the manor for some time after this is uncertain, but it eventually passed to William Sherrington, junior,[149] who died seised of it in 1711. A year later his executors, Sir Peter Mews of Hinton Admiral and Thomas Morley, sold East Hoe to Thomas Lewis,[150] lord of the manor of Soberton, and by this time owner of nearly the whole parish. The site of the manor is marked by Hoegate Farm and East Hoe Common in the extreme south-east of the parish on the borders of Hambledon and Soberton.

BERE (Beere xiv cent.; Beare xvii cent.). From early times the Wayte family had a holding in the extreme west of the parish to the north of the Forest of Bere, which they held of the bishop of Winchester as of his manor of Hambledon. In 1338 Henry Wayte dealt by fine with 2 messuages, a mill, 2 carucates of land, 10 acres of meadow, 12 acres of wood, and 30*s.* rent in Bere, near Soberton.[151] Again, in 1354 a messuage, a mill, a carucate of land, 24 acres of meadow, 30 acres of wood, and 13*s.* 4*d.* rent in Bere and Soberton were settled on Philip Wayte and Isabel his wife, no doubt on the occasion of their marriage.[152] The property is called a manor in the inquisition taken in 1363 on the death of Thomas de Wallop, who was said to hold meadow land in Soberton of Isabel Wayte as of her manor of Bere by the payment of 2*s.* a year.[153] In 1449 William Wayte died seised of the manor of Bere held of the bishop of Winchester, leaving a son and heir Edward, then aged five.[154] From Edward it passed to his son Simon, who died in 1518, leaving a brother and heir William,[155] who died in 1561 seised of the manor of Bere *alias* Wayte Bere, leaving six daughters and co-heirs, Eleanor wife of Richard Bruning, Mary wife of William Cresweller, Honor wife of William Wayte, Margaret who had married Henry Perkins, Elizabeth who had married Richard Norton, and Susan wife of William Wollascot.[156] Bere passed as her portion to Elizabeth, and from her to her son Sir Richard Norton, who died in 1612 seised of a messuage called Bere *alias* Little Bere *alias* Wayte's Bere, 100 acres of land, a cottage and an acre of land in Soberton and Meonstoke held of Thomas bishop of Winchester, his heir being his son Richard, aged twenty-six and more.[157]

WAYTE. *Argent a cheveron gules between three hunting horns sable.*

From the description of the premises it is clear that the manorial rights, if ever there were any, had by this time lapsed. The site of the manor is marked at the present day by Bere Farm, Bere Copse, and Soberton Mill in the extreme west of the parish.

Another small portion of the parish of Soberton[158] was also included in the episcopal manor of Hambledon, and in the reign of Edward III was held by Robert de Hoe and Lucy his wife, who obtained from Adam bishop of Winchester a grant of two purprestures in the waste by Hipley and the moor of Hoe, containing 28 acres of land, and of two pieces of waste land there, containing 14 acres, with licence for them to inclose. The bishop moreover granted to them common of pasture for all their beasts and cattle in the waste of the manor where the other tenants of the manor had it. For this holding they were to pay the bishop £2 a year, with a double rent by way of a relief.[159] They must have been people of position, for some years later they acquired a life interest in the manor of Meonstoke Waleraund.[160]

At the time of the Domesday Survey there were four mills in the parish—three in the royal manor[161] and one in the manor held by Herbert the Chamberlain.[162] Two of them seem to have fallen early into decay, and after the fourteenth century two mills only are mentioned in the parish. There was a mill belonging to the manor of Bere in the fourteenth century,[163] and a water-mill is also included in an extent of the manor belonging to Richard de Winton in 1383.[164] A water-mill and a fulling-mill were included in the property purchased by the earl of Southampton from Walter Bonham in 1549,[165] and in the manors owned by Humphrey Minchin in 1791.[166] At the present day there are two water-mills in the parish: Soberton mill in the south-west worked by the Meon, and Rudley mill in the south-east.

CHURCHES

The church of *ST. PETER, SOBERTON*, has a chancel 28 ft. 6 in. by 15 ft. 9 in., with north chapel of equal length and 9 ft. 6 in. wide; nave, 42 ft. 6 in. by 7 ft. 6 in., with north and south aisles; south transept, 16 ft. by 23 ft.; south porch and west tower partly overlapped by the aisles, 12 ft. 6 in. square, all measurements being internal. The chancel arch not being parallel to the east wall of the chancel or the west wall of the nave, the lengths of nave and chancel here given are the mean lengths, taken on the axis.

The building shows traces of a long series of developments, which seem to have been somewhat as follows. The first church of which any evidence still exists may have been of pre-Conquest date, and in plan like Boarhunt, with a chancel 14 ft. wide, nave about 30 ft. by 17 ft. 6 in., and a western chamber of the same width and 10 ft. long.[167] To the nave of this

[148] Feet of F. Hants, Hil. 17 Jas. I, and Mich. 19 Jas. I; Recov. R. Hil. 17 Jas. I, rot. 31; Close, 17 Jas. I, pt. 7, No. 33. In the indenture of sale the premises are described as follows:—The manor or lordship of Hoe *alias* Hoo, with appurtenances in Hoe, Soberton, Meonstoke, Hambledon, and Droxford; waste ground called Common Deane in Hoe; waste of pasture, moor, and wood called Hoe Moor, Hoe Wood, and Ridley; and common of pasture for all manner of cattle, and mast and pannage for hogs in the forest o East Bere *alias* South Bere *alias* Porchester.

[149] Recov. R. Hil. 9 Anne, rot. 48; he may have inherited it from his father, William Sherrington, sen.

[150] Recov. R. Mich. 11 Anne, m. 15; Feet of F. Hants, Hil. 11 Anne.

[151] Feet of F. Hants, East. 11 Edw. III. In the thirteenth century it was held by the family of de la Bere. Richard de la Bere obtained a grant of a messuage and 5 acres of land in Soberton in 1219 (Feet of F. Hants, 3 Hen. III) and Simon de la Bere and his wife Euphemia dealt by fine with a carucate of land in Soberton in 1272 and 1279 (Feet of F. Div. Cos. Hil. 56 Hen. III, and Trin. 7 Edw. I).

[152] Feet of F. Hants, Mich. 26 Edw. III, and Mich. 27 Edw. III.

[153] Inq. p.m. 36 Edw. III, pt. 2 (1st Nos.), No. 76.

[154] Chan. Inq. p.m. 26 Hen. VI, No. 9.

[155] Ibid. (Ser. 2), vol. 33, No. 83.

[156] Ibid. 3 Eliz. No. 181.

[157] Ibid. vol. 332, No. 170.

[158] The boundaries of the parishes have since changed, and this portion is now in the parish of Hambledon.

[159] Pat. 11 Edw. III, pt. i, m. 35.

[160] q.v. *supra*.

[161] *V.C.H. Hants*, i, 452. [162] Ibid. 500.

[163] Feet of F. Hants, Mich. 26 Edw. III.

[164] Inq. p.m. 7 Ric. II, No. 107.

[165] Feet of F. Hants, Trin. 3 Edw. VI.

[166] Ibid. Trin. 31 Geo. III.

[167] The dimensions of Boarhunt are:—chancel, 15 ft. 3 in. by 14 ft. 6 in.; nave, 27 ft. by 18 ft.; western chamber, 12 ft. by 18 ft.

church a north aisle was added *c.* 1200, and about thirty years later the aisle was lengthened westward, the side walls of the western chamber pierced with arches and its east wall pulled down, a west tower built, and a south aisle added, being returned on the west outside the line of the west wall of the chamber. The side walls of the tower were also pierced to give a free passage 5 ft. 6 in. wide across the west end of the church,[168] and in the west wall of the chamber were three arches, throwing the passage open to the body of the church. The two eastern bays of the south arcade seem to have been the last part of this scheme of enlargement. About 1270 a south transept was added, 16 ft. wide from east to west, its east wall being about a foot further to the east than the corresponding wall of the nave, and its west wall a little to the west of the east side of the first pillar of the south arcade. The intention seems to have been to accommodate the transept to the first bay of the arcade.

The chancel arch was rebuilt about 1300, its southern respond being set a little further to the east, so that it might be exactly abutted by the east wall of the transept, and it thus became out of square with the nave walls. About 1330 the south wall of the chancel was rebuilt on the line of that of the nave, and just outside that of the former south wall. The chancel was, as it seems, lengthened eastward at the same time, and a vestry added on the north-east, but the north wall was probably not rebuilt, as the old line was retained, and the chancel arch was thus thrown out of centre with the chancel. Little was done to the church in the fifteenth century beyond the heightening of the south wall of the south aisle, but early in the sixteenth century the north chapel was added, filling the space between the north vestry and north aisle; the north wall of the north aisle was taken down for some two-thirds of its height, and rebuilt of less thickness on the remains of the old wall, and the present west tower built round the old tower, the east wall of which was incorporated in the east wall of the new tower. This latter was made to project as little as might be beyond the west wall of the thirteenth-century church, evidently for the same reason which had dictated the piercing of the side walls of the former tower, namely, that the lengthening of the church had brought its west wall up to the western boundary of the churchyard. This made it impossible to find room for a procession path round the outside of the church while still keeping within the limits of the churchyard, and the expedient adopted to provide such a way was the piercing of the north and south walls of the tower in the manner already described. The south doorway was also set at the extreme west of the south aisle, on the line of the passage, and made of unusual width, but there is no evidence that there was ever a north-west doorway to correspond, as the scheme seems to demand. On the contrary, the north doorway of the church seems to occupy about the same position as that of the early church, though of course more to the north.

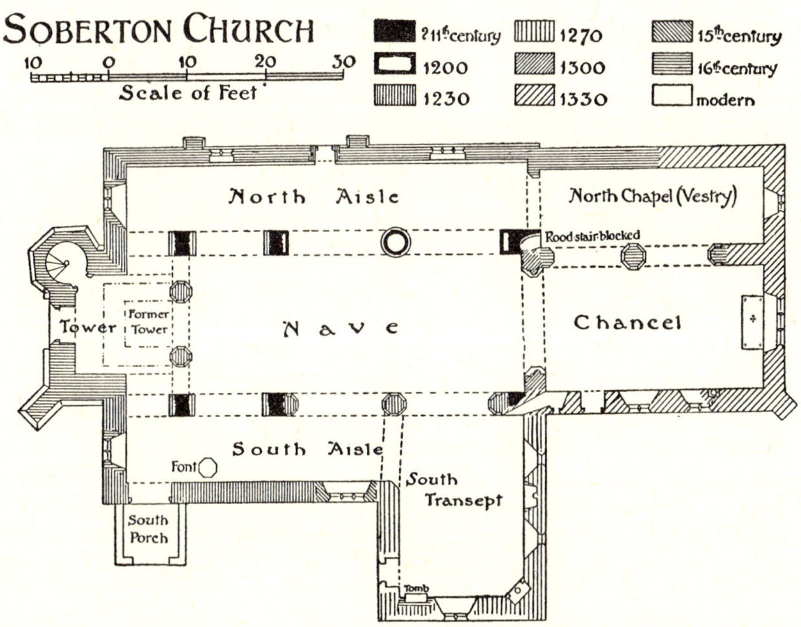

The chancel has an east window of three lights with net tracery, *c.* 1330, and in the south wall are two windows of the same date, each of two trefoiled ogee lights, and a small trefoiled low side window at the south-west angle, with an internal rebate, and a squint from the south transept in its west jamb. To the east of this window is a plain doorway. In the north wall of the chancel are two early sixteenth-century arches, with octagonal moulded capitals and bases opening to a north chapel, now, and probably in part from the first, used as a vestry. Its east window is of the date of the chancel, of two trefoiled ogee lights.

The chancel arch is of two orders, the outer with an edge-roll, and the inner chamfered with a moulded label, and in the jambs are engaged half-round shafts with moulded capitals and bases; its irregular setting and date have already been noticed.

The nave is of three bays, the two eastern bays of the north arcade, *c.* 1200, having a central round column, with plain bell capital and square abacus, pointed arches of a single square order with chamfered labels, and plain square responds. The third bay of the arcade has a later thirteenth-century arch of two chamfered orders, the inner order springing from moulded corbels, and there is a similar but narrower arch on the same line over the west aisle. The south arcade has a like arrangement at the west, but its two eastern bays have half-octagonal responds, an octagonal central column with moulded capitals, and pointed arches of two chamfered orders. Their date can be but little later than the work at the west.

The north aisle opens to the chapel by a modern arch, over which is a small two-light window, also modern. The rood-stair, now blocked, is in the

168 See below for the reason for this treatment of the tower and western aisle.

south-east corner of the aisle, with its doorway towards the east, and at the eastward of the aisle are laid two mediaeval coffin-lids of Purbeck marble. The north wall of the aisle, as already noted, is sixteenth-century work on a thirteenth-century base, and is lighted by two sixteenth-century square-headed north windows, one of three uncusped lights and one of two. Between them, and about mid-way in the aisle, is the north doorway, its jambs being of the thirteenth century with an edge-roll, while its head is four-centred and of the later period. The west window of two lights is also of the sixteenth century, its south jamb being widely splayed to light the western aisle. The south aisle wall has been raised in the fifteenth century, the weathering of the former roof showing on the west wall of the transept, and a three-light window of that date is inserted near the east end ; the west window is of two lights and perhaps the same date. The south door, as already noted, is unusually wide, and plain work of the thirteenth century ; over it is a modern porch.

The south transept, known at various times as the Curll or Minchin Chapel, and formerly the Lady Chapel, is of late thirteenth-century date, and has in its east wall a tall central recess with a pointed head containing pierced tracery, and shafts in the jambs, between two trefoiled lights with cinquefoiled rear arches. The central recess has a flat sill, below which is a narrower recess with splayed sides, in which is a shaft carrying a large carved corbel in the form of three human heads among foliage beneath a moulded shelf. The top of the shelf is level with the floor of the upper recess, and has pin-holes in its upper side. The carving of the corbel is very good, and the foliage suggests a somewhat earlier date in the thirteenth century than that of the transept, and from the way in which part of the carved work, which shows traces of colour, is buried in the wall, it would seem to have been intended for some other position. There was doubtless an altar here, the mensa of which, however placed, would have hidden the corbel completely if it had then occupied its present position. In the upper recess is now the monument of Sir Walter Curll, bart., 1678. A good deal of mediaeval wall decoration remains, both bands of scrolled foliage and masonry patterns, and on the splays of the windows are figures of female saints, St. Anne with our Lady and St. Katherine in the northern of the two east windows, and St. Margaret and another saint in the southern. In the south-east angle of the transept is a large stone aumbry set diagonally across the angle, with a piscina drain in its sill, and a shelf above. Its head is made of slabs with moulded edges turned inwards. The south window is an eighteenth-century insertion, as is the west doorway of the transept, and the south wall is faced outside with eighteenth-century brickwork. Near the south-west angle of the transept is a marble tomb of sixteenth-century type, with panelled base and shallow canopied recess over it, in the back of which are pin-holes for brasses. This is doubtless the tomb of John Newport, 1521, and his wife Elizabeth, 1527, the will of the latter providing for her burial in the church of Soberton in the Lady Chapel beside her husband.

In this transept is now kept a large stone coffin of Roman date, dug up in the parish.

At the west end of the nave is an arcade of three arches, *c.* 1230, with octagonal columns and moulded capitals and bases, the central arch being wider than the others. Above on the east are seen the quoins of the east wall of a small thirteenth-century tower, and on the west side the springing of the arches which spanned the passage through its north and south walls. The present tower, built round the other, was probably begun about 1520, its details, though still Gothic, being of the latest character. Its side walls are likewise in part pierced with arches, so as to leave a procession path at the west, and it has a west doorway, and a newel stair in an octagonal turret at the north-west. The west window is of three uncusped four-centred lights, and over it is a two-light window in the second stage, while the three-light belfry windows have the same late details, but are filled in with pierced stone slabs with excellent effect. The cornice below the battlements is enriched with carved bosses and shields which give valuable evidence as to the date of the work. On the south side is a rose parted with a pomegranate, between the arms of Newport and Kingsmill, and on the east face a pelican between the arms of Newport impaling a maunch, and a second impaled coat which is much weathered, but seems to have a fesse nebuly on the sinister half. The central bosses of these two sides, referring to Katherine of Aragon and Bishop Fox of Winchester, give the limits of date as between 1501–2, the time of Katherine's marriage with Prince Arthur (or more probably 1509, the date of her marriage to Henry VIII), and 1528, that of Fox's death. The Newport arms point to a share at least in the building being due to John Newport, *ob.* 1521, and two of the bells mention his name and that of his wife. On the west side of the tower is a curious central carving of a skull between a bucket (or purse) and a key and two human heads, which has given rise to a legend that the tower was built by the dairymaids and butlers of the neighbourhood, and on the strength of this many subscriptions were obtained at a late repair of the tower from domestic servants in the county.

KINGSMILL. *Argent crusilly fitchy sable with a cheveron ermine between three mill-rinds sable and a chief ermine.*

The nave and south aisle retain their old roof timbers with arched braces, and the chancel roof, which has an arched plaster ceiling, may be old. All roofs are covered with red tiles, except that of the north aisle, which is leaded. The south transept has a flat plaster ceiling, probably eighteenth-century, and retains some cut-down pews of that date, said to have been used by Lord Anson when he lived here.

The altar rails are good seventeenth-century work, with heavy posts, moulded top rail, and balusters, and in the vestry is a seventeenth-century altar table with turned baluster legs.

In the south-west window of the chancel is a shield with the arms of England of early sixteenth-century date.

The font, near the south doorway, is octagonal and of recent date.

There are eight bells, the first four by Warner, 1878, the fifth of 1640, inscribed 'In God is my hope,' and the tenor is by Ellis Knight, 1623,

Soberton Church : The Tower from the North-west

inscribed 'Prayes ye the Lord.' The sixth and seventh bear identical inscriptions in black letter capitals and smalls :—

ORATE PRO ĀĪABUS IOHIS NEWPORT ET ELIZABET UXORIS EIUS.

They date presumably after Elizabeth Newport's death in 1527, and probably were set here soon after the completion of the tower. They bear no cross or founder's mark by which their origin might be traced. Grooves made by the bell-ropes are to be seen not only on the west face of the middle of the three arches under the east wall of the tower, but also in the north face of the thirteenth-century arch across the south end of the western aisle. As they do not show in the sixteenth-century arch above, they must belong to a time before it was built, and point to the fact that a bell must have hung outside the former tower on the south, presumably in a small bell-cote over the western aisle.

The plate is an interesting set of 1706, consisting of communion cup and cover paten, two flagons, an alms dish, and a standing paten.

Among the church possessions is a seventeenth-century white damask table-cloth, with the story of the Good Samaritan and the inscription LUCAE X, i.e. the tenth chapter of St. Luke's gospel, and there are also some white diaper towels found in 1880 in the church roof, together with some leaves of late sixteenth-century printing.

The registers begin in 1538, the first book, which is of paper, being of more than usual interest from the fact that it was written by the parish clerk, William Middleton, from its commencement to 1588, and contains a number of additional details. He notes, on 12 May, 1549, 'this tyme began the Ingles s'vice,' and mentions outbreaks of plague in 1546 and 1564. An entry in 1580 shows that there was a priest's house near the church, not occupied by the parson, and there are several notes of marriages 'at iiij ye cloke in ye morning,' or 'an oure before day breke by licence frõ the chancelar.' In 1580 and 1589 are instances of the christening of sick children by the midwife, and twins are noted as 'halfe a child and the other halfe chylld.' This book contains burials to 1627, and baptisms 1547–1623. The second book has baptisms 1623–1775, and marriages 1540–1660, the entries from 1621 to 1654 being lost. The third book begins in 1662, and has baptisms to 1680, marriages to 1665, and burials to 1670. The next has baptisms 1695–1767, marriages 1696–1754, and burials 1678–1775 ; the next baptisms from 1756, and burials from 1775 up to 1812, and the next marriages 1754–1812.

The church of the *HOLY TRINITY*, *NEWTOWN*, erected in 1850, is a building of flint and stone in the Early English style. The registers date from the year of erection.

ADVOWSONS Soberton was a chapelry dependent upon the parish church of Meonstoke until quite modern times.[169] The living is at the present day a rectory in the gift of the bishop of Winchester.

In the reign of Henry III, Thomas de Windsor granted to the prior and convent of Southwick, in free alms, the tithes of all his lordship of Soberton from corn, sheep, pigs, cheese, and wool. This he did for the soul of his lord and father Gervase, who was buried at the church of Southwick, for his own salvation and that of Lady Amice his mother and Agnes his wife.[170]

In 1262 the abbot and convent of Beaulieu agreed to pay Geoffrey de Faring, rector of the church of Meonstoke, and his successors every year on the day of St. Peter ad Vincula in the church of Soberton £3, instead of tithes of milk, wool, lambs, calves, and pigs from their property in the parish of Soberton.[171]

At an early date there was a chapel in Hoe dependent on the parish church of Meonstoke, and in the reign of Edward I a dispute arose between the parishioners of the chapel on the one side, and Walter de Cumba, rector of the church of Meonstoke, and Roger, lord of Hoe, on the other, respecting a chantry in the chapel. The question was referred to the bishop of Winchester, who in 1282 decided that the chaplain who for the time being administered divine service in the chapel should receive all the oblations, obventions, and small tithes of every description appertaining to the altar of that chapel, reserving to the rector of Meonstoke and his successors all the great tithes of corn and the chief bequests or mortuaries within the manor of Hoe and his jurisdiction among the said parishioners. The chaplain was to have a manse with a garden adjacent, the whole of the land which William de Hoe, father of Roger, assigned to the chantry, the land which belonged to Herbert Pollard assigned by the same, fifty sheep in pasture with the sheep of Roger on the north side of the chapel, twelve pigs of his own rearing in pannage with the pigs of Roger, and six cart-loads of wood annually in the wood of Roger, and was to celebrate mass and the service for the dead three times a week for the souls of Roger, his successors and heirs. The bishop also decided that the chaplain should defray all the ordinary expenses of the chapel, viz. ornaments, books, vestments, covering of the chancel, &c., and ordered that the parishioners of Hoe once a year, viz. on the Feast of the Assumption of the Blessed Virgin Mary, should hear divine service and make their offerings personally at their mother church of Meonstoke.[172]

The living of Newtown is a vicarage, net yearly value £140, with 10 acres of glebe, in the gift of the bishop of Winchester.

There is a Free Methodist chapel in the parish, rebuilt in 1902, and situated a little to the north of Soberton Heath.

CHARITIES In 1759 William Mourn by his will, proved in the peculiar court of Hambledon, gave to the poor of the parish £100 to be placed out at interest. The legacy (with accumulations) is now represented by £117 15*s*. 11*d*. consols with the official trustees, by whom the dividends are remitted to the governing body, of which, by an order under the Local Government Act, 1894, two are elected by the parish council.

In 1867, by an award made upon the inclosure of Soberton Heath and other open lands in the parish, three pieces of land, each containing 2 acres, were allotted unto the churchwardens and overseers in

169 *Pope Nich. Tax.* (Rec. Com.), 211.
170 Add. MS. 33285, fol. 177.
171 Harl. MS. 6603, fol. 148.
172 Add. MS. 33285, fol. 175.

trust as an allotment for the labouring poor of the parish subject to a clear yearly rent-charge of £3.

By the same award 4 acres were allotted, as a place for exercise and recreation for the inhabitants of the parish and neighbourhood. The allotments for the poor are let to parishioners in plots varying from 20 to 40 poles at the rate of £1 per acre, producing about £6 a year, and the grazing of the recreation ground is let for £3 a year.

WARNFORD

Upwarneford (xi cent.); Warnesford (xiv cent.); Wanford (xvii cent.).

The parish of Warnford, covering about 3,178 acres, lies south of Kilmeston and Hinton Ampner, north-east of Exton, and west of West Meon, and falls naturally into two parts: the comparatively low-lying land bordering the River Meon on the south and east through which runs the main road from West Meon to Droxford, and the down-country on either side, Wheely Down and Beacon Hill reaching the heights of 500 ft. and 659 ft. respectively. A road to Winchester branches off from the main road at the south end of the village, climbing up from about 250 ft. above the sea-level to about 550 ft. by Wind Farm in the extreme western angle of the parish. From here a fine view opens out of the low-lying parishes to the north—Beauworth, Kilmeston, Hinton Ampner, and Cheriton.

RUINED BUILDING IN WARNFORD PARK

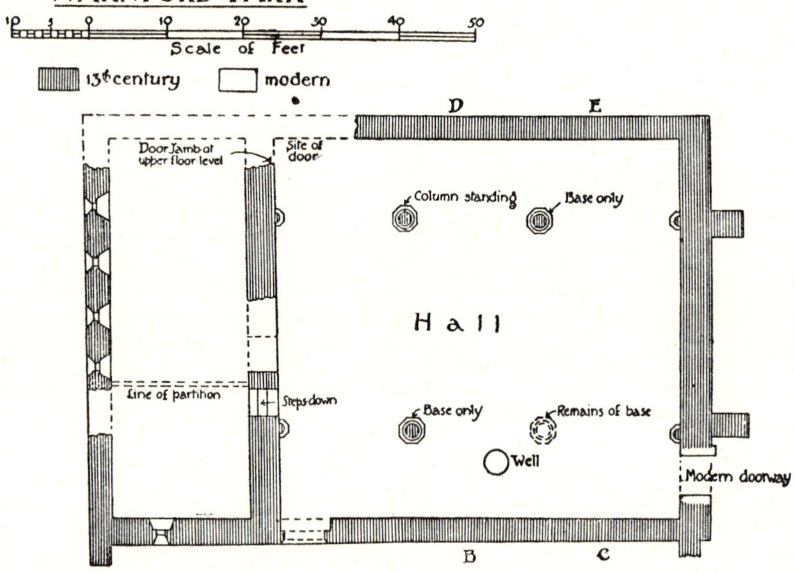

The village of Warnford lies in the east of the parish, mainly along the road leading from West Meon to Droxford, which follows the line of the River Meon, crossing it close to the gates of Warnford Park. A little way up the stream from the bridge is the site of the mill, with a large mill-pool above it, and the inn and the small group of houses which form the village stand close by, mostly on the north side of the road. On the south the river runs through Warnford Park, the house and church on the east bank being quite hidden from the road by the trees with which not only the park, but the whole neighbourhood of the village, abounds. The rectory, a large white house standing on high ground well back from the road, lies a little to the south of the village. Warnford House at the present day is of little architectural interest. The west wing is probably of some antiquity, and the site has been occupied for a considerable time, as the older house whose ruins stand in the park to the east of the church was already a ruin in the time of James I, as witnessed by Norden's map of Hampshire of 1610. The park, through which the river runs, is very well timbered. There is an amusing account of it in the *World* (afterwards the *Morning Post*) of 29 September, 1789, when Henry, twelfth Lord Clanricarde, lived here, mentioning the buildings in the gardens — 'the Gothic building, with the bath under it of Lady Mary; the Hermitage (always a miserable bauble), the wax figure in it with the apology for the Church of England in its hand, are bad works the late lord had to answer for.' After giving some advice to the then lord as to necessary improvements in the matter of landscape gardening, including the spreading of some gravel, 'cost what it will, or at least some sand,' the account continues: 'The water is the best feature of the place, very well coloured, half a mile long, 30 ft. wide. There are twelve acres of mowing, the kitchen garden is bad, the greenhouse and hothouse are small and new, and they will not be old who live by them, if there is not care, for the situation seems to want what makes men ague-proof.'

The church is in the park, surrounded and hidden by trees, a little south of the house, and to the east of it are the ruins of the old house of the St. Johns, now commonly called King John's House. In seventeenth and eighteenth-century documents it is called merely The Old House, as distinct from the present mansion, which is usually styled The Place House or Belmont.[1] It is a building of quite exceptional interest, being part of a substantial house of *c.* 1230, and consists of a hall 52 ft. long by 48 ft. wide, divided by columns into a central span 25 ft. wide, and north and south aisles. At the east end are no remains of adjoining buildings, but at the west is a block originally of two stories, of the same width as the hall, and 18 ft. long.

[1] Close, 7 Will. and Mary, pt. 12, m. 5–7; 28 Geo. II, pt. 12, m. 10–12; 5 Geo. III, pt. 15, m. 39–42.

It seems to have been divided into two rooms on the ground floor, entered by separate doors from the hall, and has four narrow windows remaining in the west wall of its north room, and one in the south wall of the south room. At the first-floor level in the north-east angle of the north room are traces of a doorway opening to a staircase or perhaps a gallery at the west of the hall, and the hall itself seems to have had the normal arrangement of a screened passage at its western or lower end, entered by doors on north and south, of which the latter still remains, and the former is shown on eighteenth-century plans. The columns of the hall were circular, on octagonal bases, with foliate capitals, and were no less than 25 ft. high, one in the north range still standing entire. They probably carried the roof-beams and no arches of masonry, though the account from the *World* above-quoted speaks of 'four fine columns and four arches,' and in the east and west walls the small half-round responds still exist. Old plans show two windows in each side of the hall, but no trace remains of them now. They may have been destroyed for the sake of their wrought stone, and their places built up in rubble when the hall was turned into a barn. In the south aisle of the hall is a well, perhaps not ancient, as the position is an unlikely one.[2]

Riversdown, a possession of St. Cross, is a hamlet on the Downs, two miles north-west of the village. Bere, about two miles north of the village, until about thirty years ago was held by the Major family, who succeeded the Lockes, who held it for several centuries. At the present day it belongs to Corpus Christi College, Oxford.

The parish contains 1,545 acres of arable land, 1,407 acres of permanent grass, and 271 acres of woods and plantations.[3] The soil is chiefly loam, the sub-soil principally chalk. The chief crops are wheat, barley, and oats. The land was formerly nearly all arable, but the present proprietor has established several dairies and cheese-making establishments. Watercress is also cultivated extensively. The River Meon affords good trout-fishing. The manufacture of paper was carried on in the parish in the eighteenth century.[4] The following place-names are found in the sixteenth century:—'Hurst Down and Walys lands,' both in Wheely;[5] 'Parson's Platt, Rook Grove,[6] Sir William's Mead, Coulson's Meadow, Walsdown, the Woollands, the Wynnells, and Wynnell's Coppice'[7] are found in a deed of the eighteenth century.[8]

MANORS Earl Brygwyn, with King Ethelred's permission, granted *WARNFORD* or *UPWARNFORD* with eight hides, which he possessed by right of inheritance, to Hyde Abbey, Winchester.[9] In the reign of Edward the Confessor Alward and Ketel held Warnford, which was assessed at eight hides, of Hyde Abbey. At the time of the survey it was held of the same abbey by Hugh de Port.[10] For the manors held by Hugh from the abbey he owed it, according to the return of 1212, the service of six knights.[11] At the time of the survey the same Hugh also held Warnford, which was assessed at two hides less one virgate, Ulvric and Olward having held it in parage of King Edward.[12] Before the Conquest, therefore, there seem to have been two manors of Warnford—one held by Hyde Abbey and the other by King Edward. At the time of the Domesday Survey Hugh de Port held them both. Naturally, therefore, they soon coalesced and came to be looked upon as one manor, the property of the Port family and their descendants.

The manor of Warnford remained in the family of Port until the thirteenth century, when William son of Adam de Port and Mabel de Aureval, heiress through her mother of Roger de St. John, took the name of St. John.[13] It continued in the St. John family until the year 1355,[14] when Edmund son and heir of Hugh de St. John dying a minor, it fell to the share of his sister Isabel, wife of Sir Luke de Poynings.[15] On her death in 1393 the manor passed to her son Sir Thomas de Poynings,[16] who died seised of it in 1429,[17] when it was assigned to his granddaughter Alice, who married first John Orell, and secondly Sir Thomas Kyngeston.[18] In 1439 the manor was granted by Alice to Thomas Gloucestre and Thomas Batell (possibly related to John Batell, the husband of Elizabeth, eldest daughter of Alice) for their lives, with remainder to her son Thomas, then aged three and a half, in fee-tail, with contingent remainder to her daughters Elizabeth, Eleanor, and Margaret.[19] Thomas Batell died in 1457, Thomas Gloucestre the co-lessee having pre-deceased him.[20] The manor then reverted to Thomas Kyngeston, who died seised in 1506, his heir being his kinsman John Kyngeston, aged sixteen.[21] John died in 1514, and was succeeded by his brother Nicholas,[22] on whose death, without issue, two years later, the manor passed to his sister Mary, the wife of Thomas Lisle,[23] whose only son Francis died without issue. Mary died seised of the manor in 1539, and on the death of her husband, three years later, the property which she had inherited from her brothers, and they in their turn from Thomas Kyngeston, was divided among the descendants of the two sisters of Mary's father, John Kyngeston, who died in 1497, viz. (1) William Gorfen, son and heir of Margaret Gorfen sister of John; (2) Margery, wife of John Cope and daughter of Katherine Malory sister of John; and (3) Katherine wife of Thomas Andrewes, and Margaret wife of Thomas Boughton, daughters of Dorothy Malory daughter of Katherine Malory.[24] By an indenture of partition (24 June, 1543) the manor and the advowson of the church of Warnford were assigned to

2 Much of this account is from information kindly given by Mr. N. C. H. Nisbett, to whom also the plan is due.

3 Statistics from the Bd. of Agric. (1905).

4 Close, 28 Geo. II, pt. 12, m. 11 and 12.

5 Chan. Inq. p.m. (Ser. 2), vol. 94, No. 51.

6 This is the name of a grove in the north of the parish.

7 Winnell's Copse is in the south of the parish.

8 Close, 28 Geo. II, pt. 12, m. 11 and 12.

9 Dugdale, *Mon.* ii, 436.

10 *V.C.H. Hants*, i, 471*a*.

11 *Testa de Nevill* (Rec. Com.), 239.

12 *V.C.H. Hants*, i, 481*a*.

13 *The Genealogist*, xvi, 1–13.

14 Inq. p.m. 3 Edw. I, No. 88; *Feud. Aids*, ii, 307, 336; Inq. p.m. 3 Edw. III (1st Nos.), No. 67; 11 Edw. III (1st Nos.), No. 49; Close, 11 Edw. III, pt. 1, m. 29.

15 Inq. p.m. 29 Edw. III (1st Nos.), No. 55.

16 Ibid. 17 Ric. II, No. 45.

17 Ibid. 7 Hen. VI, No. 69. His only son Hugh had died in 1426, leaving three daughters and co-heirs, Joan, Constance, and Alice.

18 *Feud. Aids*, ii, 372; Inq. p.m. 17 Hen. VI, No. 22.

19 Inq. p.m. 17 Hen. VI, No. 22.

20 Ibid. 35 Hen. VI, No. 4.

21 Exch. Inq. p.m. (Ser. 2), file 961, No. 6.

22 Inq. p.m. (Ser. 2), vol. 29, No. 42.

23 Chan. Inq. p.m. (Ser. 2), vol. 30, No. 44; Memo. R. L.T.R. East. 30 Hen. VIII, rot. 12.

24 Exch. Inq. p.m. (Ser. 2), file 991, No. 13; Memo. R. L.T.R. Hil. 35 Hen. VIII, rot. 32.

William Gorfen as his share.[25] On his death, in 1547,[26] his sister and heir Alice immediately took possession, without any proof of age or livery of her inheritance, but was pardoned and received licence to enter in February, 1551.[27] In Michaelmas of the same year the manor was settled on Alice for life with remainder to Chidiock Paulet[28] and his issue.[29] In this way the manor of Warnford came into the family of the Paulets, who were descended from Constance the elder sister of Alice Kyngeston, and one of the granddaughters and co-heirs of Sir Thomas de Poynings, who died in 1429. Alice Gorfen must have died before 1562, for in that year Chidiock, Lord Paulet, obtained licence from Queen Elizabeth to alienate his manor of Warnford to Peter Tichborne and Thomas Pynder,[30] no doubt for purposes of settlement. Chidiock died seised of the manor in 1574,[31] and was succeeded by his son William, who in 1577 granted the manor and advowson of Warnford to William Neale and Agnes his wife in return for various annuities.[32] In spite of this arrangement, however, William Paulet is still described as seised of the manor at the time of his death in 1596.[33] William Neale, who was one of the auditors to Queen Elizabeth, died seised of the manor in 1602, leaving a son and heir Thomas, aged thirty-six,[34] who was afterwards knighted and was auditor to King James I. On his death in 1620 Warnford passed to his son and heir Thomas,[35] the author of a little treatise entitled *A Treatise of Direction how to Travell Safely and Profitably into Forraigne Countries*, published in London in 1643.[36]

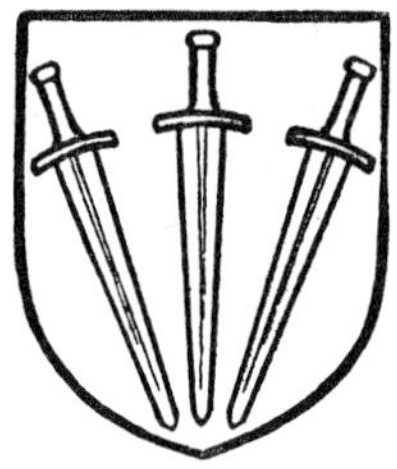

PAULET. *Sable three swords in pile with golden hilts and pommels.*

In 1678 Thomas sold the manor to Richard Woollaston, from whom it was purchased a year later by Sir Richard Stephens for £2,000 down and two further payments of £3,500 and £5,500. Sir Richard, however, failed to pay the purchase-money at the times agreed upon, and the matter was referred to Chancery, which decided against him. He then appealed to the House of Lords, but his appeal was dismissed, and by Act of Parliament passed in 1695 Hannah Woollaston, widow of John Woollaston the son and heir of Richard Woollaston, and Jonathan Woollaston were enabled to sell the manor for the payment of debts and legacies according to the will of Richard Woollaston. In pursuance of the Act they sold to Edward Silvester,[37] who by will left the manor to his grandson, George Freeman, the son of his only daughter Elizabeth, who had married Ralph Freeman.[38] George died without issue, and was succeeded by his sister Elizabeth the wife of Sir Christopher Bouverie, who was the second son of Sir Edward Bouverie.[39] On the death of Sir Christopher, Warnford passed to his son and heir Freeman Bouverie, who died without issue in 1734, his heir being his brother John, who also died childless in 1750 leaving two sisters and co-heirs, Elizabeth Bouverie and Anne wife of John Hervey.[40] In 1754 the manor was settled upon Elizabeth, her heirs and assigns for ever.[41] At that time Smith de Burgh, eleventh earl of Clanricarde, held the manor as a tenant. He seems to have purchased it shortly afterwards, for in 1765 it was settled upon him for the term of his life, with remainder in tail-male to his eldest son Henry de Burgh, Lord Dunkellin, with contingent remainder in tail-male successively to his second son John Thomas and his daughters Lady Hester Amelia and Lady Margaret Augusta.[42] Smith de Burgh, eleventh earl of Clanricarde died in 1782 and was succeeded by his son Henry, twelfth earl of Clanricarde, who died without issue in 1795, his heir being his brother John Thomas.[43] The manor, however, was for some time retained by Urania Anne, widow of the twelfth earl, who married Sir Joseph Sydney Yorke in 1815, and it was not until 1826 that she released her life interest[44] to Ulick John, fourteenth earl of Clanricarde,[45] son and heir of John Thomas, thirteenth

BOUVERIE. *Party fessewise or and argent an eagle sable with two heads bearing on his breast a scutcheon gules with a bend vair.*

DE BURGH, Earl of Clanricarde. *Or a cross gules with a lion sable in the quarter.*

[25] Chan. Inq. p.m. (Ser. 2), vol. 94, No. 51. Two years later Henry VIII granted to him the lands and tenements in the parish formerly belonging to the priories of Montacute (co. Somers.) and Boxgrove (co. Suss.) (Pat. 36 Hen. VIII, pt. 1, m. 48).

[26] Chan. Inq. p.m. (Ser. 2), vol. 94, No. 51.

[27] Pat. 5 Edw. VI, pt. 1, m. 2.

[28] This Chidiock was governor of the town of Southampton and the castle of Portsmouth in the reigns of Mary I and Elizabeth (Pat. 1 Mary, pt. 11, and 1 Eliz. pt. 9).

[29] With contingent remainder to Giles Paulet and his issue, with contingent remainder to the right heirs of William Paulet, earl of Wiltshire. Pat. 5 Edw. VI, pt. 1, m. 16; Memo. R. L. T. R. 14 Eliz. rot. 58; Feet of F. Hants, Mich. 5 Edw. VI.

[30] Pat. 5 Eliz. pt. 5, m. 36.

[31] Chan. Inq. p.m. (Ser. 2), 17 Eliz. only pt. No. 120.

[32] (1) An annuity of £50 for the term of the joint lives of Frances late wife of Lord Chidiock Paulet, and Thomas Paulet son of Chidiock and Frances; (2) an annuity of £50 during the life of Thomas Paulet, the first payment being due at the feast (either of the Annunciation of the Blessed Virgin Mary or of St. Michael the Archangel) which should first fall after the death of Frances; and (3) an annuity of £50 during the life of Frances, the first payment being due at the feast (either of the Annunciation of the Blessed Virgin Mary or of St. Michael the Archangel) which should first fall after the death of Thomas. (Notes of F. Hants, Mich. 19 & 20 Eliz.; Com. Pleas Deeds Enr. Mich. 19 & 20 Eliz; Memo. R. L. T. R. East. 20 Eliz. rot. 106).

[33] Chan. Inq. p.m. (Ser. 2), vol. 247, No. 86.

[34] Ibid. (Ser. 2) 44 Eliz. pt. 2, No. 114.

[35] W. and L. Inq. p.m. (Ser. 2), bdle. 32, No. 129.

[36] The foreword to the reader is dated from 'his house at Warneford,' 3 Feb. 1642, and the whole work is dedicated to his brother William.

[37] *Hist. MSS. Com. Rep.* xiii, App. pt. v, 275; Close, 7 Will. and Mary, pt. 12, m. 5–7.

[38] Stowe MS. 845, fol. 98; Recov. R. Hants, Mich. 4 Anne, m. 67.

[39] Manning and Bray, *Surrey*, ii, 208.

[40] Ibid.

[41] Feet of F. Div. Cos. Trin. 26 Geo. II; Close, 28 Geo. II, pt. 12, m. 10–12; Recov. R. Hil. 27 Geo. II, m. 283.

[42] Close, 5 Geo. III, pt. 15, m. 39–42; Recov. R. Trin. 5 Geo. III, m. 147.

[43] Recov. R. Hil. 38 Geo. III, m. 17.

[44] Feet of F. Hants, East. 6 Geo. IV.

[45] He succeeded to the earldom in 1808, was created marquis of Clanricarde (peerage of Ireland) 1825 and Baron Somerhill 1826. He was Under-Secretary for Foreign Affairs 1826–7, Ambassador at St. Petersburg 1838–40, Postmaster-General 1846–52, Lord Privy Seal 1858, and Lord Lieutenant of county Galway, &c.

earl of Clanricarde, who sold it some time afterwards to Mr. W. Abbott. From the latter it passed by purchase to Mr. Edward Rose Tunno,[46] who died seised of the manor in 1863, his heir being his kinsman Mr. Charles Sartoris, who sold it two years later to Mr. Henry Woods, for many years member of Parliament for Wigan. On his death the manor passed to his son and heir Colonel William Woods, J.P., the present lord.

Woods of Warnford. *Argent a cheveron nebuly gules with drops argent between three martlets sable.*

WHEELY (Weleg, xii cent.; Weologhe and Weleye, xiv cent.; Wulhaye, Wylhay, Welleigh and Wellehigh, xvi cent.). The land of Warnford called Wheely was granted to the prior and convent of Montacute (co. Somers.) early in the twelfth century by Henry de Port when lord of the manor of Warnford,[47] and seems to have developed into a small manor by the fourteenth century.[48] In the reign of Henry VIII the prior and convent were seised of £2 4*s.* rents from certain lands in Wheely by Warnford.[49] Some time after the dissolution of the priory in 1545, Henry VIII granted a messuage and lands in Wheely to William Gorfen, lord of the manor of Warnford.[50] Since then Wheely has formed part of the manor of Warnford.[51] It is at the present day represented by Wheely Down and Wheely Farm.

CHANTRY LANDS Early in the thirteenth century William de St. John, when lord of the manor of Warnford, granted a virgate of land with a messuage and other appurtenances which Owen held of him in the vill of Warnford to the prior and convent of Boxgrove (co. Suss.) in free alms.[51a] A few years later, the prior and convent, in return for two marks of silver, granted the land to William son of Theobald de Warnford to be held by the rent of a mark of silver, a further condition being that he and his heirs should whenever necessary find suitable lodging for the prior and his men, together with sufficient litter and forage.[52] In the reign of Henry VIII the prior and convent were seised of 13*s.* 4*d.* rents from a tenement and a virgate of land in Warnford called Chantry Lands.[53] Some time after the dissolution of the priory, viz., in 1545, Henry VIII granted them to William Gorfen, lord of the manor of Warnford,[54] since when they have descended with the manor of Warnford.

There were three mills in the parish at the time of the Domesday Survey.[55] In the reign of Edward VI two water-mills are mentioned in connexion with the manor,[56] whereas only one is included in the extent of the manor made on the death of Thomas Kyngeston in 1506.[57]

In 1752 a water-mill and a paper-mill belonged to the manor,[58] and they were still standing in 1826.[59] A group of cottages called Paper Mills possibly marks the site of the paper-mill, while the other was worked by the large mill-pool mentioned in the description.

CHURCH The church of *WARNFORD*, of unknown dedication, has a nave and chancel of equal width and without any structural division, 72 ft. long by 28 ft. wide, with south porch, and west tower 17 ft. 3 in. square, all measurements being internal. The tower walls being a little less than 4 ft. thick, its external dimensions are about 25 ft. each way.

On the east face of the tower are the marks of abutment of a narrower nave, about 22 ft. wide over all, with an internal span of 17 ft. Part of the weather moulding of its roof still exists, and the bonding of the quoins of its internal angles is to be seen in the tower wall. The foundations of its north and south walls have been traced in the course of some recent repairs for about 40 ft. without finding any sign of an east wall or a narrower chancel. Its walls were 2 ft. 6 in. thick, and though there is no absolute evidence to prove that it is older than the tower, it is probable that the tower was added to it about 1175–80.

Over the south doorway of the present nave, and over the place of its now destroyed north doorway, are inscriptions recording the rebuilding of the church by Adam de Port, who held Warnford from 1171 to his death in 1213,[60] and it seems that he must have built the tower soon after his coming into possession and have rebuilt the nave in the last years of his life. The tower was designed to go with the narrow nave, its ashlar-faced masonry extending up to its walls on north and south, and they probably co-existed for some twenty-five years. Then the present nave and chancel were built round the old church, their west wall overlapping the tower and being bonded to its eastern buttresses, and the stone weather mould of the new roof was let into the east wall of the tower and in part is still to be seen. The walls of the nave have been heightened and the pitch of the roof lowered at a comparatively modern date, and the east wall of the tower has been partly rebuilt in brickwork, destroying the upper parts of the old weather moulds.

The church has a three-light east window with pretty tracery of fourteenth-century style, set in a wide, round arched recess, the jambs of which may be of thirteenth-century date, and perhaps inclosed a group of three lancets. In the north wall are five

46 There is a monument to his memory in Warnford church.

47 *Bruton and Montacute Cartularies*, (Somers. Rec. Soc.), 126. His gift was confirmed by King Stephen (ibid. 122), King Henry II (ibid. 124), his son John de Port (ibid. 156), Adam de Port son of John de Port (ibid. 157), William de St. John son of Adam de Port (ibid. 157), and finally by Sir John de St. John son of Sir John de St. John in 1316 (ibid. 169).

48 In the Ministers' Accounts of 18 Edw. II, the exits of the lands and tenements of the prior of Montacute in the manor of Wheely are accounted for (Mins. Accts. Hants, 18 Edw. II, bdle. 1126, No. 19).

49 Mins. Accts. Somers. 30 & 31 Hen. VIII, No. 128, m. 33.

50 Pat. 36 Hen. VIII, pt. 1, m. 48.

51 Ibid. 5 Edw. VI, pt. 1, m. 16; Feet of F. Hants, Mich. 5 Edw. VI, and Trin. 6 Edw. VI; Feet. of F. Div. Cos. Mich. 4 Edw. VI.

51a Cott. MS. Claud. A. vi, fol. 32. His gift was confirmed by the archbishop of Canterbury in 1223 (ibid. fol. 62).

52 Ibid. fol. 136.

53 Mins. Accts. Sussex 28 & 29 Hen. VIII, No. 109, m. 5.

54 Pat. 36 Hen. VIII, pt. 1, m. 48.

55 *V.C.H. Hants*, i, 471 and 481.

56 Pat. 5 Edw. VI, pt. 1, m. 16.

57 Exch. Inq. p.m. (Ser. 2), file 961, No. 6.

58 Feet of F. Hants, Trin. 26 Geo. II.

59 Ibid. East. 6 Geo. IV.

60 The story of his banishment in 1172 is a mistake arising from a confusion with him of an Adam de Port of Herefordshire.

lancets, three evenly spaced to light the chancel, and the other two set more widely apart in the nave, the blank space between them having once contained the north doorway. West of the third window from the east is a small doorway, probably once connected with the rood-loft stair. In the south wall the same arrangement of windows exists, with a priest's door below the second lancet, and between the two in the nave is the south doorway, which is pointed, of two chamfered orders, with square abaci, and looks to be *c.* 1190, but may be of the same date as the windows in spite of its detail; or it may have been moved from the wall of the older nave. Above it is the inscription on a stone panel :—

+FRATRES ORATE PRECE VESTRA SANCTIFICATE
TEMPLI FACTORES SENIORES AC JUNIORES
WLFRIT FUNDAVIT BONUS ADAM ME RENOVAVIT.

Above the inscription is a circular sun-dial on a square stone, with leaves carved at the corners, like that at Corhampton, and probably also of Saxon date. It is now covered by the south porch, which seems to be of the thirteenth century, with a plain pointed outer arch and stone benches, and has two incised sun-dials on its east quoins.

On the north of the nave, over the position of the destroyed north doorway, is a second inscription :—

+ADAM DE PORTU BENEDICAT SOLIS AB ORTU
GENS CRUCE SIGNATA PER QUEM SUM SIC
RENOVATA

The tower is of two stages, with a plain brick parapet and broad ashlar-faced clasping buttresses at the angles. It has a plain inserted fourteenth-century west door, with a blocked recess near it on the outside, probably for a holy-water stoup. The ground stage is lighted by three round-headed windows, that in the west wall being more elaborately treated, with pairs of nook-shafts having foliate capitals.

The upper or belfry stage, reached by wooden ladders in the south-west angle, is lighted by narrow round-headed lights with, at a higher level, pairs of large circular openings surrounded by chamfered labels. Above these openings the walls are rebuilt in red brick, and the greater part of the east wall of the tower above the tower arch has been thus treated. The tower arch is pointed, of two square orders with a chamfered string at the springing, and is at present blocked by a wooden screen made up of seventeenth-century paneling and carved details.

The roofs of the church have lately been repaired and covered with red tiles, and the fittings and paving generally set in order. The double truss in the roofs marks the old line of division between nave and chancel, and the screen which now defines their limits is an interesting piece of work dated 1634, with carved upper and middle rails and a line of turned balusters between them, the panels below the middle rails being solid. On the east side of the screens are two inclosed eighteenth-century pews, in which older woodwork is used up, and on the west of the screen is a large squire's pew, taking up the whole of the north side, so that the pulpit, &c., are moved to the south of the central gangway. Against the north wall of the chancel are three fifteenth-century misericorde seats, and the altar rails are eighteenth-century work, the balusters in them being modern. On the north side of the chancel is a double stone locker in the wall, now containing two funeral helms. The benches in the nave are plain and solid, perhaps of the end of the sixteenth century, and the south door is seventeenth-century work.

On either side of the altar table are monuments against the east wall, that to the north being to William Neale, 1601, of marble and alabaster, with a panelled base on which stand two Corinthian columns supporting a pediment with the arms of his house. On the south side is the large monument of Sir Thomas Neale, 1621, and his two wives, their alabaster effigies lying beneath a panelled canopy with a broken pediment, on which are the arms of Neale between alabaster figures of Faith and Charity. On the base are kneeling figures of two sons and seven daughters, four of the latter holding skulls to show their death in their parents' lifetime.

NEALE of Warnford. *Argent a fesse between two crescents in the chief and a hunting horn in the foot all gules.*

In the nave floor west of the chancel screen are two coffin lids, one of the thirteenth and one of the fourteenth century; the former having been moved here from the north of the nave in 1905.

The font at the west of the nave is a very interesting late twelfth-century example, in Purbeck marble, with a square bowl, with more elaborate carvings than usual in this type of font, but unfortunately in very bad condition. It stands on a central and four angle-shafts of marble, and has on the east face of the bowl an Agnus Dei between two beasts, on the north three birds displayed, on the south two large beasts facing each other, and on the west a defaced carving between two birds.

There are six bells, the treble and second of 1635, by John Dauton of Salisbury, with the Neale arms on the treble, the other four being by John Wallis, the third made in 1599 and inscribed

THO GULLE QUI OBT 4 MAII ;

the fourth of 1598, the fifth of 1600, and the tenor of 1603.

The plate consists of a chalice and cover paten of 1685, a chalice and paten of 1843, and a pewter flagon.

The first book of the registers contains baptisms, 1541–1771, marriages, 1604–1764, and burials, 1617–1771. The second has baptisms 1783–1812, marriages 1735–1800, and burials 1782–1812, the baptisms and burials 1771–1783 being lost. The third book has marriages 1800–12.

ADVOWSON

There was a church in Warnford at the time of the Domesday Survey.[61] In 1292 the church was worth £21 6*s.* 8*d.* a year,[62] while in the reign of Henry VIII its annual value was £21 9*s.* 3½*d.*[63] The advowson

[61] *V.C.H. Hants*, i, 481*a*.
[62] *Pope Nich. Tax.* (Rec. Com.), 212.
[63] *Valor Eccl.* (Rec. Com.), i, 23.

Warnford Church : The Tower from the North

of the church followed the descent of the manor (q.v.) with few exceptions[64] until about 1850, when it was purchased by the Rev. John Wynne, the father of the present patron, the Rev. John Wynne, M.A., rector of Warnford.

There is a Primitive Methodist chapel in the parish. The schools were built in 1877 for eighty children.

CHARITIES In 1617 John Knight by his will charged his lands in Alton Eastbrook, called Amery Farm, with an annual payment of £2 for the poor of this parish. The sum of £2 (less land tax) is paid by Mr. G. Gathorne Wood of Shalden manor, the owner of the property charged, and is distributed among three or four poor people in money.

64 Thomas de Aspale, canon ot Salisbury, presented for this time only between 1346 and 1366 (Egerton MS. 2033, fol. 37). Thomas Baccayle, citizen and mercer of London, presented during Waynflete's episcopacy (Egerton MS. 2034, fol. 65). In 1771 Admiral Griffin presented Philip Griffin (Inst. Bks. P.R.O.), while in 1731 Robert Vincent, sen., presented his son, Thomas Vincent (Inst. Bks. P.R.O.), who died in 1733, 'in which short time he rebuilt the parsonage-house. Before he came to this place he had exercised his ministry for fifteen years in London. He had one peculiar felicity and he esteemed it such in these days to have no public dependencies, being presented to this living by his own father, a worthy citizen of London.'

THE HUNDRED OF BISHOP'S WALTHAM

CONTAINING THE PARISHES[1] OF

BISHOP'S WALTHAM
BURSLEDON
DROXFORD
DURLEY
EXBURY (WITH LEPE)
FAWLEY
ST. MARY EXTRA, OTHERWISE WESTON
UPHAM

The hundred of Waltham was at first identical with the manor of Waltham, which consisted of 38 hides acquired in 904 by the bishop of Winchester from King Edward the Elder in exchange for 40 hides at Portchester.[2] This grant was afterwards confirmed by King Edgar, who describes the land as consisting of 28 *cassae*.[3]

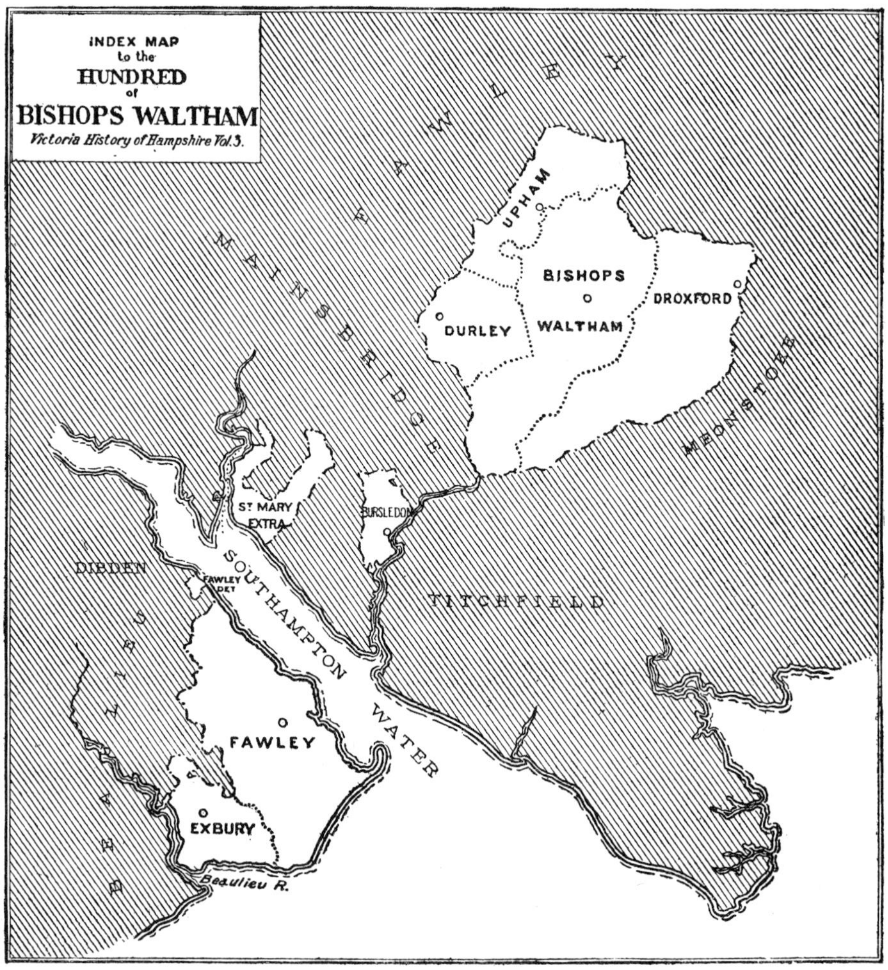

There is no mention of the hundred as such until the Domesday Survey, which gives Waltham as the only place within it. Waltham was then held by the bishop of Winchester, and was reduced to 30 hides.[4] Of the

[1] According to the *Pop. Ret.* 1831.
[2] Kemble, *Cod. Dipl.* v, 161.
[3] Birch, *Cart. Sax.* iii, 411, No. 1157.
[4] *V.C.H. Hants*, i, 460.

other parishes now in Bishop's Waltham Hundred which are mentioned in Domesday, Droxford was in Droxford Hundred;[5] Fawley, with the manors of Langley, Hardley, Stone, and Stanswood, was in Redbridge Hundred;[6] and Woolston (in St. Mary Extra) was in Mainsbridge Hundred.[7] There is no mention of Exbury in Domesday, but 'Gatingeorde' in Redbridge Hundred has been conjecturally identified with Gatewood in the parish of Exbury.[8]

A court held at Bishop's Waltham in 1236 had jurisdiction over the following tithings: Durley, Bursledon, Mincingfield, Curdridge, 'How' (presumably West Hoe), Wintershill, Upham, Woodcott, and Ashton;[9] showing that at this date Waltham manor (still co-extensive with the hundred) included what were later the separate parishes of Upham, Durley, Bursledon, and Bishop's Waltham.

An attempt to enlarge the jurisdiction of Bishop's Waltham Hundred was made in 1284, when it was granted to the bishop that the men of his manors of Bitterne, Fawley, Ower, and Stoneham should henceforth attend the hundred court of Waltham instead of that of Sweyneston in the Isle of Wight.[10] The change was probably proposed with a view to convenience, but apparently even Bishop's Waltham was found to be too distant, for the inhabitants of the above places invariably attended a separate court at Bitterne.[11] Though Fawley is duly entered as a part of Bishop's Waltham Hundred in 1316,[12] there is no evidence that the inhabitants of Fawley ever actually attended the hundred court at Waltham.

The entries of 1316 also show that Holbury, Hardley, Butsash, and Langley (all in Fawley parish) were attached to the New Forest Hundred at this date, as were also Exbury and Leap.[13] Droxford, however, had become a part of Bishop's Waltham Hundred,[14] the incorporation being exemplified on a court roll of the year 1337,[15] on which the tithings of Droxford, Swanmore, Shedfield, and Midlington are added to those already noticed in the year 1236.

In 1551 Bishop Poynet surrendered the hundred of Bishop's Waltham to Paulet the Lord Treasurer.[16] It was granted by the crown the following month to the earl of Wiltshire,[17] and restored to the bishopric by Queen Mary in 1557.[18]

The court rolls continue through the sixteenth, seventeenth, and eighteenth centuries, the parishes practically included in the jurisdiction of the hundred being apparently Bishop's Waltham, Upham, Durley, Bursledon, and Droxford.[19] The parish of St. Mary Extra never appears on the Waltham court rolls, the reason being that practically all the land was included in the manor of Bitterne. Fawley and Exbury are also absent, but some time between 1785 (the last court roll extant)[20] and 1831 all these three outlying parishes must have been formally incorporated into the hundred of Bishop's Waltham.

[5] *V.C.H. Hants*, i, 466.
[6] Ibid. 454, 467, 509, 513.
[7] Ibid. 501.
[8] Ibid. 513.
[9] Eccl. Com. Ct. R. bdle. 77, No. 6.
[10] *Cal. of Pat.* 1281–92, p. 122.
[11] Eccl. Com. Ct. R. bdle. 73, No. 35; bdle. 74, No. 1.
[12] *Feud. Aids* (Rec. Com.), ii, 307.
[13] Ibid. ii, 317.
[14] Ibid. ii, 307.
[15] Eccl. Com. Ct. R. bdle. 73, No. 35; cf. bdle. 77, No. 6, and bdle. 88, No. 7.
[16] Pat. 5 Edw. VI, pt. 6, m. 20.
[17] Ibid. pt. 4, m. 39.
[18] Pat. 4 & 5 Phil. and Mary, pt. 7, m. 20.
[19] Eccl. Com. Ct. R. bdle. 89, No. 7; bdle. 78, No. 24; bdle. 102, No. 2; bdle. 105, No. 5.
[20] Ibid. bdle. 107, No. 9.

BISHOP'S WALTHAM

Waltham Woolpit (xv–xvii cent.); Waltham Westputt (xvii cent.); also called South Waltham to distinguish it from various other places of the same name.

The parish of Bishop's Waltham, together with the former tithing of Curdridge, comprises the whole of the Hamble valley from its source to the head of the estuary at Fairthorne, and also those spurs of the South Downs at the foot of which the two branches of this river rise. The transition from the down lands to the woods of the valley is very marked, and divides the county into two distinct geological portions, the downs being of chalk formation and the valley chiefly clay. The meeting of these two formations is the cause of some curious springs close to the town.[1]

Entering the parish from the north or east (that is to say, over Stephen's Castle Down or Bishop's Down), the slope down to the valley is steep, the town lying not more than 120 ft. above sea-level, whereas Stephen's Castle Down attains at one point a height of 389 ft. The name Stephen's Castle Down is supposed to date from the days of King Stephen, during whose war with the Empress Maud some earthworks are said to have been here erected. Over this down runs the old road from Waltham to Winchester; the new one (opened in 1830) strikes west from the town and approaches Winchester up the Itchen valley. A continuation of the old Winchester road leads through Curdridge to Botley, and maintaining a fairly high level gives a good view of the Hamble country, with the Hamble itself on the right hand and one of its tributaries on the left. The whole valley is well wooded, the road being bordered by oaks and pines, through which fields of wheat, oats, barley, and occasionally strawberries, may be seen. As the road approaches Botley station, Curdridge church is passed on the right hand. Here a few cottages behind the church constitute the village of Curdridge. 'Curdridge Common' consists of a few fields with patches of furze and heath, sloping up from the road opposite the church. In 1894 Curdridge was constituted a civil parish, 2,174 acres being deducted from the original 8,325 acres of Bishop's Waltham. Of these, 2,189¾ in Bishop's Waltham and 715¼ in Curdridge are arable land; 1,641½ in Bishop's Waltham and 730½ in Curdridge are permanent grass; and 160¼ in Bishop's Waltham and 267¼ in Curdridge are woods and plantations.[2] The chief crops are wheat, barley, oats, and clover; and the cultivation of fruit is on the increase.

Botley station in this parish was opened by the London and South Western Railway Company in 1832. A single line of railway from Botley Junction to Bishop's Waltham, with a station at the latter place, was opened in 1863. A steam rail-motor has recently replaced the ordinary train service for passengers on this line.

The best view of the town of Bishop's Waltham, which stands on the left bank of the Hamble stream about half a mile below its source, is from the hill on the opposite side of the valley. Immediately below lies the station, the head of the single line which runs up the valley. Beyond the station is the Abbey Pond and Mill, and beyond these again rise the ruins of the old palace of the bishops of Winchester. To the north of the palace lies the little town, red-tiled and compact, with the church at its east end. On the west side of the valley, facing the town, is a large clay-pit, and the brick and tile works which are the chief industry of the place. Terra-cotta used to be included, but, like the matting and tanning trades, has been discontinued of recent years.

On the west side of the valley the groups of houses known as 'Newtown' have arisen within the last thirty years, chiefly along the Winchester road.

The principal street of the town is the High Street, running north and south, and ending southwards in the square. Two streets run parallel to it on the east, Houghten Street and Basingwell Street, and at the north of the town Bank Street meets them at right angles, a narrow street in continuation of Houghten Street leading to the church. There are no buildings of unusual interest in the town, but a good many examples of eighteenth-century brickwork, and a few timber fronts of older date, notably a gabled house in the west of the square with a moulded beam below the gables, an almost exact replica of which, dated 1613, is to be seen in Petersfield. The Crown Inn is an old house, with latticed windows, and a picturesque yard behind it.[3] Near the entrance to the churchyard is an early eighteenth-century house with good detail.

There used to be stocks at the entrance to St. George's Square,[4] standing back from the road on a little plot of grass which may still be seen. Until about thirty years ago a maypole stood behind the church on a plot of grass which still bears the name, but the old dances were discontinued in the seventeenth century. Tradition says that the present High Street runs through what was once the village green. The old market-house, which used to stand in the centre of the square, was pulled down about the year 1841, a good deal of the material being used in the construction of the present fire-engine house. Under the market-house, which was built on arches, was the cage or lock-up for prisoners.

Dr. Samuel Ward, one of the translators of the authorized version of the Bible, was buried at Bishop's Waltham in 1629, and several other interesting persons have been connected with the town and neighbourhood. Vernon Hill House, which stands on the hill of the same name to the north-east of Bishop's Waltham, was built by Admiral Vernon just after the capture of Porto Bello, and Emerson once visited here. Northbrook House was the residence of Parry the Arctic explorer, and here Lieutenant Cresswell brought him the news of the finding of the

[1] *Hants N. and Q.* vi, 65.

[2] Statistics from Board of Agriculture, (1905).

[3] After the battle of Trafalgar, when some two hundred French prisoners were sent up to Bishop's Waltham, Admiral Villeneuve and Ambrose Louis Garneray, the artist (who painted several of his sea pictures here from memory), were both quartered at the Crown Inn.

[4] Said to have been named after four tradesmen of the name George, who lived in the square in the early nineteenth century.

north-west passage. The Priory, a large red-brick house at Newtown on the hill overlooking the valley, was built some fifty years ago for an infirmary, the land being given by Sir Arthur Helps, a great benefactor to the neighbourhood. Prince Leopold laid the foundation stone in 1864, and Sir Frederick Perkins presented a statue of the Prince Consort. But owing to the circumstances in which Sir Arthur Helps died, the building was claimed by his creditors and sold as a private house. Sir Frederick Perkins therefore sent to take back the statue, but the villagers objected strongly, and a fray was fought which came to be called the 'Battle of Bunker's Hill.' The statue is now in Southampton.

A particularly beautiful seat, in what is now the parish of Curdridge, is Fairthorne Manor. Miss Mitford, after visiting Cobbett here, wrote:[5] 'Cobbett showed the same taste in the purchase of his beautiful farm at Botley—Fairthorne. To be sure he did not give the name, but I always thought it unconsciously influenced his choice in the purchase. The fields lay along the Bursledon River,[6] and might have been shown to a foreigner as a specimen of the richest and loveliest English scenery.' The place is also interesting as having been the site of a Roman villa.[7] At high tide barges are punted up here as far as Botley Bridge. Charles II contemplated making the river navigable for vessels right up to Bishop's Waltham, and an Act was passed in 1664[8] with this intent, but never carried into effect.

The Inclosure Act for the open fields of Bishop's Waltham was passed in 1759.[9] The inclosure of Curdridge Common was effected under the Act of 1856,[10] and that part of Wintershill Common which lies in this parish was inclosed in 1870.[11]

The following place-names occur, among others, in this parish:[12] Gyves, Playstones, Cokes Croft, Paine Meade, Downers, Penny Acre.

MANORS

The manor of *BISHOP'S WALTHAM* formed parcel of the lands of the see of Winchester from the year 904, when King Edward the Elder effected an exchange of lands with Denewulf, bishop of Winchester.[13] The king acquired Portchester, and granted to Denewulf in return 'that part of the lands of the king called by the people Waltham; to have, hold, and possess it with fields, woods, meadows, fisheries, and everything belonging to the same.' The land was to be held by the bishop and his successors of the king and his heirs.[14] King Edgar renewed the grant shortly before the Norman Conquest.[15] The Domesday Survey states that 'the bishop himself holds Waltham in demesne; it has always belonged to the bishopric,' assessing it at 20 hides, 'though there be 30 hides in number,' with a rateable value of £30.[16] The bishops of Winchester continued to hold the manor among the other possessions of the see until 1551,[17] when Bishop Poynet conveyed the property to Paulet the lord treasurer (as representative of the crown) in return for a fixed annual income.[18] The king granted the manor to William earl of Wiltshire the following month.[19] Queen Mary, however, restored it to John White bishop of Winchester in 1558,[20] and his successors continued to hold the manor until the sale of the bishops' lands in 1647. Bishop's Waltham was then purchased by one Robert Reynolds for the sum of £7,999 14*s.* 10¼*d.*[21] Reynolds's name appears as the holder of a court at Waltham manor in 1653.[22] At the Restoration, Bishop's Waltham was restored to the bishops of Winchester, who retained their hold upon it until the Bishops' Resignation Act of 1869 vested all the 'lands, tithes, hereditaments, and endowments then belonging to the bishopric of Winchester' in the hands of the Ecclesiastical Commissioners.[23]

SEE OF WINCHESTER. *Gules St. Peter's keys crossed with St. Paul's sword.*

The palace of Bishop's Waltham[24] was originally built by Henry de Blois bishop of Winchester during the twelfth century,[25] and was shortly afterwards the scene of two important councils: in 1182 when the barons met Henry II and granted him supplies for the second crusade; and in 1194 when Richard I held a council here preparatory to his last expedition to France.[25a] The palace seems to have been a favourite residence of the bishops, and to have been frequently visited by royalty. The wills of both Henry II and William of Wykeham are dated at Waltham, and Wykeham spent his last days here. Cardinal Beaufort in his will bequeathed to Queen Margaret of England his 'blue bed of gold and damask at his palace at Waltham, in the room where the Queen used to lie when she was at that palace, and three suits of the arras hangings in the same room.' William of Waynflete also made his will and died at Bishop's Waltham palace.[26] The State Papers of the reign of Henry VIII contain many references to the visits of that king and of Wolsey and Thomas Cromwell to Bishop's Waltham palace;[27] and in 1512 it was the scene of the convention between king and emperor which came to be known as the Treaty of Waltham.[28] Within a few years of this date Leland described the palace as 'a right ample and goodly Maner Place moted aboute, and a praty Brooke renning hard by it.'[29] Later in the sixteenth century, when the manor and palace of Waltham were in the hands of the crown, Edward VI described the palace as 'a fair old home,

5 Miss Mitford, *Recollections of a Literary Life.*

6 ? Hamble.

7 *Hants N. and Q.* vi, 46.

8 *Hist. MSS. Com. Rep.* x, 1799.

9 *Parl. Papers*, 32 Geo. II, No. 57.

10 *Parl. Blue Bks. Inclosures*, 148.

11 Ibid. 158.

12 Chan. Proc. (Ser. 2), vol. i, bdle. 37, No. 19; Eccl. Com. Ct. R. bdle. 78, No. 24.

13 See account of Bishop's Waltham Hundred.

14 Kemble, *Cod. Dipl.* v, 161.

15 Birch, *Cart. Sax.* iii, 411.

16 *V.C.H. Hants*, i, 460.

17 Add. MSS. 26093; Inq. a.q.d. 18 Edw. II. No. 103; *Feud. Aids*, ii, 335, 357; *Cal. of Pat.* 1381–5, p. 169.

18 Pat. 5 Edw. VI, pt. 6, m. 20.

19 Ibid. pt. 4, m. 39.

20 Pat. 4 & 5 Phil. and Mary, pt. 7, m. 20.

21 *Coll. Top. et Gen.* i, 2.

22 Court Roll of Waltham Manor, *penes* Mrs. Pleydell-Bouverie-Campbell-Wyndham.

23 *Lond. Gaz.* 1 April, 1870.

24 Rev. C. Walters, *Hist. of Bishop's Waltham*; Rev. G. W. Minns, 'Bishop's Waltham,' *Woolston Weekly News*, 7 July, 1906; Canon Vaughan, 'Bishop's Waltham,' *The Treasury*, April, 1904, *Proc. Hants Field Club*, June, 1900.

25 *Angl. Sacr.* i, 299.

25a *Chron. Rog. Hoveden* (Rolls Ser.), iii, 250.

26 Chandler, *Life of Waynflete*, 218.

27 *L. and P. Hen. VIII*, iii, 2440, 2364; ix, 884.

28 Ibid. iii, 2455.

29 Leland, *Itin.* (3rd ed. T. Hearne), iii, 115.

in times past of the bishops of Winchester, but now my Lord Treasurer's.' The great Civil War saw the destruction of Bishop's Waltham palace, which after a gallant defence by 200 cavaliers under Colonel Bennett surrendered to General Brown, on 9 April, 1644. On the 11th a cavalier wrote: 'Waltham House in ashes.' Bishop Curll, who was resident in the palace at the time, is said to have effected his escape in a dung cart. For some time after this anyone who required building stone helped himself from the palace ruins. In 1869 the property passed into the hands of the Ecclesiastical Commissioners, who sold the site and ruins of the palace to Sir William Jenner. Since the latter's death in 1898, his widow Lady Jenner has owned the place.

The ruins of the palace are still imposing, though little is left but the shell of the north wing. The house was probably foursquare, with an inner court, and a gateway in an outer court on the north-east, round which the offices were built. The whole was defended by a moat, which remains very perfect on the north and east, and a large space south and west of the moated site is inclosed by a picturesque brick wall, built by Bishop Langton (*ob.* 1501), with a square two-story garden-house remaining at its south-eastern angle. Through it a stream runs north-west towards the Hamble, leaving the inclosure at a second red-brick garden-house in the north-west angle, which has served as a latrine. In the western part of the inclosure stands the house known as Place House, owned by Lady Jenner, part of which may be of seventeenth-century date, but its chief attractions are its garden and the view of the ruined palace.

Part of the arrangement of the palace building is still to be made out, though the site is much overgrown and heaped with fallen rubbish. The south front is 180 ft. long, with a square tower at each end, projecting beyond the line of the main wall. The general appearance of the work is that of a fifteenth-century building, but in reality a great deal of twelfth-century walling and detail exists, especially in the western part. In the centre of the range stands the hall, with tall two-light windows on the south, the inner or north wall being in this part entirely destroyed. At the east end are the kitchen and offices, and at the west of the hall are living rooms. Along the west wall of the hall are remains of a twelfth-century wall arcade, and in the room immediately adjoining it a large twelfth-century window remains in a fair state of preservation. The other wings of the house are completely ruined, but the remains of the chapel, a small twelfth-century apsidal building, were excavated some years since, and are still to be seen, though much overgrown, to the south of the hall. Parts of the outer gatehouse exist at the north-east angle of the inclosure, the side walls only being left, with fireplaces in what must have been the porter's lodgings. At the south-east angle of the inclosure is a long building standing east and west, and formerly of two stories. At the east end is a large fireplace, and the building was probably a bakehouse, brewhouse, or the like, and is of late fifteenth-century date.

The large pond to the south of the palace, separated from the southern arm of its moat by the high road, is an artificial pool made to work the mill at its west end. Below the mill are the banks of a second pool, now dry, and there seems to have been a third bank further down stream. All the pools no doubt served as stew-ponds for the use of the palace.

PARK The park of Bishop's Waltham, which was attached to the palace, formerly extended for over 1,000 acres.[30] It was bounded by the 'Lug,' a mound 16½ ft. broad and some 6 ft. high, with trees planted on the top to form a barricade.[31] After the destruction of the palace, Dr. George Morley (bishop of Winchester 1662–84), being in need of money for the repair of Farnham Castle,[32] conceived the idea of dividing up the park into farms. He therefore obtained the royal assent to an Act enabling him to lease out 'the two parks and other demesnes at Bishop's Waltham,' in July, 1663.[33] A year later the place was spoken of as 'the great disparked park of Bishop's Waltham,'[34] which very accurately describes it at the present day.

The land known as Waltham Chase was probably included in the original tenth-century grant to the bishopric, but the Chase is only specifically mentioned at the time of its acquisition by the Lord Treasurer in the sixteenth century, and the subsequent grant to the earl of Wiltshire and regrant to Bishop White.[35] It stretched away to the south and east of the park, and was practically an outlying portion of the Forest of Bere. Originally the hunting-ground of the bishops, the chase became famous in the eighteenth century as the haunt of a gang of deer-stealers, who were known from their blackened faces as 'The Waltham Blacks.' It was in consequence of their doings, and at the instigation of Bishop Trimnell, that the Black Act of George I was passed in 1722, though apparently it was never enforced. Some twenty years later, Bishop Hoadly, on being asked to re-stock the chase with deer, refused, saying that it 'had done mischief enough already.' Waltham Chase was inclosed in 1870,[36] since when the timber has been entirely cut down,[37] though the name forest still clings to the locality.

The earliest reference to a market at Bishop's Waltham is in the reign of Edward I, when it was reported by some inquisitors that 'the market of Titchfield and Waltham is to the damage of the market of . . . . which is held on a Saturday.'[38] This was in all probability a joint market, held alternate weeks at either place, and dropped in consequence of the inquisitors' report, which would account for the entirely new grant by Elizabeth in 1602 to the bishop of Winchester and his successors of the right to hold a market at Bishop's Waltham on Friday in each week.[39] When the main line through Botley was opened in 1832, Botley became a more convenient centre than Bishop's Waltham, and the

30 The boundaries are given by Mr. Houghton in *Hants N. and Q.* vi, 65.

31 Bayley's *Dictionary* defines Lug as an old English rod, viz. 16½ ft. or 5½ yds., an average deer leap.

32 Grose, *Antiquities*, v, 90.

33 *Hist. MSS. Com. Rep.* x, 171*a*.

34 Ibid. 180*a*.

35 Pat. 5 Edw. VI, pt. 6, m. 20, and pt. 6, m. 39; Pat. 4 & 5 Phil. and Mary, pt. 7, m. 20.

36 *Parl. Blue Bks. Inclosures*, 157.

37 Cf. William Cobbett, *Rural Rides*, ii, 261.

38 *Hund. R.* (Rec. Com.), ii, 224.

39 Inq. a.q.d. 44 Eliz. No. 3. T. W. Shore, however, in his *Hist. of Hants*, p. 151, considers this grant of Elizabeth to be the earliest sign of a market at Bishop's Waltham, and comments upon the fact.

Bishop's Waltham : The Palace from the North-west

market was transferred thither, where it was held alternate weeks with Fareham.

Queen Elizabeth's grant to the bishop in 1602 included the right to hold two fairs in Bishop's Waltham, one on the vigil of St. Philip and St. James, and the other on the first Tuesday in Lent. By 1792 there were four annual fairs, viz.: the second Friday in May, the thirtieth day of July, the first Friday after Old Michaelmas, and the tenth day of October.[40] The last-named appears to have lapsed before the year 1848,[41] and by 1888 all had ceased with the exception of a small pleasure fair which is still held annually in August.

Of the three mills mentioned in the account of Waltham in Domesday Book,[42] two are in the present parish of Waltham,[43] viz.: Abbey Mill on the palace pond,[44] and Waltham Mill on the Fareham road. The former was rebuilt in 1862 after a fire. On a court roll of Queen Anne's reign mention is made of 'one mill called a paper mill in the tithing of Curdridge.'[45] This was the 'Frog Mill' on the Hamble River, just below Durley Mill. Having long been disused, it was pulled down some twelve or fifteen years ago, with the exception of a small portion now used as a barn.

There is no indication that the so-called manor of *FAIRTHORNE*[46] (Fayerthorne, Fayrethorne, xvi cent.) was ever anything more than an estate included in Bishop's Waltham manor. The land is possibly to be first traced in the 'one messuage and one carucate of land in Hulle' acquired in 1296 by William de la Hulle and Agnes his wife,[47] but the name Hulle or Hill is so common in Hampshire that this identification cannot be more than conjectural. In 1332 William de Overton and Joan his wife held 'one messuage and one carucate in Hulle and Titchfield,'[48] and in the following year this same tenement is described as lying 'in Southwaltham and Hulle near Botley,'[49] which clearly identifies it with the Hulle or Fairthorne of later times. From this date the descent of the property can be fairly traced. In 1361 Thomas de Overton, son of the above William de Overton, died seised of 140 acres of land in Hulle.[50] His heir was his son William, presumably the father of that Isabella whose marriage with Sir William Tanke[51] brought the Hulle property into the hands of the Tankes. Hull is not mentioned by name in 1393 and 1394 among the lands 'in Waltham' held by Robert Tanke and Elizabeth his wife,[52] but a Robert Tanke was holding the 'Manor of Hylle beside Botley' in 1431.[53] This date is noticeable as the first occasion on which the term manor is applied to the tenement. In 1504 William Tanke died seised of 'lands in Bishop's Waltham held by the bishop of Winchester.'[54] He left two daughters, the elder of whom, Joan, became in turn the wife of Richard Ryman and Edward Bartlett,[55] and under a settlement of 1542 Joan and her second husband were to hold the manor during their lives, with reversion to the children of Joan by her first husband.[56] Joan died in 1561,[57] and Humphrey Ryman her elder son in 1568.[58] John, the son and heir of Humphrey, succeeded to the property on the death of his uncle William Ryman, who had only had a life interest in it. John Ryman was still holding in 1573[59] and 1579,[60] but in 1600 Francis Serle was in possession.[61] The Serles seem to have been closely connected (probably by marriage) with the Bartlett and Ryman family, for the name appears on family settlements of the years 1542[62] and 1576,[63] and John Serle and Francis Serle apparently acted as successive trustees of the manor.[64] The descent of Fairthorne is very obscure in the seventeenth century, but by 1684 the manor was in the hands of Wriothesley Baptist Noel, descendant of Thomas first earl of Southampton, who acquired the manor of Titchfield after the Dissolution. Wriothesley's daughter Elizabeth married Henry first duke of Portland, and the Portlands were holding Fairthorne with their Titchfield property in 1734[65] and in 1762.[66] When they parted with it is uncertain.[67] The next known fact concerning Fairthorne is that about the year 1806 William Cobbett 'purchased Fairthorne Farm of about 300 acres, and around it he planted a broad belt of trees.'[68] On the site of Cobbett's summer-house, as it was called, the present house was built about fifty years ago. It is now the residence and property of Mr. R. A. Burrell, who purchased it from Sir Thomas Freke in 1878.

TANKE. *Argent a text T gules and three wreaths vert in the chief.*

BENTINCK, Duke of Portland. *Azure a cross moline argent.*

CHURCHES

ST. PETER'S CHURCH, BISHOP'S WALTHAM, has a chancel, nave of four bays with aisles and south porch, south-west tower, and at the west end of the north aisle a vestry with gallery over. There is also a large gallery in the west bay of the nave. The repairs and alterations of the last three centuries have

[40] *Parl. Blue Bks. Market Rights and Tolls*, i, 168.
[41] Kelly, *Directory*, 1848.
[42] *V.C.H. Hants*, i, 460.
[43] For the third mill see Durley Parish, note 1.
[44] There were originally two ponds, the mill standing between them. The lower pond was dammed up when the new road to Winchester was constructed.
[45] Eccl. Com. Ct. R. bdle. 106, No 7.
[46] The name Fairthorne is not applied to this manor until the reign of Eliz. (Feet of F. Hants, Mich. 18 Eliz.), after which the place is called Fairthorne *alias* Hulle or Hill, up to the nineteenth century, when the name Fairthorne completely supersedes that of Hill.
[47] Feet of F. Hants, Mich. 25 Edw. I.
[48] Ibid. East. 6 Edw. III.
[49] Ibid. East. 7 Edw. III.
[50] Chan. Inq. p.m. 35 Edw. III, pt. 2, No. 17.
[51] Berry, *Hants Genealogies*, 234.
[52] Feet of F. Hants, Trin. 17 Ric. II; ibid. Trin. 18 Ric. II.
[53] Early Chan. Proc. bdle. 12, No. 22.
[54] Chan. Inq. p.m. (Ser. 2), vol. 18, No. 4.
[55] Chan. Inq. p.m. (Ser. 2), pt. 1, No. 15.
[56] Feet of F. Hants, Trin. 34 Hen. VIII.
[57] Exch. Inq. p.m. bdle. 1002, No. 10.
[58] Chan. Inq. p.m. (Ser. 2), No. 141.
[59] Recov. R. East. 15 Eliz. rot. 147.
[60] Ibid. 21 Eliz. rot. 105.
[61] Com. Pleas Recov. R. Mich. 42 & 43 Eliz. m. 22.
[62] Feet of F. Hants, Trin. 34 Hen. VIII.
[63] Ibid. Mich. 18 Eliz.
[64] The name Serle in connexion with the tithing of Curdridge appears on the Waltham Ct. R. as late as 1703.
[65] Recov. R. Trin. 8 Geo. II.
[66] Ibid. 2 Geo. III.
[67] The duke of Portland sold Botley in 1775.
[68] William Cobbett, *Rural Rides, Introd.* p. xxxiv.

been extensive, and little early work remains. The capitals and arches of the north arcade of the nave date from the beginning of the thirteenth century, and from the evidence of windows discovered in 1868 in the north wall of the chancel it appeared that the chancel was also of thirteenth-century date. It was, however, remodelled in the fifteenth century, or in the late fourteenth, and to that time its earliest features now belong. The tower is recorded to have fallen 31 December, 1582, and to have been rebuilt in 1584–9; the north aisle was rebuilt in 1637, and the south aisle in 1652. The south arcade of the nave was destroyed in 1798 to make place for a gallery over the aisle, the wooden posts carrying this gallery and the nave roof being replaced in 1822 by Tuscan columns in Portland stone. In 1894 these in their turn gave way to a modern arcade in fourteenth-century style, and the gallery was removed. The church generally was restored in 1864–8, and again in 1894, and in 1849 the west end of the nave was rebuilt. The nave roof was 'new made' in 1669, and the west gallery was set up in 1733 to hold the organ. The chancel has a three-light east window with fifteenth-century tracery, and a rose on the crown of the rear arch, a fifteenth-century north window of two lights at the west, and two like windows on the south, the eastern of which has modern tracery; between them is a plain priest's doorway. The roof is old, low-pitched, and open-timbered, with arched braces, and the altar-rails are a pretty example of seventeenth-century work with turned balusters and a carved top rail. The altar-table is also of the seventeenth century, with carved legs. The quire seats and marble pavement date from 1894. In the same year the chancel arch, which is of two continuous chamfered orders, was made symmetrical, its south jamb having been at some time cut back and the arch widened in a clumsy manner on one side only. The extent of the widening is still to be seen, as the lower part of the cut-back jamb is preserved, a space being left between it and the new jamb, and the result might easily be mistaken for a mediaeval squint.

The north arcade of the nave has plain octagonal capitals and pointed arches of two chamfered orders in Bonchurch stone, with half-round responds in chalk at either end. The circular columns were of the same material till 1894, but being out of the perpendicular they were then rebuilt as they now appear, with new bases on a slightly different line from the old. Of the capitals only those to the responds are old. At the east end of the north aisle is preserved a large late twelfth-century scalloped capital, perhaps from the old south arcade, and worked to fit a round column. With it is the stem of a twelfth-century pillar piscina with zigzag ornament, which has been re-used in the fifteenth century as part of the shaft of a canopied niche.

The north aisle, known as the Ashton aisle, and said to have been built with the stones of Ashton chapel, which stood near Chapel Farm, has a three-light east window with a curious and clumsy attempt at fifteenth-century tracery, doubtless dating from the rebuilding of 1637, and is lighted on the north by three square-headed windows each of three cinquefoiled lights of better style. The gallery over the vestry at its west end was formerly used as the school, and is reached from the west by a stair in a projecting buttress, dated 1637. It is lighted on the north by a four-light window with uncusped four-centred lights, and gives access on the south to the west gallery of the nave. This preserves its panelled front of 1733, a good specimen of its kind, but no longer holds the organ, which is now in the east end of the south aisle.

The south aisle has an east window of the same kind as that in the north aisle, and in its south wall three three-light windows, also like those in the north aisle. It is faced with wrought stone externally, a good deal of which looks like twelfth-century material re-used. Over the east window is a stone dated 1652, with the initials of the churchwardens, then as now four in number. Before 1894 there were dormer windows on the south with stone tracery, set up in 1867 to light the south gallery, and replacing wooden dormers. In the west bay of the aisle is the south door and porch, with detail of sixteenth-century character, and a panelled door dated 1613, while on its large key is the date 1681. The doorway may perhaps be of the same date as the door, as the west wall of the porch, which is also of late Gothic character, is built against and is therefore later than the south-east buttress of the tower, and this latter is recorded to have been rebuilt in 1584-9. The rebuilding, however, may not have been from the foundations. In any case, there must have been a re-use of old material in the seventeenth-century work, and it is not likely that the whole of the window tracery is of the same date as the poor stuff in the heads of the east windows of the two aisles.

The tower is of three stages, with square-headed windows of two uncusped four-centred lights in each stage on the west face, and in all four faces in the belfry stage. At the south-west angle is a newel stair, with a plain circular turret, probably of eighteenth-century date, rising above the parapet of the tower. The tower opens to the south aisle by a four-centred doorway, and has a west doorway of brick to the churchyard. In the south wall of its ground story is a locker rebated for a door and with a groove for a shelf, removed from the chancel in 1867, and in the north wall is a second recess, probably in situ, and dating from the rebuilding of the tower. A list of ringers' rules, dated 1766, and renewed in 1835, is kept here.

The west front of the nave, dating from 1849, has a four-light window of fifteenth-century style, and below it a west doorway.

The nave roof, as already noted, was 'new made' in 1669, and the aisle roofs are probably of the same date, though both may contain older timbers re-used. The pulpit in the north-east angle of the nave is a great ornament to the church, and dates from *c.* 1600. It is hexagonal with a panelled body on a stem, the panels inclosing arches with strapwork borders, under pediments. Over the pulpit is a very fine tester, relegated to the tower in 1867, but repaired and replaced in 1894, with strapwork cresting and pendants, and a panelled soffit, in the centre of which is a rose.

The font, at the south-west of the nave, is modern, and has a square bowl worked with shallow tracery patterns.

There are no monuments of importance, the best being that of Thomas Ashton, 1629, on the north wall of the north aisle. It is said to have been brought from Ashton chapel, and is a pretty alabaster panel with a half-length figure under a pediment; it has lately been redecorated. Below it is a marble panel, with the arms of Kerby, to the 'much lamented pious charitable good catholic' Mary Kerby, 1716, and on the north wall of the chancel is a black marble tablet in an alabaster frame, to Anna Cruys, 1634.

A few mediæval tiles, found during repairs, are kept in the north aisle.

There are six bells, the treble recast 1901, formerly dated 1724, the second of 1712, the third of 1651, the fourth formerly of that date, but recast in 1901, the fifth of 1599, and the tenor of 1597. The two last bear the initials of John Wallis of Salisbury.

The church possesses a fine set of silver-gilt plate; an Elizabethan communion cup without hallmarks, having two bands of engraved ornament on the bowl, a small paten and a flagon of 1747, a second flagon of 1629, and a large standing almsdish of 1669, though recorded to have been given in 1665.

The first book of the registers, 1612–68, contains a note of the fall of the tower and the rebuilding of the aisles; the second goes from 1669 to 1736, and the third from 1736 to 1812, the marriages ending in 1754 and being continued to 1812 in two more books.

Parish accounts are preserved from 1759, and there are notes of briefs down to 1823. The record of a curious disturbance in 1688 is preserved at length, and tells how the parish clerk and one churchwarden being excommunicate, for some reason not set down, withheld the key of the church from the parishioners, who eventually defeated the adversary by getting episcopal permission to break open the church door and have a new lock made.

A homily book of 1683 is kept in the vestry, which having been originally the property of the church, was lost in course of time, but in 1869 was discovered by Mr. A. V. Walters, who bought it and gave it back to the church.

The church of *ST. PETER, CURDRIDGE*, replacing an older building near the same site, was erected in 1887, its tower being added in 1894. It is of flint, with stone dressings. The register dates from 1835.

ADVOWSONS It is recorded in Domesday Book that 'Ralf the priest holds the two churches of this manor, with two and a half hides.'[69] The first of these two churches was the parish church of Bishop's Waltham, in the gift of the bishop of Winchester, lord of the manor. Henry de Blois (bishop of Winchester, 1129–71) granted the advowson of this church to the hospital of St. Cross, Winchester, some time during his tenure of office.[70] The hospital had, however, lost it before 1284, in which year, under an agreement between the bishop of Winchester and the monks of St. Swithun concerning certain advowsons, the monks gave up their claim to Bishop's Waltham in favour of the bishop.[71] The living, which is a rectory, subsequently remained in the bishop's hands.[72] In 1533 the curate of Bishop's Waltham wrote a pathetic letter to Lady Lisle to ask for a gown cloth which she had promised him: 'you have so many whelps pertaining to you that poor Thomas Gylbert shall be forgotten.'[73] In 1551 Bishop Poynet surrendered the advowson of Bishop's Waltham, together with the hundred and manor, to the crown.[74] They were granted to William, earl of Wiltshire, the same year,[75] and eventually restored to the bishopric by Queen Mary.[76] Since this latter date the living has remained in the gift of the bishop.[77] Bishop's Waltham was a peculiar benefice. The first reference to this is in the fourteenth century,[78] and it is again recorded in the reign of Henry VIII.[79] There is also an entry in the parish registers of the year 1736, saying that mortuaries are due from Bishop's Waltham, Hamble, and Bursledon, to the minister of Bishop's Waltham, 'as having a peculiar jurisdiction there.'[80]

Several theories have been put forward for the identification of the second church recorded in Domesday.

Of these the principal are:[81] (1) That the second church was at Ashton, where the road to Upham meets Ashton Street, on the spot now occupied by a smithy; the site was at one time occupied by a little chapel of ease. (2) That Bursledon was this second church, the old Waltham registers showing that at one time the rector of Waltham exercised a peculiar archidiaconal jurisdiction over Bursledon.[81a] (3) That this second church was at Upham or Botley.

Curdridge was formed into a district chapelry, out of the parish of Bishop's Waltham, in 1838.[82] The patronage of the living, which is a vicarage, was transferred in 1880 from the rector of Bishop's Waltham to the bishop of Winchester, in consideration of a further endowment of Curdridge out of the revenues of Bishop's Waltham.[83] Between 1892 and 1893 the advowson passed from the bishop to the dean and chapter of Winchester.[84]

There is a Congregational chapel (built 1862) at Bishop's Waltham, and a Primitive Methodist mission room. There is a mission hall at Ashton, and an iron chapel at Curdridge.

CHARITIES The charities in the ancient parish of *BISHOP'S WALTHAM* were by a scheme established by an order of the Charity Commissioners, dated 14 February, 1896, consolidated under the title of 'The Combined Charities,' whereby—as modified by a further order of 14 October, 1898—provision was made for their future administration, in equal parts, as educational and eleemosynary. By an order of the said Commissioners the following charities were specifically allocated for educational purposes, viz.:—

1. The Educational Institute in Bank Street, erected with moneys arising from accumulations and from a grant of the Hampshire County Council on a site conveyed by deed of 30 September, 1898.

2. Bishop Morley's Charity, deed, 1679, being an annuity of £10, part of a fee-farm rent of £51, issuing out of the site of the late priory of the Holy Trinity of Mottisfont, and other manors and lands.

69 *V.C.H. Hants*, i, 461*a*.
70 Harl. MS. 1616, fol. 9.
71 Add. MSS. 29436.
72 Winton Epis. Reg. (Egerton MSS. 203–4); De Banc. R. 358, m. 130; *Valor Eccl.* (Rec. Com.), ii, 22, and App.
73 *L. and P. Hen. VIII*, vi, 780.
74 Pat. 5 Edw. VI, pt. 6, m. 20.
75 Ibid. pt. 4, m. 39.
76 Pat. 4 & 5 Phil. and Mary, m. 20.
77 Inst. Bks. P.R.O.
78 Winton Epis. Reg. (Egerton MSS. 2031–4).
79 *Valor Eccl.* (Rec. Com.), ii, App.
80 Extract from Par. Reg. iii.
81 *Proc. Hants Field Club*, June 1900; *Addenda Hist. of Bishop's Waltham*, Rev. C. Walters.
81a Both Bursledon and Hamble owed mortuaries to Bishop's Waltham.
82 *Lond. Gaz.* 30 Mar. 1838.
83 Ibid. 9 July, 1880.
84 *Clergy Lists.*

3. Mary Bone's Charity for education, will, 1732, a rent-charge of £20 issuing out of a farm and lands known as Lomer in the parishes of Corhampton and Warnford.

4. A sum of £500 consols with the official trustees of charitable funds to an account entitled 'The Hampshire County Council Repayment Fund,' which may be claimed in certain contingencies by the County Council ; and

5. A sum of £1,360 Great Eastern Railway Company £4 per cent. consolidated preference stock, which includes £1,195 stock representing investment of proceeds of sale in 1882 of land belonging to Robert Kerby's charities.

The income of the educational branch, amounting to £96 18*s.* a year is applied in support of the institute, which is open without distinction of creed to all young persons of the civil parishes of Bishop's Waltham and Curdridge, and so much of the civil parish of Swanmore as was included in the ancient parish of Bishop's Waltham upon payment of such fees as the trustees may fix ; but the buildings are by the scheme reserved to the free use on Sundays by the rector for the purposes of religious education in respect of Mary Bone's charity.

The Combined Eleemosynary Charities consist of the following charities, viz. :—

1. The Almshouse Charity, almshouses sold in 1882, now £44 of above-mentioned railway stock.

2. Poor's Stock Money, being £854, other part of said railway stock.

3. Mary Bone's Charity for poor widows, will, 1732, formerly rent-charge of £6 out of Stakes Farm in this parish, redeemed in 1902 by transfer to the official trustees of £240 consols, forming part of £1,237 17*s.* 8*d.* consols mentioned below.

4. Bishop's Palace Charity, consisting of rent-charge of £8 on Palace House, Bishop's Waltham, and of £28 of said railway stock.

5. Thomas Grant's Charity, rent-charge of £2 issuing out of a messuage in the High Street.

6. Elizabeth Penford's Charity for poor of Bishop's Waltham, £372 of said railway stock.

7. Elizabeth Penford's Charity for poor of Curdridge, will, 1842, £186 like stock.

8. Unknown Donor's Charity, £81 like stock.

9. £1,400 Great Eastern Railway £4 per cent. preference stock, forming part of £2,760 like stock with the official trustees, which comprises the several sums of railway stock above-mentioned ; and £1,237 17*s.* 8*d.* consols, also with the official trustees representing balance of accumulations, and £240 consols, Mary Bone's charity for poor widows above-mentioned.

The income of the Eleemosynary Branch, amounting to £96 18*s.* 8*d.* a year, is applicable under the scheme for the benefit of necessitous poor in the area above mentioned in such manner as the trustees may consider most conducive to the formation of provident habits, in aid of the funds of provident clubs or societies, contributions towards provision of nurses, &c., also in pensions to old people. In 1905 £80 was expended in providing parish nurses, and six old persons received pensions.

Poor's allotments consist of 8 acres, deed, 1832 ; the rents, about £12 16*s.*, a year, are carried to the poor rate.

By an award, 1870, 4 acres were acquired as a recreation ground, the rent of 'feed' being carried to the highway rates.

The Wheat Charity.—5½ sacks of wheat to poor yearly charged on the rectory.

The National Schools.—See article on schools, *V.C.H. Hants*, ii, 396.

Curdridge

The Combined Charities.—See Bishop's Waltham.

Gravel Pit Allotment consists of 3 acres acquired by award, 1856, rent applied in aid of highway rate.

The National Schools.—See article on schools, *V.C.H. Hants*, ii, 398.

Sir Henry Jenkin's Memorial Scholarship Fund consists of £304 10*s.* 4*d.* London County Consolidated Stock which the official trustees raised by subscription. By scheme of 31 August, 1901, the dividends are applicable for maintenance of a scholarship for a boy or girl who has been a scholar in a public elementary school in Curdridge or Botley.

Poor's Allotment consists of 3 acres award, 1856, subject to a yearly rent-charge of £3.

Recreation Ground.—By an award, 1856, 4 acres were acquired for this purpose, regulated by schemes of the Charity Commissioners of 25 August, 1885, and 9 March, 1887.

Reading Room.—By deed, 1884, a site and building thereon, together with a cottage, were dedicated for the use of the parishioners—an income of about £12 16*s.* is derived therefrom.

BURSLEDON

Brixenden (xii cent.); Burstlesden (xiv cent.); Bristelden (xvi cent.).

The parish of Bursledon is a beautiful little tract of country, 1,100 acres in extent, on the right bank of the Hamble River, which is here tidal. The north-west boundary of the parish touches the eastern side of Netley Hill, on a southern spur of which stands an old ivy-covered windmill which serves as a landmark for miles round. On the upper slopes of Netley Hill is a tract of moorland covered with bracken and heather; thence the country slopes rapidly down to the sea, and is thickly wooded to the water's edge. The main road from Fareham to Southampton, crossing the river by a wooden bridge immediately to the north of Bursledon village, strikes across the parish in a north-westerly direction, cutting it into two nearly equal portions. The bridge was built by private enterprise about 1783, and is subject to a toll. With the exception of this road, communication in Bursledon parish is by winding lanes overhung with trees. The London and South-Western Railway line from Netley to Fareham enters the parish at the south-west, and running north-east has a station on the river bank below the village, crossing the Hamble by a bridge a little above the toll bridge.

The village of Bursledon stands on steeply-rising wooded ground on the east bank of the river, which here turns sharply to the south-east and again to the south-west. The steepness of the path and the combination of woods and tidal water recall a Devonshire sea-side village. At the north end of the village stands the church, called by the villagers 'Jerusalem,' from its position above them. Immediately below it, set against the steep bank on the river's edge, is a group of houses known as the Salterns, in distinction from the upper village, which is called Old Bursledon. Between the church and the southern part of the village, where the vicarage stands, is Elm Lodge, the residence of Capt. Shawe-Storey, in well-wooded grounds. South-west of the village, where the ground falls again to a tributary stream of the Hamble, is another group of houses called Hungerford. About a mile inland, higher up the course of the same stream, and just below the point where it is crossed by the Southampton road, lies the much larger village of Lowford or New Bursledon, a red-brick suburb raised within the last twenty years.

From its position midway between the inland forests and the harbour of Southampton Water, Bursledon was a natural ship-building centre in the days of wooden warships.[1] The narrowness of the creek moreover at this point diminished the danger of attacks from French privateers. It is said that two eighty-gun ships were built at Bursledon in the time of William IV,[2] and certainly Mr. Philemon Ewer had a private ship-building yard here early in the eighteenth century. Among other ships he built the *Anson*, of sixty guns, called after Admiral Anson, afterwards baron of Soberton. Mr. Ewer's monument, on which there is a model of the battleship of the period, is in Bursledon parish church. At the latter end of the same century Mr. Henry Parsons employed shipwrights at Bursledon, launching among other ships the *Elephant* (seventy-four guns), in which Nelson sailed to the battle of Copenhagen. The ships used to be launched on the top of high-water, and towed round to Portsmouth Harbour, where they were sheathed in copper. The ship-building trade has long ago vanished, but traces of the old docks may still be seen close to the present railway station. The inhabitants are now chiefly engaged in strawberry-growing. Other crops are wheat, oats, and barley. There are 292 acres of arable land in the parish, 341 of permanent grass, and eighty-one of woods and plantations.[3] The soil is light and sandy.

The common lands in Bursledon, known as 'the waste lands of Bishop's Waltham Manor,' were inclosed in 1857.[4]

MANORS There was no separate manor of *BURSLEDON*, but the lands formed part of the ancient manor of Bishop's Waltham (q.v.). From the year 1235 onwards the name occurs regularly as one of the tithings of Bishop's Waltham on the Court Rolls of that manor.[5] In 1328 John Milyr, parson of the church of Eversley, conveyed to John Screeche and Ellen his wife one messuage, twenty acres of wood, 20*s.* rent, and half a carucate of land, in Bonewode, Titchfield, Bursledon, and Botley, with remainder to William le Wayte and his heirs.[6] William le Wayte was holding this piece of land in 1339.[7] In 1541 Walter Chandler conveyed a tenement in Bursledon to Sir Thomas Wriothesley,[8] who had been possessed of the lands of Titchfield Abbey in this county since 1537.[9]

CHURCH The church of *ST. LEONARD, BURSLEDON*, has a chancel with south organ chamber and vestry, north and south transepts, and nave with wooden west porch and bell-turret. Its later history has been that in 1833 two transepts were built, and in 1888 they were replaced by those now existing, the organ chamber and vestry being added at the same time, and the nave lengthened westward about 8 ft. The west porch and bell turret are also of this date, and the whole building was repaired and the roofs covered with red tiles. The architect was Mr. J. D. Sedding.

The chancel walls and parts of the nave are therefore the only ancient portions of the church, and they appear to date from *c.* 1230. The east window of the chancel is of three lights in fifteenth-century style, but only the jambs are old, and on them are traces of painting. In the north wall is a small thirteenth-century lancet, discovered in 1888; the head has been renewed. The chancel arch is also of the thirteenth century, of two chamfered orders, with alternate voussoirs of dark and light stone, and was taken down and reset at a higher level in 1888. The inner order springs from moulded corbels with short

1 From the *Naval and Military Record*, 16 April, 1808, as quoted in *Bursledon Parish Mag.* for 1905.

2 *A Companion in a Tour round Southampton* (2nd ed. 1801).

3 Statistics from Bd. of Agric. (1905).

4 *Parliamentary Blue Books, Inclosure Awards*, 150.

5 Eccl. Com. Court R. bdle. 77, No. 6.

6 Feet of F. Hants, Trin. 1 Edw. III.

7 Feet of F. Hants, Mich. 13 Edw. III.

8 Feet of F. Hants, Mich. 33 Hen. VIII.

9 Feet of F. Div. Cos. Mich. 29 Hen. VIII.

shafts resting on human heads. In the nave the thirteenth-century north and south doorways, with segmental rear arches, remain, but are blocked, and the two windows to the west of them on each side of the nave are in modern stonework. The external arch of the south doorway, with a roll label, remains perfect, but of the north doorway only part of the west jamb, with an edge roll, survives. The west window, likewise modern, is of four lights, and below it is a large modern wall-painting of the Maries at the tomb of Christ. The west doorway opens to a charming wooden porch, covering the west end of the church, and from it a path runs to a modern lych-gate on the north side of the churchyard.

The font in the south-west angle of the nave is of the twelfth century, with a round bowl ornamented with an arcade of narrow arches, which for nearly half the circumference are round-headed and intersect each other, while the rest are pointed and do not intersect. It stands on a round shaft and base, both modern.

The monument of Mr. Philemon Ewer, the shipbuilder, who died in 1750, is in the north transept, and records that he built 'seven large ships-of-war for his Majesty's service during the late war with France and Spain . . . . gaining the reputation of an ingenious artist, an excellent workman, and an honest man, dying with a fair character and a plentiful fortune.'

There are two bells, the treble by I. H, 1652, with the usual inscription 'In God is my hope,' while the tenor, by Thomas Mears, 1838, was given to the church in 1889 by Commander T. W. Oliver.

The plate consists of an Elizabethan communion cup, a silver-gilt paten of 1890, a silver paten of modern French make, and a spoon of 1895.

The first book of registers runs from 1653 to 1717, the second contains the marriages for 1754–1836, and the third the baptisms and burials 1792–1812. The incompleteness of the list is accounted for by the fact that many Bursledon entries are made in the registers of Hamble.

ADVOWSON The name of Bursledon does not occur in Domesday Book, nor is it found in the registers of the bishops of Winchester. Bursledon was probably a chapelry dependent upon the priory of Hamble (itself a cell of the Benedictine monastery of Tirou in Chartres), the lands of which were purchased in 1391 by William of Wykeham to assist in the foundation of Winchester College.[10] Bursledon is not expressly mentioned among the lands of Hamble Priory at this date, but in a subsequent lease by Winchester College (dated 1 Henry V) of the lands of Hamble Priory, the tithes of Bursledon are mentioned as appurtenant.[11] Subsequently the chapel was held by Winchester College until 1849, when Bursledon was formed into a separate parish, the advowson being in the gift of the bishop. The history of Bursledon chapel cannot therefore be carried back beyond the fourteenth century, unless a conjectural identification of Bursledon with Brixenton be accepted.[12] A charter of Henry de Blois (1129–1171) to St. Cross Hospital, Winchester, makes a grant of 'the church of St. Peter of Waltham, with the church of Upham and with the chapel of Durley, and with the "capella de curia," and with the chapel of "Brixentona," which the monks of Hamble hold of the said Hospital for a yearly rent of two shillings, with all tithes, etc.'[13] The monks of Hamble moreover are known to have possessed the tithes, services, and dues arising from a hide of land at 'Brixedone,' which they had under a grant from Henry de Blois made with the consent of the parson of Bishop's Waltham, to which church these tithes had belonged.[14]

Another theory is that Bursledon is the second of the two churches of Bishop's Waltham Manor recorded in Domesday.[15] This theory is borne out by an entry in the Bishop's Waltham parish registers, dated 1736, in which it is stated that 'Mortuaries are due in the parishes of Hamble and "Busseldon" to the Minister of Bishop's Waltham.'[16]

There is a Congregational chapel here, built in 1860.

CHARITIES The school. — See article on Schools, *V.C.H. Hants*, ii, 397.

The parish has been in possession of about eight acres of land for a long period. The land is let for a market garden. The rent of £16 a year is carried to the church expenses fund.

DROXFORD

Drokeneford (ix cent.); Drocheneford (xi cent.); Drokenesford (xiv to xv cents.).

The parish of Droxford lies in the Meon valley, the River Meon, which here runs due north and south, flowing just within its eastern boundary for nearly three miles. The western boundary of the parish runs along the chalk downs on the west side of the valley, the highest point being 400 feet above sea level. The village is built along the main road from Fareham to Alton, which here runs parallel to the river on the west, taking an undulating course on the lower spurs of the downs. The church, manor house, and rectory stand in the middle of the village, a little to the east of the road, and at the bottom of a dip between two ridges; the houses of the village being to the north, west, and south. Hazleholt Park, the residence and property of Mrs. A. Taylor, occupies some 280 acres in the north-west corner of the parish, in a depression of the down land. Droxford parish (exclusive of the now separate parishes of Swanmore and Shedfield) comprises 2,469 acres, of which 906¼ are arable land, 401 permanent grass, and 357¾ woods and plantations.[1] The chief crops are wheat, oats, and barley. The common lands of the parish were inclosed in 1855.[2]

In the latter part of the thirteenth century Droxford

[10] *Cal. of Pat.* 1288–92, p. 433; *Cal. Pap. Let.* iv, 440; *V.C.H. Hants*, ii, 106.

[11] Winchester Coll. Muniment Room. From information supplied by Rev. T. F. Kirby.

[12] Paper on Bursledon Church by Rev. C. E. Matthews, who mentions in support of this theory that the name is given as 'Brisselden' in the Admiralty Records of the Corporation of Southampton.

[13] Harl. MS. 1616, fol. 9.

[14] *Arch.* l, 251.

[15] *Durley Parish Mag.* July, 1900, and March, 1901.

[16] Extract from Par. Reg. iii, 1736.

[1] Statistics from Bd. of Agric. 1905.

[2] *Parl. Blue Books, Inclosure Awards*, 151.

comes into notice as the native place of an interesting person, John de Drokensford. He was keeper of the wardrobe to Edward I, and accompanied that king on some of his Scotch campaigns. He afterwards became bishop of Bath and Wells, and Lord Chancellor of England. John de Drokensford is said to have been the son of the local squire, and an effigy of a lady in the south side of Droxford church has been supposed to be that of his mother.[3]

JOHN DE DROKENSFORD, Bishop of Bath and Wells. *Quarterly azure and or with four (?) heads of croziers countercoloured.*

The connexion of Izaak Walton with Droxford has recently been emphasized by Canon Vaughan. Walton's son-in-law Dr. Hawkins, prebendary of Winchester Cathedral, was instituted rector of Droxford in 1664, and held the office till his death in 1691. Walton passed the last years of his life with his daughter and her husband, and a passage in his will says: 'I also give unto my daughter all my books at Winchester and Droxford, and whatever in these two places are, or I can call mine.' Mr. John Darbyshire, who was Dr. Hawkins's curate, and Mr. Francis Morley, were Droxford residents and great friends of Walton.[4]

The civil parish of Swanmore was formed out of parts of Bishop's Waltham and Droxford in 1894,[5] the name having originally been borne by a tithing in Droxford manor.[6] The present parish consists of 2,362 acres, of which 1,457$\frac{3}{4}$ are arable land, 598$\frac{1}{2}$ permanent grass, and 162$\frac{1}{2}$ woodland.[7] The chief crops are wheat, barley, oats, and roots. The north-west portion is a continuation of the down land of Droxford, and on this high land stands Swanmore House, the residence of Mr. Myers, M.P., one of the principal landowners in the parish. To the south, at a lower level, lies the village, at the junction of the chalk with the clay, the change of soil being marked by the existence of brick-works. The southern part of the parish, which is bounded on the south-east by the Meon River, was formerly all comprised in Waltham Chase. The bishop of Winchester being lord of both Bishop's Waltham and Droxford manors, the queston arose in 1761 as to whether the tenants of Waltham, as intercommoners with the tenants of Droxford, had a right to cut bushes and underwood 'in that part of the common that is within the manor of Droxford.' It is interesting to note that this document gives to Waltham Chase its other name of 'Horderswood Common,' the two names being clearly stated to be interchangeable.[8] The wood called 'Bishops Wood' lies across the boundary between Swanmore and Shedfield. It is so called from the fact that when Waltham Chase was inclosed in 1870, this was the only part left to the bishop. It has since been sold by the Ecclesiastical Commissioners to Major Daubeney.

Shedfield, also a former tithing of Droxford, was created a civil parish in 1894.[9] The chief natural feature is an outlying spur of the downs called Shirrell Heath, 250 ft. above sea-level. It is well wooded on the north and east slopes, and a farm called 'Hawk's Nest' lies on the eastern side. On the summit are several houses, including a convalescent home. The water-works for Gosport are also in process of erection here. From its isolated position, Shirrell Heath commands a magnificent view of the Hamble and Meon valleys, with the blue hills of the Isle of Wight on the horizon. Shedfield village consists of a few houses, with church and school, lying on either side of a cross road in the fork formed by the branching of the Fareham road to Bishop's Waltham and Botley respectively. The common behind the school, though called Shedfield Common, is really in Wickham parish. Three fine estates in this parish are Hall Court, Shedfield House, and Shedfield Lodge, owned and occupied respectively by the Rev. A. Murray-Aynsley, Lady Phillimore, and Mrs. Franklyn.

The parish comprises 2,003 acres, of which 801$\frac{3}{4}$ are arable land, 691$\frac{1}{2}$ permanent grass, and 158$\frac{1}{2}$ woods and plantations.[10] The soil is sandy loam, and the chief crops are wheat, barley, and oats. Fruit is also cultivated.

Traces of the old tithing of Hill[11] are to be seen in the place-names Hill Place (the residence of Major Daubeney), Hillpound, and Hill Grove.

MANORS

The manor of *DROXFORD*, like its neighbour Bishop's Waltham, was one of the manors of the see of Winchester. The first grant of the land was in 826, when King Egbert, 'in gratitude to God for his coronation as king of all England,' gave the vill of 'Drokeireford' to the prior and monks of St. Swithun, Winchester.[12] In 953 King Eadwig granted twenty *mansae* of land in Droxford to the noble lady Ædelhild, who probably held as a tenant of the monks.[13] According to the Domesday Survey Droxford was among the lands held by the bishop for the support of the monks of Winchester.[14] It was then assessed at 14 hides, in contrast to the 16 hides of the time of Edward the Confessor. In 1284 the manor passed wholly to the bishop, the monks renouncing 'all right and claim which they have or shall have in the said manor, for ever.'[15] This agreement marked the termination of a long series of disputes between successive bishops and priors. The credit for the peace was due to Bishop John of Pontoise, who in return for the manor of Droxford (*inter alia*) granted to the monks certain advowsons and rights. In the same year Edward I granted to the bishop the return of all writs within the manor of Droxford.[16] After this Droxford remained in the hands of the bishops of Winchester until the reign of Edward VI, when in 1551 Bishop Poynet surrendered the whole hundred of Waltham, including Droxford manor, to the crown.[17] Thence it passed the following month to William, earl of Wiltshire.[18] Queen Mary, however, restored it in 1558 to the bishopric.[19] The bishops retained the manor until the great Civil War, when the Long Parliament found a purchaser for

3 Information supplied by Canon Vaughan.
4 John Vaughan, *Wild Flowers of Selborne.*
5 Loc. Govt. Bd. Order 31854.
6 Eccl. Com. Ct. R. 10 Ric. II.
7 Statistics from Bd. of Agric. 1905.
8 Book of Customs of Droxford manor, in the hands of Mr. Gunner, Bishop's Waltham; cf. Eccl. Com. Ct. R. bdle. 77, No. 23.
9 Loc. Govt. Bd. Order 31854.
10 *Agricultural Returns*, 1905.
11 Eccl. Com. Ct. R.
12 Dugdale, *Mon.* i, 205.
13 Birch, *Cart. Sax.* iii, 134.
14 *V.C.H. Hants*, i, 466*a*.
15 Add. MSS. 29436, fol. 49.
16 Chart R. 12 Edw. I, m. 5.
17 Pat. 5 Edw. VI, pt. 6, m. 20.
18 Ibid. pt. 4, m. 39.
19 Pat. 4 & 5 Phil. and Mary, pt. 7, m. 20.

Droxford in one Mr. Francis Allen, who gave £7,675 13*s.* 7*d.* for it.[20] On the Restoration, the bishops recovered their possessions, and Droxford remained attached to the lands of the Winchester see until the Bishops' Resignation Act of 1869.[21] Droxford then passed to the Ecclesiastical Commissioners, who have since continued to be lords of the manor.

In 1376 John de Garton of Erehutte, late citizen of London, died seised of lands and rents in *MIDDLETON* held of the bishop of Winchester, with suit of court to the manor of Droxford.[22] This is evidently the same as Midlington, a tithing in Bishop's Waltham Hundred.[23] There is no descent traceable of the owners of this property, and the lands seem to have been split up. At a court baron held at Droxford Manor in 1761, it was presented that 'all lands that did heretofore belong to the manor of Midlington have no right of common in Waltham Chase.'[24] Midlington is now owned and occupied by Mr. F. H. Christian.

Steeple (? Stepple **xv** cent.[25]), now represented by *STEEPLE COURT*, is a well-wooded piece of land situated on the right bank of the Hamble, before it widens to an estuary. It formed a part of Droxford parish until 1884, when it was transferred to the parish of Botley by order of the Local Government Board.[26] In the reigns of Mary and Elizabeth, Steeple Court was called a manor,[27] which seems to have owed suit to the parent manor of Droxford. At a court baron held at Droxford in 1761 it was decided that 'Steeple Court farm has no rights of common in Horderswood'[28] (Waltham Chase). In the sixteenth century Steeple Court was in the hands of the family of Faukener,[29] a name which is found in connexion with the neighbouring parish of Swanmore as early as the thirteenth century.[30] By the eighteenth century it belonged to the family of Warner,[31] which had long owned land in South Hampshire, particularly in Titchfield, Waltham, and Botley.[32] The Rev. Henry Jenkyns, canon of Durham Cathedral, bought Steeple Court from Mr. William Warner about 1875. It is now the property of Lady Jenkyns.

CHURCHES The church of *OUR LADY AND ALL SAINTS, DROXFORD*, has a chancel 28 ft. 3 in. long by 15 ft. 6 in. wide, north and south chapels of equal length, 13 ft. 7 in. and 13 ft. 2 in. wide respectively, nave 45 ft. 2 in. by 19 ft. 6 in., with north and south aisles 8 ft. 8 in. wide, south porch, and west tower 13 ft. 3 in. square—all measurements being internal.

The earliest details belong to 1150–60, at which time the church possessed an aisleless nave and chancel, whose walls still stand for the most part, though pierced with arches opening to the aisles and chapels. The chancel arch of this church remains intact, and the north and south doorways of the nave, though not in their original positions, are part of it. The chancel had two small round-headed windows on each side, and remains of those on the south are still to be seen. Towards the end of the twelfth century a north chapel was added to the chancel, and a north aisle to the nave, and in the first half of the thirteenth century a south aisle was built. At the beginning of the next century the north chapel was rebuilt, probably on a larger scale, and the south chapel either newly built or enlarged from a previously existing building.

The aisles of the nave were widened in the late years of the fifteenth or the beginning of the sixteenth century, and in 1599 the present tower was built, leaving no evidence of the size of its predecessor, if it had one. In the eighteenth century the church was fitted with new roofs and ceilings, and the clearstory windows of the chancel remodelled. The walls of the church are of flint rubble with ashlar dressings, and the roofs are red-tiled.

The chancel has a fifteenth-century east window of three cinquefoiled lights with tracery in the head, and is also lighted by two clearstory windows on north and south, the internal masonry of which is probably of fifteenth-century date, but externally they are of the eighteenth century. The chancel opens to the chapels by wide arches, that on the north of late twelfth-century date, being of one order pointed, with a chamfered label and an edge-roll towards the chancel, and a plain chamfer towards the chapel. At the springing are square-edged strings, hollow-chamfered beneath, and the edge-roll of the arch continues down the southern angles of the jambs. Over the south arch are remains of two round-headed lights, the original south windows of the chancel, with wide internal splays.

The north chapel, *c.* 1300, has an east window of three trefoiled lights, and two two-light north windows, with cusped piercings in the head. In the south-east corner is a locker with a shouldered lintel, and rebated for a door, with a shelf-groove, and to the west of it a piscina recess with a plain arched head. The chapel opens to the north aisle by a late fifteenth-century pointed arch of two hollow-chamfered orders, the outer dying out at the springing and the inner carried by half-octagonal moulded corbels. The south respond of this arch is the north-east angle of the original nave, and preserves its quoin-stones unaltered.

The south chapel, probably built at the same time as the north chapel, has an east window of three trefoiled lights with intersecting tracery in the head, the openings being cusped. In the south wall are two two-light windows like those in the north chapel. Near the south-east angle is a trefoiled piscina, and north of the east window is a large canopied and crocketed niche for an image, with a panelled base. The arch at the west end of the chapel is of the same date and design as that in the north chapel; but the corresponding east angle of the aisleless nave has been cut back and the original quoins destroyed.

The chancel arch is semicircular, of two orders on the west face, the outer with a large roll, and the inner with a good zigzag pattern and an edge-roll, and of one plain order on the east face. The outer

[20] Dugdale, *Mon.* i, 203.
[21] *Lond. Gaz.* 1 April, 1870.
[22] Chan. Inq. p.m. 50 Edw. III (1st Nos.), No. 27.
[23] Eccl. Com. Ct. R.
[24] Ledger of Droxford Manor, in hands of Mr. Gunner, Bishop's Waltham.
[25] Feet of F. Hants, East. 8 Hen. IV; ibid. Hil. 11 Hen. IV.
[26] Loc. Govt. Bd. Order 16412.
[27] Feet of F. Hants, East. 4 & 5 Phil. and Mary; ibid. Hil. 14 Eliz.
[28] Bk. of Customs of Droxford Manor in hands of Mr. Gunner, Bishop's Waltham.
[29] Feet of F. Hants, 4 & 5 Phil. and Mary.
[30] Ibid. East. 37 Hen. III.
[31] There is a slab in Botley Church to James Warner of Steeple Court (1784–1857).
[32] Chan. Inq. a.q.d. 37 Edw. III (2nd Nos.), No. 16; Chan. Inq. p.m. 9 Hen. IV, No. 27.

order on the west has nook-shafts with foliate capitals, and small shafts with scalloped capitals are worked on the western angles of the inner order.

The nave is of three bays, with a north arcade of wide pointed arches of a single order springing from plain rectangular piers, with square-edged chamfered strings at the springing. All arches have a plain chamfered label towards the nave, and the eastern arch has an edge-roll on arch and jambs, the other having plain chamfered angles.

The south arcade has pointed arches of two chamfered orders without labels, the outer order dying into the walls at the east and west of the nave without responds, while the inner is carried on half-round moulded corbels of mid-thirteenth-century character. There is a clearstory on the north side only, of two three-light windows, a pointed light between two square heads; on the south the roof is carried without a break over the nave and south aisle.

The north aisle has two square-headed north windows of late fifteenth or early sixteenth-century date, each of two cinquefoiled lights with pierced spandrels, and in the west wall is a plain square-headed two-light window of the date of the tower. The wall in which it is set is in part of late twelfth-century date, the original north-west quoins of the former aisle being visible and showing the extent to which the aisle was widened at the later rebuilding. The blocked doorway in the north wall was formerly the north doorway of the aisleless twelfth-century church, and like the contemporary south doorway must have been twice moved and reset. Both have semicircular arches of two orders with a chamfered label, the label enriched with tooth-moulding on the upper member and a zigzag on the chamfer, while the outer order has a beaded cable mould and three rows of horizontal zigzag, and the inner order is plain. The outer order has nook-shafts in the jambs with moulded bases, and capitals scalloped in the north doorway and simply foliate in the south. On the east jamb on the south doorway is an incised sun-dial.

The south aisle has the same arrangement of windows as the north, of the same detail and dates, and in its west wall is similar evidence of widening. The west tower, built in 1599, is finished with modern red-brick battlements, the north and south windows of the upper stage being of two lights in brick, while the east and west windows are of modern stonework, with four-centred heads to the lights. In the middle stage is a square-headed window of three lights, and another in the ground stage over the west doorway. The stonework is nearly entirely modern here, and over the latter window is a tablet with the date 1599, also in modern stonework. At the north-west angle of the tower is a projecting rectangular stair turret.

The roofs of the church seem to have been entirely renewed in the eighteenth century, when plaster cornices and ceiling were added, and the chancel roof was tiled and hipped at the east. Plaster coved eaves were added to the north and south chapels, and a cornice with mutules to the chancel, and there are traces of internal painted decoration of this date. The altar rails are an interesting example of seventeenth-century date, with heavy rails and posts crowned by finials in two cases, and balustrades of turned shafts. The other fittings of the church are modern, the panelling round the east end of the chancel being a very good piece of work. In the north chapel on the south and east walls parts of an eighteenth-century masonry pattern decoration remain in red lines, with floral sprays in each block.

The font is modern, of twelfth-century design, with a square bowl on a central and four angle pillars.

In the north chapel is a brass plate with an inscription to Edward Searle, farmer, 1617, and close to it a marble slab with the indent of an inscription plate. In the south chapel is the effigy already referred to, a poor figure in Purbeck marble of a lady in long gown with hanging sleeves and a jewel hung round her neck.

There are four bells, the treble of 1606, the second recast 1899 from a bell of 1631, and the third and tenor of 1672.

The plate consists of a silver cup and paten of 1737, and a cup, paten, and flagon of 1632.

The registers begin in 1633, the first book going to 1736, but the marriages end in 1701 and the burials in 1727. The second book is of burials in woollen, 1678–1739, and the third has baptisms 1778–1812, marriages 1732–54, and burials 1740–1812. The fourth and fifth have marriages 1754–90 and 1790–1812.

The church of *ST. BARNABAS, SWANMORE*, erected in 1845, is of stone and flint, in twelfth-century style, the south aisle and tower being added in 1876–7. The register dates from 1845.

The church of *ST. JOHN THE BAPTIST, SHEDFIELD*, built in 1875, replaces an older structure on the same site, the tower of which still stands in the churchyard. The register dates from 1829.

ADVOWSONS The earliest mention of Droxford church is in 1280, when the king presented to the living because of a vacancy in the see,[33] the usual patron being the bishop of Winchester.[34] The advowson was surrendered with the manor to the crown by Bishop Poynet in 1551,[35] was granted by the king in the same year to William earl of Wiltshire,[36] and restored to the bishopric in 1558.[37] The living is a rectory, and was entered in the Valor Ecclesiasticus among the 'peculiar benefices' of the bishop,[38] in whose gift it still remains.[39]

Swanmore was constituted a consolidated chapelry and ecclesiastical district in 1846.[40] The living is a vicarage in the gift of the bishop of Winchester.

In 1829 Shedfield was constituted an ecclesiastical parish. The living is a vicarage in the gift of the rector of Droxford. There is a Primitive Methodist chapel at Droxford, built in 1886; another on Shirrell Heath (now in Shedfield parish), built in 1864; and another at Swanmore, built in 1863.

CHARITIES Henry Collins, by will 1679, charged a close called Clever's Close in Bishop's Waltham with the payment of 30*s.* a year, 5*s.* to be paid to each of six of the poorest people in Swanmore yearly for ever on the Thursday before Easter.

33 *Cal. of Pat.* 1272–81, p. 416.
34 Winton. Epis. Reg. Egerton MSS. 2031–4.
35 Pat. 5 Edw. VI, pt. 6, m. 20.
36 Pat. 5 Edw. VI, pt. 4, m. 39.
37 Pat. 4 & 5 Phil. and Mary, pt. 7, m. 20.
38 *Valor Eccl.* (Rec. Com.), ii, App.
39 Inst. Bks. P.R.O.
40 *Lond. Gaz.* 21 April, 1846.

John Arthur, by will 1722, gave to the poor of the tithings of Droxford and Hill £30; John Dee, by will 1749, gave to the poor of this parish £50; and the Rev. James Cutler, formerly rector of the parish, by will 1782, left £50. These sums, with accumulated interest, were laid out in the purchase of £215 1*s.* consols, now held by the official trustees, the dividends, amounting to £5 7*s.* 4*d.*, are applied with the next mentioned charity.

In 1850 James George Boucher, by will, bequeathed to the rector and churchwardens a sum now represented by £190 18*s.* 7*d.* consols, with the official trustees, for the benefit of the poor of the parish. The dividends, amounting to £4 15*s.* 4*d.*, were together with the charities of John Arthur and others applied in 1905 as follows: to the vicar of Shedfield £4 3*s.* 8*d.*, to the vicar of Swanmore £3 5*s.* 6*d.*, to be distributed in those districts, and £2 13*s.* 6*d.* was given in money to ten poor persons of Droxford.

Poor's Allotments. By Inclosure Award of 9 May, 1855, two allotments of 4 acres each (numbered respectively 213 and 284) were allotted for the use of the poor of Shedfield, the rents whereof, amounting to about £25 a year, are applied for public uses, subject, however, to a yearly rent-charge of £3 5*s.* and of £3 respectively. Under the same award 5 acres of land were allotted as a recreation ground.

By deed of 1880 a site and buildings thereon were conveyed for the purpose of reading and recreation rooms.

For the school and its endowments see article on 'Schools,' *V.C.H. Hants*, ii, 404.

Swanmore. For the combined charities see Bishop's Waltham.

Poor's Allotments. By the Inclosure Award of 1855 an allotment of 7 acres was allotted for the use of the poor of Swanmore, producing about £10 a year, which is subject to a yearly rent-charge of £6. Under the same award 5 acres were allotted as a recreation ground.

For the school and its endowments see article on 'Schools,' *V.C.H. Hants*, ii, 405.

DURLEY

Durlye, Durle (xiv cent.); Dyrle (xvi cent.).

Durley is a parish of 2,497 acres, lying between the upper waters of the Hamble River and its tributary Ford Lake, the latter forming its western boundary. The levels fall from 250 ft. at the north to 60 ft. at the south. In the north-east corner of the parish, where the boundaries of Durley, Upham, and Bishop's Waltham meet, is the old Robin Hood posting-house, on the southernmost point of the hill on which Wintershill stands; it commands a fine view of the Hamble valley. About half a mile south-east of the Robin Hood is another piece of high ground, on which is Durley Manor Farm, but except at these two points the parish nowhere rises to more than 200 ft. above sea level. It is intersected by winding lanes, their surface covered in many cases with a loose shingly sand, which in wet weather has earned for the parish the nickname 'Dirty Durley.' The only road of any size or definite direction is Durley Street, which strikes north-east across the parish, with a gradual rise to the Robin Hood Inn, whence it dips sharply to meet the new Waltham to Winchester road at the foot of Wintershill. Along Durley Street, between the schools at the west and the inn at the east, lies the village, in scattered groups of cottages, its two extremes more than a mile apart. At a short distance to the east of the school, a road turns southwards to a group of newer-looking houses and some saw-mills, quite a modern growth in comparison with the rest of the village.

The church and rectory stand near each other to the north-west, quite half a mile away from the nearest point of the village, and approached by a narrow lane which leads northwards from Durley Street and eventually joins the Waltham to Winchester road at Lower Upham. To the north of the church is Greenwood, the residence of Lady Jenner. In the field now used as a playground, across which a short cut can be taken from church to school, the old stocks are said to have stood. South of Durley Street, where the road falls quickly to the River Hamble, a lane leads to Durley Mill, one of the prettiest parts of the district.[1] The stream has here been widened, and the lane crosses it by a low bridge above the mill, passing under the branch railway line to Bishop's Waltham, and continuing southwards to join the Botley road.

From its position in a low-lying valley, sheltered by the South Downs on the north-east, the parish of Durley is very fertile, the surface soil being a sandy loam. There are 1,102 acres of arable land, the chief crops being wheat, oats, and barley; 1,046½ acres are occupied by permanent grass, and 328¾ acres by woods and plantations.[2] The saw-mills tell of plentiful timber in the district. That part of Wintershill Common which lies in this parish was inclosed in 1858.[3]

Gilbert White, the naturalist, became curate of Durley in September, 1753, and held the curacy for a year and a half. He did not, however, reside at Durley, but had lodgings at Bishop's Waltham, paying to Mr. Gibson, the rector of that place, £20 for one year's board. His biographer notes that during his tenure of this curacy White's expenses exceeded his stipend by nearly £20.[4]

MANORS The earliest mention of *DURLEY* is in a grant of land to the abbey of Newminster by Edward the Elder in 900.[5] In this grant the boundaries of Durley (then called Deorlaage) are given, and it is interesting to note that these are in part identical with the boundaries of the parish at the present day.[6] Whatever rights over Durley were signified in this grant, they soon became obsolete, for Durley became the property of the bishops

1 It seems not unreasonable to suppose that this is one of the three mills mentioned in Domesday as belonging to Waltham Manor; for though without the park boundary, Durley was within the manor lands.

2 Statistics from Bd. of Agric. 1905.

3 *Parl. Blue Bks. Inclosure Awards*, 158.

4 R. White, *Life and Letters of Gilbert White*, i, 48.

5 Birch, *Cart. Sax.* ii, 245.

6 *Durley Parish Mag.*, July 1900, March 1901.

of Winchester, as part of their manor of Bishop's Waltham. The history of Durley is therefore the history of Bishop's Waltham (q.v.).

Among the tenants of the bishop in Durley, the family of Wodelot or Wodelok were holding a considerable amount of land in the fourteenth century,[7] and possibly it was the same estate which was in the hands of Sir John Phylpot, knt., in 1508.[8] In 1575 a moiety of lands and tenements in Durley was possessed by one Francis Perkins,[9] who in 1586 conveyed the 'Manor of Durley' to Francis Fortescue.[10] The house attached to this so-called manor would be that now known as Durley Manor Farm. Early in the seventeenth century the estate came to the family of Hersent,[11] whence it passed by descent to John Hersent Thorpe in 1778,[12] and thence to the Heathcotes of Hursley.[13] Durley Manor Farm was sold by that family towards the close of the nineteenth century, and is now the residence of Mr. Cross.

PHYLPOT. *Sable a bend ermine.*

It is said that Richard Cromwell's daughters, the granddaughters of the Protector, lived for a time at Durley Manor Farm.[14] This coincides perfectly with some of the marriage connexions of the Hersent family in the seventeenth century. The connexion with the family of Barton is not very clear, but it is believed that Jane, the wife of Peter Hersent, was the daughter of John Barton, whose wife (afterwards the wife of Nicholas Pescod) was sister to Richard Major of Hursley.[15] If this was the Richard Major of Hursley whose daughter married Richard Cromwell,[16] the presence of the Misses Cromwell at Durley Manor Farm would easily be accounted for.

HEATHCOTE. *Ermine three roundels vert with a cross or upon each.*

Wintershill, partly in this parish, is sometimes called a manor, the old manor house of which, Durley Hall Farm, stands within the boundaries of Durley. The present Wintershill Hall is in the parish of Upham (q.v.).

CHURCH The church of the *HOLY CROSS*[17] has a chancel 25 ft. by 14 ft. 6 in., with north vestry, north and south transepts 17 ft. 6 in. east to west, the north transept being 11 ft. deep and the south 12 ft. 6 in., and the nave 49 ft. 3 in. by 18 ft. 3 in., with south porch and wooden bell-turret at the west.

The south doorway of the nave, *c.* 1200, is the oldest detail remaining, and the nave walls are probably of this date. The chancel shows evidences of thirteenth-century work, and the transepts are additions of the early part of the fourteenth century. Externally the church is covered with rough-cast, and the roofs are red tiled, the western bell-turret being boarded and its roof shingled.

The chancel has an east window of three lights with fourteenth-century tracery, but the lower part of the external north jamb seems to be of thirteenth-century masonry, part of an earlier window here. Below the window on the outside is a dwarf buttress, which with the whole of the walling is probably of thirteenth-century date. In the south wall is a square-headed window of two trefoiled lights, —*c.* 1340, except the heads of the lights, which are modern—and in the north wall is a corresponding window, having on its west splay traces of a painted figure holding a scroll and standing under a trefoiled arch. At the south-west of the chancel is a blocked doorway, probably of thirteenth-century work, and the chancel arch is modern, of thirteenth-century style.

Both transepts have widely splayed single-light windows on the east, that in the north transept having on its north splay the painting of a ship, with a man climbing up to the yard. There is a small square-headed recess near this window on the south side. The north transept has a north window of two uncusped lights with a pierced spandrel, and the south transept has a like window on the south, and below it a wide arched recess, probably for a tomb, and of early fourteenth-century date. There is also a piscina at the south-east of this transept.

The nave is lighted only by dormers on the north and south, but has a two-light window in the west wall, and below it a doorway which may be fourteenth-century work; the south doorway of the nave, as already noted, is *c.* 1200, and has a slightly pointed arch with an edge chamfer, and a label chamfered above and below. There is a recess for holy water east of it within the church. The roofs of chancel and nave are old, of plain design, and the bell-turret at the west stands on old posts coming down to the floor of the church. The south porch is modern.

The pulpit is a good specimen, octagonal with two tiers of panels, the upper with arabesque ornament, and the lower arcaded. Over it is an octagonal tester with a panelled soffit, incribed AW · ED · TC · 1630.

The font is of late twelfth-century type, with a square Purbeck marble bowl on a central and four angle shafts; on each side of the bowl are four shallow round-headed arches. It stands near the south door of the nave.

There are three bells, the treble uninscribed, while the other two bear the names of John and Robert Cor, Aldbourne, bell-founders, and are dated 1730.

The plate consists of a communion cup and paten of 1721, given to the church in 1722, and a flagon of 1841. There is also a plated almsdish.

The first book of the registers goes from 1599 to

7 Feet of F. Hants, Hil. 11 Edw. III.; Feet of F. Hants, East. 2 Ric. II.

8 Chan. Inq. p.m. (Ser. 2), vol. 16, No. 100.

9 Feet of F. Hants, East. 17 Eliz.

10 Feet of F. Div. Cos. East. 28 Eliz.

11 From information supplied by Rev. E. Heathcote; Feet of F. Hants, Mich. 28 Geo. II.

12 Recov. R. East. 18 Geo. III, rot. 219.

13 Feet of F. Div. Cos. Hil. 23 Geo. III; cf. Berry, *Hants Geneal.* 82; Feet of F. Div. Cos. Trin. 26 Geo. III.

14 Another theory is that it was the sisters of the Protector who lived here. *Hants N. and Q.* vi, 45.

15 The arms of the Hersents were formerly identical with those of Barton; and the arms of John Barton's widow were in a window, now destroyed, in Durley Manor Farm. It is possible that John Barton once owned the place (from information supplied by Rev. E. Heathcote).

16 *Harl. Soc.* xxxviii, 434.

17 William Hazell, 1410, wills his body to be buried in *Capella Sanctae Crucis de Durley.* Will in Muniment Room of Winchester College.

1728, with a gap in the marriage entries between 1647 and 1661; the Commonwealth registrations were doubtless kept in a special book now lost. The second book has baptisms and burials 1731–1812, and marriages to 1735, and the third marriages 1754–1812.

In the churchyard on the south is a very large yew, evidently of great age, even if the conventional thousand years claimed for it be more than its due.

ADVOWSON Until 1853 Durley was a chapelry of Upham, the living being a curacy in the gift of the bishop of Winchester.[18] In the twelfth century the advowson of Durley went, together with that of the mother church, to the hospital of St. Cross, Winchester, in accordance with a grant made by Henry de Blois, bishop of Winchester, to that body.[19] In 1284 however Upham was among the advowsons concerned in the dispute between the bishop of Winchester and the monks of St. Swithun's, when the latter finally renounced their claim in favour of the bishop.[20] The grant to St. Cross cannot therefore have been more than temporary. As a chapelry of Upham, the patronage of Durley was transferred from the bishop of Winchester to the bishop of Lichfield in 1852[21]; and it remained in the gift of Lichfield after the separation of Durley from Upham in 1853. In 1890 the patronage of Durley was transferred to the Lord Chancellor. Since the separation the living has been a rectory.

There is a Wesleyan chapel at Durley, built in 1851. There is also a mission room, the private property of Captain Thresher, R.N., who is a considerable landowner in the parish. (For school, see article on 'Schools,' *V.C.H. Hants*, ii, 398).

CHARITY By an award of 25 June, 1858, an allotment of 3 acres on Wintershill Common was set out for the benefit of the poor of this parish; the rents amounted to £5 5*s.* a year.

EXBURY

Ekeresbur (xiii cent.); Eukeresbury (xiv cent.).

Exbury parish is a low tract of fertile wooded land in the valley of the Beaulieu River, whose estuary curves round the parish, bounding it west and south, where it meets the Solent. Down the eastern boundary runs the Dark Water, a narrow stream with steep high banks which are covered with trees, heather, and bracken. Of the 2,593 acres of which this parish consists there are 829 of arable land, 683 of permanent grass, and 365 of woods and plantations.[1] The soil is loam, and the chief crops are wheat and barley. The occupations of the inhabitants of this secluded corner of the country are purely agricultural, and there are less than 300 persons in the whole parish. The only main road enters the parish on the north-west, and runs down to the south coast, and the nearest station is Beaulieu Road in the New Forest, nine miles from Exbury village. The other means of communication are sandy lanes or tracks across the fields, while the steep valley of the Dark Water is a great obstacle to access from the east.

The little village of Exbury stands amid thick trees on the left of the main road from Dibden or Beaulieu. The church on the east, and Exbury manor house on the west, are on the main road, the rest of the village straggling for a little way down a broad lane which turns eastward. Following the road to the coast, Lower Exbury Farm stands high up on the banks of the Beaulieu River, overlooking it as it curves eastward to meet the Solent. Here can be seen the site of the chapel of St. Katherine, the remaining stones of which are now used for pig-styes. This chapel was served by the Cistercians from Beaulieu Abbey, the tradition being that the monks used to cross the river from St. Leonard's, on stepping-stones. The chapel was not pulled down until 1827, when the present chapel at Exbury was built.

Turning westward along the coast we come to Lepe, which now consists of a few cottages and a coast-guard station, though Wise wrote of it in 1866 as 'a fishing village.' Possibly he was referring to the oyster trade, large heaps of oysters being formerly stacked here to purify. Lepe House, once an old inn, has been beautified and enlarged till it is quite unrecognizable. It is now occupied by Mr. H. W. Forster, M.P., lord of the manor of Exbury and Lepe. Both Lepe House and Inchmerry House (the residence of the Dowager Countess De La Warr) command beautiful views facing the Isle of Wight. All this coast district is very liable to floods.

MANORS There is no record of holders of land in *EXBURY* previous to the thirteenth century, when there are various traces of the family of Foliot (Faflet, Fallet, or Follet). In 1244 Richard Foliot, a minor, was holding land in Exbury in chief of the crown,[2] and at the end of the century Walter Foliot held two carucates there by knight's service.[3] On the death of Robert Foliot his lands were divided between his two daughters and coheirs: Maud, who was possessed of one messuage and one carucate in Exbury and Lepe, which she conveyed in 1304 to Andrew de Grymstead[4]; and Mabel, who apparently married Robert le Gras.[5] The Grymstead moiety was held by Andrew de Grymstead in 1316.[6] Andrew died in 1324,[7] and in 1336 his son John settled it upon Eleanor his wife for life.[8] Eleanor survived her husband many years, holding her moiety of the manor as part of the inheritance of Reginald Perot, who, in default of male issue of the Grymstead line, had become heir to the property.[9] On the death of Eleanor, in 1363, a dispute arose. Ralph Perot was a minor, and as tenant-in-chief of the crown the custody of his lands was assumed by the king, who committed it to Robert de Beverley.[10]

18 *Wykeham's Reg.* (Hants Rec. Soc.), i, App. 391.
19 Harl. MS. 1616, fol. 9.
20 Add MSS. 29436.
21 *Lond. Gaz.* 4 June, 1852.
1 Statistics from Bd. of Agric. (1905).
2 *Excerpta e Rot. Fin.* (Rec. Com.), i, 426.
3 *Testa de Nevill* (Rec. Com.), 235 *b*.
4 Feet of F. Hants, Hil. 32 Edw. I.
5 *Cal. of Close*, 1323–7, p. 361.
6 *Feud. Aids*, ii, 317.
7 Chan. Inq. p.m. 18 Edw. II, No. 49.
8 Chan. Inq. a. q. d. 10 Edw. III (2nd Nos.), No. 40; *Cal. of Pat.* 1334–8, p. 251; Feet of F. Hants, Hil. 10 Edw. III.
9 Chan. Inq. p.m. 12 Edw. III (1st Nos.), No. 37; Chan. Inq. p.m. 37 Edw. III (1st Nos.), No. 28; Hoare, *Hist. of Wilts*, i, 202.
10 *Abbrev. Rot. Orig.* (Rec. Com.), 320*a*; *Cal. of Pat.* 1377–81, p. 423.

John de Bettesthorne, however, claimed that the reversion of this moiety of the manor had been sold to him before the death of John de Grymstead.[11] This had undoubtedly been the case, and John de Bettesthorne made good his claim.[12]

With respect to the other moiety of the manor, viz. that which passed to Mabel le Gras, there is an interesting record extant of a covenant between Robert le Gras and his freemen of Exbury in the time of Edward I.[13] It was then agreed that 'Estwode and Wynesle' should be inclosed; that the men might have common of pasture for their animals all the year round, with litter for these animals in the whole demesne of Exbury outside the inclosures; and that any of Robert's men convicted in his courts should be assessed by their peers and not otherwise. Six marks were payable to Robert for damages, and, in the event of any infraction of the agreement, £60 should be paid to the queen. This second moiety of the manor was held by Mabel le Gras in 1316,[14] after which it passed through various hands[15] until finally purchased by John de Bettesthorne in 1381.[16] The descent of the two holdings is henceforward the same.

Bettesthorne. *Argent a saltire gules with five stars or thereon.*

On the death of John de Bettesthorne in 1399 his inheritance passed to his daughter Elizabeth and her husband Sir John de Berkeley, knt.[17] It remained in the hands of the Berkeley family throughout the greater part of the fifteenth century.[18] In 1484 the entire estates of Sir William Berkeley were handed over by the king to John Hoton, esquire of the body, 'for his good service against the rebels.[19] This grant was apparently only temporary, for in 1489 a dispute was in process between the relatives of the late Sir William Berkeley over his lands.[20] The manor was recovered by Sir William's sister Katherine and her husband John Brewerton,[21] and thence descended to the Comptons of Compton Wyniates, Warwickshire,[22] who held it for the next two hundred years.[23] In 1718 Henry Compton and his wife Eleanor conveyed the manor to William Mitford,[24] whence it descended to his grandson William Mitford the historian of Greece.[25] On the latter's death, in 1827, his grandson Henry Reveley Mitford succeeded to the property.[26] He sold it, in the early eighties, to Major John Forster, whose son, Mr. Henry William Forster, is the present lord of the manor.

Berkeley. *Gules a cheveron between ten crosses formy argent with the difference of a border argent.*

It is possible that the moiety which fell to Mabel le Gras in the fourteenth century became a separate manor of *LEPE* (Lupe, Hupe, Lehupe, Lope, Leope, xiv cent.; Leepe, xv cent.; Leape, xvii. cent.), and that the two manors were kept separate even after they had passed into the same hands. It seems, however, more probable that the division in the fourteenth century was one of land only, and that only one court was held, the manor being frequently called the 'manor of Exbury and Lepe.'

Compton. *Sable a leopard or between three helms argent.*

CHURCH The church, of no known dedication, consecrated in 1827, is a rectangular building of yellow brick, with three round-headed windows on the north and two on the south, the middle of the south wall having been formerly occupied by a 'three-decker' pulpit. It has a west gallery and bell-turret, and a flat plaster ceiling, and is entered from the west. Its builder was William Mitford the historian, and to the east of the church is the family vault of the Mitfords.

The font is of Purbeck marble, *c.* 1200, with a shallow square bowl with chamfered angles, and probably cut down. It stands on a circular shaft, and probably had formerly four angle columns.

In the bell-turret is a small bell, uninscribed.

The plate consists of a communion cup of rather unusual type, *c.* 1600, with a band of ornament on the lip, a curved base to the bowl, and a trumpet-shaped stem; a paten of 1902, its ornament copied from the cup; and a plated flagon and almsdish.

The register dates from 1756.

ADVOWSON Exbury was a chapelry of Fawley until 1863. The earliest mention of the chapel is in 1291, when 'Master Nicholas de Audeby' held the church of Fawley with the chapel of Exbury.[27] The next reference is in 1494.[28] In 1863 Exbury was separated from Fawley, the curate-in-charge becoming rector, while the living remained in the gift of the bishop of the diocese. In 1840 there was an agreement for the commutation of tithes, in which document Exbury is distinctly spoken of as a parish.[29] There are no dissenting chapels in this parish.

[11] *Parl. R.* (Rec. Com.), ii, 353; Chan. Inq. Misc. 3 Ric. II, No. 115.

[12] Feet of F. Div. Cos. Mich. 35 Edw. III, No. 87; Chan. Inq. p.m. 22 Ric. II, No. 6.

[13] Harl. R. E. 9; *Cal. of Pat.* 1272–81, p. 181.

[14] *Feud. Aids*, ii, 317.

[15] Feet of F. Hants, East. 5 Edw. III; *Cal. of Pat.* 1334–8, p. 520; Chan. Inq. p.m. 41 Edw. III, No. 23; *Abbrev. Rot. Orig.* (Rec. Com.), 338*a*; *Cal. of Pat.* 1377–81, p. 152.

[16] *Cal. of Pat.* 1377–81, p. 598.

[17] Chan. Inq. p.m. 22 Ric. II, No. 6.

[18] L.T.R. Mem. R. 166, m. 173; Feet of F. Div. Cos. Hil. 7 Hen. IV; Chan. Inq. p.m. 6 Hen. VI, No. 50; Chan. Inq. p.m. 38–9 Hen. VI, No. 57.

[19] *Cal. of Pat.* 1476–85, p. 514.

[20] De Banc. R. Hil. 4 Hen. VII, m. 405.

[21] Chan. Inq. p.m. (Ser. 2), vol. 10, No. 156.

[22] *L. and P. Hen. VIII*, iv (2), p. 1942; Exch. Inq. p.m. (Ser. 2), file 978, No. 7; *Arch.* xliii, 63.

[23] Exch. Inq. p.m. (Ser. 2), file 992, No. 1; Chan. Inq. p.m. (Ser. 2), No. 37; Com. Pleas Recov. R. Mich. 1649, m. 20, 21; Recov. R. East. 13 Anne, R. 23.

[24] Feet of F. Hants, East. 4 Geo. I.

[25] Recov. R. Mich. 6 Geo. III, R. 258.

[26] Burke, *Hist. of the Commoners.*

[27] *Cal. Pap. Let.* i, 546.

[28] Chan. Inq. p.m. (Ser. 2), vol. 10, No. 156. In this the advowson is entered as belonging to Katherine Brewerton, lady of the manors of Exbury and Lepe. It is difficult to reconcile this with the otherwise continuous possession of the advowson by the bishop.

[29] Information from Rev. J. Gillibrand.

FAWLEY

Falegia (xi cent.) ; Fallele (xii–xiv. cent.) ; Falle (xiv cent.).

Fawley parish is a low tract of land 9,850 acres in extent, stretching from the eastern limit of the New Forest to Southampton Water. It is separated from the true forest country by the table-land of Beaulieu Heath, the spurs of which extend into Fawley. Arable and pasture land, with fine woods of oak and pine, characterize the coast districts, but a large tract of uncultivated moorland stretches eastward from the banks of the Dark Water and occupies the centre of the parish. The larger portion of this moor bears the name 'Badminston Common' ; further west it is called 'Hugh's Common.' The latter is the name sometimes applied to the little inclosed plot of land, right in the centre of the moor, which from time to time has been sold in small allotments since about the year 1858. Mud cottages were at first erected, but these have been replaced by small red-brick houses. The settlement forms a sharp contrast to the surrounding country. Its usual name is 'Blackfields.' On the outskirts of the moor are several large farm-houses, which indeed characterize the whole district. In some cases a few cottages have sprung up in the neighbourhood of these farms, but except in the cases of Fawley and Langley there is nothing which can claim to be called a village. There are 2,544½ acres of arable land in the parish, 1,779¾ of permanent grass, and 1,211 acres covered by woods and plantations.[1] The soil is sandy, and the chief crops are oats and barley. The district is sparsely populated, and the means of communication bad, the roads being in many cases only tracks across the fields, while the nearest railway station is Beaulieu Road in the New Forest. The best mode of access is the road which runs down the parish from Hythe to Fawley, and on to Hillhead. A motor-bus service, opened by the London and South-Western Railway Company on 13 August, 1906, and running from Totton to Fawley, promises to open up the country by making it more accessible to visitors. The combination of moor, wood, and cornfield, with the glimpses of the sea and the hills of the Isle of Wight in the near distance, makes the country peculiarly attractive. The Cadland estate, which stretches down the coast of Southampton Water for nearly eight miles, is the residence of Mr. Drummond, who owns nearly all the land in the parish. The house was built in 1773, but was greatly enlarged by Mr. A. R. Drummond in 1836. Forest Lodge, the residence of Mr. Baring, is chiefly notable for its beautiful surroundings. It can also boast the possession of a Chinese pagoda and bridge in the grounds, and an observatory from which a fine view over Southampton Water is obtained. Eaglehurst, the residence of Mr. Huth, is also prettily situated, and the house itself is somewhat of a curiosity, part of it having been built, according to local report, in imitation of the tent which its first owner had used while on active service. The rectory house is of several dates, and stands in a charming garden, the mildness of the climate being witnessed to by the camellia-bushes which flourish in the open air.

The nucleus of the parish is the little village of Fawley. A quarter of a mile to the west of the village stands the parish school. Here the road forks, that on the right hand leading to the inn, the post office, the parish hall, and the few shops which constitute the village. The left-hand road leads past the high wall of the rectory garden to the church, which overlooks Southampton Water. Of many little paths leading down to the shore, one lane leads to Ashlett, where a natural creek has led to the establishment of yacht stores on the site of the old Fawley Mill. Ships of 100, or even 150 tons can be brought up here at high tide, and are unloaded at 'Victoria Quay.'[2] There is a tradition that lepers at one time lived in Fawley village, and the fact that an old farm building, pulled down some fifty years ago, and now the site of a hayrick, was called 'Lazarus' is given as a corroboration of the tradition ; but it is one not to be easily credited, as leper-houses as a rule were not founded in villages. A mile and a half south of the village, the 'Floating island' used to be an object of great interest, but the drainage of the surrounding bog has now robbed it of its floating capacities.

At Fawley village the road turns sharply southward, and runs parallel with Southampton Water, past Ower Farm, until it reaches Hillhead, the Fawley beach. Here a narrow strip of shingle connects the mainland with Calshot Castle, a small fort built by Henry VIII with stones from the ruins of Beaulieu Abbey. The arms of Queen Elizabeth, and the letters 'E.R.' on a waterspout, witness to later work on the castle. The unstable character of the shingle on which it stands causes a displacement of as much as a foot at spring tides. From the commanding position of Calshot at the entrance to Southampton Water, the view both up that harbour and down Spithead is a particularly fine one.

In sharp contrast to the rest of the parish is the detached portion which contains the little fishing village of Hythe. From its close connexion with Southampton by an hourly steamboat service, Hythe is the natural gate to Fawley. The club-house of the Hythe Yacht Club stands at the end of the pier. The manor courts of Cadlands were held at the 'Anchor in Hope' in this village until they lapsed two years ago. There were formerly stocks in the village.

The common lands of Fawley were inclosed in 1814.[3]

MANORS In Domesday Book *FAWLEY* is given among those lands which were held by the bishop of Winchester for the support of the monks of Winchester.[4] In 1284, when various agreements were concluded between the bishop and the monks, the latter gave up all their rights in Fawley to the bishop,[5] and the king ratified the agreement.[6] There seems to have been a close connexion between Fawley Manor and the manor of Bitterne, which also belonged to the bishops of Winchester. The two

[1] Statistics from Bd. of Agric. 1905.

[2] Restored by the parish of Fawley in commemoration of Her Majesty's Diamond Jubilee, 1897.

[3] Under Act of 50 & 51 Vic. cap. 64.

[4] *V.C.H. Hants*, i, 467*b*.

[5] Add. MS. 29436.

[6] *Cal. Chart. R.* ii, 274.

are generally spoken of as 'Bitterne with Fawley.'[7] It is probable that the bishop's tenant at Fawley did suit of court at Bitterne. In 1546 John Skullard was tenant at Fawley Manor,[8] which remained in the hands of that family until 1681.[9] In 1705 the manor was conveyed to Edward Peachey,[10] and a family settlement concerning Fawley Manor was made by William and Erlysman Peachy in 1765.[11] In 1801 the manor was conveyed by John and Philip Lockton, and spinsters Catherine, Elizabeth, Harriet, and Sophia Lockton, to Mr. Robert Drummond of Cadlands.[12] Fawley thus became annexed to the neighbouring manor of Cadlands (q.v.), and separate courts for Fawley ceased to be held. Mr. Drummond owns by far the greater part of the land, but there are a few copyholders who still pay in their quit-rents to Bitterne Manor.[13] Except for this, the rights of the bishops of Winchester over Fawley seem to have entirely lapsed. There is, however, one rather curious trace of them. The tradition runs that King John and the bishop of Winchester were once riding together in the New Forest when the king laughingly told the bishop that he might have 'as much land as he could crawl round.' The bishop, who was stout, had a machine made wherewith to support himself, and so managed to 'crawl' round a considerable piece. This was the Bishop's Ditch or Purlieu, near the present Beaulieu Road station. When the London and South-Western Railway Company built their line over it, all the copyholders in Fawley were compensated, and certain rights of common over the dyke still remain to them.[14]

In the thirteenth century Roger de Scures was lord of the manor of *CADLANDS*, which was attached to the lordship of the Isle of Wight.[15] In 1241 Eva de Clinton, his daughter and heiress, granted the manor to Isaac abbot of Titchfield, to be held by him in frankalmoign of herself and her heirs,[16] Reginald d'Albemarle being lord of the Isle of Wight at the time.[17] During the time that Isabella de Fortibus, countess of Devon and Albemarle, was lady of the island (1256–1292–3) she sold the over-lordship of the manor to Edward I.[18] The manor remained in the hands of Titchfield Abbey until the dissolution of the monasteries.[19] In 1537 John Salisbury, suffragan bishop of Thetford and commendatory and abbot of Titchfield Monastery, surrendered the possessions of the abbey, including the manor of Cadlands, to Henry VIII,[20] who granted it in December of the same year to Thomas Wriothesley, first earl of Southampton.[21] In 1546 Wriothesley gave the manor to Thomas Pace, who held it jointly with his wife Elizabeth until his death in 1560.[22] Alice, his daughter and heir, married George Powlett,[23] and their son, William Powlett, sold Cadlands in 1608 to Sir Walter Longe of Draycot Cerne, Wiltshire.[24] The Longes held it until 1626 or 1627, when Sir Walter Longe sold it to Nicholas Pescod.[25] In 1641 Pescod granted a ninety-nine years' lease of the manor lands to Peter Cardonell, a Norman merchant from Caen,[26] and also married his daughter and heir Mary to Adam Cardonell, probably a son of Peter. In the hands of these Cardonells the manor fell into two moieties, one inherited, the other originated by sale. Mary the granddaughter of Adam and Mary Cardonell—and by her brother's death sole heir of her father, Adam Cardonell the younger—married William, Lord Talbot, baron of Hensol, son of Charles Talbot, the chancellor of George II.[27] In 1741 a moiety of Cadland Manor was settled upon her and Lord Talbot and their children.[28] In 1772, however (ten years before Lord Talbot's death), this moiety was in the hands of Mary and Catherine, holding in their own right as the wives respectively of Joseph Small and Joseph Gibbs.[29] They quitclaimed to the Hon. Robert Drummond, a younger son of William Drummond, fourth Viscount Strathallan. His descendant Mr. A. C. Drummond is the present lord of the manor, and resides at Cadlands.

LONGE of Draycott Cerne. *Sable crusilly and a lion argent.*

DRUMMOND. *Or three bars wavy gules.*

The other moiety apparently carried no manorial rights with it, but consisted simply of the Rollstone Farm estate, which Adam de Cardonell and Mary his wife (daughter of Nicholas Pescod) conveyed to William Stanley of Paultons in 1657.[30] In 1693 the Stanleys were in possession of 'a moiety of the manor of Cadlands,'[31] and there are subsequent references to this moiety in the eighteenth century.[32] Mr. Cyril Hans Sloane Stanley of Paultons Park, Romsey, is owner of Rollstone Farm at the present day.

The first trace of *HOLBURY* Manor is in 1312, when Roger Bernerall and Gilbert de Shupton

7 Add. MSS. 29436; Eccl. Com. Court R.

8 Feet of F. Hants, Mich. 38 Hen. VIII. It is practically certain that the application of this reference to Folley Manor in Bramshott parish, Alton Hundred, is a mistake; *V.C.H. Hants*, ii, 494.

9 Chan. Inq. p.m. (Ser. 2), bdle. 2, No. 192; Feet of F. Hants, Hil. 8, Chas. I; Chan. Proc. (Ser. 2), bdle. 172, No. 8; Recov. R. Mich. 33 Chas. II, rot. 271.

10 Close, Trin. 4 Anne; Recov. R. Trin. 4 Anne, rot. 82.

11 Feet of F. Div. Cos. Hil. 6 Geo. III.

12 Feet of F. Hants, Trin. 41 Geo. III.

13 Bitterne passed from the bishop of Winchester to the hands of the Eccl. Com. in 1869.

14 Chiefly shooting rabbits and wild fowl, and cutting turf.

15 Sir F. Madden, Coll. for Cadlands, Add. MSS. 33284.

16 Feet of F. Hants, 25 Hen. III, No. 258.

17 Add MSS. 33284.

18 Ibid.; G. E. C. *Peerage*.

19 *Testa de Nev.* (Rec. Com.), 241*b*.; *Feud. Aids*, ii, 322, 340, 354; *Abbrev. Plac.* (Rec. Com.), 209*a* and *b*; *V.C.H. Hants*, ii, 184; *Cal. of Pat.* 1345–8, p. 461.

20 Feet of F. Div. Cos. Mich. 29 Hen. VIII.

21 *L. and P. Hen. VIII*, xii, g. 1311 (40); Mins. Accts. Relig. Ho. 135, m. 68.

22 Chan. Inq. p.m. (Ser. 2), pt. 2, No. 73.

23 Ibid. pt. 1, No. 133.

24 Feet of F. Div. Cos. Mich. 6 Jas. I; Com. Pleas, Deeds Enr. Mich. 6 Jas. I, m. 14.

25 W. and L. Inq. p.m. (Ser. 2), bdle. 13, No. 44; Recov. R. Hil. 19 Jas. I, rot. 94; Feet of F. Div. Cos. Hil. 19 Jas. I; Feet of F. Hants, Hil. 2 Chas. I.

26 Pat. 15 Chas. II, pt. 7, m. 20.

27 *Great Governing Families of England*, i, 264; Edmondson, *Baronagium Geneal.* iii, 303, vi, 53, 82.

28 Close, 15 Geo. II, pt. 12, m. 1 and 2; Feet of F. Hants, Hil. 15 Geo. II.

29 Feet of F. Hants, Trin. 12 Geo. III.

30 Close, 9 Chas. II, pt. 29, m. 26.

31 Recov. R. 5 Will. and Mary, rot. 204.

32 Recov. R. Hil. 18 Geo. II, rot. 53; Feet of F. Div. Cos. Trin. 21 Geo. III.

obtained licence of the king to 'grant land in Holebury to the abbey of King's Beaulieu.'[33] Holbury remained in the hands of the abbots of Beaulieu until the dissolution of that monastery in 1538.[34] Four years later Henry VIII granted it to Robert Whyte in exchange for a manor and lands in Middlesex.[35] Holbury was to be held as one-twentieth of a knight's fee for a rent of 14*s.* 6½*d.* There is no mention of Whyte heirs in the grant, and some time between this date and 1560 the manor fell into the hands of Thomas Pace.[36] From the death of Thomas Pace onwards, Holbury Manor followed the same descent as Cadlands (q.v.), being last spoken of as a whole manor when Nicholas Pescod granted a lease of the site to Adam de Cardonell.[37] As in the case of Cadlands, one moiety passed to Lady Mary Talbot,[38] and thence in 1772 to the Hon. Robert Drummond.[39] Whatever lands were signified in the conveyance of this moiety would be included in the Cadlands estate. The other moiety was in the possession of William Stanley of Paultons in 1693,[40] and his descendant, Mr. Cyril Hans Sloane Stanley, is the present owner of Holbury Farm.

BEAULIEU ABBEY. *Gules a crozier enfiled with a royal crown or and a border sable billetty or.*

Domesday Book records two tenements in *LANGLEY* held by the king's thegns; of these the smaller was held by Cola the huntsman,[41] the larger by Hugh de St. Quintin.[42] In 1372 John Baron of South Langley[43] and Julia his wife were seised of a messuage and land in South Langley.[44] Thence the tenement passed indirectly to Richard Goolde and his wife Joan in 1413.[45] This Joan afterwards became the wife of William Soper, and on being left for the second time a widow conveyed her holding to John Ludlowe in 1482.[46] In 1500 the right of the Ludlowes to hold the manor (here so called for the first time) was fiercely disputed in the Court of Chancery by one William Fletcher.[47] The Ludlowes, however, evidently made good their claim, for in 1609 Sir Edward Ludlowe sold the manor of Langley to Sir Walter Longe. This united the manor of Langley to the manors of Cadlands and Holbury, all three following the same descent henceforward. Langley, like the other two, fell into two moieties in the seventeenth century. Of these, one went to the Drummonds in 1772,[48] and coalesced with Cadlands. The other, as in the case of Holbury, is first mentioned in 1693, among the possessions of William Stanley of Paultons.[49] This latter moiety is represented by the ownership of Langley Farm by Mr. Cyril Hans Sloane Stanley at the present day.

LUDLOWE. *Argent a cheveron between three bears' heads razed sable.*

HARDLEY was assessed in Domesday at a hide and 3 virgates attached to the New Forest.[50] After this there is no further trace of it until the fourteenth century, when William Chippe held lands there.[51] In the sixteenth century the estate assumed the title of a manor in the hands of William Buckett, who held it from at least 1531 to 1579.[52] After this it changed hands rapidly[53] until finally conveyed to Richard Pittis, attorney of the King's Bench in 1628.[54] There is no further trace of Hardley as a separate manor, but a moiety of lands there is mentioned among the possessions of the Stanleys of Paultons in 1693,[55] 1745,[56] and 1781.[57] The land now forms part of the property of Mr. Drummond of Cadlands. During the tenure by one Thomas Tracie in the sixteenth century of a lease of Hardley Farm from William Buckett, an amusing incident occurred.[58] Peter Kembridge and a man named Oglander wishing to rob Tracie of some of his possessions, arrested him, Oglander impersonating the sheriff's bailiff. Carried by force to an alehouse at Dibden, Tracie, who describes himself as 'a poor plain simple creature,' was compelled 'to seal and deliver certain writings, but to what effect he himself knoweth not.' Tracie's wife meanwhile followed her husband, and 'made moan' for him outside the chamber. On gaining his freedom, Tracie appealed to the Court of Chancery.

Domesday records a manor of *STANSWOOD* in Fawley, reduced by the encroachments of the New Forest from two hides to one. It was then worth £7, and was included in the sources of the king's ferm which he had from the Isle of Wight.[59] There is no subsequent trace of any separate manor of Stanswood, which probably at an early date became merged in one of the neighbouring manors of Cadlands, Holbury, or Langley. Appurtenances in Stanswood belonging to Cadlands manor are mentioned in the inquisition on Thomas Pace's death, taken in 1560,[60] and in several subsequent extents of Cadlands before it fell into two moieties.[61] Land in Stanswood belonging to the Stanleys of Paultons is also mentioned in those documents of 1693,[62] 1745,[63] and 1781,[64] which deal with their possession of the moieties of the three manors. The land now forms part of Mr. A. C. Drummond's estate. A mill in Stanswood is men-

[33] Inq. a.q.d. 1312, No. 88.
[34] Chart. R. m. 3, No. 6; Pat. 33 Hen. VIII, pt. 8.
[35] Pat. 34 Hen. VIII, pt. 8, m. 15.
[36] Chan. Inq. p.m. (Ser. 2), pt. 2, No. 73.
[37] Pat. 15 Chas. II, pt. 7, No. 20.
[38] Close, 15 Geo. II, pt. 12, Nos. 1 and 2.
[39] Feet of F. Hants, Trin. 12 Geo. IV.
[40] Recov. R. East. 5 Will. and Mary, rot. 204.
[41] *V.C.H. Hants*, i, 509*b*.
[42] Ibid. 510*a*.
[43] Usually so called to distinguish it from neighbouring Langleys.
[44] Chan. Inq. p.m. 45 Edw. III, No. 19.
[45] Feet of F. Hants, Mich. 1 Hen. V.
[46] *Cal. of Pat.* 1476–85, p. 317; Chan. Inq. p.m. (Ser. 2), vol. 5, No. 71.
[47] Early Chan. Proc. bdle. 202, No. 24.
[48] Feet of F. Hants, Trin. 12 Geo. III.
[49] Recov. R. East. 5 Will. and Mary, rot. 204.
[50] *V.C.H. Hants*, i, 513*b*.
[51] Close, 1323–7, p. 212.
[52] Chan. Proc. (Ser. 2), bdle. 177, No. 47; Feet of F. Hants, Mich. 20 and 21 Eliz.; Feet of F. Hants, East. 21 Eliz.
[53] Feet of F. Hants, Mich. 27 and 28 Eliz.; Ibid. East. 11 Jas. I.
[54] Ibid. Mich. 4 Jas. I.
[55] Recov. R. East. 5 Will. and Mary, rot. 204.
[56] Recov. R. Hil. 18 Geo. II, rot. 53.
[57] Feet of F. Div. Cos. Trin. 21 Geo. III.
[58] Chan. Proc. (Ser. 2), bdle. 40, No. 32; bdle. 177, No. 47; bdle. 180, No. 43.
[59] *V.C.H. Hants*, i, 454*a*.
[60] Chan. Inq. p.m. (Ser. 2), pt. 2, No. 73.
[61] Com. Pleas, Indentures Enr. Mich. 6 Jas. I, m. 14; W. and L. Inq. p.m. (Ser. 2), bdle. 13, No. 44; Feet of F. Hants, Hil. 2 Chas. II.
[62] Recov. R. East. 5 Will. and Mary, rot. 204.
[63] Recov. R. Hil. 18 Geo. II, rot. 53.
[64] Feet of F. Div. Cos. Trin. 21 Geo. III.

tioned in Domesday, and is possibly referred to in some of the documents.[65] A mill stood in this locality until comparatively recently.

Domesday Book gives *STONE* in Fawley among the lands of the king's thegns, and mentions that its value had sunk since the time of Edward the Confessor from 60*s.* to 5*s.*[66] The tenement is not called a manor until the sixteenth century. In the fourteenth century William Chippe, and his son Robert Chippe after him, were holders of a messuage and land in Stone.[67] In 1346 one-twelfth part of a knight's fee in Stone, formerly in the tenure of Aymer de Valence, was held by Thomas West,[68] who was evidently one of the same family which early in the fourteenth century was united to the De La Warrs;[69] for in 1547 Thomas West, Lord De La Warr, was holding the manor of Stone.[70] In 1608 Thomas Fashion died seised of this manor, bequeathing it by will to West Fashion his son.[71] West Fashion in 1639, and his son Thomas the following year, died seised of the manor of Stone; the heir of Thomas was another Thomas, his son.[72] The family of Fashion was of Guernsey;[73] when they parted with Stone is not clear, the next trace of that manor being in 1704, when William Bulkley conveyed it to Samuel Mason.[74] Some time between this date and 1740 Stone came into the hands of the Mitfords of Exbury (probably about 1718 when William Mitford purchased Exbury of Henry Compton). In 1740, 1765, and 1774 family settlements concerning Stone were made by the Reveleys and Mitfords.[75] The estate now forms part of the property of Mr. Drummond of Cadlands.

West. *Argent a fesse dancetty sable.*

CHURCHES

The church of *ALL SAINTS, FAWLEY*, has a chancel 30 ft. 6 in. by 15 ft. 4 in., with north and south chapels, nave of the same width, 59 ft. 3 in. long, with north and south aisles 11 ft. 8 in. wide, south-east tower, and west porch.

As it stands to-day, without taking into account the modern details, the church seems to belong to two main periods, *c.* 1170–1210, and 1300–1340. But it is evident that its present plan, which is, roughly speaking, a rectangle 100 ft. long by 50 ft. wide, has only been reached by a long series of developments, some of which at least may be conjectured from existing evidence. The north wall of the tower, 2 ft. 3 in. thick, as against 3 ft. in the other three tower walls, is clearly the south wall of a nave older than the tower, and probably of the same date as the thin east (2 ft. 1 in.) and north walls of the nave (2 ft. 3 in.). The equality of width between nave and chancel suggests that the latter has been built round an older and narrower chancel, and above the east face of the chancel arch are the marks of a roof belonging to a narrower building. The evidences therefore of a small aisleless church, consisting of chancel about 11 ft. wide, and nave 15 ft. 4 in. wide, are demonstrable, but its east and west dimensions can only be suggested from the analogy of other examples: 13 ft. for the chancel and 35–40 ft. for the nave are probably near the mark.

The chancel built round the early chancel at some date in the twelfth century difficult to fix was probably at first aisleless, a length of string-course on the north wall, west of the present arcade, pointing to the fact that the wall is older than the arcade. It was also probably some 8 ft. shorter than the present chancel. About 1170–80 a north aisle to the chancel was built, probably narrower than the present aisle and of equal length with the chancel, and some thirty years later a south aisle of like dimensions was added.

The tower at the south-east of the nave must have been begun about the same time as the north aisle of the chancel, and the lengthening of the nave and addition to it of north and south aisles was probably determined on, but, from the evidence of the details, carried on very slowly. The two eastern bays of the north arcade have been altered, if not rebuilt, in the fourteenth century; and this, together with some evidence of the former existence of an east wall to the north aisle, suggests that some transeptal arrangement balancing the tower may have been originally intended. Unless the west arch of the tower has been tampered with, the width of the south aisle of the nave must always have been as now; and since the north aisle is of exactly the same width, it also may preserve its original plan. The first part of the fourteenth-century enlargements probably began with a lengthening, *c.* 1300, of the chancel, and some thirty years later the aisles were similarly lengthened and also widened, the north aisle to the width of that of the nave, and the south aisle to the width of the tower. The work in the nave, beyond the alterations to the south arcade already noted, involved no changes in the plan. The chief repairs to the building of modern date are those of 1840 and 1866.

The chancel has an east window of three trefoiled lights with intersecting mullions, and a plain circle in the head, an interesting piece of early tracery, *c.* 1300. Beneath its sill on the outside is a small round-headed recess with a pedimented seventeenth-century slab with an inscription to Elizabeth Light, the back of the recess being also part of a seventeenth-century tombstone. The north arcade of the chancel is of two bays with pointed arches of a single order, round shafts, and square capitals scalloped; the bases are moulded and have angle-spurs; all details being much worked over in cement. The south arcade is evidently of a later date, though of the same general design, and has plain leaf-work on the bells of the capitals. The north chapel has a three-light east window with net tracery, *c.* 1330, the mullions being modern, and in the north wall two square-headed three-light windows, much repaired. On the north of the east window is a plain image-bracket, in the south wall a trefoiled fourteenth-century piscina.

In the south wall of the chancel is a modernized

65 Feet of F. Hants, Hil. 2 Jas. I.
66 *V.C.H. Hants*, i, 509*a*.
67 *Abbrev. Rot. Orig.* (Rec. Com.), 15*b*; Chan. Inq. p.m. 18 Edw. II, No. 68; De Banc. R. 292, m. 164.
68 *Feud. Aids*, ii, 327.
69 G.E.C. *Peerage*, viii, 102.
70 Feet of F. Hants, Mich. 1 Edw. VI.
71 W. and L. Inq. p.m. 1–6 Jas. I (Ser. 2), bdle. 2, No. 27.
72 Chan. Inq. p.m. 15 Chas. I (Ser. 2), No. 40; W. and L. Inq. p.m. 5 Jas. I, bdle. 33, No. 27.
73 *The Genealogist*, vii, 236.
74 Feet of F. Hants, Hil. 3 Anne.
75 Close 14 Geo. II, pt. 7; Recov. R. Mich. 6 Geo. III, rot. 258; Feet of F. Hants, East. 14 Geo. III.

trefoiled piscina and a square locker, the back of which has been cut through and now opens to the south chapel, the east end of which is used as a vestry. It has east and south windows corresponding to those in the north chapel, and at the south-west a small pointed doorway of late twelfth-century date with a continuous edge-roll on its outer face. At the west is a modern arch to the tower, and at the south-east an arched piscina recess with a small trefoiled recess, also with a drain, below it. North of the east window is an image bracket, on which rests a stone with roughly-cut fourteenth-century tracery on it. In the east window are the arms of Henry VIII in a garter, and several loose pieces of fifteenth-century glass are kept here, one being part of a crucifixion, and another having a figure of St. Nicholas. The chancel arch is semicircular, of one square order, with a moulded and chamfered abacus of late twelfth-century detail. The wall in which it is set is only 2 ft. 1 in. thick, and it probably succeeds an early and narrower arch.

The nave arcades are of plain character, with pointed arches of one order, circular columns, and square capitals with the angles cut back. The general details are of thirteenth-century style, except in the two east bays of the north arcade, where the detail of capitals and bases looks like fourteenth-century work. The tower at the south-east of the nave is of late twelfth-century date, with a plain round-headed light in the south wall of its ground story, and modern round-headed arches on the north and west. The north-west pier also has been rebuilt, but the responds of the arches are old, with scalloped capitals and moulded bases with spurs. The capital of the south respond of the west arch has curious foliate detail, resembling that at South Hayling, but of earlier type. On the south and east walls is a modern wall arcade, with memorial inscriptions of the Drummond family. The upper part of the tower is a fifteenth-century addition or rebuilding, and has a plain parapet and two square-headed lights on each face of the upper stage. In the second stage are trefoiled windows on the north and east, and on the south side is a rain-water head dated 1743.

The north aisle of the nave has four trefoiled fourteenth-century lights in its north wall, partly modernized, and the west window, of two trefoiled lights, is modern. The south aisle has similar windows, but in place of the second from the east is a plain fourteenth-century doorway.

At the west end of the nave is a gallery lighted by a modern three-light window, and beneath it a west door of good twelfth-century style, and looking earlier than the other twelfth-century work. The semicircular arch has a plain inner order, and an outer order ornamented with a roll and zigzag, springing from nook-shafts with scalloped capitals. Its south jamb and part of the arch are in large stones of later date than the rest, perhaps fifteenth-century work, and the arch has doubtless been moved from its original position, which may have been in the south wall of the nave. Over it is a porch of 1844 in twelfth-century style.

The roofs of the church are ceiled, except in the north chapel, and at the east end of the south chapel is a fourteenth-century truss. The nave walls have a line of stone corbels on both sides at plate level, and corbels which carried part of the rood-loft remain in the east angles of the nave.

The font, at the west end of the south aisle, is modern, octagonal with panelled sides.

The pulpit is octagonal, the upper part of good early seventeenth-century work, with arched panels and a projecting book-board carried on scrolled brackets; no other wood fittings are old, and the only monument of interest is a brass plate on the south side of the chancel to Henry Audley, 1606, a copy of whose will is kept among the church papers.

There are four bells, the treble by Joshua Kipling, 1737; the second by Richard Flory of Salisbury, 1677; the third, of 1603, inscribed 'Give God the glory,' R.B.; and the tenor by Warner, 1867.

The plate includes an interesting pre-Reformation paten, $5\frac{5}{8}$ in. diameter, parcel gilt, with a vernicle in a six-lobed depression. Its date is *c.* 1520. There is also an Elizabethan communion cup of 1562, a flagon of 1834, a standing paten of 1844, two silver-topped glass cruets, and an old pewter plate.

The first book of the registers runs from 1677 to 1759, but there are two loose pages with entries of marriages 1674–7, and burials 1673–7. The second book is the marriage register 1754–92, and the third contains baptisms and burials 1759–98. The fourth continues the baptisms and burials, and the fifth the marriages, to 1813 and 1812 respectively. There are two pages of churchwardens' accounts for 1681, and consecutive accounts for 1725–1818.

The church of *ST. JOHN THE BAPTIST, HYTHE*, erected in 1874, is of red brick, with Bath stone dressings, in thirteenth-century style. The register dates from 1823.

ADVOWSONS A chapel in Fawley is mentioned in Domesday Book.[76] The living is a rectory, and has always been in the gift of the bishop of Winchester. There is a chapel of ease at Langley licensed for divine service. Exbury was a chapelry of Fawley until 1868. The two formed one of the 'peculiar benefices' of the bishop of Winchester.[77] Hythe was separated from Fawley in 1841,[78] and formed into an ecclesiastical parish. The living is a titular vicarage in the gift of the rector of Fawley.

Fawley contains a Primitive Methodist chapel and a Wesleyan chapel, and there is a Baptist chapel at Blackfields, and a Congregational chapel at Hythe.

CHARITY Mary Trattle by will, proved 1868, bequeathed a legacy and a share of residuary estate, now represented by £1,068 9*s.* 2*d.* consols (with the official trustees) upon trust that the income should be applied, one-half in the distribution of beef to the poor at Christmas, and the other half in providing them with blankets or articles of clothing.

The annual dividends, amounting to £26 14*s.*, are duly applied.

[76] *V.C.H. Hants*, i, 467*b*.

[77] *Valor Eccl.* (Rec. Com.), ii, App.

[78] *Lond. Gaz.* 21 Dec. 1841.

ST. MARY EXTRA

The ancient parish of St. Mary Extra, together with that of Sholing, was in 1903 formed into the civil parish of Itchen.[1] At the time of the last Ordnance Survey St. Mary Extra comprised 2,177 acres, and Sholing 597 acres. The parish is bounded on the west by the estuary of the Itchen and the upper reaches of Southampton Water, and runs some two miles inland, the levels sloping gently from a height of about 130 ft. on its eastern boundary to the tidal waters on the west. The coast district is practically an outlying portion of Southampton, which threatens to encroach still further in this direction. This, together with the circumstance that much of the inland county is of a barren character, makes it not surprising that the proportion of agricultural land to the whole is very small: there are only 322 acres of arable land, 433 of permanent grass, and 70 of woods and plantations.[2] The soil is sandy, and what crops there are consist of wheat, oats, and barley. The London and South Western Railway passes through the parish from north-west to south-east, and the road which leads to Southampton by way of the Itchen Ferry follows the same general direction as the railway, traversing Weston and Sholing Commons. Both these commons were included in the Inclosure Act of 1814 for South Stoneham and St. Mary Extra.[3] Weston Common is a piece of waste land surrounded by groups of red-brick houses, one of which, known as Newtown (i.e. New Netley) is close to the railway. Another little group, in a hollow of the common, is called Botany Bay. Behind Botany Bay is Sholing. Continuing westward along the Southampton road, Itchen lies on the north, and Woolston on the south. The continuation of the road is the double ferry known as the 'Floating Bridge' (opened 1836) which connects these places with Southampton, of which they are practically suburbs. In the seventeenth, eighteenth, and early nineteenth centuries, Itchen was a little fishing village, and up to the end of the eighteenth century the fishermen kept the festival of St. Peter by carrying an image of the saint in procession through the village. The inhabitants are said to have been always very peculiar, and chary in their dealings with natives of other parts of the country. They used to be notorious smugglers, but have so far changed with the times as to be now famous as yachtsmen. The modern growth of Woolston dates from the opening of the Portsmouth road in 1834, and from the establishment of a ship-building yard in 1876. The tanning trade once carried on here is now extinct. 'The Paddock,' the residence of Lady Longmore, occupies the site of the former 'Woolston House,' which, originally a farm-house, was enlarged and beautified in the eighteenth century and pulled down in the early part of the nineteenth. The chief historical interest connected with Itchen is the building of Jesus Chapel on Ridgway Heath in the seventeenth century. The enterprise was a private one, the result of the efforts of Captain Richard Smith of Pear Tree, governor of Calshot Castle, who urged the necessity of a church nearer than that of St. Mary, Southampton, from which the inhabitants of St. Mary Extra were separated by 'the great river Itchen, where the passage is very broad and often dangerous.' Licence to build a chapel was granted on 23 February, 1617, and the chapel was consecrated 17 September, 1620, by Lancelot Andrewes, bishop of Winchester, the form of service then used being that which has formed the basis of all consecration services since used in the Church of England.[4]

The heath called Ridgway Heath at the time of the consecration included the present 'Pear Tree Green.' The pear tree which later gave its name to the Green was already planted, though at what date is unknown. It is still standing, and in 1850 Mrs. Preston Hulton of Barnfield caused a young pear to be planted by its side, that the name might be perpetuated.

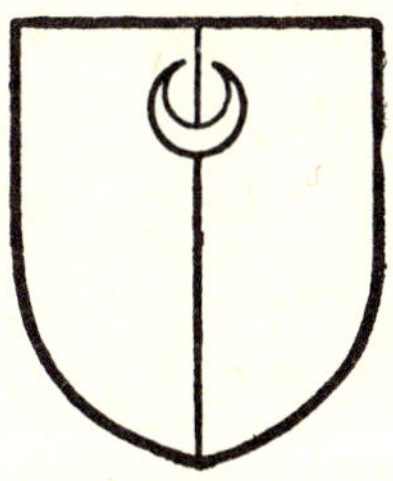

Waldegrave, Lord Radstock. *Party argent and gules with the difference of a crescent sable.*

Turning southward down a wooded lane which runs at right angles to the Portsmouth road, and passing Mayfield, the residence of Lord Radstock, on the right hand, the little village of Weston is reached, the spot being remarkably rural and secluded considering its vicinity. Before reaching the village the road passes under two arches, both built by Mr. William Chamberlayne early in the last century, one of them in commemoration of the battle of Waterloo. In 1810 Mr. Chamberlayne also erected an obelisk as a memorial to Charles James Fox. On Mr. Chamberlayne's death in 1829, that portion of the Weston Grove estate on which the obelisk stood was included in the land which passed to Mr. Wright, of Oak Bank, Itchen, who built Mayfield upon it in 1856. Mr. Wright's son, a captain in the 4th Dragoon Guards, buried two favourite horses near the obelisk and had their names engraved upon it. Lord Radstock, however, who purchased Mayfield in 1883, has had these removed. The present Weston Grove estate extends from Mayfield to the coast, and is the residence of Mr. T. W. Chamberlayne. The house was built in 1801. The small village of Weston itself consists of a few thatched cottages and some newer-looking houses nearer the coast. The moss-covered building, now a Sunday School, was used for divine service between 1855 and 1865, when the present church was consecrated. Both buildings were the gift of the Rev. P. Hulton. 'The Cliff' overlooking Southampton Water was built by the Rev. G. W. Minns in 1882, there being then no vicarage attached to the benefice. On the coast is a curious old hut, entirely roofed with matted seaweed and said to be of considerable antiquity.[5] Altogether Weston

[1] L.G.B. Order, 44465.
[2] Statistics from Bd. of Agric. 1905.
[3] *Parl. Blue Bk. Inclosure Awards*, 156.
[4] Rev. T. L. O. Davies, 'Historical Notes,' published in the *Southampton Times*.
[5] *Papers and Proc. Hants Field Club*, iv (3).

justifies the remark of William Cobbett: 'To them that delight in water scenes this is the prettiest place that ever I saw in my life.'

MANORS

A considerable portion of the land in the north of St. Mary Extra parish lies within the manor of Bitterne,[6] but the remainder constitutes the manor of *WOOLSTON* (Olvestune, xi cent.; Wolveston, xiii cent.). One hide of land in Woolston, held by Tovi of Edward the Confessor, was held at the time of the Survey by Rainald the son of Croch from the king, its value having depreciated from 10*s.* to 5*s.*[7] Two centuries later Hugh de Chikenhull was seised of half a carucate of land here, which on his death in 1257 descended to his son Alan.[8] It was still held of the king in chief by the serjeanty of maintaining one footman with bow and arrow in the king's army in Wales, for forty days annually.

From Alan the Woolston estate descended to his son Hugh,[9] and on the death of the latter in 1317 passed to John de Chikenhull,[10] who settled the manor of Woolston upon a certain John Seyntcler and Henry de Wayte for life, with an ultimate remainder to Isabella de Inkpenn, sister of Henry.[11]

The manor passed into the possession of Isabella prior to 1350, when she died, leaving as heir her son John, who died in 1362.[12] Robert his son succeeded to the estate in 1375 on the death of his brother John without issue,[13] and on his marriage in 1389, settled Woolston upon his wife Margery.[14]

The settlement was made without the king's licence, and on the second marriage of Margery with John Benet, after the death of Robert Inkpenn in 1406,[15] controversy arose concerning the validity of the deed. She was eventually allowed to hold the manor till her death,[16] when it reverted to her son Richard Inkpenn, who conveyed the estate in 1424 to his daughter Alice, wife of Ralph Chamberlayne, and her issue.[17]

CHAMBERLAYNE. *Gules a cheveron engrailed or between three scallops argent.*

The history of the manor during the next two hundred years remains in obscurity. Sir George Rivers, who held Woolston in 1631, conveyed the estate to Nathaniel Mill,[18] and nine years later Joseph Debertine and his wife Alice, possibly heiress to Nathaniel Mill, sold it to Henry Pitt.[19]

In 1701 Thomas Macham and John Gilbert held the manorial rights,[20] but whether by inheritance or purchase is not clear, and quitclaimed to Nicholas Winkworth.[21] In 1766 Woolston manor, together with the adjoining manors of Netley and Hound,[22] was held by Thomas Dummer, and has descended with them from that date to the present day,[23] the present lord of the manor being Mr. Tankerville Chamberlayne, whose residence, Weston Grove, is within Woolston manor.

One of the ancient rights attached to this manor was that of the ferry over the Itchen waters, to Southampton,[24] where the old 'Floating Bridge' now stands.

A mill is mentioned in an extent of Woolston manor in 1317, but no further reference to it is found after this date.[25] It is probably identical with Weston Mill, which Mr. Taylor obtained from Thomas Lee Dummer, lord of Woolston manor, about 1762, for the establishment of his machinery for making ships' blocks. The water at the mill often proving deficient, the works were moved to Wood Mill, on the Itchen, and Weston Mill was abandoned.[26]

Pear Tree House was built in the opening years of the seventeenth century by Mr. Mylles of Bitterne manor, and remained in the hands of that family throughout the seventeenth and eighteenth centuries, passing by marriage to the family of Waring in 1792. In 1871 Miss Margaret Waring bequeathed the estate to Mr. George Atherley, a banker in the town, whose son sold it to Mr. Cruickshank.

CHURCHES

JESUS CHAPEL as first built was a little building '20½ ft. broad by 50½ ft. long, fitted with a wooden chancel screen, a Holy Table, a font, a pulpit, seats on the floor and gallery, and a bell.' In Captain Smith's will of 1630 it is called 'Jesus Chappell at Ridway.' It has been enlarged and repaired again and again, till nothing but part of the west end of its original building remains. In 1821 it was repaired, the south transept, west porch and gallery being built; in 1847 a north aisle and vestry were added; in 1866 additions were made on the east side of the south transept, and in 1882 a new chancel with a south aisle was built. Of its old fittings only the altar table remains, and the old pulpit has been used up as wainscoting in the vestry. The old bell, which is said to have come from Netley Abbey, but is of much later date, is blank, and not now hung, and in the western bell-cot is its successor, hung in 1870.

The church stands in a crowded little churchyard, its west end facing on to the open green where grew the pear tree from which the district is named, and is of more historical than architectural interest; it was doubtless a very plain little building at the first, and the successive enlargements, made as occasion served, have not tended to produce unity of design.

The church plate consists of chalice, paten, and two flagons, all dating from the seventeenth century. The chalice and paten have no inscription, and the former no hall-mark, but it seems probable that they date from some time between the years 1620 and 1630. The offertory, amounting to £4 12*s.* 2*d.*, which was collected on the day of the consecration of the chapel (17 September, 1620), was ordered by the bishop to be converted into a chalice, and this, with its cover (i.e. paten) would almost certainly be the 'church plate' to which Captain Richard Smith refers in his will of 1630. The two flagons bear the

[6] See South Stoneham.
[7] *V.C.H. Hants*, i, 501*a*.
[8] Chan. Inq. p.m. 41 Hen. III, No. 22.
[9] Chan. Inq. p.m. 45 Hen. III, No. 9.
[10] Ibid. 10 Edw. II, No. 33.
[11] Pat. 2 Edw. III, pt. 2, m. 29.
[12] Chan. Inq. p.m. 23 Edw. III, pt. 2, No. 116; ibid. 35 Edw. III, pt. 1, No. 123.
[13] Ibid. 48 Edw. III, No. 41.
[14] *Cal. of Pat.* 1388–92, p. 171.
[15] Chan. Inq. p.m. 7 Hen. IV, No. 48.
[16] *Cal. of Pat.* 1388–92, p. 171.
[17] Ibid. 1422–29, p. 195.
[18] Feet of F. Hants, East. 6 Chas. I. An extent of the manor at this time gives 8 messuages, 7 gardens, 150 acres of land, 50 acres of meadow, 60 of pasture, 35 of woodland, 45 of furze, and the passage over the River Itchen to Southampton.
[19] Ibid. Hil. 15 Chas. I.
[20] Ibid. Trin. 12 Will. III.
[21] Ibid.
[22] Feet of F. Hants, Trin. 6 Geo. III.
[23] Recov. R. Trin. 1 Will. IV, No. 163. See Netley and Hound.
[24] Feet of F. Hants, Hil. 15 Chas. I; ibid. Trin. 12 Will. III.
[25] Chan. Inq. p.m. 10 Edw. II, No. 33.
[26] *Proc. Hants Field Club*, iv, 3.

inscription 'The gift of Mrs. Katherine Palmer to Jesus Chapel,' and her coat of arms. Mrs. Palmer died before 1674, and the hall-mark on the flagons is 1665–6. It should be added that in an old list of benefactors, drawn up early in the eighteenth century, it is said that flagons, chalice, and paten were all bequeathed by Mrs. Palmer to Jesus Chapel, but this was probably an error made by the vicar who drew up the list.

Its earliest registers are transcripts from South Shoreham, having one entry of 1671, and then a series from 1681 to 1699. The first complete book runs from 1699 to 1708, and the second is a copy of it continued to 1712, with scattered entries afterwards—one of 1713, three of 1717, several from 1723 to 1729, and four marriage entries between 1733 and 1741. The third book has entries 1733–43, and the fourth 1743–1812, no marriages being registered after the passing of the Act of 1753.

The church of the *HOLY TRINITY, WESTON*, is a stone building in fourteenth-century style. The register dates from 1866.

The church of *ST. MARY, SHOLING*, a building of stone, in the thirteenth-century style, was erected in 1866, and the register dates from the same year.

ADVOWSON Jesus chapel, later known as Pear Tree Church, from its site on Pear Tree Green, has never been formally separated from the mother church of St. Mary's, Southampton. The living was a curacy in the gift of the founder, Captain Richard Smith of Pear Tree, governor of Calshot Castle. In 1685 the patronage was sold to Mrs. Mylles of Pear Tree House, from whom it descended by marriage to the family of Davies. In 1881 Mrs. Davies transferred the patronage to the rector of St. Mary's Southampton, in return for an annual endowment of the living out of the tithes of that church. In 1896 a scheme was sanctioned by the Ecclesiastical Commissioners for the further endowment of Jesus Chapel out of the revenues of St. Mary's, the result of the arrangement being the transference of the patronage to the bishop of Winchester, the diocesan, in whose hands it still remains. The living is now a vicarage.[27]

Until 1855 Pear Tree Church was the only one in that part of the parish of St. Mary's Southampton which lies on the left bank of the River Itchen. In that year, as before mentioned, the Rev. P. Hulton erected a building now used as a Sunday school at Weston, to act as a chapel of ease to Pear Tree Church. He supplemented this a few years later by building a church, consecrated in 1865 as the church of Holy Trinity, Weston. His son, who succeeded him as vicar in 1870, accepted a grant for the augmentation of the living from the Ecclesiastical Commissioners, and this involved the transference of the patronage of the benefice to the bishop of the diocese.[28] The ecclesiastical parish was formed in 1866.[29]

Sholing was formed into a consolidated chapelry in 1867, out of the parishes of Hound and St. Mary Extra. The living is a vicarage in the gift of the bishop of Winchester.

There is a Congregational chapel, built in 1838, in St. Mary Extra parish. At Sholing there is a mission room, and chapels for the Primitive Methodists, Baptists, and Plymouth Brethren.

CHARITIES Charity of Nathaniel Mill. See Southampton Municipal Charities.

The following payments are made out of the dividends of a sum of £1,525 £2 10*s.* per cent. annuities, held by the official trustees in trust for this charity, namely, £1 14*s.* 4*d.* to the minister of Jesus Chapel, 17*s.* 4*d.* for repair of same chapel, £1 14*s.* 4*d.* for the poor of this parish, and 13*s.* 8*d.* for a coat or gown to a poor person.

UPHAM

The parish of Upham consists of 2,883 acres, of which approximately 1,596 are arable land, 1,018¾ permanent grass, and 556½ woods and plantations.[1] It lies on the southern slope of the downs, and is some four miles long from north-west to south-west, its greatest width being about two miles at the upper end, while the southern portion varies from a mile and a quarter to half a mile in width. The levels rise from a height of 130 ft. on the southern boundary of the parish, to about 420 ft. at the north-east, on the slopes of Millbarrow Down. As in the case of the parishes of Bishop's Waltham and Droxford, the country falls geologically into two portions, the chalk of the down land and the clay of the valley. The old road from Waltham to Winchester crosses the north of the parish, passing Belmore House, the residence of Mr. Kinnard, and running through a splendid grove of beech trees near the north-west boundary of the parish. Except on Stephen's Castle Down the country is beautifully wooded, the lanes being thickly shaded with oaks. Some two and a half miles to the south-west, the new road from Waltham to Winchester traverses the south end of the parish in a parallel direction to the old road; the two are connected by a third, which runs north-east and south-west up the middle of the parish, with smaller roads branching off on either side. On this central road, on an outlying spur of the downs, stands the main portion of the village, including the church, the vicarage, the manor-house, the 'Brushmakers Arms,' and the school, which occupies the site of the old brush factory. To the north-west is Stroudwood Common, inclosed in 1860,[2] and on the south-east the outlying houses of the village are set at irregular intervals down the thickly wooded lane to its junction with the new Winchester road, where is a little group of newer-looking houses in more open country called 'Lower Upham,' at a distance of over a mile from the village proper. In the south-east corner of the parish is the hill called Wintershill, with the house which bears its name;

27 From information supplied by Rev. T. L. O. Davies, vicar of Woolston.

28 Rev. T. L. O. Davies, *Hist. Notes*, published in the *Southampton Times*.

29 *Lond. Gaz.* 27 June, 1873.

1 Returns of Bd. of Agric. 1905. The return includes lands in adjoining parishes.

2 *Parl. Blue Books Inclosure Awards*, 156.

the land attached to the estate extends into the adjoining parishes of Bishop's Waltham and Durley. Previous to the building of the Droxford Union there was a poor-house (now cottages) at Upham, the following being one of the rules for the conduct of its inhabitants: 'That all persons, both men, women, and children, shall attend Divine Service every Sunday morning at eleven o'clock, or else go without a dinner; except such as are not able by infirmity or age.'

The industry of brushmaking, which at one time occupied the villagers, has now become extinct, and the work of the people is purely agricultural. The chief crops are wheat, oats, and barley.

Edward Young, the author of 'Night Thoughts,' was born at Upham Rectory in 1684, but left the village when quite a boy.

MANORS There has never been a separate manor of *UPHAM*, the lands in the modern parish of Upham forming part of the ancient manor of Bishop's Waltham,[3] which passed from the bishop of Winchester to the Ecclesiastical Commissioners in 1869.[4] The house known as Upham Manor House was built in the latter part of the nineteenth century, on the site of the old one, by Mr. J. C. Stares.

The *WINTERSHILL* estate was also included in the lands of Bishop's Waltham manor, and there were never separate manorial courts for Wintershill. The earliest record of the name is in 1420, when John Fromond de Spersholte conveyed land in 'South Waltham, Cleverly, Upham, Durley, Wintershill, Mincyngfield, and Botley,' to Margaret, widow of one John Tank.[5] This estate, or part of it, was next found in the possession of Edward Upham,[6] after whose death an amusing dispute arose between his widow, Iseult, and the trustees of the property.[7] The account relates that Iseult, who apparently had married again, sent her son to one of the trustees 'with a release from his mother Iseult, and required him (the trustee) to seal the said release, and thereto he said, "Nay—I was enfeoffed in the said lands to the use of the heirs of Upham, and not of Barnevyle, and to them will I release and to none other, to die for it or to be drawn with wild horses." Afterward the said Iseult came to him, and asked him why he had not sealed the release that she sent unto him, himself answering that it was not his duty so to do, and not well. Whereupon the said Iseult said unto him, "Thou beggar! Then keep my land against my will!" He saying again unto her, "Thou mare! wouldst thou make me damn my soul?" And so departed in great anger.' From the year 1500 onwards the estate was dignified by the name of manor,[8] and up till at least 1766 passed through exactly the same hands as did the manor of South Ambersham (q.v.). A certain Nicholas Taillard and Alice his wife, who was holding in her own right, quitclaimed the land to John Onley in 1500,[9] and in 1538 Thomas Onley sold it to Katherine Percy, dowager countess of Arundel.[10] She sold it three years later to the Yongs of Petworth, in Sussex,[11] and this family were still holding in 1629, when the estate was made over to Sir Thomas Bilson.[12] In 1733 and 1766 Wintershill was in the hands of the Caprons of Sussex,[13] after which no connected descent of the holders is traceable.

It is interesting to note that the original manor-house of this so-called manor was the old farm-house now known as Durley Hall Farm, standing about a quarter of a mile away from the upper lodge of Wintershill Hall, and within the parish of Durley.[14] This house is now the property of Dr. Maybury, and has no connexion with the Wintershill estate. Wintershill Hall was built by Mr. G. H. Stares in 1852, and the larger portion of it rebuilt in 1902 by Mr. J. S. Moss, the present owner and occupier.

There is an interesting entry in the churchwardens' accounts for 11 April, 1642: 'For cleansing the church against Christmas, after the troopers had abused it for a stable for their horses, 2*s.* 6*d.*'

CHURCH The church (dedication unknown) has been so much repaired that it shows little appearance of age, but a small amount of thirteenth-century work remains. The chancel walls may be of this date, as their eastern angles have quoins of thirteenth-century character (on the southern of which is an incised sundial), and at the east end of the north aisle is a thirteenth-century arch, though it is not in its original position.

The chancel, which has a modern vestry and organ chamber on the north, has a three-light east window and a single-light south window, both with modern tracery of fifteenth-century style, though the rear arch of the latter appears to be old. There are two sedilia and a double piscina of doubtful date; and the chancel arch is a somewhat nondescript specimen with clustered shafts and a moulded arch. The chancel was restored in 1877, and its present appearance of comparative newness is doubtless due to that event. The north aisle of the nave was rebuilt in 1881, with an arcade of three bays, having hollow-sided octagonal columns and moulded capitals; the aisle has a doorway at the north-west and a west and two north windows, all modern. At its east end is the thirteenth-century arch already noted, with half-round responds, moulded capitals and bases, and pointed arch of two chamfered orders.

The south arcade, much taller than the north, is of fifteenth-century style but doubtful date, with slender octagonal columns and an east respond with clustered shafts corbelled off at some distance from the floor. The windows of this aisle, each of two cinquefoiled lights under a square head, preserve some old stonework of fifteenth-century date, but the south doorway has a plastered arch, and shows no signs of age. Over it is a modern south porch, and the aisle is prolonged westward to the west face of the tower, and has a two-light west window with a trefoiled circle over, and a single cinquefoiled light on the south.

3 Suitors from Upham are found attending the Courts Baron of Bishop's Waltham manor. Eccles. Com. Ct. R.

4 *Lond. Gaz.* 1 April, 1870.

5 Feet of F. Hants, Mich. 8 Hen. V.

6 Feet of F. Hants, Mich. 31 Hen. VI.

7 Early Chan. Proc. bdle. 44, No. 121.

8 It is rather perplexing to note that the appurtenances of Wintershill manor after this date are quite different from those in the earlier documents. But the descent has no possible connexion with that of Wintershill in Bramley, Surrey.

9 Feet of F. Div. Cos. Mich. 16 Hen. VIII.

10 Feet of F. Div. Cos. Hil. 29 Hen. VIII.

11 Com. Pleas. Deeds Enr. Trin. 33 Hen. VIII, m. 1 *d.*

12 Feet of F. Div. Cos. Mich. 5 Chas. I.

13 Feet of F. Hants. East. 6 Geo. II; Feet of F. Div. Cos. Hil. 6 Geo. III.

14 From information supplied by Mr. Stares, of Upham Manor House.

The west tower is in great part a rebuilding in brick, on its north face being a stone with the date 1700. It has a plain pointed east arch, a plastered west doorway, and over it a round-headed window.

In the vestry is a panel of slate in a frame, dated 1756, and recording the names of the 'singers' of that time.

There are six bells of 1761, all by Thomas Swain.

There are two chalices, a paten, a flagon, and an alms dish of Sheffield plate, also a silver chalice 1901, and paten 1898, and a silver-mounted glass flagon of 1897.

The registers down to 1812 are contained in three books, the oldest having baptisms and burials 1598–1734, with a gap in the burials from 1602 to 1640, and marriages 1622–1734. The second runs from 1734 to 1772, and the third from 1773 to 1812.

The churchwardens' accounts for 1640–60 are preserved.

ADVOWSON Upham being a part of the manor of Bishop's Waltham, the advowson of the church was in the hands of the bishop of Winchester, lord of the manor,[15] being one of his 'peculiar benefices.'[16] As in the case of all the churches in this manor, Henry de Blois, bishop of Winchester (1129–71) made a grant of Upham advowson to the hospital of St. Cross, Winchester.[17] Upham was, however, once more in the hands of the bishop by 1284, being among those advowsons to which the monks of St. Swithun, Winchester, finally agreed to renounce all claim in favour of the bishop.[18] After this date Upham continued to follow the history of Bishop's Waltham manor, the advowson being specifically mentioned in the grant by Edward VI to William, earl of Wiltshire, of those manors, &c., which had fallen to the crown by the surrender of Bishop Poynet.[19] In 1852 an exchange of benefices was effected between the bishops of Winchester and Lichfield, and the patronage of Upham was transferred to Lichfield.[20] In the following year Durley, which had hitherto been served by a curate as a chapelry of Upham, was separated from it. In 1890 the patronage of Upham was transferred to the Lord Chancellor, in whose gift it still remains.

There is a Bible Christian Chapel at Lower Upham.

15 Winton Epis. Reg. Egerton MSS. 2031–4; *Wykeham's Reg.* (Hants Rec. Soc.), i, App. 561.

16 *Valor Eccl.* (Rec. Com.), ii, App.

17 Harl. MS. 1616, fol. 9.

18 Add. MSS. 29364.

19 Pat. 5 Edw. VI, pt. 4, m. 39.

20 *Lond. Gaz.* 4 June, 1852.

THE HUNDRED OF FAWLEY

WITH THE

LIBERTY OF ALRESFORD

CONTAINING THE PARISHES OF

OLD ALRESFORD
AVINGTON
BISHOPSTOKE
CHERITON WITH BEAUWORTH
CHILCOMB
EASTON
EXTON
HINTON AMPNER
KILMESTON
MARTYR WORTHY WITH CHILLAND
MEDSTED
MORESTEAD
OVINGTON
OWSLEBURY WITH BAYBRIDGE
PRIVETT
TICHBORNE
TWYFORD
WEST MEON
WIELD
WINNALL[1]

THE LIBERTY OF ALRESFORD

At the time of the Domesday Survey the hundred of Fawley (Falelie, Falley) included Alresford, Kilmeston, Twyford, Owslebury, Easton, Bishopstoke, Chilcomb (which included Winnall and Morestead), and Avington; the amount of the land assessed was 89 hides, Alresford alone being rated at 42 hides.[2]

West Meon and Exton, afterwards in Fawley Hundred, were at this time in Meonstoke Hundred; and Ovington, part of Wield, and Hinton Ampner were part of Mainsbridge. The land in these five places was assessed at 38 hides. Privett, Tichborne, Cheriton, Martyr Worthy, and Medsted are not mentioned in the Domesday Survey; but Privett was probably included in West Meon, Medsted and the rest of Wield in Alresford, and Tichborne possibly in Twyford.

By 1316 the hundred had practically assumed its modern proportions except that Havant and Alverstoke were assessed as part of Fawley.[3] Havant was still rated in Fawley in 1465, for in that year the tithing-man of Havant paid a fine at the hundred court of Fawley to have release from suit of court of four men until Michaelmas.[4] In an exactly similar way, Old Alresford, Medsted, and Wield, which formed part of Alresford liberty (q.v.), still continued to be assessed with Fawley, and sent tithing-men to the Fawley hundred court. Consequently, therefore, when the bishop ceased to hold his Alresford hundred courts, Old Alresford, Medsted, and Wield were again reckoned in Fawley Hundred, and the term 'Alresford liberty' was taken to comprise merely the borough of New Alresford, as in the population returns for 1831.

[1] The extent of the hundred as given in the *Population Returns* of 1831.
[2] *V.C.H. Hants*, i, 459, 464.
[3] *Feud. Aids*, ii, 320.
[4] Eccl. Com. Ct. R. bdle. 80, No. 1. The fine was 10*d.*

In 1841 Headbourne Worthy parish was included in the hundred of Fawley,[5] and still remains so. Medsted and Wield, on the other hand, had become separated from Fawley and attached to Bishop's Sutton Hundred;[6] Privett was included in East Meon,[7] and West Meon and Exton in Meonstoke Hundred.[8]

In the reign of Edward III a tax of a fifteenth and a tenth levied on the country produced £28 from the hundred of Fawley,[9] a similar tax levied in 1558 produced £28 8*s.* 1*d.*,[10] and in 1623 the same amount.[11]

The hundred of Fawley was held by the prior and convent of St. Swithun, and by a charter of 1284, confirmed in the following year

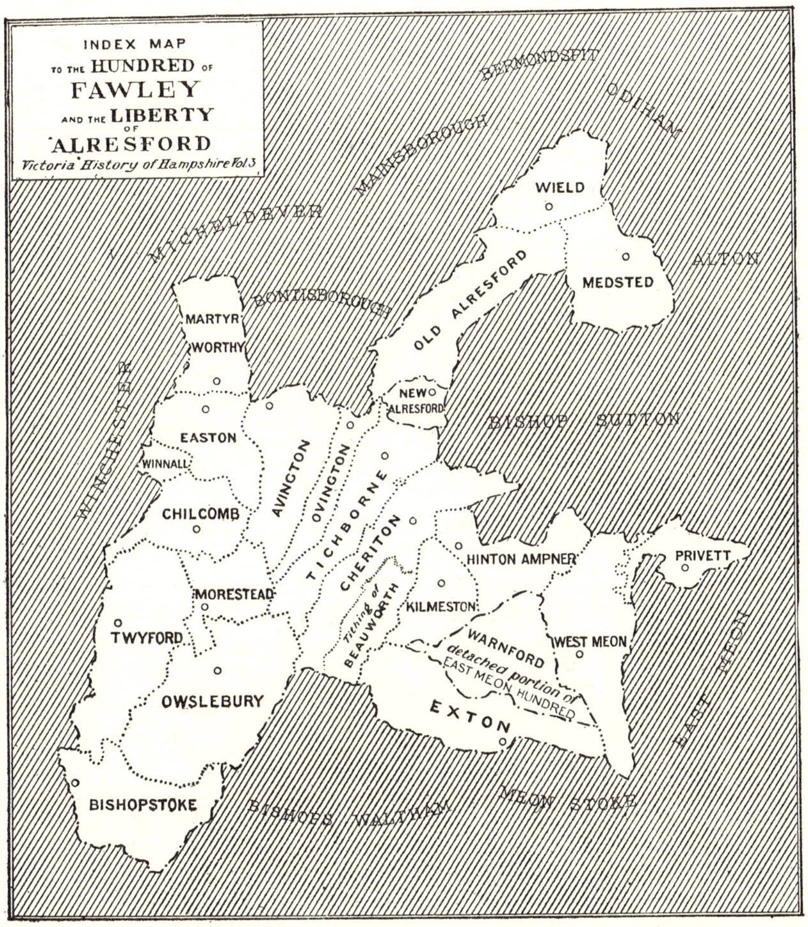

by King John, the bishop of Winchester gave up for himself and his successors all claim to the hundred.[12] The bishop nevertheless seems sometimes to have held the hundred court,[13] and after the Dissolution it evidently passed into his possession.

[5] *Population Returns* for 1841, p. 283.
[6] Ibid. 272.
[7] Ibid. 278.
[8] Ibid. 275.
[9] Lay Subs. R. Edw. III 178/98.
[10] Ibid. 1 Eliz. 174/366.
[11] Ibid. 21 Jas. I, 175/499.
[12] Chart. R. 13 Edw. I, No. 98.
[13] Eccl. Com. Ct. R. 5 Edw. IV, 159, 465 (2), bdle. 80, No. 1; *V.C.H. Hants*, ii, 108.

OLD ALRESFORD

The parish of Old Alresford covers a long sweep of rolling country of about 3,671 acres,[1] generally rising from south to north, from a height of 200 ft. above the sea level in the south near the valley of the River Alre and the village of Old Alresford, to a height of 600 ft. in the north-east near Woodridden Wood. The arable and pasture land is for the most part in the west of the parish ; the woodland, Upper and Lower Lanham Copse and Woodridden Wood, lying away to the north. About two miles south-east of Old Alresford, in the parish of Bishop's Sutton, the River Alre 'beginnith of a great Numbre of fair Sylver Springes,' which 'resorting to a Botom make a great brode Lak, communely caullid Alsford Pond.'[2] This pond, the reservoir from which the Itchen is for the most part supplied, was formed by Bishop Godfrey de Lucy towards the end of the twelfth century in order to render the River Itchen navigable from Alresford to Winchester as well as from Winchester to Southampton (see under New Alresford). Entering the parish from New Alresford, immediately north of the pond, Old Alresford Park stretches to the east, in the north-west of which stands Old Alresford House, best known to fame from its connexion with Admiral George Brydges Lord Rodney (1719–92), who considerably enlarged and improved the original house during his residence. It is a large white brick mansion finely situated with its grounds gradually sloping down to the lake. Colonel Richard Norton, 'idle Dick Norton,' the farmer of the manor of Old Alresford, resided at Old Alresford House during the Commonwealth, and Oliver Cromwell paid several visits to him there. In the most westerly corner of the park, seeming almost to be within its boundaries, is the church of St. Mary surrounded by a churchyard. A large eighteenth-century house of red brick, north of the church, was till recently the rectory. It has lately been sold, and is now known as Old Alresford Place. The present rectory is a white building standing east of Old Alresford Place and opposite Upton House. The main block of houses, however, is some yards higher up the road, which rises slightly as it goes north. Here are the smithy, the village green—an irregularly-shaped plot of grass, the post office, an iron foundry, and the national school, built in 1846 by the Onslow family. There is also a group of almshouses, built to house three destitute couples in 1852 by the Misses Onslow in memory of their mother. Some yards still further north is an industrial home (Primitive Methodist), which was in existence by the middle of the nineteenth century.

Rodney, Lord Rodney. *Or three eagles purple.*

Manor Farm lies west of the village, and still further west, near the Itchen Stoke border line, is Fob Down Farm. About a quarter of a mile east of the village, reached by Kiln Lane, which cuts across the fields east and west, is Upton Hamlet, consisting of a few scattered farm buildings, and including Upton Farm and Upton House. The latter was occupied by a younger branch of the Onslow family during the early nineteenth century, but is now occupied by Mr. J. F. Christie, J.P.

Armsworth tithing covers the north-west corner of Old Alresford parish. It consists of Armsworth House, the seat of Mr. Thomas Alderman Houghton, J.P., and two or three cottages within Armsworth Park. The house is a modern building, standing a short distance to the west of the site of an older house, of which nothing but some outbuildings of comparatively modern date remains. An upper room in these buildings has for more than seventy years been used as a chapel, served from Old Alresford, and in it is an altar table of 1620, with a movable top and carved baluster legs, formerly in Old Alresford church. In the present house is preserved a very interesting fourteenth-century pix of copper gilt, found on the estate at a spot called Wield Row, and a set of silver coins of Mary, Elizabeth, James I, and Charles I, also found here.

As in New Alresford the principal industry is water-cress growing, the best beds lying up stream beside the Bighton road.

The soil is mainly gravel on the lower levels round the streams ; but higher up it is loam on chalk. The chief crops are wheat, oats, and turnips.

Parts of the parish of Old Alresford (Nythen Common) were inclosed in 1801–2.[3]

The tithe map is with the parish clerk. The tithes were commuted in 1843 for £747.

The following place-names occur in early records : Gooseland[4] (xv cent.), Fysshewareclose, Glen Pytts,[5] and Yardmanligh[6] (xvi cent.), and Pieway, Pingleston Lane, The Nythyn,[7] Bishopp's Meade, and The Cadefeild[8] (xvii cent.).

MANOR The manor of *OLD ALRESFORD* was included in the grant of the 40 *mansae* at Alresford made by Kinewald, king of the West Saxons, to the church at Winchester. Its history is given under Alresford Liberty[9] (q.v.).

A sixteenth-century perambulation of the manor, preserved at the Public Record Office,[10] shows what a large area it covered. 'Beginning at the bridge of New Alresford at the end of the great weir, and thence west where the stream runs to the southern angle of Fobdowne, thence north to the angle of the manor of Abbottystone near a fulling-mill there, thence east to Harymsworgate,[11] and thence north to Bugner Corner[12] and thence to the park of Welde, and round the park east to the common of Weld, thence to Dedhob,[13] from Dedhob to Weldbayle, thence . . . to Bentworth Holt, thence to Howpenn Corner . . .

1 Containing 2,276½ acres of arable land, 827 acres of permanent grass, and 314 acres of woods and plantations (Statistics from Bd. of Agric. 1905).

2 Leland, *Itin.* (ed. Hearne), iii, 88.

3 Loc. and Pers. Acts of Parl. 42 Geo. III, cap. 29, and 43 Geo. III, cap. 67.

4 Eccl. Com. various, bdle. 57, No. 159460$\frac{2}{2}$.

5 Eccl. Com. Ct. R. bdle. 136, No. 1.

6 Ibid. bdle. 85, No. 3.

7 Ibid. bdle. 115, No. 10.

8 Close, 24 Chas. I, pt. 3, m. 16.

9 Dugdale, *Mon.* i, 210.

10 Eccl. Com. Ct. R. bdle. 136, No. 1.

11 Armsworth, a tithing in the parish of Old Alresford.

12 Bogmoor Hill in Godsfield.

13 Deadhob Copse in the south of Wield parish.

and thence to a certain road near the Dell there . . . and then the way stretches south to another angle on the east of Lister's wood called Ron Downe, and abutting upon the way opposite Rede Busshes . . . and then stretches south between Rede Busshes[14] on the west and the common of Chawton on the east . . . thence even to a void plot of land called Fowremarkes[15] near Cookemere and called Fowremarkes because the four tithings abut together there—Medsted, Ropley, Faryngdon, and Chawton, thence west . . . even to the Greane Dene, thence west . . . to Gullett Mere[16] and thence between the land called Solrydg[17] on the north and the land of the warden of New College on the south to the great trench in Ramscombe wood,[18] and thence west over Pyewey to Byckton Down, thence north to the Pounde Post, thence north to Myll Oke, and from Myll Oke to Hangyng Beche, and by a lane leading to Layneham Downe,[19] and thence west by Bykwodd and Byckton Feld even to Cokeslane, and by the said lane even to London wey and over the way to the east of the Nythen, and thence south to Furdley Dyche Corner, and thence west on the south of the great pond even to the bridge where began the perambulation.'

From these boundaries it is clear that the manor comprised the whole of the modern parishes of Old Alresford and Medsted, and part of the parish of Wield. The bishop derived a large income from his property, his chief sources of wealth apart from the rents of assize being the woods and copses, the great pond, fisheries, and mills.

In the reign of Edward VI woods and copses in the manor comprised an area of 464 acres made up as follows: Le Lawnde Copys 30 acres, Great Haywodd Copys 36 acres, Peked Haywodd Copys 18 acres, Fyncheley Copys 60 acres, Bradley Copys 7 acres, Burley Copys 3 acres, Stancombe Wood by Hangyngbeche 34 acres, Little Stancombe by Stancombe Gate 21 acres, Stancombe Hill 81 acres, Le Holte 96 acres, and Ramscomb 78 acres.[20] Pannage of pigs in these woods was an important asset. They were looked upon as so valuable that the surveyor sent down from London to survey the whole bailiwick of Bishop's Sutton previous to its purchase by Sir John Gate in the reign of Edward VI advises him as follows: 'Thoughe your lordship like not to take the holl bailiwicke, yet I wold you forsooke not Old Alresford and Sutton for the wodds' sake and the comodities and gretness that shall ensew to your tenaunts of Ludshett.'[21] He adds as a further inducement: 'The tenants at Alresford have no woods in the lords' woods but by byinge for their money and otherwyse they do not medyll there . . . But the tenants desyre to bye some nowe or els they shall dye for could this winter.'[22]

The next source of income, the great pond, increased the bishop's revenue in various ways. It was his custom from early times to farm out the reeds and flags growing in it for 8*s.* a year.[23] An additional sum of £1 6*s.* 8*d.* was paid every year for the privilege of catching eels called 'S
rigges' and water-fowl in the pond.[24] The fishery in the pond was worth another £1 a year when it was farmed out.[25] When the bishop failed to find a tenant he committed it to the charge of a servant, who, however, was not allowed to help himself to the fish, a certain John Colson being fined heavily in Elizabeth's reign for appropriating pikes and perches from the pond and giving them to his friends.[26]

The bishop also had various other fisheries in the manor: the fisheries of Boblesham or Bubblesham and Burrow which were farmed out for 6*s.* 8*d.* and 8*d.* respectively, a fishery from Dean Bridge to Jening's Mill, and from thence to Broadwater and Mousewater, which was let with the mill, and a fishery called the Compe from the Bonte to the Compehole which was leased together with New Mill.[27] Other fisheries mentioned in the deed of sale of Old Alresford manor to Thomas Hussey in 1648 are the Shittles and a fishery at Andrewes Mills and from them to the borough.[28] These fisheries also indirectly augmented the bishop's income from the manor, the bailiff of the borough of New Alresford paying 1*s.* 4*d.* every year for 'lez fysshestalles' in the market place of New Alresford.[29] To pass on to the mills, which were another valuable asset. In 1086 there were no fewer than nine in the manor of the annual value of £9 2*s.* 6*d.*,[30] and there is frequent mention of mills in subsequent documents. Of these the most important were two water corn-mills called Burrowe Mills, two fulling-mills called Andrewes Mills, a fulling-mill called Jening's Mill or Jones Mill or Black Mill, a fulling-mill called the New Mill, and a water-mill called the Weir Mill,[31] and in the ministers' accounts and court rolls there are also mentions of various other mills the names of which are not given.[32] In the course of the seventeenth century the cloth-trade declined, and a hint of this is afforded by an entry in a court roll of 1612 to the effect that Henry Perrin paid a fine for licence to destroy an old fulling-mill called Jening's Mill or Black Mill, and to take the timber thence to his own use.[33] About the same time Andrewes Mills were converted into corn-mills, and consequently four corn-mills called Burrowe Mills or Town Mills or Andrewes Mills were included in the sale of Alresford Liberty to Thomas Hussey in 1648.[34] The lord of the manor derived a good income from the various mills, the Town Mills alone being farmed out at £10,[35] but he was sometimes forced to disburse a considerable

14 In the extreme east of Medsted parish are Roe Downs, Redhill Copse, and Red Bushes.

15 Now partly in Medsted, and partly in Ropley.

16 Gullett Wood and Gullett Lane are in the northern extremity of Ropley parish.

17 Upper and Lower Solridge Farm are in the extreme south of Medsted parish.

18 Rampscomb Farm in the north of Ropley parish.

19 Upper and Lower Lanham Copse are in the north of the parish of Old Alresford.

20 Eccl. Com. Ct. R. bdle. 136, No. 1.

21 Duchy of Lanc. Rentals and Surv. bdle. 8, No. 22*a*.

22 Ibid. No. 22*b*.

23 Ibid. Eccl. Com. Ct. R. bdle. 136, No. 1; bdle. 85, No. 3; bdle. 115, No. 10; Eccl. Com. various, bdle. 56, No. 159460$\frac{1}{2}$.

24 Mins. Accts. bdle. 6112, No. 366; Eccl. Com. various, bdle. 57, No. 159460$\frac{2}{2}$.

25 Eccl. Com. various, bdle. 56, No. 159460$\frac{1}{2}$.

26 Eccl. Com. Ct. R. bdle. 90, No. 5.

27 Eccl. Com. various, bdle. 56, No. 159460$\frac{1}{2}$; Eccl. Com. Ct. R. bdle. 115, No. 10; Close, 24 Chas. I, pt. 3, No. 16.

28 Close, 24 Chas. I, pt. 3, No. 16.

29 Eccl. Com. Ct. R. bdle. 136, No. 1.

30 *V.C.H. Hants*, i, 459.

31 Eccl. Com. Ct. R. bdle. 115, No. 10; Eccl. Com. various, bdle. 56, No. 159460$\frac{1}{2}$; bdle. 57, No. 159460$\frac{2}{2}$; Mins. Accts. bdle. 6112, No. 366; Eccl. Com. Ct. R. bdle 136, No. 1.

32 For instance, in a minister's account of the reign of Hen. VI there is mention of a mill formerly belonging to Nicholas Miller, a mill recovered from William Overton by the church of Winchester, and two other fulling-mills (Eccl. Com. various, bdle. 57, No. 159460$\frac{2}{2}$. See also Mins. Accts. bdle. 1141, No. 8).

33 Eccl. Com. Ct. R. bdle. 115, No. 10.

34 Close, 24 Chas. I, pt. 3, No. 16.

35 Eccl. Com. various, bdle. 56, No. 159460$\frac{1}{2}$; bdle. 57, No. 159460$\frac{2}{2}$.

sum in repairing them, as may be seen from a study of the various ministers' accounts. For instance, the farmer of Old Alresford in 1399 gave in great detail the debts he had incurred in repairing the various mills, including the hire of four men to bring a new mill-stone for the mill of the borough from Portsmouth to Alresford.[36] Only two of these mills now survive—Weir Mill and a disused fulling-mill built across the Alre.

CHURCH The church of *OUR LADY* was entirely rebuilt in 1753, a west tower was added in 1769, and in 1862 the eighteenth-century work, except as regards the tower, was Gothicized, and a south transept, north organ-chamber, and vestry added. As a result the building is of very little architectural interest, though the tower is a good specimen of its kind, of red brick with round-headed western doorway and belfry windows, and finished with a parapet carrying stone ball finials at the angles.

The only thing of note in the church is the monument of Mrs. Jane Rodney on the north wall of the nave, dated 1757, a fine piece of eighteenth-century work in white marble with figure sculpture. Her husband afterwards became the famous admiral, Lord Rodney, and in the church are monuments to the second and third lords.

There are six bells, by Wells of Aldbourne, dated 1769 and 1770, a tablet on the west face of the tower recording their casting, as well as the building of the nave and tower.

The plate comprises an undated seventeenth-century communion cup and paten, a standing paten of 1679, a flagon of 1717, and a small bowl of 1845.

The first book of the registers contains baptisms 1556–1727, marriages 1559–1729, and burials 1562–1701. The second has the burials in woollen, 1678–1728, and the third runs from 1728 to 1779, the marriages only to 1752. The fourth and fifth have baptisms and burials 1780–1812, and the sixth marriages 1754–1812.

ADVOWSON At the time of the Domesday Survey there were three churches in Alresford worth £4[37]; one of these churches possibly became later the parish church of Medsted, the other two the parish church of Old Alresford with the chapelry of New Alresford attached. The church of Old Alresford with the chapel were of considerable value at an early date; for in 1291 they were valued at £26 13*s.* 4*d.*,[38] in 1340 the ninths came to £8 16*s.* 4*d.*,[39] and by 1535 the rectory of Old Alresford alone was valued at £50.[40]

The advowson of St. Mary's Church at Old Alresford has always been in the hands of the bishop of Winchester. The living is now a rectory in the gift of the bishop.

Peter Heylyn, the distinguished theologian and historian, became rector of Old Alresford in 1633. He lived at New Alresford, and while there was a good friend to smiths and carpenters, saying that 'he loved the noise of a workman's hammer, for he thought it a deed of charity as well as to please his own fancy by often building and repairing to set poor people a work and encourage painful artificers and tradesmen in their honest callings.'[41] At the time of the Commonwealth he was voted a delinquent, and his goods, chattels and livings sequestered, but in 1662 he was restored to his living. He died, however, shortly afterwards. Another distinguished rector was the poet and dramatist John Hoadly,[42] youngest son of Benjamin Hoadly, bishop of Winchester, who was presented to the living in 1737.

CHARITIES In 1642 John Pinth gave £10, and John Edgur (date unknown) gave £10 for the use of the poor. The two gifts were united, and by accumulations amounted in 1822 to £30, which was laid out towards building two tenements, in respect of which 30*s.* a year is distributed in half-crowns to indigent persons.

In 1705 Christopher Perin by his will devised 17 perches of land and cottages thereon for the occupation of poor widows. The cottages are let at weekly rents to poor persons, and after payment of rates, insurance, and repairs, about £2 10*s.* a year is distributed among the poor.

In 1886, 1 a. 0 r. 24 p. and buildings thereon, was conveyed to trustees for the establishment of an institution for the orphans of Primitive Methodists and others. In the event of the determination of this trust, the trustees are empowered to sell the premises and apply the proceeds for the benefit of the Connexion.

AVINGTON

Avintun (xi cent.); Avintun, Yabyndon, Abingdon, (xiv cent.).

The parish of Avington lies to the east of Winchester, the land rising southward from the west bank of the Itchen to Cheesefoot Head, which attains a height of some 600 ft. above the sea level, and tops the chalk downs stretching to the east from Winchester. The area was extended in 1889 by the addition of detached portions of Easton, Itchen Abbas, and Itchen Stoke, and now contains 26 acres of water and 2,927 acres of land, of which 1,107½ acres are arable land, 914 acres permanent grass, and 388 acres woodland.[1]

Avington Park, with its fine stretches of undulating country and its magnificent trees, described by Cobbett in 1830 as 'one of the very prettiest spots in the world,'[2] covers nearly the whole of the north of the parish, extending over about 300 acres. Avington House, the seat of the Shelley family, stands almost in the heart of the woodland. The western corner of the park is in Easton parish, from which direction a narrow winding road runs south-east across the park to the eastern gate. As the road curves to the south a few yards past the western lodge Avington House lies to the left, with its background of dark woodland and with the lake, a narrow strip of water about a mile long on the north and north-west, in the foreground. Cobbett describes how the high road through the

[36] Mins. Accts. bdle. 6112, No. 366.
[37] *V.C.H. Hants*, i, 459.
[38] *Pope Nich. Tax.* (Rec. Com.), 211.
[39] Lay Subs. R. 14 Edw. III, $\frac{173}{13}$.
[40] *Valor Eccl.* (Rec. Com.), ii, 9.
[41] For life of Peter Heylyn see *Dict. Nat. Biog. sub nomine.*
[42] Ibid.
[1] Statistics of Bd. of Agric. (1905).
[2] Cobbett, *Rural Rides*, 335

park goes very near the water, and adds, 'We saw thousands of wild ducks in the pond or sitting round on the green edges of it, while, on one side of the pond, the hares and pheasants were moving about upon a gravel-walk on the side of a very fine plantation.'[3] The house itself is a fine red-brick mansion, and was used as a residence by Charles II when his palace at Winchester was being built. The stone pillars of the original hall still remain, and form the supports of the modern conservatory.

Past the eastern gates the road across the park turns north-west near by Pits' farm, and passing the schools, which lie well back from the road on the right, and curving sharply down hill by two or three cottages which lie behind a low hedge on the left, becomes the main village street. Thus the small thinly-populated village nestles almost in the centre of the park, and seems to be closely dependent on Avington House, bringing back a semblance of old manorial life. A few simple cottages and the original and now dilapidated small square graveyard are on the southern side of the road. A high wall of the park, hiding Avington House from sight, runs along the opposite side of the road as far as the church, which lies well back behind a narrow modern graveyard. The rectory, a square white building, stands immediately south-east of the church. The road continues through the parkland, branching both north to cross the lake by a rustic bridge and lead on to Itchen Abbas, and north-west through a long stretch of the park to the saw-mills, which stand at the head of Avington lake, and from thence south to Ovington. South of the park the centre of the parish is covered with thick woodland, Hampage Wood and Little Hampage Wood, of which mention is made as far back as the year 1306, when licence was granted to the prior and convent of St. Swithun, who then held the manor, to inclose their wood called 'Hemepynge Wood in Avington parish,' saving the right of the rector to drive his cattle into it.[4]

A legend also connects Hampage Wood with a still earlier date. When Winchester Cathedral was being built, Bishop Walkelin being in need of timber asked William the Conqueror for the gift of as much timber as he could carry away from Hampage Wood in four days and nights. The king consented, and the bishop, having collected all the woodmen from the surrounding country, managed to clear the wood with the exception of the one tree under which St. Augustine was said to have preached. The hollow shell of a tree, kept together by iron bands and protected by an iron fence, still stands in the wood, and is known locally as Hampage or Gospel Oak.

In the southern part of the parish is a picturesque dell called Temple Valley, the lower end of which is thickly wooded; while to the south of the valley lies Cheesefoot Head, from which fine views of the country can be obtained, Winchester lying away to the north-west, the Itchen valley to the north, and to the south and east undulating down country and dark woodland. The soil is loam and chalk; the subsoil clay. The chief crops are wheat, oats, barley and turnips.

MANORS The earliest mention of *AVINGTON* seems to be in the year 961, when King Edgar granted land here to the monastery of St. Peter and St. Paul at Winchester,[5] afterwards called St. Swithun's Priory.[6]

At the time of the Domesday Survey it was held by the bishop[7] in demesne, and the assessment had risen from £6 in the time of King Edward to £10.[8] Avington was confirmed in 1205, and again in 1285,[9] to the prior and monks of St. Swithun's and remained in their hands until the time of the Dissolution.[10]

In 1291 Avington was numbered among the St. Swithun's temporalities, and was valued at £9 13*s*.[11]

It was valued at £22 7*s*. 8*d*. in 1535, and was in the hands of William Basing, cook and keeper of the priory granary.[12]

After the dissolution of St. Swithun's Priory Avington was granted to the dean and chapter of Winchester.[13] It was one of the five manors which were charged with the maintenance of six students in theology at Oxford and six at Cambridge; and which the king compelled the dean and chapter to surrender in 1545[14] (*vide* West Meon). It was thereupon granted, together with Hampage Wood, to Edmund Clerke and his wife Margaret, to be held in chief for the fortieth part of one knight's fee.[15] Edmund Clerke died seised of it in 1586,[16] leaving a son and heir Thomas, who died in 1617, when the estate passed to his son Henry.[17] It was conveyed by Henry, probably for the purpose of a settlement, to Sir Nathaniel Napper in 1634.[18] Some time, however, before 1689 the manor was purchased by George Brydges, M.P. for Winchester, who in that year was granted an exemption from having officers or soldiers quartered on his manor-house of Avington, and from having his horses impressed.[19]

CLERKE. *Azure a cheveron between three swans argent.*

In 1702 it was in the possession of George Rodney Brydges,[20] and remained with the Brydges family, who in the eighteenth century became dukes of Chandos, until the death of James Brydges, duke of Chandos, without male heirs in 1789,[21] when the male line of the Chandos family being extinct, Avington and other estates passed from Ann Eliza, daughter of the last duke of Chandos, to the Grenville family, on her marriage with Richard Grenville marquis of Buckingham, who assumed the name of Brydges, and was created duke of Buckingham and Chandos in 1822.[22]

3 Cobbett, *Rural Rides*, 335.
4 Inq. p.m. 34 Edw. I, No. 117.
5 Birch, *Cart. Sax.* iii, 291; Add. MSS. 15350, fol. 114.
6 *V.C.H. Hants*, ii, 108.
7 There was apparently no distinction in early times between the lands of the bishop and the lands of the monastery (see *V.C.H. Hants*, ii, 108).
8 *V.C.H. Hants*, i, 464.
9 *Cal. of Chart. R.* 1257–1300, p. 288.
10 *Cal. Pap. Letters*, i, 21; Dugdale, *Mon.* i, 211.
11 *Pope Nich. Tax.* (Rec. Com.), 213.
12 *Valor Eccl.* (Rec. Com.), vi, 8. In 1346 Nicholas de Wodelock held one-eighth of one fee in Avington which had been held before by Richard de Warener (*Feud. Aids* [Rec. Com.], ii, 334).
13 Pat. 33 Hen. VIII, pt. 9, m. 34–40; *L. and P. Hen. VIII*, xvi, 417.
14 *Winton Cath. Docs.* (Hants Rec. Soc.), i, 171.
15 Pat. 38 Hen. VIII, pt. 7, m. 29.
16 Chan. Inq. p.m. 29 Eliz. No. 167.
17 Ibid. 15 Jas. I, vol. 367, No. 37.
18 Feet of F. Hants, Mich. 9 Chas. I.
19 *Cal. of S.P. Dom.* 1689–90, pp. 32, 36.
20 Stowe, Add. MSS. 845, fol. 91.
21 Burke, *Extinct and Dormant Peerages.*
22 Information supplied by Lady Shelley.

The declining fortunes of the Buckingham and Chandos families are a matter of recent memory. In the great sale of the late duke's possessions in 1848 Avington Manor passed to Mr. (afterwards Sir John) Shelley, in whose family it still remains;[23] the present lord of the manor being Sir John Shelley.

BRYDGES. *Argent a cross sable with a leopard's head or thereon.*

In 1301 a grant was made to the prior and convent of St. Swithun of free warren in their demesne lands of Avington.[24] In 1809 the Grenvilles held courts leet, courts baron, view of frankpledge, and rights of free warren in Avington.[25]

In 1655 the Commissioners for the Sale of Bishops' Lands sold the capital messuage or manor-house called *YAVINGTON HOUSE* in the parish of Avington, possession of John Unwin, whose estate had been forfeited by treason, to Edward Keate.[26] This is the only mention of the so-called manor of Yavington.

GRENVILLE. *Vert a cross argent with five roundels gules thereon.*

CHURCH The church of OUR LADY was built 1768–71 by Margaret marchioness of Carnarvon, and is a plain red-brick building of chancel, nave and west tower, chiefly interesting from the fact that it preserves its original arrangements with little alteration. Nothing of the former church remains.

Internally it is plastered, with a moulded cornice and arched ceiling, and is fitted with high pews and a pulpit with a domed tester on the south wall of the nave, the 'squire's pew' being as usual large and important, on the north side. By a treatment characteristic of the time, the details of the panelling within the pew are more ornamental than those on the outside.

There is a good panelled reredos at the back of the altar-table, which is inclosed by gilded wrought-iron rails. At the west of the church is a large gallery with the royal arms, dated 1771, on its front, and the font of grey marble has a small bowl on a baluster stem.

On the north of the altar-table is the monument of Margaret marchioness of Carnarvon, 1768, and on the south that of George Brydges, 1751. Other monuments are those of Anna duchess of Buckingham and Chandos, 1836, on the north wall, and of John, only brother of Percy Bysshe Shelley, 1866, on the south, and there are several hatchments in the church.

SHELLEY. *Sable a fesse engrailed between three shells or.*

There are six bells of 1771 by Pack & Chapman of London.

The plate consists of a silver communion cup, a large and small paten, and a flagon, each inscribed 'Avington Church, 1829.'

The first book of the registers contains all entries from 1609 to 1812, except those of the marriages from 1754 onwards, which are in a separate book.

ADVOWSON At the time of the Domesday Survey there was a church at Avington in the possession of the bishop.[27] The advowson is now and always has been in the hands of the bishops of Winchester.[28] Avington rectory was numbered among the bishop's spiritualities. In 1291,[29] 1354,[30] and 1535[31] it was valued at £12.

At the present day the living is a rectory of the net yearly value of £145, including 24 acres of glebe, with residence, in the gift of the bishop of Winchester.

CHARITIES In 1761 Mrs. Anne Brydges by her will left £1,000 to be invested, and directed that £20 should be paid to the rector for the time being on condition of residence in the parish, or in default to be distributed among poor and decayed old housekeepers living in the parish or adjoining parishes in the discretion of the trustees. In satisfaction of this legacy a sum of £666 13*s.* 4*d.* consols is in court under the title of Attorney-General *v.* Rodney, the dividends of which are regularly received by the incumbent.

BISHOPSTOKE

Stoke, Stoches (xi cent.).

The parish of Bishopstoke, as originally constituted, covered about 3,430 acres of land rising from west to east from the arable lands round Great and Little Eastley farms, a height of 40 ft. to 50 ft. above the ordnance level, to the woodland round Fair Oak Park, a height of 190 ft. to 220 ft. However, in 1894, Fair Oak, the eastern part of the parish, was formed into a civil parish of 1,680 acres independent of Bishopstoke. In 1899 Stoke Park was also separated and made a civil parish of 1,250 acres, of which two are water, leaving the original parish with an area of only 500 acres, of which thirteen are covered by water.

The main road from Winchester to Southampton, passing through Fair Oak, leaves to the west the low-lying ground composing the modern parish of Bishopstoke. A road branching off westward leads from the main road through fields and meadows to the village. About a quarter of a mile east of the village this road turns sharply northward for a few yards to the National School built in 1895, then east again past Manor Farm and across the bridge, to enter the village near Bishopstoke (corn) Mill, which is said to be on the site of the mill of Domesday. North of the mill, almost on an island formed by two branches of the Itchen, is the Manor House with its enormous fish

23 Information supplied by Lady Shelley.

24 Chart. R. 29 Edw. I, m. 12, No. 54.

25 Feet of F. Hants, Trin. 49 Geo. III.

26 Close, 1655, pt. 22, No. 35; Stowe MS. 845, fol. 91.

27 *V.C.H. Hants*, i, 464.

28 Inst. Bks. (P.R.O.).

29 *Pope Nich. Tax.* (Rec. Com.), 211.

30 *Cal. Pap. Pet.* i, 263.

31 *Valor Eccl.* (Rec. Com.), ii, 10.

pond. The greater number of the older houses of the village with the two inns, 'The Anchor' and 'The Angler,' are grouped here and higher up the road beyond the old church of St. Mary (rebuilt in 1825, now disused) and the Rectory. Many modern red-brick cottages are now in process of building at both ends of the village to supply the needs of the men who are employed in the Eastleigh Railway Works, which are rapidly increasing in size. The new church of St. Mary, opened in 1891, is north of the village, close to the new church schools. Further north, its well-wooded grounds of about 100 acres stretching away west to the River Itchen, is The Mount, the residence of Mr. Thomas Atkinson Cotton. The house, which is surrounded by a fine park in which a herd of deer is kept, is modern and has a tower at one end. The grounds contain a fine collection of conifers, many rare plants, and a rock garden, while in the house is a large collection of British birds numbering over a thousand specimens. There is also a clock tower in the grounds containing a clock with carillon chimes which play fourteen tunes. Longmead, another fine house, the residence of Mr. Gubbins, stands east of the village in a park and grounds of about 46 acres. Longmead Farm is on the edge of the estate. Stoke Lodge, the residence of Mr. George Young, is north-east of The Mount near Stoke Common.

The soil of the parish is mixed clay, loam, and sand; subsoil, clay and sand. The proportion of land in the parish is as follows: 13¼ acres of arable land, 175 acres of permanent grass, and 8 acres of woods and plantations.[1] The chief crops are wheat, barley, oats, peas, and beans. The following place-names occur: 'the High Bridge and Davis,'[2] 'Mortimers and Crowdhill' (name still preserved);[3] Mayles Thomas and Strowdelonde;[4] The Reeve's Gore, Lower Beddemeade, Breathfield,[5] Woodrowes Purrockes,[6] and 'Maveland.'[7]

Stoke Common itself is the hamlet which is the nucleus of the small parish of Stoke Park. It is reached from Bishopstoke by the road running north-east from the village, and consists of a few scattered houses, a Bible Christian Chapel, a smithy, and an inn, 'The Foresters' Arms.' Stoke Park Farm lies away to the east, surrounded by a belt of arable land which stretches away to woodland, Upperbarn Copse, Crowdhill Copse in the east, and Stoke Park Wood in the south. The meadow land west of Stoke Common is often flooded, as the Itchen, which here divides into many branches, overflows its banks during the rainy season. On the lower part of the river is Withymead Lock, where the several branches of the river meet in one, and Stoke Lock still lower, where the Itchen Navigation joins the River Itchen.

The village of Fair Oak consists of widely scattered houses and farms reaching from Crowdhill on the north to Horton Heath on the south. From Crowdhill, part of which is in Fair Oak, a fine view can be gained of the surrounding country, the Itchen valley stretching away to the south-west towards the Solent, and the chalk downs which lie round Winchester sweeping away to the north. A Wesleyan chapel and two or three houses belonging to Crowdhill are in the north in Fair Oak parish. In the north of Fair Oak village itself is Stocks Farm, south of which are the houses of the village grouped round the church of St. Thomas erected in 1863. Close by are the church schools, the smithy, and the inn. A few cottages are scattered along the road to the south towards Knowle Hill, which rises to a height of about 160 ft. above the ordnance datum. Horton Heath, a detached portion of Fair Oak village, lies round the four cross roads formed by the road known as Burnett Lane as it crosses the main road from Winchester. Here is a Union Chapel, Hammersley Farm, the Rising Sun Inn, and the post office. Fair Oak Park, the residence of Mr. George Pember, stands east of the village; the house commanding a fine view of the well-wooded park and grounds, which cover about 120 acres. On the northern edge of this estate is Hall Lands House. Stroudwood is to the north-east. Fair Oak Lodge, the property of Sir Arthur Grant, bart., of Monymusk, N.B., lies south-west of the village. The estate covers about 120 acres, and in the park is a lake of about seven acres in extent called Quableigh Pond, the home of several varieties of water fowl.

MANORS

The earliest reference to *BISHOPSTOKE* seems to be in the year 948 when King Edred granted 11 *mansae* at Stoke to the thegn Ælfric.[8] Sixteen years later King Edgar[9] endowed Winchester Cathedral with lands at Bishopstoke, together with numerous other manors in Hampshire, and at the time of the Domesday Survey the bishop was holding Bishopstoke in demesne as he had formerly done; it was assessed at 5 hides and was worth £8.[10] In 1284 the king gave up to John bishop of Winchester and his successors all his right in the manor of Bishopstoke.[11] The manor remained in the hands of the bishop from this date[12] until the sale of the bishops' lands in 1650,[13] when it was sold to Dr. Thomas Cox and Malachy Dewdney for £1,601 4*s.* 6*d.*,[14] and five years later the site of the manor also was sold to Dr. Cox for £479 3*s.* 4*d.*[15] Bishopstoke was restored to the see of Winchester at the Restoration and remained in the bishop's possession[16] until the year 1869, when the lands belonging to the bishopric were vested in the Ecclesiastical Commissioners, who are lords of the manor at the present day. The bishop of Winchester had a park here at an early date. In 1305, and again in 1334, certain persons were indicted for hunting in the bishop of

1 Statistics of Bd. of Agric. (1905).

2 Eccl. Com. Ct. R. 159507$\frac{2}{3}$ (2) $\frac{73}{34}$.

3 Ibid. 158030$\frac{115}{8}$.

4 Ibid. 158826$\frac{137}{2}$.

5 Close, 1650, pt. 1, m. 21.

6 Eccl. Com. Ct. R. 151857$\frac{140}{7}$.

7 Ibid. 158878$\frac{143}{5}$.

8 Birch, *Cart. Sax.* iii, 7.

9 King Edgar also granted a small piece of land at Stoke, probably Bishopstoke, to his kinsman Osward in 975 (Birch, *Cart. Sax.* iii, 468).

10 *V.C.H. Hants*, i, 460.

11 Chart. R. 12 Edw. I, m. 5.

12 *Feud. Aids*, ii, 320; Eccl. Com. Ct. R. 159510 (1).

13 The bishop occasionally leased small pieces of land in Bishopstoke to various tenants; for instance, John Philpott held land in Bishopstoke at his death in 1503 (Chan. Inq. p.m. [Ser. 2], vol. 16, No. 100). The Philpotts seem to have held land in Bishopstoke for a considerable period, for in 1650 Edward Bosden begged that an inquiry might be made concerning his right to lands at Bishopstoke purchased by his father in 12 Chas. I from Henry Philpott and then conveyed to Benjamin Hiborne (*Cal. of Com. for Compounding*, ii, 997).

14 *Coll. Top. et Gen.* i, 24; Dugdale, *Mon.* i, 203–4.

15 Close, 1650, pt. 1, m. 21. In 1597 this had been leased by Thomas bishop of Winchester to Queen Elizabeth for 50 years at a yearly rent of £8 6*s.* 8*d.*

16 Thomas Walker and his wife Anne held a lease of the site of the manor of Bishopstoke in 1787, and conveyed it in that year to John Ramsay and others (Feet of F. Hants, Hil. 27 Geo. III).

Winchester's park at Bishopstoke.[17] At the sale of the bishops' lands Stoke Park was sold to Dr. Cox and Malachy Dewdney for £221 18*s.* 4*d.*[18]

At the time of the Domesday Survey there was a mill in Bishopstoke worth 10*s.*[19] In 1523 Nicholas Poule was miller and chief toll collector in Bishopstoke,[20] and in 1594–6 Thomas Carpenter, miller of Bishopstoke, claimed to have a right of way by the bridge called Cutbridge, 'in order to repair the weirs by the water-course.'[21] In the following year Francis Serle and his heirs were enfeoffed of one toft, one corn mill, and one fulling mill in the tithing of Bishopstoke.[22] 'The waste soil near the mill' is spoken of in 1648[23]; at the present day there is a (water) corn-mill in the parish. In 1709 Robert Smith was holding a fishery in Bishopstoke.[24]

CHURCHES The church of *ST. MARY, BISHOPSTOKE*, now disused, was rebuilt in 1825 in the lifeless Gothic of the time, with a west tower. No part of the older church remains.

The modern church, also dedicated in honour of St. Mary, was built in 1891 of shaped flints with quoins and dressings of Bath stone, and consists of a chancel with vestries and an organ chamber on the north, and a nave and south aisle with baptistery at the west end.

There are three bells, the treble of 1600 by John Wallis of Salisbury, inscribed 'Seeke the Lord'; the second of 1598 by R.B., an unknown founder, bearing 'Geve thanks to God'; and the tenor, also by Wallis, 1589, with 'In God is my hope.'

The plate includes a communion cup and paten of 1749, a flagon and almsdish of the same date, and a paten of 1706.

The first book of registers runs from 1650 to 1700, and the second from 1700 to 1781, the marriages ceasing in 1753. The third book contains baptisms and burials 1781–1812, and the fourth marriages 1754–1812.

The church of *ST. THOMAS, FAIR OAK*, built in 1863, is of brick with stone dressings, in Early English style, consisting of apsidal chancel and nave, and turret containing one bell. The register dates from 1871.

ADVOWSONS At the time of the Domesday Survey there was a church at Bishopstoke.[25] In the fourteenth century the church rendered a pension of 40*s.* annually to Hamble Priory; this pension was afterwards received by Winchester College, to which the priory was given by William of Wykeham in 1391.[26]

The advowson of Bishopstoke has always been in the hands of the bishops of Winchester[27]; except for a time in the fourteenth century, when John bishop of Winchester alienated it in mortmain to the four chaplains celebrating divine service daily in the chapel of St. Stephen and St. Lawrence at Marwell, in lieu of the sum of money which they used to receive in alms from the bishop's exchequer at Wolvesey.[28] In 1291 the church of Bishopstoke was assessed at £8,[29] but by 1535 the value had risen to £14 4*s.* 8*d.*[30]

In 1558–9 the rectorial tithes of the church of St. Mary at Bishopstoke were granted to the notorious 'fishing grantees' William Tipper and Robert Dawe.[31] The living is now a rectory in the gift of the bishop of Winchester.

The living of St. Thomas, Fair Oak, is a vicarage, with residence, also in the gift of the bishop of Winchester.

CHARITIES In 1632 Richard Dummer charged a close called 'Five Acres' with the payment of 40*s.* annually for the use of the poor at Michaelmas and Lady Day. In 1653 Thomas Dummer charged certain copyhold land with 40*s.* a year for the poor at Easter and Christmas. The annuities are duly paid out of a close known as the Poor Close.

In 1630 Mrs. Joan Bassett by her will left £20, interest to be distributed amongst the poor sort of the inhabitants at Easter for ever, now represented by £20 9*s.* 8*d.* consols with the official trustees.

In 1834 Henry Twynam by deed charged four acres of copyhold land at Stoke Common with the annual payment of 40*s.* to be applied on 21 December in every year in the distribution of fuel and clothes among the poor on the west side of the parish. The donor, by the same deed, granted to trustees a messuage, garden, and orchard situated at Fair Oak, the net rents to be applied in the same manner for the benefit of the poor on the east side of the parish. The annuity is duly paid, and the messuage and premises now consist of five cottages, known as Everett's, which are let to weekly tenants, producing £26 a year.

In 1846 George Twynam, by a codicil to his will, bequeathed £200, income to be applied in the distribution of bread or fuel amongst poor residents of the parish. The legacy was invested in £208 13*s.* consols, held by the official trustees. By an order made in 1896 under the Local Government Act, 1894, the parish councils of Fair Oak and Bishopstoke have elected representatives on the governing body, by whom the income of the several charities is applied in the distribution of coal and other articles in kind.

[17] Pat. 33 Edw. I, m. 17*d.* and 8 Edw. III, pt. 1, m. 7 *d.*
[18] *Col. Top. et Gen.* i, 286.
[19] *V.C.H. Hants,* i, 460.
[20] Eccl. Com. Ct. R, 159510 (1), bdle. 84, No. 15.
[21] Ibid. bdle. 83, No. 17.
[22] Ibid. 159507 $\frac{3}{8}$ (2), bdle. 73, No. 34.
[23] Ibid. 155760, bdle. 99, No. 8.
[24] Ibid. 158878, bdle. 143, No. 5.
[25] *V.C.H. Hants,* i, 460.
[26] *Wykeham's Register* (Hants Rec. Soc.), i, 77; ii, 608. In 1398 twenty years' arrears of this pension was owing to the warden of Winchester College.
[27] Ibid. i, 77; Inst. Bks. (P.R.O.).
[28] *Cal. of Pat.* 1330–4, p. 165.
[29] *Pope Nich. Tax.* (Rec. Com.), 210.
[30] *Valor Eccl.* (Rec. Com.), ii, 6.
[31] Pat. 31 Eliz. pt. 5, m. 31.

CHERITON

Cherytone (xii cent.); Churton Chyritone (xvi cent.).

The 3,264 acres of land comprised in the parish of Cheriton are made up of high down country sloping in every direction towards the village, which lies in a river valley almost in the centre of the parish.

Cheriton Wood lies away to the north-west of the parish, while stretching west of the wood is the wide plain on which the Battle of Cheriton was fought on 29 March, 1644—the battle which, as Clarendon says, 'broke all the measures and altered the whole scheme of the king's counsels.'[1] The Royalists under Hopton were quartered at New Alresford, whither Waller was advancing from East Meon. Leaving Alresford, Hopton marched south and met Waller on the plain near Lamborough Field. 'The king's horse never behaved themselves so ill as that day,' writes Clarendon, and though the foot 'behaved gallantly,' and withstood not only the attack of Waller's foot but also 'two or three charges from the horse with notable courage and without being broken,' yet as evening drew near Hopton was forced to retire to Reading.

The village of Cheriton, described by Cobbett in his *Rural Rides* as 'a little hard iron village where all seems to be as old as the hills that surround it,' is at the present day one of the best cared for and most progressive villages in the district.

The main road from Winchester to Petersfield runs through to the south of the parish and a lane branching off a few yards past Hockley House leads in a north-easterly direction to the village. As it approaches down-hill, a small unobtrusive house lying back on the south side of the road is known as the Flower Pots Inn. Beyond this are two or three groups of thatched cottages facing south-west, while along the north side of the road runs the high wall of the rectory garden. At the end of this wall at the bottom of the hill the road turns sharply north past the gates of the rectory into the middle of the village. Immediately in the foreground is the village green, through which flows a tributary of the Itchen, running a north-westerly course through the parish, intersecting the village with many branches and crossed by several light bridges. In the centre of the green and on either side are several old thatched and tiled cottages, some half-timbered, for the most part picturesquely grouped behind narrow well-cultivated gardens. North-west of the green a narrow wooden bridge leads over one of the small streams to an open field, across which a well-trodden pathway runs south to the low white gate of the churchyard and to the low square-towered church of St. Michael, which stands here immediately west of the village. The rectory, a fine red-brick house dating from the early years of the eighteenth century, stands close to the church on the south. On the east side of the village is a Congregational chapel, built in 1862, near by which are the Board Schools, built in 1876.

Leaving the green and the river and the cottages around it, close by the inn which bears the sign of the Prince of Wales' Feathers, and calls itself the Hampshire Hunt Inn, the main village street continues in a circuitous north-easterly direction running east of the river, between picturesque low-thatched cottages, the Bricklayers' Inn, and two or three obtrusive modern villas, to that part of the village which is known as North End, and from here continues north through Tichborne parish to New Alresford. As the road leaves the parish Cheriton Mill, with the Mill Cross, stands away on the river to the east.

South of the green and village, the village street curves slightly to the south-east to meet the main road from Winchester to Petersfield on Lane End Down, over which the main road descends to an outlying portion of Cheriton known as Lane End hamlet, which is also approached from Cheriton by a narrow lane through the water meadows.

Here the watercress industry is in full progress, since the river with its luxuriously growing watercress beds makes a detour between and behind the several cottages grouped here on its way north-west to Cheriton. Immediately beyond Lane End hamlet the road enters Hinton Ampner parish and so passes on east towards Petersfield.

The soil of the whole parish is chalk and clay, with a subsoil of chalk, producing wheat and oats and green crops. Of the total acreage 1,660 acres are given up to arable land, 470 are permanent grass, and 370 woodland.[2] Of the woodland Shorley Copse in the south-east of the parish covers the widest stretch of country, and close to the wood are the Shorley Pottery Works, which afford a special source of employment for some of the villagers.

The following place-names occur in 1605: Shoredrane, Holifield, and Charkers[3]; in 1611, 'Torshawe';[4] in 1620–24, 'Somerfield';[5] in 1648–51, The Breach, Cowdown Close, Eastwood, Brookfurlong, Burrow Land, and Londonway[6]; in 1704–12, Sheeremead, Kemen Coppice, and Ruffolds.[7]

Beauworth, now a civil ecclesiastical parish, was formerly the south-eastern corner of Cheriton parish, and was separated from Cheriton by Order in Council of 4 February, 1879.[8] In 1888 a detached portion of Kilmeston was added to Beauworth,[9] the whole area now being 1,508 acres. It covers a sweep of high country reaching some 530 ft. above the ordnance datum near the Fox and Hounds Inn on Millbarrow Down.

From here can be seen fine views of the surrounding district, and it is not surprising that the land is being developed for building purposes. Several new houses have already been built and many plots of ground have been marked out for sale.

A narrow road leads down from Millbarrow Down towards the village, which lies in the north of the parish, shut off from Cheriton by thick woodland country. At the entrance to the village is the smithy, beyond which is the white manor-house, now untenanted, standing in fine grounds. The manor

[1] Clarendon, *Hist. of Rebellion*, iii, 338.

[2] Statistics from Bd. of Agric. (1905).

[3] Eccl. Com. Ct. R. 158821. bdle. 136, No. 2.

[4] Ibid. 158030, bdle. 115, No. 8.

[5] Ibid. 158826, bdle. 137, No. 2.

[6] Ibid. 155760, bdle. 99, No. 8.

[7] Ibid. 158878, bdle. 143, No. 5.

[8] Ord. in Council.

[9] Local Govt. Bd. Order, No. 22375.

farm with its scattered outbuildings, several very picturesque half-timbered cottages grouped round the village green with its tall pine trees, and the modern church of St. James with the village school lying immediately west, make up the rest of the village. Behind the manor-house is a field called the 'Church Lytton', the site of a former church or chapel and graveyard. It was here that the great hoard of silver pennies of William the Conqueror, known as the Beaworth Hoard, was discovered.

The soil of the parish is chalk and clay with subsoil chalk, producing the ordinary green crops, and wheat and oats on the 443¼ acres of arable land. Dur Wood in the south of the parish is the largest stretch of woodland, of which there are altogether 292½ acres, while 467¼ acres are permanent grass.

The following place-names occur: Hillonds and Hooke Close,[10] Hornswood Coppice, St. Cross Mill, Brown Down, Milbarrowe Down, Weely, Nibden Bottom, Rackdowne, the Rakes, the Parke Reade, Homedown, Northall, and Cowleys.[11]

MANORS From a charter of Ethelred about 984 it is found that amongst the lands given to Winchester Cathedral there were at Easton four hides, at Avington five hides, at Ovington five hides, at Kilmeston five hides, and at 'Tichebourne' twenty-five hides.[12] It is noticeable that the lands at Tichborne are of far greater extent than those elsewhere; and it is quite possible that *CHERITON*, which is not mentioned in the Domesday Survey, was included in these twenty-five hides. Probably a new church was built, within the bounds of Tichborne, and the inclosure in which it stood acquired the name of Cheriton, which has since distinguished the whole district. In 1284 the king surrendered any rights which he had in Cheriton to the bishop of Winchester,[13] who was holding the vill in 1316;[14] and from this time the lordship of the manor remained vested in the bishop.[15]

At various dates from 1280 to the middle of the seventeenth century lands in Cheriton were leased to different tenants, the most important being the Inkepennes, who held estates here from 1353 to 1597.[16]

Philip le Wayte[17] and his wife Isabel conveyed two messuages and lands in Cheriton to John Inkepenne in 1353,[18] who died possessed of land in Cheriton in 1361,[19] leaving a son John, who at the time of his death in 1374 held nine virgates of land there, his heir being his brother Robert, then aged forty-one,[20] who died in 1405 seised of land in Cheriton, which he left to his wife Margery and his son Richard. The former survived him, and married John Beneyt as her second husband;[21] three years later John Beneyt and Margery gave up their land in Cheriton to Margery's son, Richard Inkepenne.[22] In 1441 Robert Inkepenne (probably son of this Richard), who came of age in 1410,[23] and his wife Elizabeth held land in Cheriton, which was granted to them by Richard Umfray and John Bukke, probably trustee for a settlement,[24] and this Robert, together with John Tichborne, represented the tithing of Cheriton at the bishop's manor court in 1465.[25] He was followed by his son John Inkepenne, who died in 1514, leaving as his heir his son Richard, then aged three weeks,[26] who was a free suitor at the bishop's court in 1574.[27] In 1597 Adrian, William, and Francis Inkepenne, Richard's sons, conveyed their lands in Cheriton, described for the first time as the manor of Cheriton, to Edmund Anderson, Chief Justice of the Bench.[28] In 1651 Robert Reynold was holding the manor on a lease from the bishop,[29] but this is the last record of land in Cheriton being held by under-tenants of the see of Winchester.

Inkepenne. *Gules two gimel bars or and a chief indented ermine.*

The Ecclesiastical Commissioners took over Cheriton in 1869 from the bishop, and they are lords of the manor at the present day.

There was a water-mill at Cheriton first mentioned in 1408, when it was conveyed by fine from John Beneyt and Margery his wife to Richard Inkepenne,[30] and William Inkepenne was in possession in 1518.[31] At a court held at Cheriton in 1606 an order was issued for the water stream 'from John Hobbsmead' until the mill to be cleansed every man against his land' under penalty of 3*s.* 4*d.*, while an entry at the same court records that 'Thomas Hart is a common miller and took toll to excess. Fined 8*d.*'[32] In 1631 Benjamin Tichborne died possessed of a water-mill at Cheriton, but after this date no further record of it can be found.[33]

The following entries in the ministers' accounts for the year 1323 give some idea of the annual working expenses of the manor. Iron and steel bought for four ploughs, 3*s.*; in payment of smith nothing, because he gives iron as his customary service; two horse-shoes bought, 10*d.*; two ploughs, 12*d.*; binding same with iron, 4*d.*; mending ploughs, 3*d.*; wages of herdsman, 4*s.*; tyres for cart, 4*d.*; wages of

[10] Eccl. Com. Ct. R. 158030, bdle. 115, No. 7.

[11] Close, 24 Chas. I, pt. 8, m. 41–2, No. 5.

[12] Eccl. Com. Ct. R. 158878, bdle. 143, No. 5.

[13] Chart. R. 12 Edw. I, No. 77.

[14] *Feud. Aids*, ii, 320.

[15] Feet of F. Hants, Hil. 5 Edw. III.

[16] Stephen le Fraunkelyn of Cheriton and his wife Alice held a messuage and 19½ acres of land in Cheriton in 1280, which they granted to Richard le Wayte of Cheriton (Feet of F. Hants, Hil. 9 Edw. I). In the same year Walter de Warener and Alice his wife held 17½ acres of land which they conveyed to William le Brayboeuf.

[17] In 1313 Robert le Wayte called 'of Cheriton' entered a complaint concerning lands in Enedhelle and Hamele (*Cal. of Pat.* 1313–17, p. 60).

[18] Feet of F. Hants, 27 Edw. III. Four years later the bishop of Winchester, who was also rector of Cheriton at that time, received seisin from William de Overton of three messuages and land in Cheriton and other places (*Abbrev. Rot. Orig.* [Rec. Com.], ii, 246.)

[19] Inq. p.m. 35 Edw. III, No. 123.

[20] Ibid. 48 Edw. III, No. 41.

[21] Ibid. 7 Hen. IV, No. 48. In 1406 dower was assigned to Margery in the Cheriton lands in spite of her late husband's forfeiture (Inq. p.m. 8 Hen. IV, No. 51).

[22] Feet of F. Hants, East. 9 Hen. IV.

[23] Inq. p.m. 12 Hen. IV, No. 50.

[24] Feet of F. Hants, Trin. 19 Hen. VI.

[25] Eccl. Com. Ct. R. 159465, bdle. 80.

[26] Chan. Inq. p.m. (Ser. 2), vol. 25, No. 15. William Inkepenne granted land in Cheriton and Alresford to Thomas Inkepenne and others in 1518 (Feet of F. Hants, Mich. 16 Hen. VIII, No. 27). They were probably brothers and not in the direct line.

[27] Eccl. Com. Ct. R. 158960, bdle. 87, No. 6.

[28] Feet of F. Hants, East. 40 Eliz.

[29] Eccl. Com. Ct. R. 155760, bdle. 99, No 8.

[30] Feet of F. Hants, East. 9 Hen. IV.

[31] Ibid. Hants, Mich. 10 Hen. VIII.

[32] Eccl. Com. Ct. R. bdle. 87, No. 12.

[33] Chan. Inq. p.m. 6 Chas. I (Ser. 2), pt. 1, No. 69.

carter, 18*d.*; fan for dairy, 2*d.*; wages of dairymaid, 12*d.*[34] Other entries in the court rolls for the reign of Elizabeth are :—'No tenants to permit their horses or sheep to pasture in the low down called "le Marsh" for the winter under penalty of 20*d.* each. All the tenants of Cheriton to make palings for the park of Waltham as tenants, this side of Pentecost under penalty of 40*d.* each. Tenants to make sufficient hedges round their cornfields before the Feast of St. Andrew next under the same penalty. Edmund Newbury is to forfeit one messuage and one virgate of land to the lord because he cut down without licence 20 oaks value 6*s.*'[35]

BEAUWORTH (Beworth, Buworth xiv cent.) was originally a tithing in the parish of Cheriton. The earliest mention of it seems to be in the year 1265, when the men of Beauworth paid 26*s.* 8*d.* at the bishop's court.[36] In 1316 Beauworth was held by the bishop.[37] In 1635 it was leased to Richard Bassett, his son Richard, and his daughter Elizabeth for the term of their lives for a yearly rent of £5 19*s.* 8*d.*[38] At the sale of the bishops' lands in 1648 the manor and the site of the manor was sold to Christopher Mercer for £6181;[39] but it was restored to the bishopric at the Restoration, and after this there seems to be no further record concerning Beauworth manor, the manorial rights of which probably lapsed. Mr. Walter Long is the principal landowner in the parish at the present day.

John Gater and his wife Sarah sold the site of the manor to Richard Eyre in 1767,[40] in whose family it remained until 1816, when Henry Eyre and Edward Foyle conveyed it to Thomas Westcombe.[41]

CHURCHES

The church of *ST. MICHAEL, CHERITON*, built on a mound to the west of the village, is in the main a thirteenth-century building. It has a nave and chancel of equal width, 19 ft. 6 in., the chancel being 39 ft. 6 in. long and the nave 47 ft. 3 in., but the former has been lengthened in the fifteenth century. The nave has arcades of three bays, and aisles 8 ft. wide, with a south porch and west tower, all originally of thirteenth-century date, but the tower and aisles have been repaired and partly rebuilt in the eighteenth century and later.

The chancel, the added eastern bay of which is built on the east slope of the mound, has a four-light east window with fifteenth-century tracery, and at north-east and south-east two-light transomed windows of the same date, with the difference that in the north window the lights below the transom are cinquefoiled, and in the south they are shouldered and have rebates for wooden frames. The western part of the chancel is lighted by a pair of thirteenth-century lancets on each side, and there is a small priest's door of the same date to the east of those on the south side. The external masonry of all the thirteenth-century work has been renewed. At the south-east is a trefoiled piscina with a shelf and two brackets, but no drain; it is of thirteenth-century work probably moved eastward to its present position.

The chancel has a decided lean to the north from the axis of the nave, probably due to an error in setting out when building round an older chancel. The nave preserves the width of the older and probably aisleless nave to which the former chancel belonged, the arcades of three bays dating from *c.* 1220 (the date at which, it may be presumed, the aisles were added). They have pointed arches of two chamfered orders, and round columns with moulded capitals and bases with spurs, the latter all modern except part of that of the first column from the east in the north arcade.

Both aisles have square-headed two-light east windows of the fifteenth century, but all the others are of modern date with wooden frames.

The south porch has a thirteenth-century outer arch with moulded capitals, the inner doorway having a modern wood frame, and the north door of the nave being of like character, but blocked with masonry. On the east jamb of the outer arch of the south aisle is an incised sundial, and on either side of the opening are pieces of elaborately traceried fourteenth-century stonework, built into the walls.

The tower has a thirteenth-century eastern arch of two square orders with a string at the springing, but externally shows no mediaeval work, being faced with eighteenth-century brick and flint work. It has a south door of this date. The roofs of the church are modern and red-tiled, that of the nave being carried in one span over nave and aisles.

The font, near the south door of the nave, is modern, as are all the internal fittings, including a stone pulpit.

There are six bells by Warren recast from the old ring of five, four of which were by John Stares, 1746.

The church of *ST. JAMES, BEAUWORTH*, built in 1838, is a rectangular room with lancet windows, a south porch and bell turret on the west gable, containing two bells by Mears, of the date of the church. The fittings are of the same period, with a west gallery, and a small marble bowl on a wooden pedestal, doing duty as a font.

The plate of Cheriton church consists of a silver communion cup of 1621, a paten of 1698, and a modern paten. At Beauworth there is a modern set of electro-plate.

The first two books of the Cheriton registers, including Beauworth, contain all entries from 1577 to 1740, and 1656 to 1779, respectively. The third book is the marriage register 1754–1812, and the fourth that of baptisms and burials 1742–1822.

A book of accounts of the overseers of the poor for Beauworth, beginning in 1732, is kept at Kilmeston.

ADVOWSONS

The church of Cheriton, one of the most valuable livings in the diocese of Winchester, has always belonged to the bishops. In 1284 the king gave up to John bishop of Winchester and his successors all his right in the advowson of Cheriton.[42] As early as 1291 Cheriton rectory was taxed at £40,[43] and in 1535 the value had increased, and it was assessed in the *Valor* at £66 13*s.* 4*d.*[44] Such a living was of course one of the prizes of the diocese, and was usually held by men of local if not of wider celebrity; it is

34 Mins. Accts. bdle. 1141, No. 16.

35 Eccl. Com. Ct. R. bdle. 87, No. 12.

36 Ibid. 159294, bdle. 24.

37 *Feud. Aids*, ii, 330.

38 Close, 24 Chas. I, pt. 8, m. 41–2, No. 5.

39 Ibid. Dugdale, however, says that the manor was sold to Stephen Estwicke in December, 1648, for £748 6*s.* 6*d.*, but no further record of this can be found. Dugdale, *Monasticon*, i, 204. He was probably a trustee of the bishop's lands.

40 Feet of F. Hants, Trin. 8 Geo. III.

41 Ibid. Hil. 57 Geo. III.

42 Chart. R. 12 Edw. I, No. 5.

43 *Pope Nich. Tax.* (Rec. Com.), 211.

44 *Valor Eccl.* ii, 9.

45 *Dict. Nat. Biog.* xvi, 386. The manor and the rectory were therefore in the same hands.

not surprising, therefore, that Bishop William of Edendon was rector of Cheriton at one time.[45]

From 1606 to 1618 the rectory was held by John bishop of Oxford, who in the former year was fined 4*d.* for neglecting to pay suit at the bishop's court of Cheriton.[46] On his death in 1618 the king claimed the next presentation by promise of the late rector, and 'jure prerogative nostre regie seu alio quocumque legali modo pro hac vice spectandum.'[47]

The king then granted the rectory and church of Cheriton together with the chapels of Tichborne and Kilmeston to Richard Meredith.

From 1644 to 1646 the curious situation is presented of the rectory being held by two incumbents, the appointments having been made by the bishop and Parliament respectively. In 1646 a petition was presented by Heritage Harford asking Parliament 'to confirm him in the rectory of Cheriton, to which he had been appointed by the Committee for Sequestration in 1644, but which had been granted by the bishop of Winchester, a delinquent, to Hugh Haswell, prebend of Winchester, also a delinquent.' The latter presented a counter petition stating that he was of an ancient family, that he had been brought up to learning in the university of Oxford, that he was Fellow of All Souls and had been Proctor of the University, that he had been presented to the parsonage of Codford, Wilts. which he enjoyed till the trouble of these times and the reducing of that part of Wilts. under the king's power, that the living of Cheriton which lay more under the authority of Parliament being vacant he resigned his university appointments and was appointed thereto in 1644 by the bishop, who he conceived had full power to make the appointment, and that he had never been guilty of delinquency. He appealed to Parliament to oust the respondent.[48] A day was appointed for hearing the case, but Parliament being 'too much occupied' to consider the matter in question, and there being no further record of the dispute, it may be assumed that it was settled privately in favour of the bishop, who certainly continued to present.

Except for this short period the advowson, until the last few years, has always belonged to the bishopric of Winchester. At the present day the living is a rectory with the chapelry of Tichborne annexed in the gift of the crown; the chapels of Kilmeston and Beauworth were also annexed to Cheriton until 1879, when they were separated by an Order in Council dated 4 February, 1879, and they now form a distinct ecclesiastical parish, and the patronage of the joint living belongs to the crown.

CHARITIES In 1718 the Rev. Morgan Jones, rector, by a codicil to his will, left £100 to be laid out in land, the annual rent to be for ever paid towards the schooling of the children of the poor of the parish. A piece of land called Northpits in the parish of Chawton was purchased containing about four acres, producing £10 a year or thereabouts.

In 1828 Elizabeth Goodrich, by will proved this date, directed her trustees to purchase sufficient stock to produce £20 a year, interest to be applied for the benefit of the poor of the parish. The legacy (after payment of duty) is represented by £600 consols with the official trustees.

CHILCOMB

Ciltecumbe (xi cent.); Chiltecumbe (xiv cent.).

The parish of Chilcomb, chiefly divided into down and arable land, lies on the eastern outskirts of Winchester and contains 2,667 acres of the sweep of chalk down country which rises south and east of the city. Of the whole parish 947½ acres are arable land, 1,131¾ are pasture land, and 3 acres only are woodland. Owing to the growth of the city over the north-west corner of the parish on the estate called Highcliff and on Magdalen Hill after the year 1881, Chilcomb was in 1894 divided into two civil parishes, Chilcomb Within being this north-west part, included in the municipal borough of Winchester, and Chilcomb Without the rest of the parish[1] with the addition in the same year of the rural parts of Milland, St. John, St. Peter Cheesehill, and Winnall.[2] In November, 1900, part of Chilcomb Without was annexed to Chilcomb Within.[3] Chilcomb Within is necessarily the most populous corner of the parish, forming quite a suburb to Winchester, with its new red-brick houses and shops, and with the recent laying-out of the 'Highcliff Park Estate' off the Petersfield Road the houses are extending east to the borders of Chilcomb Without. Owing to the increase of population and the distance of the old parish church in the narrow valley away over the downs, the new church of All Saints was erected and completed in 1891, the modern rectory was built near by in 1892, and the schools, given by the bishop of Guildford, in the next year. While thus Chilcomb Within has become a modernized suburb, Chilcomb village, or as it is locally called Upper Chilcomb, the nucleus of Chilcomb Without, remains unchanged, a calm old-world village.

About half a mile or so from Highcliff a lane branching south from the main road to Petersfield, which cuts across the parish, climbing the down-land, leads through thick luxuriant hedges to the low-lying village. As the lane approaches the village it joins with another lane which comes from the south-west from Winchester and then curves slightly west past the picturesque outbuildings of Chilcomb Farm which, lying to the left, mark the beginning of the village. A few yards beyond the farm the lane forks south and south-west, the two branches curving to meet again some yards further on. In the north of the island so formed by the two lanes are two or three groups of low thatched and timbered cottages, some lying back behind typical cottage gardens, while the old rectory, now a private residence known as 'St. Kilda,' stands in a wide garden almost in the middle. South of the island the lane rises steeply southwards to the small church of St. Andrew, which lies to the left with a background of high down and

[46] Eccl. Com. Ct. R. bdle. 87, No. 7.

[47] Pat. 16 Jas. I, pt 12, No. 24.

[48] *Hist. MSS. Com. Rep.* vi, 110*a*, 117*a*, 131*a*.

[1] Local Govt. Act, 56 & 57 Vic. cap. 73, sect. 36.

[2] Local Govt. Bd. Order, No. 31853, Sept. 1894.

[3] Ibid. No. 1604, Nov. 1900.

woodland, since Beacon Hill rises to the south to a height of nearly 500 ft. above the sea level.

Skirting this high down-land Chilcomb Lane continues south as a rough pathway to meet the Roman road from Bishop's Waltham to Winchester on the southern border line of the parish. From here the Roman road runs for some distance between the two parishes, then turning to the north and west enters Winchester at Bar End. As it turns north a rough road known as Bull Drove branches off westward through down-land and arable land to the River Itchen, and crossing the bridge leads through a shady lane between the flooded water meadows into Winchester. South of this road rises St. Catherine's Hill, a well-known landmark, encircled by traces of an ancient fortification, and crowned by a clump of fine trees[4] which mark the site of the ancient chapel dedicated in honour of St. Catherine. This chapel, once annexed to the rectory of Chilcomb, had been suppressed before Leland visited Winchester (1536–42). Thus he says 'Ther was a very fair chapelle of S. Catarine on an hill scant half a mile without Winchester town by south. This chapel was endowid with landes. Thomas Wolsey, cardinal, causid it to be suppressid, as I hard say.'[5]

On the summit of the hill also, east of the supposed site of the chapel, is a maze which, with the school song 'Domum,' College tradition ascribes to the ill-fated Winchester scholar who, having cut the maze and written the song, died of a broken heart and pointed a moral against depriving boys of holidays. At least the maze is of some considerable age, dating back to the early seventeenth century, since such mazes are of Dutch origin and came to England with the Stuarts. On the south side of the hill immediately rising from the narrow valley are the Twyford Downs, while away to the west over the Itchen valley and the quiet meadows and village of St. Cross, with its square-towered Norman church, is down-land sweeping away to a group of trees silhouetted against the sky line, known as Oliver's Battery. To the north and west over the stretch of low-lying water meadows appear the roofs and towers of Winchester, the square cathedral tower and the delicately-turreted college tower rising behind a thick foreground of trees. To the north-east runs the railway bank of the Great Western Railway, east of which are sweeps of rolling arable land, in the distance the houses of Chilcomb Within, and rising behind them St. Giles's Hill, and again stretches of down-land.

Of the other hills in Chilcomb, both St. Giles's Hill (which is only partly in the parish) and St. Mary Magdalen Hill (locally known as Magdalen or Morn Hill) are in the north. The road from New Alresford, cutting through wonderful down-country, rises steadily over Magdalen Hill, and skirting the northern slopes of St. Giles's Hill enters Winchester. On the summit of Magdalen Hill a large group of tumuli can be seen to the south of the road, while to the north is the Victoria Hospital for infectious diseases, behind which is the site of the original hospital of St. Mary Magdalen. This hospital, founded probably in the twelfth century,[6] was used for Dutch prisoners of war by Charles II, who in 1665 ejected the master and inmates, obliging them to seek lodgings in Winchester. The hospital was not pulled down until 1788, but it had been entirely spoilt and the inmates never returned. The charity still exists, the houses now occupied by the recipients being a group of small, low houses in St. John's parish, Winchester.

Twice in the twelfth and thirteenth centuries Magdalen Hill was the scene of historic incident. Henry de Blois, bishop of Winchester, went out to meet Empress Maud on Magdalen Hill 2 March, 1141, and from thence conducted her into the city in solemn procession.[7] In 1214 the downs of Magdalen Hill were the meeting-place of Archbishop Langton and other of the bishops and clergy with King John, who 'at the sight of them fell on his knees and shed many tears.' From thence the king was conducted to the cathedral, though he could not enter there until he had been absolved.[8]

The site of the ancient chapel of St. Giles is without the boundaries of Chilcomb parish, which only contains the southern portion of the hill, including the site of the celebrated St. Giles's Fair of old days.

The soil of the whole is calcareous loam with a subsoil of chalk, difficult of cultivation, but producing most kinds of grain and green crops. Hence the chief employment of the inhabitants is agriculture, while the lime works at Bar End and west of the village of Upper Chilcomb have become quite an industry.

MANORS Before the time of the Domesday Survey *CHILCOMB* was the name given to a large tract of country round Winchester, comprising nearly 100 hides, and called 'the Hundred Hides of Chilcomb,'[9] the whole of which is said to have been granted to the cathedral church of Winchester by Kinegyls between the years 608 and 634.[10]

The manor was evidently taken away from the church afterwards, but was restored about 856 by Athulf, king of the West Saxons, who also granted a confirmation of certain privileges to Winchester Cathedral for the land at Chilcomb,[11] and land and privileges alike were confirmed to the church by subsequent kings.[12] The origin and early history of this vast estate has been discussed by Professor Maitland, who rejects as spurious all the royal charters relating to it earlier than Ethelred's writ, which Kemble accepted as genuine, but the details of which as to the constituents of Chilcomb the Professor questions.[12a]

At the time of the Domesday Survey Bishop Walkelin held the manor of 'Barton and Buddlesgate' in Chilcomb, Winnall, Morestead, St. Faith, Compton, Weeke, Littleton, and Sparsholt[13] for the support of the monks of St. Swithun.[14] Chilcomb was assessed at one hide with land for sixty-eight ploughs; seven tenants held land of this hide from

[4] These trees were planted about the middle of the eighteenth century by Lord Botetourt, who commanded the Gloucestershire Militia, then quartered at Winchester.

[5] Leland, *Itin.* (2nd ed.), iii, 87.

[6] For its foundation and early history see *V.C.H. Hants*, ii, 197–200.

[7] Milner, *Hist. of Winchester*, i, 160, quoting from William of Malmesbury and Trussel; Round, *Geoffrey de Mandeville*, 57–62. Mr. Round places the meeting at Wherwell.

[8] Ibid. 180, quoting from Trussel and Matthew Paris.

[9] The Hundred Hides included the modern parishes of Avington, Easton, Ovington, Tichborne, Kilmeston, Stoke, Otterbourne, Twyford, Coldhannington, Nursling, and Brambridge hamlet.

[10] Dugdale, *Mon.* i, 210; Leland, *Coll.* i, 613.

[11] Birch, *Cart. Sax.* ii, 96.

[12] Ibid. ii, 282, 419; iii, 413.

[12a] *Dom. Bk. and Beyond*, 449–50, 496–9.

[13] The large manor of 'Barton and Buddlesgate' was an honour including the smaller manors, which latter paid suit at the court of 'Barton and Buddlesgate.'

[14] *V.C.H. Hants*, ii, 108.

the bishop.[15] The whole manor of Chilcomb was valued in the time of Edward the Confessor at £73 10*s.*; in 1086 the amount held by the monks was worth £80, and that held by the tenants £24.[16]

The manor of Chilcomb, together with many other manors and lands, was confirmed to the prior and monks of St. Swithun in 1205,[17] and again in 1285,[18] and remained in their possession until the time of the Dissolution.[19]

In 1535 the manor of Chilcomb was included among the St. Swithun's temporalities, and was assessed at £48 11*s.*[20] Upon the dissolution of the priory Chilcomb manor was granted to the dean and chapter of Winchester,[21] and remained in their hands until about the year 1893, when it was purchased by Mr. George Parker of Winchester, the present owner.[22]

At the time of the Domesday Survey there were four mills in Chilcomb worth £4, but there seem to be no later records concerning them.[23]

CHURCHES The church of *ST. ANDREW* is a small building with chancel 17 ft. 4 in. by 13 ft. 6 in., and nave 30 ft. 6 in. by 17 ft. 8 in., with south porch, and a wooden bell turret over the west end of the nave. It is a plain little country church of about 1130–40, standing on the side of the down above the village, and in its essential features not much altered from its original condition. The chancel arch is semicircular of one square order with chamfered strings at the springing, ornamented with zigzag on the vertical faces. The north window of the chancel, a plain, round-headed light, remains untouched, but on the south is a tall and narrow thirteenth-century lancet and a square-headed fifteenth-century window of two cinquefoiled lights, with a little old white and gold glass in the heads. The east window, of two square-headed lights with a quatrefoil over, is probably of no great age in its present condition, and at the west end of the north wall is a low-set round-headed opening, now blocked. At the north-east angle is a plain recess with a pointed arch, and the chancel arch is filled with a wooden screen of very rough Gothic design, perhaps of early seventeenth-century date. In the chancel floor are some good fifteenth-century glazed tiles with impressed slip patterns of usual types, lions, griffins, eagles, fleurs-de-lis, &c.

The nave has two small round-headed north windows, with internal rebates, the western of the two being set higher in the wall than the other, and its sill cut off by a late mural monument. In the south wall is a single round-headed window, widened and modernized, and a plain, round-headed south doorway of original date. The north doorway is of the same character, but blocked, all the twelfth-century work being in Binstead stone.

The west window is of the fifteenth century with two cinquefoiled lights and a cinquefoil in the head, and over the chancel arch are two pointed openings cut square through the gable, which probably held bells. The walls are of flint rubble, originally plastered over, but now stripped and pointed, the chancel walls being still plastered, and the roofs are red-tiled, the nave roof being hipped at the west. On the south-east quoin of the nave is an incised sundial.

The south porch is modern.

The roofs of nave and chancel are old, with trussed rafters, as are the main timbers of the bell-turret, which has weather-boarded sides and a red-tiled roof.

All internal fittings are modern, the font, with a small bowl on an octagonal shaft, standing on a marble coffin-lid with a much damaged cross of fourteenth-century date.

There are two bells, but pits for three, in the turret. The treble is of 1628, inscribed 'In God is my hope,' with the founder's initials I H (possibly for John Higden) and G R on the waist, and the tenor is a fifteenth-century bell from the Wokingham foundry bearing the characteristic cross, groat, and lion's face, but no inscription.

The plate consists of a communion cup and cover paten of 1569, a paten of 1683 bought with a bequest of 40*s.* made in 1680, and a pewter flagon and two alms dishes. All Saints' church possesses a silver gilt set of plate, consisting of two chalices, two patens, and a flagon, of modern date.

The first book of the registers contains all entries, 1556–1798, the second has baptisms and burials, and the third marriages, 1799–1812.

The modern church of *ALL SAINTS* already mentioned is of rough flint and brick, in thirteenth-century style.

ADVOWSON At the time of the Domesday Survey there were nine churches in Chilcomb, seven of which evidently belonged to the seven smaller manors which were included in Chilcomb, and the remaining two to Chilcomb itself.[24] Of these one became the parish church, and the other a dependent chapelry attached to it. In 1284 the king gave up to John bishop of Winchester and his successor all his right in the advowson of Chilcomb with the chapel of St. Catherine.[25]

At the time of Pope Nicholas's taxation the church of Chilcomb, together with a chapel attached, was assessed at £6 13*s.* 4*d.*,[26] and by 1535 the value of the rectory of Chilcomb had risen to £10.[27] At the same date St. Swithun's prior owned a pension of £1 6*s.* 8*d.* from Chilcomb church.[28]

In 1657, in accordance with the Act providing that no living should have a stipend less than £100 a year, the parishes of Chilcomb and Morestead with benefices of the value of £60 and £40 respectively were united for a time under one incumbent, the presentation being made jointly by the patrons of the two churches. The services were held alternately at either church.[29]

Since 1284 the advowson of the church of St. Andrew has been in the hands of the bishop of Winchester.[30]

[15] The lands held by these seven tenants were most probably the seven small manors of Winnall, Morestead, St. Faith, Compton, Weeke, Littleton, and Sparsholt included in Chilcomb at this time.

[16] *V.C.H. Hants*, i, 463.

[17] *Cal. Pap. Letters*, i, 21.

[18] *Cal. of Chart. R.* 1257–1500, p. 288.

[19] *Feud. Aids*, ii, 320. In 1280 Alice and Joan, daughters of Geoffrey de Chilcomb, granted one messuage and 40 acres of land in Chilcomb to the prior and convent for the rent of 20*s.* and two corrodies (Feet of F. 9 Edw. I).

[20] *Valor Eccl.* (Rec. Com.), vi, App. vi.

[21] Pat. 33 Hen. VIII, pt. 9, m. 34–40; *L. and P. Hen. VIII*, xvi, 417; Mins. Accts. 32 & 33 Hen. VIII, R. 109, m. 45, 46.

[22] Information supplied by Mr. Parker.

[23] *V.C.H. Hants*, i, 463.

[24] Ibid.

[25] Chart. R. 12 Edw. I, m. 5.

[26] *Pope Nich. Tax.* (Rec. Com.), 210.

[27] *Valor Eccl.* (Rec. Com.), ii, 6.

[28] Ibid. vi, App. 10; Dugdale, *Mon.* i, 218.

[29] Aug. of Ch. Livings, vol. 991, fol. 464.

[30] *Wykeham's Reg.* (Hants Rec. Soc.), i, 39; Inst. Bks. (P.R.O.).

EASTON

Eston, Estune (xii cent.) ; Istune (xiv cent.).

The parish of Easton lies to the north-east of Winchester, and covers 2,172 acres of undulating country falling in the north to the valley of the Itchen, which flows through the low country in the north of the parish and forms the boundary between Easton and Martyr Worthy. Of the whole area 19 acres are water, 1,976½ are arable land, 671¼ are permanent grass, and 94 woodland and plantation.[1] The south-west of the parish consists wholly of farmland and open fields ; Larkwhistle Farm and Pitt Barn are in the south-east, but the village itself lies in the north of the parish where the land falls away to the Itchen valley. The hilly road from Winchester approaching from the south between low quickset hedges commands a wide view to the north over the Itchen valley to King's Worthy and Abbot's Worthy, Worthy Park standing up in fine relief against a dark background of woodland. After a last steady rise uphill the road descends into the village and curving to the east becomes the main village street. Here at the entrance to the village a road turns north towards the river, between a group of low, old-fashioned cottages, and the obtrusive newly built inn 'The Cricketer's Arms.' From this a narrow branch road turns uphill to the west, leading past the manor farm, which is on high ground to the south, to the church, which stands on the lower side of the road as the ground sweeps down to the river. West of the church is the small school, built in 1840, and still further west is the rectory. Beyond this the road becomes a rough path across the fields. The main village street turns east past a line of thatched cottages which stand on the south side of the road behind a low brick lichen-covered wall, and again past other thatched and timbered cottages until it turns sharply down hill to the left to the quaint Chestnut Horse Inn with its tiled lichen-covered roof and hanging sign. From here until the end of the village is reached the road turns east again, leading past groups of thatched deep-roofed cottages, with here and there more modern buildings, between which, on the left, glimpses can be caught of the water meadows traversed by the Itchen, and of Martyr Worthy church and village, which lie on the slope of the hill rising from the opposite side of the valley.

THE CHESTNUT HORSE INN, EASTON

The soil is chalk and loam ; the subsoil chalk. The chief crops are wheat, barley, oats, and turnips.

MANORS EASTON The earliest recorded mention of *EASTON* seems to be in 871 when Alfred bishop of Winchester granted 8 hides of land at Easton on the River Itchen to Cuthred the Dux and his wife Wulfrith for three lives.[1a] Thus from early times Easton was in the hands of the bishops of Winchester, and the right of the bishopric to it seems to have been confirmed by a grant made by King Edgar to his kinsman Brihthelm bishop of Winchester in 961 of 7½ *mansae* at Easton on the River Itchen.[2]

At the time of the Domesday Survey the bishop held Easton in demesne as he had done in the time of Edward the Confessor from him. Turstin held 52 acres of the demesne which had been held before by Aelfeth ; Geoffrey held 3 hides of this manor which Brictric had held from the bishop in parage in King Edward's reign ; and Alwin held 1 hide and 1 virgate which he had held in the time of King Edward.[3]

It appears from a bull of Innocent III that Easton was granted and confirmed to the prior and monks of St. Swithun's, Winchester, in 1205,[4] who held it of the bishop by the service of one-third of a knight's fee,[5] and by a charter of 1284, confirmed in the following year by Edward I, John bishop of Winchester gave up for himself and his successors all rights in the manor, saving his rights of overlordship, to the prior and convent,[6] who had already acquired land in Easton by grant of James Hansard in 1243.[7] Easton manor was included among the temporalities belonging to St. Swithun's in 1291, and was assessed at £38 12*s.* 4¾*d.*[8] Licence was granted to the prior and convent by Edward II to acquire further land and rent to the value of £50, and in 1330 and in part satisfaction of this right 6 acres of land in Easton

[1] Statistics of Bd. of Agric. (1905). Lands outside the parish are included in this return. [1a] Birch, *Cart. Sax.* ii, 162.

[2] Ibid. iii, 303.

[3] *V. C. H. Hants*, i, 460.

[4] Dugdale, *Mon.* i, 211 ; *Cal. Pap. Letters*, i, 21.

[5] Coram Rege R. No. 86, m. 7.

[6] Chart. R. 13 Edw. I, No. 98.

[7] Feet of F. Hants, 27 Hen. III, No. 281.

[8] *Pope Nich. Tax.* (Rec. Com.), 213.

was granted to them by John de Madhurst.[9] It remained in the hands of the prior and convent until the time of the Dissolution,[10] and was granted in 1541 to Sir William Sidney ;[11] from him it passed to his son Henry, who held it in 1564.[12] Sir Henry was succeeded by his son, the famous Sir Philip Sidney, who married Frances daughter of Sir Francis Walsingham ; and their only daughter, Elizabeth, married Roger earl of Rutland.[13] In 1600 Robert earl of Essex and his wife Frances (Sir Philip Sidney's widow) and Roger earl of Rutland and his wife Elizabeth made a settlement of the manor of Easton,[14] which they conveyed five years later to Thomas Antrobus.[15]

SIDNEY. *Or a pheon azure.*

Thomas Antrobus died seised of the manor in 1612, which passed under a settlement to his son Thomas, and Elizabeth the son's wife.[16] This second Thomas sold the manor to William Rolfe before his death in 1624, leaving to his daughters Elizabeth and Mabel tenements in tail male, with remainder to Thomas Antrobus of Clifford's Inn.[17] William Rolfe still held Easton manor in 1640, and conveyed it in that year to Hugh Windham and Edward Abbott.[18] At a survey of the manor taken in 1647 it was valued at £5 2*s.* 3*d.* per annum, there being no timber or woods.[19]

At the sale of the bishops' lands in 1649 Easton manor was sold to Adoniram Byfeild for £352 15*s.*[20] At the Restoration, however, the manor was restored to Edward Abbott, who conveyed it in 1673 to Richard Coleman.[21] Between 1673 and 1741 the manor seems to have been divided among five coheiresses ; for in the latter year Edward Hooker and his wife, James Battin and his wife Hannah, Anne, Mary, and Dulcebella Hooker conveyed it to John Morgan, evidently for a settlement ;[22] and in 1745[23] and 1751[24] James Battin and Hannah made conveyances of a fourth part in right of Hannah.

By 1773 the whole manor had passed to James Brydges, duke of Chandos,[25] and from this date Easton follows the descent of Avington (q.v.).

At the time of the Domesday Survey there were two mills in the parish of Easton worth 30*s.* ;[26] but there seems to be no trace of a mill at the present day.

In 1301 a grant was made to the prior and convent of St. Swithun of free warren in their demesne lands at Easton.[27] Hugh Rolfe held a free fishery and view of frankpledge in Easton in 1640, and conveyed his rights in that year to Hugh Windham and Edward Abbott.[28]

CHURCH

The church of *OUR LADY* is a very valuable example of a small parish church of *c.* 1170, simple in plan, but of good scale and detail, with a square vaulted chancel and eastern apse, a nave 50 ft. by 20 ft., and a western tower.

The apse has been too thoroughly 'restored' and its windows widened, and the transverse arches at east and west of the chancel, owing to insufficient abutment, have spread, but otherwise the chancel is in very good preservation. The transverse arches are pointed, of two orders with keeled edge rolls and chamfered labels, and spring from clustered responds with foliate capitals of excellent design. The vault is quadripartite, with moulded ribs, and the apse vault has similar ribs springing from shafts between its three windows. These have been spoilt by widening and are modernized, but are still of very good effect, with banded shafts in the jambs, and round arched heads with an outer order of large zigzag ornament, and a banded roll on the inner. On the south of the chancel is a similar window, entirely

EASTON CHURCH : THE TOWER

[9] *Cal. of Pat.* 1327–30, p. 501.

[10] *Feud. Aids*, ii, 320. In 1317 Alice de Durnegate, an idiot, was holding a messuage and 20 acres in Easton. Inq. p.m. 10 Edw. II, No. 47. *Cal. of Close*, 1313–18, p. 420. In 1346 John de Madhurst held one-eighth of one fee in Easton which had belonged to the heir of John de Boulogne and of Robert Poterel (*Feud. Aids*, ii, 335).

[11] Pat. 33 Hen. VIII, pt. 2, m. 28.

[12] Ibid. 6 Eliz. pt. 6, m. 15.

[13] G. E. C. *Complete Peerage*, iii, 285.

[14] Feet of F. Hants, East. 42 Eliz.

[15] Ibid. Hil. 2 Jas. I. Robert earl of Essex died and his wife Frances married as her third husband Richard earl of Clanricarde (G. E. C. *Complete Peerage*, ii, 258), and with him conveyed any right that she had left in the manor of Easton to Roger earl of Rutland (Feet. of F. Div. Cos. Hil. 3 Jas. I), evidently in confirmation of the title of Thomas Antrobus.

[16] Chan. Inq. p.m. 8 & 9 Jas. I (Ser. 2), bdle 5, No. 234 ; ibid. 21 Jas. I, vol. 400, No. 77, and *Harl. Soc. Publ.* xxii, 123.

[17] Chan. Inq. p.m. 21 Jas. I, vol. 400, No. 77.

[18] Feet of F. Hants, Trin. 15 Chas. I.

[19] *Coll. Top. et Gen.* iii, 28.

[20] Close, 1649, pt. 24, m. 6 ; *Coll. Top. et Gen.* i, 289.

[21] Feet of F. Div. Cos. Mich. 25 Chas. II.

[22] Ibid. Hants, Hil. 15 Geo. II.

[23] Ibid. East. 18 Geo. II.

[24] Ibid. Mich. 25 Geo. II.

[25] Ibid. East. 14 Geo. III.; Recov. R. East. 14 Geo. III, m. 59.

[26] *V. C. H. Hants*, i, 460.

[27] Chart. R. 29 Edw. I, No. 54.

[28] Feet of F. Hants, Trin. 15 Chas. I.

Easton Church : The Chancel

Easton Church : South Doorway of Nave

modern, and on the north is the organ and a modern vestry.

The nave retains its two original north windows, narrow round-headed lights widely splayed inwards, with a keeled roll at the inner wall face ; at the sill level a moulded string runs round the walls. The southern windows have given place to square-headed fifteenth-century windows of two cinquefoiled lights, and between them is the south doorway, with a richly worked semicircular arch of three orders and trebly-banded shafts with foliate capitals. The north doorway is blocked, and quite plain. On the east jamb of the south doorway is a sunk cross, perhaps a consecration cross, which may have been inlaid in cement or the like for effect.

The tower arch is pointed, of one square order with a chamfered string at the springing, and has above it a plain round-headed doorway which once gave access to the space within the original roof. At the south-east angle is a projecting stair, and the tower is finished with a very picturesque shingled spire ; the whole of its external masonry has been renewed, but the internal chalk quoining and masonry is original.

The nave roof is a well-designed piece of work, with arched braces to the collars and wind-braces to the purlins, and the pulpit, on a modern stone base, is of early seventeenth-century date, with arabesque ornament. Close to it at the north-east of the nave the upper and lower doors of the fifteenth-century rood stair remain, the stair being in a projecting turret. All other fittings of the church are modern, including a tall oak chancel screen, and the font, at the west of the nave, of twelfth-century design.

On the south wall of the chancel is a pretty monument, set up in 1595, to Agatha, wife of Bishop Barlow of Chichester, and to two of her sons and five daughters.

There are three bells, with pits for four. The treble, a late fifteenth-century bell, has an interesting inscription, the whole of which the bell-founder was unfortunately unable to get on to the bell, so that it runs thus, the words being set in groups as shown : 'Jhū have mercy . . . uppon the sowlis of T . . . homas Stooker & . . . of Septēb . . . ye yere of o^r lord.' The date is thus crowded out. The second bell, by Roger Landon, is inscribed 'Ave Maria,' with the founder's marks of a lion's head, groat, cross, and shield with R.L. The tenor of 1614, by a founder R. B., bears 'In God is my hope.'

The church plate is modern, consisting of a silver chalice, paten, and alms dish of 1850, and a plated flagon.

There are no registers of an earlier date than the seventeenth century, the first book now preserved containing the baptisms from 1692 to 1754, the marriages from 1694 to 1759, and the burials from 1693 to 1812. The second book contains the baptisms from 1754 to 1812, and the marriages for the same period, there being no separate printed marriage register from 1754 onwards, as is usually the case. There is a book of churchwardens' accounts, covering the period from 1655 to 1819, and after a break of ten years they are continued to 1870.

ADVOWSON At the time of the Domesday Survey there were two chapels at Easton in the possession of the bishop [29] The advowson of Easton was in the hands of the bishop of Winchester until the year 1885. From 1885–8 the living was in the gift of the bishop of Lichfield ;[30] and since 1888 the Lord Chancellor has held the right of presentation.[31]

Easton was assessed in 1291 at £10,[32] but by 1535 the value of the rectory had so much increased that the assessment amounted to £26 13*s* 4*d*.[33]

The living is now a rectory, net income £344, with residence and 4 acres of glebe in the gift of the Lord Chancellor.

There is a small Primitive Methodist chapel in the parish.

CHARITIES There is a small piece of land in this parish called 'the Church Halves,' containing about an acre, but there are no documents showing how the parish became possessed of it. The rent is applied for church purposes.

EXTON

East Seaxnatune (x cent.) ; Essentune (xi cent.) ; Exton (xii cent).

The parish of Exton covers a long sweep of high ground of about 3,567 acres, of which 1,208¼ are arable land, 460½ permanent grass, 591 woodland, and 6 water.[1] Part of Corhampton, including Preshaw Park, the high ground north and west of Exton village, was transferred to Exton parish in March, 1894,[2] and from this part of the parish fine views can be obtained of the low-lying parishes to the north, Beauworth, Kilmeston, Hinton Ampner, Cheriton, and Tichborne. The south and centre of the parish through which the River Meon flows is lower country, and is the most fertile part of the parish, where the bulk of the arable land lies, while the River Meon affords good trout fishing.

The village itself is in the extreme south of the parish, immediately north of Corhampton. The three villages of Exton, Corhampton, and Meonstoke lie so near together as almost to form one village. Exton is approached most easily by a road which branches west from the main road from West Meon to Droxford, and runs for some way parallel with the river, beyond which to the south of the village is a wide stretch of low-lying marsh land. A large grey stone house, formerly the manor-house, but now used only as a farm, stands at the entrance to the village on the north side of the road. A few yards beyond is the small stone church of St. Peter and St. Paul, and opposite on the south of the road are some quaint thatched cottages in strange contrast with the little red-brick schoolhouse which stands near the church. Beyond the school, on slightly higher ground, is the rectory, a handsome house in fine grounds, near which are The Grove and Exton Cottage. Further south, on the road which connects Exton with the main

29 *V. C. H. Hants.* i, 460.
30 *Clergy List*, 1885–88.
31 Ibid. 1888–1904.
32 *Pope Nich. Tax.* (Rec. Com.), 211.
33 *Valor Eccl.* (Rec. Com.), ii, 10.
1 Statistics of Bd. of Agric. (1905).
2 Local Govt. Bd. Order, No. 16412.

Corhampton road, is another small group of houses, including the little general shop and the Shoe Inn, and close by, on the right bank of the river, is the old mill-house which has now fallen into picturesque decay. The soil of the parish is chalk and clay, subsoil gravel, chalk, and stone. The chief crops are wheat, oats, and barley.

MANORS

The first mention of *EXTON* is apparently in 940, when a grant was made by King Edmund to his thegn Ethelgeard of 12 *mansae* at 'East Seaxnatune' or Exton, on the River Meon.[3] Between 940 and 1086 Exton must have passed into the hands of the priory of St. Swithun, for which it was held by the bishop of Winchester as it had been in the time of King Edward. Formerly it had been assessed at 12 hides, but in 1086 at 8 hides only. Its value, it is said, had fallen from £16 in the time of King Edward to £12; and though by 1086 the value had only risen to £20 the land was subject to a tax of £30, which was a burden heavier than it could bear. For twenty years Lening had held 2 hides of this land and a mill worth 2*s.*[4]

Exton was confirmed to the priory of St. Swithun at Winchester in 1205, and again in 1285, and remained to the prior and convent until the dissolution of the monasteries.[5] In 1291 Exton was numbered among the St. Swithun temporalities, and was assessed at £20 13*s.* 10*d.*[6] After the Dissolution the manor was granted in 1542 to the dean and chapter of Winchester,[7] to whom it was confirmed by James I in 1605.[8]

At the sale of the dean and chapter's lands in 1649 the manor of Exton was bought by William Collyns and Neville Larymore for £1,518 16*s.* 8*d.*,[9] but at the Restoration it was recovered by the church, and in 1682 it was still a possession of the cathedral church of Winchester. The present lord of the manor is Col. William Woods of Warnford Park (in Bishop's Waltham), who succeeded his father, Mr. Henry Woods, in 1882.

WOODS OF WARNFORD. *Argent a cheveron nebuly gules with drops argent between three martlets sable.*

At the time of the Domesday Survey there were two mills in Exton worth 20*s.*[10] After the Dissolution there is an entry on the ministers' accounts for the farm of one water-mill worth £5,[11] and at the sale of the dean and chapter's lands in 1649 a water-grist mill was sold to William Collyns and Neville Larymore.[12] There is a ruined mill in the parish at the present day. A grant of free warren in their demesne lands of Exton was granted to the prior and convent of St. Swithun in 1301,[13] and in 1649 a free fishing in 'the river of Exton' passed with the manor to William Collyns and Neville Larymore.[14]

CHURCH

The church of *ST. PETER* and *ST. PAUL* is a small building with chancel 22 ft. by 18 ft. 10 in., north vestry, and organ chamber, nave 56 ft. 8 in. by 21 ft. 5 in., south porch, and wooden bell-turret over the west end of the nave. It has undergone very thorough repair, and its details are for the most part modern. The chancel, which dates from *c.* 1230, has a marked southward deviation from the axis of the nave, and the latter may contain work of an earlier date, though no architectural features remain to prove it.

In the east wall of the chancel are two large lancets with a quatrefoil over, in the north wall a single lancet with a wide internal splay, and in the south wall two similar lancets. All have external reveals, but only in the north window is any old stonework preserved. A heavy moulded string runs round the interior of the chancel below the window sills, and at the south-east is a double trefoiled piscina recess with a modern oak shelf. The masonry of the chancel arch is partly modern and partly retooled. The nave has four windows on each side, the eastern window on the north being a thirteenth-century lancet with old stonework, while the next to it and the western window on this side are similar lancets in modern masonry. The remaining window of three cinquefoiled lights is of the fifteenth-century style, and retains a little masonry of that date. On the south side the eastern window is of two lights in fifteenth-century style, while the other three are single lancets; none have any old stonework. Between the second and third windows on this side is the south doorway, with a plain round arch of uncertain date, under a modern porch, which follows the lines of the probably thirteenth-century porch at Warnford.

The west end of the nave appears to be entirely modern, and the west window is a single lancet.

The roofs and other woodwork are likewise modern, together with the bell-turret, which can only be reached by means of a long ladder from within the church. The west end of the nave is screened off to form a vestry, and near the south door is the modern octagonal font of thirteenth-century style.

On the south wall of the chancel is the marble monument of Dr. John Young, dean of Winchester, who died in 1642, the date being given in a chronogram—

VenI VenI MI IesV IVDeX VenI CIto.

There are two bells, the treble bearing only 'fecit 1829,' the founder's name being left out, while the other is an interesting mediaeval bell, bearing a reversed inscription in black letters—

+ Ricardus + Ricardus Puinter + Neuport. The third word is doubtful.

The plate consists of a silver cup of 1648 and a paten, and a plated paten and flagon.

The first book of the registers contains all entries from 1579 to 1720; the second, baptisms and burials 1720–80, and marriages to 1754; the third and

[3] Birch, *Cart. Sax.* ii, 484.

[4] *V.C.H. Hants*, i, 466. This was evidently not a manor, but part of the demesne with which it was geldable. William son of Gilbert held of the bishop half a knight's fee in Exton in 1166, which William de Exton formerly held (*Red Bk. of Exch.* i, 206).

[5] *Cal. of Chart. R.* 1257–1306, p. 288; Dugdale, *Mon.* i, 211; *Cal. Pap. Letters*, i, 21.

[6] *Pope Nich. Tax.* (Rec. Com.), 213.

[7] Pat. 33 Hen. VIII, pt. 9, m. 34–40. Its value at this time was £39 7*s.* 6d. yearly (Dugdale, *Mon.* i, 217). The firm of the site of the manor was assessed at £14 3*s.* 4*d.*

[8] Pat. 2 Jas. I, pt. 23, m. 37.

[9] Close, 1649, pt. 16, m. 16.

[10] *V.C.H. Hants*, i, 466.

[11] Dugdale, *Mon.* i, 217.

[12] Close, 1649, pt. 16, m. 16.

[13] Chart. R. 29 Edw. I, m. 12.

[14] Close, 1649, pt. 16, m. 16.

fourth are the printed marriage registers 1755–99 and 1800–11; and the fifth the baptisms and burials 1780–1812.

ADVOWSON

In 1086 there was a church at Exton which, together with the manor, was in the hands of the bishop of Winchester.[15] In 1284 the king gave up all claim in the advowson of this church to the bishop.[16] In 1291 the church owed a pension of 8 marks to the hospital of St. Cross at Winchester,[17] but this pension appears to have lapsed before 1535. The bishop of Winchester is still patron of the church.

CHARITIES

This parish is entitled to benefit from the schools in Corhampton.

HINTON AMPNER

Hentune (xi cent.); Henton (xii cent.); Hinton Ampner or Amner (xiii cent.).

The parish of Hinton Ampner contains 2,378 acres of land rising gradually from west to east to a height of more than 400 ft. above the sea level.

Hinton Park, covering an area of 66 acres, in which is Hinton House, the seat of Mr. Henry John Dutton, fills up the whole of the north-west of the parish; immediately east of the park is the village, and from here the parish stretches eastward in a long irregular tract away to Brookwood in the south-east. 'Brookwood' is the residence of Mr. Daniel Meinertzhagen, and stands in a finely wooded park of 86 acres through which the house is approached by two good drives. As the main road from Winchester to Petersfield sweeps over Lane End Down and leaves Cheriton parish at Lane End hamlet, the Jolly Farmer Inn, standing on the south of the road, seeming locally in Cheriton, marks the beginning of Hinton Ampner parish. North of the road is the low-lying country of Hinton Marsh, a few yards south of which the Itchen tributary, which runs through Cheriton, has its beginning. Along the south side of the road are the rising grounds of Hinton Park, up which winds one of the carriage drives to Hinton House, though the house itself, standing further south-west among the trees over the brow of the hill, is hidden from the road. About a quarter of a mile east of the 'Jolly Farmer' a steep lane branches south from the main road, and here and there on either side of this, as it runs uphill between high banks and overhanging trees parallel with the grounds of Hinton House, the cottages of the village for the most part lie. Several, one group especially which lies back behind long narrow gardens, are half timbered and thatched and most picturesque in appearance. At the top of the hill beyond the rectory, which stands high on the left hand, the road branches south-east to Brookwood and south-west towards Kilmeston. Here, close on the road to the west, but actually within the grounds of Hinton House, is the church of All Saints, still west of which, half hidden from view by the thickness of the trees, is Hinton House itself. From here the ground falls away to the south, so that the house, standing on the slope nearly 400 ft. above the ordnance datum, commands a wide view, with Kilmeston immediately in the south, while away to the south-west beyond Kilmeston rises Millbarrow Down. Several cottages and farm buildings lie east of the church along the road which runs south-east to Brookwood.

Apart from the main group of houses thus clustered near the church and manor-house, as the turnpike road runs east to Petersfield, between wide stretches of green sward bordered by copper beeches and other fine trees, or past occasional clearings with high stacks of brushwood, every here and there scattered along the road are other cottages belonging to Hinton Ampner village. Here also south of the road, about midway between Bramdean and Hinton Ampner, is the schoolhouse, a red-brick building dating from 1861, near which is the police station, facing a fine clump of tall pine trees.

The inhabitants are mostly employed in agriculture, since the soil is clay loam with a subsoil of chalk producing ordinary root and green crops.

The greater proportion of the 1480¼ acres of arable land are in the centre of the parish intermingled with the 561½ acres of permanent grass land. Of the 151½ acres of woodland the largest group is in the south of the parish close to Kilmeston.

Joan's Acre, Whitehill, Broomwood, and Lamborough Road are still existing place-names which were mentioned in a Close Roll of 1650,[1] and undoubtedly date back to a much earlier time.

MANORS

The manor of *HINTON* or *HINTON AMPNER* was held by the bishop of Winchester at the time of the Domesday Survey, it had always belonged to the Church; the manor was assessed at eight hides and was worth 100*s*.[2]

Hinton Ampner was among the manors confirmed to the prior and convent of St. Swithun, Winchester, in 1205, and again in 1285.[3] The manor was appropriated to the office of almoner of St. Swithun's (hence the name Ampner which is a corruption of almoner); it defrayed the expenses of the almoner's office and the almoner held the manorial courts either in person or by his bailiff.[4]

STEWKELEY. *Checky argent and sable a fesse and a border gules.*

The manor remained in the possession of the priory of St. Swithun until the Dissolution[5] when it passed with the other manors belonging to the priory to the dean and chapter of Winchester, by whom it was leased for a term of 21 years to Sir Thomas Stewkeley in 1637.[6] At the sale of the dean and chapter's lands in 1650 it was bought by Sir John Hippesley for the sum of £2,587 17*s*. 5½*d*. There was then a capital messuage called Prior's Hinton or the manor-house consisting of a large hall, two parlours, and twenty-one

15 *V.C.H. Hants*, i, 466.
16 Chart. R. 12 Edw. I, m. 5.
17 *Pope Nich. Tax.* (Rec. Com.), 211.
1 Close, 1650, pt. 5, m. 43.
2 *V.C.H. Hants*, i, 467.
3 Dugdale, *Mon.* i, 211; and *Cal. Pap. Letters*, i, 21; *Cal. of Chart. R.* 1257–1303, p. 288.
4 *Obedientiary Rolls of St. Swithun's* (Hants Rec. Soc.), 76.
5 *Feud. Aids*, ii, 320. In 1535 the manor of Hinton Ampner was worth £26 13*s*. per annum, *Valor Eccl.* (Rec. Com.), v, App. ix.
6 Pat. 33 Hen. VIII, pt. 9, m. 34–40; ibid. 2 Jas. I, pt. 23, m. 37.

chambers, with brewhouse, malthouse, stables, barns, a hop garden and bowling green. More than 700 acres of land were attached to the manor, including a common containing 100 acres.[7] Hinton Ampner was recovered by the Cathedral Church at the Restoration and was again held by the Stewkeleys, who must have obtained the fee-simple of the manor about this date; although no record of this has been found.[8] From the Stewkeleys it passed to the Stawells, by the marriage in 1719 of Mary, daughter and heiress of Sir Hugh Stewkeley, with Edward, fourth and last Baron Stawell.[9] Lord Stawell left a daughter and heiress Mary, who was created baroness Stawell in 1759; she married as her first husband the Hon. Henry Bilson-Legge, who became Baron Stawell in right of his wife;[10] and from this time onwards the descent of the manor follows that of Bedhampton (q.v.).[11] The manor was held by paying a septennial fine, which was enfranchised by the Hon. John Dutton in 1863.[12] The lord of the manor at the present day is Mr. Henry Dutton. View of frankpledge and rights of free warren in Hinton Ampner were granted to the dean and chapter under the grant of the manor to them in 1542.[13]

BILSON-LEGGE. *Azure a hart's head argent,* for LEGGE, *quartered with Azure a rose argent parted with a pomegranate or having a stalk and leaves vert,* for BILSON.

CHURCH The church of *ALL SAINTS* has suffered from 'restoration' more severely than many of its neighbours,[14] but is still of great interest as preserving its pre-Conquest plan and a few details of that date. It has a chancel 15 ft. 8 in. wide by 21 ft. long, and a nave 21 ft. 10 in. wide by 47 ft. with walls 2 ft. 6 in. thick of flint rubble with ashlar dressings. There is a north-west vestry to the nave, a west bell-turret, and a south porch, all being modern. The chancel shows little traces of age, all its details having been reworked. It has a pair of lancets in its east wall, two in the north wall, and two in the south, and at the south-west a priest's door and a low-set lancet window, all of thirteenth-century style. At the south-east is a double piscina with a shelf and a recess in the back below the shelf. The chancel arch is modern, as are all the windows of the nave, of which there are four on the north, three on the south, and two at the west, with a trefoiled opening between them. The south doorway is also modern.

DUTTON. *Quarterly argent and gules, the gules fretty or, with the difference of a crescent.*

The remains of pre-Conquest work are as follows: part of the north-east quoin of the nave, two pilaster strips in the nave walls, one on the north and one on the south, set at 6 ft. westward from the eastern angles, and a doorway now leading to the modern north-west vestry, and formerly the south doorway of the nave, its position being further eastward than the present south doorway. The doorway has square jambs without a rebate, long and short quoins, and a round arch with a chamfered label, which may have been recut, the doorway not being in its original position. All this early work is in Binstead oolite, used in pre-Conquest work at Corhampton, Tichborne, Hambledon, and elsewhere. The vestry door has panels with mitred mouldings on one panel, with an inscription recording that 'Nicholas Lacy gave this doore February, 1643.' No other woodwork in the church is ancient, and the font, near the south door of the nave, is modern.

The monuments are interesting. On the south wall of the chancel, east of the piscina, are some small brass plates to the memory of William son of Sir Thomas Stewkeley, 1606, Katherine daughter of Sir Humphrey Drewe of Little Gidding, 1599, and Edward Drewe, 1601. On the north wall is a brass plate to Sir Hugh Stewkeley, 1612, with a shield of arms above it, and others to Thomas his son, 1638, Elizabeth his daughter, 1667, and Elizabeth, widow of Sir Thomas Stewkeley, 1648. On the north wall also is a painted marble and alabaster monument with the effigy of an infant son of the Stewkeley family, 1638, and on the south wall is the monument of an infant son of Thomas Stewkeley, 1601. At the south-west corner of the nave is a large white marble mural monument to Henry Bilson-Legge, 1764.

There are three bells, the treble inscribed: 'Serv God I W 1603.,' the second 'Fere God I W, 1603.,' and tenor 'In God is my hope, 1610.' The latter is by the unidentified founder I.H. (possibly John Higden), the other two by John Wallis of Salisbury.

The plate consists of a cup of 1745, with a paten of 1879, both bought in 1880; a flagon, *circa* 1704, and an almsdish of 1740. The old communion plate was sold in 1880, and is now in a private collection. The present cup and paten were bought from the proceeds of the sale.

The first book of the registers contains baptisms and burials 1541–1774, and the second marriages 1561–1754. The third continues the marriages to 1813.

ADVOWSON At the time of the Domesday Survey there was a church in Hinton Ampner which was worth 40*s*., but was assessed at 50*s*.[15] In 1284 the king gave up to John, bishop of Winchester, all his right in the advowson of this church.[16] In 1291 the church was taxed at £6,[17] and by 1535 the value had risen to £22.[18]

The bishop presented to the living of Hinton Ampner until nearly the end of last century,[19] when the dean and chapter of Winchester became the patrons.[20]

The living is now a rectory, net yearly value £300, with residence and 118 acres of glebe.

CHARITIES Charity of William Blake for Charity School.—In 1738, William Blake by his will proved in the P.C.C. founded and endowed a charity school in this

7 Close, 1650, pt. 5, m. 43.
8 Add. MSS. Stowe, 845, fol. 41.
9 Banks, *Dormant and Extinct Baronetage*, iii, 675–6.
10 Ibid.
11 Information supplied by Mr. Henry Dutton.
12 Ibid.
13 Pat. 33 Hen. VIII, pt. 9, m. 34–40.
14 Some 60 years since; information from Rev. E. C. Peake.
15 *V.C.H. Hants*, i, 467.
16 Chart. R. 12 Edw. I, m. 5.
17 *Pope Nich. Tax.* (Rec. Com.), 211.
18 *Valor Eccl.* (Rec. Com.), ii, 11.
19 Inst. Bks. (P.R.O.). Jonathan Edwards, who became rector in 1681, figured prominently in the Socinian and Antinomian controversies. *Dict. Nat. Biog.*
20 *Clergy List*, 1895.

parish.[21] The endowments consist of school, schoolhouse and premises in hand; a farm at Sheet in the parish of Petersfield, of 53 acres of arable land, and 6 acres of meadow; 11 acres or thereabouts of common allotted under Sheet Inclosure Award in respect of the above lands; a farm at Noah Hill in the parish of Newton Valence, consisting of 81 a. 2 r. 29 p. of arable land, 4½ acres of coppice, and 5¼ acres of pasture. The farms produce an annual income of about £145. The official trustees also hold £288 17*s.* 10*d.* consols arising in part from sale of land and in part from investment of accumulations.

The trust is administered under a scheme approved 1 May, 1890.

Charity of William Blake for Poor.—The same testator by his will directed that £200 should be laid out in the purchase of land, the yearly income to be applied for the benefit of the poor of the parish. This was laid out in the purchase of 10½ acres at Rogate, Sussex, let at £15 a year. The official trustees also hold a sum of £120 6*s.* 10*d.* consols in trust for this charity. The income is applied in the distribution of coal, 5*s.* being paid to the sexton for tolling the church bell as per will of donor.

In 1861 the Hon. Honora Legge by will left £100 consols for the benefit of the poor, which is held by the official trustees. The dividends are given in equal shares to two poor labourers with large families, or to two aged widows.

In 1898 Mrs. Honora Augusta Cowper-Coles, by will and codicil proved this date, bequeathed £120 £2 10*s.* per cent. annuities, income to be applied by the officiating minister in the distribution of warm winter clothing to poor women. The stock is held by the official trustees.

KILMESTON

Chenelmestune (x cent.); Chelmestune (xi cent.); Culmiston Gymminges, Kilmeston Gymminges, Culmiston Plugnett, Kilmeston Plunkenet (xiii, xiv, xv cent.); Culmeston, Kympston (xvi cent.).

The small parish of Kilmeston containing 1,670 acres of land lies on the chalk down country south-east of Winchester, the land rising generally from north to south from under 300 ft. near Hinton Ampner to over 500 ft. in the south-west near the high down country in the north-west of Exton parish.

The long straggling village of Kilmeston lies almost in the centre of the parish. As the road from Hinton Ampner, leading south, rises towards Kilmeston village a sudden turn to the west leads past the vicarage, which stands on high ground south of the road, on to the church of St. Andrew, which stands also on the south of the road opposite the fine old manor-house. Past the church the road branches north to College Farm, and south to the scattered cottages, the smithy and the school composing the rest of the village.

Dean House, the residence of Mr. Charles Naylor, stands in good grounds to the east of the village.

Westwood, a large copse stretching for about half a mile along the western boundary line of the parish, together with a wood called Broomwood in the east, comprises the greater part of the 81 acres of woodland in the parish. The 553 acres of permanent grass are mostly in the south and south-west of the parish, where there are stretches of low downland known as Kilmeston Downs. The 911½ acres of arable land lie mostly in the north and north-east. The soil is clay with a subsoil of chalk, producing the ordinary crops of wheat, oats, and barley.

The manor-house is an interesting building, partly of brick and partly of timber construction. It has a central hall, and wings on the north and south, the latter being of half timber, hung with tiles and containing the kitchens and offices. On the east side is a court and terrace leading to the entrance to the hall, but the principal entrance is at the north-west. On the west side are two early seventeenth-century gables of cut and moulded brickwork with an enriched cornice and projecting pilasters of very good detail, and the main building is probably of this date, though the timber part may be earlier. The main block is of two stories, the hall having had a flat ceiling with rooms over it; the detail in this part of the building belongs to the first half of the eighteenth century. The hall ceiling has been taken down, throwing it open to the upper floor, round which a gallery runs. In the north wing is a good Jacobean angle chimneypiece, but this part of the house was remodelled early in the nineteenth century to accommodate George IV, then prince regent, who lived here for some time, and is credited with having written with a diamond on one of the lattice panes in the kitchen window a few lines of verse, which have, however, the appearance of being before his time.

MANORS Land at *KILMESTON* was in the possession of the cathedral church of Winchester as early as the tenth century; for in 961 King Edgar, under a licence from the bishop of Winchester, to whom the land belonged, granted 10 *mansae* at Kilmeston to the thegn Athulf for three lives. On the death of the last survivor the land was to return to the church of St. Peter at Winchester.[1]

At the time of the Domesday Survey the 10 *mansae* were divided equally and formed two manors of 5 hides each, both belonging to the bishop, one being held by Edred, apparently in right of his wife, and the other by Godwin.[2] These manors became known as Kilmeston Plunkenet and Kilmeston Gymming from the names of the families who afterwards held them.

The manor of *KILMESTON PLUNKENET*, sometimes called half the manor of Kilmeston, was evidently granted by the bishop to the de la Beres; and about 1230 Richard de la Bere enfeoffed Alan de Plunkenet of the manor,[3] and he in 1295, together with his wife Joan, granted it to Alan de Plunkenet, junior, and his wife Sybil, to be held for the rent of a rose, with reversion (in case of the failure of heirs to

[21] *V.C.H. Hants.* ii, 'Schools.'

[1] Birch, *Cart. Sax.* iii, 304.

[2] *V.C.H. Hants.* i, 459, 460.

[3] *Cal. of Close*, 1227–31, p. 346; De Banco R. No. 270, m. 96 *d.*

the younger Alan)[4] to the heirs of Alan de Plunkenet, senior.

Before the death of Alan de Plunkenet, junior, his sister and heir Joan de Bohun, who died *s.p.*, appears to have disposed of her claim to the estate to Walter de Woodlock, and although she attempted subsequently to repudiate her grant the right of Walter was established.[5]

PLUNKENET. *Ermine a bend engrailed gules.*

Walter Woodlock was succeeded by his son Nicholas, who held Kilmeston Plunkenet in 1346,[6] and after his death his widow Joan was seised in fee tail of the manor. She granted it to certain trustees for their lives and died leaving an infant heir, her grandson Thomas.[7] Sir Almaric de St. Amand claimed the custody of the manor and the heir on behalf of the feoffees, but was successfully sued by William, bishop of Winchester.[8]

WOODLOCK. *Sable a cheveron between three lions argent looking backwards.*

From the Woodlocks the manor evidently passed to William Spershute or Sparsholt, who was holding it in 1428 and 1431,[9] but no record of this transfer can be found.

After 1431 no mention of the manor of Kilmeston Plunkenet has been found until the early part of the sixteenth century, by which time it had been divided into two parts, one being in the hands of the Skillings, and the other in the possession of the Bengers.

Mary Skilling was the widow of Walter Skilling, of Draycott, and daughter of John Ernelay of Marwell.[10] The Ernelays had a good deal of land in Sparsholt near Romsey ; it is therefore quite probable that they were in some way connected with William de Sparsholt or Spershute, who was holding Kilmeston Plunkenet in 1431. There may have been a marriage connexion, though no trace of one can be found, or William de Sparsholt may have been a member of the Ernelay family ; in support of this theory is the fact that both William de Sparsholt and John Ernelay were called 'of Marwell.' The half of Kilmeston Plunkenet manor held by the Skillings was granted to Richard Badger by Mary Skilling in 1570, probably as a settlement,[11] and in 1585 William, Mary's son, was holding half the manor and made a settlement of it in that year.[12] In 1605 William Skilling and his wife Margery, Swithun Skilling his brother and his wife Jane, and Edward Skilling sold half the manor of Kilmeston Plunkenet to William Lacie.[13] From this time onwards the descent of this half of Kilmeston Plunkenet manor becomes the same as that of the manor of Kilmeston Gymming (q.v.). John Benger died seised of the other half of the manor of Kilmeston Plunkenet in 1520, leaving as his heir his grandson Richard, a boy of thirteen.[14] On the death of Richard, in 1530, the manor passed to his widow Katharine,[15] and subsequently to her second husband, John White, and his heirs. The other heirs of Richard surrendered their claim,[16] and from this time until 1660 the estate followed the same descent as Southwick (q.v.).

SKILLING. *Argent two cheverons gules and a chief gules with three bezants therein.*

Richard Norton was still holding the manor in 1660, evidently in conjunction with the Lacies, who were also holding the other moiety of Kilmeston Plunkenet and the manor of Kilmeston Gymming,[17] and from this time the two moieties of the manor are reunited and the whole follows the descent of Kilmeston Gymming (q.v.), with which it finally became amalgamated.

The manor of *KILMESTON GYMMING* was apparently granted at an early date by the bishop of Winchester to the Gymming family, from whom it took its name, for in 1282 Nicholas de Gymming died seised of half the manor of Kilmeston leaving a son and heir John, aged eighteen.[18] In 1307 a licence was granted to Simon de Fareham and Robert de Harvedon, who were evidently trustees for the Gymming estates, to alienate the manor of Kilmeston Gymming in mortmain to Richard de Bourne, provost of the chapel of St. Elizabeth at Winchester,[19] and the manor remained in the hands of the provosts of this chapel until the Dissolution, after which it was granted (in March, 1544) to Thomas Wriothesley, together with all customary services ;[20] it was held by him until the following June, when he conveyed it to Anthony Cope,[21] who received licence in 1579 to alienate the manor to John Tichborne and his heirs.[22] A little later in the same year John Tichborne conveyed the manor to William Lacie, in whose family it remained for 160 years.[23] William Lacie died in 1595 seised of the manor of Kilmeston Gymming charged with annuities to Nicholas and Henry Tichborne. He left a son William, who died in 1614.[24]

William Lacie son of the last William[25] was sequestered in 1645,[26] but he recovered his estates and his family held the manor for nearly another century.

[4] Feet of F. Hants, Hil. 23 Edw. I.

[5] De Banco R. No. 270, m. 96 *d.* There were several tenants holding small pieces of land in Kilmeston about this time. The most important of these was John de Inkepenne, who died seised of land there in 1374 (Inq. p.m. 35 Edw. III, No. 123). Walter Woodlock evidently granted the manor of Kilmeston Plunkenet to Roger de Heywood, who conveyed it back to him by fine in 1340, probably as a settlement. (Feet of F. Hants, Mich. 14 Edw. III.)

[6] *Feud. Aids*, ii, 334.

[7] *Wykeham's Reg.* (Hants Rec. Soc.), ii, 537.

[8] De Banco R. Mich. 3 Hen. IV, m.201.

[9] *Feud. Aids*, ii, 357, 362. John de la Bere sued William Spershute for the manor of Kilmeston Plunkenet in 1429, as the great-great-great nephew of Alan de Plunkenet, senior, who had granted the manor to Alan de Plunkenet, junior, in 1295 with reversion to himself and his heirs ; but he failed to win the case, as William de Spershute was still holding in 1431. (De Banco R. Mich. 8 Hen. VI, m. 241.)

[10] Sir T. Phillipps, *Visit. of Wilts.*

[11] Feet of F. Hants. Hil. 12 Eliz.

[12] Ibid. Div. Cos. East. 27 Eliz.

[13] Ibid. Hants. Hil. 3 Jas. I.

[14] Chan. Inq. p.m. 11 Hen. VIII (Ser. 2), vol. xxxiv, No. 29.

[15] Ibid. 21 Hen. VIII, (Ser. 2), file 982, No. 3.

[16] Feet of F. Hants, Mich. 38 Hen. VIII.

[17] Recov. R. Trin. 12 Chas. II, m. 122.

[18] Inq. p.m. 10 Edw. I, No. 53.

[19] *Cal. of Pat.* 1307–13, p. 20.

[20] Pat. 35 Hen. VIII, pt. 9, m. 7.

[21] *L. and P. Hen. VIII*, xix (i), 812 (114).

[22] Pat. 21 Eliz. pt. 6, m. 41.

[23] Feet of F. Hants, East. 22 Eliz.

[24] Chan. Inq. p.m. 2 Jas. I (Ser. 2), pt. 2, No. 65 ; 11 Jas. I (Ser. 2), pt. iii, No. 56.

[25] Ibid.

[26] Petty Bag Cert. No. 4.

Kilmeston Manor House: A Gable on the West Front

Owslebury Church from the South-west

About the year 1677 it became united with Kilmeston Plunkenet, and in 1739 Henry Lacie and his wife, John Caryll, William Lacie, and George Lacie sold the manor of Kilmeston Gymming or Plunkenet to George Ridge.[27] The Ridges apparently held the manor for some time, and ultimately sold it to Robert Westley Hall, from whom in 1810 it was bought for £19,152 8s. 5d.[28] by Edmund Smith, £13,000 of the purchase money being raised by a mortgage on the estate to Richard and John Sparkes and Sarah Shurlock.[29]

LONG OF THE HOLT. *Sable a lion between four crosslets argent with two flaunches argent each charged with three crosslets sable.*

Walter Long purchased the whole manor from Edmund Smith and the mortgagees in 1812,[30] and it has remained in his family ever since; Mr. Walter Long of The Holt, Beauworth, being lord of the manor at the present day.

CHURCH The church of *ST. ANDREW* is in plan a simple rectangle with a modern south aisle and north porch, and any ancient features which it may possess are hidden by plastering and ivy. There is no structural division between nave and chancel. With the exception of the east window of the chancel, which has modern three-light tracery of fourteenth-century style, all the windows in the church, two in the chancel and five in the nave, are single lancets of decidedly modern appearance. The north door has a plain chamfered pointed arch, covered with plaster, and impossible to date, and the south arcade of the nave is of two bays in modern brickwork, with a vestry at the west of the aisle. The roof is tiled, and at the west is a wooden bell-turret with a leaded spire, containing one bell dated 1772 without further inscription.

The font is urn-shaped, of the eighteenth century, and there are no old fittings in the church, except that below the south window of the chancel is a piscina and a square locker.

The plate includes an interesting and perhaps local cup, with a trumpet-shaped bowl, on which is a band of incised ornament, and a spreading conical foot. It is without marks, and in spite of the incised band of ornament is probably of the latter part of the seventeenth century. There is also a standing paten of 1700.

The first book of the registers, which contains a memorandum that it was bought 1 June, 1671, at Winchester, runs from 1661 to 1812, and there is also an overseer's book of accounts beginning in 1691.

ADVOWSON There was a chapel in Kilmeston at the time of the Domesday Survey,[31] which was annexed to the rectory of Cheriton, and the advowson therefore followed the descent of Cheriton (q.v.). By an order in council, however, dated 4 February, 1879, the chapelries of Kilmeston and Beauworth were separated from the old rectory of Cheriton and formed into a distinct parish for ecclesiastical purposes. The living is now a vicarage in the gift of the crown.

CHARITIES In 1706 Dame Mary Sadlier by her will proved this date in P.C.C. bequeathed £100 to be laid out in land or otherwise, profits to go towards teaching poor children to read and write. A moiety of the legacy was lost through the insolvency of the holder, the remaining £50, with accumulations, was in 1803 invested in £124 19s. 11d. consols, held by the official trustees. The dividends are now applied in connexion with the National School.[32]

MARTYR WORTHY

Wurdia la Martre, Wordia, Worthi Martre (xiii cent.).

The parish of Martyr Worthy cum Chilland covers about 2,060 acres, rising from the low-lying ground near the Itchen in the south, to the high ridge of down land which stretches north of the Itchen valley. Of the whole area 1,438 acres are arable land, 400½ are permanent grass, and 220½ are woodland.[1] The north of the parish, through the north-west corner of which runs the Roman road from Winchester to Basingstoke, is one long stretch of down land and open field, with here and there a tract of woodland, including Brentwood and Schroner Cottage Wood. Budgitts Farm is on high ground, almost in the centre of the south. Further south, running from east to west, is the railway line of the Alton branch of the London and South-Western Railway, on which is Itchen Abbas station, about half a mile east of Martyr Worthy village. South of and almost parallel with the railway line runs the main road from Winchester to Alresford, passing south of Worthy Park, the residence of Captain Charles Fryer, M.P., as it enters the parish from the west. The house of Worthy Park, a fine mansion of white stone, standing in the midst of well-wooded country, is in this parish, although much of the estate stretches into Abbot's Worthy. South of the main road, nearly a mile east of Worthy Park, is the village of Martyr Worthy, on a branch road, almost a lane, leading down to the Itchen. The church of St. Swithun stands on the west, well sheltered behind thick-growing trees. North-west of the church are the schools and the old rectory, a square red-brick house, from which a fine view can be obtained to the south, across the Itchen valley, over the village of Easton, away to the down land and the dark woodland of Avington Park. Four or five groups of thatched and timbered cottages compose the village, several being actually in the meadow land close to the river, over the several tributaries of which narrow bridges lead to Easton.

Half a mile up the river, east of the village, is Chilland Mill, close by which are the offices of the Itchen Trout Breeding Association. The little hamlet of Chilland itself lies on the slope north of the mill, and consists of a few cottages and several modern houses, lying for the most part along the narrow road which leads up from the mill to the main road. A picturesque modern house, with grounds sloping down

27 Notes of F. Hants, Mich. 13 Geo. II.
28 Recov. R. Hil. 52 Geo. III, m. 90.
29 Ibid.
30 Ibid. m. 96.
31 *V.C.H. Hants*, i, 460.
32 Ibid. ii, 'Schools.'
1 Statistics of Bd. of Agric. (1905).

to the river, stands west of the mill. Chilland House is in the north-east, close to the main road from Winchester to Alresford. The soil of the whole parish is clay loam with a subsoil of chalk, and the chief crops are wheat, barley, oats, and turnips.

The place-name 'Ashdoun,' not now traceable, occurs in an Exchequer Deposition of 1716.[2]

MANORS There are several entries relating to land at *WORTHY* in Anglo-Saxon charters, but as there are five Worthies in Hampshire, all situated within a few miles of one another, identification is difficult. The 'land at Worthy' mentioned in the grant made by King Egbert to the monastery of St. Peter and St. Paul at Winchester in 825[3] is probably Martyr Worthy, for among the boundaries mentioned are Igtun (possibly Avington), Easton, and the high road to Alresford; and of all the Worthies Martyr Worthy lay nearest to these three places. It is not mentioned in the Domesday Survey. It remained part of the possessions of the prior and monks of St. Swithun's, who in 1205, and again in 1285, obtained a confirmation of their ownership of land at Worthy.[4] In 1251 the prior dealt with the manor and advowson,[5] and by a charter of 1284, confirmed by Edward I in 1285, the bishop quitclaimed for himself and his successors all right in the manor.[6] Martyr Worthy remained in the hands of the prior and convent until the Dissolution,[7] after which the manor was granted to the dean and chapter of Winchester.[8]

The manor must have been sold by the dean and chapter during the eighteenth century to the family of Sheldon, probably to the William Sheldon who in 1728 owned part of the manor of Bereleigh, in East Meon (q.v.). In 1773 his grandson Edward Sheldon sold Martyr Worthy to Sir Chaloner Ogle, bart., whose successor, Sir Charles Ogle, bart., built a mansion here in 1820, which he sold five years later, together with the manorial rights, to Mr. Samuel Wall. The latter died before 1848, being followed by Mr. G. A. E. Wall, who was still holding in 1875. Between this latter date and 1880 the manor passed to Capt. C. G. Fryer, the present owner.

OGLE. *Argent a fesse between three crescents gules.*

There seem to be only two separate references to the tithing of *CHILLAND*, which was usually included in Martyr Worthy.[9] In 1763 William Dale and his wife Elizabeth conveyed the so-called manor of Chilland to Philippa Venables,[10] and in 1789 Elizabeth Gale (possibly Dale), widow, sold it to John Doswell.[11]

CHURCH The church of *ST. SWITHUN* has an apsidal chancel of twelfth-century style built in 1865, a nave 46 ft. by 17 ft. 6 in., and a wooden bell-turret at the west. The nave dates from *c.* 1140–50, its north and south doorways being original work. The north doorway is somewhat more richly treated than the south, and though not now the principal entrance, may at one time have been so. It is roundheaded, of two orders with jamb-shafts, the outer order having a line of horizontal zigzag with a label of billet ornament, while the inner is plain, and the capitals are carved with simple foliage. The south doorway has a label with hatched ornament, a moulded outer order, and a plain inner order; on its east jamb is cut a large cross, perhaps a consecration cross. East of this doorway is an original window retaining its semicircular rear arch, but with a cinquefoiled light of fifteenth-century style, of modern stonework, in place of its former opening. On the north side of the nave is a window corresponding to this, but entirely modern, the twelfth-century rear arch and the fifteenth-century light being alike copied in the new work. Towards the east end of the nave are two-light fifteenth-century windows on north and south, with renewed tracery, and there is another two-light window in the west wall, with a cinquefoil in the head. At the south-east of the nave is a piscina with a groove for a shelf.

MARTYR WORTHY CHURCH

Over the east end of the nave the roof is of lower pitch than elsewhere, with plain heavy timbers in two bays with carved bosses at the intersections and a moulded wall-plate of fifteenth-century style. This appears to be an example of a ceiling over the rood.

The bell-turret dates from 1871, and contains three bells, the treble an early sixteenth-century bell with Roger Landon's marks, inscribed 'Sancte Luce or.'; the second of 1632, inscribed in black-letter smalls, 'In God is my hope'; and the tenor, with the same inscription in Gothic capitals, of 1681

[2] Exch. Dep. 3 Geo. I, No. 7.
[3] Birch, *Cart. Sax.* i, 539. This afterwards became known as the priory of St. Swithun.
[4] *Cal. of Pap. Letters*, i, 21; *Cal. of Chart. R.* 1257–1300, p. 288.
[5] Feet of F. Hants, 35 Hen. III, No. 389.
[6] Chart. R. 13 Edw. I, m. 27.
[7] Inq. p.m. 9 Edw. III (2nd nos.), No. 55.
[8] Pat. 33 Hen. VIII, pt. 9, m. 34–40. In 1557 a mansion house with barns and stable, being the property of 'Robarte Daye, husbandman, and Jane his wife of Marten Wourdye,' was burnt to the 'utter discomforde and undoynge' of the said Day, his wife, and six children, who are commended to the charity of all Christian people. Anct. D. (P.R.O.), A. 6471.
[9] Pat. 33 Hen. VIII, pt. 9, m. 34–40.
[10] Feet of F. Hants, Hil. 4 Geo. III.
[11] Ibid. Mich. 29 Geo. III.

(probably for 1631), both by the founder I H., possibly for John Higden.

The font, near the south door, is modern, with an octagonal bowl on a panelled stem, and there are no ancient fittings in the church.

The plate consists of a silver chalice and paten of 1851, and a modern plated cup, paten, and flagon.

The first book of the registers, on paper, runs from 1539 to 1624 (baptisms 1542–89, marriages 1550–84, burials 1539–80 and 1597–1624); the second from 1633 to 1807, the marriages not after 1753; the third is the printed marriage register 1754–1812, and the fourth contains baptisms and burials 1808–12.

ADVOWSON The earliest mention of a church at Martyr Worthy is in the year 1251, when John la Martre conveyed the advowson of the church to the prior and convent of St. Swithun.[12] In 1535 the church was assessed at £16.[13]

The advowson of the church followed the descent of the manor until the Dissolution, since which time it has been in the hands of the bishop of Winchester.[14] The living is a rectory.

Paul Clapham, vicar of Martyr Worthy, in 1639 was charged with defrauding the parishioners by compounding with excommunicated persons. Other accusations were brought against him, one being 'that he thought it lawful for a man to have as many wives as his estate would keep.'[15]

CHARITIES In 1589 Alderman Pranell, by his will (confirmed by deed 1592 by Agnes Pranell his widow), charged his great messuage and houses in Hart Street, city of London, with an annual payment of £6 13*s.* 4*d.* for the maintenance of a schoolmaster to teach ten poor children born in the parish until the age of sixteen years. The rent-charge is applied in connexion with the National School of the parish.[16]

MEDSTED

The parish of Medsted, covering an area of 2,484 acres of land, lies on the high country which rises north-east of Alresford and south-west of Alton, and slopes down towards the north-west to Preston Candover. Generally speaking the land of the parish rises from south to north, though the highest ground—697 ft. above the ordnance datum—is near the village, which lies more to the west than the north. The main road from Winchester to Alton cutting through the town of New Alresford runs on through Bishop's Sutton to Ropley, and gradually climbing towards Medsted enters the south-eastern corner of the parish, forming its south-eastern boundary line for about a mile. As it enters the parish it sends off a branch road north-west towards the village, passing under a railway bridge on the Alton branch of the London and South Western Railway, which runs through the parish for about a mile and a half, north of and parallel to the main road to Alton. There is a station at Medsted on this line, near the spot locally known as Four Marks, north-east of the bridge.

Leaving the railway bridge and winding between fields and meadows the road continues north by the small iron Congregational chapel standing on the west side and between the several cottages and houses which form that part of the village known as South Town. Then curving slightly east it again turns sharply north and runs between the village green, with its scattered gorse bushes, which stretches to the east, and the trim burial ground hedged in by a thick line of well-growing fir trees. This burial ground was formed and consecrated in 1884 at a cost of £150, and is under the control of a Burial Board of nine members. Past the green and the cemetery the road branches east and west, the eastern branch running towards Alton, the western forming the main village street. Along this the unpicturesque low slated cottages are grouped, with the small village shops and the post office which lies on the south side of the road. Nearly opposite the post office is the old Congregational church, built in 1850, now used as an oil store. Here at the west end of the village a narrow branch curves to the north from the main road, and after sending off a branch north-east towards Bentworth circles round to meet the main road again some few yards up. On the island so formed is the church, standing comparatively near the road in the midst of several fine yew trees; the schools, which stand immediately west of the church; and two or three cottages, which stand behind the church, two facing north, two facing west. On the outer side of the circling road are two or three cottages; the Castle Inn, a plain-fronted house standing behind a narrow courtyard; and the parish hall, consisting of two rooms, erected by the late Mr. Thomas Nuller.

West of the church, on the south side of the main village street, behind a high garden wall, stands Medsted House, round the grounds of which the road curves to the south, downhill towards Bighton. On the north side of the road as it curves stands the rectory, round the east side of which a branch road curves north-west towards Wield, sending off a branch road south-west towards the small tithing of Hattingley about three-quarters of a mile from Medsted village.

Both from Medsted House and from the rectory, and from the high sloping fields which fall away to the west, a panoramic view stretches north and west. To the north over Wield and Preston Candover parishes is seen the dim outline of the high country round Nutley and Farleigh Wallop, and from this running west a fine line of undulating country rising against the horizon, Juniper Hill, Bogmoor Hill, Abbotstone Wood, and Abbotstone Down.

The lane leading to the two farm-houses and the three or four cottages composing Hattingley runs downhill between fields and meadows, beyond which as they stretch away to the north can be seen a long blue line of distant country. Passing one group of thatched cottages on the left the lane approaches the high tiled wall which surrounds the garden of Pullinger's Farm, with its square white farm-house and outbuildings lying on the north side of the road. Nearly opposite, standing back from the road, is

[12] Feet of F. Hants, 35 Hen. III, No. 389.

[13] *Valor Eccl.* (Rec. Com.), ii, 10.

[14] Inst. Bks. (P.R.O.).

[15] *Cal. S.P. Dom.* 1639, p. 182.

[16] *V.C.H. Hants*, ii, 'Schools.'

Hattingley Farm with its substantial farm-house and outbuildings. Some yards on are the two other groups of cottages, standing north and south of the road, which compose the rest of Hattingley. Beyond these the road continues towards the few cottages composing the small hamlet of Heath Green, which lie west of it as it branches north and south near the western border line of the parish.

There are several ancient wells in the village, but owing to the great depth of all they are seldom used, many of the inhabitants being supplied with water from an underground tank. On high ground north of the village are the remains of a circular entrenchment, and there are several barrows in the parish.

The soil is chalk and clay with a subsoil of chalk, producing crops of wheat and oats on the 1,278¼ acres of arable land. The parish is sparsely wooded, the whole 36½ acres of woodland being covered by Boynes Wood in the north-east. Everywhere, however, between the arable fields is rich meadow land, and this with the down land in north and west makes up the 1,069¼ acres of permanent grass.

There is no inclosure award for Medsted. Goatacre Farm preserves one of the old place-names, among which, occurring at least in the sixteenth and seventeenth centuries, are 'Croftpytte,' 'Mayegate,' [1] 'Tennacres,' 'Pitacre,' 'Penland,' 'Layneham Down,' [2] 'Whitewey,' and 'Greenwayes.' [3]

MANORS

Although there is no separate mention of *MEDSTED* either before or at the time of the Domesday Survey, nevertheless, if the identification of place-names that occur in an eighth-century charter of King Ine be correct, Medsted must have been included in a grant of 40 *mansae* of land at Alresford made by that king to Winchester Cathedral in 701, in confirmation of an earlier grant by Kinewald.[4] It consequently formed part of Alresford Liberty (q.v.) and the manor of Old Alresford (q.v.), and is most probably included in the entry under Alresford in Domesday Book.[5] That this is so is supported by a perambulation of the manor taken in the reign of Edward VI,[6] by the fact that the tithing of Medsted sent a tithing-man to the old Alresford court-leet,[7] and also by the circumstance that Anthony Browne, an agent sent down from London to report on the whole bailiwick of Bishop's Sutton [8] previous to its purchase by Sir John Gate in the reign of Edward VI, included in his survey the parish of Medsted, reporting as follows:—'Midsted adjoyning on the sowthest side of Wild and parcell of Old Alresford manor is verie well wodded with great beches and some oks onn everie side the greate wodds thereof, which from the village roun a mile and a haulf of Alton, and onn the west side from the ferme of Alresford downe to the commen felds of Medsted and on the sowth side to London hieghwaie that leadeth from Alresford to Alton, and onn the northe side to the mannor of Wild.' [9]

The parish still forms part of the manor of Old Alresford.

The history of a holding in Medsted, afterwards known as *MEDSTED COURT*, can be traced from the fourteenth century. As late as 1316 the bishop occurs as lord of the vill of Medsted without mention of any sub-tenants of the manor,[10] but in 1346 Richard Houtot, probably a descendant of a family which had held small parcels of land in the parish as early as 1202,[11] was holding a knight's fee here which had belonged to Andrew Houtot,[12] and seven years later Martin de Hertham and Isabel his wife, sister and heiress of Andrew Houtot, conveyed lands, rents, and half a knight's fee in Medsted to William de Overton.[13] He was followed by his son William, who held one fee in Medsted and Tadelyng in 1428 which Richard Houtot had formerly held; [14] and three years later Thomas de Overton, William's son, held the manor of Medsted, a liberty of the bishop of Winchester, by the service of the fourth part of one knight's fee.[15]

In 1501 John Wayte of Titchfield recovered seisin of the manors of Sutton and Medsted against Eleanor Courte; [16] and in 1530 this John Wayte conveyed the manor of Medsted to Richard Lyster,[17] who, however, sold all his right in it to Sir John Leigh in 1556.[18]

LEIGH. *Gules a cross engrailed and a border engrailed argent.*

Sir John Leigh [19] died seised of the manor in 1575,[20] leaving an infant son and heir John, aged one year,[21] who died in 1612, and was succeeded by his son Thomas, a child of six at the time of his father's death.[22] Thomas Leigh died in 1640, leaving a son and heir Philip, aged eleven, who evidently succeeded to the estates on the death of his mother.[23] Philip Leigh still held Medsted in 1653,[24] but between that date and 1699 the manor changed hands, for in the latter year John Henley conveyed it to Joseph Mayor.[25]

In 1748 Edward Rookes was holding Medsted, though whether by purchase or by inheritance is uncertain, and sold it in that year to Sir William Jolliffe for £1,400.[26] After this date no further record of this property has been found.

In the fourteenth century we have records of another holding in Medsted, which after being leased to various tenants was conveyed to Nicholas de Hany-

[1] Eccl. Com. Ct. R. 155967, bdle. 85, No. 3.

[2] Ibid. 158821, bdle. 136, No. 2.

[3] Ibid. 155760, bdle. 99, No. 8.

[4] Birch, *Cart. Sax.* i, 148.

[5] *V.C.H. Hants*, i, 459.

[6] Eccl. Com. Ct. R. bdle. 136, No. 1.

[7] Ibid. bdle. 85, No. 2, &c.

[8] Consisting of the Liberty of Alresford and the hundred of Bishop's Sutton.

[9] *Duchy of Lanc.* Rentals and Surv. bdle. 8, No. 22 *a*.

[10] *Feud. Aids*, ii, 320.

[11] Feet of F. Hants, Trin. 4 John; ibid. 47 Hen. III.

[12] *Feud. Aids*, ii, 334.

[13] Feet of F. Hants, Trin. 27 Edw. III.

[14] *Feud. Aids*, ii, 357.

[15] Ibid. ii, 363.

[16] De Banco R. 17 Hen. VII, m. 249.

[17] Feet of F. Hants, Trin. 22 Hen. VIII. The property at this date became known as the manor of Medsted Court; Eccl. Com. Ct. R. bdle. 136, No. 1.

[18] Ibid. Hil. 3 & 4 Phil. and Mary.

[19] Edward Fitzgarrett and his wife Agnes, daughter of Sir John Leigh, John Leigh, John Glastocke, and Edward Welshe conveyed the manor of Medsted to John More and Richard Bostock in 1565, evidently as a settlement (Feet of F. Div. Cos. East. 9 Eliz.).

[20] In 1571 Thomas Wayte, son of John Wayte, sought to regain possession of land in the manors of Sutton and Medsted, which ought to have descended to him at the death of his father, but of which Sir William Kingsmill had wrongfully possessed himself (Chan. Proc. 13 Eliz. bdle. 195, No. 80).

[21] Chan. Inq. p.m. 18 Eliz. (Ser. 2), pt. 2, No. 82.

[22] W. and L. Inq. p.m. 10 Jas. I, bdle. 45, No. 97.

[23] Chan. Inq. p.m. 16 Chas. I (Ser. 2), pt. 2, No. 85.

[24] Recov. R. Hil. 1653, m. 65.

[25] Feet of F. Hants, Mich. 11 Will. III; Recov. R. Mich. 11 Will. III, m. 243.

[26] Feet of F. Hants, Mich. 22 Geo. II.

ton in 1333.[27] Two years later Nicholas de Hanyton was granted a licence to alienate this land in mortmain to the prior and convent of St. Swithun at Winchester,[28] who retained it until the dissolution of the monasteries.[29] In 1541 it was granted to Sir William Sidney,[30] and subsequently it seems to have become amalgamated with his other lands, as there is no further separate record of it.

CHURCH The church of *ST. ANDREW* has a chancel 22 ft. by 13 ft. 8 in., and a nave 45 ft. by 17 ft., with north transept and aisle, a north-west vestry and south porch, and wooden bell-turret. The whole building was modernized and enlarged in 1833, the nave being lengthened at the time, a west tower destroyed, and the south doorway of the nave blocked up.

Though so completely modernized the building probably preserves the dimensions of its twelfth-century nave and chancel (the lengthening of the nave excepted), the oldest work now existing being the north arcade of the nave, *c.* 1160, of two bays with semicircular arches of a single order chamfered on the angles, square scalloped capitals, and round columns with moulded bases, the whole liberally whitewashed over. The chancel has a modern east window with net tracery, and fourteenth-century trefoiled lights in the north and south walls, the chancel arch being modern, as are all other features of the nave. The vestry and north transept are also modern, but the north aisle retains its original width of 5 ft. 7 in. The font, near the south door, which is to the west of the older blocked doorway, is also modern, and near it is the poor-box on a curious stone bracket, a corbel of three engaged shafts with foliage more like fourteenth-century French work than anything English ; it appears to be ancient, and was formerly an image bracket, on the north side of the east window of the chancel.

There are three bells, the treble by Samuel Knight, 1705, the second and tenor being of 1655 and 1660 respectively.

The plate consists of a communion cup of 1563, with an incised band of ornament on the bowl and another on the foot, and a flat paten, probably of local make, with the date 1680 upon it. The church also possesses a brass cross of Abyssinian workmanship from King Theodore's chapel at Magdala.

The first book of the registers begins in 1560, the baptisms continuing till 1732, the marriages till 1723, and the burials till 1702. The second book runs from 1732 to 1779, and the third from 1780 to 1812, while the fourth is the printed marriage register 1754–1812.

ADVOWSON At the time of the Domesday Survey there were three churches at Alresford,[31] and as Medsted was probably included in Alresford, possibly one of these churches became later the parish church of Medsted. Until quite recently the church of Medsted was attached to that of Old Alresford, and the advowson has therefore followed the descent of Alresford, and was from earliest times in the hands of the bishop of Winchester.

A few years ago the churches were separated, and since then the living of Medsted has been in the gift of the Lord Chancellor.

At the present day the living is a rectory with 7 acres of glebe and residence.

CHARITIES In 1875 Henry Joyce Mulcock, by will proved this date, left £500 to be invested and income applied in the distribution of articles in kind among the poor, the charity to be called 'The Parish of Medsted Trust Fund.' The legacy was invested in £528 15*s.* consols, with the official trustees.

MORESTEAD

The small parish of Morestead, covering an area of 1,701 acres, is on high ground south-east of Winchester, the Roman road from Bishop's Waltham to Winchester forming the northern part of its western boundary. The village lies on comparatively low ground in the south-west of the parish at the junction of the Roman road to Winchester, which forms the main village street, with a narrow lane running across the fields from Twyford, which here crosses the main road and continues a north-westerly course, as Fawley Lane, over Fawley Down to meet the main road from Petersfield to Winchester, just outside the boundaries of Morestead parish. The few cottages that comprise the village, with Complin's Farm, Burgers' Farm, and the church and rectory, lie south of the junction, the church, near which is a reputed Roman well, lying to the east of the main road. South-east of the church is the rectory surrounded by a beautiful old-world garden. On either side the land rises from the village, Morestead Down sweeping away north-east of the Roman road, which cuts its way north between the down and a thick belt of hedgerow. Again to the south-west is Hazely Down, while north and east are Fawley Down and Longwood Warren, where there is a rabbit warren of some local fame. Patches of woodland, St. John's Copse, Grove Copse, and Old Down Copse, mingle with the open country to the south between the village and Old Down Farm, which lies in the furthest south-west corner of the parish. Immediately south of the village, on a branch road leading to Owslebury, is Morestead Farm, south again of which is Morestead House, the property of Mr. R. Eden Richardson, whose large game farm supplies many of the neighbouring estates with birds. To the south-west is a fine house 'The Firs,' the residence of Mr. Joseph Storey Curtis, who owns a large training stable and to whom the lately-inclosed 'No Man's Land,' consisting of about five acres in the extreme south of the parish, belongs.

The soil being loam on chalk is very poor, and although there are 515 acres of arable land as compared with 340 of permanent grass and 35 of woodland, much of the arable land is now being rapidly

[27] Feet of F. Hants, Trin. 7 Edw. III ; ibid. Mich.

[28] Pat. 9 Edw. III, pt. 1, m. 30.

[29] Misc. Bks. 389, 94, fol. 92 ; Chapter House Bks. 26 Hen. VIII, A, bdle. 6, No. 1.

[30] Pat. 33 Hen. VIII, pt. 1, m. 32.

[31] *V.C.H. Hants*, i, 459.

converted into pasture. A considerable number of sheep are reared on the downs, and these with the game farm and racing stable furnish occupation for the inhabitants.

The common lands were inclosed on 10 February, 1859.[1] The tithe map is at the vicarage. Some field names in the parish were 'Suffle, Barrow Croft, Hern Croft, Dungerts, and Winderane.'

MANORS There seems to be little doubt that *MORESTEAD* was originally one of the eight sub-manors in Chilcomb mentioned at the time of the Domesday Survey; and one of the nine churches included in Chilcomb at this date probably became the parish church of Morestead.[2] The bishops of Winchester seem to have retained possession of Morestead until nearly the end of the thirteenth century; for Morestead is not mentioned by name in the charter of 1205, under which various manors in Hampshire passed into the hands of the prior and convent of St. Swithun, Winchester;[3] but by 1284 the manor was in the possession of the prior and convent, and owed suit at the bishop's court.[4] In 1316 the vill of Morestead was in the hands of the prior of St. Swithun's,[5] and there are a few records of leases by him. In 1338 Philip Marmyon conveyed a messuage, a carucate of land, 20 acres of wood, and 8*s.* rent in Morestead to John Sauncere and his wife Julia, to be held by John and Julia and the heirs of Julia;[6] and in 1525 John Dyker conveyed the manor of Morestead, together with lands, tenements, and rent in Morestead, to William Thorpe and others.[7]

After the dissolution of the monasteries Morestead with many other lands formerly belonging to St. Swithun's became part of the endowment of the dean and chapter of Winchester Cathedral;[8] they granted Morestead Manor to Richard Lyster, who died possessed of it, held of the dean and chapter, in 1558.[9]

CARNEGIE, Earl of Northesk. *Or an eagle sable with a naval crown or on his breast and the word* TRAFALGAR *in the chief.*

Richard Lyster had sold a great deal of his land to Sir John Leigh in 1556;[10] and the Leighs evidently bought Morestead Manor, for it was in their possession in 1567.[11] In 1612 Sir John Leigh, son of the Sir John Leigh mentioned in 1556, died seised of the capital messuage of Morestead, which he held from the dean and chapter of Winchester, as of their manor of Barton formerly Chilcomb.[12]

In 1682 Morestead was in the possession of the cathedral church of Winchester,[13] which continued to hold it until the middle of the nineteenth century. At some date between 1859 and 1866 the earl of Northesk must have bought the property, his grandson, the present earl, being lord of the manor.[14]

CHURCH The church (no dedication known) is a small building with a twelfth-century nave 14 ft. 8 in. wide, a modern chancel of 1873, a modern south porch and western brick bell-cot, and a brick building dating from 1833 set against the west wall of the nave, which has served its turn as a school, and is now disused. Its site is said to have been occupied by the old rectory pulled down in 1833. The chancel is lighted by modern round-headed windows, and has a modern chancel arch springing from corbels, while the nave has one north and two south windows, likewise modern. Its walls are 2 ft. 5 in. thick, and the north doorway, which has a plain round head with a chamfered string at the springing, is of mid-twelfth-century date, while the south doorway has a head which may be of the same period but reworked, its jambs being modern. At the west end of the nave is a pointed window blocked up. The nave roof with its tie-beams is old, but all other fittings in the church are modern except the font, which stands near the south door, and is of a common late twelfth-century type, of Purbeck marble, with an octagonal bowl on a central and smaller flanking shafts, each face of the bowl being worked with two pointed arches.

The single bell bears in rough lettering I H 1616.

The communion plate is modern, consisting of a chalice of 1872 with flagon and paten of the preceding year.

The first book of the registers, a parchment copy apparently made about 1656, begins in 1549 and goes to 1811, the marriages not being entered after 1754. The second book is a copy of the baptisms and burials 1800–11 taken from the first book, and the third is the marriage register 1760–1811. There is also a book of the overseers of the poor, 1813–35.

ADVOWSON Morestead church was probably among the nine churches mentioned in Domesday as belonging to the manor of Chilcomb[15] (q.v.). The advowson is now, and always has been, held by the bishop of Winchester.[16] In 1285 the prior and convent of St. Swithun received confirmation of a charter by which they received the Easter offerings and a pension from the church of Morestead.[17] In 1291 the church was assessed at £5;[18] and by 1535 the value had risen to £6 3*s.* 8*d.*[19] In 1658 Morestead was temporarily united with Chilcomb parish by order of the Trustees for the Maintenance of Ministers.[20] The living is now a rectory.

Joseph D'Arcy Sirr, D.D., rector of Morestead 1859–68, was the author of *A Memoir of Archbishop Trench* and the *Life of Archbishop Usher*.[21]

1 *Parl. Accts. and Papers*, vol. 71, 485–523.
2 *V.C.H. Hants*, i, 463.
3 *Cal. Pap. Letters*, i, 21.
4 Add. MS. 29, 436, fol. 59; Eccl. Com. Ct.R. bdle. 80, No. 1. It is stated in the St. Swithun charters that Morestead, a possession of the prior and convent, owed, together with eight other manors, certain services to the bishop of Winchester, about which services a compromise was made.
5 *Feud. Aids*, ii, 320.
6 Feet of F. Hants, Mich. 12 Edw. III.
7 Ibid. East. 17 Hen. VIII. The extent of the manor at this date is given as 2 messuages, 500 acres of land, 200 acres of pasture, 100 acres of meadow, 10 acres of wood, and 40*s.* rent.
8 Pat. 33 Hen. VIII, pt. 9, m. 34–40; *L. and P. Hen. VIII*, xvi, 505.
9 Chan. Inq. p.m. 1 Eliz. (Ser. 2), pt. 3, No. 222.
10 Feet of F. Hants, Hil. 3 & 4 Phil. and Mary.
11 Ibid. East. 9 Eliz.
12 W. and L. Inq. p.m. 10 Jas. I, bdle. 45, No. 97.
13 *Winch. Cath. Doc.* (Hants Rec. Soc.), ii, 185.
14 *P.O. Dir.* 1848, 1855, 1859, 1867, 1875, 1880, 1885.
15 *V.C.H. Hants*, i, 463.
16 *Cal. Pap. Letters*, ii, 206; Inst. Bks. (P.R.O.).
17 *Cal. of Chart. R.* 1257–1300, p. 288.
18 *Pope Nich. Tax.* (Rec. Com.), 210.
19 *Valor Eccl.* (Rec. Com.), ii, 6.
20 *Cal. S.P. Dom.* 1657–8, p. 376.
21 *Dict. Nat. Biog.*

OVINGTON

Edintune (xi cent.) ; Edyneton (xiii cent.).

The parish of Ovington, covering 1,288 acres of the country which stretches southwards from the valley of the Itchen to become part of the ridge of down land which stretches south and east of Winchester, is long and narrow, being about four miles in length and barely a mile in breadth at its widest part. Approaching the village from Itchen Stoke a pathway along the river bank between two branches of the Itchen leads to a ford over the widest part of the river, from which the first houses of the village of Ovington, lying on the slope rising to the south from the valley, can be seen. The uphill road leads past the Bush Inn, a small unobtrusive house lying to the west near the river, on past the smithy, two or three modern houses and several low-thatched cottages, one of which serves as the post office, to the church of St. Peter, which stands to the east of the road. Near by the church is a group of tiled half-timbered cottages, on one of which is a tablet G.F.H. 1847. The rectory is almost opposite, south of Ovington Park Farm. South of the church low white gates lead up a short drive to Ovington House, the seat of Mrs. Hewson, lady of the manor, which stands in the midst of finely-wooded country, beyond which Ovington Park stretches away to its boundary, the main road which leads from Winchester through Chilcomb and Tichborne to New Alresford. Beyond the main road the south of the parish is one long sweep of down land, rising to a height of over 500 ft. above the sea level near Longwood Warren. Ovington Down Farm and Ovington Down Cottages lying along Rodfield Lane, which is a continuation of the village street across the down land, are the only traces of human existence in the midst of this lonely country.

The soil of the parish is clay, the subsoil chalk, and since this is so and since most of the country is down land there are only 561 acres of arable land and 13 acres of woodland as compared with 328½ acres of permanent grass. Ordinary crops—wheat, oats, barley, and roots—are produced. The common lands were inclosed in 1811–12.[1]

MANORS There are two entries in Domesday with reference to the manor of *OVINGTON*[2] ; in the first it was held by the bishop[3] ; in the second it is said to be in the possession of the abbey of St. Mary at Winchester, for whom the bishop evidently held it. It had previously been held by Archbishop Stigand. Formerly Ovington had been assessed at one and a half hides ; in 1086 the whole of the revenue was appropriated to the support of the nuns.[4]

Between 1086 and 1316 the nuns were constantly in pecuniary difficulties[5] ; it is probable that in order to raise money they sold the manor to St. Swithun's before 1284, as in that year John bishop of Winchester gave up all his right in the manor to the prior and convent of St. Swithun.[6] The manor evidently remained in the possession of St. Swithun's until the Dissolution ;[7] and in 1542 Ovington Manor lately belonging to St. Swithun's was granted to the dean and chapter of Winchester ;[8] it was in the possession of the cathedral church of Winchester in 1682 ;[9] and in 1701 the dean and chapter of Winchester were still lords of the manor.[10]

In 1855 and 1859 the manorial rights were the subject of a dispute between the bishop of Winchester and the Baroness van Zandt of Ovington Park, who had inherited the estate from her father, Mr. James Standerwick. Between 1859 and 1866 this estate passed to Captain G. F. Hewson, whose widow, Mrs. Hewson, is the present owner.

At the time of the Domesday Survey there was half a mill in Ovington worth 7*s.* ;[11] there is no mill in the parish at the present day.

CHURCH The church of *ST. PETER*, entirely rebuilt in 1865–6, consists of a chancel with north vestry, north and south transepts, a nave with south-west tower, the ground stage of which serves as an entrance porch. In the porch is preserved an ancient holy-water stone. The font is of Purbeck marble, with a bowl ornamented with shallow arcades, after a late twelfth-century fashion, but there is nothing else in the church with any pretensions to antiquity.

There are four bells, the treble by Warner, 1881 ; the second and tenor by the same founder, 1866 ; and the third by Mears, 1820.

The plate consists of a cup of 1807, with paten and flagon of 1811, all presented in July 1811 by George Lowther.

The first book of the registers contains all entries from 1591 to 1738, and the second baptisms and burials 1738–85, and marriages to 1754. The third has marriages 1755–1812, and the fourth baptisms and burials 1786–1813.

ADVOWSON There is no mention of a church in *OVINGTON* at the time of the Domesday Survey. One, however, existed before 1284, as in that year the king gave up to John bishop of Winchester and his successors all his right in the advowson of the church of Ovington.[12] In 1291 Ovington church was valued at £5,[13] and by 1535 the value had risen to £12.[14]

The bishop of Winchester was patron of Ovington until about the year 1870,[15] when the advowson passed into the hands of the bishop of Lichfield,[16] and remained in his gift for some fifteen years. From 1890 to the present day the Lord Chancellor has presented to the living.[17]

CHARITIES There were formerly in this parish about two acres of land considered to belong to the church which became intermixed with private property, and could not be identified. In 1820 Sir Thomas Richard Dyer, bart. (who by marriage had come into possession of the

1 *Local and Pers. Acts of Parl.* 52 Geo. III, cap. 41.
2 It was in Mainsbridge Hundred at this date.
3 *V.C.H. Hants*, i, 462.
4 Ibid. i, 474.
5 *Feud. Aids*, ii, 320.
6 Chart. R. 13 Edw. I, m. 27.
7 Ibid.
8 Pat. 33 Hen. VIII, pt. 9, m. 34–40. *L. and P. Hen. VIII*, xvi, 878 (1).
9 *Winch. Cath. Doc.* (Hants Rec. Soc.), ii, 182–5.
10 Add. MSS. Stowe, 845, fol. 53.
11 *V.C.H. Hants*, i, 462.
12 Chart. R. 12 Edw. I, m. 5.
13 *Pope Nich. Tax.* (Rec. Com.), 211.
14 *Valor Eccl.* (Rec. Com.), ii, 9.
15 Inst. Bks. (P.R.O.).
16 *Clergy List*, 1865–70.
17 Ibid. 1890–1906.

property in question), entered into an agreement with the parishioners to pay 40*s.* a year to the churchwardens to be applied towards the repairs of the church.

There are also belonging to the church about three acres of land in the parish. The annual sum of 40*s.*, together with the rents of the land, is carried to the churchwardens' general accounts.

OWSLEBURY

Oselbury (xiv. cent.) ; Owlesbury (xiv cent.).

The parish of Owslebury consists of 22 acres of land covered with water and 5,412 acres of land which rises gradually from south to north, reaching the greatest height, with the exception of the rise on Green Hill in the west of the parish, near the village, which stands on the crest of a hill towards the north. The main road from Winchester to Bishop's Waltham, passing south-east through Morestead, sends off a branch road directly south towards Owslebury. Rising on to high ground this road then descends steeply into Owslebury parish. At the bottom of the hill two or three thatched cottages and the Shearer's Inn standing on the right-hand side make up the outlying portion of Owslebury, known as Owslebury Bottom. A few yards on as the land begins to rise the road curves slightly east round by the Cricketers' Inn and winds up the hill, curving sharply south-west into the village. Entering the village, the blacksmith's shop, a low tiled picturesque building, stands on the north side of the road facing wide sloping fields which stretch away to the south. As the road continues uphill, past two or three thatched cottages and outbuildings, the old windmill, near which is a new mill which supplies the pumping power for the Owslebury waterworks, stands in a high field to the north, marking the crest of the hill. Beyond this the greater number of the cottages and houses composing the village are grouped. On the south side of the road are the village schools, immediately west of which is the square-towered church of St. Andrew, standing on high ground overlooking the valley as the ground falls away to the east and south-east. Immediately to the east over the valley lies Baybridge, beyond which the high land which sweeps away to Millbarrow Down rises in the distance ; to the south-east, over the stretches of woodland which lie in the south-east of Owslebury parish, lies the parish of Upham, beyond which rises the high ground round Winter's Hill House. South-west of the church is the vicarage, to which a pathway from the church leads across the square inclosed recreation ground of about four acres. The village stocks stood at the churchyard gate until recent times, but have now disappeared. As the long village street continues to run south-west down the slope of the hill beyond the church and vicarage, several picturesque thatched cottages lie on the left, while others lie on either side as at the further end of the village the road forks north to Twyford and south to Marwell Hall, round a small triangular green. On the north side as the road forks stand two tiled lichen-covered cottages, known as Yew-tree Cottages, in front of which grow two large yew trees, shaped like the trees of a toy Noah's Ark. Beyond these cottages is the Ship Inn, a low, thatched, timber-framed house, which has some good panelling within, and the date 1681 on the tap-room fireplace. Marwell Manor Farm, the manor farm of Owslebury parish, stands on the site of the ancient palace of Marwell, which was probably destroyed[1] in the sixteenth century, after the grant to Sir Henry Seymour, who already had a house in the adjoining manor of Marwell Woodlock. The site is marked by a large moated inclosure within which the present dwelling-house stands, but such old masonry as is now to be seen is said to belong rather to the college of priests founded here than to the episcopal house. Beyond the moat to the south is a small early sixteenth-century building now used as a cottage.

Marwell Hall, the manor-house of Marwell Woodlock, now the property and residence of Captain William Standish, J.P., belongs for the most part to the nineteenth century, having been almost rebuilt about 1816 by Mr. William Long, on the site and in the style of the former building. It retains, however, in its central portion, once the hall of an H-shaped house, a certain amount of old work. A very fine wooden chimney-piece with the Seymour crest, and a stone panel of their arms now above the fireplace in the entrance hall, are from the old building. The house has a fine position in about seven acres of well-wooded grounds, the western edge of which extends along the crown of the sloping fields that rise east of Hensting hamlet in the south-west of the parish. Tradition asserts that the old house, built probably in the early part of the sixteenth century, was the scene of the marriage between Henry VIII and Lady Jane Seymour, the sister of the lord of Marwell. Edward VI is also said to have visited Marwell Hall, and the initials E. R. were carved in stone over the porch of the old house. Tradition of another kind makes Marwell Hall the scene of the well-known 'Mistletoe Bough' tragedy.[2]

The hamlet of Baybridge, consisting of a small group of cottages, a Primitive Methodist chapel, and the farm-houses and out-buildings of Baybridge and Lower Whiteflood Farms, lies about a mile, as the crow flies, south-east of Owslebury village. It is approached from Owslebury by a branch road leading south from the road which runs north-east from the village to Longwood House, and the cottages and farms stand about three-quarters of a mile along the branch road at the corner where it sends off a branch south-west to Marwell.

The hamlet of Hensting lies in the south-east of the parish, and is approached from Owslebury village by a downhill lane which branches south-west from the narrow road which turns off north towards Twyford by the Ship Inn at the west end of the village. This lane, passing between fine stretches of meadow and plough-land, comes to the outbuildings and the long thatched barn of Hensting Farm, behind which stands the farm-house on high ground. Passing on it curves more directly south between the cottages and farmyards of Hensting and runs on to the high pine woods which slope from the north towards Fisher's Pond, the long narrow stretch of water which runs along the south

[1] Duthy, *Sketches of Hampshire*, 307.

[2] For full description of Marwell Hall see Duthy, *Sketches of Hampshire*, 308–14.

side of the road, and gives its name to the small hamlet which lies immediately south-west. Woods also rise from the south side of the pond, which is thus one of the most beautiful spots in the neighbourhood. Water fowl of all sorts haunt the banks of the pond, and the deep water affords good fishing which is carefully preserved. West of the pond goes the main road from Winchester to Botley, and on the east side of this stands the Queen's Head Inn and the two or three cottages composing Fisher's Pond hamlet. Continuing from Fisher's Pond the main road rises to Crowd Hill, on the top of which on either side of the road are grouped the cottages and farms composing the hamlet of Crowd Hill, the southern portion of which belongs to Fair Oak (see under Bishopstoke). From the top of Crowd Hill remarkably fine views open out on almost every side. To the north-west is the fine woodland surrounding Cranbury House, followed by the high down land that composes the north-west of Compton parish; to the north over Twyford village are the fine curves of Twyford Downs, stretching away towards the east to the high country round Chilcomb. Colden Common, formed into a separate ecclesiastical parish in 1843, is for civil purposes included partly in Owslebury and partly in Twyford.

Formerly there was an iron foundry in Owslebury parish; but all traces of this have disappeared except a few specimens of the work, dated in the latter part of the seventeenth century. The soil of the whole parish is clay with a subsoil of chalk on which crops of wheat, barley, oats, turnips, and sainfoin are grown.

The tithe map is at the vicarage.

The common lands were inclosed in 1851.[3] Of the 5,399 acres of land in the parish, 2,520 are arable land, 1,570¼ are permanent grass, and 827 are woodland.[4] Owslebury Down and part of Colden Common were inclosed in 1861.[5]

The following place-names occur in 1400: Varlonde, Waddene, Tichehurst, Okheltislade, le Hurst, and Grenewey.[6]

MANORS

As early as 964 King Eadgar granted lands in Owslebury to the bishop of Winchester,[7] and at the time of the Domesday Survey the bishop held the manor of Owslebury under the name of Twyford. It was held under the bishops in the time of Edward the Confessor by Wulfric, the under-tenant in 1086 being Elded wife of Oswald.[8]

In 1284 the king gave up to John bishop of Winchester and his successors all his right in the manor of Twyford with Marwell,[9] the name by which this manor in Owslebury was known. There are occasional notices of the ownership of Owslebury by the see of Winchester. In 1313 Bartholomew of Widehaye who held under the bishop conveyed two messuages and two carucates of land in Owslebury held of the bishop to William de Overton and Joan his wife;[10] and after this date, though the name of the parish remained Owslebury, the name of the manor in the parish became *MARWELL* or *MARWELL WOODLOCK*. A pardon was granted to William Woodlock[11] in 1316 for acquiring in fee without licence land in the manor of Marwell from Henry late bishop of Winchester. The land and tenements were to be subject to a rent of 55*s.* 4*d.* payable to the bishop; and service was due at the bishop's court of Marwell.[12]

Bishop Fox, who founded Corpus Christi College, Oxford, in 1515–16, endowed it with the demesne lands round Owslebury, which the college retains at the present day.[13]

In 1520 Lionel Norreys held half the manor from the bishop;[14] and in 1523 William Holgyle held the remainder and conveyed it by fine to Richard Wotton.[15]

When John Poynet was granted the see of Winchester in 1551 one of the conditions attached to his appointment was that he should surrender all the episcopal manors in exchange for a fixed income of 2,000 marks, and thus Marwell passed into the hands of the crown.[16] In the same year the manor and the advowson of the vicarage were granted to Sir Henry Seymour, the king's uncle.[17] The manor of Marwell, among other lands, was restored by Queen Mary to the bishopric of Winchester; but Sir Henry Seymour evidently compounded with John bishop of Winchester for Marwell, as in 1577 he died seised of it, leaving a son and heir John,[18] who died in 1618 and was followed by his son Edward.[19]

SEYMOUR. *Gules a pair of wings or.*

In 1625 Sir Edward Seymour and Henry Seymour conveyed the manor with all appurtenances to Susanna Holliday widow,[20] daughter of Sir Henry Rowe; who married as her second husband Robert earl of Warwick.[21] In 1626 she and her husband conveyed the manor of Marwell to Sir Henry Mildmay and his wife Anne, the latter being Susanna's daughter by her first husband.[22] The manor then descended in the male line. On the death of Carew Mildmay of Shawford House, Hants, at the end of the eighteenth century, it passed to his daughter Jane, who had married Sir Henry Paulet St. John, bart. In 1786 the latter obtained licence to use the name and bear the arms of Mildmay

MILDMAY. *Argent three lions azure.*

[3] *Local and Pers. Acts of Parl.* 14 & 15 Vict. cap. 54.

[4] Statistics from Bd. of Agric. (1905).

[5] *Parl. Accts. and Papers*, vol. 71, 485–523.

[6] *Cal. of Pat.* 1399–1401, p. 396.

[7] Birch, *Cart. Sax.* iii, 412.

[8] *V.C.H. Hants*, i, 460.

[9] Chart. R. 12 Edw. I, m. 5.

[10] Feet of F. Hants, Trin. 7 Edw. II.

[11] Walter Woodlock obtained licence to inclose land in Marwell in 1310, this licence being confirmed in 1400 (*Cal. of Pat.* 1399–1401, p. 396).

[12] Pat. 9 Edw. II, pt. 2, m. 3; *Feud. Aids*, ii, 320.

[13] In 1535 its rents from lands in Owslebury amounted to £3 3*s.* 5½*d.* (*Valor Eccl.* [Rec. Com.], ii 245) and at the same date Lionel Norreys rented lands in Marwell Woodlock from Corpus Christi for £13 6*s.* 8*d.* per annum. In 1648 Sir John Arundel was lessee of the Corpus Christi lands in Owslebury and compounded as a recusant. *Cal. of Com. for Comp.* i, 105.

[14] Feet of F. Hants, East. 12 Hen. VIII.

[15] Ibid. Trin. 25 Hen. VIII.

[16] Pat. 5 Edw. VI, pt. 6, m. 20.

[17] Ibid. pt. 5, m. 29.

[18] Chan. Inq. p.m. 20 Eliz. (Ser. 2), pt. 2, No. 64.

[19] Ibid. 16 Jas. I (Ser. 2), pt 2, No. 39.

[20] Notes of F. Hants, Mich. 1 Chas. I.

[21] G.E.C. *Complete Peerage*, viii, 67.

[22] Feet of F. Hants, Hil. 2 Chas. I; Recov. R. East. 52 Geo. III, m. 27; ibid. East. 54 Geo. III, m. 74.

as well as his own.[23] Sir Henry left his Hampshire estates to be divided between his widow and his thirteen children. Marwell remained in the possession of the Mildmays until 1858, when it was sold to Mr. J. E. Robinson of Pontefract, who transferred the manorial rights to Mr. Bradley, the present owner.[24]

There are occasional references to the bishop of Winchester's *PARK of MARWELL.* In 1280 an order was issued to William de Hamilton, guardian of the bishopric of Winchester, for the immediate deliverance of five oaks from the park of Marwell granted by Nicholas late bishop of Winchester to the sacristan of St. Swithun's Priory, for the works of the priory.[25] In the Ministers' Accounts for the manor of Twyford for the year 1322 the following occurs: '39*s.* 6*d.* for animals pastured in the park of Marwell till Trinity.'[26] In the sixteenth century a complaint was entered by William bishop of Winchester that Aumary St. Amand with others hunted in his park at Marwell where he had free warren.[27] A park existed down to the middle of the seventeenth century, for in the court rolls for 1651 reference is made to the 'park of the President and Scholars of Corpus Christi College, Oxford, called the Coney Park.'[28]

At the time of the Domesday Survey there were two mills in Owslebury,[29] and among the appurtenances belonging to the manors of Twyford and Marwell in 1625 and 1626 were two mills, a free fishery, view of frankpledge, and rights of free warren.[30] At the present day there is only one mill.

BRAMBRIDGE, a hamlet in the civil parishes of Twyford and Owslebury, became part of the newly-formed ecclesiastical parish of Colden Common in 1843.

Upon the foundation of Corpus Christi College, Oxford, in 1515–16, Brambridge, as part of Owslebury parish, probably passed into the possession of the college under the endowment by Bishop Fox, for in 1535 Corpus Christi College was receiving an annual rent of 24*s.* from land here.[31] In 1609–10 Brambridge was granted to John Peirson together with the lands belonging to the recusants Ursula Uvedale, Richard Bruning, and Thomas Welles.[32] Charles I granted Brambridge to Gilbert Welles in 1636,[33] and his widow married Sir William Courtenay, who was a recusant and compounded for his Brambridge estates in 1648.[34] Brambridge remained in the Welles family until towards the end of the eighteenth century, when in accordance with the will of Henry Welles (2 August, 1762) it passed to his cousin Walter Smythe, second son of Sir John Smythe, bart., of Acton Burnell, Shropshire[35] (see under Boyatt in Otterbourne). Walter Smythe's eldest daughter was the famous Mrs. Fitzherbert, wife of George IV, who spent the early years of her life, before and after her education in France, at Brambridge until her marriage to Edward Weld of Lulworth Castle, Dorset. She is also said to have lived at Colden Common, in a cottage which still exists, during her first widowhood.[35a] During the nineteenth century Brambridge House (see under Twyford) was the residence of the Fairbairns family. It is now occupied by Major Cecil du P. Powney.

The earliest mention of *BAYBRIDGE* (Baberigge, Babbrigge, Barbridge, xiv cent.), a hamlet in Owslebury parish, seems to be in a grant made in 1324 by Henry bishop of Winchester of a messuage and half a virgate of land in Baybridge, near Owslebury, to William son of William de Overton, in confirmation of a grant made to him by John late bishop of Winchester of the land formerly held by Henry le Carter.[36] In 1377 the abbot and convent of Titchfield were holding land in Baybridge.[37]

In 1441 Thomas Sands died seised of lands in Baybridge held under lease from the bishop of Winchester, leaving an infant heir, William, aged three.[38] The Sands continued to hold the reputed manor[39] of Baybridge until 1610,[40] when Sir William Sands sold it to Thomas Ridley, LL.D.[41] Nine years later, in 1619, the Ridleys were still holding Baybridge,[42] but after this date no mention has been found of it until the year 1802, when Sir Henry Paulet St. John Mildmay, John Clerk of Worthy, and George William Ricketts of Lainston were holding it in right of their wives Jane, Ann, and Letitia,[43] the daughters and co-heirs of Carew Mildmay of Shawford House.[44] It must therefore have been acquired by the Mildmay family in addition to their manor of Marwell (q.v.). After 1802 it evidently became amalgamated with the Marwell estate and followed its descent (q.v.).

SANDS. *Argent a ragged cross sable.*

The capital messuage of *LONGWOOD FARM*, originally part of the possessions of the bishopric of Winchester, was granted to Edward Vaughan and Thomas Ellys in 1589.[45] Eight years later Longwood was in the possession of Richard Garth, who died seised of it in 1597.[46] In 1648 Longwood Warren and Lodge were sold by the Trustees for the Sale of Bishops' Lands to Thomas Hussey and his heirs.[47]

Longwood House is now the property of the earl of Northesk and the residence of Lord Aberdare. It stands in the north-east of the parish in wide grounds which extend north-east into the neighbouring parish of Tichborne. When Duthy wrote in the early part of the nineteenth century this house was known as Rosehill. About the beginning of the eighteenth century General (afterwards Lord) Carpenter, the ancestor of the earls of Tyrconnel, lived at Rosehill, then called Longwood, which is thus its original name.

[23] Debrett, *Illustrated Baronetage*, 557.
[24] Information supplied by Colonel Mildmay.
[25] *Cal. of Close*, 1279–88, p. 11.
[26] Mins. Accts. bdle. 1142, No. 13.
[27] Early Chan. Proc. bdle. 68, No. 127.
[28] Eccl. Com. Ct. R. bdle. 84, No. 23.
[29] *V.C.H. Hants*, i, 460*a*.
[30] Feet of F. Hants, Mich. 1 Chas. I; ibid. Hil. 2 Chas. I.
[31] *Valor Eccl.* (Rec. Com.), ii, 245.
[32] Pat. 6 Jas. I, pt. 3, m. 19.
[33] Ibid. 11 Chas. I, pt. 2, m. 23.
[34] *Cal. of Com. for Comp.* iii, 1841–2.
[35] Recov. R. Trin. 19 Geo. III, m. 156; Hil. 21 Geo. III, m. 73.
[35a] Wilkins, *Mrs. Fitzherbert and George IV*, i, 7, 16 & 17.
[36] *Cal. of Pat.* 1321–4, p. 400.
[37] Inq. p.m. 51 Edw. III (2nd Nos.), No. 42.
[38] Inq. p.m. 20 Hen. VI, No. 35.
[39] So-called for the first time in 1493 (De Banco R. East. 9 Hen. VII, m. 21).
[40] Corpus Christi College, Oxford, received 49*s.* rent from Baybridge in 1535 as well as rents from Owslebury of the gift of Bishop Fox (vide Marwell Manor). *Valor Eccl.* (Rec. Com.), ii, 245.
[41] Feet of F. Hants, Mich. 11 Jas. I.
[42] Ibid. Trin. 17 Jas. I.
[43] Ibid. 42 Geo. III.
[44] Berry, *Hants Gen.* 228–9.
[45] Pat. 32 Eliz. pt. 23, m. 25–31.
[46] Chan. Inq. p.m. 40 Eliz. vol. 255, No. 169.
[47] Close, 24 Chas. I, pt. 2, m. 23.

CHURCH The church of *ST. ANDREW* has a chancel 28 ft. by 16 ft. 3 in., nave with aisles 33 ft. 8 in. long by 38 ft. wide, and west tower 10 ft. by 11 ft., all measurements being internal.

The chancel appears to be the earliest part of the church, dating from the first quarter of the fourteenth century, and the building has at one time been cruciform, but in the latter part of the seventeenth century the nave and tower were remodelled, and in spite of later repairs a good deal of work of this date yet exists.

The chancel has an east window of three lights with modern tracery of geometrical style, the rear arch being old. On north and south are single uncusped lights with modern heads, and below that on the north a tomb recess, apparently of early fourteenth-century date, as are the old parts of the windows. The chancel arch is pointed, of two chamfered orders, with seventeenth-century capitals of classic design.

The nave is covered by a central roof running east and west, and pairs of gabled roofs on each side, running north and south, a single cast-iron column on each side supporting the wall plates. It is lighted by two north and two south windows, of which all but the south-east window are of three uncusped lights with tracery, of seventeenth-century date, the remaining window having trefoiled lights under a transom and trefoiled tracery over. In the west wall on either side of the tower is a doorway, that to the north having a pointed head of two moulded orders and a label, and that to the south a modern shouldered arch.

The tower is of three stages, embattled, with a west window in the ground stage of two trefoiled lights, curious work which is dated by a panel over it bearing the initials of the churchwardens for 1675. The tower arch appears to be of the same date. In the second stage and belfry stage are windows of fourteenth-century style but modern stonework.

The roofs of the nave are of the trussed rafter form, and the panels from destroyed seventeenth-century pews, with carved top rails, are fixed as wainscoting round the nave walls. The altar rails are eighteenth-century balusters, and in the chancel is an ancient iron-barred chest with three locks, made from a solid log.

Below the east window are four quatrefoiled stone panels inclosing blank shields, of fifteenth-century date; on one shield is a dent to which the tradition attaches that it was made by a bullet which killed the priest who celebrated the last mass here in the sixteenth century.

The font, at the west end of the nave, is octagonal with a moulded base to the bowl, and perhaps of fifteenth-century date, but much re-tooled.

In the chancel are some large marble mural monuments to the first and second Lords Carpenter, 1731 and 1749; and to the last earl of Tyrconnel, 1853.

There are six bells, the first three by Mears and Stainbank, 1905; the fourth, formerly of 1674, recast by Taylor in 1900; and the fifth and tenor, of 1622 and 1619, by the founder I H (possibly for John Higden), with the usual inscription, 'In God is my hope'; on the fifth is the founder's mark of Roger Landon, re-used.

The church possesses a very fine and early communion cup of 1552, inscribed 'The Communion Cup of Owsylbury,' and an almsdish with the inscription 'This with my soule I dedicate to God—Alice Mildemay, June the 8th, 1680.'

The first book of the registers is of burials in woollen, 1678–1812; and the second contains the baptisms 1696–1812 and the marriages 1696–1704, 1722, and 1744–54.

Bishop Henry of Blois founded a small college of secular priests, called later a chantry, in the church or chapel of Marwell Park, Owslebury, between 1129 and 1171,[48] to which were attached four chapelries.

The site of the episcopal house at Marwell Park is marked by a square moat inclosing a large area, at the north-east corner of which stand the remains of the college buildings, now of little importance, and serving as out-buildings to the present dwelling-house, which though in itself of no architectural interest, is built with fragments of the old work. No details appear to be older than the fifteenth century. It was suppressed under the Act of Edward VI for the dissolution of such foundations.

ADVOWSON The earliest mention of the present church of St. Andrew seems to be in the year 1551, when the advowson of the vicarage of Marwell, the site of the ancient chapel in Marwell Park, and the manor, were granted to Sir Henry Seymour.[49] The advowson was annexed to the manor of Marwell until 1836, since which date it has been in the hands of the vicar of Twyford.[50]

CHARITIES In 1840 Mrs. Alice Long, by will proved this date, directed (*inter alia*) that sufficient stock should be purchased to produce £30 a year to be applied by the incumbent in payment of her usual subscriptions to the parochial school, and subject thereto in the purchase of fuel, blankets, clothing, or provisions for the benefit of the deserving poor.

£1,000 consols was set aside in satisfaction of this legacy, and forms part of a larger sum held by the Corporation of Winchester in trust for this and other charities founded by this donor. By an order made under the Board of Education Act, 1899, a sum of £400 consols has been determined to be the proportion of the charity applicable for educational purposes.

48 *V.C.H. Hants*, ii, 211.

49 Pat. 5 Edw. VI, pt. 5, m. 29.

50 *Clerical Guide*, 1836–41; *Clergy List*, 1845–1904.

PRIVETT

Pryvet (xiv cent.) ; Pryvate (xvi cent.).

The parish of Privett, containing about 1,279 acres, 31¼ acres of which are arable land and 30¼ acres permanent grass,[1] lies east of Winchester on high ground which rises to nearly 600 ft. above the sea level in several parts of the parish. The village is in the south of the parish, and consists mainly of a number of scattered farms and cottages grouped for the most part at Filmer Hill in the west, at Bailey Green, and at the junction of the road from West Tisted to Petersfield with a branch road coming from Froxfield. Holy Trinity Church with the vicarage and schools is in this latter group, the nucleus of the village, the church standing in a fine situation on high ground overlooking the Meon valley south of the Froxfield road, while the vicarage is to the north. The schools lie away a few yards to the south, to the west of the road to Petersfield, which here makes a rapid winding descent to the south to meet the main road from Winchester to Petersfield. The Wheatsheaf Inn and the smithy are situated in the midst of pine trees near Filmer Hill.

Privett station on the Meon Valley line lies north of the village a few yards east of the Alton road. After passing the railway station the Alton road runs parallel to the railway line, which is, however, hidden by high hedges and pine trees. One of the entrances to Basing Park (which is in Froxfield parish, though some of the copses and farms in the southern part of the estate are in Privett) is on the right of this road, which leaves the parish after passing Basing farm.

The soil is varied : on the chalk-hills it is loam and stiff clay, in the valleys it is stiff clay. The subsoil is chalk. The chief crops are oats, wheat, barley and beans.

MANORS There is no manor of *PRIVETT* at the present day ; and there is no reference to a manor in Privett before the seventeenth century.

Privett seems to have been merely part of the manor of West Meon ; for in 1391 the chapel of Holy Trinity at Privett in the parish of West Meon is mentioned,[2] and it is mentioned as part of the manor of West Meon in the valuation of the lands lately belonging to St. Swithun's monastery, which were granted by Henry VIII to the dean and chapter of Winchester.[3] From this time the descent of Privett follows that of West Meon manor (q.v.).[4]

CHURCH The modern church of the *HOLY TRINITY, PRIVETT*, is a fine flint structure with Doulting stone dressings in thirteenth-century style. It consists of a chancel, a clearstoried nave of four bays with aisles, transepts, and north porch, and a western tower with a spire, containing eight bells, cast in 1878.

The church was built in 1876–8, from the designs of J. L. Pearson, and occupies the site of the old church, of which nothing now remains. It is a very fine specimen of Pearson's work, its tall spire being a landmark for miles around.

The plate is modern (1878), and consists of chalice and paten and credence paten with a silver-mounted glass flagon.

The first book of registers contains the baptisms 1538–1632, marriages 1545–1626, and burials 1552–1632. The second contains all entries from 1653 to 1714, and a note of briefs 1705–12. The third runs from 1712 to 1776, the marriages ceasing in 1752, and the fourth has baptisms and burials 1776–1812. All entries between 1632 and 1653, and the marriage registers 1753–1812, appear to be missing.

ADVOWSON The earliest mention of a chapel in Privett is in the year 1391, when an indulgence was granted to penitents who gave alms to 'the fabric' of the chapel of Holy Trinity at Privett, in the parish of West Meon.[5]

The chapelry of Privett continued to be attached to the church of West Meon[6] (q.v.) until 1874, when it was formed into a separate[7] ecclesiastical benefice ; the church was rebuilt in 1834.[8]

The living is now a vicarage in the gift of Mr. William Nicholson of Basing Park, who bore the expense of the last rebuilding.

TICHBORNE

The parish of Tichborne, containing 3,049 acres of land, rises from north to south from the valley through which the River Itchen wanders to the high downland rising in the far south, and stretches down to the borders of Morestead and Owslebury.

As the two main roads from Winchester to New Alresford, the one coming through the Worthies and Itchen Abbas, and the other over Magdalen Hill and through Avington and Ovington, meet about a mile from New Alresford, a branch road turns off south towards Tichborne, and following the course of the River Itchen, which runs through the meadows on the east, leads circuitously to the picturesque village.

Along the east side of the road, which now begins to leave the river, are the grounds of Tichborne House sloping up from the river to the east, while on the west side are thatched cottages and farm buildings, behind which the ground rises up to the square-towered church of St. Andrew, which can be seen from the entrance to the village standing on high ground to the west. Beyond the first group of cottages, having passed Tichborne House, which stands close down by the river on the east, the road makes a still greater divergence from the river, turning uphill to the south-west. Here on the left up the hill is the low thatched 'Tichborne Arms,' opposite which is a group

[1] Statistics from Bd. of Agric. (1905).
[2] *Cal. Pap. Letters*, iv, 356.
[3] *Winch. Cath. Doc.* (Hants Rec. Soc.), i, 91.
[4] Recov. R. Mich. 16 Chas. II, m. 102; ibid. East. 13 Geo. III, m. 347.
[5] *Cal. Pap. Letters*, iv, 356.
[6] *Conspectus Dioc. Winton.* 1854, p. 16.
[7] *Clergy List*, 1874.
[8] *Conspectus Dioc. Winton.* 1854, p. 16.

of four half-timbered thatched cottages, the first one being the village post-office, perhaps one of the most picturesque cottages in the district. Beyond these is another group round which a rough road curves north-west, crossing the fields into Ovington parish, while the main road turns south-east, and passing by several thatched cottages and farm buildings, branches south-east to Sevington Farm and south-west uphill to Gander Down.

Tichborne House, the seat of Sir Henry Doughty Tichborne, was built in the beginning of the last century in place of the old house, which is known to have existed as early as the time of Henry III. It is surrounded by a well-wooded park of 116 acres. A Roman Catholic chapel is attached to the house. In the south-west corner of the park is a large fish-pond which is formed by the River Itchen. Vernal Farm, Goodwin Farm, and the Home Farm lie to the north; and Grange Farm and Sevington Farm are situated south of the village. The north-east corner of the parish is composed of downland called Tichborne Down, on which lies Tichborne Down Farm. In the centre of the parish is Gander Down, on the southern slopes of which stands Gander Down Farm; still further to the south lie Warren Farm and New Warren Farm. Altogether there are 1,762½ acres of permanent grass as compared with 1,341¾ acres of arable land. The extreme south of the parish is thickly wooded country, comprising most of the 281½ acres of woodland, in the midst of which stand Honeyman Farm and Longwood Farm.

There is no inclosure award for the parish. The soil is clay and chalk; the subsoil chalk. The chief crops are wheat, barley, and oats.

The following place names occur: in 1602 'Wales and Wickhurst,'[1] in 1611 'Ewfards,'[2] and in 1648 'Ruddlersdell, Hasards, Rowdich, and Gorings.'[3]

MANORS The descent of the manor of *TICHBORNE* is interesting because it has been held by the Tichborne family under the bishops of Winchester from the twelfth century to the present day. King Edward granted land at Tichborne to Denewulf, bishop of Winchester, for three lives in 909;[4] Athelstan, however, did not renew this grant, but instead gave 25 *mansae* at Tichborne to the monks of St. Peter and St. Paul at Winchester in 938;[5] and in 964 King Edgar granted Tichborne to Winchester Cathedral.[6] There is no entry with regard to Tichborne in Domesday Book; but it is possible that some of the land at least was included in Twyford, which was assessed at a very large amount at the time of the Survey.

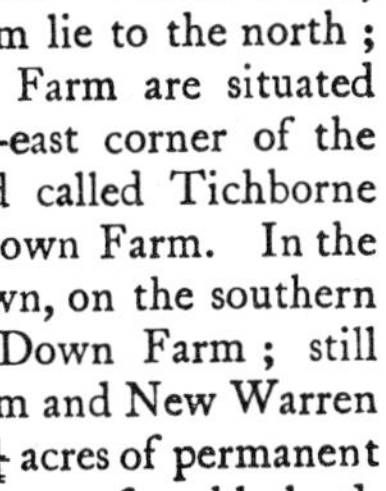

TICHBORNE. *Vair a chief or.*

Walter de Tichborne held two knights' fees from Henry, bishop of Winchester, in 1135; and his son Roger who succeeded him held one and a half fees from the bishop in 1166.[7] Bartholomew de Wydehaye conveyed the manor to John de Tichborne[8] and his wife Amice, evidently as a settlement, in 1320; the reversion was settled on Roger, John's son.[9]

Roger de Tichborne succeeded his father, and in 1346 was holding one fee in Tichborne which had belonged to John de Tichborne.[10] John de Tichborne, Roger's grandson, held Tichborne in 1428,[11] and died seised of the manor in 1499, leaving a son and heir William.[12]

Francis Tichborne was holding Tichborne manor at the time of his death in 1565; before he died he had settled it on his wife Joan with remainder to his half-brother Benjamin;[13] this Joan evidently married William Page as her second husband, for in 1571 Joan wife of William Page granted her life interest in Tichborne to Benjamin,[14] who died in possession of Tichborne manor in 1631, leaving a son and heir Richard.[15]

A few years later, in 1639, Richard Tichborne granted the manor to his brother Benjamin for the term of his own life.[16] After the death of Richard the estate, heavily burdened with debt,[17] passed to his son Sir Henry, who held it until his death in 1689.[18]

He was succeeded by his son Henry, who made a settlement of Tichborne manor in 1718.[19] Henry died in 1743 without male heirs, and the Tichborne estates passed to a cousin, Henry Tichborne of Frimley,[20] who held it until 1778.[21]

From 1778 until the present day the manor of Tichborne has remained in the same family; the present lord of the manor being Sir Henry A. J. Doughty Tichborne, of Tichborne Park.

Among the appurtenances belonging to Tichborne manor in 1654 were a water-mill, free warren, and free fishery in the waters of Tichborne;[22] and again in 1717, when Sir Henry Tichborne held the manor of Tichborne, free fishery and free warren are mentioned.[23]

At the present day there seems to be no trace of a water-mill in Tichborne.

CHURCH The church of *ST. ANDREW*, on the higher ground north-west of the village, is prettily situated in a churchyard with an eastward fall, commanding a beautiful view over the valley. There is a fine yew tree in the south-west of the churchyard. The church has a chancel 16 ft. by 11 ft. 8 in., nave 29 ft. by 17 ft. 6 in., with north aisle 10 ft. wide, south aisle 7 ft. 9 in. wide, south porch and west tower.

The chancel is an interesting piece of early building,

1 Eccl. Com. Ct. R. 158821, bdle. 136, No. 2.
2 Ibid. 158030, bdle. 115, No. 8.
3 Ibid. 155760, bdle. 39, No. 8.
4 Birch, *Cart. Sax.* ii, 289.
5 Ibid. ii, 443.
6 Ibid. iii, 407.
7 *Red Bk. of Exch.* i, 205.
8 John de Tichborne was a man of some eminence; he was sheriff of Hampshire, Dorset and Somerset in 14 Edw. II; and he was knight of the shire for Hampshire, warden of the Castle of Salisbury and one of the judges of assize.
9 *Cal. of Close*, 1318–23, pp. 338, 632.
10 *Feud. Aids*, ii, 334.
11 Ibid. ii, 363.
12 Chan. Inq. p.m. 14 Hen. VII (Ser. 2), vol. 13, No. 16.
13 Feet of F. Div. Cos. Hil. 4 Eliz.; Chan. Inq. p.m. 7 Eliz. (Ser. 2), vol. 141, No. 12.
14 Feet of F. Div. Cos. Trin. 13 Eliz.
15 Chan. Inq. p.m. 6 Chas. I, vol. 455, No. 69.
16 Feet of F. Hants, Mich. 14 Chas. I.
17 *Cal. of Com. for Comp.* iv, 2531.
18 Berry, *Hants Genealogies*, 28. Sir Henry fought at Cheriton with two of his uncles, and tradition still points out the Tichborne oak in which he was supposed to have hidden himself. He was also implicated in the Popish Plot, and was imprisoned for a long time, but was released in 1685.
19 Feet of F. Hants, East. 4 Geo. I; Recov. R. East. 4 Geo. I, m. 203.
20 Berry, *Hants Genealogies*, 28–32.
21 Recov. R. Mich. 18 Geo. III, m. 112.
22 Ibid. Mich. 1654, m. 227.
23 Ibid. East. 4 Geo. I, m. 203.

probably belonging to the middle of the eleventh century. It has pilaster strips at the eastern angles, and in the centres of the north, south, and east walls of Binstead stone in regular courses, and much wider than the ordinary type of pre-Conquest pilaster, those at the angles being nearly 2 ft. wide on each face, and the others 13 in. Their projection from the wall face, which is of thickly plastered flint rubble, is 2½ to 3 in. The original east window of the chancel has been replaced by one of three lights with net tracery, *c.* 1330, but in the north-east and south-east are single round-headed lights, double splayed, with a central stone slab pierced with a narrow round-headed opening, the masonry being well and accurately worked, with none of the roughness characteristic of work of the end of the eleventh century.

The original chancel arch, which was doubtless narrow, has been removed, and the wall above is now carried by a plain pointed arch of the full width of the chancel, perhaps of fourteenth-century date, and contemporary with the east window. The roof, which is hidden by a canted plaster ceiling, has a moulded wall plate of fourteenth-century detail, and is probably of the same date.

The nave, though having no features like those in the chancel, probably preserves its eleventh-century plan. In the latter part of the twelfth century a south aisle was added to it, and plain-pointed arches of a single order, with a central octagonal pier, were cut through the wall. In the north wall similar arches, probably of later date, but without any detail of a decisive character, open to the north aisle, which is the chapel of the Tichborne family, and is inclosed by modern cast-iron railings. It has a square-headed east window of three lights with engaged nook-shafts in the jambs, of early fourteenth-century date, but much modernized, having a stone image bracket to the north of it, and a piscina with projecting bowl on the south. Below is a seventeenth-century altar, with a thick wooden slab, moulded on the front and sides. The roof is of seventeenth-century date, and there is a small north doorway. The south aisle has a two-light window at the east, originally of fourteenth-century date, but with the west and two south windows here it is much modernized. The south door and porch are also of eighteenth-century date, and the red-brick west tower is dated 1703 on a cast-iron slab let into its south face, on which is also a modern sundial.

On the outer face of the east gable of the nave two blocked pointed arches are to be seen, which may have held bells, like those at Chilcomb. In the west face of the east respond of the south arcade is the doorway to the rood stair, which is continued in the thickness of the wall; the door itself is probably original, and of fifteenth-century date.

The font at the west end of the south aisle has a large bowl originally octagonal, but cut back to circular form; it is ancient but of uncertain date, and stands on a modern shaft and a plastered brick base. In the nave are some good seventeenth-century pews, with the Tichborne arms on those at the south-east, and the Tichborne chapel contains several monuments of the family, the oldest being a brass plate to Anne wife of Richard Tichborne, 1519. Against the north wall is a fine alabaster monument to Sir Benjamin Tichborne, 1621, and Amphillis, his wife, with their effigies in alabaster and figures of four sons and three daughters on the panelled base. Above are the Tichborne arms quartering Azure three bars wavy argent (Martin); Gules a saltire between four boars' heads or (de Racke); and Party gules and sable a crosslet fitchy between four fleurs de lis or (Rythe).

To the west is the monument of Richard son of Sir Richard Tichborne, 1619, and there are others of later date, several hatchments, a helm and a bracket for carrying a helm.

There are six bells, the treble and tenor by Thomas Mears, 1799 and 1798, the second, third, and fifth by Richard Phelps, 1737, and the fourth by Warner, 1887.

The plate consists of a cup of 1569 with cover paten of 1567, with a band of ornament at the lip and three scrolls below it; a paten of 1874, two glass cruets, one of which is silver-mounted, and a plated dish given 1859.

The earliest register book, dated 1704, contains an entry of 1667 and one of 1670, and runs to 1812, with marriages to 1744. The second book is the marriage register 1754–1813.

ADVOWSON The chapel of St. Andrew at Tichborne is annexed to Cheriton, and the descent of the advowson, therefore, is the same as that of Cheriton rectory (q.v.).

The joint net yearly value of the living is £530, with 150 acres of glebe, now in the gift of the crown.

There was also a chapel belonging to the manor in the sixteenth century,[24] and at the present day there is a Roman Catholic chapel attached to Tichborne House, with a chaplain and missionary priest.

The chapel of Tichborne is reputed to have been the scene of one of Henry VIII's marriages.

A chantry was founded in the manorial chapel of Tichborne by Roger Tichborne, son and heir of John Tichborne, 'to the intent to have a priest to celebrate and do the divine service in the chapel of Tichborne, and to have for his stipend yearly £4 out of the manor of Bromden in the county of Southampton, which manor is parcel of Maudelyn College in Oxford.'[25]

It was described as 'within a chapel situated within the manor place of Tichborne a quarter of a mile from the parish church,'[26] and was maintained at the cost of the Tichborne family.[27]

The chapel of Monk Sherborne held some land belonging to the Tichborne chantry; the profits of which 'the warden of the Queen's College in Oxford receiveth, yet by what right it is unknown.'[28]

[24] Chant. Cert. 51, No. 18.
[25] Ibid.
[26] Ibid.
[27] *Valor Eccl.* (Rec. Com.), ii, 9.
[28] Chant. Cert. 51, No. 18.

TWYFORD

Twyford, one of the most beautiful villages in Hampshire, often called 'the queen of Hampshire villages,' is situated on the River Itchen about three miles south of Winchester, and about a mile distant from Shawford Station, which is a junction for the London and South Western and Great Western Railways, both of which run through parts of the parish.

The parish of Twyford is five miles in length and two miles in breadth, and contains 43 acres of water and 4,229 acres of land, of which 2,074½ acres are permanent grass, 1,883 acres arable land and 185½ acres woodland.[1] Morestead and Owslebury lie on the east.

Brambridge and Colden Common are in Twyford and Owslebury civil parishes. The whole of the north of the parish consists of downlands which stretch northwards to the foot of St. Catherine's Hill and are bounded on the east and north-west by the Roman road, which runs through Chilcomb Without. Hockley Farm and Down Farm lie under the shelter of these downs. The River Itchen flows through the parish of Twyford, forming the western boundary, and is famous for its trout fishing.

The village of Twyford lies in the west of the parish; it is long and straggling but very picturesque, and contains two or three fine houses. On entering the village from the north, Twyford Lodge, the residence of Mr. Alexander P. Ralli, lies to the right in the valley of the Itchen, surrounded by beautiful grounds which slope down to the water's edge. Further south is Twyford House, a fine mansion built in the Elizabethan style, in which Dr. Franklin is said to have written his well-known autobiography while on a visit to Dr. Jonathan Shipley, then bishop of St. Asaph.

Close to Twyford House stands St. Mary's church and the vicarage; in the churchyard is a fine yew-tree, which according to local tradition is between four and five hundred years old. A little farther down the village street, surrounded by extensive play-grounds, stands Twyford School, a large preparatory school for boys under fifteen. In the centre of the village stands the institute and reading room, an iron building erected in 1892. Near to the River Itchen a short distance below Twyford Bridge is a group of houses called Seagar's Farm or Seagar's 'buildings,' in which during 1697 Pope received part of his education.

At the southern end of the village lies the old Manor House Farm, and to the east, surrounded by wooded grounds, stands Littlebourne House, the residence of Mr. Athol Maudsley. On the edge of this estate are the remains of a Roman villa.

About three-quarters of a mile to the west stands Shawford House, once the residence of the Mildmays, and now the property of Lieut.-Colonel Sir Charles Edward Frederick, surrounded by beautiful grounds and a large wooded park which slopes down to the River Itchen. The estate is almost encircled by water, the Itchen running along the eastern side, and a stream from the river to Itchen Navigation or canal, on which stands Shawford Mill, inclosing the southern and western sides.

FREDERICK, baronet. *Or a chief azure with three doves argent therein.*

About a mile south of Twyford is Twyford Moors, the residence of Mrs. Conway Shipley. Still further south is Brambridge House and Park, once the possession of the Welles family, and during the last century the residence of the Fairbairns. (See Owslebury.) The old house was burnt down in 1872. The modern house is a long low white building approached from the east by a double avenue of lime trees, and situated in a park of about fourteen acres; the River Itchen flows along the north side of the park, Brambridge Lock being at the junction of several of its tributaries. One of the rooms in the old Brambridge House was fitted up as a Roman Catholic chapel in the latter part of the eighteenth century by the Smythe family. Later, when the Relief Acts made it possible, they built a small chapel in the village, endowed about 1782 by Mrs. Fitzherbert.[1a]

The soil is chalk in the north of the parish, and loam and clay in the southern part; the subsoil is

SHAWFORD HOUSE, TWYFORD

[1] Statistics of Bd. of Agric. (1905).

[1a] The priest's house in the village is now held by a nurseryman. In one of the rooms there are traces of the ancient chapel. Wilkins, *Mrs. Fitzherbert and George IV*, i, 8 & 9.

chalk. The chief crops are wheat, barley, oats, and turnips.

Twyford Common was inclosed on the 13 December, 1855.[2]

The following place-names occur: in 1523, 'Jevonesland, Godwynscroft, Germaynelond, and Modyes,'[3] and in 1540, 'Blaklond, Medelond, Lokesbridge, and Coledown Heath.'[4]

There are certain stones at Twyford lying close to the River Itchen to the south of the church supposed, but with little probability, to be druidical remains.

About a mile to the east of Brambridge Park lies the village of Colden Common, which was formed into a separate ecclesiastical parish in 1843, with 1,618 acres formerly belonging to the parishes of Twyford and Owslebury. The church of the Holy Trinity stands on the borders of the two parishes, and was only erected in 1844. There is a Bible Christian chapel in the parish built in 1866.

The chief industry carried on in the village is brick-making.

MANORS As early as 964 King Edgar granted land in Twyford to Winchester Cathedral.[5] At the time of the Domesday Survey the bishop himself held Twyford in demesne as he had always held it; it was assessed at the time of Edward the Confessor at twenty hides, but in 1086 at only fifteen hides: there were four mills in Twyford worth £4.[6] In 1284 the king surrendered to John, bishop of Winchester, and his successors, all his right in the manor of Twyford,[7] and it continued to belong to the see of Winchester until the middle of the sixteenth century,[8] the bishops making grants of the manor or of land in it from time to time.

When John Poynet was made bishop of Winchester in 1551, he surrendered the manor of Twyford to the crown in exchange for other lands (vide Marwell manor), and it was at once granted by Edward VI to his uncle, Sir Henry Seymour.[9]

From this time until 1857 the descent of the manor of Twyford is the same as that of Marwell in Owslebury parish (q.v.) In 1857 the manor with land in Owslebury was sold to Mr. Humphrey Francis St. John Mildmay, from whom it passed to Mr. Francis B. St. John Mildmay, M.P. for the Totnes division of Devon, the present lord of the manor.[10]

In the grant of the manor to Sir Henry Seymour in 1551 the bishop's warren of Long Wood, in the bailiwick of Twyford, was excepted. In 1552–3 John Williams, who appears to have been granted the remainder of the non-expired lease of the land held by the late earl of Southampton, complained that Sir Henry Seymour had entered a part of his warren, called Harley in Twyford, and carried off his 'erthes.' In 1605 Thomas, bishop of Winchester, leased the warren and lodge to William Brock for the lives of Anne and Elizabeth, his wife and daughter respectively, for a yearly rental of £9 6*s*. 8*d*.[11] In 1648 this warren was sold by the Commissioners for the Sale of Bishops' Lands to Thomas Hussey for £351 3*s*. 4*d*.[12] In the Ministers' Accounts for 1323 mention is made of another park in Twyford called Suthnolnesmed, the sale of the pasture from which produced 18*s*. 6*d*., 'as all the park was mown in that year.' 19*s*. 7½*d*. was paid in wages to the park keeper at the rate of 1½*d*. per day.[13]

At the time of the Domesday Survey there were four mills in Twyford parish;[14] and for some time there are entries in the Court Rolls for the farm of four mills in Twyford, called 'Cumton Mill,' Schaldeford Mill, Brambridge Mill, and North Twyford Mill.'[15]

In 1323 20*s*. and five eels were paid for the farm of the mill of Brambridge; 6*s*. 8*d*. for the farm of the mill of Compton that Robert de Shernecombe held by charter of the lord Henry the bishop; 13*s*. 4*d*. and two quarters of barley were received from the issues of the mill of North Twyford; the custom of this mill being 8*s*., and the miller's portion of the farm 8*s*.; 5*s*. was paid for twenty men for two days to repair part of the mill which was broken by the watercourse—i.e., each man 1½*d*. per day. From Shaldeford Mill, 6*s*. 8*d*. and two quarters; three bushels of barley were received from the issues of the mill, price per quartern 6*s*. 8*d*.; the miller's portion of the farm was 4*s*. Total received from all the mills, 18*s*. 2¾*d*.[16]

When Sir John Seymour died seised of Twyford manor in 1618 he also possessed a mill called 'Shalford' Mill,[17] and in 1824 among the appurtenances of Twyford manor, which then belonged to Dame Jane St. John Mildmay, was a corn-mill at Shawford.[18] At the present day there is a water corn-mill at Shawford, part of which is so old that it is believed locally to have belonged to the original mill mentioned in Domesday.

Besides this mill the Seymours and the Mildmays claimed free fishery and free warren in Twyford.[19]

The following entries in the Ministers' Accounts for the year 1323 are of interest. 18*s*. from men collecting toll from the river; 181 skins of lambs received for customs; received from the excutors of the late lord bishop, according to custom, two cart-horses, 10 horses, 38 oxen, 295 sheep, 4 rams, 250 ewes and 181 lambs. Items of expenditure are: iron and steel bought for five carts, and wages of smith who repaired the same, 12*s*.; binding same with iron, 2*d*.; shoeing eleven horses, 10*s*.; wages of carter, 18*d*.; wages of two keepers of horses, 4*s*.; mending two broken ploughs, 2*d*. beyond agreement; one quarter of oats for provender for horses, 4*s*.; one quarter of oats for forage for servants, 4*s*.; one cloth for dairy, 5½*d*; ewers and earthern pans, 3*d*.; two bushels of salt, 8*d*.; wages of one keeper of lambs, 2*s*.[20]; perquisities of the court, £64 17*s*. At a court held in 1526 those tenants who had lands on the watercourse of the river of the lord were requested to clean out their parts before the next term under penalty of 4*s*. each. In 1540 it was presented that

[2] *Parl. Accts, and Papers*, vol. 71, 485–523.
[3] Eccl. Com. Ct. R. 159510 (1), bdle. 84, No. 19.
[4] Ibid. 155967, bdle. 85, No. 3.
[5] Birch, *Cart. Sax.* iii, 412.
[6] *V.C.H. Hants*, i, 460.
[7] Chart. R. 12 Edw. I, m. 5.
[8] *Abbrev. Plac.* (Rec. Com.), 276*b*; *Pope Nich. Tax.* (Rec. Com.), 215; *Feud. Aids*. ii, 320; *Abbrev. Rot. Orig.* (Rec. Com.), ii, 246.
[9] Pat. 5 Edw. VI, pt. 5, m. 29.
[10] Inform. from Col. Mildmay.
[11] Star. Cham. Proc. bdle. 11, No. 4.
[12] Close, 24 Chas. I, pt. 2, m. 23.
[13] Mins. Accts. bdle. 142, No. 13.
[14] *V.C.H. Hants*, i, 460.
[15] Eccl. Com. Ct. R. 159270, bdle. 22, and 159280, bdle. 22.
[16] Mins. Accts. bdle. 1142, No. 13.
[17] Chan. Inq. p.m. 16 Chas. I, bdle. 59, No. 39.
[18] Recov. R. Hil. 5 & 6 Geo. II, m. 11.
[19] Notes of F. Hants, Mich. 1 Chas. I; Recov. R. Trin. 17 & 18 Geo. II, m. 303.
[20] Mins. Accts. bdle. 1142, No. 13.

the bridge of Fokesbridge was in decay, whereupon the whole tithing was ordered to repair it by a fixed date under a penalty of 6*s.* 8*d.*, the lord supplying the timber. At the same court the tenants of North Twyford were requested to mend their hedges around[21] fields sown with barley, while those of South Twyford were to make hedges in 'Golden Lane.'

CHURCHES The church of *OUR LADY, TWYFORD* was rebuilt in 1876–7, some features of the former building being re-used in the new work. The present church consists of a chancel with north-east vestry and north and south chapels, nave with aisles, and a tower with a spire at the north-west. The site falls from east to west, and the chancel is raised considerably above the nave level, and is fitted with good oak stalls and screen, and an elaborate reredos. The nave has arcades of five bays, with painted arches of two orders, the round columns which carry them, with their octagonal capitals and moulded bases, being for the most part of late twelfth-century date; the capitals are of several different designs, with scallops, flutes, and foliage. The clearstory above likewise preserves some old stonework in its square-headed windows of two trefoiled lights. The east window of the south chapel is of the fifteenth century with three cinquefoiled lights and tracery over; it was formerly the east window of the old chancel.

The monuments from the old church have been relegated to the north chapel, behind the organ, and are of no particular note, the most interesting being that of Dulcibella Welles, 1616, of alabaster with a bowed front, and black marble panel for the inscription.

In the church is hung a plan of the seating made in 1698, showing the front seats on either side of the nave assigned as the vicar's pew and the churching pew; the side seats in the back blocks on the north side are apportioned to 'poor housekeepers,' and those corresponding to them on the south to their wives.

In the tower are eight bells, the treble and second by Taylor, 1899; third by Mears, 1833; fourth, fifth, sixth, and tenor by Lester & Pack, 1766; and seventh by Chapman, 1780.

The plate, with one exception, is modern, consisting of two chalices and patens, and a flagon; there is also an old pewter flagon and almsdish. The old piece is a paten of 1692, given by Mr. Anthony Leger; it was sold, together with an old communion cup, some time since, but has fortunately been recovered, though the cup has not.

The first book of the registers runs from 1627 to 1712, and the second from 1713 to 1812, the marriages ceasing in 1754. The third book contains the burials in woollen 1714–1812, and the fourth is the printed marriage register, 1754–1812.

The church of *HOLY TRINITY, COLDEN COMMON*, built in 1844, is a small building of flint with stone dressings in Transition style, consisting of chancel, nave, south porch, and open bell-turret with one bell. The register dates from 1843.

ADVOWSON At the time of the Domesday Survey there was a church in Twyford worth 5*s.*, which was in the possession of the bishop,[22] and in 1284 the king surrendered to John, bishop of Winchester, and his successors all his right in the advowson of this church.[23] In 1291 Twyford vicarage was assessed at £10,[24] and in 1535 it was assessed at £14.[25]

The advowson of the vicarage was in the hands of the bishop until 1551,[26] when John Poynet, bishop of Winchester, gave up all the episcopal manors to the crown in exchange for a fixed income of 2,000 marks;[27] and the manor and advowson of Twyford were at once granted to Sir Henry Seymour the king's uncle.[28]

From this time until about 1825 the advowson of Twyford followed the descent of the manor (q.v.), which in 1824 was in the possession of the Mildmay family.

From 1829 until the present day Emmanuel College, Cambridge, has nominated to Twyford vicarage,[29] but the St. John Mildmays have presented to the living.[30] The rectorial tithes of Twyford were appropriated to the hospital of St. Cross founded by Bishop Henry of Blois, founded about 1136,[31] and after the dissolution of the monasteries passed into the possession of the lords of the manor.[32]

The living of Holy Trinity, Colden Common, is a vicarage, net yearly value £183, with residence and 2 acres of glebe in the alternate gift of the vicar of Twyford and the vicar of Owslebury.

CHARITIES In 1780 Richard Wool directed his executors to lay out £500 in the public funds, the dividends to be paid to a schoolmaster for teaching all the poor children of Twyford. The legacy was invested in the purchase of £877 3*s.* 10*d.* consols.

In 1839 Archdeacon Clark (who died in 1841) by his will bequeathed (subject to the life interest of his widow, who died in 1871) £1,000 consols, dividends to be applied towards the support of the school, in augmentation of the provisions made by Richard Wool. The legacy, less duty and expenses, was invested in £896 5*s.* 3*d.* consols. The two sums of stock are held by the Official Trustees of Charitable Funds.[33]

In 1855, by an award made on the inclosure of Twyford Down, 4 acres were allotted as a recreation ground, afterwards sold to the Didcot Railway for £150, which sum was laid out in 1891 in the purchase of 4 acres in Hazeley Down, about a mile from the village.

In 1855, by an award, 2 acres were allotted for garden allotments (subject to a rent-charge of £3 a year) for the poor of Colden Common. The allotments produce about £8 11*s.* 6*d.* a year, which is applied in maintaining and improving the same. The rent-charge has been redeemed out of surplus rents.

In 1897 Mrs. Jane Mary Smith-Dampier, by deed, conveyed to trustees a house and site as a residence for a nurse for this parish and Compton. See hundred of Buddlesgate.

21 Eccl. Com. Ct. R. bdle. 85, No. 3.
22 *V.C.H. Hants*, i, 460.
23 Chart. R. 12 Edw. I, m. 5.
24 *Pope Nich. Tax.* (Rec. Com.), 210.
25 *Valor Eccl.* (Rec. Com.), ii, 6.
26 *Wykeham's Reg.* (Hants Rec. Soc.), i, 45.
27 Pat. 5 Edw. VI; pt. 6, m. 20. See also Marwell.
28 Ibid. pt. 5, m. 29.
29 *Clerical Guide*, 1829–41; *Clergy List*, 1845–1904.
30 Information supplied by Colonel Mildmay.
31 *V.C.H. Hants*, ii, 20.
32 Feet of F. Hants, Mich. 30 Geo. III.
33 *V.C.H. Hants*, ii, 'Schools.'

WEST MEON

Menes (xi cent.) ; Meones (xiii cent.).

The parish of West Meon covers 3,772 acres of hilly country, through the centre of which the River Meon runs east to west, while the land rises north and south from the valley, reaching a height of over 600 ft. above the ordnance datum in the south and of 500 ft. in the north near the Three Horseshoes Inn. The main road from Petersfield to Alton runs through the parish in a south-westerly direction, and crossing the main road from Petersfield to Winchester in the north, close by the George Inn, climbs a ridge and comes down into the low-lying ground of the Meon valley to become the main street of the village. Along a branch road from East Meon which approaches the village by the river bank from the south-east are several outlying houses and cottages, including Hall Farm, Hall Place, and Lynch House, which lie south of the road and river, and Shaft's Farm which lies to the north. Following the course of this road as it cuts across the main road, where the majority of the houses are grouped, and continues in a north-westerly direction towards Hinton Ampner, the village schools stand on the left close on the road. Beyond the schools is the church of St. John standing on high ground, from which the land falls away to the Meon valley to rise again beyond the river and become a long sweep of downland and woodland. Past the church the road goes uphill to Lippen Cottages, with their long trim gardens, and from here passing through fine woodland it reaches the high ground north of the parish, from which good views of the village and of the surrounding country can be obtained.

In the centre of the village at the junction of the two roads is a square piece of ground inclosed by a railing, in the middle of which is a stone cross surrounded by several seats, and shaded by some fine trees. A stone slab in front of the cross states that this ground was given to the West Meon Parish Council for the use of the parishioners for ever by the lord of the manor, Henry Johnson, 1898. On the south face of the cross an inscription tells that another cross (probably a market cross) originally stood on this spot, and other inscriptions on the east and west faces relate that the modern cross was put up in 1901 by the last surviving of the sixteen children of George Vining Rogers (1777–1846), for more than forty years medical practitioner in West Meon, and Mary Anne Rogers his wife (1783–1873). As the main road goes downhill from here past the village inn, the Congregational chapel, and the various groups of houses, shops and cottages composing the village, it crosses the river close by the mill, then turns sharply west near by the modern Queen Victoria Institute, erected in 1887, to run parallel with the river through peaceful pastoral country to Warnford parish. Here also, close by the smithy, a branch road turns south-east, past the rectory and several outlying cottages, to the railway station on the Meon valley line. There is no inclosure award for the parish. The soil is various, the subsoil chalk. The chief crops on the 1,192½ acres of arable land are wheat, barley, and oats. Of the whole parish 680¾ acres are permanent grass and 296¾ are woodland.

West Meon : View in Village

During the Civil War West Meon was the scene of several skirmishes previous to the battle of Cheriton (29 March, 1644). Major-General Brown with the London Brigade was directed by Waller to take up quarters at West Meon, three miles from the main body, on the night of 25 March. There they found, according to an eye-witness who was with the brigade, 'a partee of the enemies horse . . . which occasioned some action, though not much considerable.' The next day, Tuesday, 26 March, continues the narrator, 'we lay still, onely our scouts brought in some prisoners, 6 troops incountring with 16 of the enemies, put them to flight and brought away 3 of them prisoners.' The day following the enemy took some few of their men who 'were straggling from their colours, and soon after appeared in a great body upon the hill on the left hand, the Town intending (as some prisoners confessed) to take us at church, it being the Fast Day.' However, 'this godly body of Londoners' had already kept the fast on the Wednesday before and were therefore 'provided to entertain' the enemy and drew their forces into a body near the town. Then marching out 'in the Forlorn-Hope expecting the enemy every hour to fall upon us' they were 'forced to make a stand a mile or so from the town in extream danger' till joined by Waller's forces coming from East Meon.[1]

A Roman building in Lippen Wood has been excavated in 1905–6, and proved to be of an interesting type. In plan it was a rectangle of 140 ft. by 60 ft., standing nearly north and south. The entrance was by a gateway on the east, opening to a central courtyard, on the north side of which was the dwelling-house, and on the south the outbuildings. The principal rooms in the house were arranged from east to west on either side of a central hall or corridor 11 ft. wide; at the east end the corridor opened to two rooms with well-preserved mosaic floors, each room about 21 ft. by 11 ft. The two largest rooms flanked the corridor immediately to the south of the first two, and both were about 20 ft. by 18 ft. 6 in., but had lost their flooring. At the north-west angle of the house was a room with a channelled hypocaust, and opposite to it, on the south of the corridor, were two small rooms. A good deal of painted plaster was found, and the house was evidently one of some importance. The south-west corner of the courtyard was at a lower level than the rest, and in it were three chambers, two of them apsidal, with pillared hypocausts; all were probably bath-rooms. The remaining buildings, in the south-east part of the inclosure, were too fragmentary to be identified.[1a]

MANORS There are several references in the Anglo-Saxon Charters to grants of land 'on the river Meon to the king's thegns and relations'; but it is impossible to identify any of them with the manor of *WEST MEON*, which was held by the bishop in 1086, and which according to the Domesday Survey had always belonged to the church.[2]

The manor of West Meon together with other manors and lands was confirmed to the prior and convent of St. Swithun, Winchester, in 1205,[3] and by a charter of 1284 John, bishop of Winchester, gave up for himself and his successors all rights in the manor saving the right of overlordship.[4] It was numbered among the St. Swithun temporalities in 1291, being assessed at £31 16*s.*[5]

West Meon was still in the hands of the prior and convent at the time of the Dissolution; and it was then assessed at £65 8*s.* 2*d.*, more than double its former value.[6]

After the Dissolution the manor with the other possessions of the priory was granted in 1541 to the dean and chapter of Winchester by Henry VIII[7] for a yearly rent of £178 16*s.* 5½*d.*,[8] West Meon, together with four other manors, being charged with the maintenance of six students in theology at Oxford and six at Cambridge.[9] The king, however, compelled the dean and chapter to surrender the five manors in 1545; and the maintenance for the students ceased.[10] In consideration of this surrender Queen Elizabeth in 1567 commuted £18 4*s.* 9½*d.* of the annual rent paid by the bishop, and in 1674 Charles II for the sum of £2,402 9*s.* 8*d.* granted £160 11*s.* 8*d.*, the residue of the rent, to George, bishop of Winchester.[11] In 1544 West Meon was granted by letters patent to Thomas Wriothesley, earl of Southampton, who died seised of the manor in 1550, leaving an infant son, Henry, aged three years,[12] who as the second earl of Southampton held the manor until his death in 1581. He was succeeded by his son Henry, third earl of Southampton, who died in 1624, leaving a son Thomas.[13]

WRIOTHESLEY. *Azure a cross or between four falcons close argent.*

Sir Thomas Wriothesley, earl of Southampton, became one of the most trusted advisers of Charles II, and he remained in close attendance upon him until his death in 1667.

Shortly before this time, Sir Thomas, who left no male heir, must have sold the manor of West Meon to Thomas Neale, for he was holding it in 1664[14] [15]; and in 1677 sold the manor to Isaac Foxcroft.[16]

Nearly a century later West Meon was still in the possession of the Foxcroft family; for in 1773 Henry Foxcroft was holding the manor together with all lands and tenements in West Meon, free warren and view of frankpledge.[17] In the same year, however, he sold it for the sum of £5,350 [18] to Charles Rennett, who was still lord of the manor in 1802. He was followed by John Dunn, formerly his steward, who held the manor until the marriage of his only daughter with Captain Aubertin; and by this marriage West Meon passed to the Aubertins, from whom it was purchased in 1894 by Mr. Henry G. Johnson, the present lord of the manor.[19]

At the time of the Domesday Survey there were

1 King's Pamphlets, E. 40, No. 1.

1a For an account of the excavations see *Arch. Journ.* lxvi, 1.

2 *V.C.H. Hants*, i, 461.

3 *Cal. Pap. Letters*, i, 21.

4 Chart. R. 13 Edw. I, No. 98.

5 *Pope Nich. Tax.* (Rec. Com.) 213. Licence was granted to the prior and convent in 1333 to impark their woods in West Meon (6 Edw. III, pt. 1, m. 13). A licence was granted to William of Wykeham, bishop of Winchester, to alienate to the prior and convent in 1383 certain lands and tenements in West Meon, held for the rent of one rose and the service of one man working for a day in autumn; and the reversion of other lands and tenements after the death of Elizabeth Langrish, who had held them in dower since the death of her husband William Atte Halle. This grant was made in part satisfaction of £50 worth of land which the prior and convent had licence to acquire in mortmain by letters patent from the late king (Pat. 16 Ric. II, pt. 3, m. 7). The bishop is mentioned as holding West Meon for the prior and convent in 1383 (Inq. p.m. 6 Ric. II, No. 160).

6 *Valor Eccl.* (Rec. Com.), v, App. ix.

7 Pat. 33 Hen. VIII, pt. 9, m. 34–40; *L. and P. Hen. VIII*, xvi, 878 (1).

8 Pat. 21 Chas. II, pt. 2, m. 12.

9 *Winch. Cath. Doc.* (Hants Rec. Soc.), i, 171.

10 Pat. 21 Chas. II, pt. 2, No. 12.

11 Ibid.

12 W. & L. Inq. p.m. 4 Edw. VI (Ser. 2), vol. 5, No. 103.

13 Ibid. (Ser. 2), 22 Jas. I, bdle. 41, No. 120.

14 Recov. R. Mich. 16 Chas. II, m. 102.

15 In 1675 Thomas Neale conveyed the manor to Sir John Norton, John Garrard, and others (Feet of F. Div. Cos. Trin. 27 Chas. II) evidently as a settlement.

16 Feet of F. Div. Cos. East. 29 Chas. II.

17 Recov. R. Trin. 13 Geo. III. m. 42; ibid. East. 13 Geo. III, m. 347.

18 Close, 13 Geo. III, pt. 14, m. 19, No. 11.

19 Information supplied by Mr. Johnson.

two mills in West Meon, worth 10*s.*[20] In 1664 when Thomas Neale was holding the manor there were three mills.[21] In 1301 a grant was made to the prior and convent of St. Swithun of free warren in their demesne lands at West Meon.[22] View of frankpledge was granted to the dean and chapter of Winchester in 1542,[23] and the Foxcrofts held view of frankpledge and rights of free warren in 1773.[24]

The reputed manor of *HALL PARK* in West Meon is first mentioned in 1550, when it was in the possession of Thomas Wriothesley, earl of Southampton, who also held the main manor of West Meon.[25] Hall Park subsequently followed the descent of the manor of West Meon (q.v.). A fine house called Hall Place and Hall Place Farm now stands on the site of the so-called manor.

The earl of Southampton was also holding the so-called manor of *COOMBE* at the time of his death in 1550;[26] it is always mentioned with West Meon and follows the descent of that manor (q.v.) until the end of the eighteenth century, after which no further record of it has been found. It may possibly have become amalgamated with the main manor, though there is no place of this name at the present day in West Meon; or possibly the tithing of Coombe, now in West Meon, may mark its site.

In 1677 occurs the first separate mention of the so-called manor of *WOODLANDS*,[27] a name given to a porton of West Meon manor, with which its history is identical. It subsequently became merged in that manor; and its site is now occupied by the Woodlands estate and farm.

The earliest mention of *PUNSHOLT* (Punsold, xiv cent.; Poundesolte, Ponsholt, xvi cent.; Punsholes, Punsalls, xvii cent.) is found in 1341, when Walter de Ticheborne and his wife Agatha were holding in right of the latter half the manor of West Tisted and 40*s.* rent in Bramdean and Punsholt.[28]

Again, in 1511 William Tisted, lord of the manor of West Tisted, died seised of the reversion of two tenements, forty acres of land, twenty acres of pasture, and six acres of woodland in Punsholt which he held of the priory of St. Swithun as of the manor of West Meon.[29] It seems probable therefore that Punsholt followed the descent of West Tisted (q.v.).

On the death of William Tisted's brother and heir, Thomas, a few years later, these tenements were divided among his four sisters and co-heirs and their descendants.[30] Three of them sold their shares to Richard Norton,[31] whose descendant, Richard Norton, died seised of the so-called manor or capital messuage of Punsholt in West Meon and Privett in 1584, leaving a son and heir, Anthony,[32] who ten years later granted three-fourths to his sister, Isabel Norton.[33]

Isabel married Thomas Lovedean of East Meon, and owing to his recusancy two-thirds of his lands and tenements, including a messuage called Punsholt, were granted in 1608 for a term of forty-one years[34] to John Casewell, Christopher Stubbs, and Thomas Hutchinson.

On the death of Thomas and Isabel, Punsholt descended to Anthony Lovedean, on whose death in 1635 it was described as a messuage or tenement, and a virgate of land in the parish of West Meon held from Thomas Neale as of his manor of West Meon by a rent of 26*s.* 8*d.*[35] His heir was his son Sebastian, aged ten and a half years, who was a recusant like his grandfather.[36]

After this the only record concerning Punsholt seems to be in the year 1791, when Thomas Marchant and John Marchant and Ann his wife were holding a moiety of the so-called manor of Punsholt, which they conveyed to Richard Pratt and John Greene.[37]

Punsholt Farm in the north of West Meon parish now indicates the site of the manor of Punsholt.

CHURCH The church of *ST. JOHN* was rebuilt in 1843–6 to the north of the former church, nothing of the older building being preserved. It is a fine building in geometrical style, of carefully faced flint with stone dressings, and has a chancel with north vestry and organ chamber, a nave of five bays, with an embattled porch, and a tall western tower. The roofs are covered with blue slates. The old font was removed at the rebuilding, and is now in St. Edmund's, Lombard Street; its successor stands at the west end of the nave, and is octagonal, of thirteenth-century design. There are eight bells, six of 1850 and two of 1897.

The plate includes a set given in 1846, consisting of two chalices and patens, a larger paten, a flagon and two alms dishes. There is also a gold dish given in 1844, and a plated chalice and paten given in 1900.

The first book of the registers contains all entries from 1542 to 1639, the second runs from 1640 to 1688, the third from 1690 to 1733, the fourth from 1675 to 1733, and the fifth from 1733 to 1812. The sixth and seventh are the printed marriage registers, 1745–1817.

There are some entries of burials as early as 1536, two years before the passing of the Act for the keeping of parish registers.

ADVOWSON At the time of the Domesday Survey there was one church in West Meon to which was attached one hide of land; the church paid 50*s.* towards the farm of the manor.[38] In 1284 the king gave up to John, bishop of Winchester, and his successors all right and claim in the advowson of the church of West Meon with the chapels.[39]

In 1291 the church was assessed at £20,[40] and by 1535 the value had risen to £31 5*s.* 4*d.*[41]

The advowson, except during the Commonwealth, has always been in the hands of the bishop of Winchester.[42] The living is a rectory.

In 1391 there was a chapel of the Holy Trinity

20 *V.C.H. Hants*, i, 461.

21 Recov. R. Mich. 16 Chas. II, m. 102. Two of these mills may possibly have been in West Meon, as Hall Park and Privett were included in West Meon.

22 Chart. R. 29 Edw. I. No. 54.

23 Pat. 33 Hen. VIII, pt. 9, m. 34–40.

24 Recov. R. Trin. 13 Geo. III, m. 42.

25 W. & L. Inq. p.m. 4 Edw. VI (Ser. 2), vol. 5, No. 103.

26 Ibid.

27 Feet of F. Div. Cos. East. 29 Chas. II.

28 Ibid. Hants, Trin. 11 Edw. III.

29 Chan. Inq. p.m. (Ser. 2), vol. 26. No. 13.

30 Berry, *Hants Genealogies*, 29.

31 Vide Feet of F. Hants, Mich. 11 Hen. VIII.

32 Chan. Inq. p.m. (Ser. 2), vol. 351, No. 82.

33 Add. MSS. 38278, fol. 131*b*.

34 Pat. 6 Jas. I, pt. 3, No. 15.

35 Chan. Inq. p.m. 11 Chas. I, vol. 476, No. 71.

36 *Cal. of Com. for Comp.* iii, 1788.

37 Feet of F. Hants, Mich. 34 Geo. III.

38 *V.C.H. Hants*, i, 461.

39 Chart. R. 12 Edw. I, m. 5.

40 *Pope Nich. Tax.* (Rec. Com.), 211*b*.

41 *Valor Eccl.* (Rec. Com.), ii, 22.

42 Inst. Bks. (P.R.O.).

in West Meon, and an indulgence was granted to those penitents who visited and gave alms to the 'fabric of the chapel.' The same indulgence was also granted to those penitents who gave alms towards the chapel of St. Mary the Virgin in Punsholt.[43]

CHARITIES In 1846 William Butterworth Bayley by deed conveyed to trustees schoolhouse, master's house, and three acres of playground, and by a deed in 1853 Miss Mary Touchett endowed the school with three tenements, blacksmith's shop, and coach-house. In 1897 the blacksmith's shop was pulled down and upon the site an institute called the 'Queen Victoria Institute' was built at a cost of £377, provided by voluntary contribution. The income is about £17 a year.[44]

In 1867 a village green was granted by the lords of the manor for the use of the inhabitants.

In 1872 Hannah Batten by will, proved this date, left £100 consuls, income to be divided yearly among three poor widows on last day of January by the rector and churchwardens.

In 1873 Elizabeth Sibley, by will proved this date, left £5 a year for the daily ringing of the church bell, to denote certain hours and the day of the month. The funds consist of £166 13*s.* 4*d.* consols. The sums of stock are held by the official trustees.

WIELD

Walde (xi cent.); Welde, Wolde (xiv cent.).

The parish of Wield, covering an area of 2,104 acres, lies in the open down country that rises north-east of Old Alresford and south-east of Preston Candover. The land, generally speaking, slopes upward from north to south, reaching a height of 576 ft. above the ordnance datum in the south-east as the road leads from Upper Wield to Medsted.

The village of Upper Wield, the nucleus of the parish, lies in the south, and is reached from the north-west from Preston Candover by a steep rough lane which rises for about a mile between thick hedges, plough-land, and pasture land, from 450 ft. above the ordnance datum to over 550 ft. near the village. On the approach to the village a farmhouse stands north of the road, which here makes a more distinct curve to the south round the house and thatched out-buildings of a small farm which lies in the west, and runs past the village pond on the opposite side of the road to the groups of thatched cottages which lie on either side. A branch road to the west leads down to the church, which, being approached by a narrow pathway leading north, stands in a fenced-in churchyard, and on the north side of the road immediately behind a group of thatched cottages. South-west of the church is a small Primitive Methodist chapel dated 1818. The main road continues south for a few yards beyond this branch leading to the church, a few thatched cottages lying on the west side, while opposite is a rough uninclosed green. At the end of this green the road branches east and west, the western branch leading to Alresford, the eastern to Lower Wield. A few yards along this eastern branch as it leads down hill the village schools stand on the north side, while beyond the schools are a few outlying thatched cottages, and at the corner as a branch road goes north-west to Lower Wield is the thatched vicarage. Lower Wield, lying away towards the north of the parish, is about a mile as the crow flies from Upper Wield, and is on much lower ground. It consists of three farms, Lower Wield Farm, Nicholas' Farm, and Pitter Farm, with a few scattered

Wield Village

[43] *Cal. Pap. Letters*, iv, 356.

[44] *V.C.H. Hants*, ii, 'Schools.'

cottages which always seem to appear round each corner of the lane known as Berry Wood Lane as it winds down hill in a more or less northerly direction towards Bradley. North-west of Lower Wield, Windmill Hill rises to a height of about 490 ft. above the ordnance datum.

The soil of the whole parish is clay with a subsoil of chalk, and crops of wheat, oats, and turnips are grown on the 1,191 acres of arable land which make up the best part of the parish. Only 304 acres are given up to permanent grass, while Wield Wood and Barton Copse in the south-west of the parish cover nearly the whole of the 215 acres of woodland.

MANOR The southern portion of the parish formed part of Alresford Liberty, and is most probably included in the entry under Alresford in Domesday Book.[1] That this is so is supported by a perambulation of the manor taken in the reign of Edward VI,[2] by the fact that the tithing of Wield sent a tithing-man to the Old Alresford court leet,[3] and also by the circumstance that an agent sent down from London to report on the whole bailiwick of Bishop's Sutton[4] included in his survey part of the parish of Wield, reporting as follows: 'Your Wild is but a baron ground whereupon be to littell copices and one small comen thynn sett with greet trees.'[5]

The overlordship of the remaining portion, the so-called manor of *WIELD*, belonged from a very early date to the bishops of Winchester, under whom it was held by various tenants. Durand held it of the bishop at the time of the Domesday Survey, and two freemen had been the tenants in the reign of Edward the Confessor.[6]

From 1270 to 1316 the Wintershulls held Wield from the see of Winchester, for at the earlier date Gerard la Grue conveyed a messuage and two carucates of land at West Wield to William de Wintershull,[7] who died seised of the manor[8] in 1286, his heir being his son John,[9] who was still holding in 1296.[10] In 1306 William de Wintershull, John's son, conveyed the reversion of the manor, two-thirds of which was held by his mother Mary for life, and the remaining third by his grandmother Beatrice in dower, to John de Drokensford and his heirs.[11] John de Drokensford must have died almost immediately, for in the same year (1306) Peter de Courtenay and his wife Margaret claimed the manor as next heirs of John de Drokensford on the ground that John de Drokensford, Mary and Beatrice de Wintershull were dead, and that a certain Nicholas de Valence had entered into possession of the manor of Wield, which ought by right to have descended to Margaret as daughter and heiress of John de Drokensford.[12]

The record of the result of this suit has not been found, but Nicholas de Valence probably proved his claim to some of the property,[13] and was succeeded by his son John and by his grandson another John, for in 1340 the latter entered a plea for the restoration of the lands in Wield of which his father[14] had been deprived for 'feloniously breaking the mill of the prior of Southwick, and for having stolen a grindstone worth 40*s.* and 1½ quarters of wheat found there of the price of 6*s*,' for which offence he had died in prison.

The lands had been taken into the king's hands, but after it had been proved by inquisition that the Valences' lands in Wield were held of the bishop[15] and not of the king in chief, they were restored.[16] Six years later John de Valence was holding half a fee in Wield which had formerly belonged to Beatrice de Wintershull.[17]

The Holts evidently succeeded to part of the Wintershulls' estate, for in 1428 Richard Holt and his co-parceners were holding half a fee in Wield formerly held by John de Valence.[18] After this date there seems to be no mention of Wield until 1569, when the manor was settled on Thomas Sackville, Lord Buckhurst, and his wife Cecilia, daughter of Sir John Baker of Sissinghurst in Kent.[19] [20]

Seven years later it was conveyed by them to Ralph Henslowe,[21] who died seised of the manor of Wield in 1578.[22] His son and heir Thomas conveyed the estate to Thomas Burye in 1591,[23] who sold the manor in 1598 to Arthur Wilmott,[24] in whose family it remained for thirty-six years and was then sold by Edward Wilmott to Constance Lucy, widow, and her son Sir Richard for £1,200.[25]

The manor remained in the possession of the Lucy family for about 140 years,[26] and then passed to the Rodneys,[27] though whether they held by the right of inheritance or by purchase it is difficult to discover. Mr. Earle was the owner of the manor from about 1874 to 1886, when he sold it to Mr. Wood, brother

1 *V.C.H. Hants*, i, 459.
2 Eccl. Com. Ct. R. bdle. 136, No. 1.
3 Ibid. bdle. 85, No. 2.
4 Including the hundred of Bishop's Sutton and Alresford Liberty.
5 Duchy of Lanc. Rentals and Surv. bdle. 8, No. 22*a*.
6 *V.C.H. Hants*, i, 463. Two freemen also held one hide worth 20*s.* in 1086. In 1167 the bishop returned account for half a mark. (*Pipe R.* [Pipe R. Soc.] 13 Hen. II, rot. 12, m. 1.)
7 Feet of F. Hants, Mich. 54 Hen. III.
8 So called for the first time.
9 Inq. p.m. 15 Edw. III, No. 15. The property then consisted of a capital messuage with garden worth per annum 30*s.*; 252 acres of arable land worth 6*d.* per acre, total £6 6*s.*; separate pasture for six horses, twenty oxen, and eight cows, price per head for all horses 12*d.*, for oxen and cows 6*d.*, sum 20*s.*; separate pasture for 168 sheep price per head 1*d.*, sum 14*s.*; one windmill worth 10*s.* per annum; rent of freemen 7*s.* 6*d.*; four cottars paying per annum 6*s.* and a cock at Christmas worth 8*d.*; customs of said cottars worth per annum 10*d.* Sum of whole extent of the manor £11 7*s.*
10 Feet of F. Hants, East. 22 Edw. I.
11 Ibid. Mich. 34 Edw. I.
12 De Banco R. Mich. 34 Edw. I, No. 575, m. 235. Mary de Wintershull was certainly not dead as the claimants asserted, she was still living in 1316, and in that year made a settlement of land in Wield. (Feet of F. Hants, Mich. 9 Edw. II.) This fine seems to point to some relationship between the Valences and the Wintershulls.
13 Most probably John de Drokensford conveyed the manor to Nicholas before his death, though no trace of such a conveyance can be found.
14 This John after his conviction had been delivered to Adam, bishop of Winchester, and had died in prison at Wolvesey.
15 At this date the bishop was receiving 20*s.* 4*d.* from the manor twice yearly. Mins. Accts. bdle. 1142, No. 19.
16 Close, 13 Edw. III, pt. 2, m. 31.
17 *Feud. Aids*, ii, 334.
18 Ibid. ii, 357. William Wynbrode and Christine his wife owned a small estate in Wield about 1368. (Feet of F. Hants, East. 42 Edw. III.)
19 Feet of F. Hants, Hil. 11 Eliz.
20 It seems probable that the manor remained in the hands of the bishop of Winchester until the middle of the sixteenth century, when it passed into the possession of Sir Richard Sackville as patentee of the bishop of Winchester's lands. It was by him settled on his son Thomas, Lord Buckhurst; but it seems impossible to verify the truth of this conjecture, a document which might throw some light on the subject (Com. Pleas Enr. 34 Eliz.) being unfit for production.
21 Feet of F. Hants, Hil. 18 Eliz.
22 Chan. Inq. p.m. 20 Eliz. (Ser. 2), pt. 2, No. 59.
23 Feet of F. Hants, Mich. 33 & 34 Eliz.
24 Ibid. 39 & 40 Eliz.
25 Ibid. Trin. 9 Chas. I.
26 Ibid. 33 & 34 Geo. II.
27 Recov. R. Trin. 18 Geo. III.

Wield Church : East End of Nave

of Mr. Gaythorne Wood of Thedden Grange, Alton, who in his turn sold it to Mr. Barnes Wimbush, from whom it was bought in 1900 by Count D. Beaumont Gurowski, the present lord of the manor.[28]

There is a mill mentioned among the appurtenances of the manor in 1286[29] and in 1569,[30] which probably gave its name to Windmill Hill in the north-west of the parish. There was a park at Wield from an early date. In 1279 complaint was made that certain persons had broken into the park of the bishop of Winchester, hunted therein and carried away deer.[31] Among the entries in the Ministers' Accounts for Wield for 1323 is 'Payment made by the park-keeper of 2*s.* each for 6 carts during the winter.'[32] Beyond these references no record of the park can be found.

CHURCH The church of *ST. JAMES* has a chancel 20 ft. 4 in. by 14 ft., and nave 34 ft. 8 in. by 19 ft. 8 in., with a bell-turret at the west. There was formerly a western tower, but this was destroyed in 1812, when the turret was set up, which contains a single bell.

Externally the building is covered with rough-cast, and has red-tiled roofs. The nave walls are of twelfth-century date, probably *c.* 1150, and those of the chancel, though showing no twelfth-century features, are probably co-eval with them. The chancel has a modern three-light east window of geometrical style, the north and south walls being blank; and the chancel arch is semicircular, of two orders, slightly chamfered on the west face, with a chamfered string at the springing, which is continued up to the angles of the nave. On either side of the arch, which is 5 ft. 8 in. wide, large openings have been cut through the wall.

The nave has two windows on each side, but none at the west; all are apparently the original twelfth-century windows, altered and enlarged in the fifteenth century, single trefoiled or cinquefoiled lights being inserted in three of them, and in the fourth, that at the south-east, two trefoiled lights. There is a blocked south doorway, which, like the chancel arch, is of the twelfth century, its semicircular head with a label showing on the outside. The entrance to the church is by a west doorway with a square head, dating from 1812. The roof timbers are old, with a modern painted wooden ceiling fitted to them; and at the west of the nave is a wooden gallery, also modern. The fittings are also modern, and very good of their kind; a second altar has been set up at the north-east of the nave, and very well furnished. The font, at the west of the nave, is of Purbeck marble, with a shallow square arcaded bowl on a central and four angle shafts, of late twelfth-century date; it was dug up in a garden in the Close at Winchester, and lately given to Wield church.

Below the north-east window of the nave is a trefoiled fourteenth-century recess, connected with the nave altar whose successor has lately been set up here, but the chancel shows no remains of piscina or sedilia, their place being occupied by the large monument of William Waloppe, 1617, whose alabaster effigy, with that of his third wife, lies on a panelled tomb of alabaster under a canopy on which are cherubs holding emblems of mortality. Above the effigies in the recess beneath the canopy are the arms of Wallop quartering Fisher of Chilton Candover.

The plate consists of a communion cup of 1569 with a modern foot, and a very interesting pre-Reformation paten, *c.* 1500, and very like that at Bishop's Sutton, with a silver-gilt edge, and engraved I H S in the centre. It has, however, at some time been beaten inside out, so that the hexagonal central depression has been flattened and the I H S is now on the underside.

The registers are also of more than ordinary interest, the original small paper book of 1538 being preserved. To each year a heading is written, giving the regnal year also, and in the time of Edward VI the full royal titles. There is a gap from 1552 to 1560, but from 1560 to 1562 the same form of heading is retained, the entries to this date being in Latin. From 1562 onwards the heading is dropped, and English used till 1597, when Latin occurs again, the entries of baptisms, &c., being from this time kept separate. The baptisms are entered in two sections, 1597–1663 and 1655–95; the burials in one, 1597–1648; and the marriages likewise, 1597–1678. The book also contains a register of briefs, 1707–13. The second book, likewise of paper, is supplementary to the first, containing baptisms 1568–98, marriages 1563–98, and burials 1561–97.

In a wood at some distance from the village is the site of a destroyed house, known as the Castle. It was probably a house of the Wallop family, but nothing of it now remains, its masonry having been, according to local report, carried off for building material in the village.

ADVOWSON At the time of the Domesday Survey there is no mention of a church in Wield,[33] and the earliest mention seems to be in the year 1280, when the presentation to the church was in the hands of the king during a vacancy of the see of Winchester.[34]

In 1306 the priory of Newark (co. Surrey) acquired the advowson of the church of Wield,[35] by grant of John, bishop of Winchester, and this grant was confirmed by letters patent.

The advowson remained in the hands of the prior and convent until the Dissolution, when the rectory was valued at £4 6*s.* 8*d.*[36]

From this time until about the beginning of the nineteenth century the advowson follows the descent of the manor. From 1817 until the present day presentations to the living have been made by the earls of Portsmouth,[37] whose ancestors, the Wallops, had held the rectorial tithes of Wield since 1586.[38]

CHARITIES In 1872 Miss Jane Ewen by her will proved this date left £100, the interest to be paid yearly to the poor of Lower Wield, under the direction of the incumbent. The legacy (less duty) was invested in £97 0*s.* 9*d.* consols with the official trustees. The dividends are distributed in coal to the cottagers.

28 Information supplied by Count Beaumont Gurowski.
29 Inq. p.m. 15 Edw. I, No. 15.
30 Feet of F. Hants, Hil. 11 Eliz.
31 Pat. 7 Edw. I, m. 5.
32 Mins. Accts. bdle. 1142, No. 19.
33 *V.C.H. Hants*, i, 463.
34 Pat. 8 Edw. I, m. 20.
35 Inq. a.q.d. 34 Edw. I, No. 115; Pat. 34 Edw. I, m. 13.
36 *Valor Eccl.* (Rec. Com.), ii, 33.
37 *Clerical Guide*, *Clergy List*, 1817–1906.
38 Recov. R. Trin. 28 Eliz. m. 63.

WINNALL

Wynhale, Wylehall (xiv–xv cent.); Wynhall, Winnall (xvi–xvii cent.).

Winnall is a small parish of about 533 acres lying to the north-east of Winchester, at the foot of St. Giles Hill, seeming to be locally part of Winchester. The village lies in the south, the few cottages being grouped along a road which is a continuation of Water Street (Winchester). This road runs north through the downland which composes the rest of the parish, directly to Easton.

The small picturesque church of St. Martin stands at the upper end of the village street on the west almost immediately opposite the rectory, and a little to the east of the church lie Winnall Farm and the manor-house. The Didcot, Newbury, and Winchester Branch of the Great Western Railway runs along the eastern side of the parish, with its nearest station at Winchester. The River Itchen, as it curves south below the Worthies, flows along the western borderline of the parish through low-lying meadows which are constantly flooded.

Since the extension of the boundaries of the borough of Winchester the greater part of Winnall has been included in the borough, and since the Local Government Board order, dated September, 1894, the rural parts of Winnall have become part of the parish of Chilcomb Without.

MANOR *WINNALL* was probably one of the seven small manors included in Chilcomb (q.v.) in 1086.[1]

It was evidently confirmed to the prior and convent of St. Swithun in 1205, together with Chilcomb and most of the land round Winchester,[2] and it remained in their possession until the time of the Dissolution,[3] when the manor, together with the rectory, was granted by Henry VIII to the dean and chapter of Winchester;[4] it has now become absorbed in the borough of Winchester.

In 1651 the Commissioners for the Sale of Bishops' Lands sold 13 acres of arable land in the parish of Winnall to Nicholas Love.[5]

CHURCH The church of *ST. MARTIN* was rebuilt in 1858 of flint and stone in thirteenth-century style. It consists of a chancel, nave, south porch, and western turret containing one bell by W. and R. Cor of Aldbourne, 1713.

The plate is a modern set, consisting of silver chalice, paten, flagon, and almsdish of 1872, given by the Misses Knight. There are also two plated almsdishes and a pewter flagon.

The register of baptisms dates from 1680, of marriages from 1699, and of burials from 1697.

ADVOWSON The church of St. Martin, Winnall, was probably one of the nine churches included under Chilcomb in the Domesday Survey.[6] In 1291 it was assessed at £8,[7] but by 1335 the rectory was only valued at £3 6*s.* 8*d.*[8]

The advowson is now and always has been in the hands of the bishop.[9] The rectorial tithes were confirmed with the manor to the prior and convent of St. Swithun in 1205,[10] and remained in their possession until the Dissolution. In 1541 they passed with the manor to the dean and chapter of Winchester.[11]

CHARITIES In 1859 Henry Knight, by will proved this date, left £150 consols, income to be applied by minister and churchwardens on 20 February in each year (the anniversary of his birthday) in distribution of bread, fuel, or money, among the necessitous poor of the parish.

THE LIBERTY OF ALRESFORD

Kinewald, king of the West Saxons, on his conversion to Christianity about the middle of the seventh century, granted forty *mansae* at Alresford, afterwards forming the *LIBERTY* of *ALRESFORD*, to the church at Winchester free from all secular service except the *trinoda necessitas*.[1]

This grant was confirmed by King Ine in 701,[2] and again by King Egbert between 825 and 831.[3] Towards the end of the ninth century Bishop Denewulf leased the forty hides at Alresford to his kinsman Alfred for life.[4] However, a charter of 909 shows that Alfred during his tenure was indicted for crime, and the estate was therefore forfeited and only redeemed by Denewulf at the cost of a valuable offering.[5] Further, to prevent the recurrence of such a scandal King Edward decreed that no layman should be granted a lease of church property. However in 956 King Edwy was prevailed upon by Ælfric son of Alfred to restore to him the forty hides at Alresford;[6] but this grant was annulled in 964 by King Edgar, who restored to the church of Winchester 'with most humble devotion land seized from the said church by money-lovers.'[7] After this the bishop remained in quiet possession of his liberty, and was holding it in 1086, as forty-two hides, of which seventeen were leased to various tenants.[8] The boundaries of the liberty, as given in early charters, are somewhat difficult to trace,[9] but the entry in

1 *V.C.H. Hants*, i, 463.
2 Dugdale, *Mon.* i, 211; *Cal. of Pap. Letters*, i, 21.
3 *Feud. Aids*, ii, 320.
4 Pat. 33 Hen. VIII, pt. 9, m. 34–40.
5 Close, 1651, pt. 37, No. 18.
6 *V.C.H. Hants*, i, 463.
7 *Pope Nich. Tax.* (Rec. Com.), 210.
8 *Valor Eccl.* (Rec. Com.), ii, 5.
9 *Wykeham's Reg.* (Hants Rec. Soc.), i, 31, 177, 219; Inst. Bks. (P.R.O.).
10 *Cal. of Pap. Letters*, i, 21.
11 Pat. 33 Hen. VIII, pt. 9, m. 34–40.

1 Dugdale, *Mon.* i, 210.
2 Birch, *Cart. Sax.* i, 148.
3 Ibid. i, 554.
4 Ibid. ii, 280.
5 Ibid. ii, 291.
6 Birch, *Cart. Sax.* iii, 115.
7 Ibid. iii, 404.
8 *V.C.H. Hants*, i, 459.
9 In the charters the following occur as boundaries:—Cendefer, Hremmescumbes geate, Dregtune, Ticieburnan, and Icenan. They can be identified respectively as Brown Candover, Rampscombe Farm, Drayton Farm, Tichborne, and the Itchen.

Domesday Book shows quite well that it comprised the modern parishes of New Alresford, Old Alresford, and Medsted, and perhaps that of Wield, for no less than three churches are included in the extent representing the churches of New and Old Alresford and Medsted, and leading to the inference that New Alresford and Medsted were settled villages with separate churches.

A statement in a book of customs of the hundred of Bishop's Sutton of the time of Henry III to the effect that Alresford great pond belonged not to the hundred of Bishop's Sutton but to the hundred of Alresford [10] furnishes an additional proof that Old Alresford was in Alresford Liberty, for the pond was parcel of the manor of Old Alresford.[11] The bishop held hundred courts twice a year at Martinmas and Hocktide for both New Alresford borough and Old Alresford manor,[12] including the tithings of Old Alresford, Medsted, and Wield,[13] and the latter likewise paid tithing-pence or cert-money at the hundred court.[14] Owing to some confusion, however, Old Alresford sometimes sent a tithing-man to Fawley hundred court,[15] and Old Alresford, Medsted, and Wield were usually assessed with the parishes of Fawley Hundred for the payment of taxes.[16] Hence it followed that when the bishop ceased to hold his Alresford hundred courts, Old Alresford, Medsted, and Wield were included in Fawley Hundred, as in the population returns for 1831, while Alresford Liberty and New Alresford borough came to be looked upon as interchangeable terms.

The liberty remained in the possession of the bishops of Winchester until 1551, when it was among the possessions of the bishopric which were surrendered by John Poynet to the crown on his accession to the see.[17] In the same year Edward VI granted it to Sir John Gate,[18] but it was restored with the other episcopal property in 1557,[19] and remained in the possession of the see of Winchester until, under the Root and Branch Bill, it was sold in 1648 to Thomas Hussey for £2,683 9*s*. 1¼*d*.[20] Alresford came back to the bishopric at the Restoration, and remained part of its possessions until 1869, when the lands of the see of Winchester were taken over by the Ecclesiastical Commissioners, who are the owners at the present day.

The modern parish of *NEW ALRESFORD* comprises about 693 acres of arable and pasture land, sloping gradually north and south to the valley of the River Alre, which becomes the southern boundary line between New and Old Alresford. The town is in the extreme north-east of the parish on high ground, the streets sloping gradually up to the Market House, which stands almost in the centre of the parish, where West Street, East Street, and Broad Street meet.

The road from Southampton to London cuts through the parish, forming the main street of the town, approaching it from the west through a long avenue of fine old trees.[21] At the end of the avenue the road dips downhill, where it is called Pound Hill, since the pound originally stood here on the north side of the road, and again sharply uphill into the town, taking the name of West Street as far as the market-place. Here it starts downhill again, and is known as East Street, becoming narrower and bearing to the south as it leaves the town and goes towards Bishop's Sutton. Branching north from West Street by the market-place is Broad Street, a wide short stretch of road which sweeps gently down towards the river. At the lower end of Broad Street two smaller roads branch off to the north, the more easterly one leading to Old Alresford across a small bridge, probably identical with the stone bridge mentioned by Leland in his *Itinerary*. It has now been widened on the south side, but on the north its original pointed arch, which dates from the latter part of the fourteenth century, can be seen from the garden of the house near by, and is in perfect condition. The span is barely six feet, the stream which it crosses being a small one, dammed up just below the bridge to work a mill.

West Street itself, with its numerous inns—the 'Running Horse,' the 'White Horse,' the 'Dolphin,' the Swan Hotel, and the Bell Inn—combines memories of old coaching days with the modern days of the motor-car. It has all the quiet picturesqueness of a market town of the old days, yet its peacefulness is continually disturbed by the noise of motor-cars on their way from London.

Although the plan of the modern town is almost identical with that of the original town as it was rebuilt by Bishop Godfrey de Lucy in the thirteenth century, the houses only date back for the most part to the eighteenth and early nineteenth centuries, since the town suffered from fire both in the seventeenth and eighteenth centuries. However, just to the north of the place where the most disastrous fire began in 1689, at the lower end of Broad Street, are several older houses, one containing some early seventeenth-century panelling and chimney-pieces, of rather rough and simple workmanship, but interesting specimens of the ornament employed in small houses of the time.

The church of St. John the Baptist, standing behind the market-house and approached by a narrow passage from West Street, suffered severely in the fire of 1689, and was described by Duthy in 1839 as 'a plain neat substantial structure . . . possessing no monuments of any particular interest,' and 'better calculated to afford accommodation to its congregation than materials to the topographer.'[22] The rectory is some distance from the church, standing in wide grounds south of the Alresford railway station, which is on the Alton branch of the London and South-Western Railway as it runs through the parish south of the town.

[10] Duchy of Lanc. Rentals, bdle. 8, No. 26.

[11] This is clear from the court rolls and ministers' accounts of Old Alresford manor.

[12] A series of these rolls is preserved at the Public Record Office.

[13] Old Alresford and Medsted tithings always sent tithing-men to the Old Alresford court, Wield only occasionally (Eccl. Com. Ct. R. bdle. 85, No. 2; bdle. 94, No. 2; bdle. 99, No. 8).

[14] Mins. Accts. bdle. 1141, No. 8.

[15] e.g. to the hundred courts of 1465 and 1486 (Eccl. Com. Ct. R. bdle. 80, Nos. 1 and 2).

[16] Exch. Lay Subs. R. Hants, bdle. 173, Nos. 23, 200, 221.

The contributions of New Alresford borough on the other hand were sometimes returned with those of the parishes of Bishop's Sutton Hundred, and sometimes with those of the other Hampshire boroughs.

[17] Pat. 5 Edw. VI, pt. 6, m. 20.

[18] Ibid. pt. 5, m. 20.

[19] Ibid. 4 & 5 Phil. and Mary, pt. 7, m. 24.

[20] Close, 24 Chas. I, pt. 3, m. 16.

[21] On either side of this avenue are strips of land called Avenue Common, which are the property of the town trustees, who received them as successors of the bailiff and burgesses, the latter having acquired them by gift from the bishop of Winchester, lord of the manor.

[22] Duthy, *Sketches of Hants*, 108.

Of the several houses of note in the parish, Arlebury House, or New Place, is a fine house built in Italian style, standing west of the town and north of the main road to Winchester. Charles Kingsley is said to have frequently stayed here, probably when he was rector of Eversley. Miss Mitford, the authoress of *Our Village*, is said to have been born in a house in Broad Street, which bears a tablet recording the fact.[23] On the south side of West Street, near a house called St. John's, there formerly stood a meeting-house of the Quakers and a cemetery. The meeting-house was standing in 1750, but has since been pulled down, and no trace either of it or of the graveyard now remains.

The parish contains 244¼ acres of arable land and 283¾ acres of permanent grass.[24] The soil is chalky loam, the subsoil chalk. The chief crops are wheat, oats, turnips, and watercress.[25]

Among place-names can be mentioned Bouerewey, Abourewey, Houlendelle, Basteletyn, La Floudeland, Jagonslane, and Le Hankysburgh[26] (xv cent.); and Sewelsebryge[27] and Boltings[28] (xvi cent.).

The following sixteenth-century perambulation of the vill of New Alresford is preserved at the Public Record Office: 'Perambulation there beginning at the bridge to the north of the vill there and stretching east to Utley Dych and Furley Dych, and thence stretching south to the east of Shiplond over the way leading to Sutton, and thence on the western part of Swetley to Appledowne, and so by the hedge from New Alresford even to a certain ditch, and by the ditch to the southern end of Le Merchis and by the hedge to a stream, and thence north by the stream to Tottenmede, and thence east by the great stream coming out of Alresford Pond to the eastern part of Brodmed, and thence by the land of Roger Crope to the north of the mill called Townemyll and thence to the bridge.'[28a]

BOROUGH OF NEW ALRESFORD

According to local tradition the early existence of New Alresford as distinct from Old Alresford and Medsted was due to a defeat inflicted by the Saxons on a party of Danes near the village of West Tisted about five miles east of Alresford. The Saxons granted quarter to the defeated enemy on condition that they went to the ford over the River Alre to be baptized. In commemoration of the victory a statue of the Virgin was then erected in the churchyard of Old Alresford.[29] New Alresford was certainly a separate village in the reign of William the Conqueror, though less important than the village of Old Alresford,[30] and it would doubtless have remained in this subordinate position had it not been for the exertions of its lord Godfrey de Lucy bishop of Winchester (1189–1204), who often resided in the neighbouring palace of Bishop's Sutton, and was naturally anxious to promote its welfare. In the first place, he made the Itchen a navigable waterway for barges and flat-bottomed boats from Southampton to Winchester as well as from thence to the very head of the river, by throwing up a great dyke at Alresford, by which means the water from two or three local streams was gathered into a great lake now called Alresford Pond, and a reservoir of water provided for supplying the navigation.[31] In reward for this scheme undertaken at his own expense King John gave the bishop the royalty of the river, and in addition granted him free licence and authority to collect, receive, take, and apply to his own proper use and benefit . . . all fines, tolls, taxes, and customs from goods and merchandise conveyed up or down the River Itchen.[32] In the second place, having obtained a charter from King John in 1200 granting to him a weekly market in Alresford on Thursday,[33] he made a spacious market-place, causing all the buildings to be taken down and rebuilt with the square in the centre, the market-house at one end and the great corn-mills and public ovens and boulting-house at the other. According to Camden he altered the name of his town to New Market, with respect perhaps to Old Alresford adjoining, but this name continued not long with the common people, the best preservers of language.[34] In 1202 King John granted Godfrey de Lucy a fair at Alresford for three days, on the Feast of the Nativity of St. John the Baptist and the two following days.[35] This grant was confirmed by Edward I in 1282, and by Richard II in 1380,[36] and an additional fair was added on the Feast of the Ascension of our Lord some time later.[37]

New Alresford was now well equipped as a market town, and by means of the canal was linked with Winchester and Southampton. Henry III increased its trade still more when he connected it with Alton by a royal highway instead of the hitherto only means of communication—a narrow road passing through a continuation of woods where foresters and shepherds had committed all sorts of depredations. The bishops of Winchester and Oxford, together with Robert de St. John and others, met before the king's justices in 1269, and surrendered all their title and claims in these woodlands in order that they might be grubbed up and brought into a state of cultivation, and immediately afterwards the king by deed granted his own demesnes in the neighbourhood in order that a royal road, spacious, wide, and good, might be forthwith made from Alton to Alresford.[38] It seems probable that the old road, which runs from Alton by Chawton Wood and several solitary farms through Bighton, and enters Old Alresford over the causeway at the head of the pond, is the royal road of

23 The whole question of her birthplace was discussed in *Hants N. and Q.*

24 Statistics from Bd. of Agric. (1905).

25 This latter industry dates from very early times, there being many mentions of 'Cress pytts' in the sixteenth-century borough court rolls.

26 Duchy of Lanc. Rentals and Surv. bdle. 8, No. 21.

27 Eccl. Com. Ct. R. bdle. 85, No. 3.

28 Eccl. Com. Various, 57, No. 159460$\frac{2}{2}$.

28a Eccl. Com. Ct. R. bdle. 136, No. 1.

29 *Hants N. and Q.* iii, 66. The author adds that two or three circumstances give some probability to the story, such as the existence of four barrows in Burrow Lane, West Tisted; also of a hillock in Old Alresford churchyard, which is said to contain the ruins of an ancient chapel, but that the story looks suspiciously like the account of the defeat of the Danes by Alfred at Edinson.

30 *V.C.H. Hants*, i, 459.

31 Dugdale, *Mon.* i, 196.

32 Ibid.

33 Chart R. 1 John, m. 10. This grant was confirmed to Godfrey bishop of Winchester in 1378 (ibid. 2 Ric. II, m. 7).

34 Camden, *Mag. Brit.* (1789), i, 117. His statement is probably based on the words 'Item forum innovatum est apud Halresford per Godefridum de Lucy episcopum Wintoniensem appellavitque nomen ville novum Forum,' in a cartulary of Waverley Abbey (*Ann. Mon.* [Rolls Ser.], ii, 252).

35 Chart. R. 4 Ric. II, No. 1.

36 Ibid.

37 Eccl. Com. Ct. R. bdle. 73, No. 7; Eccl. Com. Various, bdle. 57, No. 159460$\frac{2}{2}$. A court of piepowder was held by the bailiff of the borough on the fair days. The rolls of the courts held in 1420 are preserved at the Public Record Office.

38 Duthy, *Sketches of Hants*, 88; Chart. R. 53 Hen. III, m. 10.

New Alresford

New Alresford : The Old Bridge

Henry III. With these advantages it is not surprising that the trade of New Alresford flourished. In the fourteenth century it was reckoned as one of the ten great wool markets in England, and its prosperity may be gauged from the fact that in the reign of Edward III a contribution of ninths produced £2 15*s.* from New Alresford as compared with £9 from Southampton and only 8*s.* 6*d.* from Portsmouth.[39] The manufacture of cloth was also carried on vigorously by the inhabitants, at one time there being no fewer than four fulling-mills within a mile of the town.[40] A further proof of its importance is afforded by the fact that in the reign of Edward I it gained the right of representation in Parliament, sending two burgesses to the Parliaments of 1295, 1300–1, and 1306–7,[41] and one to the Parliament of 1306.[42] Although the town seems never to have received a charter of incorporation, the inhabitants from a very early date possessed certain privileges, as is shown by a charter of 1256 whereby Ethelmar, bishop-elect of Winchester, granted to the burgesses of Francheville or Newtown in the Isle of Wight all the liberties and free customs which were enjoyed by the burgesses of Taunton, Witney, Alresford, or Farnham.[43] The king's grant also in 1302 of pavage to the bailiff and good men of Alresford seems to point to the nucleus of a corporation,[44] and if the town had prospered as it had begun it seems probable that a charter of incorporation would have been granted to it at no distant date. But linked up as it was with Winchester, the prosperity as well as the adversity of the inhabitants of New Alresford depended to a great extent on that of the former city, and when, after enduring the calamities of hostile incursions and destructive pestilence, Winchester sank under that ordinance of Edward III which sapped the foundation of its trade by removing the wool-staple thence to Calais, the prosperity of New Alresford declined. A fire of 1440 and a pestilence in the reign of Edward IV completed the ruin of the town,[45] and in the latter reign the place was so deserted and the survivors reduced to such distress that the bailiff found it impossible to collect his quit-rents.[46] However, under the Tudors the town recovered to some extent from its depression. It made considerable advances in the trade and manufacture of cloth, other officers, such as ale-tasters, tax-collectors, leather-sealers, and constables, began to be elected in the court leet of the borough,[47] and a statement of the reign of Edward VI to the effect that the inhabitants of New Alresford held in common to the use of the poor of the town a house or upper room built over the Churchway at the gate of the churchyard, a close called the Town Close, and half an acre of land lying in Downegate Furlong,[48] seems to indicate the existence of the municipal governing body which afterwards consisted of the bailiff and eight burgesses.[49] A further proof that it already existed and held the borough at fee-farm of the bishop seems to be afforded by the report of a surveyor sent down by Sir John Gate before his purchase of the bailiwick of Bishop's Sutton. His language is not very clear, but he states: 'The boroughe of New Alresford standeth all upon quite rents,' 'The boroughe is the worst rent within the hooll bailiwicke, as I take it, becawse of the contynual reparations,' and again 'Alresford is clerely gevin bi the bisshopp to one of the porters of the towne, as I have lernd, which must be considered upon your purchase if it be not remedied.'[50] All this seems to point to the same conclusion that the borough was farmed out for a fixed rent, nearly all of which the bishop had to spend on the town, while the words 'if it be not remedied' seem to hint that the right was only a prescriptive one. At length, on 10 December, 1572, Robert Horne bishop of Winchester by charter granted the borough to the bailiff and burgesses to hold of him at a fixed annual rent of £16 14*s.* 2¼*d.*, viz. £15 15*s.* 6¼*d.* farm of the borough, 12*s.* picage and stallage of fairs and markets, and 6*s.* 8*d.* farm of a tenement called Bultings in the north of the town.[51] From this date the income of the borough was applied in pursuance of resolutions passed at meetings of the bailiff and eight burgesses.[52] At these meetings also the bailiff and the other officers of the borough, such as constables, ale-conners or beer-tasters, and kerners of flesh and fish, were elected and vacancies among the burgesses filled up, but at each election the bailiff, burgess, or other officer was presented and sworn in at the court leet of the borough.[53] The corporation also was accustomed to exercise a legal jurisdiction within the borough, and held a law-day court every three weeks for the trial of inferior actions of debt, trespass, &c., but it was discontinued after the burning down of the council-house in 1689.[54] Such was the constitution of the borough during the seventeenth and following centuries.

Its prosperity during this time was repeatedly checked by outbreaks of fire.[55] The first of these took place in 1644, after the battle of Cheriton, when the royal troops, under the earl of Forth and Lord Hopton, being forced to leave the town, set fire to it at both ends as they marched out, knowing the republican tendencies of the inhabitants. Owing, however, to the exertions of the victorious Roundheads who were quickly on the scene, the ravages of the fire were stayed before much damage was done.[56] About 1689 almost the whole town, including the church, market-house, and council-house, was destroyed by a more disastrous fire, attributed by some to a party of soldiers who had just marched through the town.[57] According to the testimony of an Irishwoman, however, Mary Collins by name, the incendiaries were a company of sixty-seven Irishmen and six Irishwomen, who pretended themselves to be distressed Protestants, forced out of Ireland, but whose real object in coming to England was to set

39 *Inq. Non.* (Rec. Com.), 124.
40 Duthy, *Sketches of Hants*, 104.
41 *Return of Members of Parl.* pt. i, 5, 14, 25.
42 Ibid. 23.
43 *Vide* Chart. R. 13 Edw. I, m. 2.
44 Pat. 30 Edw. I, m. 14.
45 Duthy, *Sketches of Hants*, 104.
46 Eccl. Com. Various, bdle. 57, No. 159460⅔. In this series there are six ministers' accounts of Alresford borough previous to the reign of Henry VII. On each of these accounts there is a long list of sums of money owing to the bishop from various bailiffs.
47 Eccl. Com. Ct. R. bdle. 85, No. 3.
48 Ibid. bdle. 136, No. 1.
49 *Parl. Pap.* 1880, vol. 31, p. 8.
50 Duchy of Lanc. Rentals and Surv. bdle. 8, No. 22*a*.
51 Eccl. Com. Various, bdle. 56, No. 159460½.
52 *Parl Pap.* 1880, vol. 31, p. 8.
53 Ibid.
54 Duthy, *Sketches of Hants*, 108.
55 The inhabitants' fear of fire is clearly shown by the heavy fines inflicted upon persons for having dangerous and insufficient flues in their houses (Eccl. Com. Ct. R. bdle. 99, No. 8.)
56 Woodward, *Hist. of Hants*, ii, 28.
57 Ibid.; *Cal. S. P. Dom.* 1689–90, pp. 94, 121.

towns and houses on fire. She declared that they were all well armed and that the women carried fire balls, that they intended to burn Winchester, and that they had already set fire to several houses near Sherborne, and in addition gave the names and descriptions of five of the company.[58] At this lapse of time, however, it is difficult to test the truth of this story.

It seemed that the prosperity of the town, recovered during the preceding century, was lost for ever ; but within fifteen years, owing to the industry of the inhabitants and the willing help which poured in from the neighbouring gentry and a royal brief for assistance,[59] there was but one person, an old and crippled female, who received support from the parish,[60] and the town had begun to prosper once more. However, another fire, which also proved disastrous, owing possibly to the number of thatched houses in the town,[61] broke out in 1736. It began in a brewhouse and spread quickly along the thatched roofs, enveloping the streets before many of the inhabitants could save any of their goods.[62] But the same spirit of determination in the inhabitants, helped by various relief funds, again reinstated and rebuilt the town on the lines of its modern existence. In 1753 the new London road was made, and the town became a great posting centre, and so continued till the coming of the railway.[63] Defoe's *Tour* (ed. 1778) speaks of Alresford as having 'now a very great market every Thursday, particularly about Michaelmas, for sheep, corn, etc., and a small market-house standing on wooden pillars.' The town is now important as the centre of an extensive agricultural district, much stock being brought in on market day, and especially on the last Thursday in July and the Thursday after 11 October, on which days the fairs are now held, and its trade is still further increased by its position on the main road from London to Southampton. The corporation continued until March, 1886, when by the operation of the Municipal Corporations Act, 1883 (46 & 47 Vic. cap. 18), it was dissolved. In 1890 its property was vested in the town trustees, who administer the revenues of the borough at the present day.

CHURCH

The church of *ST. JOHN THE BAPTIST* was burnt in the fire which destroyed so much of the town in 1689, the tower and walls of the nave alone remaining. The chancel was rebuilt of the same width as its predecessor, but 10 ft. shorter from east to west, the nave arcades being replaced by wooden posts which were boarded and painted. In 1897–8 the late seventeenth-century building was replaced by modern Gothic work, the chancel being entirely rebuilt and extended to its former length, the wooden posts replaced by stone arcades, and the whole church thoroughly renovated, except the tower.

The oldest remaining feature in the building, with the exception of part of a twelfth-century font found during the repairs, is a thirteenth-century lancet at the west end of the south aisle, partly overlapped by the west respond of the south arcade, which is set to the south of the line of the mediaeval arcade, as a weathering on the east face of the tower shows. The lower part of the tower is of fourteenth-century work, but the earlier developments of the plan are naturally difficult to trace. The nave evidently had a south aisle in the thirteenth century, which must have been narrower than the present, and parts of two large thirteenth-century bases, preserved with other pieces of old stonework at the west end of the north aisle, belong to an arcade of that date. The east window of the north chapel has part of a late thirteenth-century nook-shaft in its south jamb, witnessing to work done at that time, but it is not in its original position. In the fifteenth century both aisles were probably set out to their existing width, and several pieces of fourteenth and fifteenth century detail show that a good deal of building went on in this period. The north and south doorways of the nave and parts of the aisle windows are of the fifteenth century, the traces of previously existing work having been carefully followed at the late repairs. The south doorway is now blocked, and the north has lost a porch which formerly sheltered it.

The upper part of the tower is of red brick, embattled and crowned by a large vane, the belfry windows having oak frames with two trefoiled lights. In the ground stage is a modern west doorway, and above it an ogee-headed fourteenth-century trefoiled light. There are similar windows on the north and south in this stage, and the tower arch is of the same date, of three chamfered orders with repaired jambs. Above it, but below the weathering of the old roof, is a square-headed opening, and there is another like it above the old roof line, but blocked, ranging with similar windows on the other faces of the tower. In the north side of the ground story is a blocked eighteenth-century doorway in red brick with a semicircular head.

The font is modern, but parts of two of its predecessors have been found : the twelfth-century fragment already noted and part of the shaft of a fourteenth-century font.

The modern fittings of the church are very good, and the five-light east window of the chancel is filled with excellent modern glass, the subject being Christ in glory.

There are eight bells of 1811, by Mears of Whitechapel.

The plate consists of a cup of 1564, a standing paten of 1695, a second paten of 1729, and a large flagon, 14¼ in. high, of 1728.

The earliest register book runs from 1678 to 1734, containing the burials in woollen, and there are scattered entries, eleven of 1714 and one of 1722, on the fly-leaf, four pages with baptisms and burials 1724–5 and marriages 1724–32, and on a loose leaf a few baptisms ranging between 1726 and 1735.

The second book contains baptisms and marriages from 1736 to 1768, and burials copied from the first

[58] *Hist. MSS. Com. Rep.* x, App. vi, 185.

[59] A verbatim copy of the royal brief is printed in *Hants N. and Q.* viii, 47–9. Owing to the fact that more than three years elapsed before the inhabitants applied for and obtained the brief, the collection did not amount to so much as was expected. The whole of the amount collected after all expenses were paid did not exceed 12*s.* in the £ in their several losses (*Hants N. and Q.* vi, 133).

[60] Duthy, *Sketches of Hants*, 107.

[61] The reeds that grow so plentifully in the old Alresford pond were formerly used for thatching.

[62] Duthy, *Sketches of Hants*, 107 ; Woodward, *Hist. of Hants*, ii, 30.

[63] Woodward, *Hist. of Hants*, ii, 30. Even before the making of the new road the town was a posting centre, as may be seen from the petition of Francis Barnard, innkeeper of New Alresford, in 1661 for renewal of his patent that his house might be the post house from Southampton to Winchester towards London, and he himself might be continued postmaster (*Cal. S.P. Dom.* 1661–2, p. 125).

book, and continued to 1768; the third book is a copy of Nos. 1 and 2, with baptisms and burials continued to 1812, and the fourth book is the printed marriage register 1754–1812.

ADVOWSON New Alresford was formerly a chapelry attached to the rectory of Old Alresford (q.v.). In 1291 the church of Old Alresford, together with the chapel, was valued at £26 13*s.* 4*d.*,[64] but in 1535 New Alresford chapel was valued separately at £3 6*s.* 8*d.*[65]

The chapelry of New Alresford remained attached to the church of Old Alresford and followed its descent (q.v.) until the year 1850, when it was separated and formed into a distinct ecclesiastical benefice.[66] The living is now a rectory in the gift of the bishop of Winchester.

In the parish of New Alresford there was a brotherhood or fraternity called the brotherhood or fraternity of Jesus,[67] endowed with a tenement in New Alresford called Jesus House, a shop and another tenement situated near the porch of the parish church of New Alresford,[68] 'towardes the fyndynge of a priest called the brotherhed priest to the intent that he should synge within the parishe churche of New Alresford as well for the ayde and helpe of the curate as also for the ease of the inhabitauntes there.'[69] The brotherhood was erected within the parish church of New Alresford, and was of the yearly value of £3 14*s.*, of which the priest received £2 10*s.* 8*d.*[70] On its suppression in the reign of Edward VI its possessions became the property of the crown. Part were granted by Queen Elizabeth in 1589 to Richard Branthwaite and Roger Bromley,[71] while the rest remained with the crown until 1618, in which year James I granted them by letters patent to James Ouchterlong and Richard Gurnard.[72] Jesus House was the property and residence of James Apsdale in 1774,[73] but the further history of these tenements has not been traced.

CHARITIES The Town Trust.—The Town Trust property now consists of the fire-engine house and site let to the overseers for £6 a year; tolls arising from fairs and markets averaging £80 a year; a building known as the Hurdle House in the Fair Field; and two strips of copyhold land at Pound Hill used as a recreation ground. Also £205 17*s.* 7*d.* consols with the Official trustees of Charitable Funds, who also hold £60 3*s.* 8*d.* consols received towards the repayment of a loan of £200 to Henry Perin's School.

The administration of the trust is regulated by a scheme made under the above-mentioned Act in 1890 (modified by a scheme in 1894), whereby trustees were appointed, who were authorized to contribute out of the income a yearly sum of £20 for the public benefit of the inhabitants of the parishes of Old Alresford, New Alresford, and of Pound Hill, and the maintenance of trees in Broad Street, and a yearly sum of £25 to Perin's School, and to apply the balance towards the improvement of the water supply or other public purpose.

The trustees of the Town Trust also administer the income of the following charities, namely:—

Charity of James Withers (1680), consisting of a rent-charge of £5 received annually in respect of land taken in 1861 for the purposes of the railway, and £99 12*s.* consols, arising from the sale of the remainder of the land allotted on the inclosure in 1806, and an annual sum of 8*s.* received in respect of property on the Dean.

Charity of John Pink (1642), consisting of an annual rent-charge of £10 received in respect of land taken in 1861 for the purposes of the railway, and £234 11*s.* 9*d.* consols arising from the sale of the remainder of the land allotted in 1806.

Susanna Eliza Coney's Charity for Poor (will 1885), consisting of £177 6*s.* 9*d.* consols; and

Susanna Eliza Coney's Charity for Education, consisting of £206 11*s.* 10*d.* consols.

The several sums of stock are held by the Official Trustees of Charitable Funds; and by a scheme, dated 21 July, 1893, the income of the last-mentioned charity is directed to be applied in the maintenance of exhibitions tenable at Perin's School or other place of higher education to deserving children bona fide resident in New Alresford.

Church Trust.—From time immemorial the town was entitled to common rights for the benefit of the church in respect of which 1 r. 36 p. was allotted on the inclosure in 1806, which was sold in 1865 for £60; a plot of garden ground containing 2 r. 8 p. situated in the Dean was also held by the churchwardens, which was sold in 1888 for £150. The purchase moneys are now represented by £218 18*s.* 11*d.* consols with the official trustees.

In 1696 Henry Perin by his will founded and endowed a grammar school in this parish.[74] By a scheme under the Endowed Schools Acts, approved by Her Majesty in Council, 7 October, 1899, provision is made for the establishment of foundation scholarships, each entitling the holder to exemption, total or partial, from the payment of tuition fees at the rate of not more than one scholarship for every five scholars, to be awarded to boys and girls of the parishes of New Alresford, Old Alresford, Bishop's Sutton, and Cheriton (with a preference as to one-third for boys and girls of the parish of New Alresford) qualified as therein mentioned.

The present endowment of the school consists of the school, master's house, and garden in hand, 51 a. 3 r. 36 p. of land at New Alresford let at £41 12*s.* a year; a rent-charge of £5 on land at Bishop's Sutton; and a yearly sum of £25 out of the income of the New Alresford Town Trust.

Certain works of improvement in the school buildings were effected in 1901 at a cost of £358 10*s.*, whereof £150 was provided by the Hampshire County Council, and the governors of Perin's School were authorized to borrow £200 from the Town Trust at 3½ per cent. to be repaid in fifteen years (see above).

William Todd (1681) gave £3 per annum to be distributed in the church porch on Good Friday. The rent-charge is duly received and applied.

In 1831 Mrs. Jenny Harris by deed declared the trusts of a sum of stock to produce £10 a year to be applied for the benefit of the poor in bread or

64 *Pope Nich. Tax.* (Rec. Com.), 211.
65 *Valor Eccl.* (Rec. Com.), ii, 9.
66 Woodward, *Hist. of Hants*, ii, 24; *Clergy List*, 1850.
67 Eccl. Com. Ct. R. bdle. 136, No. 1.
68 *Vide* Pat. 16 Jas. I, pt. 13, m. 14.
69 Chant. Cert. 52, No. 23.
70 Ibid.
71 Pat. 31 Eliz. pt. 11, m. 27.
72 Ibid. 16 Jas. I, pt. 13, m. 14.
73 Robert Boyes' MS. History of Alresford (1774) *penes* Lord Swaythling.
74 *V.C.H. Hants*, ii, 387, 391.

other provisions on 1 January. The fund consists of £333 6*s.* 8*d.* consols with the official trustees.

In 1853 William Wilkinson by will left to the vicar and churchwardens £100, the interest to be applied on St. Thomas's Day in the distribution of articles in kind to the poor. The legacy (less duty) was invested in £94 14*s.* 9*d.* consols.

In 1862 John Dunn by will directed his executors to purchase a sum of consols sufficient to produce £5 a year to be applied on Candlemas Day in the distribution of bread amongst needy and deserving poor. The legacy is represented by £166 13*s.* 4*d.* consols.

In 1882 Christopher Cooke, by will proved this date, bequeathed £5 a year for the distribution of food, clothes, fuel or money among the poor, subject to the deduction of £1 for the minister for a sermon on 26 June, when that day shall fall on a Sunday. The legacy is now represented by £200 2½ per cent. annuities with the official trustees.

THE HUNDRED OF BERMONDSPIT

CONTAINING THE PARISHES OF

DUMMER WITH KEMPSHOT
ELLISFIELD
FARLEIGH WALLOP
HERRIARD
NUTLEY
PRESTON CANDOVER
SOUTH WARNBOROUGH
UPTON GREY
WESTON CORBETT

At the time of the Domesday Survey the hundred of Bermondspit consisted of the parishes of Candover, Herriard, Ellisfield, Nutley, Farleigh, Dummer, and 'Sudberie.'[1] Of these Sudberie only remains unidentified.[2] It was held, according to Domesday, by Ednod and Edwi of King Edward. After their deaths, Cola, their kinsman, redeemed this land of Earl William of Here-

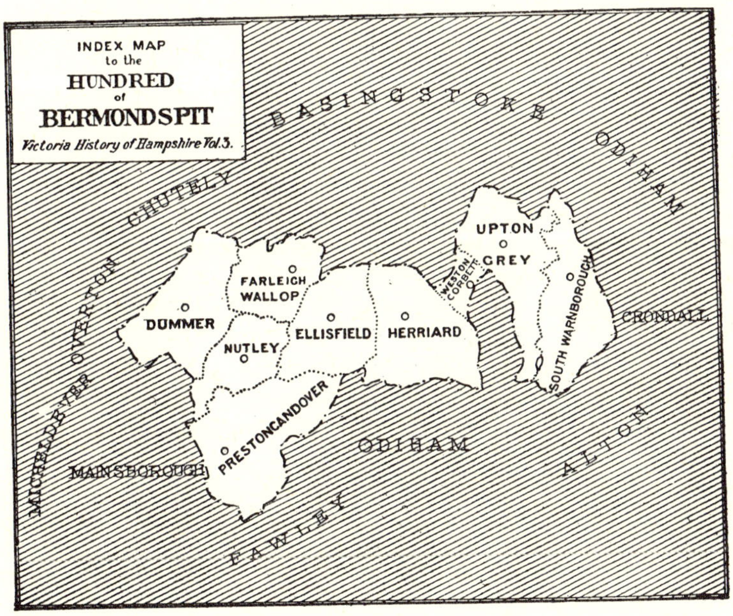

ford. Walter, at the time of the Survey, held it in pledge from the son of Cole of Basing.[3]

The other parishes afterwards included in the hundred, namely, Upton Grey[4] and South Warborough, with Hoddington,[5] and Weston (Patrick)[6] (now in Odiham Hundred) were at the date of the Domesday Survey part of a hundred named Odingetone which derived its name from Hoddington in

[1] *V.C.H. Hants*, i, 477, 482, 486, 490, 493, 500, 504, 505.
[2] Ibid. 505.
[3] Ibid. 505.
[4] Ibid. 482.
[5] Ibid. 496.
[6] Ibid. 468.

Upton Grey, but before the eleventh century this hundred had been merged into that of Bermondspit.

The returns of the Feudal Aid for 1316 include Hoddington (Hodegeton), Upton, Weston Corbett, Herriard (Herehyrde), Dummer, Nutley, Ellisfield, (Hulsefelde), Farleigh, Candover, within the hundred of Bermondspit.[7] 'Southwarneborough' appears in the hundred in 1346.[8] Since this date there has been very little variation in the extent of the hundred. The lay subsidies of the reigns of Henry VIII[9] and Elizabeth[10] show that the hundred still contained the same parishes as in the fourteenth century.

Bermondspit being a royal hundred came under the Parliamentary Survey of the crown property in the time of the Commonwealth. According to the returns of this Survey the hundred still contained the same parishes, Weston Corbett only being unmentioned. It appears that the courts-leet and law-day sheriff's turn courts for the hundred were held about Hocktide and St. Martin's Day, the parish of Nutley being the place in which the court was usually held.[11]

The parishes included since the returns of 1831 within Bermondspit Hundred are Bentworth, Bradley, Dummer, Ellisfield, Farleigh Wallop, Herriard, Lasham, Nutley, Popham, Preston Candover, Upton Grey, Weston Corbett, and Weston Patrick. With the hundred of Hoddington (Hodeketone) and others Bermondspit belonged to the royal manor of Basingstoke. Edward I appears to have had cause of complaint in that due payment had not been rendered from the hundred, and John de St. John, powerful in Bermondspit as elsewhere, did not permit the king's bailiffs to make distraint for the debt in his fee.[12] The same king is found calling a tenant in Bermondspit to account, since the villeins of the prior of Southwick had failed to render suit at the hundred of Bermondspit, as was their duty. The prior put the onus of the offence upon William de Valence, who had hindered the suit due to the king.[13] Likewise also Edmund earl of Cornwall was summoned to see that his men of Dummer rendered suit at the royal hundred of Bermondspit.[14]

[7] *Feud. Aids*, ii, 313.
[8] Ibid. 330.
[9] Lay Subs. 37 Hen. VIII, $\frac{174}{272}$.
[10] Ibid. 31 Eliz. $\frac{174}{404}$, and 39 Eliz. $\frac{174}{422}$.
[11] Parl. Surv. Hants, 1.
[12] Hundr. R. 2, 3 Edw. I.
[13] *Plac. de Quo Warr.* (Rec. Com.), 768.
[14] Ibid. 772.

DUMMER WITH KEMPSHOT

Dummere (xi cent.); Dumare (xiii cent.); Dommere (xiv cent.).

The parish of Dummer, with Kempshot added in 1876 for civil purposes, contains 2,774 acres of hilly country generally rising from west to east, and reaching a height of over 660 ft. above the ordnance datum in the east of the parish.

The main road from Winchester to Basingstoke, leaving the high ground near Popham church, continues north, and running downhill enters the parish of Dummer about half a mile south of the Wheat Sheaf Inn. Thence it continues north, forming for about a mile and a half the western boundary of the parish, until suddenly turning east it cuts across the parish north-west of Kempshot, and skirting the grounds of Kempshot House, the residence of Mr. Henry Gourlay, continues towards Basingstoke. Three-quarters of a mile north of the Wheat Sheaf Inn a road from North Waltham runs across the main road, and goes east to the village of Dummer, between banks and fields and hedgerows covered in the early spring with masses of primroses and violets and lilac-coloured 'milkmaids' or lady-smocks. Curving slightly north the road enters the village, past two or three more or less modern cottages lying back behind hedges and gardens, to the more old-world thatched and half-timbered cottages, farms and farm buildings, which lie for the most part along the north side of the street, and along the branch road which leads south from the west end of the village. On the south side of the road, nearly half-way along the village street, beyond a line of tall young spruce firs, a square tiled and now dilapidated roof, supported on four wooden pillars, forms the covering for the village pump. A few yards on, on the opposite side of the road, is the small village pond, beyond which are the schools, built in 1816. Beyond the schools a low brick wall encircles an old well-kept graveyard, entered from the street by an iron gate, and east of which runs a narrow grass inclosure. The church, the manor-house, and the rectory are grouped together at the east end of the village, the rectory, a grey stone house, standing on the north side of the road, facing west on the lane that turns off towards Kempshot, among well-grown trees which are much frequented by rooks. The simple quaint church, west of which a lane leads off south to Tidley Hill, stands opposite behind a low brick wall, in front of which several fine beech and horse-chestnut trees grow by the side of the road. Immediately south-east, almost behind the church, is the manor-house, a large square white building, the residence of Sir Richard Nelson Rycroft, bart. It is in the main a good specimen of early eighteenth-century date, with excellent details of panelling, staircases, and chimney-pieces. Parts of the building are, however, of earlier date, and there is some Jacobean panelling in some of the first-floor rooms. In front of the house on the north side of the short wide drive, spreading over the road is a fine horse-chestnut tree. From here the road winds east, generally uphill, through the parish, then, curving slightly north, enters Farleigh Wallop. As it rises towards Farleigh, climbing the side of the downland which rises to the east, fine views of the whole parish and of the surrounding country can be seen on the north and west and south from between the low hedges, and from the open fields which stretch on either side. Away to the north-west is the dark woodland surrounding Kempshot House, followed by undulating country, stretching away west and south to North Waltham parish, and over North Waltham to the misty outline of the woods which adjoin Steventon manor-house, and to the dark outline of Steventon Warren, which rises further south. Following on still further south beyond Tidley Hill another long stretch of woodland lies north of Woodmancott. Dummer Grange Farm, which was for some centuries before the Dissolution the property of Waverley Abbey, is near Tidley Hill in the south of the parish. Kempshot House stands in a well-wooded park of about 150 acres, north of the village and parish. The soil of the whole parish is clay with a subsoil of chalk, and hence on the 2,131¼ acres of arable land good crops of wheat, barley, oats, and turnips are produced, while only 654 acres are given up to permanent grass, and those mostly in the east of the parish. The 268½ acres of woodland are for the most part included in Kempshot manor, and encircle the grounds of Kempshot House. A small wood which extends mostly into Nutley parish lies in the south-east. Several disused chalk-pits, a familiar feature in most parts of Hampshire, exist in the parish.

MANORS The manor known in the sixteenth century as *EAST DUMMER* or *POPHAM DUMMER* may be identified with the five hides of land in Dummer held at the time of the Survey by Odo of Winchester, and under him by Hunger.[1] Odo's lands subsequently became part of the honour of St. Valery, which, having escheated to the crown in the reign of Henry III,[2] was regranted by that king to Richard earl of Cornwall. On the death of Richard's son Edmund without heirs his estates, including the honours of St. Valery and Wallingford, once more came into the king's hands,[3] and the overlordship of Dummer by a confusion, not unusual about this date, seems to have been transferred to Wallingford honour and henceforth the overlordship followed that descent.[4]

At the time of the Survey one Hunger held these five hides as a sub-tenant of Odo. Three 'hagae' in Winchester which paid a rent of 2*s.* were annexed to the property.[5] It is possible that this Hunger may have been the ancestor of the family of Dummer, for between the years 1107 and 1128 a certain Henry Dummer possessed rents from three houses in Winchester,[6] possibly the three 'hagae' of Domesday Book, and Ralph Dummer, probably a son or grandson of Henry, held a rent of 5*s.* 7*d.* from lands in Tanner Street, Winchester, in 1148. In 1198 his son Robert gave half a hide of land in Dummer to his brother Geoffrey, parson of the church; and it may be assumed that the property in Dummer passed through his son

[1] *V.C.H. Hants*, i, 504*b*.
[2] *Cal. Inq. p.m.* 56 Hen. III, No. 32.
[3] Chan. Inq. p.m. 28 Edw. I, No. 44.
[4] Ibid. 21 Ric. II, No. 44; ibid. 10 Hen. IV, No. 22, &c.
[5] *V.C.H. Hants*, i, 504*b*.
[6] Liber Winton, 532.

Richard who was living in 1248, to John Dummer of Easton, co. Leicester, who died seised of the manor in 1304. Robert Dummer, son of John, was succeeded by his daughter Alice, from whom the estate passed to her husband John Astwick of co. Beds.[7] He appears to have been a 'King's merchant,' and was probably that John Astwick, who, when summoned to appear before the council at Westminster, sought protection on the ground that his person was liable to be seized on account of certain debts.[8] He was succeeded by his son John, whose daughter Agnes married John de Drayton, and in 1368-9 they conveyed all their right in the manor of Dummer to Sir John Popham of the adjoining hamlet of Popham.[9] From Sir John it passed to Philip Popham, possibly a younger son, and Elizabeth his wife, who were succeeded in 1397 by a second Philip and Elizabeth.[10] The latter survived her husband some years, and her son Philip dying a minor in the king's wardship in 1414 left as co-heiresses two sisters, Margaret and Matilda, aged fourteen and thirteen years.[11] Dummer seems to have been allotted to Margaret, who married as her second husband Edward Wayte of Draycot[12] (Wiltshire), and thirdly Robert Long of Wraxall[13] (Wiltshire), who held one fee in Dummer in 1428,[14] and was succeeded by his son John, who had married Margaret Wayte, heiress of the family of Wayte, who held the manor in 1484.[15] For the next century it is impossible to trace any connexion between the owners of the manor. In 1529 Robert Drury and Alice his wife quitclaimed the manor of Dummer to William Barentyne, while fifteen years later it passed by fine from Walter Bonham and Alice daughter of John Dale to William Dale. In 1577 Richard Kingsmill and Robert Brinnage were each in possession of half the manor, while in 1591 Nicholas Venables conveyed half by fine to John Millingate. Six years later the latter was in possession of the whole estate, and it remained in the Millingate family until the middle of the seventeenth century, when it passed into the family of Terry. It remained in their possession until 1864, when the manor-house and a considerable part of the parish was sold to the Rev. T. J. Torr, and ten years later to the late Sir Nelson Rycroft, bart., whose son, Sir Richard Nelson Rycroft, bart., is the present lord of the manor.

The manor known in the sixteenth century as *WEST DUMMER* may probably be identified with the 5 hides of land held at the time of the Domesday Survey by one of the men of Hugh de Port.[16] The overlordship of this manor passed with Hugh's other estates to his descendants the St. Johns.[17]

The first mention of a sub-tenant of the De Ports in Dummer after the time of the Domesday Survey occurs early in the thirteenth century,[18] when William Dummer was called upon to do homage for two knights' fees in Dummer.[19] In 1294-5 the abbot of Waverley recovered seisin against John son of William Dummer of common pasture in Dummer, which the abbot alleged belonged to his free tenement, and of which he had been unjustly dispossessed.[20] This Sir John Dummer appears to have been a man of considerable local importance. He represented Somerset in the Parliaments of 1306 and 1313, and in the latter year obtained a writ *de expensis* with John de Beauchamp for £21 12*s.* at the rate of 4*s.* per day for attendance.[21] He was probably that John Dummer referred to in the order issued to the sheriff of Somerset in 1289 'to cause a coroner for that county to be elected in the place of John de Dummer lately elected, whom the King has caused to be amoved from office since he cannot conveniently attend to the duties of the office because he is of the household of John de St. John who is now staying continually with the King.'[22] In 1316 Thomas son of Sir John Dummer held one half of the vill of Dummer. As his father was then living it is probable that he granted it to his son on his marriage shortly before this date.[23] From Thomas the estate, then said to be worth 100*s.*, passed to his son, also Thomas,[24] who appears to have been the last heir male of the family; and his daughter Ellen having married Nicholas atte More, her descendants assumed the name of Dummer, and continued to possess the manor until the death of William Dummer in 1593.[25] In 1579, however, William, who had married Kenborough Brydges, granted the reversion to Humphrey Brydges, possibly a cousin, with reversion to John Millingate,[26] and seven years later the manor was conveyed by fine from Humphrey Brydges to John.[27] It remained in possession of the Millingate family until the middle of the seventeenth century, and its later history is identical with that of East Dummer (q.v.).

DUMMER *alias* ATMORE. *Argent two bars vert with six martlets gules over all.*

The *GRANGE OF DUMMER* was granted to the abbey of Waverley by Stephen, and this grant was afterwards confirmed by John[28] and Edward II. In 1291[29] its value is given as £2, but by 1535 it had increased to £2 10*s.* It remained in possession of the abbey[30] until the suppression of the latter in

7 *Feud. Aids*, ii, 330.

8 *Cal. of Pat.* 1343-5, p. 225; ibid. 1345-8, p. 248.

9 Close, 42 Edw. III, m. 30.

10 Chan. Inq. p.m. 21 Ric. II, No. 44.

11 Ibid. 12 Hen. IV No. 10.

12 Ibid. 2 Hen. V, No. 15.

13 Chitty, *Family of Long*, 14.

14 *Feud. Aids*, ii, 344.

15 Chitty, *Family of Long*, 16.

16 *V.C.H. Hants*, i, 482*b*.

17 Inq. p.m. 3 Edw. III, No. 67. Early in the thirteenth century two knights' fees in Dummer were said to be held of Henry Hosato, but Henry probably merely represented Adam de Port, with whose family he was connected by marriage; *Abbrev. Plac.* (Rec. Com.), 736; *Suss. Arch. Soc.* viii, 46, 47.

18 If, however, it be a fact that the Dummers were really holding of the honour of St. Valery in this parish in the twelfth century, it is also possible that they acquired the de Port 5 hides at an early date, or indeed it may even be the case that the man of Hugh de Port who held of Hugh at the time of the Survey was that Hunger who was the ancestor or predecessor of the St. Valery tenants. In this case the two holdings probably followed the same descent until the division of the property between the two sons of Ralph about the year 1198.

19 *Abbrev. Plac.* (Rec. Com.), 73*b*; and see *ante* note 17.

20 *Abbrev. Rot. Orig.* (Rec. Com.), 91.

21 *Parl. Writs* (Rec. Com.), i, p. xxviii.

22 *Cal. of Close*, 1288-96, p. 25. Though this does not prove that John Dummer was holding Dummer of John de St. John, yet in the light of later evidence this is extremely probable.

23 Plac. de Banco, Mich. 14 Edw. II, m. 332.

24 Inq. p.m. 3 Edw. III, No. 67.

25 *Som. Arch. Soc.* 1871-3, p. 106.

26 Pat. 21 Eliz. pt. 6.

27 Feet of F. Hants, East. 28 Eliz.

28 *Chart. R.* (Rec. Com.), 7 John, 61.

29 *Pope Nich. Tax.* (Rec. Com.), 215.

30 *Cal. of Pat.* 1340-3, p. 294.

1536, and in the following year the abbey and its possessions were granted to Sir William Fitz William, treasurer of the king's household.[31] It appears to have been acquired by the Dummer family before the end of the sixteenth century, and from that date followed the descent of West Dummer (q.v.).

The Grange is a good early seventeenth-century house, with a central block and two gabled wings projecting on the east side, the southern of the two having some good cut brickwork with Ionic pilasters at the angles and a blank scutcheon in the apex of the gable. The house contains a stair with an early seventeenth-century balustrade, and parts of it are probably of greater age. A coin of Henry V, among other things, has been found here. In front of the house is a large farmyard, the south side of which is formed by a fine barn built of oak timber, of large scantling and in excellent preservation.

CHURCH The church of *ALL SAINTS* consists of a chancel 23 ft. 6 in. by 16 ft., and nave 39 ft. by 21 ft. 3 in., with west porch and wooden bell-turret over the west end of the nave.

The south doorway of the nave dates from the end of the twelfth century, and the nave walls may be of this time; the chancel belongs to the first quarter of the thirteenth century, and has three lancet windows of that date in both north and south walls, and a small blocked north doorway between the second and third windows. A roll string runs round the chancel at the level of the sills of the windows, breaking up over the head of the doorway. The east wall was rebuilt in 1893, and contains three lancet windows of that date, and to the south of the windows is a small trefoiled recess of thirteenth-century date. On the splays of the eastern lancet in the north wall, and of that next to it, are traces of a masonry pattern in red, with a rose in each square. The roof timbers are modern, but the altar rails have good twisted balusters of the eighteenth century. The chancel arch is of the date of the chancel, of one pointed order edge-chamfered, and only 7 ft. wide; on the west face it has a chamfered label, cut away above the springing for the fitting of the back beam of the rood-loft floor. On either side of it are squints from the nave, that on the south being round-headed and blocked with brickwork, so that it does not show towards the nave, while the other, a smaller round-headed opening, is cut irregularly through the back of a square-headed fourteenth-century recess marking the position of a former nave altar. The recess has a flat sill, and cinquefoiled ogee tracery with pierced spandrels in the head, with a label which is cut back like that of the chancel arch, and for the same reason.

Over the chancel arch is a large wooden coved canopy, panelled in squares with moulded ribs having carved and gilded bosses of foliage at their intersections; the background is painted a dark blue, and the canopy rests on a rough cambered beam, on which are traces of diagonal bands of colour on either side, and some other indistinct colouring in the middle. These probably were backgrounds to the three figures on the rood-beam, and the canopy is a rare and remarkable instance of a 'ceiling over the Rood' preserved almost intact.

The nave is lighted at the north-east by a fifteenth-century square-headed window of three trefoiled lights, and there is a like window at the south-west, but without cusps and of sixteenth-century date. In the east jamb of the former window is a chase to take the end of the front beam carrying the rood-loft, and below the sill is a fourteenth-century tomb recess with a low moulded segmental arch containing a Purbeck marble grave slab; it is partly blocked with masonry, as the wall is very shaky at this point. The south doorway of the nave has a semicircular head with an edge-chamfer; it is blocked and fitted with a wooden lattice frame, and to the west of it is a plain two-light window of the sixteenth century or later, with four-centred uncusped lights. The west half, or rather more than half, of the nave is taken up by a large west gallery set in front of the wooden posts carrying the belfry, and having a good seventeenth-century balustrade in front. In the gallery are the arms of Charles II, dated 1672. The west doorway of the nave is of the fifteenth century, with a four-centred head and a cinquefoiled niche above it; the porch is of the same date, with a wooden outer arch, a north window of two cinquefoiled lights, and a single light on the south side. Over the doorway, but only visible from inside, is a blocked round-headed opening, too little of which is at present exposed to give any clue to its date or purpose. The nave roof is old, plastered below the timbers, and, like the chancel roof, is covered with red tiles. The bell-turret also has a red-tiled roof, and its sides are covered with modern weather-boarding, except in one part, where the older flush boarding remains. The nave walls are in somewhat unsound condition, and have brick buttresses at the four angles.

The octagonal font, at the south-west of the nave, is modern.

On the east wall of the chancel, north of the east window, is a slab with the brass figures of William at Moore *alias* Dommer and Katherine (Brydges) his wife, kneeling at a desk, and their son kneeling behind his father. The inscription recounts William's birth in 1508, and that he was clerk of the mayor's court and controller of the chamber of London fifty years, but the date of his death has never been inserted. Above are the arms of Dummer, with helm and mantling, between shields of Dummer impaling Brydges, and Brydges. With the Dummer arms are quartered a cross engrailed and billetty a crescent. At the south-east of the nave is a brass to William Dommer and Elena his wife, 1427, with an inscription of six leonine hexameters; and at the south-west is a palimpsest brass plate, originally commemorating Robert Clerk, chantry chaplain of Peter Habiller's chantry, founded in this church, and afterwards used for 'Alys Magewik of Dumer wedow,' 1591.

There are five bells and a sanctus, the last being blank. Of the rest the treble is by James Wells of Aldbourne, 1811; the second by Thomas Swain, of Longford, Middlesex, 1759; and the other three by Joseph Carter, of Reading, 1590, 1599, and 1597. Each bears on the waist the name or initials of John Myllyngate or Milingat, and the fourth also has Carter's founder's mark, a bell on a shield between I C. Below the bell chamber, on the west wall of the nave, are painted in seventeenth-century black-letter type a set of ringers' rules of the usual character, an early example of the kind, and it seems that they

[31] Dugdale, *Mon.* v, 240, 243.

are painted over a still earlier version of the same thing.

The plate consists of a large communion cup and cover paten of 1570; another cup and paten and flagon; and a pewter flagon and almsdish.

The first book of registers runs from 1540 to 1741, and the second from 1740 to 1812. There is also a marriage register 1760–1812.

ADVOWSON There was a church at Dummer in 1086,[32] and it is probable that the advowson always formed part of the Dummer estate. In 1198 Geoffrey son of Ralph Dummer was parson of the church, and a half-hide of land in Dummer was given to him by his brother Robert, to be held in free alms by his successors.[33] Two generations later a dispute arose between Sir John Dummer and his cousin, John Dummer of Aston, joint-holders of the manor, respecting the advowson of the church, and it was ultimately agreed in 1275 that the heirs of each should present alternately.[34] This arrangement continued until the two moieties of the manors were acquired by the Millingate family in the sixteenth century, after which the histories of the manor and advowson are identical.

CHARITIES Charity of John Millingate for the poor.—In 1607 John Millingate, by deed, charged his close, called Leedgar's Close, in this parish, and nine acres of arable land lying in the open fields (inclosed in 1742) with 20*s.* yearly for the poor. In 1905 half-crowns were given to eight recipients. Charity of John Millingate for school and charity of John Henshaw thereto (1759).[35]

In 1710 Michael Terry, by will, devised his manor of Popham in Dummer and other lands in the open fields with 20*s.* for the poor at Michaelmas, which sum is distributed in half-crowns to eight recipients.

John Marriott, by will (date unknown), gave to the parish £20, for the raising of an annuity of 20*s.*, to be employed for the buying of three Bibles for three poor children. The Bibles are duly distributed.

— Adams gave £86 14*s.* 10*d.* consols (with the official trustees), dividends to be applied in aid of funds of provident club, etc., by scheme of Charity Commissioners of 31 July, 1891. The annual dividends amounting to £2 3*s.* 4*d.* are distributed in coal.

ELLISFIELD

Esewelle, Domesday; Ulesfeld, Hulsefelde (xiii cent.); Essefeld, Elsefeud (xiii cent.); Elsefeld (xii, xiii, xiv cent.).

The 2,349 acres comprising the parish of Ellisfield are part of the high sweep of country that rises south-west of Basingstoke and reaches its greatest height at Farleigh Wallop. Ellisfield, lying south-east of Farleigh, is practically in itself a hill, the ground rising to over 640 ft. above the ordnance datum almost in the centre of the parish between the two outlying groups which compose the village, the church and manor farm, which lie together towards the north-west, and the Fox Inn, and the various farms which are grouped together in the south-east. Although the parish is intersected by lanes and narrow roads, there is no main road running through it, the most important being that which enters the south-east corner, about a mile from Herriard Station, and runs a generally north-westerly course through the parish to Farlington and Cliddesden. This road mounts uphill, past Bushy Leaze Copse and College Farm, the Fox Inn, and Cooper's and Merritt's Farms and their outbuildings, then curves west past Widmore House, now known as Ellisfield Manor, the residence of Mr. Harry Hoare. At this point, the highest in the parish, the road divides, one branch running north-east, the other northward downhill to the church and manor farm, which both lie west of the road, the farmhouse, a square white stone house with a dark tiled roof, being immediately south-west of the church. Forming a foreground for the church and farmhouse, as the road approaches from the south-east, is the farm pond. On the opposite side of the road are two low flint cottages.

The chief charm of Ellisfield is not in its scattered village, but in the wonderful sweeps of woodland country that rise on every side. Every lane seems to run between or through copses carpeted in early spring by masses of primroses and wild anemones, and inhabited by rabbits and pheasants, which start up everywhere. Of the cluster of copses lying north of the parish the chief are Kingsmore Copse, Allwood Copse, Whinkney Copse, and Fryingdown Copse, while in the east are Park Field Copse, Smart's Copse, and Withy Copse, south of the manor farm and in the south-east, Great Reid's Copse, Warwick's Row Copse, Berry Down Copse, and Highwood. These cover the best part of the 562 acres of woodland in the parish. Crops of wheat, oats, and roots are produced on the 766 acres of arable land lying on the chalk soil and subsoil of the parish, 483½ acres are given up to permanent grass, and 562 to woods and plantations.

MANOR In the time of Edward the Confessor Auti had held *ELLISFIELD* as an alod, but at the date of the Conqueror's Survey it formed part of the great possessions of the bishop of Bayeux, of whom it was held by Hugh de Port,[1] with whose descendants the overlordship remained, passing to the St. Johns in the thirteenth century.[2] The family of Sifrewast held as mesne lords under the St. Johns except in 1386, when half of the manor was held directly of the St. Johns and the other half partly of Bernard Brocas and partly of John Bremshott. Richard de Sifrewast,[3] holding of Robert de St. John, was lord of Ellisfield in 1255, and owed suit at the courts of Basing and Sherborne. Of his grandson Roger Sifrewast[4] Ellisfield was held in

[32] *V.C.H. Hants*, i, 482*b*.
[33] Feet of F. Hants, 10 Ric. I, No. 8.
[34] Ibid. Trin. 3 Edw. I.
[35] See article on 'Schools,' *V.C.H. Hants*, ii, 398.
[1] *V.C.H. Hants*, i, 486*a*.
[2] Feet of F. Hants, East. 40 Edw. III.
[3] Feet of F. Hants, Hil. 33 Hen. III.
[4] Chan. Inq. p.m. 35 Edw. III, 164, No. 36.

Herriard House : The West Front

Dummer Church : Chancel Arch and Canopy

1361, and of John Sifrewast[5] in 1496. In the reign of James I, however, the manor was held of the heirs of Sir Edward Marvyn.[6]

The history of the manor cannot be traced earlier than the reign of Edward II, although the Pipe Rolls and Fines show tenants in the parish[7] at an earlier date. In the reign of Henry III, Nicholas son of Ralph held half a carucate and half a virgate in Ellisfield, and also a capital messuage, which seems to imply a not inconsiderable estate, the third of which, and of a wood called 'Wodehull,' and lands named 'Homcroft' and 'Middelcroft' (the latter forming part of the half-virgate), he leased to Peter de Chevelegh and his wife Sarah for their lives.[8]

Robert Cusyn and Joan his wife seem to have been landowners in Ellisfield in the same reign, since of them John son of Thomas de Beckering held a house and land, paying a yearly rent of two capons.[9] In the reign of Edward I Henry and William de la Stonhupe are mentioned in connexion with a house and land in Ellisfield and Herriard,[10] but none of these early tenants can be connected with the two joint lords of Ellisfield in the reign of Edward II. In 1316 the vill of Ellisfield was the joint possession of the priory of Southwick and Roger de Fyfhide;[11] in 1346 the prior was still holding, and Roger had been succeeded by William de Fyfhide.[12] The priory owned two-thirds and William the remaining third, the latter's portion being described as having formerly belonged to Hugh de Spaigne.[13]

In 1361 William de Fyfhide died possessed of land in Ellisfield,[14] and his son William, a minor at his father's death, had seisin of his estates in or about 1382.[15] He died four years later without issue, and the manor of Ellisfield descended to his cousin Joan, wife of Sir John Sandys.[16] Sir Walter Sandys[17] succeeded as lord of the manor, and died 16 June, 1435. He was followed by his son Sir Thomas, who held the manor until 1443,[18] when he was succeeded by his son Sir William,[19] whose son, also Sir William, inherited the manor in 1496.[20] This second Sir William enjoyed the favour of Henry VIII, who made him his lord chamberlain and created him Baron Sandys. His son Thomas, Lord Sandys, held the manor at the time of Elizabeth's accession,[21] whose grandson William, the third Lord Sandys, was in possession of Ellisfield until 1624.[22] In 1657 William, fifth Lord Sandys, son of Colonel Henry Sandys, who was mortally wounded in the service of Charles I at Cheriton fight, sold the property. The manor house, site of the manor, and land in Ellisfield were sold for £3,300 to Robert Stocker of Basingstoke.[23] For £736 the Berrydown portion of the demesne lands went to John Oades, yeoman of Preston Candover,[24] and for £150, £550, £65, and £266 10*s.* other parts of the estates were bought by Hugh White, Richard Wither, and William Beck, and Nicholas Merriott, husbandman, and Edward Panford, respectively.[25]

SANDYS. *Or a fesse dancetty gules between three crosslets fitchy gules.*

Robert Stocker was still holding the manor in 1668, but no further mention of him occurs, and the manor appears to have been divided, for in 1675 Henry Lincbrey and William Moleyns were parties to a fine concerning half the manor of Ellisfield,[26] and in 1685 another fine between Michael Terry and Robert Searle and Anne his wife deals also with half the manor and half the advowson.[27] The moiety held by William Moleyns under the conveyance of 1675 must have remained in his family, though details of the descent are not known, for in 1704 Mary and Anne Moleyns, spinsters, each held a fourth of the manor.[28] In 1756 one of these fourth parts was held by William Saltmarsh,[29] who was probably a descendant of one of these sisters, he being the son of Philip Saltmarsh, who had married Anne, daughter of William 'Mullins'[30] of Skervill Court, Hants.[31] As the bulk of the family property lay in Yorkshire William Saltmarsh sold his Hampshire property to Michael Terry of Dummer in 1756.[32] From the Terrys of Dummer the manor passed by purchase to the earls of Portsmouth,[33] John Wallop, earl of Portsmouth, holding the manor in 1789.[34] What became of the other scattered portions of the manor is nowhere shown. Possibly the Terrys had acquired more than the fourth part of William Saltmarsh, at any rate the lands of the earl of Portsmouth in 1789 are described, not as a portion of, but as the manor of Ellisfield. The lordship of the manor is still held by the earl of Portsmouth.

Earlier mention, however, of the Wallop family in

[5] Chan. Inq. p.m. 12 Hen. VII, No. 110.

[6] W. & L. Inq. p.m. 21 Jas. I, bdle. 59, No. 200.

[7] In the Pipe R. of 1166 there occurs a note of a payment in Ellisfield. 'Elsefeld Henricus reddidit compotum de xx solidis.'

[8] Feet of F. Hants, Hil. 33 Hen. III.

[9] Ibid. 41 Hen. III.

[10] Ibid. East. 14 Edw. I.

[11] *Feud. Aids*, ii, 313.

[12] Ibid. ii, 330.

[13] Ibid.

[14] Inq. p.m. 35 Edw. III, pt. 1, No. 88; Pat. 6 Ric. II, pt. 1, m. 4, 5.

[15] Ibid. In the same year, 1361, also died Roger de Syfrewast, overlord (Chan. Inq. p.m. 35 Edw. III, vol. 164, No. 36). The extent of the manor at this date comprised a capital messuage, a dove-cot, 2 carucates of land containing 300 acres, a pasture for 200 sheep, and another pasture called 'Cockesmede,' together with woodland, rent, and profits of court.

[16] Sir T. Phillips, 'Hants Visitations'; Feet of F. Hants, East. 15 Ric. II; Chan. Inq. p.m. 10 Ric. II, No. 17. Sir William, last of the male line of the Fyfhides held, it appears, half his manor of Lord St. John, it representing half a knight's fee; the other half was held of Bernard Brocas (as of his manor of Boadley), and of John Bremshott.

[17] Chan. Inq. p.m. 13 Hen. VI, 33. In 1428 he was described as holding a third part of a knight's fee (*Feud. Aids*, iv, 45).

[18] Chan. Inq. p.m. 20 Hen. VI, 35.

[19] Ibid.

[20] Chan. Inq. p.m. 12 Hen. VII, No. 110.

[21] Ibid. 2 & 3 Eliz. (Ser. 2), pt. 1, 143.

[22] Chan. Inq. p.m. (Ser. 2), vol. 402, 131.

[23] Close, 1657, pt. 27, No. 35; ibid. 1659, pt. 4, No. 39.

[24] Ibid. 1657, pt. 27, No. 34; ibid. 1659, pt. 4, No. 35.

[25] Ibid. 1659, pt. 4, Nos. 26–33, 29, and 30.

[26] Feet of F. Hants, Hil. 27–8 Chas. II.

[27] Feet of F. Hants, Mich. 1 Jas. II. Michael Terry described as Cursitor of Court of Chancery, and Robert Searle as merchant. There appears to be no other document to reveal the purport of this fine.

[28] Feet of F. Hants, Mich. 3 Anne; Recov. R. 3 Anne, 98; ibid. Trin. 5 Anne, 19; Close, 5 Anne, pt. 2. Mary Moleyns appears to have held the manor-house or capital messuage then occupied by Cornelius Pyle.

[29] Com. Pleas Recov. R. Hil. 30 Geo. II, 77. In 1756 William Saltmarsh had married Lady Anne Plunkett, daughter of the earl of Fingall, when settlement was made of his property.

[30] Variant of Moleyns probably.

[31] Foster, *County Families of Yorks.*

[32] Com. Pleas Recov. R. Trin. 30 & 31 Geo. II, m. 18.

[33] Ex inform. Rev. Botry Pigott.

[34] Recov. R. Hil. Geo. III, rot. 223.

Ellisfield occurs, for Robert Wallop, regicide, forfeited, with the manor of Farleigh Wallop, a farm called 'Dyer's Farm,' with lands in Ellisfield and Nutley,[35] which with Farleigh Wallop evidently descended to his son, as for upwards of two hundred years the Wallops have held lands in this parish [36]

Besides the manor held by the Fyfhides there was, in early times, a second manor held by the prior of Southwick. Before 1284 Bartholomew Pecche had granted, together with part of the advowson, a house, a carucate of land, woodland, and rent to the priory.[37] According to the taxation of 1291 a manor, 'apud Elleswelde,' was taxed at 15*s.* 11*d.*[38] In the reign of Edward II the prior appears as joint lord of Ellisfield,[39] and, moreover, in the same reign free warren was granted to the prior and convent in their demesne lands in Ellisfield by royal charter,[40] which was later confirmed by Richard II.[41] In 1346 the prior was said to hold two parts of a knight's fee,[42] and in 1337 and 1348 held with John de Roches one fee of Edmund and Hugh de St. John.[43]

In 1428 the prior was still holding his two parts of a fee in Ellisfield, but later than this there is no mention of the priory's land.

In 1218 Maud de Munfichet appears to have granted to Beatrice de Bovill, William de Bremlessete, and Robert de Chinham 22 acres in Ellisfield.[44] The name Chinham then spelt Chunham occurs again in 1272, when Herbert Pecche died seised of 60 acres of land in Ellisfield, which he held of William de Chunham.[45] He left an heir in his son Bartholomew, who was probably that Bartholomew Pecche who made the grant of land and advowson in Ellisfield to Southwick Priory.[46] In 1284 John de Foxle, John de St. John, and Michael de Chillham (another variation probably of Chinham) were guardians of the lands and heir of Bartholomew Pecche.[47] In 1327 part of rents in Ellisfield and Bromleigh which were granted by Sir John Pecche to his mother Dame Joan was due from the prior [48] of Southwick.

Connected also with the priory as early landowners in Ellisfield were the family of De Roches, who probably acquired their lands and the advowson through the marriage of Geoffrey de Roches with Emma, daughter of Walter Fitz Roger, and heiress of her brother.[49]

In 1329 John de Roches held a knight's fee in Ellisfield of John de St. John, described as worth £6 14*s.*,[50] and eight years later the name of John de Roches occurs with that of the prior of Southwick as joint holder of a knight's fee worth £10,[51] it being held of Hugh de St. John, and in 1348 they held the fee of Edmund de St. John.[52] Nothing more is known of the De Roches property, which no doubt passed to Sir Bernard Brocas with the advowson on his marriage with Mary de Roches at the end of the fourteenth century.

Property in Ellisfield was also held under the Sifrewasts by the prioress of Wintney. Avis, the prioress, in the reign of Henry III, held ½ a carucate by grant of Richard de Sifrewast,[53] of whom also Lucy, the prioress, held 3 carucates later in the same reign.[54] In the reign of Edward III the nuns of Wintney held 100 acres of pasture of Roger Sifrewast.[55] After the dissolution of Wintney Priory the land in this parish, including what is now Merritt's Farm, held with Herriard Grange, was allotted to Sir William Paulet,[56] and remained with Lord Bolton's family till 1851, when it was sold to F. J. E. Jervoise.

CHURCH The church of *ST. MARTIN* has a chancel, nave, south porch, and west tower. The tower was built in 1884, and the rest of the church underwent a most unsympathetic 'restoration' in 1870, which obliterated nearly everything of interest. The chancel seems to have been lengthened at this time, and is lighted by modern lancets on north and south, and a modern three-light east window, on either side of which are plain corbels for images, re-used, and at the south-east is a length of moulded string-course, which is old work. Parts of the nave walls probably date from the first quarter of the twelfth century, the label and tall semicircular rear arch of a south doorway of this date being left in the wall above the present south doorway, which is plain work of fourteenth-century date, and opens to a brick porch now used as a vestry, its outer arch being built up. The chancel is of the same width as the nave, separated from it by a modern chancel arch, and was probably built round a smaller chancel, contemporary with the nave, at some time in the thirteenth century. At the north-east of the nave is a lancet window, which may be in part of this date, the wall at this point being cut back to give more room for a former altar here.

Externally the nave walls show some early-looking flint masonry, and there is some trace of the former existence of a north doorway, a modern window now taking its place. A blocked lancet window or thirteenth-century date shows on the outer face of the south wall of the chancel, and a few quoin stones mark the line of the former east wall, partly hidden by modern buttresses.

The tower has a curious vane shaped like a pineapple, which was once on the tower of Long Ditton church, whence it was taken and set up over the stables of Cawley Priory, finally coming to Ellisfield.

In the tower are five bells, without any inscription, but with an unusual number of lines on the crown, shoulder and sound bow; they are said to be Spanish.

The plate consists of two communion cups and a paten, with a pewter almsdish.

The first book of registers begins in 1668 and goes to 1812, the second being the printed marriage register 1756-1812.

35 Pat. 13 Chas. II, pt. 20, m. 10.

36 Ex inform. Rev. Botry Pigott.

37 De Banco R. No. 60, 12 *d.* Mich. 13 Edw. I.

38 *Pope Nich. Tax.* (Rec. Com.), 213.

39 Nomina Villarum.

40 Chart. R. 14 Edw. II, m. 8, No. 3[illegible].

41 Maddon, 33280.

42 *Feud. Aids*, ii, 330.

43 Chan. Inq. p.m. 11 Edw. III, No. 49; ibid. 21 Edw. III, No. 57.

44 Feet of F. Hants, East. 3 Hen. III.

45 Chan. Inq. p.m. 57 Hen. III, No. 4.

46 De Banco, No. 60, 12 *d.*; Mich. 13 Edw. I.

47 Ibid.

48 Burrows, *Family of Brocas*, 398; Feet of F. Hants, Trin. 3 Edw. III.

49 Burrows, *Family of Brocas*, 323. In 1227 Henry son of Roger and Alice, daughter of Roger, evidently relatives of the wife of Geoffrey de Roches, recognized the right of Emma and Geoffrey in a carucate of land at Ellisfield (Feet of F. Hants, 12 Hen. III).

50 Chan. Inq. p.m. 2 Edw. III, No. 67.

51 Chan. Inq. p.m. 11 Edw. III, No. 49.

52 Ibid. 21 Edw. III, No. 57.

53 Feet of F. Hants, Hil. 33 Hen. III.

54 Ibid. East. 40 Hen. III.

55 Chan. Inq. p.m. 35 Edw. III, 164, No. 36. In 1337 the prioress and convent granted to Sir Thomas Coudray 6 marks rent from their lands in Ellisfield and Herriard for the foundation of a chantry in the chapel of Shirbourne Coudray.

56 Ex Inform. Mr. F. H. T. Jervoise; *L. and P. Hen. VIII*, xi, 385(3).

South-east of the rectory is the site of a chapel, belonging to the fraternity of the Holy Ghost at Basingstoke ; it is still known as the Litton, and foundations of walls and graves have been found there. Near to it stood till recent years a small Jacobean house with cut brickwork details, now entirely destroyed.

ADVOWSON The advowson of Ellisfield can boast of a longer descent than the manor. A church existed at the time of the Domesday Survey, but by the reign of Henry III there were two churches, one dedicated to the honour of St. Martin, the other to All Saints.

In 1284 a suit was brought against the prior of Southwick by John de Foxle and his wife Constance for the recovery of land and of a third of the advowson of the church of 'Ellisfield.'[57] The prior it seems was able to produce a charter in witness that the property had been granted to him by Bartholomew Pecche. It is not certain to which of the two churches in Ellisfield this grant referred, nor is there any subsequent record of the ownership of the advowson by the prior of Southwick.

The churches of St. Martin and of All Saints were at the end of the thirteenth century in the patronage of the De Roches family,[58] members of the same family also having filled the living, Geoffrey de Roches being rector of Ellisfield in 1284 and Hugh de Roches in 1305.[59] Between 1282 and 1304 Hugh de Roches presented, and in the fourteenth century the name of John de Roches occurs as patron of both churches.[60] John de Roches, whose only son William was an idiot, settled in 1338 the advowson of All Saints upon his daughters, Alice and Mary, after the decease of himself and his wife Joan, the latter daughter being then wife of Sir John Boarhunt.[61] On the death of Joan, Mary, widow of Sir John Boarhunt, inherited the advowson,[62] her sister Alice having predeceased her mother.

Her second husband was Sir Bernard Brocas, who towards the end of the fourteenth century was patron.[63] In the year 1383 the two churches of All Saints and St. Martin's were united[64] on the petition of Sir Bernard Brocas and William Fyfhide, lord of the manor, who appears to have shared the advowson, as had his father before him,[65] and had presented to St. Martin's towards the end of the fourteenth century.[66] The plea was made on the ground of the poverty of the churches, All Saints being then a ruin.[67]

The Brocas family continued to share the advowson with the lords of the manor, the names of Sandys and Brocas occurring alternately,[68] until the manor was sold to Robert Stocker, to whom the advowson must have passed also, as he presented in 1668.[69] On the subsequent partition of the manor the advowson was also split up and was held by owners of portions of the manor successively.[70] In 1661 Thomas Taylor appeared as patron ; his name had before occurred in 1634 and 1648 in conjunction with that of Brocas.[71] In 1783 Thomas Brocas, in 1734 Thomas Terry, and in 1785, and 1830 Richard Willis presented.[72] In the reign of George III the advowson descended to the natural son of Bernard Brocas of Beaurepaire, Bernard Austin, who had assumed the name of Brocas.[73]

Bernard Brocas of Beaurepaire was the last of the Brocases to hold the advowson. He married first Anne Dolly, daughter of Paynton Pigott, and secondly, Miss Raymond Barker, who sold the advowson about 1870 to Mr. Henry and Mr. Alfred Welch-Thornton. Upon the death of the Rev. Richard Paynton Pigott, brother-in-law to Bernard Brocas, the Messrs. Welch-Thornton presented the present rector, the Rev. Botry Pigott, in 1885. The trustees of the latter have since bought the advowson.

CHARITIES In 1736 Thomas Ellisfield by his will gave to the poor £20 to be put out for their use, and directed that 20*s.* a year should be paid for ever for the use thereof. The principal sum of £20 has been lost.

In 1737 Stephen Terry by deed charged his farm and lands called Tilbroughs in this parish with a clear yearly rent of £3, of which 40*s.* was to be paid to a schoolmaster or school dame for teaching six poor children, boys or girls, to read and say their prayers and the catechism, and 20*s.* in buying two Bibles and other religious books to be given to the best scholars. The annuity is paid by the earl of Portsmouth.

In 1896 a scheme was established by the Charity Commissioners, whereby the £3 a year is to be applied in granting prizes or rewards, not exceeding 10*s.* each, to children bonâ fide resident in the parish attending elementary schools, including the gift of a Bible.

57 De Banco R. No. 60, 12 *d.* Mich. 13 Edw. I.

58 Egerton MS. 2031.

59 Burrows, *Hist. of Brocas Family*, 322.

60 Egerton MS. 2031, 2032 once ; Thos. Tayllard presented to St. Martin's.

61 Feet of F. Hants, Mich. 12 Edw. III.

62 Burrows, *Hist. of Brocas Family*, 329, 330.

63 Egerton MS. 2033. He presented to St. Martin's in right of his wife Lady Mary.

64 *Wykeham's Reg.* (Hants Rec. Soc.), i, 144.

65 Chan. Inq. p.m. 10 Ric. II, No. 17; Pat. 6 Ric. II, pt. 1, m. 4, 5.

66 Egerton MS. 2033. The De Roches family were evidently joint patrons with the Fyfhides of both churches. John de Roches, according to his fine of 1338, held the advowson of All Saints' and a third of the church of St. Martin. The inquisition of William Fyfhide stated that he (William de Fyfhide) held two presentations to All Saints' (the heir of John De Roches holding the third) and the advowson of St. Martin's. At the end of the fourteenth century Lady Joan de Roches presented and in 1403 or 1404 Joan, heiress of the Fyfhides, and Sir Thomas Skelton, her second husband, were patrons.

67 *Wykeham's Reg.* (Hants Rec. Soc.), i, 144 ; the instrument of the union declared, 'quod nulli omnino liceat locum dictae ecclesiae Omnium Sanctorum, in quo modo stat ipsa ecclesia, cum processu temporis diruta fuerit aut prostrata, nec solum adjacentis cimiterii dedicati in quibus jacent corpora defunctorum humata, vendere nec quocunque alio titulo in personam aliquam laicalem transferre valeat quoquomodo.'

68 Egerton MS. 2034. Lady Rose Wallop once presented by grant of Lord Sandys.

69 Inst. Bks. P.R.O.

70 The fourth of the advowson of Ellisfield was sold to Michael Terry in 1756, by William Saltmarshe (Com. Pleas Recov. R. Trin. 30–1 Geo. II, m. 18). The Moleyns family had before this also held a fourth of the advowson (Close, 5 Anne, pt. 12 ; Feet of F. Hants, Mich. 3 Anne).

71 Inst. Bks. P.R.O.

72 Ibid.

73 Recov. R. East. 3 Geo. IV, rot. 258 ; Close, 3 Geo. IV, pt. 21.

FARLEIGH WALLOP

Ferleye (Domesday); Farley, Farlega (xiii cent.); Farlegh (xiv cent.); Farlegh Mortymer, Farle Mortymere, Farley Mortimer (xiv cent.; xv cent.; xvi cent.); Farley Wallop (xvii cent.).

The small parish of Farleigh Wallop contains 1,725 acres of hill country which reaches its greatest height, of over 680 ft. above the ordnance datum, in the centre of the parish, where the main road which climbs up north from the Candovers meets the branch road which cuts across from the north-west of the parish and runs east by the lodge and grounds of Farleigh Park to the village. From here, after rising again by Broadmere, the ground gradually falls away towards the north of the parish, reaching only a height of about 400 ft. as the main road leaves Farleigh and enters Cliddesden.

Farleigh House, the residence of Mrs. Routh, with its wide stretching grounds and park, occupies most of the south-west corner of the parish. The house itself lies immediately south of the village, the out-buildings and stables becoming part of the village, and the high garden wall running along the south side of the village street. The village itself, lying on high ground, consists only of a few farmhouses and buildings with one good thatched house, and one or two cottages which stand lower than the road as the ground slopes away on the north side. At the east end of the village, near Park Farm, which, with its thatched out-buildings and farm-yard, in which is a gigantic horse-chestnut tree, stands on the left, a narrow lane known as Pigeon House Lane leads sharply downhill to the north. From here over the meadows to the north can be seen the church of St. Andrew, lying away at the top of a rising field, about a quarter of a mile from the village. It is served by the rector of the neighbouring church of Cliddesden.

The soil of the parish is clay with a subsoil of chalk, on which the ordinary green crops and wheat, barley, and oats are grown on the 708½ acres of arable land. There are 286 acres of permanent grass in the parish and 270 acres of woodland. The latter is almost wholly in the south of the parish, where in the south-east the Great Wood stretches south of Farleigh Park; and in the south-west Inwood Copse sweeps away to the west of the main road, covering the track of country that lies between the main road and that leading from the parish of Dummer.

MANOR The overlordship of *FARLEIGH WALLOP* was held at the Conquest by the king,[1] and in the fifteenth and sixteenth centuries by the prior of St. Mary of Southwick;[2] after the Dissolution it appears to have been held of the crown as of the hundred of Basingstoke.[3]

In the time of the Saxon king Edward, Ulvera or Wulfgifu held Farleigh,[4] her successor after the Conquest being Siric, the chamberlain, who held of the king.[5] Farleigh was subsequently held by a family who took their surname from the place. Henry de Farley, in the reign of Edward I, is found alienating his manor of Farleigh to Robert[6] de Mortimer and Joyce[7] his wife, at whose death it passed to his son, Hugh de Mortimer of Richard's Castle, son of this Robert (or Roger as he is sometimes called).[8] He died without male heir in 1304, leaving Joan and Margaret, daughters and co-heiresses. In 1316 Roger de Mortimer of Richard's Castle held the vill of Farleigh[9] and in 1328 made settlement of the manor on William de la Zouche, of Assheby.[10] Robert son of William de la Zouche was lord of the manor in 1346,[11] and was still in possession in 1371.[12] Early in the next century, however, the manor of Farleigh Mortimer must have been alienated by the Zouches, since it was held in 1428 and in 1431 by John Wyntreshulle of Surrey.[13] The Wyntreshulles did not long hold Farleigh, as in 1486 John Wallop died seised of the manor of Farley Mortimer.[14]

[1] *V.C.H. Hants*, i, 505.

[2] Chan. Inq. p.m. (Ser. 2), ii, 31; ibid. (Ser. 2), xvii, 31.

[3] Chan. Inq. p.m. 41 Eliz. pt. i, No. 6.

[4] *V.C.H. Hants*, i, 505.

[5] Ibid.

[6] Or Roger.

[7] *Abbrev. Plac.* (Rec. Com), 199.

[8] Pat. 25 Edw. I, pt. 2, m. 8; Feet of F. Div. Cos. East. 26 Edw. I.; ibid. Mich. 25 Edw. I. A little before his death he had alienated Farleigh to John de Drokenesford in the reign of Edw. I (Chan. Inq. p.m. 32 Edw. I, 48).

[9] *Feud. Aids*, ii, 313.

[10] Feet of F. Hants, Trin. 2 Edw. III. According to Dugdale, Robert de Mortimer, of Richard's Castle, had two sons, Hugh, who died 1304, and William, called la Zouch of Mortimer, from his property in Ashby de la Zouch. This Roger de Mortimer of Richard's Castle, holding Farleigh in 1316 and 1328, may possibly have been another son, to whom the property, when John de Drokenesford's time of tenure was over, may have reverted (Dugdale *Baronage*, i, 152–3).

[11] 'Robertus de la Zouche tenet in Farle dimiduum feodis quod fuit Johannis de Drokenesford.' *Feud. Aids.* ii, 330.

[12] Feet of F. Hants, Trin. 45 Edw. III.

[13] *Feud. Aids*, ii, 344, 364. The alienation probably took place about 1389, for at that date a fine occurs between William Pant, parson of the church of Farley Mortimer, and Thomas de Illeston and his wife, Margaret, by which the latter conveyed the manor to William Pant. The conveyance was evidently for the purpose of sale or re-settlement. In 1371 Robert, son of William de la Zouche, had settled the manor upon himself and his wife Margaret and their issue. Possibly this Margaret, wife of Thomas de Illeston, may have been identical with that Margaret, wife of Robert de la Zouche, she having married again on her husband's death, or, which is perhaps more likely, she may have been a daughter of Robert de la Zouche.

[14] Chan. Inq. p.m. (Ser. 2), ii, 31. According to Millard and Baigent (*Hist. of Basingstoke*, 247) and Stevens (*Hist. of St. Mary Bourne*), also Berry (*Hants Genealogies*), Farleigh descended to the Wallops from the De Valoignes, Sir Thomas Wallop having married Margaret daughter and heiress of Nicholas de Valoignes, and having obtained with her the manors of Cliddesden Hatch and Farleigh. This marriage took place in the reign of Henry V (*vide* Stevens, *Hist. of Basingstoke*), but John Wyntreshulle held Farleigh or Farleigh Mortimer in 1431 when Henry VI reigned. Possibly the Valoignes had for time past owned land in this parish separate from the Mortimers' manor. (Stevens says that Farleigh manor-house was the seat of Sir William de Valoignes *temp.* Hen. III.) It is noteworthy that the hamlets of Hatch and Cliddesden, of which with Farley Mortimer John Wallop died seised in 1486, were in 1316 held by Nicholas de Valoignes, although Farleigh at that time was owned by Roger de Mortimer. In 1346 John de Valoignes held half a fee in Cliddesden, and in 1428 William 'Fachell' held half a fee there late in possession of John Valence (*Feud. Aids*, ii, 344). It was between 1447 and 1486 that William 'Vachell' appeared as one of the patrons of 'Farleye' church, and the fact that he who was the lord of Cliddesden in 1428 was a little later patron of Farleigh seems to indicate a common ownership of the two parishes about that date. This theory depends upon the identification of 'Farleye' with Farleigh Mortimer. The name of Wyntreshulle does not appear among those who presented to the church. It may be that they alienated the manor to the De Valoignes. In 1420 Jno. Wyntreshulle held the half knight's fee that had before been held by Robert de la Zouche, but in 1431 he held his manor of Farleigh Mortimer for the fourth part of a knight's fee.

His son and heir, Richard Wallop, who was sheriff of Hampshire in 1502, succeeded him, surviving him seventeen years.[15] Sir John Wallop owned Farleigh Mortimer in the reign of Edward VI.[16] Farleigh Wallop was favoured by a visit from Queen Elizabeth, who visited the first Sir Henry Wallop there in the September of 1591.[17] He had been knighted by Elizabeth in 1569, and she had no servant more honest. After years of service in Ireland, after the loss of his second son, shot by Irish rebels, and when he himself was old and ill, he prayed to be relieved of his task, but died the day before his successor arrived. Sir Henry's views on free trade are of interest, for being at one time commissioner for restraining the transport of grain from Surrey, he disagreed with his fellow commissioners in declaring that markets should be free for all men, as 'yt ys most reasonable that one contrye shoulde helpe an other with soche comodytes as they are able to spare.' During his descendant's lifetime in 1667 the manor house of Farleigh Wallop was destroyed by fire and the family muniments perished.[18] His son Sir Henry Wallop was granted free warren in the manor then known as Farleigh Wallop by James I.[19] The favour of royalty, however, was withdrawn from Sir Robert Wallop, who succeeded his father in 1642. He took the side of the Parliament in the Civil War, and sat in judgement upon Charles I.[20] He was one of the few regicides who escaped the death sentence only to undergo a worse ordeal. For his sentence of perpetual imprisonment in the Tower involved also the cruel degradation of being taken once a year to and under the gallows, there to stand with ropes about his neck.[21] He made sorrowful petitions to the king, but never regained his liberty and died in the Tower in 1667, aged 66.[22] He had married the Lady Anne, a daughter of Henry Wriothesley, earl of Southampton, and a sister of Thomas Wriothesley, the lord treasurer.[23] In 1661 Charles II granted to Thomas, high treasurer of England and earl of Southampton, the manor of Farleigh Wallop and other property, all of which had been confiscated upon the attainder of Sir Robert Wallop, and he conveyed the same to the Lady Anne and her son and the family of Robert Wallop.[24]

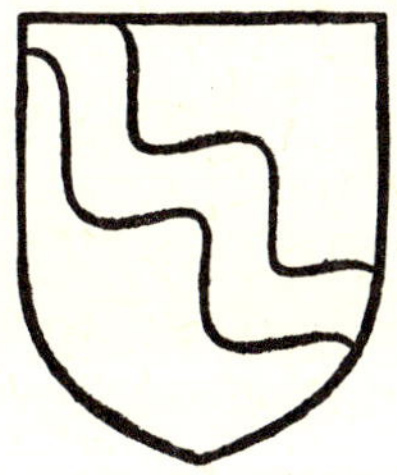

WALLOP. *Argent a bend wavy sable.*

The son of Robert Wallop succeeeded to his father's estates,[25] since which time the Wallop family have held the manor,[26] the earl of Portsmouth being the present owner.

FARLEIGH HOUSE was burnt in 1667 and not rebuilt till 1731 by Viscount Lymington. It is a large rectangular building fronting to the north, in flint and stone, the masonry being of excellent quality. In the middle of the north front is a projecting porch, over which is a large shield of many quarterings giving the alliances of the Wallops. There is a central entrance hall from which the series of ground-floor rooms open, and in the middle of the south or garden front, which commands a beautiful view, is a stone-faced bay of two stories. This looks on to a rectangular garden which with the sloping field to the south covers the site of the old house, whose foundations still exist in part. It probably had a central courtyard, with a terraced garden to the south, and there are traces of what looks like a round bastion at the south-west angle. To the west of the house is an eighteenth-century well-house with a large wheel, and to the east a low range of offices into which two large early seventeenth-century mullioned and transomed windows are built; they are of very good workmanship and doubtless formed part of the old house.

Farther to the east are the stables, a long two-story range standing north and south, substantial flint-faced buildings of eighteenth-century date, having the Wallop arms on a cartouche over one door, and the same quartering three bends wavy and a chief over another.

The walled kitchen garden lies to the south-east, and in its centre at the intersection of four paths is the base of a cross which is perhaps of thirteenth-century date, with part of an oblong shaft set in it.

CHURCH

The church of *ST. JOHN, FARLEIGH WALLOP*, is a cruciform building of flint and stone with a west tower. It was entirely rebuilt in the middle of the eighteenth century, in a very dull Gothic style, and the west tower dates from 1873. The east window of the chancel, and those in the north transept, are of three lights with arched heads and tracery, all the rest being square-headed, with three cinquefoiled lights. The interior is absolutely uninteresting as far as the fittings are concerned, the only woodwork of any merit being the altar rails with their twisted balusters of eighteenth-century date. There are a large number of floor slabs to members of the Wallop family, and two large mural monuments of eighteenth-century date in the south transept. On the south side of the chancel is an altar tomb of sixteenth-century date with quatrefoiled panels, in one of which is the Wallop coat: on the tomb is a Purbeck marble slab with indents of the brass figures of a man and his wife, with what may have been a figure of the Trinity over, and four shields at the angles. At the west end of the nave is the indent of another late brass on a broken slab, the remainder of which is in the chancel floor within the altar rails.

The octagonal stone font is modern, and replaces one of wood.

There are three bells by Mears and Stainbank, 1872.

For plate see Cliddesden.

The register was included with that of Cliddesden until 1813.

ADVOWSON

The descent of the advowson of Farleigh Wallop has always followed that of the manor. There was a church in the parish in the reign of Edward I[27] the advowson of which in 1279 was granted with the manor to Robert de Mortimer by Henry de Farley.[28] This Robert and Joyce his wife brought suits against

15 Chan. Inq. p.m. (Ser. 2), xvii, 13.

16 W. and L. Inq. p.m. 5 Edw. VI (Ser. 2), vi, 51.

17 Stevens, *Hist. of St. Mary Bourne*, 164. This Sir Henry Wallop was son of Sir Oliver Wallop.

18 *Dict. Nat. Biog.*

19 Pat. 14 Jas. I, pt. 25, m. 8.

20 Stevens, *Hist. of St. Mary Bourne*, 170.

21 Ibid. 173.

22 Ibid. 174–5.

23 Ibid. 169, 170.

24 Pat. 13 Chas. II, pt. 20, m. 10.

25 Stevens, *Hist. of St. Mary Bourne*, 176.

26 Recov. R. Trin. 1 Geo. I, rot. 83. Recov. R. East. 13 Geo. II, 316; ibid. Mich. 4 Geo. III, rot. 52.

27 *Pope Nich. Tax.* (Rec. Com.), 212*a*.

28 *Abbrev. Plac.* (Rec. Com.), 199.

Nicholas bishop of Winchester and Henry de 'Farley,' both of whom appear not to have recognized their right of patronage.[29] In the fourteenth century Roger de Mortimer[30] and Robert le Zouche[31] presented. In the following century the patrons were William Vachell[32] and John Wallop.[33] In the family of the last-named patron the gift of the living has ever since been vested.[34] The rectory is annexed to Cliddesden, and the earl of Portsmouth, the direct descendant of John Wallop, owns the right of presentation.

CHARITIES In 1736 Thomas Fellowes by will gave to the poor of Cliddesden £30.

In 1766 the Rev. Benjamin Woodroffe, the then rector of Cliddesden cum Woodroffe, invested a sum of £131 8*s*. 9*d*. (including probably the said sum of £30 and moneys given by an unknown donor) in £150 Old South Sea Annuities—now represented by £164 14*s*. 8*d*. consols with the official trustees, producing £4 2*s*. 4*d*. a year.

There is also a schoolhouse and a messuage in Cliddesden, formerly used as a schoolhouse, let at £12 a year.

An annual sum of £10 a year is paid by the earl of Portsmouth for educational purposes.

By a scheme of the Charity Commissioners, dated 25 April, 1899, the income is applicable in the proportion of three-fourths for Cliddesden and one-fourth for Farleigh Wallop, and the educational part made applicable in apprenticing, and in encouraging attendance at the schools.

HERRIARD

Henert (xi cent.); Herrerd (xiii cent.); Hereyard (xiv and xvi cent.).

The parish of Herriard covers an area of 2,978 acres of high country, which rises on every side from near the centre of the parish, where the ground is lowest and where the houses are mostly grouped. Even here the lowest ground is 500 ft. above the ordnance datum, yet the general impression is that the parish lies low, since the high ground round Ellisfield and Farleigh Wallop rises to the west to more than 600 ft., and in the south-east the land stretches away towards Shalden, rising to over 680 ft. near Shalden Green. From Basingstoke, however, the main road to Alton running south-east gradually climbs up to Herriard, entering the parish in the extreme north-west. From here it runs for about a mile and a half along the western boundary of the beautiful woodland country of Herriard Park, which fills up the whole of the north-east of the parish, and extends into the parish of Tunworth. Curving gently towards the south-east between the park and ploughed fields and meadows the road comes to the lodge gates of Herriard House, which stands in the south-west of the park, quite hidden from the road. South of the lodge gates, also on the east side of the road, is the church, standing behind a low wooden, lichen-covered fence, and approached by an avenue of Irish yew trees. Almost directly opposite the park gates an oak tree surrounded by a triangular wooden seat heads a rough narrow lane which runs south-west into Bagmore Lane, passing some cottages and the manor farm which stands on the north side of the lane. The farm-house, behind which runs a fine tall line of elm trees, stands well back from the road, while the thatched outbuildings and farm lands stretch away west and south. The rest of the village consists of cottages and houses which lie quite apart from the church and manor farm. For another half-mile the road leads on between the south-western boundary of the park and field and meadow land, until it comes to the schools, dated 1851, which lie on the west side. Beyond the schools the road runs across Bagmore Lane coming from Weston Patrick, leads south-west to Herriard Station on the Alton branch of the London and South Western Railway, and to the few cottages which lie round the station and on the north side of the lane as it goes to Preston Candover. Meanwhile the main road continuing south-east curves more directly south by Elderfield House (now used as the vicarage), which stands back on the west side of the road, and passing the blacksmith's shop runs between Hyde's Farm, which stands on the east, and the small village pond, by the New Inn, a modern slated building, and a small group of old cottages, one of which is the village post-office, all standing on the west side of the road. Beyond these the road continues south towards Lasham. A lane curving to the south-east by Hyde's Farm leads to the thatched cottages and houses lying for the most part on the west side of the road, composing the quiet little hamlet of Southrope. Lee Farm lies further north-east, while The Grange, the residence of Mr. A. T. E. Jervoise,[1] occupies the site of the grange that once belonged to the nuns of Wintney. The soil of the whole parish is clay and chalk with a subsoil of chalk, and crops of wheat, oats, and roots are grown on the 902 acres of arable land. The greater part of the parish is, however, given over to permanent grass, which covers 1,266 acres. Of the 729 acres of woodland, Hen Wood with Cowdray's Copse,[2] and Honey Leaze in Herriard Park cover the widest extent, while in the south-west are the Herriard Beeches and Herriard Common Wood, and in the south-east is Brick-kiln Common, adjoining Weston Common.

MANOR HERRIARD. Erlenc, before the Conquest, held Hugh de Port was lord at the time of the Domesday Survey,[3] the overlordship being held by his descendants William, John, and Edward de St. John in the reigns of Henry III and Edward III.[4] Holding from the St. Johns were the Fitz Peters, Herbert Fitz Peter in 1235[5] being followed by Sir Reginald Fitz Peter[6] in 1251, Matthew

[29] De Banco, Nos. 7, 27 *d.*; ibid. Nos. 3, 35; ibid. Nos. 9, 19 *d.* and 45. Assize R. 1341, m. 33.

[30] Egerton MS. 2032.

[31] Ibid. 2033; *Wykeham's Reg.* (Hants Rec. Soc.), i, 7.

[32] Ibid.; he presented to 'Farleye.' The suffix of 'Mortimer' is not in this case given.

[33] Ibid. 2034.

[34] Ibid.; Inst. Bks. P.R.O.; Pat. 13 Chas. II, pt. 20, m. 10; Recov. R. Trin. 1 Geo. I, rot. 83; ibid. Mich. 4 Geo. III, rot. 52.

[1] Mr. Jervoise has the bailiff's accounts for the farm from the reign of Edward II.

[2] Cowdray's Copse recalls the name of the early lords of Herriard.

[3] *V.C.H. Hants*, i, 482.

[4] Feet of F. Hants, Mich. 20 Hen. III; Chan. Inq. p.m. 3 Edw. III, No. 67; ibid. 21 Edw. III, No. 57.

[5] Feet of F. Hants, Mich. 20 Hen. III.

[6] Chan. Inq. p.m. 36 Hen. III, No. 42*a*.

Fitz Peter[7] in the reign of Edward III, and Herbert Fitz Peter[8] in 1526.

It must have been very early in the thirteenth century when John de Heryerd was lord of this land. His son Richard de Heryerd died in 1221 leaving as his heiress his sister Maud,[9] who married Richard de Sifrewast. By this marriage the latter acquired Herriard and held it for the service of a knight's fee and a half of Herbert Fitz Peter in 1235.[10] Maud de Heryerd and Richard Sifrewast had sons Nicholas and Roger, and Richard Sifrewast, son of the latter, married the mother of Fulk de Coudray.[11] To this Fulk de Coudray (the stepson of her grandson Richard), Maud de Heryerd, then a widow, and Nicholas her son agreed to give in perpetuity the manor of Herriard in exchange for the manors of Sherborne in Hampshire and Padworth in Berkshire.[12] Fulk de Coudray died in possession of the manor in 1251 leaving a son and heir, Peter de Coudray, aged fourteen.[13] Upon Sir Thomas de Coudray[14] the manor settled in 1297, he being succeeded by his son Sir Thomas, who died in 1349.[15] Sir Fulk, son of the latter, died childless and was succeeded by his cousin, Sir Henry[16] (holding in 1354), who in turn dying without issue, was succeeded by his nephew Edward Coudray in 1365.[17] The manor then passed from father to son, Peter, Edward, and again Peter de Coudray, holding during the fifteenth century.[18] On the death of the last Peter the male line of the family ended. He predeceased his wife, Dorothy Coudray, who died in 1528 without male issue. Her heiresses were her three daughters, Joan, Elizabeth, and Margery.[19] Of these Joan became wife of Peter Kydwelly,[20] and Margery wife of William Riche,[21] while Elizabeth married Richard Paulet.[22] Joan and Margery and their husbands granted their thirds of the manor to Elizabeth and Richard Paulet, who thus became possessed of the whole.[23] Their son, John Paulet, died in September, 1579, during the lifetime of his mother, who had by that time married her third husband George Puttenham[24]; he left a son, Richard Paulet, who held Herriard manor some few years later.[25] With the death of this son, Sir Richard Paulet, Herriard passed from the male line of the family, and was settled upon his daughter Lucy, wife of Sir Thomas Jervoise, who followed Sir Richard in the reign of James I. Sir Thomas Jervoise received his knighthood from James I. He represented Whitchurch (Hants) in the Short and Long Parliaments of Charles I, and was a staunch supporter of the Parliament during the Civil War.[26] The family of Jervoise held in succession in the male line as follows: three lords of the manor of the name of Thomas Jervoise, the son, grandson, and great-grandson of the husband of Lucy Paulet, during the seventeenth and eighteenth centuries. The first of these followed in his father's footsteps in his adherence to the Parliament, and he and Captain John Jephson were described by Clarendon as 'the two eldest sons of two of the greatest rebells.' Tristram Huddlestone Jervoise held in 1776, and George Purefoy Jervoise in 1792. Here the male line terminated. From Mary Purefoy Ellis Jervoise, sister of the last male heir, the manor passed to her son Francis Jervoise Ellis Jervoise, who held it in 1849. From his son Francis Michael Ellis Jervoise the manor passed to his son and heir, Francis Henry Tristram Jervoise, the present owner.[27]

Coudray. *Sable ten billets or.*

Paulet. *Sable three swords set pilewise with their hilts or.*

Jervoise. *Sable a cheveron between three eagles close argent.*

The present house was built in 1704, and is a large brick building covered with plaster, containing some good eighteenth-century panelling, and later work of the Adams period; there is also a little early seventeenth-century panelling from a former house. There is a good deal of excellent seventeenth and eighteenth-century furniture, some inlaid cabinets

7 Chan. Inq. p.m. 3 Edw. III, No. 67.

8 Ibid. 20 Hen. VIII (Ser. 2), vol. 48, No. 168.

9 From copies of Ct. R. lent by Mr. F. H. T. Jervoise. Entries upon the Pipe R. concerning the de Heryerds occur as follows 'Henricus de Heriet reddit compotum de xl solidis' (*Pipe R.* 13 *Hen. II* [Pipe R. Soc.], 187), and 'Henricus de Heriet reddit compotum de xx solidis,' (*Pipe R.* 14 *Hen. II* [Pipe R. Soc.], 179).

10 Feet of F. Hants, Mich. 20 Hen. III. The usual quarrel occurred between the underlord and his intermediate lord; Richard de Sifrewast complaining that William de St. John had demanded service from him which Fitz Peter should have rendered. The Sifrewasts were demesne lords of Herriard and overlords of Ellisfield, q.v.

11 From copies of the Ct. R. lent by Mr. F. H. T. Jervoise.

12 Ibid.; Maud de Heryerd died in 1245. An inquisition which was probably taken on her death shows that Richard son of Robert Sifrewast was her heir. Robert probably represents Roger.

13 Inq. p.m. 36 Hen. III (42*a*). The grant made by 'the dame Maud de Heryerd' to Fulk de Coudray was confirmed by Reginald son of Peter, of whom Fulk held Herriard (ex inform. Mr. F. H. T. Jervoise). The grant was also confirmed by Richard de Sifrewast grandson of Maud de Heryerd; ibid. To a Lewis de Heryerd and Matilda his wife, Peter de Coudray, at the end of the reign of Henry III, granted one virgate and a half of land and some woodland in Herriard. From this land a rent was due to the prior of Hamele (Hamble) under a grant of Richard de Heryerd (Feet of F. Hants, Hil. 56 Hen. III).

14 Feet of F. Hants, Hil. 26 Edw. I.

15 Ex inform. Mr. F. H. T. Jervoise. The manor was alienated before 1346 to Sir Robert Achard and Agnes his wife, for term of their lives with reversion to Sir Thomas de Coudray (Feet of F. Hants, East. 22 Edw. III; De Banco R. 354, m. 321). In 1346 Robert Achard held a knight's fee in Herriard (*Feud. Aids*, ii, 330).

16 Of whom mention occurs in Assize R. No. 1476, m. 4.

17 Ex inform. Mr. F. H. T. Jervoise.

18 Ibid.

19 Chan. Inq. p.m. 20 Hen. VIII (Ser. 2), vol. 48, No. 168.

20 Feet of F. Hants, Trin. 32 Hen. VIII.

21 Ibid. East. 34 Hen. VIII. 22 Ibid.

23 Feet of F. Hants, Trin. 32 Hen. VIII; ibid. East. 34 Hen. VIII.

24 Chan. Inq. p.m. 22 Eliz. pt. 2 (Ser. 2), No. 79. Her second husband was William, Lord Windsor. Feet of F. Hants, East. 1 Mary.

25 Recov. R. Hil. 29 Eliz. rot. 36; Feet. of F. Hants, Hil. 30 Eliz.

26 W. and L. Inq. 21 Jas. I, bdle. 38, 199*a*; *Ancestor*, No. 3, pp. 2, 3.

27 Ex inform. Mr. F. H. T. Jervoise; Feet of F. Div. Cos. Mich. 16 Jas. I; ibid. East. 13 Chas. I; ibid. Trin. 22 Chas. I; Recov. R. Hil. 17 Geo. III, rot. 245; *Ancestor*, No. 3, p. 5.

being particularly fine, and there are a large number of portraits, including an early panel picture, belonging to a class of royal and other portraits of which there is a good series in the library of the Society of Antiquaries.

SOUTHROPE (Sudtrop, Suthorp, Sudetrope, Suderope, xiii cent.) was held of the crown.[28] An inquisition taken in the reign of Henry III shows that Richard le Malle was granted the hamlet of Southrope by Henry II for the serjeanty of keeping the king's falcons.[29] In 1221, however, Maude de Heryerd and her husband Richard de Sifrewast paid a fine when they entered upon the land of Richard de Heryerd in Southrope.[30] During the reign of Henry III the lady of Herriard was summoned to show by what warrant she held the hamlet, which the king appeared to regard as his property.[31] Her title must have been found good, as Fulk de Coudray held Southrope with the manor of Herriard in 1251,[32] the hamlet evidently having formed part of the grant to Fulk from Maud de Heryerd. Thence onwards the hamlet follows the descent of the manor.[33]

The De Heryerd family were benefactors of Wintney Priory. A charter of Edward I confirmed a charter of Richard son of Richard de Heryerd, which in its turn confirmed the gift of Richard Makerel to the nuns of Wintney of 1½ virgates of land in Southrope, afterwards known as *WINTNEY HERRIARD GRANGE*, which had been granted to John and Thomas Makerel by his father Richard de Heryerd.[34] Maud de Heryerd also had alienated rent to the nuns.[35] King Henry III attempted to obtain a virgate in Southrope from the prioress as part of the royal manor of Odiham alienated without licence.[36] Richard de Sifrewast was called to warrant the prioress's right, which he did.[37] However, the matter ended well for the nuns, as Edward I made them a grant in free alms of a virgate of land and 5 marks rent, 'which the king lately demanded against them.'[38] In 1428 the grants made to Wintney represented half a knight's fee in Herriard.[39] At the Dissolution all lands in Wintney Herriard which had belonged to the priory were granted to Sir William Paulet, first marquis of Winchester, comptroller of the household of Henry VIII, and brother of the Richard Paulet who married Elizabeth Coudray.[40] The Paulets held the manor of Herriard Wintney[41] until 1851, when Lord Bolton sold it with the advowson to F. J. E. Jervoise, grandfather of the present owner of Herriard.[42]

In 1337 the prioress and convent of Wintney enfeoffed Sir Thomas Coudray of rent from their land in Herriard and Ellisfield for the endowment of a chantry chapel in Sherborne Coudray for the benefit of the souls of Sir Thomas and his ancestors.[43] From 'the outgoing' of the manor of Herriard Wintney Richard Paulet paid £4 to the chantry priest at the Vyne in the reign of Edward VI.[44]

CHURCH The church of *OUR LADY* is a very valuable example, built about the year 1200, of excellent style and detail, preserving, in spite of decay and repair, much of its original character. It has a chancel 26 ft. by 16 ft. 6 in., with modern north vestry, a nave 47 ft. 4 in. by 20 ft. 2 in., with a modern north aisle and a modern west tower.

The east window of the chancel is a fifteenth-century insertion of three cinquefoiled lights with tracery, probably replacing a group of three lancets. The side walls preserve the original arrangement of three lancets, a pair coupled in the eastern part of the wall, and a single light farther west.[45] Externally these are quite plain, but have an edge roll at the inner angle, and a moulded string at the sill level. At the north-east of the chancel was a small vestry, part of the original design, which is now destroyed, but traces of its roof-line and door are yet to be seen. In a drawing of 1828 in the possession of Mr. F. H. T. Jervoise this doorway is shown complete under the second lancet on the north. Below the east window, and now hidden by the altar table, are two large square locker recesses, of original date, rebated for doors, and under the first window in the south wall is a round-headed piscina recess with a modern bowl, and a square locker to the west of it. Their nearness to the floor shows that the levels have been raised in modern times. Near the south-west angle of the chancel is a square-headed low side window of fourteenth-century date, the lower part blocked up; it now contains a few pieces of old glass, including a pretty fifteenth-century figure of St. Margaret in white and gold glass, formerly in the tracery of the east window of the chancel, above the south main light.

The chancel arch, which before the repairs of 1876–7 had spread dangerously and was cracked and distorted, is a very fine feature, 14 ft. 8 in. in span, with three moulded orders and a dog-tooth label. In the jambs are short engaged shafts with foliate capitals, the two belonging to the inner order and the south capital of the outer order being ancient, all the rest, with the bases and much of the stonework of the arch and jambs, dating from 1876. The nave had in the first instance three lancets on each side, with doorways between the second and third. The north wall has been destroyed by the addition of the aisle and its place taken by an arcade of three bays with octagonal shafts and capitals, but in the south wall two of the original lancets remain, the place of the third, the eastern of the three, being taken by a three-light fifteenth-century window, inserted to give more light to the south nave altar. Another window of this kind now takes the place of the south doorway, having been put here in 1876; before that date it was at the north-east of the nave in a corresponding portion to the other. The original south doorway has completely disappeared; it had a brick porch over

[28] *Excerpt. e Rot. Fin.* (Rec. Com.), i, 72; Chan. Inq. 36 Hen. III, No. 42*a*.
[29] Chan. Inq. p.m. (Ser. 1), 30 Hen. III, No. 14.
[30] *Excerpt. e Rot. Fin.* (Rec. Com.), i, 72. According to the Pipe Rolls of the twelfth century, 'Robertus filius presbiteri de Suthrop reddere compotum debet dimiduum marcum sed mortuus est'; *Pipe R.* 14 *Hen. II* (Pipe R. Soc.), 179. A grant of a virgate of land in Southrope was made to Geoffrey and William de Langelegh by Richard de Sifrewast and Maud his wife; Feet of F. Hants, Mich. 15 Hen. III.
[31] *Abbrev. Plac.* (Rec. Com.), 120.
[32] Chan. Inq. p.m. 36 Hen. III, 42*a*.
[33] This hamlet, although in Herriard parish, lies within the hundred of Odiham.
[34] Dugdale, *Mon. Angl.* v, 722.
[35] Chan. Inq. p.m. (Ser. 1), 30 Hen. III, 14.
[36] Cur. Reg. R. No. 168, m. 8.
[37] Ibid.
[38] *Cal. of Pat.* 1272–81, p. 463.
[39] *Feud. Aids*, ii, 344.
[40] *L. and P. Hen. VIII.* xi, 385 (3).
[41] Pat. 21 Eliz. pt. 7, m. 45; Recov. R. Mich. 44 Geo. III, rot. 47.
[42] Ex inform. Mr. F. H. T. Jervoise.
[43] Pat. 11 Edw. III, pt. 1, m. 14.
[44] Chant. Cert. Hants, 54, No. 6.
[45] Only the east jamb of that on the south is old.

Herriard Church : The Chancel Arch and Jervoise Pew before Restoration

it in 1828, but no drawing of it seems to be extant. By a rather unusual treatment the inner jambs and rear arches of the fifteenth-century windows have been made to harmonize with the thirteenth-century lancets, having a similar edge roll worked on them.

The west tower is of three stages with a plain parapet and a north-east stairway, and serves as a porch to the nave. The jambs of its eastern arch are in part of old stonework, and the entrance is from the south through a fine pointed doorway, formerly the north doorway of the nave, of two moulded orders with a dog-tooth label, and nook-shafts with foliate capitals. Several small crosses are scratched on its jambs. Before the building of the tower there was a square wooden turret at the west of the nave, and an external brick stair to a square-headed door in the west wall leading to a gallery. Under the gallery was a square-headed window of three lights. Externally the ashlar clasping buttresses of the south angles of the nave are preserved, but the chancel has added diagonal angle buttresses. On the nave buttresses are a considerable number of incised sundials.

At the east end of the north aisle is the organ, screened by the re-used materials of a fine pew which used to stand in the south-east angle of the nave. It has high panelled sides surmounted by open arcades with a carved cornice and turned finials. On the heads of the posts are the initials of Peter and Dorothy Coudray, Richard and Elizabeth Paulet, John and Katherine Paulet, Richard and Anne Paulet, Sir Thomas and Lucy Jervoise, and Sir William and Anne Young, and the dates 1635 and 1819, the latter marking a repair.

The font, of serpentine, is at the west end of the nave, and is modern, as are all the other fittings of the church.

In the west window of the north aisle is a little old heraldic glass, with the arms of Popham—there was a Coudray-Popham marriage in the fifteenth century. Below is the upper part of a second shield, per pale indented or and gules.

At the west end of the aisle is a large slab with the indents of two shields, apparently of fifteenth-century date.

Popham. *Argent a chief gules with two harts' heads or.*

There are three bells; the treble by a late fourteenth-century London founder, probably John Langhorne, inscribed: 'Thomas vocor ego Nevile super omnia sono'; the second by John Warner, 1876; the tenor inscribed Nathaniel Hied, 1654.

The plate consists of a very fine parcel-gilt cup of 1562, unusually richly ornamented, with an inscription recording its repair in 1850; a modern paten (1849) engraved to match the cup; a second paten of 1887, and a plated flagon.

The first book of the registers begins in 1666, and goes to 1731, the second goes from 1736 to 1792, and the third from 1791 to 1812.

ADVOWSON Under the Taxation of Pope Nicholas the church of Herriard was assessed at £16 13*s.* 4*d.*[46] The Coudray family were patrons until 1333,[47] when Thomas de Coudray granted the advowson in mortmain to the prioress and convent of Wintney.[48] The nuns held the patronage until the Dissolution,[49] when it was granted by letters patent to Sir William Paulet,[50] in whose family it remained for over three centuries. Lord St. John presented in 1664, the marquis of Winchester in 1683, Charles, duke of Bolton in 1736 and 1742, Harry, duke of Bolton in 1758, Lord Bolton 1802, William Paulet or Lord Bolton in 1830, and again Lord Bolton in 1835.[51] In 1851 Lord Bolton sold the advowson to Mr. F. J. E. Jervoise,[52] whose grandson Mr. F. H. T. Jervoise is the present patron.[53]

NUTLEY

Noclei (Domesday); Nutleye, Nuclega, Nutelegha (xiii cent.); Nuttele, Nutleghe, Nottele (xiv cent.); Nutle, Nutes (xv cent.).

The parish of Nutley, containing only 1,524 acres of land, lies between Farleigh Wallop and Preston Candover on the slope of the high ridge of downland which sweeps down from the north, from a height of over 600 ft. above the ordnance datum at Farleigh to less than 300 ft. in the north of Preston Candover. The main road from the Candovers climbing this high country towards Farleigh cuts through the centre of Nutley parish, entering it from the south at Axford, which, with its two fine old thatched farm-houses of the farms of Upper and Lower Axford, is partly in Nutley and partly in Preston Candover. Leaving Axford Lodge, the residence of Captain Richard Purefoy, R.N., and the Crown Inn on the east, the road curves slightly west between rising fields and downland, and then turning due north again approaches the quiet village. To the east, behind short front gardens, is a group of two or three thatched cottages, beyond which a sloping field, rising to the sky-line, runs along the side of the road to the low brick wall which, curving with the road to the east, incloses the farmyard with its pond and some of the thatched outbuildings of the Manor Farm. Opposite, along the west side of the road, run other long straight barns and outbuildings of the farm, while the house itself, a substantial

[46] *Pope Nich. Tax.* (Rec. Com.), 212.

[47] Egerton MSS. 2031, 2032.

[48] Pat. 8 Edw. III, pt. 1, m. 28.

[49] Egerton MSS. 2032, 2033, 2034; *Wykeham's Reg.* (Hants Rec. Soc.), i, 83. In 1403–4 the nuns received a certificate exonerating them from the moiety of the tenth, since 'the priory is a house of poor nuns heavily encumbered.'

[50] *L. and P. Hen. VIII*, xi, 385 (3).

[51] Inst. Bks. P. R. O.

[52] Ex inform. Mr. F. H. T. Jervoise.

[53] A Richard de Coudary was rector of the church of Herriard early in the fourteenth century and made an exchange with the church of Exton. The exchange was little to the liking of the parishioners of Exton, who had heard that Parson Richard had pledged himself and the goods of Herriard church for his personal debts. They therefore petitioned the authorities at Winchester to forbid Richard under pain of excommunication to do the like deeds at Exton. *Reg. Bishop Rigaud de Ass.* 475.

square red-brick building, stands on high ground immediately behind the barns. North-east of the farm on the curve of the road as it turns east is the church of St. Mary, standing behind a low brick wall. East of the church fronting on the road is a picturesque block of two thatched and timbered cottages, beyond which high downland stretches to the north-east. Up the downland the road curves, and being lost to sight from the village passes on the north between fine woodland and down country, past two or three outlying thatched cottages, out of the parish. Bermondspit House is in the south-east of the parish on the border between Nutley and Preston Candover.

The soil of the whole parish is chalk and clay with a subsoil of chalk, and crops of wheat, turnips, oats, and barley are produced on the $556\frac{1}{2}$ acres of arable land which lies for the most part south and east of the village. The $174\frac{3}{4}$ acres given up to permanent grass are for the most part in the west where the downland stretches away to Dummer. Of the $386\frac{3}{4}$ acres of woodland, Norton's Wood, bearing the name of early lords of the manor of Nutley, covers nearly the whole of the north-east of the parish, while Nutley Wood covers the north-west part of the parish that lies between the main road and the western boundary.

MANOR

At the time of Domesday Survey, Henry the treasurer held *NUTLEY*, assessed at $2\frac{1}{2}$ hides. Of this manor, Geoffrey Mareschal held $\frac{1}{2}$ a hide, and at the same time 1 virgate, but not of the manor.[1] No further information exists concerning the treasurer's lands, and probably the family of Geoffrey Mareschal, or de Venuz, obtained the whole of Nutley, as in the thirteenth century John de Venuz held Nutley by serjeanty of being marshal of the king's household.[2]

In the reign of Henry III, Constance de Venuz, daughter of the above-mentioned John, and lady of the manor, conveyed 24 acres in Nutley to Gilbert de Dene, evidently her tenant.[3] Gilbert afterwards brought an unsuccessful action against her for trespass.[4] It was through his marriage with the same Constance, heiress of Nutley, that the famous Adam Gurdon became possessed of the manor.[5] In the reign of Edward I Joan daughter of Adam Gurdon received licence from the king to enfeoff James de Norton and Elizabeth his wife of the manor,[6] described as held of the king in chief as a member of the manor of Worldham, by John de Venuz, the service due being that of great serjeanty, namely, 'that Joan together with the said John should carry a Marshal's rod yearly in the king's house.'[7] The Nortons continued in possession[8] for 400 years, ever described as holding of the crown by great serjeanty, once varied by the term 'knight service.'[9] In the eighteenth century Elizabeth Norton married Francis Paulet of Amport, and their son Norton Paulet became lord of the manor. He disposed of Nutley to Thomas Hall in 1745.[10] With Elizabeth Hall, his granddaughter, heiress of her brother Thomas Hall of Preston Candover, the manor passed to George Purefoy Jervoise of Herriard, she being his first wife.[11] His descendant, Captain Richard Purefoy Purefoy, sold it in 1905 to Mr. J. C. A. Hall and Mr. C. Wade, in whose hands the manor now is.[12]

NORTON. *Vert a lion or.*

It is evident that some property in Nutley remained to the family of de Venuz after the marriage of Constance de Venuz to Adam Gurdon, as in 1317 John le Mareschal, then lord of East Worldham,[13] granted that manor with its rent from Nutley Manor to John de Burghersh.[14] The grant was said to be only for the grantor's life; however, in 1374, John, the son of the said John de Burghersh, granted the manor of East Worldham and all lands and rent from Nutley to the crown.[15] In spite of this, Alice de la Pole, duchess of Suffolk, a descendant of John de Burghersh, petitioned Edward IV for the restoration of lands in Nutley and East Worldham 'once held by John de Venuz,' which she said had been granted to her and the duke of Suffolk by King Henry VI.[16] The same had come into the hands of Edward IV in the first year of his reign, but were regranted to the duchess upon her petition.[17]

Upon the attainder of Edmund, duke of Suffolk, these lands must again have passed into royal possession, which perhaps accounts for the fact that Humphrey Bridges (to whom a grant may have been made), holding land in Nutley of the crown, received licence to alienate the same to John Myllyngate and Anne his wife.[18] In 1669 there was a lawsuit between the granddaughters of John Myllyngate, Mary wife of John Coates, and Amy wife of William Soper.[19] The plaintiff Mary stated that her father had settled his estates upon his daughters, but that William Soper had carefully lived close to his father-in-law, and had obtained the family deeds from him as well as a settlement to the use of his wife. The defendants, however, maintained that the land had been settled upon Amy as eldest child, and that the plaintiff and her husband had been non-suited when they laid claim to the moiety seven years back, and for yielding up their claim had received money from William Soper. The defendants apparently won their case,[20] and the Sopers continued to hold their property. In 1736 Patience

1 *V. C. H. Hants*, i, 500*b*.

2 *Testa de Nevill* (Rec. Com.), 233*a*.

3 Feet of F. Hil. 3 Hen. III.

4 *Bracton's Note Bk.* 1433.

5 *Herald and Genealogist*, v, 321.

6 Inq. a.q.d. 34 Edw. I, No. 175; Pat. 34 Edw. I, m. 3.

7 Inq. a.q.d. 34 Edw. I, No. 175.

8 *Feud. Aids*, ii, 313; Chan. Inq. p.m. 44 Edw. III (1st Nos.), No. 50; ibid. 45 Edw. III (Add. Nos.), No. 91; Exch. Inq. 28 Hen. VIII, file 988, No. 8; Chan. Inq. p.m. 34 Eliz. pt. 2, No. 118; Feet of F. Mich. 8 Jas. I. Richard Norton received pardon from Henry VI for resettling his estates upon himself and his heirs without royal licence (*Cal. of Pat.* 1422–9, p. 198).

9 Chan. Inq. p.m. 44 Edw. III (1st Nos.), No. 50.

10 Feet of F. Hants, 18 & 19 Geo. II.

11 Ex inform. Capt. R. P. Purefoy.

12 Ibid.

13 *Vide* East Worldham.

14 Anct. D. (P.R.O.), A. 3254.

15 Ibid. 3250.

16 *Cal. of Pat.* 1467–77, p. 66, *vide* East Worldham.

17 Ibid. Presumably these lands were part of the dowry of the duchess. Upon the Rolls of Parliament of the reign of Edward IV careful provision is made that no Act of Resumption or other Act be to the prejudice of Alice duchess of Suffolk, or her son John duke of Suffolk, who entered into all his father's possessions (*Cal. of Pat.* 1461–7, p. 261; Parl. R. Edw. IV).

18 Pat. 21 Eliz. pt. 6, m. 38; Feet of F. Hants, Hil. 22 Eliz. This property consisted of lands called 'le Graunge or Farm of Dummer Nutley and Basing.'

19 Chan. Proc. Bridges, bdle. 55, No. 26, Coates and Soper.

20 Feet of F. Hants, Trin. 22 Chas. II.

and Frances Soper, daughters and heirs-at-law of John Soper of Preston Candover, sold to Stephen Terry of Long Sutton Dummer Grange Farm and land in Nutley and Basing and other places.[21]

In 1757 the name of Soper again occurs in connexion with Nutley and Axford, when resettlement of his lands was made upon William Soper, yeoman, and his heirs.[22]

In 1578 William Fauconer of Laverstock, Wiltshire, sold to Philip Wateridge of Axford for £400 his messuage commonly called Axford or Axor Farm, and lands in Nutley.[23] A fine in 1652 occurs between William Soper and John Wateridge concerning a messuage and 150 acres of land besides pasture, meadow, and woodland.[24] As the Soper settlement of 1757 has reference to a messuage in Axford and 150 acres of land and woodland,[25] it seems probable that Axford Farm had been sold to the Sopers by Philip Wateridge.

Glimpses of the history of Axford hamlet can be found here and there. The prior of Southwick in early times held land there,[26] and his villeins owed suit at the hundred of Bermondspit, which William de Valence, so said the prior, hindered them from paying.[27] The Valences also had land there, as Aylmer de Valence earl of Pembroke held three parts of a fee in Axore (Axford) before 1323.[28]

The family of Ingepenne held land in Axford and Nutley from the fourteenth until the seventeenth century.[29] Their land in Axford they held of John Norton in 1405 and 1410.[30]

CHURCH The church of *OUR LADY* is entirely modern, having been rebuilt with chancel, north vestry, nave, south porch, and west bell-turret, in 1845. One voussoir of a mid-twelfth-century arch, with zigzag ornament, is preserved in the vestry, as a relic of the former church. The font has an octagonal bowl, and stands near the south doorway of the nave; it is modern, together with all the fittings of the church. There is one bell without inscription, possibly from the old church.

For plate and registers see Preston Candover.

ADVOWSON The vicarage of Nutley is annexed to Preston Candover. The priory of Southwick held the advowson until the Dissolution.[31] It was then probably annexed to Preston Candover, and granted with Preston Candover to the dean and chapter of Winchester,[32] who presented in the time of Bishop Gardiner,[33] and are the present patrons.

PRESTON CANDOVER

Candevre, Candovre (xi cent.); Candeura, Candieura (xii cent.); Preste Candevere, Kandever, Kandevera (xiii cent.); Preston Candeuere (xiv cent.); Preston in Candeveresdene (xv cent.); Kandavor (xvii cent.).

The parish of Preston Candover, containing 3,457 acres, lies on comparatively low ground, south of the high country round Farleigh Wallop and Nutley, and north-west of that which rises to Wield and beyond Wield to Medsted. The ground rises generally from west to east, the greatest height, 500 ft. above the ordnance datum, being reached in the north-east near Moundsmere Farm.

The village itself lies on the lowest ground towards the west of the parish on the road which comes north-east from Northington and the two other Candovers, and runs across the parish to enter Nutley at Axford and continues uphill to Farleigh and thence to Basingstoke. As the road enters the village the farm buildings of Lower Farm lie on the east, as a branch road turns off south-east towards Godsfield and Alresford. On the west at the corner of a lane which runs north-west by the Manor Farm to Preston Copse, is the old vicarage, now a private house, north of which is the graveyard and the remains of the old church of St. Mary, now used as a mortuary chapel. As the road continues up the village, South Hall, the property and residence of Mr. C. Hall, stands back on the east, while on the west is North Hall, the manor-house of the Purefoy estate, now the property and residence of Mr. C. L. Wade.

Passing by several good cottages and houses the road comes to the modern church of St. Mary, to which, as it stands well to the east, a lychgate leads the way over a grass inclosure. Here the road curves to the north by the 'Purefoy Arms,' which stands on the west almost opposite the church, and passing by the several shops and cottages of the village, one of which on the east side serves as the post office, goes on to the schools, which stand in their inclosed playground also on the east side of the road. On high ground north-east of the schools is the modern vicarage standing in good grounds. Beyond the schools two or three thatched cottages lie east and west of the road, and a small plain tiled building, a Primitive Methodist chapel, bearing the date 1863, stands on the east. Passing on through the north end of the village, the wooden fence inclosing the well-wooded grounds of the west park of Preston House, the seat of Mrs. Hope, runs along the west side of the road, a drive at the further end leading up to the house. On the opposite side of the road are two or three thatched cottages, while from here a road branches east to Bradley and Herriard. Leaving the grounds of Preston House the main road continues north to Axford and so out of the parish.

21 Com. Pleas D. Enr. Trin. 10 Geo. II, rot. 1. She was heiress of Preston Candover manor, and married William Guidott; see Preston Candover.

22 Com. Pleas Recov. R. rot. 695, No. 45. This was a different family evidently, Soper not being an uncommon name in these parts; ex inform. Rev. Sumner Wilson.

23 Com. Pleas Recov. R. rot. 63, No. 18.

24 Feet of F. Hants, Mich. 1652.

25 Com. Pleas Recov. R. rot. 695, No. 45.

26 *Plac. de Quo Warr.* (Rec. Com.), 768.

27 Ibid.

28 Chan. Inq. p.m. 17 Edw. II, No. 75.

29 Feet of F. Hants, Mich. 27 Edw. II; Chan. Inq. p.m. 7 Hen. IV, No. 48; ibid. 8 Hen. IV, No. 95; Feet of F. Hants, East. 9 Hen. IV; Chan. Inq. p.m. 12 Hen. IV, No. 44; Feet of F. Hants, Trin. 19 Hen. VI; ibid. Mich. 10 Hen. VIII; ibid. East. 22 Eliz.

30 Chan. Inq. p.m. 7 Hen. IV, No. 48; ibid. 12 Hen. IV, No. 44.

31 Egerton MS. 2031-4, *Wykeham's Reg.* (Hants Rec. Soc.), i, ii. In the reign of Edward III the prior and convent granted licence to Sir James Norton to hear divine service in the oratory of the manor of Nutley. Egerton MS. 2032.

32 Pat. 33 Hen. VIII, pt. 9, m. 40.

33 Egerton MS. 2034. In 1636 John Young, and in 1661 Edward Griffin, esq., are found presenting (Inst. Bks. P.R.O.).

Moundsmere Farm, lying on the downs in the north-east, is the most interesting spot in the parish. When the property of Southwick Priory, including the manor of Moundsmere, passed to Winchester College by exchange with Henry VIII in 1543, the farmstead was in the very next year used as a sick-house for the Winchester scholars who were stricken down by the plague that visited Winchester in 1544. Thus new buildings appear to have been run up round the farm-house during that year, and a number of scholars were sent there both in the autumn and winter terms.[1] In 1554, on the occasion of another outbreak of the plague, scholars were again sent to Moundsmere, and, probably by means of a certain sum over from Queen Mary's largess given on her bridal visit to the college, 'the chyldren's hows at Mouseberie (*sic*) for their comfort in tyme of siknes' was repaired and the barn was fitted with bed-places and windows for their reception.[2] Mr. Kirby, in his *Annals of Winchester College*,[3] quotes an interesting clause inserted after this date in all successive leases of the demesne land of the manor, reserving to the college 'the new buildings adjoining the manor house' with all new rooms that might hereafter be built for such time only as the warden, scholars, schoolmasters, clerks, or servants of the college should 'resort, come, and remain there for the avoiding of the plague or any such pestilential sickness.' But although the tenant of Moundsmere Farm was thus obliged to receive sick scholars at any time, when the plague of 1666 made its appearance in Winchester the sick scholars instead of being sent to Moundsmere were sent to a farm-house at Cranley, and presumably from that time the tenant of Moundsmere escaped his obligation.[4]

Cobbett, in his *Rural Rides*,[5] mentions the avenue of yew trees which runs east of the road south of the village at Preston Candover, estimating it as probably a mile long, 'each containing as nearly as I can guess from twelve to twenty feet of timber.' Chalk, as he says, is the favourite soil of the yew tree, and chalk composes both the soil and subsoil of Preston Candover. Thus on the 2,498¼ acres of arable land the usual crops of wheat, turnips, and oats are grown. Preston Down in the south-east of the parish, with the downs in the north round Moundsmere, make up the greater part of the 985 acres of permanent grass.

There are numerous small copses in the west of the parish—Lilley's Copse and Preston Copse with the small Upper Barn Copse and Furze Yard Copse, and these with Inham Copse near Axford and the large stretch of woodland known as Preston Oak Hills Wood which fills up the north-east corner of the parish, make up the 405¾ acres of woodland included in Preston Candover.

MANORS

In *PRESTON CANDOVER* at the date of the Domesday Survey there were six separate estates, five of which were owned by the Conqueror's followers who had replaced the Saxon owners, whilst the sixth was still held by a Saxon priest, the pre-Conquest owner. Of these estates William Mauduit had one which in the Confessor's time had been held as two manors; Ralf de Mortimer and his under-tenant Oidelard held the second which had before belonged to Cheping; Hugh de Port, whose under-tenant was Anschitel, held the third which had been a portion of the possessions of Earl Godwin; clerks, or priests, had the fourth which had been the land of Alvric; Cheping had the fifth which was before held by Sberne of Queen Edith; and lastly, Edwin the priest held the sixth of King William as he had held it of King Edward.[6]

No connexion can be made out between these separate owners and the overlords or owners of the various manors found later in the parish, and any attempt to discover one must be conjectural, except in the case of the lands of William Mauduit which by the twelfth century were in the hands of Robert de Pont de l'Arche,[7] and in the case of the Mortimer possessions, which remained to that family, Roger de Mortimer and his son Edmund holding in Candover before 1398 and 1424 a fee worth 100*s*.[8]

Upon the Pipe Roll of 1166 an assessment for *CANDOVER SCOTLAND* was given as half a mark.[9] This was evidently the manor that, in the thirteenth century, Jordan and William Eschotland held.[10] No further trace of the Eschotland family or their manor can be found unless it can be identified with the manor of Preston Candover, which appears for the first time in the reign of Edward III held by the Hoyvilles.

In 1368 John de Hoyville, son and heir of William de Hoyville, granted to William de Wykeham, bishop of Winchester, the manor of *PRESTON CANDOVER* and lands in 'Candeveresden.'[11] In the reign of Richard II the bishop granted this manor to Thomas Warenner and his wife Joan.[12] The only child of Thomas Warenner and Joan was Agnes, to whose husband, Sir Walter Sandys, the manor descended in the reign of Henry IV.[13]

The manor remained in the Sandys family[14] until some time in the latter part of the sixteenth or early part of the seventeenth century, when it seems to have been alienated to a man of the name of Guye, since in 1636 James Guye, yeoman of Preston Candover, sold for £1,110 the manor of Preston Candover with all manorial rights to George Long.[15]

The new owner, a stout adherent of the Parliament, lived in London during the Civil War, and

1 For accounts, &c. proving this see T. F. Kirby, *Annals of Winchester College*, 259.

2 See Compotus Roll quoted by Mr. Kirby as above.

3 Op. cit. 260.

4 T. F. Kirby, op. cit. 355.

5 Wm. Cobbett, *Rural Rides*, 18, 22.

6 *V.C.H. Hants*, i, 477*b*, 482*b*, 490*b*, 493*a*, 504*b*, 505*a*.

7 'Robertus Mauduit tenuit feodum unius militis et modo Robertus de Ponte Arche' (*Red Bk. Exch.* i, 206).

8 Chan. Inq. p.m. 22 Rich. II, No. 34; ibid. 3 Hen. VI, No. 32. The earl of Arundel also held, in 1166, a knight's fee in Candover; *Red Bk. Exch.* i, 202.

9 Pipe R. 13 Hen. II. The early overlordship of this property is not known, but in the fifteenth century Walter Sandys held it of the abbey of Hyde, and his successors Thomas and Sir William Sandys held of Richard Brun and Sir Thomas Brun; *Feud. Aids*, ii, 364; Chan. Inq. p.m. 20 Hen. VI, No. 35; ibid. 11 Hen. VII, No. 110.

10 Add. MS. 33280. Another variation of the name occurs as Candover 'Scudland.' A bull of Pope Alexander confirmed the chapel of 'Candveura Scudland' to Southwick Priory, which had been granted 'in elemosinam' by Jordan Eschotland; ibid.

11 Close, 42 Edw. III, m. 16 *d*.

12 Feet of F. Hants, East. 2 Ric. II.

13 Chan. Inq. p.m. 9 Hen. IV, No. 27; *Feud. Aids*, ii, 344.

14 Chan. Inq. p.m. 20 Hen. VI, No. 35; ibid. 24 Hen. VI, No. 40; Feet of F. Hants, East. 9 Hen. VII; Chan. Inq. p.m. 11 Hen. VII, vol. 11, No. 110; ibid. 2 Eliz. pt. 1, No. 143; Feet of F. Hants, 1 Edw. VI. In the reign of Henry VI the manor seems to have comprised a manor-house, five other houses, and 160 acres of arable land, 11 acres of meadow, 150 acres of pasture, 20 acres of wood, and rent of various free tenants.

15 Close, 12 Chas. I, pt. 6.

assisted the Parliament with money.[16] When he returned home after Basing House had fallen, he found his house a ruin and his land wasted. By way of compensation the Parliament gave him a small farm in Preston Candover from the forfeited property of a recusant, Francis Perkins, the owner of another manor in Preston Candover.[17] Later, however, Mr. Perkins offering a larger amount than that paid by Mr. Long, was allowed by the Parliamentary Committee to buy back the estate for his son. Against this decision George Long petitioned in vain.[18]

The Longs, however, recovered their property later, and either this George Long or a son of the same name sold the manor in 1677 to William Soper,[19] in whose family it remained until the reign of George II, when, in 1739, Patience Soper, one of three daughters,[20] and evidently heiress of John Soper, of Preston Candover, brought the manor to her husband, William Guidott.[21] William Guidott, the famous builder of Preston House, died in 1745, and on the death of Patience in 1749 Preston Candover passed to their kinsman and heir William Woodroffe, who took the name of Guidott.[22]

In 1783 William Woodroffe Guidott sold the estate for £9,000 to John Blackburne, a merchant of London, and John Slade, in equal shares, and in 1789 John Blackburne bought Slade's moiety.[23] By his will dated 1792 he left his manor and lands to his son John.[24] He died in debt, and in 1829 an order was made for the sale of his estate to defray his liabilities.[25] Mr. Rumbold purchased the manor and sold it later to H. King, who was succeeded by his son J. H. King. The latter sold the estate in 1877 to Lord Templemore, from whom it was purchased by Mr. H. J. Hope at the end of the nineteenth century.[26] Mr. Hope died in 1905; his widow Mrs. Hope is now lady of the manor.

The earliest reference to the manor of *STEVENBURY* or *HORWOODS* is apparently on a Pipe Roll of 1166 when the name of 'Candeura Stephani' appears.[27] Probably from this Stephen, who owned Candover, the manor known in the thirteenth century as 'la Stevenbury' took its name. Robert de Watteville, lord of the manor of la Stevenbury in the thirteenth century, granted a chantry therein to the priory of Southwick.[28] Nothing more is known of this manor until the name of Horwoods occurs in connexion with it in the reign of Edward II, when Thomas de Cailly held rent in Preston Candover which he received from William de Horwode,[29] who held the manor of Stevenbury or Horwoods as member of the manor of Bradfield in Berkshire, first of the De Somerys and then of the Langfords and the Staffords, lords of Bradfield.[30]

In 1322 the same William de Horwood held this manor, which consisted of 2 carucates of land,[31] and died seised of it in 1349.[32] His son Thomas had died in the king's service at Calais two years before, and he left, as heir, his grandson, also named William, aged seven.[33] The manor variously called Stevenbury or Preston Candover manor remained in the Horwood family, the holders in tail male from 1422 being William Horwood, who left a son William,[34] and John Horwood and his wife Katherine,[35] whose son John married Elizabeth, and died in the reign of Edward IV.[36] The last John Horwood left a daughter Alianora, as heiress, but a posthumous son was born who became heir.[37] He, however, died while still a minor in 1495, when the manor of Preston Candover went to his uncle Hugh Horwood.[38] The last of the male line of Horwood died five years later, leaving as his heirs his four sisters, Joan wife of Richard Savage, Katherine wife of John Frith, Alice wife of Thomas Lende, and Christine wife of Ingilram Prior.[39] Of these Alice Lende and Catherine Frith (then Catherine Peter by her second marriage) died in the reign of Henry VIII each seised of a third part of the manor of Horwood in Preston Candover.[40] Another third part appears to have been sold by John Prior to Richard More in the reign of Philip and Mary,[41] and Sir William and Lady Elizabeth Warham in Elizabeth's reign held a fifth part of Horwoods manor. Dame Elizabeth Warham had evidently been previously married to More, by whom the scattered portions of Horwoods manor must have

16 S.P. Dom. Interreg. G. 253.

17 Ibid. 18 Ibid.

19 Feet of F. Hants, East. 29 Chas. II.

20 Com. Pleas D. Enr. Trin. 10 Geo. II, rot. 1.

21 Ex inform. Rev. Sumner Wilson; Feet of F. Hants, Mich. 13 Geo. II.

22 Ex inform. Rev. Sumner Wilson; Recov. R. East. 12 Geo. III, rot. 38. The Guidotts were originally Florentines, and settled in England in the time of Henry VIII. In 1746 Mr. Guidott's place at Candover was one of the famous country seats of England; Woodward, *Hist. of Hants*, ii, 300.

The Soper family was well known in Hampshire. William Soper was mayor of Southampton in the fifteenth century, and another William Soper and Anna his wife received licence to eat flesh in Lent, 1661 (Ex inform. Rev. Sumner Wilson).

23 Close, 24 Geo. III, pt. 22, m. 3; ex inform. Rev. Sumner Wilson.

24 Com. Pleas Recov. R. Mich. 40 Geo. III, m. 33. The estate of John Blackburne comprised Preston Candover manor and mansion house, with Lower and Middle farms, and Upper or Home farm and mansion house called Sopers, together with the manor or reputed manor or farm of Horwoods and a farm in Axford in Nutley parish. 'Sopers,' formerly the residence of the Soper family, eventually passed to the Lainsons, and now belongs to the Hopes of Preston House. The old house has long been pulled down; the site of the wrought-iron gates is still shown, and of the avenue before the house only a few elms remain (ex inform. Rev. Sumner Wilson); Com. Pleas Recov. R. Mich. 40 Geo. III, m. 33.

25 Ex inform. Rev. Sumner Wilson.

26 Ibid.

27 *Pipe R. Soc.* 13 Hen. II, 188.

28 Add. MS. 33280.

29 Chan. Inq. p.m. 10 Edw. II, No. 63. Thomas de Cailly was one of three who held rent in Preston Candover, which had before belonged to Robert de Tatteshale. His share was 17*s.* 11½*d.* His heir, according to his inquisition, was some kinsman unknown. In 1360, however, a certain rent in Preston Candover was in the hands of the king owing to the minority of Thomas de Cailly; Mins. Accts. 34 Edw. III, bdle. 119, No. 7.

30 Chan. Inq. p.m. 16 Edw. II, No. 72; ibid. 23 Edw. III, pt. 1, m. 65; ibid. 10 Hen. V, No. 11; ibid. 14 Edw. IV, No. 28; ibid. 11 Hen. VII, No. 60; ibid. 16 Hen. VII, vol. 14, No. 129; ibid. 18 Hen. VIII (Ser. 2), vol. 45, No. 115.

31 Ibid. 16 Edw. II, No. 72.

32 Ibid. 23 Edw. III, pt. 1, No. 65.

33 Ibid. The manor at this time included a manor-house and garden, 300 acres of arable land, 10 several acres of pasture, and 300 acres of wood, with rent of free and villein tenants, arrented at 33*s.* 4*d.* yearly.

34 Chan. Inq. p.m. 10 Hen. V, No. 11.

35 Ibid. 14 Edw. IV, No. 28; ibid. 11 Hen. VII, vol. 11, No. 60.

36 Ibid.

37 Ibid.

38 Ibid. 11 Hen. VII (Ser. 2), vol. 11, No. 60.

39 Ibid. 16 Hen. VII, vol. 14, No. 129.

40 Ibid. 18 Hen. VIII (Ser. 2), vol. 14, No. 115; Exch. Inq. 19 Hen. VIII (Ser. 2), file 981 (1). Alice Lende or Leynde died 4 April, 1523 or 1524. She appears, according to an inquisition of 18 Henry VIII, to have been seised of the reversion of a third of Horwoods manor which Edith Horwood held for life. Edith Horwood died in December 1525. The heir of Alice Lende was her descendant, William Somer, aged eight. The heir of the other sister, Catherine Peter, was the son of her first marriage, Henry Frith.

41 Feet of F. Hants, Mich. 3 & 4 Phil. and Mary.

been acquired.[42] From her and Richard More her son Horwoods *alias* 'Stoniburie' manor passed by sale to Thomas Dabridgecourt of Stratfield Saye[43] in Elizabeth's reign, and was held by this well-known family until 1634 when Thomas Dabridgecourt and Barbara his wife seem to have sold it to Sir Richard Harrison.[44] John Harrison[45] appears as owner of Horwoods manor in 1669, and about a year later it seems to have been transferred to Anthony Guidott by Anne Harrison, widow of Richard Harrison.[46] With the Guidott family, who already owned the manor of Preston House in this parish, Horwoods remained, forming part of William Woodroffe Guidott's property in 1772;[47] thence onwards it has followed the descent of Preston House manor with which it is now incorporated.[48]

DABRIDGECOURT. *Ermine three bars gules cut off at the ends.*

The overlordship of the property afterwards known as the manor of *BOTILLERS CANDOVER* belonged during the fifteenth century to the family of Camoys, Botillers Candover being held of Lady Joan de Camoys and her heirs.[49]

CAMOYS. *Argent a chief gules with three roundels argent.*

Early in the thirteenth century Robert the Butler or Pincerna was settled[50] in Candover, and later in the same century and the next there is evidence of ownership by the family now known as Botteleye[51] and Botiller.[52] In 1310 William le Botiller and Alice his wife held eleven messuages, 2 carucates of land, 20 acres of wood, and 30*s.* rent in Preston Candover,[53] their heirs being their children, John, William, Robert, and Elizabeth,[54] from one of whom probably the land passed to John de Kacchefrensh and Alice his wife, since they, in 1345, held eleven messuages, 2 carucates of land, 40 acres of wood, and 30*s.* rent in Preston Candover.[55] John de Kacchefrensh settled the reversion of his property upon Oliver de Bohun and Margaret his wife during their lives, with final remainder to John de Warbelton and Alice his wife.[56] Accordingly in 1368 John de Warbelton held lands called 'terra de Boteller in Candeveresden,' in reversion, he being the son of Alice then widow of John de Warbelton.[57] Katherine wife of the younger John de Warbelton died, in 1404, seised of a house and carucate of land in Preston Candover,[58] and her son William,[59] in 1405, held a manor 'called Botillers in Preston in Candeveresden.'[60] William Warbelton, who died 11 October, 1469, held the manor of 'Botelers Candevere,' and having no issue left this land to William Skulle the son of his cousin Agnes.[61]

In 1485 William Skulle apparently held the manor.[62] Here the history of Botillers Candover ceases, unless it can be identified with the manor called Purefoys.

In the June of 1495 Richard More died in possession of Preston Candover manor known later as *PUREFOYS*.[63] It is difficult to determine his title to this property unless it was conveyed to him by William Skulle, or unless some land in Preston Candover passed to the Mores from the Horwoods.[64]

The manor of Richard More, however, was not

[42] Feet of F. Hants, Mich. 3 & 4 Eliz. Thomas Tovye and Margery his wife, and James Payse and Joan his wife also appear to have held portions of Horwoods manor (*vide* Feet of F. Hants, Mich. 3 & 4 Eliz.).

[43] Ibid. Hil. 18 Eliz.; Close, 6 Jas. I, pt. 5, No. 8. In 1602 Thomas Dabridgecourt settled Horwoods upon his second son Thomas, upon whose first wife Catherine Legatt the manor was settled as her jointure in 1603. Thomas Dabridgecourt was twice married, his second wife being Barbara daughter of William Fisher of Chilton Candover (ex inform. Rev. Sumner Wilson and Close, 6 Jas. I, pt. 5, No. 8; ibid. 1 Jas. I, pt. 2; Add. MSS. 33278, No. 183).

[44] Feet of F. Hants, Mich. 10 Chas. I.

[45] Recov. R. Hil. 20 & 21 Chas. II, rot. 159.

[46] Feet of F. Hants, Hil. 22 & 23 Chas. II.

[47] Recov. R. East. 12 Geo. III, rot. 38. Horwoods appears as Stonebury and Stoners, probably a corruption of Stevenbury.

[48] The possessions of John Blackburn in Preston Candover before 1799 included, with Preston Candover (Preston House) manor, 'the manor or reputed manor, farm and farm place' named Horwoods. *alias* Stonebury or Stoners. Two centuries earlier there occurs a mention of a 'Horwooddes farm,' the site of which was leased by one John Phetyplace of Standlake, Oxfordshire, to Thomas Froste of Wield in Hampshire in the reign of Edward VI for twelve years.

[49] Chan. Inq. p.m. 5 Hen. IV, No. 15; ibid. 8 Edw. IV, No. 44.

[50] *Rot. Lit. Claus.* (Rec. Com.), i, 126, when an inquiry was ordered to ascertain whether Robert Pincerna had justly accused his wife of infidelity. Herbert Pincerna held in this century land 'in Candevere,' of the abbey of Hyde; *Testa de Nevill* (Rec. Com.), 239.

[51] In 1262 John de Botteleye granted to John de Langerude two parts of two virgates of land in Preston Candover which later were granted to Martin de Roches by John de Langerude (Feet of F. Hants, East. 47 Hen. III; Assize R. No. 1220, m. 10). Martin de Roches, dying in the first year of the reign of Edward I, was seised of two virgates of land held of John de Botteleye. He left a brother and heir, Hugh de Roches, aged forty.

[52] Feet of F. Hants, Mich. and Hil. 4 Edw. II.

[53] Ibid. Mich. 4 Edw. II.

[54] Ibid.

[55] Ibid. Trin. 19 Edw. III.

[56] Ibid. In 1346 John de Chacchefrensh and Oliver de Bohun each held a fourth part of a knight's fee in Candover, but the fourth part of John de Chacchefrensh was described as that 'quod fuit Alicie Wys de Preston,' and that of Oliver de Bohun as 'quod fuit Philippi de Hoyvill.' Oliver de Bohun therefore seems to have also held land either inherited by, or granted to him by Philip de Hoyville. This was earlier than the grant made by John de Hoyville to Thomas Warenner of his manor of Preston Candover; *Feud. Aids*, ii, 330. In 1431 John Roger of Soberton appears to have held lands and tenements called 'Botillers in Preston Candevere.' Possibly he was one of the Hoyville family, who held land in Soberton; ibid. 364.

[57] Chart. R. 42 Edw. III, No. 159. Grant of free warren was made to John de Warbelton in his demesne lands by Edward III.

[58] Esch. Inq. 5 & 6 Hen. IV, file 1719, No. 5.

[59] Ibid.

[60] Feet of F. Div. Cos. 7 Hen. IV.

[61] Chan. Inq. 8 Edw. IV, No. 44. The manor appears to have been settled upon William Warbelton and Margery his wife and male issue, with remainder in default to Elizabeth Sifrewast aunt of William Warbelton, for her lifetime, thence to descend to her daughter Agnes wife of Miles Skulle, and her issue. Both Elizabeth Sifrewast and Agnes Skulle predeceased William Warbelton, but the latter left a son and heir, William Skulle, aged thirty, to whom Botillers Candover descended.

[62] De Banco, Mich. 2 Ric. III, m. 328.

[63] Chan. Inq. 11 Hen. VII, vol. 11, No. 55.

[64] William atte More, son of John atte More, of Wytheford, and Henry atte More, were trustees of John de Horewood for the settlement of the manor of Polhampton upon John de Horwood and his wife Katherine and their issue (Chan. Inq. p.m. 11 Hen. VII, vol. 11, No. 60). A further connexion with the Horwoods is shown in an inquisition taken upon the death of Nicholas More in 1497. The document is nearly indecipherable and all that can be read from it is that Nicholas

held either of the Camoys family, or of the lords of Bradfield, as was Horwoods manor, but of Lord St. John.[65] Katherine, Richard More's widow, held the manor for life under her late husband's will, with remainder to her son John More, then aged twenty,[66] or in default of male heirs, the property, according to the settlement, was to remain to Isabel Williams, wife of John Williams, among several other heirs.[67]

There is no mention of John More being in possession of Preston Candover, but the property seems to have descended or been conveyed to Isabel Williams.[68]

Her son, Reginald Williams, next held the property, whose son John, dying without issue, was succeeded by his brother Nicholas.[69]

The title of Nicholas to the estate was disputed in Elizabeth's reign by Walter Mayhew, a husbandman of Rotherwick, who claimed the manor in right of his wife Elizabeth, who, according to Walter Mayhew's statement, was a daughter of John More, son of that Richard More who had died in 1495 seised of the manor of Preston Candover.

The defendant traced his title to his grandmother, Dame Isabel Williams.[70] The matter was, about 1566, referred to the arbitration of the bishop of Winchester and Henry Wallop,[71] and evidently Nicholas Williams won his case, as Walter Mayhew in 1579 relinquished his claim to Francis Perkins,[72] who by marriage with a daughter of Nicholas Williams[73] had become lord of the manor.[74] He died in 1617,[75] and his son, a Roman Catholic Royalist, in his old age suffered sequestration of his estate for recusancy under the Commonwealth.[76] The family held the manor until 1733, when the fourth Francis Perkins, of Preston Candover,[77] who had married the famous Arabella Fermor,[78] sold it to Thomas Hall for £1,700.[79] Elizabeth granddaughter of Thomas Hall, heiress of her brother, brought the manor to George Purefoy Jervoise,[80] who bequeathed it to his niece, Elizabeth Fitzgerald, from whose grandson, Captain Richard Purefoy Purefoy, it was purchased in 1905 by Mr. J. C. A. Hall and Mr. C. Wade,[81] the present owners.

Of William de Pont de l'Arche, in 1381, the priory of Southwick held the manor later known as *MOUNDSMERE*.[82]

In the year 1290 the prior of Southwick's manor of Candover was valued at £3 11*s.* 7*d.*[83] In the thirteenth century Robert de Pont de l'Arche confirmed the grant of his father of the church with the manor of Candover (which comprised five hides of land with wood and meadow) to the canons of Portchester,[84] and this grant was again confirmed by Henry III, Edward II, and Richard II.[85]

PUREFOY. *Sable three pairs of clasped hands in armour argent.*

The land held by the priory in this parish was increased by grants from other early benefactors—Jordan and William Eschotland—who gave to the prior and canons the chapel, with the tithes, belonging to their manor of Candover, together with some tenements for the support of the chapel.[86] Another donor appears in Walter de Passeflamberd, who gave a virgate in Candover 'of the fee of la Stavenburie.'[87] Thomas Dounton also granted land in the thirteenth century to the priory.[88] In 1316 and 1322 the prior of Southwick was described as lord of Preston Candover,[89] and the ninths due to the priory in the parish were, in 1339, of the value of 26*s.*[90] In the reign of Henry IV the prior recovered 100*s.* as damages from a neighbouring lord of the manor, William Horwood, who had impounded 300 sheep belonging to the priory, of which forty had since died of hunger.[91]

SOUTHWICK PRIORY. *Argent a chief sable with two roses argent.*

At the time of the Dissolution the property of the priory was known as the manor of Moundsmere.[92] It afterwards formed part of the dower of Anne of

More had land in Preston Candover and possibly Polhampton. As very considerable mention seems to be made of the Horwoods and settlements made by them, it may be inferred that the More family may have obtained land through some of these settlements. Also, as has been noted, the inquisition upon the death of Hugh Horwood makes no mention of the manor, but of land only, which may be indicative of certain alienation, although the manor of Horwoods still continued in the female line (Chan. Inq. p.m. 13 Hen. VII, No. 168).

65 Chan. Inq. p.m. 11 Hen. VII, vol. 11, No. 55. Later in the seventeenth century this manor, then owned by Francis Perkins, was held of Arthur Wilmot of Wield, as of the manor of Godsfield.

66 Chan. Inq. p.m. 11 Hen. VII, vol. 11, No. 55.

67 Ibid. The other heirs were Elizabeth Doyle, Maud Lethingham, Christine wife of Henry Wilkins, Alice wife of John Raff, and Anne More. A fine occurs in the reign of Hen. VII by which Katherine and John More granted the reversion, after the death of Katherine, of certain land in Preston Candover to Isabel Williams, then styled widow (Feet of F. Hants, Hil. 24 Hen. VII).

68 Chan. Proc. 1 (Ser. 2), 1558–79, bdle. 119, No. 12. Mayhew *versus* Williams.

69 Ibid.

70 Ibid.

71 Chan. Decrees and Orders, 1566–7, A. 167.

72 Feet of F. Hants, Trin. 22 Eliz.

73 Ex inform. Rev. Sumner Wilson.

74 Feet of F. Hants, East. 17 Eliz. This was the well-known family of Perkins of Ufton Court, Berks. who suffered under the monarchy for their religious views, and under the Commonwealth for their loyalty to the king; Sharp, *Hist. of Perkins of Ufton Court.*

75 Chan. Inq. 15 Jas. I, vol. 366, No. 181.

76 S.P. Dom. Interreg. G. 253.

77 Ex inform. Rev. Sumner Wilson.

78 She was the beautiful Belinda of Pope's *Rape of the Lock*, who 'to the destruction of mankind, nourished two locks, which graceful hung behind.'

79 Ex inform. Rev. Sumner Wilson and Recov. R. Trin. 7 Geo. II, rot. 53.

80 Ex inform. Rev. Sumner Wilson; Feet of F. Hants and Sussex, Trin. 52 Geo. III.

81 Ex inform. Capt. R. P. Purefoy, R.N.

82 Add. MS. 33280.

83 Ibid. 33278.

84 Ibid. 33280.

85 Ibid. and De Banco, 154, m. 118 *d.* In the reign of the last-named king the manor was said to contain 60 acres of arable land and 80 acres of pasture, and a dove-cot.

86 Add. MS. 33280. As often as these benefactors were residing at Candover the priory was responsible for the celebration of divine service thrice a week, and once a year when they were absent.

87 Ibid.

88 Ibid. This gift comprised land near 'Suwede,' and 5 acres 'by the way of Odiham,' and land upon 'Denemendona,' and 6 acres near 'the Cross of Bradley' with a pasture for animals.

89 'Nomina Villarum.'

90 *Inq. Non.* (Rec. Com.), 109.

91 Add. MS. 33280.

92 Dugdale, *Mon.* vi, 244. The name occurs in a charter roll of Edward II, when the prior and convent were granted free warren in their manor of Moundsmere; Chart. R. 14 Edw. II, m. 8, No. 32.

Cleves [93] and Catherine Howard,[94] and on the death of the latter Henry VIII granted the manor of Moundsmere, in part exchange for the manor of Harmondsworth and others, to the college of St. Mary, Winchester.[95] With the college it long remained, and was used for a hospital in the times of plague.[96] In 1906 Moundsmere was sold by the college to Mr. Wilfrid Buckley, who is the present owner.

WINCHESTER COLLEGE. *Argent two cheverons sable between three roses gules.*

The crown held a rent from Moundsmere which was granted by James I to his queen, Anne,[97] and by Charles II to Lord Hawley and others in trust for John Lindsay, who had undertaken to defray £25,384 2*s.* 1*d.* due from the crown to London city.[98] A fine between Sarah Rolle and William Parker respecting the same rent occurs in the reign of George I.[99]

The name of Oades occurs frequently in the records of Moundsmere, where that family owned land in the seventeenth and eighteenth centuries.[100] In 1639 an order was made against one James Oades of Preston Candover since he had in August, 1637, 'rhymed profanely on the Lord's prayer,' and had been accused of blaspheming the Scriptures. His punishment was a public submission in his parish church and in Winchester Cathedral, and a fine of £100.[101]

The family of Inkepenne held land in Preston Candover of the Knights Hospitallers.[102] John de Inkepenne held land there in the fourteenth century.[103] Owing to the minority of his heir, who died in wardship, the house and the carucate of land held of the bishop of Winchester and his four virgates held of the Knights Hospitallers came into the royal hands [104] until the majority of his other son Robert. Robert Inkepenne and his son Robert died seised of land in Candover in 1405 and 1406.[105] The name of Richard son of Robert Inkepenne occurs in 1407;[106] in 1410 Robert Inkepenne died seised of land in Preston Candover,[107] which in 1440 another Robert Inkepenne held.[108] In 1510 John Inkepenne held land [109] of Katherine More.[110] The name of William Inkepenne occurs in 1518.[111]

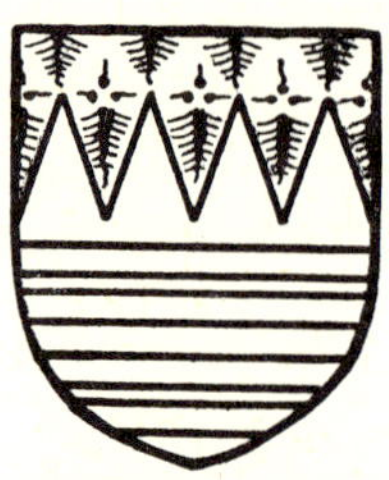

INKEPENNE. *Gules two gimel bars or and a chief indented ermine.*

The name of *CANTERTON* often appears in the church rate-book.[112] In the reign of Charles I Sir Richard Norton leased a tenement called Canterton in Preston Candover to Edward Elkins, husbandman,[113] for £10 yearly rent. Canterton is now included in Preston House estate.[114]

For several centuries a small portion of land in Preston Candover followed the fortunes of the manor of Woodcott.[115] It was evidently included in the two and a half virgates held by Miles the Porter in Bermondspit Hundred at the time of the Survey.[116] With Woodcott a hide of land in Candover was granted to Matthew de Wallop for the service of keeping the king's gaol at Winchester and mewing the royal hawks.[117] The lords of Woodcott and warders of Winchester gaol held this land worth 11*s.* in Candover, [118] from the thirteenth until the sixteenth century; Warin son of Geoffrey held it in 1227,[119] and it is last mentioned in the reign of Charles I,[120] when it was held by Anthony Bruning.

Of the old church of *OUR LADY CHURCH* the chancel only remains, though the limits of the old nave are preserved by blocks of stone marking the position of its western angles. It was burnt down in 1883, a new church being built in the middle of the village to take its place. It had no aisles, but on the north side an eighteenth-century building which contained the pew of the Guidott family, and on the west gable of the nave was a wooden bell-turret.

The chancel dates from *c.* 1190, having a north window of that date, a small pointed light with a wide internal splay and semicircular rear-arch. The east window is of doubtful date, a wide single light which was probably divided into two by tracery, which is now lost. In the south wall is a blocked doorway, built of old material re-used, and a square-headed window of two trefoiled lights, of late fifteenth-century date. The west wall is modern, there having been no chancel arch in the old church, and in it is a round-headed doorway, also made up of old material, some of it of twelfth-century date. On the gable above it is a wooden bell-cote with a small modern bell. In the floor is a slab with the brass of Katherine Dabridgecourt, 1607, the figure, inscription plate, and one shield of arms being preserved. The new church is built of red brick and stone, and has a chancel with north vestries, nave with north aisle, and a tower and spire at the north-west. No part of the old church

93 *L. and P. Hen. VIII*, xiv (2), 154.

94 Ibid. xvi, p. 716. Augmentation Bk. ccxxxv, fol. 26.

95 Pat. R. 35 Hen. VIII, pt. 8, m. 18.

96 The college also owned the first cut of grass in a portion of common meadow called Wildmoor in the parish of Rotherwick. It went with the farm of Moundsmere (Ex inform. Rev. Sumner Wilson). This is referred to in the grant of Henry VIII as 'the custom of the hay at Rotherwick.'

97 Pat. 11 Jas. I, pt. 13, m. 4.

98 Pat. 26 Chas. II, pt. 4, m. 5.

99 Feet of F. Hants, Mich. 4 Geo. I.

100 Ex inform. Rev. Sumner Wilson.

101 *Cal. S.P. Dom.* 1639–40, p. 458.

102 Chan. Inq. p.m. 48 Edw. III, No. 41; ibid. 7 Hen. IV, No. 48; ibid. 12 Hen. IV, No. 44.

103 Feet of F. Hants. Mich. 27 Edw. III; Chan. Inq. p.m. 35 Edw. III, pt. 1, No. 123.

104 Chan. Inq. p.m. 48 Edw. III, No. 41.

105 Ibid. 7 Hen. IV, No. 48; ibid. 8 Hen. IV, No. 95.

106 Feet of F. Hants, East. 9 Hen. IV.

107 Chan. Inq. p.m. 12 Hen. IV, No. 44.

108 Feet of F. Hants, Trin. 19 Hen. VI.

109 Chan. Inq. p.m. 2 Hen. VIII, vol. 25, No. 15.

110 *Vide* Purefoy's manor.

111 Feet of F. Hants, Mich. 10 Hen. VIII.

112 Ex inform. Rev. Sumner Wilson. In 1753 the rate-book gives John Savage for 'Carter's lands.' Carter's land is identified with Canterton by the Rev. Sumner Wilson. Other mentions occur.

113 Ex inform. Rev. Sumner Wilson. Canterton included lands in Downsfield, Delmandowne, Longdownfield, Blackdelfield, and the field called Wedlands and others.

114 Ex inform. Rev. Sumner Wilson.

115 *Vide* Bishop's Sutton Hundred.

116 *V.C.H. Hants*, i, 503.

117 *Rot. Chart.* (Rec. Com.), 126; *Testa de Nevill* (Rec. Com.), 237.

118 Worth 5*s.* at the time of the Survey.

119 Pat. 11 Hen. III, m. 8; Close, 11 Hen. III, m. 20.

120 Feet of F. Div. Cos. Trin. 12 Chas. I; Pat. 4 Chas. I, pt. 5, m. 18.

has been worked into the new building, and the font, though brought thence, is modern.

In the churchyard is a sundial made up of a twelfth-century capital and base, both being set upside down.

In the tower are five modern bells. In the old church there were at one time four bells, two of which were recast by Warner in 1870. The two others were recast by Warner and a fifth added in 1885, when they were moved to the new church.

The plate consists of a cup and paten of 1746, a jug-shaped flagon of 1885, and an almsdish of 1798, with the initials E.H. in the centre, probably for Elizabeth Hall, who owned land in the parish and died about 1798.[121]

The registers are in a somewhat fragmentary condition. The earliest entries are on a parchment recovered from Basingstoke church, and record the marriages from 1584 to 1695; the second portion contains the baptisms, marriages, and burials from 1724 to 1736, and the third is a book containing the baptisms for Preston Candover and Nutley, 1688–1812, marriages 1696–1754, and burials 1724–1812. The printed marriage register, 1755–1812, is also preserved.

ADVOWSON Although Domesday makes no mention of a church in Preston Candover, there seem to have been two churches besides manorial chapels in the thirteenth century. Richard de Candevere, 'Filius Wys,' granted in that century the advowson of the church of Preston Candover to the priory of Southwick,[122] and John 'de Bottel' likewise granted the advowson of a church in the same place to Matthew, prior of Southwick, in 1255.[123] The grant of his manor by Robert or William de Pont de l'Arche included a church;[124] Jordan Eschotland also granted the chapel belonging to his manor,[125] and the priory moreover held a chantry in the manorial chapel of Stevenbury.[126] The control of ecclesiastical matters in Preston Candover was therefore vested in the priors from early times, and they held sole patronage[127] until the Dissolution, when the advowson was given to the dean and chapter of Winchester,[128] who ever since have held it.[129]

A church that was not under the patronage of the priory is mentioned once only, when in 1322 there was said to be a parish church in the manor of William de Horwood of the advowson of John de Somery and worth 25 marks. There is no other reference, however, to this church.[130]

The only mention of a chantry in Preston Candover occurs in the account of a quarrel between Matthew prior of Southwick and Robert de Watteville concerning a virgate of land, tithes, and a chantry in the chapel in Robert's court in 'la Stevenburie,'[131] with the result that the virgate[132] and tithes were assured to the priory. The chantry, too, was granted to the priory, with the proviso that its priest must render fealty to the rector of the mother church of Preston Candover, and that the services, which were to be celebrated three times weekly when the lord of the manor was present, were only to be attended by the family of 'la Stevenburie' and not by the parishioners of the church of Preston Candover.

CHARITIES Robert Lipscomb, by will, 1711, gave a rent-charge of £4 per annum to the poor of this parish. The charge was upon leasehold property, and upon the determination of the lease the charity lapsed.

An unknown donor, as stated in the returns made to Parliament in 1786, gave lands to the poor, producing 10*s*. a year, and the same returns state that a sum of £5 was given by some person unknown, producing 5*s*. a year. In 1904 the sum of 15*s*. was paid by Cecil Wade, esq., out of the North Hall estate, and given to six recipients.

Thomas Hall, by will proved in the P.C.C. in 1784, founded a school and endowed it with 7 acres of land in this parish.[133]

Church lands.—Upon the inclosure of the common fields in this parish 11 a. 2 r. 27 p. were awarded in lieu of certain parcels of land formerly held by the churchwardens. The land is let at £15 a year, which is paid to the churchwardens' account.

In 1870 30 acres of land were awarded as a poor's allotment, subject to a yearly rent-charge of £5 payable to the overseers. The land is in the hands of the parish council. In 1905–6 £5 was received for letting the sporting and shooting, and £3 15*s*. from the sale of the underwood.

121 Information from Rev. Sumner Wilson, vicar.
122 Add. MS. (1), 33280.
123 Feet of F. Hants, Trin. 39 Hen. III. (probably one of the Botiller family who held Botillers Candover).
124 Add. MS. 33280.
125 Ibid.
126 Ibid.
127 Egerton MS. 2031–4.
128 Pat. 33 Hen. VIII, pt. 9, m. 40.
129 Inst. Bks. P.R.O.
130 Chan. Inq. p.m. 16 Edw. II, No. 72.
131 Add. MS. 33280.
132 This was exchanged for a pasture called 'la Breche.' The tithes were separate from those belonging to the church of Preston Candover.
133 See article on 'Schools,' *V.C.H. Hants*, ii, 403.

SOUTH WARNBOROUGH

Wergeborne (Domesday), Waregeburnae Widonis (xii cent.); Suthwarneburne (xiii–xiv cent.); Sutwarneburn, Southwargheborgh *alias* Southwargheburn (xiii cent.); Warneburn or Warnborne (xiv cent.); Warborne, Suthwarborne, Suthwermborowe or Southwarmbourne (xvii cent.); Southwanborow Southwarmeborne (xvii cent.); South Warmborough (xviii cent.).

South Warnborough is a long narrow parish covering 2,654 acres of undulating country which rises to its greatest height as the road from Upton Grey enters the parish from the north-west. The village, the only populated part of the parish, lies towards the north where the main road from Odiham to Alton running south-east meets the road from Upton Grey. South of the village the whole parish is one long stretch of open field and meadow land, the only woodland being a few copses running along the western border.

After entering the parish the road from Upton Grey runs south-east for nearly half a mile, and then curving slightly east between two or three outlying cottages and farm buildings descends sharply between high banks, on either side of which houses and thatched and tiled cottages are grouped, into the centre of the village, where are the railed-in village pond, an elm tree surrounded by a wooden seat, and the smithy. A plain low house, on the left hand as the road descends, in front of which are quaintly-clipped yew trees, representing a cock and hen, is the village police station, south of which are the modern schools, dated 1880. Opposite the schools are two groups of the most picturesque cottages in the village, with deep overhanging thatch, standing behind a long low brick wall. The big elm tree stands in the centre where the main road from Odiham to Alton crosses that from Upton Grey as it leads south-east circuitously to Long Sutton. At the north-west corner formed by the junction of the roads is the village pond, and opposite, at the south-west corner, is the low tiled smithy. Two or three thatched cottages fill up the north-east corner and continue up the north side of the road running uphill towards Long Sutton, while round the south corner, and some yards up the opposite side of this road, runs the high brick wall of the garden of South Warnborough House. A few yards up the village to the north, on the east side of the Odiham to Alton road, is the Plough Inn, a new red-brick building which replaces the old and less pretentious inn bearing the sign in former days. Opposite the inn a high brick garden wall, behind which rises a high yew hedge, shuts in the grounds of the rectory, a square red-brick house. As the Odiham to Alton road goes south along the village, a house standing close to the smithy serves as the post office, south of which are two or three cottages and houses.

On the opposite side a row of fine horse-chestnut trees edges the footpath running along before South Warnborough House, the residence of Sir Arthur James Walmesley, which stands in its fine grounds back from the road. South-west of the house is the church, approached over a small triangular green, round which a gravel path leads up to the lychgate, and thence through an avenue of horse-chestnut trees to the north door. Behind the church begin the trees of Warnborough Park, those near the church seeming to be specially chosen out by a large band of rooks who resort there every year.

South Warnborough Park stretches about a quarter of a mile in every direction, its western boundary being formed by the Odiham to Alton road as, leaving the village, it continues its south-easterly course through the parish. The soil of the parish is chalk with a subsoil of chalk and clay, and good crops are produced on the 1,934 acres of arable land. Only 376 acres are given up to permanent grass, while only $158\frac{3}{4}$ acres are woodland. Of the latter Venny or Fenny Oaken Copse and Swenchetts, now Swanshott Copse, date back their names at least to the seventeenth century.

MANOR

The manor of *SOUTH WARNBOROUGH* belonged to the crown,[1] and was held of the king by Hugh son of Baldric at the time of the Domesday Survey. It passed to his daughter on her marriage with Guy de Craon,[2] whose son, grandson, and great-grandson, Alan, Maurice, and Guy de Craon held the manor in succession.[3] Petronilla, daughter and heiress of the last-named Guy, was first married to William de Longchamp,[4] secondly to Henry de Mara, and thirdly to Oliver de Vaux,[5] and held the manor jointly with her respective husbands until her death in 1280. Henry de Longchamp, her son by her first marriage, became her heir,[6] and did homage for his manor about 1261.[7] During his lifetime he alienated South Warnborough to Philip Basset and Ela his wife[8] for the sum of £200, which was to redeem certain of his lands,[9] the alienation being for the term of Henry's life.[10]

Alice the only child and heir of Henry de Longchamp, a minor at her father's death,[11] married Roger de Pedwardyn,[12] and settled the manor on herself and her husband and their heirs male.[13] Roger Ped-

[1] *Testa de Nevill* (Rec. Com.), 233–5; Chan. Inq. p.m. 46 Hen. III, No. 5; ibid. 20 Edw. I, No. 15; ibid. 43 Edw. III, pt. 2, No. 13; ibid. 6 Hen. IV, No. 22; ibid. (Ser. 2), vol. 44, No. 112.

[2] *V.C.H. Hants*, i, 496*a*, 438.

[3] De Banco, Trin. 20 Edw. III, m. 55 *d.* The second Guy de Craon held the manor in 1167, when South Warnborough bore his name—Waregeburna Widonis. *Rot. Pipe* 13 *Hen. II* (Pipe R. Soc.), 187.

[4] Dugdale, *Baronage*, i, 412.

[5] *Testa de Nevill* (Rec. Com.), 235; Dugdale, *Baronage*, i, 526. Account was rendered of payment by Oliver de Vaux for right to marry Petronilla in 1211. Rot. Pip. 13 John, Norf. and Suff.

[6] Chan. Inq. p.m. 46 Hen. III, No. 5.

[7] Rot. Fin. 46 Hen. III, m. 14.

[8] She is called countess of Warwick, her title by an earlier marriage.

[9] Chartul. of Pedwardyn Family. Add. MS. 32101; *Cal. Chart. R.* 1257–1300, p. 116.

[10] De Banco, Mich. 12 Edw. II, m. 29 *d.* Against this Ela, Sibyll wife of Henry de Longchamp, after her husband's death, brought a suit respecting a third part of the manor (De Banco, Mich. 3 Edw. I, No. 11, m. 71 *d.*), evidently without success, as Ela was holding the park of South Warnborough three years later, in 1278 (*Cal. of Pat.* 1272–8, p. 287).

[11] Chan. Inq. p.m. 4 Edw. I, No. 91; De Banco, Trin. 5 Edw. I, m. 11; ibid. 3 Edw. I, No. 11, m. 71 *d.* She is variously stated to have been in wardship of Robt. Burnell, Walter de Betheward and of Walter and Roger Pedwardyn; *vide* as above.

[12] Dugdale, *Baronage*, i, 594.

[13] Feet of F. Hants, Mich. 10 Edw. II; *Cal. of Pat.* 1313–17, p. 391. According to statements made in the suit of Sibyll de Longchamp, Nicholas Malemayns held a carucate of land in the manor,

wardyn leased his manor for a while to Richard Berton, 'parson of the place.'[14] His son Sir Roger, and after him Sir Walter, and then Sir Robert Pedwardyn held the manor in succession,[15] but the heir and grandson[16] of the last-named alienated it, nine years after coming into possession in the reign of Henry VI, to Robert White and Margaret his wife.[17] For some years the Whites held the manor.[18] Henry VIII, by a grant about 1543, increased their estate by giving them certain lands that Crowland Monastery had once held in South Warnborough.[19] In the reign of Elizabeth licence was granted to Sir Thomas White to enfeoff Chidiock Paulet of the manor for the purpose of resettlement on Sir Thomas and his numerous sons.[20] A grandson of this Sir Thomas in 1636 sold the manor (certain lands excepted) for the sum of £11,631 2*s.* to Richard Bishop, of London.[21] The Bishops only held the manor until the reign of Anne, as William Bishop then sold it (certain lands again excepted) for £14,800 to Robert Graham of the parish of St. Paul, Covent Garden.[22] The only daughter or adopted daughter of Robert Graham was Barbara Anne Graham, who was his sole heiress.[23] She married Captain Thomas Harrison Wayne of the 10th Regiment of Foot, and the marriage, which was a runaway one, took place at Farnham, Surrey, where the regiment was quartered at the time.[24]

WHITE of South Warnborough. *Argent a cheveron gules between three popinjays vert within a border azure bezanty.*

They had no children and Captain Thomas Harrison Wayne bequeathed South Warnborough manor to Mr. Richardson Harrison, believed to be his cousin, as trustee and guardian to his (Mr. R. Harrison's) second son, Thomas Moore Harrison, with the stipulation that his son should take the name and arms of Wayne, but failing male issue the property was entailed on the elder brother, the Rev. William Moore Harrison, and his eldest son. Mr. Thomas Moore Wayne married Miss Fanny Bowyer in 1817, and they had daughters only, and therefore after the death of Thomas Moore Wayne in 1868, Mr. Thomas Harrison Wayne succeeded, his father the Rev. W. M. Harrison having died in the previous October.[25]

GRAHAM. *Sable a cheveron argent between three scallops or with a rose gules on the cheveron.*

He married Emma Tucker Messiter, and died in 1879. His widow is the present lady of the manor, and as the entail is now ended, her eldest daughter, Mary Elizabeth Harrison married to Mr. John Scales Bakewell, is her heir.[26]

CHURCH

The church of *ST. ANDREW* has a chancel 26 ft. 6 in. by 16 ft. 3 in., nave 46 ft. by 22 ft. with modern south aisle and north porch, and wooden bell-turret at the west. The walls are of flint rubble, all except the west wall of the nave and the new south aisle being covered with rough-cast externally, and the roofs are red-tiled. At the east end of the south aisle an early twelfth-century volute capital and shaft are built into the new wall, and it is probable that the nave walls belong to a building of this date, of which one window at the south-west is still to be seen. The north doorway of

then held by Ela wife of Philip Basset. Probably he was enfeoffed of the manor by the said Ela, as an inquisition of 1291 (Ela not dying until 1297) discovers a Nicholas Malemayns seised of the manor of South Warnborough which he held of the crown (Inq. p.m. 20 Edw. I, No. 15). An inquisition of the reign of Edward III shows Nicholas Malemayns, evidently the son, holding land in South Warnborough of Roger Pedwardyn (Chan. Inq. p.m. 23 Edw. III, pt. 2, No. 160). At the time when Nicholas Malemayns held the manor its extent amounted to a capital messuage with a courtyard worth 2*s.* per annum; also 10 acres of arable land, which with common of pasture were of the value of 2 marks (Inq. p.m. 20 Edw. I, m. 15). Later, in 1366, Sir William de Hoo with his wife Alice granted lands that had once belonged to Nicholas Malemayns to Sir Roger Pedwardyn (Chartul. of Pedwardyn Family, Add. MS. 32101).

14 Chartul. of Pedwardyn Family, Add. MS. 32101. This lease was a source of future trouble to the lords of South Warnborough, for Richard Berton (de Bartone) demanded a common of pasture at the end of his lease. He did not get it, nor did his successors who in turn demanded it. But parson Richard Gardiner, a man of spirit, brought an action against Sir Walter and Robert Pedwardyn concerning this pasture. The action lasted seven years, in the reigns of Richard II and Henry IV, and ended in the defeat of the parson. One parson, Thomas Saddok, in addition to clerical duties, became bailiff of the manor (seigneurie). Chartul. of Pedwardyn Family, Add. MS. 32101.

15 Feet of F. Hants, Mich. 10 Edw II; Chan. Inq. p.m. 43 Edw. III, pt. 2, No. 13; *Cal. of Pat.* 1343–5, p. 42; Chan. Inq. p.m. 6 Hen. VI, No. 22; ibid. 10 Hen. VI, No. 20. According to *Feud. Aids*, Walter Sandys of Andover held the manor by service of one knight's fee in 1431, about the time of Sir Robert Pedwardyn's death. Probably he was a lessee for a term of years. During the Pedwardyn lordship the charters of that family, as well as certain fines, disclose the names of lesser but not inconsiderable landowners in South Warnborough: Geoffrey le Froghel, owner of one virgate (Feet of F. Hants, Mich. 6 Edw. III); John Fode of Winchester who had 42 acres (Feet of F. Hants, East. 11 Edw. III), and who granted lands held by him to Sir Roger Pedwardyn (Chartul. of Pedwardyn Family, Add. MS. 32101). Moreover the family of Byflete appear as tenants of the lords of the manor (ibid. and Feet of F. Hants, Mich. 12 Edw. II; ibid. East. 8 Edw. II).

16 Chan. Inq. p.m. 10 Hen. VI, No. 20.

17 Close, 19 Hen. VI, m. 38, 36.

18 Chan. Inq. p.m. 9–10 Edw. IV, No. 25; ibid. (Ser. 2), vol. 27, No. 65; Exch. Inq. p.m. 13 Hen. VIII (Ser. 2), file 974, No. 5; Inq. p.m. (Ser. 2), vol. 44, No. 112. They appear to have let the estate at one time, as Roger Fitz died seised of the manor in the reign of Henry VII (Chan. Inq. p.m. (Ser. 2), vol. 18, No. 4).

19 Pat. 35 Hen. VIII, pt. 9, m. 34*b.* These lands included the wood of 3 acres in South Warnborough called 'Crowdale Grove.' The possessions of Sir Thomas Seymour in Hampshire included certain land in South Warnborough of which the Whites of Warnborough were in tenure. A patent of Edward VI after the execution of Sir Thomas assigned these lands, with his manors, of which they were appurtenances, to William Lord St. John, earl of Wiltshire. They had been, and were to be, held in chief.

20 Pat. 3 Eliz. pt. 2; Feet of F. Hants, Trin. 3 Eliz.; Com. Pleas D. Enr. Mich. 6–7 Eliz. No. 27.

21 Close, 12 Chas. I, pt. 3, No. 24. For documents leading up to this sale see Close, 7 Chas. I, No. 8; Feet of F. Hants, Mich. 7 Chas. I; Recov. R. East. 8 Chas. I, m. 7; Com. Pleas Recov. R. East. 8 Chas. I, m. 8; Close, 9 Chas. I, pt. 9, m. 6; Recov. R. Trin. 10 Chas. I, rot. 114.

22 Close, 3 Anne, pt. 10, No. 15.

23 Ex inform. Mrs. Harrison Wayne.

24 Ibid. Mr. Robert Graham's second wife was Lady Londonderry, who was buried under the chancel of South Warnborough church. There is a curious extract from the will of Robert Graham that runs as follows:—'A pair of white cotton stockings and a Bible to be open at the 20th Chapter of St. John on my stomach in my coffin—£100 to Mrs. Wayne to buy a piece of plate. To the poor of South Warnborough £20 to be distributed to them in bread.'

25 Ex inform. Mrs. Harrison Wayne.

26 Ibid.

the nave dates from *c.* 1160, and the chancel seems to have been rebuilt in the first half of the thirteenth century, retaining the width and perhaps some of the walling of its twelfth-century predecessor. In its east wall are three lancets under an inclosing arch, much patched with modern stone, but having remains of painted decoration, a zigzag pattern on the rear arch, and masonry patterns on the jambs. A single lancet remains at the east end of the south wall, with a foliate pattern on the head, and west of it is a modern south doorway and a modern arch to the east end of the south aisle, which overlaps the chancel. On the north is a square-headed window of three cinquefoiled lights, *c.* 1530, which has early fourteenth-century shafts reset in its inner jambs; below its sill on the outer face of the wall are three quatrefoiled panels inclosing shields with a cross, a rose, and a saltire respectively. Near the north-west angle of the chancel is another thirteenth-century lancet. There is no chancel arch, its place being taken by a fifteenth-century rood-loft, retaining the floor of its gallery, at the level of the plate of the roof, and the coved canopies beneath it on the west side; into the front beam, on which a modern embattled cresting has been set, two posts were formerly mortised on each side of the central opening, making wing screens for the nave altars. A good modern screen has been inserted on the line of the old screen under the back beam of the loft. The chancel roof is old, with trussed rafters. The nave has three north windows, *c.* 1320, each of a single ogee light trefoiled, the eastern of the three being wider than the others and having its sill carried down as a recess in connexion with the north nave altar. The north doorway, between the second and third windows, has a semicircular arch of two orders, the outer continuous, with an alternating zigzag ornament, and the inner having a moulded edge roll and a chamfered string at the springing. Over the doorway is a modern wooden porch. The west end of the nave is taken up by the posts of the wooden belfry, the lower parts of which have been cut off and replaced by stone piers; the braces and framing are a very good specimen of mediaeval carpentry, and the turret is probably of late fourteenth-century date. The west window of the nave is of three cinquefoiled lights under a square head, and dates from the fifteenth century.

Of the north wall of the old nave only a short length at the west remains, containing a single round-headed light without any ornamental detail; its probable date has been noted above. The nave roof, like that of the chancel, is old, with trussed rafters, a simple form used throughout the Middle Ages and later; its date in this instance can only be guessed at.

The font, at the west of the nave, has a modern bowl of marble, on an old base of uncertain date. The south aisle is entirely modern, but its west window seems to be old work re-used, of three trefoiled lights with net tracery, *c.* 1320.

The church is rich in monuments and heraldry. Under the north-east window of the chancel is a large altar tomb with panelled sides on the south and west, evidently not in its original position. The panels are quatrefoiled, two of those on the south side containing foliage, and the other three shields, one of which is blank. Another bears the arms of White differenced with a crescent, impaling on a cheveron between three shackle-bolts three choughs in an engrailed border charged with roundels, and the third has the latter coat, which is no doubt that of Fenrother. At the west end of the tomb are the arms of White. The top slab is of Purbeck marble, very roughly worked and too wide for the tomb; it looks as if it might be an altar slab set upside down. At the head of the tomb on the east wall is a panel with the brass figure of Robert, son of John White, kneeling, with the Trinity on a brass plate above him, and to the left a hand among clouds pointing to a scroll inscribed 'Sancta Trinitas unus deus miserere nobis.' An inscription gives the date of his death as 4th of Henry VIII, recording that he was *quondam dominus istius ville.*

On either side of the east window are image brackets, that on the north quite plain, and now carrying a helm with the White crest, the other with an embattled cresting and a band of foliage, with the White arms as on Robert White's tomb; it is probably of the date of the tomb, and on it is set a later sixteenth-century scutcheon with the same arms.

Against the wall between the two north windows of the chancel is a large tomb of late Gothic type, with a wide and shallow recess under a four-centred arch with Tudor cresting above it. On this cornice are three octagonal pedestals carrying small figures with shields which are now blank. In the recess are the kneeling figures of Sir Thomas White, 1566, and his wife Agnes, 1570, on either side of a prayer desk, with fourteen sons and six daughters behind them; the children who died before their parents hold skulls in their hands. Below are three cusped panels inclosing shields with heraldry painted on them, and now much defaced. The eastern shield has a cheveron and three birds, the central shield White impaling a coat which is now unrecognizable, while the third coat is quite destroyed by the fumes of a hideous iron stove which stands in front of the tomb. Above the figures are three panels with an inscription.

> Thomas and Agnes dye unto God and Saye: we hope to see the goodnesse of God in the lande of lyfe: they had issue fourteen sons and six daughters this sayde Sir Thomas Whyte Knight departed thys present lyfe the seconde of November and in the yeare of our Lorde God 1566. Dame Agnes yelded unto God of the workes of hys handes the 4th daye of January in the yeare of our Lorde God 1570. Lorde Jhesu take our soules unto thy mercye. Sur Thomas departed in London and my Lady in Canytebery the dayes and yeares above wryten. God save the Queen.

Above this monument is a small kneeling figure of Elizabeth Paulet, daughter of Sir Thomas White, and another monument with figures of Richard, son of Sir Thomas White, with his wife Ellen, *ob.* 1597, and her daughter Anne (Philpott).

On the south wall of the chancel is a late sixteenth-century monument, undated, with kneeling figures of two brothers, of the White family, but not otherwise identified. Each is in an arched panel, with a black-letter inscription at the back, under a cornice carried on Corinthian columns; over one figure are the White arms, and over the other the same impaling a cheveron engrailed and three lions' heads.

In the south aisle are a number of panels of heraldic glass of various dates. In the south-east window is a panel dated 1599, with White impaling a quartered coat, (1) Argent a fesse gules, and a cheveron gules in the chief, (2) Argent a crescent in a border invecked sable, (3) Blank, but should contain party or and gules, a fesse between three leopards' heads counter-coloured, (4) Argent a fesse between three hawks' hoods gules, which is the quartered shield of Kirton of Thorpe Mandeville in Northants. In the same window are three shields encircled by garters, of the first half of the sixteenth century. The first is quarterly: (1) Quarterly 1 and 4, azure a cross or between four falcons close argent, Wriothesley, 2, argent a pale indented gules in a border azure bezanty, Lensell, 3, argent fretty gules with a border engrailed sable and a quarter gules and therein a lion passant or, Dunstervile; (2) Argent a cheveron between three crows sable, with the difference of a crescent, Croton; (3) Or a lion parted fessewise sable and gules, Luftoft; (4) Sable a cheveron or between three crosslets fitchy argent, Peckham. This is the quartered shield of Thomas Wriothesley, K.G., first earl of Southampton. The second shield has a blank coat impaling azure three hour-glasses or, with below *His quoque finem*, and the third has the royal arms with a crown over the garter. In the east window are two shields, the one of England with a label of three points, in a wreath ensigned with a royal crown; on the wreath are the three feathers of Wales twice, and the rose once. This is presumably for Henry VIII as Prince of Wales. The second shield, which is in a frame of the same design and date as that first described in the south-east window, is quarterly of 8 and differenced with a crescent: (1) Argent three cheverons gules and a label azure; (2) Barry argent and gules a lion or crowned gules; (3) Argent two bars sable, a chief argent three scutcheons sable; (4) Or a pheon azure; (5) Blank; (6) Quarterly or and gules an escarbuncle sable; (7) Azure a cheveron between three molets or; (8) Argent three lions gules. This is a Barrington shield.

There are three bells, the treble by Ellis and Henry Knight, 1674, and the second and tenor, of 1603, by John Wallis of Salisbury, the former inscribed 'Feare God,' and the latter with nothing but the initials A. W.; on the shoulder of the second bell is cut A. C. 1713.

The plate consists of a silver cup and paten of 1689, and a plated flagon, paten, and almsdish.

The first book of the registers contains all entries from 1538 to 1728, and is the parchment copy made in 1598. The second has the burials in woollen 1678–1793, the third the marriages 1732–1754, the fourth the baptisms and burials 1728–1813, and the fifth is the marriage register 1755–1811. There is also a sheet with marriages for 1812.

ADVOWSON 'Upon the High Altar of St. Guthlac, Croyland,' did Alan de Craon, for himself and Muriel his wife, grant the church of South Warnborough to be subject to the church of St. James's, Freston, cell of St. Guthlac.[27] This was some time in the twelfth century, and the advowson remained with Crowland[28] until the Dissolution, when in 1544 it was granted to Thomas White, lord of the manor,[29] who was patron as late as 1562.[30]

Probably it was his next descendant who allowed the right to lapse, and King James I presented Richard Blundell to the living about 1618.[31] The Whites recovered the patronage, however, before 1633,[32] but Thomas White, through trustees, sold the advowson in 1636 to the college of St. John's, Oxford, with whom the patronage still remains.[33]

During the Pedwardyn ownership a pension of £4 was ordained to be paid to the prior and the church of Freston from the church of Warnborough.[34] The collection of the rent was a source of trouble to the priors, one rector, William de Whytyngtone, having to be sued for arrears amounting to £12, and another, Richard Gardner, for £50.[35] On another occasion Crowland had to sue the executors of the late rector, Richard de Barton, not for the pension this time, but for repairs needed both in the chancel and church buildings, the default amounting to £23 13*s.* 8*d.*[36] At the Dissolution the pension was granted to Thomas White,[37] and passed to his successors, Richard Bishop[38] and Robert Graham,[39] and is to-day paid to the lords of the manor.[40]

It is supposed to have been paid for an amount of land, part of the kitchen garden at the rectory, which was evidently in early times a common.[41]

A chantry chapel was established in St. Mary's church, South Warnborough, in 1268, by Henry de Longchamp,[42] who endowed it with lands in South Warnborough, among them 'three acres of the land of Broming.' If Henry de Longchamp and his heirs failed to provide a chaplain the bishops of Winchester were to present in their stead.

CHARITIES It appears from a list of benefactors in the parish that Sir Thomas White, knt., who died in 1566, gave £100 to the sick and needy; that Stephen White, esq., gave £50 to the honest and industrious; and that Thomas Newland, esq., who died in 1768, gave £50 to the aged and infirm. These sums were represented by £200 stock. In 1831 Mary Ann Warren, by her will, bequeathed £100 stock income to be given away to fourteen of the most aged poor. This sum of stock and that belonging to Sir T. White's and other 'charities' are now represented by £327 14*s.*

27 Pedwardyn Chartulary, Add. MSS. 32101. This charter was confirmed by both Maurice and Guy de Craon. Despite this grant of the lord of the manor, later lords, Roger Pedwardyn, and afterwards his son Roger, tried to obtain the advowson, bringing a suit against the abbot of Crowland (De Banco, Mich. 12 Edw. II, m. 29 *d.*). The abbot however won his case. (De Banco, Trin. 20 Edw. III, m. 55 *d.*)

28 Egerton MSS. 2301 and 2304; *Wykeham's Reg.* (Hants Rec. Soc.), i, 15; ibid. ii, 580 and 591; (*Winton Epis. Reg. Sendale*) (Hants Rec. Soc.), 140. With one exception, when Sir Robert Pedwardyn appears to have presented between 1404 and 1447 (Egerton MSS. 2034). Once the prior and monks of Freston seem to have made an unlucky choice of a cleric for South Warnborough, for the lords of the manor had occasion to complain of the conduct of the two monks ordained for the service of their church, they having been found guilty of permitting their parishioners to die unshriven and babes unbaptized, and moreover had committed deeds 'unfit to mention.'

29 Pat. 35 Hen. VIII, pt. 9, m. 134*b.*

30 Com. Pleas D. Enr. Mich. 6 & 7 Eliz. m. 27.

31 Pat. 16 Jas. I, pt. 5, m. 20.

32 Com. Pleas Recov. R. East. 8 Chas. I, m. 7; Close, 9 Chas. I, pt. 9, No. 6.

33 Ex inform. St. John's College, Oxon.

34 Chartulary of Pedwardyn family.

35 *Wykeham's Reg.* (Hants Rec. Soc.) ii, 580, 591.

36 Egerton MSS. 2032; Winton Epis. Reg. Sendale, fol. 79.

37 Pat. 35 Hen. VIII. pt. 9, m. 34*b.*

38 Close, 12 Chas. I, pt. 3, m. 24.

39 Ibid. 3 Anne, pt. 10, m. 15.

40 Ex inform. Mrs. Harrison Wayne.

41 Ibid.

42 Chart. of Pedwardyn family, Add. MS. 32101.

Birmingham Corporation 3 per cent. stock, producing £9 16*s.* 6*d.* a year, which was in 1905 applied in the payment of 5*s.* 5*d.* each to fourteen persons in respect of Miss Warren's charity and the balance in the distribution of coal to fifty-eight persons.

In 1808 the Rev. John Duncan, D.D., a former rector of the parish, gave £200 Old South Sea annuities towards the maintenance of a Sunday school and school of industry. The stock was converted into £253 16*s.* 2*d.* consols.

In or about 1841 a school was erected at the expense of the Rev. Thomas Alston Warren, the then rector, the site of which, together with two freehold cottages belonging to the said rector, were conveyed by a deed, dated 9 January, 1841, upon trust for the education of poor children. The cottages are let at £4 a year.

In 1843 Miss Elizabeth Warren gave £100 South Sea stock in augmentation of the endowment, which was converted into £126 18*s.* consols.

In 1849 the said Rev. Thomas Alston Warren gave a further endowment of £100 South Sea stock, which became £126 18*s.* consols.

The above-mentioned sums of consols were sold out, and proceeds re-invested in £508 17*s.* Birmingham Corporation 3 per cent. stock.

In 1898 a sum of £215 stock was sold out to defray the expense of effecting certain alterations to the buildings belonging to the National School, and the balance of the Corporation stock, amounting to £293 17*s.*, was transferred to the official trustees.

By an order of the Charity Commissioners, dated 28 June, 1898, the said sum of £215 stock so sold was directed to be replaced within twenty-five years out of the income of the charities. The amount already replaced (1906) amounts to £378 6*s.* 3*d.* stock.

For 'Schools,' see *V.C.H. Hants*, ii, 405.

UPTON GREY

Aoltone ? (xi cent.); Upetone, Upetona (xviii cent.).

The parish of Upton Grey contains 2,553 acres of undulating country, the land rising generally north-west and south-east of the village as it lies about the road which runs north-east from Herriard and Weston Patrick towards Greywell. Approaching from Weston Patrick, several outlying cottages, some thatched, others low tiled buildings, and one good-sized white house in front of which are two Scotch pine trees, lie along the north-west side of the road opposite sloping fields which rise up to the grounds of Hoddington House. Then the road makes a sharp curve round the village pond and continues north-east past the blacksmith's shop and several farm buildings, which lie on the right-hand side, towards Greywell, while a branch road curving north-west round the pond mounts up between the cottages and houses composing the main part of the village to the church. Behind a low railing on the north-west side of the pond are two or three picturesque thatched cottages, behind which is the modern school, built in 1856. Beyond the schools on the right and left are low houses and thatched cottages, some standing on high ground behind short sloping gardens, while on the left, behind

VILLAGE POND, UPTON GREY

three or four pollarded lime trees, is the rectory, facing which is a well-kept garden. A few yards higher up on the same side is the church facing an open meadow, beyond which the land sweeps away west to the high country round Herriard and Ellisfield. Past the church the ground still rises north-west as the road curves west past Upton Grey House, the residence of Mr. Charles Holme, which stands on the south side of the road as it runs across the western part of the parish to Tunworth. Hoddington House, a low long red-brick house, the seat of Lord Basing, stands on the high ground which rises immediately south-west of the village, in a fine open park, from the slopes of which wide views reach away west and south over Herriard and Ellisfield to Farleigh Wallop and Dummer, and to the east over Long Sutton and Crondall to the distant Surrey hills. A road rising south-west from the village and skirting the western boundary of the grounds of Hoddington House branches just beyond the grounds through fine open country south-east to South Warnborough and south through the length of the parish towards Alton. The manor house is an Elizabethan structure with a finely carved oak staircase and panelled rooms. For the last 100 years it has been used as a farm-house, but is now undergoing a careful restoration.

Sclater-Booth, Lord Basing. *Argent a saltire and a border azure with a quarter ermine and therein a boar's head erect and razed sable between three crescents or.*

The soil is chalk with a subsoil of chalk, producing the ordinary root crops, with wheat, barley, and oats, on the 1,522 acres of arable land. Including two or three small copses in the north-west of the parish and in the south and south-east, there are 350¼ acres of woodland in the parish, while 489 acres are permanent grass. Several disused chalk-pits are scattered about the parish.

MANORS The statement that the 'Aoltone' of Domesday held by Hugh de Port represents the Upton Grey of to-day is supported by the fact that the De Ports and their descendants remained the overlords of Upton Grey for several centuries. In the time of the Confessor it had been held by a certain Azor and was then worth £10; by the time of the Conquest it had fallen to £8, but in 1086 it had risen to its former value.[1]

There are no documents to show its history in the twelfth century, but in 1206 a certain Thomas de Ireis quitclaimed to Robert Arundel one virgate of land in Upton.[2] It is probable that the latter belonged to the Dorset or Somerset branch of the Arundel family, of whose origin there is apparently no distinct account nor any evidence to show how they became possessed of land in Upton. In 1218 Hugh Arundel, probably son or brother of Robert, with the consent of William Arundel his chief lord, gave one virgate of land in Upton to Peter son of Godfrey,[3] while later in the same reign William Arundel made a fine with Hubert prior of Merton in which he confirmed the gift of one hide of land which his father Hugh had made to that abbey.[4] In 1241 William Arundel made a promise to grant half the manor of Upton to Robert Wauchan (when the term of eight years for which it was held by Hugh de Cumbe should have expired) to hold until the coming of age of William his son and heir, to whom the half-manor was then to revert to hold with the remainder of the estate.[5] William Arundel the younger sold the Upton estate to John de Grey, Lord of Codnor, who held it as one knight's fee of John de St. John.[6]

John de Grey died in 1272, leaving a son aged seventeen, and the same year Lucy his widow made complaint that the escheator had taken into the king's hands the manor of Upton, of which she was jointly enfeoffed with her husband.[7] From John the property descended through his son Henry to Richard de Grey, to whom Edward III granted free warren in his demesne lands of Upton,[8] and from him it passed in a direct line to his great-grandson Richard de Grey, who married Elizabeth daughter of Lord Bassett of Sapcote. Richard died in 1418 seised of this manor, which he left to his son Henry, who farmed it to Humphrey duke of Gloucester.[9] His mother Elizabeth, who survived him, held the manor in dower during the lifetime of her son and minority of her grandson.[10] She died in 1451,[11] and in 1467 Sir Henry Grey and Margaret his wife sold the manor to Sir Richard Illingworth, a distinguished lawyer in the reign of Henry VI. On his death in 1476 the manor was settled upon his son Richard, and from him the property descended to his son William,[12] whose son Ralph conveyed it in 1571 to a certain Ambrose Matthew.[13] In 1606 Andrew Matthew, probably son of Ambrose, and Joan his wife and their son James conveyed all their right in the manor to Roger and John Loker.[14] The same Roger, or possibly his son, died in 1629 seised of the manor, his wife Eleanor surviving, while Barbara a minor and daughter of his son John, deceased, was heiress to the property.[15]

Grey of Codnor. *Barry argent and azure with three roundels gules in the chief.*

The manor appears to have been conveyed in 1631 to a certain Edmund Daniell for the use of Barbara, with reservation of rents to Martha and Eleanor her mother and grandmother respectively.[16]

In 1646 it was in the possession of Malachy Dudeney and Barbara his wife (possibly a married daughter of Barbara, and her husband), and they held the manor certainly until 1669. From them it passed by marriage of their daughter Barbara to Richard

[1] *V.C.H. Hants*, i, 482*a*.
[2] Feet of F. Hants, Trin. 8 John.
[3] Feet of F. Hants, Trin. 3 Hen. III, No. 46.
[4] Feet of F. Hants, 20 Hen. III No 206.
[5] Feet of F. Hants, Hil. 25 Hen. III.
[6] Chan. Inq. p.m. 56 Hen. III, No. 34.
[7] *Cal. of Inq.* Hen. III, 276.
[8] Chart. R. 8 Edw. III, m. 20.
[9] Close, 19 Hen. VI, m. 26.
[10] Chan. Inq. p.m. 23 Hen. VI, No. 35.
[11] Ibid. 29 Hen. VI, No. 34.
[12] Ibid. 4 Hen. VII (Ser. 2), file 964, No. 10.
[13] Recov. R. Hil. 13 Eliz. m. 326.
[14] Feet of F. Hants, Trin. 4 Jas. I.
[15] Chan. Inq. p.m. 5 Chas. I (Ser. 2), pt. 3, No. 67.
[16] Feet of F. Hants, East. 13 Jas. I; Chan. Inq. p.m. 5 Chas. I (Ser. 2), pt. 3, No. 67.

Opie, member of a family of considerable note in the parish, and in 1698 Nicholas Opie son of Barbara was in possession of the manor.[17] He was succeeded by Barbara Opie, his sister, who held a court as lady of the manor in 1730. The estate then passed to the family of Skinner, and in 1752 Thomas Skinner held the manor jointly with Barbara his wife. The latter survived her husband many years, and held various courts until 1784, when Adolphus Meetkerke, who had married Miss Skinner, appears in the Court Rolls as lord of the manor. From him it passed in 1800 to John Hanbury Beaufoy, who held it till 1825, and whose daughters sold it to Admiral Sir William Fanshawe Martin, bart. From his son Sir Richard Martin, bart., it passed in 1902 to Mr. Charles Holme, the present lord of the manor.[18]

In the reign of Cnut, Alwin, bishop of Winchester, gave the manor of *HODDINGTON* to the cathedral church of St. Swithun in Winchester,[19] and in Domesday it is mentioned among the lands held by the bishop for the support of the monks.[20] There is no evidence to show that it was ever farmed out or leased by the abbey, and in the reign of Edward I the prior received a grant of free warren in his demesne lands there.[21] The monastery of St. Swithun was surrendered in 1539, and in accordance with Cranmer's intention to make use of cathedral establishments as theological colleges it was decreed that twelve scholars should be maintained at the two universities by the dean and chapter of Winchester. For the support of these students the king re-granted five manors to the cathedral, one of which was Hoddington, but in the following year these manors were again surrendered to the crown.[22]

Hoddington manor appears to have been granted shortly afterwards to Thomas White and Agnes his wife,[23] in whose family it remained until 1637, when William White sold the manor to Brian Matthew.[24] In 1695 Jane Matthew, widow presumably of Brian, conveyed it to John Limbrey,[25] whom she had married as her second husband, from whom it passed in direct succession to John Limbrey, who died at the end of the eighteenth century, leaving the property to his daughter Magdalen, who had married Richard Sclater. Their son Thomas succeeded, but died without issue in 1809, after which his sister Elizabeth held the manor till her death in 1814.

Richard Sclater had married secondly Penelope Lutley of Loughton Hall, Salop, and from them the property passed through four successive generations to Lord Basing, the present lord of the manor.[26]

There are no manorial rights now existing. The Court Rolls for the seventeenth century are in the possession of the lord of the manor.

CHURCH The church of *OUR LADY* is an abnormally shaped building, having a chancel 29 ft. by 13 ft., a tower between nave and chancel 13 ft. square, an irregular nave about 28 ft. by 19 ft. with a south porch, and a large north aisle 30 ft. 7 in. by 19 ft. 2 in. The chancel and tower, which are continuous with each other, are set at an oblique angle with the nave, with a deflection towards the south, and the east wall of the nave follows their line and is clearly of the same date. The nave is very short in proportion to its width, and formerly had a south aisle, the arcade opening to which is built up in its south wall. It is of two bays with a pier 3 ft. wide between the arches, and its west respond is overlapped by the west wall of the nave, a fact which, taken in conjunction with the unusual proportion of the latter, suggests that it was originally longer from east to west. The chancel arch is tall and narrow, with plain square jambs and a semicircular head, its voussoirs ornamented with a double line of billet moulding; the stones are evidently re-used, and it seems that they are the materials of an early twelfth-century arch, which was rebuilt as it now appears in the early part of the thirteenth century, to which date the chancel and tower belong. The blocked south arcade seems to belong to the end of the twelfth century, and the history of the building appears to be that an early twelfth-century nave, longer than the present nave, received the addition of a south aisle in the end of the twelfth century; that about the year 1220 a new chancel was set out beyond the then existing chancel, being begun from the east after the usual fashion and carried westward to join on to the older work, the old chancel being destroyed as the work progressed and its site occupied by a tower; and that at some later date, apparently in the fifteenth century, the nave was shortened and a new west wall built. The large north aisle and the north arcade are eighteenth-century work, perhaps replacing an earlier aisle and arcade, and it is not clear at what time the south aisle was destroyed, whether when the west wall of the nave was rebuilt or later. The top story of the tower is an eighteenth-century rebuilding in red brick, the walls of the church are covered with plaster externally, and the roofs red-tiled.

At the south-west angle of the nave, at the springing of the west bay of the south arcade, is a stone which may take the history of the church back beyond the twelfth century; it has mouldings of pre-Conquest character, and looks like the impost of a tenth or eleventh century arch. There is, however, no reason to assume that it is in its original position.

The chancel has an east window of two lancet lights with a quatrefoiled circle over, and two single lancets evenly spaced in the north wall, the head of that to the west being modern. In the south wall also are two lancets, but set closer to each other, to give room for a south doorway to the west of the second lancet. The external stonework of this lancet is new, and the other is a 'restoration,' the jambs of a wider blocked window showing on either side of it. Close to it on the east are two thirteenth-century arched recesses, the western somewhat larger than the other, and having a drain; on either side of the pair are three pinholes arranged triangle wise, the lower holes on a level with the sills of the recesses. A beam, the ends of which remain in the walls about 8 ft. from the floor, crossed the chancel at a point between the windows.

17 Recov. R. Hil. 10 & 11 Will. III, rot. 69.

18 Information received from present lord of the manor.

19 Dugdale, *Mon. Angl.* i, 195.

20 *V.C.H. Hants*, i, 468*a*.

21 Chart. R. 29 Edw. I, No. 94.

22 *V.C.H. Hants*, ii, 61.

23 Feet of F. Hants, Trin. 3 Eliz.

24 Recov. R. Hants, Mich. 13 Chas. I, rot. 146.

25 Feet of F. Hants, Mich. (Div. Cos.) 7 Will. III.

26 Recov. R. Hants, East. 11 Geo. I, rot. 265, and information obtained from the present lord of the manor.

The east arch of the tower is pointed, of one chamfered order with a chamfered string at the springing, and on its west face remains of a painted masonry pattern in red lines, each square inclosing a rose. The west arch is as already noted, and there are traces of openings in the north and south walls, as if for arches to transepts. There is, however, no definite evidence that transepts were ever built. The opening on the south, of which only the east jamb is to be seen, would have been only 3 ft. 6 in. wide if it was set centrally with the tower, but that on the north, a few stones of the east jamb of which, with an edge roll worked on them, remain in the wall below a late fifteenth-century two-light window, may have been of ample width. On the outer face of the south wall of the chancel, just to the east of the east wall of the tower, are the toothings of a destroyed wall or buttress; they look rather too slight to have formed part of the east wall of a transept here, and such an east wall would more naturally have been set in the same line as that of the tower. The upper stories of the tower are reached by a square-headed doorway near the west angle of its south wall, at some height from the ground, access to it being by a ladder from the churchyard.

The nave has a north arcade of three bays, of eighteenth-century date, with plastered semicircular arches on octagonal columns. They stand on stone plinths which may belong to an older arcade. The north aisle is of red brick with large round-headed windows inclosing pairs of pointed lights. In the west wall is a doorway of cut brickwork with a moulded cornice, with a round-headed window over it and a small oval opening in the west gable; on the outer face of the wall a number of initials, probably contemporary, are cut in the brickwork.

In the south wall of the nave are two similar windows, set in the blocking of the arcades already referred to; the west jamb of an older window is to be seen in the west bay, showing that the blocking is at least older than the eighteenth century. Enough of the arcade is exposed to show that it had half-octagonal responds and plainly-moulded capitals with bells; the tooling of the masonry points to a date late in the twelfth century, but the details of the arcade are very advanced for such a date. The springing of the west arch coincides with the south-west angle of the nave, and has the early impost already mentioned. The south doorway of the nave has a two-centred arch with a continuous edge-roll, and opens from a modern oak-framed porch with chalk masonry between the timbers and a red-tiled roof; it was doubtless once in the south wall of the destroyed aisle.

The west window of the nave is square-headed, with two cinquefoiled lights of fifteenth-century date, and below it in the plaster are three crosses, made when the plaster was fresh; they are probably consecration crosses.

The font, which stands midway in the nave on the north side, is of the fifteenth century, and has an octagonal bowl with quatrefoiled panels and a slender octagonal stem.

In the east wall of the nave, on the south side, is a fourteenth-century recess with an ogee head, 16 in. wide, with a plastered back; it probably held the image above the south nave altar.

The chancel roof is old, with trussed rafters, and the nave has a good roof with tie beams and collars, with braces to the collars and purlins. On the second tie beam from the east is this inscription:—'This Frame was erected the 7 day of July 1608. John Clarke the minister, Thomas King and Brian Matew churchwardens.' Hanging from it by a wrought-iron bar, adorned with three sets of scrolls and flowers, is a fine brass chandelier with fourteen lights.

The north aisle is full of good contemporary oak pews, and in the nave is a west gallery, also of the eighteenth century, with a very pretty and delicately worked balustrade, small pointed arches springing from the balusters. At the angles and over the posts of the gallery are Corinthian columns ranging with the balusters.

At the south-east of the chancel is the alabaster monument of Lady Dorothy Eyre, 1650, with a portrait bust under a pediment with heraldry; the inscription is on a black marble tablet below, and in the west gallery is a wooden board with a set of verses in English to her memory.

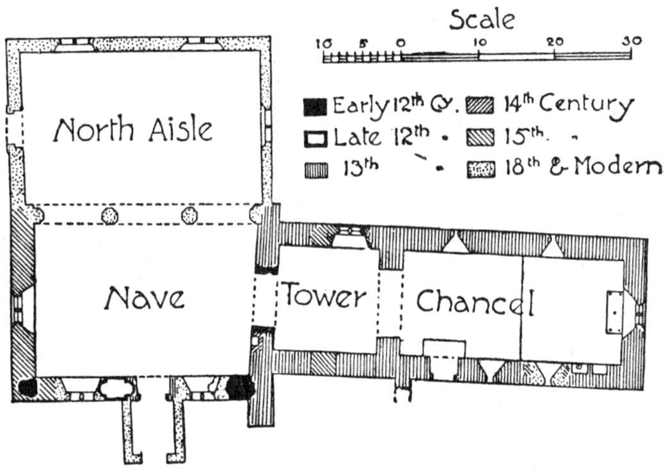

Church of Our Lady, Upton Grey

On the east wall of the nave, on the north side, is part of an inscription painted in red Gothic capitals; some twenty letters are preserved, and it appears to be in English. Most unfortunately it is too fragmentary to be read with any certainty.

There are five bells, one being a small clock bell of 1761. Of the others the treble is by Thomas Mears, 1832, the second is a mediaeval bell, by John Saunders or a predecessor, bearing the arms of the see of Winchester in a circle with four fleurs-de-lis on its circumference, and inscribed 'Sancta An ora pro nobis'; the third is of 1631, inscribed 'Prayes the Lord'; and the tenor, probably an early sixteenth-century bell, has 'Sancti blasi' in black-letter smalls.

The plate comprises a communion cup, a paten, and a large flagon, given in 1724 to the church by a former incumbent whose initials, T. G., occur on the cup and flagon; a paten given by Agnes Beaufoy; and another cup and paten given, together with a glass flagon and cruet, in 1884.

The first book of the registers begins in 1550 and ends in 1672; the second contains the burials 1680 to 1792; and the third the baptisms 1667 to 1792, and marriages 1683 to 1753. The fourth has baptisms and burials 1793 to 1813; and the fifth marriages 1754 to 1812.

ADVOWSON There was a church at Upton in 1086, and in the reign of Henry I it was granted by Henry de Port to the priory of West Sherborne, and this gift was confirmed by his son John de Port.[27] In 1294 the church of Upton paid 9 marks yearly to the priory.[28] There was a chantry attached to the church as early as 1344,[29] and issues of two acres of land to the yearly value of 8*d.* were granted to the churchwardens to maintain a light there for ever.[30]

After the suppression of the alien houses the priory of Sherborne was given by Edward IV to the hospital of St. Julian in Southampton. The latter had, however, been given by Edward III to Queen's College, Oxford, and hence the endowments of the priory were transferred to that college, which is the present patron of the vicarage of Upton.[31]

CHARITY John Limbrey by his will dated 24 April, 1801, bequeathed to the rector, churchwardens, and overseers, £500, to be invested, and income distributed for the use and benefit of such persons of the parish not receiving parochial relief as they should deem most proper. The legacy, with some interest thereon, was invested in the purchase of £858 10*s.* consols (with the official trustees). The annual dividend, amounting to £21 9*s.*, was in 1905 distributed in money among thirty-three persons.

WESTON CORBETT

The parish of Weston Corbett, covering only 513 acres, is immediately north-east of Herriard and north-west of Weston Patrick. It now forms a part of the parish of St. Lawrence Weston Patrick and consists of a stretch of meadow and arable land sandwiched between the south-eastern boundary of Herriard Park and the main road which forms the north-western boundary of Weston Patrick, and continues north-east to Upton Grey. This road, running between Weston Corbett and Weston Patrick, separates the two villages, Weston Patrick with its church, schools, and picturesque cottages lying on the south side of the road, while Weston House, the two farms, and the two cottages comprised in Weston Corbett, lie on the north side, and seem to be part of Weston Patrick. There is no church or school in the village, which is thus dependent on Weston Patrick.

Weston House lies east of the narrow lane that leads north uphill from the main road, while on the opposite side are the one or two cottages of the village and the Manor Farm. North of the farm the lane curves downhill to the west, and then turning sharply north and north-west goes off in two branches across the west of the parish towards Tunworth.

The soil of the parish is chalk with a subsoil of chalk producing crops of wheat, barley, and roots. The actual proportion of the arable land, pasture, and woodland in the parish is difficult to gauge since the return for Weston Patrick and Weston Corbett is made together, as 695¾ acres of arable land, with 299¼ acres of permanent grass, and 457 acres of woodland. Certainly little of the woodland is in Weston Corbett since, except for a thin belt of copse running along about half a mile of the western boundary, an extension of Herriard Park, there are no woods in the parish.

MANOR *WESTON CORBETT* is not mentioned in the Domesday Survey, but in 1224 it was held of the crown by Thomas Corbett from whom the manor derived its name.[1]

Thomas Corbett, who belonged to the great house of the lords of Caus, had evidently granted his land of Weston to Robert son of Madoc for life, and in 1224 recovered seisin of it, but Henry III commanded that a dowry of lands in Weston should be assigned to the wife of Robert, son of Madoc, 'for the love he bore her, in that she had been foster-mother to his niece, the daughter of Llewellyn Prince of Wales.'[2]

Corbett. *Or a corbeau sable.*

How Weston Corbett passed from the Corbetts is not known, but at some time during the fourteenth century it became the property of another great family connected with the Welsh Marches, that of De Breuse, lords of Gower.

William de Breuse, who died about 1325, held the manor.[3] He appears to have alienated this property temporarily to John de Laudimor, who in 1304 held demesne lands in Weston Corbett, and was granted free warren there by Edward I,[4] and in 1316 was described as holding the vill of Weston Corbett of the king.[5]

De Breuse. *Azure crusilly and a lion or.*

On the death of William de Breuse the manor descended in moieties to his daughter Olive, wife of John de Mowbray, and his grandson John de Bohun, son of his daughter Joan.[6]

John de Mowbray, whose wardship and marriage had been granted to William de Breuse in order that he might marry his daughter, had the misfortune to become embroiled in a dispute with the Despensers, whereby he incurred the wrath of Edward II. He was captured after the battle of Boroughbridge,

[27] Dugdale, *Mon. Angl.* vii, 1014.

[28] *V.C.H. Hants*, ii, 227.

[29] *Cal. of Pat.* 1343–5, pp. 211, 223.

[30] Chant. Cert. 52, No. 5.

[31] *V.C.H. Hants*, ii, 228.

[1] *Rot. Lit. Claus.* (Rec. Com.), ii, 24*b.*

[2] Ibid.; also 16*b*, 17*b*.

[3] De Banco R. 292, m. 25 *d.* Mich. 6 Edw. III. Wherein John de Bohun and John de Mowbray, grandsons of William de Breuse, are said to hold the manor, which had belonged to this William, their grandfather.

[4] Chart. R. 32 Edw. I, No. 103.

[5] *Feud. Aids*, ii, 313. He was evidently a Welshman as his name 'de Laudimor' indicates, and had received land in Wales from William de Breuse (Chan. Inq. p.m. 13 Edw. II, No. 32).

[6] Chan. Inq. p.m. 19 Edw. II, No. 89; De Banco R. No. 292, m. 25 *d.*; Dugdale, *Baronage*, i, 417.

1322, and hanged, 'the royal spite being so hot that burial was grudgingly granted to his corpse.'[7] Olive and her son John were imprisoned in the Tower, her late husband's lands being confiscated, and she herself having to yield up much of her own inheritance.[8]

An inquisition taken upon her death in 1336 shows that Richard de Peshale, her second husband, held half the manor of Weston Corbett as his wife's inheritance, and that upon her death it fell into the king's hands.[9] An order followed forbidding further meddling with the moiety, as the king learnt that Richard de Peshale held of Olive's inheritance, and that a daughter, born of the marriage, was living.[10] However, her son by her first husband became her heir, since John de Mowbray,[11] the younger, held half the manor in the following year,[12] and afterwards parted with it to the other co-heir of William de Breuse, John de Bohun of Midhurst, who thus became sole lord of the manor.[13] John de Bohun died in 1367[14] and left a son aged five years, of whom the wardship was granted to Thomas de Burton.[15]

This son, Sir John de Bohun, died in 1433, and his heir also was a minor.[16]

The manor passed from the Bohuns with the marriage of Mary daughter and heiress of Sir John Bohun of Midhurst to Sir David Owen, a natural son of Owen Tudor.[17] John Owen of Wootton, his descendant, sold the manor in 1558 to James Altham, alderman of London,[18] who sold it almost immediately to John Elliot, a mercer of London.[19] A slightly different account of the descent appears in a petition filed in Chancery between 1558 and 1579 by John Grene for waste committed by John Harte and Humphrey Ockley.[20] According to statements therein made, it seems that John Owen leased the moiety of the manor to John Harte and Thomasina his wife for a term of years, and sold the reversion to Mr. Elliot of London, who sold it afterwards to Mr. Alton (Altham) of London. By Alton the reversion was sold to William Cufande, who sold it to John Grene. This account of the order of the sales is incorrect, as it was Altham who sold it to Elliot, and the whole manor, not the moiety, was sold; but the truth of the sale to Cufande is attested by a fine of 1559, which seems to indicate a sale of the manor (it is here described as the manor, not as a moiety) by John Elliot to Simon and William Cufande.[21]

From another Chancery proceeding it appears that Henry Owen tried to claim the manor. According to his own account he was the son of John Owen by Isabel Catesby, and was under age when his father died in 1558. His mother then married John Prestall, described as a hopelessly dishonourable person, who obtained the young heir's property by false pretences, and even wished him to murder his mother.[22] He could have had, however, no claim, since his father had sold the manor.

There is proof of the sale to Grene in that John Grene held property in Weston Corbett (described as land, not as the manor) before his death, which occurred about or before 1587.[23] To his widow Agnes he left this land, with reversion in tail male to his cousin, John Grene of Basingstoke, and final remainder to his nephew John Grene. The widowed Agnes remarried, taking as second husband George Norton, whose right to the property was contested by John Grene, the nephew, on the grounds that in remarrying, Agnes had failed to fulfil certain conditions under which alone she could hold the property.[24]

The name of Norton is connected with the manor during the next century, as in 1678 Richard Norton of Southwick sold it to Sir Thomas Higgons for £1,645.[25] George Higgons, his eldest son, sold the manor in 1700 to Gilbert Serle, a merchant of Leghorn.[26] Peter Serle held the manor in 1738,[27] and the name of his son,[28] Peter Serle, occurs in 1784.[29] To this latter Peter Serle, Wentworth Serle, his younger brother, sold his interest in the property in 1793.[30] By his will, proved 1827, Peter Serle bequeathed his manor to the son of his sister Sukey, Sir William Oglander, who sold it to George Purefoy Jervoise.[31] In 1847 the niece of George Purefoy Jervoise, Mrs. Eliza Fitz Gerald, succeeded to the property, and in 1848 or 1849 exchanged it for other land with her first cousin, Francis Jervoise Ellis Jervoise, whose grandson, Mr. F. H. T. Jervoise, is the present lord of the manor.[32]

HIGGONS. *Vert three cranes' heads razed argent.*

The church was in ruins at the end of the sixteenth century, since which date there has been no church in the parish. The earliest mention of a

[7] *Dict. Nat. Biog.*

[8] Ibid.; also Dugdale, *Baronage*, i, 126.

[9] Chan. Inq. p.m. 5 Edw. III, No. 32*b*. The manor at this time was said to be held of Matthew Fitz Herbert, to whom probably a temporary grant had been made by Edw. II.

[10] *Cal. of Close*, 1330–3, pp. 259, 260.

[11] He was a minor at his mother's death, but in spite of that was granted seisin of the lands, which Olive had held of his hereditament, by Edw. III. Four years before Edw. III had received his homage for all lands that his father had held in chief (Rot. Fin. 5 Edw. III, m. 12; ibid. 1 Edw. III, m. 1).

[12] De Banco R. 292, m. 23 *d*.

[13] Exch. Inq. file 114, Nos. 10, 16.

[14] Chan. Inq. p.m. 41 Edw. III (1st Nos.), No. 13.

[15] *Abbrev. Rot. Orig.* (Rec. Com.), 309*b*.

[16] Chan. Inq. p.m. 11 Hen. VI, No. 33. The extent of the manor at this time includes 40 acres of pasture, each being worth 3*d*., and 5 acres of wood, worth nothing save when felled, and rent of assize of divers tenants.

[17] *Suss. Arch. Coll.* vii, 27; Feet of F. Div. Cos. Trin. 5 Hen. VIII.

[18] Recov. R. East. Phil. and Mary, rot. 544.

[19] Close, 1 Eliz. pt. 2, No. 1.

[20] Chan. Proc. (Ser. 2), bdle. 76, No. 8.

[21] Feet of F. Hants, East. 2 Eliz.

[22] Chan. Proc. (Ser. 2), bdle. 135, No. 18.

[23] Ibid. G. g. 13 Hants, No. 58. His mother was a lady said to have attained the great age of 100 years. In accordance with her husband's wish that she should 'live quietly and not be troubled with worldly business, she gave over housekeeping and betooke herself to the findinge of her sonne,' who found meat, drink, apparel, and a maid servant for her for £15 per annum.

[24] Ibid.

[25] Close, 30 Chas. II, pt. 9, No. 30. The property was then described as the manor or reputed manor of Weston Corbett and Farm of the same place. At the time of this sale it was said to have been in tenure either of Matthew Cufande or John Hockley, and then was occupied by Richard Norton. The manor at that date was probably represented by a farm and its lands.

[26] Com. Pleas Recov. R. Mich. 11 Will. III, m. 22. At this time it was said that the manor had been in the tenure of Matthew Cufande and John Hockley, and then was in occupation of Timothy Browne, yeoman.

[27] Recov. R. Mich. 12 Geo. II, rot. 16.

[28] Ex inform. Mr. F. H. T. Jervoise.

[29] Recov. R. Mich. 25 Geo. III, rot. 443.

[30] Ex inform. Mr. F. H. T. Jervoise.

[31] Ibid.

[32] Ibid.

church of Weston Corbett occurs in 1305, when John de Laudimor was patron.[33] The advowson afterwards passed to the lords of the manor. John de Bohun, father and son, both held the presentation.

The right having lapsed, Lady Ann Roos presented between 1447 and 1486.[34] Later, Richard More, of the king's household, presented.[35] The lords of the manor were again patrons in the reigns of Philip and Mary and Elizabeth, John Altham and John Elliot both holding the advowson.[36]

In or about 1586 Elizabeth, on the petition of Sir James Crofte, granted the 'free chapel of Weston Corbett, now ruined and profaned,' to Edward Wymarke, to be held in common socage and by payment of rent.[37] There is no further mention of the church.

The tithes were also given to Edward Wymarke, but in 1678 were sold with the manor by Richard Norton to Sir Thomas Higgons.[38] The tithes were subsequently held by the Serles and Sir William Oglander,[39] and are still owned by the lord of the manor.

[33] Egerton MS. 2031; Inq. p.m. 41 Edw. III (1st Nos.), No. 13; ibid. 11 Hen. VI, No. 33; Egerton MS. 2034; *Wykeham's Reg.* (Hants Rec. Soc.), i, 148. In 1374 the king presented in right of wardship of the heir of Sir John de Bohun; ibid. i, 59.

[34] Egerton MS. 2034. She was widow of Sir Robert Roos. This family has intermarried with that of De Breuse, the third wife of William de Breuse, father of Aliva de Mowbray, having been Mary de Roos.

[35] Ibid.

[36] Recov. R. East. Phil. and Mary, rot. 544; Close, 1 Eliz. pt. 2, m. 1. The advowson is also mentioned in the fine between Simon Cufande and John Elliot, when it was evidently sold with the manor.

[37] Pat. 29 Eliz. pt. 4, m. 15; 'to be held as of his manor of Estgrenewich.' Before this, in 1501, the following statement occurs in the records of the visitation of Winchester diocese concerning the church of Weston Corbett: 'Ecclesia est inofficiata, Thomas Wheler, firmarius.' Then it was probably a parish with a church, but no parish priest, and Thomas Wheler took the revenues, paying annual rent for the 'farm' thereof, but by whom it was 'farmed' out to him does not appear; ex inform. Mr. T. H. Wyatt.

[38] Close, 30 Chas. II, pt. 9, No. 20.

[39] Com. Pleas Recov. R. Mich. 11 Will. III, m. 22; Feet of F. Div. Cos. Mich. 12 Anne; Recov. R. Mich. 25 Geo. III, rot. 443; Feet of F. Hants, East. 11 Geo. IV.

THE HUNDRED OF MICHELDEVER

CONTAINING THE PARISHES OF

MICHELDEVER NORTHINGTON POPHAM EAST STRATTON

In 1831 the hundred included, locally speaking, only these four parishes, but quite recently its jurisdiction extended also over Cranborne, Slackstead in Farley Chamberlayne, and Abbots Worthy in Kings Worthy parish.[1] Of these Cranborne had been granted to the New Minster with Micheldever Hundred,[2] and both Cranborne and Worthy are separately mentioned in the Domesday Survey as being in Micheldever Hundred. Other lands also included in the hundred in 1086 were Drayton in Barton Stacey, West Stratton, and Popham, whilst Northington and East Stratton were evidently included in the abbey's lands there, though not expressly mentioned.[3] The jurisdiction of the hundred also extended over Swarraton,[4] for which the tithingman of Northington answered.[5] The hundred was assessed at 113 hides in the time of Edward the Confessor, but of these seven hides at Worthy paid no geld. The remaining 106 hides were reduced to 83 hides and half a virgate before 1086.

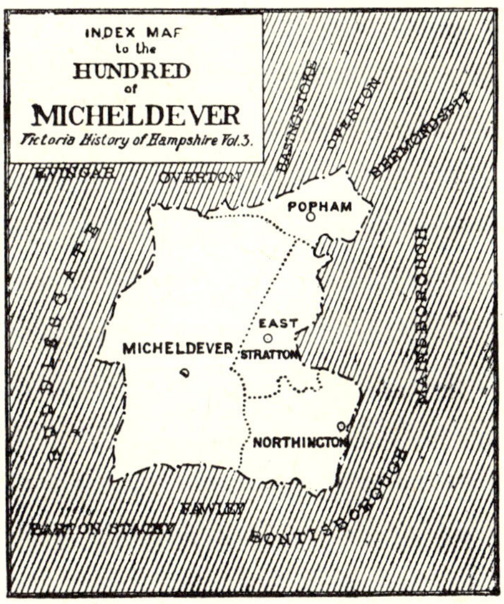

The hundred court was held at Micheldever,[6] probably in early days at the moot-house mentioned in the boundaries of Micheldever in 901.[7] The hundred was granted to the New Minster with the manor (q.v.) in the early years of the reign of Edward the Elder,[8] and its history has since been coincident with that of the manor. In 1282 the abbot complained that the mayor and bailiffs of Winchester, together with certain citizens, had entered the abbey's inclosures within the hundred with a great multitude and seized the attachments for certain trespasses there, a right which should have belonged to the abbey.[9] Assize of bread and ale was also claimed as appurtenant to the hundred,[10] and this with other privileges, such as return of writs, freedom from interference by the sheriff, and exemption from pleas, tallage, aids, geld and scot, was confirmed to Henry earl of Southampton in February, 1607–8,[11] shortly after the restoration of the hundred with his other lands.[12]

[1] See Ct. Bks. *penes* Lord Northbrook.
[2] *Liber de Hyda* (Rolls Ser.), 88.
[3] *V.C.H. Hants*, i, 469*b*.
[4] Harl. MS. 1761, No. 49.
[5] Ibid. fol. 160.
[6] Ibid.; Ct. Bks. *penes* Lord Northbrook.
[7] *Liber de Hyda* (Rolls Ser.), 86. In the English explanation of the Saxon charter it is called the manor; it is possible, therefore, that this moot-house stood on the site of the present manor farm.
[8] Kemble, *Codex Dipl.* 336.
[9] *Cal. Pat.* 1281–92, p. 47.
[10] *Plac. de Quo Warr.* (Rec. Com.), 766.
[11] Pat. 5 Jas. I, pt. 15, m. 1.
[12] Ibid. pt. 2, m. 1.

MICHELDEVER

Mycendefer (ix cent.); Mycheldefer (x cent.); Micheldeura (xii cent.); Mucheldever (xiii–xv cent.).

The parish of Micheldever, lying beyond the Worthies to the north-east of Winchester, contains nearly 7,819 acres, of which the greater part is arable land. Generally speaking the land slopes down from north and south towards the centre of the parish where the village of Micheldever lies, and where the stream called the North Brook, a tributary of the Test, rises to flow westward across the parish towards Hunton.

The Roman road from Winchester to London passing through Martyr Worthy enters Micheldever near Lunway's Inn, which lies on the right-hand side where a branch road turns off north-east towards Northington. Rising steadily the main road skirts the western edge of Micheldever Wood, with its well authenticated remains of a Roman villa[1]—the wood which Cobbett in his *Rural Rides* mentions as containing 1,000 acres, and as being 'one of the finest oak woods in England'[2]—and passes on in a north-easterly direction to form the border line between East Stratton and Micheldever. About half a mile north of Lunway's Inn a lane branching west from the main road leads between low hedges through ploughed fields and pasture land to Micheldever village. A short steep descent marks the entrance to the village past the Half Moon and Spread Eagle Inn and a few low thatched cottages lying on either side of the road. Here a turn to the north-west leads into the main village street, on either side of which are quaint thatched half-timbered houses, with only here and there a less attractive modern cottage. To the west stands the manor farm, while about half way down the main street a low gate leads to the church of St. Mary up a gravel path between grass banks covered in the early spring with masses of celandine and shaded by well-grown lime trees. Opposite the church is the village school, south-east of which is the vicarage. Immediately north of the school is the thatched cottage which serves as a post office. North of the village the road curves slightly north-west, crossing the brook to Northbrook tithing, and thence running north past Northbrook House, and for some distance east of and parallel with the railway line, branches north-west to the station on the London and South Western Railway, near the northern boundary of the parish. The tithing of Northbrook, lying about a quarter of a mile from the east bank of the railway line, consists of a Primitive Methodist chapel (1867) and a few cottages and outbuildings on either side of the road coming from Micheldever. Northbrook Farm and Northbrook House, the residence of Mr. W. G. Wittingstall, a large white house backing on the line, stand some distance from the road behind a small park nearly half a mile to the north of the cottages of Northbrook.

A road leads west from Northbrook under the railway line to the tithing of Weston Colley, which consists of several scattered groups of picturesque thatched cottages and one or two good-sized houses, including Weston House, the residence of Miss Armstrong. Near to the railway bank is the old mill house over the Test tributary, probably standing on the site of the mill mentioned in the Domesday Survey of the manor. The mill at Weston with the suit of customary tenants there was leased to John Prikehare and his wife Orenge by the abbot of Hyde late in the thirteenth century.[3]

Norsbury House near Norsbury Ring is in the south-west of the parish, and is surrounded by a small park. The soil of the whole parish is loam with a subsoil of chalk, and ordinary green crops are grown on the 4,493½ acres of arable land. Only 1,936¾ acres are given up to permanent grass, and 1,056 to woodland.[4] The woodland is mostly comprised in Micheldever Wood, formerly part of Pamber Forest. Of the smaller woods Blackwood and Upper Blackwood lying in the north-east on the borders of Popham were granted to Hyde Abbey in 1258 by Audoenus Black (le Noir) in return for maintenance of himself and his wife Alice as long as they should live;[5] while Bazeley Copse is probably identical with 'Bablysley' Copse leased to Sir Thomas Wriothesley with the rectory in 1537.[6] A cottage called The Forge was occupied by Thomas Wickham and Peter Leffe at the time of the surrender of Hyde Abbey.[7]

There is now no market or fair held in the parish, but both were appurtenant to the manor in 1685,[8] and probably originated with the liberties granted to Henry earl of Southampton in 1607. Some field names of interest are Wlfladescroft, Alwoldeslynche in Southbrook, and Smokakre.[9] There is no inclosure award.

MANORS

In Saxon times *MICHELDEVER* was a royal vill.[10] It was included in the 100 *cassati* at Micheldever granted according to the will of King Alfred to the New Minster at Winchester *c.* 900 by his son Edward the Elder.[11] In 904 Edward added ten more *mansae*, with a fishery at Micheldever on the borders of Worthy, which were intended for the support of the refectory of the abbey.[12] Ethelred the Unready granted a confirmatory charter to the abbey *c.* 984, mentioning

[1] *V.C.H. Hants*, i, 307.

[2] Cobbett, *Rural Rides* (1853), p. 71.

[3] Harl. MS. 1761, fol. 105.

[4] Information from Bd. of Agric. (1905).

[5] Harl. MS. 1761, No. 65.

[6] Mins. Accts. Hants, 30–1 Hen. VIII, R. 135, m. 30.

[7] Ibid.

[8] Recov. R. Trin. 1 Jas. II, 221.

[9] Harl. MS. 1761, Nos. 15, 52, and 120.

[10] Kemble, *Codex Dipl.* No. 286. This charter, however, is of very doubtful authenticity. It is dated from the 'royal vill of Mycendefer' A.D. 862, in the presence of King Ethelred (who ascended the throne in 866), and Bishop Swithun (who died in 862).

[11] Birch, *Cart. Sax.* ii, 596. The boundaries are given in full in *Liber de Hyda* (Rolls Ser.), 85. They can be so far identified as to prove that the grant included Micheldever, Cranborne, land at Curdridge and Durley, Farley Chamberlayne (Slackstede), the detached part of Northington east of Brown Candover and Abbots Worthy. The charter was probably made in 1000–30 possibly as an assurance of title for all the lands attached to Micheldever at that date (Inform. kindly supplied by the earl of Northbrook). The almost certainly spurious 'Golden Charter' of 903 (Kemble, *Codex Dipl.* 336) recites the endowment of New Minster with the farm called Micheldever with its hundred and appurtenances, 100 *cassati* and a church and also both vills of Stratton (i.e. East and West Stratton), Burcote, and Northington with other lands.

[12] *Liber de Hyda* (Rolls Ser.), 101.

ten hides at Micheldever and fifty more at Waltham and Micheldever.[13] These were not all of the abbey's possessions there, for under Edward the Confessor Micheldever was assessed at 106 hides.[14]

Micheldever manor was the 'caput' of the abbot's barony, the undertenants owing suit of court there for their holdings.

In 1226 there appear the first signs of a contest between the abbot and the monks as to the tenure of the manor. Abbot Selid, looking upon it as parcel of the abbot's temporalities, had granted a virgate of land there to Ralph le Clauer without the consent of the convent, and in this year an assize was held as to whether Ralph's son Walter should hold the land of the abbot and his church or of the abbot in demesne ;[15] it was finally decided late in the fourteenth century that Micheldever with its members pertained to the office of abbot,[16] and the manor was therefore seized into the king's hands on the voidance of the abbey.[17] The manorial lands were split up into numerous small holdings held of the abbot by free service.[18] Among the profits of the manor the underwood cut in Micheldever Wood was of some importance. In 1300 the king granted licence to Hyde Abbey to inclose 60 acres of the wood, for though it lay within the bounds of Pamber Forest wild beasts did not repair there much,[19] and in 1328 the abbey was granted free warren in its demesne lands at Micheldever.[20] A few years later Richard Edmund of Micheldever was fined £20 for having entered the abbey's warren and caught and carried away hares and rabbits to the value of 100*s.*[21] In 1421 the crown attempted to claim certain services from the abbey, stating that Henry I gave the monks Micheldever manor on condition that they should sing for his soul and those of his successors, and furnish a 'meete of kenettes or racches' to hunt wolves, wild cats, and other harmful animals. The abbot in reply asserted that the abbey had held the manor in frankalmoign from time immemorial.[22] Some years before the surrender of the abbey, which took place in 1538, the site of the manor with a dove-cote and a rabbit warren called Godwynesdowne was leased to John Smyth, his wife Joan and their son John for thirty-five years on condition that they should provide the abbot's steward and clerk with meat and drink and fodder for their horses twice yearly when they held courts there, and should give the steward and bailiff breakfast when they held the hundred court.[23] In 1538 the manor was taken into the king's hands on the dissolution of Hyde Abbey, and was purchased from the crown in 1544 by Thomas Wriothesley, afterwards earl of Southampton, soon after his appointment as Lord Chancellor.[24] Wriothesley already held the site of the rectory under a lease from the abbey, and also had some land called Butlers in the parish. He held the manor jointly with his wife Jane, and died seised of it in July, 1550, when his son and heir Henry was only three years old.[25] This Henry died in 1581, leaving a young son and heir of the same name,[26] who was attainted in 1601 for his share in the insurrection of the earl of Essex, but was restored to his honours in 1603.[27] His lands, including Micheldever, which had been forfeit to the crown, were restored at the same time, and in 1607 the king granted him return of writs, waifs and strays, and goods of felons, treasure-trove, assize of bread and ale, court leet, freedom from juries and assizes, and also that his tenants on the lands which had belonged to Hyde Abbey should be quit from pleas, tallage, aids, geld and scot, and should be exempt from shires, ward, and hundred-penny.[28] In 1624 he died at Bergen-op-Zoom of the pestilence, and was succeeded by his second son Thomas,[29] who was an ardent Royalist, and was rewarded with the office of Lord High Treasurer at the Restoration. After his death in 1667 his estates were divided among his three daughters, Micheldever being assigned to the second, Rachel Vaughan,[30] who afterwards married William Lord Russell, executed in 1683 as being concerned in the Rye House Plot. Micheldever manor descended to her grandson, Wriothesley, who inherited the title of duke of Bedford.[31] He was succeeded by his son John,[32] whose widow Gertrude held courts there during the minority of the heir Francis,[33] eighth duke of Bedford, who in February, 1801, sold Micheldever to Sir Francis Baring.[34] He was succeeded by Sir Thomas Baring, in whose name courts were held at Micheldever in November, 1811.[35] His son and heir Sir Thomas Baring was created Baron Northbrook in 1866, the title being taken from the tithing of that name in this parish. His son Thomas George Baring was viceroy of India from 1872–6, at the end of which period he was created earl of Northbrook. The estate has remained with his direct descendants, the present earl of Northbrook being lord of the manor.

RUSSELL. *Argent a lion gules and a chief sable with three scallops argent therein.*

BARING. *Azure a fesse or and a bear's head in the chief with a golden muzzle and ring.*

The tithing of *WEST STRATTON*, consisting of some picturesque cottages and farm-buildings, lies west of the main Winchester to London road, and of the parish of East Stratton, and north-east of Micheldever village. It is approached by a narrow lane

13 Kemble, *Codex Dipl.* 642.

14 *V.C.H. Hants*, i, 469*b*. These, however, included the above-mentioned lands at Cranborne and elsewhere, which Hugh de Port and his descendants held by knight's service.

15 *Bracton's Note Bk.* 1727.

16 Harl. MS. 1761, fol. 177.

17 Ibid. 175*b*.

18 *Testa de Nevill* (Rec. Com.), 239.

19 Inq. a.q.d. file 33, No. 3. Micheldever Wood had been afforested by Hen. II, but in 1228 the sheriff was ordered to exclude it from the ancient forest. *Cal. Close*, 1227–31, pp. 102–3.

20 Chart. R. 2 Edw. III, 17 ; ibid. 3 Edw. III, 16.

21 Harl. MS. 1761, No. 109.

22 Ibid. fol. 1*b*.

23 Mins. Accts. (Hants), 30–31 Hen. VIII, R. 135, m. 30, et seq.

24 *L. and P. Hen. VIII*, xix (2), 690 (19).

25 Chan. Inq. p.m. (Ser. 2), vol. 92, No. 78.

26 Ibid. 24 Eliz. pt. 1 (Ser. 2), No. 46.

27 Pat. 1 Jas. I, pt. 2, m. 1.

28 Ibid. 5 Jas. I, pt. 15, No. 1.

29 Feet of F. Hants, Mich. 5 Chas. I.

30 Ibid. Div. Cos. Hil. 20–21 Chas. II ; Recov. R. East. 21 Chas. II.

31 Her son Wriothesley who succeeded his paternal grandfather as duke of Bedford died during her lifetime.

32 Feet of F. Hants, Hil. 4 Geo. III.

33 Ct. Bk. of Micheldever *penes* Lord Northbrook, fol. 86 et seq.

34 Information kindly supplied by the earl of Northbrook.

35 Ct. Bk. fol. 113.

which branches west from the main road, and passing through West Stratton, goes north towards Parkhill Farm. West Stratton was granted to Hyde Abbey with Micheldever manor,[36] and was among the lands occupied by a freeman before the Conquest, and afterwards held of the abbey by Hugh de Port and his successors.[37] By the thirteenth century they had enfeoffed the Braiboeufs of Candover of this manor,[38] while the actual tenant under the Braiboeufs in 1167 was Richard de Stratton.[39] In 1199 Richard son of Robert obtained quitclaim of a virgate of land in Stratton from Lavinia Perchehaie,[40] and four years later a Richard de Stratton was pardoned six marks for scutage which he owed for a fee held of the barony of the abbot of Hyde.[41] In 1226–7 Stephen de Stratton witnessed a charter to the abbot of Hyde,[42] and later in the same century Walter de Stratton held of the abbot half a knight's fee in Stratton.[43] William de Stratton was holding a whole fee, probably the manor of West Stratton, in 1284.[44] He had a son Richard,[45] who had succeeded his father as lord of the manor before 1315.[46] He was knighted before 1325, and in that year conveyed the manor of West Stratton with a messuage and land there to Stephen de Stratton, parson of Worthy, for life, with remainder to William Wayte for life, and final remainder to the latter's son, Thomas Wayte.[47] William Wayte was in possession by 1346,[48] and his grandson John Wayte presented to West Stratton chapel in 1398,[49] and was succeeded by his son Thomas before 1403.[50] In 1428 he was said to hold one fee there.[51] Thomas Wayte was still lord of the manor in 1431.[52] His grandson William was living in 1487,[53] and in February, 1527–8, John Wayte, brother and heir of John Wayte (*sic*), sold all his Hampshire estates, including West Stratton, to his kinsman Arthur Plantagenet Viscount Lisle, for £2,000, on condition that he should have food and lodging within the viscount's house whenever he willed;[54] and again in 1530 John Wayte conveyed the same lands to Viscount Lisle, Sir Richard Lister, chief baron of the Exchequer, and many others, and the heirs of Sir Richard Lister;[55] hence it appears that Viscount Lisle's rights in West Stratton were transferred to Sir Richard Lister,[56] to whom a certain Robert Fawkenor and his wife Joan quitclaimed their rights in the manor eight years later.[57] Sir Richard evidently parted with West Stratton before his death, which occurred in March, 1553–4,[58] to his father-in-law, Thomas Wriothesley, earl of Southampton, who died seised of it in 1550.[59] Both West and East Stratton were among those of the earl's lands which were seized by the crown for payment of a debt; they were regranted to his widow in 1554, in consideration of £400 to be paid to the queen yearly until the debt should be satisfied.[60] The subsequent history of the manor is identical with that of Micheldever.

Among the holdings under Hyde Abbey was one known later as the manor of *MOTTISFONT* or Micheldever. It apparently consisted of half a hide.[61] William of Micheldever seems to have been the tenant in the thirteenth century, for a charter dated February, 1248–9, recording an exchange of land between him and the abbot makes mention of his demesne lands, while two of the crofts which he acquired of the abbey were adjacent to his 'court' in Micheldever.[62] His son Geoffrey joined with him in witnessing several grants to the abbey.[63] Geoffrey's son Philip was evidently a minor at the time of his father's death, for in 1280 John de Fraxino, called le Hyne, released all claim to the custody of Philip and his father's lands.[64] In 1304 a Robert de Micheldever was acquiring lands in the neighbouring parish of Laverstoke.[65] Simon de Micheldever witnessed a grant of land in Micheldever in 1328,[66] and in 1331 he and his wife Agnes were enfeoffed of a messuage, 10 virgates of land, 10 acres of meadow, 10 acres of wood, and £13 0*s.* 10*d.* rent in Micheldever, Southbrook, Weston, and East and West Stratton, with remainder to their son Philip.[67] The latter's son Richard had a sister and heir Thomasine, whose grandson John, son of John Mottisfont, came to Hyde on Wednesday before Easter, 1440, and in the large room of the abbot did homage for half a hide, which he held of the abbot in Micheldever, at the same time paying 14*s.* 8*d.* relief for his lands.[68] It must have been from this family of Mottisfont that the tenement gained its later name of Mottisfont. It was evidently identical with the 'manor of Micheldever' of the reversion of which William Stanesby died seised on 21 October, 1574. It was then held in dower by his mother Elizabeth, widow of Robert Stanesby.[69] William Stanesby had a brother and heir John aged twenty-two at the time of William's death; he was possibly the same John Stanesby who was in possession of a manor in Micheldever in 1622.[70] His son Robert joined with him in 1625 in a settlement of the manor of Micheldever otherwise Mottisfont, together with 16 messuages and 912 acres of land in Micheldever, Southbrook, Northbrook, Weston, and East and West Stratton.[71] Robert had succeeded to the estate before 1647, when he conveyed it by fine to William Colnett the elder.[72] This, however, was not a direct sale, for in 1684 certain lands in

36 Kemble, *Codex Dipl.* 336.
37 *V.C.H. Hants*, i, 469*b*.
38 *Testa de Nevill*, 232.
39 *Pipe R.* (Pipe R. Soc.), xiii, 190.
40 Feet of F. Hants, 1 John, 7.
41 *Rot. de Liberate* (Rec. Com.), 5 John, 75.
42 Harl. MS. 1761, No. 39.
43 *Testa de Nevill*, 232*b*.
44 *Cal. Close*, 1279–88, p. 278. A William de Stratton, knt. had witnessed a charter to the abbot of Hyde in 1258 (Harl. MS. 1761, No. 19), and again in 1278 (Cott. MS. Domit. A. xiv, 43).
45 Harl. MS. 1761, No. 103.
46 Ibid. 138. He held one and a quarter fees of the abbey. See also *Feud. Aids*, ii, 306.
47 Feet of F. Hants, 18 Edw. II, 10.
48 *Feud. Aids*, ii, 329.
49 *Wykeham's Reg.* (Hants Rec. Soc.), i, 217.
50 Ibid. 237.
51 *Feud. Aids*, ii, 348.
52 Ibid. 364.
53 *Cal. Inq. p.m.* Hen. VII, 187.
54 Close, 20 Hen. VIII, No. 35.
55 Feet of F. Hants, Trin. 22 Hen. VIII.
56 Sir Richard Lister paid 35*s.* rent of assize for a capital messuage with its appurtenances called 'Waytslands' in West Stratton, in 1539. Mins. Accts. Hants, 30–1 Hen. VIII, R. 135, m. 36*d*.
57 Feet of F. Hants, Trin. 30 Hen. VIII.
58 Chan. Inq. p.m. (Ser. 2), vol. 104, No. 67 (1).
59 Ibid. vol. 92, No. 78.
60 Pat. 2 & 3 Phil. and Mary, pt. 4.
61 Harl. MS. 1761, fol. 9*b*.
62 Ibid. No. 26. The two crofts had been held respectively by Robert Fullo and Edmund le Conde.
63 Ibid. Nos. 27, 28, 48.
64 Ibid. fol. 100.
65 Inq. a.q.d. file 45, No. 9.
66 Harl. MS. 1761, No. 141.
67 Feet of F. Hants, Hil. 5 Edw. III, 64.
68 Harl. MS. 1761, fol. 9*b*.
69 Chan. Inq. p.m. 17 Eliz. (Ser. 2), 116.
70 Chan. Proc. Jas. I, S. x, 28.
71 Feet of F. Hants, Trin. 1 Chas. I.
72 Ibid. Hil. 22 Chas. I.

Micheldever Church : The West Tower

Northbrook, Southbrook, Ridgefield, and other places in Micheldever, lately in the tenure of Richard Stanesby the elder and Richard Stanesby the younger were settled on Katherine daughter of Robert Woolley on her marriage with Robert Bristow the younger.[73] In 1743 Katherine Bristow, then a widow, entailed her Hampshire lands on her son Robert Bristow.[74] It has not been found possible to identify these lands or to ascertain their later descent.

The hospital of St. John at Winchester held 2 acres of land in Weston Colley by purchase from Hugh le Bere of Weston, made in June, 1270,[75] one in 'Brocfurlong' and the other east of 'la Stapele' and abutting on 'Mitcheiles Farm.'[76] They also had lands and a grange at Southbrook, of which the modern Southbrook House, the residence of Mr. A. Stewart, probably marks the site. This grange was purchased early in the fourteenth century and was transferred to Micheldever from Worthy in 1314–15.[77]

CHURCH The church of *OUR LADY* has a chancel, an octagonal nave with a western bay flanked on north and south by vestries, and a west tower. The nave and chancel are of brick, built in 1806 after a fire, and the only ancient parts of the building are the west bay of the nave, which has some late thirteenth-century work, and the tower, which belongs to the first half of the sixteenth century.

The east window of the chancel is of fourteenth-century style, replacing an early nineteenth-century window. On the chancel walls are several monuments of the Baring family; a large white marble monument on the north wall, with kneeling figures of angels, commemorates the first earl of Northbrook, 1904, Lady Northbrook, 1884, and Thomas Baring, 1873. The flag of H.M.S. *Captain*, lost at sea in 1870, is hung up here.

The octagonal nave, though poor in design, is effective and well lighted; its western arch, the jambs of which have been heightened to range with the octagon, is of late thirteenth-century character, with half-octagonal moulded capitals, and the arches on either side of the west bay of the nave (17 ft. 2 in. wide), between the octagon and the tower, are of the same detail.

The tower, which measures 14 ft. 3 in. by 14 ft. 9 in. within the walls, is a fine massive building, plain in treatment, but giving a very good effect. It may be compared with the contemporary, though rather more elaborate, tower of Soberton church. It has a stair in the south-west angle, and a west doorway, the four-centred head of which is modern. Over it is a square-headed window of three uncusped lights with a transom, and the belfry windows are of the same character, but with four lights filled with pierced stonework, and having in the heads panels with various devices in incised circles. On the west side there are IHS . IS . IOP . and W over a tun (a rebus); on the south side are no letters, but a grotesque face, a three-leaved flower, &c. The north and east sides have blank circles.

The east arch of the tower is of a single chamfered order on half-octagonal responds, into which the arch dies without a capital. The thirteenth-century arches in the west bay of the nave die into the wall on either side of the tower arch above their springing, their width being about two-thirds of their full span. The font, which stands on the north side in the west bay, is modern, with panelling of fifteenth-century style on the bowl. Two fragments of Purbeck marble from an older rectangular font with arcaded sides are also preserved under the tower.

There are six bells, of which two are dated 1703, forming part of a ring of that date of five bells. Three of these were recast and a new bell added in 1903.

The plate consists of a set given by Lady Northbrook in 1866, a chalice, paten, flagon, and two plates, and there is also a curious silver cup given by Rachel Lady Russell, 1703.

The first four books of the registers, which overlap one another considerably, contain all entries between 1538 and 1576, 1538–1683, 1540–1721, and 1684–1765. Another book contains the baptisms and burials, 1766–1812, and the marriages, 1754–1812, take up two more volumes.

ADVOWSON Micheldever church was included in Edward the Elder's grant of the vill to the New Minster,[78] but no mention is made of it in the Domesday Survey. In the *Taxatio* of 1291 the church was assessed at £66 13*s.* 4*d.*, and the vicarage at £10 13*s.* 4*d.*, while attached to the church there was a pension of £3 6*s.* 8*d.* besides 6 lb. of wax yearly.[79] Again in 1297 protection was granted to the vicar of Micheldever,[80] but it was not till 1302 that the abbey had formal licence from the crown to appropriate the great tithes of the church,[81] and in April, 1309, the abbot and convent obtained from the pope confirmation of the appropriation of Micheldever church made by John of Pontoise in 1293 for the use of guests and of poor and infirm people coming to the monastery.[82] The vicar's portion was regulated by Bishop Woodlock, *c.* 1308, the conditions being that the vicar should cause the church with its chapels of East and West Stratton, Northington, and Popham to be served by chaplains and provide the necessary books, ornaments, and vestments besides seven boys' surplices.[83] A dispute having arisen later in the century as to whether the fruits of the chapels appendant to Micheldever belonged to the office of abbot or to the convent generally, Bishop Wykeham wrote to the abbot in February, 1386–7, advising a compromise.[84] Under Hyde Abbey, Chancellor Wriothesley held a lease of the parsonage,[85] which he sublet to Edmund Clerk of Micheldever on condition that the lessee should give 20*d.* weekly in alms to ten of the poorest householders there, and should keep any of Wriothesley's children at the parsonage for 12*d.* a week if he wished to send them.[86] After the surrender of Hyde Abbey the advowson of the vicarage was purchased by Wriothesley with the manor.[87] Among the property exchanged by Edward VI with the

[73] Close, 17 Geo. II, pt. 8, m. 4.
[74] Ibid.
[75] Five years previous to the generally accepted date of the foundation of the hospital, see *V.C.H. Hants*, ii, 201.
[76] Harl. MS. 1761, No. 93.
[77] *Hist. MSS. Com. Rep.* vi, App. 597. It was still held by the mayor of Winchester and the master of the hospital in 1539. Mins. Accts. Hants, 30–1 Hen. VIII, R. 135, m. 830 et seq.
[78] Kemble, *Cod. Dipl.* 336.
[79] *Pope Nich. Tax.* (Rec. Com.), 210*b*.
[80] *Cal. Pat.* 1292–1301, p. 275.
[81] Ibid. 1301–7, p. 48.
[82] *Cal. Pap. Letters*, ii, 51.
[83] Harl. MS. 1761, Nos. 117, 118.
[84] *Wykeham's Reg.* (Hants Rec. Soc.), ii, 390.
[85] Perhaps it was for the parsonage that Wriothesley was granted twenty oaks from the forest of West Bere 'for his building in Micheldever' in 1534; *L. and P. Hen. VIII*, vii, 154.
[86] Ibid. ix, App. 14.
[87] Pat. 36 Hen. VIII, pt. 22.

bishop of Winchester for the manor of Twyford and other lands were the rectory and parsonage of Micheldever.[88] They were already leased to Jane countess of Southampton, and widow of Wriothesley, and in 1585 a fresh lease was made out in favour of Henry, earl of Southampton, Wriothesley's grandson.[89] His father's executors bought the reversion of the lease in 1599,[90] since which date both the rectory and the advowson of the vicarage have remained the property of the successive lords of Micheldever manor.

There was formerly a chantry chapel at West Stratton, founded in honour of St. John the Baptist.[91] In the bishop's ordination of Micheldever vicarage in 1308, it was arranged that the vicar should cause West Stratton chapel to be served by a chaplain,[92] but in 1325 the advowson of the chapel belonged to Richard de Stratton, who conveyed it to Stephen de Stratton with the manor of West Stratton.[93] Some years later, during the rule of Bishop Stratford (1323–33), William Wayte, then lord of the manor, presented to the chantry chapel of West Stratton,[94] and it was still in his gift between 1333 and 1345.[95] A few years later the bishop collated,[96] and in 1367 a commission was issued for an inquiry concerning the vacancy of the perpetual chantry of West Stratton in Micheldever parish, and the right of patronage to it.[97] Thomas Wayte presented to the chapel or chantry in 1402, and again in 1403.[98] There is now no trace of a chapel at West Stratton.

At Northbrook a Primitive Methodist chapel was built in 1867, near the cross road leading to Weston Farm. Another Methodist chapel lies due west of the station.

CHARITIES

In 1642 John Pink by will directed his executors to provide for the payment of £4 a year for the poor. The trust fund is now represented by £97 0*s*. 4*d*. consols, with the official trustees, the dividends upon which, amounting to £2 5*s*. 4*d*., are, together with 15*s*. a year received from the next-mentioned charity, applied in the distribution of coal. In 1905, 2 tons 12 cwt. were given to twenty-eight recipients.

The donors of the following charities are unknown :—An annuity of 15*s*. formerly paid by the owner of a small farm, called Garrett's Bargain. In 1894 the rent-charge was redeemed by the transfer to the official trustees of £30, £2 10*s*. per cent. annuities. An annual payment of 5*s*. formerly received in respect of a charge on land in Upton Grey does not appear to have been recently claimed.

In 1823 Dame Susannah Boothby, by a codicil to her will, proved in the P.C.C., bequeathed certain moneys for the poor of this parish, and of Ashbourne, Derbyshire. In the result of proceedings in Chancery the sum of £464 4*s*. 9*d*. consols was assigned to this parish. By a scheme made in 1871 under the Endowed Schools Acts, a sum of £268 1*s*. 11*d*. consols was sold out to provide £250, which was expended in the erection of school buildings. The dividends upon the balance of the stock, which, with accumulations, now amounts to £365 1*s*. 6*d*. consols with the official trustees, are applicable under the scheme in procuring further education for some deserving boy or girl in the schools by payment of tuition fees, exhibitions, prizes or rewards.

Southbrook House for aged and infirm persons. The Charles Pain Memorial Fund. Miss Mary Elizabeth Pain, by deed dated 29 September, 1906, gave £300 India 3 per-cent. stock (with the official trustees), dividends to be applied in sums of 2*s*. 6*d*. cash, and 2*s*. 6*d* in coals on 1 January yearly to each of the twelve inmates of this almshouse ; failing the number of twelve almspersons, poor aged persons of the parish to be selected.

NORTHINGTON

Northametone (x cent.) ; Norhampton and Nuthampton (xiii cent.); Nonehampton and Northampton (xiv cent.); Northington and Norrington (xviii cent.).

The parish of Northington, which was incorporated for ecclesiastical purposes with the neighbouring parish of Swarraton in 1849, has an area of 2,414 acres, which are still distinct from Swarraton for civil purposes. Yet locally, the two villages, separated only by the narrow Candover stream, which forms the eastern boundary line of Northington parish, seem to be one ; Northington, with its commanding modern church, its school and scattered cottages, lying on the hill-side sloping down to the river from the west, meeting the cottages and houses of Swarraton, among which is the vicarage for both parishes, as they lie along the opposite bank of the river on a lesser slope. The high down called Northington Down, on the slope of which Northington village lies, is now for the most part inclosed in Lord Ashburton's estate, Grange Park, which includes about 530 acres, covering nearly the whole of the south-east portion of the parish, and extending into Swarraton. Cobbett, in his *Rural Rides*, speaks of the inclosure and subsequent planting with trees of a 'pretty little down called Northington Down,' by Mr. Alexander Baring (created Lord Ashburton in 1835), as a sort of outwork to his park. 'But Mr. Baring,' he continues, 'not reflecting that woods are not like funds, to be made at a heat, has planted his trees *too large*, so that they are covered with moss, are dying at the top, and are literally growing downward instead of upward . . . so that the down . . . is now a marred, ragged, ugly-looking thing.' Cobbett may have been right in his day, but the sight of the finely-wooded down as the steep road descends into Northington village justifies Lord Ashburton rather than Cobbett. The Grange, the house of the estate, lies almost in the centre of the park, close to the river, which here broadens out into a long narrow lake. The old mansion, the nucleus of the present house, was a seventeenth-century square brick building, the work of Inigo Jones, without any external ornament, but

88 Pat. 5 Edw. VI, pt. 6.
89 *L. and P. Hen. VIII*, xix (1), 80 (42) ; Partic. for Leases, *temp.* Eliz. 1585, No. 5, Hants.
90 *Cal. of S.P. Dom.* 1598–1601, p. 271.
91 Egerton MS. 2032, fol. 83.
92 Harl. MS. 1761, No. 117.
93 Feet of F. Hants, 18 Edw. II, No. 10.
94 Egerton MS. 2032, fol. 83.
95 Ibid. fol. 149.
96 Ibid. 2033, fol. 38*b*.
97 *Wykeham's Reg.* (Hants Rec. Soc.), ii, 8.
98 Ibid. i, 237, 242.

cased in stone, with a magnificent portico and other classic decorations.[1] Both house and park, according to Duthy, owed their origin to the family of Henley, who resided there for many generations. Carlyle, among other of the great men of the early nineteenth century, was a constant visitor at the Grange. Thus in 1844 he wrote to Lady Ashburton, 'I am in ugly drudgery and sorrow, and shall not see the beautiful face of "The Grange" or any beautiful thing, for I know not what long months or years.'[2]

Apart from the north-west corner of the parish, which includes a part of Micheldever Wood, and covers the greater part of the 501 acres of woodland, the rest of the parish is mostly composed of arable and pasture land, covering respectively 1,331 and 684¾ acres. When Duthy wrote, early in the nineteenth century, the work of draining the water meadows was being carried on by Lord Ashburton with excellent results. Thus, though, as Duthy stated, the land with its chalk soil and subsoil is 'for the most part thin and weak in quality,' since there are 'tracts of a stronger description on some of the hills, and since the water meadows can now be turned to use as pasture land, farming is in a comparatively flourishing state in the parish, good crops of wheat, oats, and turnips being grown.' Many now disused chalk and gravel-pits are still to be seen in the fields.

There is no inclosure award.

MANORS Six hides at *NORTHINGTON* were named in the almost certainly spurious charter of Edward the Elder to the New Minster.[3] In the Domesday Survey it is difficult to distinguish Northington from the other lands of the abbey in Micheldever Hundred. It may, perhaps, have been identical with the six hides held by Alsi and his father before him.[4] In the fourteenth century three distinct holdings can be traced in Northington. These were the demesne lands of the abbey, known later as the Grange, and two reputed manors held by under-tenants, and known respectively as Northington and Totford.

The *GRANGE*, as its name denotes, was kept under the immediate control of the abbey. In 1263 Alice wife of Henry le Frankelyn released all her right in 36 acres of land in Northington to the abbey,[5] and in 1346 the abbot of Hyde was said to hold there a moiety of a hide which had been in the tenure of Henry le Frankelyn.[6] It seems, therefore, that this land was part of, or was added to, the Grange. Amongst the lessees of the Grange was Thomas (or William)[7] Turner, who obtained a thirty years' lease from the abbey, 24 May, 1519. He also farmed the glebe lands and the tithes of Northington chapel, paying for the whole £8 10*s.* yearly.[8] After the surrender of the abbey in 1538, the Grange fell to the crown with the rest of the monastic lands, and was leased successively to William Ryth and Richard Pigot. Finally, in January, 1589–90, Queen Elizabeth sold it to Richard Thekeston and Henry Best,[9] who were probably speculators, for they parted with it almost immediately to James Hunt of Popham,[10] who died seised of it in 1605.[11] His grandson of the same name sold Northington Grange and chapel, together with two mills,[12] 464 acres of land, meadow, wood, and heath in Northington and Kingsclere, and the tithes of Northington, to Sir Benjamin Tichborne in 1641.[13] Northington Grange was evidently purchased by Sir Robert Henley before 1665,[14] and added to his estate in Swarraton, which was also known as the Grange. He was buried at Northington in 1692 and was succeeded by his eldest son Anthony, whose grandson Robert was Lord Keeper and was created earl of Northington by George III.

HENLEY. *Azure a lion argent with a crown or in a border argent and thereon roundels gules.*

The title became extinct on the death of his son and heir Robert, whose sisters and co-heiresses sold the Grange in 1787 to Henry Drummond, a wealthy banker.[15] Drummond's grandson and heir, the famous follower of Irving, sold the estate in 1817 to Alexander Baring, a cousin of Sir Thomas Baring of Stratton. He also was a leading banker, and was created Baron Ashburton in 1835. In 1842 he negotiated the settlement of the boundaries between the United States and the British Territory in America, and during his lifetime many distinguished guests visited the Grange. The estate was inherited in 1848 by his son William Bingham, second Lord Ashburton, a noted philanthropist, who was succeeded by his brother in 1864. The latter's son and heir, the fourth Lord Ashburton, greatly improved the Grange estate.[16] He died in 1889 and was succeeded by the present Francis Denzil, fifth baron.

The tenement known later as *NORTHINGTON MANOR*[17] was held of the successive lords of Micheldever, and apparently had no manorial rights attached to it. It evidently included land lying near the site of the present village of Northington, its appurtenances extending into Totford and Swarraton. The tenant in 1167 seems to have been a certain Richard,[18] and late in the following century Herbert Butler (*Pincerna*) was holding three hides in Northington of the abbot of Hyde, while Richard son of Ralph also had four and a half virgates there.[19] In 1346 Henry of Northington was holding with the abbot a part of the land which had been Henry le Frankelyn's.[20] Northington was a few years later in the possession of Thomas Bifleet and his wife Alice,

1 Duthy, *Sketches of Hampshire*, 150.

2 Quoted in *A Brief Hist. of Northington and Swarraton*, by W. L. W. Eyre, rector of Swarraton.

3 Kemble, *Codex Dipl.* 836.

4 *V.C.H. Hants*, i, 469*b*.

5 Feet of F. Hants, 47 Hen. III, No. 47.

6 *Feud. Aids*, ii, 329.

7 He is called by both names in the account. Perhaps it was William Turner who obtained the lease, and Thomas Turner, his heir, who was holding it at the time of the Dissolution.

8 Mins. Accts. Hants, 30–31 Hen. VIII, R. 135, m. 44 *dorso*.

9 Pat. 32 Eliz. pt. 7, No. 1.

10 Close, 32 Eliz. pt. 20.

11 Chan. Inq. p.m. 3 Jas. I (Ser. 2), bdle. 1, No. 67.

12 One, at least, of the mills was in Kingsclere.

13 Feet of F. Hants, East. 17 Chas. I.

14 He was taxed for thirteen hearths in Northington in 1665; Lay Subs. R. 176/565. It is not mentioned in the will of his father, Sir Robert Henley, in 1655 (see Eyre's *Hist. of Swarraton and Northington*, 28), who is nevertheless stated to have been the purchaser in the memoir of the first earl of Northington by his grandson.

15 Feet of F. Hants, Trin. 27 Geo. III.

16 Eyre, *Hist. of Swarraton and Northington*, 35 et seq.

17 It was not so called till the seventeenth century.

18 *Pipe R.* (Pipe R. Soc.), xiii, 188.

19 *Testa de Nevill* (Rec. Com.), 239. Herbert Butler paid a rent of 4*s.* to the abbey, while Richard son of Ralph paid 22*s.* yearly.

20 *Feud. Aids*, ii, 329.

who were holding in her right two-thirds of a messuage, 2 carucates of land, 2 acres of meadow, 100 acres of wood, besides other land in Totford, Northington, Swarraton, and Burcot. In 1357 they granted these lands to Richard Burton and his wife Alice, together with the remainder of the other third due to Alice Bifleet at the death of John Hungerford, to hold of them and the heirs of Alice Burton for a yearly rent.[21] The grant stipulated that, failing heirs of the bodies of Richard Burton and his wife Alice, the lands should revert to Thomas and Alice Bifleet, and this seems to have occurred, for in the following century the Bifleets were seised of considerable lands in Northington.[22] Robert Bifleet held two messuages and certain land called Northington at his death 20 July, 1488.[23] He left an infant son and heir John, who evidently did not live to inherit the estate, for two years after Robert Bifleet's death a certain Thomas Bifleet died seised of land in Northington, and was succeeded by his brother John Bifleet, then aged thirty.[24] In May, 1635, Robert Bifleet, perhaps a grandson or great-grandson of this John, settled the 'manor of Northington,' in Northington, Swarraton, and Totford, on his son Thomas at the time of his marriage with Mary Speake.[25] In 1707 Francis Dickens and his wife Rachael sold the manor of Northington, with Totford and Swarraton, to Anthony Henley,[26] with whose estate at the Grange it has since descended.

TOTFORD (Totteford xii cent.)[27] is not mentioned by name in the Domesday Book, but since it was assessed at five hides in the thirteenth century it may perhaps be identical with the five hides held of the abbey in 1086 by Odo the Steward, which were then worth 50*s*.[28] William de Totford witnessed a charter to Hyde Abbey in 1191,[29] and was probably the William de Totford referred to in an inscription[30] which has been taken from the north wall of the old church. William was probably succeeded by Robert de Totford, who witnessed a grant to Roger Abbot of Hyde (1248-63),[31] and who had a son John living in 1262.[32] These were evidently members of a family which held part of the land now known as Totford. Later in the thirteenth century the whole of Totford, consisting of five hides, was held by Philip de Totford, Philip Butler, Peter de Fraxino and Henry le Frankelyn by service of one knight's fee to the abbot of Hyde.[33] Of these five hides Philip Butler held one, which was apparently annexed to the Butlers' neighbouring manor of Brown Candover (q.v.);[34] another, which was held by Peter de Fraxino, was acquired from his descendant John de Fraxino[35] before 1346 by Philip of Micheldever and Richard de Bordene, the former of whom doubtless added his moiety to his manor of Mottisfont (q.v.); Henry le Frankelyn's hide was afterwards divided between the abbot and Henry of Northington, while the remaining two hides formed the portion of Philip de Totford, and were probably inherited from him by Robert de Totford, who was living in 1272.[36] In 1314–15 John de Totford paid scutage for two hides in Totford;[37] he was living in 1341 when his name appears in the list of jurors in an inquisition concerning lands in Brown Candover and Northington.[38] He was succeeded by his son John de Totford, whose daughter and heir, Christine, was taken into the abbot's custody in 1349[39] when she was only four years old. The abbot immediately sold the marriage of Christine, together with the custody of her inheritance, to Thomas Warner of Southampton, then receiver in Winchester Castle, for 20 marks.[40] She married Richard son of Richard de Candover, clerk, who did homage for her inheritance in February, 1364–5,[41] and joined with his wife in 1387 in granting 10 marks rent from the manor of Totford to John Maydeford, clerk, and his heirs for ever.[42] Totford seems to have passed to the Tichborne family, for in 1571 Elizabeth Tichborne, widow, joined with William Rythe and his wife Margery in conveying 'Totford manor,' with its appurtenances, including a dove-cote to Richard Lee and William Sutton,[43] and in February, 1584–5 Benjamin Tichborne of Tichborne sold the capital messuage called Totford with its appurtenances in Northington and Swarraton, late the inheritance of Ambrose Tichborne of West Tisted to William Waller of Stoke Charity, saving only the estates made for life to Mary Tichborne and to Mary wife of William Rythe.[44] One-third of this property was apparently retained by the Tichbornes, while probably the other two-thirds were purchased (with the Grange estate) by Sir Robert Henley. In July, 1670, Susan Tichborne of Stoke Charity, with the consent of Sir Robert Henley, knt., of Northington Grange, conveyed to John Henley of Crawley one-third of the manor and demesne lands of Totford, then late in the occupation of Robert Soper, and one-third of Totford Inn in Brown Candover, during the life of Richard Hunt the elder of Popham.[45] This was probably the same third of Totford that was in the possession of Joseph Tichborne in 1717,[46] but the main part of the tenement was annexed to the Grange park estate, with which it has since descended.

The priory of Christchurch had two virgates of land in Northington which had been granted to it in 1249 by Matilda Breton, sister and heir of Roger Breton, in exchange for a corrody equal to the

[21] Feet of F. Hants, 31 Edw. III, file 26, No. 18.

[22] Thomas son of Thomas Bifleet was impleaded with Sir William Cobham for unjust disseisin of lands in Northington and elsewhere in 1373, but was acquitted since the land in question was at Burcot, to which he laid no claim. Assize R. 1476, m. 11.

[23] Chan. Inq. p.m. (Ser. 2), vol. 3, No. 107.

[24] Ibid. vol. 15, No. 22.

[25] Ibid. 18 Chas. I, pt. 1, vol. 498, No. 19.

[26] Feet of F. Hants, Trin. 6 Anne.

[27] In Edmund's charter concerning Basing, dated 945, part of the land was said to lie near Totdesford. *Liber de Hyda* (Rolls Ser.), 145.

[28] *V.C.H. Hants*, i, 470*a*.

[29] Harl. 1761, No. 38.

[30] 'Conceduntur et confirmantur pro anima Willelmi De Toteford 240 dies indulgencie.' For a print of the stone thus inscribed see Duthy, *Sketches of Hampshire*, 147.

[31] Harl. 1761, No. 22.

[32] Ibid. No. 50.

[33] *Testa de Nevill* (Rec. Com.), 232*b*.

[34] For the division of the five hides among the four tenants see *Feud. Aids*, ii, 329.

[35] Harl. 1761, No. 101.

[36] Ibid. 69.

[37] Ibid. 138.

[38] Chan. Inq. a.q.d. vol. 259, No. 3.

[39] Harl. 1761, fol. 173. In 1346 a John de Hampton held two hides in Totford (*Feud. Aids*, ii, 329), possibly he was this same John de Totford under another name, or he may have been holding the land during the minority of the heir.

[40] Harl. 1761, fol. 137.

[41] Ibid. 173.

[42] Feet of F. Hants, Trin. 11 Ric. II, 48.

[43] Ibid. Mich. 13–14 Eliz.

[44] Com. Pleas Deeds Enr. Hil. 27 Eliz. 13 *d*.

[45] Ibid. Mich. 22 Chas. II, 14.

[46] Recov. R. East. 4 Geo. I, 203.

allowance of one brother granted to her for life.[47] These lands were granted after the dissolution of the priory to Sir William Berkeley, 'the king's servant,' and then included a field called 'Northclose,' in the immediate occupation of the prior, together with other lands in Northington in the tenure of John Tucker.[48]

CHURCH The church of *ST. JOHN THE EVANGELIST* is a fine modern building by T. G. Jackson, R.A., standing well on a site which has a considerable fall to the east. It is of flint with stone dressings, and has a chancel with an octagonal east end, a nave with south porch, and a tall western tower with pinnacles and battlements. It is of fifteenth-century style, the treatment of the upper parts of the tower and the parapets in chequer work of flint and stone being very effective. The site of the old church is to the north-east, a little lower on the hill-side, marked by the tombstones of the old churchyard and a cross on the place where the church stood.

There are three old bells by William Cor, 1700, John Clarke, 1611, and John Wallis, 1602.

The plate of Northington and Swarraton disappeared in 1850 during a fire at the parish clerk's cottage, and the present plate is entirely modern. There are, however, two old pewter flagons with hinged lids which belong to the joint parishes.

The oldest register commences in 1579, but the first book is merely a collection of entries without order of date.[49] There are also churchwardens' books dating from 1769.[50]

ADVOWSON For many years Northington was a chapelry attached to Micheldever vicarage. A chapel was in existence at the time of the appropriation of Micheldever to Hyde Abbey, i.e. in 1308,[51] and was not separated from that church till 1847, when it was annexed to the vicarage of Swarraton.[52]

The elementary school, which lies in the village, was founded in 1864.

CHARITIES George Harding, by will proved 1879, left £200 to be invested and income applied in the distribution of bread among the poor of this parish and Swarraton. The legacy was invested in £205 7*s.* 10*d.* consols (with the official trustees). The dividends amounting to £2 5*s.* 8*d.* were in 1905 applied in the distribution of 112 half gallons of flour and in 112 half gallons of bread to fifty-six families.

POPHAM

Popeham (xi cent.).

The small parish of Popham, containing only 1,440 acres, lies north of Micheldever and East Stratton on high ground, which rises to nearly 600 ft. above the ordnance datum in the west of the parish.

The main road from Winchester to London passing west of the grounds of Stratton Park rises steadily as it enters Popham parish between thick hedges and wide stretching meadow and arable land, past the vicarage and schools,[1] which lie east of the road halfway up the hill, onwards to the simple grey stone church at the top of the hill. The several farms, farm buildings, and few outlying cottages which compose the main part of the village, lie just over the brow of the hill, immediately north and east of the church. Here to the west of the road is West Farm, a rambling old house with a front garden full of close clipped yew hedges of all shapes and sizes. To the east is the Manor Farm, through the yards of which runs the old Roman road[2] from Winchester to Silchester, which leaving the modern road as it curves slightly to the west near the vicarage runs directly north to meet the modern road again by the Wheatsheaf Inn at the cross roads near North Waltham.

The soil of the whole parish is clay and chalk, the subsoil chalk. Hence the ordinary crops, wheat, oats, and turnips, are grown on the 975½ acres of arable land, and the population is mostly engaged in agriculture; 223½ acres are given up to permanent grass. Of the 184 acres of woodland the chief copses are those in the north and Hellier's Copse in the east, near Dummer.

There is no inclosure award.

MANOR *POPHAM*, which was granted with Micheldever to the New Minster,[3] was held of the abbey before the Conquest by a freeman who was nevertheless unable to 'withdraw himself.'[4] It was among the lands held of the abbey by Hugh de Port in 1086. In the thirteenth and fourteenth centuries the St. Johns, heirs of the de Ports, succeeded as tenants under Hyde, but before the fifteenth century their rights had lapsed, while the actual tenants of the manor held it directly of the abbey. One of these tenants was Thurstan, clerk to William de Pont de l'Arche, evidently the same Thurstan who was sheriff of Hampshire in 1155. He obtained confirmation from the Empress Maud of all his land of Popham which he had held at the death of Henry I, and all his holdings within and without Winchester as he had had them on the day when Maud was received into the city, i.e. in 1141, during her triumphal progress after the capture of Stephen.[5] Henry II confirmed his mother's charter to Thurstan, and in 1157 granted him the privilege of keeping hounds to hunt hares and wolves.[6] During the next century the Braiboeufs of Cranborne and Robert de Pont de l'Arche and his successor, Sir Thomas West, knt.,[7] were tenants intermediate between the St. Johns and the actual

[47] Feet of F. Hants, 33 Hen. III, 32.
[48] *L. and P. Henry VIII*, xix (1), 812 (94).
[49] It is printed in full in Eyre's *Hist. of Swarraton and Northington*.
[50] Ibid. 65.
[51] Harl. 1761, fol. 117.
[52] Sumner's *Conspectus of Dioc. Winton*, 1854, p. 24.

[1] The school was built in 1860 and is attended also by the children from Woodmancott.
[2] The remains of two Roman villas have been discovered near Popham, though not actually within the parish boundary, one in College Wood in Woodmancott, just without the southern boundary, and the other near the Wheatsheaf Inn, in North Waltham, near the northern boundary. *V.C.H. Hants*, i, 306.
[3] In Edward the Elder's 'Golden Charter' to the abbey, mention is made of Popham with eight hides 'et dominium.' Kemble, *Codex Dipl.* 336.
[4] *V.C.H. Hants*, i, 469*b*.
[5] *Cal. Pat.* 1377–81, p. 110.
[6] Ibid.
[7] Harl. 1761, fol. 174; Cott. Domit. A. xiv, 237.

holder,[8] who was Gilbert de Popham, a successor of Thurstan the clerk.[9] Gilbert de Popham did homage for the lands of his mother Agnes in 1225 and died 4 November, 1251, leaving a son and heir Robert, aged twenty-five,[9a] who witnessed a charter to Hyde Abbey in 1277–8.[10] Robert was succeeded by John de Popham, probably his son, who was holding the manor in 1284, and did suit of court for one half of it to William de Braiboeuf at Cranborne.[11] He received a grant of free warren in Popham in 1305.[12] In 1309 he brought a suit against Hugh le Frankelyn for usurping common of pasture in Popham.[13] He was still living in 1316,[14] and in the previous year his holding in the parish was assessed at four hides,[15] but it seems likely that he died about this date, for in 1317 William de la Beere conveyed a messuage, four carucates of land, 200 acres of pasture, twenty acres of wood, and 100*s.* rent in Popham to Robert de Popham and his wife Alice,[16] and in 1346 Robert de Popham was said to hold there half a knight's fee which had belonged to John de Popham.[17] In 1360 Henry, brother and heir of Laurence de Popham, and probably son of Robert de Popham, did homage to the abbot of Hyde for four parts of a knight's fee in Popham.[18] This Henry was also sheriff of Hampshire, and in 1378, and again in 1401, obtained a royal confirmation of his predecessors' charters from the Empress Maud and from Henry II.[19] He died in December, 1417, leaving a son and heir Stephen, aged twenty-five,[20] who nevertheless did not formally enter into possession of his father's lands till January, 1422–3.[21] He had been knighted before his death in 1445, and had enfeoffed Sir John Lisle and others of his lands in trust for his four daughters.[22] The trustees conveyed Popham in 1464 to one of these daughters, Elizabeth, then wife of John Barantyne.[23] Their son John Barantyne succeeded to the manor, which was valued at ten marks at his death in 1485.[24] He left an infant son William, who was knighted before 1529, when Elizabeth wife of Robert Drury quitclaimed all her rights in the manor to him.[25] In 1552 Francis Barantyne of Haseley, in Oxfordshire, eldest son of Sir William Barantyne,[26] sold the manor to Peter Temple, Thomas Lee, and Thomas Wattys,[27] who conveyed it in the following year to Hugh Hunt of Kingsclere,[28] in whose family it remained for nearly two centuries. James Hunt, probably son or grandson of Hugh, died at Popham in 1605, and his son John inherited the manor[29] and was succeeded by a son James in 1625.[30] Another James Hunt was in possession in 1693.[31] In 1715 James, son and heir of James Hunt, conveyed the manor to John Bowen in order to bar the entail,[32] and in 1739 it was apparently purchased outright by Matthew Bowen,[33] from whom it descended in moieties to two co-heiresses, Anne Bowen and Louisa wife of Thomas Threlkeld. The latter was in possession of her moiety in 1756,[34] while the former seems to have conveyed her moiety to John fourth duke of Bedford, or his widow, Gertrude,[35] who in 1791 joined with Louisa Threlkeld, then a widow, and William Threlkeld her heir, in a settlement of the whole manor.[36] It is said to have been purchased by Alexander first Baron Ashburton, and is now in the possession of the present Lord Ashburton.

POPHAM. *Argent a chief gules with two harts' heads or therein.*

The church of *ST. KATHARINE CHURCH* was built by Lord Ashburton in 1875–8 on a new site, and contains no relic of the old church, which stood at the back of the manor farm, except a few glazed floor tiles in the vestry. The font is modern, its predecessor having been sent to North Waltham church.

In the bell turret is a single small bell.

The plate is a modern set, of chalice, paten, and flagon, given in 1878 by Lord Ashburton.

The register for 1628–1795 is preserved, but there is a gap between 1734 and 1774.

ADVOWSON The parish of Popham was originally served by a chantry chapel attached to Micheldever and endowed with certain lands. By Bishop Woodlock's ordination of Micheldever vicarage in 1308 it was arranged that the house and lands assigned of old to the chantry chapel of Popham should form part of the vicar's portion.[37] The vicar failed to perform the requisite number of services, so that Henry Popham and other inhabitants of 'the hamlet of Popham within the parish of Micheldever' impleaded the vicar before the commissary as to the provision of a chaplain to hold service daily and to perform sacraments except burial, and to dwell continually in a house at Popham ordained of old for that purpose. The vicar acknowledged the obligation and promised

[8] *Testa de Nevill* (Rec. Com.), 232*b*.

[9] Cf. Round, 'Rise of the Pophams,' *Ancestor*, vii, 59. Thurstan's son Richard was sheriff in 1159, and his brother William succeeded him in 1189. Perhaps he was succeeded at Popham by Warner de Popham and his wife Agnes who, with their heir Gerbertus (possibly a misreading for Herbertus), quitclaimed to John abbot of Hyde (1181–1222) the custody of woods on the bounds of Dummer; Harl. 1761, fol. 150. It may be noted that Warner 'the huntsman' had the custody of the heir of William son of Thurstan. An Agnes de Popham (wife of Robert de Popham) was holding four-fifths of a knight's fee in Popham late in the reign of Henry III. *Testa de Nevill* (Rec. Com.), 239.

[9a] Cal. Inq. p.m. Hen. III, 211.

[10] Cott. Domit. A. xiv, 43.

[11] Inq. p.m. (Ser. 1), file 38, No. 6.

[12] *Cal. Rot. Chart.* (Rec. Com.), 137.

[13] *Abbrev. Rot. Orig.*(Rec. Com.), i, 153.

[14] *Feud. Aids*, ii, 306.

[15] Harl. 1761, No. 138.

[16] Feet of F. Hants, Mich. 11 Edw. II, 26.

[17] *Feud. Aids*, ii, 329.

[18] Harl. 1761, fol. 174.

[19] *Cal. Pat.* 1377–81, p. 110; ibid. 1399–1401, p. 420.

[20] Inq. p.m. 6 Hen. V, 36.

[21] Harl. 1761, fol. 161*b*.

[22] Inq. p.m. 24 Hen. VI, No. 18.

[23] Ibid. 14 Edw. IV. 36. Stephen Popham left two daughters Elizabeth at his death; one was then married to John Wadham, and the other was a child of six years. It was probably the second who inherited Popham.

[24] Ibid. (Ser. 2), vol. 2, No. 22.

[25] Feet of F. Hants, Trin. 21 Hen. VIII.

[26] *Visitations of Suss.* (ed. Sir T. Phillipps), 1.

[27] Feet of F. Hil. 6 Edw. VI.

[28] Close, 7 Edw. VI, pt. 3, m. 39.

[29] Inq. p.m. (Ser. 2), vol. 289, No. 94.

[30] Ibid. vol. 414, No. 58.

[31] Recov. R. Trin. 5 Will. and Mary, m. 57.

[32] Close, 2 Geo. I, pt. 11, No. 14; Recov. R. Trin. 1 Geo. I, 50.

[33] Ibid. Hil. 13 Geo. II, m. 169.

[34] Feet of F. Div. Cos. Hil. 30 Geo. II.

[35] Anne Bowen parted with her moiety in 1765. It was acquired by Richard Woodhouse and John Griffith, who were perhaps agents in the sale to the Bedfords. Feet. of F. Hants, Mich. 6 Geo. III.

[36] Ibid. Hil. 31 Geo. III.; Recov. R. Hil. 31 Geo. III, 207.

[37] Harl. 1761, No. 117.

to fulfil it.[38] It was not till 1847 that this distant chapelry was separated from the mother church and annexed to Woodmancott.[39]

CHARITIES In 1845 William Waldron Harding by will, proved in the P.C.C., left £500 consols to the minister and churchwardens upon trust to apply the annual dividends for the relief of the poor. The sum of stock was reduced by the payment of legacy duty, and in 1867 the stock was raised to £500 consols by the gift of Mr. Jesse Vidler. The stock is held by the official trustees; the dividends, amounting to £12 10*s.* a year, were in 1905 applied in the distribution of 10 tons 17 cwt. of coals to nineteen labourers.

EAST STRATTON

Strattone (x cent.); Eastratton (xii cent.).

The parish of East Stratton, containing nearly 1,997 acres of land, lies immediately east of Micheldever, on ground which rises generally from a height of 296 ft. above the ordnance datum in the south to nearly 400 ft. in the north.

The main road from Winchester to London, following for the most part the course of the old Roman road, enters the parish north of Micheldever Wood, and about half a mile on, near one of the main entrances to Stratton Park, the seat of Lord Northbrook, sends off a branch road east towards the village. Thence it continues north and uphill towards Popham, running for a distance of nearly two miles along the western border of the well-wooded grounds of Stratton Park, and forming the western boundary of the parish. Stratton Park is indeed the chief feature of the parish, with its long stretch of woodland thickening towards the north, where Embley and Biddles Wood lead on to Rownest and College Woods, outside the northern boundary of East Stratton.

The narrow road that branches east to the village runs for about half a mile over level ground between the low wooden fence which bounds the southern stretch of the Stratton Park estate, and over which glimpses can be caught of the house and grounds, and the low hedges which encircle the arable lands lying away to the south. Then as it reaches the modern church which stands north opposite East Stratton farm it suddenly faces some picturesque thatched cottages and branches north and south, the branch to the south leading past groups of thatched cottages and the Plough Inn, which lies to the right towards Northington. That to the north sweeps sharply down past groups of thatched cottages which stand behind low brick walls and bright cottage gardens, to a low iron fence and gate which leads across the park to Stratton House. The descent is so steep that a brick gutter to carry off the surplus rainwater has been devised down the east side of the street, and this being edged by short grass, and being crossed before each house by a narrow stone plank, forms one of the most distinctive characteristics. The parsonage house is on the west side of the road, but since the living is a chapelry annexed to Micheldever vicarage, the vicar resides at Micheldever. The village school, built in 1850, stands at the bottom of the village just inside the park, east of the high stone cross which marks the site of the original church.

Stratton House is a comparatively modern building, with a central block having a tall Doric portico and wings at either end. The portico is of stone, but the rest of the house is mainly of plastered brickwork, and dates from the time of Sir Francis Baring, who bought the estate in 1801. Part of one wing is, however, of greater age, and is said to date from the latter part of the seventeenth century, and to have been inhabited by the ill-fated William Lord Russell, but no details of his time remain.

The great interest of the house lies in its pictures, although some of the best are in Lord Northbrook's London house. Two large paintings by Vandyck of Queen Henrietta Maria with the dwarf Sir Jeffrey Hudson, and of the earl of Newbury are among the best, but there are some good landscapes by Claude and Crome, and a long set of portraits, including Warren Hastings, Nelson, and Gibbon, as well as the well-known painting of the brothers Baring. In the dining-room, where are the two Vandyck pictures, is a painting by Reynolds of a sleeping girl, and a vast and ambitious view of the Fire of London by Loutherbourg, dated 1797; and a large collection of water-colours by Edward Lear, author of the *Book of Nonsense*, is preserved in the house. The stable court and offices lie at the back of the old wing, and the flower garden comes up to the house on two sides, the land rising fairly quickly behind. The soil being shallow, trees do not reach perfection, but there are many fine oaks, beeches, yews, &c., an avenue of trees showing the line of the old high road, which was diverted westward when Sir Francis Baring was improving his newly-purchased property.

The soil of the whole parish is clay and chalk, with a subsoil of chalk with Woolwich and Reading beds immediately south of the village. Thus the chief crops on the 622 acres of arable land are wheat, barley, oats, and turnips. With the exception of Dodsley Wood in the south of the parish, the 352 acres of woodland are comprised in Stratton Park and the woods adjoining. There are 344 acres of permanent grass in the parish. There is no inclosure award.

MANOR *EAST STRATTON* was granted with West Stratton to the New Minster *c.* 900, the two being then assessed at 9 hides.[1] It formed part of the portion of the prior and convent, and as such was not taken into the king's hands on the voidances of the abbey.[2] The lands were apparently held of the abbey in small parcels; for instance, in the thirteenth century one free tenant held 3 virgates there, another ½ a virgate, and a third 1½ virgates.[3] The grange or manor-house was leased with the demesne lands from time to time, the lessees in 1539 being Robert Clerke and Walter and William his sons, who rented it at £8 13*s.* 4*d.* At the same

[38] *Wykeham's Reg.* (Hants Rec. Soc.), ii, 467.

[39] Sumner, *Conspectus of Dioc. of Winton,* 1854, p. 30.

[1] Kemble, *Codex Dipl.* 336.

[2] *Cal. Pat.* 1385–9, p. 496.

[3] *Testa de Nevill* (Rec. Com.), 239.

time the perquisites of the court only amounted to 9*d.*[4] After the surrender of Hyde Abbey the manor was seized by the crown and sold in 1544 to Edmund Clerke, one of the clerks of the Privy Seal, and his wife Margaret,[5] from whom it was purchased in 1546 by Sir Thomas Wriothesley, earl of Southampton.[6] Its descent has since been coincident with that of Micheldever manor. The last earl of Southampton made Stratton Park one of his chief seats, and his son-in-law, Lord Russell, pulled down part of the hamlet and added it to his deer park.[7]

BURCOT'S FARM, which lies on the road from East Stratton to Northington, is evidently identical with 'Burcote,' which Edward the Elder granted to the New Minster *c.* 900. At that time there were 4½ hides attached to the holding.[8] Perhaps, therefore, it was at Burcot that Waleran the Huntsman held his 4½ hides of the abbey's demesne lands in 1086.[9] In 1199 Adam of Burcot held 1 hide in Burcot, the service from which was in dispute between Roger de Seures and Walter de Audeli and the abbot of Hyde.[10] Adam's nephews and heirs John of Burcot and Adam of Repling held respectively 2½ virgates and 1½ virgates of land in Burcot. In 1249 Hamo de Basing assured them in their tenure of these lands, for which they owed him certain rent.[11] Nicholas of Burcot in 1277 granted to the abbey of Hyde an annual rent of 1½*d.* from the master and brothers of St. John, Winchester, to hold for a yearly rent of a rose to John (*sic*) of Burcot,[12] and finally released all his claims to the abbot.[13] Before 1373 Burcot had passed to John Hampton in marriage with a certain Thomasine. At that date he brought a suit against Sir William Cobham and his wife Alice and others for disseisin of two-thirds of a messuage and certain lands in Northington, Swarraton, and Totford. It was decided that the tenement in question was Burcot, 'quedam mansio infra villam de Northampton,' and that John Hampton and his wife had been unjustly dispossessed of it, in consequence of which they recovered seisin against Sir William Cobham.[14] The later descent of the farm is unknown.

CHURCH The church of *ALL SAINTS* was begun in 1873 to take the place of the old church in the park, now removed, by the earl of Northbrook and the Hon. Francis Baring. It is in fifteenth-century style, from designs by T. G. Jackson, in chalk faced with flint with Chilmark stone dressings, and consists of chancel, nave, north aisle with arcade of four bays, vestry, organ chamber, south porch, and tower on the north, finished with a spire.

There is a modern ring of bells.

The plate consists of a communion cup and paten, silver-gilt, of 1709, and a silver paten, flagon, and alms-dish.

The registers are incorporated with those of Micheldever from 1540 down to 1813, but the following registers of earlier date are kept here: a book of baptisms, marriages, and burials 1719–1809, a burial book 1719–28, and a marriage book for 1760–1812. Till 1888 all burials took place in Micheldever churchyard.

ADVOWSON The church of All Saints is a chapel attached to Micheldever and in the same gift. There was a separate chapel here at the time of the appropriation of Micheldever church to Hyde Abbey.[15]

An iron building is used as a Primitive Methodist chapel.

[4] Mins. Accts. (Hants), 30–1 Hen. VIII, R. 135, m. 36 *d.*
[5] *L. and P. Hen. VIII*, xix (1), 132.
[6] Feet of F. Hants, Mich. 38 Hen. VIII.
[7] Value of the inheritance of Wriothesley, duke of Bedford, 1730, *penes* Lord Northbrook.
[8] Kemble, *Codex Dipl.* 336. It must, however, be noted that this charter is of very doubtful authenticity.
[9] *V.C.H. Hants*, i, 469*b*.
[10] Feet of F. Hants, 1 John, 6.
[11] Ibid. 33 Hen. III, 37.
[12] It seems, therefore, that Nicholas was holding the tenement of John of Burcot for the rent of a rose
[13] Harl. 1761, No. 99.
[14] Assize R. 1476, m. 11.
[15] Harl. 1761, fol. 117.

THE HUNDRED OF BUDDLESGATE

CONTAINING THE PARISHES OF

CHILBOLTON
COMPTON
CRAWLEY
Hunton Chapelry
HOUGHTON
HURSLEY
LITTLETON
MICHELMERSH
MILLBROOK
NURSLING
OTTERBOURNE
SPARSHOLT
Lainston Extra-Parochial
STOKE CHARITY
WEEKE
and
WONSTON

The above list represents the extent of the hundred at the time of the Population Returns of 1831. The parishes of Ashley and Little Somborne were added to the hundred before 1841, and probably at the same time the parishes of Chilbolton, Houghton, Michelmersh, Millbrook, and Nursling were transferred respectively to the hundreds of Wherwell, King's Somborne, Thorngate, Mainsbridge, and Redbridge.[1]

In the Domesday Survey the hundred of Buddlesgate or 'Bitelesiete,' as it is there called, included Chilbolton,[2] Crawley,[3] Nursling,[4] and part of Otterbourne.[5] The total assessment before the Conquest was $28\frac{1}{2}$ hides, which by 1086 had decreased to $21\frac{1}{2}$.[6] The parishes of Compton, Littleton, Sparsholt, and Weeke, as parcels of the great manor of Chilcomb, were probably included in the entry of that manor under the heading of the hundred of 'Falemere,'[7] which is probably an error for 'Falelie,' the modern Fawley. King's Somborne Hundred included Houghton[8] and the tithing of Awbridge in the parish of Michelmersh,[9] and Mainsbridge Hundred, the entire parish of Millbrook[10] and the tithing of Boyatt in the parish of Otterbourne,[11] while Wonston formed part of the hundred of Barton Stacey.[12] Stoke Charity is entered, perhaps wrongly, under Meon Hundred,[13] while the parishes of Hursley and Michelmersh are not mentioned. In the fourteenth century the area of the hundred had greatly increased, comprising as it did Hursley with the dependent hamlets of Ampfield, Pucknall, Merdon, Standon, Pitt, West Pitt, and Silkstead, Michelmersh with the tithing of Awbridge,[14] Stoke Charity,[15] Compton with the hamlet of Sparkford, Nursling, Weeke with the hamlet of Fullflood, Sparsholt, Littleton, Crawley with the chapelry of Hunton, and Chilbolton, parts of the parishes of Otterbourne, Millbrook, and Wonston, the tithings of Houghton Drayton in the parish of Houghton, and Bransbury in the parish of Barton Stacey,[16] and parts of knights' fees in Wishanger

[1] Cf. the Population Returns of 1831 and 1841.
[2] *V.C.H. Hants*, i, 464, 494.
[3] Ibid. 460.
[4] Ibid. 464.
[5] Ibid. 489.
[6] Ibid. 460, 464, 489, 494.
[7] Ibid. 463*b*.
[8] Ibid. 477, 480, 494, 503.
[9] Ibid. 480, 494.
[10] Ibid. 467, 487, 489.
[11] Ibid. i, 500*b*.
[12] Ibid. 467*a*, 488*b*, 504*b*.
[13] Ibid. 461*b*.
[14] *Feud. Aids*, ii, 309.
[15] Ibid. 325, 348.
[16] Ibid. ii, 309.

and Newton.[17] The vills of Boyatt, and Shirley in Millbrook, were still included in the hundred of Mainsbridge,[18] and Sutton Scotney and Norton Valery in the parish of Wonston in that of Barton Stacey;[19] Cranborne, also in Wonston, was in the hundred of Micheldever,[20] while the tithing of North Houghton in the parish of Houghton was included in the hundred of King's Somborne.[21] The area of the hundred thus underwent but little change until the beginning of the nineteenth century, the only alterations consisting in

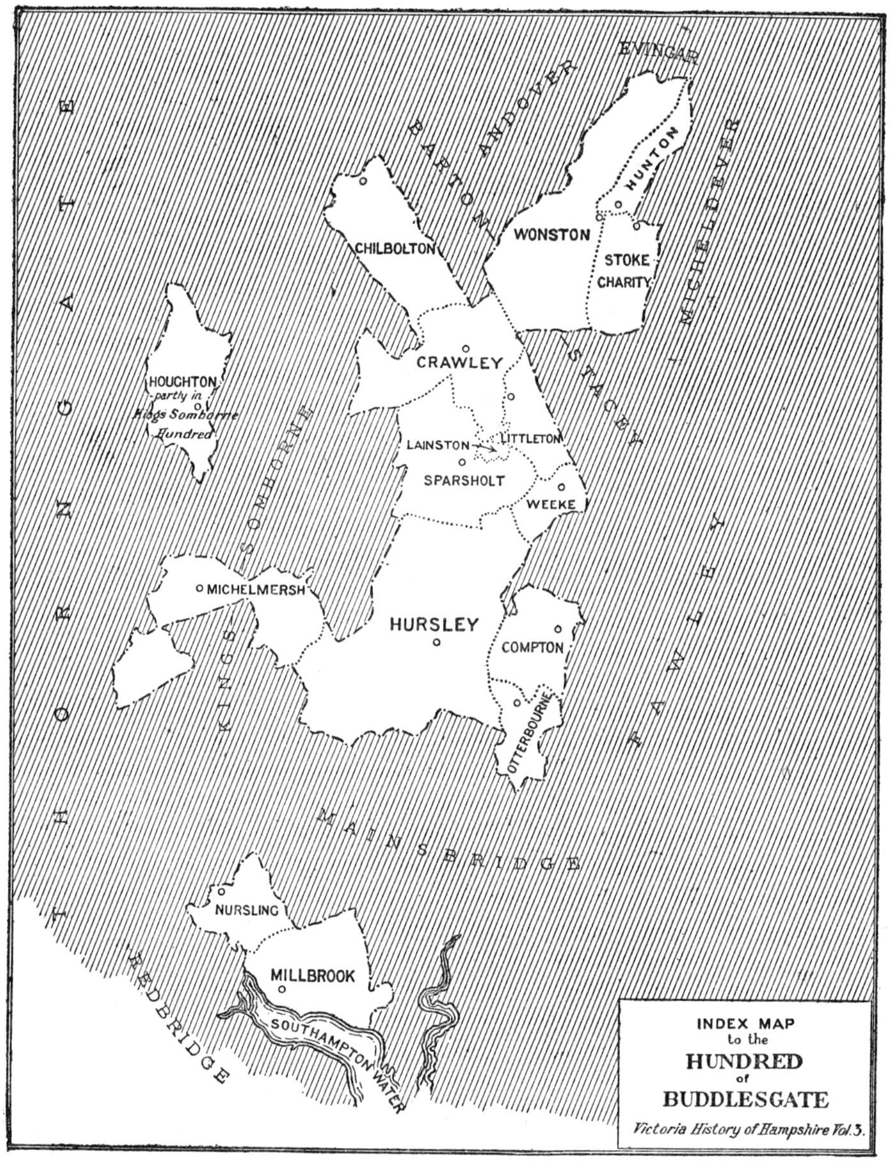

the addition of some tithings and the removal of others. In 1831 the tithing of North Houghton was still in the hundred of King's Somborne. The hundred was the property of the prior and convent of St. Swithun, Winchester,[22] and passed with much of their property to the dean and chapter at the Dissolution.

[17] *Feud. Aids*, ii, 325, 348. In 1316 the boroughs of Romsey and Stockbridge and other places were assessed under Buddlesgate although they were really in the hundred of King's Somborne (*Feud. Aids*, ii, 310).

[18] Ibid. 318.

[19] Ibid. 311, 326, 348.

[20] Ibid. 306, 329, 348, 365.

[21] Ibid. 310, 325, 351, 352.

[22] Ibid. ii, 309.

CHILBOLTON

Chelbaltone (xii cent.).

Long undulating lines of hilly country sweeping down towards the north and west to the valley of the Test make up the 3,122 acres of land which are included in the parish of Chilbolton, while the Test supplies the 12 acres of water. It is not surprising that the village lies on the edge of the valley close by the Test, where the first settlers made their encampment, valuing the Test as their water supply and the Downs as their pasture land.

The main road from Winchester to Andover, going in a north-westerly direction, leaves Barton Stacey on the east and winds uphill to the west of the low hedge that forms the north-eastern boundary line of Chilbolton. Close by Newton Cottages, which are actually in Newton Stacey parish though they seem locally in Chilbolton, a narrow lane branches to the west from the main road and passing by Gravel Hill Farm on the left turns abruptly north-west into the village. In the centre where the road broadens stands a large oak tree planted on the twenty-first birthday of Bishop Richard Durnford, whose father was rector of Chilbolton. It is surrounded by a wooden seat and a triangular grass plot. A turn to the right leads to the rectory, which is a picturesque red-brick house with hipped red-tiled roofs, H-shaped in plan. Originally an early seventeenth-century building, it was much altered and refitted at the beginning of the eighteenth century, and has much good panelling of the latter date, and a little of the former. At the back of the house is a fine avenue of about forty lime trees. Below the rectory is the village school, built in 1844 on the site of the original school, on a tenement which the lords of the manor gave 'to the rectory of Chilbolton for ever for the purpose of a school' in 1837.[1] Opposite the rectory is the church of St. Mary standing in a long and rather narrow churchyard, and behind the church is Manor Farm or House, close to the Test and on the site of the original manor-house. The houses of the village lie south-west of the church and rectory, being scattered along a straggling village street. There are now groups of modern cottages, but except for these and two or three large houses built of red brick, the village might belong to the sixteenth or seventeenth century with its low-roofed, tiled, thatched, and half-timbered cottages, their beauty heightened during the autumn months by masses of bright-coloured creepers. The River Test, separating the parish from Wherwell, forms its northern and western boundary line and runs almost parallel with the village street. Hence while the Downs stretch away behind the houses on the south-east of the village, the Test valley is on the north-west, and beyond it are the Wherwell hills. Chilbolton Common lies to the west between the village and the river. There is a difference in the soil marking the same change from hill to valley. The Downs on the south and east are mostly chalk with a chalk subsoil, but near the river the soil becomes more of a mixture of chalk and gravel, and even the subsoil is in some places gravel. Root crops are the most plentiful on this soil, though wheat and barley are also grown.

MANOR. *CHILBOLTON* was granted by King Athelstan to the church of Winchester,[2] and was said at the time of the Domesday Survey to have always belonged to the minster (*in monasterio*).[3] Five hides and 3 virgates of it were then held by the bishop for the monks, while 1 hide was held of him by Richard Sturmy.[4] In the days of Edward the Confessor the 5-hide manor of the church had been assessed at 10 hides, while the 1 hide held by Richard Sturmy had been assessed at three and had been held of the bishop by a certain Ordwald. The latter was probably the 'certain steward' of one entry who 'could not betake himself anywhere' and who held two of the hides by villein tenure (*quasi villanus*). Chilbolton was confirmed to the prior and convent in the general confirmation of their manors made by the pope in 1206 and again in 1243,[5] and Edward I gave them free warren in their demesne lands in Chilbolton in 1300.[6]

Robert de Berton and Matilda his wife received licence in 1332 to grant to the prior and convent one messuage and a carucate of land in Chilbolton, and it seems possible that this may have been the land which Richard Sturmy had held at the time of Domesday. In connexion with this transaction there is an entry on the Receiver's Roll of 1334 of an annual payment of £10 to Robert de la Berthone 'pro terris et tenementis ab eo perquisitis in manerio de Chilboltone.'[7] Evidently the manor was valuable chiefly for sheep-farming, since the Receiver's Roll of 1334 shows that while the rents from the manor were only worth 20*s.* yearly, the receipts for wool reached £37 9*s.* 11*d.*[8] Also it was evidently one of the manors where the prior went hunting. It is especially mentioned in an entry on the Receiver's Roll of the same year giving expenses for fish, flesh, and various other provisions, including salt meat for the expeditions made during that year.[9]

With the surrender of the priory in 1539 the manor passed into the king's hands to be granted in 1541[10] to the dean and chapter of Winchester. They in the usual way leased out the manor for a set term of years at an annual rent of about £23, and then seem to have cared little more about the management of the estate except to see that the rent was paid. A lease made in 1622 for twenty-one years to Edward Tutt of Chilbolton of the 'site of the manor place of Chilbolton' with the appurtenances includes all the customary services of the tenants, a parcel of ground called 'Nytherne,' a mead called Titcombe,[11] and a cottage called 'Shepheard's Coote.' During the period of the Commonwealth, when deans

1 Chilbolton Parish Register, *sub anno.* The school was enlarged in 1874, 1878, and 1894.

2 Dugdale, *Mon.* i, 210; Kemble, *Codex Dipl.* v, 215.

3 *V.C.H. Hants*, i, 464.

4 Ibid. 494.

5 *Cal. of Pap. Letters*, i, 21, 201.

6 Chart. R. 29 Edw. I, No. 94, m. 12.

7 *Obed. R. of St. Swithun* (Hants Rec. Soc.), 233.

8 Ibid. 118. The Compotus Rolls for the manor in Winchester Cathedral Library also show this very plainly.

9 Ibid. 236.

10 Pat. 33 Hen. VIII, pt. 9, m. 5–10.

11 This name occurs in the earliest Compotus Rolls from 1384, and continues through them all. In 1384 is the entry of '12*d.* de pastura in Titecumbe.' At a later date, in 1497, is an entry of 2*s.* for rent arising out of a meadow containing by estimation 2 acres called 'Tytcombe' and held by John Titcumbe of the lord of the manor. The modern survival is Testcombe Cottage, which nestles at the foot of West Down in the valley of the Test, and close to the western border line of the parish.

and chapters, canons and prebends, were abolished, and their land confiscated, the manor of Chilbolton, with the fishing, hawking, hunting, and fowling in the same, was sold to John Lisle by the commissioners appointed by the Long Parliament.[12] With the Restoration the dean and chapter lands were restored, but in 1861 the manor of Chilbolton was vested in the Ecclesiastical Commissioners, who are now lords of the manor in place of the dean and chapter.

The prior and convent had ordinary manorial rights in the manor of Chilbolton, and the Court Rolls and Compotus Rolls preserved in Winchester Cathedral Library[13] show how there, as elsewhere, they carefully guarded their rights.

The mill at Chilbolton existed at Domesday, and was then worth 15*s.* Rent from and repairs of this mill are entered duly throughout the Compotus Rolls. Thus in the earliest, that for 1384, there is a note of no rent for that year; in 1444 John Hale paid 60*s.* rent for the farm of the mill. As examples of the repairs done are accounts in 1475 and 1497. In the former year 'le courbe molendini' was renewed, 15 lb. of iron were bought for lengthening 'le spyndell' of the mill and 'le necke' of the same 'spyndell' was renewed. In 1495 new 'Flodgates' were made for the mill, the materials for which alone cost 28*s.* 4*d.*

From the first the lords of the manor had right of multure. In the late leases of the mill with the manor in the seventeenth century the dean and chapter especially reserved for their tenants the right to grind their corn at the lord's mill. The rent of the mill was worth £3 6*s.* 8*d.* in 1622.[14]

A dove-house was also one of the other valuable possessions of the prior and convent in the manor, and 100 pair of doves seem to have been the average 'ferm' from the same. The old dove-house, with its tiled roof and its interior walls composed of line upon line of chalk blocks at regular intervals, still exists.

The fishery of the manor has also played an important part in its history. The farm of 'the fishery at Titcombe' is given throughout the Compotus Rolls at rents varying upwards from 10*s.*, that given in 1384. According to the custom of the manor right of fishing in the lord's water with a rod and net called a shoe net from Testcombe Bridge (Titcombe) to Butcher's mead, and incident thereto a right of way along the river bank between these points, was always enjoyed by the copyhold tenants of the manor. Under the Inclosure Award of 1838 all these rights of fishery, with full liberty of ingress and egress for purposes of fishing, were reserved to the copyhold tenants. Incident to this was the *cause célèbre* of 1890, in which the owners and occupiers of ancient copyhold tenements, then enfranchised, failed to make good their title to these rights, since it was held they could not be claimed by prescription, and had ceased on the enfranchisement of the copyholds.[14a]

CHURCH The church of *ST. MARY* is built of flint rubble with chalk and Isle of Wight stone dressings, and has red-tiled roofs to nave and chancel, while the tower is of wood on a stone base, with a red-tiled spire. The church stands at the east end of the village, being approached through a small wooden gate leading to the south porch, and consists of a chancel 31 ft. 6 in. by 18 ft., with a modern vestry on the north; a nave 38 ft. 8 in. by 20 ft. 4 in.; north and south aisles 11 ft. 2 in. and 8 ft. 3 in. wide respectively; and a south-west tower.

The nave preserves its twelfth-century length and width, and a good deal of walling of that date; but the chancel seems to have been entirely rebuilt in the first quarter of the thirteenth century, and enlarged in both dimensions, being now only 27 in. narrower than the nave, and 7 ft. shorter. The aisles were added to the nave early in the fourteenth century, and there is nothing to show that any earlier aisles existed. The only detail of the twelfth-century work is a window set high in the wall at the south-west of the nave, having a plain round head built in plastered rubble. Its outer face is built up and cannot be seen, so that any question as to its exact date must remain doubtful, but its sill is no less than 15 ft. from the floor level, a fact which in itself suggests an early date. The rough walling, 2 ft. 6 in. thick, contemporary with this window, is clearly to be seen above the nave arcades, having been underbuilt in the usual fashion.

The chancel has three modern lancet windows at the east, a reproduction of the original arrangement, of which traces were found during repairs. The three original lancets had been replaced by a fifteenth-century window, and it in turn by a wooden frame. In the north wall of the chancel are two lancet windows, the sill of the eastern of the two being higher in the wall than that of the other, and in the south wall is a like arrangement. The heads of all four windows have been renewed, but the rear arches are original, and show traces of colour. West of the north window is a modern arch to the north vestry and organ chamber, while in a similar position in the south wall of the chancel is a plain priest's door, and to the west of it a square-headed fifteenth-century window of two cinquefoiled lights. In the north wall of the vestry is set a fifteenth-century two-light window, with a recess below it containing various architectural fragments found in the course of repairs.

The chancel arch and nave arcades of two bays are of very poor and plain detail, with pointed arches of two chamfered orders, octagonal pillars, and moulded capitals. The bases of the nave arcades point to a date at the beginning of the fourteenth century, and it is possible that all the work may be of this date, though the poverty of its detail suggests a much later period. Remains of painting, no doubt a Doom, were formerly to be seen over the chancel arch, but have now entirely disappeared.

The north aisle has an early fourteenth-century east window, of two trefoiled lights with a quatrefoil in the head, and there is another window of like detail in the north wall. West of it is a plain pointed doorway, and beyond it a single trefoiled light, the west window of the aisle being of the same description.

The east window of the south aisle is of the same design as that of the north aisle, except that the opening in the head has no cusps, and this detail also occurs in the easternmost window in the south wall. The south door is 4 ft. 7 in. wide, with a moulded arch of fourteenth-century date, and modern jambs,

[12] Close, 1650, pt. 4, No. 37.

[13] Seen by permission of the librarian, Rev. F. T. Madge.

[14] From lease made in that year to Edward Tutt.

[14a] *Law Rep.* Chan. Div. 1890, xlv, 98–126, Tilbury *v.* Silva.

Chilbolton Church : Pulpit and Screen

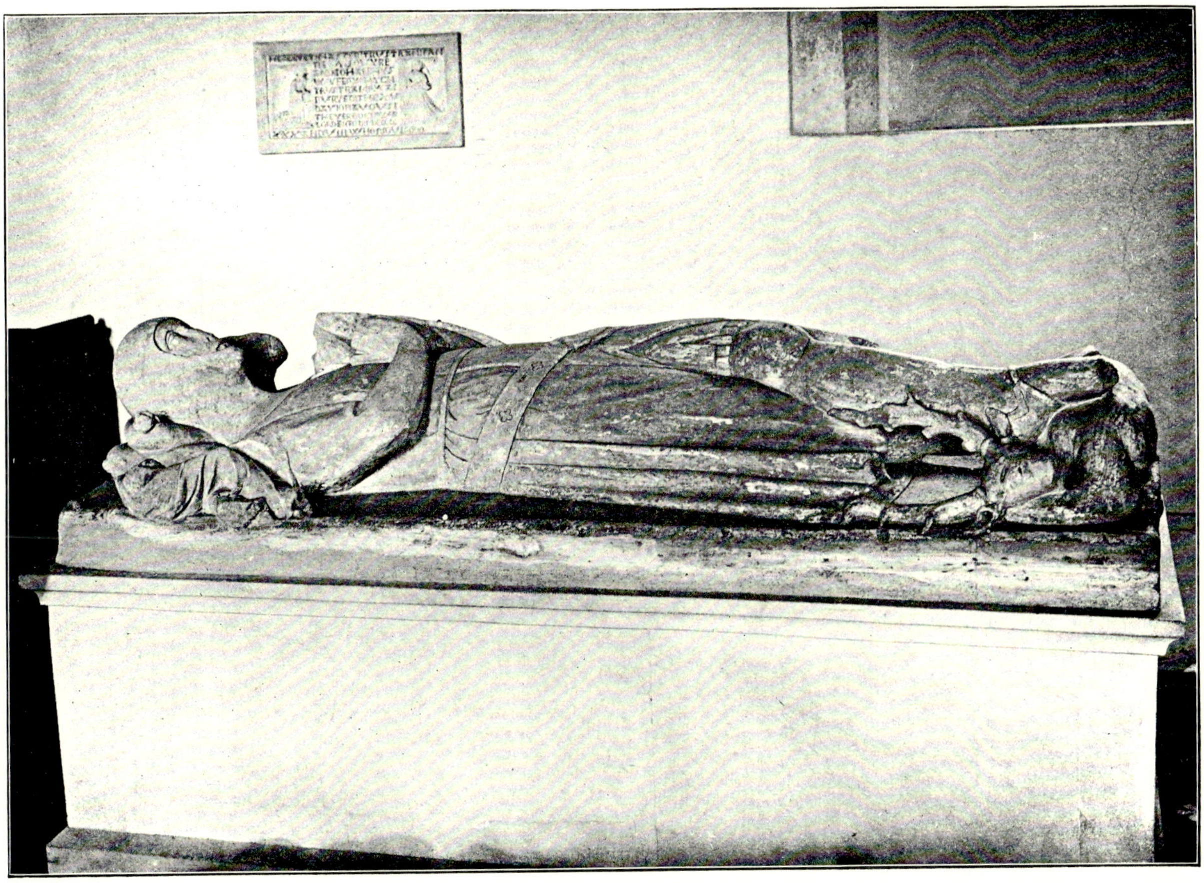

Effigy in Michelmersh Church

and over it is built a porch of plastered masonry dating from 1867. To the west of it is a single trefoiled light, as in the north aisle. The west window of the nave is of three cinquefoiled lights, with tracery of fifteenth-century style, and was, till 1893, the east window of the chancel.

The lower stage of the tower is of masonry, and of comparatively recent date, the upper stage and spire being of wooden construction. The roof of the nave is modern except for the tie-beams, and the aisle roofs are modern (1893), while that of the chancel is hidden by plaster.

The fifteenth-century stair to the rood-loft remains at the north-east angle of the nave, and at the west of the chancel is an oak screen with a central doorway, and six openings on either side with pierced tracery in the heads, the lower panels being solid. It is much patched, but in part of fifteenth-century date, and against its eastern face on either side of the central opening are set three seats with linen-panelled fronts of a late type, probably of the second quarter of the sixteenth century. The pulpit, a good specimen of early seventeenth-century work, is a half-hexagon with tall moulded and carved panels, and guilloche ornament on the styles. It has a projecting bookboard, carried by scrolled brackets, and stands on a modern linen-panelled base. At the south-east of the chancel is a plain arched piscina recess, with a stone shelf, probably coeval with the wall in which it is set, and the altar table is a good example of early seventeenth-century work, with carved ornament. At the east ends of both aisles are piscinae, that in the north aisle with a trefoiled head, and the other with an uncusped ogee head; both are probably contemporary with the aisles.

The font, near the south door, is modern, octagonal with carved panels, and none of the fittings of the church, beyond those already mentioned, are ancient.

There are three bells, the treble having an inscription common enough in itself, but notable for the badness of its lettering and spelling.

I am the forst and thof bot smal
It wil be herd abofe you al. 1641.

On the waist are the initials T.H. T.H. The second bell, cast in 1890 by Taylor, retains its former inscription: 'Rejoice in God, I. D. 1630,' the initials being those of John Dunton of Salisbury. The tenor, of about the same date, bears only 'Feare God.'

The church plate includes a good Elizabethan cup, with cover paten, undated; a very fine two-handled secular cup or posset-pot of 1659, and a plated alms dish.

The only monument in the church that has any interest is a seventeenth-century brass close by the pulpit on the north wall of the chancel, to the memory of Thomas Tutt,[15] the date of whose death is not filled in.

The earliest parish register begins with mixed entries in 1699, and continues until 1772, with a few stray entries to 1776. Inductions to the rectory and names of the rectors at a later date are inscribed in this book, and among them are Dr. Alured Clarke, dean of Exeter, prebendary of Westminster and Winchester, and rector of Chilbolton; Dr. Thomas Cheyney, dean of Winchester, inducted 1748; Dr. Jonathan Shipley, dean of Winchester, inducted 1760; and Matthew Woodford, prebendary of Winchester, inducted 1789. Evidently the living was a sinecure for the deans and prebendaries of the eighteenth century, giving them good fishing in the Test, and good hunting on the Downs. The second book is also a mixed register from 1722 to 1769. The third book gives baptisms and burials from 1774 to 1813. These fill up about one-third of the book, and the rest of it is practically a journal of 'remarkable occurrences under Crosbie Morgill, collated to the rectory in 1830.' He tells how the parish clerk was suspended for liquor, how the machinery riots of 1830 told on the nerves of the parishioners, how the cholera visited the neighbouring villages in 1832, and how influenza began as a 'national judgment' in 1837. The marriages from 1784 to 1812 are given in a separate book.

ADVOWSON The advowson of Chilbolton, with sole jurisdiction over the church,[16] has belonged to the bishops of Winchester probably from the time when Chilbolton itself was granted to the church at Winchester by King Athelstan.[17] The church existed at the time of Domesday,[18] was taxed at £23 6*s*. 8*d*. in 1290,[19] and at £30 at the time of the Dissolution.[20]

William of Wykeham changed the feast of the dedication of the church of Chilbolton from 23 August to 4 October, because at the former date the parishioners were so busy harvesting that they were unable to keep the festival.[21]

CHARITIES In 1710 the Rev. Charles Layfield, D.D., by will gave one-fourth part of his estate to the poor of Winchester, Chilbolton, Wrotham in Kent, Croston, Lancashire, and Tewin, Hertfordshire. As the result of proceedings in the Court of Chancery in 1751, the trust fund was apportioned in regard to population, and one-eighth part assigned to this parish, now represented by £273 9*s*. 2*d*. consols, and applied for the benefit of the poor.

In 1844 a building and site was conveyed in trust for a National school.

15 Edmund Tutt farmed the manor of Chilbolton in 1622. He may have been some relative of Thomas.

16 *Valor Eccl.* (Rec. Com.), ii, 507.

17 See 'Manor.'

18 *V.C.H. Hants*, i.

19 *Pope Nich. Tax.* (Rec. Com.), 210*b*.

20 *Valor Eccl.* (Rec. Com.), ii, 16.

21 *Wykeham's Reg.* (Hants Rec. Soc.), ii, 369.

COMPTON

Cuntone (xi cent.) ; Cumyngton (xvi cent.).

The Roman road from Winchester to Southampton running south-west almost parallel with the Itchen cuts through the whole length of the eastern part of Compton parish. On either side of the road are the chalk downs which rise to the south of Winchester, Compton Down on the right just outside Winchester and Shawford Down on the left beyond Compton village, which lies in the valley between the two. The whole parish consists of 2,803 acres, of which 17 are water.[1]

Compton village street crosses the Roman road as it runs south-west. The branch which runs west from the main road leads past low thatched cottages, one of which serves as the post office, to the church on the left facing the village school, while west of the church at the top of Carman's Lane is the Rectory, dating from 1780. Then the street becomes a narrow lane leading on between fields, thick hedges, and farm buildings to picturesque Dummer's Farm. From here it turns to the right and runs north over Compton Down and on to Oliver's Battery. The eastern branch of the village street leads by a group of farm buildings to the manor-house on the left-hand side of the road, and then becomes a narrow lane called Place Lane which leads down to the river and over the canal into Twyford parish. A few yards up the main road from Compton village a road leads east on to the downs to Shawford hamlet,[2] which is now the most populous part of Compton parish, although less than a hundred years ago it consisted only of a few thatched cottages.[3] It has a station on the London and South-Western and Great Western Railways on a joint line, which runs through the parish close to the western border line, and it is since the opening of the railway that Shawford has grown in importance. The modern residences of which Shawford is mostly composed are grouped on the hill on the north side of the road facing the Downs, while the village shops, the inn, and the post office are near the station. The old mill, which is generally counted locally in Shawford, is just beyond the canal, and is properly in Twyford parish, though the mill stream forms the western boundary line of Compton. Shawford House, which lies still further west, is also in Twyford parish.

Further along the main Roman road as it continues in a south-westerly direction towards Otterbourne are modern residences lately built. Oakwood House is partly in Compton, partly in Twyford. The south-westerly corner of the parish is comprised of part of the lands of the manor of Silkstead, which is a hamlet partly in Compton and partly in Hursley parish.

The soil of the parish, since it is part of the great chalk downs, is entirely chalk with a subsoil of chalk, though it seems to touch a layer of sand and gravel in the lower ground in the south-west towards Silkstead. The chief crops are wheat, barley, and turnips.

MANORS

The manor of *CHILCOMB* as granted by King Edward to the church of Winchester in 908 included land in Compton.[4] In Domesday Book Compton, though not mentioned by name, was evidently included in the entry under Chilcomb,[5] and the modern manor of Barton and Buddlesgate representing Chilcomb still comprises part of Compton parish.

One of the earliest references to the manor of *COMPTON WASSELING* is in 1250, in which year Thomas son of Herbert de Boarhunt and Emma his wife quitclaimed 70 acres of land, 10 acres of wood, 2½ acres of meadow, and 8*s.* rent in Compton from themselves and the heirs of Emma to Nicholas Wasseling in exchange for a messuage and 40 acres of land in Ropley.[6] Nicholas was succeeded by John Wasseling, probably his son, who died towards the end of the reign of Edward I seised of a messuage, 300 acres of arable land, 8 acres of pasture, a mill,[7] and rents of free and customary tenants,[8] leaving as his heirs his two daughters, Nichola wife of Henry de Sardene, and Maud widow of John de Pairok.[9] In 1303 a moiety of the manor was settled on Henry de Sardene and Nichola in fee-tail with contingent remainder to Margaret daughter of Nichola and her heirs.[10] It is probable that they died without issue and the moiety passed to Margaret, who seems to have married Robert de Thorncombe, to whom Richard de Codinge and Maud his wife, evidently Nichola's sister, quitclaimed a messuage and 1½ carucates of land in Compton, no doubt representing the other moiety of the manor, in 1315.[11] Before 1338 Robert had died, for in that year two parts of three messuages, a mill, lands and rents in Compton, and the reversion of the third part, after the death of Margaret de Thorncombe, were settled on Thomas de Thorncombe, a merchant of Winchester, and Elizabeth his wife.[12] Some time afterwards Thomas obtained licence to celebrate mass in the oratory of his manor house,[13] but soon fell so deeply into debt that in 1352 John Malweyn, citizen and merchant of London, was seised of a rent of £20 from his manor and his messuages and shops in Winchester, which were in addition burdened by an annual payment of £4 to Nicholas de Thorncombe and £2 11*s.* 8*d.* to the prior of St. Swithun.[14] The subsequent history of the manor is obscure, but it ultimately came into the Philpot family,[15] though at what date is

[1] Pop. Ret. 1901. The Ordnance Survey gives the area at 2,109 acres.

[2] In 1527 John Smythe of Shawford was amerced at the manor court of Barton for trespass on lands in Compton which belonged to the prior and convent of St. Swithun (Ct. R. in Winchester Cathedral Lib.).

[3] There was a group of about six seventeenth-century cottages near the station until about five years ago, when they were burnt by a spark from a train settling on the thatch.

[4] Kemble, *Codex Dipl.* ii, 153.

[5] *V.C.H. Hants*, i, 463*b*.

[6] Feet of F. Hants, Trin. 34 Hen. III.

[7] It was worth £3 a year, £2 18*s.* of which was paid to the bishop of Winchester.

[8] There is no mention of the parish in which the tenements are situated.

[9] Inq. p.m. 30 Edw. I, No. 16. The tenements were stated to be held of the prior and convent of St. Swithun by rent of £1 13*s.* 8*d.*

[10] Feet of F. Div. Cos. Mich. 31 Edw. I.

[11] Ibid. Hants, Mich. 9 Edw. I. During the life of Richard and Maud he was to pay a rent of 11 marks for it.

[12] Ibid. Hants, Mich. 12 Edw. III.

[13] Egerton MS. 2032, fol. 49.

[14] Inq. p.m. 35 Edw. III, pt. 2 (1st Nos.), No. 5.

[15] The Philpots were descendants of Sir John Philpot, a Kentish man who was Lord Mayor of London in 1378. It is possible that Sir John purchased his interest in the manor from John son and heir of John Malweyn.

uncertain.[16] However, John Philpot, who was sheriff of Hampshire in 1460, died seised of the manor in 1484.[17] By his will dated 24 November, 1484, he left the manor to trustees for a term of years, directing them to build a chapel to the honour of the Holy Trinity and the Virgin Mary in the east end of the parish church of Compton, where he and his wife Elizabeth should be buried in a tomb with a stone portraiture of himself and his wife and his seventeen children.[18] At the end of the term it passed to his son and heir John, sheriff of Hampshire in 1501, who died seised in 1502, leaving a son and heir Peter aged fourteen and more.[19] Peter, who was knighted some thirty years later, sheriff of Hampshire in 1524 and again in 1535, died seised of the manor in 1540, when it passed to his son and heir Thomas,[20] who remained in possession[21] until his death in 1586.[22] Sir George Philpot son of Thomas dealt with the manor by fine in 1606,[23] and died seised in 1624, his heir being his son John.[24] The latter died some ten years later, and Compton Wasseling then passed to his son and heir George,[25] who sold it in 1640 to Sir Benjamin Tichborne.[26] The manor remained in the Tichborne family for about eighty years, Sir Henry Joseph Tichborne, bart. dealing with it by fine as late as 1717.[27] It next passed to Sir Robert Worsley, bart. and Henry Worsley sons of Sir Robert Worsley, bart., of Appuldurcomb, who sold it in 1722 to William Heathcote of Hursley,[28] with whose descendants it remained until 1890,[29] in which year the trustees of the late Sir William Heathcote, bart. sold the whole of the Compton estate. The greater part of it was purchased by Mr. Edward Eames of Silkstead Priors.[30] The manor as such has long ceased to exist, the whole of the copyholds having been enfranchised many years ago.

PHILPOT. *Azure a bend ermine.*

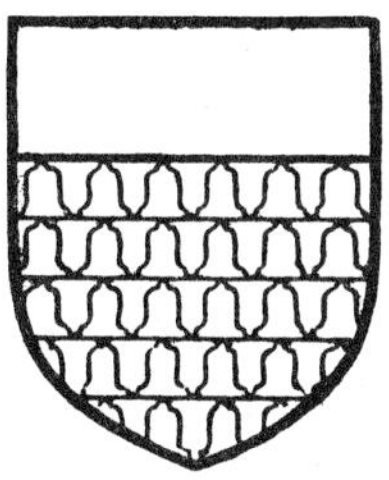

TICHBORNE. *Vair a chief or.*

CHURCH The church of *ALL SAINTS* is a small twelfth-century building of chancel 21 ft. 6 in. by 14 ft. 6 in., and nave 40 ft. 6 in. by 19 ft., which has been enlarged in 1904–5 by the process of building a large nave and chancel against it on the south side, turning the old church into a north chapel and aisle. This has been done with all due regard to the old building, and has involved as little destruction of old work as was possible under the circumstances.

The old nave retains its two original north windows, plain round-headed lights set high in the wall, the western of its southern pair of windows, its north doorway of two orders with zigzag ornament on the arch and the abaci of the jamb shafts, which have capitals of advanced detail, *c.* 1160, and high in the west wall a round-headed light like those on the north. Below it is a two-light fifteenth-century window with a transom, and in the north wall, below the eastern of the two original windows and a little further to the east, is a small cinquefoiled fifteenth-century light, probably connected with the former existence of a north nave altar.

The chancel possesses no twelfth-century features, though its plan and dimensions make it probable that its walls are in part of that date. Its east window, *c.* 1320, is of three lights, the middle one trefoiled and the others uncusped, and in the north wall are two thirteenth-century lancets, the western at a much lower level than the other. In the south wall were formerly a sixteenth-century window of two uncusped lights, and a wide thirteenth-century lancet, the former of which is now in the south wall and the latter in the north of the new chancel. A south doorway from the old chancel is now set, blocked up, in a corresponding position, in the new.

The chancel arch, *c.* 1300, springs from responds with very slender triple shafts, and has an arch of two orders, the outer with a quirked hollow chamfer, and the inner with a plain chamfer.

The new nave has in its south wall a piscina with a stone shelf, a square-headed fifteenth-century window of two cinquefoiled lights, and a twelfth-century doorway with a line of zigzag on the label, all having been moved from the corresponding wall of the old nave.

On the west end of the old nave roof is a small wooden bell-turret.

The fittings of the church are for the most part modern, but some seventeenth-century balusters are worked up in the square pulpit, and a fifteenth-century bench end in the seat at the north-west of the new chancel. The north door is also old, and in the north porch is a relic of the old order of things, now happily past, in the shape of a blue china bowl which did duty at baptisms till within modern times.

In the east splay of the north-east window of the old chancel is painted the figure of a bishop holding a crosier in his right hand, wearing a cope fastened by a quatrefoiled morse. He stands under a trefoiled canopy of thirteenth-century style, and on the right is his name S' THEOPH . . NUS. In this window are a few pieces of old glass.

16 The only evidence seems to be an early Chancery proceeding wherein John Philpot complains to the bishop of Lincoln chancellor of England that John Kent of Winchester had refused to make estate in the manor of Compton to him (Early Chan. Proc. bdle. 53, No. 78). The date of this document, however, might be either 1403 (while Henry Beaufort was chancellor), 1475 (during the chancellorship of Thomas Rotherham), or 1483 (during the chancellorship of John Russell).

17 Inq. p.m. 2 Ric. III, No. 26.

18 P.C.C. Will. 17 Logge.

19 Chan. Inq. p.m. (Ser. 2), xvi, No. 100; xvii, No. 102.

20 Ibid. lxiv, No. 152.

21 In 1563 he had a dispute with Francis Kempe of Compton Wasseling, the latter asserting that Mary wife of Thomas had 'procured him by sundrie synister meanes and wayes to marie and take to wiffe her daughter Eleanor, and besides sundry fair offers and faithful promises had promised to procure him a lease of the manor.' Thomas denied this statement, and declared that on their marriage he had settled lands of the yearly value of £20 upon Francis and Eleanor (Chan. Proc. [Ser. 2], bdle. 137, No. 2).

22 Chan. Inq. p.m. (Ser. 2), ccxiii, No. 84.

23 Feet of F. Div. Cos. Hil. 4 Jas. I.

24 Chan. Inq. p.m. (Ser. 2), ccccii, No. 129.

25 Ibid. ccccxcvi, No. 129.

26 Feet of F. Hants, Mich. 16 Chas. I.

27 Ibid. Hil. 3 Geo. I. In that year he conveyed it to Thomas Pengelly.

28 Ibid. Trin. 8 Geo. I; Close, 9 Geo. I, pt. ii, No. 17.

29 Recov. R. Hil. 16 Geo. II, rot. 243; Mich. 31 Geo. III, rot. 334; Trin. 6 Geo. IV, rot. 141.

30 Information supplied by Mr. Edward Eames.

In the churchyard are several seventeenth-century monuments to members of the Goldfinch and Harris families.

There are three bells: the treble, of the sixteenth century, bears ACHOIA in black letter; the second is by Oliver Cor of Aldbourne, 1727; and the tenor has the cross, shield, and initials of William Hasylwood of Reading, *c.* 1500.

The plate consists of a silver chalice with a plain stem and flat foot, dated 1674, a silver chalice, cover paten of the same date, a plain paten with a moulded wire edge, and a tankard-shaped flagon dated 1717.

The earliest parish register gives mixed entries from 1673 to 1813. In these the Goldfinch and the Harris families figure largely, the one as tenants of Compton manor house, the other of Silkstead Priors. In 1745 is an entry of the burial of James Lowe, a ship carpenter, 'accidentally killed by overthrow of a cart. He was a stranger passing in his way from Guernsey to London as appeared by letters found about him.' At the end of the book is an account of various briefs for the redemption of English captives in Algiers and other places on the coast of Africa, for the relief of French Protestants, and for the Protestants of Lesser Poland.

The earliest churchwardens' accounts start in 1724.

ADVOWSON The advowson of Compton church has belonged from its earliest existence to the bishops of Winchester.[31] The living is at the present time a rectory, net yearly value £234 with two acres of glebe and residence.

During the episcopacy of Adam Orlton (bishop of Winchester, 1333–45) sentence was pronounced against certain of the parishioners of Compton for withholding tithes of lambs.[32]

CHARITIES An annual sum of £3 is paid from the funds of St. John's Hospital and Allied Charities in respect of the charity of George Pemerton founded by deed, 1637 (see city of Winchester), and an annuity of £3 is paid by the governing body of Winchester College in respect of the charity of Rev. Chas. Scott, founded by will, 1760.

By order of Charity Commissioners of 22 June, 1900, representative trustees were appointed and the charities made applicable in the supply of clothes or other articles in kind, or in loans to the poor.

In 1897 a house and site was conveyed by Mrs. Jane Mary Smith-Dampier to trustees, and settled upon trust as a residence for a nurse for the parishes of Compton and Twyford.

CRAWLEY

Crawanlea (x cent.), Craule (xiii cent.).

The open chalk downs which run north-eastwards from Winchester and continue onwards to Chilbolton comprise the 3,608 acres which are included in the parish of Crawley.

The road from Winchester to Crawley running north-west branches at Weeke Mark to Littleton and through Littleton to Crawley along a steep ascent which rises to a height of about 360 ft. From the top of this hill comes a first glimpse of Crawley village as a group of houses lying away to the north-east against a background of wooded country. From here the road descends steeply and loses sight of the village, then it suddenly rises again, to swerve again sharply downhill and curve round the village pond into the village itself. North and south of the village street as it rises westwards to the church and rectory are picturesque thatched and timbered houses. The Fox and Hounds Inn stands on the left hand at the bottom of the hill, and close by is one of the oldest cottages in the village now tumbling to ruin and uninhabited. Higher up the street, on the right and left, sloping garden paths lead up to quaint deep-roofed cottages. On the left again is a clump of fir trees, and beyond these the village school built about 1835. Almost opposite the school, behind a low brick wall, is the other village inn, 'The Jolly Sportsman.' Further up the hill the road curves to the left, and on the right is the church of St. Mary almost encircled by trees, and opposite is the rectory. Behind the church is Crawley Court, a modern residence built in the grounds but not on the site of the old Crawley Court. North and east of the village are Crawley Warren and Crawley Down, the latter stretching away to the thickset hedge with its belt of hedgerow growth mingled with beech, oak, ash, yew trees and crab-apple trees, which runs along to the left of the Roman road from Winchester to Cirencester and forms the eastern boundary line of Crawley parish. South and west of the village towards the Sombornes is the arable land with only here and there a group of trees or strip of hedgerow. Close on the border-line in the south-west corner of the parish, seeming locally to be in Little Somborne, is Rookley House, known to fame as the favourite residence of George IV.[1] In the south-east corner is Northwood Park, sandwiched between the parishes of Littleton and Lainston. Northwood House is now used as a naval college.

Hunton parochial chapelry is an outlying district about five or six miles to the north-east of Crawley parish, yet it has been connected with Crawley parish since 909, when King Edward the Elder granted twenty *mansae* at Crawley and eight at Hunton to Frithstan, bishop of Winchester.[2] Hunton itself seems to have quite an individual existence, as is natural considering the distance from the mother parish. The village is in the south on the lowest lying ground of the 1,075 acres which comprise the parish, close to the Test, which forms the boundary line between Hunton and Wonston and Hunton and Stoke Charity. Hunton Lane running east from Wonston, between Hunton Moor and the Test, forks just beyond the church which lies on the right between the road and the river, the south-eastern branch leading to Stoke Charity, the north-eastern up through the length of Hunton parish and on to Basingstoke. It is at the fork in the road that the cottages of the village are grouped. At the corner facing the lane is a thatched and timbered cottage, with an overhanging upper story, with

[31] Pat. 8 Edw. I, m. 20; Chart. R. 12 Edw. I, m. 5; *Wykeham's Reg.* (Hants Rec. Soc.), i, 45; *Winton Epis. Reg.* (Hants Rec. Soc.), 265; Inst. Bks. (P.R.O.).

[32] Egerton MS. 2032, fol. 97.

[1] It was during his residence at Rookley that the existing tennis court was built at Crawley Court.

[2] Birch, *Cart. Sax.* ii, 304.

shaped brackets and moulded ends to the beams, dating back to the beginning of the seventeenth century.[3] The other dozen or so houses of Hunton are all thatched and covered with gay creepers, while the quiet peacefulness of the village, hardly broken by the drowsy hum of the water-mill on the Test, seems to tone with the picturesqueness of the houses and give the complete atmosphere of an old-world village. The red-brick manor-house, rebuilt in the eighteenth century on a site north-west of that of the former manor-house, stands to the north of the village on the right-hand side of the road. It is a pretty specimen of the smaller type of country house, with the usual accessories of moulded brickwork, good panelling and chimneypieces, and a staircase with turned balusters, while the garden in its entirety might belong to the eighteenth century, with its grass lawns and paths, cut yew-trees, and thatched mud wall. One of the dove-houses of the manor originally stood in the garden; the other, which still exists, stands among the farm buildings west of the house, and is apparently of the fifteenth century. It is practically square, measuring 21 ft. by 20 ft. outside, and built of flint with sandstone quoins, the nests being formed of chalk blocks. The original four-centred entrance doorway, now blocked, is in the east wall, and in the west wall, which has been refaced externally, is a second doorway, also blocked, near the north-west angle, leading originally into a building adjoining on the west, but now destroyed. The present entrance is by a hole broken through the south wall. The roof is not ancient, and there are no remains of a revolving ladder or other contrivance for reaching the nests. These dove-houses are noted in the various extents of the manor, together with the water corn-mill on the Test, free fishery in the river, 300 acres of heath and gorse, and 20 acres of moor as among the appurtenances. Parts of the moor and downs were the common lands of the manor, and in 1733, when the common lands were inclosed, special provision was made 'for the watering of the moor called Hunton Moor three times in every week.' The water for watering the same depended on a weir standing in the parish of Stoke Charity.[4]

The soil of the whole of the parish of Crawley, including the outlying district of Hunton, is loam with a subsoil of chalk. On this the chief crops are wheat and oats, with a small crop of barley, but of late years, here as elsewhere, much of the land has been laid down for hay.

MANORS The manor of *CRAWLEY* was granted to Frithstan bishop of Winchester by King Edward in 909 as '20 mansae in Crawanlea.'[5] The boundaries as given in the charter are almost impossible to identify. They seem to start from some point in the south-east, to go northwards, probably along the Roman road (ðonne norð to lunden haerpaðe) to Wonston parish (to Þinstanes stapole), then west and south probably along the modern Drift road, thence along the border of a forest, possibly Whiteberry Copse, on to the road from Stockbridge to Winchester, along by the shambles (to ðam scamelan), west along the valley and by the wood to Somborne (? Sþinburnam), then north from 'the heathens' burial-places' (of ðone aeþena byrigels) back across hills and valleys to the starting-point.

At the time of the Domesday Survey the bishop held the manor in demesne.[6] It was then assessed at 6½ hides, and of the manor a certain Hugh held 3 hides,[7] which Alwin Stilla had held of the bishop in parage,[8] and 'could not betake himself anywhere.' The bishop's demesne was worth £30, and what Hugh held was worth £7, while in 1291 the value of the manor was given at £31.[9]

In the year 1274 the bishop complained against the sheriff of Hampshire that, in lieu of the 500 marks owed by the bishop to the crown from a group of his manors of which Crawley was one, the sheriff had seized cattle from the various manors and had driven them to Winchester Castle, detaining them there for two or three nights. At Crawley he had seized five horses, twenty oxen, six cows, seventeen bullocks, and 350 sheep, and had detained them for two nights. As a result of this complaint the sheriff was ordered by writ to release the cattle on condition that the bishop gave sufficient security for the payment of the 500 marks.[10]

The manor remained the property of the bishopric until 1648, when it was included in the sale of the episcopal possessions, being sold to John Pigeon.[11] It was restored to the bishop at the accession of Charles II, and continued to be held by the bishops of Winchester until 1869, when the lands belonging to the see were taken over by the Ecclesiastical Commissioners.

The manor of *HUNTON* (Hundatone, x cent.) was granted as eight *mansae* to Frithstan bishop of Winchester in 909.[12] The boundaries of the land are given as starting from the river (fram ðaere ea) close by Wonston (foran gean ðaes abbodes byrig),[13] then going north along the green way to Cranborne (lang ðaes grenan weges to Crammaere).[14] The landmarks of the northern boundaries are difficult to identify, but they evidently reached to the wood in the north and then swept down again towards Stoke Charity (ðonne be slade to ðaere byrig), then to a ford over the Test,[15] and along by the river back again to Wonston.

The next reference we have to the manor is that Margaret widow of John son of Matthew held it in dower in 1286–7 of the inheritance of Matthew son of John, to whom the reversion belonged. However, in that year Matthew, with the consent of Margaret, conveyed the reversion to the king and Queen Eleanor,[16] and in the same year received it back for life, with reversion on his death to the king and queen.[17] Many other manors and lands in Devonshire and Wiltshire and the manor of Warblington in Hamp-

[3] The date 1628 has been found on some woodwork here.

[4] Inclosure Award, 6 Geo. II.

[5] Birch, *Cart. Sax.* ii, 304.

[6] *V.C.H. Hants*, i, 460.

[7] It seems just possible that these 3 hides may be Hunton (q.v.).

[8] Namely as senior thegn or king's man of the manor; cf. Pollock and Maitland, *Hist. of Engl. Law*, ii, 264.

[9] *Pope Nich. Tax.* (Rec. Com.), 215*b*.

[10] Coram Rege R. Mich. 2–4 Edw. I, No. 14, m. 1 in *dorso*.

[11] *Coll. Top. et Gen.* i, 127.

[12] Birch, *Cart. Sax.* ii, 304.

[13] This must be Wonston, which belonged to the prior and convent of St. Swithun.

[14] 'maere' might quite well be interchangeable for 'bourne.'

[15] This was evidently over the part of the Test near Stoke Charity, which is swampy marsh-land at the present day covered with osiers.

[16] Feet of F. Div. Cos. 15 Edw. I, No. 51.

[17] *Cal. of Close*, 1307–13, p. 233. Both fines were enrolled in 1309, the year of Matthew's death.

shire went with this grant, and all reverted to the crown on the death of Matthew son of John in 1309.[18] Dowry in the manor of Erlestoke (Wiltshire) was granted, on appeal,[19] to Eleanor widow of Matthew, but the manor of Hunton and the other possessions of Matthew were granted by Edward II in 1309 to Ralph de Monthermer, who had married Joan daughter of Edward I, and to his two sons Thomas and Edward, the king's nephews.[20] Evidently Matthew son of John had died leaving many debts, since in 1313 came an order to the barons of the Exchequer to supersede the demand they had made on the various lands that had belonged to Matthew, among them on the manor of Hunton, and not to molest Ralph de Monthermer and his sons on account of these debts.[21] On the death of Ralph de Monthermer in 1325 his sons made a partition of the lands that had belonged to 'Sir Thomas Matthew son of John,' and the manor of Hunton fell to the share of Edward,[22] who was holding in 1337, when he mortgaged it to Peter de la Mare.[23] Ralph de Monthermer becoming Baron Monthermer through his romantic marriage with the king's daughter, had been summoned to Parliament as baron from 1309 to 1324,[24] and had played an active part in the Scotch wars of Edward II, and thus the details of his life are fairly well known.[25] Of his son Edward, however, little is known except that he served in Scotland in 1334, and that, although he was the second son, was summoned to Parliament as baron in 1337.[26] In all probability he died unmarried soon after the latter date, and the manor of Hunton passed to his elder brother Thomas, who after seeing active service in Scotland was killed at the naval victory off Sluys in 1340.[27] The manor was held by his wife Margaret in dower until her death nine years later, when it passed to their only daughter and heir Margaret, the wife of Sir John de Montagu,[28] second son of William first earl of Salisbury. Sir John died

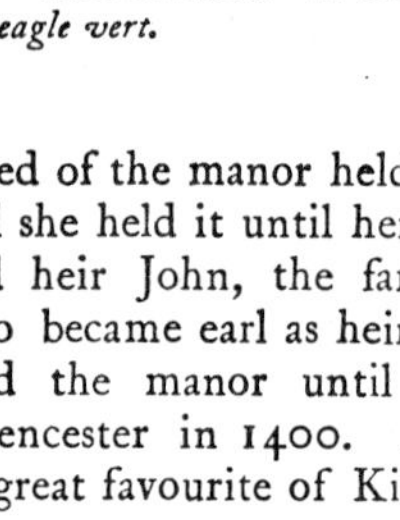

MONTHERMER. *Or an eagle vert.*

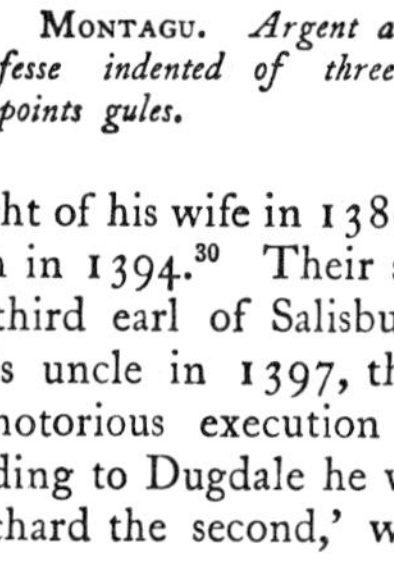

MONTAGU. *Argent a fesse indented of three points gules.*

seised of the manor held in right of his wife in 1389,[29] and she held it until her death in 1394.[30] Their son and heir John, the famous third earl of Salisbury, who became earl as heir of his uncle in 1397, then held the manor until his notorious execution at Cirencester in 1400. According to Dugdale he was 'a great favourite of King Richard the second,' who granted him the sequestered lands of Thomas earl of Beauchamp, and constituted him marshal of England in 1398.[31] When the news of Bolingbroke's arrival reached Ireland, whither Salisbury had gone in attendance on the king, he was dispatched to Conway, North Wales, to gather the Welshmen in the king's cause.[32] Their dispersion when they found that Richard tarried in Ireland is a well-known story, best known perhaps through its introduction into Shakespeare's *Richard II*.[33] Henry IV tried to win his adherence by a policy of propitiation, but in his faithfulness to Richard he 'confederated with the earls of Huntendon and Kent in designing Henry's destruction.' Under the disguise of Christmas players they came to Windsor, intending to murder Henry and his sons and restore Richard, but being discovered they fled by night to Cirencester in Gloucestershire. There the townsmen, being 'much affrighted at their coming thither with such numbers at that unseasonable time,' blocked their way and a sharp fight ensued. The conspirators yielded and were given sanctuary in the abbey, but a priest of their company having set fire to some houses as a means of escape, the enraged inhabitants, without stopping to quench the fire, brought them out of the abbey and beheaded them.[34] From the hands of this self-sacrificing supporter of Richard II, on whom an attainder was passed after his death, the manor went by the generosity of Henry IV, 'much compasionating the low estate of the widow and her children,' to his eldest son and heir Thomas.[35] The latter in 1414 appealed to Parliament to reverse the attainder passed on his father, but without avail.[36] He himself rendered Henry V much valuable service in his wars in France, was present at Harfleur and Caen, was constituted lieutenant-general of the duchy of Normandy, and remained in France until he was accidentally killed before Orleans[37] on 3 November, 1428–9.[38] He left an only daughter and heir Alice, married to Richard Nevill, who was created earl of Salisbury in right of his wife by letters patent of 1442.[39]

The new earl, although favoured by Henry VI and made warden of the West Marches,[40] was one of the first to espouse the cause of York, and, after fighting in many brilliant victories, at the Yorkist reverse at Wakefield he was taken prisoner and beheaded, and his head fixed to a pole over the gates of the city of York.[41]

On Richard's death the manor passed, when after the battle of Towton Edward earl of March had become king, to his more famous son Richard earl of Warwick, better known perhaps as 'Warwick the Kingmaker.' His life and deeds are too well known to need any record, and his death on Barnet field in 1471 is almost without historic parallel in its picturesqueness. His estates, together with those of his wife, Anne Beauchamp, were taken from the latter by Act of Parliament, 'as if she herself had been naturally dead,' and settled upon their two daughters Isabel and

[18] Inq. p.m. 3 Edw. II, No. 49.
[19] Ibid.; *Cal. of Close*, 1307–13, p. 510.
[20] *Cal. of Close*, 1307–13, p. 510.
[21] Ibid.
[22] Ibid. 1323–7, p. 492.
[23] Ibid. 1337–9, p. 103.
[24] *Parl. Writs* (Rec. Com.).
[25] See *Dict. Nat. Biog.*
[26] G.E.C. *Complete Peerage*, v, 352.
[27] Inq. p.m. 14 Edw. III (1st Nos.), No. 34.
[28] Ibid. 23 Edw. III, pt. 2 (1st Nos.), No. 90.
[29] Ibid. 13 Ric. II, No. 34.
[30] Ibid. 18 Ric. II, No. 31.
[31] Dugdale, *Baronage*, i, 650.
[32] Ibid.
[33] Act ii, scene iv.
[34] Dugdale, *Bar.* i, 650.
[35] Pat. 1 Hen. IV, pt. 6, m. 35; 2 Hen. IV, pt. 1, m. 12.
[36] *Roll of Parl.* (Rec. Com.), iv, 18.
[37] Dugdale, *Bar.* i, 653.
[38] Inq. p.m. 7 Hen. VI, No. 57.
[39] Pat. 20 Hen. VI, pt. 4, m. 3.
[40] Dugdale, *Bar.* i, 302.
[41] *Polydorus Virgil*, 510.

Anne.[42] The manor of Hunton was settled on the former, who had married George duke of Clarence, and on her death in 1476[43] it passed to her husband during his lifetime. On his death in the Tower in

NEVILL. *Gules a saltire argent and a label gobony argent and azure.*

BEAUCHAMP. *Gules a fesse between six crosslets or.*

1478, in the traditional butt of Malmsey wine,[44] Hunton passed to his son Edward earl of Warwick, who nominally held the same until attainted and beheaded in 1499. It was then granted by Henry VII to his mother, Margaret countess of Richmond, who held it until her death in 1509.[45]

In February of the next year Henry VIII granted the manor to William Arundel Lord Maltravers and Anne his wife, to hold in chief by the service of one red rose.[46] However, this grant became void in 1513 when the king created Margaret Pole, daughter of George duke of Clarence and Isabel sister of Edward earl of Warwick, countess of Salisbury, reversed her brother's attainder, and restored to her the family lands of Salisbury.[47] On her attainder in 1539 Hunton once more passed into the king's hands, until sold in 1547 to John Whitehorne and his daughter Alice, the wife of Thomas Salmon, as 'part of the possessions of Margaret countess of Salisbury, lately attainted of high treason.'[48]

In the particulars for the sale the yearly value of the manor was reckoned at £15 4*s.*, since the annual fixed rent from the free tenants was 2*s.*, from the customary tenants £12, from the farm of the dove-house 12*s.*, from the farm of the water-mill 26*s.* 8*d.*, and from average perquisites of courts 23*s.* 4*d.* There was a coppice containing 2 acres of wood of nine years' growth, 'the kynd whereof is hassyll and thorne, worth 7*s.* the acre'; also fourteen oaks appraised at 6*d.* apiece. On the side of the common forty more old oaks were growing, 'appraised at 6*d.* the piece, which cometh to 30*s.*' The 'soyll or grounde' of the manor was also yearly worth 6*d.* or 4*d.* the acre.

The purchase was made for £307 4*s.* 4*d.*, and the king discharged John Whitehorne and Alice of all encumbrances, but specially reserved all advowsons of churches, chantries, and chapels.[49]

In 1575 Thomas Salmon and Alice sold the manor to John Hunte,[50] on whose death in August, 1586, it passed to his only daughter and heir, Anne, the wife of Thomas Clerke.[51]

In December of the same year Elizabeth granted Thomas Clerke, jun., gentleman, and Anne his wife licence to alienate the manor, with free fishing, for purpose of settlement on himself and his wife.[52] Another licence to alienate to Thomas Clerke, sen., was granted to the same Thomas Clerke, jun., in December, 1592.[53]

In the same year Thomas Clerke, sen., and Thomas Clerke, jun., demised and granted the manor, excepting one messuage, tenement, and yardland 'to several persons by several leases for 3,000 years for a yearly quit rent.'[54] By the year 1746 the manor had descended in tail male to George Clerke, but the title deeds and writings belonging to the same were in the custody or possession of Thomas Dummer of Cranbury, 'or in the custody or possession of some other person or persons who had no right or title to the same.'[55]

John Pitter son of John Pitter the elder of Crawley purchased the manor in 1746, 'with all mills, dovecotes, barns, stables, &c., lying in the tything of Hunton, in the parish of Crawley.'[56] George Clerke and Thomas Dummer of Cranbury released all their rights and title to John Pitter, but it seems to have been impossible to recover all the title deeds, as it was not known in whose possession they were.[57]

John Pitter's only son and heir, the Rev. Robert Pitter, succeeded to the estate on the death of his father, and held it until his death in 1801. It then descended to his eldest son Robert Pitter, who died in 1866, leaving the estate to his son Robert Pitter, the present lord of the manor and owner of the whole parish.

CHURCHES The church of *ST. MARY, CRAWLEY*, stands on the north of the village street, the churchyard being bounded by a low wooden fence. A fine avenue of lime trees leads up to the church porch, and in the churchyard to the east are some fine yew trees, while to the west and north of the church are the trees of Crawley Court.

The church has a chancel with modern organ transept and vestry on the north, nave with north and south aisles, modern south porch, and west tower. The chancel and north vestry date from 1887, a thirteenth-century lancet window being re-used in the north wall of the former, while a good deal of defaced twelfth-century stonework is built up in the walls. The jambs of the chancel arch are the only surviving part of a church of the middle of the twelfth century, from which the present building has developed. The chancel was probably rebuilt in the thirteenth century, and the body of the church in the fifteenth, nothing of the older nave being retained, and the tower belonging to the sixteenth century. In 1887 the chancel was rebuilt and the north vestry added; the nave has been thoroughly repaired, and the top of the tower was rebuilt in 1901. The walls are of flint and stone and the roofs red-tiled.

The chancel has three lancets in the east wall, three trefoiled lancets and a doorway on the south, and in the north wall a single thirteenth-century lancet re-used.

42 *Rot. Parl.* (Rec. Com.), vi, 100.
43 Inq. p.m. 18 Edw. IV, No. 47.
44 See *Dict. of Nat. Biog.*
45 Exch. Inq. p.m. 4 & 5 Hen. VIII (Ser. 2), file 965, No. 9.
46 Pat. 2 Hen. VIII, pt. 3, m. 4.
47 See *Dict. Nat. Biog.*
48 Partic. for Grants, Aug. Off. file 1210.
49 Ibid.
50 Feet of F. Hants, Trin. 18 Eliz.
51 Chan. Inq. p.m. 29 Eliz. (Ser. 2), ccxii, No. 35.
52 Charter in possession of Mr. Robert Pitter of Hunton; see also Feet of F. Hants, Mich. 29 & 30 Eliz.
53 Charter in possession of same; and Feet of F. Hants, Hil. 35 Eliz.
54 From Abstract of Title *penes* Mr. R. Pitter.
55 Ibid. 56 Ibid. 57 Ibid.

The chancel arch has a span of nearly twelve feet, with nook-shafts having scalloped capitals, and on the east face of the north respond a few stones of the springing of the twelfth-century arch, enough to show that it had a line of zigzag and a moulded label with zigzag and pellet ornament. The existing arch is pointed, of two chamfered orders, perhaps of fourteenth-century date. To the north of the arch is a large squint from the nave.

The nave arcades are of wood, of three bays with octagonal posts and arched braces to the head beams; they afford little evidence of date, but may be of the fifteenth century. They are not set out from the same centre line as the chancel arch, but from one considerably to the north of it, and the same is true of the west wall of the nave, suggesting its rebuilding at the same time. All the nave windows and the south doorway have been retooled or renewed; in the north aisle are three of two cinquefoiled lights with square heads, and in the south aisle two of the same description, but with four-centred rear arches with rolls at the angles. The aisles are very narrow, averaging about four feet seven inches in width.

The tower is small, its internal measurements being only 5 ft. 7 in. by 5 ft. 10 in. its eastern arch being the head and jambs of a window whose sill has been cut down to the ground level. The window is apparently not older than the fifteenth century, giving a limit of date to the tower. In the belfry stage, dating from 1901, are square-headed windows of three trefoiled lights, and the west window on the ground stage is a single uncusped pointed light.

The font is of fifteenth-century style, with an octagonal bowl with quatrefoiled panels.

The most interesting monument in the church is a brass on the south wall of the chancel to Michael Renniger, D.D., archdeacon of Winchester and rector of Crawley, who died on 26 August, 1609. He was evidently exiled under Mary, but returning to England when Elizabeth succeeded to the throne, was made rector of Crawley[58] in 1560.

There are five bells: the treble by Robert Wells of Aldbourne, 1802; the second by Warner, 1900; the third by Wells, 1789; and the fourth and tenor by John Stares, 1746. The two last have large arabesque patterns on the shoulder.

The church plate consists of an old plain silver chalice and paten without date or inscription, a silver chalice, paten, and glass cruet given in 1875 by members of the Pern family, and a small silver-gilt chalice, paten, and cruet for private communion given by Arthur Percival, curate, in 1824.

The oldest parish register gives mixed entries from 1649 to 1812.

The earliest existing poor book for the parish dates from 1776 to 1797, and there is another from 1797 to 1822. The old book of churchwardens' accounts, which has lately been rescued from a book shop in Reading, dates from 1766 to 1832.

The church of *ST. JAMES, HUNTON*, stands to the south-west of the village in a fenced-off space in the middle of a field, between the River Test and Hunton Lane. It has a chancel 15 ft. 6 in. by 8 ft. 6 in. built of flint rubble with wrought-stone dressings, a brick-faced nave 43 ft. 9 in. by 19 ft. 10 in., with a south porch of brick, and a brick tower at the west end. All the windows are in modern stonework of fifteenth-century design, and the chancel arch is covered with plaster, and has a four-centred head dying into the walls at the springing. The south doorway of the nave has brick jambs, but its pointed head, worked with a hollow chamfer, looks like mediaeval work, and, with a small fifteenth-century piscina in the chancel, is the only architectural feature which is old. There is therefore practically no history to the building, and the most interesting thing which it contains is the front of a raised tomb, set in a recess in the north wall of the nave, and now half buried beneath the floor. It is of the latter part of the fifteenth century, with panels of foliage alternating with the **I h s** monogram and with that of our Lady, and is by tradition part of the tomb of Thomas Hunton, prior of St. Swithun, Winchester, from 1470 to 1498.

The west tower is very small, finished with brick battlements, and contains one bell by I. Earley of Winchester, dated 1751.

The church plate consists of an old plain silver chalice and paten, and a modern glass cruet with a silver top.

The earliest parish register contains mixed entries of baptisms from 1564 to 1773, burials from 1564 to 1753, marriages from 1575 to 1744, and burials again from 1678–9 to 1702, with two or three stray entries for 1717 and 1721. The next book contains baptisms from 1775 to 1812. There is also a book of banns from 1755 to 1810.

ADVOWSONS The patronage of the church of Crawley had always belonged to the bishop of Winchester[59] until the year 1860, when Bishop Wilberforce exchanged it with Queen's College, Oxford, for six small livings in Portsmouth and Gosport of the same aggregate value. In 1896 Queen's College, Oxford, sold the advowson to Mr. G. Bliss, the present patron.

The church existed at the time of the Domesday Survey;[60] in 1291 its annual value, together with the chapel of Hunton, was £20,[61] and in 1536, £35 13*s*. 4*d*.[62]

Fremund Lebrun, a rector of Crawley, was appointed papal chaplain in 1259 by special provision.[63]

In 1325 Pontius de Tornamira, another rector, was allowed to hold a canonry of Salisbury as well as the living of Crawley.[64]

William de Dereham, who was rector about 1330, and Nicholas de Alton, parson of Middleton, were appointed in that year to survey the jewels, goods, and chattels belonging to John de St. John of Basing, which were to be forfeited to the crown for debt. Nicholas de Alton complained that William de Dereham had seized and 'carried to the church of Crawley' jewels and goods worth £32 16*s*. 8*d*., for which he, Nicholas, had been charged 'as if he had them.' Nicholas was discharged, and a jury was formed to ascertain that William took and had the jewels, and in all probability he was obliged to forfeit the same.[65] Within two years this same William was provided

[58] 'Exul in Helvetiam migravit et inde reversus Reginae a sacris Rector fuit istius Aedis.'

[59] Chart. R. 12 Edw. I, m. 5; *Wykeham's Reg.* (Hants Rec. Soc), i, 134, 147, 238; Egerton MS. 2032, fol. 50.

[60] *V.C.H. Hants*, i, 460*b*.

[61] *Pope Nich. Tax.* (Rec. Com.), 210*a*.

[62] *Valor Eccl.* (Rec. Com.), ii, 6.

[63] *Cal. of Pap. Letters*, i, 367.

[64] Ibid. ii, 248.

[65] *Cal. of Close*, 1330–3, p. 12.

with a canonry and prebend of Chichester, although he was rector of Crawley.[66]

The church, or as it was originally, the chapel of Hunton, has always been attached to the church of Crawley, and has been under the same patronage.[67] The church of Crawley *cum capella* of 1291 means Crawley with the chapel of Hunton.[68]

CHARITIES Poor's Money.—In the year 1768 a sum of £26 12*s.* 4*d.* was due to the churchwardens and overseers from one Robert Pitter. This sum was increased by subscription in the parish to £32, which was in or about 1869 placed in a savings bank and interest distributed in bread.

HOUGHTON

The parish of Houghton, lying south-west of Stockbridge and north-west of King's Somborne, is detached from the other parishes of Buddlesgate Hundred. It comprises 33 acres of land covered by water and 2,639 acres of land, which rises generally from south-east to north-west from the low-lying country near the River Test, which flows along the east of the parish to the downland, which stretches away north to Houghton Down, behind which rises Danebury Hill in Nether Wallop parish. The main road from Romsey to Stockbridge branches north-east and north-west, south-east of Houghton parish, and immediately south-east of Horsebridge village (in King's Somborne parish). The north-eastern branch leads through King's Somborne village to the east end of Stockbridge, while the other leads to the west end of Stockbridge through Houghton village. The north-western branch, after passing through Horsebridge, over the railway line (the Andover branch of the London and South-Western Railway, which skirts Houghton parish, has a station at Horsebridge), continues through low-lying water meadows, and crossing the Test passes by the old Houghton mill, which stands on the left, and is now used for generating electric light. Winding round more directly to the north the road comes to the picturesque buildings of the village, lying for the most part on the west side of the road, and becomes the main village street. On either side of the long village street are grouped low thatched cottages, one of which on the east side serves as the post-office, while towards the north is the Boot Inn, standing on the west, and several more modern cottages and houses. Here a road branching uphill to the west leads to the church and rectory and to the Manor Farm. A high hedge on the north shuts in the rectory, a fine old eighteenth-century house, which is approached by a drive on the east running round to the north entrance. A narrow door close to the house in the west garden wall leads into the churchyard and to the church, which stands immediately south-west of the rectory near the road behind a low brick wall. In the fields opposite the church stands one of the old barns of Manor Farm, which was used for services while the church was being altered in 1882, on which is an old weather vane from the church. Manor Farm stands west of the church, a square, plain-fronted house facing east, with long rambling passages and low old-fashioned rooms. Beyond Manor Farm the road becomes a rough lane leading north-west over fields to the downland.

The main village street, curving west for a few yards at the north end of the village, turns sharply north and runs uphill past Houghton Lodge, the residence of Colonel E. St. John Daubney, which lies back from the road on the east, on to North Houghton.

The soil of the parish is loam, chalk, and peat with a subsoil of chalk producing the ordinary crops of wheat, barley, and roots. Of the total 2,639 acres of land, 1,610¾ are arable, 813¾ permanent grass, and 41 woodland.[1]

MANORS The manor of *HOUGHTON DRAYTON* belonged to the church of Winchester by the grant of King Edgar of lands at 'Horton' in the tenth century.[2] At the time of the Domesday Survey the bishop held Houghton for the monks of Winchester, and it was then assessed at 16 hides.[3] William Peverel held 1 hide of the manor, but refused to pay geld, and a certain Walter in like manner held 1 hide.[4] In 1205 and again in 1243 the pope confirmed the manor to the prior and convent,[5] and in 1301 Edward I granted them free warren in their demesne lands in Houghton.[6] From this date to the time of the Dissolution the prior and convent held the manor,[7] the annual receipts from which increased from £19 6*s.* 3½*d.* to £41 11*s.* 11*d.* during the fourteenth century.[8] In 1543 the king granted the manor of Houghton in Houghton with appurtenances in Houghton, Drayton, Dockham and Evely, with a reserved rent of £2 19*s.* 9*d.*, to Robert White of Aldershot,[9] who five years later conveyed it by fine to his father John White, gentleman and grocer of London.[10] In 1558 the manor was settled on John and his heirs on the occasion of his marriage with Katherine Greneway, widow,[11] and four years later Queen Elizabeth granted him the reserved rent of £2 19*s.* 9*d.*[12] On his death the manor passed to his son and heir Robert, who dealt with it by a recovery in 1589[13] and died seised of it in 1599.[14] His heirs were his two daughters, Ellen wife of Richard Tichborne, and Mary wife of Walter, brother of Richard Tichborne.[15] The manor of Houghton Drayton was settled on Ellen the elder,[16] and on her death in 1612 passed to her only daughter Amphyllis, who married Lawrence Hyde, son and heir of Sir Lawrence Hyde, bart., in 1619.[17] Amphyllis died before her husband

66 *Cal. of Pap. Letters*, ii, 373.
67 Chart. R. 12 Edw. I, m. 5; *Wykeham's Reg.* (Hants Rec. Soc.), i, 364.
68 *Pope Nich. Tax.* (Rec. Com.), 210.
1 Information from Bd. of Agric. (1905).
2 Birch, *Cart. Sax.* iii, 412.
3 *V.C.H. Hants*, i, 462*b*.
4 Ibid.
5 *Cal. of Pap. Letters*, i, 21, 201.
6 Chart. R. 29 Edw. I, m. 12.
7 *Feud. Aids*, ii, 309; Mins. Accts. Hants, 32 & 33 Hen. VIII, 109, m. 51.
8 *Pope Nich. Tax.* (Rec. Com.), 213; *Obed. R. of St. Swithun* (Hants Rec. Soc.), 225.
9 Pat. 34 Hen. VIII, pt. 8, m. 15–18.
10 Feet of F. Hants, East. 2 Edw. VI.
11 Pat. 5 & 6 Phil. and Mary, pt. 4, m. 13, 14.
12 Ibid. 4 Eliz. pt. 4, m. 50–3.
13 Recov. R. Hil. 21 Eliz. rot. 71.
14 Chan. Inq. p.m. (Ser. 2), cclvii, Nos. 31, 90.
15 Ibid.
16 In 1600 Walter Tichborne and Mary conveyed a moiety of the manor to Richard Weston and others, most probably for settlement on Richard Tichborne and Ellen (Feet of F. Div. Cos. Hil. 42 Eliz.).
17 Chan. Inq. p.m. (Ser. 2), 14 Chas. I, pt. 1, No. 199.

in 1632 leaving one son Robert, an infant, and three daughters, Amphyllis, Anne, and Ellen, who became co-heirs.[18] Amphyllis married Thomas Chaffin of Chettle (co. Dorset),[19] and it is probable that Ellen married John Lowe of Shaftesbury (co. Dorset), for in 1655 Amphyllis Chaffin, widow, John Lowe and Ellen his wife, and others, were dealing with the manor of Houghton and the other manors originally belonging to Robert White.[20] Houghton was evidently soon afterwards settled on John Lowe and Ellen, for Lawrence Lowe, probably their son and heir, dealt with it by recovery in 1679, no doubt on the occasion of his marriage with Lucy daughter of Thomas Pile of Baverstock (co. Wilts.).[21] He seems to have left no issue, for in 1689 his widow Lucy, in conjunction with Thomas Chaffin, Edward Lowe, clerk, and Robert Hyde, released all right in the manor to Thomas Freke,[22] who, on his death without issue in 1698, left his estates to Thomas Pile and Elizabeth wife of Thomas Freke of Hannington (co. Wilts.) for life with reversion to George Pitt of Stratfield Saye,[23] who had married Lucy, Lawrence Lowe's widow.[24] In this way Houghton came into the possession of the Pitt family, with whom it remained for a considerable period.[25] The subsequent history of the manor is uncertain, but it eventually came into the possession of the Rev. Richard Townsend, rector of Ickford (co. Bucks.). He sold it about 1860 to Mr. Charles Warner, on whose death it passed to Mr. Frederick Warner of Winchester.

PITT. *Sable a fesse checky argent and azure between three bezants.*

There were four mills worth 70*s.* in the manor of Houghton Drayton at the time of the Domesday Survey.[26] The present Houghton mill in the south of the parish probably marks the site of one, while another is possibly represented by Horsebridge mill, which although quite near the village of Houghton is locally situated in King's Somborne parish. The latter mill was certainly held of the prior and convent of St. Swithun, as appears from the inquisition taken in 1482 on the death of Sir Thomas Mylbourne, who died seised of a toft, lands, and the site of a mill in Houghton, Horsebridge, and Forton in the parish of Alverstoke, leaving a son and heir Henry.[27]

There seem to have been four estates in Houghton besides the manor of Houghton Drayton. Thus at the time of the Domesday Survey Hugh de Port held 2½ hides in Houghton which were held of him by a certain Heldered and which together with part of Awbridge in the parish of Michelmersh had been given to Hugh as one manor, as parcel of the forfeited possessions of Earl Godwin.[28] Turstin the Chamberlain also held lands in Houghton, which Algar and Edward had held of King Edward.[29] Besides Hugh de Port and Turstin the Chamberlain, Anschitil son of Osmund and Turold were also holding lands in Houghton,[30] the former of the king in chief and the latter of Roger earl of Shrewsbury. Anschitil's estate had formed part of the possessions of Earl Godwin, while Turold's lands in Houghton had been held by Osmund of King Edward.[31]

The Port estate, which was afterwards called the manor of *NORTH HOUGHTON*, was held of the Ports and their heirs by the family of Portsea in the twelfth, thirteenth, and fourteenth centuries. In the latter part of the twelfth century Baldwin of Portsea and Adeliza his wife granted 1 virgate in Houghton and pasture for one hundred sheep, six oxen, five swine, and one boar to the church of St. Denis in free alms, and their gift was confirmed by their overlord Adam de Port.[32] Andrew of Portsea, probably great-nephew of Baldwin and Adeliza,[32a] was holding half a knight's fee in Houghton in the reign of Henry III of Robert de St. John, who held in chief.[33] In 1316 the same tenement seems to have been held by Thomas de Brykevile or Brinkhale and Richard of Portsea;[34] and two years later Richard of Portsea, to whom Edward I had granted free warren in his demesne lands of Houghton in 1303,[35] died seised of 1 messuage and 1 carucate of land in the vill of North Houghton held of John de St. John by service of half a knight's fee and suit at the hundred court of Somborne.[36] His heir was his sister Alice Loveratz, aged fifty,[37] but she seems soon afterwards to have alienated her part of the vill to Richard de Ranville and Lucy his wife, who in 1323 dealt by fine with 1 messuage, 1 carucate of land, 10 acres of meadow, and 60*s.* rent in North Houghton near Stockbridge.[38] In 1346 Richard de Ranville was still holding the half-fee which had belonged to Richard of Portsea in Houghton,[39] but by 1428 it had come into the possession of John Roger, junr. of Bryanston (co. Dorset).[40] By this date also the tenement which had belonged to Thomas Brinkhale at the beginning of the fourteenth century had descended to John Brinkhale.[41] To each of these holdings was afterwards given the name of the manor of North Houghton, so that for centuries there were two manors of the same name in the parish, each with a distinct history of its own.

ROGER of Bryanston. *Argent a pierced molet sable and a chief or with a fleur-de-lis gules therein.*

The estate which John Roger had purchased came into the possession of the Webbes of Odstock (co. Wilts.) and Great Cranford (co. Dorset), but whether

[18] Chan. Inq. p.m. (Ser. 2), 14 Chas. I, pt. 1, No. 199.

[19] Hutchins, *Dors.* iii, 565.

[20] Recov. R. Mich. 1655, rot. 3; ibid. East. 1656, rot. 109.

[21] Close, 31 Chas. II, pt. 10, No. 18; Recov. R. Mich. 31 Chas. II, rot. 36.

[22] Feet of F. Div. Cos. Trin. 1 Will. and Mary. [23] Hutchins, *Dors.* iv, 89.

[24] Berry, *Hants Gen.* 101.

[25] Ibid.; Recov. R. Trin. 16 & 17 Geo. II, rot. 205.

[26] *V.C.H. Hants*, i, 462*b*.

[27] Chan. Inq. p.m. (Ser. 2), viii, No. 77.

[28] *V.C.H. Hants*, i, 480*b*.

[29] Ibid. 494*b*.

[30] Ibid. 477*b*, 503*a*.

[31] Ibid.

[32] Add. MS. 15314, fol. 85.

[32a] See under Portsea. Possibly North Houghton followed the same descent as Portsea between the death of Baldwin and the succession of Andrew of Portsea to the property.

[33] *Testa de Nevill* (Rec. Com.), 230.

[34] *Feud. Aids* (Rec. Com.), ii, 310.

[35] Chart. R. 31 Edw. I, m. 3.

[36] Inq. p.m. 12 Edw. II, No. 44.

[37] Ibid.

[38] Feet of F. Hants, Trin. 17 Edw. II. They conveyed the premises to Walter de Stapleton, bishop of Exeter, and his brother Richard, probably as trustees.

[39] *Feud. Aids* (Rec. Com.), ii, 324.

[40] Ibid. ii, 351.

[41] Ibid.

by purchase or inheritance does not appear. In 1569 William Webbe and Catherine his wife, daughter and heir of John Tourney of Motcombe and Payne's Place near Shaftesbury (co. Dorset),[42] dealt with the manor of North Houghton by fine.[43] From them it descended to their son Sir William Webbe,[44] who died seised of the manor in 1623, leaving as his heir his daughter Rachel, wife of Sir John Croke of Chilton (co. Bucks.).[45] Their son Charles Croke left an only daughter Catherine, who married John Lisle of Moyle's Court,[46] and probably brought the manor to her husband. The later history of this manor has not been ascertained.

WEBBE of Odstock. *Gules a cross between four falcons close or.*

In 1485 Richard III granted the manor or lordship of North Houghton, formerly belonging to Michael Skilling, deceased, to John Pole and Richard Pole and their heirs and assigns,[47] and judging from this, it is clear that the estate in North Houghton, which was in the possession of John Brinkhale in 1428, passed before long to some member of the Skilling family. In spite of the royal grant, however, Alice Skilling, daughter of Michael Skilling, and Robert Pistar, son and heir of William Pistar and Rebecca his wife, daughter of William Skilling,[48] dealt by fine with a fourth part of the manor in 1517[49] and 1546[50] respectively, and William Skilling was in possession of the whole in 1585.[51] From the latter it passed to George Hunt, who sold it together with a free fishery in the Test to William Symons in 1592.[52] Thirty years later it passed by purchase from William to Richard Oviatt of Highwood (co. Hants),[53] who died seised of the same in 1634.[54] By his will dated 26 January, 1632, he left the manor to his daughter Catherine[55] wife of Thomas Urrey of Gatcombe[56] in fee-tail. The subsequent history of this estate has not been discovered.

LISLE of Moyle's Court. *Azure a chief or with three lions azure therein.*

DENECOURT (Dennecourt, xiv cent.; Houghton Dencourte, xvi cent.).

In the reign of Henry III Richard de Dene was holding half a knight's fee in Houghton of the ancient feoffment of Robert de Punchard, who held of William de Beauchamp, who held of the king.[57] In 1316 William de Dene, apparently a descendant of Richard, was still holding this half-fee,[58] which by this time had evidently come to be known as the manor of Denecourt in Houghton, but he must have parted with it soon afterwards, for in 1325 it was settled on Thomas de Weston and Margaret his wife,[59] who were already owners of the manor of Marshcourt in King's Somborne.[60] Sir Thomas de Weston died seised of the manor in 1354, leaving as his heirs his daughters Eleanor and Isabel, and his granddaughters Eleanor and Isabel, the daughters of his deceased daughter Margaret wife of John Louvaine.[61] One moiety was assigned to the elder granddaughter Eleanor, who married Sir William Bourchier in 1365,[62] but what became of the other moiety at this time it seems impossible to ascertain. It does not seem to have been assigned to the other granddaughter Isabel who died without issue in 1359,[63] for, if so, on her death it would naturally have passed to her sister Eleanor as her heir, and Eleanor, at her death in 1397, was only seised of one moiety.[64] By 1428, however, it had evidently passed to a certain John Puttoun,[65] but in what manner does not appear. Eleanor's moiety on the other hand passed to John Roger of Bryanston, the purchaser of North Houghton in 1422,[66] and consequently John Roger and John Puttoun are given as the joint owners of Denecourt in 1428.[67] John Puttoun's moiety was evidently bought up by John Roger or his successors,[68] and after this the manor of Houghton Denecourt, as it was afterwards called, followed the same descent as the first-named manor of North Houghton (q.v.).

HOUGHTON EDINGTON (Edingtons, xvi cent.).

There was also another estate in Houghton—parcel of the honour of Gloucester—[69] which, in the reign of Henry III, was held by John de Waleys and Robert le Dene of Geoffrey de Lauriton who held of Robert de Mesy.[70] In 1316 Walter de Waleys was holding the moiety formerly held by John de Waleys,[71] and it is probable that by this time Thomas de Rous had succeeded Robert le Dene in possession of the other moiety,[72] although this is not expressly stated. By 1323, however, the whole seems to have been in the possession of Thomas de Byvedon and Joan his wife, who in that year conveyed seven messuages, two carucates of land, 26 acres of meadow, 50*s.* rents, and half a knight's fee in North Houghton, Stockbridge, and Longstock to Walter de Stapleton bishop of Exeter and his brother Richard,[73] probably for purposes of settlement. In 1341 the same estate, described in this case as three messuages, two carucates of land, 34 acres of meadow, and £8 rent in North Houghton, Longstock, and Stockbridge, was settled on William de Edington, or Edendon, afterwards bishop of Winchester (1346–66), by John de Cologne of London,[74] and remained in his

42 Hutchins, *Dors.* iii, 298.
43 Feet of F. Div. Cos. Hil. 11 Eliz.
44 Hutchins, *Dors.* iii, 298.
45 Chan. Inq. p.m. ccccl xxix, No. 111.
46 Berry, *Hants Gen.* 174.
47 Pat. 2 Ric. III, pt. 2, m. 16.
48 Berry, *Hants Gen.* 262.
49 Feet of F. Hants, East. 9 Hen. VIII.
50 Ibid. Mich. 38 Hen. VIII.
51 Ibid. Div. Cos. East. 27 Eliz.
52 Ibid. Hants, East. 34 Eliz.
53 Ibid. Hants, Mich. 19 Jas. I.
54 Chan. Inq. p.m. 10 Chas. I (Ser. 2), pt. 1, No. 108.
55 Ibid.
56 Berry, *Hants Gen.* 357.
57 *Testa de Nevill* (Rec. Com.), 234, 238*b*.
58 *Feud. Aids*, ii, 310.
59 Feet of F. Hants, Mich. 19 Edw. II.
60 Ibid. East. 4 Edw. II.
61 *Winton Epis. Reg.* (Hants Rec. Soc.), 619, 620.
62 Banks, *Dormant and Extinct Peerage*, i, 367.
63 Ibid.
64 Inq. p.m. 21 Ric. II, No. 10.
65 *Feud. Aids*, ii, 351.
66 Close, 1 Hen. VI, m. 21 *d*.
67 *Feud. Aids*, ii, 351.
68 William Webbe and Catherine his wife dealt with the whole manor by fine in 1569 (Feet of F. Div. Cos. Hil. 11 Eliz.).
69 The earls of Stafford held a knight's fee in Houghton by Stockbridge as a parcel of the honour of Gloucester as late as the fifteenth century (Inq. p.m. 16 Ric. II, pt. 1, No. 27; 22 Ric. II, No. 46; 4 Hen. IV, No. 41).
70 *Testa de Nevill* (Rec. Com.), 234*b*.
71 *Feud. Aids*, ii, 310.
72 Ibid. 324.
73 Feet of F. Hants, East. 16 Edw. II.
74 Ibid. Hants, Trin. 15 Edw. III.

possession until his death,[75] on which account it was in after times called the manor of Houghton Edington or Edingtons. After his death it seems to have passed to Sir Thomas Hungerford,[76] and from him to Sir Aumary de St. Amand and Eleanor his wife, with whom it remained for a considerable period, Sir Aumary at length conveying it to Robert Shotesbroke in 1401.[77] It was sold to John Roger of Bryanston (co. Dorset) together with half the manor of Denecourt in 1423,[78] and from this time has followed the same descent as the first-named manor of North Houghton (q.v.).

EDINGTON. *Or a cross engrailed gules with five cinquefoils or thereon.*

CHURCH The church of *ALL SAINTS* has a chancel 27 ft. 3 in. by 14 ft. 2 in., with a modern south vestry and a nave 38 ft. 6 in. by 14 ft. 9 in., with north aisle 10 ft. 4 in. wide, south aisle 7 ft. 3 in. wide, modern south porch, and wooden bell-turret over the west end.

Some pieces of twelfth-century detail, belonging to the first half of the century, and including the head of a small window, are built into the east wall of the south aisle, and there is other evidence that a church was on this site at the time. It was probably a small building with aisleless nave and chancel, the nave being of the same width as at present but shorter, and the chancel smaller in both dimensions than that which now stands. The first enlargement seems to have been the addition of a north chapel to the nave, and about 1200 a south aisle of three bays was built, the nave being probably lengthened at this time. Towards the end of the thirteenth century the north chapel was carried westward to the same length as the south aisle, and in the second quarter of the fourteenth century the chancel was rebuilt. The wooden bell-turret is probably of the fifteenth century, but the upper part and spire date from 1890. In 1875 the chancel was restored and the present east window set up in place of one with wooden frame and mullions. The nave was repaired in 1882, and the chancel arch rebuilt. The walls are of flint rubble with stone dressings, mostly covered with plaster, and the roofs are red-tiled.

The chancel has a modern east window of three lights, two two-light windows on the north, and two on the south, with a plain priest's door between them. With the exception of the south-west window all the stonework of the windows is modern, of fourteenth-century style. In the south-west window, which dates from *c.* 1330, it is old except the central mullion and the springing of the tracery above it. Below this window a piece of fifteenth-century canopy work is built into the outer face of the wall, upside down. At the south-east of the chancel is a pretty trefoiled piscina with a moulded label, and against the east wall the remains of a fine reredos, a good deal re-tooled, but evidently of fourteenth-century date. A band of quatrefoils runs across it and on either side of the altar are half-octagonal pedestals for image-niches; the whole has evidently been painted, and traces of colour are yet to be seen.

The chancel arch is of two chamfered orders, rising from plain square jambs which are broader than it, and probably form part of the wall of the older church. The quoins, however, are not of twelfth-century type, and may belong to the widening of the arch when the chancel was rebuilt; the arch itself has been rebuilt in modern times with old material.

On the north side of the nave are two arches, separated by a 6 ft. length of walling. The eastern arch is of irregular shape, stilted and round-headed, of two edge-chamfered orders; the responds are square, and that at the west has a twelfth-century chamfered string at the springing, a modern copy of which is in the east respond. The arch has evidently been altered, but may have been of the twelfth century in the first instance, opening to a north chapel. The western arch is pointed, of two chamfered orders, with a string of late thirteenth-century section at the springing, and has to the east of it on the north side a trefoiled piscina, marking the site of a former altar about mid-way in the present aisle. At the south-west of the aisle is a second piscina, square-headed, and a wide squint towards the chancel. The aisle is lighted by square-headed windows of two wide trefoiled lights, one at the east and two on the north, while the west window is of the same type but narrower, and near the north-west angle is a plain round-headed north doorway of uncertain date.

The south arcade of the nave, of three bays, has circular columns with plain capitals and bases moulded with two rolls; the abaci are square edged and chamfered beneath, and the arches are pointed, of two edge-chamfered orders, all the stonework having diagonal tooling. The east window of the aisle is of two lights and the south window of three, both being modern, and in the west wall is a small square-headed window of two trefoiled lights. The south doorway is probably *in situ*, though reworked, the width of the aisle, 7 ft. 3 in., being a likely one for the date; the doorway has a semicircular arch of one order with a sunk quarter-round moulding and a double chamfered label. Here and in the north aisle, there is a squint to the chancel, the southern narrower than the other. There is no clearstory, and the west window of the nave is of three cinquefoiled lights in modern stonework of fifteenth-century style. The south porch is entirely refaced, but contains some old masonry, and its moulded wall plates are of fifteenth-century date.

All the roofs of the church, except that of the north aisle, are old, the chancel having trussed rafters and a single moulded and cambered tie-beam, while in the nave the tie-beams are left in the rough, and have king posts with struts to the pole plate. At the west end are the heavy posts carrying the western bell-turret, with braces to the upper beams. Externally the turret and spire are covered with oak shingles, and have in the belfry stage modern two-light openings of fifteenth-century style.

[75] *Feud. Aids*, ii, 324; De Banco R. No. 554, m. 441.

[76] The only evidence of Sir Thomas Hungerford's tenure of the manor is a De Banco Roll of 1399, whereby Sir Aumary sued Joan, widow of Sir Thomas Hungerford, for unlawfully detaining charters and title-deeds of the manor. One of the documents in question was a deed whereby Thomas Hungerford and others put in their place Thomas Vautort to take seisin in their name of the manor (De Banco R. No. 554, m. 441).

[77] *Vide* Pat. 10 Hen. VI, pt. 1, m. 1.

[78] Close, 1 Hen. VI, m. 21 *d*. In this document it is described as lately in the tenure of Eleanor, who was the wife of Sir Aumary de St. Amand.

The font is old but reworked, with a panelled bowl and a square base of Purbeck marble. There are no other old fittings in the church. On the south-east angle of the south aisle is an incised sundial. There are three bells, the treble of 1882 by Llewellin & James of Bristol, and the second and tenor of 1742 by Robert Cor of Aldbourne.

The plate consists of a chalice, paten, and almsdish of 1796, given by William Langford, D.D.

The earliest parish register contains mixed entries from 1669 to 1713; the second from 1714 to 1738. The third register contains baptisms and burials from 1738 to 1812, and marriages from 1738 to 1750; those between 1752 and 1812 being in a separate register.

ADVOWSON The church was in the gift of the bishops of Winchester until 1852,[79] in which year the patronage was transferred on the next voidance of the see of Winchester to the bishops of Lichfield.[80] The living is now a rectory in the gift of the Lord Chancellor, the patronage having been exchanged and transferred to the crown in 1873.[81]

Dependent upon the parish church was the chapel of North Houghton, which existed at the time of the Domesday Survey.[82] It was still in existence in the fourteenth century, a certain Richard de Wotton, described as parson of the chapel of Houghton, being summoned during the episcopacy of Fox concerning a plea of debt,[83] but there is no mention of it in the *Valor Ecclesiasticus* of 1535. Its site can still be traced near North Houghton manor-house.

While John Stratford was bishop of Winchester, the parish church and churchyard of Houghton, which had been polluted by the shedding of blood, were reconciled by the bishop of Bath and Wells.[84]

CHARITIES An annual sum of £2 6*s.* 8*d.* is paid from the funds of St. John's Hospital and Allied Charities in respect of the charity of George Pemerton, founded by deed 1637. See city of Winchester.

HURSLEY

Hurseleghe (xiii cent.), Hursele (xiv cent).

The parish of Hursley, covering 6,949 acres,[1] lies south-west of Winchester. The north of the parish, being part of the girdle of bare chalk downs which surround the city of Winchester, reaches over 500 ft. near Crabwood Farm. The land falls towards the centre of the parish, where the village lies on low ground, but rises again to a moderate height in the south. The main road from Winchester to Romsey traverses the whole length of the parish, passing through the hamlets of Pitt and Standon, Hursley village, and Ampfield. Hursley village is one of the most picturesque types of the larger Hampshire villages. Entering it from Winchester, low thatched cottages are grouped on the left and right. A row of pollard limes stands in front of some low cottages on the east hand, and away on the west, behind a low hedge, are stretches of meadow, and in the distance behind a belt of trees is the church spire. Farther along the road by the 'White Horse' a sharp bend up-hill to the left leads by Collins Lane to Upper Sharland, and then the main road winds slightly west into the centre of the village. Standing well back from the road on the right is the village school; beyond is the church, and behind the church the vicarage. Facing and parallel with the low stone wall of the churchyard is a row of cottages, one of which serves as the post office, and at the end of the row is the quaint blacksmith's shop overshadowed by a tall elm tree. Beyond the church, on the right, are four or five cottages fronting on the street, tiled and timbered with latticed windows and overhanging stories belonging at latest to the seventeenth century. Lower down the street and on the opposite side of the road are more modern houses and cottages, and at the end of the street on the left, surrounded by a high wall, is Southend House, the residence of Mr. H. V. Henry. Following this wall round to the left a narrow lane branches from the main road and leads to Bunstead and on to Silkstead, which is partly in Hursley parish.

West of the village and almost parallel with the village street is Hursley Park, covering 450 acres of luxuriantly wooded country well stocked with deer. Hursley House, standing in the park, was built in 1718–20 by Sir William Heathcote, first baronet, and has been very much extended and refitted within the last few years by the present owner, Sir George Cooper. In the north of the park are the ruins of Merdon Castle, one of the palaces of the bishops of Winchester.

The Cranbury estate, including Cranbury Park and Cranbury House, a residence of Mr. Tankerville Chamberlayne, M.P., lies in the south-east corner of the parish. The thickly-wooded country which closes around the park on the east and south continues southwards to Hiltingbury Common, which is now since 1894 part of Ampfield parish, but was part of Hursley when Ampfield itself was a hamlet of Hursley. Ampfield Wood, lying to the west, stretches across from the woods which lie south of Hursley Park to the border line between Ampfield and Romsey parishes.

Ampfield village is south of the wood and consists of a number of scattered cottages brought probably into existence by the necessity for workers at the saw-mills and the gravel-pits in Ganges Wood. St. Mark's church stands on high ground north of the main road, and west of the church, about half way down the hill, is the vicarage. Ampfield House, the residence of Mr. David Faber, J.P., and Philpott's Farm are also close on the main road, but the cottages and the village school lie away to the north along a branch in the road between the church and vicarage.

The hamlet of Standon lies about half a mile north of Hursley village where the main road curves to the right towards Winchester. It consists of a group of some picturesque half-timber thatched cottages lying back for the most part behind bright cottage gardens.

Pitt hamlet nestles between two steep hills about two miles north-west from Stanton. Pitt Farm is on the right, and along a branch road to the left

79 Chart. R. 12 Edw. I, m. 5; *Cal. of Pat.* 1301–7, p. 313; *Wykeham's Reg.* (Hants Rec. Soc.), i, 76, 102, 123, 126, 133, 232; *Cal. Pap. Letters*, iv, 181; Egerton MS. 2034, fol. 166.

80 *Lond. Gaz.* 1852, p. 1578.

81 Ibid. 1873, p. 2264.

82 *V.C.H. Hants*, i, 462*b*.

83 Egerton MS. 2033, fol. 104.

84 Ibid. fol. 58.

1 Of these 10 acres are water.

are a few scattered cottages and a school chapel built by Miss Charlotte Yonge in 1858, served by the vicar of Hursley. The oldest house is at the corner of the road, a long low half-timber thatched cottage possibly dating back to the sixteenth century. There is no river in Hursley parish, but there are several lakes and ponds covering 10 acres altogether; one in Hursley Park, three in Cranbury Park (Great Pond, Upper Pond, and Lower Pond), a small one at Parsonage Farm, another at Upper Sharland, and several at Standon and Pitt. The soil of the parish varies from chalk in the north to clay, sand, and gravel with peat in the south, and the vegetation differs accordingly. The chief crops are wheat, barley, and oats, with good crops of turnips and peas.

CASTLE Although it is possible that an earthwork existed at Merdon in the eleventh century or earlier, yet there is no mention of such in Domesday, and the foundation of the castle is ascribed to Bishop Henry de Blois, who built and fortified it in 1138.[2] During the next few years, in the struggle between Stephen and the Empress Maud, the castle was doubtless of military importance, but from that time it seems to have been rather a bishop's palace than a military castle.

Like Farnham and Wolvesey it was kept in good repair, and between 1265 and 1268 in Bishop Gervase's account book an entry was made of the expense of fitting up the hall in the castle of Merdon.[3] In 1278 Bishop Nicholas of Ely was resident at the castle, and the ceremony of reinstating the prior of St. Swithun was performed there.[4] However, by the fourteenth century such parts as were useless for habitation seem to have fallen into decay, though Bishop Edendon seems to have resided there as late as 1365.[5]

The site of Merdon Castle is marked by a fine circular earthwork surrounded by a deep ditch, with traces of a second line of banks outside the ditch, and a causeway on the east leading to the central inclosure. A small length of the curtain wall remains on the south, with a tower which may be of twelfth-century date. Its walls are 7 ft. thick, and the windows and doorways have lost their architectural detail, but appear to have been round-headed.

MANOR There is only one manor in the parish of Hursley, and that bearing not the name of the parish, but of the ancient castle of *MERDON*—(Maerdune, Meredune, Meretune, Merantune (ix cent.), Mardon, Merden (xv cent. et seq.)—within the parish. Though it is difficult to state with any certainty that the 'Merantune' of the Anglo-Saxon Chronicle, the scene of Cynwulf's murder by Cynheard his kinsmen in 784, was Merdon in Hursley, yet there is much to be said for the suggestion.[6] Certain it is that the murdered king was buried at Winchester, his capital; and his visit with a small company to 'Merantune,' made evidently from Winchester, is more likely to have been a short journey to a quiet country place just outside Winchester than across Surrey. The next mention of Merantune or Maerdune is in 781, when two months after the Danes had been victorious at Basing King Ethelred and Alfred his brother fought with them at Merdon. Though for a time fortune favoured the king, yet in the end the Danes were victorious and held the place of battle.[7]

Merdon was probably included in the grant made about 636 by King Kinegils to the bishop and church of Winchester of land within a seven-mile circle of Winchester,[8] and from that time onwards to the reign of Edward VI the bishops of Winchester held the manor. In 1291 Merdon was included among the bishop's lands, and was worth £80.[9]

In 1341 Adam, bishop of Winchester, granted the office of parker or warrener in his manor of Merdon to Giles de Mansynton, subject to the confirmation of the grant by the prior and convent of St. Swithun. There is little else in the history of the manor, apart from the castle, until the reign of Edward VI, when in 1552 John Poynet, bishop of Winchester, surrendered Merdon among other lands to the king.[10] In the same year Edward granted it to Sir Philip Hoby, together with the park of Hursley, to be held in chief for the fortieth part of a knight's fee.[11] Before this time there was probably no manor-house at Merdon except the castle, and that was in decay by the fourteenth century, and it was Sir Philip Hoby who probably built the 'great Lodge.' But he had little time to enjoy his new possession, since in 1557, when Mary dared to restore the church lands, the manor of Merdon was granted to John White, bishop of Winchester.[12]

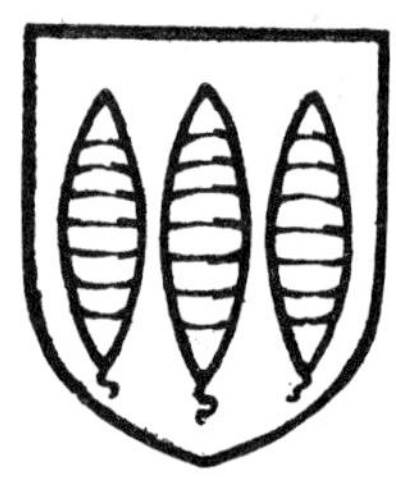

HOBY. *Argent three weavers' bottoms gules.*

An entry on the steward's roll for 1559, the year of the regrant by Elizabeth to Sir Philip Hoby's half-brother William Hoby,[13] shows that the profits of the manor, 'part of the Bishopric of Winchester before this,' were then brought into the annual account register, 'since the said manor by Act of Parliament was granted to William Hoby.'[14]

William Hoby seems, according to a monumental inscription in Hursley church, to have married as his second wife the widow of the Thomas Sternhold who in collaboration with John Hopkins first 'sounded out the Psalms of David' in metrical verse, and employed much time in singing his psalms to his organ for his own 'godly solace'.[15] On his death, probably at Hursley, in the latter part of the sixteenth century,[16] the manor descended to his son

[2] *Ann. Mon.* (Rolls Ser.), ii, 51.

[3] Quoted by Marsh, *Mem. of the Parish of Hursley*, 31 *n.*

[4] Wharton, *Angl. Sac.* i, 314. *Dictus episcopus predictum Valentinum in pristinum statum prioratus restituit die S^ti Petri ad Vincula apud Merdonam.*

[5] Winton Epis. Reg. Edendon, pt. i, fol. 129, &c.

[6] Milner in his *Hist. of Winchester* identifies it thus because of the evident nearness of the scene to Winchester, whereas Merton in Surrey, with which other writers (Lingard, *Hist. of England*, i, 164, &c.) have identified Merantune, would have been too far from the king's capital for his military forces to reach the scene of the murder before Cynheard could withdraw (*Hist. of Winchester*, 111). Woodward unhesitatingly accepted Milner's opinion (*Hist. of Hants*, i, 319). One other point that seems to sweep away many of the objections made by Marsh in his *Mem. of the Parish of Hursley* is that the spelling 'Merantune' is found in one version of the chronicle in the description of a battle which he himself gives as taking place at Merdon; *Angl.-Sax. Chron.* (Rolls Ser.), i, 140; Cott. Tib. A. iv.

[7] *Angl.-Sax. Chron.* (Rolls Ser.), i, 138–40.

[8] *Ann. Mon.* (Rolls Ser.), ii, 5.

[9] *Pope Nich. Tax.* (Rec. Com.), 215*b*.

[10] Pat. 5 Edw. VI, pt. 6, m. 3.

[11] Ibid. m. 4.

[12] Pat. 5 & 6 Mary, pt. 7, m. 24.

[13] Marsh, op. cit. 6 *n.*

[14] Ibid; quoting Steward's Roll for 1559.

[15] See *Dict. Nat. Biog.*

[16] Marsh, op. cit. 7.

Giles, who in 1600 sold the castle and manor to Thomas Clerke of Ardington in Berkshire, his father-in-law, reserving to himself and his wife a life interest in the lodge and park of Hursley.[17]

In 1602 Sir Thomas Clerke was living at Merdon, and in that year his son was married in Hursley church.[18] At this time the copyholders of the manor were still required to perform their customary services of reaping and carrying crops, and in Robert Morley's manuscript there is an account of a quarrel between the lord and his tenants on one of the 'hay dobyn' or service days. The lord was obliged to supply breakfast and dinner for the workers, and one day 'the cart brought afield for the reapers a hogshead of porridge which stunk and had worms in it.' The tenants headed by Mr. Coram, the holder of Cranbury, refused to work without better provision, and he and Mr. Pye, Sir Thomas Clerke's steward, drew their daggers, and rode at one another through the wheat. At last Lady Clerke promised to dress two or three hogs of bacon for them, and they quietly retired to work.[19] It is not difficult to imagine how much these hay dobyn days were hated by the tenants, especially as a hindrance to their own work, and Morley writes how 'a heire went for a man on hay dobyn days if able to carry a hook aforesaid.'[20] In 1606 Sir Thomas Clerke sold the manor of Merdon with the rest of his property to William Brock, 'a great lawyer,' who died in 1618, leaving his only child, a daughter and minor, under the joint guardianship of Sir Thomas Savage and Sir Richard Tichborne,[21] on whom settlement was made at the time of the sale in 1606.[22] In 1626 Anne Brock married John Arundell,[23] who in right of his wife became lord of the manor. The Arundells do not, however, seem to have lived at Hursley, but leased the manor in 1623 to Richard Lumley,[24] in 1626 to Henry Hastings,[25] and before 1630 sold it to Sir Nathaniel Napier of Crichel (Dorset).[26]

Napier of Crichel. *Argent a saltire engrailed between four cinquefoils gules.*

In the meantime, in 1621, Giles Hoby had leased the lodge and park of Hursley to Nicholas Peascod.[27] Giles died in 1626 and his wife in 1630, and thereupon the lodge and park reverted to the holder of Merdon Manor, Sir Nathaniel Napier.[28] On the death of the latter some time before 1635,[29] the manor descended to his son Gerard, who sold it in 1638–9 to Richard Major, who was, according to the description of a contemporary, a man witty and thrifty even to miserliness, and an unscrupulous oppressor of his tenantry.[30] More especially did he 'usurp authority over his tenants,' when 'King Charles was put to death and Oliver Cromwell was Protector of England and Richard Major of his Privy Council and Noll's eldest son Richard was married to Mr. Major's Doll.'[31] The marriage there referred to was that of Richard Cromwell with Dorothy Major, which brought Merdon into the Cromwell family, and gave it a part in one of the most interesting periods in English history. Richard Cromwell lived at Merdon from 1649, the year of his marriage, until he became Protector on the death of his father in 1658.

On his forced withdrawal from Whitehall in 1660, he came to Hursley for a few months, but early in the summer left England for France,[32] leaving behind him a heavy burden of debts contracted, as he himself stated, upon the public account.[33] While abroad he went by another name, 'though he did not disguise himself nor deny himself to any man that challenged him.'[34] It was thus under assumed names that he corresponded with wife and children at Hursley, where they lived in quiet seclusion, and where Mrs. Cromwell died in January, 1675–6. During her illness Cromwell wrote to his daughter Elizabeth, bidding her desire her mother to quiet her conscience concerning him and strive to be cheerful.[35] Yet the letters that follow show how little cheerfulness there was for the solitary exile. In 1680 he returned to England,[36] but not to Hursley; so the letters to his children continue. His great anxiety concerning the marriage of his son Oliver, who was of age in 1677, became quite pathetic. To his daughter Elizabeth he wrote in 1689 'it would greatly please to see your brother answer a duty both to God and his family. . . I would hope he would not dalley any longer with Providence, but take a resolution to fixe his minde.[37]' In the next year he wrote 'Pray let your brother settle, and that will be the best step for us to enjoy each other, according to what you desire.'[38] About this time there was evidently some thought of Richard joining his family at Hursley,[39] but the idea fell through and the letters continue.

Cromwell. *Sable a lion argent.*

In the meantime Oliver, on the death of his mother, had claimed Merdon in right of her marriage settlement and took possession of the estate. It was then that the customary tenants, possibly taking advantage of his youth, determined to win back some of the privileges and customs they had lost under the oppression of Richard Major. The Chancery suit was in progress in 1692, and lasted on until after the death of Oliver in 1705. In 1707 Imber, on behalf of the tenants, since the Chancery decree was 'written in chancery hand and part thereof being in Latin and therefore not able to be read and understood by the tenants,' made an English abstract of the same in

17 Feet of F. Hants, Trin. 42 Eliz.
18 Extract from parish register given in Marsh, op. cit.
19 Extracts from Robert Morley's MSS. in Marsh, op. cit. p. 9.
20 Ibid. The tenants continued to perorm these services until they were commuted in 1650.
21 Brock had married Anne Tichborne, sister of Sir Richard.
22 Feet of F. Hants, Hil. 4 Jas. I; Com. Pleas Recov. R. Hil. 4 Jas. I, m. 17.
23 Marsh, op. cit. 9.
24 Feet of F. Hants, Mich. 21 Jas. I; Com. Pleas Recov. R. Mich. 21 Jas. I, m. 10.
25 Feet of F. Hants, Trin. 2 Chas. I.
26 Marsh, op. cit. 9 and 10.
27 Feet of F. Hants, Hil. 19 Jas. I.
28 Marsh, op. cit. 7.
29 Ibid.
30 From a MSS. account of the customs of the manor written by a tenant, Richard Morley.
31 From Robert Morley's manuscript.
32 Ludlow, *Memoirs*, 360.
33 *Engl. Hist. Rev.* (1887), 152.
34 Pepys' *Diary*, 19 Oct. 1664.
35 *Engl. Hist. Rev.* (1898), 95.
36 Mark Noble, *Mem. of the House of Cromwell*, 173. He lived at Cheshunt, near London, under an assumed name of Clark.
37 *Engl. Hist. Rev.* (1899), 101.
38 Ibid. (1898), 105–6; Letter xv.
39 Ibid. Letter xvi.

order that the tenants and their successors 'might on all occasions rightly know the customs of the manor.'[40] They claimed ordinary copyholders' rights, right to demise customary lands by copy; to pay a fixed fine on admittance; to let their tenements for a year without licence; to have sole right to fell trees on their tenements except oak, and even oak for repairs; to have sole pasture and feeding on the lord's heaths and wastes, and in the three coppices of South Holme, Heale Coppice, and Holman Coppice. Oliver Cromwell had ignored these customs on several occasions, as for instance when he brought an action against Mrs. Elliot for leasing her copyhold for a year, and against Thomas Lloyd for cutting down some oak trees for repairs on his copyhold of Nevil's Close and Hiltingbury[41] In 1705 Oliver died before the suit was finished, and a dispute arose concerning the Hursley estate. Richard Cromwell, who had allowed his son's right to the manor, now disputed the right of his daughters, who considered themselves the heirs of their brother. The case was heard and decided in Richard's favour,[42] and after this he seems to have lived partly at Hursley and partly at Cheshunt.[43] In 1712 he died at Cheshunt, and was buried at Hursley with much pomp.[44] His two surviving daughters, Elizabeth and Anne, succeeded to the estate, but only lived at Merdon for a few years, selling the whole manor in 1718 to Sir William Heathcote.[45] Sir William pulled down the old mansion-house, then in ruins, and built the modern house. He died in 1751,[46] leaving his eldest son Thomas as heir. On the death of Sir Thomas in 1787 the manor descended to his son William, whose great-grandson, Sir William Percival Heathcote, sold the estate in 1899 to Joseph W. Baxendale, who sold it in 1905 to Sir George Cooper, bart., the present owner.

HEATHCOTE. *Ermine three roundels vert with a cross or upon each.*

Hursley House is a fine building, the central part of which dates from the early part of the eighteenth century, while the wings are modern additions. The great attraction of the house is the splendid oak panelling and fittings formerly in Winchester College Chapel, and most unfortunately removed at the disastrous 'restoration' of the chapel by Butterfield. The work is of the time of Charles II, the carving being, as usual, attributed to Gibbons; in this case it is at any rate worthy of him. The site of the former house lies behind the present building on lower ground, and its foundations may be seen in the turf, though no part is now above ground.

CRANBURY seems originally to have been an important hamlet of Hursley,[47] and to have consisted of many distinct tenements or copyholds,[48] but now the name belongs only to Cranbury House and Park. Of the proprietors of Cranbury, who held of course of the bishop as of his manor of Merdon, the first mentioned seems to be a certain Shoveller, who surrendered to a Roger Coram before 1580. The latter, according to Marsh, seems to have been 'a zealous assertor of the tenants' rights against the lords of the manor.'[49] On the death of this Roger Coram Sir Edward Richards seems to have held the property until 1640–3,[50] when he let it, with the lord's consent, to Dr. John Young, dean of Winchester, who lived in quiet retirement at Cranbury during the Commonwealth. His widow, Mrs. Young, was holding in 1650, and probably resigned the house to Sir Charles Wyndham, who married her daughter in 1665. Sir Charles, who seems also to have been 'a zealous assertor of the tenants' rights,' and 'of a most respectable family,' died in 1706, before his wife, who survived him until 1720.[51] On her death the house and estate were sold to Jonathan Conduit, who sold the whole in 1737 or 1738 to Thomas Lee Dummer. The latter died in 1765, leaving a son and heir Thomas, from whom the estate devolved to Sir Nathaniel Holland.[52] On the death of Lady Holland, widow of Sir Nathaniel, the estate passed into the Chamberlayne family, and is held at the present day by Mr. Tankerville Chamberlayne.

CHAMBERLAYNE. *Gules a cheveron engrailed or between three scallops argent.*

Cranbury House is a large eighteenth-century red-brick building, with a projecting entrance porch on the south front, the main rooms being arranged round a central hall and staircase. There is a good deal of fine plaster decoration in the Adam style, especially in the saloon on the south front, which has a circular domed ceiling. The house contains a good number of valuable paintings, there being one very fine Romney, of Lady Hamilton as a maenad, and several of less merit. In the rooms on the east front are a number of pictures by Richter and Westall, and a curious unfinished subject painting, said to be by Romney.

The site of the house is well chosen, the ground falling steeply on the north, in well-wooded slopes. Some way down the slope is a spring, over which a domed well-house has been built, and on the higher ground to the west of the house is a circular earthwork. To the north of this is a summer-house and a stone sun-dial, said to have been designed by Sir Isaac Newton; its gnomon is supported by a monogram in openwork, apparently I.L.C. for Jonathan Conduit. In the park, at some distance to the south-west of the house, is a gamekeeper's cottage, masked by a sham ruin made up of fragments from Netley

[40] Imber, *The Case and Customs of the Manor of Merdon.* [41] Ibid.

[42] Mark Noble, *Mem. of the House of Cromwell.* The censure passed by Mark Noble on the conduct of Richard's daughters seems justifiable on the surface. However, his correspondence with his daughters continued on friendly terms during the suit. In one letter he says: 'To trouble & tare me aboute my estate is a feeling to the flesh, but I have spirit as well as flesh . . . whoe dare to break that knot of love and faithfulness which time hath of soe many years experienced.'

[43] *Engl. Hist. Rev.* (1898), 122.

[44] Mark Noble, op. cit. 176–7.

[45] Feet of F. Hants, East. 5 Geo. I.

[46] *Gent. Mag.* (1751), xxi, 236. Here the heir is given as his eldest son William, evidently a mistake. See G.E.C. *Complete Baronetage*, v, 75.

[47] Tenements in Cranbury are included in the extent given of the manor of Merdon when granted to Sir Philip Hoby in 1551. Pat. 5 Edw. VI, pt. 6.

[48] See Marsh, *Mem. of the Parish of Hursley*, 36. Evidence of the number of houses in Cranbury having at one time reached at least eleven is here deduced from the manorial court rolls. [49] Ibid.

[50] Ibid. 37. In 1640 he was fined £20 for cutting timber in Cranbury without licence from the lord of the manor.

[51] See tablet to their memory in Hursley church. [52] Marsh, op. cit. 37.

Abbey, whose north transept was destroyed for the purpose. A set of very beautiful early fourteenth-century bosses from a vault are built into the work.

Tenements in *LONGMOOR*, which is now the name of a farm on the western borders of Cranbury Park, were included in 1551 and in later grants among the appurtenances of the manor of Merdon.[53]

The hamlets of *STANDON* (Staundone, xiv cent.; Stonden, xvi cent.) and *PITT* (Putte, xiv cent.) were given among the bishop's possessions in 1316 as the 'villa de Staundone' and the 'villa de Putte,' and were evidently quite important hamlets.[54] Tenements in both were also given among the appurtenant tenements of Merdon manor in 1551.[55] A messuage and lands in Pitt were held by Sir John Philpott, lord of the manor of Compton, on his death in 1502,[56] and remained in the Philpott family until 1623, when Sir George Philpott held the same on his death.[57]

Hursley parsonage-house and the tenement of *SHARLAND* (Shorling, xv cent. et seq.) belonged in the fourteenth and fifteenth centuries to the college of St. Elizabeth near Winchester as appropriators of the church of Hursley.[58] At the Dissolution they were granted as 'the parsonage of Hursley and a tenement and pasture called Shorlinge in Hursley' to Thomas Wriothesley, Lord Southampton.[59]

In 1562 Frances Kempe and Thomas Wilmot brought a Chancery suit against John Forster concerning a lease of the parsonage and 'the manor or tenement of Shorling.' They petitioned that Thomas Runcorne, warden of the late college of St. Elizabeth, and the chaplains of the same being lawfully seised of the house and tenement about 1539, leased the same with the consent of the bishop of Winchester for a term of forty-one or forty-two years to John Wilmot. In 1558 John Wilmot bequeathed the same to his wife Joan for her life and after her death to his son Edward Wilmot. In later days the parsonage-house and the great tithes were purchased by the Heathcote family.

AMPFIELD (Annfelde, xiv cent.; Anfield xvi and xvii cent.), civil parish, was created out of Hursley parish in 1894. Before this time it was a hamlet of Hursley, appurtenant to the manor of Merdon. In 1316 it was given among the bishop of Winchester's possessions.[60] In 1551, when, after John Poynet had surrendered the manor of Merdon among others to Edward VI, the king granted the manor to Sir Philip Hoby, lands and tenements in 'Anfield' were given among the appurtenances together with those in *PUCKNALL* (Pukenhale, xiv cent.; Puckinhall, xvi cent.); *HILTINGBURY* and *HAWSTEAD* (Horstead Field, xiv cent.).[61] The latter are now included in Ampfield parish; Pucknall Farm is in the north-west, Hiltingbury Common in the south-east, and Hawstead in the east.

CHURCHES The church of *ALL SAINTS, HURSLEY*, has a chancel with north and south chapels, a nave with north and south aisles, and a western tower, all except the tower being modern, and rebuilt by John Keble during his long incumbency, 1836–66. The work is of fourteenth-century style, but rather lifeless; the church owes its picturesque effect rather to its situation than its architecture. The tower is of three stages, faced with chequer work of flint and stone, the two lower stages being old, and apparently of fifteenth-century date. There is a pointed west doorway under a square head, with what may be a consecration cross on its south jamb, and above the doorway is a square-headed window of three cinquefoiled lights. The belfry stage is modern, and from it rises a stone spire.

KEBLE. *Argent a cheveron engrailed gules and a chief azure with three molets or therein.*

Two brasses are preserved from the old church, one of John Bowland, 1470, and another of Anne Horswell, 1559, with a quaint inscription in English. In the tower is a large monument to Mrs. Elizabeth Connell, 1731.

There are six bells: the first by Mears & Stainbank, 1880; second and third by W. Taylor, Oxford, 1835; the fourth bears the inscription 'Prayse God, I W, 1616'; the fifth 'O Give thanks to God I W, 1616,' both by John Wallis of Salisbury; the sixth is by Robert Cor of Aldbourne, 1713.

The plate is a silver-gilt set dating from 1841, consisting of a chalice, two patens, a large flagon, and an almsdish.

The first five books of registers, containing mixed entries, run as follows:—1600–39, 1640–53, 1653–66, 1665–1706, 1706–53. The sixth and seventh books contain baptisms and burials, 1755–82, and the eighth the same, 1783–1820. The ninth and tenth contain marriages, 1754–1813.

The church of *ST. MARK, AMPFIELD*, was built in 1838–40 by Sir W. Heathcote, bart., of blue brick and stone. It consists of chancel, nave, north transept, south aisle, porch and open octagonal western turret with spire, containing two bells. The register dates from 1841.

ADVOWSONS The church of Hursley was in the gift of the bishop of Winchester until the beginning of the fourteenth century when John de Pontoise founded the college of St. Elizabeth, Winchester.[62] This foundation led to the ordination of the vicarage of Hursley, the rectory of which was given by the bishop to the college.[63] The grant of the appropriation of the church, which had been made without the licence of Edward I, was confirmed to Richard de Bourne, the provost, and the chaplains and clerks by Edward II in 1307.[64] Bishop Edendon, when ratifying to the college the gift of Hursley Church,[65] contrived to secure for himself and his successors the rectory-house.[66] The possession of the rectory was, however, restored to the provost and chaplains by William of Wykeham in 1372, when the college undertook to pay an additional annual pension of 13*s.* 4*d.* to the bishop.[67] The provost and chaplains presented the vicars until the Dissolution, when

[53] Pat. 5 Edw. VI, pt. 6, m. 324.
[54] *Feud. Aids*, ii, 309.
[55] Pat. 5 Edw. VI, pt. 6, m. 3, 4.
[56] Chan. Inq. p.m. (Ser. 2), xvi, No. 100.
[57] Ibid. ccccii, No. 129.
[58] See *infra* under 'Advowson.'
[59] Pat. 35 Hen. VIII, pt. 9, m. 7.
[60] *Feud. Aids*, ii, 309.
[61] Pat. 5 Edw. VI, pt. 6, m. 3.
[62] *V.C.H. Hants*, i, 212.
[63] Ibid.
[64] Pat. 1 Edw. II, pt. 2, m. 9.
[65] Egerton MS. 2033, fol. 19.
[66] *Wykeham's Reg.* (Hants Rec. Soc.), ii, 175.
[67] Ibid. The church seems to have been already burdened by one annual pension of 13*s.* 4*d.* to the bishop (ibid. ii, 106).

the advowson fell into the hands of the king. Edward VI granted it together with the manor of Merdon to Sir Philip Hoby,[68] and from this time the advowson followed the descent of the manor.[69]

The living of St. Mark's, Ampfield, is a vicarage in the gift of the Heathcote trustees.

CHARITIES In 1720 Mrs. Wyndham left £20 in respect of which 20*s* a year was distributed among the poor on St. Thomas's Day.

By deed, 1817, the trusts of a sum of money were declared which had been raised by subscription for the purpose of providing a Sunday evening service at the church. The fund was added to from time to time, and is now represented by £1,224 18*s*. 8*d*. consols.

In 1864 James Beckley, by will proved this date, left £3,647 2*s*. 6*d*. consols to the rector and churchwardens, and directed that the income should be applied weekly to five poor widows or widowers not under the age of fifty-five, who receive 7*s*. 6*d*. a week each.

In 1893 Emma Baker, by her will proved this date, bequeathed a moiety of her residuary estate for the benefit of the poor. A sum of £318 was received in respect thereof, of which £300 was invested in £301 16*s*. 9*d*. India £3 per cent. stock, the balance being distributed among the poor together with the income accruing on the stock.

The sums of stock belonging to the charities respectively are held by the Official Trustees of Charitable Funds.

LITTLETON

The parish of Littleton, covering about 1,303 acres,[1] lies on the downs which stretch away north-west of Winchester. The road leading from Winchester to Stockbridge through Weeke village sends off two branches at Weeke Mark, where the boundary lines of Weeke and Littleton meet, one branch going north-east through Harestock, the other going north-west through Littleton village and on to Crawley. After a long descent this road rises abruptly near Flower Down and continues generally uphill until it descends to form the short village street of Littleton. From the top of the hill the roofs of the thatched cottages and farm buildings are seen in the near distance backed by high downs. The church of St. Katherine, more commonly called the church of St. Mary Magdalene, is on the right beyond most of the houses and stands on a high mound; while behind the church is the village schoolhouse. Opposite is the manor farm, in front of which is one of the few small ponds in the parish. Away north and east of the village are grass downs reaching away to the thick belt of hedgerow which lines the Roman road from Winchester to Andover and forms the eastern boundary of the parish. The soil is loam with a subsoil of chalk. The arable land producing ordinary crops of wheat, barley, and oats is mostly in the south of the parish and round the village itself.

It seems to be impossible to discover any early mention of the place-name of Harestock, which is a group of houses, mostly quite modern, in the south of the parish, although it would seem likely that it was originally a field-name.

Harestock House is the residence of Maj.-Gen. Adolphus Brett Crosbie.

Place-names in the parish that occur on the thirteenth and fourteenth-century Court Rolls and Ministers' Accounts for Littleton[2] are Woodcot, Lupenshull or Lyppinghulle, Mydle Furlonge Close, Longacre, and Basyndowne. The tithe map is in the hands of the Ecclesiastical Commissioners.

MANOR *LITTLETON* was probably included in King Kinegils' grant to the church of Winchester of land within a seven-mile circle of the city.[3] As such it seems to have been considered as part of Chilcomb and excluded from individual mention in the various charters to the church even in the confirmation of its possessions made by the pope in 1205.[4] It is first definitely noticed as a manor in 1243 in the confirmation made by the pope in that year.[5] King Edward I granted the prior and convent free warren in their demesne lands of Littleton in 1300,[6] and in the levy for a feudal aid made in 1316 the prior was returned as holding the 'vill of Littleton.'[7] In 1334 there is an entry on the Receiver's Roll for the priory of £5 for rents from the manor, but evidently, like Chilbolton, Littleton was most valuable for sheep-farming, as its yearly receipts for wool reached £15 13*s*. 1*d*.[8] The village was evidently visited by the plague in 1364, since rents from various tenements were returned on the Ministers' Accounts as unpaid, owing to the death of the tenants by the plague (*causa pestilenciae*).[9] In the description of the proceeds of the manor made in the sixteenth century there is an interesting entry among the rents from the tenants of 10*s*. rent for having common rights on 'Basyndowne.' At that time the manor was farmed by a certain Laurence Bell at an annual rent of £17. He had also the farm of the tithes of the manor, and the demesne lands valued at £1 13*s*. 4*d*. The fines, tallages, heriots, strays, and perquisites of court only amounted to 10*s*., while 6*s*. 8*d*. was due yearly for the 'farmer' of the manor *pro toga sua*.[10]

The details of a lease made in 1500–1 by Prior Silkstead of 40 acres at Littleton near the hospital or house of St. Mary Magdalene to William Atkins the custodian of the same, seem to show that at Littleton, as at Silkstead, there was a house where the brethren of St. Swithun went for country air, and it is suggested that the chimney of the old vicarage, the

[68] Pat. 5 Edw. VI, pt. 6.
[69] Recov. R. East. 42 Eliz. rot. 48; Chan. Inq. p.m. (Ser. 2), cccclxxix, No. 110; Recov. R. Mich. 2 Jas. I, rot. 246; Inst. Bks. (P.R.O.).
[1] Ord. Surv.
[2] Ct. R. and Mins. Accts. *penes* D. and C. of Winchester (Winton. Cath. Lib.).
[3] Wharton, *Angl. Sacr.* i, 285.
[4] *Cal. of Pap. Letters*, i, 21.
[5] Ibid. 201.
[6] Chart. R. 29 Edw. I, m. 12, No. 54.
[7] *Feud. Aids*, ii, 309.
[8] *Obed. R. of St. Swithun* (Hants Rec. Soc.), 224.
[9] Mins. Accts. (Winton. Cath. Lib.), 224.
[10] *Winton. Cath. Doc.* (Hants Rec. Soc.), i, 88.

present schoolhouse, represents its only surviving remains.[11]

In the ordinary sequence of events Littleton passed into the king's hands at the Dissolution, and was granted to the newly-founded dean and chapter in 1541,[12] with a special stipulation that the 6*s.* 8*d.* above mentioned should continue to be paid to the 'farmer.'[13]

CHURCH The church of *ST. MARY MAGDALENE* (originally *ST. KATHERINE*) is a small building with an irregularly-shaped nave 26 ft. by 15 ft., with a north aisle, and a chancel 18 ft. 10 in. by 10 ft. 9 in. with a marked northward inclination, having a modern vestry and organ chamber on the north side.

The nave walls are thin, 2 ft. at the east and 2 ft. 3 in. at the south, and are probably of twelfth-century date. The jambs of the chancel arch belong to the later years of this century, and are the oldest pieces of detail now to be seen. The chancel belongs to the first half of the thirteenth century, and the north aisle was added during the same period, and from that time till the nineteenth century no additions were made to the plan. The walls are of flint with stone dressings, and the roofs are red-tiled.

The chancel has an east window of five trefoiled lights under a transom, with an arched head above filled with tracery dating from 1885. In the north wall are no windows, but a wide modern arch to the organ chamber, and on the south side is a widely splayed thirteenth-century lancet and a narrower trefoiled light to the west of it. The chancel arch has old jambs with a roll worked on the angles, of late twelfth-century style, and is only 4 ft. 7 in. wide, flanked on either side by square-headed openings. The chancel arch is segmental and modern, as are the heads of the openings, and above them there is a pointed modern arch. In the east wall to the south, at some height from the floor, is a quatrefoiled opening blocked with brickwork, which may have lighted the rood-stair, but all traces of the old arrangement are gone, and the south-east angle of the nave has been rebuilt.

The north arcade of the nave is of two bays, with pointed arches of two chamfered orders and round central pillar with half-round responds; only the arches are old, the pillar and responds having been renewed. In the north aisle no old details are preserved, and the pointed south doorway of the nave is also modern, under a modern porch, as is the tracery of the only window in the south wall, of two cinquefoiled lights with a quatrefoil in the head.

The west window, with a wide round-headed light, is also modern, but has old stonework in the jambs, and over it in the west gable are two pointed arches containing two small uninscribed bells, with the date 1897 on the stonework. The font, near the south door of the nave, is the most interesting thing in the church, belonging to the last quarter of the twelfth century. It is of Purbeck marble, with a square bowl carved with scalloped and imbricated ornament, and having a circular sinking, the angles of the upper surface filled in with foliage. It stands on a central and four angle shafts, with moulded capitals and bases.

There are two bells without inscription.

The plate consists of a chalice and two patens, dated 1836, of plated metal, and the registers before 1813 are contained in a single book beginning in 1738.

ADVOWSON The church of Littleton existed at the time of the Domesday Survey, as one of the nine churches included in Chilcomb.[14] It evidently belonged to the bishop of Winchester until granted in the twelfth century by Bishop Henry de Blois to the prior and convent of St. Swithun *ad religiosos hospites suscipiendos*.[15] The church was confirmed to the prior and convent by the pope in 1205,[16] and again in 1243.[17] At the Dissolution it was granted to the dean and chapter of Winchester,[18] who are the patrons at the present day.

Its original dedication in honour of St. Katherine is recorded in Wykeham's register.[19]

MICHELMERSH

Muchelmaries, Michelmares, and Muchelmarays (xiii cent.); Michelmarsh and Mitchelmarsh (xiv cent.); Mychelmers (xvi cent.).

The parish of Michelmersh is on high ground which falls in the west to the Test valley. North and north-east are wide stretches of woodland covering about 520 acres, while in the west near the more fertile valley is the pasture land of about 1,114 acres and the arable land of 1,847 acres. The modern parish, including Braishfield, extends over an area of 4,178 acres, 35 of which are covered by the Test; but until 1877, when Awbridge was formed into a separate parish from part of Michelmersh and Romsey, the whole area was 4,246 acres.

Although the more modern and growing part of the village with its shops and modern villas is in the south of the parish near the brickworks, the older part of the village is in the north, where several detached cottages and farm-houses are grouped on either side of the steep narrow road that rises between high chalk banks and overhanging trees from a height of about 100 ft. to 273 ft. near the church and rectory. Thus from Bellropes Field opposite the rectory, from the rectory garden, and from the fields round, can be seen wide stretches of the surrounding country. To the north is Michelmersh Wood, and beyond in the distance King's Somborne parish; to the south and east Romsey is seen in the distance over Timsbury and Braishfield; and away to the west, beyond the glittering Test, the village of Mottisfont nestles in the valley with a background of hills and woodland. Michelmersh House, the residence of Mrs. A. Wheable, stands back from the road among well-wooded grounds a few yards away from the church. A walk across the field called Agincourt at the back of the rectory leads to the manor farm, which is evidently the old manor-

[11] *Winton. Cath. Doc.* (Hants Rec. Soc.), ii, 69.

[12] Ibid. i, 71.

[13] Ibid. 76; Pat. 33 Hen. VIII, pt. 9, m. 5–10.

[14] *V.C.H. Hants*, i, 463.

[15] *Winton. Epis. Reg.* (Hants Rec. Soc.), 607; *Cal. of Pap. Letters*, i, 21.

[16] *Cal. of Pap. Letters*, i, 21.

[17] Ibid. 201.

[18] Pat. 33 Hen. VIII, pt. 9.

[19] *Wykeham's Reg.* (Hants Rec. Soc.), i, 365.

house. At the back of the house are traces of fourteenth and fifteenth-century stonework, and what may possibly be the survival of an ancient chantry chapel.

A rough road from the southern part of the village leads downhill by Hunts Farm to the hamlet of Braishfield, which was made an ecclesiastical parish in 1855. About two miles from Michelmersh the road curves slightly to the north and leads round by quiet cottages and farmsteads to the main road from Romsey, along which the modern part of the village of Braishfield has grown up within the last century. The northern part of the main road branches to the right near the village inn to the church, vicarage and schools, and to the left along a shady lane to Braishfield House, the residence of Mr. Edward M. Eaton, and on to Pitt House, Pitt Farm, and Braishfield Lodge, the residence of Mr. George Deare Dietz. Nonconformity is represented in the village by a Primitive Methodist chapel and an Independent chapel a few yards apart on the west of the main road and south of the village.

The parish of Awbridge, formerly a hamlet of Michelmersh, lies for the most part on the low-lying country, stretching away from the right bank of the Test. Awbridge House, the residence of Mrs. Thurston, is in the north near the river in the midst of picturesque country, which slopes up to the high wood of Long Croft Copse in the north-west. An uphill road runs south-west from Awbridge House between field and hedgerow to fork east and west at the top of the hill, where there is a group of houses and shops, one of which serves as the post office. The western branch curves south again, passes by Awbridge Farm, and runs on to the village proper, which consists of several cottages and farms, the modern church built in 1876, and the Independent chapel built before 1874. The Awbridge Danes estate fills up most of the south-west corner of the parish. A main road to Romsey runs along to the west of Awbridge Danes, the residence of Mrs. Tragett. A branch from the road to Romsey, which cuts through the western part of the parish, curves south round the park and woodland, inclosing Awbridge Danes and a few houses.

Among place-names mentioned in records are Ruchenaye (xiii cent.),[1] Newbridge Meads[2] or Bridge Meads (xvi cent.),[3] and Tipley Hill (xvii cent.).[4]

MANOR

King Ethelred in 985 granted eleven *mansae* at *MICHELMERSH* to a certain Ælfred for the term of his life.[5] The boundaries as given in the charter are difficult to identify with but two exceptions, namely, 'feora burnan' and 'ceomman bricge,' the former being represented by the present Farburn Farm on the borders of Braishfield and the latter by Kimbridge on the Test. Michelmersh remained the property of the crown until 1043, when it was granted by Queen Emma, together with eight other manors, to the church of Winchester.[6] Like several of the manors belonging to the church, Michelmersh was not mentioned in Domesday Book. In 1205 and again in 1243 Michelmersh was confirmed to the prior and convent of St. Swithun in general confirmations of their lands made by the pope.[7] In 1285 John, bishop of Winchester, quitclaimed to them all his right in the manor,[8] and in 1301 the king granted them free warren in their demesne lands in Michelmersh and their other manors.[9] William Briwere, who founded the priory of Mottisfont about 1200, granted to it all the land which he held in the manor of Michelmersh free from suit at his hundred-court of King's Somborne, and from all other services and secular exactions, to keep the anniversary of his wife Beatrice, and his gift was confirmed by his daughter Margery de la Ferté in her widowhood.[10] The prior and canons of Mottisfont remained in possession of this land for some time, but in 1231, owing to the fact that they had erected a house upon it to the damage of the prior of St. Swithun, an agreement was made whereby Stephen, prior of Mottisfont, surrendered to Walter, prior of St. Swithun, all his possessions in the parish in exchange for a meadow called 'Ruchenaye,' and lands and rents in the vill of Drayton.[11] During the fourteenth century further grants of land in Michelmersh were made to the prior and convent,[12] while in 1332 the king gave them licence to impark their wood of Michelmersh.[13] The manor remained in the possession of the monastery until 1539,[14] when it was taken into the hands of the king.[15] Unlike the other manors that had belonged to St. Swithun, Michelmersh was not granted to the dean and chapter in 1541, but was held by the crown until 1543. In that year it was granted with a reserved rent of £5 11*s.* 3*d.* to Sir William Sidney in recognition of his services as tutor and steward of the household to Prince Edward.[16] Sir William died at Penshurst in 1554,[17] leaving as heir his eldest son Henry, who ten years later obtained a release of the reserved annual rent from the manor and park.[18] Worn out by his hard work as lord-deputy of Ireland, unrewarded as it was by the capricious Elizabeth, Sir Henry Sidney died at Penshurst in May, 1586, at the age of fifty-seven.[19] His eldest son, the poet, courtier, and soldier, Sir Philip Sidney, died at Zutphen in September of the same year, leaving his estates to his younger brother Robert, the second son of Sir Henry, on condition that he should sell so much of the lands as should pay his own and his father's debts.[20] In 1588 Sir Robert Sidney[21]

SIDNEY. *Or a pheon azure.*

[1] Feet of F. Hants, 15 Hen. III.
[2] *L. and P. Hen. VIII*, xviii, 368.
[3] Mins. Accts. Hants, 32 & 33 Hen. VIII, 109, m. 45. [4] Close, 4 Jas. I, pt. 22.
[5] Kemble, *Codex Dipl.* iii, 218–19.
[6] Wharton, *Angl. Sacra*, i, 235.
[7] *Cal. of Pap. Letters*, i, 21, 201.
[8] Chart. R. 13 Edw. I, m. 27.
[9] Ibid. 29 Edw. I, m. 12.
[10] Dugdale, *Mon.* vi, 481, 482.
[11] Feet of F. Hants, 15 Hen. III.
[12] *Rot. Orig.* (Rec. Com.), i, 206*b*; Inq. a.q.d. 7 Edw. II, No. 115; *Cal. of Pat.* 1313–17, p. 37; 1327–30, p. 501.
[13] *Cal. of Pat.* 1330–4, p. 263.
[14] *Feud. Aids*, ii, 309; *Pope Nich. Tax.* (Rec. Com.), 214.
[15] Mins. Accts. Hants, 32 & 33 Hen. VIII, No. 109, m. 45.
[16] Pat. 35 Hen. VIII, pt. 2, m. 10; *L. and P. Hen. VIII*, xviii, 368. The grant included the Outward Manor-place of Michelmersh Manor, then held at farm by John Bacon, a messuage in Awbridge, two meadows in the lordship of Michelmersh called Newbridge Meads, and the site of the lodge and inclosure of the park with herbage and pannage and warren of small game which William, Lord Sandys, was then holding on a thirty-one years' lease by indenture of 1538.
[17] Collins, *Letters and Mem. of State*, i, 82; Chan. Inq. p.m. (Ser. 2), xcviii, No. 30.
[18] Pat. 6 Eliz. pt. 6, m. 15–20.
[19] Collins, *Letters and Mem. of State*, i, 96.
[20] Ibid. 110; Chan. Inq. p.m. (Ser. 2), ccxix, No. 53.
[21] He was knighted in 1586 (Collins, *Letters and Mem. of State*, i, 114).

was made governor of Flushing, and in the same year the queen confirmed him in his estates.[22] Among these was the manor of Michelmersh, which had not been sold to pay Sir Philip's debts. During his tenure of the manor legal proceedings were taken against him by the tenants. In 1590 they complained that their 'immemorial rights of common' in a piece of waste called 'Typley Hill' had been broken by its inclosure and secret conveyance to Thomas Bacon and John Sidney.[23] Sir Robert at the same time filed a bill against the tenants that they had cut down divers great timber trees without licence, contrary to the custom of the manor and 'to the dysinherysone of Her Majesty, and the said orator and to the dangerous example of others to doe the like, yf condinge punishment be not speedily in that behalf provided.'[24] The tenants answered that by custom of the manor they had wood for house bote, plough bote, and other necessaries.[25] About the same time the tenants made another complaint that the lord of the manor did not exact the customary fine for admission of tenants, but asserted that the fines were uncertain. Judgement was finally given by decree of the Court of Chancery dated 20 May, 1598, that the fine was to be 8*s.* an acre certain, and an heriot.[26] On 7 June, 1606, Sir Robert Sidney, who had been created Viscount Lisle in 1605, was granted the reversion and remainder of the manor and park of Michelmersh.[27] Three days later he sold the same to Sir Thomas Stewkley of Hinton Ampner for a sum of £3,100.[28] Sir Thomas died in 1639, and the manor passed to his eldest son Hugh, who died in the same year as his father, leaving a son Hugh, who succeeded to the manor of Michelmersh.[29] His widow, Sarah Stewkley, married again in 1648, and lived at Michelmersh.[30] Sir Hugh held the manor until his death in 1719, when dying without heirs male he ordered the manor to be sold among his other possessions, giving his daughters preference as purchasers.[31] Michelmersh fell to his eldest daughter Mary, who in the same year married Edward, fourth Lord Stawell of Somerton.[32] She died in 1740, and was buried at Hinton.[33] Her husband survived her until 1755 when, dying without heirs male, he left Michelmersh to his only daughter Mary,[34] the wife of the Rt. Hon. Henry Bilson-Legge, fourth son of William, earl of Dartmouth, whom she had married in 1750.[35] In 1760 she was created Baroness Stawell of Somerton, with remainder of title to her heirs male.[36] Surviving her husband, by whom she had one son and heir, the baroness married Wills, first earl of Hillsborough, in 1768.[37] On her death in 1780 Michelmersh passed to her son Henry Stawell Legge, Lord Stawell, who died without heirs male in 1820.[38] Michelmersh then descended to his daughter Mary, who had married the Hon. John Dutton, only son and heir of James, Lord Sherborne.[39] The latter died in 1864, and the manor passed to his son, James Henry Legge Dutton, Lord Sherborne.[40] The present owner, Edward Lenox, Lord Sherborne, son of the latter, succeeded to the manor on the death of his father in 1883.[41]

STEWKLEY. *Checky argent and sable with a fesse and a border gules.*

DUTTON, Lord Sherborne. *Quarterly argent and gules, the gules fretty or, with a crescent for difference.*

Earl Godwin held *AWBRIDGE* (Abedric, xi cent.; Abberuge, Abbederugge, xiii cent.; Abbederygg, xiv cent.; Abrige, xvi cent.) of Edward the Confessor. After the Conquest William divided Awbridge into two portions, granting one part together with part of the parish of Houghton, which Godwin had also held, to the great Hampshire landowner Hugh de Port,[42] and the other part, which was then assessed at one virgate, to Bernard Pancevolt.[43] The part which was granted to Hugh de Port naturally followed the descent of Houghton. The other portion seems also to have lost its independence and from an early date formed part of the great manor of Michelmersh.[44] Thus in the dispute of Elizabeth's reign between Sir Robert Sidney and his tenants mention is made of the fact that the manor of Michelmersh comprised divers copyhold and customary messuages, lands, and tenements in Awbridge.[45]

BRAISHFIELD (Brayfeld, Braisfelde, xiv cent.; Brayesfeld, xv cent.) is not mentioned in Domesday Book, and its early history is somewhat obscure. In 1289 William Bonell of Braishfield granted a messuage and a carucate of land in Braishfield to Aimery de Somerset and Denise his wife.[46] Twenty years later Aimery granted a messuage, lands, and 14*s.* rent in Braishfield by Michelmersh to John de Braishfield and Maud his wife to hold of him for life by a rent of £2 10*s.*,[47] and in 1331 he granted the reversion of these tenements to Andrew Payn and Alice his wife.[48] They perhaps descended to Roger Woodlock, who in 1346 was holding the fourth part of a fee in Braishfield formerly belonging to John Brayboef,[49] though this part may possibly represent the land in Braishfield settled on Roger Woodlock and Joan his wife by Roger de la Bere in 1316.[50] In 1428 this fourth part of a fee had passed to John Emery, but in what way it is difficult to ascertain.[51] Braishfield afterwards lost its independence and formed part of the manor of Michelmersh. Thus in the dispute of Elizabeth's reign, mention is made of the fact that divers copyhold and customary tene-

[22] Collins, *Letters and Mem. of State*; Pat. 31 Eliz. pt. 1, m. 6.
[23] Exch. Dep. Hants, Mich. 32 & 33 Eliz. No. 18.
[24] Ibid.
[25] Ibid. Hil. 33 Eliz. No. 21.
[26] Chan. Enr. Dec. R. 106, No. 9.
[27] *Cal. S.P. Dom.* 1603–7, p. 320.
[28] Add. MS. 33278, fol. 165; Close, 4 Jas. I, pt. 22; Feet of F. Hants, Trin. 4 Jas. I.
[29] A. W. *Michelmersh and its Antiquities*, 7.
[30] While there she wrote a letter to the archbishop of Canterbury, dated 18 June, 1667, requesting some fit employment for her husband against the enemies of the crown (*Cal. of S.P. Dom.* 1667, p. 208).
[31] A. W. *Michelmersh and its Antiquities*, 7.
[32] G. E. C. *Peerage*, vii, 243.
[33] Ibid.
[34] A. W. *Michelmersh and its Antiquities*, 7.
[35] Ibid.
[36] G. E. C. *Peerage*, vii, 243.
[37] Ibid.
[38] Ibid.
[39] Ibid, 130.
[40] Ibid.
[41] Ibid.
[42] *V.C.H. Hants*, i, 480*b*.
[43] Ibid. 494*a*.
[44] *Feud. Aids* ii, 309.
[45] Chan. Enr. Dec. R. 106, No. 9.
[46] Coram Rege R. Hil. 17 Edw. I.
[47] Feet of F. Hants, Trin. 13 Edw. II.
[48] Ibid. Mich. 4 Edw. III.
[49] *Feud. Aids*, ii, 325.
[50] Feet of F. Hants, East. 9 Edw. II.
[51] *Feud. Aids*, ii, 348.

ments in Braishfield formed part of Michelmersh manor.[52]

Kimbridge water-mill on the Test on the borders of the parishes of Mottisfont and Michelmersh probably marks the site of the water-mill belonging to the prior and convent of St. Swithun in 1248.[53]

CHURCHES The church of *OUR LADY, MICHELMERSH*, consists of a chancel, north transept, nave with south aisle, and wooden south porch, and wooden tower at the south-west. A former south transept has been destroyed.

In 1847 a great deal of repair, not all judicious, was carried out, and as a consequence the history of the building is to some extent conjectural. The chancel is large in proportion to the nave, being 38 ft. long and 17 ft. 2 in. wide as against 48 ft. and 18 ft. 2 in. The north transept is about as wide as the nave, 18 ft. by 12 ft. deep, and it seems probable that both transepts and the chancel were additions of the middle of the thirteenth century, the former chancel having been smaller and narrower than the present, and co-eval with an aisleless nave whose general dimensions are preserved in that now existing. The south aisle may have been added in the fourteenth century.

The chancel has an east window of three lancets under an obtuse pointed arch, a north window of two similar lancets, and on the south a like window, all being contemporary with the chancel. To the east of the south window is one of *c.* 1330 of two lights with net tracery under a square head, having in its west jamb a small arched recess. The chancel arch dates from 1847, dying into the wall on both sides.

The arches to the transepts are segmental and round-headed, of a single order edge-chamfered; on that to the north transept are remains of red colouring, and part of the cross-slab of a stone coffin is built into its eastern jamb. In its western jamb is a lozenge-shaped panel containing a shield, *c.* 1520; the arms are a crescent between three human heads impaling three fleurs-de-lis. The north transept has a square-headed east window of three trefoiled lights with roll cusps, and a north window, also square-headed, of three uncusped lights. In both the stonework is old, but much patched, and its date is difficult to fix. Over the transept arch is a brass plate recording the repairs of 1847. The arch to the south transept is blocked, and a three-light window, perhaps from the south wall of the destroyed transept, is set in the blocking. The south arcade of the nave is of two bays, and of the same date and character as the chancel arch.

The nave has three tall square-headed north windows, each of three cinquefoiled lights, the western window of the three being entirely modern, while the other two retain a little fifteenth-century stonework. In the west wall is a plain doorway of uncertain date, and over it a window of two uncusped lights. The south aisle is lighted by three single trefoiled windows of fourteenth-century style with ogee heads, retaining a little old masonry, and the south doorway of a single edge-chamfered order is apparently an insertion, though its masonry may be old.

In the south wall of the nave near the west end is an opening at some height above the floor, probably a doorway to a former west gallery. At the west end of the south aisle is the font of thirteenth-century date, with human heads and well-carved foliage on the bowl and a round moulded base. There is some good early seventeenth-century panelling on the walls here, but no other woodwork in the church is old except the timbers of the chancel roof, a chest in the north transept, and the seventeenth-century altar table. The tower is old but of uncertain date, covered on the outside with weather boarding. In the south-east window of the chancel is a little fifteenth-century glass, with the heads of St. Paul, an archbishop, &c.

On the north side of the chancel is a fine freestone effigy of a knight in mail, *c.* 1320, with a mail cap, a long surcoat beneath which the quilted gambeson shows, and knee cops of leather or plate. The surface of the arms and legs is smooth, and perhaps the mail was here shown by painting instead of carving. The pommel and guards of his sword remain, hung to an ornamental belt, and on his feet are rowel spurs. On the left arm is a shield bearing two cheverons, the head rests on two cushions with seated angels on either side, and under the feet is a stag.

On the north wall behind the effigy is a very pretty little mural tablet with an inscription between the small kneeling figures, carved in low relief, of 'Trustram Fantleroy, Squyre,' 1538, and his wife, and at the west end of the south aisle is the monument of Sir William Ogle, Viscount Catherlough, 1682, a black marble tablet with a pediment on which is the coat of Ogle, Argent a fesse between three crescents gules impaling Tame, Argent a lion azure crowned gules fighting with a dragon vert.

There are three bells inscribed 'R. Wells of Aldbourne fecit 1769.'

The plate consists of one silver chalice inscribed 'For Michelmersh Church, 1635,' and one modern (1807) silver chalice and cover; one silver paten dated 1721 and a silver paten cover; two flagons, one plated, one pewter; one pewter almsdish dated 1674, one wooden almsdish with a plated edge, and one glass cruet.

The first register contains mixed entries from 1558 to 1648; the second baptisms and marriages from 1717 to 1754 and burials from 1718 to 1773; the third marriages only from 1754 to 1812; the fourth baptisms and burials from 1773 to 1812.

The churchwardens' accounts begin in 1774.

The church of *ALL SAINTS, AWBRIDGE*, consecrated in 1876, is a building of brick faced with Swanage stone, in the Gothic style, erected at a cost of £2,800, the greater part of which was subscribed by the late Rev. T. H. Tragett. The register dates from the year 1877.

The church of *ALL SAINTS, BRAISHFIELD*, was built in 1855, of red brick with tiled roof, in Gothic style, with belfry at west end containing three bells.

ADVOWSONS The advowson of the church of Michelmersh was from an early date in the hands of the bishop of Winchester,[54] and was confirmed to him by Edward I in 1284.[55] The living is at the present time a rectory

[52] Chan. Enr. Dec. R. 106, No. 9.
[53] Egerton MS. 2031, fol. 21.
[54] *Cal. of Pat.* 1272–81, p. 398; *Wykeham's Reg.* (Hants Rec. Soc.), i, 35, 115; *Winton. Epis. Reg.* (Hants Rec. Soc.), 94; Pat. 16 Jas. I, pt. 14, m. 22; Inst. Bks. (P.R.O.).
[55] Chart. R. 12 Edw. I, m. 5.

with net income £366, 58 acres of glebe, and residence, and is still in the gift of the bishop.

A certain John Cole was presented to the rectory by James I in 1621, during the vacancy of the see,[56] and in 1629 the churchwardens of Romsey presented John Mowle for saying that the 'bishops of Cant rbury and London' and two others of the lord bishops were no more able to argue in the Scriptures than 'one old Coles of Abridge who goeth about a begging.'[57]

In 1248 the prior and convent of St. Swithun and the rector of Michelmersh came to an agreement concerning the tithes of the mill and the meadows of the prior and convent in the parish.[58] The manor-farm is tithe-free at the present time.

The living of Awbridge is a perpetual curacy, net yearly value £250, with residence, in the gift of the bishop of Winchester.

The living of Braishfield is a vicarage in the gift of the bishop of Winchester.

CHARITIES In 1679 George Reeves gave £30 for education, and in 1711 Thomas Manningham, bishop of Chichester, and a former rector of the parish, gave £100; and John Cox in 1721 gave £40 for the same purpose. These sums have been invested in the purchase of £179 3*s.* 8*d.* consols, the dividends of which are applied under a scheme of the Charity Commissioners of 30 November, 1897, in granting prizes or rewards not exceeding in value 10*s.* to children qualified by attendance at a public elementary school.

MILLBROOK

The original parish of Millbrook, including Freemantle and Shirley, now suburbs of Southampton, contained an area of 3,223 acres of land, 10 acres of land covered by water, 140 by tidal water, and 140 of foreshore. However, by the Southampton Borough Extension Act of 1895, Shirley and Freemantle, already separate ecclesiastically, the one since 1836, the other since 1851, were included in the municipal borough, and together formed into a civil parish, containing altogether 2,651 acres, of which 2,047 acres are land, 8 acres land covered by water, and 100 by tidal water, and 496 acres of foreshore. Hence the modern parish of Millbrook contains only 986 acres of land, 2 of land covered by water, and 40 by tidal water, together with 191 of foreshore.

The nucleus of the original parish of Millbrook, marked by the old houses that survive among the many modern along the main road from Southampton which runs some yards from the foreshore towards Redbridge and forms the village street, is now the least important part of the district once composing the parish, so entirely have Shirley and Freemantle become the most populous and flourishing centres as suburbs of Southampton. The gradual increase in their importance, from a population point of view, dates from the middle of the nineteenth century, with the extraordinary growth of Southampton, owing to the opening of the docks in 1843. The break up of the greater number of Shirley estates, which were for the most part sold out in building allotments to the members of the Hants Freehold Land Society before 1852, was followed in that year by that of the Freemantle estate, which extended from Millbrook to Hill Hamlet near Fourposts. Sir George Hewett sold this estate to Mr. Sampson Payne, who pulled down the old hall, famous for its fine room entirely laid with slabs of marble, and, intersecting the park by nearly twenty good roads, resold to various land societies. From this time Shirley and Freemantle have been united to Southampton by a network of modern cottages and villas ever on the increase, and are being more closely linked by the service of electric trams extending now nearly the whole way up the Shirley Road as it runs north-west towards Old Shirley and Nursling. The extension of the building area continues west; Blighmont Park, the estate of 47 freehold acres that lies between Shirley and Millbrook, within the modern parish of Shirley, is now for sale, and possibly will be laid out for building. Moreover, Redbridge village, in the extreme west of the parish, with its station on both the Southampton and Andover branches of the London and South-Western Railway, with its important wharf and saw-mills belonging to the company, who have also large stores of railway plant here, is growing more especially towards the east, so that both from east and west it seems that Millbrook village, protected up to now by its number of good-sized houses, is about to be involved in modern growth.

As the main road comes from Southampton through Fourposts hamlet and Freemantle towards Millbrook village, the Southampton and Dorchester branch of the London and South-Western Railway runs south of the road along the foreshore with a station at Millbrook, within the bounds of the modern Shirley parish. Still continuing within modern Shirley the road gradually leaves the railway line and curves slightly north-west, passing the Blighmont Park estate (or, as it is locally known, Regent's Park), which lies on the north, and the rectory and old church of St. Nicholas (now disused), which stand opposite. West of Blighmont Park, also on the north side of the road, is the old churchyard of St. Nicholas. Thence, continuing west, the road enters the modern Millbrook parish at Tanner's Bridge, over the Holybrook rivulet, which runs south-west from Holybrook through Old Shirley to Millbrook, forming the western boundary of Shirley parish from Shirley Mill about a mile north. Thence, passing between several good-sized houses, among which is the manor-house lying on the south nearly opposite the new church of the Holy Trinity (built in 1873–80), which stands on the north, the road falls north-east to the little hamlet of Wimpson and north-west to Redbridge. This is one of the most picturesque corners of the village, as the small pond with its rough wooden railings lies on the left in front of the White Swan Inn. The parish hall (1859) stands on the north side of the road as it continues to Redbridge. Beyond the hall the road enters Redbridge, and, passing the village school, the railway station and several thatched half-timbered cottages scattered among the many modern houses, comes to the Ship Hotel, where the annual court leet of the manor of Millbrook is held, a quaint old house with a painted sign standing on the south

[56] *Cal. of S.P. Dom.* 1619–23, p. 358.

[57] Ibid. 1628–9, p. 587.

[58] Egerton MS. 2031, fol. 21.

side of the street. Passing thence by two or three low cottages, the road sends off a branch north to Nursling, near the modern Railway Guard Inn, and itself crossing the railway line (Andover branch), and the famous Red Bridge over the River Test, leaves the parish.

The north-eastern branch of the Millbrook road passing by the Royal Oak Inn, goes on to Yew Tree House, lying on the west, and thence to the group of cottages, the school, and the Methodist chapel composing the hamlet of Wimpson. Wimpson Farm lies to the north-west, while Upper Wimpson Farm with its thickly-grouped farm buildings is still further north-west near the border-line of Millbrook parish.

Although the extensive growth of both Shirley and Freemantle makes them impossible of description, there are still a few landmarks remaining in Shirley distinguishing Old and New Shirley, Shirley Warren, and Coxford, while Hill Farm in the south-east, now the head quarters of a dairy company, suggests the whereabouts of the manor farm of Hill. Banister's Park estate, with Banister's Court School and Cricket Ground mark the site of the so-called manor of that name.

The small rivulet called the Holybrook, running in a south-westerly direction through the parish, passes west of the fine grounds of Holybrook House, and broadens out into fine ponds at Old Shirley, on the north side of which are two or three picturesquely-situated houses. Near Shirley Ponds also are two or three of the old houses of Old Shirley, and the thatched inn 'Ye Old Thatched House,' and the modern 'Blacksmith's Arms.' Another rivulet known as Tanner's Brook also enters the ponds at the north-west corner, and as it thus joins with the Holybrook rivulet the two flow south to Shirley Mill, now a dilapidated building quite disused, and then south between Millbrook and Shirley to the Test.

Old Shirley Hill south of the pond is locally recognized as some sort of boundary-mark between Old and New Shirley. The Shirley Park estate, south of Old Shirley, is now almost wholly built over, Shirley Park Road being almost the only suggestion of the existence of Shirley Park.

The wide Shirley Road running south-east from Old Shirley into Southampton is the main feature of New Shirley. From it on either side go off branch streets and again branch streets, both wide and narrow, lined with modern cottages, shops and houses. A rather fine wide street known as Church Street goes off to the north-east to St. James's Road and to the well-built modern church of St. James, north-east of which are the church schools. There are several chapels in Shirley; Wesleyan, Baptist, Primitive Methodist, Bible Christian, and Evangelist.

Freemantle lies almost wholly south-west of the Shirley Road. The small stretch of water known as Freemantle Pond and the name Park Road alone survive to mark the site of Freemantle Park. Christ Church, Freemantle, a well-built modern church, stands in a good position south of the widest street, which is known as Payne's Road, from Mr. Sampson Payne, who, as has already been stated, converted Freemantle into a building estate. The schools are north-east of the church.

Two or three old houses and an old inn among the modern buildings mark the site of Four Posts hamlet in the south-east of Freemantle.

Among place-names found in the parish are a spring in Shirley called Colewell (xiv cent.),[1] and a plot of ground called the Conquest in Millbrook (xvi cent.).[2]

MANORS

King Eadwig in 956 granted 7 hides in *MILLBROOK* to Prince Wulfic for life,[3] and in 1045 King Edward granted the same 7 hides to Alwin, bishop of Winchester.[4] The boundaries of the land given in the two grants are almost identical, except that those of 1045 are much more fully given. They are traced from Redbridge to the River Test, and along the Test to Nursling (*on hnut scyllinga mearce*), then along the boundary to the hollow way (*holan wege*),[5] from the hollow way to Farningbrook (*on fearninga broc*), and so along to Millbrookford, and so east along the boundary to Thursley (*thunres lea*) northward, then along the way to the King's Dike (*cynges dic*), and so along the boundary to the other hollow way, thence to the weir on the river (*on ða ea se werstede*) near Redbridge, out through to the stream to the King's Wharf (*stæð*), and so along the stream back to Redbridge and the hedge (?) to Hampton, which belongeth thereto. At the time of the Domesday Survey the bishop himself held Millbrook, 'it had always belonged to the monastery,' but it was then and had been in the time of Edward the Confessor assessed at 5 hides.[6] In 1167 the prior of St. Swithun rendered account for the manor,[7] and in 1205 he received confirmation of Millbrook among his other possessions from the pope.[8] From this time till the dissolution of the monastery the manor remained in the hands of the prior and convent. Evidently from a very early period Millbrook was one of the St. Swithun's manors which were 'farmed' by villeins resident on the manor. Thus the Domesday entry states that 'villeins held it and hold it; there is no hall there.'[9] By the fourteenth century, if not earlier, the receipts from the 'farm' of Millbrook, together with that of the adjacent manor of Nursling, were appropriated to the office of warden of the works (*custos operum*).[10] Thus in 1409 John Hurst, warden of the works, received £21 15*s.* 7*d.* from the serjeant (*serviens*)[11] of Millbrook,[12] and in 1532 Walter Frost, warden of the works, received £27 5*s.* from the reeve.[13] On the suppression of the monastery in 1539[14] the manor passed into the king's hands, to be granted within the next year to the dean and chapter of Winchester, with a stipulation that its proceeds, together with those of four other manors, including Nursling, should be relegated to the support of twelve poor university students, six at Oxford and six at Cambridge.[15] However, in 1545 the dean and chapter, probably under compulsion, surrendered these five manors to the king. Millbrook and Nursling were then granted to John Mill,[16] who already owned

1 Pat. 1 Edw. III, pt. 1, m. 33.
2 Ct. of Requests, bdle. 17, No. 85.
3 Birch, *Cart. Sax.* iii, 99.
4 Kemble, *Codex Dipl.* iv, 104.
5 This may be the modern Brownhill Lane.
6 *V.C.H. Hants*, i, 467.
7 *Pipe R.* (Pipe R. Soc.)
8 *Cal. of Pap. Letters*, i, 21.
9 *V.C.H. Hants*, i, 442, 467.
10 *Obed. R. of St. Swithun* (Hants Rec. Soc.), 55.
11 *Serviens* seems to have the sense of under bailiff. Du Cange defines 'Serviens de Manerio' as 'villicus cui Manerii cura incumbuit.'
12 *Obed. R. of St. Swithun* (Hants Rec. Soc.), 114, 210.
13 Ibid. 215.
14 *L. and P. Hen. VIII*, xvi, 26.
15 Pat. 33 Hen. VIII, pt. 9, m. 5–11. *Winton. Cath. Doc.* (Hants Rec. Soc.), i, 171.
16 Pat. 37 Hen. VIII, pt. 1.

one manor in Nursling parish. From this time Millbrook and both the manors of Nursling followed the same descent. The descent has been traced under Nursling as being the more important manor (q.v.).

In the reign of Edward the Confessor Cheping held *SHIRLEY* (Sirelei, xi cent.; Schyrlegh and Shirlee, xiii cent.) of the king, and it was assessed at 1 hide. Ralph de Mortimer held in Cheping's stead at the time of the Domesday Survey,[17] and his descendants held knights' fees in Shirley as late at least as 1362.[18] By the fifteenth century, however, the manor had come to be looked upon as held of the prior and convent of St. Denis,[19] which held much property in the neighbourhood. In the fourteenth century the manor was held by the family of Shirley. Nicholas de Shirley in 1240 granted the advowson of the church of Shirley, which up to this time had no doubt gone with the manor, to the prior of St. Denis,[20] and Isabel de Shirley, widow of Roger de Shirley, and Nicholas, Roger, John, and Simon, sons of Roger de Shirley, were also benefactors to the priory.[21]

In 1272 Nicholas son of Roger, who was no doubt son of Roger de Shirley, granted two parts of a messuage, a mill, and other appurtenances in Shirley to Nicholas de Barbflete or Barnflete and Alice his wife.[22] Nicholas was a member of a family coming originally from Barfleur which had long been settled at Southampton.[23] In 1286 he was appointed by the king to collect the murage at Southampton and to apply the same towards rebuilding Southampton Castle.[24] Four years later licence was given him to grant a spring in his manor of Shirley to the Friars Minor of Southampton,[25] while in 1327 the friars received licence to make a conduit underground from this spring in Shirley, called Colewell, as far as Houndewellecrouche, and thence by King Street to their dwelling house, to lay the pipes of the conduit in such part of the street as they should find most suitable, and to repair the same as often as required.[26] Nicholas de Barbflete died seised of the manor of Shirley in 1294 leaving a son and heir Nicholas.[27] The latter died before 1311[28] and was succeeded by Richard de Barbflete,[29] probably his son, who was mayor of Southampton in 1317.[30] In 1327 Maud widow of Richard released all right in Shirley and Hill to Roger Normand and Joan his wife,[31] to whom free warren within the manor was granted ten years later.[32] Roger was a wealthy merchant[33] and one of the most prominent burgesses of Southampton at this time, being M.P. for the town in 1328, 1332, and 1338–9 and mayor in 1330.[34] He stood high in favour with Edward III, who in 1337 appointed him to man a ship called *La Coggerschippe* to take engines and other weapons to Scotland,[35] and in 1338 exempted him from further service in consideration of his having for no small time found at his own charges divers ships of war and armed men both on land and sea in defence of the realm against foreign attack.[36] He also assisted so largely in the building of the church of Holy Rood or St. Cross, Southampton, that in 1333 by decision of John bishop of Winchester permission was granted to him to be interred within it.[37] Roger died seised of the manor in 1349 leaving his grandson Giles, a minor, his heir.[38] The custody of the manor was committed to John Inkpen during the minority of Giles,[39] but the latter died in 1362 leaving as his heir his cousin Margaret, wife of John Chamberlayne.[40] It is difficult to trace the descendants of Margaret and John, but they seem to have had a daughter and heiress Alice who became the wife of Richard Beket. Hence in 1391 the charter of Edward III granting free warren in his demesne lands in Shirley to Roger Normand was confirmed to Richard Beket and Alice his wife, kinswoman and heir of Roger Normand.[41] By 1433 the manor had descended to a certain Joan wife of Robert Peny, who in that year in conjunction with her husband quitclaimed it to Robert Whitehead.[42] From Robert it seems to have passed to John Whitehead, who settled it in fee-tail upon his son Maurice and Joan his wife. Maurice died seised in 1496–7 leaving a son and heir John, aged nine;[43] but it is doubtful whether the latter succeeded to his inheritance, for George Whitehead died seised in 1520 leaving a son and heir, a minor, John,[44] whose guardianship was committed to Sir William Sandys.[45] Evidently John died without issue either during his minority or soon after he had entered into possession since his brother Augustine died seised of the manor in 1557-8 assigning it as part dower of his wife Julian.[46] His son Richard died seised of the reversion in May 1593, and on the death of Julian four months later the manor passed to Henry, son and heir of Richard.[47]

WHITEHEAD. *Azure a fesse between three fleurs-de-lis or.*

[17] *V.C.H. Hants.* i, 489*b*.

[18] Inq. p.m. 23 Edw. III, pt. 1, No. 87 and 36 Edw. III, pt. 2 (1st Nos.), No. 8.

[19] Chan. Inq. p.m. (Ser. 2), xi, No. 104 and xxxv, Nos. 38, 106.

[20] Feet of F. Hants, Hil. 25 Hen. III.

[21] Add. MS. 15314, fol. 47.

[22] Feet of F. Div. Cos. Hil. 56 Hen. III.

[23] Pat. 9 Hen. III, m. 7; 14 Hen. III, m. 9; 15 Hen. III, m. 4; Chart. R. 11 Hen. III, pt. 1, m. 13.

[24] Pat. 14 Edw. I, m. 18.

[25] Ibid. 18 Edw. I, m. 24.

[26] Ibid. 1 Edw. III, pt. 1, m. 33.

[27] Inq. p.m. 23 Edw. I, No. 26.

[28] In that year Parnel is described as 'late the wife of Nicholas de Barbflete' (Close, 5 Edw. II, m. 27 *d*.).

[29] *Feud. Aids*, ii, 318.

[30] Davies, *Hist. of Southampton*, 171.

[31] Close, 21 Edw. III, pt. 1, m. 18 *d*. In 1333 the manor was settled on Roger and Joan with remainder to their son Roger in fee-tail. (Feet of F. Hants, Trin. 7 Edw. III.) Six years later Maud released to Roger and Joan a rent of 8*d*., 2 lb. of cummin, and ½ lb. of pepper coming from a tenement which Richard de Sutton and Joan his wife formerly held of her in Hill and Shirley (Feet of F. Hants, East. 13 Edw. III).

[32] Chart R. 11 Edw. III, m. 35.

[33] Pat. 7 Edw. III, pt. 1, m. 14; Close, 13 Edw. III, pt. 2, m. 24 *d*.; 16 Edw. III, pt. 1, m. 43 *d*.

[34] Davies, *Hist. of Southampton*, 171, 200.

[35] Pat. 11 Edw. III, pt. 3, m. 11.

[36] Pat. 12 Edw. III, pt. 1, m. 7.

[37] Davies, *Hist. of Southampton*, 353.

[38] Inq. p.m. 23 Edw. III, pt. 1, No. 87.

[39] *Rot. Orig.* (Rec. Com.), ii, 202.

[40] Inq. p.m. 36 Edw. III, pt. 2 (1st Nos.), No. 8. She was the daughter of Agnes elder sister of his father, Roger Normand. The manor, however, does not seem to have passed directly to Margaret, for in 1379 Richard Monk and John Still dealt by fine with the reversion of the manor which John Sonde and Joan his wife were holding for the term of Joan's life (Feet of F. Hants, Mich. 3 Ric. II). It is possible that this Joan was the widow either of Roger or Giles Normand and that she married as her second husband John Sonde.

[41] Pat. 15 Ric. II, pt. 1, m. 5.

[42] Feet of F. Hants, Mich. 12 Hen. VI.

[43] Chan. Inq. p.m. (Ser. 2), xi, No. 104.

[44] Ibid. xxxv, Nos. 38, 106.

[45] Pat. 13 Hen. VIII, pt. 1, m. 17.

[46] Chan. Inq. p.m. (Ser. 2), cxiv, No. 26.

[47] Chan. Inq. p.m. (Ser. 2), ccxxxv, No. 97.

Henry, who afterwards became Sir Henry Whitehead, lived into the early part of the reign of Charles I. On the marriage of his son Richard with Margery daughter of John Culliford of Encombe (co. Dors.), Sir Henry and Constance his wife evidently settled the manor of Shirley on Margaret as dower, since they had dealings concerning the same in 1621 with Frances Culliford, widow of John, and her brothers Sir Thomas, John, and William Freke of Shroton (co. Dors.).[48] Sir Henry died in 1629 and Shirley and Hill accordingly passed to his son Richard.[49] The latter was sheriff of Hants in 1636 and had a hard task to collect the ship money for the county. In that year he wrote to the council complaining of the backwardness of the county, and how a constable who had failed to duly certify the defaulters, when censured by the writer, had answered that the money would never be gathered during his lifetime. For this Whitehead had committed him to prison, 'since when he has become very penitent and begs to be enlarged, promising to use his best endeavours to perform the service.'[50] During the next year Whitehead was told that the arrears, which stood at £404, must be gathered in and the service perfected,[51] but in spite of his hard work the task seems to have been almost impracticable.[52] Perhaps it was partly the ungratefulness of this task that soured him against the king's cause and made him so faithful an adherent of Parliament during the Civil War. Clarendon mentions him with Norton, Onslow, Jarvis, and Morley among the colonels of regiments composing the Parliamentary troops of Hampshire and Sussex.[53] In 1643 he was one of those appointed to extort large sums of money from the Cavaliers on pain of imprisonment at Portsmouth, and is credited with the saying that 'he had been at a great charge to build a cage at Portsmouth where many Hampton birds should sing very suddenly.'[54] Besides being present at the various attacks on Basing House under Waller's command, Colonel Whitehead, in the beginning of 1644, besieged Bishop's Waltham palace, and having obtained its surrender with the help of the London brigade under Major-General Browne, was given permission 'to pull down the house if he chose.'[55] In June of the same year he was one of those ordered by the House of Commons to take steps within a month for sequestration of the estates of Papists and delinquents of a less value than £12,000 within London and Westminster. The proceeds were to be applied to pay off arrears to the garrisons of Portsmouth and of Hurst, Southsea and Calshot Castles.[56] Few facts seem discoverable about the end of Richard Whitehead's life or for the history of the manor of Shirley during the reign of Charles II. It was probably held by his son Francis,[57] but before 1684 it had come into the hands of Richard Whitehead, either a son or brother of Francis, who in that year, probably on the marriage of his son Henry with Mary the daughter of Richard Norton of Southwick had dealings with Richard Norton and others concerning the manor.[58] Mary, the daughter of Henry and Mary, married Alexander Thistlethwayte in 1717, and the manor thus passed to the Thistlethwaytes with whom it remained for a considerable period.

In the middle of the nineteenth century however the greater part of Shirley was sold in building allotments, and consequently the manor ceased to exist.

From early times the lords of the manor of Shirley engaged in disputes with the mayor and burgesses of Southampton as to whether the east side of the manor was within the jurisdiction of the town or not. The point was disputed as early as 1528–9, the following entry occurring in the steward's account for that year: 'costs for the meeting of the Town's counsel and Mistress Whitehed for the variance of our liberties in Hill Lane.'[59] In 1596 a suit was still pending in the Court of Wards and Liveries between Henry Whitehead and the town. 'He seemeth to lay challenge,' say the court-leet jury, 'unto all or the most part of the common pasture belonging to us and others the inhabitants, leading up within our liberties and perambulation towards Cut-thorn as yet time out of memory ever enjoyed, held and occupied by the inhabitants of Southampton without any lawful challenge or impeachment.'[60] In 1600 they presented that 'the inhabitants on the east side of Hill Street ought to do their suit and service at our Law-day.' In 1611 Hill was again stated to be 'within the liberties of Southampton,'[61] and it was not until 1713 that the form 'through the village' was dropped for 'northward from the village.'[62]

THISTLETHWAYTE. *Or a bend azure with three pheons or thereon.*

A water-mill was appurtenant to the manor of Shirley and Hill from an early date,[63] but it has now fallen into disuse.

BANISTER'S COURT (Banaster Court, xv cent.; Banister's Farm, xvii cent.) was from an early date held by the Banisters of Idsworth in the hundred of Finchdean (q.v.)[64] The mayor and burgesses of Southampton long claimed that the manor was within the jurisdiction of the town, and in the middle of the seventeenth century, when Sir Edward Banister was owner of Banister's Farm, as it was then called, James Needle and James Flower, collectors of taxes in the ward of All Saints Southampton levied a distress upon it.[65] There is an entry in the town-book to the effect that the trial of the suit was ordered to be at New Sarum (co. Wilts.), the point of issue being whether Banister's Farm was in the county of Hants, or in the county of the town of Southampton, but nothing is said as to the date or the result of the trial.[66] Banister's Court and Banister's Park at the present day are included in the ecclesiastical parish of Shirley. Banister's Court is now used as a private school, while Banister's Park serves as the county cricket ground.

REDBRIDGE (Hreodbrycg) occurs as a boundary-mark as early as 956 in the charter whereby King Edwy granted land in Millbrook to Prince Wulfic.[67] According to the settlement of the bounds of the port of Southampton as returned into the exchequer in 1680, the line on the west was drawn up the stream

[48] Feet of F. Hants, Mich. 19 Jas. I.
[49] Chan. Inq. p.m. (Ser. 2), ccccxlviii, No. 92. [50] *Cal. S.P. Dom.* 1635–6, p. 392.
[51] Ibid. 1636–7, p. 233.
[52] See letters, ibid. pp. 217, 230, 337, &c.
[53] Clarendon, *Hist. of the Rebellion* (ed. Macray), iii, 410.
[54] Godwin, *The Civil War in Hampshire*, 61, quoting from *Mercurius Aulicus.*
[55] Ibid. 141, 142, quoting *ut supra.*
[56] Ibid. 157; *Com. Journ.* iii, 515.
[57] Berry, *Hants Gen.* 287.
[58] Feet of F. Div. Cos. Hil. 1 & 2 Jas. II.
[59] Davies, op. cit. 42.
[60] Ibid. 43. [61] Ibid. [62] Ibid. 44.
[63] Feet of F. Div. Cos. Hil. 56 Hen. III, and Hants, Mich. 17 Jas. I.
[64] Chan. Inq. p.m. (Ser. 2), viii, No. 113; ix, No. 32; ccxcii, No. 177.
[65] Davies, op. cit. 43.
[66] Ibid. [67] Cott. Chart. viii, 12.

to Redbridge including all bays, channels, &c., and in consequence of this award the inhabitants exercised every branch of admiralty power as far as Redbridge. In 1610 Sir Thomas West of Testwood prosecuted some licensed fishermen for fishing below Redbridge, but he was forced to withdraw his action. Again in 1658 the court-leet presented that the fishing between Southampton and Redbridge had been usurped by Thomas Knollys and others to the hurt of the place.[68]

According to an inquisition of the reign of Edward III the bridge was rebuilt by Noel, a rich merchant, for the use of the people living in the neighbourhood.[69] Owing to its position half in the hundred of Buddlesgate and the land of the prior and convent of St. Swithun, and half in the hundred of Redbridge and the manor of Testwood,[70] it was no one's business to repair it, and so when it fell into bad repair it became the custom for the king to grant pontage for varying terms of years to the men of Redbridge. This was done as early as 1276, when the king granted them pontage for five years, charging them to apply it, by view of the prior of St. Denis, to the repair of the bridge and to no other purpose.[71] In 1362 the jurors presented that a certain Robert Tots and Alexander de Compton who lived near the bridge in the land of the prior and convent had just absconded with all the money that they had collected for some time past from travellers and merchants for the repair of the bridge,[72] and the king accordingly granted pontage for five years to the inhabitants of the place.[73]

Towards the end of the fourteenth century it became the custom for a warden to be appointed to take the pontage.[74] The custom seems to have been discontinued, however, in the sixteenth century, for the money for repairing the bridge in 1581 was raised by voluntary contributions among the clergy and laity of the county.[75]

In the reign of Charles I timber for the repair of the fortifications at Portsmouth was sent by boat down the Test from the New Forest to Redbridge,[76] and there is an interesting remark in a letter written by Kenrick Edisbury to Secretary Coke in 1632 to the effect that Captain Pett would take the order about sending ships to fetch the timber from Redbridge, but that in the writer's opinion 'long ships fit for that service will hardly be gotten because they are Flemish bottoms too long to turn the narrow creeks near Redbridge.'[77]

CHURCHES The tower is the only ancient part of the church of *ST. NICHOLAS, MILLBROOK*, plain fifteenth-century work of three stages. The rest of the church was rebuilt in pseudo-Gothic style in 1824, and has a chancel with nave and shallow transepts, slate-roofed and plaster ceiled, fitted with deal pews and galleries. The font, of the same style, stands at the west of the chancel, and the whole building, no longer in regular use, is damp, dusty, and neglected.

There is one bell in the tower by Clement Tosier, 1701.

The church of the *HOLY TRINITY, MILLBROOK*, built in 1873-80 in Early English style from the designs of Mr. Woodyear, consists of a chancel with aisles, nave aisles, and a tower of Swanage stone. The spire is 150 ft. high, and contains four bells, three of which were hung in 1897 as part of the Diamond Jubilee Memorial.

The plate is modern, consisting of one silver chalice, two silver patens, and one glass silver-mounted cruet.

The earliest parish register contains mixed entries from 1633 to 1679. The second book contains baptisms from 1683 to 1695, marriages from 1689 to 1692, and burials from 1699 to 1703. The third contains mixed entries from 1695 to 1701, the fourth baptisms and burials from 1754 to 1786, the fifth mixed entries from 1780 to 1787, the sixth mixed entries from 1784 to 1802, the seventh baptisms and burials from 1803 to 1812, and the eighth and ninth marriages only from 1754 to 1792 and from 1792 to 1812.

The church of *ST. JAMES, SHIRLEY*, built in 1836, is of white brick in Transition style, and consists of a chancel nave and pinnacled western tower, which contains three bells and a clock.

The register dates from 1836.

There was originally a church at Old Shirley, supposed to have been pulled down about 1609, and its materials used to enlarge Millbrook church.[78]

CHRIST CHURCH, FREEMANTLE, built in 1866 in the Geometrical Gothic style, consists of a chancel, nave, aisles, transepts, and a high tower, with pinnacles and spire, added in 1874, and containing a clock.

The register dates from 1865.

ADVOWSONS The advowson of the church of Millbrook has from its earliest existence belonged to the bishop of Winchester.[79] The living is at the present time a rectory, net yearly value with residence £200.

There was a church in Shirley (Old Shirley) at the time of the Domesday Survey,[80] the advowson of which belonged to the lords of the manor of Shirley until 1233, in which year Nicholas de Shirley granted it in free alms to the prior of St. Denis and his successors.[81] The church was subsequently appropriated to the priory, the appropriation being confirmed by Bishop Orlton in 1334.[82] The prior and convent presented the vicars until the Dissolution, when the advowson of the vicarage and the rectory of Shirley fell into the hands of the king.[83] They remained the property of the crown until 1549, in which year Edward VI granted the rectory and tithes to Nicholas Prideaux.[84]

Soon afterwards the advowson and rectory fell into the hands of the Pagett family, James Pagett and Bridget his wife dealing with them by fine in 1574,[85] probably for purposes of settlement. Twenty-one years later James Pagett and Barbara his wife sold the advowson and the rectory to Thomas Lambert,[86] with

68 Davies, op. cit. 222.
69 Inq. p.m. 32 Edw. III (2nd Nos.), No. 97.
70 Ibid.
71 Pat. 4 Edw. I, m. 34.
72 Inq. p.m. 32 Edw. III (2nd Nos.), No. 97.
73 Pat. 32 Edw. III, pt. 1, m. 22. The following were some of the charges authorized by the grant :—Pipe of wine ½*d.*, cartload of wool 2*d.*, cartload of salted hide 1*d.*, cartload of tanned hide 2*d.*, 20 sheep ½*d.*, 20 pigs ½*d.*, cartload of iron, steel, or lead 1*d.*, cartload of oil or honey 2*d.*, cartload of fish 2*d.*, cartload of corn 2*d.*, cartload of timber 1*d.*
74 Pat. 4 Ric. II, pt. 2, m. 15; 15, Ric. II, pt. 1, m. 7; 2 Hen. IV, pt. 1, m. 9 and 7, and pt. 2, m. 24.
75 *Acts of P.C.* 1581, p. 188.
76 *Cal. S.P. Dom.* 1631–3, p. 372.
77 Ibid. p. 409.
78 White's *Dir.* 1859.
79 Chart. R. 12 Edw. I, m. 5; *Wykeham's Reg.* (Hants Rec. Soc.), 124, 144, 158, 200, 228; Inst. Bks. (P.R.O.).
80 *V.C.H. Hants*, i, 489.
81 Feet of F. Hants, Hil. 25 Hen. III.
82 *V.C.H. Hants*, ii, 162.
83 Ibid. 163.
84 Pat. 3 Edw. VI, pt. 5, m. 18.
85 Feet. of F. Div. Cos. Hil. 16 Eliz.
86 Ibid. Trin. 37 Eliz.

whose descendants they remained as late at least as 1640.[87] Their subsequent history is uncertain, but they eventually came into the Heathcote family, who owned much property in the neighbourhood, William Heathcote and Frances his wife dealing with a moiety of the rectory and advowson in 1783,[88] and William Heathcote and Frances his wife, and Thomas Gore and Sarah Amy his wife, with the whole three years later.[89] At the present time the living of Shirley is a vicarage net yearly value £316 in the gift of the Church Patronage Society. The living of Freemantle is a rectory net yearly value £250 in the gift of the bishop of Winchester.

John Wygge, while parson of Millbrook, preached a seditious sermon, for which he was committed to the Marshalsea, where he lay for a year and more. Taking advantage of his absence, John Mill, lord of the manor of Millbrook, it is stated, seized half an acre of land called the 'Conquest,' which had belonged to the parsonage of Millbrook from time immemorial, and also deprived a poor lame man called John Wygge of two houses and lands in Millbrook, because he chanced to be related to the parson. In addition, the comptroller of Southampton during his absence entered the parsonage, opened doors and gates, felled two great elms in the parsonage grounds, and one in the churchyard, and carried away 'topp, lopp and chypp,' without payment. John Wygge, on his return finding he could get no redress, brought his case before the Court of Requests, with what result, however, does not appear.[90]

CHARITIES In 1812 the Rev. William Harvest, rector, gave by will £100 consols, the dividends to be applied at Christmas in flannel for the aged poor; and also £100 consols, to provide yearly for the distribution of one blanket to each poor family having the greatest number of children under eight years of age. The trust fund has been divided, the amount belonging to Millbrook being £48 Lancashire and Yorkshire Railway £3 per cent Consolidated Preference Stock. See below, Freemantle and Shirley.

In 1822 Mrs. Susannah Pollen by her will bequeathed £10 a year to be applied in blankets and warm clothing. The trust fund for this parish consists of £79 of the like railway stock. The income of the two charities is applied together in the distribution of clothing. See Freemantle below.

In 1872 Mrs. Mary Baker by her will bequeathed £2,000 consols, the income to be applied in sums of £1 to poor and industrious parishioners, male or female, above 60 years of age on 24 December in every year. The sum of £1,788 6*s.* 9*d.* consols belonging to the charity, after payment of duty, was sold out and the proceeds invested in the purchase of £1,700 Egyptian Government Guaranteed £3 per cent. Loan (Bonds).

In 1833 Mrs. Sarah Spinks by will bequeathed £400 consols, the income to be applied in the purchase of clothing for the poor (not being paupers), on St Thomas's Day. The stock was sold out and the proceeds invested in £336 Lancashire and Yorkshire Railway £3 per cent. Consolidated Preference Stock.

In 1883 William Ross by will, proved this date, bequeathed £500, the income to be applied at Christmas in such manner as the trustees should think fit for the benefit of poor persons of 61 years or upwards. The endowment fund consists of £468 of the like railway stock, the dividends being applied in the distribution of coal.

In 1891 Miss Jemima Frances Sophia Prior by will left £200 to be invested in £2 10*s.* per cent. annuities, the dividends to be applied as to £4 10*s.* to thirty-six persons (irrespective of creed) on fifth November, 5*s.* to verger for care of tablets of Prior family in church. The legacy was invested in the purchase of £207 15*s.* 10*d.* stock.

The several securities above mentioned are held by the Official Trustees of Charitable Funds in trust for the respective charities.

Freemantle Charities.—The dividends on the sum of £50 consols and on £83 6*s.* 8*d.* consols are applied in the distribution of clothing in respect of the charities of the Rev. William Harvest and Mrs. Susannah Pollen respectively. See Millbrook, above.

Redbridge Charities.—In 1858 Miss Diana Emily Flora Doyle, in memory of her late aunt Emily Milner, by deed conveyed to the bishop of Winchester and the rector of Millbrook a piece of land and buildings thereon to be used as a Church of England school.

In 1879 the same Miss Doyle by will, proved this date, directed her executors to purchase £1,500 consols to be held and applied as an endowment of the Church of England school founded by her. The fund now consists of £1,444 Lancashire and Yorkshire Railway £3 per cent Consolidated Preference Stock held by the Official Trustees of Charitable Funds.

Shirley Charities.—The dividends on £100 consols and on £166 13*s.* 4*d.* consols are applied in the distribution of clothing in respect of the charities of the Rev. William Harvest and Mrs. Susannah Pollen respectively. See Millbrook, above.

Homes for Aged Women.—In 1876 funds were subscribed for the establishment of a Home for Aged Women, and a piece of land at Shirley Common opposite to St. James's Church was purchased and buildings erected thereon, mainly at the expenses of Mr. Andrew Barlow and Mr. Richard Dyer Ellyett. The trusts were declared by a deed, dated 31 March, 1877, under which the buildings are to be occupied by women of good character exceeding the age of 55 years who should have been previously resident for not less than one year within a radius of five miles from the Bargate, Southampton, and who had means to support themselves.

The endowment Funds of the Institution are as follows:—

£1,833 1*s.* 9*d.* consols arising from a legacy by will of Mr. Richard Dyer Ellyett, proved 8 March, 1881; £1,200 £3½ per cent. Harbour Bonds, the gift of Mr. Andrew Barlow in 1901; and £548 9*s.* 2*d.* consols, arising from the investment of £100 left in 1879 by will of Miss Frances Cecilia Marett; and of £400 bequeathed in 1883 by Miss Mary Wade; and of £50 left in 1902 by Mr. Josiah Skidder Roe. The inmates occupy the home rent-free and the income from the endowment funds is supplemented by voluntary subscriptions.

[87] In that year Charles Lord Lambert and Jane his wife, and Anthony Bourchier and Jane his wife, conveyed them to John Barton (Feet of F. Hants, East. 16 Chas. I).

[88] Feet of F. Div. Cos. Hil. 23 Geo. III.

[89] Ibid. Trin. 26 Geo. III.

[90] Ct. of Requests, bdle. 17, No. 85.

NURSLING

The parish of Nursling, covering an area of 1,508 acres of land, with 22 acres of land covered by water, and 6 acres by tidal water, lies on left bank of the Test, which as it enters the parish from the north-west divides into two main branches that run circuitously south-east through the low-lying country to the south-west of the scattered village of Nursling.

The main road from Shirley to Romsey, entering the south-east of the parish, runs north along high ground, while the fields and cottages of Nursling lie away on lower ground to the west. A road from Aldermoor to Redbridge cuts across the highroad as it enters Nursling, and going downhill to the south-west forms the southern boundary line of the parish. About half a mile from the main road the Redbridge road sends off a branch which leads in a circuitous north-easterly direction back to the main road. Along this branch the greater number of the cottages and houses of the village are grouped, for the most part on the east side of the road, the Wesleyan chapel, opposite which are the Wesleyan schools and the City Arms Inn, being nearest to the main Shirley-to-Romsey road.

Another branch from higher up the main road goes off west from the bottom of Horns Hill between the two Inns, 'The Balmoral' on the left with its closely-clipped yew trees and 'The Horns' on the right, both facing on the main road. South-west of 'The Balmoral' stands the school, built in 1871 and enlarged in 1894. Continuing west, the road known as Nursling Street leads past the Four Horse-Shoes Inn and two or three cottages standing on the south, between fields and meadows past the grounds of Grove Place, which stands north, over the railway bridge, past the Manor Farm and one or two thatched cottages, on to the church and rectory. East of the church, which stands on the north side of the road, nearly opposite the high wall of the rectory garden, is the modern red-brick church-room built in memory of Queen Victoria's Diamond Jubilee. The rectory, a large red-brick house, was built in the late eighteenth century by one of the rectors, Mr. Cramner. Beyond the church, as the road ceases, are two or three low cottages; facing west are the water meadows which slope down to the Test.

Grove Place, the seat of Mr. Clarence Wilson, is finely situated at the end of a long, wide avenue of lime trees, through which the fine chimneys and octagonal turrets of the house appear. The present fabric was built in the sixteenth century, and is not on the site of the older house, which stood some way to the south-west between the avenue and the modern railway line. The latter is the Andover and Redbridge branch of the London and South Western Railway which cuts through the parish from north to south, with a station at Nursling about half a mile south-west of Grove Place.

A road turns off south from Nursling Street immediately east of the Manor Farm, and running parallel with the west bank of the railway, passes Nursling Station. Past the station the road curves west, leaving the railway, and branches north-west to Nursling Farm, and Nursling Mill and south-east to Redbridge. Nursling Farm, with its square farm-house and low thatched outbuildings, stands on high ground south of the road. In the fields nearly opposite, one of which is known as 'The Walls,' is the site of the ancient Benedictine monastery, famous as the residence of St. Boniface during the early years of his life, but destroyed by the Danes in one of their raids about 878. Skirting these fields the road continues for about half a mile to Nursling Mill, running north-west of the water meadows, among which glisten the waters of the Test. The old mill facing south-west stands over the rushing water, and dates as it now stands from the eighteenth century. A stone in the wall states that the building stands on a frame of large beech timber given by Sir Richard Mill in 1728. The adjoining mill-house stands back from the road at the east end of the mill. Near by are two or three cottages and in front of the mill-house a small thatched dovecot. In the south-west of the parish near the Test as the road goes towards Redbridge is the tall chimney of the Test Valley Chemical Works, with its surrounding buildings, now disused.

The small hamlet of Upton consisting of one or two cottages and a smithy lies in the north-east of the parish west of the main Shirley-to-Romsey road as it rises over Horns Hill. On the opposite side of the road, lying back behind fine open grounds, is Upton House, the seat of Colonel Edward St. John Griffiths, J.P.

The soil of the whole parish is gravel, sand, and clay with a subsoil of clay and gravel, producing the ordinary crops of wheat, barley, and oats on the 714¼ acres of arable land. The greater portion of the parish is given over to permanent grass, of which there are 737¼ acres, while only 58 acres are woodland.[1]

MANORS The manor of *NURSLING* as it now exists is composed of two original manors, the one associated from its earliest history with the prior and convent of St. Swithun and called *NURSLING PRIOR* in the sixteenth century, the other taking the name of *NURSLING BEAUFO* from its fourteenth-century holders. At the Dissolution Nursling Prior passed into the hands of John Mill, who was already holding Nursling Beaufo, and hence the two practically became one. Although there is no definite history for *NURSLING PRIOR* in the eighth century, it is almost certain that it belonged to the bishops of Winchester, since in 877 Bishop Tunberht or Dunbert[2] granted 5 *mansae* at Nursling to the refectory of St. Swithun free from all charges except the *trinoda necessitas*.[3] It is difficult to identify the boundaries given in the charter, although if it were possible to trace them they would be very valuable as giving exactly the locality of the two manors in the parish. However, enough can be traced to show that the manor of the prior and convent extended into the western part of

[1] Statistics from Bd. of Agric. (1905).

[2] Dugdale, *Mon.* i, 193*a*.

[3] Birch, *Cart. Sax.* ii, 163.

the parish, with the Test River as its western and southern boundary.[4]

In 908 King Edward confirmed the manor to Bishop Frithstan in a charter confirming the grants of his ancestors to the church.[5] King Ethelred made a similar confirmation in 984.[6] In both these grants the 5 hides at Nursling were included in what was then the very large district of Chilcomb, comprising 100 hides to be assessed as one manor.[7] How long the manor was so included is doubtful, but by the time of Domesday it seems to have lost all connexion with Chilcomb and to be included in the hundred of Buddlesgate. The bishop held the manor, still rated at 5 hides, and it is said to have always belonged to the monastery.[8] In 1167 the prior of St. Swithun rendered account for the manor,[9] and in 1207 the pope confirmed him in his possession.[10] Edward I granted the prior and convent free warren in their demesne lands in Nursling in 1300,[11] and in 1330 they were licensed to acquire certain lands in Nursling from Robert de Wytton and Thomas le Boys.[12]

Although Bishop Tunberht had originally granted Nursling to the refectory of the monastery, by the fifteenth century the profits of the manor were diverted to the office of warden of the works (*custos operum*), and appear on the two extant rolls of the office of 1409 and 1532–3. In 1409 John Hurst, warden of the works, received £30 13*s.* 1½*d.* from the manor and paid the prior £4 from meadows in Nursling.[13] Walter Frost, warden of the works in 1532, received £20 5*s.* 9*d.* from Nursling and £8 7*s.* 6*d.* for the farm of the manor with the farm of Ware in Nursling.[14] On the surrender of the monastery in 1540[15] the manor passed in the natural course of events into the king's hands, and was entered in the Ministers' Accounts.[16] In 1541 it was granted to the newly-founded dean and chapter,[17] being made specially chargeable, with four other manors, for the maintenance of twelve university students, six at Oxford and six at Cambridge.[18] However, in 1545 the king evidently compelled the dean and chapter to execute a deed of surrender, by which Nursling and the four other manors were given up into the king's hands.[19] In the same year the king granted away the manor to John Mill, with land and wood in Nursling called 'Londswood.'[20] John Mill outlived his eldest son Richard, and died in 1551, leaving the manor to his second son George.[21] The latter held the manor for seventeen years, but died without issue in 1568.[22] Before his death he had settled the manor upon his brother Thomas in fee-tail on the occasion of his marriage with Alice daughter of Robert Coker. Thomas and Alice had issue one son called Richard and several daughters. As Richard was 'very sickly in his youth,' George was often minded to settle the reversion of his lands after his death on his younger brother John in fee-tail, so as to continue the same in his own name, but refrained from doing so on account of the former settlement.[23] On the death of George the estate therefore passed to Richard, who some time afterwards married Mary daughter of Sir John Savage. 'He used his sisters very kindly oftentimes affirming that the possibility of his lands would be a preferment for them in marriage he having no issue nor likely to have any,' and although his wife Mary often entreated him to disinherit his sisters he steadfastly refused, saying that the lands should descend to them in accordance with the wish of his uncle. However, Mary prevailed upon him to settle a part of his estate upon her for life, although he persisted in his determination of settling the greater part upon his sisters. Shortly afterwards 'he grew weak both in body and mind by reason of a dread palsey which he had,' and while in this state his wife Mary and her nephew Sir Thomas Savage, who waited upon him and 'mynistered phisicke' to him during his long illness, seemingly gained complete ascendancy over him, so much so that he finally conveyed the greater part of his estates to Mary about 1609,[24] and by his will left only £300 to his sisters, Anne the wife of Thomas Bilson, Alice the wife of Sir John Bingham, Elizabeth Collnett, and Bridget the wife of Thomas Barnes.[25] After her husband's death in 1613[26] Mary used 'faier words' to her husband's sisters, but nevertheless previous to her marriage with Thomas Wroughton in 1616 executed a deed granting the reversion of her property to her nephew.[27] The sisters of Richard appealed to the Court of Chancery, but the case was dismissed in 1619.[28] Sir Thomas, afterwards Viscount Savage, who had succeeded to Nursling on the death of his aunt in 1623,[29] sold the manor to Sir Thomas Cornwallis, groom porter to James I, John Scrivener, and others in December, 1624,[30] and made the first conveyance by fine in the spring of 1625.[31] In July, 1630, Cornwallis and Scrivener sold the manor to the king,[32] who granted it in August of the same year to Henry Knollys, controller of the king's household.[33] Henry Knollys died in 1638, leaving his son Henry as his heir.[34] The latter was created a baronet in 1642, but died without issue in 1648, and the baronetcy became extinct.[35] The manor then passed to his brother Thomas Knollys, and remained in the Knollys family until 1751,[36] when, on the extinction

4 The boundaries in the charter run thus :—'Aerst fram ðaem hlidgate scioteð se merc on gearnes egae. ðonne be suðen hriod eg on terstan. ðonon andlang testan on mercfrot (probably the Blackwater brook, a branch of the Test, now a part of the western boundary of Nursling parish) ðonon anlang fliotes on boddingmed. ðonon on boddanstan. ðonon ut on acleih. ðonon on stemnes peð. ðonon on grindanbroc. ðonon on heslea on ðaere byri hyrne. ðonon ut on hedenes dene. suðut on ðet hlid gaet.'

5 Harl. Chart. 43, C. 1 ; Kemble, *Codex Dipl.* ii, 153. The genuineness of this charter is doubtful.

6 Ibid. iii, 203.

7 Ibid. ii, 154 ; iii, 203.

8 *V.C.H. Hants*, i, 464*a*.

9 *Pipe R.* (Pipe R. Soc.), 1167.

10 *Cal. of Pap. Letters*, i, 21.

11 Chart. R. 29 Edw. I, No. 94, m. 12.

12 *Cal. of Pat.* 1327–30, p. 501.

13 *Obedientiary R. of St. Swithun* (Hants Rec. Soc.), 210, 214.

14 Ibid. 215.

15 *L. and P. Hen. VIII*, xv, 139 (1).

16 Dugdale, *Mon.* i, 217.

17 Pat. 33 Hen. VIII, pt. 9, m. 5–11.

18 *Documents of the D. and C. of Winton.* (Hants Rec. Soc.), i, 71.

19 Ibid.

20 Pat. 37 Hen. VIII, pt. 1, m. 27.

21 Inq. p.m. 5 Edw. VI (Ser. 2), xciv, No. 47.

22 Exch. Inq. p.m. (Ser. 2), file 1006, No. 2.

23 Chan. Enr. Dec. R. 1286.

24 Feet of F. Div. Cos. Trin. 6 Jas. I ; Close, 6 Jas. I, pt. 18, No. 8.

25 Chan. Enr. Dec. R. 1286.

26 Chan. Inq. p.m. (Ser. 2), cccxxxiv, No. 76.

27 W. and L. Inq. p.m. (Ser. 2), bdle. 35, No. 92.

28 Chan. Enr. Dec. R. 1286.

29 W. and L. Inq. p.m. (Ser. 2), bdle. 35, No. 92.

30 Chan. Inq. p.m. 16 Chas. I (Ser. 2), pt. 2, No. 97.

31 Feet of F. Hants, East. 22 Jas. I.

32 Chan. Inq. p.m. 16 Chas. I (Ser. 2), pt. 2, No 97.

33 Pat. 5 Chas. I, pt. 18, No. 2.

34 Chan. Inq. p.m. 16 Chas. I (Ser. 2), pt. 2, No. 97.

35 G.E.C. *Complete Baronetage*, ii, 170.

36 Recov. R. Hil. 7 Geo. I, rot. 26 ; Close, 7 Geo. I, pt. 19, No. 3 ; Recov. R. Hil. 21 Geo. II, rot. 223. On the death of Thomas Knollys in 1679 it passed to

of the male line with the death of Thomas Knollys, it passed to Sir Richard Mill, bart., who had married Margaret daughter of Robert Knollys.[37] Sir Richard died in 1760, and four of his sons in succession inherited the baronetcy and the estates.[38] Sir Charles

KNOLLYS. *Gules a cheveron argent with three roses gules thereon and a quarter ermine.*

MILL. *Six pieces argent and sable with three bears sable having golden muzzles and chains.*

Mill, the ninth baronet, died on 10 July, 1792, leaving two children, Charles and Mary, the former of whom, Sir Charles, the tenth and last baronet, died on 25 February, 1835, leaving the estate to Mr. John Barker, his sister's son,[39] who assumed the arms and name of Mill, and was afterwards made a baronet. The manor remained with Sir John Barker-Mill until his death without issue in 1860, when it passed to his widow Jane, who died in 1884.[40] On her death it passed to the present owner, Mrs. Vaudrey, third cousin of Sir John Barker-Mill,[41] who has recently taken the name of Mrs. Barker-Mill.[42]

There is seemingly no trace of the existence of the manor of *NURSLING BEAUFO* before the twelfth century, when in 1170 Godfrey de 'Notscilling' rendered account of half a mark for land, which was possibly the nucleus of the later manor.[43]

In 1236 Edmund Fitz William gave up all his right in a virgate of land in Nursling to Walter de Bruge, receiving in return from him an acre of meadow lying between his meadow and that of Cecily de Nursling, and ten acres on the Down.[44] The Bruge family were still settled at Nursling in 1255, in which year Edmund de Bruge granted one mill, with appurtenances in Nursling, to Adam de Bruge, to hold of him and his heirs for the rent of one penny at Easter, with reversion, in default of heirs to Adam, to Edmund and his heirs.[45] There is little or nothing to connect these last entries with the next mention of the 'tenement of Nursling,' which comes in 1276. In that year Gilbert de Teya, and Maud his wife, made a final agreement concerning a right of way claimed by John de la Haleford, son of Edmund de la Haleford, as pertaining to his tenements of Nursling and Eling.[46] The tenements are said to belong to John by hereditary right, though with the scant evidence at present obtainable it can only be a hypothetical suggestion that he was connected with the Edmund Fitz William to whom the grant was made in 1236, and who may have been his father, Edmund de la Haleford. The manor remained in the hands of the Haleford family until about the beginning of the reign of Edward III, when Margery daughter of Edmund de la Haleford, nun of Wherwell, released the manor to Richard de Beaufo (de Bello Fago) and Olimpyas his wife, sister of the said Margery.[47] Richard de Beaufo, who had become Sir Richard by 1335, settled a moiety of the manor on his son John on his marriage with Ellen the daughter of Sir Gilbert de Ellisfield,[48] and a further settlement was made after the death of Sir Richard in 1344.[49]

The manor seems next to have passed to a certain Edmund Forster of Southampton, probably by purchase, although there seems to be no record of the sale, and in 1435, on the occasion of the marriage of his daughter Joan with Peter Marmion of Thame (co. Oxon.), the manor was settled on him for life with remainder to Joan and Peter in tail.[50]

They died, according to some accounts, without issue, and thereupon Edmund settled the manor upon his daughter Christine and her husband, Thomas Hargrove, lord of the manor of Hargrove, in Stalbridge (co. Dorset),[51] in tail.[52] Towards the end of the reign of Henry VI, however, a certain Robert Marmion came forward alleging that he was son and heir of Peter and Joan, and therefore entitled to the manor, and it seems to have been awarded to him by a decree of the Court of Chancery.[53] He granted it to Peter Marmion, jun., and Peter John Marmion, jun.,[54] who in 1481 and 1482 respectively released all right in the manor to Sir William Stoner,[55] who thereupon entered into possession. By this time Thomas and Christine Hargrove had died leaving three daughters and co-heirs, Elizabeth wife of John Wells (co. Oxon.), Joan wife of Thomas Dormer of Nursling, and Alice wife of Walter Coker of Stourpaine (co. Dorset),[56] who did not submit to the loss of their inheritance without a struggle.

In 1492 Thomas Dormer and John Wells and certain yeomen servants to Sir Robert Cheyne, accompanied by 'divers riotous persons arrayed in manner of war,' marched to the manor and 'in riotous wise put out James Marks, then being tenant and servant unto Sir William,' commanding him to 'avoid the possession of the manor within four weeks after Michaelmas next or else it should cost him his life and goods,' and asserting that 'if they might meet Sir William it should cost him his life.'[57] Again, in 1494, Sir

his son Robert, who died of an accidental wound in 1701. He was succeeded by his son Henry, who died at Nursling 1746–7. His son was the Thomas Knollys who died in 1751.

[37] G.E.C. *Complete Baronetage*, i, 133.

[38] *Gent. Mag.* (1760), xxx, 249; (1770), 143; (1780), 347; G.E.C. *Complete Baronetage*, i, 133; Recov. R. Hil. 26 Geo. III, rot. 301. They were Sir Richard Mill, bart., who died in 1770, Sir John Hoby Mill, bart., who died in 1780, the Rev. Sir Henry Mill, bart., rector of Woolbeding, who died in 1782, and the Rev. Sir Charles Mill, who died in 1792.

[39] *Proc. Hants Field Club*, iii, pt. 2, 126.

[40] Ibid.

[41] Her grandfather was first cousin of Sir John Barker-Mill.

[42] Ex inform. Mrs. Barker-Mill.

[43] *Pipe R.* (Pipe R. Soc.), xv, 125.

[44] Feet of F. Hants, Hil. 20 Hen. III.

[45] Ibid. 40 Hen. III.

[46] *Cal. of Close*, 1272–9, p. 351.

[47] Anct. D. (P.R.O.), C. 141, undated.

[48] Ibid. C. 3513; Feet of F. Hants, Hil. 9 Edw. III.

[49] Feet of F. Hants, Hil. 18 Edw. III.

[50] Early Chan. Proc. bdle. 26, No. 74.

[51] Hutchins, *Dorset*, iii, 677.

[52] De Banc. R. East. 17 Hen. VII, m. 315 *d.*

[53] Early Chan. Proc. bdle. 26, No. 74.

[54] De Banc. R. East. 17 Hen. VII, m. 315 *d.*

[55] Close, 21 Edw. IV, m. 3; 22 Edw. IV, m. 27.

[56] Early Chan. Proc. bdle. 235, No. 47; Hutchins, *Dorset*, i, 310; iii, 677; *Gen.* (New Ser.), ii, 297.

[57] Star Chamb. Proc. Hen. VII, No. 45.

William Stoner brought an action against Thomas Dormer for entering into his closes and house at Nursling Beaufo.[58]

On the death of Sir William in 1494 Nursling Beaufo passed to his only son and heir, John Stoner, aged ten and more at the time of his father's death.[59] John Stoner died young without issue soon afterwards, and then there was 'great dyscencyon, dyscorde, and varyaunce moved and styred between Sir Adrian Fortescue and Dame Anne, daughter and heir-general of Sir William, and Thomas Stoner brother of Sir William,'[60] the said Thomas claiming certain manors by virtue of gifts of entail made to his ancestors and their heirs male. However Nursling Beaufo was not among the disputed manors,[61] but passed quietly to Anne and her husband Sir Adrian. The latter is a picturesque figure of the period, a warm supporter of Henry VII, by whom he was knighted on Bosworth Field, and a faithful servant of Henry VIII, who rewarded him, as so many others, by execution on a charge of high treason non proven.[62]

In 1506, six years after the last attempt made by Thomas Dormer to regain it,[63] Sir Adrian Fortescue had alienated the manor to Edmund Dudley,[64] the well-known colleague of Richard Empson, a grasping minister of a still more grasping king, whose miserliness may be justified but cannot be excused. Henry VIII on his accession brought his father's unpopular ministers to trial, and they being found guilty were beheaded on Tower Hill in 1510.[65] Thus Nursling Beaufo, among the other forfeited estates of Edmund Dudley, came into the hands of the king,[66] and was granted in the next year to Francis Cheyney.[67]

However, by the earnest petition of Edward Guildford, guardian of the young John Dudley son of Edmund, the attainder was reversed in 1513, and by special Act of Parliament John Dudley was restored in name, blood, and degree to inherit his father's lands.[68] John Dudley, who in 1525 was knighted by Charles Brandon, duke of Suffolk, general of the English army in France,[69] was sent in 1527 in the train of Cardinal Wolsey on an embassy to France.[70] In the same year he alienated the manor of Nursling Beaufo to John Mill,[71] to whom in 1545 the king granted the manor of Nursling Prior (q.v.), and from this time the two manors have followed the same descent.

The early history of *GROVE PLACE*,[72] which was a member of the manor of Southwells,[73] is obscure. It was probably granted to the dean and canons of St. George's Chapel, Windsor, by Edward III, who in 1344, according to Froissart, endowed them with a good and liberal revenue.[74] In 1442 John Grenefeld was tenant of Grove Place. In his will dated 8 June, 1448, he styles himself of 'Southwelles in the county of Southampton, gentylman,' and especially gives to Ingram Huet, 'farmer of Southwellys,' his furred gown, and to John Huet, 'my farmer of the Grove,' his black gown.[75] In 1480 John Hammond was lessee of Grove Place.[76] Thirty-three years later the dean and canons granted a forty-five years' lease to the abbess and convent of Romsey.[77] In 1536 the latter granted the remainder of the term to John Uttoft or Huttoft and Bridget his wife,[78] who at the dissolution of the monastery took another lease of fifty years.[79] In 1561 the dean and canons granted a lease for eighty-one years to James Pagett of Poulton (co. Wilts.) and his son-in-law William Paulet.[80] The latter by indenture of 1590 made over the remainder of the term to Sir Richard Mill and Mary his wife,[81] who were already lessees from the dean and canons of another tenement in Nursling called Grove Place with a garden containing 6 acres,[82] which in a document of the early seventeenth century is described as a capital messuage called the old farm of Nursling.[83] According to the statement of the plaintiffs in the Chancery suit, of which mention has already been made, Sir Richard often declared that on his death Grove Place was to go to his sister Anne with remainder to her son Sir Thomas Bilson in tail, but like the rest of the property it passed to Sir Thomas Savage.[84] From this date the leasehold estate remained with the lords of the manor of Nursling, but on the reversion of it to Sir Richard Mill, bart., in 1752, by the death of Robert Knollys without issue, there is evidence to show that the tenancy of the mansion with 88 acres became separated from that of the farm-lands, the latter being retained in the Mill family under a succession of seven years' leases till the death of Sir

[58] De Banc. R. East. 17 Hen. VII, m. 315 *d.*

[59] Chan. Inq. p.m. (Ser. 2), ix, No. 91.

[60] See *Stat. of the Realm*, 28 Hen. VIII, cap. 36.

[61] *L. and P. Hen. VIII*, x, 1091.

[62] For an account of his life see Archdall Lodge, *Peerage of Ireland*, iii, 345.

[63] De Banc. R. East. 17 Hen. VII, m. 315 *d.*

[64] Ibid. 21 Hen. VII, m. 152. See also the will of Edmund Dudley, where the Hampshire manor mentioned as purchased of Sir A. Fortescue is evidently Nursling Beaufo (*L. and P. Hen. VIII*, i, 179).

[65] Dugdale, *Bar.* ii, 218.

[66] Chan. Inq. p.m. (Ser. 2), lxxviii, No. 75.

[67] Pat. 3 Hen. VIII, pt. 2, m. 11; and pt. 3, m. 7.

[68] *L. and P. Hen. VIII*, i, 2082, 3687.

[69] Burke, *Extinct Peerage.*

[70] *L. and P. Hen. VIII*, iv (2), 3216.

[71] Feet of F. Hants, Trin. 19 Hen. VIII.

[72] Much of this account is taken from a paper read at a meeting of the Hampshire Field Club, 8 May, 1895, by Mr. B. W. Greenfield, M.A., F.S.A.

[73] In 1860 this manor consisted of Scudamore Farm, Lee, part of Toothill Street Meadow, North Romsey, Osborne House, Church Street, Romsey and Grove Place, house and premises, and covered an area of 444 a. 2 r. 15½ p. (*Proc. Hants Field Club*, iii, pt. 2, 126).

[74] *Proc. Hants Field Club*, iii, pt. 2, 115. The archives of the dean and canons have been examined regarding Grove Place, but the librarian at Windsor cannot discover how they became its possessors, as the Court Rolls date only from 1442.

[75] P.C.C. Will 35, Luffnam. In 1489 his widow Alice claimed dower from the manor, but apparently with no success (De Banc. R. Trin. 4 Hen. VII, m. 102.)

[76] *Proc. Hants Field Club*, iii, pt. 2, 115.

[77] Ibid.

[78] Mins. Accts. Hants, No, 135, m. 60.

[79] *Proc. Hants Field Club*, iii, pt. 2, 115.

[80] Chan. Enr. Dec. R. 1286. James Pagett is described as of Grove Place in a Chancery proceeding of 1561 (Chan. Proc. Eliz.).

[81] Ibid. James Pagett's second wife Bridget was only daughter of John Mill, and consequently aunt of Sir Richard Mill.

[82] So described in the paper in the archives of the dean and canons of Windsor, dated 6 July, 1560, reciting a former paper of 1523, which contains the following item:— 'Thomas Mylle generosus tenet unum tenementum in parochia de Nurslinge vocatum Grove Place cum domibus et edeficiis eidem tenemento pertinentibus cum curtilagio et gardino continente per estimationem VI acras.' Doubtless this was the old manor-house pulled down during the seventeenth century, the site of which has been traced to the south-west of the present mansion between the lime-tree avenue and the railway. But for some time the two tenements called Grove Place, distinguished sometimes as 'the New House' and 'the Old House,' existed side by side, as the probability is that the present mansion was built by James Pagett between 1561 and 1581.

[83] Chan. Enr. Dec. R. 1286.

[84] Ibid.

Charles Mill, bart., in 1835.[85] The rate-books of the parish show well the various tenants of the mansion with 88 acres during the next century, the most interesting names up to 1813 being General Sir John Clavering from 1765 to 1773, James Harris, afterwards created earl of Malmesbury, in 1775, and James Drummond in 1811.[86] About the year 1813 Dr. Edward Middleton, M.D., was dwelling at Grove Place, having taken a twenty-one years' lease, renewable on payment of a fine, of the mansion and 88 acres from the dean and canons of Windsor. He also rented the farm-lands from Sir Charles Mill the lessee, and after his death in 1835 his widow continued to do so from Sir John Barker Mill, bart.[87] Dr. Middleton converted the house and premises into a lunatic asylum, and in adapting the mansion for the purpose permanent injury was done to the interior, especially to the great dining-room and long gallery, the latter being divided off into separate chambers by wooden partitions covered with lath and plaster. Dr. Middleton died in 1826, and the tenancy and use to which the place had been turned were continued by his widow, who died in 1847 as lessee in possession.[88] Two years later the charge of the place as a lunatic asylum was undertaken by Mr. Pothecary and Dr. Symes, and so it continued till 1854, after which time the mansion remained vacant for six years.[89] In consequence of the death of Sir John Barker Mill, bart., in 1860, who some time before had conveyed to Henry John third Viscount Palmerston all his leasehold estate in the farm-lands, the dean and canons of Windsor in that year sold the whole manor of Southwells, including Grove Place, to Lord Palmerston.[90] Lord Palmerston, who died in 1865, bequeathed the property to his step-son the Right Hon. William Francis Cowper (who assumed the surname of Temple), a younger son of Lady Palmerston, by her first husband the fifth Earl Cowper. Mr. Cowper-Temple was created in 1880 Lord Mount-Temple. He died in 1888 without issue, and was succeeded by his nephew the Hon. Anthony Evelyn Ashley, who sold Grove Place with 65 acres

Cowper. *Argent three martlets gules and a chief engrailed gules with three rings or therein.*

Temple. *Argent two bars sable with three martlets or upon each.*

of land to Captain Bulmer de Sales La Terriere in 1895. It was bought by Mr. Clarence Wilson, the present owner, in 1906.

Grove Place is a pretty specimen of an Elizabethan house of red brick with stone dressings, fronting to the south, with a main block standing east and west, and wings projecting southward at either end, with tall octagonal staircase turrets set in the angles formed by the wings and the main block. The entrance doorway is central, and opens to the screens of the hall, the kitchen and offices lying to the west. The house is of three stories, with a red-tiled roof, and many of the windows retain their original stone mullions and transoms, though some have been replaced by eighteenth-century sashes. The hall is on the ground floor, and some of the original oak panelling remains in position at its east or upper end, the screens being made up of woodwork removed from the passage on the first-floor of the east wing. It has a large fireplace in its north wall with a four-centred head, the spandrels of which have modern

Grove Place, Nursling: The South Front

[85] *Proc. Hants Field Club*, iii, pt. 2, p. 123.

[86] Upon the restoration by Act of Parliament of the family honours which were forfeited in 1746 by his ancestor for his adhesion to the fortunes of the young Pretender, James Drummond became 8th Viscount Strathallan and Baron Drummond.

[87] *Proc. Hants Field Club*, iii, pt. 2, p. 124.

[88] Ibid. 125.

[89] Ibid.

[90] Ibid.

carving and the dates 1565 and 1895, the latter recording a late repair, and on the hearth is a cast-iron fireback of 1687 with the royal arms. The ceiling is of plain plaster panels with moulded ribs and bosses at the intersections. At the south-west angle is the octagonal stair, more carefully treated than its fellow at the other side of the courtyard, and having evidently served as the chief stair of the house. To the east of the hall is a room with a fine plaster ceiling with the royal arms and initials of Elizabeth in a garter, and roses and fleurs-de-lis; its original panelling has been replaced by good eighteenth-century work. Adjoining it and taking up the south end of the east wing is a large room with panelling and ceiling of eighteenth-century date, but the corresponding room in the west wing retains a plastered ceiling of geometrical design with the arms of Pagett of Poulton in Wiltshire, who bore Argent a cheveron erminees between three talbots passant sable; Farringdon, whose arms were Sable three running unicorns argent; Sherington of Lacock in Wiltshire, whose shield was Gules two crosses formy or voided sable between two flaunches checky argent and azure; Mill of Hampton, to whom arms—Six pieces sable and argent with a fox's head proper between two bears argent with muzzles and chains or in the chief and a like bear between two like foxes' heads in the foot—were granted in 1533.

There is a fine arabesque frieze, and below it a plain band with the arms of Sherington, Talbot, and others. The walls have contemporary oak panelling below the frieze. The fireplace on the east side has a flat-pointed arch with carved spandrels and a plasterwork chimney-piece with the arms of James I beneath a projecting cornice enriched with a vine pattern and carried by pairs of Ionic columns. Below the panel with the royal arms are the arms of Talbot, flanked by leopards and fleurs-de-lis.

The first floor rooms over this part of the house are bedrooms, and on the plastering in one of them are some roughly sketched designs in red with the date 1576. The western room on this floor in the main block has a fine plasterwork ceiling and frieze with the following shields:—Pagett; Farringdon; Sherington; Wilford, whose arms were Gules a cheveron ermine between three leopards' heads or; Cooke of Giddea Hall in Essex, who bore arms Quarterly of 6: 1, Or a cheveron checky gules and azure between three cinquefoils azure impaled with Malpas, Sable a fesse between three pheons argent, (2) Or an eagle azure with two heads, for Montgomery, (3) Azure three eagles set bendwise between two bends argent, for Belknap, (4) Gules a fesse checky argent and sable between six crosses formy fitchy or, for Boteler, (5) Or two bends gules, for Sudeley, (6) Bendy of ten pieces or and azure, for Mountfort; Bacon of Redgrave, whose arms were Gules a chief argent with two pierced molets sable therein, quartered with Barry or and azure a bend gules, for Knaplod, with the difference of a crescent. The adjoining room takes up the rest of the first floor of the main block, and has a fine early eighteenth-century moulded ceiling; a passage has been partitioned off from it on the south side, cutting into the ceiling, and connects with that down the west side of the east wing, from which the panelling has been removed. The north room in this wing, adjoining the large room just described, is quite plain, but that next to it on the south has an Elizabethan plaster ceiling like that below it on the ground floor, and eighteenth-century oak panelling. To the south is a room without any ornament, opening to that at the south end of the wing, which has an Elizabethan ceiling with two-headed eagles, leopards and fleurs-de-lis; the crests of Bacon—a boar passant, and of Paulet—a falcon rising from a branch, are also introduced. The third story is an attic, divided into small rooms, but originally formed a long gallery over the main block and west wing, with a coved plaster ceiling adorned with all the arms which occur elsewhere in the house. It remains in a fair state over the main block, but very little is left in the west wing. The stair turrets are carried above the roofs and finished with embattled parapets, their upper stages being lighted by square-headed two-light windows, and the chimney stacks which project from the outer faces of the walls have lost their original brick shafts, all the existing shafts being modern. On the west side of the house is a walled garden, with the stables to the south-west, and a fine avenue of limes leads from the road to the south front of the house.

From early times a water-mill was appurtenant to the manor of Nursling Beaufo, being mentioned as early as 1255.[91] It is probable also that there was another mill in the parish appurtenant to the manor of Nursling Prior, for one is included in the extent of 'Notesselinge' (representing Nursling Prior) in Domesday Book.[92] In the Chancery decree of 1619 two water corn-mills and three 'fullingstocke' thereunto adjoining called Nursling Mills are mentioned as having been leased to Andrew Mundy by Sir Richard Mill.[93] One of them seems to have fallen into disuse by the beginning of the eighteenth century,[94] and there is now only one water-mill in the parish.

A several fishery in the River Test was appurtenant to the manor of Nursling Prior. The prior sometimes had some difficulty in maintaining his rights. Thus in 1387 he brought an action against John Goldsmith of Southampton, William Fisher, Robert Goudyer, and Richard Lobbe for fishing in his fishery at Nursling and carrying off 200 lampreys, 300 salmon, 200 trout, 4,000 eels, and other fish to the value of £40. John Goldsmith, who was at this time holding the manor of Testwood on a nine years' lease from Sir Thomas West, asserted that the fishery in the Test between 'Asshedych' on the north and 'Dodepole' on the south was common to the lords of the manors of Nursling Prior and Testwood, and that therefore he and his servants were justified in fishing therein. The case was therefore adjourned for further evidence, but with what result does not appear.[95]

CHURCH The church of *ST. BONIFACE* has a chancel 22 ft. 3 in. by 12 ft., with a large south chapel 16 ft. 9 in. wide by 14 ft. 4 in. long, a nave 43 ft. 10 in. by 25 ft. 4 in., and a south porch carried up as a tower. In the thirteenth century the nave had a south aisle, which seems to have been destroyed in mediaeval times. The building in its present form appears to date from the first quarter of the fourteenth century, but includes part of the thirteenth-century church. In 1881 the church was repaired by Street, and a thir-

[91] Feet of F. Hants, Hil. 40 Hen. III.
[92] *V.C.H. Hants*, i, 464*a*.
[93] Chan. Enr. Dec. R. 1286.
[94] Recov. R. Hil. 7 Geo. I, rot. 26.
[95] De Banc. R. Mich. 11 Ric. II, m. 211.

Grove Place, Nursling: Fireplace in Dining-room

teenth-century window-head, found during the pulling down of the north wall of the chancel at that time, is preserved in the porch. The chancel probably retains its thirteenth-century plan, and has on the south side a plain pointed arch with a string of thirteenth-century section in its west respond, that in the east respond being cut away. The east window, of two trefoiled lights with a quatrefoil in the head, has tracery of early fourteenth-century style : in the north wall is a window of two trefoiled lights with a trefoil over, the head of which is fourteenth-century work reset, and in the south wall, to the east of the arch already mentioned, is a single trefoiled fourteenth-century light. Under this window is a wide segmental arch serving as the sedilia, the panelling at the back of it being of Street's design, and in the north wall is a credence of the same date (1881). The chancel arch is sharply pointed, of two chamfered orders, the inner springing from moulded half-octagonal corbels of early fourteenth-century section ; on either side of the arch on its west face, some 4 ft. above the springing, are hooked corbels for the rood beam. The south chapel is lighted on the south by a square-headed fifteenth-century window of three cinquefoiled lights, and opens to the nave by an arch formerly at the east end of the south aisle, but now divided by the south wall of the nave, its southern half being blocked in the masonry. The plan and probably part of the walling of the chapel may be of thirteenth-century date, like the chancel. The nave is of unusual proportions, being more than twice as wide as the chancel, and appears to be entirely of the fourteenth century. Before its building, which involved the destruction of the south aisle, there must have been a south arcade on the same line as the south wall of the chancel, dating from the thirteenth century or possibly earlier. It probably stood on the line of the south wall of an earlier aisleless nave of small size, the chancel of which had been built round and destroyed when its thirteenth-century successor was set out. If, as must be assumed, the nave was on the same axis as the present chancel, its width could hardly have been greater than 12 ft. 6 in., and its widening would very naturally suggest itself to later builders. To avoid throwing it out of centre with the chancel, it would be necessary to pull down the south arcade, and to encroach on the area of the south aisle, and this is what actually happened, the width thus obtained being sufficient without the addition of aisles. The south wall of the thirteenth-century aisle was therefore pulled down, and the southern half of its eastern arch blocked up as it now appears. Traces of the bonding of the destroyed wall are to be seen not only in the west wall of the south chapel, but in the east wall of the south porch, and in the latter case can only be explained by supposing that the wall in question incorporates the west wall of the destroyed aisle, probably giving thereby the line of that of the early nave, whose dimensions would be about 30 ft. by 12 ft. 6 in.—a very usual size. The nave has two north windows, each of two trefoiled lights and fourteenth-century date, but the eastern of the two has geometrical tracery of an earlier kind than the flowing tracery of the other window. In the south wall are two windows identical with those in the north, except that the geometrical window is the western of the two. In the west wall is a fourteenth-century window with three lights and net tracery, having below it a contemporary doorway of two chamfered orders. Of the tower only the lower part is in stone, the upper stage being of wood, with a shingled wooden spire ; its inner and outer doors are of plain fourteenth-century style, and the whole is doubtless of this date, except so much of the east wall as may have belonged to the thirteenth-century aisle. The walls are plastered externally, and the roofs red tiled ; the timbers of the nave roof are probably mediaeval, and a beam with the date 1675 over the south doorway may refer to repairs done at that time. To the east of the south doorway is a holy-water niche, and the font, which is modern, stands near by, having an octagonal bowl on marble shafts. There are a few old floor tiles in the church of common type, and on the east gable of the nave is an old gable cross. In the south chapel, at the south-west corner, is the large monument of Richard Mill, 1613, with effigies of himself and his wife, the latter on a lower level, beneath a tall canopy with heraldry and pierced strap-work, the scrolls on either side of the central cresting ending in lions' heads, as on the contemporary Uvedale tomb at Wickham. There is also a curious mural monument to Andrew Mundy, 1632, a brass plate engraved with allegorical devices, a sun and sphere, a skull, a book, stars and clouds, and on a lozenge a chronogram :—

LeX aeternI LVX MVnDI = 1632.

The brass plate is set in a stone frame inscribed with a second chronogram :—

Vt CererI fVnVs aC phoenICI CInIs
Vesper apoLLInI sIC MIhI fInIs = 1632.

There are three bells of 1769 by Wells of Aldbourne.

The plate consists of a silver cup, paten, and flagon of 1727, repaired in 1879.

The first book of the registers begins in 1617 and runs to 1735, and the second from 1736 to 1797. The third is the marriage register 1754–1812, and the fourth the baptisms and burials 1797–1812.

ADVOWSON There was a church in Nursling at the time of the Domesday Survey.[96] The living has always been in the hands of the bishop of Winchester,[97] and is at the present time a rectory, net yearly value £325 with 10 acres of glebe and residence.

CHARITIES In 1880 Mrs. Jane Collett Langley by her will left £100, the income to be applied for the benefit of such nine poor widows, or other persons, as the incumbent should select. The legacy was invested in the purchase of £104 3*s.* 3*d.* consols, and the income is applied in accordance with the trusts.

96 *V.C.H. Hants*, i, 464.

97 *Wykeham's Reg.* (Hants Rec. Soc.), i, 134, 178 ; Inst. Bks. P.R.O.

OTTERBOURNE

The small parish of Otterbourne, covering roughly an area of 1,412 acres, of which 1,385 are land and 27 land covered by water, lies about four and a half miles from Winchester at the base of one of the chalk downs which rise south-west of the city. From the comparatively low-lying village, which is in the north of the parish, the ground rises to a height of 237 ft. above the ordnance datum at Otterbourne Hill at the south end of the village, and then falls again in the south and south-east of the parish to the low ground west of Allbrook which is traversed by the Itchen.

The road from Winchester to Southampton cutting through the parish forms the main village street. As it runs downhill from Shawford towards Otterbourne a group of three or four houses near by the lane which leads north-west to Silkstead and Hursley seems to mark the beginning of the village, but is in reality in Compton parish, and Otterbourne only begins at the bridge over the narrow river—a branch of the Itchen—which feeds a water-cress bed a few yards away north of the road.

Beyond the bridge is a small group of well-worn cottages, some of which were built of the stones from the old church when it was rebuilt by Keble in 1837–9. Here the road curves slightly to the west past the vicarage with its quaint chimneys, up a slight incline to the main group of cottages and houses composing the village, some thatched and half-timbered, others red brick and modern. A large white house standing in good grounds on the east side of the road is Otterbourne House, the residence of Mrs. Christian. The village inn stands well back from the road on the west side, and so a small front courtyard is formed in which stands the familiar sign of the 'White Horse.' Higher up the road on the opposite side is 'Elderfield,' where Miss Charlotte Yonge the authoress lived for many years. The house is now the property of Mr. G. Norsworthy, by whom it has been much modernized and enlarged. On the west, close by the entrance to Cranbury Park (see under Hursley) at the bottom of Otterbourne Hill, stands the church of St. Matthew, half hidden from the road by high shrubs and trees planted inside the churchyard wall. The village school, erected in 1874, is north-east of the church.

From the base of Otterbourne Hill the soil changes from clay to gravel. At the top of the hill on the east is the village green, round which roughly grouped in a half circle the cottages of this part of the village used to stand. Now, however, the cottages here are mostly modern, and the name Maypolefield, applied to some allotments here, suggests that this was once the scene of the yearly maypole dance. From the top of the hill a fine view opens to the south over woods and hills to the distant Southampton Water, beyond which is the dim outline of the Isle of Wight. Passing over the hill the main road continues towards Southampton over the stretch of woodland country, comprising Otterbourne Park, on the southern outskirts of which is 'The Grange,' the residence of Mr. Jones Bateman. Almost opposite the church of St. Matthew a lane, known as Kiln Lane, branches east from the village street, and passing the pound, near which the stocks originally stood, leads to Otterbourne Farm, and to a rough stile which leads across a field to the ruins of the original parish church, the chancel of which is still standing. An effort has been made during the last few years to utilize this chancel for gild and other services. At the back of the ruined church runs the London and South Western Railway main line from London to Southampton, the rush and roar of the trains contrasting sharply with the sense of quiet and decay and desolation that seems to hang around this bit of grey weatherbeaten building standing in the midst of old headstones, round which grow rank grasses and weeds. Across the water-meadows that stretch to the south a short lane leads up to the old moated manor-house, that is now no longer even a farm-house, the house being dilapidated and the moat choked with weeds and rushes. The old panel picture representing a battle, possibly between Turks and Austrians, was removed from the house a few years ago.[1] Parallel with and east of the railway line as it cuts from north to south through the parish, the River Itchen, one branch of which is here diverted into an aqueduct, runs down to Allbrook, and after taking a circuitous course to the east goes south to Bishopstoke, and thence to Southampton Water.

Allbrook itself, once a hamlet of only one or two cottages, has now become quite a flourishing modern village, owing to the success of its saw-mills, which are at the extreme east of the village near the railway line. Monotonous modern cottages, small provision shops, and a small school-chapel compose the village. Allbrook Farm is on the north side of the street near the saw-mills, and close by is the village school, built in 1874. Passing out of the village to the west the road curves north-west, uphill past 'Rookwood,' a modern house, the residence of Mr. Coombes, owner of the saw-mills, to Boyatt Farm, becoming a rough narrow lane between ploughed fields and hedges. At the back of the farm-house, which is a square red-brick building, dating from the seventeenth century, are the Boyatt brickworks. Until 1840 a pound and stocks stood opposite the farm-house. Boyatt Wood and the lands west and south of the farm are in a detached portion of South Stoneham parish.

To the east of Allbrook is Highbridge, where is another small hamlet, half in Otterbourne, half in Twyford. Here was the small Roman Catholic chapel, where tradition places the secret marriage between George IV and Mrs. Fitzherbert, though modern research has definitely proved that the marriage took place in London.[1a]

The soil of the parish is gravel, with a subsoil of gravel and chalk, and on the 438¼ acres of arable land crops of wheat, barley, and turnips are grown. A belt of woodland, including Freemantle Copse and Great Moorlands Copse, stretches away to the west of the parish, and this, together with Peverell's Wood, which is in the extreme south-west, makes up the 227 acres of woodland. The greater part of the

[1] For a description of this and for much valuable and detailed information concerning Otterbourne, see Miss Charlotte Yonge's *John Keble's Parishes.*

[1a] See W. H. Wilkins, *Mrs. Fitzherbert and George IV*, i, 96 et seq.

parish, however, 627¼ acres, is given up to permanent grass.[2]

Otterbourne Common, which covers the top of Otterbourne Hill, was inclosed under the general Inclosure Act by the award of 24 June, 1837.

Among place-names mentioned in extant records are Millands or Millhouse[3] and Aldermoore and Boyton Mead[4] (xviii cent.).

MANORS

Lands in *OTTERBOURNE* as parcel of the district of Chilcomb were granted by King Edgar to the church at Winchester about 978,[5] and were confirmed to the church by King Ethelred in 984.[6] In the reign of King Edward the Confessor Cheping held Otterbourne of the bishopric of Winchester, and 'could not withdraw himself from the church.'[7]

At the time of the Domesday Survey the manor had been alienated from the church, and belonged to Ralph de Mortimer,[8] whose descendants held half a fee in Otterbourne as late as the fifteenth century.[9] In 1212–13 Richard Ferebraz alienated 1 virgate of land in Otterbourne with appurtenances to Henry de Capella.[10] This virgate evidently became parcel of the manor of Otterbourne, and passed from Henry de Capella to his son Bartholomew in 1248.[11] In 1253 the king licensed Bartholomew de Capella to inclose his wood of Otterbourne, called Parc, which was within the royal forest of Ashley.[12] Bartholomew died seised of the manor of Otterbourne in 1258, held of Sir Brian de Brampton in chief of the fee of Roger de Mortimer.[13] Joan de Capella his daughter and heir was a minor only one and a half years old, and the guardianship of the lands of Bartholomew, granted in 1259 to Eubold de Montibus, probably included Otterbourne.[14] She seems to have married John de Bohun, for in 1279 John and Joan quitclaimed the manor of Otterbourne from themselves and the heirs of Joan to Simon the draper, sometimes called Simon de Winton, to hold of them by the annual payment of a pair of gilt spurs.[15] In 1280 Simon was summoned to show cause why he amerced his men at his court of Otterbourne against their will.[16] From Simon the manor passed to his grandson, Richard de Winton, son and heir of Richard de Winton,[17] who was holding the same in 1316.[18]

There is no inquisition on the death of Richard, but the manor evidently passed to his son or kinsman, John de Winton,[19] who died seised of it in 1361.[20] His brother and heir, Richard de Winton, conveyed the manor for life in 1378 to Hugh Craan or Crane of Winchester and his wife Isabel.[21] However there seems to have been some flaw in the transaction, since two years later Hugh Crane petitioned against Richard de Winton and Agnes his wife that they had with certain others schemed to dispossess him and his wife of the manor, and had forged a recognizance of the statute of merchants for £550 purporting to have been made in 1348 during the life of John de Winton, and had caused a certificate to be delivered in Chancery for obtaining execution in respect of the manor and other lands belonging at that date to John de Winton.[22] However, Hugh Crane was evidently successful in his petition, and in 1386 Thomas de Winton, son and heir of Richard, who had died in 1383,[23] released to Hugh Crane all right in the manor.[24] Richard de Winton's wife Agnes survived her husband, and seems to have married (2) Nicholas Brus[25] and (3) Richard Caas; and after the death of Hugh Crane she and her husband Richard Caas made claim to a third part of the manor of Otterbourne against Isabel the widow of Hugh. The suit was begun in 1404 and lasted until 1405. Agnes claimed the third in dower by donation of Richard de Winton, but Isabel maintained that Agnes had no right to dower in the same since Richard de Winton had not been seised of the manor until after his marriage to Agnes, and this seems to have been the case, since his brother John had held it until 1361.[26]

The result of the suit is not given, but unquestionably the right lay with Isabel. Except for this third, which Isabel evidently had in dower for her life, Otterbourne had been sold by Hugh Crane to William of Wykeham in 1386.[27] Within the next few years William of Wykeham granted the manor to his great-nephew William Perot, who took the name of Wykeham.[28] William Wykeham had been admitted to New College in 1387, but probably owing to ill-health had left the same year.[29] In 1396 he married Alice Uvedale, the daughter of John Uvedale of Titsey (co. Surrey), sheriff of Hants from 1388 to 1399 and a great personal friend of the founder.[30] On the death of William Wykeham and Alice his wife at an early age without issue Otterbourne passed in tail male to his second brother Thomas, to whom reversion had been granted in 1400.[31] Thomas Wykeham, who was knighted early in the century, had also been at New College, admitted in 1390 and leaving in 1394.[32] Surviving both his brothers he became William of Wykeham's sole heir-at-law on his death in 1403. Several years before his death, which occurred in 1443 or 1444,[33] he evidently settled the manor of Otterbourne on his eldest son William,

WYKEHAM. *Argent two cheverons sable between three roses gules.*

[2] Statistics from Bd. of Agric. (1905).
[3] Chan. Inq. p.m. (Ser. 2), ccccii, No. 129.
[4] Chan. Enr. Dec. R. 1819, No. 4.
[5] Kemble, *Codex Dipl.* iii, 153.
[6] Ibid. 203.
[7] *V.C.H. Hants*, i, 489*a*.
[8] Ibid.
[9] *Vide* Inq. p.m. 22 Ric. II, No. 34, and 3 Hen. VI, No. 32.
[10] Feet of F. Hants, 14 John.
[11] *Excerpta e rot. Finium* (Rec. Com.), ii, 31.
[12] *Hist. MSS. Com. Rep.* viii, 263.
[13] Inq. p.m. Hen. III, file 20, No. 19.
[14] *Excerpta e rot. Finium* (Rec. Com.), ii, 296.
[15] Feet of F. Hants, Mich. 7 Edw. I.
[16] Assize R. Mich. 8 Edw. I, rot. 9.
[17] Richard died in 1296 in the lifetime of Simon, leaving a son and heir Richard aged fourteen. (Inq. p.m. 24 Edw. I, No. 21).
[18] *Feud. Aids*, ii, 309.
[19] Feet of F. Hants, 16 Edw. III, No. 10.
[20] Inq. p.m. 36 Edw. III, pt. 2 (1st Nos.), No. 78.
[21] Pat. 4 Ric. II, pt. 1, m. 10 *d.*
[22] Ibid; Pat. 4 Ric. II, pt. 2, m. 13*d.*
[23] *Vide* manor of Soberton in the hundred of Meonstoke.
[24] Close, 10 Ric. II, m. 50 *d.*
[25] *Vide* manor of Soberton.
[26] De Banc. R. East. 5 Hen. IV, m. 446 *d.* and East. 6 Hen. IV, m. 417.
[27] *Hist. MSS. Com. Rep.* viii, App. 263. Documents belonging to Magdalen College, Oxford. Feet of F. Hants, Mich. 10 Ric. II.
[28] *Hist. MSS. Com. Rep.* viii, App. 263.
[29] Kirby, *Annals of Win. Coll.* 93.
[30] See *Surrey Arch. Coll.* iii, 83.
[31] Feet of F. Hants, Trin. 3 Hen. VI.
[32] Kirby, *Annals of Win. Coll.* 93.
[33] Inq. p.m. 22 Hen. VI, No. 16.

probably on his marriage, and in 1440 William himself settled the manor on his younger brother Thomas and Agnes his wife.[34] Nevertheless Sir Thomas seems to have lived at Otterbourne until his death, as there is an entry on the Compotus Roll of Winchester College for 1444 marking a land transaction made between Warden Thurburn and Sir Thomas, and noting 9*d.* for wine brought and sent to the latter at Otterbourne.[35] William his eldest son died in 1457 leaving a daughter and heir Margaret, who on the death of her uncle Thomas without issue became possessed of Otterbourne.[36] This Margaret married William Fiennes, Lord Saye and Sele, who sold the manor to William Waynflete, bishop of Winchester, in 1458.[37]

MAGDALEN COLLEGE, OXFORD. *Lozengy sable and ermine a chief sable with three garden lilies therein* which are the arms of William Waynflete.

In 1464 Lord Saye and Sele publicly declared his sale to the bishop by his own declaration and that of Thomas Danvers his attorney, probably before the bishop granted the manor to Magdalen College, Oxford.[38] In 1535 Magdalen College was seised of the manor, which was charged with an annual payment of £4 to the chamberlain of Winchester and a fee of a noble to the bailiff.[39] The president and fellows of the college are still lords of the manor. The court of the manor was held at the old moated manor-house by the president of Magdalen on progress until the early half of the nineteenth century.

BOYATT (Boviet, Boneta, Bometa xii, xiii, and xiv cents.) in Otterbourne was held by Godric in the time of Edward the Confessor and was then assessed at two hides. At the time of the Domesday Survey it was held of the king by Herbrand, and was assessed only at half a hide.[40] In 1167 William son of Martin rendered account of half a mark for Boyatt.[41] Between that date and 1189 it was granted to Waverley Abbey, since at the later date the farm or grange of 'Bomata' was confirmed to the abbey by Richard I,[42] while King John made a similar confirmation in 1206.[43] In 1219 Adam abbot of Waverley granted one messuage, 11 acres of land, and two of meadow in Boyatt, to Nicholas Malherbe to be held of the abbot and his successors for an annual rent of 12*d.*[44] Nine years later the abbot granted him common of pasture in his foreign pasture, namely outside his wood, and arable land, while Nicholas quitclaimed to the abbot all right in the common of pasture in the arable land of the abbot in Boyatt.[45] Boyatt continued in the possession of Waverley until the sixteenth century, and in 1535 its rents had risen to £13 18*s.* 0½*d.*, while its perquisites of court were worth 6*s.* 8*d.*[46] Hence by this time the messuage and 11 acres of former times had come to be considered as a manor, and after the suppression of Waverley it was granted in 1537 as 'The Manor of Roviat' (*sic*) to Sir William Fitzwilliam, together with the site of the late monastery and most of its possessions.[47] Sir William, who was Comptroller of the King's Household,[48] was created earl of Southampton in 1537.[49] In 1539, as lord admiral, he conducted Anne of Cleves to England. His letters to the king and Cromwell give an account of the voyage, of the numerous delays caused by contrary winds 'which blew as all would have gone asunder,'[50] and give some picture of Anne herself with her distaste for court ceremony, and yet her princesslike manner.[51] The earl died in 1542,[52] and Boyatt passed by virtue of a settlement made in 1538 to his widow Mabel, with contingent remainder to his half brother Sir Anthony Browne, Master of the Horse.[53] The latter died in 1548,[54] two years before the widow,[55] and the reversion passed to his son Anthony, who in 1554 was created Viscount Montague.[56] In Elizabeth's reign he was very active in furnishing horse and men against the Spanish Armada,[57] and won the queen's friendship, although he favoured the old religion.[58] Unlike the other estates which had passed into the Browne family on the death of the first earl of Southampton, Boyatt was alienated during the lifetime of this first Lord Montague, who obtained licence to convey to Gilbert Welles in 1566,[59] and made conveyance by fine and recovery within the next few months.[60] Gilbert Welles was the first recusant member of a family whose endurance for the sake of their religion was to be well tried within the next century. It was reported in March, 1594, that two Jesuits were harbouring with him, and he was ordered by the council 'with divers other recusants of Hampshire to confine himself to Ely.'[61] In May of the same year Grafton, 'a learned Jesuit,' was

BROWNE, Viscount Montague. *Sable three lions passant bendwise between double cotises argent.*

WELLES. *Sable a cheveron ermine between three martlets argent.*

34 Close, 18 Hen. VI, m. 9.
35 Kirby, *Annals of Win. Coll.* 182, 184.
36 See S.P. Dom. Eliz. xc, No. 5. Sir Richard Fiennes here claims his right and sole right to the privilege of Founder's kin through his descent from Margaret, since 'it is clear from many evidence, that Thomas de Wykeham, sonne to Sir Thomas de Wykeham, left no male issues,' and he quotes a recovery made by one of his ancestors who made good his claim to the manor of Gerbston because Thomas de Wykeham had died without heirs.
37 *Hist. MSS. Com. Rep.* viii, App. 263.
38 Close, 4 Edw. VI, m. 13 *d.* 26.
39 *Valor Eccl.* (Rec. Com.), ii, 285.
40 *V.C.H. Hants*, i, 500*b*.
41 *Pipe R.* (Pipe R. Soc.), xii, 178.
42 Dugdale, *Mon.* v, 242; Cart. Antiq. S. No. 20.
43 Chart. R. 7 John, m. 4.
44 Feet of F. Hants, 3 Hen. III, No. 61.
45 Ibid. 12 Hen. III, No. 160.
46 *Valor Eccl.* (Rec. Com.), ii, 35.
47 Pat. 28 Hen. VIII, pt. 2, m. 9 and 10.
48 Ibid.
49 See *Dict. Nat. Biog.*
50 *L. and P. Hen. VIII*, xiv (2), 693.
51 Ibid. 677.
52 G.E.C. *Complete Peerage.*
53 Exch. Inq. p.m. 3 Edw. VI (Ser. 2), file 994, No. 2.
54 Ibid.
55 G.E.C. *Complete Peerage.*
56 *Cal. S.P. Dom.* 1547–80, p. 63.
57 Ibid. 1581–90, p. 510.
58 Ibid. 1591–4, p. 97. Elizabeth visited him at Cowdray Park (Sussex), and was entertained there for six days in 1591.
59 Pat. 8 Eliz. pt. 4, m. 15.
60 Feet of F. Hants, Mich. 8 & 9 Eliz.; Recov. R. East. 9 Eliz. rot. 148.
61 *Cal. S.P. Dom.* 1591–4, p. 463.

OTTERBOURNE : CHANCEL ARCH OF THE OLD CHURCH

supposed to be 'at the house of Welles a confirmed recusant.'[62] On the death of Gilbert in 1598 his son and heir Thomas held Boyatt, until in 1605, in accordance with the statute against recusants of 1605,[63] two parts of the manor were seized towards the non-payment of the £20 a month which had been inflicted on popish recusants in 1581;[64] 'whereas' the letters patent ran, 'he hath of late tyme absented himself from the church and refused to come to divine service and other spiritual exercises . . . . and doth continue his recusancie contrarie to the form of divers good laws and statutes,' two parts of his estates were forfeited and granted to John Pierson for a term of forty-one years.[65] In 1613 these two parts of the manor of Boyatt were granted to John Gray for the term of twenty-one years by reason of the continued recusancy of Thomas Welles and his mother Elizabeth.[66] During the same year the third part of the manor was alienated, probably mortgaged, by Thomas to George Dowse and Francis Perkins,[67] and in 1627 came a similar mortgage to Henry Manfeld and others.[68] In 1630 Thomas Welles died and all his right in the manor passed to his son Gilbert, who in 1634 received the whole manor for a term of forty-one years.[69] Boyatt remained in the Welles family until towards the end of the eighteenth century,[70] when, in accordance with the will of Henry Welles dated 2 August, 1762, it passed to his cousin Walter Smythe,[70a] second son of Sir John Smythe, bart., to hold for life, with remainder to his son and heir Walter Smythe.[71] The further history of this manor has not been ascertained.

ALLBROOK FARM, described as a 'very good house' in 1726, with lands belonging to it called Aldermoor, Boyton Mead, and Otterbourne Mead, was owned by John Wybarne, who died intestate about 1717. In 1715 he had conveyed it to Thomas Goodwin to dispose of it by sale and to pay his debts from the proceeds. After the death of John Wybarne Walter Curll offered £680 for it, and entered into possession, alleging that his money was in London. For six years he remained in possession without payment, and was consequently ordered to pay an additional £185 8*s*. by the Court of Chancery in 1726.[72]

CHURCHES The church of *ST. MATTHEW* was built in 1840, and has an apsidal chancel, north and south transepts, a nave with north aisle, and a bell-turret containing two bells on the west gable. It is in a poor Gothic style, and has but little architectural interest, but the low screen at the west of the chancel, formerly in a Premonstratensian abbey in Flanders, is in its way a remarkable piece of seventeenth-century woodwork, being adorned with carvings, the subject of which is the adoration of the Holy Sacrament, with kneeling figures of men on the north side, and of women on the south. The top rail is carved with flowers and fruit, and there are cherubs holding bunches of grapes and ears of corn, with figures of saints on the uprights dividing the bays of the screen; on the south side St. Dominic and St. Norbert, and on the north St. Clara and St. Anthony of Padua.

At the north-east angle of the churchyard stands the modern schoolhouse, the east doorway of which is a fine piece of thirteenth-century work, with a pointed arch of two orders enriched with dog-tooth ornament.

There are two bells of 1838.

The church plate is silver-gilt, and consists of a chalice of foreign make, with foliage round the base of the bowl, a paten of 1641, and an almsdish with indistinct date letter. There is also a spoon of Norwegian manufacture.

The first book of registers contains all entries from 1648 to 1653, the second runs from 1690 to 1746, and the third from 1747 to 1812. There are marriage registers also from 1754 to 1786, 1786 to 1812, and 1747 to 1812, and burial registers from 1654 to 1666, 1666 to 1695, and 1805 to 1812.

The old church of Otterbourne stood at some distance to the south, on lower ground; its chancel is all that is now left. This is of thirteenth-century date, with two lancets on the south side, and a two-light east window with a quatrefoil in the head. The chancel arch is part of the thirteenth-century work, and is small, with a single chamfer on the pointed arch; on either side of it are contemporary arched recesses but little narrower than the arch itself, having an inner order with jamb shafts and moulded capitals and bases. These recesses have flat sills, and both they and the chancel arch are filled in with modern brickwork. They were not pierced, but formed backings to the nave altars.

The eighteenth-century altar rails remain in the chancel, which is seated with chairs, but there are no other fittings of interest. The walling is of flint with good limestone ashlar dressings, and under the east window parts of a Purbeck marble coffin slab are built in. Part of another marble slab lies in the churchyard.

ADVOWSON Otterbourne was a parochial chapelry dependent upon Hursley until 1876, when by order in council dated 23 August, 1876, it was constituted a separate ecclesiastical parish and perpetual curacy.[73] The advowson at the present time belongs to Mr. Anthony Gibbs.

The Rev. John Keble, M.A., author of the *Christian Year*, who was vicar of Hursley from 1836 to 1866 built the present vicarage-house. There is a stone to his memory in Otterbourne churchyard.

CHARITIES 'The Touchet Charity' was founded by Miss Clara Olivia Elgie and Miss Edith M. C. Elgie, who by deed dated 4 September, 1891, settled a sum of £181 16*s*. 4*d*. consols upon trust that the dividends should be applied as to three-fifths for repair of the grave of their brother-in-law John Hastings Touchet in the churchyard, one-fifth for the benefit of a Working Men's Club, and the remaining fifth in aid of the Charitable Institutions in the parish.

[62] *Cal. S.P. Dom.* 1591–4, p. 511.
[63] *Stat. of Realm*, 3 Jas. I, cap. 4.
[64] Ibid. 23 Eliz. cap. 1, § 4.
[65] Pat. 6 Jas. I, pt. 3, No. 19.
[66] Pat. 11 Jas. I, pt. 21, No. 8.
[67] Feet of F. Hants, Trin. 11 Jas. I.
[68] Ibid. Div. Cos. Mich. 3 Chas. I.
[69] Pat. 11 Chas. I, pt. 2.
[70] Feet of F. Hants, East. 13 Chas. I; *Cal. of Com. for Compounding*, v, 3287; Recov. R. Trin. 8 Geo. II, rot. 43.
[70a] Mrs. Fitzherbert, the wife of George IV, was the eldest daughter of this Walter Smythe, and spent the early years of her life at Brambridge House (q.v. Fawley Hundred), her father's Hampshire residence.
[71] Recov. R. Hil. 21 Geo. III, rot. 73; Trin. 19 Geo. III, rot. 156.
[72] Chan. Enr. Dec. R. 1819, No. 4.
[73] *Lond. Gaz.* (1876), 4654.

In 1901 Miss Charlotte Mary Yonge by her will, proved this date, left £100 to the vicar for the time being for the benefit of the parish schools so long as they should be voluntary Church of England Schools.

The legacy was invested in the purchase of £96 10*s.* New South Wales 3½ per cent stock.

The above-mentioned sums of stock are held by the Official Trustees of Charitable Funds in trust for the respective charities.

SPARSHOLT

Speresholte (xii and xiii cents.) ; Sparshall, Spershott (xvi cent. et seq.).

The parish of Sparsholt including the modern parish of Lainston covers an area of 3,672 acres. The whole of the parish is on high ground, which reaches its greatest height towards the centre of the parish, where the village of Sparsholt and Lainston House lie. The road from Winchester to Stockbridge branches south-west about two miles from Weeke, cuts across Lainston Avenue, passes Upper Dean Farm, and turns up a steep hill into the village. On the right-hand side behind a high hedge is the vicarage, and a few yards higher up where the village street forks is the church of St. Stephen. The road to the left leads down between thatched and half-timbered cottages to Ham Green, to a smithy and group of cottages taking the name of the green. That to the right leads past some cottages and houses to Merecourt Farm. A shady lane to the right leads up another steep rough lane to Westley and the picturesque buildings of Westley Farm. Half a mile east of the village is Lower Dean Farm and the cottages and farm buildings forming the small hamlet of Dean. Lainston House, north-west of the village, stands in the midst of well-wooded country on high ground with an eastward fall. It is a fine H-shaped brick building with stone dressings, dating generally from the early years of the eighteenth century, but part of the east front belongs to an Elizabethan house. The main entrance is on the west through a picturesque forecourt with wrought-iron gates. To the north is a red-brick pigeon-house lined with chalk. Opposite the iron gates is a hexagonal walled garden which, with its long gravel paths, sun-dial, and rose gardens, seems to incorporate past centuries, and to go back to the days when the notorious Elizabeth Chudleigh was married in the now ruined church of St. Peter, which stands almost hidden among the trees to the south of the house. Stretching away to the west is the famous lime avenue, about three-quarters of a mile in length. Fine views can be obtained from Lainston : away to the south, over down and pasture land, Winchester is seen in the distance, and away to the north another long sweep of downland stretches away towards Littleton and on to Crawley. The south-west corner of the parish is thickly wooded, and the woods slope gradually upwards to the track of the Roman road which forms the southern boundary of the parish. Crab Wood, Burrow Copse, and Cow Down Copse are three of the best-known woods. Among place-names in the parish mentioned in the sixteenth century are Goose Acres, Floodfield, and Berksdeane.[1]

MANORS

The manor of *CHILCOMB* as granted by King Edward to the church of Winchester in 908 included lands in Sparsholt.[2] Stigand bishop of Winchester, probably between 1050 and 1060, granted one hide at Sparsholt to Athelmar for his own life and that of Simon his son for such payment as he could make. As witnesses to the grant came Stigand and his following from the Old Minster and Alfwin the abbot and his monks from the New Minster and all the thegns of the shire.[3] In the Domesday Survey Sparsholt, though not mentioned by name, was evidently included in the manor of Chilcomb, the later manor of Barton and Buddlesgate, and one of the nine churches pertaining to the manor was probably the church of Sparsholt.[4] The manor of Barton and Buddlesgate still comprises part of Sparsholt parish.

Lands in Sparsholt were held independently, it would seem, of those held by the prior and convent, by Godfrey de Caritate in the reign of King Henry II.[5] On his death they descended to his son John de Caritate, who was employed in King John's service in 1215 and 1216.[6] Owing partly to some jealousy between the de Caritate family and the family that took the name of Sparsholt and held other lands in the parish,[7] the lands held by the de Caritate family seem to have been separated from Sparsholt probably by the beginning of the thirteenth century and to have become a manor known later as the manor of *LAINSTON*.[8] Unfortunately it seems impossible to gather any definite imformation concerning Lainston until 1342, when Sir Henry de Harnhulle conveyed by fine one carucate in Lainston and the advowson of the church of Lainston, held by Henry de Laverstoke for the term of his life, to John de Winton and Joan his wife.[9] John de Winton died seised of the same in 1361, leaving a brother and heir Richard de Winton,[10]

[1] Exch. Dep. Mich. 33 & 34 Eliz. No. 9.

[2] Kemble, *Codex Dipl.* ii, 153.

[3] Ibid. iv, 170.

[4] *V.C.H. Hants*, i, 463*b*.

[5] Cur. Reg. R. No. 65, m. 1 *d.* ; *Pipe R.* (Pipe R. Soc.), xi, 187.

[6] *Rot. Lit. Pat.* (Rec. Com.), i, 136*b*, 188.

[7] See Fromond's Court and Westley below.

[8] This seems to be a possible conjecture, although it is difficult to give any tangible proof. The jealousy between the two families is certainly shown in the suit given in Cur. Reg. R. No. 65. The eleventh juror in the suit moreover stated that Godfrey de Caritate built a church of stone on the site of a traditional wooden chapel, and it seems possible that this church, which could hardly have been on the site of the church belonging to the prior and convent, was the present ruined church of Lainston. Otherwise the origin and existence of that second church in the parish is difficult to explain, as Lainston is certainly not a hamlet. It follows that if the church that Godfrey de Caritate built was the church of Lainston it was built to avoid attending the church of Sparsholt, and the greater probability is that it was built on his lands in Sparsholt, which were the nucleus of the manor of Lainston.

[9] Feet of F. Hants, 16 Edw. III, No. 10. It is possible, however, that it descended to him from Sir Robert de Harnhulle, whose confessions William de Corfe, a Franciscan, was granted licence to hear in 1322 (*V.C.H. Hants*, ii, 16).

[10] Inq. p.m. 36 Edw. III, pt. 2 (1st Nos.), No. 78.

who was evidently in financial difficulties,[11] for he raised £200 on the manors of Soberton and Lainston in 1383,[12] but this was not enough to satisfy his creditors, and nine months later he was ordered to be imprisoned and his property valued in order that his debts might be paid.[13] He died, however, the same year, and immediately afterwards his widow Agnes married Nicholas Brus.[14] Nicholas and Agnes Brus dealt with the manor by fine in 1384,[15] but after this there seems to be a gap in the descent of the manor, which, however, ultimately passed to Michael Skilling, who presented to the living in 1445.[16] He was succeeded by John Skilling, either his son or grandson, who presented to the living during the episcopacy of William Waynflete.[17] He died seised of the manor and advowson in 1512, leaving as his heir his son John aged forty and more.[18] The manor remained in the possession of the Skilling family until 1613,[19] in which year Edward, Richard and Michael Skilling sold it to Anthony Dawley.[20] The latter died seised of the manor in 1616 leaving a son and heir Walter,[21] who died sixteen years later, his heir being his son Henry aged twelve.[22] Anthony Dawley, grandson of Henry, high sheriff in 1707, sold the manor in 1711 to Sir Philip Meadows,[23] from whom it passed by purchase in 1721 to John Merrill,[24] whose granddaughter Mary married Dr. Bathurst. Their son and heir, dying without issue, left the manor to his paternal uncle General Henry Bathurst, who dying unmarried left the property by will to Selina, the daughter of his eldest sister Lady Elwill, who married Sir William Freemantle.[25] The manor remained with their descendants the Harvey-Bathursts until a few years ago, when it was sold to the present owner Mr. Samuel Bostock.

Skilling. *Argent two cheverons gules and a chief gules with three bezants therein.*

Bathurst. *Sable two bars ermine and three crosses formy or in the chief.*

From an early date, as has been shown, the family of Sparsholt held lands in the parish side by side with the de Caritate family. In 1258 Richard de Sparsholt, chaplain, granted one virgate of land in Sparsholt to Stephen Fromond and his heirs.[26] From Stephen this property descended to Richard Fromond of Sparsholt, the bishop's bailiff for the hundreds of Highclere and Overton, probably his son or grandson, who in 1318 in conjunction with Alice his wife acquired from Richard Beaupel one messuage, two carucates of land, 200 acres of pasture, 6 acres of wood and 60*s.* rent in Sparsholt.[27] These tenements must have been equivalent to the manor of *SPARSHOLT*, sometimes also called *FROMOND'S COURT*,[28] in the oratory of which he obtained licence to hear service during the episcopacy of John Stratford.[29] In 1337 John de la Berton, parson of the church of Farleigh, and Henry de Asshe, chaplain, quitclaimed 6 messuages, 3 carucates of land, 36 acres of meadow, 40 acres of wood and 16*s.* 6*d.* rent in Sparsholt and Stockbridge to Richard and Alice.[30] It is probable that this was a settlement on them of lands which they already possessed, but is just possible that it marks the acquisition of the reputed manor of Westley (q.v.). Richard was succeeded by John Fromond, to whom William Edendon bishop of Winchester granted licence to have mass celebrated in the oratory within his house of Sparsholt.[31]

The subsequent history of the manor is somewhat uncertain, but it was probably included in the twenty-eight messuages, 4½ carucates of land, 28 acres of meadow, 1,000 acres of pasture, 60 acres of wood and 2*s.* 2*d.* rents in Sparsholt and neighbouring places which in 1433 were settled on Sir William Goushill and Julia his wife, widow of John Esteney,[32] for the life of Julia with remainder to Michael Skilling and his heirs.[33] John Skilling died seised of the manor of Fromond's Court in 1512,[34] and from this time the manor of Sparsholt, as it was afterwards more usually called,[35] has followed the same descent as Lainston (q.v.).

The origin of the reputed manor of *WESTLEY* is uncertain. It is possible that it was included in the property in Sparsholt and Stockbridge acquired by Richard Fromond and Alice his wife in 1337, but it seems more probable that it originally belonged to the Sparsholts, passed from them with the manor of Coldrey to the Coldreys,[36] and descended from Thomas Coldrey to his daughter and heir Christine, wife of Richard Holt. In support of this latter theory the following documents can be adduced : a fine of 1253, whereby the manor of Coldrey and rents in Lainston were settled on Philip Sparsholt for life with remainder to William Sparsholt,[37] and a fine of 1333, whereby a messuage, a carucate of land, 8 acres of meadow, 10 acres of wood and 40*s.* rent in Bentley and Lainston were settled on William de Coldrey and Alice his wife,[38] but whether these tenements represent the later manor of Westley is a debatable point. However, they descended to Christine wife of Richard Holt,[39] were granted by her to John Esteney and Julia his wife in 1427,[40] and were included in the lands settled

[11] He owed Hugh Crane £100 in 1377 (Inq. p.m. 7 Ric. II, No. 107).

[12] Feet of F. Hants, Hil. 6 Ric. II.

[13] Inq. p.m. 7 Ric. II, No. 107.

[14] Close, 7 Ric. II, m. 31 *d.*

[15] They conveyed it to Thomas Wolvele and John King, chaplain (Feet of F. Hants, Hil. 7 Ric. II).

[16] Egerton MS. 2034, fol. 48.

[17] Ibid. fol. 80 *d.*

[18] Chan. Inq. p.m. (Ser. 2), xxviii, No. 14.

[19] Ibid. xliv, No. 129. Notes of F. Hants, Mich. 7 & 8 Eliz. and East. 27 Eliz.

[20] Feet of F. Hants, East. 11 Jas. I, and Recov. R. East. 11 Jas. I, rot. 45.

[21] Chan. Inq. p.m. 14 Jas. I, pt. 13, No. 10.

[22] Ibid. (Ser. 2), ccccclxxi, No. 95.

[23] Close, 10 Anne, pt. 7, No. 6.

[24] Feet of F. Hants, East. 7 Geo. I.

[25] *Ex inform.* the Rev. Evelyn Heathcote.

[26] Feet of F. Hants, Trin. 42 Hen. III.

[27] Ibid. Trin. 11 Edw. II.

[28] Chan. Inq. p.m. (Ser. 2), xxviii, No. 14.

[29] Egerton MS. 2032, fol. 75.

[30] Feet of F. Hants, East. 11 Edw. III.

[31] Egerton MS. 2033, fol. 64.

[32] Early Chan. Proc. bdle. 12, No. 32.

[33] Feet of F. Hants, Mich. 12 Hen. VI.

[34] Chan. Inq. p.m. (Ser. 2), xxviii, No. 14.

[35] Recov. R. East. 11 Jas. I, rot. 45 ; Chan. Inq. p.m. (Ser. 2) ccccclxxi, No. 95 ; Recov. R. Trin. 2 Anne, rot. 1.

[36] *V.C.H. Hants*, ii, 503.

[37] Feet of F. Hants, Hil. 37 Hen. III.

[38] Ibid. Trin. 6 Edw. III.

[39] *V.C.H. Hants*, ii, 503.

[40] Feet of F. Hants, Mich. 6 Hen. VI

on Julia for life in 1433 with remainder to Michael Skilling and his heirs.[41] John Skilling died seised of a capital messuage and 5 acres of land in Sparsholt, a tenement in Crawley and a tenement in Westley in 1512.[42] It is probable that to these tenements was afterwards given the name of the manor of Westley, the descent of which has been identical with that of Lainston.

CHURCHES

The church of *ST. STEPHEN, SPARSHOLT*, has a chancel 24 ft. 6 in. by 19 ft. 6 in. with modern organ chamber and vestry on the north, nave 36 ft. by 19 ft. 6 in. with north and south aisles and south porch, and west tower 9 ft. square, all measurements being internal. The walling is of flint rubble with stone dressings, and the chancel and south aisle have red-tiled roofs, while the nave and north aisle are leaded, and the tower has a wooden upper story with a steep shingled roof.

The plan has developed from an aisleless nave and chancel church of twelfth-century date, part of the nave walls of which, including the north-west angle, still exist. About the year 1200 a south aisle was added to the nave, and in the fourteenth century the chancel was rebuilt on a larger scale, becoming of equal width with the nave. The tower is a fifteenth-century addition, built against the old west wall of the nave. In modern times the chancel has been lengthened 8 ft. eastwards, a north aisle added to the nave, and a north vestry and organ chamber to the chancel, under the direction of Mr. Butterfield.

The chancel has an east window of three cinquefoiled lights with fifteenth-century tracery, moved to its present position when the chancel was lengthened. In the south wall is a two-light window with tracery of the same date, but a new mullion, and just to the east of it a blocked priest's door of the first half of the fourteenth century. There are modern sedilia and a credence, and in a glazed wooden case against this wall a pewter coffin chalice and paten, taken from the grave of a priest found in the church, and probably dating from *c.* 1250. The chancel arch is four-centred, of two continuous moulded orders, with plain late fifteenth or early sixteenth-century detail, but the masonry of the jambs up to 5 ft. 7 in. from the floor is of quite different character from the rest, and seems to be twelfth-century work moved outwards at the widening of the arch, and cut to the later section.

The nave has arcades of three bays, that on the north being Butterfield's work; the two eastern bays have arches of two chamfered orders with clustered columns, while the west bay has a plain arch, the break between it and the other bays being caused by the passage of the flue of the heating apparatus. The south arcade has semicircular arches of two chamfered orders, and round columns with plain capitals and moulded bases, good and simple work of *c.* 1200; the nave clearstory has three three-light windows and one single light on the north side, all modern, and no windows on the south.

The south aisle has an east window of two lights, all modern except the fifteenth-century tracery in the head, two square-headed south windows of two and three lights, both modern, and a two-light west window with fifteenth-century tracery and modern jambs. The south doorway, moved by Butterfield into the west bay of the aisle, dates from 1631, having a semicircular head above which is a panel with the churchwardens' names and date of its insertion, and preserves its contemporary door, a very pretty piece of woodwork with square panels and strapwork in low relief filling its arched head. The south porch is modern, of wood on a stone base. The tower is of three stages, having an eastern arch with continuous mouldings like those of the chancel arch, and a west window in the ground story of two cinquefoiled lights with a quatrefoil in the head, which seems to be old work much patched with new stone. At the south-west angle is a large diagonal buttress, added at some time to counteract a failure of the foundations, some signs of which are yet to be seen on the tower. The belfry stage is of wood and modern, and contains pits for five bells, though only four are now in existence. The treble, third, and tenor are of 1742, by Robert Catlin, and the second by Thomas Mears, 1820.

During the alterations to the church a good many remains of wall paintings were found, among them being a figure of St. Stephen under a mutilated stone canopy. The paintings have perished, but the canopy is now set over the inner face of the south doorway of the nave.

All the fittings of the church are new, except for a good eighteenth-century organ screen on the north side of the chancel, with pillars carrying a moulded cornice.

On the south-east angle of the south aisle is an incised sundial.

The plate consists of a communion cup and cover paten of 1826, given by the Rev. William Masters, vicar of Sparsholt; a flagon of 1869, given by the Rev. Edward Stewart; an almsdish of 1766, given in that year by the Rev. Richard Barford; a standing paten of 1715, the gift of Philip Eyre; and two glass cruets, silver mounted.

The plate belonging to the ruined church of Lainston is also kept here, and consists of a cup and cover paten of 1628, with the monogram of the maker, T.F., whose mark occurs on a number of fine pieces of plate from 1609 onwards, and a standing paten or bread-holder of 1723, given in that year by John Merrill. It bears the mark of the famous goldsmith, Paul Lamerie.

The registers for Sparsholt and Lainston are contained in a single book, and record the baptisms from 1607, marriages from 1630, and burials from 1628, down to 1812. During the summer of 1666 the village was scourged by the plague, over a score of entries in the register for that year showing how men, women, and children died and were buried in their own gardens. The churchwardens' accounts begin in 1818.

The ruined church of *ST. PETER, LAINSTON*, is a simple aisleless building, the north, south, and west walls still standing. Enough remains to show that it was of late twelfth-century date, but its windows are later insertions, none of the early lights being preserved.

There was originally a separate register for Lainston Church taken to London during the trial of Elizabeth Chudleigh in 1776, and never recovered.

41 Feet of F. Hants, Mich. 12 Hen. VI.

42 Chan. Inq. p.m. (Ser. 2), xxviii, No. 14.

ADVOWSONS One of the nine churches mentioned in Domesday Book as pertaining to the manor of Chilcomb was probably the church of Sparsholt.[43] The advowson from early times belonged to the prioress and convent of Wintney,[44] and it is just possible that it was granted to them by a member of the Coldrey family, for the Coldreys were benefactors to this priory,[45] and as has been shown above owned property in the parish.

After the Dissolution the living remained in the gift of the crown,[46] notwithstanding Queen Mary's grant to the bishop of Winchester in 1558,[47] and under the Tudors was leased out with the rectory to various persons.[48] It is at the present time a vicarage, net yearly value £177 with residence in the gift of the Lord Chancellor.

The rectory of Sparsholt was at an early date appropriated to the priory of Wintney.[49] Anne, prioress of Wintney, in 1534, granted a forty years' lease of it to William Abbott.[50] Notwithstanding this, Henry VIII, in 1539, granted the rectory for life to his servant John Cook,[51] and his gift was confirmed by Queen Mary, who in 1553 granted it to him during her good pleasure without account or payment.[52] However, William Abbott was reinstated in 1561, in which year Queen Elizabeth granted to him the rectory and advowson to hold for twenty-one years at a rent of £10.[53] Nine years later Elizabeth granted the reversion of the rectory and advowson after the expiration of the lease to Robert Jones,[54] who sold all his interest in the premises to Walter Sandys,[55] on whom Elizabeth settled them in 1587 with remainder to his wife Mabel with remainder to his son William for life.[56] Walter Sandys was the farmer of the rectory in 1591,[57] notwithstanding Elizabeth's grant to Henry Best and John Welles earlier in the year,[58] and died seised of the same in 1610.[59] After the death of Sir William Sandys in 1628[60] the rectory and advowson reverted to the crown in accordance with the settlement of 1587. The advowson, as has been shown, remained with the crown, but the rectory was afterwards granted to the Heathcote family and remained with them for a considerable period,[61] Sir William Heathcote, bart., finally alienating it to the Ecclesiastical Commissioners.

The church of Lainston, as has been shown, probably owed its origin to the jealousy between the de Caritate and Sparsholt families.[62] The advowson has followed the descent of the manor[63] with but few exceptions.[64] The living is at the present day a rectory, of the yearly value of about £54 in the gift of Mr. Samuel Bostock.

The question of tithes was dealt with by the Court of Exchequer in 1591.[65]

CHARITIES The Parliamentary Returns of Charities for the poor, dated 1786, mention that Richard Bricknell, — Sims, and — Wade gave £5 each for the poor. These sums have been invested in the purchase of £16 15*s.* 5*d.* consols.

In 1875 the Rev. Edward Stewart by his will left £50, the income to be applied for the benefit of the poor, invested in £52 19*s.* 5*d.* consols.

The same testator left another sum of £50, invested in £53 0*s.* 10*d.* consols. The dividends are applied in the distribution of clothing in pursuance of the trusts declared by deed, dated 22 December, 1875.

STOKE CHARITY

Stockes (xi cent.); Eledderstoke (xiii cent.); Ouldstoke (xv cent.); Ouldestokecherytie (xvi and xvii cents.).

Stoke Charity is a small parish of only 1,841 acres, three of which are water supplied by the Test, a tributary of which forms the northern boundary line between Stoke Charity and Hunton. The village lies in the north close to the river, and from here the parish is one long southward sweep of rolling country, rising to its highest point at Waller's Ash and continuing onwards to Kings Worthy parish.

The road from Wonston, the parish which lies due west, runs downhill into Stoke Charity village, and passing by some farm buildings on the left becomes the uphill village street. On either side are thatched and half-timbered cottages grouped most thickly at the top of the hill where the road branches to Hunton, Micheldever and Winchester. The village school, built in 1815, is at the corner formed by the branching of the roads to Micheldever and Winchester, and on the right higher up the branch to Micheldever is the rectory. This is in part a sixteenth-century timber building to which in the latter part of the seventeenth century additions were made, including a very good panelled entrance hall with a carved cornice. In a field opposite the rectory is the church of St. Michael, and in the meadow called 'Pretty Meadow' north-west of the church, the sixteenth-century manor house originally stood. To the left of the site of the manor house is a large fish-pond

43 *V.C.H. Hants*, i, 463*b*.

44 *Wykeham's Reg.* (Hants Rec. Soc.), i, 82, 108, 134, 364; Egerton MS. 2031, fol. 103; 2034, fol. 88.

45 *V.C.H. Hants*, ii, 149.

46 Inst. Bks. (P.R.O.).

47 Pat. 5 & 6 Phil. and Mary, pt. 4, m. 6.

48 *Vide infra.*

49 *Wykeham's Reg.* (Hants. Rec. Soc.), i, 364.

50 Pat. 3 Eliz. pt. 2, m. 10.

51 *L. and P. Hen. VIII*, xiv (1), p. 594.

52 Pat. 1 Mary, pt. 9, m. 14.

53 Pat. 3 Eliz. pt. 2, m. 10.

54 Ibid. 12 Eliz. pt. 5, m. 16–17.

55 Ibid. 29 Eliz. pt. 2, m. 10-11.

56 Ibid.

57 Exch. Dep. Mich. 33 & 34 Eliz. No. 9.

58 Pat. 33 Eliz. pt. 3, m. 7–14.

59 W. and L. Inq. p.m. (Ser. 2), bdle. 12, No. 96.

60 Chan. Inq. p.m. (Ser. 2), ccccliviii, No. 141.

61 Recov. R. Hil. 16 Geo. II, rot. 243; Mich. 31 Geo. III, rot. 334; Trin. 6 Geo. IV rot. 141.

62 Cur. Reg. R. No. 65, m. 1*d*.

63 *Wykeham's Reg.* (Hants Rec. Soc.), i, 5. Egerton MS. 2032, fol. 140; 2033, fol. 22; and 2034, fol. 48. Inst. Bks. (P.R.O.).

64 Philip Aubyn, citizen of Winchester, presented in 1316, 1317, and 1318 (*Winton Epis. Reg.* [Hants Rec. Soc.], 138, 157, and 346), but whether as lord of the manor is uncertain. A certain Charles Bulkeley presented between 1531 and 1535 (Egerton MS. 2034, fol. 167).

65 Exch. Dep. Mich. 33 & 34 Eliz. No. 9.

supplied with water from the Test tributary. Old Farm, which is probably the farm attached to the original manor house, lies in the meadows east of the church. Stoke Farm lies well away from the village on the left hand side of the road to Winchester, while across country to the west is West Stoke Farm.

The soil of the whole parish is loam with a subsoil of chalk, and the chief crops are wheat, barley, and turnips.

William Cobbett, 'the homespun politician' of Surrey, visited Stoke Charity in 1829 and in his *Rural Rides* (1830) used 'that obscure village' as an illustration of the decay of parishes in the early nineteenth century. 'Formerly,' he says, 'it contained ten farms, but now only two which are owned by Mr. Hinton Bailey and his nephew, and therefore may probably become one. There used to be ten well-fed families in the parish, these taking five to a family made fifty well-fed people. And now all are half starved except the curate and the two families' (i.e. the farmer and his nephew). The blame for this miserable state he attributed not to the landowners but to 'the infernal funding and taxing system which of necessity drives property into large masses in order to save itself, which crushes little proprietors down into labourers and . . . make them paupers.'

MANOR It seems probable that the lands which afterwards became Stoke Charity parish were granted as part of the manor of Micheldever to Hyde Abbey by Edward the Elder in 904.[1] However, it would seem that the Abbey had parted with the land by the time of the Domesday Survey if the 'Stockes' held by the bishop of Winchester and entered wrongly under Meon Hundred can be *STOKE CHARITY*.[2] Then of the land of the manor a certain Geoffrey held four hides held of him by villeins.

By the thirteenth century the manor had passed into the hands of Henry de Caritate or de la Charité and was held of him by John de Windsor while only scutage was owing to the bishop of Winchester.[3] John de Windsor before his death in 1284 enfeoffed his son Geoffrey de Windsor of the manor of Stoke Charity[4] and Geoffrey in right of this enfeoffment made fine of 16 acres of land with appurtenances to Richard de la Rude and Margaret his wife in 1287.[5] However, the heirship of the manor passed to John de Windsor's granddaughter Alice, daughter of his eldest son Hugh who had seisin of the same when she came of age in 1297.[6] Alice married first John de Alneto, who died in 1323,[7] and secondly John Everard. She seems to have had one son at least and possibly a daughter by her first husband, since in 1330 she conveyed part of the manor to Thomas de Alneto who was evidently her son, and the other part to John de Lutershall and Cecilia his wife, who may have been her daughter, with reversion to Thomas.[8] In 1333 Thomas de Alneto who was about to sell the manor recovered seisin of the same to ensure all rights against Alice and her second husband John Everard, Stephen son of John de Alneto, who may have been another son of Alice, and John de Lutershall and Cecilia his wife.[9] In proceedings for this purpose Alice and John Everard stated that on Alice's death the manor must revert to the nearest in blood to John de Windsor, that is undoubtedly to Thomas de Alneto eldest son of Alice.[10] During the next year, 1334, Thomas de Alneto sold the manor to John de Hampton who was knight of the shire of Southampton from 1336 to 1344.[11] He was holding the manor as 'half a fee in Oldstoke' in 1346,[12] but died before October, 1357,[13] leaving a son and heir Thomas de Hampton who was also knight of the shire of Southampton in 1362 and was sheriff of the county from 1361 to 1365. In 1370 this same Thomas presented to the living of Stoke Charity.[13a] The manor passed on his death before 1384 to his son and heir John de Hampton, also knight of the shire in 1394. In 1384 the manor was said to be held by John son of Thomas de Hampton, of the bishopric of Winchester by the service of two knights' fees.[13b] An inquisition *ad quod damnum*, taken in 1392, ensured the right of John de Hampton in the manor of 'Eldestoke,' held 'of the Bishop of Winchester for unknown services,' against all claims put forward by Hyde Abbey.[14] This same John seems to have died about 1433 in which year his wife Margaret was assigned dower in his lands in Stafford.[15] His son and heir John Hampton knight of the shire in 1432,[16] and esquire of the body to Henry VI in 1454, was in his turn succeeded in the manor by his son Thomas Hampton, but at what date is uncertain. Thomas Hampton died in October, 1483, and was buried in the church of Stoke Charity.

HAMPTON. *Argent a cheveron gules between three cinquefoils azure with three bezants on the cheveron.*

From the effigies on his tomb in the church it is evident that he and his wife Isabel, who died in 1475, had eight children, two sons and six daughters, four married and two unmarried as is shown by their head-dress. But only the four married daughters survived their father and became his co-heirs.[17] Elizabeth the eldest, wife of Richard Wallop, died after her husband without issue in 1505, the second daughter Juliana wife of William Frost of Avington also died after her husband and without issue in 1526, the third, Anne wife of Morris Whitehead of Tytherley died likewise, at what date is uncertain. Thus the manor came into the possession of Joan, the youngest of the four, and wife of John Waller. He survived her and became lord of Stoke Charity, or rather Oldstoke, as it was still called, in her right. He died in 1525–6, leaving as heir his grandson Richard, the eldest son of his only

[1] Birch, *Cart. Sax.* ii, 245, 256, 260; *Liber de Hyda* (Rolls Ser.), 101. Edward granted the manor of Micheldever to the abbey in 901, is supposed to have confirmed this grant in the Golden Charter of 903, and made a further grant of lands in Micheldever in 904. In this latter grant the lands are said to stretch across and down to the Worthies, and would seem to include Stoke Charity.

[2] *V.C.H. Hants*, i, 461.

[3] Inq. p.m. 13 Edw. I, No. 22.

[4] Ibid.

[5] Feet of F. Hants, Mich. 15 Edw. I, No. 149.

[6] *Abbrev. Plac.* (Rec. Com.), 293*b*.

[7] Inq. p.m. 17 Edw. II, No. 41.

[8] See Pat. 7 Edw. III, pt. 2, m. 13.

[9] Ibid.

[10] Ibid.

[11] *List of Members of Parl.* (Parl. Papers).

[12] *Feud. Aids*, ii, 325.

[13] Montagu Burrows, *The Family of Brocas*, 342. Several deeds relating to lands in Stoke Charity, especially a meadow known as 'Brocas mede' are printed among the Brocas deeds (op. cit. pp. 341–4).

[13a] Winton Epis. Reg. Wykeham, i, fol. 38, 74.

[13b] Montagu Burrows, op. cit. 307.

[14] Inq. a.q.d. 16 Ric. II, pt. 1, No. 143.

[15] Inq. p.m. 12 Hen. VI, No. 8.

[16] *Parl. Writs.* (Rec. Com.).

[17] Inq. p.m. 12 Hen. VI, No. 8.

Stoke Charity Church : The Chancel Arch

son Richard.[18] In his will he desired to be buried in Oldstoke church 'before the altar of St. Thomas,' and his monument still stands in its original site against the north wall of the Hampton chapel. Richard Waller, his grandson, came of age in 1536 and held the manor of 'Old Stoke Charity' until his death, 7 September, 1551,[19] according to his inquisition, although the parish register states that he was buried 4 September, 1552, possibly following the date given on his mutilated brass in Stoke Charity church. William Waller his eldest son succeeded his father when a minor only fourteen years old. He seems to have involved himself in many pecuniary difficulties, and as a result his estates were nearly all mortgaged at the time of his death to his brother John Waller of Compton Monceaux and others. Thus in 1575 he leased the manor of 'Ouldestokecherytie otherwise Stokecherytie' to Nicholas Saunders for a term of years, and in 1617 made lease of the manor to his brother John for ninety-nine years as security for £2,000 spent by John in payment of his debts. William's co-heirs were his daughters, Charity the wife of Thomas Phelipps and Susan wife of Sir Richard Tichborne. Charity inherited the reversion in fee of the manor and on the death of her uncle John in 1618 she received the rents and profits from the manor during the remainder of the lease made by her late father. Moreover, if she should discharge and acquit his executors and estate of all bonds and encumbrances entered into between him and his late brother her uncle forgave and remitted the above-mentioned debt of £2,000.[20] Thomas Phelipps, created baronet in 1619–20,[21] held the manor by right of his wife until his death in 1626.[22] Dame Charity survived him and before 26 May, 1627, she had married Sir William Ogle, the guardian of her eldest son Thomas. The latter never held the manor of Stoke Charity, as he was slain while fighting for the Royalist cause in March, 1644–5, just seven months before his mother's death. Her royalist husband Sir William Ogle held Winchester Castle against the Parliament from 1643 until Cromwell besieged the city and castle and forced him to surrender in October, 1645. Cromwell gave Dame Charity special permission to leave the castle and seek safety, but worn out by her long and troubled life she died when only a few miles away from Winchester. Her body was taken to Stoke Charity, where a tablet in the south wall at the west end of the north aisle of the church commemorates her death on 5 October, 1645. Her only surviving son and heir Sir James Phelipps, third baronet, succeeded to his mother's estates before the December of that year. In his petition to the Parliamentary Commissioners, dated 20 December, 1645, begging that he may compound for delinquency, he states that 'by compulsion he joined, as Captain, Sir William Ogle, who married his mother and held a garrison for the king,' but he himself surrendered to Sir William Waller before the castle was besieged. He also notes that 'his mother's estate has now come to him.' His fine, set at £700 in 1646, was finally reduced to £646 in May 1649.[23] In the October of 1652 he died,[24] and was buried in Stoke Charity church under the altar tomb at the west end of the north aisle. His wife Elizabeth, who survived him until 1693, was his first cousin, since she was third daughter of his aunt Susan, Lady Tichborne, and Sir Richard.[25] Their only surviving son and heir James, fourth baronet, baptized in 1650, married in 1674 to Marina Michell,[26] held the manor until his death in Ireland in 1690. His only son James had died in infancy and was buried at Stoke Charity in 1675, so that his nearest relative was his sister Elizabeth Phelipps of Winchester, to whom he left his real estate by will dated 1688.[27] She married George Colney of Testwood (co. Hants), with whom it remained until 1726, in which year he sold it to Dame Lydia Mews, the widow of Sir Peter Mews.[28] The latter sold the manor two years later to William Heathcote of Hursley,[29] and from this time it remained with the Heathcotes until 1890, in which year it was sold to the present owner, Mr. Henry John Elwes, J.P., of Colesborne Park, Gloucestershire.

PHELIPPS of Barrington and Stoke Charity. *Argent a cheveron between three roses gules.*

ELWES. *Or a fesse azure with a bend gules over all.*

Within the manor Martin de Roches held two virgates of John de Windsor on his death in 1276–7.[30] His son and heir, John de Roches, died in 1311[31] leaving a son and heir, John. Joan the widow of John held the lands until her death in September, 1362, when they passed to her daughter Mary, widow of John de Boarhunt. Mary married as her second husband Bernard Brocas, who survived her and held her lands in Stoke Charity, extended at one messuage and 72 acres held of John de Hampton for unknown service.[32] On 24 June, 1383, Bernard Brocas obtained licence to use this said messuage and 72 acres together with 6 marks of rent from the manor of Hannington to form a chantry in the church of 'Clyware' (Clewer, co. Berks.) for the sake of his own soul and that of his present wife Catherine, and for that of his late wife Mary.[33]

CHURCH The church of *ST. MICHAEL* is a building of more than common interest, not only on account of its fine series of monuments, but also for its architectural details and the difficulties they offer to anyone studying the history of the church.

The plan, though irregular in setting out, is comparatively simple, consisting of a chancel with a large

18 Exch. Inq. p.m. 18 Hen. VIII (Ser. 2), file 979, No. 1.
19 Inq. p.m. 6 Edw. VI (Ser. 2), xcvii, No. 98.
20 Will of John Waller of Compton Monceaux, 1618. P.C.C. 106, Meade.
21 G.E.C. *Complete Baronetage.*
22 Inq. p.m. 3 Chas. I (Ser. 2), pt. 1, No. 130.
23 *Cal. of Com. for Compounding*, i, 105 *d.*
24 Parish Register.
25 Tablet in Stoke Charity church.
26 Parish Register.
27 Will of Sir James Phelipps, fourth baronet, 1690; P.C.C. 113, Dyke.
28 *Vide* Close, 2 Geo. II, pt. 9, No. 4.
29 Ibid.
30 Inq. p.m. 5 Edw. I, file 17 No. 8.
31 Ibid. 5 Edw. II, No. 44. The lands in Oldstoke are not mentioned in the inquisition.
32 Ibid. 7 Ric. II, No. 137.
33 Ibid.

north chapel, a nave with north aisle and south porch, and a wooden bell-turret at the west end. The chancel arch and the two bays of the north arcade of the nave date from *c.* 1160, the walls in which they are set being 3 ft. 2 in. thick. The arcade, with its heavy octagonal central pillar and half-octagonal responds, and its round arches of a single square order on scalloped capitals, gives the impression of having been cut through an older wall, and it may well be that the north and east walls of the nave contain masonry older than the middle of the twelfth century, belonging to an aisleless nave which measured about 30 ft. by 15 ft. within the walls, and had a small chancel, now entirely destroyed. The present chancel appears to have been set out, with a slight lean to the south, in the first half of the thirteenth century, and the nave seems to have been lengthened westward and its south wall rebuilt about 100 years later. The north chapel is a fifteenth-century addition, opening by an arch of that date to the chancel, but in its west wall is a plain round arch, edge-chamfered, with a chamfered string at the springing, which suggests a date not later than the twelfth century for some building formerly on the site of the chapel. This is very difficult to bring into line with the rest of the history of the church, and it has even been suggested that the arch belongs to a pre-Conquest building, having opened to its chancel. But the details, such as they are, do not give the slightest ground for the idea, nor indeed has the masonry any of the character of normal twelfth-century work. The north aisle, to which it opens, seems to be a late mediaeval re-building of a former aisle, and the twelfth-century doorway at its north-east angle is clearly not in its original position, so that it may well be that the western arch of the chapel is of a much later date than at first sight it would seem to be.

The chancel has a fifteenth-century east window of three lights with tracery and a transom, and in the south wall two widely-splayed lancets, the eastern of which dates from *c.* 1220, while the second has been widened, the outer stonework of both being comparatively modern, though the jambs and rear arches are old. The sills of both are carried down, the one to serve as a sedile, and the other for a low side window. On the north side of the chancel is a pointed arch of two hollow-chamfered orders, on splayed and recessed jambs with moulded capitals, of fifteenth-century date ; it opens to the north or Hampton chapel, which has a square-headed north window of three cinquefoiled lights, and an east window of two lights with tracery and a moulded rear arch, on the label of which is a shield with the arms of Hampton.

The chancel arch is a very pretty piece of twelfth-century work, round-headed and of two orders, the inner plain and the outer with a roll and a band of horizontal zigzag, and having a moulded label. The capitals are foliate, and there are nook-shafts to the outer order with spreading moulded bases. To the north of the arch is a wide squint opening both to the north chapel and the chancel.

The north arcade of the nave has been already noted, and at the south-east of the nave is a two-light window of *c.* 1320, with a four-centred tomb-recess partly below its sill and partly to the west of it. The south door is plain fourteenth-century work of two chamfered orders, under a modern porch, and from it four steps lead down to the floor of the nave. The west window of the nave is like that on the south, the tracery in both having been repaired. The north aisle has a square-headed west window of two quatrefoiled lights, which looks like fourteenth-century work renewed, and a modern north window of two lights. The doorway already mentioned at the north-east angle is round-headed, with a line of zigzag in the head.

The nave roof is in two bays, with moulded wall-plates and arched principals, to which are fixed turned pendants of seventeenth-century style ; this probably shows the date of the roof. The west bay of the nave is taken up with the beams of the bell-turret, which do not come down to the floor, though they may have done so in the first instance. The roof of the north aisle is plain, but preserves some old timbers, while that of the north chapel is a good piece of fifteenth-century work, of low pitch with arched principals and a deep embattled cornice on the north side, with two rows of carved bosses ; the corresponding cornice on the south side has been cut away. In the east wall of this chapel is a plain image bracket to the north of the site of the altar, which was that of St. Thomas of Canterbury, and in the north-east angle a fine piece of fifteenth-century carving representing the mass of St. Gregory. The saint stands at the north end of an altar, with his server in a cope at the south end, and over the altar is a large figure of Christ under a canopy, typifying the Real Presence, which the story was intended to vindicate.

On the sill of the north window of the chapel is a square twelfth-century foliate capital with angle volutes, and a vine-trail pattern below. It is made to fit a round shaft 6½ in. in diameter, and has on the top a sinking 7 in. square by 3½ in. deep. There being no drain, it has not been part of a pillar piscina, but may be an early example of a holy-water stone. At the south-west of the chapel is part of a fifteenth-century canopied niche and pedestal, not in position, and part of a second pedestal, and in the east window of the chapel is a little old glass, with our Lady and Child, and a border with the letters T and H, for one of the two Thomas Hamptons who were lords of the manor here in the second half of the fifteenth century.

The font at the west end of the north aisle has a plain round bowl and stem, the top of the bowl being cut to an octagon ; it is old but of uncertain date, the bowl looking as if it had been cut down.

There are six incised sundials on the south window of the nave, and two on the south-east angle, and at the south-west angle of the chancel, just beneath the eaves, a stone carved with a small bearded head is inserted in the wall.

Beneath the arch opening to the Hampton chapel, and against its eastern respond, is set the altar tomb of Thomas Hampton, 1483, and Elizabeth (Dodington) his wife, 1475, having on a Purbeck slab their brass effigies with those of their two sons and six daughters. The lower half only of Elizabeth's figure is preserved. On scrolls from the mouths of the principal figures are 'patꝰ de celis miserere nobis' and 'scā tĩitas un⁹ de⁹ miserere nobis,' and above them a fine representation of the Trinity. Below the figures is an inscription giving the record of their deaths on St. Simeon and St. Jude's Day and St. Andrew's Day

Stoke Charity Church : St. Gregory's Mass

in the years noted above, and at the four corners of the slab are shields with the arms of Hampton and Dodington.

The sides of the tomb are panelled, with shields in the panels, bearing on the north side (1) a cheveron between three owls (Frost); (2) Wallop quartering paly wavy a chief with a saltire; (3) Hampton impaling Dodington; (4) Hampton. On the west are (1) on a bend cotised three walnut leaves (Waller); (2) a fesse between three fleurs-de-lis (Whitehead); and on the south are two blank shields and two panels without shields. The arms other than those of Hampton and Dodington refer to the marriages of Thomas Hampton's daughters. On the wall east of the tomb is a projecting iron, probably to carry a helm.

In the east arch of the north arcade of the nave is a second altar tomb, all of Purbeck marble, with panelled sides of late fifteenth or early sixteenth-century character, inclosing quatrefoils. On the south side the two eastern panels are blank, probably because this part of the tomb adjoined the north nave altar. There is nothing to show to whom it belongs. Against it on the north a second tomb has been built at a lower level, with a Purbeck marble slab, and sides made of chalk blocks; it also has no arms or inscription.

Against the north wall of the Hampton chapel is the tomb of John Waller, 1525, with a recessed canopy on which are the arms of Waller and Hampton, and a base with paintings of St. Thomas of Canterbury and our Lady and Child. In front of this tomb on the floor is the gravestone of his grandson Richard Waller, 1552, and at the north-west of the chapel is the raised tomb of Sir Thomas Phelipps, 1626. At the west end of the north aisle is the monument of Sir James Phelipps, 1652, and of his mother Charity, wife first of Sir Thomas Phelipps and then of Sir William Ogle, 1645.

In a recess at the south-east of the nave is an altar tomb with a slab having indents for four shields, only one of which is preserved. It bears the arms of Waite, argent a cheveron gules and three bugle horns sable impaling Skilling, argent two cheverons gules and in chief gules three bezants.

In the churchyard is the tomb of the Rev. Joshua Reynolds, 1734, uncle and godfather of the painter.

There are three bells, the tenor of 1606, by a founder R.B. and inscribed 'God be our Gvyd'; the second a fifteenth-century Wokingham bell, with the marks of the cross, lion's face, and groat, and the inscription 'Sancta Trini Tas (*sic*) ora pro nobis'; and the treble, also mediaeval, probably by John Sanders, bears the arms of St. Swithun's Priory, Winchester, and 'Sancta Catarina ora pro nobis.'

The church plate consists of a silver chalice dated 1568 with a cover used as a paten and two almsdishes, one of pewter, the other of brass.

The early parish register is the original paper book of mixed entries, dating from 1540.[34] This, at least, is the first distinct entry, though there is a fragment of a first page preserved which if intact would probably take the register back to 1538. In 1595 there is an entry that Thomas Gillson of Olde Stoke Charity did 'reade the articles of religion at morninge prayer after sermon made at morninge prayer the 20th day of July in the church of Old Sook before the congregation.' Another entry states that John Clarke 'having before wandered here and there in povertye and extremitye was founde dead in Stoke fielde the 20th day of March, 1596, in which day beinge before viewed by the inhabitants of the same parish he was in the churchyarde buried.' The entries continue until 1812.

The early churchwardens' accounts, now in the possession of Corpus Christi College, Oxford, are complete from 1549 to 1728, with entries for 1541–3; the oldest poor book dates from 1753 to 1837.

ADVOWSON At the time of the Domesday Survey a certain Mauger held the church of the manor.[35] However, by the fourteenth century, and probably before, the advowson was attached to the lordship of the manor and was held by Alice de Windsor in 1330.[36] From this time it followed the descent of the manor[37] (q.v.) until the end of the seventeenth century. It is now a rectory in the gift of the dean and chapter of Winchester.

WEEKE (OR WYKE)

Weeke was formerly one parish containing about 1,093 acres, but under the Local Government Act of 1894[1] it was divided into two civil parishes, Weeke Within comprising about 90 acres and Weeke Without containing about 1,004 acres,[2] the former being included within the boundaries of the city of Winchester. The growth of the city to the north-west during the last twenty years has changed Weeke Within from field and arable land to a thickly populated district, since newly-built cottages and villas extend almost to the boundaries of Weeke Without. The Winchester station of the London and South Western Railway is in Weeke Within, and close to the station is the church of St. Paul's, formerly a chapel of ease to Weeke Without.

The upper Stockbridge road comes straight out of the city through Weeke Within, and rises steadily to a height of 282 ft. before descending between high banks into the little village of Weeke Without. On the right a short line of pollard limes stands before plain-fronted houses; on the same side behind a low brick wall almost hidden by trees is the little church of St. Matthew or St. Mary the Virgin, a pathway of tombstones leading up to the church porch. Beyond the church are two or three low thatched cottages and the village pond, and beyond are farm buildings and Weeke Farm itself. Almost opposite the church is the manor-house, the residence of Col. Thomas Burnett Hitchcock, J.P., standing among well-grown trees which line the garden wall as it runs along the village street.

Fine stretches of down country away to the south and west, Weeke Down and Teg Down, the property

[34] An excellent transcript was made of this register by one of the late rectors of Stoke Charity.

[35] *V.C.H. Hants*, i, 461*b*.

[36] Pat. 5 Edw. III, m. 15

[37] *Wykeham's Reg.* (Hants Rec. Soc.) i, 40, 102; Egerton MS. 2033, fol. 32; 2034, fols. 40, 142, 154, 172.

[1] Stat. 56 & 57 Vict. cap. 73.

[2] Ord. Surv.

of the Ecclesiastical Commissioners, make up the rest of the parish. Teg Down Farm is on the south side of Teg Down on the right-hand side of the old Roman road from Winchester to Old Sarum. The soil of the parish is chalk and loam with a subsoil of chalk and produces ordinary crops of wheat, barley, and oats.

MANOR *WEEKE* was included in the grant made by King Kinegils to the church of Winchester when he endowed it with land within a seven-mile circle of the city.[3] It was held by the prior and convent not as a separate manor, but as part of the manor of Barton.[4] Hence in the inventory of the estates of the prior and convent made in the sixteenth century the rents and farm of Sparsholt, Weeke, and Fullflood were given as parcel of the manor of Barton at £32 19*s.* 6*d.*, while the fines, tallages, and perquisites of court of the same were rendered at 20*s.*[5] There was also a special rent of 33*s.* 4*d.*, called 'Downe Silver,' from Weeke.[6] In 1541 the manor of Barton with other possessions of the dissolved house was granted with all its dependent manors to the dean and chapter of Winchester,[7] who since that time have been lords of Weeke and the owners of 889 acres, 2 roods, and 5 perches of land in the parish.[8] In a list of the possessions of the dean and chapter made in 1682, Sparsholt and Weeke were bracketed together and their returns given as one sum, but no longer as part of the manor of Barton.[9]

CHURCH The church of *OUR LADY* is a small building of very simple character, the oldest part dating from the end of the twelfth century. It consists of a chancel and nave, with a modern vestry on the north of the chancel, and a south porch and west bell-turret to the nave. The roofs are red tiled and the walls covered with roughcast. The chancel is 14 ft. 6 in. in length, and the nave 32 ft. 7 in., both being of the same width, 13 ft. The chancel has been rebuilt, probably in the fifteenth century, outside the lines of the former chancel, and has an east window of that date of three cinquefoiled lights under a square head with a four-centred rear arch. In the south wall are two square-headed two-light windows rebated for wooden frames, and in the north wall a small trefoiled recess of thirteenth-century date, and a modern door to the vestry.

The chancel arch is pointed, of two chamfered orders with square abaci at the springing, the angles of the upper member and of the jambs being cut back, probably at a comparatively modern date.

The nave is lighted by four small square-headed windows, two on the north and two on the south, which may be eighteenth-century insertions, and has a west window of three lights of similar character. The south doorway has a plain semicircular head with square abaci, and, with the chancel arch, belongs to the earliest work now to be seen in the church. It is to be noted that the tooling of the masonry in the doorway is of the normal diagonal type, that in the chancel arch is vertical and perhaps slightly later in date.

The timbers of the chancel roof are modern, and the nave has a canted plaster ceiling. At the west end is a gallery framed to the wooden posts of the bell-turret, and reached by a stair on the south side. The font stands at the west end of the nave, and has an octagonal bowl on a round stem; it shows no traces of antiquity, having been entirely retooled. There are a few pieces of fifteenth-century glass in the east window, but otherwise the fittings of the church are modern.

On the north wall of the nave, opposite the south doorway, is a slab of Purbeck marble with an inscription plate and a figure of St. Christopher in latten above it. On the plate is engraved this inscription:—

> Here lieth Willm̃ Compton & Annes his wife ye[e] whiche Willm̃ decessid ye[e] xxi day of mayi ye yere of oure lord mcccclxxxxviij. Also this be ȝe[e] dedis yt[t] ȝe[e] said Willm̃ hath down to this Church̄ of Wike yt[t] is to say frest dedycacion of ye[e] church xl[s] & to make new bellis to ye[e] sam church x[li] also gave to ye[e] halloyeng of ye[e] grettest bell vj[s] viij[d] & for ye[e] testimonyall of the dedicacion of ye[e] sam church vj[s] viij[d] on whos soules Ihū have mercy Amen.

The St. Christopher above the inscription is perhaps a substitute for the usual painting on the wall opposite the principal doorway, so often found in mediaeval churches.

In the north wall of the chancel is a stone slab inscribed,

> Here lyeth Mr. Docter Harpesfeeld parson here 1550. Apri. iii.

and in front of the altar are slabs to the Goodwin family. Thomas Goodwin, 1776, is commemorated by a monument in the south wall of the nave.

There are three bells, the second and tenor by Ellis and Henry Knight, 1673, and the treble a mediaeval bell, probably one of those to whose casting William Compton gave ten pounds, inscribed, 'Sancte Laurenti ora pro nobis.' It bears three marks, a cross paty, a w reversed, and a Latin cross on a shield. It is by William Hasylwode of London.

The plate consists of a communion cup and paten, a flagon and a standing paten. The cup is dated 1705, but the paten, which is of silver parcel-gilt, is a piece of the very greatest rarity and interest, being one of a very small group of early patens *c.* 1200, of which others have been found at Canterbury and Chichester. It has an Agnus Dei engraved in a central circular sinking, inclosed in a larger octofoil depression, with engraved foliage of late Romanesque type in the spandrels, and on the outer rim is an inscription, 'Cuncta creo vvirtute rego pietate reformo.'

The first book of the registers contains all entries from 1573 to 1645, and the second baptisms and burials from 1675 to 1769, and marriages from 1674 to 1753. The third continues the baptisms and burials to 1812, and the fourth is the printed marriage register from 1754 to 1812.

ADVOWSON Weeke was a chapelry dependent on the parish church of St. Mary of the Valleys near Winchester[10] until early in the fifteenth century, when Henry Beaufort, bishop of Winchester, united the church and chapel to the parish church of St. Anastasius without the walls of the city of Winchester.[11] Towards the end

[3] Wharton, *Angl. Sac.* i, 288.

[4] *Obedientary R. of St. Swithun* (Hants Rec. Soc.), 224. The profits from Weeke are included under the entry for the manor of Barton.

[5] *Winton Cath. Doc.* (Hants Rec. Soc.), i, 86.

[6] Ibid.

[7] Pat. 33 Hen. VIII, pt. 9, m. 5–10.

[8] F. J. Baigent, *Hist. of Parish Church of Weeke.* In 1857 and 1859 much of the dean and chapter's property in Weeke was made freehold, as the dean and chapter bought up the leasehold interests.

[9] *Winton Cath. Doc.* (Hants Rec. Soc.), ii, 182.

[10] *Pope Nich. Tax.* (Rec. Com.), 210; *Inq. Non.* (Rec. Com.), 107; *Winton Epis. Reg.* (Hants Rec. Soc.), 495.

[11] F. J. Baigent, *Hist. of Parish Church of Weeke.*

of the fifteenth century, however, the churches were in such a ruinous state, and the parish so destitute of parishioners, that the chapel of Weeke was made a rectory, continuing in the gift of the bishop of Winchester, and the other two churches pulled down.[12] In the reign of Henry VIII the church was of the annual value of £12 19*s.* 0½*d.*[13] The living is at the present day a rectory, net income £230, with 2 acres of glebe, and is still in the patronage of the bishop of Winchester.

CHARITIES The Parliamentary Returns of Charities for the poor dated 1786 mention that — Godwin gave £40 for the poor. In 1729 William Blake by his will left £100, the income to be disposed of among the poor on 22 July yearly, in memory of his wife's death, the clerk to have 5*s.* for his pains. The principal sums were lent on the security of a promissory note, and eventually lost. In the year 1892 the endowments were made good by Miss King, by the transfer to the Official Trustees of Charitable Funds of £41 3*s.* 2*d.* India £3 per cent. stock, and £102 19*s.* 2*d.* like stock, in trust for the respective charities.

In 1895 General Henry Nott by will proved this date directed that a sum of £250 2½ per cent. annuities should be purchased in the name of the Official Trustees of Charitable Funds, the dividends to be remitted to the vicar and churchwardens of Weeke or Wyke St. Mary, and applied by them in keeping in repair the vestry of the parish church and the monument erected therein to certain members of his family.

WONSTON

The parish of Wonston covers an area of 5,493 acres, of which 8 are covered by water. The greater part of the land is included in the northern slope of the high ridge of downland which rises north-west of Winchester and slopes down towards the north to the tributary of the Test as it runs a generally north-western course through the centre of Wonston parish. The parish boundaries from east to west narrow near the river, and here is the village of Wonston, west of which is the closely dependent, but now larger and more important, village of Sutton Scotney. North of Sutton Scotney are Cranborne and Norton Farms, the centres of the original manors of Cranborne and Norton, the lands of which, making up the rest of the parish, stretch away in a long narrow piece of land of about two miles of open field and downland to a dark clump of woodland which covers the north-east corner of the parish and joins the south-eastern edge of the Freefolk Woods as they run west and form the northern boundary of Wonston. Two roads from Winchester lead to Wonston; one the road which runs north-west from the city through the Worthies and Stoke Charity and approaches Wonston village from the east; the other, the main Roman road to Andover, which runs north-west from the city and, skirting Flower Town east of Littleton, sends off a branch road north over the north-eastern part of Wortley Down, through Sutton Scotney village, and thence east towards Wonston. The latter road after climbing Wortley Down rises on Cow Down and thence descends sharply between a clump of fine trees standing on the west side of the road and two or three detached houses lately built on the opposite side, running along through open country over which the buildings and plough-lands of South Wonston Farm lie to the east. Continuing over hilly country for about a mile and a half north, the road rises to a house which standing to the west at the top of the hill is the first sign of Sutton Scotney village, and from here the road curves east sharply downhill past outlying thatched cottages and farm buildings into the village. Here it branches west to Stockbridge, north to Whitchurch, and east past the railway station[1] over the railway bridge to Wonston village. The branch running north to Whitchurch becomes the chief village street, standing east of which at the corner of the road leading to Wonston is the Victoria Diamond Jubilee Institute with its clock tower. Beyond this on the same side of the road is the small wooden chapel of ease for Wonston church. But the chief features of the village, apart from its numerous picturesque thatched cottages, its small provision shops and post office, are the two old inns which stand on the west side of the road in the centre of the village, the 'White Swan' with its stuffed bird representing its sign in a dusty glass case over the north entrance, and the yellow-painted 'Coach and Horses,' which stands close by on the north side of the small courtyard-like space which separates the two.

The manor-house of Sutton Scotney, lately dismantled and rebuilt, stands to the west of the village.

Leaving Sutton Scotney at the south end of the village and turning east to Wonston, the road leads between thick hedges and field and plough-land, slightly uphill to the outbuildings of Wonston Farm on the north of the road. From here, past a steep rough lane leading south, the road rises between several thatched cottages and farm buildings to the 'Wonston Arms' standing north of the road, west of which a lane runs north downhill across the river towards Norton Farm, sending off a branch to the east a few yards north of the village and river, known as Hunton Lane. Past the 'Wonston Arms' the road continues again for several yards between thatched cottages and farm-buildings, with one or two larger houses, towards the east end of the village, where, as the road curves to the south, high thick hedges and tall spreading trees, following the curve of the road, run for several yards along its north side and shut in the beautiful old rectory and the church, which stands immediately east of the house.

The old rectory to the west of the church, now known as 'The Old House,' occupied by Lady Laura Ridding, is a very interesting mediaeval building of two stories, the oldest parts of which are of late fourteenth-century date. It stands north and south, with a central hall, formerly open to the roof, but now in two stories, with screens at the south end and a porch over the east doorway; on the south is a block projecting east and west, and containing the old

[12] F. J. Baigent, *Hist. of Parish Church of Weeke.* [13] *Valor Eccl.* (Rec. Com.), ii, 6.

[1] The Sutton Scotney station is on the Great Western Railway line, which cuts across the parish in a north-westerly direction from Winchester.

buttery and pantry with the kitchen passage between them. To the south again are modern buildings on the site of the old kitchen, which here, as in many instances, has entirely disappeared, and may have been of wood. At the north or upper end of the hall is a north cross wing, containing the drawing-room, &c., and projecting northward from its western half is a contemporary building which had an outer stair at its north-east angle. A range of modern date runs along the west side of the house, and in this is the principal entrance.

Very few of the old features are left, but there are several single-light windows in the north block, three on the ground floor and two on the first floor, which are of mediaeval date, and the upper and lower doorways to the staircase which formerly adjoined the north-east angle of the north rooms yet remain. There is some good panelling in the hall screens, but otherwise nearly everything has given way to eighteenth or nineteenth-century work, the old windows being replaced by square-headed sash windows. A bay window has been added to the drawing-room in modern times, and the east porch is modern. The roof over the hall is not the original one of open timber, but seems to date from after the insertion of an upper floor in the hall. The building projecting northward from the main north wing is an unusual feature, and is known as the priest's room; it seems to have consisted of a living room with a chamber over, but there is no real evidence in favour of its current name. The original main stair perhaps occupied the same position at the west end of the north wing as the present stair, but the many alterations which the house has undergone must make the arrangements of its upper floor conjectural only.

The new rectory, built within the last few years by the present rector, the Rev. R. F. Biggwither, stands on high ground over the meadows to the north-west of the church and north of Hunton Lane.

At the north end of Sutton Scotney village a road branches east, crosses the river near a house called Egypt, the residence of Dr. Charles Wickham, and continuing in a north-easterly direction for about three-quarters of a mile, reaches the one or two outbuildings and cottages which with Cranborne Farm and Cranborne Cottage, the residence of Miss Childers and Miss Carta Sturge, compose the whole of Cranborne. Cranborne Cottage, representing the union of two or perhaps three small cottages, stands on the west side of the road in a long peaceful garden which stretches away north-west to the adjoining fields of Norton Farm. Cranborne Farm stands a few yards higher up the road on the opposite side. The old house, round which run the traces of a moat, is in all

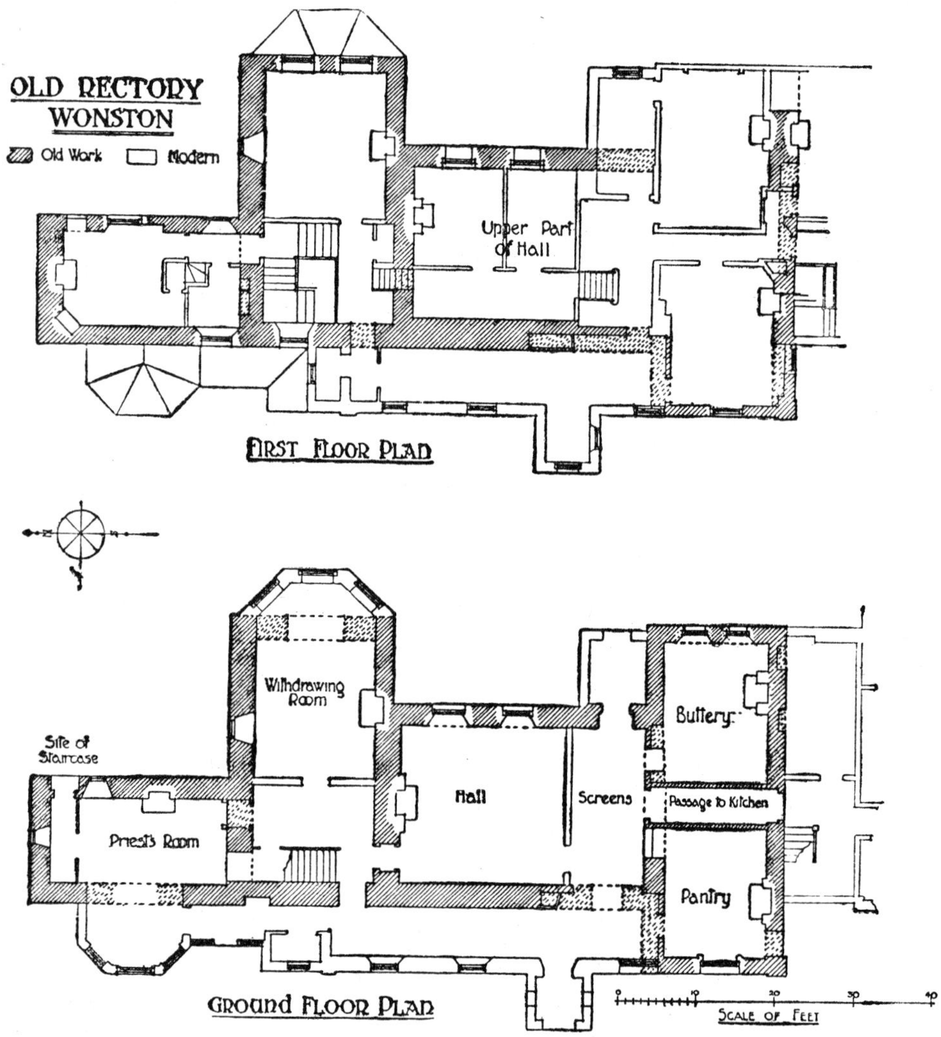

probability on the site of the original manor-house of Cranborne, though it is now only an ordinary farm-house. Norton Farm, the original manor-house of Norton manor, lies north-west of Cranborne and is reached by a narrow road leading north-west from Wonston, and another leading east from the main road from Sutton Scotney to Whitchurch. It is a picturesque red-brick and flint building, mainly of early eighteenth-century date, with brick pilasters at the angles, having moulded capitals and the unusual feature of a band of yellow and blue Dutch tiles set in the necking of the capitals. The roof is red tiled and hipped, and has wide projecting eaves which add much to the dignity of the building. The entrance is from the north, the gardens lying on the west and south, and the stables and offices on the east. There is a central hall with a good eighteenth-century staircase at the south end, the hall itself being panelled with early seventeenth-century panelling formerly in one of the upper rooms. This goes to show that part of the interior is of older date than the exterior would suggest. The present owner of the house, Mr. George Hampton, has fitted it up in excellent taste, and the gardens, with a large pond on the west, are very prettily laid out.

The soil of the whole parish is loam with a subsoil of chalk, and the chief crops grown on the $3,964\frac{3}{4}$ acres of arable land are wheat, barley, oats, and turnips. Although the parish is generally speaking well wooded, there is very little woodland, only $148\frac{1}{2}$ acres, and that mostly in the north-east corner, while $1,003\frac{1}{2}$ acres are given up to pasture land.[2]

MANORS Like the other manors in Buddlesgate Hundred that belonged from the first to the church at Winchester, and passed at the Dissolution to the dean and chapter, the manor of *WONSTON* has little history. The actual grant of the manor to the church does not appear, but according to Domesday it always belonged to the minster (*in monasterio*), was held by the bishop at the time of the Survey, and was assessed at 7 hides.[3] In 1205, and again in 1243, it was confirmed to the prior and convent by the pope,[4] and right of free warren in their demesne lands was granted them by Edward III.[5] In 1334–5, and again in 1337, the profits of the farm of the manor were entered on the Receiver's Roll at £10 and £6 respectively.[6] By 1539, the year of the suppression of the monastery, the farm had reached the value of £13.[7] In 1541 the manor was granted to the dean and chapter of Winchester, who at the present day hold the manor, and have one farm in the parish.

SCOTNEY. *Argent a cheveron between three scallops azure.*

At the time of the Domesday Survey there were two manors of *SUTTON*, one assessed at $2\frac{1}{2}$ hides, held by Odo of Winchester, the other assessed at the same, held by Robert son of Gerold. Earl Godwin had held both, probably as one five-hide manor, in the time of Edward the Confessor, and of him Alward and Tovi had held. The extents of the manors as given in the Survey are identical.[8] The half that was held by Robert son of Gerold passed to the Scotney family in the thirteenth century. The first mention of them in connexion with the manor is in 1235–6, when Robert son of Alan surrendered five virgates of land in Sutton to Walter de Scotney,[9] a member of the Sussex and Lincolnshire family of Scotney.[10] Walter was the son of Peter and Mabel de Scotney,[11] and grandson of another Walter,[12] and both his father and grandfather had been important men in Sussex, and benefactors to the priory of Hastings.[13] During the reign of Henry III Walter himself held $14\frac{1}{2}$ knights' fees of the manor of Hastings,[14] and the lands which he held in Sutton were held as belonging to the manor of Crowhurst as of the manor of Hastings.[15] However, Walter de Scotney is best known to fame not as the holder of large fees, but as the perpetrator of an attempt to poison Richard earl of Gloucester and William de Clare, by the instigation, it is said, of William de Valence. Richard earl of Gloucester escaped with a severe illness and the loss of his hair and nails, to be finally poisoned three years later by another tool of William de Valence. However, William de Clare died, and Walter de Scotney was consequently sentenced to death and hanged at Winchester on 23 May, 1259.[16] An inquisition taken on his death shows that

NORTON MANOR HOUSE, WONSTON

[2] Statistics from Bd. of Agric. (1905).
[3] *V.C.H. Hants*, i, 467*a*.
[4] *Cal. of Pap. Letters*, ii, 21, 201.
[5] Chart. R.
[6] *Obedientiary R. of St. Swithun* (Hants Rec. Soc.), 226, 244.
[7] *Doc. relating to the D. and C. of Winchester* (Hants Rec. Soc.), i, 90.
[8] *V.C.H. Hants*, i, 488, 504.
[9] Feet of F. Hants, East. 29 Hen. III.
[10] See *N. and Q.* (Ser. 4), iii, 332.
[11] Inq. p.m. 28 Hen. III, No. 8.
[12] *Coll. Top. et Gen.* vi, 105.
[13] Ibid.
[14] *Testa de Nevill* (Rec. Com.), 224.
[15] Inq. p.m. 44 Hen. III, No. 6.
[16] Dugdale, *Bar.* i, 676.

his lands in Sutton, now termed 'half the manor of Sutton,' were then held by his mother Mabel as belonging to Crowhurst, to revert to the lord of Crowhurst after her death.[17]

The family of Sutton were at this time holding lands in the parish of the manor of Cranborne,[18] and it seems evident that on the death of Mabel de Scotney they gained possession of the whole moiety that had belonged to the Scotneys. Hence in 1316 Edmund (sometimes called Peter [19]) de Sutton was holding the vill of Sutton jointly with Robert Harwedon (who was at that date holding the other manor),[20] and in 1324 Edmund and Alice his wife settled the reversion on Ralph de Monthermer and Isabel his wife,[21] who was daughter of Hugh le Despenser and widow of John Hastings of Abergavenny.[22] On the death of Alice de Sutton in 1330 [23] the escheator took the manor as 'a moiety of the manor of Sutton' into the hands of the king, but in 1331 he was ordered to intermeddle with it no further,[24] and it consequently passed to Isabel de Hastings, who had survived her husband. By an inquisition *ad quod damnum* taken in 1332 it was adjudged a damage to the king if Isabel should be allowed to grant this moiety of the manor to her son Thomas de Hastings, since if he reconveyed it to Isabel the king would lose possible wardship and marriage of the heir of Thomas if under age.[25] However, later in the same year the required licence was given; Thomas de Hastings was to be enfeoffed as tenant in chief to regrant the same to his mother for life.[26] Isabel died seised in 1335, and Sutton passed to Hugh de Hastings, brother of Thomas, who had predeceased his mother.[27] Eight years later, in 1343, Hugh de Hastings was given licence to grant his manor to Nicholas Devenish of Winchester, reserving to himself 2 acres of plough-land called Hentechele.[28] In 1346 Nicholas was holding the half-fee in Sutton which had belonged to Edmund de Sutton,[29] and two years later Margery widow of Hugh de Hastings claimed from him the third part of the manor of Sutton Scotney as dower from her late husband, with what result does not appear.[30] Nicholas died seised of the manor in 1350 leaving a son and heir Thomas,[31] to whom the escheator was ordered to deliver up the manor in 1351.[32] On the death of Thomas in 1373 the 'moiety of the manor' came into the king's hands by reason of the minority of his son and heir John.[33] John evidently died within the next few years and Thomas his younger brother became his father's heir. The latter also died while a minor in 1382, leaving a sister and heir Nichola.[34] It seems probable that Nichola was first married to Sir John Englefield of Warwickshire and afterwards to John Golafre of Blakesley (Northants). Certainly Sir John Englefield, who lived about the reigns of Richard II and Henry IV, married a certain Nichola,[35] and John Golafre married as his second wife a 'Lady Inglefield,' [36] while in 1404 John Golafre and Nichola his wife settled the manor of Sutton Scotney on themselves for their lifetime with reversion to William Englefield, who was the son of John Englefield and would seem to be Nichola's son. On the death of William Englefield the reversion was to go to the right heirs of John and Nichola.[37] John and Nichola do not seem to have had any children, therefore the manor probably went to distant kinsmen of Nichola—John Skilling of Lainston and Elizabeth wife of Richard Norton.[38] John Golafre was still holding the manor in 1428,[39] but by 1464 it had descended to Elizabeth wife of John Wynard,[40] most probably identical with Elizabeth the kinswoman and heir of John Skilling, who as widow of Thomas Wayte conveyed the manor to trustees in 1482.[41] They sold it the same year to the prior and convent of the Blessed Mary of Southwick, in whose possession it remained until the Dissolution.[42]

Southwick Priory. *Argent a chief sable with two roses argent therein.*

The manor remained in the hands of the king until 1540, in which year he granted it as part of her jointure to Anne of Cleves on his marriage with her.[43] A year later he granted it for life to Catherine Howard, in whose hands it remained until her execution.[44] The king next granted it to his servant John Leigh,[45] who sold it in 1544 to John Fisher of Overton [46] (co. Hants). From the latter it passed by purchase in 1545 to John Twyne of Norton, being settled on him and his heirs by his first wife Christine.[47] John by will dated 23 April, 1554, left the manor of Sutton Scotney to his son Richard, who was under age at the time of his father's death a month later.[48] The manor was accordingly in the wardship of the crown for some time, but Richard had succeeded to his inheritance by 1566, in which year he engaged in a dispute with Thomas Kewen and Joan his wife concerning their right to a messuage and lands called Hawkins,

17 Inq. p.m. 44 Hen. III, No. 6.
18 q.v. *infra*.
19 Feet of F. Hants, East. 5 Edw. III.
20 *Feud. Aids*, ii, 311.
21 *Cal. of Pat.* 1321–4, p. 413; Inq. a.q.d. 17 Edw. II, No. 220; Feet of F. Hants, Trin. 18 Edw. II.
22 G.E.C. *Complete Peerage*, iv, 179.
23 Inq. p.m. 5 Edw. III, No. 19.
24 Close, 5 Edw. III, pt. 1, m. 20.
25 Inq. p.m. 6 Edw. III (2nd Nos.), No. 28.
26 Pat. 6 Edw. III, pt. 2, m. 25.
27 Inq. p.m. 9 Edw. III (1st Nos.), No. 44.
28 Inq. p.m. 17 Edw. III (2nd Nos.), No. 56; Feet of F. Hants, Mich. 17 Edw. III. These 2 acres remained the property of the Hastings family until 1403–4 (Inq. p.m. 21 Edw. III, No. 52, and 2 Hen. IV, No. 60), in which year Sir Edward Hastings, brother of Hugh Hastings, released all his right in them to Henry IV (Anct. D. P.R.O. A. 3243).
29 *Feud. Aids*, ii, 326.
30 De Banc. R. East. 22 Edw. III, m. 238 *d.*
31 Inq. p.m. 24 Edw. III (1st Nos.), No. 61.
32 Close, 25 Edw. III, m. 22.
33 Inq. p.m. 47 Edw. III (1st Nos.), No. 10.
34 Ibid. 5 Ric. II, No. 19.
35 *Harl. Soc.* xii, 123.
36 Baker, *Northants*, ii, 22.
37 Pat. 6 Hen. IV, pt. 1, m. 28; De Banc. R. Mich. 6 Hen. IV, m. 400 *d.*; Feet of F. Div. Cos. Mich. 6 Hen. IV.
38 *V.C.H. Hants*, ii, 506.
39 *Feud. Aids*, ii, 348.
40 Feet of F. Div. Cos. Hil. 4 Edw. IV. It is probable that John Wynard was the son of William Wynard, third recorder of Exeter in 1404, and founder of the almshouses in Magdalen Street, Exeter (Ellacombe, *Hist. of the Parish of Clyst St. George, Devon*, 67).
41 Close, 22 Edw. IV, m. 14.
42 In 1500 a writ was issued to inquire into the prior's right of title, and it was found that the late prior had been pardon edentry without licence by letters patent of 1484 (Chan. Inq. p.m. (Ser. 2), xv, No. 13). At the Dissolution the annual net value of the manor was £4 6*s.* 6*d.* (Mins. Accts. Hants, 29 & 30 Hen. VIII, No. 113, m. 25)
43 *L. and P. Hen. VIII*, xiv (2), 432.
44 Ibid. xvi, p. 716.
45 Ibid. xix (i), 80 (20); Pat. 35 Hen. VIII, pt. 10, m. 33.
46 *L. and P. Hen. VIII*, xix (1), p. 385; Pat. 36 Hen. VIII, pt. 25, m. 16.
47 Pat. 37 Hen. VIII, pt. 8, m. 30.
48 Chan. Inq. p.m. (Ser. 2), ci, No. 107.

Mannyngfords, Byrdes, and Barkelettes, parcel of the customary lands of the manor of Sutton Scotney.[49] He died seised of the manor of Sutton Scotney in 1597, leaving a son and heir John aged twenty-two.[50] Licence to the latter to enter into possession of the manor of Sutton Scotney was enrolled in the patent roll of 1602,[51] but within two years he died and the manor descended to his son and heir John,[52] who alienated it in 1606 to Thomas Warburton.[53] Nine years later Thomas Warburton and Anne his wife sold the manor to Robert Harward,[54] who was still holding in 1622,[55] and apparently also in 1639.[56] The subsequent history of the manor is difficult to trace owing to the many changes of ownership during the eighteenth and nineteenth centuries. A certain William Smith dealt with the manor by recovery in 1740,[57] and his descendants seem to have retained it for a considerable period, Thomas Assheton Smith being lord of the manor in 1799,[58] but it is not known when they parted with it. They seem however to have been succeeded in the lordship by Richard Meyler, who was killed by a fall from his horse. Benjamin Heywood Bright was lord of the manor in 1841, and on his death Sutton Scotney passed to Henry Bright, who was in possession in 1852.[59] Edward Burtenshaw Sugden first Lord St. Leonards, Lord Chancellor of Great Britain, purchased Sutton Scotney in 1868,[60] and on his death seven years later it descended to his second son the Hon. and Rev. Frank Sugden, on whose death in 1886 it passed to his nephew Edward Burtenshaw Sugden second Lord St. Leonards.[61] The latter sold the manor to Mr. Percy Tarbutt.

Evidently the overlordship of the half of Sutton that belonged to Odo of Winchester at the time of the Domesday Survey passed like Norton Valery (q.v.) to the family of St. Valery,[62] and from them to Richard earl of Cornwall[63] and so to the crown. Like Norton Valery also the actual possession of the manor passed to the college of St. Elizabeth near Winchester in 1313,[64] was granted with Norton in 1544 to Thomas Wriothesley[65] and was sold by him the same year to John Twyne, together with Norton.[66] John Twyne by his will dated 23 April, 1554, left the hamlet of Sutton Scotney, formerly belonging to the house of St. Elizabeth, to his son Nicholas in fee-tail.[67] There is no inquisition on the death of Nicholas, and it is probable that on his death the hamlet reverted to John Twyne son and heir of his brother Richard, and became merged in the other manor of Sutton Scotney, the original portion of Richard.[68]

The manor of *NORTON* or *NORTON ST. VALERY* was held by Odo of Winchester at the time of the Domesday Survey. Fulchi had held it in the time of King Edward and could betake himself whither he would. Then it was assessed at five hides, but by the time of the Survey at only two hides one virgate.[69] Possibly on the death of Odo the manor was granted to Roger de Ivrey and became part of the barony of Ivrey.[70] Hence when this barony was granted to Guy de St. Valery by Henry I, Norton passed into the St. Valery family, and when the honour escheated to the crown in the reign of Henry III the overlordship of the manor remained with the honour, passing to Richard earl of Cornwall by grant of Henry III, and after him to his son Edmund, and on his death in 1300 to the king as his cousin and heir.[71]

St. Valery. *Or two lions passant gules.*

The family of St. Valery were in actual possession of the manor in the early part of the thirteenth century. Thus in 1214 John granted Thomas de St. Valery full seisin of the manor which had belonged to Henry his brother.[72]

By 1231 Thomas had been succeeded by Henry de St. Valery, probably his son, who in that year engaged in a dispute with the abbess of Bertocurt or Bertancourt (Somme, France) concerning customs in Sutton and Norton.[73] In the beginning of the fourteenth century Richard de St. Valery alienated the manor to Walter de Langton, bishop of Coventry and Lichfield, who received pardon for acquiring the manor from Richard in 1307.[74] Three years later the king had evidently seized the manor from the hands of the bishop and granted it for life to Robert Fitz Pain, one of the stewards of the royal household, with a special condition that if the king should resume the manor Robert should receive compensation.[75] In September, 1312, the manor of Kingsbury with other property in Somerset was granted to Robert, since the king had restored the manor of Norton to the bishop.[76] Shortly afterwards the bishop conveyed the manor to trustees, Robert de Harewedon and William de Staunford,[77] who in February, 1313, received licence to alienate the same to the provost and chaplains of the chapel of St. Elizabeth near Winchester.[78] Two months later the provost and chaplains were pardoned the service of a sore sparrow-hawk for the manor of Norton St. Valery,[79] and in May the king confirmed it to

49 Chan. Proc. (Ser. 2), bdle. 106, No. 17.

50 Chan. Inq. p.m. 39 Eliz. pt. 2, (Ser. 2), No. 18.

51 Pat. 44 Eliz. pt. 16, m. 9–12.

52 Chan. Inq. p.m. (Ser. 2), cclxxxiv, No. 23.

53 Feet of F. Hants, Trin. 4 Jas. I.

54 Ibid. Hil. 13 Jas. I.

55 Ibid. Trin. 20 Jas. I.

56 *Cal. of S.P. Dom.* 1639, p. 283.

57 Recov. R. Trin. 13 & 14 Geo. II, rot. 221.

58 Information furnished by Mr. Spencer Clarke of Whitchurch.

59 Ibid.

60 Ibid.

61 Burke, *Peerage.*

62 Cf. *Rot. Lit. Claus.* (Rec. Com.), i, 161, where full seisin is granted to Thomas de St. Valery in the lands in Sutton which had belonged to Henry his brother.

63 Cf. *Testa de Nevill* (Rec. Com.), 234*b*, where Hugh de Foresta is said to hold one fee in Sutton of the earl of Poitou (one of the titles of Richard earl of Cornwall) of the honor of Wallingford (St. Valery).

64 *Feud. Aids.* ii, 326, 348.

65 Pat. 35 Hen. VIII, pt. 9, m. 5–7.

66 *L. and P. Hen. VIII*, xix (1), p. 641.

67 Chan. Inq. p.m. (Ser. 2), ci, No. 107.

68 John Twyne son and heir of Richard certainly succeeded to the rent of the fourth part of 1 acre of underwood and 5*s*. from the manor of Norton Valery and the annual share of a meadow called Myllmead (Chan. Inq. p.m. [Ser. 2], cclxxxiv, No. 23), left to Nicholas by his father John (Exch. Inq. p.m. [Ser. 2], file 999, No. 25), and it is probable that he succeeded to the hamlet of Sutton Scotney also.

69 *V.C.H. Hants*, i, 504.

70 Lipscombe, *Hist. of Bucks.* i, 367.

71 Inq. p.m. 28 Edw. I, No. 44.

72 *Rot. Lit. Claus.* (Rec. Com.), i, 161.

73 Close, 15 Hen. III, m. 19*d.* and 2 *d.*

74 Pat. 35 Edw. I, m. 30.

75 Pat. 3 Edw. II, m. 21.

76 Pat. 6 Edw. II, m. 17.

77 Feet of F. Hants, Mich. 8 Edw. II.

78 Pat. 6 Edw. II, pt. 1, m. 1.

79 Pat. pt. 2, m. 15.

them in free alms quit of every service.[80] The manor remained with the college until the Dissolution,[81] when it fell into the hands of the king, who granted it in 1544 to Sir Thomas Wriothesley Lord Wriothesley to hold of him and his successors by rent of £2 13*s.* 4*d.*[82] In the same year Wriothesley obtained licence to alienate the manor to John Twyne, yeoman, and his sons William and Nicholas.[83] John Twyne, by will dated 23 April, 1554, left the manor to his son William Twyne the elder in fee-tail, and died shortly afterwards.[84] On the death of William in 1559[85] the manor passed to his son and heir Thomas,[86] who held the manor until 1566, when he died leaving a widow Barbara and two infant daughters named Margery and Anne.[87] Barbara married William St. John of Farley Chamberlayne, 'a man of great countenaunce and credyt,' as her second husband,[88] and in 1582 the two daughters Margery and Anne with their respective husbands William Skilling and William Fisher gave up their moieties of the manor to William and Barbara.[89] John Twyne, who died in 1554, had by will left to his widow Agnes two quarters of wheat and two quarters of malt yearly during her widowhood, and the depasturing and feeding of two kine with grass and fodder upon the lands of his manor of Norton while she remained unmarried.[90] She remained a widow for seven years, at the end of that time marrying John Kent of Catherington, blacksmith, but no payment was ever made to her, and in 1591 her husband 'having nothinge ells to relive himself withall being utterly waste and consumed by means of his marriage with the foresaid Agnes,' sued William St. John and Barbara his wife for £200 which had been awarded to Agnes in lieu of the annual payments by Sir William Kingsmill and Sir Oliver Wallop just before the death of William Twyne,[91] but most probably without success.

In 1609 William St. John died during his wife's lifetime, leaving the reversion of the manor after the death of Barbara, according to a settlement of the year 1600, to his son and heir Henry and Ursula his wife, daughter of Hugh Stewkley,[92] to whom Payne Fisher, probably son and heir of William Fisher and Anne his wife, quitclaimed a moiety of the manor in 1619.[93] Henry died seised of the manor in 1621 leaving a son and heir John[94] aged seven, who five years later, in conjunction with Sir Thomas Stewkley his maternal uncle and most probably his guardian, conveyed it to Dr. Nicholas Love,[95] head master of Winchester College in 1601, warden 1613, canon of Winchester 1610, and chaplain to James I. On his death in 1630 the manor passed to his son and heir Nicholas,[96] who early in 1644 obtained from the Parliament a grant of the office of one of the six clerks in Hampshire, and is said to have made £20,000 out of the post.[97] He is best remembered, however, as one of the judges of Charles I, being present in Westminster Hall when sentence was delivered. On his own showing he advised that 'conference might bee had before any further proceeding,' and consequently refused to sign the death-warrant, whereupon he 'was violently opposed By Oliver Cromwell, Ireton and others, and clamorously reviled as an obstructer of that black designe.'[98] At the Restoration Love escaped to the Continent, and he was absolutely excepted in the Act of Indemnity, December, 1660. In October of the some year Edward Penruddock, who had paid £10,000 for the place of clerk in Chancery, and had only held it three years, having been ousted by Nicholas Love in 1644, petitioned for a lease of Norton Farm in the parish of Wonston,[99] while at the same time Dr. Joseph Rhodes, chaplain to the king, who had been sequestered for loyalty and conformity for many years, and whose brother Richard Rhodes had spent £3,000 or £4,000, his whole fortune, in the royal cause, prayed for a free grant of Norton Farm near Winchester, late the estate of Nicholas Love.[100]

Norton Farm is now the property of Mr. G. Hampton of London.

Lands in *CRANBORNE* (Cramburnan, x cent.; Gramborne, xi cent.; Cramburn, xv cent. et seq.) were granted by Edward the Elder to Hyde Abbey as part of the hundred and manor of Micheldever. The boundaries of Cranborne are given, and would seem to extend beyond the bounds of the later manor, although it is difficult to identify any of the boundaries except that they begin 'at the stream of Micheldever that runneth before the church field of Wonston' meaning the River Test.[101] At the time of the Domesday Survey Cranborne was held by Hugh de Port of the abbey of Hyde, whereas in the days of Edward the Confessor a freeman had held it of the abbey, and could not withdraw himself from the abbot's jurisdiction.[102] The St. Johns in the thirteenth and fourteenth centuries, and the Paulets in the fifteenth century, as the heirs of Hugh de Port,[103] held knights' fees in Cranborne of Hyde Abbey and the abbot of the king.[104]

The Brayboef family held of the St. Johns in the twelfth and thirteenth centuries. Hence in 1215 King John commanded the sheriff of Hants to give seisin to Elias the mayor of Winchester (Elije Majori Wint̃) of the land in Cranborne which had belonged by his gift to Henry de Brayboef.[105] In the reign of Henry III Robert de Brayboef, who was seemingly a son of Henry and a minor in 1215, held one fee in Cranborne 'de veteri feoffamento' of Robert de St. John, and he of the abbot of Hyde, and the abbot

[80] Pat. 6 Edw. II, pt. 2, m. 11.

[81] *Feud. Aids*, ii, 326, 348.

[82] *L. and P. Hen. VIII*, xix (1), 278 (74); Pat. 35 Hen. VIII, pt. 9, m. 5–7. This rent was still paid to the crown in 1667, in which year Charles II granted it by letters patent to his kinsman George, duke of Albemarle (Pat. 19 Chas. II, pt. 8, No. 19).

[83] *L. and P. Hen. VIII*, xix (1), p. 641.

[84] Chan. Inq. p.m. (Ser. 2), ci, No. 107.

[85] He hanged himself according to Ct. of Requests, bdle. 49, No. 34.

[86] Exch. Inq. p.m. (Ser. 2), file 999, No. 25.

[87] Exch. Inq. p.m. (Ser. 2), file 1005, No. 5.

[88] Ct. of Requests, bdle. 49, No. 34.

[89] Feet of F. Hants, East. 24 Eliz. and Mich. 24 & 25 Eliz. In 1589 William Fisher and Anne his wife again quitclaimed their moiety of the manor to William St. John (Feet of F. Hants, East. 31 Eliz).

[90] Ct. of Requests, bdle. 49, No. 34.

[91] Ibid.

[92] W. and L. Inq. p.m. (Ser. 2), bdle. 5, No. 185.

[93] Feet of F. Hants, Mich. 17 Jas. I.

[94] W. and L. Inq. p.m. (Ser. 2), bdle. 32, No. 40.

[95] Feet of F. Hants, Mich. 2 Chas. I. He was the third son of John Love of Basing Park in the parish of Froxfield.

[96] Berry, *Hants Gen.* 267.

[97] *Cal. of S.P. Dom.* 1660, p. 343.

[98] *Hist. MSS. Com. Rep.* vii, 119.

[99] *Cal. of S.P. Dom.* 1660, p. 343.

[100] Ibid.

[101] Birch, *Cart. Sax.* ii, 245–6; *Liber de Hyda* (Rolls Ser.), 89.

[102] *V.C.H. Hants*, i, 470.

[103] See Norton in Selborne.

[104] *Testa de Nevill* (Rec. Com.), 232; Inq. p.m. 12 Edw. I, No. 13; 3 Edw. III, No. 67; 11 Edw. III, No. 49; 17 Edw. IV, No. 31.

[105] *Rot. Lit. Claus.* (Rec. Com.), i, 235.

of the king in chief.[106] William de Brayboef, who was evidently the heir of Robert, died in 1284 seised of the manor held of John de St. John.[107]

On William's death Henry de Bray, escheator, was ordered to deliver 12*s.* 6*d.* in the manor of Cranborne, to be received from the villeins thereof,[108] to Joan de St. Martin, widow of William de Brayboef. This order was however cancelled, and instead she was assigned in dower the chief messuage of the manor extended at 6*s.* 8*d.* with a moiety of the manor extended at £6 14*s.* 11*d.*[109] The remainder went to Hugh de Brayboef, son and heir of William,[110] who became seised of the whole on Joan's death. According to the subsidy return for 1316 Hugh de Brayboef was holding Cranborne in that year,[111] while in 1329–30 he held a fee in Cranborne worth 100*s.* of John de St. John,[112] and in 1337 he was said to hold four knights' fees in Cranborne and other places valued at £40 yearly of William son of Roger de Melebury, who held of Hugh de St. John.[113] There is no inquisition on the death of Hugh, but his widow Joan[114] held the manor in 1346[115] and 1349.[116]

It is doubtful whether William, son and heir of Hugh and Joan,[117] or Hugh, son and heir of William,[118] ever succeeded to the manor, for as early as 1367 Sir Hugh de Camois, who was no doubt holding the manor in right of his wife Joan, daughter and heir of Hugh,[119] obtained a grant of free warren in his demesne lands of Cranborne.[120] In 1380 Sir Hugh received confirmation in his favour of the charter of Edward III,[121] and two years later leased the manor 'from Michaelmas next to the morrow of Michaelmas next thereafter' to Sir John de Montagu, lord of Werk, and Sir John de Montagu his son.[122] He had died before 1395, for in that year his widow Joan dealt with the manor by fine[123] for purposes of settlement. Cranborne next passed to Elizabeth, daughter and heir of Hugh and Joan, who married first Sir John Hamely or Hamelyn of Wimborne St. Giles[124] (co. Dors.), and secondly Thomas Wake of Winterborne Stoke[125] (co. Wilts.). By her first husband, who died in 1398, she had a daughter and heir Egidia,[126] to whom the manor passed after her mother's death, which took place after 1431.[127] Egidia married first Robert Ashley,[128] and secondly Sir Thomas Thame of Hampshire, and died in 1476.[129] Before her death she had settled the manor upon a certain Robert Ashley, probably her son, and Isabel his wife.[130] Robert, however predeceased Egidia, and in 1477 his widow Isabel was holding Cranborne as a free tenement for the term of her life with reversion to Edmund Ashley, son and heir of Egidia, and his heirs.[131] In 1554 Henry Ashley, great-grandson of Edmund, sold the reversion of the manor after the deaths of John Nicholson of Cranborne and Alice his wife to John Twyne, yeoman, of Norton in the parish of Wonston.[132] Within the year John Twyne died, leaving the manor to his sons by his first wife Christine, William and Nicholas, 'to be held between them without any contention, strife or variance during the term of their lives' with reversion to John and William the younger, his sons by his second wife Agnes.[133] William the elder died in 1559,[134] and his brother Nicholas probably some time afterwards. There is no inquisition on his death, but it must have been before 1579, in which year John Twyne settled an annuity of £50 from the manor of Cranborne upon his natural son John.[135] Two years later William the younger sold his moiety of the manor to Sir Richard Norton,[136] who conveyed it in 1582 to John Twyne the owner of the other moiety.[137] The manor remained in this branch of the Twyne family until 1621,[138] when John Twyne and Anne his wife sold it to Robert Payne and William Payne.[139]

The history of this manor during the next century is obscure. Hugh Willoughby seems to have been lord in the reign of Charles II, and dealt with it by recovery in 1682.[140] By the middle of the next century it was held by Sir Martin Wright, justice of the court of King's Bench, who died in 1767, in which year Andrew Gother was dealing with the manor.[141] Sir Martin was succeeded by his son William Wright, who, dying without issue in 1814, devised his property to Lady Frances Elizabeth, daughter of the earl of Aylesbury and wife of Sir Henry Wilson, M.P.[142] The latter by will left all her property in Hampshire to Frances Elizabeth, daughter of Captain Christopher Wilson and wife of Colonel Sir Michael M'Creagh.[143] Their son Major Michael M'Creagh married Eva Helen Emma, granddaughter of Bache Thornhill of Stanton-in-Peak (co. Derb.), and obtained by royal licence in 1882 permission to take in addition the name and to quarter the arms of Thornhill on her succession to the Stanton-in-Peak estate by the death of her brother, Henry Francis Hurlock Thornhill.[144] He died in 1902 leaving a son and heir Michael Christopher M'Creagh-Thornhill, and his widow is at the present time lady of the manor of Cranborne.

The family of Sutton from an early date held lands in *CRANBORNE* and *SUTTON* of the manor of

106 *Testa de Nevill* (Rec. Com.), 232.
107 Inq. p.m. 12 Edw. I, No. 13. In 1281 William Strecche and Selina his wife had quitclaimed to him the third part of a messuage, 2 virgates of land and 1 acre of meadow in Cranborne Brayboef, and all that tenement in the same vill which Parnel wife of William le Franklin once held in dower of the inheritance of Selina. (Feet of F. Hants, Trin. 9 Edw. I.)
108 *Cal. of Close*, 1279–88, p. 277.
109 Ibid. 278.
110 Inq. p.m. 12 Edw. I, No. 13.
111 *Feud. Aids*, ii, 306.
112 Inq. p.m. 3 Edw. III, No. 67.
113 Ibid. 11 Edw. III, No. 49.
114 De Banc. R. Hil. 20 Hen. VI, m. 314.
115 *Feud. Aids*, ii, 329.
116 Close, 23 Edw. III, pt. 1, m. 17, 18 *d.*
117 De Banc. R. Hil. 20 Hen. VI, m. 314.
118 Ibid.
119 Ibid.
120 Chart. R. 41 Edw. III, No. 11.
121 *Cal. of Pat.* 1377–81, p. 437.
122 Anct. D. (P.R.O.), B. 3718.
123 Feet of F. Hants, Trin. 18 Ric. II. She granted it to John, vicar of the church of Basingstoke, in fee-tail, with contingent remainder to Henry Popham and Joan his wife.
124 Hutchins, *Dorset*, iii, 579.
125 Hoare, *Wiltshire*, v (3), 35.
126 Inq. p.m. 22 Ric. II, No. 25.
127 *Feud. Aids*, ii, 348, 365.
128 Hutchins, *Dorset*, iii, 579.
129 Inq. p.m. 17 Edw. IV, No. 31.
130 Ibid.
131 Ibid.
132 Chan. Inq. p.m. (Ser. 2), ci, No. 107.
133 Ibid.
134 Exch. Inq. p.m. (Ser. 2), file 999, No. 25.
135 Com. Pleas D. Enr. Hil. 21 Eliz. rot. 11 *d.*
136 Feet of F. Hants, Mich. 23 & 24 Eliz.
137 Ibid. Hil. 25 Eliz.
138 In 1586 John Twyne mortgaged the manor to Robert Pyncke and William Hanyngton (Com. Pleas Recov. R. Hil. 28 Eliz. rot. 9 *d.*). In 1587 Margery Heath, widow, niece of John gave up all her right to a moiety of a third part of the manor (Feet of F. Hants, Mich. 29 & 30 Eliz.).
139 Feet of F. Hants, Trin. 19 Jas. I; Recov. R. Mich. 19 Jas. I, rot. 139.
140 Recov. R. Mich. 34 Chas. II, rot. 252.
141 Ibid. Mich. 8 Geo. III, rot. 442.
142 Information supplied by Mr. Michael Christopher M'Creagh-Thornhill.
143 Ibid.
144 Burke, *Landed Gentry*.

Cranborne by a rent of 6*s.* 8*d.*, suit at Cranborne court and an animal as heriot.[145] In 1243 Adam de Sutton granted lands in Sutton to Andrew of Winchester,[146] and in 1247 Geoffrey son of Alexander and Olympia his wife settled a virgate of land in Sutton on Robert

M'CREAGH. *Or a battled fesse between three stars in the chief and a lion in the foot all gules with a sword lying in the fesse having its hilt and pomel or.*

THORNHILL. *Gules two gimel bars argent and a chief argent with a voided lozenge sable therein, a crosslet for difference.*

de Sutton.[147] By the beginning of the fourteenth century Robert had been succeeded by Richard de Sutton, senr., who in 1315 settled half a messuage and lands in Sutton Scotney and other places on Richard de Sutton, junr.,[148] no doubt his son. Further settlements of lands in Sutton Scotney and Cranborne were made on Peter de Sutton and Alice his wife in 1330 and 1341.[149] Peter seems to have been succeeded in a great part of the premises by John de Sutton, who was seised in fee-tail of 3 messuages, lands, and 20*s.* rent in Sutton Scotney and other places. The property seems to have been entailed upon his son Thomas, but in spite of this on the death of John another son Alan succeeded,[150] who was seised of a close called 'Wythygers' and other lands in Cranborne held of the manor of Cranborne in 1442, and in that year sued William Godale, bailiff of Thomas Thame, who was at that time lord of the manor of Cranborne, for seizing six horses in lieu of rent.[151] On his deathbed Alan repented of his action in ousting Thomas, and delivered up the deeds showing that the estates were entailed on him to his wife Ellen, charging her solemnly to give them to his brother. However Ellen gave them instead to her daughter Alice, 'whom she loved better than Thomas,' and about 1460 she and her husband Robert Sherrard were summoned by Thomas for refusing to give them up.[152]

CHURCH The church of the *HOLY TRINITY* consists of chancel, nave with north aisle and south porch, and west tower. The north aisle is a modern addition, but the plan of the chancel and the nave, without the aisle, appears to date from the early years of the thirteenth century.

The church was burnt in 1714, the nave being more damaged than the rest of the building, but several of the old features survived the fire, and the walls are in large measure ancient.

The chancel has a three-light east window of fifteenth-century design with modern tracery, and two lancets in the north and south walls, the heads of which are trefoiled internally, but uncusped on the outside; the cusping is probably a later addition.

At the eastern angles of the chancel are spreading plinths of thirteenth-century character, and the chancel arch is an interesting piece of thirteenth-century work, with a pointed arch of two rounded orders, and pretty foliate capitals, that of the south respond showing traces of Romansque feeling in its detail. The bases are modern. The nave has two windows on the south side, the eastern of which is of the fifteenth century, though much patched and renewed, with three cinquefoiled lights and tracery over. The other is a single cinquefoiled light with little if any old masonry. Between the windows is the south doorway, with a semicircular head of two orders of the rounded section which occurs in the chancel arch, and doubtless of the same date; it has a modern label. On the jambs are three incised sundials; the doorway now opens to a modern wooden porch.

The tower is of three stages with an embattled parapet and a stair at the south-east. It dates from the early part of the sixteenth century, and has two-light belfry windows of plain character, and a west window of three cinquefoiled lights with tracery, beneath which is a west doorway of two hollow-chamfered orders. A window in which a fifteenth-century cinquefoiled head is re-used has been in modern times inserted near the south-west angle of the ground stage, which is screened off from the nave and used as a vestry. The font is modern, as are all the fittings of the church; the nave roof is dated 1714, the year of the fire.

There are five bells, the third, fourth, and tenor by James Wells of Aldbourne, 1802, the other two being blank and probably by the same founder.

The plate is a fine set, silver-gilt, given by Thomas Newry, rector, in 1717, and bearing the London hall-mark for 1716. It consists of chalice with cover paten, flagon, and almsdish. There is also a silver-gilt bowl of 1815 for use at baptisms, given in 1816 by Honora wife of the Hon. Augustus George Legge, rector.

The first book of the registers contains all entries from 1570 to 1718, and a list of burials in woollen 1678-1717, together with a record of 595 births between 1683 and 1767, and the names of fourteen persons touched for the king's evil, 1684–1713. The second book contains all entries 1718–62, the third baptisms and burials 1763-1812, and the fourth is the printed marriage register 1754–1812.

Between 1655 and 1672 the registers are very imperfect, and there is a note of explanation that 'the registrar deputed for the purpose had not what was due to him for it.'

ADVOWSONS There was a church in Wonston at the time of the Domesday Survey[153] the advowson of which belonged to the bishop of Winchester.[154] In 1333 John

145 *Vide* de Banc. R. Hil. 20 Hen. VI, rot. 314.

146 Feet of F. Hants, 27 Hen. III.

147 Ibid. East. 31 Hen. III.

148 Ibid. Mich. 9 Edw. II.

149 In 1330 a messuage and lands were settled on Peter and Alice in fee-tail with contingent remainder in fee-tail successively to John son of Hugh de Sutton, Alan son of Richard de Sutton, junr. and Joan daughter of Alan de Sutton, senr. (Feet of F. Hants, Trin. 4 Edw. III). In 1341 3 messuages and land were settled on Peter de Sutton in fee-tail with contingent remainder in tail-male successively to Alan son of Richard de Sutton and Robert son of Hugh de Sutton (Feet of F. Hants, East. 15 Edw. III).

150 Early Chan. Proc. bdle. 28, No. 112.

151 De Banc. R. Hil. 20 Hen. VI, m. 314.

152 Early Chan. Proc. bdle. 28, No. 112.

153 *V.C.H. Hants*, i, 467*a*.

154 Pat. 26 Hen. III, m. 13; Chart. R. 12 Edw. I, m. 5; Egerton MS. 2032, fol. 87; Pat. 5 Edw. III, pt. 1, m. 23.

Stratford, bishop of Winchester, obtained licence to appropriate the church, then valued at £40, to the prior and convent of St. Swithun. Out of that sum £25 19*s.* 4*d.* was to be paid yearly to the hospital of St. Mary according to the prescription of Henry Woodlock, bishop of Winchester, and a perpetual vicar was to be appointed.[155] The appropriation, however, was never carried into effect,[156] probably owing to the fact that, immediately after the licence, Stratford was succeeded in the episcopacy by Adam Orlton. The living is at the present day in the gift of the bishop of Winchester and is a rectory, net income £580 with 20 acres of glebe and residence built from the proceeds of the sale of the old rectory house and glebe.

Dependent on the parish church of Wonston was the chapel of Sutton Scotney,[157] probably representing one of the two churches of Sutton Scotney mentioned in Domesday Book.[158] It was probably desecrated early in the seventeenth century, as in 1639 Robert Harward, who was at this time lord of the manor of Sutton Scotney, and Ambrose Beach were referred to the bishop of Winchester to inquire as to who was answerable for the profanation of the chapel and to report thereon to the Court of High Commission.[159]

In the fourteenth and fifteenth centuries there was also a chapel in Cranborne. Thus in March, 1397–8, John Frere and John Kyngestone were licensed to confess penitents and administer the Eucharist in the hamlet of Cranborne at the impending season of Easter, saving the rights of the parish church of Wonston.[160] Again, in March, 1401–2, William of Wykeham granted licence to John Kyngestone, chaplain, to perform divine service in the chapel of Cranborne and to administer the sacraments to his servants and tenants, John Pyperwhyt and Joan his wife, during his good pleasure.[161]

CHARITIES In 1710 Thomas Sayer by will gave £30 for the benefit of the poor. In 1779 John Wickham by will gave £5 yearly towards educating poor children of the parish. In satisfaction of the legacy, a sum of £166 13*s.* 4*d.* Old South Sea annuities was purchased, subsequently augmented by investment of accumulations of income. By a scheme of the Charity Commissioners of 22 March, 1867, the two charities were merged, and the income applied towards the maintenance of the parochial school. The present endowment consists of £278 14*s.* 10*d.* consols with the Official Trustees of Charitable Funds.

In 1863 the Hon. Honora Legge, widow, by will proved this date, left £100 consols (part of a sum of £400 consols directed to be transferred to the Official Trustees of Charitable Funds) the dividends to be applied by the officiating minister as a marriage portion for the daughter of a resident labourer under the age of twenty-five years, she and her husband to be members of the Church of England, or, failing a suitable person, to a deserving labourer having the most children dependent upon him, or to two of the oldest and poorest residents, widows in preference. See also parish of Hinton Ampner (hundred of Fawley) and parish of Bramdean (hundred of Bishop's Sutton).

In 1898 Mrs. Honora Augusta Cowper–Coles, by a codicil to her will proved this date, bequeathed £120 £2 10*s.* per cent. Bank Annuities to the officiating minister of Wonston, the income to be employed in providing warm winter clothing for respectable poor women of the parish.

155 Pat. 7 Edw. III, pt. 2, m. 12; *Cal. Pap. Letters*, ii, 381.
156 *Valor Eccl.* (Rec. Com.), ii, 17.
157 Chart. R. 12 Edw. I, m. 5; Egerton MS. 2034, fol. 176.
158 *V.C.H. Hants*, i, 488*b*, 504*a*.
159 *Cal. of S.P. Dom.* 1639, p. 283.
160 *Wykeham's Reg.* (Hants Rec. Soc.), ii, 480.
161 Ibid. 537.

THE HUNDRED OF MAINSBRIDGE

CONTAINING THE PARISHES OF

NORTH BADDESLEY — CHILWORTH — HOUND WITH NETLEY
BOTLEY — HAMBLE LE RICE — NORTH STONEHAM
SOUTH STONEHAM[1]

At the time of the Domesday Survey Mainsbridge Hundred covered a much larger area than it does at present, for in addition to the above parishes it also contained Shirley in Millbrook, Redbridge, Boyatt, and Woolston. Hound, although nominally belonging to Warnford in King's Somborne Hundred, paid geld in Mainsbridge, with the men in the adjoining vill of 'Letelie' or Netley.[2] At this period the total assessment of the hundred was 25 hides, showing a decrease of 7 on the assessment of the hundred made before the Conquest.

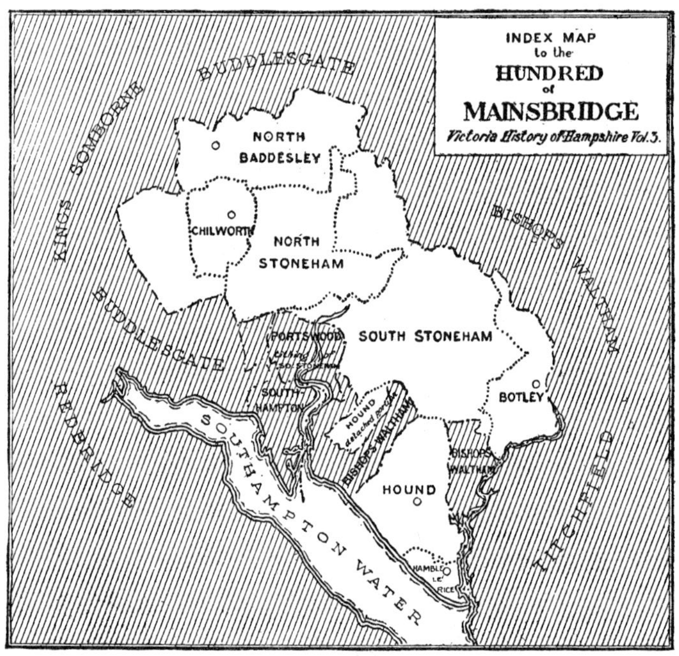

Mainsbridge was a royal hundred and until the fifteenth century remained, so far as is known, entirely in the hands of the crown. In 1280 an inquiry was made into the right of the men of the abbot of Netley to freedom from doing suit at the king's hundred court. It was proved that the abbot had received a grant from Henry III releasing his villeins in the tithings of Hound, Shotteshal (Satchell), and Sholing in Hound, from all service at the shire and hundred courts, and from payment of all scot and geld, and tolls,[3] a privilege which the tenants of the abbey seem to have always claimed from this date. In 1467 John Davy was granted the hundred court with all its issues and profits for life in return for an annual rental of 40*s.* 8*d.* payable to the king.[4]

The hundred court was customarily held under an ash-tree in Swaythling in South Stoneham at Martintide.[5]

[1] This list is taken from the *Population Return of* 1831.
[2] *V.C.H. Hants*, i, 481.
[3] *Plac. de quo Warr.* (Rec. Com.), 763.
[4] *Cal. of Pat.* 1461–67, p. 337.
[5] Parl. Surv. (Aug. Off.), No. 7.

NORTH BADDESLEY

Bedeslei (xi cent.) ; Baldisle (xiv cent.).

The parish of North Baddesley, in the New Forest division of the county, lies on open heath country, north and south of the road from Romsey to Portsmouth.

Its total area, including the almost detached portion in the south-west, is nearly 2,584 acres, and its population in 1901 was 245. This isolated portion, together with neighbouring parts of the parishes of Romsey Extra and Nursling, was in 1897 formed into the new civil parish of Rownhams, whose population is 498. The land is well wooded, but here and there are wide stretches of bog-land.

The soil is not fertile, and is sand or loam with a subsoil for the most part clay or gravel, and although a small amount of wheat, oats, and barley is raised, the greater part of the land is given over to woods and plantations.[1] Tanners Brook flows in a southerly direction through Rownhams, and a small tributary of the Itchen forms the eastern boundary of the parish for a short distance.

The main road from Romsey to Botley crosses the south-west corner of the parish, and a branch from it communicates with North Baddesley village, which consists of a few small cottages scattered on either side of the road.

Approaching from the west, the manor-house lies to the south, standing a little way back from the road. Farther on, to the north, is the small parish church of St. John, and opposite to it the vicarage, on the site of the preceptory 6f the Hospitallers. Part of the house is probably mediaeval, incorporating some remains of the preceptory.

The village of Rownhams, in the extreme south of North Baddesley parish, consists of a single street of small houses. In the centre of the village is the church of St. John the Baptist, built in 1856, and the vicarage and elementary schools, built at the same time by Mrs. Colt, are near to one another. St. John's Convalescent Home, erected in 1876 by Lady Helena Trench and the Rev. R. F. Wilson, M.A., lies to the north of Rownhams, where are several fine residences. Rownhams House, a large brick mansion occupied by Mrs. Keates, stands in a park of 40 acres, and Lords Wood, the residence of General Sir Neville Chamberlain, lies in the south.

There is a small recreation ground in the parish granted when North Baddesley common was inclosed in 1867,[2] and sixteen small garden allotments let to the poor at 1*s.* 6*d.* each, given to the parish at the same time.

Mr. Tankerville Chamberlayne, lord of the manor, collects the tithes in North Baddesley and Rownhams, and has the tithe map in his possession. The following place-names occur :—Nutburn, Scrag Hill, and Zionshill, where is a farm reputed to have belonged to the knights of St. John.[3]

MANOR The manor of *NORTH BADDESLEY*, assessed at two hides at the time of the Domesday Survey, belonged to Ralph de Mortimer, holding of the king in chief,[4] and the overlordship rights passed down through the Mortimer family[5] until they lapsed at the close of the fourteenth century.[6] The manor was probably alienated to the Knights Hospitallers before 1167, for, at this date, they were settled at Baddesley,[7] where was a cell belonging to the preceptory of the knights at Godsfield.[8]

MORTIMER. *Barry or and azure a chief or with two pales between two gyrons azure therein and a scutcheon argent over all.*

Before the year 1365, however, the latter migrated to North Baddesley and made that preceptory their head quarters.[9]

At the time of the dissolution of the monasteries, in 1536, Baddesley, still held by the Knights of St. John, and valued at £131 14*s.* 1*d.*,[10] fell to the crown, but was immediately afterwards granted to Sir Thomas Seymour, the king's brother-in-law, who, nine years later, was tried and beheaded for high treason.[11]

THE KNIGHTS HOSPITALLERS. *Gules a cross of Malta argent.*

This placed Baddesley once more at the disposal of the crown, and Edward VI, in 1552, granted the preceptory with its appurtenances to Sir Nicholas Throckmorton.[12]

On the accession of Queen Mary Baddesley was restored to the Knights Hospitallers,[13] but was confiscated by Elizabeth, who, in 1558, restored the manor to John Foster, who had purchased it from Sir Nicholas Throckmorton in 1553.[14]

John died in 1576, leaving as his heir his son Andrew, the estate being charged with annuities payable to his daughter Jane, wife of William Fleming, and to Thomas Sharpe and Margaret his wife.[15]

Andrew was succeeded in 1595 by his son John,[16] who dying without issue in 1597, left the estate to his brother Barrow,[17] who, before 1600, conveyed the manor and rectory of North Baddesley to his cousin

1 Statistics from Bd. of Agric. (1905).
2 Commons Inclosure Awards.
3 Harl. MS. 6603.
4 *V.C.H. Hants*, i, 491.
5 Chan. Inq. p.m. 32 Edw. I, No. 63.
6 Ibid. 22 Ric. II, No. 34. At this date Roger Mortimer earl of March had half a knight's fee in Baddesley, held of him by the master of the Hospital of St. John there.
7 Pipe R. 13 Hen. II. No trace of the grant by the Mortimers to the Hospital can be found.
8 *Feud. Aids*, ii, 318.
9 *V.C.H. Hants*, ii, 187.
10 *Valor Eccl.* (Rec. Com.), 26.
11 Dugdale, *Mon.* vi, 800.
12 Pat. 5 Edw. VI, pt. 3, m. 31. This grant was made 'in reward for services done by him, more especially bringing the first news of victory over the Scots' (Battle of Pinkie). The Baddesley estate was given to him instead of an annuity of £100 previously granted.
13 Dugdale, *Mon.* vi, 807.
14 Feet of F. Hants, Trin. 1 & 2 Phil. and Mary.
15 Chan. Inq. p.m. 18 Eliz. (Ser. 2), pt. 2, No. 65.
16 Ibid. 37 Eliz. (Ser. 2), pt. 1, No. 79.
17 Ibid. 40 Eliz. (Ser. 2), pt. 1, No. 44.

Thomas Fleming, the king's solicitor-general, son of his aunt Jane, wife of William Fleming.[18] He and his son Thomas sold the estate in 1603 to John More, serjeant-at-law,[19] whose heir John died seised in 1622,[20] leaving no children, and on the partition of his property between his sisters, Dowsabella wife of Samuel Dunch, and Anne wife of Edward Hooper, Baddesley fell to the share of the former.[21]

DUNCH. *Sable a cheveron between three castles argent.*

Samuel was succeeded by his son John Dunch, who died in 1668, and by his grandson Major Dunch, successively. On the death of the latter in 1679, his son Wharton inherited Baddesley, and he, dying without issue in 1705, left the estate to his sister Jane, wife of Francis Keck.[22] By the will of the latter, North Baddesley Manor passed to Anthony Chute,[23] and his brother and heir John Chute, of the Vine, sold it to Thomas Dummer, of Cranbury, in 1767, for £5,500.[24]

His extensive property in Hampshire was left by his will, in 1781, to Mr. Thomas Chamberlayne, who subsequently married Mr. Dummer's widow. On the death of her third husband, Sir Nathaniel Dance-Holland, in 1811, the estates passed to the Chamberlayne family,[25] and they are now held by Mr. Tankerville Chamberlayne of Cranbury Park, Winchester, who is lord of the manor.[26]

CHURCH

The church of *ST. JOHN THE BAPTIST* has a chancel and nave of equal width, 15 ft. 9 in., the chancel being 19 ft. 10 in. long to the screen, and the nave 33 ft. 2 in.; at the west of the nave is a small tower, 5 ft. 10 in. by 5 ft. 2 in. within the walls, and over the south doorway of the nave is a porch.

The chancel has been rebuilt at some time in the fifteenth century, and made of the same width as the nave, the junctions with the older masonry being clearly to be seen. The chancel walls are built with good-sized pieces of Bonchurch or some kindred stone, and have a chamfered plinth at the base, which is wanting in the nave. There are no architectural details in the nave earlier than the latter part of the fourteenth century, but the north and south walls may well be older than that time, and it is to be noted that in the porch floor, near the north-east angle, is part of an octagonal shaft of twelfth-century date ornamented with zigzag, perhaps a relic of the former church. Its present position, nearly buried in the floor, may be due to its re-use as the pedestal of a holy-water stone here. The west wall of the nave and the west tower were rebuilt in 1674, as appears from a stone panel in the south wall of the latter bearing this date, with the initials of Major Dunch and the arms of Dunch impaling More.

The chancel has a fifteenth-century east window of three cinquefoiled lights, and on the north and south single square-headed windows of the same date, each of two cinquefoiled lights with a quatrefoil over between pierced spandrels. To the east of the south window is a blocked four-centred doorway, and there are no sedilia or piscina. The roof is of wagon form with moulded ribs and shields at their intersections.

The nave has two windows on the north, the eastern of the two being a modern copy of the other. This is of late fourteenth-century date, and has a square head, with two trefoiled lights and a quatrefoil over. In the south wall are two windows, the eastern of which is a very charming specimen of late fourteenth-century work, of two cinquefoiled lights with a six-foiled opening in the arched head, and an external label with angels at the springing. The other window, west of the doorway, is of two lights under a square head, and set high in the wall to light the west gallery, and of seventeenth or eighteenth-century date. The doorway is plain work, probably of the fifteenth century, of two continuous hollow chamfered orders with a four-centred head. The porch may be contemporary with it, and has low stone walls on east and west carrying a timber framework with uncusped ogee-headed openings, now boarded up. Its south gable is filled in with brickwork. The nave roof, though of the same width as that of the chancel, is slightly the higher of the two; its timbers are modern.

The west tower, the top of which is but little above the ridge of the nave roof, is of red brick with an embattled parapet and narrow slits in the upper stage, and was built in 1674. Below, a modern west window of fifteenth-century style has been inserted, and above it is a panel with the initials of the churchwardens for 1674, Simon Tredgo and Thomas Compton. The eastern arch is tall, narrow, and round-headed, and access to the bells is by a ladder only.

The screen between chancel and nave is inscribed 'TF 1602,' for Sir Thomas Fleming, and is a very pretty piece of work of the date, panelled below, and with an open balustrade above, carrying a carved and moulded top rail. The head of the central doorway is framed in between the posts, some 2 ft. below the top rail, and the space between is filled with small balusters. Local tradition has it that this screen came from North Stoneham, and Sir Thomas Fleming's initials would not be against the theory. The width of nave and chancel at North Stoneham is 7 in. less than that at Baddesley, but there is some new work at the ends of the screen, and the width of the old work is almost exactly 15 ft. 2 in., which would fit the Stoneham position. The pulpit is also of early seventeenth-century date, with inlaid panels and octagonal tester; an hour-glass stand was formerly fastened to it. The west gallery has an eighteenth-century panelled font, and in the chancel on the north side is a shelf to which a Bible of the 1611 edition is fastened by a chain.

Against the north wall of the chancel is set a raised tomb with panelled sides and a Purbeck marble top slab. It is clearly not in its original condition. The slab, 6 ft. 5½ in. long, is complete, but the panelled

18 Feet of F. Hants, Trin. 43 Eliz. He did not gain possession through the death of Barrow, for he was living in 1605; see Recov. R. Hil. 3 Jas. I, rot. 102.

19 Add. MS. 3328, fol. 185*b*; Feet of F. Hants, East. 1 Jas. I.

20 W. and L. Inq. p.m. 19 Jas. I (Ser. 2), bdle. 33, No. 87.

21 Ibid.

22 John Marsh, *Mem. of Parishes of Hursley and North Baddesley*, 1808; Feet of F. Div. Cos. Trin. 5 Anne.

23 Somers. Ho. 14, Abbot.

24 Close, 7 Geo. III, pt 13, No. 6.

25 John Marsh, *Mem of Parishes of Hursley and North Baddesley*, 1808.

26 Information supplied by Mr. T. Chamberlayne.

North Baddesley Church : Interior looking West

Botley : The Market Place

sides have been shortened at each end to fit it, showing that the slab was no part of the original tomb. The sides have quatrefoiled panels, with shields bearing the cross of the Hospitallers, and between each pair of such panels a narrower panel with a smaller quatrefoil above a shield charged with three chapes on a bend. The same coat occurs in old glass in the east window, the tinctures being gules with the bend or and the three chapes azure. In the window and on the tomb the letter T also occurs, as a capital letter only on the tomb, and both as capital and small in the window. The tomb is clearly that of a Hospitaller, and of the first half of the fifteenth century, but the arms do not help to an identification of the person.

MORE. *Ermine a cheveron sable between three Moors' heads sable with two swords argent on the cheveron.*

In the north-east angle of the chancel is the mural monument of John More, 1620, and his son who died two years later, aged twenty. The inscription is on a tablet framed by Tuscan columns carrying a rounded pediment with heraldry, and below is a medallion with a putto on a skull, holding a winged book in his right hand. In the chancel floor are several slabs to the Dunch family, and at the south door of the nave is a Purbeck marble coffin slab. In the nave floor is a large marble slab, 8 ft. 6 in. by 3 ft. 10 in., with indents for an inscription plate and a heart-shaped sinking.

The font, which stands a little to the east of the south door of the nave, is of Purbeck marble, with an octagonal bowl, stem, and base. The details of the base suggest a fourteenth-century date.

There are two bells, the treble being blank, and the second inscribed 'RB 1595.' They are hung to shallow stocks which have a long projection at one end to which the bell-rope is fastened.

The communion cup and cover paten are of 1618, and there is a standing paten of 1716, inscribed 'For ye Communion Table in Badsly 1716,' and two modern cruets.

The first book of the registers runs from 1682 to 1816, the marriages not being entered in this book after 1754. The churchwardens' accounts are complete from 1674, the building of the west tower being noted in the first year.

ADVOWSON The church of North Baddesley is mentioned in the Domesday Survey; but, like the manor, it had passed into the possession of the Knights of St. John of Jerusalem before 1167,[27] although no particulars of the grant can be found. The church remained with the Knights Hospitallers until the dissolution of the monasteries, and was granted with the manor to Sir Thomas Seymour in 1539.[28] Since that date the history of the advowson is identical with that of North Baddesley Manor (q.v.).

There are no endowed charities.

BOTLEY

Botelie (xi cent.); Bottele (xiii cent.).

The parish of Botley, comprising nearly 2,037 acres, of which 23 are covered by water, is situated in the Fareham division of the county. The ground is slightly undulating, having an average altitude of 50 ft., but at one point in the west, and another in the north of the parish, at Braxell's Farm, it rises as much as 100 ft. above the ordnance datum.

The greater part of the land is under cultivation, 667 acres are permanent grass, and 245 acres are occupied by woods and plantations.[1]

The principal crops raised are wheat, barley, oats, and roots. Strawberry-growing is the principal industry of the place, which provides the markets at London and Southampton. In the extreme south are clay-pits which formerly supplied material for the Hoe Moor brickworks, now closed, and the gravel pits in the east of the parish are now no longer used.

The two small wharves which constitute Botley Harbour are now almost deserted, for the timber trade which originally made it important has vanished. Formerly timber used to be brought into the mills and either sawn up or roughly dressed and floated down the river to the waiting ships. The hoop-making trade, which employed a number of hands, has disappeared, and the old paper-mill near Curdridge, known as Frog's Mill, where the paper for the *Morning Post* was formerly manufactured, is now disused.

Just above the bridge is a large mill, reputed to be the largest in Hampshire, the wheel of which is turned by a stream which rises beyond Bishop's Waltham. This is evidently the mill referred to by William Cobbett in his *Rural Rides*, when describing a mill turned by fresh water which falls into the salt water, as at Beaulieu.

The small market town of Botley stands on the River Hamble, which is here tidal and navigable for barges, at the junction of the high roads from Winchester and Fareham, and is for the most part built along a main street running east and west, widening out to a market-place, and continued eastward over the river. In the market-place are a few large buildings, the most important being the Market Hall, originally built by the Farmers' Club in 1848, and now vested in trustees nominated by the club or the parish. It stands on the south side, with a portico in front, and a turret with a clock above, and though in itself of no particular merit, gives an air of importance to the place, and groups with several good red-brick buildings in a very satisfactory manner.

One side of the market-place belongs to the lord of the manor, who used to collect the tolls there at the fortnightly markets, which are no longer held. These tolls are now leased to the Market Hall trustees, who have also charge of the public weigh-bridge. There is a yearly root show held by the Farmers' Club.

From the north-east corner of the market-place the road to Winchester branches off, bordered with houses for some little distance. One of these, on the east side, is a pretty seventeenth-century timber building with a projecting upper story. On this road is a

[27] Pipe Roll, 13 Hen. II.

[28] Dugdale, *Mon.* vi, 800

[1] Statistics from Bd. of Agric. (1905).

Congregational chapel. In the main street are the schools erected in 1855, and now capable of accommodating 190 children.

On the south side of the road, opposite the schools, is the parish church of All Saints, erected in 1836 to replace the old church about a mile to the south of the village, of which now only the chancel remains. The Church Farm, close to the old church, is in part an old timber-framed building, and has on the first floor, at the back of the kitchen chimney, a large smoke-room for curing bacon.

In the north, situated near the river, is a brewery belonging to Messrs. Edwards Limited, supplied from a malt-house in Church Lane, on the south side of the village.

A few mud cottages on an uninclosed common, tenanted by labourers and squatters, have, since the inclosure of Botley Common in 1863, become the populous and thriving village of Hedge End, which contains the church of St. John the Evangelist, built in 1874, and endowed two years later by the Ecclesiastical Commissioners, a vicarage adjoining the church also being built.

The ecclesiastical parish thus formed was constituted a civil parish in 1894, containing 1,694 acres.[2] Botley Grange, standing in a deer park, and Netley Firs are seats in Hedge End.

Botley Hill in the south is the seat of R. A. Bayford, K.C., and in its grounds is the site of the house in which Cobbett lived for many years. Steeple Court, standing on some rising ground above the parish wharf, once the residence of the Warners, lords of the manor, is occupied by the widow of the late Admiral Colomb.

Admiral Rowley lives at Holmesland, a renovated farm-house on the Swaythling road, opposite the vicarage.

The following place names occur :—Mattocksford, Boorley, Wildern.

In 1889 fragments of tiles and tessellated pavement were found at Fairthorn, south of Botley, pointing to its having been the site of a Roman villa.[3]

MANOR *BOTLEY*, which had been a royal manor held of King Edward by a certain Cheping, belonged to Ralf de Mortimer at the time of the Domesday Survey,[4] and remained in the Mortimer family until the early part of the fourteenth century, when the overlordship rights apparently lapsed.[5]

In the thirteenth century the manor was held of the Mortimers by a family which took the name of Botley. In 1263 John de Botley obtained 1½ virgates of land there by a deed of gift from Thomas de la Durhirde and Alice his wife,[6] John de Langrude releasing to him his title to the same land, in exchange for land in Preston Candover.[7] Four years later John de Botley[8] obtained a royal grant of a weekly market, an annual fair, and free warren in his manor.[9] Brian de Botley, who probably succeeded John, further increased his property here in 1281 by the acquisition of land and wood from Thomas le Moyne and Margery his wife.[10]

Thomas de Botley, who held Botley manor with its appurtenances at the beginning of the next century, granted his whole estate here in 1304 to John bishop of Winchester, Robert de Harwedon, and Simon de Fareham,[11] probably under a trust for the endowment of the chapel of Saint Elizabeth without Winchester, to which, three years later, the estate was conveyed (by licence for alienation in mortmain).[12]

From this time until the dissolution of the monasteries Botley remained in the possession[13] of the college.

Thomas Wriothesley, earl of Southampton, at this time obtained by royal grant many of the lands formerly held by the religious houses of Hampshire ; among others, Botley manor and church.[14] He died in 1550, leaving a son and heir Henry, then a minor.[15] The latter died in 1582,[16] when the estate passed to his son Henry, third earl of Southampton, who died whilst abroad on the king's service in 1624.[17]

Thomas his son and heir became Lord High Treasurer in 1660, and held the manor until his death without heirs male in 1667. Elizabeth, wife of Edward Noel, first earl of Gainsborough, the elder of his two daughters and co-heirs, inherited most of his property in Hampshire, including the manor of Botley. On the death of their only son without issue, Botley descended to their granddaughter Elizabeth, wife of William Bentinck, first duke of Portland.[18] It remained in her possession until the year 1775, when it was sold to the Rev. Richard Eyre, whose son succeeded him in 1823. Ten years later the manor once more changed hands, when it was purchased by James Warner, the famous agriculturist, and friend of William Cobbett.[19] These two were the original founders of the Botley and South Hants Farmers' Club, and a statue to the memory of the former stands in the Market Hall of Botley.[20] On the death of James Warner the manor passed through the Warner family to Mr. J. C. Warner, solicitor, of Winchester, who now holds it.[21] The market, fair, and right of free warren, granted to John de Botley in the thirteenth century, were confirmed to St. Elizabeth's College later in 1447, by Henry VI, and at the Dissolution were granted with Botley manor to Sir Thomas Wriothesley,[22] and the market held until recently on every alternate Monday was a survival of the ancient grant of Henry III. Record is found of certain holders of small portions of land in Botley in the fourteenth and fifteenth centuries,[23] but none attained to any importance, and it is impossible to identify these small holdings at the present day. A messuage called 'The Sign of the Swan,' with land in Botley, formed the subject of a Chancery suit in

[2] Information supplied by Rev. R. E. Payne, vicar of Hedge End.
[3] *V.C.H. Hants*, i, 310.
[4] Ibid. i, 490*a*.
[5] Chan. Inq. p.m. 11 Edw. III (1st Nos.), 49 ; ibid. 21 Edw. III, No. 57 ; ibid. 22 Ric. II, No. 34.
[6] Feet of F. Hants, 47 Hen. III, No. 533.
[7] Ibid. No. 546.
[8] *Testa de Nevill* (Rec. Com.), 233*b*.
[9] Chart. R. 51 Hen. III, No. 7.
[10] Feet of F. Hants, 9 Edw. I, No. 62.
[11] Ibid. East. 32 Edw. I.
[12] *Cal. of Pat.* 1307–13, p. 20.
[13] *Feud. Aids*, ii, pp. 318, 351.
[14] Pat. 35 Hen. VIII, pt. 9, m. 6, 7.
[15] Chan. Inq. p.m. 4 Edw. VI, pt. 1 (Ser. 2), No. 103.
[16] Ibid. 24 Eliz. pt. 1 (Ser. 2), No. 46.
[17] *Dict. Nat. Biog.*
[18] Ibid. See also Titchfield Manor.
[19] Information supplied by Mr. J. C. Warner.
[20] Certain manorial rights have now been virtually given over to the trustees of the Market Hall.
[21] Information received from Mr. J. C. Warner.
[22] Pat. 35 Hen. VIII, pt. 9, m. 6 and 7.
[23] Feet of F. Hants, Trin. 3 Edw. II ; ibid. Trin. 5 Hen. VI ; ibid. Mich. 11 Hen. VI.

the middle of the sixteenth century, but no trace of it now exists.[24]

At the dissolution of the monasteries, Wherwell Abbey held among other lands *MATTOCKESFORD* in Botley,[25] which was granted with them to Lord De La Warr. In 1579 Mattockesford was in the possession of the marquis of Winchester,[26] and remained in his family until 1629,[27] when it was sold by George Paulet to John Forde.[28] No further record is to be found of the place, but Maddoxford Farm, in the north-east of the parish of Botley, is probably a relic of this so-called manor of Mattockesford.

CHURCHES Of the old church of *ALL SAINTS* only the chancel is now left standing. It measures 31 ft. by 16 ft. 6 in., and is of thirteenth-century date, built of freestone rubble with a red-tiled roof. It has a fifteenth-century east window of three cinquefoiled lights under a square head, and in the north and south walls are three windows, a square-headed two-light window with modern tracery between two small lancets. Between the second and third windows on the south was a small doorway, now blocked, the entrance to the chancel being now from the west, by a doorway made up of twelfth-century fragments, set in a rough blocking wall which takes the place of the chancel arch. The roof retains its old trussed rafters, and on its west end is a small wooden bell-cote containing a single bell.

The church now in use, in the main street of the village, was built in 1836, and has a shallow chancel added in 1859, with a south vestry, and a wide nave, to which a north aisle was added in 1892, and in 1895 a west porch of the full width of the nave. The tower at the south-west, of yellow brick, is part of the 1836 work.

The building is an uninteresting specimen of its time, which has been to some extent gothicized by the later alterations; the only ancient features which it contains are the font, a monument in the south wall, and the bells.

The font, which is said to have been dug up on the river bank, is a roughly-shaped round bowl, its base cut back to a hexagonal shape at some later time. Its ornament is equally rough, and though doubtless of twelfth-century date, is probably not quite so early as it looks. A band of cable moulding runs round the top of the bowl, and a band of lozenge ornament lower down, the space between being divided into panels by vertical lines of lozenge or cable moulding, in which are round arched arcades—in one case of three interlacing arches, and in the others of two arches side by side. The tomb recess in the south wall, *c.* 1330, has a cinquefoiled arch with a crocketed label, and contains the contemporary effigy of an unknown civilian. He is clean-shaven, with long curled hair, and wears a close-fitting tunic over which is a full-sleeved gown reaching half-way down the leg. His feet rest on a lion. The effigy has been supposed to represent John de Botley, but must be some fifty years later than his time.

There are three bells, all with marks of Wokingham bell-founders, and probably dating from *c.* 1420. The treble bears the marks of a groat, a lion's face, and a cross; the second has the two latter marks, and an inscription, 'Sancte Petre or̄,' while the tenor, with the same marks, has 'Sancta Anna ora pro nobis.' There is also a small clock bell dated 1784.

The plate comprises a communion cup, paten, flagon, and almsdish of 1772, and modern copies of the cup and paten made in 1871.

The first book of registers goes from 1679 to 1778, the marriages stopping at 1754; the second has marriages 1754–1812, and the third baptisms and burials 1779–1812.

ADVOWSON The church of Botley, with the manor, belonged to Ralf de Mortimer at the time of the Domesday Survey.[29] Thomas de Botley, holding the manor at the beginning of the fourteenth century, also held with it the advowson, both of which were alienated to the chapel of St. Elizabeth, near Winchester. Until the eighteenth century the advowson shares the same history as the manor, but it was not sold with the manor of Botley by the first duke of Portland, but remained as a possession of successive dukes until 1855,[30] when it was purchased by Mr. H. Lee. He presented the living in 1856 to the late Rev. J. Morley Lee, canon of Winchester, who also inherited the patronage a little later.[31] It is a rectory now in the gift of, and since 1903 has been held by, the Rev. E. C. Osborne, M.A.

CHARITIES In 1842 Elizabeth Penford by will bequeathed £500 consols, one moiety for certain poor of the parish and one moiety for Curdridge (see Bishop's Waltham combined charities). The sum of £250 consols belonging to this parish is held by the official trustees. The dividends, amounting to £6 5*s.*, were in 1905 applied in gifts of £1 0*s.* 10*d.* to each of six recipients.

In 1890 Mrs. Sophia Kidgell Warner by will left £60 £2 10*s.* per cent. annuities for keeping in order the churchyard of the old parish church.

In 1904 Mrs. Elizabeth Warner by her will left £100 consols, the dividends to be added to the church repair fund. The two sums of stock are held by the official trustees.

The Market Hall and yard were acquired by deeds of 29 September, 1858, and 25 August, 1884. In 1905 the income derived from rent of the hall, hire of tables, &c., amounted to £40, of which £20 was expended in insurance, repairs, &c., and superintendent's salary, and the yearly balance had accumulated to £161.

In 1887, by deed dated 31 December of that year, and made between Henry Jenkins of the one part and James Clark and Alfred Pern of the other part, 4 acres of land were conveyed for the purposes of a recreation ground. By an order of the Charity Commissioners dated 27 September, 1898, the parish council of Botley were appointed trustees, and a scheme established for its administration.

For Sir Henry Jenkins's memorial scholarship, see Curdridge in Bishop's Waltham.

Parish of Hedge End.

The poor's allotment consists of 2 acres, producing £3 10*s.* a year, which—subject to a rent-charge of £2—is applied in the repair of the fences, &c. There are also 3 acres used as a recreation ground.

24 Early Chan. Proc. bdle. 57, No. 96.
25 *V.C.H. Hants*, i, 137*a*.
26 Pat. 21 Eliz. pt. 7.
27 Chan. Inq. p.m. 42 Eliz. (Ser. 2), vol. 262, No. 125; Feet of F. Hants, East. 43 Eliz.; W. and L. Inq. p.m. 20 Jas. I (Ser. 2), bdle. 35, No. 90.
28 Feet of F. Hants, Hil. 4 Chas. I.
29 *V.C.H. Hants*, i, 490*a*.
30 Inst. Bks. P.R.O.
31 Information supplied by Rev. J. Morley Lee.

CHILWORTH

Celeworda (xi cent.), Cheleworth (xiv cent.), Chylworth (xv cent.).

The parish of Chilworth, covering about 1,540 acres, with a population of 245, is situated in the New Forest division of the county, about five miles north of Southampton.

Tanners Brook is the only natural waterway in the parish, and forms part of the western boundary. The land, which has an average height of 150 ft., slopes up gradually to the centre of the parish, which is 200 ft. above the ordnance datum. It is fertile and densely wooded. Lords Wood in the south and Chilworth Common in the south-east cover a considerable portion of the parish. There are 785 acres of wood, 312 acres of arable, and 287 acres of permanent grass land.[1]

The soil is loam or sand, the subsoil gravel, and that portion which is cultivated yields rich crops of wheat, barley, and oats. It is, however, especially favourable for the production of oak, which here grows in great luxuriance.

The village of Chilworth is very small, and consists of a few thatched cottages and barns in a little hollow, on the main road from Romsey to Botley. The small parish church stands to the north of the village on higher ground. The children from this village attend the schools at North Baddesley.

In the south of the parish, towards Southampton, are Chilworth Manor, owned by Mr. J. E. A. Willis Fleming; Chilworth Towers, which belongs to Miss Fortescue; and Ingersley, the property of Mr. H. E. Sugden. Near Chilworth Court, the residence of Mr. C. Simpson, is an old gravel-pit, but this, like the clay-pit in the east, is now disused.

MANOR At the time of the Domesday Survey *CHILWORTH* belonged to Bernard Pauncefoot, to whom it, with four other manors in Hampshire, had passed from Earl Godwin. Then, as in the time of King Edward, it was assessed at two hides, and amongst its appurtenances were three houses in Southampton.[2]

The overlordship of the manor passed from the crown to the Bohuns, earls of Hereford and Essex, before the middle of the thirteenth century,[3] and remained in that family until the end of the succeeding century,[4] after which no trace of their retaining any title to Chilworth is found, and it seems probable that their rights had lapsed.[5]

Agnes Peverel was holding lands in Chilworth as early as 1230, when a dispute concerning the boundary between her estate and that of the abbot of Hyde in North Stoneham[6] was settled by a perambulation. She still held the same, for half a knight's fee, in 1270,[7] and her son Thomas, who died in 1306, left Chilworth to his grandson and heir, William Peverel.[8]

BOHUN. *Azure a bend argent cotised or between six lions or.*

William's property in Chilworth is described in the inquisition taken at his death in 1337 as a manor, which descended to his son Henry.[9] He died in 1363,[10] and two years later Chilworth Manor was sold by his son Thomas to Thomas Tyrell, knt., of Essex,[11] who prior to the year 1372 conveyed it to John Daccombe,[12] in whose family the manor remained for the next century. It was held by Thomas Daccombe in 1477,[13] and sixty years later it was purchased from his son John by John Dowse,[14] who, dying in 1558, left it to his youngest son Thomas, in tail-male.[15] During the latter half of the sixteenth century Thomas and Richard Dowse, grandsons of John Dowse, succeeded in recovering a sum of £300 from John Daccombe, which they claimed under the agreement made between John Daccombe and John Dowse at the date of the sale of the manor.[16]

Richard, who in 1602 succeeded to the Chilworth estate on the death of his father,[17] shortly afterwards conveyed the estate to John More, serjeant-at-law,[18] who died in 1620.[19] His son and heir survived him only a few months, and Chilworth passed to a younger daughter, Anne wife of Edward Hooper, of Hurn Court,[20] and from them to their son Sir Edward Hooper, who held the manor in 1676,[21] the entail having been barred in 1671.[22] Before 1714, however, the manor, with the advowson, had passed to Gilbert Serle,[23] probably by purchase, although the exact date of the transfer cannot be found. The Serles continued as lords of the manor for the next century.[24] Peter Serle, who succeeded his father Peter in 1782, was a philanthropist who endowed many charities in the parish of Chilworth and the surrounding districts, and rebuilt the church in 1812.

In 1825 he conveyed the Chilworth estate to John Fleming, who was to enter into possession on Peter's decease, subject to the payment of a jointure of £600 to Charlotte Malazena Serle.[25] Mr. Fleming obtained the manor in 1827, and it is now in the possession of his grandson, Mr. John E. A. Willis-Fleming.

1 Statistics from Bd. of Agric. 1905.

2 *V.C.H. Hants*, i, 491*a*.

3 *Testa de Nevill* (Rec. Com.), 231.

4 In 1306, however, it is stated in an inquisition taken at the death of Thomas Peverel that Chilworth was held of Robert de Hauvile (Chan. Inq. p.m. 34 Edw. I, No. 51), and in 1337 Chilworth was held of Robert's son Alan de Hauvile.

5 Chan. Inq. p.m. 46 Edw. III, No. 792.

6 *Cal. of Close*, 1227–31, p. 407.

7 *Testa de Nevill* (Rec. Com.), 231.

8 Chan. Inq. p.m. 34 Edw. I, No. 51; *Feud. Aids*, ii, 318.

9 Chan. Inq. p.m. 10 Edw. III, No. 43.

10 Ibid. 36 Edw. III, pt. 2 (1st Nos.), 24.

11 Close, 38 Edw. III, m. 32, 28.

12 Chan. Inq. p.m. 45 Edw. III (2nd Nos.), 48.

13 Feet of F. Hants, East. 16 Edw. IV.

14 Ibid. Mich. 1 Edw. VI.

15 Chan. Inq. p.m. 1 & 2 Eliz. (Ser. 2), vol. 999, No. 30.

16 Chan. Proc. (Ser. 2), bdle. 52, No. 11. Between 1560 and 1591 there are several documents recording settlements of the manor by Thomas Dowse; Recov. R. East. 3 Eliz. rot. 621; ibid. 5 Eliz. rot. 740; Feet of F. Hants, East. 10 Eliz.; ibid. 16 Eliz.; ibid. 33 Eliz.

17 Chan. Inq. p.m. 44 Eliz. pt. 2 (Ser. 2), No. 105.

18 Feet of F. Hants, Trin. 7 Jas. I.

19 W. and L. Inq. p.m. 18 Jas. I (Ser. 2), bdle. 31, No. 31.

20 Ibid. 19 Jas. I (Ser. 2), bdle. 33, No. 87; Lay Subsidy Rolls, 15 Chas. II, $\frac{176}{563}$; Recov. R. East. 22 Chas. II, R. 168.

21 Close, 27 Chas. II, pt. 15, No. 23.

22 Ibid. 22 Chas. II, pt. 18, No. 19.

23 Feet of F. Div. Cos. Mich. 12 Anne.

24 *Ex inform.* F. H. T. Jervoise; Recov. R. Mich. 12 Geo. II, rot. 16.

25 John Fleming's Estates Act, 1854.

CHURCH The church (? dedication unknown), built by Peter Serle in 1812, the first stone being laid on 16 September, has a chancel, shallow transepts, nave and west tower in a dull and plain 'Gothic' style, the whole covered with Roman cement outside and plaster inside, and having a wood and plaster vault. The transepts were built to contain the comfortable pews of the period, and had fireplaces, and the fittings generally were such as might be expected. The stained glass of the east window, representing the four evangelists, cost £160. Nothing of the former church is preserved except the font, which has a square shallow bowl of Purbeck marble, of late twelfth-century date, and formerly much deeper; on the underside are the capitals of the four angle shafts on which, with a central shaft, it stood. The shafts are lost, and the bowl is now balanced on a wooden post.

In the tower are two small bells, both blank, but of very early type, with domed crowns, straight sides, and a sound bow of angular section on the inner face. They may date as far back as the twelfth century, and are probably the two oldest bells in the county. Bells of this early type are to be met with here and there at very wide intervals all over England, but that two such bells should have survived together is an event of the greatest rarity.

The plate, given by G. F. Pitts about the time of the rebuilding of the church, consists of two cups, a flagon, a standing paten, and an almsdish, all plated.

The first book of the registers begins in 1721, and contains the baptisms to 1800, the marriages to 1769, and the burials to 1799. The second has the baptisms and burials 1760 to 1812, and the third the marriages 1744–1811.

ADVOWSON The church of Chilworth is mentioned in Domesday among the lands of Bernard Pauncefoot. Probably the church passed into the possession of the Bohuns in the same way as the manor of Chilworth.[26] It was certainly held by Humphrey de Bohun in the reign of Edward I, for he then confirmed the gift made by his father of the church of Chilworth, with its appurtenances, to St. Denys' Priory, Southampton.[27] The priory continued to hold the church until the Dissolution, after which, in 1550, it was sold by the crown to Nicholas and Roger Prideaux,[28] and before the year 1591 had passed into the possession of Thomas Dowse, lord of the manor.[29] Since that date the advowson and manor of Chilworth have always been held together.[30]

CHARITIES In 1828 George Frederick Pitts by will left £100, interest to be applied in the distribution of bread on Easter Day and Christmas Day. After payment of legacy duty and expenses the balance of the legacy was applied in the purchase of an annuity of £4 charged upon a close known as Smith's Close, now belonging to Mr. John Edward Arthur Willis-Fleming, of Chilworth Manor. The annuity is duly paid and applied.

In 1853 the Hon. Richard George Quin by his will left £800 stock—now represented by £781 18*s.* 10*d.* consols with the official trustees—one moiety of the dividends to be applied in the distribution of clothing, and the other moiety in providing medical aid for the poor of the parish. The dividends, amounting to £19 10*s.*, are applied one-half in clothing and the other half in payment of a doctor's fees.

HAMBLE-LE-RICE

Hamele, xiii cent.

The parish of Hamble-le-Rice, one of the smallest in Hampshire, comprising nearly 950 acres, of which more than half is tidal water or foreshore, lies in the extreme south of the county. It is roughly triangular in shape, and occupies the tongue of land between the mouth of the Hamble River and the eastern bank of Southampton Water. The southern extremity, called Hamble Spit, is a long mud-bank which is completely covered at high tide. Behind the spit lies the common, a flat and barren stretch of about 20 acres.

The village itself, situated in the north-east of the parish, consists of a single street of small river-side cottages, which rises abruptly from the river landing-place to the top of the hill, on which are the church and a few modern villas. The church and vicarage are situated close to the site of the ancient priory, while opposite is Hamble House, the residence of the Rev. Joseph Curling, M.A.

As far back as the fifteenth century the place was famous for its oysters, 20,000 of which the prior of Hamble rendered at mid-Lent to the monks of St. Swithun's as a corrody.[1] An extensive trade is still carried on in shellfish—principally lobsters and crabs—which are imported from Devon and Ireland, and fattened for the market. The majority of the inhabitants are employed in the yacht-building yard situated on the river just above the landing place. The industry is a growing one, the place being peculiarly suitable, for, besides being perfectly sheltered, there is ample accommodation for the laying-up of boats on the excellent mud-berths, where they can be left safely without any fear of their becoming foul.

There is a little general farming, and the soil, which is light, on a gravel subsoil, is suitable for growing small crops of wheat, oats, and barley. There are 380 acres of arable land, and 297 acres of permanent grass in the parish.[2] Hamble, however, is residential rather than agricultural, owing to its salubrity.

A little higher up the river than the village is anchored the *Mercury*, a training ship financed by Mr. C. A. R. Hoare, one of the well-known banking firm, in which boys are trained for the navy and army or the mercantile marine service.

On the Netley road, which connects Hamble with the parish of Hound, stands Sydney Lodge, the seat of the earl of Hardwicke, while the Hon. Mrs. Eliot

[26] Cf. Hist. of manor.
[27] *V.C.H. Hants*, ii, 160.
[28] Pat. 3 Edw. VI, pt. 5, m. 18–21.
[29] Feet of F. Div. Cos. East. 33 Eliz.
[30] Ibid. Mich. 1664, 16 Chas. II; ibid. 12 Anne; Recov. R. Mich. 12 Geo II, rot. 16.
[1] *Arch. Journ.* vii, 158–9.
[2] Statistics from the Bd. of Agric. (1905).

Yorke lives at 'Hamble Cliff,' near to Netley Hospital. 'Ravenswood' is a large house facing the river, owned by Mr. A. G. Beale, and in School Lane is the house of Sir John Fullerton, late captain of the royal yacht. Other important houses are the manor house, occupied by Colonel Dugmore, J.P., 'The Copse,' occupied by Mr. H. Emmons, and Grantham Cottage, the residence of the Hon. Alexander Yorke.

MANOR

There is no mention of *HAMBLE-LE-RICE* in Domesday, but by the middle of the twelfth century monks from the great Benedictine abbey of Tiron were settled here, having obtained the land from William Giffard, bishop of Winchester (1100–38).[3]

Hamble remained a cell of the abbey of Tiron for more than two centuries, during which period the prior probably leased the manor to laymen.[4]

Edward I in 1294 seized most of the alien priories in England owing to the war with France. At that time the possessions of Hamble Priory do not seem to have been considerable, and the total annual value is given at £18 14*s.* 8*d.*[5]

The French at this time made an expedition against England, and wrought considerable havoc on the south coast towns of Hampshire.[6] The possessions of the Hamble monks suffered so severely that exemption from the payment of farm rent was granted them, that they might rebuild and repair.[7]

In 1391 William of Wykeham, bishop of Winchester, bought Hamble-le-Rice with its appurtenances, for the endowment of St. Mary's College, Winchester,[8] with which it still remains.

WINCHESTER COLLEGE. *Argent two cheverons sable between three roses gules.*

The wardens of the college did not come into full possession until later in 1401, on the death of Sir Bernard Brocas and Tidman the monk, on whom Hamble had been settled for their lives during the French war by the king.[9]

A considerable sum of money was then spent on improvements, and the manor was provided with a new dovecote.[10]

CHURCH

The church of *ST. ANDREW* has a chancel and nave of equal width, 19 ft., and approximately equal length, about 43 ft. in each case. The unusual proportion is due to the fact that the chancel was the church of the alien priory of Hamble, while the nave served for that of the parish. There is a modern vestry on the north of the chancel, and a large modern chapel on the south-west, and the nave has a north-west porch and a west tower. At the junction of the nave and chancel are north and south doorways, the latter now opening by a curved passage to the south chapel, and the former blocked; it seems to have led into a small square porch or turret which had a doorway at the west. Traces of what seems to have been a second instance of this may be seen at Idsworth. The nave and west tower are of twelfth-century date, while the chancel belongs to the thirteenth century, and was probably rebuilt about 1250 round an older and narrower chancel. It has a fine east window of three uncusped lights with cusped circles in the head, two quatrefoiled and one septfoiled; the rear arch is moulded and has engaged shafts in the jambs. On the north side is a widely-splayed lancet at the east, and a pair of similar windows at the west, with the modern vestry door between them; to the west of the single lancet is a wide arched recess in the wall rebated for a door. The south wall had a pair of lancets at the east, of which one yet remains perfect, but the other has been partly destroyed in building the new south chapel; below the remaining lancet is a very fine cinquefoiled piscina recess with two drains, and a single sedile, quite plain except for an edge chamfer; both are of the date of the chancel. The nave has a single twelfth-century round-headed light at the north-east, and no other window in this wall, but on the south are a pair of wide round-headed lights, splayed like the pair of lancets in the chancel, but with nook-shafts and capitals of late twelfth-century detail, the middle capital being foliate. To the west are two more lancets under a single head with a plastered rear arch. The north and south doorways at the east end of the nave are of twelfth-century date, the southern having a plain round head and the other a line of zigzag on its inner order. The turret or porch into which it opened was of the same date, the south jamb of its western doorway, with a foliate capital, still remaining on the nave wall. The principal doorway of the nave is at the north-west, close to the west end, under a fifteenth-century porch, and has a segmental arch with a label and zigzag on the outer order, the inner order being plain and slightly pointed, while the outer is round-headed. In the jambs are single nook-shafts with foliate capitals, and the abacus of the east jamb is moulded in late twelfth-century style, while the other is plain and has been recut. There is a recess for holy water inside the nave to the east of the doorway. The north porch is probably of the fifteenth century, with a chamfered outer arch.

The tower is of three stages, faced with small ashlar stones; it is probably not later than 1140, and has had plain round-headed belfry windows, into which cinquefoiled fifteenth-century heads have been inserted; the plain parapet is also of the fifteenth century. In the second stage on the west is a wide round-headed window with zigzag in the arch and nook-shafts with foliate capitals of fairly early style; its opening has probably been widened. At the base of each of these stages is a string with billet moulding. In the ground stage are blocked archways, 4 ft. wide, cut straight through the wall, in the north and south walls; that on the north has a semicircular head, while the other is segmental; they may have been made for the purpose of a procession path round the west end of the church, and the existing west boundary of the churchyard supports the idea, if it occupies the ancient line. The arch opening from

[3] The original charter is not extant, but from the names of the witnesses to a confirmation of the grant now among the Winchester College muniments, it could not have been later than 1140; *V.C.H. Hants*, ii, 221–6.

[4] *Arch.* l, 251–62. One lease bearing the date 1320 between Prior Beaumont and one John Poussant, of all services and customs at Hamble Manor, is still preserved at Winchester.

[5] *V.C.H. Hants*, ii, 222*a*.

[6] *Cal. of Pat.* 1377–81, p. 535.

[7] Ibid.

[8] Ibid. 1388–92, p. 433.

[9] Pat. 10 Ric. II, pt. 1, m. 37.

[10] *V.C.H. Hants*, ii, 223*a*.

Hamble Church from the North

nave to tower is tall and of a single order, with a semicircular head and a chamfered string at the springing; it is to be noted that it is entirely in the nave wall, and that there is a taller arch built against it on the west with a straight joint, which carries the east wall of the tower. There can be but little difference of date between the two, but the tower and nave are separate buildings, and the east wall of the tower is much thinner than its other walls, presumably for the reason that the support of the west wall of the nave made an equal thickness unnecessary.

A site at a little distance to the south-east is pointed out as that of the monastic buildings of the priory, but no vestige of them remains above ground. It would be natural to suppose that some part of them adjoined the church, but there is little to suggest that this was the case, and the building of the new south chapel may have destroyed some evidence. The western part of the south wall of the nave has no window in it, and on the outer face is an arched recess, 6 ft. 7 in. wide, which has somewhat the appearance of the wall-rib of a vault running in a southerly direction, but there are no other traces of the abutment of a building here. Excavations would doubtless throw light on the matter, and until they are undertaken the question must remain unanswered.

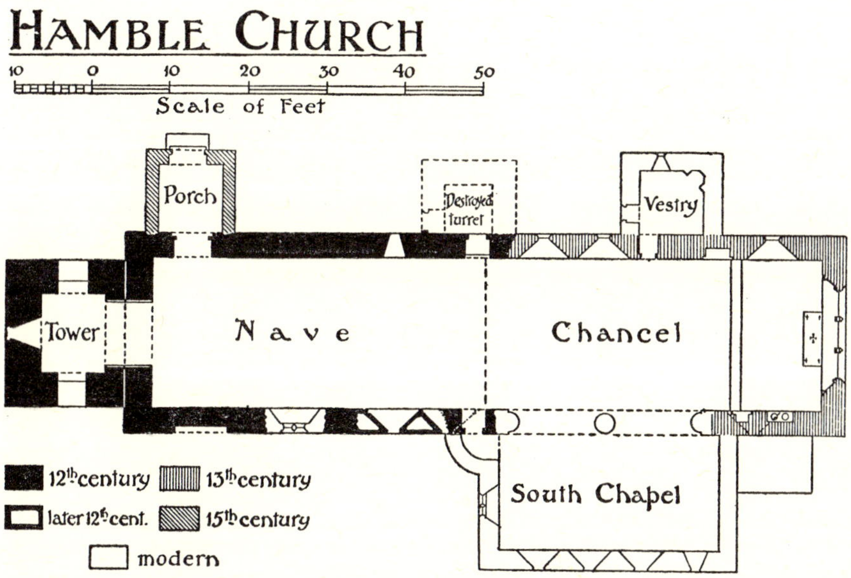

The timbers of both nave and chancel roof are old; they are of the trussed rafter form with tie-beams, king posts, and pole pieces. The north door of the nave is also old, but within the church are no ancient wood fittings. If there was anything in the nature of the *pulpitum* of a monastic church between the chancel and nave it has left no trace, but that some substantial division existed there can be little doubt.

The arrangement of the doorways at the east angles of the parochial nave is interesting, and it may be that a passage ran between them, with the parish altar immediately to the west, the stalls of the monastic quire being returned against the east side of the passage.

The font, which stands under the tower, is modern and of the same design as that in Littlemore Church, Oxfordshire.

There are three bells, the treble and second by Clement Tosier, 1715, and the tenor, a fifteenth-century bell inscribed 'Ave Gracia' in Gothic capitals. The inscription on the treble, like that on the treble at Chilbolton, is a model of bad spelling :—

> Tho I ham but lettel and small all (*sic*)
> I will be hard above tham all.

The plate consists of a cup of 1651, inscribed 'For the church of Hamble, James Carter churchwarden'; a standing paten of 1710, another of 1873, and a flagon of 1863, given 1865.

The oldest register book contains the entries for 1660 to 1715 and 1760 to 1763 for the parishes of Hound, Sachell, Netley, and Sholing; the second contains the Hamble baptisms and burials, 1674–1717; the third the same entries for Hamble, Hound, and Bursledon, 1720–60; the fourth the marriages for the same parishes, 1754–95; the fifth the Hamble marriages, 1759–1801; the sixth the baptisms and burials for Hamble, Hound, and Bursledon, 1760–91; the seventh the Hamble marriages, 1792–1812; and the eighth the same for Hamble, Hound, and Bursledon, 1795–1812.

ADVOWSON The church of Hamble-le-Rice was confirmed to the abbot of Tiron in 1147 by Pope Eugenius III, and again in 1175 by Pope Alexander III.[11] The church was held from this date by the Benedictine monks of the priory of Hamble until the year 1391, when it was sold with the other possessions of the priory to William of Wykeham, to assist in the foundation of his college at Winchester.[12]

From this time the advowson has always been held by the wardens of St. Mary's College.[13]

CHARITIES In 1854 Mrs. Margaret Lind Henville by her will bequeathed to the vicar for the time being a legacy for the poor to be applied in clothing. The trust fund consists of £166 7*s*. 6*d*. consols with the official trustees. The dividends, amounting to £4 3*s*., were in 1905 expended in warm clothing among seven poor persons.

[11] *V.C.H. Hants*, ii, 221*b*; Merlet, *Cartulaire de l'Abbaye de Tiron*, Charters 182, 262, 291, 292, 326, 328.

[12] *Cal. of Pat.* 1388–92, p. 433.

[13] Inst. Bks. P.R.O.

HOUND WITH NETLEY

Hune (xi cent.) ; Howne (xiv cent.) ; Letelie (xi cent.).

The parish of Hound, covering an area of 4,271 acres, of which 301 are foreshore and 458 tidal water, with a population of 4,548 inhabitants, is situated north of Hamble parish, on the peninsula formed by the Southampton Water and the Hamble River with its tributary Badnam's Creek.

In the extreme south is the tithing of Satchell, which is served by the chaplain of the training ship *Mercury*, anchored in the river opposite Hamble village.

The land near the coast is low, and part of the shore which is submerged at high tide consists of a long stretch of mud-bank. There is a gradual slope to the north, however, which is over 100 ft. above the ordnance datum.

There are no natural waterways of any size in the parish, but in the west are two sheets of water, used in earlier times by the monks of Netley as fish-ponds. These were reclaimed by Mr. Chamberlayne, predecessor of the present lord of the manor, at the beginning of the nineteenth century,[1] and are now inclosed in the grounds of 'The Hermitage' and 'The Fishponds.'

The soil is sandy, with a gravel subsoil, and gravel-pits are still worked in many parts. Small crops of wheat, oats, and barley are grown, the land being principally arable, although there are 373½ acres of wood and 357⅓ of permanent grass.[2] A small fishing industry is carried on, the produce of which is mainly absorbed by the hospital.

Hound village, in the centre of the parish, on the outskirts of Butlock's Heath, is a small group of old farmsteads and cottages, surrounding the ancient parish church of St. Mary, said to have been built by Hamble Priory about 1230.

Old Netley, a mile due north of Hound, is a picturesque hamlet of timber-framed cottages with trim old-fashioned gardens.

Netley village, which is rapidly increasing in size, stretches along the sea-front from Netley Abbey, in the vicinity of which are many good houses, to the Royal Victoria Hospital, built in 1856, which with its quarters for officers, grounds, and observatory extends more than half a mile inland. It has also a cemetery attached of about 17 acres, and a recreation ground was presented in 1900 by Mr. Tankerville Chamberlayne in commemoration of the Diamond Jubilee. On a knoll overlooking the abbey ruins stands the new church of St. Edward the Confessor, while between the abbey and the shore is Netley Castle, a large castellated building which is for the most part modern, occupying the site of the fort built here in the sixteenth century. It is now the residence of the Hon. H. Crichton. A little further up the Woolston road, on the north side, is Abbey House, belonging to Miss Rashleigh, and near by is the vicarage. 'The Towers,' a large white house at the other end of the village, the residence of Mrs. Jarrold, has now no claim to its name, as the tower has been pulled down. Netley Market Hall, a large new building of Portland stone, erected by the late Mr. Whitchurch, is used for meetings and assemblies.

The London and South Western Railway passes through the parish from east to west, and has a station at Netley midway between the villages of Hound and Netley Abbey.

There are no inclosure awards : Butlocks Heath in the centre and Netley Common in the extreme north of the parish are wide tracts of open heath country.

At Butlocks Heath, on which are a few modern cottages, there is an elementary school with accommodation for 245 children, and at Netley Abbey there is room for about 113 children. The following place names occur :—Shotteshale (Satchell), Sholing (now in St. Mary Extra).

A hoard of third-century coins was found here in 1867 during excavations at Netley Hospital.[3]

Netley Abbey was first inhabited in 1239 by a colony of Cistercians from Beaulieu, and the foundation having been adopted by Henry III it is probable that sufficient funds were available for the buildings,[3a] and that their construction was pushed on without interruption, so far at least as was necessary for the accommodation of their inmates.

The eastern parts of the church, the chapter-house and dorter range, and the frater with the warming-house and kitchen, were all included in the first work, together with part of the southern end of the western range, the quarters of the lay brothers. The church was not finished till the early years of the fourteenth century, and in the first half of this century the western range of the claustral buildings was completed, and certain alterations made in the novices' room under the great dorter. From this time to the suppression there is no evidence of any important building work, if the vaulting of the south transept of the church be excepted, but the gap might be supplied if some of the detached buildings, of which nothing now remains, such as the infirmary and abbot's house, were to be excavated.

The general plan as set out in the thirteenth century seems to have been carried out without alteration, except as regards the western range, and a great deal of the original work is still standing, giving much information about the arrangements of the house. This is the more valuable because of the late date of the foundation, Netley being in point of date the second of the three great royal Cistercian houses of the thirteenth century [Beaulieu 1204, Netley 1239, and Hailes 1246], the last to be founded in England with the exception of Newnham in Devonshire, 1246, Vale Royal, founded by Edward I, 1277, Rewley, by Richard king of the Romans, 1280, and St. Mary Grace's by the Tower of London, set up in 1349 by Edward III.

The site is well chosen and still very beautiful, though it can no longer be called secluded. The buildings stand in a wooded recess on the east bank of Southampton Water, sheltered by high ground on the north and east, and open only towards the west

[1] William Cobbett, *Rural Rides in Hants*, ii, 255.

[2] Statistics from Board of Agric. (1905).

[3] *V.C.H. Hants*, i, 345.

[3a] Pat. 29 Hen. III, m. 6.

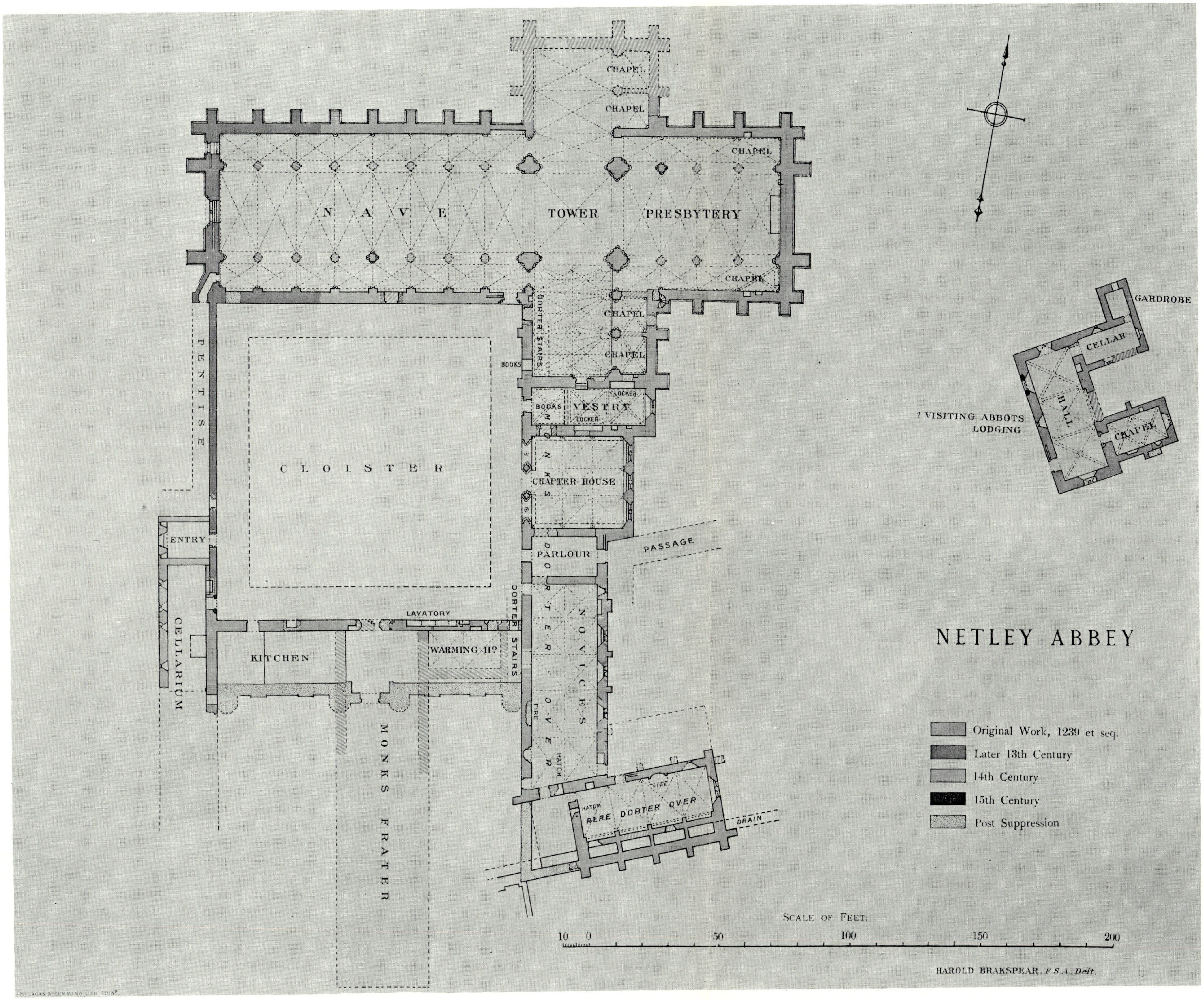
NETLEY ABBEY
CHAPEL
CHAPEL
CHAPEL
NAVE
TOWER
PRESBYTERY
CHAPEL
CHAPEL
CHAPEL
DORTER STAIRS
BOOKS
BOOKS
VESTRY
LOCKER
LOCKER
PENTISE
CLOISTER
MONKS
CHAPTER HOUSE
PARLOUR
PASSAGE
ENTRY
CELLARIUM
LAVATORY
KITCHEN
WARMING H?
DORTER STAIRS
DORTER
NOVICES
OVER
FIRE
HATCH
MONKS FRATER
HATCH
FIRE
RERE DORTER OVER
DRAIN
GARDROBE
CELLAR
HALL
CHAPEL
? VISITING ABBOTS LODGING
Original Work, 1239 et seq.
Later 13th Century
14th Century
15th Century
Post Suppression
SCALE OF FEET.
10 0 50 100 150 200
HAROLD BRAKSPEAR, F.S.A. Delt.
MCLAGAN & CUMMING, LITH. EDINR

and south-west. Netley Castle, standing between the abbey and the water, now shuts off the view on the west, and the main road runs close to the church and cloister on the same side, while houses are springing up on all sides, though hidden from view by the ring of trees which grows on the high bank inclosing the precinct. The bank looks as if it was partly artificial, cut back to make a steeper boundary and to gain more room on the somewhat restricted site, and there is no trace, here or elsewhere, of a stone boundary wall, though such a wall almost certainly existed.

The church stands to the north of the cloister, close to the northern boundary of the site, and is cruciform, its extreme dimensions being 237 ft. by 136 ft. The eastern arm or presbytery has north and south aisles and is of equal width with the nave, 57 ft. within the walls and 60 ft. from east to west, divided into four equal bays. Like all the rest of the church it was designed for a stone vault, and is square-ended, the aisles running as far east as the main span. The walling is of rubble, originally plastered, the columns, responds, windows, &c., being worked in wrought stone, partly from the Isle of Wight and partly Caen stone, the two being used indiscriminately. The aisles are lighted on the north and south by pairs of lancets in each bay, and single lancets at the east, while the great east window of the main span is of four lights, with uncusped lancet heads, having a foiled circle over each pair of lancets and a larger circle in the head. In the inner splay there have been four detached marble shafts, with marble rings of which the bonding ends remain, and the arch is of four moulded orders. All the aisle windows are rebated for wooden frames, but the east window has glass grooves, and is clearly of later date than the wall in which it is set. The arcades, of which only the eastern responds remain, were of three chamfered orders, with round engaged shafts on the cardinal faces of the piers, and moulded capitals and bases; the single respond shafts in the aisle walls being of the same character. Above the main arcades was a three-light clearstory, and at the level of the string at the base of the clearstory sprang the vault, from short marble vaulting shafts resting on foliate corbels in the spandrels of the arches. The vaults were quadripartite with chamfered ribs and rubble fillings, those in the eastern bays of the aisles still remaining in part, while all the rest have fallen.

The section of the ribs in these two bays is different from that elsewhere in the presbytery, having a single wide chamfer instead of a double chamfer, the change of detail marking either a pause in the work or a rebuilding of the vaults. The high vaults belonged to the second type. Below the east window the base of a large altar is still left, with a large fifteenth-century corbel to the north of it, and part of the altar in the south aisle also remains. There is here a double piscina in the south wall with small recesses in its east and west jambs, 12 in. high from the sill, and to the west of it a locker rebated for a door, and having a shelf. In the moulded string, which runs at the level of the window sills, are pinholes at the eastern angles of the aisle, and the same thing occurs in the north aisle. There are no remains of the altar in the north aisle, but at the north-west of the east bay is a rebated recess with a shelf like that opposite, and in the north-east respond of the north arcade a T-shaped groove as if for a wooden bracket, 5 ft. 10 in. above the old floor level.

Of the tower which stood over the crossing only the stumps of the piers are left, the inner orders of the western arch having evidently been corbelled back at some height from the floor level, to give room for the stalls of the monks' quire. There is a curious irregularity in the east side of the south-east pier. The 'foundation stones' of three of the four piers are yet visible. On the north-east pier is *H. dī gra rex angl*, with a shield of England and a cross, for Henry III, on the north-west pier a crown surmounted by a cross, perhaps for the queen, and on the south-west a plain shield with a banner above.

The north transept has been almost entirely destroyed, and parts of it are now set up as a landscape gardener's ruin in Cranbury Park, but its plan was the same as that of the south transept, which is the best preserved part of the church. It is two bays deep, with an eastern aisle formerly divided by thin masonry walls into two chapels, and in the angle formed by the presbytery and transept is a stair in a square turret. The chapels are vaulted, and remain in a fairly perfect condition, the southern of the two being lighted by an east window of two lights under a semicircular head. The northern chapel has only a single lancet on the east, being partly overlapped by the stair turret, and a modern door has been cut through below the window. In the south wall of the south chapel is a piscina, and to the west of it an opening broken through to the vestry. Two bays of the eastern arcade of the transept remain complete, with equilateral arches of three chamfered orders, and moulded capitals and bases; above them is the clearstory with windows of three lancet lights in each bay, and rear arches with engaged shafts in the jambs. The sills of the windows are kept up to clear the former lean-to roof over the chapels, and there is no continuous wall passage here, but each bay was entered through a doorway from the chapel roof. The thirteenth-century vaulting shafts remain in the spandrels of the arcade, being here of coursed stone and not of marble, but the contemporary vault has been replaced—if, indeed, it was ever completed—by an elaborate fifteenth-century vault, of which the embattled springers and southern wall-rib remain, all the rest having fallen.

The outer order of the main arcade on the east side is carried as a blank wall arcade round the other two sides of the transept, and the arrangement of the clearstory on the west is like that on the east, except that the passage is here continuous and the window sills are brought down nearly to its floor level, there being no external roof to block them. On the south wall the clearstory stage is treated as an arcade of two bays, each divided into two arched openings with a blank quatrefoil over, and in the spandrel above the bays is a large circular sixfoiled panel. The night stair to the dorter filled up the south-west part of the transept, opening to a doorway in the south wall at the level of the clearstory. It came to the ground close to the small recess in the west wall of the north bay, which perhaps held a cresset, and the doorway next to it on the south belongs to the post-suppression house, being built up of old materials. In the south wall is a doorway to the vestry. The south gable of the transept stands almost complete, though in the destructive clutch of the ivy, and has a wide lancet opening above the vault, formerly of three lights, which existed within the last thirty years, and on the outer face a small stone bell-cot, the bell in which must have been rung from the north end of the dorter.

The nave is of eight bays, and retains the walls of its aisles and its west wall, but as in the case of the chancel its arcade and clearstory have been entirely destroyed. In each bay on the south side is a wide arched recess, having in the head, above the line of the cloister roof, a window of three trefoiled lights. There is a similar recess in the east bay on the north side, but not in the other bays, and the windows on the north, the first three of which from the east retain their tracery of three trefoiled lights, are longer than those on the south because of the absence of any building on the outside. The recesses on the south side are caused by the thickening of the wall to take the thrust of the aisle vaults, a row of external buttresses like those on the north being impossible here on account of the cloister. At Beaulieu and Hailes the recesses are on the outer face of the wall, towards the cloister. In the south wall are remains of three doorways, the largest being in the east bay; it was the principal entrance to the church from the monastic cloister, and had an arch of three orders with pairs of marble shafts in each jamb. It was mutilated and blocked up after the Suppression, and a second doorway cut in the fourth bay. Of the third or western procession doorway in the eighth bay very slight traces are to be seen, and nothing can be said as to its details.

In the west wall of the nave is a wide central doorway, which has had double doors, and over it a large window which has lost its mullions and tracery.[3a] The gable wall over it has been rebuilt with a level top in red brick. At the ends of the aisles are small west doorways, that on the north with a chamfered arch and moulded label, while the other opens to a diagonal passage opening southwards to a former passage along the west wall of the cloister. Above each door is a trefoiled two-light window, with a quatrefoil in the head. It seems that the aisle vault in the west bay of the north aisle was never built, owing to a change of design in the process of building, and it may be that none of the vaults of the aisles were completed. The evidences of slow and intermittent building are clearly to be seen in the church, by the changes in details. The presbytery and east piers of the tower belong to the earliest work, and the south transept was next begun. In addition to the differences in the profiles of the bases, the later date may be seen in the vaulting shafts, the foliate corbels to those on the west side of the transept being of late thirteenth-century style. The five eastern bays of the south aisle followed, and then the western piers of the crossing, the north transept, and five bays of the north aisle. The two western bays of the nave and the west front belong to the end of the thirteenth century and early part of the fourteenth.

Very slight traces of the actual arrangements of the church remain. The monks' quire was partly under the tower, but did not come as far as the eastern piers, and the destruction of the nave arcades has made it impossible to say how far it extended down the nave.

The lay brothers' quire must have been in the western part of the nave,[4] and their approach to the church was by the passage outside the west wall of the cloister and through the south-west doorway. By the time that the church was being finished they were a far less important item of a Cistercian house than in the twelfth century, and the provision made for them here at Netley may be instructively compared with that at Fountains or Furness. After the Suppression the nave and south transept were turned into living rooms, the first three bays of the nave becoming a large hall, with a doorway from the cloister in the fourth bay and another opposite to it in the north aisle. The arrangement suggests that the screens were here, with the kitchen, &c. to the west, and there are marks of a stone bench, 3 ft. high from the floor, in three of the four western bays of the south aisle. The south-east doorway of the nave was walled up, and that in the south transept made instead of it, and there are traces of the bonding of a brick wall, apparently the east wall of the hall, just west of the line of the western crossing piers. The south transept shows many marks of damage caused by the insertion of floors, and the marks left by the western screens of the chapels are easily to be distinguished from the careless hacking of the later workmen. On the other hand it must be noted that the arcades in the south transept, and the tracery of the windows in the three east bays of the north aisle of the nave, owe their preservation to the fact of their inclusion in the sixteenth-century house.

The cloister, on the south side of the church, is approximately a square of 115 ft., being a little wider on the west than the east. No traces of the inner walls of its four alleys are now to be seen, but they were covered with wooden pent roofs, many of the corbels for which remain. On the east side of the cloister are the south transept, vestry, chapter-house, inner parlour, and novices' room, with the great dorter over. There are two book cupboards, one in the west wall of the south transept, and partly underlying the night stair to the dorter, the other, of much larger size, taking up the west bay of the vestry, and originally cut off from it by a masonry wall 15 in. thick, of which the traces are still to be seen on the plaster of the north and south walls. It opened to the cloister by a pointed doorway with a large pierced trefoil over, inclosed in a moulded arch with roof shafts. The vestry is vaulted in three bays, the wall cells and cross-ribs being nearly semicircular, and has an east window of two lancets under a semicircular head, with wide internal splays and a segmental rear-arch. In the east bay is a tall recess on the north side, rebated for a wooden frame, and on the south side a trefoiled piscina with recesses in the jambs on each side, and a square rebated locker to the west of it. On the east wall below the window are marks of the altar formerly here, and its plan is marked on the floor in broken mediaeval tiles. In the second bay is the door from the church on the north side, and on the south a wide recess like that in the east bay, rebated for a frame; both recesses contained wooden cupboards for vestments, &c. The south wall of the west bay has been broken through in post-monastic

[3a] See below, p. 476.

[4] See Mr. Brakspear's plan of Hailes Abbey in *Arch. Journ.* lviii, 350.

[H. Brakspear, photo.

NETLEY ABBEY CHURCH : THE SOUTH TRANSEPT

[H. Brakspear, photo.

NETLEY ABBEY CHURCH : THE SOUTH TRANSEPT

[H. Brakspear, photo.

NETLEY ABBEY : ENTRANCE TO CHAPTER-HOUSE

[H. Brakspear, photo.

NETLEY ABBEY CHURCH : EAST BAY OF SOUTH AISLE OF PRESBYTERY

times, and a doorway inserted opening to a passage which ran along the west side of the eastern range.

The chapter-house has three two-light windows on the east, each with a sixfoiled opening in the head under a pointed inclosing arch, all being rebated for wooden frames. It was vaulted in three spans and three bays, being 19 ft. square, and had stone benches round the walls on which the vaulting shafts rested; these with their capitals and bases were of Purbeck marble, the vault-ribs being of simple chamfered section. The vault has fallen, and the benches and shafts have been cut away on the north and south sides, but on the east there are seats in the sills of the windows. Towards the cloister there are the usual three openings, beautiful moulded arches with quatrefoiled piers and Purbeck marble capitals and nook-shafts, the central opening having been the doorway, and the other two being originally filled with low walls, carrying open arcades of two arches with central marble shafts. These have now been removed, the low wall remaining only in the southern opening. In the south wall of the west bay of the chapter-house are traces of an original doorway opening to the parlour, and to the west of it, partly destroying it, was a sixteenth-century doorway as in the vestry.

The parlour has a plain round-headed barrel vault without ribs, and pointed chamfered archways at east and west, that on the east having been fitted with a door, opening to a wooden pentise from which a branch ran north-east towards the isolated thirteenth-century building described below as the visiting abbot's lodging. It is probable that between it and the parlour lay the infirmary, approached by this passage, but nothing of it is now above ground. It is to be noted that there is a masonry joint between the east wall of the parlour and its north and south walls, the east wall being built first.

The novices' room, vaulted in five bays of two spans, joined the parlour on the south, and was entered from the cloister at the north-west by a small doorway which has lost the moulded stonework of its head. The door close by, leading to the parlour, is a post-suppression insertion. The vault, which has fallen, had chamfered ribs, and round-headed wall cells as in the vestry; it sprang from moulded corbels which remain in the walls. The room was lighted on the east by four lancet windows, of which that in the south bay remains, but the other three have been replaced by wider windows of two trefoiled lights with a transom, *c.* 1330, all having internal rebates for frames. The wall at the north-east angle has been rebuilt, and contains a sixteenth-century window and fireplace, but part of the rear arch of a small thirteenth-century window remains; it would have opened under the pentise which was set against the east face of the wall. At the south-east angle is a thirteenth-century doorway, and part of a later doorway to the north of it; there are traces of a third doorway, probably original, partly destroyed by the inserted fourteenth-century window in the next bay. The southern half of this wall seems to have been masked by a sixteenth-century staircase, now destroyed. In the west wall of the novices' room are two fireplaces, one in the southern bay, with a doorway close to it in the south-west angle, and the other in the next bay. It was the larger of the two and had a stone hood, but is now destroyed. A little distance to the north was a thirteenth-century cupboard or recess, nearly obliterated by the making of a later cupboard, so that only two stones of its head remain. Below the line of vault corbels ran a band of painted decoration, which still shows faintly. It is probable that this room was divided up by wooden partitions, the south bay and perhaps the north being cut off in this way. The dorter extended on the first floor from the south transept to the south end of the novices' room, and, besides its night stair already mentioned, was reached by a day stair from the south-east angle of the cloister, both the lower and upper doorways of this stair being still in existence. It was lighted on both sides by rows of small square-headed windows, a good many of which are still to be seen blocked with masonry, having been replaced after the Suppression by wider mullioned openings. Part of the cornice remains on the east side, with plain rounded corbels under a flat soffit, and the steep pitch of the roof shows on the transept wall. The east ends of the vestry and chapter-house, projecting beyond the line of the east wall of the dorter, formed separate rooms, the former having a barrel vault and a roof gabled from north to south, and the latter a lean-to roof in continuation of that of the dorter; the east wall of the dorter ran right up to the transept, being carried on arches over the chapter-house and vestry. The room over the vestry has two small square-headed windows on the east, one of them a later though mediaeval insertion, and a doorway on the south towards the narrow room over the east end of the chapter-house. Its position and its stone vault suggest that it may have been a treasury or strong-room. The narrow room to which it opens had two small square-headed windows, which were reset higher in the wall after the Suppression; it can hardly have been other than a passage.

At the south end of the dorter, running in a north-easterly direction, probably to suit the line of the stream which flushed its drain, is the rere dorter, on the same level as the dorter, with the latrines on the south side, lighted by small square-headed loops. Its east window is gone, and the north wall is rebuilt in red brick. It overlapped the south end of the dorter for half its length only, and in the space to the west of it was a one-story pent-roofed building, through the south side of which the drain is continued, which was a small kitchen, or perhaps a wood-shed. It opened on the north to the novices' room, and at the north-east to the ground floor of the rere dorter; on the right hand of each doorway is a small hatch, with one side widely splayed towards the kitchen, through which small articles could be passed.

The room under the rere dorter is vaulted in four bays, the vault still standing, though its ribs have fallen. It is in a very shaky condition, covered with earth and bushes, and not proof against heavy rain, and is likely to fall at any moment. The room has a widely splayed east window of two lights with a quatrefoil over, and has been lighted on the north by two single lancets, between which is a fine hooded fireplace. The eastern of the two lancets has been widened, but is now blocked, and below the second lancet is a plain chamfered doorway. The fireplace is part of the original work, and has lamp brackets on either side of the hood, and a fine back of herring-bone brickwork. On the south side of the room, masking the pit of the drain, are four wide recesses, their back walls now in part broken away, and in the west bay is a small door which led to a latrine. Mr. Brakspear suggests that the room may be the infirmary of the novices, the recesses being for beds, and in this case the use of the pent-roofed building to the west as a kitchen seems probable. There is a cupboard recess in the north wall of the west bay, and in the west wall traces of a second doorway, blocked and apparently of two dates. In the sixteenth century the west wall of the dorter and the south wall of the rere dorter were prolonged, making a two-story block on the site of the kitchen, and traces of other foundations running south and west from their junction are yet to be seen.

In the southern range of claustral buildings were the warming-house, frater, and kitchen, all pulled down in the sixteenth century, except their north wall and part of the west wall of the kitchen. At the east end, between the warming-house and the dorter, was the day stair to the dorter, the arch by which it was reached from the cloister still remaining, with a sixteenth-century arch below it; the upper doorway into the dorter also exists, but the stairs are entirely destroyed. The warming-house was vaulted in two bays, being entered from the north-east, and having a locker in its north wall; the fireplace was probably at the west. Above it was a room lighted by a square-headed window from the cloister side, of which nothing more can be said. Between the warming-house door and the frater door was the lavatory, with four vaulted compartments under a wide relieving arch; at its east end is a sixteenth-century arched recess partly overlapping it. The east jamb of the frater door still exists, but the rest of it has been destroyed by a wide four-centred sixteenth-century doorway, the gatehouse having been made here after the destruction of the frater. Part of an original cupboard recess remains to the west of the doorway on the south face of the wall, and above the doorway a few stones of the north window of the frater, though there is no trace of a gable towards the cloister, as at Beaulieu. The frater was 20 ft. wide, and according to excavations made some time since, about 134 ft. long. The north and west walls of the kitchen still stand, showing that there was a room over the kitchen with three small north windows, the walls of this room having been heightened. On the site of the kitchen is the present caretaker's house. The south wall of this range of buildings is of sixteenth-century brickwork, and has had a projecting central gateway flanked by octagonal turrets, and similar turrets at either end of the range; the south ends of the east and west ranges of the claustral buildings were left standing to form two sides of a forecourt, while the cloister made the inner or principal court of the house. On the west side of the cloister the monastic buildings were of no great importance, and for two-thirds of the length from the south wall of the church there was nothing but the boundary wall of the cloister, with a pentise to the south-west doorway of the church running along its west side. Near the south-west angle was an entry of fourteenth-century date, against which the pentise returned, and running southwards from it a contemporary building of the same width, of which only the lower story with a few single lights is preserved. It seems to occupy the site of a thirteenth-century building, probably the lay brothers' frater, and its small size and probable use as a storehouse witness to the gradual extinction of this section of the community, which in the twelfth century had been one of the great sources of strength to the Cistercians. A doorway opens to the storehouse from the cloister, its jambs being fifteenth-century insertions, and the door to the entry is of late date set within older jambs. Against the north wall of the entry is a mass of red brickwork, apparently part of a large sixteenth-century oven.

The detached thirteenth-century building to the east of the main block, already referred to as the visiting abbots' lodging, is an interesting dwelling-house, with a vaulted hall of three bays on the west, a chapel on the south-east, and a cellar and latrine on the north-east. The entrance is from the south-west, and there may have been a fireplace in the east wall of the middle bay of the hall, but the wall is here broken away. The hall has north and south windows, and in the west wall a three-light fifteenth-century window and an original lancet light. The cellar has had a barrel vault, and the chapel has a rib vault of two bays and the remains of an east window of two lights and of one or two windows on the south, destroyed by later work. In the north wall is a locker, and the west door from the hall is set to the north of the centre line of the chapel, perhaps in order to be on the east side of a screen crossing the west bay of the hall from the south-west door. There has been a second story over the whole building, of which little can be said, and the position of the stair which led to it is not certain, but may have been in the angle formed by the chapel and hall. The general arrangements of the house which was built here after the suppression have been noted as far as they can be seen. Browne Willis, writing about 1718,[4a] says that the M—— of H—— 'converted the west end of the chapel below the cross isle into a kitchen and other offices, keeping the east end of it for a chapel, in which state it continued till about fifteen years ago, when Sir B—— L——[5] sold the whole fabrick of the chapel to one Taylor a carpenter of Southampton, who took off the roof (which was entire till then) and pulled down great part of the walls.' Willis further tells us that Taylor, who, to add to his other sins, was a Dissenter, had forewarnings of personal catastrophe in dreams during his sacrilegious doings, and these were effectually fulfilled, for as he was hacking at the west wall of the church, the tracery of the great west window fell on him and put a stop to his destructions.

MANORS

The manor of *HOUND* does not appear in the Domesday Survey in Mainsbridge Hundred, but is included in Meonstoke Hundred as belonging to Hugh de Port's manor of Warnford, not, however, paying geld with Warnford, but with the lands in Mainsbridge Hundred.[6] In 1242 Robert de St. John, as heir of the Ports, granted land to the abbey of Netley, which Henry III had built and founded in the parish three years before.[7] From this time until the dissolution of the smaller monasteries in 1536 Hound remained in the possession of the abbey.

In 1251 Henry III granted the abbot and convent free warren in their demesne lands of Netley, Hound, Shotteshal (now Satchell), and Sholing, and also made

[4a] *Mitred Abbeys*, ii, 205. [5] Sir Berkeley Lucy. [6] *V.C.H. Hants*, i, 481*a*. [7] *Cal. of Pat.* 1232–47, p. 333.

[H. Brakspear, *photo.*

NETLEY ABBEY CHURCH : WESTERN BAYS OF SOUTH AISLE OF NAVE

[H. Brakspear, *photo.*

NETLEY ABBEY : EAST END OF CHAPTER-HOUSE

a grant of a market to be held every Monday in their manor of Hound.[8]

On the suppression of the smaller monasteries the monks from Netley migrated to the larger Cistercian abbey of Beaulieu, from which their predecessors had originally come, and Hound manor, with its windmill, and other lands in Shotteshal and Sholing, in this parish, were granted by the crown to Sir William Paulet, kt., Baron Beauchamp, and first marquis of Winchester.[9] He took an important part in the politics of his day, became controller of the king's household and treasurer, and cleverly managed to retain his position through the reigns of the three successors of Henry VIII until his death in 1572.[10] He was succeeded by his son John, who mortgaged the manor of Hound with its appurtenances in the same year.[11]

PAULET. *Sable three swords set pilewise with their hilts or.*

John died in 1576, and his son William inherited the estate and held it until his death in 1598, when it passed to his son Thomas.[12] The latter was soon involved in financial difficulties, and in 1602 sold his manors of Netley and Hound and his other property in Hound parish to Edward Seymour, earl of Hertford,[13] who remained seised until his death in 1621.

His grandson William, who inherited the estates, married Frances daughter of Robert earl of Essex in 1618,[14] and settled the manors of Netley and Hound on her for life. He survived his wife and lived until 1660, when the dukedom of Somerset was restored to his family.[15] William his grandson, who succeeded to the estates in 1660, died in his minority eleven years later, when his sister Lady Elizabeth inherited the property and the titles went to his uncle. Lady Elizabeth did not long remain in possession, for in 1676 the two manors were purchased by the marquis of Worcester.[16]

SEYMOUR. *Gules a pair of wings or.*

The descent of the manors cannot be ascertained for the next forty years, but they had passed before 1718 into the possession of Sir Berkeley Lucy,[17] probably by purchase from the marquis or his heirs. Mr. Thomas Lee Dummer of Cranbury purchased Netley and Hound, with all the lands and mills belonging to them in Shotteshal and Sholing, from Sir Berkeley Lucy before the year 1765, when a pamphlet entitled *The Ruins of Netley Abbey* was dedicated to him and printed at his expense.[18] The next year he sold his possessions in Hound parish, which included the two manors of Netley and Hound, to William Chamberlayne,[19] who died in 1775, leaving a son William as heir. At his death, without issue, in 1830, these manors passed to his cousin Thomas, father of the present owner, Mr. Tankerville Chamberlayne of Cranbury Park.

At the time of the Survey *NETLEY* was held by Richard Puingiant. In King Edward's time Alward had been the holder, and it was then assessed at 3 hides. Under Richard it was assessed at 1 hide, but its value had risen from 60*s.* to 100*s.*[20]

In 1241 Netley manor was the property of Geoffrey the Chamberlain, who that year granted it to Robert the abbot and the monks of the newly founded monastery in Netley, in exchange for lands in Mildenhall.[21]

The grant was confirmed by Henry III in the following year[22] and again in 1251, when the king also granted to them free warren in their manor and the site of their monastery in Netley.[23] This grant, which included other possessions in the parish of Hound, was again confirmed by Edward I in 1285,[24] by Henry IV in 1400,[25] and later still by Henry VI.[26]

With the dissolution of Netley Abbey in 1536, its possessions went to the crown, and in 1537 the site of the monastery, with the manor and grange of Netley, was granted with the manor of Hound to Sir William Paulet.[27]

From this date the histories of the manors of Netley and Hound (q.v.), with the exception of the mortgage of Hound in 1572, have been identical.

FORT.—In 1545 a small fort was built by Sir William Paulet within the grounds of Netley Abbey at the request of Henry VIII, for the protection of the coast and the approach to Southampton. Certain manors and lands were granted to him for the upkeep of the fort and its garrison, which consisted of a captain, two soldiers, a porter, and six gunners.[27a] This garrison was still maintained in 1627,[27b] but the fort, known as Netley Castle, was shortly afterwards enlarged and turned into an ordinary residence, occupied at the present day by the Hon. H. Crichton.

CHURCHES The church of *OUR LADY* is a plain rectangle measuring externally 84 ft. 3 in. by 20 ft. 4 in., divided into nave and chancel by a wall 24 ft. from the east end, and 3 ft. 8 in. thick, the other walls of the church being only 2 ft. 7 in. thick. The reason for this extra thickness, unless intended to take a masonry bell-turret, is not evident. There is no trace of such a turret, and the bells hang at the west of the nave in a wooden turret carried on posts coming down to the floor of the church. The general structure belongs to the first half of the thirteenth century, the chancel having an east window of three lancet lights under an inclosing pointed arch, the rear arch being round, and two rather high-set lancets in each side wall. At the south-west is a fifteenth-century cinquefoiled light at

[8] *Cal. of Chart.* 1226–57, p. 354. At the beginning of the fourteenth century the abbot acquired a considerable amount of land in the parish by grant from Roger atte Felde and the But family, and also a salt-pit from Ric. de Morilun and Christina his wife, licence for the alienation of which property in mortmain was granted in 1311.

[9] Dugdale, *Mon.* v, 676; Pat. 28 Hen. VIII, pt. 3, m. 12.

[10] *Dict. Nat. Biog.*

[11] B.M. Chart. Add. MS. 16153.

[12] *Dict. Nat. Biog.*

[13] Feet of F. Hants, Hil. 44 Eliz.; B.M. Add. MS. 33278, fol. 167.

[14] Feet of F. Hants, Trin. 15 Jas. I.

[15] G.E.C. *Complete Peerage.*

[16] Feet of F. Div. Cos. Trin. 28 Chas. II.

[17] Willis, *Mitred Abbeys*, ii, 205; Feet of F. Hants, Trin. 9 Geo. I.

[18] B.M.

[19] Feet of F. Hants, East. 6 Geo. III.

[20] *V.C.H. Hants*, i, 495*a*.

[21] Feet of F. Hants, 25 Hen. III, No. 272.

[22] *Cal. of Pat.* 1232–47, p. 333.

[23] *Cal. of Chart.* 1226–57, p. 354.

[24] Chart. R. 13 Edw. I, No. 78.

[25] *Cal. of Pat.* 1399–1401, p. 329.

[26] Ibid. 1422–9, p. 315.

[27] Pat. 28 Hen. VIII, pt. 3, m. 12.

[27a] Pat. 1 Edw. VI, pt. 3, m. 37, 38, 39.

[27b] *Coll. Arch.* 1881 vol. xii.

a lower level, and just east of it a small blocked priest's doorway. The chancel arch is pointed, of two chamfered orders, with half-round shafts to the inner order, and moulded capitals and bases. The nave has at the north-east a small modern vestry, and three lancets in the north wall. On the south side are two lancets and a plain pointed doorway under a modern porch, and at the south-east a wide two-light window to light the south nave altar, with a piscina recess below it, but no drain. There is a plain west doorway. The north side of the church is overgrown with ivy, hiding any traces of a north door to the nave, if such existed. The roofs are old, with trussed rafters, collars, and tie-beams with king-posts from which the pole plates are strutted. Externally they are red-tiled, the bell-turret being boarded, with a slate roof. At the north-west of the nave stands a Purbeck marble font with octagonal bowl, much retooled, with two pointed arches sunk on each face; it has an octagonal central and four smaller shafts, and dates from *c.* 1200.

There are pits for four bells in the turret, but only three bells, all of 1607; the tenor has the founder's initials R.B.

The plate consists of a cup of Elizabethan type, but without hall-marks, with initials and date IL IB 1689, the initials being those of the churchwardens; a paten of 1723, given in 1724 by an unknown benefactress; a modern chalice and paten of 1879 and 1880 respectively, two silver-mounted glass cruets, and a plated flagon.

The earliest register preserved is the burial register for 1792–1812. For earlier entries see Hamble.

To the south of the church is a fine yew tree, and the churchyard, which is entered by a stone lichgate at the north-west, has been lengthened westward from the line of the west wall of the nave.

The modern church of Hound and Netley stands to the south of the site of Netley Abbey, in remembrance of which it is dedicated in honour of *ST. EDWARD THE CONFESSOR.* It was built from the designs of J. D. Sedding in 1886, and consists of chancel with north vestry and organ chamber, a tower of three stages with an eastern chapel on the south side of the chancel, and a nave with chapels of two bays on the north-east and south-east, and a western narthex or baptistery. It is a very attractive example of Sedding's work, and its fittings and colouring are excellent. Under the tower are two stones from Netley Abbey—one a small Purbeck marble effigy of a knight in mail, with shield and sword, of thirteenth-century date, which probably covered a heart-burial or the like, and the other a fifteenth-century incised slab with the figure of a Cistercian monk in his habit. It has had an inscription, of which only the word Johēs is left. In the tower is a ring of eight bells of 1886.

ADVOWSON

No mention of a church at Hound occurs in the Domesday Survey, although the existence of Netley chapel is recorded.[28] Tradition states that Hound church was built by Hamble Priory about 1230, ten years before the founding of Netley Abbey.[29] Neither Hound nor Netley church is entered among the possessions of the priory in the Ministers' Accounts of 1325, but in 1344 the king, who owing to the French wars had the possessions of Hamble-le-Rice and other alien priories in his hands, presented Richard de Montserrel to the church of Hound,[30] which must therefore have been acquired by the priory before 1344. In 1391 the possessions of the priory were all sold, and William of Wykeham acquired the church of Hound for his college of St. Mary, Winchester. From this date the warden and governors of the college have always held the advowson.

A chapel at Netley is mentioned in Domesday,[31] but since there is no further mention of it with the manor, it is possible that the prior and monks acquired it at the same time as they did the church of Hound, and that with it it passed to Winchester College.

CHARITIES

In 1882 Henry Usborne, in the chapelry of Scholing or Sholing St. Mary, formerly part of Hound, by deed, gave a sum of £100 consols, income to be applied for the benefit of the poor. The stock is held by the official trustees, and the dividends are remitted to the vicar and churchwardens for application.

28 *V.C.H. Hants*, i, 495.

29 Information obtained from the vicar, Rev. W. A. Chevalier.

30 Pat. 14 Ric. II, pt. 2, m. 1.

31 *V.C.H. Hants*, i, 495*a*.

NORTH STONEHAM

Ad Lapidem (x cent.)[1]; Staneham (xi cent.); Stanham Abbatis (xiii cent.)

The parish of North Stoneham, comprising over 5,026 acres, thirty-two of which are covered by water, is situated in the New Forest division of the county, north-east from Southampton, and south-west from Eastleigh.

In the east is the River Itchen, which forms the boundary between North and South Stoneham, and one of its tributaries, Monk's Brook, traverses the parish from north to south. The land is fertile and well wooded; there are 896 acres of wood, 1,485 of arable, and 1,088 of permanent grass-land.[2]

The soil is red loam with a gravel or clay subsoil, and the inhabitants, mostly engaged in agriculture, cultivate wheat, oats, and barley.

The main roads from Southampton to Winchester, and from Romsey to Botley, cross the parish.

There is a gradual slope of the land from the north-west, where the average altitude is 200 ft. above the ordnance datum, to the south-east and south, where is the River Itchen, and where the altitude is only 50 ft. Most of the centre of the parish is occupied by North Stoneham Common and North Stoneham Park. The latter surrounds the Manor House, now unoccupied, and covers 500 acres. The grounds are well laid

1 *Antoninus Iter. Brit.* (B.M. Reading Room, 984, G. 12) gives a place Ad Lapidem, 6 miles from Winchester and 4 miles from Clausentum (Bitterne). Ven. Bede, *Eccl. Hist.* iv, xvi, relates the martyrdom of two sons of Aliwald, king of Isle of Wight, 'ad Lapidem,' near the mouth of the Itchen.

2 Statistics from the Bd. of Agric. (1905).

out, and are used by the members of the North Stoneham Club for games and athletic sports of all kinds. There are also two fine fishponds, now used for boating. The church of St. Nicholas stands just within the park, while opposite is the rectory.

There is no village of North Stoneham, but about half a mile north of the church is the little hamlet of Middle, consisting of a farm and a few cottages, the Cricketer's Arms Inn and the post office.

North End is a hamlet in the extreme north of the parish, near Chandlersford, and comprises a few picturesque old cottages, and a farm called the Home Farm. Chandlersford was formed into a separate civil parish in 1897, from portions of North Stoneham, North Baddesley, and Ampfield. A few years ago it contained only a few small cottages, but it is now rapidly developing into a favourite residential neighbourhood, owing to its healthy situation and charming scenery. The iron church and schools erected in 1889 lie to the north of the village. Chandlersford Railway Station on the Eastleigh and Salisbury branch of the London and South Western Railway is in North Baddesley parish, according to the boundaries of 1895. Bassett, a group of large modern residences, lies on the southern border of the parish and contains the fine new church of St. Michael and All Angels, opened in 1897.

Saxholme, to the north of the village, is the residence of Sir Alfred Wills, Ridgemount is the property of W. Erasmus Darwin, J.P., and Red Lodge, in the south-west of the village, is owned by Sir Harold Hewitt.

The old canal from Alresford, which still forms part of the parish boundary, is now disused and practically dry.

The village stocks have disappeared, but they were formerly on the road to Chandlersford near the pound, close to the gates of North Stoneham Park.

Lord Hawke, the victor of Quiberon Bay, formerly lived in this parish, and is buried in the church.

MANOR

King Athelstan, in the year 932, at the Witenagemot at Amesbury, granted certain land in *NORTH STONEHAM* to the thegn Alfred,[3] who in 941 gave the same land to the abbey of Hyde, Winchester.[4]

In Domesday North Stoneham is given as one of the possessions of St. Peter's Abbey of Hyde, 'to which it has always belonged.' Then, as in the time of King Edward, it was assessed at 8 hides, and there were considerable lands belonging to the manor.[5]

In 1329 the abbey of Hyde was granted free warren in its demesne lands in North Stoneham.[6]

The property of the abbot here had been increased three years before by a grant of one messuage and land from John de Chekenhull and Beatrice his wife, for the maintenance of a chaplain who every day should pray for the souls of the donors and their ancestors.[7]

At the dissolution of the monasteries North Stoneham manor, with many of the other possessions of Hyde Abbey, was granted to Thomas Wriothesley, earl of Southampton.[8] He was succeeded on his death in 1550 by his son Henry, then a minor.[9] Henry died in 1582 and left as his heir a son Henry, then only eight years of age.[10] Shortly after attaining his majority he sold the North Stoneham estate to Thomas Fleming,[11] whose descendants are the present owners. His son Thomas, who succeeded him in 1623,[12] died in 1639, leaving a son Edward as his heir. He also left a daughter Katherine, who afterwards married Daniel Eliot.[13]

Edward's grandson died unmarried, and the male line of the Fleming family became extinct. The estate of North Stoneham then passed to Thomas Willis, great-grandson of Katherine and Daniel Eliot, who assumed the surname Fleming. He died without heirs, and was succeeded by his half-brother John, who also took the name Fleming, but died without issue in 1802. The property then devolved upon his cousin John Barton Willis, great-grandson of Browne Willis the antiquary by Katherine Eliot, daughter of Daniel Eliot and Katherine Fleming, who became John Barton Willis Fleming.[14] His grandson,

Fleming. *Gules a cheveron between three owls argent with an ermine tail on the cheveron.*

Willis. *Argent a fesse between three lions gules and a border gules bezanty.*

Mr. John Edward Arthur Willis Fleming, holds the manor at the present time.

Two mills are mentioned in Domesday among the possessions of Hyde Abbey in North Stoneham.[15] No such buildings exist here at the present day, although there are two in the neighbouring parish of South Stoneham, one called the 'Wood Mills' at Swaythling, the other called 'West End Mills,' a little above the old Mansbridge, on the River Itchen.

In the extent of North Stoneham, as granted to Hyde Abbey in 941, the boundary extended as far as the River Itchen in two places, at 'Swathelyngford,' and at 'a mylle place by Northe Mannysbrygge,'[16] from which it seems conclusive that the mills now in South Stoneham are those formerly in North Stoneham, having been transferred from one parish to the other by a change of boundary, especially as there is no river or stream in North Stoneham capable of turning a mill. In the time of George I the sheaves for the blocks of the men-of-war were turned in the Wood Mill, some of the Hanoverian bodyguard being given employment at the work. Now, however, it is a flour mill worked by Messrs. A. & F. Ray, roller millers, of Southampton. 'West End Mill' is now a corn mill, the property of Mr. John Gater, whose family have held it for over a century. It was formerly a paper mill, belonging in 1686 to the com-

[3] Birch, *Cart. Sax.* No. 692.
[4] Ibid. No. 649.
[5] *V.C.H. Hants*, i, 471*b*.
[6] Chart. R. 3 Edw. III, m. 16.
[7] Pat. 19 Edw. II, pt. 2, m. 21; Inq. a.q.d. 19 Edw. II, No. 68.
[8] Pat. 37 Hen. VIII, pt. 1, m. 9.
[9] W. and L. Inq. p.m. 4 Edw. VI (Ser. 2), bdle. 5, No. 103.
[10] Chan. Inq. p.m. 24 Eliz. pt. 1 (Ser. 2), No. 46.
[11] Feet of F. Hants, East. 42 Eliz.
[12] W. and L. Inq. p.m. 22 Jas. Cap. I (Ser. 2), bdle. 40, No. 97.
[13] Chan. Inq. p.m. 15 Chas. I, pt. 2 (Ser. 2), No. 118.
[14] Burke, *Landed Gentry*.
[15] *V.C.H. Hants*, i, 471*b*.
[16] *Liber Mon. de Hyda* (Rolls Ser.), 126.

pany of White Papermakers. Nine of the fifteen members of the company were French refugees, and in 1702 Gerard de Vaux, 'frenchman,' was living at South Stoneham Mill. Here he was joined by another Huguenot, Henry Portal, who afterwards set up for himself at Laverstoke, and in 1724 obtained the contract for making bank-note paper, which his descendants still hold.

North Stoneham Park is of great antiquity, and in the fourteenth century was a fine deer park belonging to the abbot of Hyde.[16a]

The messuage granted to the abbot by John de Chekenhull in the fourteenth century was conveyed with North Stoneham manor to Thomas Wriothesley at the dissolution of the monasteries,[17] and shares the same history as that manor.[18] Traces of this messuage possibly still exist in Chickenhall Farm.

CHURCH The church of *ST. NICHOLAS* has a chancel 25 ft. long, and of equal width (15 ft. 2 in.) with a nave of 35 ft. 9 in., aisles of the full length of nave and chancel, 11 ft. 5 in. and 11 ft. 2 in. wide respectively, a west tower 10 ft. by 9 ft. 6 in., a north porch and a south vestry.

The various additions and alterations which have brought the church to its present symmetrical plan have destroyed all evidence of any work earlier than the fifteenth century, with the exception of the west window of the tower, which is a beautiful triplet of thirteenth-century lancets, re-used here, as it seems, when the tower was built in the sixteenth century.

The nave arcades, of three bays with octagonal pillars, simply moulded capitals, and arches of two chamfered orders, are probably fifteenth-century work, while the two bays on either side of the chancel are of curious pseudo-Gothic character, and apparently of late eighteenth or early nineteenth-century date. They are of different section, and may perhaps be intended as copies of mediaeval work formerly existing here, but if this be the case the copying is not sufficiently close to give grounds for assuming the date of the former arcades.

The east window of the chancel is of fifteenth-century style, of three cinquefoiled lights with tracery, and flanked on the inside by modern niches for images; it is filled with painted glass made in 1826 by Edwards of Winchester, the subject being an adaptation of Raphael's Transfiguration; the result is not happy.

The aisle windows are of late Gothic character, and probably in no case earlier than the sixteenth century; they have been a good deal repaired, modern cusping being inserted, so that their dates are chiefly matter of conjecture. Both aisles have three-light east and west windows, the east window of the south aisle having image brackets on either side of it; in the north aisle are four north windows, the eastern of two cinquefoiled lights with tracery under a pointed head, the next two square-headed, of three and four cinquefoiled lights respectively, and the fourth also square-headed, of three cinquefoiled lights. Between the third and fourth windows is a round-headed north doorway with a plain quarter-round moulding of uncertain but not ancient date.

In the south aisle the south windows are all square-headed, of three or four lights. The details of the windows are not uniform, the west window of the south aisle, and the four-light window in the north aisle, being of better style than the rest.

The tower is of three stages, with a stair at the north-east angle. It is probably of sixteenth-century date, but externally its details are hidden by ivy; the east arch is of a single pointed order, edge-chamfered. The west window, as already noted, is a beautiful piece of thirteenth-century detail: a triplet of lancets under a segmental rear arch with engaged shafts to the lights and rear arch, having moulded capitals and bases and bands at half height. The rear arch and lights are also moulded, and the date of the whole is about 1230; the bonding of the masonry shows that it has been carefully re-used in the tower at the time of its building in the sixteenth century.

All the roofs and wood fittings of the church are of modern date, but a seventeenth-century altar-table with twisted baluster legs stands at the east end of the south aisle. The organ is at the east end of the north aisle, and the font, which has an octagonal bowl of Purbeck marble on a modern stone stem, is under the east arch of the tower. The bowl looks like fifteenth-century work, but may be an older bowl refashioned at that time.

In the middle of the chancel floor is a bluish limestone slab, 6 ft. 8 in. by 3 ft. 8 in., formerly in the north aisle, which was perhaps its original position. On it is a shield charged with a double-headed eagle surrounded by foliage of foreign Gothic type, and round the edge of the slab runs a marginal inscription with the evangelistic symbols at the four angles—

SEPULTURA DE LA SCHOLA DE SCLAVONI AÑO DÑI MCCCCLXXXXI

There appears to be no record of any connexion of North Stoneham with these Slavonians, who doubtless came to Southampton with the Venetian fleet. The Rev. G. W. Minns[18a] suggests that the slab may have been brought here from the destroyed church of St. Mary, Southampton, *c.* 1550, as it is said that some of the material of this church found its way to North Stoneham. At the east end of the south aisle, on the south side, is the monument of Sir Thomas Fleming, Lord Chief Justice, who died in 1613, with his effigy in scarlet robes, and that of his wife, and kneeling figures of the six sons and two daughters who survived him. Two sons and one daughter died before their father, and are not represented on his tomb. The inscription is in two panels on the base, and above the effigies are the arms of Fleming, gules a cheveron between three owls or, an ermine spot on the cheveron, between Fleming impaling James (his wife's family), and James, gules a dolphin or, quartering per fesse sable and or a lion or and gules.

Opposite to the Fleming monument, on the north side of the aisle, is a mural tablet to John Serle, 1576, his wife Christine, 1561, and their son John, 1575.

In the south aisle also is a monument to Lord Hawke, 1781, with a sea piece carved in white marble of very good style.

A wooden screen now in North Baddesley church, bearing Sir Thomas Fleming's initials and the date 1602, is said to have been brought from North Stoneham. It has been, as it seems, lengthened a few inches, and its original size, 15 ft. 2 in., is precisely that of the

[16a] Pat. 8 Edw. III, pt. 1, m. 2 *d.*
[17] Pat. 37 Hen. VIII, pt. 1, m. 9.
[18] Chan. Inq. p.m. 24 Eliz. pt. 1 (Ser. 2), No. 467.
[18a] *Proc. Hants Field Club*, ii, 363.

width of North Stoneham nave and chancel, so that the tradition may be correct.

There are six bells by Taylor of Loughborough, 1893. The former ring was of three, by I H., 1651, Antony Bond, 1623, and a Salisbury founder, *c.* 1400.

The plate consists of a silver-gilt cup of 1702, with a cover paten, inscribed 'ΤΑ ΣΑ ΕΚ ΤΩΝ ΣΩΝ anno domini 1702,' and a standing paten of the same date, the gift of Margaret and Thomas Fleming, bearing the Fleming arms, and Fleming with Bland on a scutcheon of pretence.

The flagon, which has no marks but that of the maker Ro—perhaps Philip Rollos of London—was given in 1703, and is inscribed 'Humbly offered by Richard Dummer.' There is also a modern paten, silver-gilt, and two glass cruets, with silver-gilt mounts.

The first book of the registers runs from 1640 to 1716, and the second, which bears on the cover the date 1716, and has lost a few pages, runs from 1722 to 1812, the marriages ceasing in 1754, and being entered in a third book which carries them to 1812.

ADVOWSON A chapel evidently existed in North Stoneham as early as the tenth century, for besides the grant of Stoneham by Aelfrid the thegn to Hyde Abbey, it also received from King Athelstan 6 hides of land at 'Stanham,' together with the chapel thereto pertaining and the vestments.[19]

The abbey held the church with the manor at the time of the Domesday Survey, and in 1330 the abbot received licence in fulfilment of a grant to his convent by Edward I to appropriate the church as well as hold the patronage.[20] The advowson continued in the gift of the abbot until the Dissolution, when it was granted with the manor to Thomas Wriothesley, since which time it has always been held by the lord of North Stoneham manor (q.v.)

CHARITIES In 1720 Edward Dummer, by his will proved in the P.C.C. charged his manor and lands in Swaythling with the yearly payment of £5 for a schoolmaster for teaching boys and girls to write and read.

The Poor's Money, the gifts of various donors, formerly consisted of £168, which, it is understood, was laid out on some cottages, now forming part of the North Stoneham estate belonging to John Fleming, esquire, by whom the sum of £6 15*s.*, being interest at £4 per cent., is paid annually and distributed on Easter Thursday by the rector and churchwardens. In 1906, sixty-eight cottagers received from 1*s.* to 2*s.* each.

SOUTH STONEHAM

Stonham, Stanham, xi and xiii cent.

South Stoneham, in the southern division of the county, is a very large and scattered parish stretching along the banks of the River Itchen from Southampton just above Northam Bridge to Eastleigh, a distance of about six miles. Its total area, including the tithings of Allington, Barton, Pollack, Shamblehurst, and Portswood, is 8,007 acres, with 50 acres of water and 50 of foreshore. Since 1891, however, a large part of these tithings has been incorporated with newly-formed civil parishes, and the area of South Stoneham proper in 1901 was 1,296 acres of land and 26 acres of inland water.[1]

The land is very fertile and well watered by the Itchen and its smaller streams, the former being navigable as far as Winchester.

The soil is sandy, with either a gravel or clay subsoil, and considerable crops of wheat, oats, and barley are raised. The ground slopes down gradually to the river side, and is mostly low-lying and flat, especially near the mouth of the Itchen.

There is no village bearing the name of the parish, the church and a few adjacent houses are situated near Swaythling, a pleasant village on the right bank of the river just where it receives the tributary Monk's River. Swaythling is now practically a suburb of Southampton, and is a favourite residential quarter.

The church of St. Mary, South Stoneham, lies to the south of Swaythling village, just beyond South Stoneham House, formerly the manor house, built in the early part of the eighteenth century, now the residence of Sir Samuel Montagu, created Lord Swaythling in 1907. To the south of the grounds surrounding the house, and above the Wood Mill, is a salmon pool, probably a relic of the fishery mentioned in Domesday, and the home of the salmon for which the Itchen was once so famous.

In the north of the village is the Grange, an old house reputed to be the manor house of the manor of Mainsbridge, now the property of Lord Swaythling, and Sheppard's Farm which was once probably Swaythling manor house.

MONTAGU, Lord Swaythling. *Or a pile azure with a tent argent thereon between two palm trees torn up by the roots.*

Just outside the modern parish boundaries is Swaythling railway station on the London and South Western Railway, and opposite is the Mason's Arms Hotel. Portswood, formerly a tithing in South Stoneham parish, was united in 1894 with part of Bitterne tithing, to form a separate civil parish in the municipal borough of Southampton. The western portion of Portswood, which includes Bitterne Park, Bevois Mount and Valley, is in the ecclesiastical district of St. Denys, the church being situated on the right bank of the river, opposite the remains of St. Denys' Priory. The Cobden Free Bridge which crosses the Itchen at this point is a fine structure, opened in 1883, consisting of five spans. Bitterne Station, on the Netley and Fareham branch of the London and South Western Railway, is in the extreme south, almost in Bitterne parish.

The eastern part of Portswood, known as Highfield and Westwood Park, is in the ecclesiastical district of Christ Church, formed in 1844, and is mainly a residential suburb of Southampton, consisting of modern villas with several large houses.[2]

[19] Cott. MSS. Vesp. D. lx, p. 113; ibid. Plut. xxiv, G. 30*a*, 31*b*.

[20] Pat. 4 Edw. III, pt 1, m. 40.

[1] Ordnance Survey.

[2] The total area is 1,120 acres, and it has a population of nearly 10,000 inhabitants.

Bitterne village and tithing, formed into a separate parish out of South Stoneham in 1894, is situated on the east bank of the estuary of the Itchen, and communicates with Southampton by means of Northam Bridge, near the Roman station, Clausentum.

The High Street, part of the main road from Southampton to Botley, passes through the village from east to west. North of this road the land is high, and owing to its healthy situation the place has become a suburb of Southampton.

There are several large houses facing the West End Road, including Heathfield, belonging to Mrs. Raymond ; Bitterne Lodge, the residence of Mrs. Martin ; and Mersham, the property of Mr. C. Noke. Lady Macnaghten lives at Bitterne Manor House, but the estate itself has been largely cut up into building plots. Freemantle Common was awarded to the parish in 1812, but is now in St. Mary Extra.

Parts of the tithings of Shamblehurst and Allington in South Stoneham were made into the civil parish of West End in 1894. Allington Farm, the old manor-house, is in the extreme north, while in the east is Townhill House, formerly the manor-house and now the residence of Miss Cooper. The village of West End is entirely residential owing to its splendid situation on a high ridge, whence fine views of the Itchen valley may be obtained, and it contains many good houses. The main road from Romsey to Botley divides the parish into the northern and southern portions.

The parish church of St. James, an edifice of red brick and Weldon stone, erected in 1838, is situated in the south of the village at the top of Church Hill.

The elementary schools are situated on the north side of the Botley road, and were built in 1838 for 192 children. A few yards farther on are the library and reading room, and nearly opposite is the cemetery, on the south side. In the extreme east of the village is the South Stoneham Union, in Shamblehurst tithing, a large red-brick building erected in 1848, enlarged in 1887, and again, by the addition of an isolation hospital, in 1894. The principal houses in the neighbourhood are Harefield, the residence of Mrs. Edward Jones ; Hatch Grange, the property of Mr. R. Warnford Fletcher ; Thornhill Park, belonging to Colonel Willan, J.P. ; and Townhill Park, owned by Mr. Henry Bessemer. The total area of West End is nearly 3,000 acres, and it has a population of 1,778, including the officers and inmates of the workhouse.

The most northerly portion of South Stoneham, including the tithings of Barton Peverel, Eastleigh, and part of Boyatt, was separated in 1894, and formed into the civil parish of Eastleigh.

Its growth to a town within recent years is due to the extensive works of the London and South Western Railway, in which nearly all the inhabitants are employed. All kinds of machinery are made here, besides coaches, wagons, and other railroad fittings.

The town itself consists of several long straight streets, uniformly laid out, a crescent, and a few blocks of houses. The church of the Resurrection, erected in 1868, stands in the crescent at the north end of the town, next to the elementary schools, built in 1870, and enlarged in 1882 and 1889, to accommodate 478 children—girls and infants. The boys' school is in Chamberlayne Road and will accommodate 580 boys.

The Institute, erected by the company for the use of those employed on the railway, contains a reading room, an extensive library, a large hall, and a billiard room.

In the extreme north is the recreation ground facing Withymead Lock. On the River Itchen, a little farther down, is a mill, near Barton Farm, both of which are part of the ancient manor of Barton Peverel. There is excellent trout and salmon fishing in this reach.

Eastleigh Station, on the London and South-Western Railway, is an important junction, where several branches leave the main line. One called the Eastleigh and Salisbury line runs due west, while the Gosport and Stokes Bay line passes to Portsmouth in a south-easterly direction.

West End Mill, South Stoneham

MANORS

SOUTH STONEHAM, occasionally called Bishop's Stoneham, at the time of Domesday was held by the bishop of Winchester, and its revenues were appropriated to the clothing of the monks of St. Swithun's. It possessed two fisheries, and was then valued at £8 as against its value of £7 in the time of King Edward.[3] In 1167 the manor was still in the hands of the bishop,[4] whose overlordship is mentioned at intervals[5] until 1478,[6] after which date it has been found twice only, in 1636 and 1741.[7]

The tenants who held of the bishop appear to have taken their name from the lands, for in 1236, and later in 1249, Gregory de Stoneham or South Stoneham had possessions there.[8]

[3] *V.C.H. Hants*, i, 467*a*.

[4] Pipe R. 13 Hen. II.

[5] In 1284 the king transferred his rights in the manor of South Stoneham (probably claims to services) to the bishop of Winchester, and in the same year the men of Stoneham manor were exempted by royal charter from attendance at the hundred court of Sweynston, and were allowed instead to answer at the bishop's court with his hundred at Waltham (Chart. R. 12 Edw. I, m. 77 and *Cal. of Pat.* 1281–92, p. 122). In 1316 the *Feudal Aids*, ii, 318, give the abbey of Hyde as owner of the vill of South Stoneham. They may have been overlords under a lease from the bishop.

[6] Chan. Inq. p.m. 17 Edw. IV, No. 7.

[7] Ibid. 11 Chas. I, pt. 3, No. 51 ; Close 14 Geo. II, pt. 7, No. 11.

[8] Feet of F. Hants, Hil. 20 Hen. III. ; ibid. Hil. 33 Hen. III. His property is described as 1 hide of land except 4 acres of land.

South Stoneham House : The Garden Front

South Stoneham : The Salmon Pool

In 1315 Nicholas the son of Guy de South Stoneham held the manor,[9] and the same family was still in possession in 1348, when Thomas de Stoneham settled it upon himself and his wife Alice.[10]

Twenty years later the manor of South Stoneham was held by five heiresses,[11] who may possibly have been daughters of this Thomas. They quitclaimed in 1367 all right which they had to Adam le Chaundler and his heirs for ever.[12]

The descent during the next century is somewhat obscure. In 1436, however, the manor, then in the hands of Nicholas Fitz John, was released by him to William Nicholl[13] and others.

In 1478 it was in the possession of Thomas Payne, to whom it had been demised by John Langhorn. On the death of Thomas the manor reverted to William son of this John,[14] and remained in his family until 1553, when Stephen Langhorn, or Langher, sold it for £140 to John Capelyn.[15] He was still in possession in 1600, but in that year it was purchased by William Conway,[16] and once more changed hands in 1612, when it was bought from him by Edmund Clerke.[17] His son, who succeeded to Stoneham in 1634,[18] survived him only two years, and in 1636 the estate passed to his grandson Edmund, then 8½ years of age.[19] This Edmund was apparently sheriff of the county in 1671,[20] and clerk to the Signet. He married the daughter of one Giles Frampton,[21] and dealt with South Stoneham manor in 1705.[22]

Before 1740 South Stoneham had passed into the possession of William Nicholas,[23] for in that year it was purchased from him by William Sloane,[24] who was sheriff of Hampshire in 1749.[25]

John Lane acquired the manor in 1811,[26] and he, together with Susan his wife, sold it eight years later to John Fleming.[27] Since the beginning of the nineteenth century the manorial rights have not been exercised. The manor was sold in 1878 by Mr. Thomas Fleming to Captain Daveson, and ten years later was purchased from his executors by the present owner, Lord Swaythling, who resides at South Stoneham House.[28] The old bridge called Mans Bridge gives its name to the hundred in which it lies and to two manors situated close to it.

The manor of *MAINSBRIDGE* (Manesbrigge, xii cent.)[29] *alias TOWNHILL* in the thirteenth century was held of the king in chief.[30] That portion held by the Sandfords was divided between the coheiresses of Gilbert de Sandford, who married respectively Robert de Vere, earl of Oxford, and John de Rivers.[31] The son of the former purchased that share of the manor which had passed to John de Rivers in 1317,[32] and in 1329 granted the whole of the Sandford estate to the abbot and convent of Netley for the purpose of supporting a chantry of two monks to pray there for the souls of himself, his ancestors, and descendants.[33]

In 1167 Thomas de Mainsbridge owned land in Mainsbridge,[34] and in 1217 the rent paid to the king for the same by John de Mainsbridge was granted to William Brewere.[35] John died in 1244 without issue, when his lands were divided between his sister Agnes Peverel and Juliana daughter of his sister Clementia.[36]

Mainsbridge accrued to the former and then passed down in a direct line through the Peverel family until 1365,[37] when it was purchased from Thomas Peverel, with several other Hampshire manors, by Thomas Tyrell, kt., of Essex.[38] He sold it almost immediately to Thomas Daccombe, and from him it was bought by John Smyth before 1372.[39] The estate was forfeited to the crown for alienation without licence, although in an inquisition taken in 1372 the jurors declared that it would be no damage to the king if Smyth were allowed to receive back his lands.[40] The lands, however, were retained by the crown.[41]

In 1464 the custody of all possessions 'late of John of Mainsbridge,' in that place, was granted for life to John Davy.[42]

No trace of the manor after this date, however, can be found, but it seems probable that it was purchased from the crown by Netley Abbey, who already held one moiety, granted to it by Robert de Vere in 1329. After this date the manor of Mainsbridge *alias* Townhill is known only under the latter name.[43] At the Dissolution Townhill was granted with other lands of Netley to William Paulet, kt., marquis of Winchester.[44]

His son John, who succeeded to the property in 1572,[45] mortgaged this manor in the same year, but died four years later. His son William then became third marquis of Winchester and earl of Wiltshire.

During his lifetime this manor was granted, with several other Paulet lands, to 'the fishing grantee' William Tipper.[46] He failed to make good his claim however, for in 1605 the marquis sold the manor of Townhill to Gideon Amondsham and others.[47]

Nine years later it was purchased by John Serle,[48] and at his death in 1624 passed to his brother.[49]

Before 1665 it had passed into the possession of John Dunch,[50] lord of North Baddesley manor, and with it Townhill descended to Francis Keck.[51]

9 Feet of F. Hants, Hil. 8 Edw. II.
10 Ibid. Trin. 21 Edw. III.
11 Thomas de Sandwich and Ellen his wife, Agnes sister of Ellen, Isabel sister of Agnes, Edith sister of Isabel, and Thomas atte Parke and Ena his wife.
12 Feet of F. Hants, Mich. 40 Edw. III.
13 Close, 14 Hen. VI, m. 17.
14 Chan. Inq. p.m. 17 Edw. IV, No. 7.
15 Feet of F. Hants, Mich. 6 Edw. VI.
16 Ibid. Div. Cos. Trin. 42 Eliz.
17 Ibid. Hants, Trin. 9 Jas. I.
18 Chan. Inq. p.m. 9 Chas. I, pt. 2, No. 182.
19 Ibid. 11 Chas. I, pt. 3, No. 51.
20 *List of Sheriffs* (P.R.O.), 54.
21 Berry, *Hants Genealogies*.
22 Feet of F. Hants, Hil. 3 Anne.
23 Close, 14 Geo. II, pt. 7, No. 11; Recov. R. Hil. 14 Geo. II, rot. 156.
24 Feet of F. Div. Cos. Mich. 15 Geo. II.
25 *List of Sheriffs* (P.R.O.), 54.
26 Feet of F. Hants, Hil. 51 Geo. III.
27 Ibid. Mich. 59 Geo. III.
28 Ex inform. Lord Swaythling.
29 Pipe R. 13 Hen. II.
30 Chan. Inq. p.m. 28 Hen. III, No. 37; *Cal. of Inq. p.m.* Hen. III, No. 386.
31 G.E.C. *Complete Peerage*.
32 B.M. Add. Chart. 55, D. 28.
33 Pat. 2 Edw. III, pt. 1, m. 9; Chan. Inq. a.q.d. 2 Edw. III, No. 19. The manor was to be held subject to the payment of an annual rent of £26.
34 Pipe R. 13 Hen. II.
35 *Cal. of Pat.* 1216–25, p. 106.
36 Chan. Inq. p.m. 28 Hen. III, No. 17.
37 See Chilworth for details of descent which Mainsbridge follows.
38 Close, 38 Edw. III, m. 32 and 28.
39 *Abbrev. Rot. Orig.* (Rec. Com.), 318.
40 Chan. Inq. p.m. 45 Edw. III (2nd Nos.), 48.
41 Mins. Accts. fol. 983, m. 10.
42 Pat. 4 Edw. IV. pt. 1, m. 7.
43 At this period the manor included 20 acres of great oakwood and a fishery in the River Itchen, both of which still exist.
44 Pat. 28 Hen. VIII, pt. 3, m. 12.
45 B.M. Add. Chart. 16153.
46 Pat. 31 Eliz. pt. 5, m. 31.
47 Feet of F. Hants, Hil. 2 Jas. I.
48 Ibid. Mich. 11 Jas. I.
49 Chan. Inq. p.m. 21 Jas. I (Ser. 2.) pt. 13, No. 98.
50 Lay Subsidy R. 15 Chas. II, $\frac{176}{565}$
51 Recov. R. Mich. 24 Chas. II, rot. 210; Feet of F. Div. Cos. Trin. 5 Anne.

In 1750 it was purchased by John White,[52] and by him conveyed to Nathaniel Middleton, sheriff of Hampshire in 1800. Middleton sold Townhill in 1799 to William Cator *alias* Gater,[53] and it remained in his family until sold by Mr. Caleb William Gater of Salisbury to Lord Swaythling, who now holds it.[54]

Another manor bearing the name *MAINSBRIDGE alias SWAYTHLING* was held by the De Lisles of Hyde Abbey[55] by doing suit at the abbot's court of Stoneham. The earliest mention which can be found of the ownership of the manor by the De Lisles occurs in 1304 in an inquisition taken on the death of John son of William de Lisle.[56] The De Lisle family held it in a direct line from father to son[57] until the death of John de Lisle in 1471.[58] By his will dated 1468 he left his manor of Throckleston and Mainsbridge to his son Nicholas.[59] Nicholas by his will dated 1496 directed that after his death the issues from Swaythling, probably identical with Mainsbridge, were to be set aside for three years for the payment of legacies made in his will.[60] It appears to have then passed to the Philpotts, Elizabeth sister of Nicholas having married John Philpott.[61]

De Lisle. *Gules a cheveron between three burdock leaves or.*

Thomas his son, who was seised in 1556,[62] died in 1587,[63] and the estates of the De Lisles which had descended to him passed to his son George, afterwards created a knight,[64] who died in 1624. His son John, who inherited the estates, was also knighted, and became a staunch royalist.[65] His son Sir George Philpott took an important part in the Civil Wars of the reign of Charles I and was a noted recusant. He died leaving no male issue, and his two daughters had previously become nuns at Pontoise.[66]

Philpott. *Azure a bend ermine.*

In 1691 a fourth part of the manor of Swaythling was in the hands of Charles Holt and Anne his wife,[67] evidently one of four co-heiresses, and was sold in that year for £4,680 to Humphrey Wyrley and Charles Jennens.[68]

The remaining three-fourths of the manor[69] was conveyed by the co-heiresses, Ann Clobery widow, Ann wife of Sir Charles Holt, bart., Susan wife of Sir Thomas Trollope, and Maria Noel widow, to Edmund Dummer in 1712, but was held by Dummer Andrews for life until 1773.[70] Edmund's daughter, who had married Dennis Bond, son of her stepfather, inherited on the death of Dummer Andrews, and in 1821 this manor with Pollack was sold to John Fleming.[71]

All manorial rights have been lost, and in the schedule of the Fleming estates, of 1843,[72] Swaythling is referred to as a farm, and Sheppard's Farm is reputed to be the site of the manor-house.

POLLACK[73] formed part of the Hampton Park Estate, which was recently purchased from the Flemings by Mr. H. K. Grierson. His title deeds however shew no trace of manorial rights.

The manor of *BITTERNE* was granted to the bishop of Winchester by Edward I in 1284,[74] and later in the same year permission was given for the men in the bishop's manor of Bitterne to answer at his hundred court at Waltham, instead of at that of Sweynston, as had formerly been their custom.[75]

From this time until the middle of the sixteenth century Bitterne remained a possession of the See of Winchester.

See of Winchester. *Gules Saint Peter's keys crossed with Saint Paul's sword.*

In 1552 Bitterne with other manors was surrendered by the bishop, John Poynet, in exchange for other property, chiefly churches and their advowsons, in Hampshire.[76] Three months later these lands were granted to William earl of Wiltshire, Lord High Treasurer,[77] but they were restored by Queen Mary to the See of Winchester,[78] and Bitterne was held by the successive bishops until 1869, when, on the resignation of Bishop Sumner, it was vested in the Ecclesiastical Commissioners, who at the present time are lords of the manor.[79]

At the beginning of the nineteenth century Nathaniel Middleton of Townhill, sheriff of Hampshire, purchased a part of Bitterne manor, which he called Midanbury; it now belongs to his descendant Mr. H. B. Middleton of Dorchester.[80]

In 1330 certain lands in Swaythling, worth £20 a

52 Feet of F. Hants, East. 23 Geo. II.

53 Ibid. Trin. 39 Geo. III.

54 Information supplied by Lord Swaythling.

55 It seems probable that this manor under the name of Swaythling formed part of the grant to Hyde Abbey, by Alfred the thegn in 941. Birch, *Cart. Sax.* ii, 328.

56 Chan. Inq. p.m. 32 Edw. I, No. 60.

57 Free warren in Mainsbridge manor, among others, was granted to John de Lisle in 1306, Chart. R. 34 Edw. I, m. 99, and confirmed to his descendant John de Lisle in 1390. *Cal. of Pat.* 1388–92, p. 282. In 1339 Bartholomew de Lisle was exempt from the provision of defence for Hampshire, the guardianship of the Isle of Wight having already been committed to him. *Cal. of Close*, 1339–41, p. 117.

58 Chan. Inq. p.m. 11 Edw. IV, No. 59.

59 P.C.C. Will 3, Wattys.

60 Ibid. 7, Adeane.

61 P.C.C. Will 3, Wattys.

62 Recov. R. East. 2 & 3 Phil. and Mary, rot. 10 and 11; Feet of F. Hants, Mich. 18 & 19 Eliz. In 1563 Thos. Philpott had to apply for a writ against William Gibbons and Henry Palmer, who had seized his manors of Barton and Swaythling on the strength of certain 'evidences and other writings concerning the said premises, which had casually come to their hands and possession.' Chan. Proc. (Ser. ii), bdle. 146, No. 4.

63 Chan. Inq. p.m. 29 Eliz. (Ser. 2), No. 84.

64 Ibid. (Ser. 2), vol. 402, No. 129.

65 Ibid. 17 Chas. I (Ser. 2), pt. 2, No. 129.

66 *Herald and Genealogist*, iii, 412.

67 Feet of F. Div. Cos. East. 2 Will. and Mary

68 Ibid.

69 It is possible that the other ¼ part became the manor of Pollack, so called, which appears at this date and descends with Swaythling until purchased by Mr. H. K. Grierson (q.v.).

70 Recov. R. Mich. 11 Geo. I, rot. 45; ibid. East. 13 Geo. III, rot. 281.

71 Feet of F. Hants, Hil. 1 & 2 Geo. IV.

72 Fleming Estates Act, 1854.

73 See Swaythling.

74 Chart. R. 12 Edw. I, m. 5, No. 31.

75 *Cal. of Pat.* 1281–92, p. 122.

76 Pat. 5 Edw. VI, pt. 6, m. 26.

77 Ibid. pt. 4, m. 39.

78 Ibid. 4 & 5 Phil. and Mary, pt. 7, m. 19.

79 Information supplied by the Ecclesiastical Commissioners.

80 Information supplied by Mr. H. B. Middleton.

year, were held by Ingelram Berenger.[81] The extent of these lands appears to have been 10 acres of great oakwood, and £1 9*s.* 6*d.* rent, held of the king in chief, the rent being paid to the sheriff of the county.[82]

John son of Ingelram succeeded his father in 1337, and died seven years later leaving two sons and a daughter Christina as co-heirs, and his wife Emma, who afterwards married Edmund Hakeluyt.[83]

Nicholas, the sole survivor of John's children,[84] inherited the estate, which on his death in 1405 was divided between his two daughters, Joan wife of Peter Stantor, and Anastasia wife of Stephen Bodenham.[85] The latter survived her sister and became her heir.[86] By her second marriage to Thomas Semeley she left no children, and the lands at Swaythling, at this date called the manor, descended to Robert Bodenham, the son by her first marriage.[87]

During his lifetime he settled Swaythling and Shipton Berenger manors upon his sister Anastasia for life, but she predeceased him, and at his own death in 1467 they passed to Richard Bodenham his grandson, aged nine months.[88] Before 1480, however, the manor had become the possession of John Hall, who died in that year, leaving Swaythling to his son William.[89] Proceedings were taken against the latter in 1501, by John Pace, presumably on behalf of the Dudleys, to obtain possession of the manor, and Hall failed to maintain his right.[90]

Swaythling then became the property of Edmund Dudley, the notorious minister of Henry VII,[91] and was sold by his son John in 1538, to John Mill,[92] in whose family it descended in a direct line to Richard Mill,[93] who in 1609 settled it among other manors upon his wife Lady Mary Mill for life, reverting at her death to Thomas Savage, son of her brother John.[94] Thomas Savage entered into possession in 1623,[95] having been created a baronet. He also inherited Nursling (q.v.), the history of which Swaythling shares from this date.[96]

SAVAGE. *Argent six lions sable.*

ALLINGTON (Ellatune xi cent.; Aldington xiii cent.) at the time of the Domesday Survey was held by William Alis, it was then assessed at two hides, had a church and two mills worth 20*s.*[97] It was later held of the honour of Wallingford, parcel of the Duchy of Cornwall.[98]

A grant of the tithes of land in Allington with pannage to the newly founded priory of St. Denys, by William Alis, was confirmed by Bishop Godfrey de Lucy in 1204,[99] and a little later a further grant of rents from Allington manor was made by Thomas Alis, with the consent of Roger his father.[100] Roger was still seised in 1223,[101] but before 1304 the male line of the family apparently ceased with the death of William Alis, who left his estate to his two daughters, Isabella and Margaret, wives of Robert le Helyon and William le Rolleston, Juliana his widow, who survived him,[102] having a life interest. The moiety inherited by Margaret passed in 1306 to Richard Woodlock,[103] who died in 1318 and was succeeded by his son William and Margaret his wife.[104] The former apparently predeceased his wife, who was in possession of this portion in 1347,[105] which on her death passed to John Woodlock and Agnes his wife, who were seised in 1379.[106]

It is evident that John Woodlock died without male issue, for before 1408 this portion of Allington had passed into the possession of his daughter Joan, wife of William Oysell,[107] and later the wife of William Park.[108] She transferred this property in this year to John Fromond, steward of Winchester College, who died in 1420, and by his will left all his property in Allington, subject to his wife's life interest,[109] to the college to assist in clothing the choristers. In 1306 Robert le Helyon, who had married Isabel, co-heiress of Margaret Alis, purchased a certain messuage and land from Valentine de Chaldecote and Ellen his wife.[110] This, together with his wife's moiety of Allington manor, descended in 1326 to Thomas his son,[111] who apparently died shortly afterwards, for in 1330 Walter held Robert le Helyon's lands here.[112]

The descent of this moiety for the rest of the fourteenth century is obscure, but it seems probable that it passed in the female line to Amice wife of John More, who was holding it with her husband in 1408, when they granted a portion to John Fromond,[113] who left it with the other part of Allington manor to Winchester College (q.v.). From Henry their son and his wife Christine the remaining moiety of John More's lands in Allington passed to Nicholas,[114] who died in 1496, when it was divided between his two daughters Joan and Christine, then infants.[115] The former survived her sister, who married John Dawtrey and died without issue.[116] Joan therefore inherited the whole estate. She married first William Ludlow, by whom she had a son George, and secondly Robert Temmes. She survived him also and at her death in

[81] Pat. 4 Edw. III, pt. 1, m. 6. They had previously been forfeited owing to his adherence to the duke of Kent, at the beginning of Edw. III's reign, but were restored.

[82] Chan. Inq. p.m. 10 Edw. III, No. 29.

[83] Ibid. 17 Edw. III (1st Nos.), 56.

[84] Ibid. 23 Edw. III (2nd. Nos.), 140.

[85] Ibid. 6 Ric. II, No. 17.

[86] Ibid. 9 Ric. II, No. 57.

[87] Ibid. 8 Hen. V, No. 110.

[88] Ibid. 7 Edw. IV, No. 34.

[89] Ibid. 19 Edw. IV, No. 33.

[90] De Banco. R. Trin. 16 Hen. VII, m. 355.

[91] Esch. Inq. p.m. (Ser. 2), vol. 962, No. 16.

[92] Feet of F. Hants, Trin. 19 Hen. VIII.

[93] Recov. R. Mich. 6 Jas. I. rot. 161; Feet of F. Div. Cos. Trin. 6 Jas. I.

[94] Chan. Inq. p.m. 11 Jas. I, pt. 1, (Ser. 2), No. 76.

[95] Ibid. 20 Jas. I (Ser. 2), bdle. 35, No. 92.

[96] See Nursling. Swaythling manor was held by the king in 1631, but after that date all Savage lands were granted to Sir Francis Knollys, and the manorial rights apparently ceased or were transferred to Nursling.

[97] *V.C.H. Hants*, i, 498*a*.

[98] Chan. Inq. p.m. 11 Edw. II, No. 3; ibid. 2 Hen. VI, No. 23; ibid. 5 Chas I. (Ser. 2), bdle. 18, No. 26.

[99] *V.C.H. Hants*, ii, 160.

[100] Anct. D. (P.R.O.), B. 28.

[101] Close, 7 Hen. III, pt. 2, m. 7.

[102] Feet of F. Hants, 34 Edw. I.

[103] Ibid.

[104] Chan. Inq. p.m. 11 Edw. II, No. 3.

[105] Bk. of Aids, 20 Edw. III.

[106] Feet of F. Hants, 2 Ric. II. John Woodlock and Richard acknowledged the right of the church of St. Denys to certain rents in Allington in 1385.

[107] Feet of F. Hants, 10 Hen. IV.

[108] Chan. Inq. p.m. 2 Hen. VI, No. 23.

[109] His widow evidently did not die till over twenty years later, for the college did not obtain licence to hold this manor with others left by John Fromond, in mortmain, until 1442.

[110] Feet of F. Hants, 34 Edw. I, No. 279.

[111] Chan. Inq. p.m. 19 Edw. II. No. 45.

[112] Bk. of Aids, 1330.

[113] Feet of F. Hants, 9 Hen. IV.

[114] Early Chan. Proc. bdle. 219, m. 76.

[115] Chan. Inq. p.m. (Ser. 2), vol. 11, No. 57.

[116] Ibid. 5–6 Eliz. (Ser. 2), vol. 1002, No. 7.

1563 her son George Ludlow became her heir.[117] His son Sir Edmund succeeded him in 1580,[118] and obtained a grant from the king of free warren in his lands here and elsewhere in 1618.[119] Four years later, however, Allington manor was purchased by John Major of Southampton for £900.[120] Major died in 1630, and was succeeded by his son Richard.[121] He left Allington to his nephew Major Dunch, who had also inherited Baddesley and Townhill manors before 1672.[122]

From this date Allington manor follows the same descent as the manor of Townhill (q.v.).

The manor of *BARTON* in South Stoneham is called *BARTON PEVEREL*, from the family of Peverel, which appears to have held it from a very early date.

Andrew Peverel inherited lands there in 1227 on the death of his father Robert.[123] On Andrew's death it passed to his son Thomas, who died in 1306,[124] being followed by his son Andrew,[125] who died in 1328,[126] and his grandson, another Andrew, successively.

The latter died without issue in 1376,[127] when Barton Peverel was divided between his two great nephews, Edward Fitz Herbert and John Brocas, grandsons respectively of his sisters Lucy and Alice.[128]

On the death of John Brocas without issue in 1377–8 Edward acquired the whole manor,[129] which in 1387, subject to the life interest of his widow Joan, passed to his sister Alice, wife of Thomas West.[130] Her son Thomas,[131] and his two sons, Thomas[132] and Reginald, afterwards Lord De La Warr,[133] held it successively.

From Reginald it passed to Richard,[134] and thence to Thomas West,[135] who in 1539 sold Barton Peverel manor to Peter Philpott,[136] in whose family it descended, like Swaythling (q.v.), until 1636, when Henry Philpott, a noted recusant, sold it to Edward Bosden.[137]

Shortly afterwards it was acquired by Benjamin Wybarne on a lease for thirteen years, but owing to his recusancy it was sequestered in 1645. Edward Bosden appealed to the crown on the expiration of the term and obtained the discharge of the estate.[138] He apparently disposed of all claim in Barton Peverel manor to his lessee, Wybarne, whose son John held the manor and its water-mill in 1719.[139]

In 1759 Katherine Wybarne held the manor,[140] but in 1764 the property was purchased by Thomas Lee Dummer,[141] and from this date has followed the descent of the manors of Netley and Hound,[142] Mr. Tankerville Chamberlayne being the present lord of the manor.

The manor of *EASTLEIGH*, in South Stoneham, is given in the Domesday Survey as the property of Henry the Treasurer, and a former possession of Earl Godwin.[143]

The overlordship of the manor during the next two centuries is difficult to trace. In 1260 Herbert son of Peter answered for the Eastleigh fee, but in 1306 it was held by the Beauchamps of the king in chief by the service of being chamberlain of the king's exchequer.[144] The Beauchamp estates passed by marriage to Richard Nevill, earl of Warwick, the king-maker. His wife was a Beauchamp, and survived both her husband and her two daughters.

At the beginning of the reign of Henry VII she granted the whole of the Warwick estates to the king and his heirs male.[145] From this date the manor of Eastleigh has been held directly of the crown.[146]

In 1167 Ralph de Eastleigh held lands here,[147] being followed by his son Hugh, who in 1219 increased the estate by the purchase of other lands from Richard son of Guy, and John de Venoiz, from whom he was to hold the same by the service of a third part of a knight's fee.[148]

At the latter end of this century Eastleigh had passed into the possession of William de Roos and Eustacia his wife.[149] In 1271 they conveyed it to William de Wyntershull and Beatrice his wife, to hold of William de Roos and his heirs by a rent of a pair of gold spurs.[150] Eastleigh became the property of John de Wyntershull, son of William, in 1287,[151] and at his death passed to his brother Walter, who was holding in 1295[152] and 1316.[153]

William, who died in 1362, demised it to Thomas his brother,[154] who died in 1388,[155] and was succeeded by his son, another Thomas, on whose death in 1417 the manor passed to Thomas de Wyntershull his son.[156] He died without issue in 1420, when the manor was divided between his sisters, Joan wife of William Catton, and Agnes wife of William Basset.[157] Agnes

117 Chan. Inq. p.m. 5–6 Eliz. (Ser. 2), vol. 1002, No. 7.

118 Ibid. 22 Eliz. pt. 2, No. 122.

119 Pat. 15 Jas. I. pt. 15, m. 14.

120 Close, 20 Jas. I, pt. 8. m. 21.

121 Chan. Inq. p.m. 5 Chas. I. pt. 18, No. 26.

122 Recov. R. Mich. 24 Chas. II. rot. 210.

123 *Excerpta e Rot. Fin.* (Rec. Com.), 162. These lands were held of the king in chief.

124 Chan. Inq. p.m. 34 Edw. I, No. 39. Thomas was seised of a moiety of the manor only. The property included a water-mill.

125 *Feud. Aids*, ii, 318.

126 Chan. Inq. p.m. 1 Edw. III (2nd Nos.), 20; ibid. 2 Edw. III, No. 53.

127 Ibid. 49 Edw. III, pt. 2 (1st Nos.), 26.

128 Ibid.

129 Ibid. 1 Ric. II, No. 4; ibid. 2 Ric. II, No. 93. This document refers to a water-mill and inclosed (*separalis*) water.

130 Chan. Inq. p.m. 10 Ric. II, No. 18; ibid. 16 Ric. II, pt. 1, No. 10. Joan died in 1393.

131 Ibid. 19 Ric. II, No. 49.

132 Ibid. 7 Hen. IV, No. 26.

133 Ibid. 4 Hen. V, No. 28.

134 Ibid. 29 Hen. VI, No. 21.

135 Ibid. 16 Edw. IV, No. 62.

136 Feet of F. Hants, Hil. 30 Hen. VIII.

137 Recov. R. Trin. 12 Chas. I, rot. 22.

138 *Cal. of Com. for Compounding*, 996–7.

139 Recov. R. Hil. 6 Geo. I, rot. 84.

140 Com. Pleas Recov. R. Hil. 3 Geo. II, m. 6.

141 Ibid. Hil. 4 Geo. III, m. 69.

142 See Hound.

143 *V.C.H. Hants*, i, 500*a*.

144 Chan. Inq. p.m. 34 Edw. I, No. 13; ibid. 11 Ric. II, No. 54.

145 G.E.C. *Complete Peerage*.

146 Chan. Inq. p.m. 41 Eliz. pt. 2 (Ser. 2), No. 36; ibid. 6 Chas. I, pt. 2 (Ser. 2), No. 121.

147 Pipe R. 13 Hen. II. In 1200 licence was given to a certain William Brewer for the building of a castle either at Stoke or Eastleigh in Hampshire (Rot. Chart. 2 John, m. 28; Duchy of Lanc. Misc. Bks. xi, 3), but the fact that there is no subsequent allusion to a castle proves that his choice did not fall upon the latter place.

148 Feet of F. Hants, 3 Hen. III; ibid. Mich. 4 Hen. III.

149 Feet of F. Hants, Mich. 56 Hen. III.

150 Ibid.; Close, 15 Edw. I, m. 5.

151 Chan. Inq. p.m. 15 Edw. I, No. 15.

152 Feet of F. Hants, East. 24 Edw. I.

153 *Feud. Aids*, ii, 318.

154 Chan. Inq. p.m. 35 Edw. III, pt. 2, No. 82.

155 Ibid. 11 Ric. II, No. 54.

156 Ibid. 5 Hen. V, No. 52.

157 *Feud. Aids*, ii, 351.

sold her share in the estate to the children of her sister,[158] and Eastleigh then became the property of William Weston, son of Joan by her first marriage, and subsequently, on his death without issue, of his sister Margaret, wife of Thomas Welles.[159] She, on her death in 1513,[160] left her son John Welles as heir, and from him Eastleigh passed to his son Thomas,[161] and in 1553 to his grandson Gilbert Welles.[162] Gilbert[163] died in 1598,[164] and was succeeded by his son Thomas, and afterwards in 1631, by his grandson Gilbert,[165] whose lands were confiscated for recusancy during the life of his sons Charles and Swithun, the family of Welles being notoriously recusant and royalist.[166] Their lands were, however, subsequently restored, and Eastleigh came into the possession of Thomas Welles and his son Henry successively. In 1734 Henry, Charles, and Alexander Welles sold Eastleigh manor with two water-mills, court leet and court baron, free warren and fishery, to James Ryder,[167] and before the end of the eighteenth century the whole estate had passed into the possession of Walter Smythe, who purchased the manor with the attached farm and mills from Peter Rorke and John Prujean in 1779.[168] Two years later he mortgaged Eastleigh to Thomas Bennett for £2,000.[169]

From this date no further trace of Eastleigh is to be found, and it is probable that it was incorporated with the adjoining manor of Barton Peverel;[170] for Mr. Tankerville Chamberlayne, lord of that manor, holds Eastleigh farm and Great Eastleigh House with it, although no rights are attached to either. Any rights that formerly existed must have fallen into abeyance in the early part of the nineteenth century.

In 1124 Henry I founded in *PORTSWOOD* the priory of St. Denys, and in the foundation charter granted to it a parcel of land between Portswood and the River Itchen which formerly paid 11*s.* 6*d.* yearly to the king.[171] In 1189 the priory received a further grant from Richard I, of Kingsland, and a wood called Portswood which gives the name to the surrounding district,[172] and in 1305 Elias Starie granted to the monks 25*s.* rent from land in Portswood.[173] These lands and rents were held by the prior until the Reformation,[174] when the value of the 'manor' of St. Denys with its grange is given as £13 6*s.* 8*d.*[175] In 1538 the site of the priory and the adjoining grange, with about 374 acres of land and 90 acres of wood, were granted by the king to Francis Dawtrey.[176] A manor of Portswood mentioned in a list of his property made at his death in 1569 is probably identical with this priory manor.[177] This had been previously settled on his wife Elizabeth for her life, with reversion on her death to Richard Knight.[178] John Knight, son of Richard, was seised in 1615, and Portswood was apparently in the same hands in 1658, when a map of the manor gives John Knight as the owner. This map shows the demesne lands to comprise the priory site and buildings, a conduit, paddock and orchard, and to the south-east of the church a weir for the taking of fish from the Itchen, which supplied the ancient convent.[179] The Morgans were in possession of Portswood manor in 1689[180] and 1693, and it descended under the will of Richard Morgan to Thomas Wood, who was seised in 1776.[181] From Thomas Wood, junr., who held the manor in 1812,[182] it has passed by many conveyances to Mr. T. A. Skelton.[183] He sold the site of the priory to Mr. W. H. Baigent in 1878, and it has recently been disposed of for building purposes.

At the present time it appears that there are no manorial rights here, nor can record of any be found. No courts are now held, as the Portswood men have always attended the Southampton court since the time of Richard II, being within the borough.

In the thirteenth century record is found concerning land in *SHAMBLEHURST* in South Stoneham. In 1219, 1 carucate of land in that place was granted by a certain John son of Peter to the prior of St. Denys, near Southampton, who was to hold the same by payment of a rent of 1 lb. of cummin.[184] At this same period half a carucate of land was held by Svelfus son of Walter, who in 1219 conveyed it to Matthew de Wellop.[185]

Thirteen years later a certain Matthew Turpin and Anne his wife held the same amount of land here.[186]

John Biset held the manor at his death in 1241, and on the division of his estates among his three co-heiresses Margaret his daughter, wife of Richard de Rivers, obtained possession of this manor,[187] which was held of Robert de Vere, earl of Oxford, who purchased from John de Rivers in 1317 all his rights in Townhill and Shamblehurst.[188]

No mention of Shamblehurst is to be found among the lands of the De Veres after 1317, and since at the

158 Close, 14 Hen. VI, m. 6. The Basset family were to receive in recompense from the heirs of Thomas Welles £4 yearly rent in perpetuity.

159 Feet of F. Hants, Mich. 4 Edw. IV.

160 Chan. Inq. p.m. (Ser. 2), vol. 27, No. 62; She had married as her second husband—Appisley.

161 Ibid.

162 Ibid.

163 He appears to have leased out the manor during his lifetime to Robert and William Leyse.

164 Chan. Inq. p.m. 41 Eliz. pt. 2, (Ser. 2), No. 36, Feet of F. Div. Cos. Trin. 11 Jas. I.

165 Chan. Inq. p.m. 6 Chas. I, pt. 2, (Ser. 2), No. 121.

166 *Cal. of Com. for Compounding*, pp. 184, 3138, 3287. The value of Charles Welles' land in Eastleigh was £45 per annum. His grandmother Isabel, and his mother Mary, who had married Sir William Courtney, both held certain lands in Eastleigh for life in dower.

167 Feet of F. Hants, East. 7 Geo. II.

168 Com. Pleas Recov. R. Trin. 19 Geo. III, m. 228; ibid. Hil. 21 Geo. III, m. 73.

169 Ibid. m. 156.

170 In 1831 Barton and 'Eastley' formed a tithing of the parish of South Stoneham; *Pop. Ret.*

171 *V.C.H. Hants*, ii, 160, Dugdale, *Mon.* vi, 213.

172 B.M. Add. MS. 15314, fol. 99*b*, 100; *V.C.H. Hants*, ii, 160*b*; Pipe R. 13 Hen. II.

173 Pat. 33 Edw. I, m. 24.

174 Occasional leases of land in Portswood by the prior are found; see Anct. D. (P.R.O.), B. 29, 36.

175 Dugdale, *Mon.* vi, 213.

176 Pat. 30 Hen. VIII, pt. 6, m. 4.

177 Chan. Inq. p.m. (Ser. 2), vol. 152, No. 140.

178 Ibid.

179 *Hants Field Club Proc.* vol. 3, pt. 2. It was one of the customary duties for the men of Portswood manor to keep this king's weir in repair.

180 Recov. R. Trin. 1 Will. and Mary rot. 72.

181 Feet of F. Vill Southampton, Trin. 16 Geo. III.

182 Recov. R. East. 52 Geo. III, rot. 399.

183 *Hants Field Club Proc.* vol. iii, pt. 2.

184 Feet of F. Hants, 3 Hen. III, No. 16. This grant was confirmed forty years later by Walter of Shamblehurst, on condition that he received from the prior for his life a daily allowance of one white loaf and two ordinary loaves, and one gallon of beer, with a cart-load of wood yearly. Feet of F. Hants, 33 Hen. III, No. 53.

185 Ibid. 5 Hen. III, No. 27.

186 *Cal. of Pat.* 1231–4, p. 127.

187 *Excerpta e Rot. Fin.* (Rec. Com.), i, 358.

188 B.M. Add. Chart. 55, D. 28.

Dissolution Shamblehurst farm with Townhill manor was in the possession of Netley Abbey, it seems probable that the grant of Robert de Vere of Townhill to Netley Abbey in 1329 included Shamblehurst.[189]

The lands of Netley Abbey in Shamblehurst were granted by Henry VIII, in 1537, to Sir William Paulet, kt.,[190] and two years later, by a similar grant, he received that part of Shamblehurst which had formerly belonged to St. Denys' Priory, and is described as the grange.[191] In the inquisition taken on the death of Sir William Paulet's grandson in 1599–1600, Shamblehurst is no longer called a manor, but merely a farm held with Townhill.[192] Later than this no trace of manorial rights can be found, and if any such had existed it is evident that the Paulets allowed them to fall into abeyance. The history of the farm of Shamblehurst from this date is the same as that of Townhill manor (q.v.).[193] Shamblehurst was not sold with Townhill, however, to Lord Swaythling, but still remains in the possession of Mr. Caleb W. Gater of Salisbury, and is occupied by Mr. N. Baxendale.[194]

CHURCH The church of *OUR LADY* has a chancel 24 ft. by 15 ft. 6 in. with south vestry, nave 52 ft. 4 in. by 20 ft. 4 in. with small north and larger south transepts, and a west tower.

The plan of the nave and chancel seems to belong to the end of the twelfth century, and the chancel arch and walls of the chancel and perhaps a little of the nave walls are of this date.

The east window of the chancel is of the fifteenth century, with three cinquefoiled lights and tracery over, and in the north wall are three single lights, the middle window higher in the wall than the others, and round-headed, being of the date of the wall, the lancets on either side of it being thirteenth-century additions. On the south side the same arrangement formerly existed, but the west window of the three is not now to be seen, probably because it has been blocked by the modern vestry. The small pointed doorway opening to the vestry appears to be a thirteenth-century priest's door. In the east wall of the chancel, north of the altar table, is a rebated recess with an arched head, and in the north wall a second recess, but without a rebate.

The chancel arch of two pointed orders with a roll on the western angles, and large moulded label and abaci, has detached jamb-shafts to the outer order, and keeled engaged shafts to the inner. The latter have hollow-fluted capitals and spurred bases, while the capitals of the outer order are carved with plain foliage.

Hardly any features of ancient date remain in the nave, which has two windows on the north and one on the south, and is fitted with a west gallery. The north transept has modern two-light windows on east and west, and opens to the nave by a modern arch of twelfth-century style, but the jambs of the arch are of old stonework, perhaps of fourteenth-century date.

The south transept opens to the nave by a tall arch with a poor imitation of twelfth-century detail, and is of modern date.

The tower is apparently of the sixteenth century, with two-light belfry windows uncusped, and an embattled parapet. Over the west doorway, which is a modern imitation of twelfth-century work, is a niche, and the west doorway of the nave, on the east of the tower, is of uncertain date though probably mediaeval, with a plain chamfered arch. The roofs of the church are red tiled and the internal woodwork is nearly all modern. In the vestry is a seventeenth-century table, and on the south side of the chancel arch a good carved chest of much the same date. Over the chancel arch are the royal arms of Charles II, dated 1660, and above the belfry window on the south face of the tower is a sundial dated 1738.

The font, at the north-east of the nave, is of Purbeck marble, of late twelfth-century date, with a square bowl having four round-headed arches on each face inclosing wedge-shaped objects in relief. The upper surface of the bowl has foliage in the angles, and the bowl is carried on a central and four outer shafts, the latter being modern, while the base stone is old.

There are several interesting monuments. On the north wall of the chancel, below the middle window, is a pretty recessed tomb of *c.* 1540, with a panelled base in three divisions, each bearing a blank cartouche in a wreath, while on the upper part, which has a four-centred canopy with panelled soffit of Gothic detail, flanked by pilasters of Italian style carrying an arabesque cornice, are three other panels, the two outer with blank cartouches, and the middle one having a tablet engraved with the initials F.D., B.D.

On the south side of the chancel, opposite this tomb, is that of Edmond Clerke, 1632, and his wife Anne: their figures kneeling under a canopy, with those of four sons and eight daughters on the base of the monument. The north wall of the north transept is entirely occupied by the large grey and white marble monument of Edmund Dummer, 1724.

There are three bells, one by Gillett and Bland of Croydon, 1880, and the others of 1603 and 1619.

The plate consists of a silver cup of 1630, a second cup with a paten given in 1704 by Mrs. Amy Clarke, another cup and paten given in 1756 by Mrs. Elizabeth Shoare, a salver of 1828, given by Mrs. Mary Jones, and a pewter flagon, the gift of the Rev. W. D. Harrison.

The first book of registers goes from 1663 to 1713, the second to 1754, and the third, containing baptisms and burials only, to 1793. The fourth book continues these entries to 1812, while the marriages from 1754 to 1812 are entered in two other books.

ADVOWSON *SOUTH STONEHAM* church at the time of the Domesday Survey was the property of Richer the clerk, who held this, with two dependent churches near Southampton, of the bishop of Winchester.[195]

In the Valor of 1535 South Stoneham rectory is described as an appropriation of St. Mary's Church, Southampton,[196] and both churches were peculiar

[189] Chan. Inq. a.q.d. 2 Edw. III, No. 19. See Townhill.

[190] Pat. 28 Hen. VIII, pt. 3, m. 12.

[191] Pat. 31 Hen. VIII, pt. 5, m. 5.

[192] Chan. Inq. p.m. (Ser. 2), vol. 262, No. 125.

[193] See Townhill.

[194] Information from Lord Swaythling.

[195] *V.C.H. Hants*, i, 467 *a*. At this date the tithes of South Stoneham and 1 hide of land there were appurtenances of the church.

[196] As early as 1291 in the Taxatio of Pope Nicholas a chapel attached to St. Mary's Church is mentioned, but South Stoneham church is not included by name. *Pope Nich. Tax.* (Rec. Com.), 210.

benefices, in the gift and under the special jurisdiction of the bishop of Winchester.[197]

During the past three centuries the living has been in the gift of the rector of St. Mary's, Southampton, who still holds the right of presentation.[198]

Of the ecclesiastical property belonging to South Stoneham, the tithe-rent charges were transferred from St. Mary's to the church of Portswood in 1863,[199] while later still, in 1879, a grant of some of the lands was made to the bishop of the diocese as endowment.[200]

CHARITIES By an order of the Charity Commissioners of 12 May, 1905, a scheme was established for the administration of the three following charities, viz.:—

James Serle's Charity gift, about 1680, endowment £50 19*s.* 1*d.* consols, income to be divided between two poor widows of the tithing of Allington and two of the tithing of Shamblehurst.

George Alexander Fullerton, will, proved P.C.C. 1847, £360 consols, income to be distributed amongst the distressed poor of the ancient parish of South Stoneham, and Harriet Louisa Crabbe, will, proved P.C.C. 1848, £90 consols, income to be distributed at Christmas in each year among poor persons of the ancient parish of South Stoneham. The several sums of stock are held by the official trustees, and the dividends thereon, amounting together to £12 10*s.* a year, are applied by the administering trustees appointed by the above-mentioned order proportionately in respect of each of the charities.

In 1689 the Rev. John Dummer gave to the vicar and churchwardens an annuity of 40*s.* payable out of his estate called Barn's Land, to be divided between two poor of the village of Swaythling and two of West End. The rent-charge is paid by R. Warneford Fletcher, esq. In 1905 10*s.* was given to each of four persons.

In or about 1863 Miss Janet Hoyes gave a sum of £109 17*s.* 9*d.* consols, the income to be applied, subject to repairs of monument, in the distribution of clothing among the poor of the parish. The stock is held by the official trustees and the dividends, amounting to £2 14*s.* 10*d.*, are duly applied.

Chapelry of Bitterne.—By deed, dated 11 June, 1868, Stewart Macnaghten, as the residuary legatee of the late Miss Janet Hoyes—after reciting that in order to carry into effect the intention of that lady he had at his own expense placed a clock in the tower of the church of St. Saviour's and that a sum of £55 had been subscribed by various donors towards winding and keeping in proper repair the said clock—transferred to the Official Trustees of Charitable Funds £100 reduced £3 per cents. (now £100 consols), the charity to be known as 'The Janet Hoyes Memorial Clock Charity.'

The Wesleyan Chapel founded by deed, 1826—By an order of the charity Commissioners of 25 May, 1886, a scheme was established vesting property in trustees thereby appointed on trusts of 'The Wesleyan Chapel Model Deed.'

Portswood, tithing of.—In 1879 Charles Twynam by will, proved at London, left to the vicar of South Stoneham £100 upon trust to invest and to apply the income for the benefit of the poor of the tithing of Portswood residing within one mile from the parish church. The legacy was invested in £100 5*s.* consols with the official trustees.

In 1883 William Ross by will, proved at Winchester, bequeathed funds to the incumbent and churchwardens of Christ Church, Portswood, upon trust to invest and divide the income at Christmas amongst poor persons of the district apparently of the age of sixty-one years or upwards. The legacy was invested in £493 16*s.* 5*d.* stock, now consols, with the official trustees.

197 *Valor Eccl.* (Rec. Com.), ii, Appendix.

198 Inst. Bks. P.R.O. Occasionally the right of presentation for one turn was sold by the rectors, e.g. Inst. Bks. P.R.O. 1626, 1631, 1743.

199 *Lond. Gaz.* 15 Sept. 1863.

200 Ibid. 7 Mar. 1879.

BOROUGH OF SOUTHAMPTON

Pleasantly situated on the banks of the Southampton Water, on a tongue of land with the mouth of the River Itchen to the east, and on the west a fine bay formed by the outflow of the River Test, Southampton has grown, especially within recent years, far beyond its ancient proportions.

Southampton. *Party fessewise argent and gules with three roses countercoloured.*

Leland[1] heard on his visit to Southampton before 1546 that the town did not originally stand where it now does, but in the immediate neighbourhood of St. Mary's Church, some quarter of a mile or more to the north-east of the walled town, whence it stretched away to the river side. Camden,[2] some thirty years after, heard the same account, and excavations of the last century go some way to confirm the tradition which these writers have handed down.[3] The growth of the town on its present stronger and better site probably belongs to the earlier part of the eleventh century in the settled time before the death of Canute in 1035. By the end of that century there is evidence that the town stood where it does now; while the tokens of the population would seem to indicate an occupation of the old site till about the period suggested. The movement was but within the same civil and ecclesiastical district, and it seems likely that there is evidence of the relationship between Old and New Hampton in the traditionary ecclesiastical connexion between the churches of the borough.[4]

The mediaeval plan of the town is a parallelogram stretching north and south, following the line of the western shore. Its fortifications are still to be traced on every side, and partly on the north and almost entirely on the west they exist to this day in good preservation, affording a unique and striking example of ancient defences. The parallelogram was divided by several principal streets. English Street, the modern High Street, runs due north and south from the Bargate on the north: French Street, which still retains its old name, runs parallel to it on the west, and farther to the west is the ancient Bugle or Bull Street. The last two run no farther northwards than St. Michael's Square, the north-western quarter

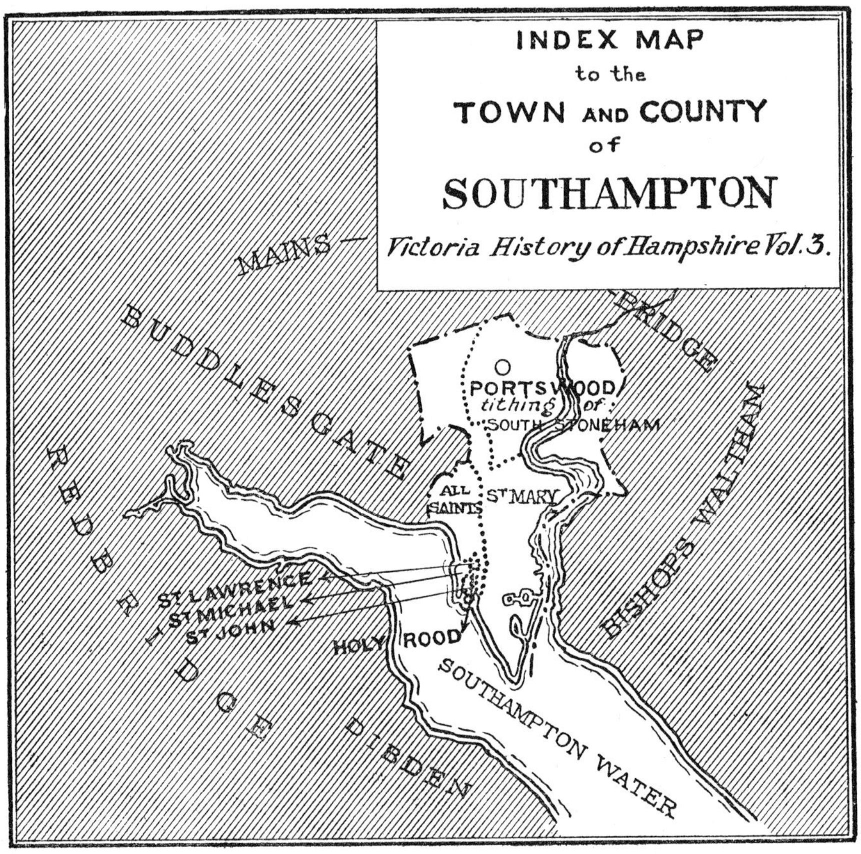

[1] *Itin.* (ed. Hearne), iii, 90, 91.
[2] *Brit.* (ed. 1590), 190.
[3] *V.C.H. Hants*, i, 395–6.
[4] See below under St. Mary's.

of the town being in great part taken up by the castle inclosure. West Street leads from Bugle Street, through the West Gate, still existing, to the western shore. East Street, which retains its ancient name, ran from near the north end of High Street to the East Gate, now destroyed, and so into a suburb of old standing. Lower down the east side of High Street the modern Bridge Street, which leads to the railway station and floating bridge, is an expansion of an ancient lane which ended at a postern in the town walls. Still farther south exists with but slight alteration the ancient Winkle Street, which passes the entrance to God's House and through the South Castle Gate, still existing.

On the east side of the old town the long streets or alleys running north and south, called Back of the Walls and Canal [5] Walk or the Ditches, mark exactly the fortifications on that side.

At the south of the town an ancient quay at the bottom of High Street has been transformed into the appliances of electric trams and other facilities. At the present time the population of the borough and county of the borough is estimated at 108,000.

In spite of prosperity and growth of population, which are so often fatal to the older buildings of a town, Southampton is rich in remains of mediaeval houses and the vaulted cellars on which they commonly stood. Besides the well-known 'King John's House,' elsewhere described, there are several pieces of twelfth-century work, the best being a house on the south of St. Michael's Church, and 'Canute's Palace' in Porter's Lane. The former has a large vaulted cellar with a central round-headed entrance, and on the ground floor two semicircular-headed doorways, all of late twelfth-century date. Only the lower part of the early house remains, but at the back are many traces of later mediaeval work. On the west side of St. Michael's Square is the fine timber-built house now called 'Henry VIII's Palace,' and probably to be identified with that built by Henry Huttoft in the

'Henry VIII's Palace,' Southampton

wide modern platform with pier and quays, and farther to the east lie the spacious docks and railway station, while on the west of the town the mediaeval quay outside West Gate, the ancient scene of traffic, has entirely changed its purpose and given way to a broad esplanade of land reclaimed from the sea outside the walls, connecting the southern quays with the railway station of Southampton West.

To the north-east the ground connecting the ancient town with the old suburb of Northam has been built over. To the north Portswood must be included, and to the west Freemantle. Fortunately there are beautiful public parks, the inheritance of ancient days in one form or other; and there is the Southampton Common, a lovely piece of forest scenery approached from the town by a wide avenue of old elms. This large extent of busy life is well connected and held together with all the modern early years of the sixteenth century, and mentioned by Leland. It has four projecting gables towards the square, being of two stories and an attic, with a row of large mullioned windows on the first floor. It runs back some distance from the street, and includes parts of an older building. A little to the north of the square is Simnel Street, where the vaulted basement of an early fourteenth-century house has been preserved from the general demolition which has here taken place. It is a good example, vaulted in two bays with excellent details, and has a stone-hooded fireplace on the east with brackets for lights, and two windows and a doorway on the south. Parts of the house attached to it yet stand, with the pit of a large garderobe.

Leland mentions the timber houses of Southampton, and no doubt the majority of the mediaeval town buildings were so constructed, standing on masonry

[5] So called from the abortive canal brought through the East Ditch of the town in 1795 which opened into the Southampton Water through an archway under God's House spur work (see below).

basements. Such basements, stone vaulted, remain in a good many places, as at Nos. 91 and 111, High Street. On the latter is an ancient timber building, now faced with cement in imitation of stonework, and other timber buildings, now brick-fronted, are the Nag's Head and Red Lion Inns in High Street. Next to Holy Rood Church is another timber house, faced with tiles which are made in imitation of brickwork, and there are several other examples of this, both in white and red tiles, in various parts of the town.

A great deal of good wood and iron work of later date exists, as at Nos. 1, 17, 90, 111, and 150, High Street, at Bugle House in Bugle Street, and elsewhere. A chimney-piece at 17, High Street is dated 1605, and bears the initials of James I. The many eighteenth-century projecting bay windows are a prominent feature, those of the Dolphin Inn in High Street being conspicuous examples, and a good deal of pretty red brickwork of this time has so far escaped destruction in favour of something more showy.

The modern buildings of Southampton are neither better nor worse than the general run; the Hartley Institute is the best of them, and has a front to the High Street of some distinction.

The ancient boundaries of Southampton are said to date from the reign of King John,[6] and though they cannot with certainty be traced further back, yet it is not to be supposed that the borough was without an ample extent of land from the very first. In documents of 956 and 1045 we read of a haye or inclosure, which could hardly have been other than the western boundary of the town's land.[7] Again, in 1180 (26 Hen. II), William Briwer[8] was made forester of the forest of Bere with power to arrest transgressors there between the 'bars' of Hampton and the gates of Winchester; and these 'bars' almost certainly formed the northern boundary of the town's liberties, considerably to the north of, and not to be confounded with, the present Bargate, the core of which then existed. Moreover it is distinctly stated that land granted to the canons of St. Denys within the area in question, as early as 1174 (see below), formed a portion of that for which the town paid its annual fee-farm,[9] so that, in spite of the town tradition, it is fair to conclude that these liberties of the borough existed before any grant of King John, if such there were, and that whatever he may have done in this respect could only have been in confirmation.

In 1254 the bound and limit between the forest of Bere and the King's Majesty's town of Southampton was declared to be 'from Acard's (now Four-post) bridge as the way lies northward by the crosses to Cut-thorn,[10] and from Cut-thorn to Burle stone, and from Burle stone to the water course of Furse-welle as it goes down to the River Itchen.'[11] Within these bounds the canons of St. Denys held a certain wood called Portswood by a grant from King Richard in free, full, and perpetual alms. For this wood and the land called Kingsland the aforesaid king remitted 100*s.* of his farm of the town of Southampton.[12] In 1488 almost identical but more elaborate boundaries were given.[13]

'The perambulacion of the franchise of the toune of Suthampton graunted by King John and confermed by mayny other noble kings his successours.'

'Item, first fro Barred-gate unto Acorn [otherwise Acard's] brig and crosse, west-north-west: and fro the Acorn brig and crosse unto the Hode crosse, north, thorough the village called Hill: and fro the Hode crosse to the Cutted-thorne crosse, suth suth est: and fro the Cutted-thorne crosse to the Berell stone crosse, est, at Burger's strete ende: and so along Burger's strete and thorough Kinghern [otherwise Langherne] yate unto Haven stone in Hilton upponne the water side, est: and fro Haven stone along as the water lyeth unto Hegstone [later Millstone] at Blackworth, suth: and fro Hegstone as the water lyeth to Ichenworth [i.e. by the existing Cross house] suth: and fro Ichenworth as the water lyeth to the Mesynedue [Maison Dieu] yate of Suthampton, west.'[14]

It is difficult to reconcile what were till lately the municipal and Parliamentary limits of the borough county with those given in the documents above. From these it would appear that the western boundary was through the village of Hill, including a considerable amount of property, with Banister's, all of which was in fact ultimately excluded, as a glance at the map will show. This boundary was long in dispute. In 1528 (20 Henry VIII) an entry occurs of a 'meeting of the Town's counsel and Mistress Whitehede for the variance of our liberties in Hill lane.'[15] In 1600,[16] 1611,[17] 1651,[18] and again in

[6] See below, perambulation of 1488 and a similar document of the reign of Hen. VIII, in which the liberties are said to have been granted in John's first year (1199). 'The copy of our perambulacon graunted by King John, the ffyrst yere of his reigne, of the circuyte of our fraunchese.' Boke of Remembrances, Corp. MSS. last leaf.

[7] Birch, *Cart. Sax.* iii, 99; Kemble, *Codex Dipl.* No. 781.

[8] Dugdale, *Bar.* i, 700.

[9] Anct. Town Accts.; Madox, *Hist. of Exch.* i, 409.

[10] Here till within the last two centuries the town held its court leet by a well known and traditional tree—probably a holly—recalling the memories of early English jurisdiction. It was an inclosure near the north boundary of the common, and to the right of the Winchester road, deriving its name from some traditional 'cutted-thorn,' where the most ancient criminal court was held; and not far from it to the west, and now covered by a reservoir, stood the ancient gallows, last used in 1785; the natural appendage of the borough jurisdiction from time immemorial.

[11] 'De ponte de Acardo sicut via extendit per cruces versus Aquilonem usque Cuthorne, et a Cuttethorne usque ad Burlestone usque ad aqueductum de Fursewelle sicut descendit in Ychens;' Oak Bk. (Corp. MSS.), fol. 56.

[12] Ibid.

[13] Lib. Remembranc. BB. fol. 1*b*.

[14] Corp. MSS.

[15] The details of the dinner, over which the lady of the manor and the lawyers discussed the point, are given; lastly comes the fee, 'Item, to master Wintershull for his labour hither V*s.*' What transpired does not appear; but the dispute dragged on and the court leet continued presenting their grievances and defining their claims, which they generally did in the terms of 1488.

[16] In this year they find 'the vanes at Hill bridge doe not stand as in times past . . . . We challenge our liberties on the east side of Hill street and the inhabitants there ought to do their suit and service at our Law day, as we suppose, our perambulation considered and regarded which leadeth us hereunto.'

[17] Then they added a presentment, as they had done before, of their need of a 'court of survey' for viewing their lands and writings 'that they may not only know but enjoy their rights.'

[18] Already 'Banisters' was an important part of the disputed area. As early as 1474 a dispute is hinted at by an entry of the sum of 8*s.* given to the town clerk 'to pay unto Whitehede for the matter of Banestres court'; in 1651 a suit was commenced by Sir Edward Banister against the town to try whether Banister's farm was in the county of Hants or in that of the town. The trial was ordered by the Upper Bench of Westminster to be at New Sarum. The town in maintenance of its ancient boundaries produced before Lord Justice Rolle the perambulations given above among other evidences not specified; but it is said that the town lost its case.

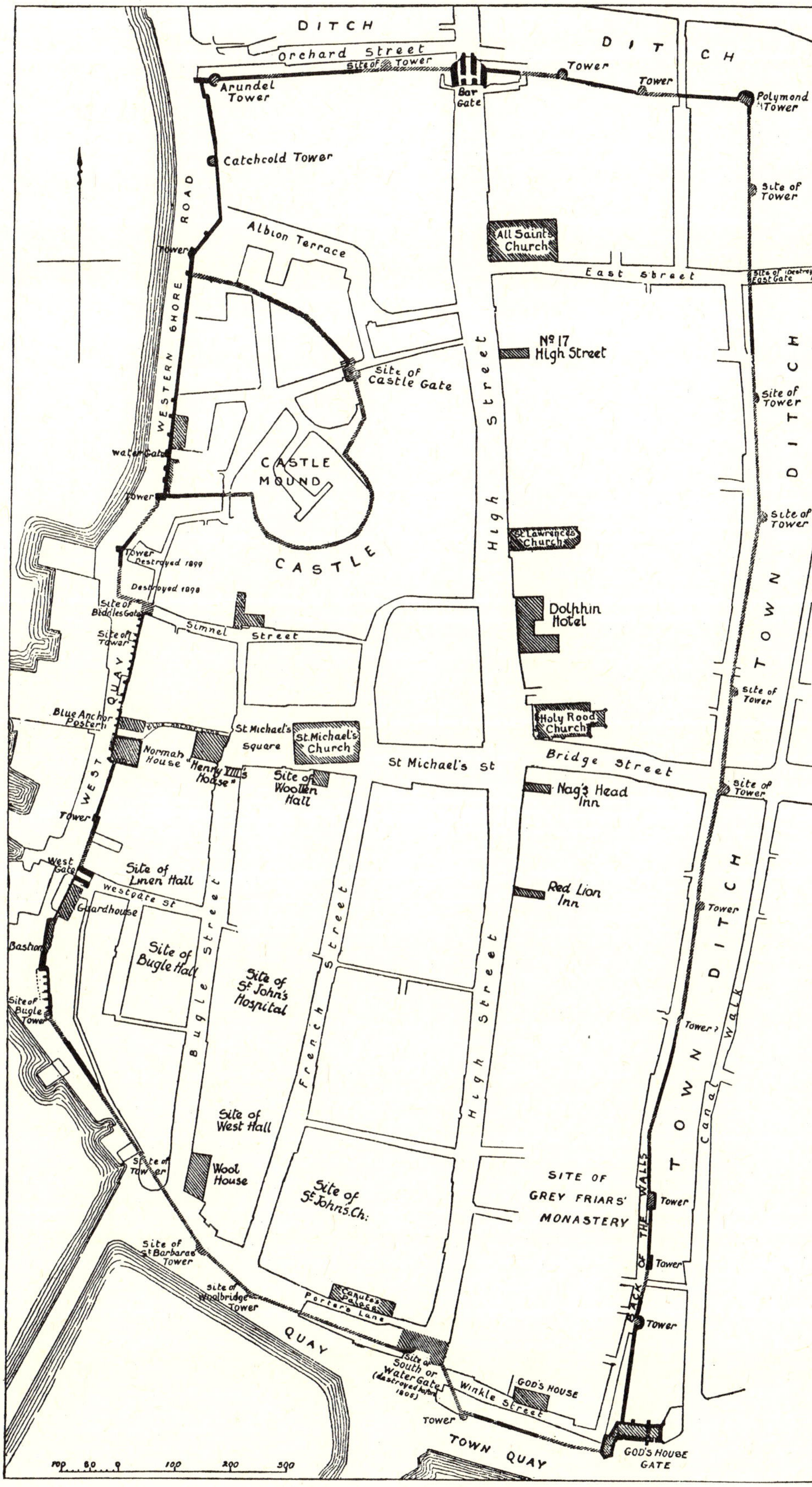

Plan of Southampton, showing the Walls, Castle, etc.
(From a plan belonging to the Society of Antiquaries)

1652[19] the town persistently made claims in maintenance of its ancient boundaries, but the claims became relaxed early in the next century. From 1704 the town presents that the 'metes and bounds *ought* to extend *through* a village called Hill etc.' In 1748 the name of Sidford is added, and afterwards the bounds were presented as extending northward 'from a village called Hill and Sidford.' But there was hesitation to the last. The Parliamentary Boundary Commissioners of 1832 took the larger limit; on the other hand the Municipal Corporation Commission of 1835 excluded the disputed district; this the commissioners of 1868 followed, and the matter at length rested.

At the north-west angle of the old borough limits was another loss. At this point there seems to have been hedging and ditching about 1577 not altogether to the satisfaction of the court leet. They present (1579): 'That whereas of late daies theare hathe bin a peece of our comon and heathe ditched and hedged and enclosid in and planted wth willows under the name of a shadow for our cattel wch have hitherto many yeres past prosperid verie well as the comon was beefore; wherefore we dessire yt may be pulled down agayne and levelid as before; for we doubt that in short time yt wilbe taken from the common to some particuler man's use, wch weare lamentable and pitieful and not sufferable; for as our auncestors of theire great care and travell have provided that and like other many benefyts for us theire successors, so we thinck it our dwetie in conscience to keep, uphold and maintain the same as we founde yt for our posteritie to come without diminishing eny part or parcel from yt, but rather to augment more to yt yf yt may be.' This hedging and ditching, for some reason or other, had left the ancient Hode cross, which is mentioned in every description of the franchises, standing as it does now, some 100 paces from the corner of the inclosed common; and the jury immediately continue: 'Also wee fynd that theere ys a great peice of our sayd comon and heathe leaft unclosed from the rest by Hood crosse, for what purpose wee know not, but we doubt that in continuance of tyme yt will be quit lost, and so by litell and littel we shall loose and diminish oure Lyberties wch we so long have enjoyed wch weare greate pitie.' Similar presentments and warnings continued to be made for many years; but no teps seem to have been taken, and in time this portion became abandoned and the Parliamentary Commissioners of 1832 drew the boundary along the inclosure on the evidence of the latest perambulations.

At the north-eastern limit the ancient inquisitions and the court-leet books describe the boundary line as passing the Burle or Borell stone along Burgess Street to Langherne gate, and thence to Haven stone; and there is evidence that the corporation exercised jurisdiction within these limits.[20] However the modern perambulations had been confined to the shorter route by the Burle stone, and along the stream there to the River Itchen; and in accordance with this the boundary was drawn by the commissioners of 1832, in which they were followed by those of 1868. It is a matter now of small moment since the alterations of 1895; and the discussion of the old boundaries serves but to illustrate the methods of the past. There can be little doubt that the old borough-county limits had in time somewhat shrunk from their ancient dimensions. The area till 1895 comprised the parishes of All Saints, Holy Rood, St. Lawrence, St John, St. Michael, so much of the parish of St. Mary as lies west of the Itchen, the tithing of Portswood in the parish of South Stoneham and Southampton Common, which is extra-parochial.

The existing boundaries as settled[21] in 1895 are much more extended. Three large wards have been added on the west, the Shirley, Freemantle, and Banister wards, the greater part of which were formerly comprised in the urban district of Shirley and Freemantle;[22] while on the east a large addition was made to the Portswood ward consisting for the most part of the Bitterne Park estate in the South Stoneham rural district on the opposite side of the Itchen, which is crossed by the Cobden bridge, opened in 1883. The wards are now thirteen in number, viz., the Town, St. James's, St. Mary's, All Saints', Trinity, Northam, Nichols Town, Newtown, Bevois, Portswood, Banister, Freemantle, and Shirley wards. And the acreage of the whole, as against the old boundaries of 2,817 acres, or, excluding mudlands, 2,004 acres, is now 5,295 acres, or, excluding mudlands, 4,416¾ acres. The population of the borough-county immediately prior to the alteration was estimated to be 71,750, immediately after, 94,150; while at the last census the population of the enlarged borough was found to be 104,911; it is now estimated at 108,000. The extension order expressly provides that the whole area included within the altered boundary shall be 'the Borough and also the County of the Borough of Southampton and shall be the County Borough for the purposes of the Act of 1888.'[23]

Southampton Common, an important member of the above precincts, demands a special notice. It is first mentioned in 1228, when the burgesses of Southampton, represented by John de Lillebane, were in contention with Nicholas de Scherleg or Surlie (Shirley) concerning the moiety of a messuage in Southampton, and battle[24] in the court was pending

[19] In this year the burghers not only made claim to their ancient boundary but complained of the many annoyances arising within the precincts 'for want of an officer within this Towne anciently called the lord Mayor of the Buckinges, wherefore wee desire that suche an officer be yearly choasen at the accustomed tyme accordinge to the ancient custom of this towne etc.' No trace of such an officer has been discovered.

[20] Thus in 1488 repairs were made at the crosses in that locality, and in 1594 a man was fined £5 for tampering with the Haven stone. In 1600 'the postes and vanes at Langthorne gate' were ordered to be repaired and painted, as also at Haven stone by Hilton; they also fined Sir Michael Blunt, who held Stonage (Stoneham) Farm, 12*d.* for a path by the Haven stone which was 'so moyry' as not to be passable. So late as 1819 a new boundary stone bearing the arms and monogram of the town was placed at Langherne where it now stands; and in the same year, on the aldermen of Portswood giving notice that the Haven stone 'dividing the county of the town from the county of Hants' had been taken away and converted to the use of South Stoneham Mill, the Corporation, after strict inquiry, finding the act to have been that of a vagrant without authority, were satisfied with an ample apology and the placing of a new stone.

[21] By virtue of the Southampton Order, 1895, confirmed by the Local Govt. Board's Provisional Orders Confirm. Act, 1895 (No. 16), sess. 2. *Ex inform.* Mr. R. R. Linthorne, town clerk of Southampton.

[22] See above under 'Millbrook.'

[23] *Ex inform.* Mr. R. R. Linthorne.

[24] 'Unde duellum vadiatum et armatum fuit inter eos in prefata curia.'

between the two, when a final concord was arranged in the king's court, John de Lillebane quitclaiming all his right or possible right to Nicholas. Upon this, Nicholas, at the instance of John, granted the burgesses one piece of land without the town of Southampton to remain to the burgesses; neither party was to have rights on the other's common, but each to have free way to and from his own.[25] Although it is impossible to identify the thirteenth-century boundaries with those of the present day, there is little doubt that the extent of the common remains as in the sixteenth century.

Of the remaining ancient common lands and their modern transformations, 'The West and East Marlands' (corrupted from Magdalens) represent property formerly belonging to the Hospital of St. Mary Magdalene,[26] and Houndswell and Hoglands are transformed into a zone of park and recreation grounds on the north and east of the town, or rather, as it will soon be, in the centre of the extending population. To the south of the town a tract of land, partly lammas but chiefly common, known as the saltmarsh, stretched from the old bowling green outside God's House gate to Cross house and chapel; the western or lammas portion of this, which belonged till recently to Queen's College, Oxford, is now represented by Queen's Park, opened in 1885.

Having dealt with the territory we pass to the town itself and its fortifications. A wall of varying thickness some 25 ft. to 30 ft. in height inclosed the mediaeval town in its irregular parallelogram, measuring on the north side about 217 yards, on the east 786 yards, on the south from east to west as far as the site of Bugle Tower about 435 yards, and from that point to the north-west angle of the town some 543 yards. The wall was strengthened at unequal intervals by twenty-nine towers.

These fortifications belong in part to the Norman period. Of this range of date are the core of the Bargate, with a portion of the present walls, some existing works below the castle, and domestic buildings in the line of the western wall, forming part of its original circuit and subsequently adapted for defence.

There were eight gates, four of which remain. These are the north or Bargate, God's House or South Castle Gate, West Gate, and the postern called Blue Anchor Gate. Those which have disappeared were East Gate, Biddles' Gate on the west, and the South or Water Gate. In addition to these was a Castle Water Gate, now to be seen in the face of the wall on the western shore, having been discovered in 1887; there was also a postern near the friary, the site of which is lost. The insertion called York Gate in the north wall east of the Bargate is of the eighteenth century.

The chief periods of construction will be indicated by the aids granted for the purpose. In 1202–3 and the following year John allowed £100 each year out of the farm towards the walling of the town.[27] During the latter part of the reign of Henry III two murages were granted, the former on 30 November, 1260, for ten years, the latter on 12 November, 1270, for five years. A considerable number of tolls is scheduled on these grants.[28] In April, 1282, a murage had been recently granted, and in March, 1286, another was allowed for five years from Easter of that year.[29] In 1321 a murage was granted for three years,[30] after which a renewal was petitioned for.[31] By this time the flanking towers, to be mentioned presently, had been added to the Bargate. The Quayages and Barbican duty, granted from 1323 to 1346 (see below) should also be mentioned as having an immediate connexion with the fortifications. To this period may be assigned the arcade work described below. The next efforts of construction were called forth by the invasion of the town in 1338 (see below). It appears that in spite of murages the town was not entirely walled. The enemy are supposed to have landed at 'the gravel' (see below) or in that immediate neighbourhood, and the weak quarter was now ordered to be strengthened. By the advice of his council the king issued a mandate for the building of a stone wall as quickly as possible towards the sea,[32] Stephen de Bitterle being commissioned on 30 March, 1339, to find all necessary timber, and governors were appointed with a special view to the fortification of the town and the reassurance of the inhabitants. A writ in aid of the inclosure was issued in 1340.[33] On 20 May, 1345, a murage of considerable length was granted for six years,[34] and ten years later the burgesses received a further grant for ten years, in the usual form of a penny in the pound, a halfpenny in ten shillings, and a farthing in five shillings on all goods brought into or carried out of the town, whether by land or water, by their own burgesses or not, in aid of the walls. This was dated 28 June, 1355.[35]

Further repairs were ordered in April, 1369, and contributions were exacted from all persons according to their means, workmen being employed at the wage of the community.[36] Accordingly, in 1376, the poor commons and tenants prayed the king to take the town into his hands and forgive them the farm for the

[25] Feet of F. Hants, 12 Hen. III, No. 137. The land was thus described, viz. 'from the corner and fence of William Wolgar as the land stretches in length [northward] as far as Kottesthorne below (*sub*) the highway from Acard's bridge to the aforesaid thorn of Kottesthorne; and all the land in breadth within the highway which leads from the aforesaid thorn to Barlestone cross, which is upon the great Southampton and Winton road; and all the land in length [southward] from Berlestone cross as far as the corner and fence of land formerly belonging to John Chopin, as the great road leads from Winton to Suhampton; and all the land in breadth from the same corner and fence [its southern boundary] to the corner and fence of Wolgar's land aforesaid.' A similar fine, of the same date and place, but not identical, except as to the boundaries, describes the litigation as concerning the common pasture of the town of Southampton lying on the north part of the lands of William Wolgar, John Blancbully, Amise Fortin, and of land which belonged to John Chopin. Nicholas quitclaims to the burgesses all his rights or possible rights to the land, which is defined as in the last deed. Liber Niger, Corp. MSS. fol. 107.

[26] For account of this and the other religious houses in the borough, namely the priory of St. Denys, of which the merest fragment remains, the convent of Friars Minor, latterly Observants, of which no distinguishable remains exist, and the Hospital of St. Julian or God's House, see *V.C.H. Hants*, ii, 160–3, 193, 202–6.

[27] Pipe R. 4 & 5 John, m. 6.

[28] Pat. 45 Hen. III, m. 22; 55 Hen. III, m. 28.

[29] Ibid. 10 Edw. I, m. 17; 14 Edw. I, m. 18.

[30] Ibid. 14 Edw. II, pt. 2, m. 8.

[31] *Rot. Parl.* (Rec. Com.), ii, 439.

[32] *Rot. Orig.* (Rec. Com.), ii, 130.

[33] Ibid.

[34] Pat. 19 Edw. III, pt. 1, m. 12.

[35] The corporation possesses an exemplification of this grant dated 10 Feb. (39 Edw. III), 1365, made at the request of the burgesses.

[36] Pat. 43 Edw. III, pt. 1, m. 22.

last two years, which sum, together with £1,000 besides, they had expended on fortifications. The town was but half inhabited, they stated, owing to the above burdens, and those who remained were preparing to go. They also petitioned for soldiers to defend the town and neighbourhood, being themselves unable to hold the place against the force prepared by France.[37] They obtained no relief at the time, but evidently there had been considerable outlay on the walls. In the first year of Richard II, under the immediate apprehension of invasion, the mayor and bailiffs were ordered to look to the walls and compel necessary contributions, 8 December, 1377; and a few months later, 9 April, 1378, provision was made for the reconstruction of the castle-keep. Sir John Arundel had been appointed governor in the preceding July. In 1386 the defences of the town were ordered to be surveyed in view of the threatened invasion of the French; walls and ditches were to be repaired and fortified.[38]

In 1400 (1 Henry IV) a grant of £200 per annum, during the royal pleasure, £100 out of the duty of wool in the port of the town, and £100 out of the fee-farm for the first year, but after that entirely from the latter source, was made in aid of the fortification, provided the inhabitants raised among themselves another £100 each year for the like purpose. This £300 per annum was to be spent under the supervision of Richard Mawardyn, king's esquire, of the mayor, and controller of the port.[39] By this time the beautiful octagonal projection had been added to the front of the Bargate.

Henry V, in 1414, released 140 marks (£93 6*s.* 8*d.*) from the fee-farm for ten years, with licence to purchase lands in mortmain to the value of £100 in aid of the fortifications.[40] At this period possibly, or not long after, the spur-work and tower outside God's House Gate were added. Under the act of resumption of 1482 grants for repairs of the walls were especially saved to the town;[41] but at this very period we have a note of their miscarriage. Thus the Steward's Book of 1483 (rather 1484) contains an account of the town's suit 'ayeynste Roger Kelsale,[42] Elizabeth Sorell, and Thomas Nutson, as to the xl *li* the which was graunted to the reparacon of the walles by Kynge Edwarde for vij yeres; and they and Richard Wystard have take alowance of the same as for iiij yeres, and have not paid hit to the towne.'

In 1493 (8 Henry VII) the king granted £50 out of the fee-farm towards repairing the walls on the west side, several private persons contributing at the same time.[43]

On 9 November, 1486, licence had been given to export thirty sacks of wool, free of custom, in aid of the maintenance of the walls, stathes, and quays of the port; and again in February, 1511, the corporation obtained licence to export 100 sacks of wool, free of custom, towards the repair of the town walls inundated by the sea.[44]

Some provision against this danger to the wall-footings had been made from early times. In 1469 the town purchased 'a grove of wood' from the abbot of Netley for 53*s.* 4*d.* for piling the shore for the purpose. The lightermen of the town had also by ancient custom to bring their lighter-loads of stone yearly from the Isle of Wight or elsewhere, to shoot between the piles; receiving for 'every lighter of 20 ton a barrell of beer, and under 20 ton a verkyn.' There was, too, of old time, a ferry from Hythe to the western shore, by virtue of which the corporation claimed of the ferrymen their service of a boat or lighter-load of stone every half-year to be deposited between the piles.

Such were the chief periods of construction. It now remains to deal with such of the fortifications as demand notice in connexion with town history.

The Bargate is a fine structure of various periods in two stages, the upper part of which is occupied by the Gildhall, arranged as a court of justice for the petty sessions of the borough; and the lower pierced by a principal or central archway, with a postern of modern construction on either side—that to the east belonging to 1764, that to the west to 1774. The original gate of the twelfth century had a plain semicircular arch about 10 ft. wide, of three orders, and there was probably an upper story over the arch. This arrangement seems to have remained with but little alteration till the fourteenth century, in the early part of which two towers[44a] were built on either side of the north face of the gate, and about 1330 the south front was added, and carried to the east and west beyond the lines of the old gate, giving a much larger room space above, on the first floor. About the end of the century, or a little later, the north front was enlarged by the addition of a projecting forebuilding with its east and west angles canted off, a fine and imposing structure, with its battlements carried forward on large corbels, and a central gateway between a pair of boldly designed buttresses. Above the arch is a band of panels with heraldry, and a central loop-hole flanked by two narrow slits.

The south front is of very different character, with a flat face divided into two stages. In the upper stage are four two-light fourteenth-century windows, with a canopied niche between the middle pair, now containing a statue of George III in classical garb, and in the ground stage are three archways, that in the centre being of the fourteenth century, and the two others eighteenth-century insertions. Beyond them on either side are original entrances to stairs, that on the east leading up to the Gildhall over the gate, while the other is blocked. It formerly led to the old Bargate prison, mentioned in the Steward's Book of 1441 and afterwards. The central archway beneath has been pared and cut away to make the opening as wide as possible, and comparatively recently the roadway has been deepened 20 ins. to give headway to the electric tram-cars. Under the archway may still be traced the loopholes, one on either side, which commanded the ditch, and also those which

[37] *Rot. Parl.* (Rec. Com.), ii, 346*b*.

[38] Pat. 10 Ric. II, pt. 1, m. 34, 26 Aug. on the general preparations; cf. Froissart, Bk. iii, cap. 37.

[39] This document is printed in Madox, *Firma Burgi*, 290.

[40] *Rot. Parl.* (Rec. Com.), iv, 53; Pat. 2 Hen. V, pt. 3, m. 13.

[41] *Rot. Parl.* (Rec. Com.), vi, 201.

[42] He was M.P. in 1477–8, and again 1482–3 (22 Edw. IV), was attainted with other known Southampton men and others in 1 Ric. III (1483), when he is described as yeoman; reversal of attainder in 1485 (1 Hen. VII); he was customer of Southampton with John Sorell; Steward's Bk. 1486.

[43] Steward's Bk. (Corp. MSS.), 1493.

[44] *Materials for Hist. of Hen. VII* (Rolls Ser.), ii, 38; *L. and P. Hen. VIII*, i, 1474.

[44a] The Corporation has most laudably opened to view and is repairing the tower on the west side, having removed a public-house which stood against it.

Southampton : Town Walls on the Western Shore

Southampton : Vaulted Room in Simnel Street

still earlier, from the basement of the flanking towers. defended the Norman gate.

It is possible that the alterations to the Bargate on the south side in the first half of the fourteenth century may have been carried out to provide a fixed Gildhall, or there may have been no such hall till after the octagonal work was projected. In the earlier history of the gate the space required for working the portcullises and drawbridge would have left little room for civic purposes; but after the addition on the north side the regulation of the defences may have been confined within the projection, and thus sufficient room left for the hall.

The ordinances of the gild-merchant[45] (see below) make no reference to a Gildhall. The gild meetings were held at different places (ord. 4); the community assembled for business 'in a place provided,' as if perhaps for each occasion (ord. 32); the common chest, with the treasure and muniments, was kept in the chief alderman's (i.e. really the mayor's) house, or in that of the seneschal (ord. 35); in much later times it was ordered to be kept in the Gildhall or audit house. In the steward's book of 1441, under the heading 'Bargate,' the first observed notice occurs of a 'townhall' in repairs to the lead of the roof; mention is also made of a new key for the 'tresory dore in the hall.' A few years after (1468) we find the hall made a receptacle for guns in an account of the distribution of artillery among the various towers of the fortifications. 'Fyrst, in ye Guyld halle over ye Bargate j gonne of Bras chawmbred of hymself. Item in the same place ij gonnes and v chawmbres wt tressels to ye sam. Item in the same plas ij gonnes wt owght chambres The whiche ij gonnes lay in ij towres the whiche beth next to ye seyd Bargate eastward to Seynt Denys towr.'[46] The Gildhall in its present condition dates from 1852 and measures about 52 ft. by 40 ft.

It is impossible, with the space at command, to go into the history of what the court-leet books call 'the monuments of Bargate'[47] the lions,[48] Sir Bevis and Ascupart[49] or of the heraldry,[50] paintings, niches, statues, and watch-bell.[51]

Following the westward course of the walls, at about 100 ft. from the gate a half-round tower existed which, in 1468, seems to have been furnished with 'ij gonnes wt ij chawmbres.' A few yards beyond this the wall, destroyed to this point in 1854, is traced behind the houses on its way to Arundel, or as it is often called, 'Corner tower next Hill.' This is a drum now in ruins, at the north-west angle of the walls, 22 ft. in diameter, and from 50 ft. to 60 ft. high. The level within the walls here is some 30 ft. or more above that of the beach or road below. About 130 ft. from the north-west angle southward is 'Catchcold,' which, with the adjacent curtain for some feet, Mr. Clark[52] considered to be a fifteenth-century addition to what seems to be a fourteenth-century wall. 'Catchcold' is a half-round tower, about 20 ft. in diameter, and 30 ft. in height, with machicolations at the level of the curtain. South of this the wall, in substance Norman, runs obliquely to a rectangular buttress, heading a salient, the angles of which are crossed with low pointed arches pierced as garderobes. Some 20 ft. to the south of this, the north wall of the castle bailey struck the town wall, a plain rectangular buttress marking the junction. The wall, probably of Norman date, and about 38 ft. high, now continues southward some 380 ft., being common to the town and to the castle, as far as the remains of a tower at the south-west angle of the castle bailey.

Town Walls, Western Shore, Southampton

Somewhat more than half-way some broken bonding occurs, to the south of which is a series of six rectangular buttresses, the first three being additions to the Norman wall; the fourth contains the late fourteenth-century Castle Water Gate, disclosed in 1887. Immediately to the north of this is a vaulted chamber, lying north and south, 55 ft. long by 19 ft. wide, and 23 ft. in height, the only indication of which from without since ancient times was a narrow loop hole, now somewhat enlarged. The floor is on a higher

45 These are printed in full in Rev. J. Silvester Davies, *Hist. of Southampton*, 132–51; in the *Arch. Journ.* xvi, 283–96, 343–5, and in Gross, *Gild Merchant*, ii, 214–31.

46 It is not possible to identify all the towers round the walls. Such as may be considered well-established are marked on the plan given above, p. 493. The towers were generally leased out by the corporation, 'except,' as it is sometimes stated, 'in time of war.' Thus we have towers named after individuals or trades, and the same tower may have gone under different names from time to time.

47 Davies, op. cit. 65–71.

48 Formerly one on each side of Freebridge, now set back against the gate. First observed notice, 1619.

49 Panels of Sir Bevis of Hampton and his giant esquire, mentioned in 1635 (Court Leet Bk.), &c., as in decay. Subsequently repainted, supposed to perpetuate work of the early fourteenth century.

50 Cross of St. George of England, cross of St. Andrew for Scotland, shields of Noel Visc. Campden, Paulet Marq. of Winch. Tylney, De Cardonnel, Fleming, Leigh of Testwood, Mill, Wyndham, Newland—insertions of close of seventeenth century, representing M.P.'s and benefactors. (For identification of coats, see Mr. Greenfield's paper, *Proc. Hants Field Club*, iv, pt. 2, 97.

51 In 1579 the court-leet desired that a bell should be set up in this position to answer the castle watch-bell in sounding alarms, watches, &c., 'for that yt is a comfortable hearing.' The present bell bears date 1605.

52 See a paper by the late G. T. Clark F.S.A., on 'The Ancient Defences of Southampton,' *Builder*, 28 Dec. 1872; *Arch. Journ.* xxix, 370, and *Mediaeval Mil. Architecture*, ii, 475.

level than the ground outside, and the chamber is covered with a barrel vault, which formerly had ashlar [53] ribs at intervals springing from twelfth-century corbels, of which a few yet remain.

A doorway to the north of the loop opened westward, but it had been carefully walled up with ashlar and no trace of it was to be seen till recently, when an archway with door admitting to the vault was inserted. Adjoining the water gate at the south, the wall exists in two stages, divided by a plain string, for about 32 ft. as far as the sixth and last buttress: and from the indication of a couple of round-headed windows above, and two narrow apertures below, it is evident that chambers existed behind. Outside this part of the wall was the castle quay of which frequent mention is made in the close rolls of John and Henry III; and the buildings may have served partly for stores and cellarage of the king's prisage wines, and may well have been those for the protection of which the quay was so frequently ordered to be kept in repair. From this point the castle wall turns nearly due east. Portions of this wall, of late twelfth-century date, have been recently disclosed by the removal of buildings. At about 110 ft. from the south-west angle, the wall crossed Castle Lane (south). Here was the south gate of the bailey, demolished about 1770. Beyond this the wall continued some 40 ft. till it struck the lofty mound of the keep round which it continued for about 400 ft., the mound's diameter being 200 ft.; it then ran north-east for about 60 ft., then north-west for another 85 ft., crossing at this point Castle Lane (north), where was the principal gate of the castle, destroyed also in the last century, though a fragment may still be seen on the north of the lane, at the judge's entrance to the county court. Beyond this the wall made a curve to the north-west till it struck the curtain as before described. A considerable length of the substructures of this bailey wall remains. The wall stood at a good elevation with a deep ditch at its foot, but towards the end of the eighteenth century the surface was very materially lowered, and the wall's foundations exposed to view. These, now denuded of earth, stand up as an arcade of fourteen or more perfect arches, some of them slightly pointed, on square piers, at a height of about 12 ft. above the present level: the span of the arches averaging 9 ft., and the piers about 7 ft. square. Some of the ashlars of the battlemented wall above this foundation may still be detected.[54] The area thus inclosed was surrounded by a ditch, and the changes of line in the town walls north and south of the bailey are no doubt an evidence of the positions of its north and south ends.

Of the buildings within the castle precincts there is but too scanty information. As soon as the Normans became possessors of the soil, their first step was probably to throw up the castle mound with material from the deep and wide double ditch drawn along two sides of the town—very probably an enlargement of a former ditch—placing on this mound a circular stockaded fort.[55] This must have been succeeded by a fort or keep of stone; for it is quite improbable that, while during the Norman period there is ample evidence of their stone work in the town walls and other buildings, wood should have been perpetuated here. This reconstruction may have occurred before we have any accounts.

The first mention of the castle is found in the articles of agreement [56] in 1153 between King Stephen and Prince Henry, settling the succession on the latter, when it was arranged that the bishop of Winchester [57] should give security for delivering the fort or castle (*munitio*) of Southampton, and the castle (*castrum*) of Winchester, to Prince Henry in the event of the king's death: like pledges being required of the keepers of the other royal fortresses.

The early Pipe Rolls from 1156 constantly refer to the castle, its repairs, its bridges, the bailey bridge, the chapel, the houses, the king's houses, king's chamber and cellar, the storage for his prisage wines, the gaol, the castle quay: and among these notices we get a few hints at construction, but they do not help us much.

In 1156 repairs at the castle cost £7. In 1157 works on the castle bridge £4 13*s.* 4*d*; on the chapel and bailey bridge £3 12*s.* 4*d.*; a parapet ('bretesce') for the bridge 10*s.*; further for bridge and chapel £1 11*s.* 3*d.* In 1161 Richard son of Turstin, sheriff of the shire, was charged with the payment of Milo of Hamton (£7 6*s.* 8*d.*) in fortifying (*in munitione castelli*). In 1162 the 'vicecomitissa' of Rouen [58] paid 14*s.* 4*d.* and Richard, the shire official, spent £16 on repairs at the castle. In 1172–3 works were going on there, and on the castle well, by writ of Richard de Lucy, justiciar, and under view of John the controller, Fortin, and Walter of Gloucester (£7 1*s.*). In 1173 and 1174 the castle was receiving and transmitting warlike apparatus and royal treasure, and it was garrisoned by five knights. In 1183 work on the gaol cost £24. In 1192–3, when William Briwer was governor, the sum of £40 15*s.* was spent on the castle, in the next year £68 3*s.*, and in the following year £24 6*s.* It is stated that in 1286 the castle was in ruins, and dues were assigned for its restoration.[59] But there seems to be no detailed account till the rebuilding of the keep in 1378 and 1379 under Sir Richard Arundel the governor. This keep of the fourteenth century was a shell of masonry encircled by an embattled wall surmounting the escarpment. The patent of 1378 directed Henry Marmesfeld, John Pypering and Richard Baillyf [60] to cause the erection as quickly as possible of a certain tower on the 'old-castell-hill' [61] with two gates, a mantelet and barbican of stone, that is, an encircling wall about it with an outwork before the gate. The patent of the next year required the tower to have four turrets, three gates and three portcullises, a bridge also was to be constructed. Timber was to be procured from the New Forest, and material provided at the king's cost, necessary masons and workmen being taken from the neighbouring counties, and kept at work as long as needful at the king's wages.[62] In November 1378 John Polmont (or Polymond) and William Bacon,[63] two well-known burgesses who both for some years

[53] The ribs were destroyed about 1775.

[54] Three of these arches may be seen at the end of Maddison Street: the rest are hidden amongst buildings and inclosures.

[55] Cf. J. H. Round, 'The Castles of the Conquest,' *Arch.* lviii (1), 313.

[56] Rymer, *Foedera*, i, 13, 14.

[57] Henry de Blois, 1129–71.

[58] See below.

[59] Pat. 14 Edw. I, m. 18.

[60] Possibly Richard May, bailiff of the town.

[61] That is on the old mound which had always been fortified.

[62] Pat. 1 Ric. II, pt. 6, m. 7 (Apr. 1378); 2 Ric. II, pt. 2, m. 42 (Jan. 1378).

[63] Described as of Bristol, but who subsequently seems to have lived in St. Michael's parish, Southampton.

represented the borough in Parliament, were commissioned to carry out the works under the survey and control of John de Thorpe, king's clerk.[64] Bad work was to be punished by imprisonment. The keep must have been finished in 1380; as we find that year a grant of the custody of 'the gate of the king's new tower;'[65] and there can be little doubt it was brought into immediate use.[66] Next there is the survey of the mantlet and 'pavement' round the new tower under William Bacon the elder,[67] and control of Thorpe.[68]

The remaining works were hurried on especially under a lively apprehension of a French invasion.[69] The king's clerk, Thorpe, seems to have been generally superintendent; but in July 1386 occurs the appointment of Thomas Tredyngton, chaplain, to serve the king in his new tower, both in celebrating divine service for his good estate and keeping the armour, artillery, victual and guns therein for its garrisoning and defence, to do everything necessary for its safe custody, and to control all the king's works within the castle. His salary was to be £10 a year from the town's custom of wool; but being retained for this service expressly as an expert in guns and the management of artillery the appointment was not to be drawn into a precedent to burden the king with finding a chaplain therein who might not be so skilful in these matters.[70] Later in this year (November) John Polymond and William Bacon, burgesses, and William Hughlot one of the tellers of the Receipt, were directed to take the muster of men-at-arms and archers at the king's wages in the castle, reckon with them and certify accordingly to the Exchequer.[71] At this time the king's brother, Thomas earl of Kent, was keeper of the castle and town, Sir John Sondes, kt., being his deputy.[72]

The buildings as reconstructed at this time seem to have remained substantially the same till the castle's decline.[73]

A chapel, doubtless within the keep, had existed from the first, the chaplains, as we have seen, drawing their 'wages' with the other officials. This arrangement was succeeded or supplemented later by the chapel of St. George, which stood apparently towards the north-west of the bailey inclosure, since we find it occasionally mentioned in the beat of the town watch.[74] The chaplains were practically endowed, as stated above, from the time of Richard II; and being appointed by patent they are mostly known but cannot here be noticed. Their duties became those of chantry priest to celebrate for the good estate of the king and the souls of his progenitors: but the commissioners of the sixteenth century could not discover the origin of this foundation and contented themselves with the return of the salary as £10 in ready money from the king's customs in the town.[75] In 1553 the then incumbent received a pension of £6.

Leland in 1546 tells us 'The Glorie of the castelle is in the dungeon (keep) that is both larg, fair and very stronge, both by worke and the site of it.'[76] Queen Elizabeth dates from the castle in 1569. Speed, writing at the end of the same century, describes it as 'most beautiful, in forme circular, and wall within wall, the foundation upon a hill so topped that it cannot be ascended but by stairs.[77]

Hortensio Spinola in his report on the southern ports in 1599 speaks of the castle as being strong with sixty pieces of artillery and 100 soldiers.[78] However, in spite of these accounts, it appears that some dismantling of the bailey had occurred as early as the end of the fifteenth century. In 1550 the 'castle green' had fallen into utter neglect; in 1591 it had been let to the butchers for some years by Captain Parkinson, the governor, and the court leet presented that the sheep had spoiled the hill—i.e. of the keep—'most ruinously: and they begged no more sheep or cattle might be allowed there; moreover the windows and gates of the castle tower lie open to all the inhabitants, whereof they desire reformation.'[79] The condition of the building became more and more deplorable and in July, 1618, the ruined castle, its site and ditches, passed by a grant of James I, for £2,078 to Sir James Ouchterlony and Richard Garnard,[80] citizen and clothworker of London, who in the next month (10 August) consigned their interest to William Osey,[81] of Basingstoke, who in his turn made it over to George Gollop of Southampton, merchant, in July 1619. In 1636 George Gollop obtained the royal grant[82] of the castle and its ditches at the yearly rent of 13*s.* 4*d.* In the next year we find him plaintiff against several who had already converted the ditches into gardens.[83] The property remained in the Gollop family for some few years. In 1650 Peter Gollop was in possession, and 11 October that year he gave permission to Major Peter Murford (of whom later), commandant of the town, to take such stone from the castle as he might think needful for the fortifications.[84]

In later times the site became encroached upon by houses and gardens. In the last quarter of the eighteenth century a windmill made out of the old tower had given place to a summer house. In 1804 the castle hill was purchased from Mr. Watson by Lord

64 Pat. 2 Ric. II, pt. 1, m. 20.

65 Pat. 4 Ric. II, pt. 1, m. 28 (4 Aug.)

66 The story was told however that a rich Genoese merchant sought permission to store his goods in the newly built castle, and that he was killed through the jealousy of the London merchants. Walsingham, *Hist. Angl.* i, 407; Stow, *Chron.* under 1379, 1380.

67 Burgess and M.P.

68 Pat. 7 Ric. II, pt. 1, m. 11 (Nov. 1383).

69 Pat. 6 Ric. II, pt. 3, m. 3 (June, 1283); 9 Ric. II, pt. 2, m. 15 (May 1386).

70 *Cal. Pat.* 1385–9, p. 198.

71 Ibid. 236.

72 Ibid. 177. See also commission of 26 Aug. (same year) to Sir John Sondes, kt., and John Polymond, burgess, to inquire into the defences of the town, and to repair and fortify the walls and ditches against the threatened invasion of the French.

73 A very fair idea of the keep is given in the French plan of Southampton in Add. MS. 11546, taken about 1630. It does not, however, seem to be an original authority, but rather an enlargement from Speed.

74 Lib. Remembranc. 14, 27.

75 Chant. Cert. 51, No. 1. But in the appointment of John Pereson in 1461 the salary and duties (chantry) are said to be in accordance with the original grant by Richard II. Pat. 1 Edw. IV, pt. 3, m. 9 (22 Nov.).

76 Leland, *Itin.* (ed. Hearne), iii, 107.

77 Speed, *Theatre of Gt. Brit.* (reprint 1650), 13.

78 *Cal. S.P. Dom.* 1598–1601, p. 179.

79 Court Leet Bk. (Corp. MSS.) for 1591; see also 1566, 1569, 1574, &c.

80 Or rather Gurnard, son of Bryan Gurney or Gurnard. He was kt. bart. and Lord Mayor of London in 1642, but discharged from his office by Parliament and committed to the Tower, where he died in 1647. Pat. 16 Jas. I, pt. 13, m. 9, No. 7.

81 Close, 16 Jas. I, pt. 4, No. 37.

82 Pat. 11 Chas. I, pt. 8, m. 12.

83 Exch. Dep. East. 13 Chas. I, No. 3. About this time a traveller (1635) describes the building as an 'old ruinated castle on a high mounted hill, environed with a sound strong wall' (Duthy, *Sketches of Hampshire*, i, 441, quoted from Lansd. MS. 213).

84 From Journal of that year (Corp. MSS.).

Wycombe, afterwards marquis of Lansdowne, who by degrees created an extensive castellated mansion of brick and stucco upon it, which appears to have contained some slight remnant of the old fortress. He died in 1809, and in July 1816 the property was put up for sale for building material together with the freehold site of the castle, having a river frontage of 377 ft.[85] The mansion was taken down in 1818 and the mound lowered;[86] and in 1824 Zion Chapel, converted since to several uses, and in 1904 made a store for chemicals, &c., was erected on the site of the Norman keep.

To return now to the town walls. From the south-west angle of the castle bailey, the wall on a lower level and fragmentary in condition ran south-west at an angle of about eighteen degrees to a small tower which headed the salient at about 100 ft. distance from the bailey. It then ran southward for about 80 ft. and re-entered sharply to the east so as to cover Biddles' Gate, set some 50 ft. back. All this was removed in 1898 and 1899 under a scheme of improvement by the corporation, a clearance being made of all the houses and courts in the vicinity for a considerable extent, including a large part of Simnel Street. Happily the interesting fourteenth-century vaulted room (34 by 22) which was beneath a house on the north side of that street has been preserved.

Immediately below the site of Biddles' Gate the defences for a distance of 260 ft. are composed of the walls, some 4 ft. thick and 30 ft high, of Norman buildings of a domestic and mercantile character, which can never have been very suitable for defences, and have in consequence been strengthened on the outside by a series of nineteen arches, probably of fourteenth-century date, and of sufficient depth to provide a rampart walk defended by a battlemented wall along their entire length, and connecting with a similar walk on the north and south.

Between the arches and the wall behind a chase is left at intervals something like the groove for a portcullis, but in this case much wider, forming a series of machicolations. This arcade appears to have been strengthened by three towers; one by Biddles' Gate, the second in front of the fourth arch, and the third beyond the ninth arch.

The first of these was no doubt 'Pilgrims' Pit' tower,[87] close to Biddles' Gate, deriving its name, as did the gate itself sometimes, with a garden and its surroundings, from the Pilgrims' Pit, perhaps some well connected with the pilgrimages[88] to the tomb of St. Thomas of Canterbury.

The buildings to the rear of this part of the wall have been removed by the corporation, who have erected on the north of what was Blue Anchor Lane a large lodging-house for single men, immediately to the north of which a twelfth-century well was discovered and still exists. The corporation has also erected a considerable building let out in flats, the clearance of the site having involved the destruction of the remains of a small Norman house on the north of Blue Anchor Lane, close to the postern, some ancient substructures only having been preserved. This postern, called for many years Blue Anchor, but formerly Lord's Lane Gate, and more anciently simply Postern, has been much pared away in former times to obtain width, but the groove of its portcullis remains in the head of the arch.

Immediately to the south of the postern and behind the last three bays of the arcade is the twelfth-century house called locally 'King John's Palace.' It is in two stages, and measures on the south side 44 ft., on the east 41 ft., on the west along the town wall, of which it forms a portion, 35 ft., and on the north, along Blue Anchor Lane 43 ft. On the first floor is a large room with an original fireplace and chimney, and five original windows, one a mere loop and four of two lights each, all in the west or outer wall excepting one two-light window on the north facing the lane and the site of the destroyed Norman house opposite. On the same floor a wall passage started at the middle of the east side and led round through the south side to the town wall. This passage, or what remains of it, is now hidden by a lean-to roof constructed within the eastern half of the house. The ground-floor has two Norman doorways; one in the lane, the other in the archway next to the postern.[89]

From this point all the houses which were in front of the walls have been removed as far as the southern entrance of Cuckoo Lane—some 800 ft., two insertions flush with the walls alone remaining; the former of these a small tenement immediately south of the Norman house, the latter the Royal Standard Inn adjoining the north side of West Gate. A little further to the north, just beyond the entrance to what was Collis's Court, the picturesque fragment of a tower is seen, three sides of an octagon, the front carried upon a broad rectangular buttress having its hollow angle crossed by a squinch supporting the side above and pierced in the usual way for a garderobe.

West Gate, 'West-hethe-zate' as it is called in 1441, is a plain rectangular work flush with the outer face of the walls 23 ft. broad and 30 ft. deep. It is in three stages, the lowest being pierced by a roadway 10 ft. broad covered by a low-pointed vault. The entrance was formerly defended by a heavy door and two portcullises; there are also traces of other defences and modes of worrying a foe. The tower is embattled and capped by a tiled roof.

From West Gate the wall stretches for about 250 ft. with a south-westerly inclination to the site of Bugle Tower, so called from the ancient Bull or Bugle Hall which stood above it on the east.

In the rear of this wall, and only divided from West Gate by a stairway to the rampart walk on the walls, is a fifteenth-century timber building on a stone basement, built against the town wall, but leaving space for the rampart walk. It is now called the

[85] *Hants Telegraph*, 24 June, 1816. This was only a portion of the old river frontage, the entire length of which was about 380 ft.

[86] In 1822 a silver penny of Offa was found at the Castle Hill. It is now in the museum of Hartley College.

[87] In 1348 Agnes de Horder bequeathed a tenement in the parish of St. Michael in the street called 'Pilgrims' pit'; Add. MSS. 19314, fol. 85*b*. The name 'Pylgrymes pit' occurs in an inquisition taken at Southampton in 1367. In 1441 there is mention of the 'West gate next the castle called "Pylgrymys pit"'; and in 1468 of the 'towr at Pylgryms pit' which carried 'j gonne wt iij chawmbres.' Steward's Bk. *sub annis*.

[88] Starting from here the pilgrims made their first halting place at Winchester in the close. The hall devoted to this purpose is still existing, and one of the canons' houses has been built into part of it.

[89] This house passed some few years ago into the possession of Mr. F. G. Spranger, by whom a portion of it has been restored and put in order, and is carefully maintained.

'guard room.' Its length is about 60 ft.; its width, exclusive of the rampart walk, about 20 ft. It is now covered with weather-boarding externally, but preserves much of the wattle-and-daub filling between its original timbers. It has an open timber roof with cambered tie-beams and arched windbraces.

To the south of the 'guard room' the wall projects westward some 9 ft. and continues southward for about 50 ft., and is then succeeded by a bastion 40 ft. broad, behind which are remains of masonry, showing that the rampart walk was here carried on arches. From this bastion the wall—which has been much rebuilt here in consequence of the breach made in it by the early eighteenth-century house of the Maretts (the late Madame Maes), pulled down in 1898—continues for nearly 70 ft. to the vestiges of what was Bugle Tower; this stretch having been occupied by an arcade of five arches, two of which, next to the Bugle Tower, still remain. At this point the ancient shore or quay, which commenced at the sharp re-entering angle of the town wall outside Biddles' Gate, seems to have ended.

From the vestiges of Bugle Tower the wall, now exposed, exists in ruins or is to be traced south-east by east for 300 ft., as far as the remains of what appears to be called in the town books 'Square Tower' or 'Corner Tower,' at the entrance to Cuckoo Lane adjoining the Royal Southern Yacht Clubhouse. Behind this wall and just south of Bugle Tower was the Spanish prisoners' burial ground of the eighteenth century, close to the garden of the adjacent Roman Catholic nunnery.

A little short of 'Square Tower' were to be seen till the recent clearances the arms of the town under a Tudor moulding, together with some huge gun stones worked into a piece of rebuilding, in memory, as was supposed, of the direful French invasion of the fourteenth century, the foe having landed in this quarter, which was formerly called the 'Gravel.'

From 'Square Tower' the wall passed the ends of Bugle Street and French Street, joining the Water Gate which crossed the High or English Street. This line of walling was taken down in 1803, but a portion of it appears in front of Canute Hotel near where it joined the Water Gate.

In its convex sweep of 600 ft. from Square or Corner Tower, in which were included two towers, St. Barbara's and Woolbridge, the wall passed some notable buildings. Just behind the wall, commencing at the mouth of Bugle Street and passing that of French Street, ran Porter's Lane, at one time called le Cheyne, and sometimes Wool Street, from wool stores existing there. At its ancient mouth at the south-east corner of Bugle Street stands a stone building about 80 ft. by 40 ft., with heavy cylindrical buttresses along the west wall, called the 'wey-hous' and 'wolhous' in the fourteenth century.[90] It appears to be of early fourteenth-century date, and was used in the latter part of the eighteenth century as the 'Spanish prison,' hence its more recent name. Its south front, towards the harbour, has been nearly rebuilt at a late date. Adjoining this building on the east and all along the south quay are traces of handsome stores of considerable importance. In Porter's Lane are the remains of a twelfth-century house called since the beginning of last century 'Canute's Palace.' It is in two stories, and had originally a frontage of 111 ft., with a central doorway and two windows on the first floor.

Water Gate crossed the High Street a few feet to the rear of the machicolations still to be observed on the front of Castle Hotel, and slightly to the north of the present entrance to Winkle Street. It was a deep and wide structure with a low pointed arch and the usual defences to its opening. Above was a boldly projecting parapet with seven machicolations; all the windows on the second stage faced the town.

The Wool House, Southampton

This gate was probably not erected much before the reign of Richard II. It is referred to in a patent of his first year, but is still called new in his twentieth.[91] On its west side the gate was recessed and protected by the rounded curtain or flanking tower, the machicolations of which exist, while on the east its approach was completely covered, as was also much of the quay outside, by the town wall, which here struck out boldly to sea as a salient, south-east by south for about 110 ft., to a lofty round tower—Watch Tower—on the sea line. This is now marked by the bow window of the Sun Hotel, which stands on its basement.

Inside the wall was Winkle Street, entered by a narrow passage to the east of the gate either through the archway of the ancient custom house or that of a house adjoining, the lessee[92] of which obtained permission (1439) to construct solars above, provided he

[90] D. of R. Mascall, 1365; R. Bechefounte, 1388 (West Hall D. &c.).

[91] Pat. 1 Ric. II, pt. 6, m. 16; Quitclaim from W. Brugis and Gilb. Harry, chaplains, to Walt. Nicoll and Elena his wife, of a cellar and bakehouse 'in venella jacente inter novam portam vocatam Water gate et portam lanarum.' The premises were thus in Porter's Lane. Date 21 Oct. (1396), 20 Ric. II. Corp. MSS.

[92] W. Soper, lease (Corp. MSS.). He or his immediate descendant was possibly the builder of the ships *Holy Ghost* and *Grace Dieu* in 1414.

left a highway (*via regalis*) 13 ft. broad with a headway of at least 16 ft. to admit of the passing of carts and men-at-arms and their serving-men with lances and arms. The 'kynges custom hows'[93] was 'by ye water gate,' and 'j gret gonne upon wheles' stood before it. The present entrance to Winkle Street was due to a breach in the town wall made towards the end of the eighteenth century to facilitate business on the quay. Finally in 1804 the gate and ancient buildings flanking it were removed.

From Watch Tower below Water Gate the wall, some vestiges of which remain, passed eastward with a southerly inclination for about 250 ft., when it touched the south flanking of God's House Gate. This portion of the wall did not exist at the end of the thirteenth century, as we have proof that the south side of the quadrangle of God's House (see below) was exposed to the sea.

God's House Gatehouse is a plain oblong structure of two stories, 23 ft. deep and 30 ft. broad, its south end projecting with an obtuse angle beyond the line of the town wall. A lofty vaulted roadway, 10 ft. wide, piercing its north end leads into Winkle Street; and no other ancient opening occurred in the basement, which was used as a dungeon. The somewhat awkward position of this gateway passage was governed by the abutment of the town wall; it may also be noticed that the gatehouse was in existence some 100 years before the erection of the adjacent gallery and tower, which have in effect thrust the old entrance into a corner. These latter buildings belong to the close of the fourteenth or beginning of the fifteenth century, their object being not only an increase of the accommodation, but the securing an extensive flank defence for the gate and the protection of the sluices of the ditch over which the tower was constructed.

This work projects about 85 ft. The two-story gallery connecting the gate with the tower is about 55 ft. in height by 30 ft. in breadth. The lower story had no opening on the south or outside, and was originally covered with a vaulted roof. The tower is in three stages crowned by a battlement with only one wide-splayed embrasure on each side adapted for fire-artillery.

Since 1775 it had been used as the town gaol, the Bridewell having been settled over the gateway since 1707. The felons' gaol was within the gallery, the debtors' prison in the tower. In 1835 the whole condition was very bad.[94] The buildings themselves had become misused, injured, and dilapidated: but when their use for prison purposes had been abandoned in 1855, and when again in 1875 the gatehouse and gallery were needed for storage accommodation, a careful repair of the whole surface was carried out, and a curious garderobe was discovered at the north-west angle of the second floor, carefully blocked by clear masonry at least 2 ft. thick.[95] Close by the tower was the 'Millhouse,' which was probably the gallery adjoining. In 1468 labourers were paid to 'sette owte the gonnes' there. Among its several guns in store was one called 'Thomas with the beard'—'the whiche seyd gonne called Thomas wt ye Berd new bowned and pencylled, as in yis sam bok shewt, wt ij holle chawmbers to ye sam, wt viij gonne stones and viij tampons to ye same were delyvered by Master Andrew James, leftenaunte, ye xxx day of May, Ano. viij R. E. iiij, to my lord Scales by endenture as y onderstond.' In connexion with these buildings frequent mention is made of the 'Longhouse before God's house,' which was no doubt the early fifteenth-century building the remains of which we see in that position with the town wall behind it.

From the north-west corner of the spur-work just described the wall runs 160 ft. to a half-round tower, 23 ft. in diameter. This tower in 1468 carried two guns. Ninety feet farther on are the remains of a small rectangular tower, 22 ft. broad, which at the same date was furnished with two guns with chambers. At another 90 ft. was a second square tower, 30 ft. broad, which had two guns and six chambers. The wall is traceable most of the way, but nothing remains of

GOD'S HOUSE TOWER, SOUTHAMPTON

the other towers as far as East Gate. In this line from God's House Tower to East Gate there were altogether eight towers, two rectangular and six drums or half-drums; though the muster book of 1544 enumerates only seven, possibly omitting one as too small for special defence.

East Gate was a heavy structure with bold side towers and a front thrown well forward beyond its flankings. There was a chapel above the gate dedicated to St. Mary to which Agnes le Horder[96] left a bequest in 1348. In 1641 we find this same chapel leased out with a tenement and garden close by. It had been for many years used as a warehouse.[97] Between East Gate and St. Denys Tower some 145 ft. from the gate was a small tower.

St. Denys or Polymond Tower at the north-east angle of the town, a drum 28 ft. in diameter and in three stages, mostly demolished in 1828–9, still presents some considerable remains. In 1468 it was

[93] Steward's Bk. 1468.

[94] *Rep. on Munic. Corp.* (1835).

[95] Among the military stores of this tower in 1460 were a broken gun, two whole guns and one 'serpentine.' A large spruce chest contained 'xix chawmbres longyng to ye Orgons after specifyed. Item in the sam chest j baner steyned upon lynyne cloth wt ye kinges armes and order. Item in ye same towre iij hold polaxis. Item .... iij qrtes of barell gonne powder. Item .... gonne stones of dyvers sorts.' Stewards' Bks.

[96] Add. MS. 15314, fol. 85, 86.

[97] Steward's Bk. 1641–2.

Southampton : God's House Tower and the Spur Work

(From an old print)

furnished with a gun and eight chambers. Subsequently heavy ordnance was provided for it. In 1654 there was a great gun on its top, the carriage of which was found to be rotten, as likewise the whole staging was in danger of sudden collapse; and another great gun 'on the rampier by the said tower' was half buried in the ground.

Turning westward towards Bargate much of the wall remains behind the houses; there are also remnants of two half-round towers, the former with a diameter of 16 ft. at a distance of 160 ft. from St. Denys Tower; the latter about 120 ft. farther with a diameter of 22 ft. Another distance of 120 ft. brings us to Bargate.

Such is, as slightly as possible, the history of the walls and towers; it may be of interest to show how the various towers were to be defended and to whom they were appointed, at least in 1544, by order of the mayor and his brethren.[98]

Arundel Tower and the little tower towards Bargate were assigned to the shoemakers, curriers, cobblers, and saddlers. Bargate Tower with the next to the east were to be held by the town. The next small tower and Polymond's were assigned to two burgesses, William Knight and John Capleyn. The next little tower towards East Gate and the gate itself were entrusted to the goldsmiths, blacksmiths, lockiers, pewterers, and tinkers. Next came the seven towers enumerated from East Gate to God's House Tower. The first five were known by the names of those opposite whose gardens they stood, the sixth was over against the friars; the seventh next to God's House Tower; for the keeping of these no appointment had as yet been made. God's House Tower, the Watch Tower, and Water Gate Tower were kept by the town. The tower by the wool-house was given to the mercers and grocers; St. Barbara's and 'Corner' or Square Tower, 'next to Beaulieu selde,' were assigned to the brewers and bakers. That behind Bull Hall was given to the coopers; West Gate to Mr. Baker; the Tower behind Thomas Marsh's house to the vintners, mariners, and lightermen; that against Mr. Huttoft's to the weavers, fullers and cappers, and the tower next Biddles Gate to the butchers, fishers, and chandlers. The last three were evidently the towers in front of the arcade (see above). It will be noticed that Catchcold[99] Tower on the north and the destroyed salient to the south of the castle area are not included in the enumeration.

The town is stated by Leland (1546) to have been double ditched,[100] and Speed's map (1596) shows the same, excepting that by his time the portion to the west of the Bargate had been filled in and also as far as the first tower on the east. There were archery butts, approached from the north, on the bank along the middle of the ditch, which were frequently the subject of presentment, as also were those on the Castle Green. They were constantly out of order, and men were said to be obliged to shoot in Houndswell or the Salt marsh in consequence. The ranges can hardly have been satisfactory, but there is no doubt they were there.[101] The counterscarp of the moat on the north side was apparently at what is now the south side of Hanover Buildings, that is at a distance of about 120 ft.

On the west and south sides of the walls, when the tide did not wash their footings, were the shores and quays.

The Platform, outside God's House Gate,[102] dates in a very incipient stage from the end of the thirteenth century. Subsequently it was adapted for fire-artillery. In 1457,[103] under the apprehension of invasion—it was the year when Sandwich was burnt—there was some activity along the shore-line between God's House Gate and Itchen Cross (Cross-house), where in the eighteenth century, in Southampton's fashionable days, was a lovely and far-famed drive with its row of elm trees, some of which remain.

With 'Castle Quay' we have already dealt, as also with the shore from Biddles Gate to Bugle Tower. But what was specifically the 'West Quay,' the centre of life and trade in mediaeval Southampton, was in front of West Gate. A quayage in the usual form was granted in aid of the repairs to this quay for one year in 1323 (17 Edward II); two years later, 1326 (19 Edward III), in consideration of the labour of the burgesses on the quay and inclosure of the town by royal mandate, a similar grant was made for seven years. In the following year, 1327 (1 Edward III), what was really a confirmation of the previous quayage for six years was obtained.[104] Further, in connexion with these works on the quay the burgesses had constructed a barbican of wood, and were now proposing to build it in stone for the better security against hostile invasion: in consequence of this they obtained in 1336 (10 Edward II) a grant of a penny in the pound on all merchandise for five years, and on the expiration of this term in 1341 secured a renewal for a similar period.[105] But the jealousy of neighbours had eyed the concessions with alarm, and in 1339 a controversy with the men of Winchester about the payment of this barbican duty was settled by a release to them from this impost for five years.[106] West Quay was sometimes called 'Galley Quay' in the eleventh century. In the middle of the eighteenth it served for the Channel Islands trade, which was considerable, the Guernsey and Jersey vessels always anchoring off it.

Judging from documents of 1411, it would seem that South or Water Gate Quay was then of recent construction, and had not been carried out without opposition from the merchants of Winchester and New Sarum.[107] A patent of that year sets forth that the burgesses, with the assistance of Thomas Mydlington, one of their number, had constructed at great cost a certain bank called a 'wharf' with a crane upon it, at 'la Watergate,' in aid of the fortification and merchandise of the place, and for receiving custom; and that they had incurred the wrath of many who had been accustomed to evade or purloin the dues: the king therefore desired the work might be maintained henceforth, and authorized such tolls from all parties using the wharf or crane as were levied in London or other ports where such accommodation

[98] Muster Bk. (Corp. MSS.).

[99] It is mentioned however, with other towers in the same muster book in the provision made for manning the walls, where we find that there were all round the town 465 loops or crenellations to be defended, or as the *summa totalis* is given 470, but numbers do not quite tally.

[100] Leland, *Itin.* (ed. Hearne), iii, 91.

[101] Steward's Bk. 1485; Court Leet Bks. 1555, 1559, 1567, 1573, 1587, &c.

[102] Davies, op. cit. 455, 456.

[103] Steward's Bk.

[104] Pat. 17 Edw. II, pt. 1, m. 9; 19 Edw. II, pt. 2, m. 17; 1 Edw. III, pt. 1, m. 5.

[105] Pat. 15 Edw. III, pt. 1, m. 39.

[106] Indenture among Corp. MSS.

[107] Inq. a.q.d. 12 Hen. IV, No. 5.

(*ripa et crana*) existed.[108] The growth of the quay can be traced from the town books.

Leland and Speed in the sixteenth century speak of the two quays as large, fair, and stately. In the time of Charles II their dimensions are thus given officially:[109] Water Gate Quay was 223 ft. in length, with a breadth at the gate and wall of 190 ft., and at the head of the quay 63 ft. It had three pairs of stone stairs, one at the head and two on the east side. West Quay was 225 ft. in projection, its width by the gate and wall 58 ft., and at the end 37 ft. Water Gate Quay was therefore by this time the more important structure.

The development of these quays, no longer of offence or defence, belongs to comparatively recent times, and its result must be given later. We now turn to the history of the borough.

Southampton was in all probability the home of Saxon invaders of the late fifth and early sixth century, the first of whom were Cerdic and Cynric his son in 495.[110] As soon as the raiders began to have a hold on the land the site of the later town undoubtedly became a basis from which new conquests were made, securing as it did a hold on the river and a key to the upper country.[111] Although the town does not appear by name until the ninth century, it was of importance at an earlier date than Winchester, since it gave its name to the shire as early as the eighth century, when in 755 Sigebryht remained under-king of *Hamtunscire*, though deprived of the rest of the kingdom by Cynewulf and the West Saxon Witan.[112]

The earliest remarkable mention of Southampton by name is as the landing-place of the Danes in 837 and again in 860.[113] The next notice is of more peaceful character. In the year of Athelstan's accession, 925, the town is mentioned as having two mints among burhs which had a mint or mints assigned to them in the constitutions of the synod of Greatley, which gave the earliest English laws about coinage. The mints were appointed as follows: At Canterbury, seven minters or coiners, four for the king, two for the bishop, and one for the abbot; at Rochester, three, two for the bishop, and one for the abbot; London, eight; Winchester, six; Lewes, two; Hampton, two; Wareham, Exeter, Shaftesbury, each two; Hastings and Chichester, each one; and 'other burhs' one.[114] This list affords some notion of the relative position taken by the town at this time. The name of Southampton occurs on coinage from the reign of Eadmund in 940 to that of Stephen, under the forms of H., Ha., Ham., Amtd., Han., Hamt., Hantv., Hamtun, after which period it occurs no more.[115]

In 980 and 981 the town was ravaged by the Danes,[116] and in 994 was made the head quarters of the Danish and Norwegian forces under Sweyn and Olaf. Canute was at Southampton in 1016,[117] and tradition has placed here the well-known story of his rebuke to his courtiers.[118] At least there is little doubt but that the town revived under his strong rule. On the death of Canute, Edward (afterwards the Confessor), the son of Ethelred by Emma, hastened over from Barfleur to Southampton with forty ships as a competitor for the crown; and in his disappointment is said to have returned whence he came not without plunder.[119] After this there is little to record of Southampton for many years.[120]

There can be little doubt that the Norman Conquest brought prosperity and enlargement to Southampton. At the time of the Domesday Survey[121] the king had in the borough seventy-six men in demesne who paid their tax as under the Confessor; these were no doubt the original burgesses, the resident burgage holders fulfilling their duties in scot and lot, taxation and service, probably supplemented by the ninety-six French and English mentioned below, whose location in the town became known as French Street. Besides these were eight who held land or houses free of claims by grant of King Edward, and who, no doubt, so continued to hold with certain specified exceptions. Thus Cheping, a wealthy holder of old days, formerly had three houses free, which were now held by Ralph de Mortimer, a relative of King William on the mother's side, and one of his commanders; and Godwin, another ousted proprietor, formerly had four houses in which he had been succeeded by Bernard Pancevolt. Three of these houses are referred to in the entry about Chilworth,[122] where they are called 'hayes in Hantune,' showing that there was inclosed ground around them. There were also sixty-five French and thirty-one English born settled here by King William. And a list is given of certain who received the custom of their houses by grant of King William. They were mostly great landowners, and the houses they held,[123] forty-eight in all, were presumably inhabited by the burgesses, the resident trading population, who subsequently obtained supreme authority and government in the towns owing to their enrolment in strong trading gilds, and who when they had purchased the ferm of their towns passed in due time by an almost natural process into the more modern 'corporations.'

None but the most general inference can be drawn from the Domesday entry as to the size and population of Southampton. Besides the forty-eight there were many houses, if such they might be called, of the poorer classes of which no account could be taken, whose occupiers enjoyed few or no privileges. Still, though the borough may compare disadvantageously

108 Pat. 12 Hen. IV, m. 12.

109 *Guide to Merchants*, &c. (1730), 105.

110 *Angl.-Sax. Chron.* (Rolls Ser.), *sub anno*; Guest, *Early Engl. Settlements in S. Brit.* 180; Green, *Making of Engl.* 87.

111 *Angl.-Sax. Chron.* (Rolls Ser.), *sub anno*. Probably it was from Southampton that the conquest of the Isle of Wight was undertaken in 530; ibid. *sub anno*.

112 Ibid.

113 *Angl.-Sax. Chron.* (Rolls Ser.), *sub annis*.

114 Wilkins, *Leges Angl.-Sax.* 59. It will be observed that the burhs mentioned are all south of the Thames, in the Wessex of the tenth century.

115 Ruding, *Ann. of Coinage*, i, 251; iii, 35.

116 *Angl. Sax. Chron.* (Rolls Ser.), *sub annis*; see also Will. of Malmesb. *De Gestis Regum*, ii, cap. 10.

117 Flor. Wigorn. *Chron.* (Engl. Hist. Soc.), i, 173; Sim. Dunelm, *Opera* (*sub* 1016), (ed. Twysden), col. 173.

118 Henry of Huntingdon, who died in the middle of the twelfth century, puts the story under 1036 (Canute died 11 Nov. 1035), but does not venture on any locality for the occurrence; Henry of Hunt. *Hist. Angl.* (Rolls Ser.), 189.

119 See Lingard, *Hist. of Engl.* i, 319, and refs.

120 A Danish vessel, 130 ft. long, clinker-built, with timbers of large size and flanking of three thicknesses, existed in the Hamble mud above Bursledon Bridge till blown to pieces now many years ago. A vessel also found at Southampton in 1848 seems to have been of similar character. See Davies, op. cit. 25.

121 A full translation of the entry is given in *V.C.H. Hants*, i, 516.

122 Ibid. 494*b*.

123 Ibid. 516; Merewether and Stephens, *Hist. of Boroughs*, i, 201, 207, 221; Morgan, *Engl. under the Norman Occupation*, 159.

with some others, there can be no doubt that it had started on its upward growth. Amid much decay of town life at this period Southampton, in common with the other few ports leading to the Continent, showed distinct signs of prosperity. The growing importance of the place may be seen in the number of powerful barons and other wealthy folk who possessed houses or lands within its limits.

After Domesday the earliest notices of the town and its life occur in connexion with the payment and administration of its fee-farm.

The Pipe Rolls are the most valuable authority. From the earliest extant of these which touches Southampton the town was being farmed in 1156 by Roger the son of Folcher, whose account for the third part of a year stood thus :—In the treasury, £25 2*s.* ; payment to the chaplain of the castle for the last year, £1 3*s.* 4*d.*, and for the present year by writ, 9*s.* 8*d.* ; fixed payments to the porter and watchmen, 19*s.* 4*d.* ; to John the controller,[124] 19*s.* 4*d.* ; transport service by king's writ, £2 7*s.* 6*d.* ; balance of king's farm for third part of the year, £68 8*s.* 10*d.*[125] In the next account, that of William Trentegeruns, sheriff,[126] fixed tenths amounting to £18—a payment of much earlier origin—were assigned to the monks of Lire and Cormeilles, who already had houses in the town free of dues ; and an annual assignment of 13*s.* 4*d.* was made in favour of the Templars, who had only been introduced into England in Stephen's reign. The usual payments go on to the chaplain, porter, and watchmen of the castle ; for transport of the king's treasure, cages for his hawks, &c., in transport service of the king and queen ; for the queen's board when she came from Normandy (about February, 1157), and for the king's when he came from Barfleur a couple of months later. The next account of the same sheriff gives a settlement during life of 3*s.* land tax on Wimarch,[127] the mother of Nicholas ; payment for the king's board at Brockenhurst, £16—he had evidently been enjoying himself in the New Forest ; payment for catching and carrying the king's deer, for carriage of his wines and various transports by his writ.[128]

For the next five years the 'vicecomitissa' of Rouen rendered account for the farm. In 1160 the queen's last passage cost £16 12*s.* 6*d.*, and a good deal of wine was bought for her, £3 1*s.* 1*d.*[129] In 1163 the 'vicecomitissa' paid £8 15*s.* for the transport of the king's cows, and 10*s.* 9*d.* for their keep while here ; for wounded clerks, 12*d.* ; and for conducting the king's daughter, 6*s.* 4*d.*[130] For the next five years three burgesses accounted for the farm—Roger son of Milo, Fortin, and Robert of St. Lawrence[131]—but towards the end of their time they protested vigorously that they did not hold the town at farm. In their second year (1165) the 'vicecomitissa' rendered her final account for the old farm (£1,423 9*s.* 2*d.*), and nothing further was to be required of her.[132] In 1166 there is payment for the 'esnecca' in which the king crossed in Lent, £7 10*s.*; the same sum is paid by writ for the passage of the king of Scotland, while the Lord Geoffrey, the king's son, requiring two ships, besides the 'esnecca,' drew on the farm for £10.[133] For the last quarter of 1167 Richard of Limesey took up the farm.[134] At this period a change occurs. When the fee-farm first appears under Henry II it is the enormous sum of £300 'blanch,' a sum only equalled by that which London had paid, and twice as large as was paid by Winchester. But for whatever reason, from 1167 the farm seems to have become settled on a basis of £200 'blanch,' which continued so till the purchase of the farm by the town, to be mentioned presently. In 1168 an aid of £29 13*s.* 4*d.* for the marriage of the king's daughter was charged to the burgesses,[135] and in 1171 and 1172 they owed £2 13*s.* 4*d.* for arrears thereof.[136] In 1173 Robert of St. Lawrence[137] claims allowance for land in the town itself, given to the lepers[138] of Southampton, worth £1 3*s.* 2*d.* per annum, by writ of the king,[139] and in 1174 for land at Portswood worth 7*s.* 2*d.*, given to the canons of St. Denys.[140]

A memorable royal visit occurred on 8 July 1174, when King Henry landed from Barfleur to perform his vow as pilgrim to the city already famous for reported miracles at Becket's shrine.[141] On Good Friday, 1176, the two princes, Richard—afterwards king—and Geoffrey, were here on their way to join the king at Winchester ; and the same year the king's daughter, the Princess Joan, sailed for Sicily in the 'esnecca' (£7 10*s.*) with seven ships in consort (£10 12*s.*), to be married to the king of Sicily. Henry II was here apparently for the last time in April, 1186. He died 6 July, 1189. Before the coronation of the new king on 3 September that year the port was alive with the transit of great folk and preparations of various kinds ; and Geoffrey the son of Azo, who rendered account for the shire, was charged, among other things, with £6 1*s.* for repairs to the houses within 'the tower' of Southampton, probably those generally called 'the king's houses,' as if for the accommodation of the court and its supplies.

The return of Gervase, reeve (*prepositus*) of Southampton, shows that the royal 'esnecca' made six passages before the coming of King Richard, the charge being £45.[142]

William Briwer accounted for £106 13*s.* 8*d.* of the town farm in 1192–3, and in 1198–9 the sheriff of the shire accounted for the same amount.[143] It appears that Hugh de Bosco, the sheriff, had offered King John 20 marks to hold the town to farm till Michaelmas next after the coronation ; upon which it had been intimated to William Briwer that

124 His office was to check the prepositus of the town on the amounts paid to the king ; see Madox, *Exch.* i, 202 ; and note on Ric. of Leicester.

125 *Pipe R.* 1155–6 (Rec. Com.), 53.

126 Turstin was sheriff of Hants at this time, William being the appointed officer in the borough.

127 For Wimarch see Madox, *Form. Angl.* 252 ; Morgan, op. cit. 211.

128 *Pipe R.* 1555–8 (Rec. Com.), 107.

129 Ibid. (Pipe R. Soc.), ii, 23.

130 Ibid. vi, 56.

131 Ibid. vii, 27.

132 Ibid. viii, 45.

133 Ibid. ix, 109.

134 Ibid. x, 189.

135 Ibid.

136 Ibid. xvi, 43 ; xviii, 88.

137 Five years later his wife Cecilia renders account for him (1178–9). Exemp. of Town Accts. from Exch. R. 10 Apr. 3 Hen. IV (1402), *penes* Corp. Southt.

138 See below, St. Mary Magd. Hosp. for Lepers.

139 *Pipe R.* (Pipe R. Soc.), xix, 53.

140 Ibid. xxi, 134.

141 This was the earliest notable pilgrimage from this town to be followed in constant succession by devotees from Normandy, Anjou, and Brittany. The starting point may perhaps be detected in the name Pilgrims' pit, near 'Biddlesgate,' which was close to the ancient quay at which they would land, as will be seen later.

142 For further details concerning the royal 'esnecca' see Davies, op. cit. 31.

143 Exemp. of Town Accts. from Exch. R. 10 Apr. 1402 (3 Hen. IV), *penes* Corp. Southt.

if he wished to retain the town so long he must pay the 20 marks offered by Hugh. This he evidently declined, as Hugh was charged the 20 marks and held the office.[144]

The beginning of the thirteenth century—always a period of advance in borough history—was the time when the town, possibly through the agency of its gild merchant (see below) purchased its fee-farm, obtaining it (1199–1200), together with that of the port of Portsmouth and all that belonged to the farm of Southampton, in the time of King Henry, for the fine of £100, and the annual rent of £200, payable at the Exchequer each Michaelmas Day.[145] Thus in 1204 the burgesses rendered account by the hand of Azo, who was perhaps alderman of the gild and whose son in all probability was mayor a few years later, for the £200 farm of Southampton with Portsmouth. In 1208 they did the same. In 1210 they rendered account for two years together (£400), claiming abatement each year for land at Portswood and Kingsland given by King Richard (8 September, 1189) to the canons of St. Denys; but they appear to have been charged to King John 40 marks (£26 13*s.* 4*d.*) and two tuns of wine of Aucerra.[146] In 1216 Richard of Leicester answered for the town's farm; he had been, in and before 1199, controller of the town as his ancestors before him, but had in that year been ousted from office by Robert Hardwin, who had fined for it with the king.[147] In these troublous times the burgesses and their officials must often have been perplexed as to who should be their masters. On 27 October, 1217, the sheriff (shire) was directed to cause the king's uncle, William Longespee, earl of Salisbury, who had returned to his allegiance and obtained restitution of his estates several months before, to have in peace the town of Southampton;[148] on 29 November the same year a writ to the earl required him to remove his bailiffs, the town being taken into the king's hands; this is repeated to the bailiffs of the town by writ of the same date, who are required to account for the farm as usual at the Exchequer. At this period the town, or city as it is called, is stated to be entirely in the king's demesne, and settlements were held there directly of the crown.[149] A little later (6 October, 1226) the burgesses received in aid of their farm the customs of salt at Pennington, which Henry of Pont Audemer held, but which belonged to their town.[150]

In 1276 the farm was raised. The town, which had been seized into the king's hands by judgement of Exchequer for certain transgressions of the burgesses, was only restored upon a fine at the usual farm with an increment of forty marks (£26 13*s.* 4*d.*),[151] a circumstance referred to in 1531, up to which date the increment remained.[152] Apparent occasional exceptions to this amount till that date are generally capable of explanation. Releases sometimes came on special grounds, e.g. the cost of maintaining the fortifications (see below), or on woful representations of the town's financial straits. Thus Edward IV and Richard III at the commencement of their reigns remitted arrears of the fee-farm, among other matters, in general pardons to the mayor and burgesses.[153] In the early years of the next century the borough seems to have been systematically two or three years behind in its payment.

Before finishing the account of the farm some notice of the charges on it may be of interest. The practice of drawing on it by writ continued; soldiers and archers had to be paid, the king's chambers had to be repaired, wine orders to be executed, presents to be made. Alms and settlements on religious houses continued; the college of St. Mary and All Saints, Fotheringhay, founded by Henry IV in 1411, succeeded in due time to the assignment to Lire; and Shene Priory, commenced by Henry V in 1414, obtained that formerly given to Cormeilles.[154]

Again, the queens of England often obtained the fee-farm in part dowry. In 1286 Eleanor, the king's consort, had an interest in the customs of the town (30 March), and in the same year (23 June) Eleanor, the king's mother and widow of Henry III, obtained the farm for life together with the prise of wine.[155] She died in 1291, and in 1299 (10 September) the king endowed his second wife, Margaret of France, at the church door, with the farm which was to yield her £201 3*s.* 2*d.*; he also gave her a long list of manors, castles, and towns, among which was the castle

PROVENCE. *Or four pales gules.*

OLD FRANCE. *Azure powdered with fleurs-de-lis or.*

of Southampton.[156] In 1331 when Queen Isabel was deprived of her possessions the fee-farm was granted, with the assent of Parliament, to Queen Philippa,[157] but in 1340 was again in possession of Isabel, who dated her rights back from the burning of the town (October, 1338).[158] She was afterwards dispossessed and died in August, 1358. Joan of Navarre,

144 *Rot. de Oblatis* (Rec. Com.), 19; *Rot. Cancellar.* 254.

145 Madox, *Exch.* i, 402; also below under charters.

146 Exemp. of Town Accts. *penes* Corp. Southt.; Madox, op. cit. 409; *Rot. de Oblatis* (Rec. Com.), 1208, p. 433.

147 *Abbrev. Plac.* (Rec. Com.), 23; Madox, op. cit. 202.

148 Close, 1 Hen. III, pt. 1, m. 1.

149 *Testa de Nevill* (Rec. Com.), 236; *Rot. Lit. Claus.* (Rec. Com.), i, 345.

150 *Rot. Lit. Claus.* (Rec. Com.), i, 472.

151 Exemp. of Town Accts. *penes* Corp. Southt.; Pat. 4 Edw. I, m. 23, 27.

152 *Stat. Realm* (1510–45), p. 351. Among the petitions to Parliament of 18 Edw. I (1290), 'Gilbertus Canon, Ballivus qui exequendo preceptum Regis in villa Sutht' verberatus, vulneratus usque ad mortem, per homines ejusd. ville, pro qua transgressione villa capta fuit in manus Dni. Regis et finem fecerunt, et firmam suam exaltaverunt ad xx *li.* Petit quod provideat ei sustentationem in aliqua abbatia' (*Rot. Parl.* [Rec. Com.], i, 58*a*). But it is quite certain from the subsequent town accounts, as well as from the Act referred to above, that the increment of 40 marks was exacted. Gilbert's statement is as inaccurate as the description of his own condition.

153 Bdle. of Pardons (Corp. MSS.).

154 Stewards' Bks. (Corp. MSS.), 1457, 1485, &c.

155 Pat. 14 Edw. I, m. 23 sched.; Pat. 19 Edw. I, m. 26 (17 Sept. 1291), issues for a certain time to queen's executors.

156 Rymer, *Foed.* ii, 854; Exemp. of Town Accts. (Corp. MSS.).

157 Pat. 4 Edw. III, pt. 2, m. 1 (1 Jan. 1331).

158 *Rot. Orig.* (Rec. Com.), ii, 141.

queen of Henry IV, had a jointure of 150 marks on the farm in 1400.[159] She died in 1437. Margaret of Anjou was endowed (May, 1444) out of the customs of Southampton (£1,000), and in 1454 obtained an annuity of £100 from the fee-farm.[160]

HAINAULT. *Or a lion sable* for FLANDERS *quartered with Or a lion gules* for HOLLAND.

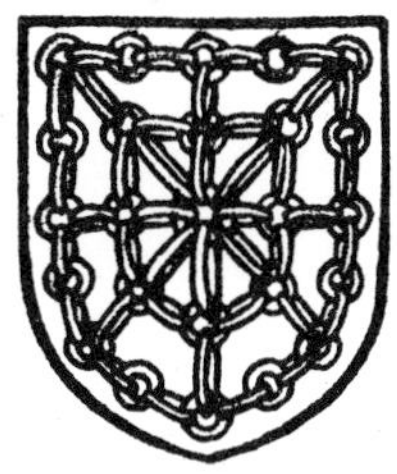

NAVARRE. *Gules a double orle, a cross and a saltire of chains or all conjoined.*

Elizabeth, queen of Edward IV, received £46 per annum from the farm (1467),[161] and three years later the mayor had to borrow £7 to make up the allowance,[162] for the town always made an effort to pay the queens with some kind of regularity, even when lapsing into a chronic state of arrears. In the reign of Henry VIII similar payments were made, and in 1605 James I made the same settlement on his queen.[163]

Again, payments were often made to great nobles. Thus, not to mention smaller amounts of an earlier date, in 1461 (14 December) an annuity of £154 from the farm was confirmed to Richard Nevill, the stout earl of Warwick; and payments were continued till he fell at Barnet, Easter Day, 1471, though not

ANJOU. *Old France in a border gules.*

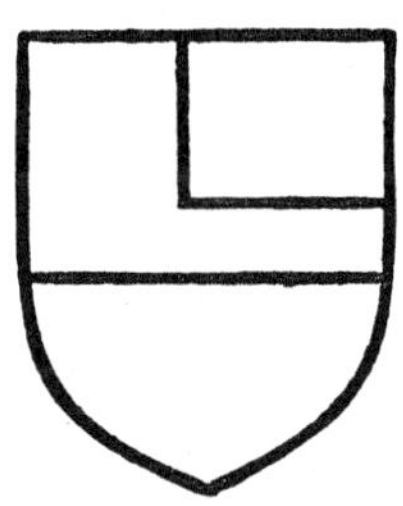

WYDVILE. *Argent a fesse and a quarter gules.*

without the usual confusion and delay. On one occasion the mayor had to ride to London (1469) 'to rekyn wt the erle of Warwicke.' He was there twelve days and spent 50*s.* 6*d.*, and it appears he had to borrow money in 'contentacion of the fee-ferme.'[164] The next settlement (£154) was made on William Fitz Alan, earl of Arundel, and payments were made to him in numerous small instalments till his death in 1487. Payment was sometimes tendered in wine, sometimes the earl would draw on the town for his friends. Occasionally his letters are quite pathetic as to his non-payment, always expressing the moderation of his demands, and begging 'his right trusty and well beloved friends and neighbours, the mayor and his brethren' to bear in mind his great charges (January-November, 1482). Two years later he urges his expenses in 'setting forth to the sea his right entirely beloved son, Sir John Arundel' at the king's command, and having to furnish so many men 'diffensibly arrayed' when needed for the royal service (April, 1484).[165]

Charges for the king's household, varying considerably, were also made on the farm from time to time;

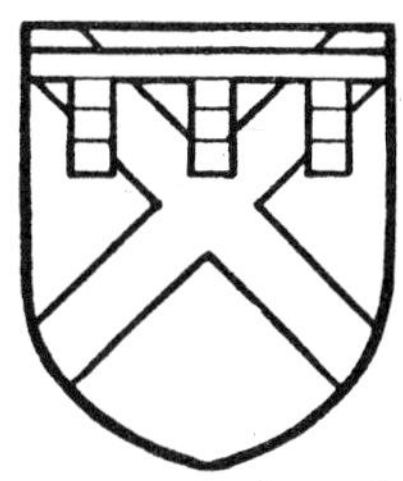

NEVILL. *Gules a saltire argent and a label gobony argent and azure.*

FITZ ALAN. *Gules a lion or.*

thus £26 18*s.* 6*d.* in 1450;[166] £133 6*s.* 8*d.* in 1461;[167] £154 in 1495.[168]

It will be gathered that the town was occasionally in difficulty about its rent. It was frequently obliged to resort to loans and gifts[169] from private individuals. Sometimes its burgesses suffered in person for the debts of the community. Thus in 1461 we find one of the chief burgesses thrown into the Fleet at the suit of John, Lord Wenlock, of the Privy Council, for the 'rerage' of the fee-farm; and on 24 July 'Symkyn Patrycke[170] and John Gryme' rode to London by commandment of the mayor and burgesses 'to labour for the worship of the town and the welfare of Richard Gryme,[171] the which was in the prison of the Fleet for the debt of the said town.'[172] The sum of £20 was paid for his deliverance, to be considered apparently as a loan by Richard.[173]

Returning now to the amount of the fee-farm: a permanent reduction of 40 marks (£26 13*s.* 4*d.*) was made in 1530–1 on urgent petition of the

[159] She was deprived of her dower estates on an absurd charge of sorcery in 1419, but restored in 1422; indentures between the queen and the town as to her payment exist, bearing date 12 Nov. that year. Corp. MSS.

[160] *Rot. Parl.* (Rec. Com.), v, 120, 133*b*, 259, 262.

[161] Lib. Remembranc. H. (Corp. MSS.); *Rot. Parl.* (Rec. Com.), v, 626.

[162] Steward's Bk. (Corp. MSS.), 1470–71.

[163] Town Journ. (Corp. MSS.).

[164] Lib. Remembranc. H. fol. 32–3; Steward's Bk. (Corp. MSS.). On indemnity by Edw. IV for payments to late earl of Warwick, see *Hist. MSS. Com. Rep.* xi, App. iii, 100; and on grant of £20 from fee-farm to Thomas Raynold, late sheriff of the town, 1469, ibid. 98.

[165] Steward's Bk. and letters affixed; Lib. Remembranc. H. fol. 149*b*. (Corp. MSS.).

[166] *Rot. Parl.* (Rec. Com.), v, 174*b*.

[167] Lib. Remembranc. H. fol. 32 (Corp. MSS.); *Hist. MSS. Com. Rep.* xi, App. iii, 16.

[168] *Rot. Parl.* (Rec. Com.), vi, 499*b*.

[169] Stewards' Bks. (Corp. MSS.) afford details.

[170] Sheriff in 1451.

[171] Sheriff in 1458, mayor 1459. This visit of the burgesses falls in fairly with the old gild ordinance which provided that any gildsman in prison, in whatever part of the kingdom, should be visited at the common expense, and his release procured if possible. Richard Gryme certainly returned safely to enjoy the sweets of freedom in his garden in East Street, and some years after he appears as lieutenant of Hampton; Stewards' Bks. 1474.

[172] Steward's Bk. 1461, and loose paper containing details of journey, &c. (Corp. MSS.).

[173] 'Payd for lyverance of Rychard Gryme, what tyme he was in Flete at sewte of lord Wanlok for the rerage of the fee-farm of the Towne, xx*li*' (Steward's Bk. 1461–2); 'Item lent to Ric. Gryme for his delyverans ayenst my lord Wenlok, xx*li*' (Lib. Remembranc. H. fol. 25*b*).

burgesses;[174] but in 1533 the corporation wrote to Cromwell urging again their great charges, stating that they had derived no benefit from past favours, and begging that their arrears might be 'stalled.' Their letter received small attention, and in 1537 matters had got so much worse that the mayor in fear of a process at the Exchequer, and seizure of the town's liberties, had recourse to the merchant Nicholas Dogra, called also Demagrine, who came to his temporary relief and advanced £200 for the farm, receiving in security[175] West Hall, a locally noted tenement which stood in Bugle Street on the site of the buildings formerly occupied by the grammar school. By 1549 the sum of £1,844 1*s.* 6*d.* was owing to the Exchequer; of this total the amount of £1,044 1*s.* 6*d.* was remitted in the following year on the corporation entering into a bond for £1,000 to pay the remaining £800 at the rate of £100 a year.[176] In 1552 the farm was reduced under certain conditions to £50, and in consideration of the present poverty of the town, 'as well on account of the repairs of the walls and forts called "bulwerkes" now in a ruinous state and demanding attention, as also on account of the town being a frontier lying on the sea-coast towards Normandy, France, and other southern ports,' all arrears were also remitted.[177] Yet in September, 1561, the town was in debt to many persons in various sums, and especially to John Caplen, who at the request of the corporation undertook to receive and administer all moneys that might be due to the town within the next two years, and from them to pay the fee-farm, officers' wages, and other ordinary charges, to satisfy the other creditors, and 'of his good nature and accustomed goodness' to be 'contente that his own dette shalbe laste payed.' No repairs were to be carried out for the town, or any money transactions negotiated without cognizance of John Caplen.[178] Loans from the burgesses in payment of the farm not uncommonly occur. The conditions of the reduction of the farm to £50, which were confirmed by the last governing charter of 1640,[179] were that the petty customs should not have amounted in any year to £200, that no ships called 'carracks of Genoa' or 'galleys of Venice' should have visited the port, and that a certificate accordingly should be sent each year to the lords of the Treasury and the barons of the Exchequer. Certificates of the amount were regularly sent, but in 1803 an Act of Parliament was passed[180] abolishing the payment of petty customs to the corporation, and giving them instead one-fifth of the port-dues to be received by commissioners created under the new Act. But when on 9 November, 1804, the corporation transmitted a certificate reciting this Act to the Treasury and Exchequer, it was rejected for want of stating the amount received in lieu of petty customs until fourteen days afterwards another was forwarded giving the required details.[181] The reduced farm of £50 was paid to the crown from the time of Edward VI to the death of Charles I. It was sold under the Commonwealth 29 September, 1650, together with the fee-farm of the city of Hereford (£42) by the commissioners appointed for selling the fee-farm rents of the late crown of England under the Act of the then present Parliament, to Azariah Husband and his heirs for £785 11*s.* 8*d.*[182] After the Restoration this, with other crown properties, was resumed; and on 20 October, 1674, was sold to Sir Robert Holmes.[183] In 1681 it passed to John Garland and his heirs, being sold and conveyed by the Trustees for Sale of the Crown Fee-farm Rents.[184] It was afterwards conveyed to Thomas Osborne, first duke of Leeds, in whose family it remained till 1737, when it was sold for £1,500 by Thomas, duke of Leeds, great-grandson of the above, to Ann, countess of Salisbury, widow, for the purpose of endowing a charity school which she had lately founded.[185] By 1835 this settlement had been forgotten, since the municipal corporation commissioners of that year conjectured that the fee-farm rent of £40 2*s.* paid annually to a charity called 'Hatfield's Charity' might be the remains of the old fee-farm transferred at one time probably from the crown to the charity, but could not find that anyone knew more of the matter. Yet the connexion of the payment with the 'Hatfield Charity School' appears clearly in the Journal of 28 October, 1825.[186] At the end of the petty customs certificate of Michaelmas, 1836, the entry occurs: 'ordered that the Treasurer of the Borough do pay to the Trustees of Hatfield's charity the sum of £40 2*s.* the remainder of the fee-farm rent, land tax deducted.' The origin of the payment was rightly inferred, its direction still a matter of confusion. A similar order to the above occurs 24 November, 1837. The payment is of course continued.

OSBORNE. *Quarterly ermine and azure a cross or.*

The early history of the government of the town can best be learnt from the history of the gild as deduced from the earliest gild ordinances,[187] for the gild was, in the case of Southampton, the nurse of its corporation. The earliest charter, that of Henry II, shows that the 'men of Hanton,' that is the burgesses, 'had their gild' by the time of Henry I; that is from the beginning of the twelfth century. Some six versions of the gild ordinances are extant, versions made from time to time as changing circumstances demanded, dated from the opening of the fourteenth to the latter half of the seventeenth century, with alterations running on a century later.[188]

174 *Stat. Realm*, iii, 351–2.

175 Boke of Remembrances, fol. 37, 41*b*. (Corp. MSS.).

176 Bond (among pardons) Audit House, Southt.

177 The charter is enrolled, Pat. 6 Edw. VI, pt. 6, m. 3, &c. The corporation possesses an exemplification made at the request of John Capelyn, mayor, and Thomas Mylle, recorder, dated 27 April, 7 Edw. VI.

178 Boke of Remembrances, fol. 90 (Corp. MSS.).

179 Yet the Town Journ. 3 Oct. 1656, states that Roger Pedley, the sheriff, was compelled by writ of Exchequer to demand a levy of £200 for the fee-farm. There must have been some informality on the town's part.

180 Stat. Realm, 43 Geo. III, cap. 21.

181 Town Journ. (Corp. MSS.), 9 Nov. 1804, &c.; *Rep. on Municipal Corps.* 1835. The certificate is still prepared in the same way every year, and each 9th of November it is humbly signified in the prescribed quarters that no ships called 'carracks of Genoa' or 'galleys of Venice' have arrived at the port.

182 Counterpart D. of sale of Fee Farm Rents, bdle. H, i, No. 17.

183 Sale of Fee Farm Rents, Enrolments, vol. 244, fol. 77 (Land Rev. Off.).

184 Close, 33 Chas. II, pt. 14. No. 6.

185 Ibid. 11 Geo. II, No. 16.

186 Town Journ. (Corp. MSS.).

187 See above, n. 45.

188 The earliest version, which went by the name of 'Paxbread,' is in French, and probably dates from the early fourteenth century. It is contained in the Oak Book, one of the most interesting of the town books. The next version is a free

Evidently by the early fourteenth century, the date of the earliest version,[189] the identity of the borough government was merged in that of the gild, since the ordinances profess to regulate both.

The officials of the gild, in many cases, had certainly functions which were beyond those of the original gild merchant, and nothing remained to show the distinction between gild and borough, so completely had the gild dominated over the old borough idea. But whenever it was that the gild became settled as the supreme authority—and it may have been from its first existence by charter (probably in the time of Henry I)—there then entered an element of restriction alien from the more ancient government of the town. The privileges of the borough communities were no longer shared by all the free, that is unservile, town dwellers who bore their part in the public burdens, but were henceforward restricted to the few, and these remained so until the Act of 1835, which restored the meaning of the word 'burgess' to something more like the original.

The alderman or chief alderman of the town,[190] assisted by two bailiffs and twelve sworn men, was head of gild and town. The 'twelve assistants,' as they were afterwards termed, were elected each year by the whole community, and themselves the same day elected the two bailiffs. There were also four sworn men, discreets of the market, and twelve aldermen of wards who had the view of frankpledge in their wards, and controlled the police and sanitary regulations of the town. The seneschal or steward acted as treasurer under the direction of the chief alderman, and the four 'skavyns'—as the word was usually written and pronounced—probably served under him as chamberlains in his department.[191] The usher gave warning of town meetings and was perhaps the mouthpiece of the gild in proclamations.

The gild did not always meet in the same place, perhaps in this respect preserving the old tradition of the gild-merchant, which was not even confined to town-dwellers, and there is no mention of a gildhall.[192] The meetings, solemn no less than festive, were to be held twice in the year, the Sunday next after St. John Baptist's Day (24 June), and that after St. Hilary (13 January).

The gildsman or burgess, with certain exceptions in the case of honorary members, was of necessity a resident of the town and held his membership, which involved the widest possible privileges, by right of inheritance or purchased it by fine. The one important restriction on his rights was that he could not barter away or sell his position. After the gildsman comes the man of the franchise, who, dwelling within the liberties of the town, bore his part in duties and taxation, and was admitted to trade by the enabling and essential permission of the gild. The stranger or foreigner was not necessarily, or indeed, generally, a foreign subject, but dwelt without the town liberties and was only admitted to the markets or even into the town on sufferance. The expression 'man of the town,' sometimes met with in the ordinances, is evidently a comprehensive term including both gildsman and franchiser.

It was in comparatively recent times that the name of gild was finally given up. The entries in the 'Burgess book' of 1496 record admissions 'into the gilde' or into 'the libertie of the gilde.' One or other of these forms occurs without a variation till the admission of Bishop Horne in 1562, whose name is the last thus entered. After this there is a marked change in the style. The next and most of the subsequent admissions are 'to be one of the burgesses,' or in the latest times till 1835, 'admitted and sworn a burgess.' Still in 1597 there is an admission 'to be one of the burgesses and gilde'; and the same or similar form of 'gild and burgess' occurs not infrequently till 1704; after which the name does not appear in documents, and only remains in the word 'gildhall.'

Of the town charters the earliest, that of Henry II (quoted above), is known only by Inspeximus. It was probably given in the first year of his reign (1154–5), and granted to his men of 'Hanton' their gild liberties and customs by land and by sea 'in as good, peaceable, just, free, quiet and honourable a manner as they had the same better, more freely and quietly in the time of King Henry I.'[193] Richard I, by a charter of 1189, known by Inspeximus, granted the burgesses freedom from toll,[194] passage and pontage both by land and water, both in fairs and markets, and from all secular customs ('de omni seculari consuetudine') in all parts of the king's dominions on both

translation from the Old French text made by William Overey, the town clerk, in 1473. He is described in the prologue as son and heir to 'Willian Overey, some time mayor,' in 1474, and as having succeeded by inheritance to his father's burgess-wick, which is a little difficult to understand, since his father was alive in 1474. Subsequently, by free election, he was chosen town clerk and sheriff, 15 September, 1473. This version, which shows certain omissions and additions, was presented to the mayor and his brethren, burgesses of the gild, and to the inhabitants of the town in 1478. The town copy now existing, however, is not the original, but was written after the beginning of the reign of Henry VIII. Two other versions belong to the same century; the latter of them being found in the Burgess Book of 1496. This was in use till superseded by a version written in the time of Charles I, about 1630. The ordinances of this last version are considerably modernized, the word 'burgess' always appearing instead of 'gildsman,' and there are several additions. The last version is that contained in the book of 'Oaths of Office,' now in use, commenced by Richard Stanley, town clerk, 1648–53. The ordinances of this copy, though presenting certain variations from the last, are substantially the same. There are, however, some considerable additions. All these versions, excepting the first, have attached to them the oaths of the numerous town officials as needed from time to time; and we have here presented the growth and movement of the borough constitution as far as contained in the ordinances from about 1300 to the period when the corporation had assumed the shape in which the Municipal Reform Act of 1835 found it.

[189] And it must be remembered that the ordinances in many cases represent a much earlier date.

[190] Namely, the alderman (originally) of the gild-merchant, as distinguished from those of the wards.

[191] In a document of 1368 (31 Dec. 42 Edw. III), the mayor, the four scabini, the two bailiffs, the steward (mentioned in this order), and several burgesses, representing the whole community of the town, are partners to an agreement with the bishop of Winchester (Corp. MSS.) The four scabini kept the accounts of the gild-merchant at King's Lynn (*Hist. MSS. Com. Rep.* xi, App. pt. iii, 226); also *Engl. Gilds* (Early Engl. Text Soc.), 46, 'four skevaynes . . . for to kepyn and reseyven the goodes and the katal of the gilde.'

[192] See above, under Bargate, p. 496.

[193] Inspeximus 1 Edw. III, 7 Ric. II, &c., in hands of the corporation.

[194] Constant feuds occurred among the mediaeval towns, as was inevitable, from the practice of granting immunity from the payment of toll and custom throughout the kingdom. Notable controversies of the kind arose between Southampton and other places, e.g. with Marlborough and Portsmouth 1239, Bristol 1260, Netley Abbey 1288–90, bishop of Winchester 1312, Lymington 1324, New Sarum 1329, Coventry 1456. For a list of towns free from the toll, brocage, pontage, petty customs, &c. see Rev. J. Silvester Davies, op. cit. 229, 230.

sides of the sea. This is confirmed in the oldest extant charter given by King John in June, 1199.[195] Three days later came the grant of the fee-farm (see above).

Henry III confirmed all the above grants in 1227,[196] and in 1252 forbade the barons of the Cinque Ports to take 'Karke'[197] within the port of Portsmouth, which was held at farm from the king (as above), to execute attachments, or do any injury to the men aforesaid contrary to their liberties and customs as granted by the king; but ordered them to permit the purchase of the king's wines from the barons' ships within the port of Portsmouth. In 1256 Henry granted the burgesses freedom from arrest in their persons or goods for debts of which they were not themselves the sureties or principal debtors; unless the debtors were of their community and capable of satisfying their debts in whole or in part, and the burgesses had failed in doing justice to the creditors.[198]

From the reign of Henry III to Henry VI various charters of inspection and confirmation[199] were given, that of 1401 (2 Henry IV) granting further to the mayor[200] and bailiffs cognizance of all pleas of whatever kind to be held in the gildhall ('guyhalda') and there finally determined, the right of holding court leet[201] and practically self-government.

In 1445 (23 Henry VI) came the incorporation charter setting forth as usual the heavy charges of the town and its great impoverishment, and incorporating it under the title of a mayor, two bailiffs, and burgesses. Provision was made for the election of mayor and bailiffs, who were also made controllers of the staple granted by this Act, on the Friday before St. Matthew's day each year, and in case of death or deposition, &c., within fifteen days of such vacancy. The mayor was to be the sole escheator with right of attachment like the sheriff of London. Further, the town and the port of Portsmouth, 'which port is within the liberty of the said town of Southampton,' were exempted for ever from obedience to the constable marshal or admiral of England, or the steward, and marshal or clerk of the market, who should not enter the town to hold pleas, or hold pleas out of the town concerning matters within the same. The mayor was to be clerk of the market, and strangers were prohibited from buying of, or selling to, strangers.

Two years later came the charter of Henry VI creating the county, granting that since the merchants and mariners of the town were incommoded by the sheriff of the county serving writs on them, and in consideration of the heavy fee-farm of 340 marks (£226 13*s.* 4*d.*) 'our said town, with the port and precinct thereof, and the port of Portsmouth, which is now called "the town of Suthampton and its precincts," shall be one entire county, incorporated in word and deed, separate and distinct from the county of Southampton for ever, and shall be called "our county of the town of Suthampton."'[202]

The sheriff, who was to hold a county court, was to be chosen from among the burgesses each year on the Friday before St. Matthew's Day and certified by the mayor to the barons of the Exchequer; in case of death, &c., a new one was to be chosen within ten days and certified as above. In 1451 a further confirmation charter gave an additional right to the mayor to perform all acts belonging to the office of steward and marshal of the household, and admiral of England, within liberties of the town and county.

In spite of the foregoing charters, in the following year notice occurs of a dispute with the justices of the county concerning mulcts ('emendas') from the assize of bread and ale and fines from various tradespeople and artisans, which belonged by right to the townsmen of Southampton, but which the justices were about to appropriate. The right of the townsmen was maintained by royal writ except that any fines or amercements of artisans or dyers arising within the aforesaid town were to be levied to the king's use under the present commission.[203] In 1461 further privileges, including court of pie powder and authorized resistance to the king's officers, were given by Edward III. In 1468, 1480, 1484, 1510, and 1515 further confirmation charters were given, to which in 1553 was added that of Edward VI, regulating and limiting the payment of the fee-farm (see above).

Various confirmations were given by Philip and Mary (1557–8), by Elizabeth (1564), and by James I (1616). The last governing charter was given by Charles I in 1640.[204] It rehearsed and confirmed former charters with certain variations, ordered the appointment of a common council to consist of mayor, recorder, aldermen, bailiffs, and sheriff, and all who have held these offices, to assist the mayors, with power to make statutes, by-laws, &c.; also the appointment of a court of orphans and of a town clerk or common clerk of the town, to be clerk of the peace and sessions and have fees. Four serjeants-at-mace were also to be appointed and fines were to be levied for refusal to take office. Power to tax

195 *Penes* Corp. Southt.

196 *Cal. Chart R.* 1226–57, p. 35.

197 'Karke,' on this word see Gloss. to *Liber Albus Lond.* 331. The charge was that the barons had been 'molesti vi capiendo karkas in navibus vestris de hominibus volentibus transfretare in porto suo de Portesmuth quem de nobis tenent ad firmam, et faciendo atachiamenta,' &c.

198 By gild ord. 27 securities for debts were to be investigated and ratified, and this ratification may have been thought to make the members of the gild responsible for the debts, a responsibility here limited; or the charter may refer to a custom which seems to have prevailed according to which a corporation, a member of which had a claim upon a member of another corporation, seized the goods of every freeman of the latter found within the jurisdiction of the former 'in Withernam' until the corporation to which the debtor belonged, or the debtor himself, made satisfaction. *Rep. on Munic. Corp.* (1835).

199 All these charters, some original, some known only by inspeximus, with all those that follow, are in the possession of the corporation.

200 The first notice of a mayor in the charters; but for the early use of title see below.

201 Clearly only a confirmation, but the first mention of such.

202 This on the surface would seem to include Portsmouth within the county of the town. Evidently it was locally thought so. On the margin of this charter is written in a later hand, 'Note how farre the countie of the Town doth strech,' and just below, 'The porte of Portismouthe is parte of the countye and of the town of Suthampton.' But the charter in its last clause has a word for Portsmouth, and provides that 'no prejudice, under pretence of this our grant, shall accrue to the bailiffs etc. of Portsmouth with regard to any privileges granted to or used by them in time past.'

203 No king's name is specified, only the regnal year is given. (From transcript by Dr. Speed in his MS. *penes* Corp. Southt.)

204 The cost of this charter was £219 17*s.* Town Journ. 1641, fol. 308. It appears to have been read in the House in English for the first time on 2 Sept. 1640. After reading it was put into the great chest with the English paper copy. This last seems to have long disappeared.

the inhabitants was given to the corporation ; piccage and stallage were ordered to be paid by strangers ; one or more prisons were to be kept in the town ; a corn market was to be held every Thursday. The mayor and corporation were to take tolls, while no person who had been mayor was obliged to bear arms in person. For the benefit of sailors and fishermen and the bettering of navigable streams, the mayor might cleanse all creeks and rivers within the liberties where the tide flows, and take the soil. The most important item on the charter, however, was the clause by which a judgement in the court of the Exchequer which had been given against the town in 1635 was reversed.[205] The liberties, franchises and privileges which had then been taken into the king's hands by reason of their exercise without warrant or royal grant[206] were now restored to the town, and the mayor, bailiffs, and burgesses were freed from all penal consequences which had been involved in this judgement.

It appears that soon after the Restoration, in May, 1661, the town considered the advisability of renewing this last, or procuring a fresh charter,[207] a question periodically mooted. In December the same year the Corporation Act[208] was passed with a view to capturing the boroughs ; and in the following February (1662) commissioners, consisting of the mayor, aldermen, and others were appointed by letters patent to administer the Act. But towards the end of the reign, November, 1683, the town was again compelled to deal with the charter. The attempt of the crown to obtain control over all municipal elections involved a correspondence with Sir Leoline Jenkins, Chief Secretary of State, in which the town avowed its willingness to surrender, but pleaded utter poverty—'the late rebellion had robbed the chamber of all public money—the plague had consumed their inhabitants, the Dutchmen had spoiled them of nearly all their ships, their looms were useless owing to the late Act of Prohibition,[209] their revenues had sunk, their burdens increased, let his sacred majesty be assured that the true cause of their tardiness in delivering up their charter was want of money, not of loyalty.' Meanwhile they determined, should the king desire it, to yield up their charter at once without waiting for a *quo warranto*, and get a new charter on the best terms they could. In December the reply from Sir Leoline came ; the king would require the town to surrender its franchise of being a separate county, and to be united to the body of Hampshire, all other liberties being saved and restored ; on such terms he would consent to their having a new charter for nothing, if they could not afford half fees, the rate at which other poor corporations had renewed.

The town swallowed this bitter pill, professing to be grateful, and on 6 September, 1684, the instrument was sealed surrendering the charter with all that went under it. In November a commission was appointed to negotiate a new one ; bnt owing to the king's death in the following February the matter fell through. James II followed the policy of the preceding king in regard to the corporations. A *quo warranto* bearing date 28 November, 1687, but not produced to the mayor till 23 January, was issued against the town requiring the presence of the mayor and bailiffs at Westminster to answer for their franchises. On this a correspondence ensued with the Attorney-general. They would make no defence, but humbly submit their charter to His Majesty's mercy ; nothing but their poverty had prevented their seeking renewal before, and the same was their plea now ; thus they begged that suffering judgement to pass by default might not be interpreted unfavourably, as they had been advised to that course as most submissive to the king, least troublesome to the Attorney-general, and easiest for themselves. Towards the end of the year it was understood that the matter would not be pressed, and on 5 November, 1688, the recorder was desired to employ some one 'to see that a nolle prosequi be entered upon the quo warranto brought against the town,' and for this they were ready to disburse.

Meanwhile a 'new charter,' destined to be a dead letter, had been prepared, and is said to have been lodged in private hands at Southampton to be produced at the proper time. The preamble states that the ancient franchises of the town had, for various abuses, been seized into the king's hands by a judgement on *quo warranto*, and that a new charter was granted on petition of the inhabitants. A common council was provided to consist of the mayor, recorder, thirteen aldermen, and twelve burgesses, one supervisor of the customs, and one common, i.e. town clerk. The mayor, recorder, four senior aldermen, and four burgesses were to be justices. But the significant variations were these :—The king was empowered under seal of privy council to remove any officer or burgess, and to appoint others mayor, aldermen and burgesses within twenty days, to elect person or persons named in royal letters mandatory to vacant offices, however small the number of burgesses attending, and all officers and burgesses were dispensed from taking the oaths of supremacy and allegiance, and that contained in the Corporation Act, from receiving the Sacrament of the Lord's Supper after the Anglican Rite, and from subscribing the declaration in the Popish Recusants Act (25 Chas. II, cap. 2). Moreover, no recorder or town clerk was to be admitted without royal consent under seal. A rectification of the governing charter (16 Chas. I) in some particulars was occasionally contemplated ; and on 6 September, 1723 (10 George I) a petition for a new charter received the town seal. But nothing came of this action, and the charter of 1640 continued in force till the Municipal Corporations Act of 1835.

Of the officers of the town the prominent persons in Southampton before and during the thirteenth century were the king's bailiffs,[210] to whom he directed his writs on matters concerning the town and the royal fiscal requirements. The earliest names of bailiffs to be found in this century are :—In 1205, William of St. Lawrence and Thomas de Bussuse ;[211] in 1209, Goce ;[212] in 1212, Roger Swein and William the Englishman. These two bailiffs (*ballivi*), together

[205] Exch. K.R. Trin. Chas. I, No. 37.

[206] It seems not unlikely, as Dr. Speed has suggested (MS. *penes* Corp. Southt.) that this *quo warranto* may have been incurred by their having neglected to certify to the Exchequer the amount of petty customs in that year, no account of which appears.

[207] Town Journ. (Corp. MSS.), 8 May, 13 Chas. II.

[208] Stat. 13 Chas. II, Stat. 2, cap. 1.

[209] Probably Stat. 29 & 30 Chas. II, cap. 1, 70, &c.

[210] See above, under fee-farm ; *Cal. Close*, 1227–31, p. 159.

[211] *Cal. Close*, 1226–57, p 61.

[212] *Hist. MSS. Com Rep.* vi, App. i, 551–69 ; God's House Comptus R.

with six principal men of the town—Simon of St. Lawrence, Robert the Controller (*talliator*), Denys Fortin, Walter Fleming, Roger Bonheit, and Thomas de Bulehus[213]—were called upon to answer for the town's trespass in appropriating certain money from Ireland belonging to the king.[214]

The bailiffs are referred to in the laws of the gild, where their election is provided for by the 'twelve discreets' (see above). In the course of time their duties varied and the status of their persons. They were bound by oath to serve the town court, to see that common right was ministered, as well to strangers as to Englishmen, and generally to advance the good of the town. In 1571 an alderman was chosen as bailiff; in 1587 it was ordered that henceforth the senior alderman should be bailiff of the court, and that the junior bailiff should preside at Trinity Fair, and be at the charges thereof. In the eighteenth century it had become usual to choose the bailiffs from the younger burgesses who had not served the office before. The senior was bailiff of the court, the junior, water-bailiff.[215] Until 1835 the bailiffs were, jointly with the mayor, judges of the civil court of Pleas; and with the mayor were also the returning officers at the election of members of Parliament.[216]

As well as the office of bailiff that of mayor certainly existed early in the thirteenth century. There was a 'mayor' about 1217;[217] and Benedict, the son of Azo, or Ace, ruled in that capacity and under that name (*major*) at least from January, 1235[218] to 1249.

At the end of this long tenure of office, for some reason probably connected with the rise of the gild,[219] to which the title of alderman came more naturally, the burgesses obtained by royal patent (22 October, 1249) the curious grant[220] that neither they nor their successors should at any time be governed by a mayor.[221] Futile as the grant was in the long run, Matthew Gese, the next head officer whose name is known (1260), was styled 'alderman,'[222] and his successors the same till 1323, when Hugh Sampson appears in deeds both ways. But the title of alderman continued usual[223] till Lawrence de Mees in 1334, when the older title was finally dropped and 'mayor' prevailed.

According to the charter of 1445 (see above) the mayor and bailiffs were to be elected by the burgesses on the Friday before St. Matthew's Day, 21 September each year, no doubt in accordance with ancient precedent.

However, a patent given[224] fifteen years later (1460), called forth by riotous proceedings threatening bloodshed at the choice of a mayor, shows that the method of election was in reality much more restricted. By a custom there, reported to have been immemorial, the outgoing mayor on the Friday before St. Matthew's Day, in the presence of the bailiffs and burgesses, in the gildhall, nominated two burgesses, one of whom was to be chosen as his successor by the assembly.[225] However, in spite of this nomination the mayor himself might be re-elected. A variation on this custom, which seems capable of being dated from about the middle of the sixteenth century, and is mentioned in 1587, consisted in what was called 'the private nomination.' On the Friday before St. Bartholomew's Day (24 August) the mayor and aldermen met in the Audit House and put two aldermen and two junior burgesses or any four burgesses in nomination for mayor; and on the morning of the day of election, the Friday before St. Matthew's Day, they struck off two names, and proposed to the burgesses the decision between the remaining two by ballot. It was usual, however, for the outgoing mayor to suggest the name, and the ballot was generally a matter of form. The ceremony was attended with considerable formality, the gildhall being decorated with flowers and duly strewn with rushes, the aldermen attending in their scarlet gowns, and the mace and oar being carried before the mayor. Before the Act of 1835 it was usual to put in nomination the two senior aldermen who had not occupied the mayoralty twice, and the two senior burgesses who had served as sheriff but not as mayor. This custom of private nomination was continued till the passing of that Act, under which, according to a uniform rule for all boroughs, and extended by the Act of 1882, the mayor is elected by the council each 9 November from among the aldermen or councillors or persons qualified to be such; so that previously to election the mayor need not have been a member of the corporation.

In the earlier centuries, as in later times, the burden of municipal office, like that of parliamentary representation, was not unfrequently avoided. In November, 1414, Thomas Armorer, who had been M.P. for the last two years, and had served as bailiff from 1404 to 1414, appeared before the mayor, John Mascall, three aldermen, his fellow bailiff and others of the *prodes-hommes* in assembly, and produced letters patent of the late king (15 February, 1412),

213 Probably the same as the former bailiff. 'Bussuse' may be a mis-writing and 'Bulehus' more correct. Bull or Bugle Hall became a locally noted place.

214 Madox, *Firma Burgi*, 158.

215 The duties of this last officer were originally to attend the mayor when performing any duty in the capacity of admiral.

216 At the municipal elections (9 Nov. 1904) objection was raised on the formal re-appointment, involving a solemn declaration of these and other ancient offices, which had become simply titular; and the matter was referred to the Parliamentary committee.

217 'Major et omnes fideles homines de S. to Peter,' bishop of Winchester, and Hubert de Burgh, justiciar (*Letters of the Time of Hen. III* (Rolls Ser.), i, 8.

218 On 14 Jan. 1235, royal confirmation was obtained to his election; Pat. 19 Hen. III, m. 15. 'Pro majore Suht. Rex eleccioni facte de Benedicto Ace in Majorem Suhampton regium assensum adhibuit et favorem. Et mandatum est probis hominibus Suht. quod eidem Benedicto quam diu fuerit Major ville predicte in omnibus que ad officium suum spectant intendentes sint et respondentes. Teste Rege apud Clarendon, xiiij die Jan.' For his mayoralty under 1237 see Madox, *Form. Angl.* pp. 196, 279; Add. MSS. 15314, fol. 53; Anct. D. (P.R.O.), B. 3308, 3368, 3383. D. 121, &c.

219 The title of mayor is only once mentioned in the Gild Ordinances, namely in the burgher's oath prefixed to the early version of the Ordinances.

220 Pat. 33 Hen. III, m. 2. 'Rex omnib. &c. sciatis quod concessimus Burgensibus de Suhampton quod ipsi et eorum heredes aliquo tempore non habeant Majorem in predicta villa nostra de Suhampton. In cujus, &c.'

221 In this same year (1249) the bailiffs of Southampton (and parts adjacent) were summoned by the king to Winchester Castle in consequence of numerous robberies committed in those parts, all the king's wines sent in advance of him having been stolen. As a result of the inquiries about 100 people were hanged; Matt. Paris, *Hist. Minor* (Rolls Ser.), iii, 47.

222 Document in *Arch.* l, 260.

223 But the title 'mayor' occurs in the dispute with Lymington in 1324 (Madox, *Firma Burgi*, 220), and in the agreement with New Sarum in 1329 (Oak Bk.).

224 Pat. 39 Hen. VI, m. 13 (1 Dec. 1460).

225 That is 'curiam assemble vulgariter nuncupatam' (1413).

granting him freedom from serving the office of mayor, a compliment possibly otherwise awaiting him, or coroner, or filling any other corporate office for the rest of his life.[226]

The dignity and importance of the mayor's office grew with the privileges of the town and with its charters: and generally, as the high functionaries from without were debarred from entering the town so the mayor ascended in their stead. For instance, by charter of 1445 he was made escheator, &c.; charter of 1447 creating the town and port a county gave him a further rise; that of 16 Charles I (1640), the governing charter till 1835, regranted all particulars.

Previously to 1835 the mayor continued to be appointed to offices which had long fallen into abeyance. These will be mentioned with others at the end of this section.

Formerly, like the members of Parliament, the mayors received remuneration. Until 1481 we find £10 assigned to the mayor of old custom. In 1579 the allowance was increased to £20, and in 1617 to £50; again, in 1623, it fell, from prudential motives, to £30, namely £20 the older sum, and £10 in lieu of making a burgess. In 1725 this old allowance of £20 for table money was taken away[227] till the town should have again at least £400 at interest. Table money, however, though to no great amount, was frequently voted; and the privilege, which can be traced from 1501, of making one burgess during the year of office and retaining the admission fee seems always to have remained. The mayor had also some small port dues on corn and coals. In 1802, when these dues were discontinued, the mayor was allowed twenty-five guineas per annum. In the depression of 1830 all dinners, perquisites, and even the daily newspaper hitherto taken in for the mayor, were stopped.[228]

The mayor has no perquisites at the present day, but it would be lawful for him to receive such remuneration as the council might think fit. The quaint oaths of mayor, &c, which are not given here, are no longer taken as oaths, but as solemn declarations.

The mayor is now invested with the chain of office, the gift of Bercher Baril in 1792, as anciently with the tippet. He also receives, 'that he may always have money in his pocket,' the £5 of quaint coins given under the will of Andrew Meares of Millbrook some time before 1639.[229] The coins are preserved in the Audit House.

The Common or Town Council.—Next to the mayor we place the town council; and we are now dealing with the close government of the town and gild which prevailed with small variation till the last century.

The 'twelve assistants' of the chief alderman ot the gild (see above) were the original mayor's or town or common council. They had of course been sworn, as the ordinance provides, from the beginning, although the oath taken at the earliest period is not extant. From that which belongs to the far later period of about 1650 we gather that the title of 'assistant' was being dropped. In the heading, as also in the body of the oath which bound them to attendance in 'the counsell-house,' the word 'assistants' was replaced by 'comon councill men,' whose office at this period, and no doubt long before, was strictly annual. It becomes a little difficult to state in what particular this body was assistant to the mayor and when he might be left to act, as he often did, *motu suo*, or how far again originally the council was itself assisted by and virtually comprised others, e.g. the aldermen of wards or other chief officials; whether in fact the common title 'the Mayor and his brethren' connoted only these 'twelve discreets,' or included other selected burgesess, certainly the bailiffs could not have been excluded; or what indeed in any accurate definition 'constituted the Assembly' or 'the house' in the early days.

Under the charter of 1640 the common council was appointed to consist of the mayor, recorder, aldermen, bailiffs and sheriff, and all past holders of these offices who were empowered to make such by-laws, the mayor always being present, as in their 'sane discretion' should be salutary for the government of the burgesses, artisans, and inhabitants, and to punish the breach of them.

This constitution of all the town council remained as here provided till the alterations of 1835. At the present time, under the county extension of 1895, the councillors are thirty-nine in number.[230] They act collectively and in eighteen committees.

The Recorder.—The earliest observed notice of this officer occurs in 1457, when we find his wages were £5 a year; he had also, as was usual, his livery gown at Christmas made of five yards of 'musterdyvelyg' at 3*s.* 4*d.* the yard.[231] This continued to be his payment for a considerable time. It may be that in the earlier period he and the town clerk were identical, and that the offices were separated under the pressure of town business. In 1649 he was allowed £20 per annum, so long as he should live in the town. In 1688 it was determined that his fee should be £5 per annum. But presents of wine and new year's gifts of sugar, spices, and olives were frequently made, as special and delicate attentions.

The oath of the recorder required him to 'minister common right after the common law of England, and the laudable customs of this town, to every person that shall duly require the same, as well to poor as rich,' and give 'true counsel to the mayor and his brethren,' and be in attendance when reasonably expected. The duties of the recorder here, as everywhere else, are now regulated under the Consolidating Act of 1882.

The Town Clerk must have been in existence from a very early period, if not under that name. He first appears in 1315, when William Fowell,[232] the 'town clerk,' received a bushel of wheat from God's House for professional assistance. Again, in 1321 John le Barbur, 'town clerk,' received a quarter of wheat under the same circumstances, by the advice of John le Flemyng, the late alderman. The 'wages'

226 Liber Niger (Corp. MSS.), fol. 23*b*.

227 This parsimony went sadly against the grain. But not seldom some disinterested friend would give an aid to the town's good cheer. So when in Sept. 1761, Mr. Dawkins, M.P., presented two turtles—he gave more turtles the next year—the town council quickly passed Mr. Mayor's little bill of £47 14*s.* 6*d.* for 'dressing' them, as also for £1 6*s.* the hire of the 'Assembly Rooms' where the turtle feast was held; Journ. *sub anno.*

228 Particulars from Town Journ. *sub anno.*

229 Earliest observed notice is 2 Oct. 1640, when the late mayor delivered to his successor the £5 gift of Mr. Andrew Meyres, deceased; Town Journ. (Corp. MSS.).

230 See above.

231 Steward's Bk.

232 Riley, *Hist. MSS. Com. Rep.* ii, 137; Rep. on Queen's College, Oxford.

of the town clerk, as of the recorder, were £5 a year, with a varying allowance for paper, parchment, and ink: he had also his five yards of 'musterdyvelyg' (1457) for his gown and tippet of fur. His duties were to 'see that true records are kept and due processes made between party and party, and true judgements given, as nigh as he could, in the Mayor and Bailiffs' behalf': to minister, 'if required, common right after the common law of England and the laudable customs of this town'; to give good advice to 'the Mayor and his brethren,' and to keep 'their counsel.' No declaration is now required by law of the town clerk.

The Aldermen existed in name from a very early period (see above). Among the officials under the chief alderman, who was in fact the mayor, the ordinances of the gild-merchant mention twelve aldermen who had view of frankpledge and controlled the order and sanitary regulations of the five wards. The first charter which refers to aldermen is that of 1401, when power was given or confirmed to elect four aldermen for the purposes therein named. The last governing charter (1640) speaks of six aldermen, but probably the number was indefinite, and nothing is said of their election. Previously to the Act of 1835 the aldermen were those who had served the mayoralty, and they became such without any election; their number at the passing of the Act was nineteen, including the mayor. Under the above Act they became ten in number, but at the extension of the county in 1895 their number was increased to thirteen, six or seven of whom go out of office every third year, but may be re-elected. They hold office for six years, and are chosen from the councillors or persons qualified to be such: the councillors themselves being thirty-nine in number, three being elected by each of the thirteen wards. They have a property qualification, and hold office for three years.

The succession of burgesses was arranged for by the gild ordinances, but from an early period irregularities occurred in their appointment from without. For instance, in 1303, John de London of Bordeaux was granted burgess-ship by royal letters, which in 1312 were extended to his wife Blanche and their sons and daughters in every particular.[233] Admissions also on the part of the town were sometimes a little arbitrary. In 1509 one was admitted, with surely a reflection on the townsmen, because he was 'an honest man and good of name'; another because 'he hath been always a helper to the town'; another, from the Isle of Wight, on promising (1520) to reside and 'victual the town with his fish.' In 1543 two barber-surgeons were admitted free on promising to be 'ready at the commandment of the mayor and burgesses' to exercise their 'craft or science' when required 'without excess taking for the same.' In 1545 burgess-ship was prohibited to any more Guernsey or Jersey men without a special vote: a point strongly urged (1550) by the court leet. It seems that a few years later the making burgesses 'for friendship' had become too common, and was said to have lowered the office in public estimation. Hence in 1561 (September) it was ordered that the fine of £10 should be exacted, except from 'prentices, or such that be men of honour and worship that shall so request for their pleasure for no gain of the petty customs and men's children which ought of right to inherit their father's room, according to the Paxbread.' Again, in 1600, the court leet presented that 'gentlemen and others' were admitted to burgess-ship without being obliged to undertake the offices of constable, steward, or bailiff, but enabled at once to advance to the dignity of sheriff, and so of mayor.

Burgesses lost their status under certain circumstances. Residence was required, and absence from the town for 'a year and a day' was a cause of their being 'disgraded,' 'discharged from the gild,' and so forth; but exceptions were allowed occasionally. Again, offences against the peace by fist, sword, or dagger, or by abusive words were constantly visited with expulsion. In 1495 one was degraded for assault upon another 'whom he did streke with his fiste.' Those who had been degraded were frequently re-admitted on a fine. Sometimes burgess-ship was forfeited, but not the freedom of the town (a distinction made in the ordinances). In 1602 an alderman was disburgessed and so expelled the corporation, but he did not lose his freedom. Other offences against town-laws were similarly visited.

Certain sumptuary laws affected the burgesses. In 1559 (2 Elizabeth) it was ordered that all burgesses from the sheriff upwards should provide and use 'one right honest gown of crimson or scarlet cloth' on certain days, under a penalty of £10, the crimson being relieved by a black velvet tippet. By a minute of 4 August, 1569, their wives also were to be clothed in scarlet under a like penalty, according to old custom, and the husbands were desired to see the gowns provided and worn. The alderman whose wife did not possess such a gown was to be fined £10, and those whose wives, though possessing, did not wear them were to forfeit 10*s.* each day. All the gowns were to be ready against the queen's coming under pain of £10, and the ladies were to wear with their scarlet gown 'frentche whoddes' (French hoods).[234] Fines on such matters were frequently exacted, and the dignity of the corporation duly maintained. In 1613 it was ordered that the burgesses and their wives should be placed according to their degrees in all public assemblies and at church, and one of the serjeants was to see to this. All burgesses were expected to attend the mayor (1637) in state on the days of assembly; and in 1594 it had been presented as a discredit that they should go on foot to the law day at Cut-thorn, and were ordered to attend Mr. Mayor on horseback.

The feasting and good fellowship encouraged by the old gild ordinances never went out of fashion. It would be easy to give an idea of many a good gild dinner. A menu of 1457 includes a dozen capons, a dozen 'pestelles of porke,' nine 'legges of beffe,' a dozen 'cople conyngges,' and many lighter refreshments, red wine, tent, muskadell, malvesy-almonds, dates, &c. This, with kitchen help, and ten capons borrowed from my master the mayor and four players from St. Cross to enliven the feast, cost the town £2 3*s.* 5½*d.*[235] In contemplating such lists one has to remember that much was given away in charity; the capacity of the burgesses themselves was but mortal. Passing to much later times it was the custom for burgesses to give a feast on being sworn,

[233] Pat. 31 Edw. I, m. 44; 6 Edw. II, pt. 1, m. 12; 18 Edw. II, pt. 2, m. 17.

[234] Lib. Remembranc. (Corp. MSS.), fol. 101*b*.

[235] Steward's Bk. (Corp. MSS.).

and these entertainments (1753) were to be made separately.[236] This was very well for good cheer, but the expense became an objection to the honour of burgess-ship, and moderation was enjoined (1767). Years after a composition in money payment was made in lieu of entertainments.

In the middle of the seventeenth century (1652), a sorry period for the town, the offices could scarcely be filled for lack of burgesses. A similar complaint was made after the Restoration, when it was ordered (1660) that every resident whom the mayor and common council should think fit to nominate gratis as serving burgess should accept the office under penalty of £20. From one cause or other a like scarcity was felt again towards the end of the eighteenth century, when, 13 October, 1788, the corporation made a spirited appeal to the grand jury at Quarter Sessions with a view to replenishing their ranks. The appeal, which is very lengthy, spoke of the 'complicated wickedness of the inferior class of inhabitants,' the shameless indecencies and blasphemies were such as 'all the watchfulness of the magistracy would not be able to prevent or punish without the concurrence of those of superior rank.' Very much more to this effect was urged; they gave their own origin, defended their utility as a corporation, and urged the necessity for strengthening the arm of authority. The appeal was remarkably successful. Forthwith two knights and eleven esquires joined the corporation, and others quickly (17 &c. October) followed, being all elected as serving burgesses. It does not appear that the town suffered again from lack of serving burgesses.

The oath which the burgesses took formerly savoured of the gild ordinances and the early charters. They were to maintain the franchises, customs, and ordinances of the town, contribute to all charges within the same —summons, watches, wards, contributions, taxes, tallages, lot and scot; not to colour or bear the name of foreigners' goods; to warn the mayor of foreigners trading within the town; not to sue an inhabitant out of the town; to take no apprentice for less than seven years, and within the first year to cause his enrolment, and to further his advantage at the end of his time; to attend the mayor on all public occasions; to warn him of any possible breach of the king's peace, or of the ordinances of the town; to keep all counsel faithfully.

Honorary burgesses were in fact provided for by the gild ordinances, and had records survived we should no doubt have been in possession of interesting examples. As it is, the first observed occurs in 1490 when 'my lord of Winchester' was 'made burgess' 'free of charge, but of his gentilnes he pardoned us for the same the fyne of the pavelyne[237] and all other costes longing to the same with the homage for that yere.'[238] At the same time the abbot of Beaulieu, Sir Edward Berkeley, and William Middleton, esquire, were admitted. Again, in 1514 Thomas Skevington, bishop of Bangor and abbot of Beaulieu, was admitted. He had been a donor of some of the town plate. But it would not be practicable to deal with the very copious entries of honorary burgesses, or the regulations made concerning them.[239] From the end of the seventeenth century the roll of burgesses consists very largely of non-townsmen and men of position. These honorary or out-burgesses were not admitted to the common council, but could vote at the election of a mayor and of members of Parliament. The election of burgesses previously to the Act of 1835, whether serving or honorary, was by the common council, nine being a quorum. The serving burgesses were inhabitants, bankers, merchants, or the higher tradespeople, the honorary persons, generally speaking, living away, who had either done some good to the town, or from whom the town expected benefit. In 1831 it was resolved that no one should be elected as honorary burgess who lived within any of the town parishes. Within the ten years immediately preceding the Act of 1835 fifty-three burgesses had been elected, forty-seven honorary, and six serving, there being in the corporation just previously to passing the Act twenty resident or serving burgesses, and about one hundred and sixty non-resident, chiefly honorary. By the Act of 1835 the admission to burgess-ship by gift or purchase became illegal, but by Act of 1885 the boroughs can now admit to honorary freedom.[240]

The exclusive trading privileges enjoyed by burgesses had long since ceased: the only privilege which remained to them being that, whether resident or not, they equally with the inhabitants paying scot and lot were electors of members of Parliament for the borough. The qualification for burgess-ship is now universally regulated under the modern Acts of Parliament, and no further notice is needed.

The grant of a Sheriff from among the burgesses, to be sworn before the mayor and certified by him to the barons of the Exchequer, was made under charter of 9 March, 1447, by which the borough was constituted a county (see charter above). Accordingly on 1 May that year Henry Bruyn was elected first sheriff. The sheriff continued to be elected as specified by the charter, and was invested with the powers of a county sheriff: he attended at the assizes when held for the town and county of the town, and at the sessions, for both of which he summoned the juries. He held a county court when necessary, and executed writs from the superior court, which were directed to him immediately. He is now appointed next after the mayor each 9 November, being invested with a chain of office, and has the powers of a county sheriff, which indeed he is, continued to him.

The Seneschal or Steward, and more recently the Treasurer, held an office in many ways identical, but with a different status in reference to the corporation. The appointment of seneschal or steward was ordered by the gild ordinances (No. 1). The chief receipts and disbursements of the borough passed through his hands, and the stewards' books, many of which are extant from 1433[241] to the time of Charles II, are of considerable interest. The treasurer now holds office during pleasure; he is appointed by, but cannot be himself a member of, the town council.

The election of Coroners, of whom there were generally two, from among the burgesses for pleas of the crown was authorized by charter of 14 July, 1256. The earliest local oath of the coroners appears in Overey's Ordinances (1473), where their duties are set forth in the usual way: viz. to sit with a jury *super visum corporis* in every case of violent death: to

[236] Town Journ. (Corp. MSS.).

[237] The Pavilion Court of Winchester. See below, also under Winchester.

[238] Temp. Thome Overy, 3rd year, *sub anno*, Corp. MSS.

[239] Entry of burgesses for 1496 to 1704.

[240] Stat. 48 & 49 Vict. cap. 29.

[241] The book assigned to 1433 really belongs to 1457.

determine what forfeitures might belong to the king, and what to the town in consequence: to give attendance at the sessions, assizes, and shire court (of the town), 'especially when any exigent is to be called, or any to be outlawed, thereon to give judgment for the king's advantage and for the town.'

Mayor and Constables of the Staple.—Previously to the Act of 1835 the incoming mayor always was, and the two senior resident aldermen generally were, elected to these obsolete offices by the town council in practice, and not, as specified by the charter of 1445, by the burgesses.

The Petty Customer took oath to deal truly with the town's customs and tolls by water, of all manner of goods, according to ancient use. There was also a receiver of customs and brokage at Bargate, who was also sworn (see below).

The four Aldermen of Wards (see above) were sworn officers, probably identical originally with those appointed under charter of 1401.

The Alderman of Portswood was a sworn officer, the earliest observed notice of whom occurs under 1469, when he makes payment to the steward on the law day 'for divers alewytes xxij*d*,' and similar but varying payments in other years. He is still appointed every year, following ancient custom, but has no duties.

Four 'discreets of the market,' formerly sworn officers (see above), are now appointed from the borough police, but have no duties to perform.

The four Serjeants-at-mace.—These sworn officers are mentioned in the gild ordinances. They were formerly elected by the 'twelve men at the common assembly in the Guildhall,' and could only be removed by the same power (1548);[242] in the next century they appear as 'biddelles.' Before the Act of 1835 two of them were gaolers, one of the debtors', and the other of the felons' prison; the third collected the tolls of the vegetable and poultry market, and the fourth was water-bailiff. There are now two serjeants-at-mace who, with the crier, are attendant upon the corporation and justices.

The Brokers were sworn to their office between merchant and merchant (Ord. 59 etc.); and were especially to 'make a stay' of 'things forren boughte and forren solde' until the pleasure of the mayor and his brethren should be known.

Porters, Bearers, and Packers.—Officers of this description are referred to in the gild ordinances. Their position was confirmed by charter 1445.[243] The porters existed as a company and were possibly already associated together as the *beremanni Suhamptonie* in 1225, when they were directed to be paid for storing wine.[244] When we know more of them they were seven in number, exclusive of their steward. This number had been arranged at least from 1501. They found security to pay the town their rent. They possessed a common stock-in-trade in horses and carts, and the takings for the week were divided every Saturday night by their steward. They were bound to provide four able horses for the service of the merchants, each horse being worth at least 26*s*. 8*d*. (1547).[245] They bought and sold their places, but were only admitted or discharged by the town council, who also fixed their rates of carriage. The company was in existence in 1835.

Before the Act of 1835, besides the offices mentioned above, the following were also held by the corporation, but not named in any charter.[246] One weigher of wool, whose duties had become nominal; one aulnager; four keepers of the keys of the gates—these were always the mayor, the late mayor, and two senior resident aldermen; besides these, warders of the gates were formerly appointed; two keepers of the keys of booths—these were supposed to have reference to booths erected at the fair above Bar; three keepers of the keys of the great chest (where the minutes were locked up)—these were the mayor and bailiffs, but the mayor really kept the keys; supervisors of lands—the mayor and aldermen indefinite in number, but they had no duties as such, the property of the corporation being managed by the common council; one crier, who attended quarter sessions, kept the weights and scales, and keys of the market gates, and acted as crier for those who paid him; besides the water-bailiff (of whom above) there were sand-walkers, indefinite in number, who formerly watched for waifs and wrecks, and their appointment had been an object of desire during the French War as a protection against impressment[247]—there were latterly from twenty to thirty of these; two wardens of Sendy's gift; auditors of accounts, indefinite. There were also fourteen beadles of wards, and extra beadles indefinite; two constables; measures of corn and coal, indefinite; one scavenger.

Besides the above there were also anciently the town gunner, an official who appears in the earliest consecutive town records. In 1457, under a hasty menace to the town from French ships, are several interesting entries[248] concerning the gunner and his work. His wages were 6*d*. a day; his office to superintend the handling and repair of the guns, and the making of gunpowder. In 1512 (4 Henry VIII) a townsman offered his services as gunner at the yearly salary of 26*s*. 8*d*. and a gown. He was to receive 2*d*. for the making of every gunstone, and 7*d*. a day 'when he workyth yn makinge of gun-powder,' and 4*d*. a day for every man employed by him. A few years later he was ordered to serve the town in peace and war at 10*s*. per annum, receiving also an allowance of four yards of cloth at 3*s*. 4*d*. for his livery. In 1657 the town gunner and the town drummer each received as annual wages 18*s*. 4*d*.

There were also the town carpenter and the paviour; of the paviour's work we first hear in 1384.[249] In 1457 we find him paving along the middle of the street assisted by 'the pavyer of London.' He had a good house assigned him, and a yearly gown, his work being to 'serche the pavement' and pave where necessary.[250] The chimney sweep was a sworn official, new in 1654. The town brick-maker has the price of his bricks given him in 1623 at 9*s*. 6*d*. per thousand; a little later it was 10*s*. In 1704 the assize of bricks, according to ancient custom, was said to be 10 in. in length, $4\frac{3}{4}$ in. in breadth, and $2\frac{1}{2}$ in. in thickness.

There was a cowherd who superintended the common lands, with whom were four overseers and twelve drovers of the common.

242 Boke of Remembrances, fol. 53.

243 *Hist. MSS. Com. Rep.* xi, App. p. 45.

244 *Rot. Lit. Claus.* (Rec. Com.), ii, 44 (4 June, 1225).

245 Lib. Remembranc. H. fol. 87*b*.

246 See also *Rep. on Munic. Corp.* (1835), xxiv.

247 See Town Corp. MSS. 10 May, 1804.

248 Davies, op. cit. 214–15.

249 Pat. 8 Ric. II, m. 31.

250 Lib. Niger (Corp. MSS.), fol. 1*b*.

A common carrier compounded for his place with the town and received from them the tariff of his charges. In July, 1593, he was forbidden to enter the gate of the town by himself or servants with his cart for fear of plague-infection, the sickness daily increasing.[251]

In 1602 his fine was £10. Some years later (1637) he was allowed to increase his charges, his trade having fallen off from the scare of plague.[252] A foot-post, between the town and London, wore a silver badge with the town arms, and usually started on Monday or Tuesday each week (1637).[253] And of course there were town minstrels who received regular wages and a livery. In 1433 they appear to have been but three in number.[254] Independently of these, strolling companies under the protection of some great lord or important town were constantly visiting the place, and receiving the town's wages. But after enjoying high favour for many generations minstrelsy fell into discredit. In 1623 we find the town musicians, who were apparently five in number, asking for their liveries, which they received with a broad hint to ask no more, but take what was given them.[255] A few years later silver badges with the town arms were distributed to them by the mayor. In this connexion may be mentioned stage-players. The town does not seem to have had any recognized company, but permitted the use of the Gildhall until 1624, when for certain adequate reasons it was forbidden.[256]

Further, at all events in 1615, there was a town-cook, who on condition of being allowed a monopoly of the oyster beds in the haven, covenanted to supply the town with good oysters at 2*d.* the hundred at most, to keep the beds in good order, and to bring in 500 oysters for the mayor's fish dinner yearly.[257]

Lastly, at the opposite end of man's needs, there was the gild or mayor's priest. For the old gild-merchant not only regulated the trade and civil government, but preserved a certain eleemosynary and religious character, and had its chaplain with a definite position and allowances (see Gild Ord. 1, 2). Subsequently the chaplains, who seem to have been appointed permanently, received a fixed stipend of £3 6*s.* 8*d.* per annum, with a gown and hood worth generally about 13*s.* 4*d.* Thus[258] in 1457 Sir William and in 1478 Sir Harry were paid. Passing rapidly towards the changes of the sixteenth century, Sir William, who sang for Holmage (see below, chantries), was also gild priest in 1501 and 1509. In 1543 Sir Hector was mayor's chaplain and received for his 'hatte, gowne and typpate' 24*s.* After this the office disappears from the town books, and in the following century it became usual to bestow a gratuity on the rector or vicar of the parish in which the mayor resided for the performance of such duties as might be required.[259] At the commencement of the nineteenth century the 'chaplain of the Corporation' with his allowances of £5 5*s.* per annum re-appears in the town books.[260] At the present time the office is purely honorary.

The Parliamentary representation of the borough commences in 1295, and the returning officers were the bailiffs, other burgesses being bound as manucaptors or bailsmen for the appearance of the elected members at the appointed day and place.

Until the time of James I, when the custom was broken through, the members elected were bona fide burgesses of the town. There was an attempt to restore this more ancient way in 1624 and 1625; the burgesses[261] being warned by order of the corporation not to give their voices for any one who was not already an in-burgess of the town, on pain of forfeiting their condition. This regulation was observed at first, but was soon again interrupted, and after the Restoration persons of a certain position, irrespective of their dwelling, who had done, or might be expected to do, something for the town were generally chosen; but even so, the form of previous election to burgess-ship was observed.

In the early days, here as elsewhere, and through the Middle Ages, the town paid their burgesses of Parliament; in later times occasionally, it may be feared, the burgesses paid the town. Their 'wages' were 2*s.* per day each man, the usual rate of payment perhaps from the earliest period for borough representatives, and fixed at that amount in 1322.[262] A writ for expenses, tested 20 January, 1306–7 (25 Edward I), was issued in favour of the Southampton members;[263] the next known was in 1313.[264]

There were symptoms, especially in the earlier period, of no great eagerness to serve at the great council of the nation and no great readiness on the part of the towns to make return to the sheriff's writ.

The first instance of such remissness on the part of Southampton occurs in 1300–1, when no return was made by the bailiffs; other instances soon followed; the meaning probably being that the town shirked the expense consequent on such return, a negligence which appears to have been provided against by statute of 1445–6.[265]

It is not so easy to state what was exactly the electing body. Broadly it was no doubt the burgesses, those who in after times were called the in-burgesses, strictly resident and performing their parts in duties and taxation; but how far they acted uniformly, whether sometimes in meeting assembled, at another by delegation to a smaller body, or whether the governing body at times assumed the function of the whole, can hardly as yet, it seems, be determined. Passing to a later period, in October, 1584, the nomination of one of the burgesses was given to the earl of Leicester 'according to his honour's request,' the town nominating the other. They were to be at their own charges and receive nothing from the town.[266] In 1624 the in-burgesses were the electors (see above), as in 1658-9[267] and subsequent years. In 1661 the corporation invited two gentlemen to accept burgess-ship with a view to their representing the town, and they were elected accordingly.[268] In 1689 the election was by the mayor, bailiffs, and select burgesses, but this was overthrown on petition,

251 Boke of Remembrances, fol. 174*b*.

252 Town Journ. 15 May, 1637.

253 Ibid. 6 Feb. 1623–4.

254 Steward's Bk. (Corp. MSS.).

255 Town Journ. 19 Dec.

256 Ibid.

257 Ibid. 25 Aug. 1615.

258 Steward's Bk. (Corp. MSS.), *sub annis.*

259 Town Journ. Sept. 1638.

260 Ibid. Jan. 1805; Dec. 1880; May, 1835.

261 Ibid. 9 April, 1624; 15 April 1625.

262 Stubbs, *Const. Hist.* ii, 235 and ref.

263 Prynne, *Parl. Writs*, pt. iv, 27.

264 Ibid. ii, p. cclvi.

265 Stat. 23 Hen. VI, cap. 14. No returns to this Parliament are now known to be extant excepting in the case of Norfolk. (*Ret. of Members of Parl.*)

266 Boke of Remembrances, *sub anno.*

267 Town Journ. 7 Jan. 1658–9.

268 Burgess Bk. and Journ. Mar. April, 1661.

and the House decided 31 December that the right of election was vested in the burgesses and inhabitants paying scot and lot.[269] Hitherto practically, there can be little doubt, the elections were very much managed by the corporation ; but the right of all was re-affirmed by the House of Commons, 17 March, 1695–6,[270] and finally the Act of 1835 secured uniformity of election in all constituencies.[271]

Of the borough courts, the court leet or law day, the most ancient local criminal court here as everywhere else, was opened with considerable ceremony. It was held before the mayor, aldermen and discreets on Hock Tuesday, i.e., the third Tuesday after Easter Sunday, most anciently at Cut-thorn (mentioned before), but afterwards frequently in the Gildhall, the town clerk being steward and judge of the court, the sheriff foreman of the jury, the latter being summoned anciently from the burgesses alone, but subsequently with greater latitude.

The duties of the court were to take the pledges of freemen, who all with certain exceptions, above the age of twelve years, were bound to be sworn and enrolled, to inquire periodically into the condition of roads, watercourses, boundaries, to be vigilant against encroachment, keep watch and ward in the town, to overlook the common lands and adjust all rights, to guard against adulteration of food, inspect weights and measures, to look generally to the morals of the people and their attendance at divine worship, to have a remedy for every inconvenience. Beyond this the court leet took cognizance of every felony at common law, larceny, murder, treason, &c., the jury acting in these cases as indictors, when action was taken accordingly. But for the greater number of cases brought before the leet the remedy was summary by amercement or fine.

The Court Leet Book of 1550, the earliest extant, shows that the court had no respect of persons. 'Mr. Maire kepith a sowe in his Backsyde whiche is brought in and oute contrary to the ordenaunce[272] of the Towne, wherfore be yt comanded to hym and all other that they kepe no hoges within the Towne to the annoyaunce of theire neighbours, upon payne' &c. Under 1576 minute regulations occur as to the apparel not only of the ladies, but of the mayor himself and the grave town officials.[273] In the next year many presentments were made as to the particulars of each offence, e.g. Walter Earl wears guards of velvet on his hose ; John Delisle's wife has a petticoat guarded with velvet. In 1579 a complaint of witchcraft having been made against Widow Walker, the jury prescribed the following test : 'We desire yr worships to examine hir before you, and to permyt five or six honest matrons to se hir strippidd to thend to se wheather she have eny bludie marks on hir bodie wch is a comon token to know all witches by and so either to stop the mouthes of the people or els to proceade farder at yr worships pleasure.' In the same year the great need of a 'cucking stoole' upon the ditches, as had been accustomed, was presented ; and in 1587 the pillory, the stocks above Bar, and those in East Street were found out of repair contrary to the statute ; about this period every householder was to have his club ready in his house against a fray. In 1594 the town was suffering from overcrowding, and in 1603 greedy landlords were taken to account who, to the great destruction of the town, were admitting too many under-tenants.

The law of fencing between properties we find perpetually laid down in the books. The local custom was for the south to fence the north, and the east the west, and towards the highway everyone was required to make his fence.

The court leet has been practically obsolete at least since 1819, but it meets annually, when 'presentments' are made, and its old festive accompaniments are not forgotten.[274]

The town court or common court of the town, a civil court of pleas of ancient date, is first mentioned in charter of 1256. It was ordered by charter of 1461 to be held in the gildhall before the mayor and bailiffs every Tuesday on personal pleas, and on pleas of lands and tenements on Tuesday once a fortnight. Town court books are extant from 1482, but Liber Niger contains a more ancient note of the court in ordinances by the mayor, aldermen, and community for the amendment of its procedure, dated 17 October, 22 Edward III (1348).[275]

Before the Act of 1835 the common court was held on every Tuesday for the first three weeks after the election of each new mayor, and on alternate Tuesdays afterwards.

The county or sheriff's court followed upon the erection of the town and its liberties into a county in 1447, when it was ordered that the county court be held every month on a Monday, and all business which might lawfully be brought before county courts was to be transacted in it. This court had no relation with the modern county court.

The court of quarter sessions, the justiciary court of the town, has varied in form at different times. Under the ordinances of the gild-merchant,[276] the whole community elected twelve discreets, who with the two bailiffs executed the king's commands, kept the peace, protected the franchise, maintained the right between man and man. The charter of 1401 empowered the election of four aldermen, three or two of whom, together with the mayor and with four, three, or two of the more honest and discreet persons of the community, to be chosen yearly by the mayor and community, were to hold the office of justices of the peace in full and ample manner, but were not to proceed in felonies without special commission. The charter given by Edward IV in 1461 added a person 'skilled in the law' to the court of justices, which was otherwise composed of the mayor, four aldermen, and four other burgesses. The charter of 1640 made the mayor, the bishop of Winchester, the recorder, and ex-mayor, together with five aldermen and two of the more discreet burgesses, to be the court, the mayor

269 Beatson, *Chron. Reg. of both Houses of Parl.* iii, 307.

270 Resolved that out-living burgesses as well as the burgesses (inhabitants) paying scot and lot had a right to vote. (Ibid.)

271 A list of the Parliaments to which Southampton sent representatives, together with their names, will be found in *The Return of Members of Parliament.*

272 See Gild Ord. No. 43, a provision continued through the latest versions.

273 Davies, op. cit. 234–6.

274 In ancient times a perambulation of the liberties formed part of the ceremony of the law day, when the mayor and his brethren rode to Cut-thorn in their 'formalities' ; and it was considered a discredit to the town and a mark of decaying times when the procession fell off, or the proper gowns were not worn. The stewards' books also bear ample evidence that considerable feasting attended these occasions.

275 *Hist. MSS. Com. Rep.* xi, App. iii, 9.

276 No. 32.

and recorder being always of the quorum; but previously to the Act of 1835 it was not the practice for the bishop or the burgess justices to attend. The court had cognizance of all offences triable at county quarter sessions, and also of capital felonies, but seldom exercised jurisdiction in these latter, removing them where possible to the assizes of the county of Hants, or in case of removal being barred, petitioning the Home Office or the judges of the Western Circuit for a commission of assize made out to the county of the town.

A court of orphans was instituted by charter of 1640, which gave power to the mayor, recorder, aldermen, bailiffs, and sheriff to hold the same for the town and county, with authority over their persons and goods, as in the case of the lord mayor and aldermen of London. The court[277] was obsolete by the middle of the eighteenth century.

The charter of King John granting the town of Southampton to the burgesses to farm, together with the port of Portsmouth, probably involved some maritime jurisdiction, by reason of which the town assumed extensive rights before the formal grant of admiralty. In 1239 the burgesses claimed rights not only within the port but in the town of Portsmouth, the claim on the water only being finally maintained.[278] In 1285 they destroyed a weir at Cadlands, constructed by the abbot of Titchfield, as hurtful to navigation.[279] In 1302 they granted a lease of customs over a wide extent which was clearly identical with the port, the members demised being Portsmouth, Hamble, Lymington, Scharprixa (on the east side of the Lymington river, south of Walhampton), Keyhaven, and Redbridge.[280] In 1324 it was set forth that from Hurst to Langstone was within the port of Southampton.[281] In 1432 the customer at Southampton was desired to appoint deputies at Lymington, Newport, and Portsmouth.[282] The charter of 1451, which first formally granted the admiralty jurisdiction, gave the limits as of old, i.e. Langstone on the east, including the port of Portsmouth, and from Hurst on the west, including Lymington, together with all tidal harbours, rivers, creeks, &c., within the boundary line. All this was confirmed by the last governing charter of 1640. But according to the settlement of the bounds of the port of Southampton as returned into the Exchequer in 1680 the line on the west was drawn from Christchurch Head, thence south-east to the Needles, then eastward to the west end of the Brambles, thence to Hill Head on the mainland at the south of the Southampton Water, and so up to the town quays, and thence up stream to Redbridge, so that Portsmouth was excluded at this time, though in the settlement of that port it is described as 'a member of the port of Southampton,' as is also the port of Cowes.[283] The court incident on this jurisdiction stood upon charters of 1445 and 1451.[284] The charter of 1640 enjoined that the court should consist of the mayor, recorder, and four aldermen, or three of them, the mayor or recorder being one; to these a civil lawyer might be added. Cognizance and power were given in all admiralty causes, with authority to choose officers of the court, registrars, notaries, attorneys, scribes, proctors, marshals, servants, &c., appeal being allowed to the Lord High Admiral. The earliest record[285] now existing in the town books is dated 14 July, 1493, when the court assembled at Keyhaven; on 15 July it was held at Lepe, when the jury, who presented the rescue by the servants of the abbot of Beaulieu of a Portuguese barque that had been seized on behalf of the mayor, was composed of men representing Hythe, Lepe, Pennington, Ower, Exbury, Hardley, and Cadlands. On 24 September it met at Hamble in the accustomed place on the sea-shore. The number of jurors at these courts varied greatly. At Hamble in April, 1508, it consisted of no less than thirty-six persons, Itchen, Netley, Hamble, Botley, Warsash, Satchell, and Bursledon being represented. From the early part of the seventeenth century the courts were held at irregular periods. In 1707 and 1708 they were held at Lymington, the corporation apparently asking leave to erect their booth on the quay, and to carry their oar erect through the borough.[286] In 1756 the admiralty circuit, which had been omitted some time, was ordered 'to be gone' by the corporation, and the recorder[287] was to receive a 'handsome grantuity' if he attended. Before the courts met the corporation of Lymington objected to a booth being erected on their quay for the purpose without permission having been first obtained. The corporation of Southampton replied that they could find no precedent for such a course, but consented to ask, and eventually marched through Lymington with their trumpeter and silver oar erect. The records of these courts are the last in the books. They were held at Southampton in the gildhall on 20 September, 1756, when the boundaries of the admiralty jurisdiction were defined at some length: at Lymington, 21 September; at Lepe, 22 September; at Hamble, 23 September. It had been intended to hold an admiralty court in 1798, partly with a view of preserving rights; but it was finally resolved to suspend it 'until the corporation purse shall be so replenished as to admit of so expensive a mode of asserting so valuable a prerogative.'[288] The opportunity does not seem to have occurred, and all rights of admiralty were finally extinguished by the Municipal Corporation Act of 1835.

Pie-powder courts[289] were held with the fairs. There can be no doubt that from ancient time Southhampton had possessed a fair.[290] The most important

277 Though granted apparently for the first time by the above charter, the principle on which the court rested had been long recognized, and belonged to the idea of the gild. In 1562 a burgess bequeathed a piece of plate to the town, beseeching 'the maior and his brethren to be as fathers to his children'; Liber Niger, fol. 99. In the same year the same authorities became answerable for silver plate belonging to other children, a trust which they duly fulfilled; Boke of Remembrances, fol. 93.

278 Oak Bk. fol. 28; see also Davies, op. cit. 225–6.

279 *Abbrev. Plac.* (Rec. Com.), 209.

280 Indenture *penes* Corp.

281 Madox, *Firma Burgi*, 220.

282 *Rot. Parl.* (Rec. Com.), iv, 417.

283 *Modern Practice of Exch.* (1730), 40, 95, 105.

284 See Chart. R. 23 Hen. VI, No. 22; 30 Hen. VI, No. 27; 1 Edw. IV, pt. 2, No. 11.

285 Lib. Remembranc. BB. fol. 15*b*.

286 King, *Old Times in Borough and Parish of Lymington*, 106.

287 The composition of the court must have been relaxed since 1640.

288 Town Journ. (Corp. MSS.), 12 June, 1798.

289 The 'Pavilion' court of St. Giles's Fair, Winchester, should be mentioned, as the Southampton town books bear frequent witness to the connexion of the borough with that fair and court. See Davies, op. cit. 243–5. See also *Cal. of Chart. R.* 1226–57, p. 445.

290 See Gild. Ord. No. 20; but no charter can be produced; see Chart. R. 35 Hen. III, m. 10.

of the four fairs of later years was Trinity or Chapel Fair, which was in existence at least by 1461, and which was confirmed by a grant of 19 July, 1496.[291] The profits were divided between the town and the chapel, a place of some honour with pilgrims.[292] The opening of the fair was attended with certain 'solemnities,' the whole body of burgesses being bound to attend Mr. Mayor to the 'proclamation'; the watch and guard of halberdiers being set, and the bailiff ready with his pie-powder court. After the proclamation,[293] which was somewhat lengthy and quaint, a pole was raised on which was fixed a large glove, or rather gloved hand, still existing. The senior bailiff then took possession of the fair, as chief magistrate for the time within its precincts and president of its court, and duly entertained the corporation in his booth. The glories of the opening day began to fade about 1840 and finally became extinguished; and the fair, now reduced to one day, is held in the cattle ground near the railway. The three remaining fairs were Shrovetide, held on the Tuesday and two following days before Shrove Sunday; Above Bar Fair, held on St. Mark's Day (25 April) and two days following; and St. Andrew's, kept on the Tuesday before St. Andrew's Day (30 November) and two succeeding days. These fairs with pie-powder courts stood on a patent of Elizabeth[294] (1600), probably but a grant of confirmation; at least as regards Shrovetide and Above Bar Fairs, since the court-leet book of 1596 calls attention to them. Above Bar Fair was abolished in 1875; the two other fairs had disappeared, after a lingering existence, before 1834.

There have been several official seals of the town, most of which bear the characteristic one-masted ship, generally with a star and crescent on the mainsail of the vessel or elsewhere, the earlier having a steerage oar at the side, a rudder appearing towards the middle of the fourteenth century.[295] A fine obverse, presented[296] in 1587, shows a magnificent three-masted ship in full sail, with the newly given town arms on the mainsail; the older obverse was a one-masted vessel, no ship in England having had more than one mast till about 1514. On the forecastle were two men blowing with trumpets. The legend on the newer obverse is *Sigillum commune villae Southamptoniae.* The original reverse, still in use, bears in a central canopied niche the Virgin and Child; within a niche on either side is a figure in adoring attitude; the legend is 'Mater Virgo Dei tu miserere nobis.' Casts of these and of various other official seals are in the Hartley Museum.

The present arms of the borough were granted by patent, 4 August 1575, with a crest of a golden castle on a green mount, 'out of the castell a quene in her imperial majestie, holding in the right hand the sword of justice, in the left the balance of equitie.' The supporters are two lions or standing in the fore part of two ships upon the sea. The patent states that the town had borne arms since its incorporation by Henry VI. The regalia of the borough consists of six maces,[297] the silver oar, the badge of admiralty, and a two-handed sword of state; the chain and the coins belonging to the mayoralty have already been mentioned.

The great prosperity of Southampton, which commenced with the Norman Conquest, probably continued till the loss of the French possessions in 1451–3, and the town seems to have taken third place in mercantile rank in 1204–5, when its fifteenths amounted to £712 3*s.* 7*d.*, being only distanced by those of London, £836 12*s.* 10*d.*, and those of Boston, £780 15*s.* 3*d.*[298]

The wine trade was settled here at the beginning of the period. The early Close Rolls abound in writs to the bailiffs concerning the wine trade generally or the king's wines, whether prisage or otherwise, or the wines of wealthy folk, all which must have kept the port alive. Wine was the chief import, but beer was at least an occasional export.[299] Coeval with this early trade are many of the vaults and cellars in the older parts of the town.[300]

The wool trade was on orderly footing here in the reign of Edward I; and it appears from a suit of 1275 that the custody of the town- or weighing-beam was in the hands of the earl of Warwick, who held a tenement in the town by service of weighing.[301] In 1299 Nicholas de Barbeflet,[302] a wealthy burgess, obtained by royal grant the tronage and pesage of wools for export from Southampton for six years at the rent of 40*s.* per annum.[303] In 1316 a grant of the pesage, which had belonged to Guy, earl of Warwick (d. August, 1315), was made to William Mauncel, at the above rent.[304] In 1327 the collectorship of wool in the port of Southampton and along the coast as far as Weymouth was in the hands of Geoffry Hogheles, and for some years we find the townsmen holding the collectorship. The Beauchamp family retained their office. Earl Thomas died in 1369, seised among other possessions of two messuages in Southampton

BEAUCHAMP, Earl of Warwick. *Gules a fesse between six crosslets or.*

[291] Original grant *penes* Corp., also Pat. 11 Hen. VII, pt. 2, m. 10 (12).

[292] It was here in the 'chapel of our Lady of Grace' that Henry VIII made his offerings of half a mark in August, 1510, and of 10*s.* in August, 1516 (*L. and P. Hen. VIII*, ii, pp. 1447, 1472), and hither Mold Petis was desired to come on pilgrimage to secure the effect of certain powders (ibid. iv (3), 5293). A vestige of the ancient chapel or hermitage may still be detected at 'chapel.' Davies, op. cit. 232.

[293] Book of Oaths and Ordinances, 1478 (end of first part).

[294] *Hist. MSS. Com. Rep.* xi, App. iii, 53.

[295] The earliest seal showing rudder appears to belong to 1338–43. On the date of rudder, see Nicholas, *Hist. of Royal Navy*, i, 370–2.

[296] Town Journ. (Corp. MSS.), 23 Aug. 1587.

[297] The more ancient of these are shown in the Hartley Museum. The making of one is detailed in the steward's book of 1482–3. See Hope & Jewitt, *Corp. Plate*, i, 260.

[298] Madox, *Exch.* i, 772.

[299] Close, 8 June, 9 Hen. III (1225).

[300] A vaulted apartment, though of somewhat later date, in Simnel Street should here be mentioned.

[301] *Abbrev. Plac.* (Rec. Com.), 188, 190.

[302] Nic. de Barbeflet or de Shirley was the originator of the town water-works by granting to the Friars Minor of Southampton (1290) his spring of Calwell or Colwell in the manor of Shirley, whence the water was to be taken, in method specified, to the house of the Friars. In 1311 the Friars granted some use of this water to the town; but being too poor to keep the water system in repair they conveyed 'le conduit hede' to the town in 1420. In 1594 Roger Pedley undertook to improve the water-works. But in 1739 the town applied to Parliament, and the management of the water was vested in a commission. An Act of 1836 repealed all former, and fresh works were commenced. Subsequently other Acts, both of Parliament and of the town, have contributed to the favourable condition of the water-supply at the present day. See Davies, op. cit. 114–19.

[303] *Rot. Orig.* (Rec. Com.), i, 109.

[304] Ibid. 196.

and the office of pesage there, and its possession was in the family for some generations.[305] The office of pesage in the town was the more important in the Middle Ages, since by an injunction[306] of Edward II in 1320 Southampton was one of the ports from which alone wool could be shipped, and under the statute of the staples[307] in 1353, staple goods from Winchester had to be weighed a second time at Southampton, wools also after 1465 were to be shipped only from Southampton and such other places where the king's beam was kept.[308]

The Venetian trade is untowardly introduced by the notice of an affray between the mariners of five Venetian galleys on the one side and the townspeople on the other in April, 1323. Blood was shed and property destroyed, but by desire of Edward II the mayor and community forbore from pressing the quarrel with these wealth-bearing strangers, and the matter was patched up by a money compensation.[309] The prosperity of the port increased, and eventually, it seems, incurred the jealousy of the London merchants.[310] In 1378 special inducement was held out to the Levant trade by Act of Parliament,[311] which gave Genoese, Venetian, Catalonian, and other merchants a privilege of freely trading at 'Hampton,' or elsewhere, provided they paid the dues they would pay at the staple of Calais; provided also they carried their exports of wool, woolfells, &c., westward to their own countries and no farther eastward than to Calais 'if they desired to go there.' As a matter of fact the offer of these advantages, and of a shortened voyage, brought the ships to 'Hampton'; and from the date of the above grant they came with the regularity of the seasons for the next 150 years, from three to five galleys being commissioned by the Doge each season, and the port remained the centre of the Venetian trade in the kingdom; but the hindrance to the foreign purchase of wool towards the middle of the sixteenth century[312] soon involved the loss of the galleys, though the town books note the presence of some few Venetian ships very occasionally as late as 1569.[313]

In the reign of Henry V much shipbuilding was carried on at Southampton. Here he built his famous ships, the *Holy Ghost* in 1414 and the *Grace Dieu*[314] in 1417. The trade had never been unknown here, and was occasionally revived, as in the reign of Elizabeth, and rather conspicuously in the time of George III, and though no ships of war are now built here, the building and repair trade of a smaller class is carried on; and on the Woolston side of the Itchen the important works of Messrs. Thornycroft & Co. are established in succession to those of Messrs. Moody, Casney & Co. In the fifteenth century Southampton was also the great emporium for tin. In 1453 it was all arrested and required to be sold towards the cost of the army to be sent into Guienne. The tin-house is mentioned in the ordinances of 1478 and subsequently.[315]

A tailors' petition of 1474, direful enough in itself, bears witness to the constant presence in the port of 'carracks, galleys and ships' of Spain, Portugal, Germany, Flanders, Zealand, and others, which all, of course, brought their treasures and would carry away wool and other goods from Southampton.[316]

In spite then of shipping detentions, hindrances from war and invasion, piracies, and the other mishaps which waited on mediaeval commerce, Southampton prospered in the fourteenth and fifteenth centuries. It was a brisk centre still for its old trades, and a staple for metals[317] (1492); it could advance heavy loans on national requirements or become security for them.[318] But by the end of the first quarter of the sixteenth century we find the townspeople complaining of ill times, as they had never done before excepting possibly when suing for some fresh charter privilege.[319] Trade was falling off; and the bishop of Bangor[320] writes to Wolsey on his elevation by the king to Winchester, thereby becoming earl of Southampton, that the townspeople were expecting great things from him in their now smaller resort of shipping.[321] In 1533 the carracks and galleys were not coming as they used.[322] But in truth, from whatever cause, decay had been slowly creeping over the port. It is referred to in an Act of 1495,[323] again in 1523, while in 1531 the loss of trade was successfully alleged in abatement of the fee-farm.[324] At the middle of the century (1551) the expediency of establishing a free mart in England for cloth and tin was debated, and the experiment was to be tried at Southampton. Nothing came of this, but shortly after the town obtained a monopoly in the landing of sweet wines,[325] a privilege at least partially confirmed by Elizabeth in 1563, and worth at least 200 marks a year. The settlement of foreign refugees in 1567 did something in the long run for trade, though the town was loth to own it. Twenty years later Southampton is classed with Bristol and other best towns as falling to decay.[326] In the year of the Armada (1588) the mayor was unable to furnish the two ships and pinnace re-

305 See the several ref. in Davies, op. cit. 250.

306 Anderson, *Hist. of Commerce* (1787), i, 231.

307 Stat. 27 Edw. III, 2, cap. 1.

308 Stat. of Realm, 4 Edw. IV, cap. 2. So in 1554 wools to the Levant were only to be shipped at Southampton. *Hist. MSS. Com. Rep.* xi, App. iii, 49.

309 *Cal. S.P. Venetian*, 10 April, 1323. Such frictions were of constant occurrence; e.g. see Davies, op. cit. 475.

310 See above.

311 Stat. 2 Ric. II, 1 cap. 3 (1378).

312 See e.g. Stat. 22 Hen. VIII, cap. 1 (1530–1); 37 Hen. VIII, cap. 15 (1545).

313 See Dr. Speed in Davies, op. cit. 251. It is to be presumed the 'ships' were not considered 'galleys,' or their visits might have been scarcely agreeable as endangering the reduction of the town's fee-farm. (See above under Fee Farm and Charters.)

314 The name at least was continued. The *Grace Dieu* was stationed at Southampton in 1460 when the master received from the mayor £31 10*s.* 10*d.* In September, 1461, he was paid £68 5*s.* 10*d.* for victualling and safe custody of the ship for a whole year. In 1470 and subsequently Edward IV by sign manual directs payment to the purser and his three fellows for keeping the ship. They were also allowed a house on shore (see *Hist. MSS. Com. Rep.* xi, App. iii, 185, 95, &c.). The name was probably not uncommon. There had been a *Grace Dieu* in 1337 (ibid. 219).

315 The Tin-office was next to Holy Rood Church (See Davies, op. cit. 255, 261–2). The tin-house or warehouse or cellar was in Westgate Street on the north side near the gate, where are 'premises still bearing the name of the Linen-hall and Tin-cellar'; Englefield, *Walk through Southampton* (ed. Buller), 38.

316 Liber Niger (Corp. MSS), fol. 13. For similar petition of 1468 see *Hist. MSS. Com. Rep.* xi, App. iii, 87.

317 See *Letters of Ric. III and Hen. VII.* (Rolls Ser.), ii, 373.

318 Davies, op. cit. 256, &c.

319 Cf. Charters, 1445, 1461.

320 Thomas Skevington; he was also abbot of Beaulieu, and was admitted burgess of Southampton in 1514.

321 *L. and P. Hen. VIII*, iv (2), 4927.

322 Ibid. The Town of Southampton to Cromwell, Sept. 1533.

323 11 Hen. VII, cap. 5.

324 See above under Fee Farm.

325 *Hist. MSS. Com. Rep.* xi, App. iii, 49, 50.

326 *Cal. of S.P. Dom.* 1581–90, p. 402.

quired. Nor do the town books of the period impress us with the concerns of the merchants at this time. The vessels were of small tonnage, the ownership divided: thus, among others, the *Mayflower* of 28 tons was let out in four several holdings.[327] Later on, in 1619, the mayor with difficulty provided £150 out of £300 required towards the suppression of piracy, and the complaint of burdens again falls heavily on the ear. Much of the town shipping was employed in the middle of the sixteenth century in the Newfoundland fishery,[328] which also made its impress on the later town ordinances,[329] but a hundred years later had migrated to Poole. The Channel Islands trade was settled in the town from early in the sixteenth century,[330] wool being exported to the islands for the manufacture of stockings which came back to England for sale. The wine trade continued together with much smuggling.

It is not to be supposed that the depression of the town was suffered without an effort on the part of the townsmen. After the Fire of London the Corporation advertised the attractions of Southampton with its many very good houses with cellars and warehouses then standing vacant. The London sufferers, being men 'of credit and reputation,' were invited to throw in their lot with Southampton and open up fresh trade.[331] In the next century a similar offer, with that of free burgess-ship, was made to 'merchants of credit and substance' if they would come and help revive decaying fortune.[332] But the turn of fortune was not to come yet.[333]

Meanwhile turning to the interior trades of the townsfolk in the fifteenth, sixteenth, and seventeenth centuries, they are found to be of the usual kind, and mostly gathered into corporations, craft gilds, or companies, with a common hall, admitting their members by fine, and having relation to the town corporation, by which they were all supervised. The usual arrangement was for one half of admission fines to go to the particular craft or trade, and the other half to the town. The articles of these corporations were to be read publicly among themselves at least once a year. Thus in 1441 all the bakers were fined by the town.[334] In 1517 they were formed into a company with usual powers of self-government; two years later (1519) certain members of the craft having engrossed the making of ship-biscuits, all were ordered to bring their portions of biscuit into the hall over the market-place, there to be sold by the masters of the craft indifferently; any evasion of the order, which was agreed to before the mayor and his brethren, was to be visited by a mulct of 10*s*., namely, 6*s*. 8*d*. to the town and 3*s*. 4*d*. to the light of St. Clement; for further offence the loss of liberty in the craft corporation was awarded.[335] They had always to report to the town what stock of grain they had ready for the supply of the public; the same applies to brewers. In 1584 the fine charged for admission into the bakers' corporation was 26*s*. 8*d*., half going to the town, and half to the craft.[336]

The fine for barber-craft, which embraced common surgery, besides 'trimming' or hair-cutting, was also (1512) 26*s*. 8*d*., half to the town, and half to the craft.[337] The relations between the town and the barbers, who were often 'of a froward mynde,' were sometimes strained, but the following entry deals with conflicting jurisdiction. In 1638 a barber surgeon with episcopal licence having been amerced by the leet jury—he was not a Southampton product—and called before the House, said he had no respect for the House and never got 6*d*. by it, 'which proud and peremptorie language of soe meane a fellow in this place is not to be indured. It is therefore this day ordered that he finde sureties for his appearance at the next sessions of the peace there to answer etc.'[338]

Brewing was a popular trade and was constantly being regulated. In 1488 the fine for admission to beer brewing by the year seems to have been 10*s*. each man.[339] In 1531 for the avoidance of gambling and idleness, 'by reason that every other house is a bruer or tapper,' the number of brewers and tappers was strictly apportioned, and the brewers were forbidden to serve their customers otherwise than in the gross, on the principle, often repeated, 'that one may lyve by another,' the tapper being the retail dealer.[340] The beer supplied was of several strengths, all regulated and charged for according to a standard set ultimately by the town corporation, which otherwise looked after the brewers. They were allowed no iron on their cart wheels; such wheels not only meant 'decay' to the pavement, but caused 'the spurging of theire beere so that their barrels cannot come full to their customers.'[341] However, it had been the practice to bring round 'filling beer' to make up deficiencies, until the regulation came out (1579) that they must supply twenty-one barrels as twenty, and be particular that they all went out full.[342] The 'tipplers' i.e. the beer-house keepers may here be mentioned. They were being constantly regulated both corporately and individually; and in 1581 were ordered not to receive into their houses any of the common drunkards of the town, the names of some being given.[343]

In 1457 the butchers, whose chief market was by the Friars Gate, paid 4*s*. per annum for each stall, but 1*d*. if only taken for a day.[344] They were constantly being regulated, and seem to have had some unpleasant customs.[345] In 1555 they were formed into a company on the usual plan. In 1575 we find slaughter houses forbidden within the walls. In connexion with the butchers, bull-baiting should be mentioned. The bull-ring was in the upper part of the High Street; its use was supposed to make the meat more wholesome; its disuse in 1496 was visited by a fine of two loads of faggots.[346]

In 1507 two chandlers sufficed, who bound themselves to supply the town with tallow candles at ¾*d*. per pound. In 1576 we find the same number—early hours were kept; they were appointed for twenty-one years, one to serve the parishes of Holy

327 Liber Notationum under 1576, &c.
328 Lib. Remembranc. H. fol. 204*b*.
329 Ordinances, *circa* 1630, p. 69.
330 Lib. Remembranc. fol. 16, and Davies, op. cit. 263.
331 Town Journ. 2 Nov. 1666.
332 Ibid. 19 June 1761.
333 See a curious poem called 'The Vision' given as Appendix to *Batt upon Batt* by a Person of Quality (Dr. Speed) (ed. vi), 1711.
334 Steward's Bk. Corp. MSS.
335 Boke of Remembrances (Corp. MSS.), fol. 18.
336 Ibid. fol. 141*b*.
337 Lib. Remembranc. H. fol. 180.
338 Town Journ. (Corp. MSS.), 14 Decem. 1638.
339 Steward's Bk. (Corp. MSS.).
340 Boke of Remembrances, fol. 29.
341 Ibid. fol. 92*b*; Court Leet Bk. 1577, 1579.
342 Boke of Remembrances (Corp. MSS.), fol. 135*b*.
343 Ibid. fol. 139.
344 Steward's Bk.
345 Davies, op. cit. 269.
346 Lib. Remembranc. H. fol. 12.

Rood, St. Michael, and St. John, the other the parishes of All Saints and St. Mary. The butchers were to supply the tallow which was to be divided equally; and no form or regulation was too minute in this as in other trades. At the end of the period there was but one 'town-chandler,' who in 1598 was dismissed from his office, bitterly complaining of the terms set him by the town; but another was appointed.[347]

In 1504 the wardens and company of clothworkers (shearmen) came before the mayor and his brethren complaining of the infringement of their liberties by certain galley men, when several arrangements were made.[348] A hundred years later (1608) usurpers of their trade were again encroaching; they were made to pay the usual fine, half to the town and half to the company, for their privilege.[349] In 1616 a company of clothworkers was formed or reformed; and in 1629 they were fined £5 for not having read among themselves the articles of their incorporation.[350]

The fine of admission to the cappers (1502) was one mark divided equally, as usual, between the town and the master of the craft.[351] Early in the same century the cobblers were fined for breaking the rules of their corporation by giving strangers work.[352]

The coopers probably existed as something of a community from early times; but at all events in answer to a petition concerning infringements of rights in 1486 they received a charter from the corporation; no one was permitted to exercise the craft without having made fine in the usual way, under penalty of £5 to be levied by the mayor's command and divided equally between the town and the craft company.[353] In 1608 the admission fine was £4, one half to the town, the other to the society.[354]

Very similar to the petition of the coopers was that of the tailors in 1474 against the encroachment of strangers and foreigners, such as galley-tailors, &c. They received the desired concessions and gave the town £5 for them.[355] In 1616 the company was partially reconstituted, but as usual in all money payments, whether of admissions or of amercements, the interests of the town and the company were equally consulted.[356]

The shoemakers' (corvesers, cordwainers) company existed here at least in 1488, when the town steward acknowledges dues from the masters of the craft.[357] In 1550 seven fishmongers were appointed for the town, the arrangement being annual.[358] In 1553 the linen-hall which was in West Street was ordered to be used under severe penalties, a custom having arisen of stowing away linen cloth contrary to good order.[359]

The mercers had their craft company here before 1486, admission to which was in the usual way.[360] A company of serge-makers, serge weavers, and wool combers was formed in 1609, dissolved in 1620, and re-formed in 1657.[361]

Tobacconists were here before 1629. In 1632 retail tobacconists to the number of seven were licensed for the town.[362] Other trades of course there were, such as the bowyers in the earlier time, the vintners or wine-sellers at all times: but whether or not gathered into gilds or fraternities, they were equally held in the iron grasp of the corporation, not without at least occasional protest.

A 'sisterhood' for wool-packing consisting of thirteen women, two being wardens, existed here in the sixteenth century. They were sworn and their regulations are given at length. The employment of women in this capacity is said to have been customary from old times.[363]

A revival of the town may be dated from the commencement of the last century. From the rôle of a fashionable watering-place which Southampton was enjoying about the middle of the eighteenth century—with its distinguished company, its retired naval and military gentlemen, the occasional presence of warlike equipments and of royalty; its balls and concerts, and master of the ceremonies, its spa, and archery, its sea bathing,[364] its libraries, its theatre, its unrivalled coaching and beautiful drives—the Act of 1803[365] for abolishing the 'petty customs,' making convenient docks, and calling the harbour board into existence, aroused her and may be said to have been the harbinger of Southampton's prosperity. The Act was amended by that of 1810,[366] but the formation of the docks was still in abeyance owing to the demand on capital by harbour and quay improvements already being carried out under the board. It was not until 1836 that the dock company was incorporated by Act of Parliament, the construction of docks being commenced in 1838. Meanwhile, the formation of a railway to London, which had been contemplated as far back as 1825, was taken in hand in 1830 and following years, the works being actually commenced in March, 1836; but it was not until 1840 that the whole line was opened from London to Southampton.

The docks were now rapidly advancing in construction. The great tidal dock, then the largest in England, which had been commenced in October, 1839, was opened in August, 1842. It contains a surface of 16 acres of water, 18 ft. deep at low water of spring tide, the average rise of tide being 13 ft.; its entrance 150 ft. wide. An inner or close dock with a surface of 10 acres of water, 28 ft. deep, was opened in 1851. The Itchen extension quay, with a frontage of 1,720 ft. and a depth of 20 ft., now deepened to 28 ft. at low water spring tides, was opened in 1876, and formed the first instalment of the Empress Dock, opened by Queen Victoria in 1890, and containing a surface of 18½ acres of water with a depth of 26 ft. at spring tide low water, and entrance 165 ft. wide. The first graving or dry dock was opened in July, 1846, entrance gates 66 ft. wide, length 400 ft., depth over blocks 21 ft.; the second, opened in 1847, entrance 51 ft., length 280 ft., depth 15 ft.; the third, finished in 1854, entrance 80 ft., length 521 ft., depth

[347] Boke of Remembrances, fol. 198*b*.
[348] Lib. Remembranc. H. fol. 12.
[349] Town Journ. (Corp. MSS.).
[350] Ibid. 4 Sept.
[351] Lib. Remembranc. H. fol. 6*b*.
[352] Ibid. fol. 140*b*.
[353] Liber Niger, fol. 60.
[354] Town Journ.
[355] Liber Niger, fol. 13.
[356] Town Journ. (Corp. MSS.), 6 Sept.
[357] Steward's Bk.
[358] Boke of Remembrances, fol. 58.
[359] Ibid. fol. 68.
[360] Lib. Remembranc. H. 1 Hen. VIII.
[361] Town Journ. *sub annis*.
[362] *Hist. MSS. Com. Rep.* xi, App. iii, 28; *Cal. S.P. Dom.* 1629–31, p. 99.
[363] Lib. Remembranc. B.B. fol. 26*b*.
[364] Dr. Speed wrote a Latin treatise on sea-bathing at Southampton which afterwards appeared in English; see also Count Kilmansegg's Diary in 1761 (*Athenaeum*, No. 3914, 1 Nov. 1902), and the 1778 edition of Defoe's *Tour*.
[365] Stat. 43 Geo. III, cap. 21.
[366] Stat. 50 Geo. III, cap. 168.

25 ft.; the fourth (1879), entered from the Itchen, width 56 ft., length 450 ft., depth 25 ft. Since the purchase of the docks by the London and South Western Railway Company (1892) there have been constructed the 'Prince of Wales' graving dock, opened August, 1895, width at entrance, 91 ft., length 750 ft., depth to blocks, 32½ ft.; and the Trafalgar (graving), opened October, 1905, width at entrance 90 ft., length 875 ft., depth 33½ ft. Another open dock, contracted for in August, 1907, will have a depth at low water of 35 ft., to be increased to 40 ft., area 16 acres. The new quay extensions in the Itchen and the Test—the Prince of Wales Quay 2,000 ft. long, and South Quay 430 ft., have each a depth alongside of 28 ft. at low water, and the Test Quay, 1,600 ft. long, a minimum depth of 32 ft. No expense has been spared by the railway company to bring the docks to the highest efficiency, and to secure to the port the pre-eminence it now enjoys. The docks, the capabilities of which were experienced in the late South African War, have also the natural advantage of their position within one of the finest harbours of England, with a deep-water channel 5 miles long from Calshot Castle at its entrance to Southampton. The double tide [367] also at this port is of extreme value to shipping, the second high tide occurring about two hours and a quarter after the former, the fall between the two being only about 9 in., so that practically high water is stationary for nearly four hours.

In this connexion should be mentioned the splendid work of the harbour board on the quays and channels, and special notice should be made of the new pier, said to be the finest in the south of England, with ten landing stages, opened by the duke of Connaught, 2 June, 1892, in place of the older pier opened by the late queen when Princess Victoria in 1833. Part of this remains, but has been entirely reconstructed and is devoted to mercantile traffic, while the new pier is reserved for passenger business.

CHURCHES The church of *ST. MARY, SOUTHAMPTON.* There is no mention in Domesday of any church within the borough of 'Hantune.' But it does not follow that there was none. The church of St. John certainly existed, and there is some reference to the ecclesiastical position of the town under the account of the manor of South Stoneham. That manor belonged to the bishop and was appropriated for the clothing of the monks of St. Swithun, Winchester; but the manorial church was held by Richer, the clerk, with two other churches near Southampton dependent on it as the mother church. Adjoining the church was a hide of land, and Richer, further, in right of his benefice owned all the tithes of the town of Southampton and also of Kingsland.[368] Probably this manorial church was no other than St. Mary's, Southampton.[369] In favour of this view is the fact that the precentors or rectors of St. Mary's have possessed the rectory of South Stoneham and presented to its vicarage as early as we have any records on the matter.[370] St. Mary's, Southampton, has its valuable glebe about the church; it possessed all the tithes of the town, together with those of the whole district probably here described. It should be observed that the tithings of Eastleigh and Allington, which are now comprised within the parish of South Stoneham, are not included in that manor in the Domesday record, but are described separately, Allington moreover having a church. The bishop's manor therefore assigned for the clothing of the Winchester monks was probably Bitterne, which had always belonged to the bishops till it passed to the Ecclesiastical Commissioners in 1869. The king's land of which Richer had the tithes was no doubt Portswood, which we know to have been royal property, and which was afterwards granted to the monks of St. Denys.[371] The site of the 'two other churches near Hantune' which belonged to the manorial church probably cannot be determined. The present church of St. Mary, South Stoneham, was not then in existence, and a church on its site could hardly have been called near Southampton.[372]

Passing from the eleventh to the twelfth century we find Henry II granting his 'chapels' of St. Michael, St. Cross (Holy Rood), St. Lawrence, and All Saints within the borough to the monks of St. Denys [373]; but these chapels must have had relation to a mother church which was, no doubt, this manorial church without the walls.

In the time of Bishop Godfrey de Lucy (1189–1204) the clergy of 'Hampton' were in controversy with the canons of St. Denys; the settlement of which dispute was, by order of the bishop, postponed till the return from the school at Paris of Stephen of Reims, the superior of these clergy, who at once recognized the right of the canons, spoke of 'my clergy of Hampton,' [374] and was very probably the priest of the mother church with whom these clergy were living in a community.

A few years later an inquiry instituted (1225) by desire of Pope Honorius at the instance of Philip de Lucy, 'rector or warden (*custos*) of the church of Southampton,' who set forth that the town was within the limits of his parish, resulted in establishing the rights of St. Mary's against the prior and convent of St. Denys over the churches or chapels within the town, the chaplains being required to swear in the rural chapter at St. Mary's—Philip de Lucy happening to be rural dean,[375] as his successors frequently were—to preserve the honour of the church of St. Mary.[376] The parishes of the town were at

[367] A phenomenon noticed by Bede, bk. iv, cap. 16.

[368] *V.C.H. Hants*, i, 516.

[369] Moody, *Domesday of Hampshire*, 47.

[370] The earliest list (1282) of the deanery of Southampton (Winton Epis. Reg. Pontoise, fol. 157) includes under St. Mary's 'all the chapels of Aldinton,' the next entries being 'capella de Esteley,' and 'capella B. Marie Suht,' which may have been the chapel of our Lady of Grace. In 1308 the warden (*custos*) of St. Mary's presents to the church of South Stoneham (ibid. Woodlock, fol. 5*b*), and in 1379 to the vicarage of the church or chapel of St. Mary, South Stoneham (ibid. Wykeham, i, fol. 104*b*).

[371] See above.

[372] The present church of South Stoneham dates from about the end of the twelfth century, the chancel containing some good original work. This church is probably to be identified in Bishop Pontoise's list with one of the 'chapels of Aldinton' dependent on the church of St. Mary, Southampton. There is no separate mention of it, nor does it occur in the Taxation of 1291, nor in the official list of the rural deanery till late, being probably always included under St. Mary's, Southampton.

[373] Dugdale, *Mon.* vi, 216, charter given at large.

[374] Add. MS. 15314, fol. 43.

[375] See further, Davies, op. cit. 329–35.

[376] The office of rural dean was of considerable importance. He granted probate of wills, and his seal was often sought, like that of the mayoralty, to strengthen documents. The seal of the dean of Southampton is frequently found in this connexion, e.g. in 1267.

this time in an inchoate state. There were certain understood limits and districts belonging to the several chapels, in common, however, with those of St. Andrew and Holy Trinity[377] without the walls, whose rights or districts never advanced to the further dignity. The churches are called 'parochial chapels,' i.e. chapels of ease, such chapels being created 'parochial' by the bishop, though dependent on the mother church, while enjoying certain privileges of their own. The chaplains of the town made no question of their relation to St. Mary's; the controversies past and to be renewed[378] were about the adjustment of rights and dues which had been acquired by or conceded to the chapels or others which it was endeavoured to obtain, and about the amount of canonical obedience due to the chief of the mother church.

As little is known of the origin of the religious community at St. Mary's as of its suppression. It may be, if there is anything in the tradition of Leland, that the community is to be traced from the time of Henry I before 1118.[379] It seems to have consisted of four priests, at all events latterly, besides clerks and the chanter, who, in the place referred to, is called the 'curate.'[380] The rector and clerks were acting as a community (see above) in 1225. In 1251 the title of chanter is found attached to the *custos* or rector.[381] In 1258 the warden, chaplains, and clerks are one party in a legal inquiry.[382] In 1278 the precentor, chaplains, and clerks of St. Mary's join in an exchange of land with the convent of St. Denys.[383] Similarly we find 'the warden and clerks,' 'the precentor or chanter or warden, chaplains and clerks,' and in 1460 'the precentor and fellows' (*socii*).[384] In 1526 the precentory or church of St. Mary in the deanery of Southampton was valued at £37 5*s.* 5*d.*, while the 'chantry of St. Mary' stood at £6 13*s.* 4*d.*[385] In the *Valor Ecclesiasticus* of 1536, Dr. Capon being precentor, the precentory was valued in oblations, tithes, &c., at £44 13*s.* 4*d.* less deductions to the amount of £7 8*s.* 1*d.*, leaving a net of £37 5*s.* 3*d.*, paying its tenth of £3 14*s.* 6½*d.* A little after this, when reporting in 1547 on the 'chantry houses' which stood on the site of, or close to, the present deanery, the commissioners of Edward VI stated that they could discover neither by whose devotion the 'chantry' had been founded, nor exactly what property belonged to it; they were only able to say that what were commonly called the 'chantry lands,' as well as the house which had always been known as the 'chantry house,' were let at the rate of £13 6*s.* 8*d.* per annum; but they note that neither Dr. Capon the rector nor his farmer appeared before them, so that their survey was less accurately made.[386] The inquiry must have been otherwise abortive, as according to a letter of September, 1529, to the customer of Southampton about the chantry lands the chantry had been dissolved many years.[387] This chantry may have been of different foundation from the old precentory, though always held by the parish priest, who was thus variously styled warden, precentor, chanter or rector.

Besides this chantry of unknown origin a chantry for the soul of Nicholas Beket, who died before 1287, and of Agnes his wife was settled here, the warden of St. Mary's from time to time being bound to find a fit chaplain.[388] In 1462 Johanna, widow of Nicholas Holmage or Holmehegg, mayor in 1454, devised certain properties to the mayor and corporation for the establishment of a chantry at St. Mary's for her husband, herself, her parents and ancestors. Her chanter's stipend was to be £6 13*s.* 4*d.*—he always received and paid for the town seal to his appointment—and on the day of her obit £1 6*s.* 8*d.* was to be distributed, namely to the mayor 3*s.* 4*d.*, to the seneschal 2*s.*, and the remainder to the priests, clerks, and poor of St. Mary's. She also provided for the support of the tenement devised for the purposes of her foundation.[389] The mind of Thomas Smale and Joana his wife was kept here yearly on 9 April; 5*s.* 6*d.* to the chanter, 4*s.* 6*d.* to the bedesmen.[390]

Of the fabrics, the earliest church must have been of Saxon origin; it was possibly represented in Leland's time (1546) by the chapel of St. Nicholas, 'a poor and small thing' which stood immediately to the east of the then existing church.[391] It was succeeded by the 'great church of Our Lady' of Leland's time, which may possibly be dated from the reign of Henry I. This church, which contained the memorials of many of Southampton's worthies, appears to have been destroyed by the town about 1549 or 1550,[392] to remove from French cruisers the direction[393] of a well-known and lofty spire, and in the latter year the stones and rubbish of the church were carted away to mend the roads.[394] The chancel, however, may have been preserved for its sacred purposes. Speed (1596) speaks[395] of a 'small unfinished chapel' as having replaced the great church; this probably refers to the building carried out in 1579,[396] which could hardly have been more than a restoration of the ruined chancel.

For many years the church remained in a miserable condition.[397] A 'fair house,' doubtless a predecessor of the present deanery,[398] seems to have been also constructed from the ruins. In 1650 the church was repaired in a niggardly fashion.[399] In 1711 a nave was fitted to the old chancel by Archdeacon Brideoake, and in 1723 he rebuilt the chancel. This church, substantially built, for the repairs of which Dr. Hoadly the next rector left a benefaction,[400] was

377 These two chapels were in the immediate vicinity of St. Mary.

378 As in 1331; Winton. Epis. Reg. Stratford, 55, 57, 65; also in 1370, ibid. Wykeham, ii, 386, and other instances.

379 'This Queen Matilda, or some other good persons following, had thought to have made this a collegiate church, but this purpose succeeded not fully.' Leland, *Itin.* (ed. Hearne), iii, 105.

380 Steward's Bk. (Corp. MSS), 1543.

381 Add. MS. 15314, fol. 76*b*.

382 Ibid. fol. 75*b*.

383 Ibid. fol. 76.

384 Winton. Epis. Reg. Waynflete, i, fol. 105*b*.

385 Ibid. Fox, v, towards end.

386 Chant. Cert. R. 52, No. 54.

387 *L. and P. Hen. VIII*, iv (3), 5933.

388 Winton. Epis. Reg. Woodlock, fol. 47, 106, 175.

389 Lib. Niger, fol. 71; Chant. Cert. R. 51, No. 1.

390 Steward's Bk. (Corp. MSS), 1457.

391 Leland, *Itin.* (ed. Hearne), iii, 90.

392 Davies, op. cit. 338.

393 Speed, *Theatre of Gt. Brit.* (ed. 1650), 13.

394 Court Leet Bk. (Corp. MSS), 1550.

395 Speed, loc. cit.

396 Lib. Remembranc. (Corp. MSS), fol. 135.

397 In Bishop Andrews' 'Form of Consecration of Jesus Chapel' in 1630 we read: 'Juxta Southampton. villam ecclesia B. Marie collapsa cernitur, solis cancellis ad sacros ritus superstitibus.'

398 Destroyed in 1641, rebuilt in 1686 by Dr. Clutterbuck, burnt down in 1706, when the registers and documents were consumed; rebuilt by Archd. Brideoake in 1712; burnt down in 1801; subsequently rebuilt, it occupies part of the site of the old chantry building.

399 Journ. 30 Dec. 1650.

400 Davies, op. cit. 345.

transformed in 1833 under the pressure of a growing population, the result being the creation of the hideous fabric which the present generation cannot have forgotten. This gave place to the existing church in the style of the thirteenth century, consisting of chancel and nave continuous without arch, north chapel, aisles throughout, transepts and vestries, the first stone of which was laid by the Prince of Wales on 12 August, 1878, in memory of Bishop Wilberforce, whose son, the present archdeacon of Westminster, was then rector. The walls were already 20 ft. high, and the church was consecrated on 21 June, 1879, and finished[401] according to the designs of the architect, the late Mr. Street, with the exception of the tower and spire, in 1884.

The church tower has not yet been built to its full height, and there are at present no bells. The plate now in use is modern, the older plate being deposited elsewhere for safety.

The early registers of the church have unluckily been destroyed in the disastrous fires which have twice wrecked the chantry or rectory-house. The entries in the register book from 1650, the earliest date, to 1706 are incomplete, being made only from notes taken by the clerks and churchwardens.

The revenues of St. Mary's, which are considerable, and are derived from the rectory of South Stoneham, commuted in 1845 at £1,430, and from the valuable rectorial property of St. Mary's in the town and neighbourhood, have been on the whole very much employed to the advantage of the neighbourhood. Even as far back as the Long Parliament we find the tithes, which had been sequestrated from the lessee of the rectory (Lord Lambert) as a delinquent, committed by order of the Committee for Plundered Ministers to the mayor and aldermen, on their petition, for distribution among the ministers of the town, whose maintenance was very inadequate.[402] Accordingly we find £40 per annum appropriated to Jesus Chapel, belonging to St. Mary's, across the Itchen, and the remaining profits of the chantry, at that time about £250 per annum, distributed in equal portions among the ministers of Holy Rood, St. Michael's, St John's, St. Lawrence's, All Saints', and St. Mary's. And subsequently to this we find the 'chantry money' directed to the payment of the various ministrations of the town until the Restoration. But especially within the last half-century the emoluments have been employed for the endowment of the many new districts in St. Mary's and within the rectory of South Stoneham, under the arrangement of the successive bishops of the diocese and with the concurrence of the rectors. Among ancient bequests Agnes le Horder, January, 1348–9;[403] William of Wykeham by will 24 July, 1403, left £20 to the precentors and a pair of vestments and chalice to the church;[404] John Renawd (1422) to the fabric 20*s*. Dr. Hoadly's bequest (1763) has been mentioned. Mary Baker, widow, by will proved 21 March, 1872, made a bequest to the poor of St. Mary's and of Milbrook.

THE HOLY AND UNDIVIDED TRINITY, North Front, Kingsland.—This church was erected in the pseudo eleventh-century style in 1829: and in view of assignment of district enlarged and consecrated in 1847. It has been improved of late years. The register commences in April, 1842. The benefice is a new vicarage in the patronage of the bishop. There is a good vicarage house. This parish has an interest in the Toomer bequest (see under Holy Rood).

ST. LUKE'S NEWTOWN (new vicarage).—District assigned in 1851. Ecclesiastical parish by Order of Council, 1853. Church erected 1852–3; enlarged 1860; chancel added and consecrated 1873; other improvements are being carried out. Register commences December, 1854. Patron, the bishop. There is a vicarage house.

ST. AUGUSTINE OF CANTERBURY, Northam Road (new vicarage).—The church of this parish, a miserable erection of 1854 under the designation of Christ Church, has now given way to a handsome church under the above invocation in the style of the thirteenth century from the designs of Mr. Woodyer; consecrated in 1884. It consists of nave and aisles, apsidal chancel, south chapel, and vestries. District arranged in 1851, formed by Order of Council 1853. Patron, the bishop. There is a good vicarage house.

ST. JAMES, Bernard Street (new vicarage).—District arranged in 1851, formed by Order of Council 1853. Church in the style of the thirteenth century, built and consecrated in 1858, with accommodation for 830. It has been since much improved. Population 7,314. Register commences in 1858. Patron, the bishop.

ST. MATTHEW'S, St. Mary's Road (new vicarage). Parish formed in 1866. Church in style of thirteenth century, built in 1870, enlarged 1874. Accommodation 730. Population 800. Patron, the bishop. This parish has an interest in the Toomer bequest.

Parishes formed from South Stoneham within the town and county of the town are:—

CHRIST CHURCH, PORTSWOOD, in Highfield Road (new vicarage). District formed in 1848. Church built in 1847. After many alterations, especially in 1878, the building presents the unusual appearance of a double nave flanked by an aisle on either side, the wide chancel with its aisles being fitted on to the two naves so that the easternmost pillar of the mid-nave arcade stands exactly in the middle at the entrance of the chancel. This bold plan was accepted and approved by the late Mr. Street. There is a large vicarage house. The bishop of Winchester is patron.

ST. DENYS, St. Denys Road, District Parish. Parish formed in 1867. Church of handsome character, 1868. Patron, the bishop.

To these must be added:—*ST. BARNABAS*, Lodge Road, Avenue. District formed in 1893 from the parishes of St. Luke, Newtown, and Christ Church, Portswood. Church consecrated 14 November, 1903. There is a parsonage house. Patron, the bishop.

HOLY ROOD or *ST. CROSS*.—The church of this parish stood originally in the middle of the High Street in front of its present position. Having fallen into decay in the early part of the fourteenth century, Thomas de Bynedon, a prominent burgess, fined with the crown (1318) for permission[405] to grant to the prior and convent of St. Denys a new site; and in

[401] During the rebuilding a leaden sepulchral cross with the inscription of the thirteenth century was found, and is, of course, preserved; *Proc. Soc. Antiq.* (1905).

[402] Journ. 17 July, 11 Sept. 1646.

[403] Add. MS. 15314, fol. 85*b*.

[404] Will of Will. of Wykeham.

[405] Pat. 14 Edw. II (30 Dec. 1320), pt. 1, m. 1, exemplified by desire of convent 20 June, 1409.

1320 the church was rebuilt where it now stands, the old site becoming in after times occupied by the Audit House. Soon after the church was opened a cause was moved between the precentor or rector of St. Mary's and the 'rector' or chaplain of St. Cross on the right of interment within and without the church. The claim of the precentor was entirely upheld (4 December, 1333), but the rector of St. Cross obtained permission for his own burial within the church and that of his successors, and certain other persons named. But the dues were to go to St. Mary's; all other sepulture being forbidden.[406]

The taxation of Pope Nicholas (1291) gives the revenue of the church as £4 6*s.* 8*d.* per annum, its tenth being 8*s.* 8*d.*[407] Soon after the rebuilding of the church the convent made an arrangement for the increase of the benefice, and in 1408 the church having become, with the church of St. Michael, appropriated (1405) to the convent, certain further arrangements were made between the priory and the perpetual new vicar[408] for the improvement of the vicarage;[409] and in 1474 the poverty of the cure was further considered[410] and payment from the convent advanced from £8 to £10.[411] By the valuation of 1535–6 the church was worth £15 10*s.* 0½*d.* or less procurations £12 1*s.* 9*d.* net, paying its tenth, £1 4*s.* 2¼*d.*, to the king. In 1683 Bishop Morley made a benefaction of £20 per annum in augmentation of the benefice under certain conditions. In 1751 Mr. Richard Taunton left £21 per annum for a double daily service. The benefice received an augmentation of £20 per annum through Queen Anne's Bounty. In 1706 Queen's College, Oxford, the patrons of the living, provided, in conjunction with the corporation, a vicarage house in lieu of the ancient vicarage house[412] which had been alienated, and in later times annexed the stewardship of God's House to the benefice, which brought in £21 per annum, besides a good house[413] for the steward, but of late the vicars have been appointed as chaplains only. The living is now valued at about £220 per annum. There is no available vicarage house. The patronage was originally granted to the priory of St. Denys, who presented till the Dissolution. From 1548 to 1574 it was in the gift of John Capelyn, burgess, and afterwards of Anthony Lisle, esq. From 1611 to 1871 the patronage was with Queen's College, Oxford, who in the latter year gave it over to the bishop of Winchester in exchange for other livings. The bishop is now the patron.

Queen's College, Oxford. *Argent three eagles gules.*

Holy Rood has been considered the 'town' church, and episcopal and archidiaconal visitations have been usually held in it. It was here that Philip of Spain heard mass (20 July, 1554) on the day of his arrival in the port. A Thursday evening lecture was formerly held here, and in 1607 was filled by the town lecturer (Mr. Hitchcock) subject to the bishop's approval. Subsequently it was agreed (1615) that the incumbents of the town should hold the lecture here, and the parishes were put under contribution accordingly.[414] Documents of some interest exist concerning this lecture under the Commonwealth.[415] It was the practice of the town clergy to keep up a daily service at Holy Rood, and in September, 1661,[416] they were begged to revive that ancient and laudable custom; a practice broken through probably before 1752, since Taunton's bequest that year for the same purpose was confined to the vicar of Holy Rood, or on his failing in the duty the bequest was to go to St. Lawrence, and on failure there to return to Holy Rood, and so from one to the other for ever. In 1781 Holy Rood is described as the fashionable church of the town, with service twice a day.[417] The old custom of houseling cloth over the rails at the Holy Communion has been retained at this church.

From an early period the western porch or cloister which existed here till the last rebuilding was used for town proclamations, and was called the 'proclamation-house,'[418] and accordingly was repaired by the corporation. At this church, too, the assembly bell for the town was rung in the early morning and the curfew at night.[419] In 1742 the churchwardens were ordered to remove the lock from a certain pew, and deliver it to the owner with the message that if he sent his cook-maid or other servant to sit there again, the parish would dispose of the pew to some other family.

In 1848 a faculty was obtained for pulling down and rebuilding the church. Fortunately the old tower was preserved, but the nave, aisles, and chancel were rebuilt (1849–50) strictly on the old plan, and partly on the original walls. The tower, which had been in danger of reconstruction in 1791, is of good proportions and crowned with a spire. It stands at the south-west angle. The interior of the church was much improved (1883) by the removal of the lateral galleries constructed at the rebuilding, and in 1901 the western gallery was removed. The fifteenth-century font has an octagonal panelled bowl and stem, with angels below the bowl, and the lectern, of the same date, represents an eagle on a globe supported by a tower; beneath the claws of the eagle a dragon raises its head to dart at her breast. The pedestal stands on a triangular base carried by three lions. The chancel contains some ancient stalls with the motto of Bishop Fox, 'Est Deo gratia,' in bold relief. The pulpit was given in 1900, and a memorial window to a late vicar (Whitlock) in 1903.

There are eight bells; the treble, second, fourth,

406 Winton. Epis. Reg. Stratford, fol. 87*b*, 88.

407 *Pope Nich. Tax.* (Rec. Com.), 210*b*.

408 'Perpetuus Vicarius modernus.' Compare the title 'new rector' or 'new vicar' for the titular rectors and vicars under Bishop Wilberforce's Act.

409 Add. MS. 15314, fol. 44*b*.

410 Winton. Epis. Reg. Waynflete, ii, fol. 130*b*.

411 However, the value of the benefice had been returned at £10 in 1428; *Feud. Aids*, ii, 342.

412 In this ancient house the town Audit was held with accompanying festivities 3 Aug. 1441; Steward's Bk.

413 In the quadrangle of God's House.

414 Town Journ. (Corp. MSS.).

415 Davies, op. cit. 359.

416 Town Journ. (Corp. MSS.).

417 Ford, *Guide* (1781).

418 As noticed above, the Audit House with its accompaniments stood in front of this church. A rather amusing entry occurs of the green stocks, standing by this church, being removed one night and tied to the bull ring. Whereupon the chief watchman at New Corner, being unable to give any account of the matter, was ordered to the stocks; Town Journ. 24 June, 1609.

419 Steward's Bk. 1456, 1461, &c. The hours in 1569 were 4 o'clock in the morning and 8 o'clock at night.

and sixth by Lester of London, 1742; and the third, fifth, seventh, and eighth by Mears of London, 1843–7.

The plate comprises two chalices and patens of 1626, the gift of Ann wife of John Major, alderman, to 'Holirudes,' 1627, a plate of 1685, inscribed 'Christ is the living Bread which came downe from heaven,' two flagons of 1765, and an almsdish of the same date given by Robert Bradsell, vicar. There are also a pewter dish given 1662 by Henry Embris and two pewter plates without inscription.

The registers commence in 1653. Churchwardens' accounts are complete from 1699.

The following chantries were settled in this church:—For William Nycoll and Annys and Alice his wives, and for Richard Thomas and Thomas Payne, founded after 1452. As originally founded by William Nycoll it was worth £8 13*s.* 4*d.*, the stipend of the priest being £6 13*s.* 4*d.*, an obit £1 6*s.* 8*d.*, and the remaining 13*s.* 4*d.* for repairs.[420] The anniversary was kept on 25 April. Subsequently the foundation was enlarged by his wife or wives for two stipendiaries receiving £6 and £6 13*s.* 4*d.* respectively; and the worth of the whole foundation was £15 13*s.* 4*d.*[421] Under 1553 we find pensions of £6 and £5 paid respectively to the stipendiaries at Holy Rood.

William Gunter, apparently after 1493, founded a chantry here worth £7 for the souls of his parents and himself. His priest was to receive £6, and £1 was reserved for repairs to tenements belonging to the chantry.[422]

John Renawd, burgess, in 1422 left 10 marks for a chaplain to celebrate here, and a penny in bread or silver to every poor man coming to his anniversary.[423]

The mind of John Mascal and Margery his wife was kept here on 10 November at the annual cost of £1 0*s.* 9*d.*[424]

John James, burgess, by his will (2 September, 1471) gave legacies to all the churches and to Alice his wife a life interest in certain properties on condition of her holding his anniversary here. On her death the property was to pass to the corporation with the same condition.[425] The mind of Margery Marsh was also kept here. The mayor and burgesses held land for the purpose of this and the preceding obit, worth £1 3*s.* 4*d.*[426]

THE FRENCH CHURCH.—Within the parish of Holy Rood in Winkle Street is the hospital of St. Julian or God's House, an ancient foundation which has been dealt with above.[427] The only remains of the ancient buildings are the chapel and the entrance gateway adjoining it on the west. These form the frontage to Winkle Street, and being of late twelfth-century date are part of the original buildings of the hospital. They have, however, lost nearly every ancient feature by 'restoration.' Till 1861 great part of the remaining buildings of the same date was standing. The tradition of the French congregation having been settled here in the time of Edward VI, though alleged in a law case of 1749, appears to be incapable of proof.[428] The earliest notice is probably to be derived from a petition to the corporation[429] in (May ?) 1567 by a body of Walloons who had obtained permission from Queen Elizabeth to settle in the town; they beg that they may have a church assigned for their worship, that they may have leave to exercise their trade of whatever kind in the town, or at least 'such misteries and occupacions' as had not been practised in the country, with permission to employ in the same their own people, as unskilled labour would be prejudicial to their work, and so to the town. The petition, which contained other points, concluded with a request for the good offices of the corporation with the Queen's Council and the bishop of Winchester, out of the 'humanity' they bore 'towards the afflicted for the Gospel's sake,' and with an assurance that their settlement in the town would soon be found a public benefit.

The answer of the corporation was but half encouraging: they might exercise trades hitherto unknown, but workmen from their own countries could not be permitted; as for other trades, shoemakers and tailors, there were too many in the town already; for other points raised they must apply elsewhere. Accordingly they appealed to Bishop Horne, who recommended the case to Cecil on 30 June and again 19 September, 1567; after which the Council replied that 'twenty families of strangers might be permitted to settle in the town, with ten servants to each household, on condition that each took and instructed two English apprentices in their science for seven years and that after seven years for every two strangers they kept one Englishman. During seven years they should pay but half strangers' subsidies for wares made in Southampton, to be carried out only from the port; and were to have the same privileges as the strangers at Sandwich.[430]

We find this congregation of Walloon strangers settled in God's House chapel before December, 1567, at which period the register of the church commences; and as we learn from the register the same year was that of their admission into 'Hampton.'[431] The occupation of the chapel was, under authority, by permission of Queen's College, Oxford, to which body the entire hospital and so the chapel of the house belonged. The settlers appear mostly to have come from Lisle, Valenciennes, and other places in the Low Countries, from Normandy and the Channel Islands. Their early history is to be gathered from the register, but cannot be detailed here;[432] but various names of subsequent interest in town history begin to appear. The family of Saravia were settled among the early refugees. In the communicants' list of July, 1569, we find Christopher de Saravia and his wife, the father and mother of the celebrated Adrian de Saravia, who was master of the grammar sehool before February, 1576.[433] In an entry of June, 1571, Saravia is described as 'minister,' and it is possible he may have officiated as pastor of the congregation at this time. The discipline of the church was strict, and the records are full of interest. On 4 September, 1591, Queen Elizabeth visited Southampton with her whole court, remaining till the 7th about mid-day, when the strangers, having been

420 Chant. Cert. 51.

421 Ibid. 52; Boke of Remembrances, fol. 91*b*; Steward's Bk. 1486.

422 Chant. Cert. 51.

423 Madox, *Form. Angl.* 431.

424 Steward's Bk. 1457.

425 Liber Niger, fol. 71; see also for this and Margery Mascal, Chant. Cert. 52, No. 60, but in the town book next cited the name is given as Margery Marsh.

426 Boke of Remembrances, fol. 91*b*.

427 *V.C.H. Hants*, ii, 202.

428 Davies, op. cit. 403, &c.

429 Cott. MSS. Vesp. F. ix, fol. 259.

430 *Cal. S.P. Dom.* 1566–79, pp. 31, 32.

431 Orig. Reg. (Somerset House).

432 Davies, op. cit. 405, &c.

433 Temp. T. Overey, sub-canon.

afforded no opportunity before, placed themselves in her way outside the town, determined on an interview to thank her for the protection she had afforded them in that town for more than twenty-four years.[434] This again points to the period of their arrival. After the revocation of the Edict of Nantes (22 October, 1685) a considerable addition was made to the foreign community here; and not long after this it appears that the town council had applied for aid to the administrators of the foreign refugee fund to enable the settlement of a silk manufacture after the fashion of Tours and Lyons: help was promised (1694) on the corporation receiving[435] a sufficient number of families to carry on the silk trade, commencing with thirty looms as a beginning. The trade was settled in the town for some time and carried on in Winkle Street.[436]

Turning to ecclesiastical relations the congregation was put formally into communion with the Anglican church in March, 1712. We cannot follow the details and reasons of a political nature which had this result. No doubt the leanings of M. Cougot the minister, who must have been in Anglican orders, having been instituted by Bishop Mew so far back as 20 June, 1702, to the rectory of Millbrook,[437] must have had their influence; but the step was by no means approved by the French church in London, and together with other troubles[438] caused a division in the Southampton congregation, a secession which came to an end apparently in 1725.

By the terms of their conformity in 1712 they had been permitted to retain their consistory, the choice of their minister, and the distribution of their charities. And finally, after a short period of abeyance in appointment to the ministry the elders or trustees sought the advice of the Charity Commissioners in April, 1856, when new trustees were appointed and a scheme adopted by order of Chancery dated 7 July the same year. Under this the old provisions were as far as possible affirmed; the minister must be a priest in orders of the Church of England and be appointed by the trustees; and the proper direction of the funds was provided.

In 1864 the college, under their corporate seal, renewed permission for the use of the chapel by the French congregation, 'at such times as the said chapel may not be required for the use of the brothers and sisters of the Hospital of God's House.' The vicar of Holy Rood as chaplain of the hospital is always one of the trustees.

ST. LAWRENCE and *ST. JOHN, UNITED PARISHES.*—The church of St. John was granted by William Fitz Osbern, earl of Hereford, to the abbey of St. Mary of Lire, which he had founded in the diocese of Evreux; he also gave a rent-charge of £9 5*s.* together with a burgage in 'Hampton' to the same monastery.[439] This must have been soon after the Conquest, when he had probably himself received the grant from the king. He died in 1071.

The abbot and convent of Lire presented to the rectory till 1373, when we find the temporalities of the abbey in the king's hands on account of the war. The convent, however, presented again through the prior of Carisbrook, their proctor, in 1400; soon after which the patronage passed into the royal hands.[440] Neither St. John's nor St. Lawrence's occurs in the Taxation of 1291. In the *Valor* of 1536 the church of St. John appears worth altogether £5 6*s.* 8*d.*, its tenth to the king being 10*s.* 8*d.*[441] In 1723 it stood in the king's book at £6 13*s.* 4*d.*, but only gave the clear value of £2.

The benefices of St. Lawrence and St. John were held together in 1614, and have so continued from that date. A more complete union was attempted owing to the poverty of the town benefices in 1663, when the town council approached the bishop with a view to the union of the churches of St. Lawrence and St. John with Holy Rood, and that of All Saints with St. Michael's.[442] No action was, however, taken in the matter, though practically the benefices were frequently held together. But the church of St. John having fallen into ruinous condition and its poverty considered, it was proposed at the beginning of the following century to take advantage of the Act of 1665[443] 'for uniting churches in cities and towns corporate' and obtain an ecclesiastical union of the parishes of St. Lawrence and St. John, their joint value not exceeding £12 per annum. Accordingly after action by the town council and the vestry the parishes were united under a faculty from Bishop Trelawney dated 3 September, 1708.[444] After this the church of St. John, which stood in French Street, was pulled down under the faculty, the parishioners being bound henceforth to support the church of St. Lawrence. The area of St. John's Church, in shape an irregular cross, measuring 90 ft. 10 in. from east to west, and 70 ft. at the transepts, then became appropriated as a burial ground for the united parishes, the walls being made up to the height of 8 ft. all round in September, 1721.[445] On 23 March, 1539, Abbot John Bradley was consecrated bishop suffragan of Shrewsbury in this church. In the angle formed by the transept and aisle wall on the south are buildings in St. John's Court belonging to the church and said to have been the ancient parsonage. Within the site of the church is a Tudor monument, quite defaced; there are also memorials of Richard Taunton, the benefactor of the town, who was buried here 7 April, 1752, and many others.

The church of St. Lawrence being granted by Henry II to the priory of St. Denys, the patronage of this church was exercised by the convent till its dissolution; after which the first presentation by the crown was exercised 26 April, 1543. The benefice continued in the royal patronage except for the intrusion of Nathaniel Robinson, a Presbyterian, about 1648,[446] and is now in the gift of the Lord Chancellor.

This church possesses churchwardens' accounts dating from 1567, a minute book, and some ancient deeds, fourteen in number, from which notices of the

[434] French Reg.

[435] Undated orig. letter to be assigned to 1694; Davies, op. cit. 410.

[436] For information on the paper-making carried on by the refugees at Woodmill in the neighbourhood of Southampton, see *Some Account of the Settlement of the Refugees at Southampton*, by Sir William W. Portal, a direct descendant from one of the chief families.

[437] Book of Institutions (Rec. Off.).

[438] Davies, op. cit. 415, &c.

[439] Dugdale, *Mon.* ii, 906, 985, 987.

[440] Davies, op. cit. (from Epis. Reg. &c.), 380, 381.

[441] In 1428 its value had been returned as xx*s.* per ann. while that of St. Lawrence was given as vj marks vj*s.* viij*d.* *Feud. Aids*, ii, 342.

[442] Town Journ. 3 Apr. 1663.

[443] Stat. 17 Chas. II, cap. 3; Town Journ. 25 Feb. 1705–6.

[444] Town Journ. 22 Oct. 1708.

[445] St. Lawrence's Churchwardens' Bk. 18 Sept. 1721.

[446] See below All Saints.

parish and of the fabric of the church may be obtained.[447] The registers are not extant before 1751; for a lengthened period before this the registrations were made in the books of Holy Rood, with which church the united parishes were held from 1660 to 1750.

There are two bells, the treble by Pack and Chapman of London, 1780, and the tenor by Thomas Mears, 1801.

The plate consists of an undated chalice and paten, with engraved ornament, two patens, also without a date from the hall-marks, but having the names of the churchwardens for 1844, a second chalice given in 1847 by certain parishioners, a paten given in 1629 by Anne Baker, and a modern flagon of Sheffield make. All the plate is inscribed as belonging to St. Lawrence's church, only the paten of 1629 being of an earlier date than the union of the two parishes.

The parish owns a house on the west side of the High Street, number 145; it formerly possessed one on the opposite side of the street, number 25, but this was alienated under the approval of the Charity Commissioners in 1862.

The old church was, as so commonly, disfigured by various tenements built against it. A couple of shops were attached to the west wall, one each side of the porch, which in 1572 were rented at 1*s.* each. In 1727 they were pulled down by order of vestry, the churchwardens being desired to fit up the front of the church in a decent manner. The vestry room was also leased out at least from 1586 to 1626. The ancient parsonage adjoined the church on the south side. This old rectory or priests' house became latterly inhabited by the parish clerk, and was, with the consent of the bishop, the patron, and rector, pulled down in 1837, when the church itself, which had become an incongruous and inconvenient mass of patching, was removed; the present church of white brick being erected on its site, and consecrated 31 March, 1842. A good broach spire was added to the tower in 1861.

The present rectory house is situated in St. Peter's parish. The rector possesses in right of his rectory a farm at Little Somborne. He also received the dividend of £100 three per cent. consols standing in the name of the corporation of Romsey, believed to have been given by Brigadier Windsor[448] for the administration of a monthly sacrament in St. Lawrence's Church.

The following obits were settled here: of Adam March[449] (bailiff in 1435) and Joane his wife yearly on the Sunday after St. Lawrence (10 August), probably worth 8*s.* per annum; of Robert Mylles,[450] who (probably early in the sixteenth century) bequeathed property for an annual obit which seems to have been worth 13*s.* 4*d.*

ST. MICHAEL'S.—The church of this parish is architecturally the most interesting in the town. Its patronage was with the convent of St. Denys;[451] it is now in the gift of the crown. It was valued in the Taxation of Pope Nicholas (1291) at £4 6*s.* 8*d.*, its tenth being 8*s.* 8*d.*; a pension settled here was worth £3 and paid its tenth of 6*s.* In 1405 the church was appropriated to the priory, when, as compelled by law, a provision was made for the vicar.[452] In the *Valor Ecclesiasticus* the vicarage appears worth £13 6*s.* or with deductions £12 11*s.* 8½*d.*, paying a tenth of £1 5*s.* 2½*d.* In 1723 it stood in the king's books at £12 11*s.* 10½*d.*, and was said to be worth £20 per annum. It is now worth about £133 per annum. The population is about 1,820.

This church suffered in the French invasion of October, 1338, when part of the south-western quarter of the town was burnt. The flames seized upon certain wooden buildings attached to the church, and the sacred edifice itself became a scene of terror, violence, and bloodshed. The church having thus become polluted was reconciled by the bishop of Sarum under a faculty from Bishop Orlton, dated 11 June, 1339.[453] In 1351, the church becoming similarly defiled, though under what circumstances does not appear, Bishop Edendon issued a faculty to the rector dated 27 November, empowering him to get any bishop of the province or the archbishop of Nazareth, suffragan of Canterbury, to perform the needful office.[454]

Among the earliest notices of this church in the town books, we find in 1456[455] and subsequent years the parish clerk paid as a town official for keeping the clock and chimes in order. Later on (1575) the court leet presented the irregularity of the chimes, and in 1594 one of the town gunners, who attended to the callivers in the Audit House and had 'promised to alter the chymes into so good a note and tone as shalbe liked by all the towne, and into good harmonie,' was employed to do so.[456] Afterwards the office fell to the sexton, whose duties in the seventeenth century were to provide and dress the church with boughs, to wash the linen, scour the eagle, cleanse the plate, and, somewhat disastrously, to write the church books and registers.[457]

The controversies of the sixteenth century were not unrepresented at St. Michael's. In 1548 Thomas Hancock,[458] who for an inflammatory sermon at Salisbury had, with certain of his friends, been bound over for his good behaviour, came to Southampton with a letter from the duke of Somerset to the Lord Chief Justice, Sir Richard Lyster, begging the discharge of the bonds. While he was with Sir Richard the bells rang out for the sermon which it seems Hancock had been asked to preach. This, however, Sir Richard entirely forbade, and, after some altercation with Hancock, sent for the mayor and his brethren, before whom Hancock professed that he was as glad to hear the word of God as to preach it himself. Whereupon Mr. Griffith[459] preached, and to Hancock's delight 'challenged' Sir Richard, who was present, that he being chief justice of the law did suffer the images in the church, the idol hanging on a string over the altar, candlesticks and tapers on them upon the altar,

447 Davies, op. cit. 372–8.

448 Andrews Windsor, fourth son of Thomas earl of Plymouth, born about 1679; brigadier-general 11 Feb. 1711 (see also below under All Saints').

449 Steward's Bk. 1486; Chant. Cert. Edw. VI (58).

450 Undated extract from will; Davies, op. cit. 377, 426.

451 See above.

452 In 1428 its annual value was declared xij marks vj*is.* viij*d.* *Feud. Aids*, ii, 342.

453 Winton. Epis. Reg. Orlton, i, fol. 70.

454 Ibid. Edendon, ii, fol. 24.

455 Stewards' Bk. (Corp. MSS.).

456 Boke of Remembrances, fol. 177.

457 Churchwardens' Accts.

458 Suspended in 1546 by Bishop Gardiner for breaches of the Six Articles, but licensed to preach by Cranmer in 1548; Hancock, *Autobiog.* (Camden Soc.), 75, &c.

459 No doubt John Griffith, vicar of Holy Rood.

and the people honouring the idol, contrary to the law, with much other good doctrine.[460]

The court leet book of 1576 shows that the vicars of St. Michael's and St. Lawrence' and the rector of All Saints' at least were slow to adopt recent changes. They were presented for habitually administering the sacrament 'with wafer or singing bread,' contrary to the statute and Book of Common Prayer, which 'for the avoiding and taking away of superstition,' the court urges, prescribed the finest 'white bread' that may be gotten, and 'such as is usually accustomed to be eaten at men's table.'

During the Puritan time St. Michael's continued to be held by the vicar, John Toms, M.A., who was instituted 4 October, 1628, and was buried as minister of the parish on 2 July, 1652.[461] On his death Giles Say, a Presbyterian, seems to have been intruded, who not being a member of the Church of England, much less in episcopal orders, and unwilling to receive ordination, was ejected in 1662.[462]

The registers commence with 8 April, 1552. In the first year the burial of Sir Richard Lyster (see above), who had a 'very fair' [463] house in the parish, is recorded on 17 March, 1552–3.

Against 1560 a royal visit is recorded. The queen came from Netley Castle to Southampton on 13 August and left for Winchester on the sixteenth of that month.

In September, 1603, King James and his queen had sought the town as the healthiest refuge from the plague; the books of St. Michael's, however, under 1604 record an abnormal number of burials, very many being notified as from plague.

Under 1791 (16 November), the vicar notes the total destruction by fire of Bugle or Bull Hall, formerly the residence of the earls of Southampton, a building of great interest and quadrangular in form, with an extensive front along Bugle Street, and bounded on the north by West Gate. The hall was adorned with wainscoting and stained glass.

The churchwardens' accounts, commencing in 1686, contain an account of houses which formerly belonged to the parish, some of which still do so. The earliest document relating to these is a lease of 1575.

The church consists of a shallow chancel, a central tower with stone spire and a nave, with north and south aisles, running the whole length of the church from east to west, the general plan being a rectangle measuring 113 ft. by 66 ft. The earliest part of the building is the tower, which is probably not later than the year 1100. The church to which it belonged was cruciform, but from the evidence of the masonry it would seem that the rest of the building must at first have been of a temporary character, as there are no traces of bonding at the angles of the tower, as far as they are exposed. But, as the south-east angle of the chancel proves, the construction of a permanent building must have been undertaken after no great interval, probably before 1120, and the presumption of the existence of an earlier chancel is strengthened by the fact that the internal width of the present chancel is within a few inches equal to the external width of the tower; that is to say, it would seem to have been built round an earlier chancel of the same width as the tower, the normal plan in a cruciform church. The building of the transepts and nave must have followed, perhaps without a break, on that of the chancel, and the dimensions of the twelfth-century church, which was probably complete about 1140, can be laid down from the existing remains in the north and south walls of the transepts and the west wall of the nave. The nave had aisles in the twelfth century,[463a] and the building as a whole was of considerable size, its greatest length and breadth being those of the present building, though its area was less, and from what is left of its old masonry it seems to have been faced throughout with wrought stone. The first alteration to its plan seems to have been made in the second half of the thirteenth century, when chapels were added on both sides of the chancel, probably of the same dimensions as those now existing, and opening to the chancel by the arches which still remain. The east walls of the transepts must have been either pierced with arches or completely taken down at this period. At the same time a large east window was inserted in the chancel, the rear arch and inner jambs of which are still in place.

Towards the end of the fourteenth century the eastern two-thirds of the north aisle were built, of the same projection as the north transept, the west wall of the transept being pulled down. At the same time the three-light windows in both transept-ends were inserted.

The south aisle, though now much altered, seems to belong to the fifteenth century, and the eastern chapels were probably remodelled at the same time, the tracery of the three east windows of the church being originally of this date. The upper story of the tower seems to have been rebuilt and a stone spire added in the fifteenth century; the spire again was rebuilt in 1745 and heightened in 1877; at the latter date the present belfry windows were also added. In the early part of the sixteenth century a chantry chapel was added on the south side of the south chapel. It is now destroyed, but the arch by which it opened to the south chapel remains.

Disastrous structural alterations to the church took place in 1828, when the nave arcades were destroyed and replaced by the present flimsy pillars and arches; the aisle walls were also raised and the north aisle lengthened westward. The three-light windows in the south aisle belong to this time.

These extensive alterations were not destined to last. With the coming of a new vicar in 1870 it was found that serious repairs were needed, and it was determined again to restore the church. In 1872 roof and fabric were made firm, the pewing and the galleries were turned out, and the walls cleaned down. The church was re-seated with open oak benches, the font removed from the tower to the west end, the chancel renovated, and quire seats placed under the arches of the tower. The mayor's or north chancel was fitted up as a morning chapel; the canopied tomb

[460] Hancock, *Autobiog.* 76. Hancock was bound over by the mayor of Salisbury under 1 Edw. VI, cap. 1, 'an act against such as shall unreverently speak against the Sacrament,' &c. A proclamation founded on the above and dated Dec. 1547 threatened anyone who should 'revile,' &c. the 'said Sacrament by calling it an idol' as Hancock had done, and as Griffith did here. Unfortunately Sir Richard Lyster's comments on this sermon do not appear.

[461] Winton. Epis. Reg. Neile; Par. Reg. St. Michael's.

[462] See further on his work in the town, &c., Davies. op. cit. 385.

[463] Leland, *Itin.* (ed. Hearne), 93.

[463a] Sir H. Englefield mentions the 'Saxon Columns' in 1801, showing that the twelfth-century nave arcades existed till then.

of Sir Richard Lyster [464] was removed from an inconvenient position between this and the central chancel to the west end of the north aisle, where at least the recumbent effigy lies in the usual direction, which it did not before. The walls throughout the church are still in their rugged state, so that every change in the history of the fabric may be detected. Mediaeval architects never intended their surfaces to be left in this condition, but in the present instance it can hardly be regretted.

The chancel is 22 ft. 6 in. by 21 ft. long, and has a five-light east window with late thirteenth-century rear arch and fifteenth-century tracery. Its walls are in substance of early twelfth-century date, and the external south-east angle retains its wide jointed ashlar masonry, with an engaged shaft, and a billet moulded string. The north and south walls were heightened, probably when the arches to the chapels were added, towards the end of the thirteenth century. At the east end of the south wall is a piscina, and in the north wall a locker.

The north chapel has a four-light east window with renewed fifteenth-century tracery, and a three-light window of the same date in the north wall towards the west, its west jamb being on the line of the destroyed north-east angle of the twelfth-century north transept. This chapel is known as the mayor's or corporation chapel, the mayors of Southampton having formerly been sworn here. At the east end of its south wall is a piscina. Of the north transept only part of the masonry of the north wall remains, refaced externally, but within the church the straight joint where the north aisle abuts against it is visible. The three-light window in this wall is of good detail of the end of the fourteenth century, being set to the west of the centre line of the transept, perhaps on account of the small doorway to the east of it, which falls just within the lines of the transept, and though now of the fifteenth century with a four-centred arch under a square head, probably takes the place of an older doorway. It is now blocked up, and cannot be seen on the inside. A thirteenth-century piscina in the south-east angle of the transept is evidence of an altar here.

The south chapel has a four-light east window with modern tracery like that in the north, and in its south wall is the blocked arch 15 ft. wide, which opened to the sixteenth-century chapel formerly standing at the south-east angle of the church, but destroyed in the last century. The south chapel is now used as a vestry, and inclosed by screens made of fifteenth-century woodwork brought from other parts of the church. The south transept is filled by the organ, and inclosed by a wooden screen on the west. The wooden stair to the upper stages of the tower occupies its north-east angle. The south wall is in part original, and contains a three-light window like that in the north transept. The tower is 15 ft. 6 in. square within the walls, which are 4 ft. thick, and opens to the chancel, transepts, and nave, with semicircular arches of a single square order, irregularly planned ; none of the arches being in the centre of their respective sides, or exactly opposite to each other. It is built of wide-jointed ashlar, and is of the plainest description on the ground stage, the only projecting feature, a soffit string at the springing of the arches, having been cut away. The second stage is plain externally, except that on the west ; facing the nave is a blank arcade of three round-headed arches, whose sills are carved with early looking diaper patterns. It is possible that this arcade may have been designed to contain the rood between our Lady and St. John—if so it is an interesting early instance. The interior of the stage, now hidden from below by the floor of the ringing chamber, has triple blank arcades on each face, and was probably meant to be seen from below, though as it never had any windows, and was masked on all sides by the roofs of chancel, nave, and transepts, traces of which are still clearly to be seen, it would have been very dark, unless top-lighted from the third stage.

The third stage contains the bells, and is of later date than the other two, having perhaps been rebuilt in the fifteenth century, but it is now much altered by later patchings, the single-light windows in each face being inserted in 1877, and the tall stone spire which covers it rebuilt and altered as before noted.

The nave arcades are of four bays, wretched thin pseudo-Gothic of 1828, with a flat-pitched roof of the same date, and no clearstory, but the west wall is in part that of the twelfth-century church, and contains a fifteenth-century west doorway, and over it a modern five-light tracery window of fifteenth-century style.

The north aisle has a blocked fifteenth-century north doorway, with a recess for a holy water stone inside the church to the east, and two late fourteenth-century two-light north windows with sharply pointed arched heads. The west end of the aisle, with the three-light window in the west wall, dates from 1828, but the three-light window at the west end of the north wall may be the old west window of the aisle re-set.

The south aisle contains towards the east a blocked doorway with a four-centred arch under a square head, of the fifteenth or sixteenth century, but its two south and one west window are modern, probably of 1828. Both aisle walls were at that time heightened and the present roofs put on.

Beyond the woodwork in the south chapel the church has no ancient fittings except the lectern and the font. The former is of brass of the fifteenth century, with an eagle on a globe carried on a circular shaft with moulded capital, annulet, and base ; the feet are three lions. The font belongs to the type of which the finest example is in Winchester Cathedral. It is of black marble, with a bowl 3 ft. 4 in. square at the top, carried on a thick central shaft, and four of less diameter, set close against the central shaft, but having separate bases. It is described and illustrated at pp. 245–6 of volume two of this history.

In the south chapel, now the vestry, is a press with an inscription, dated 1646, formerly in the north chapel, also a chest of the same period, and another of 1741. At the west end of the north aisle is a desk with four chained books ; two volumes of Foxe's *Book of Martyrs* and two of Annotations on the books of the Old and New Testaments printed by John Leggatt, 1651.

There is no ancient glass.

On the east jamb of the north window in the north

[464] The tomb is in an imperfect condition, though not more so than in 1719. It was erected some years after Sir Richard's death by his widow, as we gather from what is left of the inscription on the frieze ; 'et dicta Elizabeth hoc in viduetate sua curavit 18 die Marcie 1567.' At the back of the monument, below the canopy and over the recumbent figure, is a shield of arms with the date 1567 over, and the initials R. L. beneath it.

chapel is a merchant's mark, and near this window an early gravestone of a bishop or abbot[465] in mass vestments holding a crozier, probably of the twelfth century, the lower part being broken away; there is also a thirteenth-century coffin-lid with a floriated cross. The only noteworthy monument is that of Sir Richard Lyster, already mentioned, being the mutilated remnant of a canopied altar tomb with effigy, erected in 1567. He died in 1553.

There are eight bells: the first and second by Warner, 1878; the third of 1693, and the fourth, fifth, seventh, and eighth of 1664, are by unknown makers, while the sixth, by William Tosier of Salisbury, is of 1733.

The plate comprises a rare and interesting Edwardian covered chalice of 1551, a modern jewelled chalice and paten, two rather ugly chalices, given *c.* 1830 by Rear-Admiral John Stiles, a large paten of 1733, given by Sir William Heathcote, and an oval almsdish of 1791. There is also a very beautiful silver-gilt tazza of 1567, chased and embossed, with the story of Isaac and Rebecca in the bottom of the bowl. The outside of the bowl has an engraved border of strapwork, in which are introduced two foxes, a rabbit, a grasshopper, a lizard, and a snake. Below are six embossed scutcheons with bunches of fruit and flowers. The stem has a knot of vase-like form enriched with embossed ornament of the same character as that on the bowl, with a gadrooned base standing on a circular drum. The foot has a frieze of sea monsters. The cup is fully described and illustrated in the *Arch. Journ.* lix, 326.

The vicar seems at first to have been indifferently lodged. Under 1469 and subsequent years we find him paying rent for the house constructed over St. Michael's prison which was close by.[466] In 1497, with the bishop's consent to the arrangement, he leased a house in Fish Street, in the immediate neighbourhood, from the patrons, the prior and convent of St. Denys.[467] In and before 1686 there was a parsonage house in St. Michael's Square, which was rebuilt for the second or third time in 1853, but in 1879 a more suitable vicarage was obtained, 9, Portland Terrace, on which is a charge of £5 per annum to All Saints' parish.

Opposite the west end of the church is the timber-framed Tudor house already noticed,[468] and nearly adjacent are the extensive lodging-houses built by the corporation for the accommodation of the working-classes in lieu of dingy courts and houses removed.

The following 'mynds' were settled here: of William Maylmeslle[469] (the name afterwards appears as Maunsell), mayor in 1378, and Margaret his wife, kept each 2 September, worth about £1 11*s.* 8*d.*: and of Robert Florans,[470] or Floryse, bailiff in 1436, and Ellen his wife, kept yearly 22 February.

There was also a small foundation[471] worth 4*s.* 2*d.* for two obits, by Thomas Crikelwood and Robert Floryse (or Florans): also to maintain two obits, a foundation by William Mawnsell[472] and Robert Flores worth £1. Also there had been a foundation worth £1 a year in 1273 for one mass each day at the altar of St. Theobald for Alice, daughter of Walter Fleming, and wife of Robert Bonhayt.[473]

ALL SAINTS.—The church of this parish was originally in the patronage of the convent of St. Denys; it is now in the gift of the bishop.

It is not mentioned in the Taxation of 1291 but a settled pension there of £1 6*s.* 8*d.* yielded its tenth of 2*s.* 3*d.* In 1428 its annual value was stated at 6 marks. In the Valor of 1536 the benefice was worth £9 10*s.*, which, after deduction for the pension and other matters, gave a yearly value of £8 1*s.* 0½*d.*, paying its tenth of 16*s.* 2¼*d.* In 1723 it stood in the king's books at £8 1*s.* 10½*d.* and was of the clear annual value of £18. It is now worth about £350 per annum with a residence. Notices of the church are scanty. In April, 1461, we find payment[474] for guarding a man who had taken sanctuary there; but no details are given. On 17 March, 1463–4, an ordination was held here, the rector at that time being William Westcarre, bishop of Sidon, suffragan of Winchester.

The ejectment of Mr. Nathaniel Robinson from the benefice in 1662 claims some notice. He was in the town in 1643; and in January, 1646–7, was objected to by the corporation as not being 'an ordained minister.'[475] In October, 1648, we find he had been intruded into St. Lawrence's, and was moved, apparently a year after, to All Saints'. After the ejection of Mr. Robinson in 1662 his history became bound up with that of the Congregation Above Bar.[476]

The old church consisted of chancel and nave with north aisle, at the west end of which was an included tower of good form in three stages. There were originally five bells, but from a curious notice[477] of September, 1682, we learn that three of these had been stolen by night. The fabric having become ruinous and the accommodation being insufficient, the church was rebuilt on an enlarged scale under certain authorities[478] in 1792, and consecrated on 12 November, 1795.

The new building, a vast parallelogram with catacombs underneath, was from designs of John Reveley, and occupied the whole available space. It is in two stages throughout, having galleries on three sides within. It has a pedimented front of over 66 ft. in the High Street with three entrances into a vestibule, and adorned in the upper stage with five empty niches. The north side is built against houses, the south pierced with sixteen windows, in two ranks, the lower to give light under the gallery. The sanctuary is recessed, and a rather handsome cupola of stone is constructed over the arch which covers the altar. The building is otherwise of stuccoed brick. The chief feature is the roof, which is framed together without any support of columns over a width of 61 ft., and is adorned with sunken panels. This church was more admired formerly than now. Much money has, however, been spent on it in recent years and it has been greatly improved.

The rectory house was in East Street in the early part of the fifteenth century.[479] This property was sold in 1858, and the present rectory house in Anglesea Place provided.

There is one bell of 1828, by Warner of London.

The earliest register book commences 29 September, 1653. It records several marriages by the mayor and others, marriage at this time being regarded simply as

[465] In *Gent. Mag.* (1830), 218, it is said to be mitred. [466] Steward's Bk.

[467] Add. MS. 15314, fol. 68*b*.

[468] Lately acquired and well restored by Mr. W. F. G. Spranger.

[469] Steward's Bk. The mayor and steward each got 2*s.* and the five curates of the town 15*s.* 6*d.*

[470] Steward's Bk. 1457.

[471] Chant. Cert. Edw. VI (1547), No. 59.

[472] Ibid. [473] Add. MS. 15314, fol. 68*b*.

[474] Steward's Bk. [475] Town Journ.

[476] See below, under 'Above Bar Church.' [477] Town Journ.

[478] Davies, op. cit. [479] All Saints D.

a civil contract. Births, however, are entered from May, 1650.

District parishes separated from All Saints' :—

ST. PAUL'S.—The church of this parish was the first projected of the new churches in the town, and the corporation was prepared (March, 1824), to subscribe 100 guineas ; it was, however, carried out as a proprietary chapel in 1828. A conventional district was arranged in April, 1860, and the parish formed 3 February, 1863 ; subsequently to which, on 18 October, 1863, the church was consecrated. Originally a brick and stucco building in the Gothic of the period, in 1862 it was completely transformed by the addition of a chancel and by many great alterations ; and since that date has been further improved.

There is a vicarage house situated in Carlton Crescent.

The baptismal register dates from 1860 ; that for marriages from 1863. The benefice is in the gift of the bishop.

ST. PETER'S.—This parish was formed 4 February, 1861, from which time the registers date. The church of St. Peter, Commercial Road, in the adapted early twelfth-century style, was finished in 1845. The church is well placed and has been improved of recent years. The living is in the gift of the rector of All Saints'.

Churches which have been brought into the borough-county by the addition of 1895.

ST. NICHOLAS'S, MILLBROOK.—This, the old parish church of Millbrook, will be found noticed with the present parish church under 'Millbrook.'[480]

ST. MARK'S, Archer Road.—Taken from Shirley and formed into a parish in 1892 ; its church erected and consecrated 1891.

NONCONFORMIST CHURCHES

St. Joseph (Roman Catholic), Bugle Street, originally built in 1830, chancel by Pugin in 1847 ; the church was completed in 1850–1. In 1888 the nave was rebuilt. There are residence and schools attached.

St. Edmund, with convent, a fine building in the Avenue, erected in the style of the fourteenth century, and opened 20 November, 1889. The church consists of nave, aisles, chancel, Lady chapel, and vestries.

Above Bar Congregational Church, formerly called Above Bar Chapel, represents the oldest Nonconformist body in the town. It had its origin soon after the passing of the Act of Uniformity of 1662, and was due to the labours of the Reverend Nathaniel Robinson,[481] a Presbyterian, formerly intruded into the rectory of All Saints. The society met first in private houses as occasion offered ; but after the statutory relief to Protestant Dissenters a congregation was organized, Mr. Robinson being pastor, on 3 August, 1688; Mr. Robert Thorner, the founder of the Thorner Almshouses, being one of the elders, and Isaac Watts, the father of Dr. Watts, one of the deacons.[482] The first meeting-house was in front of the site of the present chapel, and was built or adapted for worship by Mr. Thorner, who eventually (31 May, 1690) bequeathed the remainder of his lease to the use of the congregation. The freehold, together with adjacent ground, was purchased in 1719, but the chapel becoming inadequate, a more commodious building was erected in 1727. This, after various changes, was removed in 1819 to make way for a much larger fabric in the rear of the old site, the first stone of which was laid on 1 April, 1819, and on 20 April, 1820, as a finished structure was devoted to God. This chapel has now been entirely reconstructed at a cost of nearly £6,000 ; a memorial stone having been laid on 23 April, and the re-opening service held on 6 November, 1889. The building stands well back from the street, and presents a handsome front of modern design.

Albion Congregational Chapel.—This congregation was originally formed from Above Bar Chapel in 1844. The present spacious chapel, adorned with a classical pediment, was erected in 1848, and has lately been restored.

The Avenue Congregational Church, erected in 1898.

Kingsfield Chapel, West Marlands, formed from Albion Chapel in 1853. The present building was erected in 1861.

Belvedere Independent Congregation, formed in 1847, moved into this chapel in 1854.

Baptist Chapel, East Street.—Notice occurs of a Baptist congregation in Southampton in 1689 and 1703, but the history of the present church dates from about 1750. After changes, both of building and site, the existing chapel was opened in 1818.

Portland Chapel.—The congregation (Baptist) was formed in 1840, chapel erected 1840–4.

Carlton Chapel.—An offshoot from Portland Chapel; building erected in 1865.

The Particular and Calvinistic Baptists have also meeting places, as have also the Bible Christians.

St. Andrew's Presbyterian Church of England.—Congregation organized in 1849, church erected in 1853.

The Society of Friends have their meeting-house in Ordnance Road, erected in 1882. They have possessed their burial-place in the Avenue since 1680.

The Jews' Synagogue is in Albion Place.

Wesleyan Chapel, East Street.—A congregation is believed to have been formed in the town by John Wesley in August, 1787. The present handsome chapel was built in 1850.

There is a chapel in Bevois town ; an Independent Wesleyan, Kingsland ; Primitive Methodist in South Front.

Irvingite Catholic and Apostolic Church in Southampton Street ; congregation formed in 1834.

The Church of Christ, undenominational, Above Bar, built in 1880.

Church of the Saviour (Unitarian). A congregation first met in St. Michael's Square in 1846. Subsequently after various changes the present church was built at the corner of Belle Vue Road, and opened in March, 1860.

PUBLIC BUILDINGS

Of the public buildings the following may be noticed :—

The Audit House, High Street. After Holy Rood Church had been removed farther back in the early part of the fourteenth century, an audit house was erected in its

[480] See above.

[481] See under St. Lawrence and All Saints. He lived to an advanced age, and in 1694, two years before his death, a copastor was elected. He was buried at All Saints 27 May, 1696.

[482] The Watts Memorial Hall, erected behind Above Bar Chapel, and opened in 1875, commemorates one of Southampton's worthies. Dr. Isaac Watts was born on 17 July, 1674, in French Street, and educated at the Grammar School under the Rev. John Pinhorne, B.A., rector of All Saints, to whom he afterwards expressed great obligation ; Adkins, *Brief Rec. of Independent Denom.* (1836), 101, 125.

place. It was in two stages, as usual, the lower being available for market or shop accommodation. Notices of this building occur in 1457,[483] and it is mentioned by Leland. This building, after much patching from time to time, was finally removed, and the present Audit House built (1771–3) farther down the street (on the site of a house and garden), with a wide Doric façade of Portland stone in two stages. Improvements and additions have been made according to requirements, but a new pile of municipal buildings has been long talked of. Here are the council chamber and other rooms and offices of the borough; the valuable municipal archives and official regalia, &c. are kept here.

The Hartley University College.[484]—A handsome structure of Grecian character in three stories, built and founded from the remains of the bequest of Henry Robinson Hartley, who died in 1850. Established by order of Chancery in 1859, the first stone was laid in 1860, and the opening ceremony performed in 1862, both by Lord Palmerston. The building shows a façade to the High Street of about 74 ft. with triple entrance, flanked by caryatides, opening into a spacious hall. Here are a museum, library, lecture theatre, class rooms, and every appliance for its manifold purposes as a university college.

Ordnance Survey Office, near the entrance to the Avenue. This is the head quarters of the Ordnance Survey. Established here in 1841, on the site, and partly in buildings occupied by a branch of the Royal Military Asylum, finally removed to Chelsea in 1840. In 1855 an extensive new wing was added, and in 1873 the old main buildings were removed, and the whole remodelled. The office now presents an extensive pile of fine modern buildings occupying a site of some two acres.

The Grammar School.[485]—Removed from its position in Bugle Street, on the site of the ancient West Hall.[486] The first stone of the present building in the West Marlands was laid 2 September, 1895, and it was opened 9 September, 1896. It is a handsome and commodious edifice of modern architecture, erected at a cost of between £12,000 and £13,000 from designs of Mr. Gutteridge.

The Free Public Library.—Established in 1889 is a fine building erected on the site of an old residential property, well situated for its purpose in the main street from Above Bar, at the corner of Bedford Place. It is managed by a committee of the town council.

CHARITIES Originally these were in part provided for under the ancient Gild Ordinances[487] after the manner of the times; regulations belonging in some part possibly to the twelfth and thirteenth centuries.

Later on the alms of the town were settled on a plan and lists kept of the weekly recipients of charity.[488] Following upon this the charities bore the impress of the various statutes made in reference to the poor.[489]

The first almshouse was founded by the mayor, Richard Butler, in 1564; the first workhouse in 1630 under the will of John Major, a former mayor.

Of the modern medical charities, a Dispensary was started in 1809, the corporation subscribing £5 5*s*. annually. The Royal South Hants Infirmary was established in 1838, and has been considerably improved and enlarged, being the chief hospital for this part of the county of Hants. There are also various dispensaries, smaller hospitals, and nursing institutions which endeavour to keep pace with the population.

Among special benefactions are the following:—

Lawrence Sendy, burgess, gave (about 1564) £20 in trust to the corporation to pay the interest to the almshouse occupants. William Sendy (1533) gave £100 to the corporation for certain objects now obsolete, in lieu of which £10 per annum is given to the Grammar School.

Sir Thomas White (1566) made Southampton one of twenty-four towns to receive a benefaction in rotation. This, amounting to £97 10*s*., was last paid in 1902, and transferred from the Grammar School to the Taunton School fund.[490]

William Wallop (1616), £100: interest in loans to young men.

William Lynch's gift (now £210 stock), accounts of which begin 1641, for similar loans.

John Steptoe, alderman (1667): certain property in trust for loans for 'young beginners' and for other purposes. This and the two preceding charities are dealt with under scheme of 1862.

John Cornish, alderman (1611), £100: gowns annually to poor persons.

George Gollop or Gallop (1650), £200: cloth gowns annually 'of some sad colour.'

Catherine Reynolds (1615), £50. In lieu of annual shilling doles £4 per annum is now paid to the Grammar School.

Bridget Parkinson (1635), £20. In lieu of doles the interest is now paid to the Grammar School.

Alexander Rosse[491] (1653), £100: partly to the Grammar School, partly otherwise: the whole interest is now paid to the Grammar School.

Mrs. Delamotte, 30*s*. annually to fifteen widows: now paid to the Grammar School; also 30*s*. annually to the vicar of Holy Rood.

Mr. Bradsell, 24*s*. annually to the vicar of Holy Rood.

Mr. Jacomin, £50: the interest to 100 poor people: now given to the Grammar School.

Nathaniel Mill, (1638), £42 per annum, from the residue of which, land tax deducted (£38 2*s*. 6*d*), payments are made to the Grammar and Taunton's Schools, and for other purposes.

Peter Seale, alderman (1654), £100: for apprenticing poor children: now paid to Taunton's School.

Peter Seale, jun. £5 annually for apprenticing: now paid to Taunton's School.

Mrs. Avis Knowles (1634), £50: for apprenticing two town-born children: now paid to Taunton's School.

Richard Taunton (1752), the founder of Taunton's School: benefaction of £21 per annum to the vicar of Holy Rood under conditions: benefaction for decayed aldermen, &c.

Richard Searle (1738), interest of £30 for charitable purposes.

483 Steward's Bk.; Davies, op. cit. 125–8.
484 *V.C.H. Hants*, ii.
485 Ibid.
486 Davies, op. cit. 320.
487 See ordinances 4, 7, 22.
488 Steward's Bk. 1441.
489 Davies, op. cit. 294, &c.
490 For an account of these, as of the other schools of the place, see *V.C.H. Hants*, ii.
491 This learned writer was master of the Grammar School 1616, vicar of Holy Rood and rector of All Saints 1628, and subsequently one of the royal chaplains and vicar of Carisbrook.

Mr. Alderman Knight (1762), benefaction [492] now carried to charity fund.

William Freeman (1780), £100 : for doles in casual sickness : now carried to charity fund.

Silena Fifield (1769) : the income of this charity (£44 4*s*.) is spent on the poor of the six ancient parishes of the borough.

Richard Vernon Sadleir (1810), £350 : for certain Easter gifts.

George Pemerton (1632), £150 for distributing £9 annually as his gift.

Paul Mercer (1661), interest of £100 to the French and English poor.

Sarah Spinks, the dividends on £270 3*s*. 2*d*. annually in clothing to the poor of St. Michael's.

Sloane Gibbons (1826), the dividends of £692 13*s*. 4*d*. to the pensioners of God's House, £3 being carried to the charity fund.

Elizabeth Bird (1820), £6 6*s*. per annum to each of six aged women.

Charles D'Aussey (1781), annuities of £10 each to persons who have lived with credit and are fallen into decay.

Charles Hilgrove Hammond (recorder 1800-30), annuities as last. D'Aussey's and Hammond's gifts now provide thirteen persons with annuities of £10 each.

Robert Thorner [493] (1690).—Thorner's Almshouses, Anglesea Place, were built in 1787 under his will from accumulations, and have since been largely increased. Additional almshouses have also been added in Polygon Road, the total number of widows accommodated being about fifty-nine, who each receive 5*s*. per week. The trustees also spend £25 per annum in apprentice fees and gifts to boys of the town.

Charities belonging to the church of Holy Rood:—

Katherine Wulfris by her will (30 December, 1665) gave the yearly rent of an orchard worth 40*s*. per annum, with all improvements which should be made on it, to the churchwardens of Holy Rood for the clothing and placing out of one poor maid. The property has much increased in value and charity extended. It is now worth some £700 per annum and is administered under a scheme of Charity Commissioners of 14 April, 1899.[494] The Wulfris Charity property is in Brunswick Place.

John Bishop, a baker, by will (18 November 1796) proved in 1800, left a benefaction for decayed tradesmen, especially bakers, which is worked according to a scheme.

Sarah Purbeck, by will dated 17 May, 1821, and proved 9 August same year, gave the interest of £1,000 3 per cent. to pay £5 per annum to the poor of Broughton, Wiltshire, and on the death of certain annuitants £5 per annum to four annuitants from either of the parishes of All Saints, St. Lawrence, Holy Rood, St. John, and St. Michael, Southampton; the remaining £5 per annum for expenses and casual charity. This charity, now represented by £883 6*s*. 8*d*., is held by 'The official Trustee of Charitable Funds,' and is applied in accordance with the will.[495]

Mary Trim, 10*s*. annually to the churchwardens of Holy Rood for the repair of her father's tomb (Cornelius Trim, died 14 March, 1823) in St. Mary's churchyard.

Ann Lance Hill, widow of the Rev. Hugh Hill, D.D., vicar of Holy Rood, by will proved 21 October, 1848, left £500 consols, from the interest of which to keep in repair a tomb in St. Mary's churchyard, as also a tablet in Holy Rood Church, and after these purposes the remainder to the poor.

Edward Cushen by will proved 10 April, 1837, left a benefaction for the distribution of bread in eight-gallon loaves each 8 December in the parishes of Holy Rood and St. Michael.

Miss R. Toomer by will dated 1885, and proved the same year, bequeathed the residue of her estate to the following four churches in Southampton, viz. Holy Rood, All Saints, Trinity, St. Matthew (and to the rectory of Southam, Warwickshire), in equal proportions. After litigation in Chancery a scheme was finally settled, before December, 1888, by which the capital in each case, about £1,000, was invested in the name of the rector, or vicar, and churchwardens, the income to be applied to the maintenance of the fabric and providing for the services.

The parish has also an interest in Mills', Gibbon's, Bradsall's, and Delamotte's gift, also in the charities of Henry Smith, of Silver Street, London. For Taunton's bequest see above, and under town charities.

Charities belonging to the French church in the parish of Holy Rood :—

Paul Mercier (6 June, 1661), a share in the interest of £100 placed with the corporation for the French and English poor.

Philibert d'Hervart, baron d'Huningen (1721), £12 per annum to the minister and £2 10*s*. to poor.

M. de Belleau (1738), £150 sterling to the church; a legacy never realized owing to the insolvency of the person with whom it had been placed.

David Roque (1742), the interest of £150 for the minister.

François Fradin (1746), the interest of £50 for the minister.

Madame Anne Castanier (1746), the interest of £100 for the minister.

Isaac Gignoux (1754), the interest of £150 for the French poor.

Jacques Dulamon (1761), the interest of £150 stock to the French church here and French hospital in London.

Charities belonging to the parish of All Saints :—

Mrs. Alice Palmer bequeathed (5 September, 1709) an annuity of £5 on her orchard in the parish called Moxins for the use of the poor. The site of this orchard is now occupied by St. Michael's vicarage, which is charged with the above annuity.

The Hon. Andrews Windsor conveyed to the corporation [496] (1 May, 1749) certain property at Breamore for the benefit of the rector of All Saints, on the performance of certain conditions ; but nothing is now known of the gift.

In 1893 Miss Dumaresq of Cumberland Place bequeathed £1,000 to the vicar and churchwardens to pay the annual interest to ten spinsters of the Church of England of at least the age of fifty years. Distribution is made in December.

This parish has part in certain town charities.

[492] Davies, op. cit. 304.

[493] Cf. Davies, op. cit. 307, 308.

[494] Extract from *Independent*, 13 Sept. 1902.

[495] Letter of Char. Com. dated 2 Aug. 1884.

[496] Conveyance, &c. in possession of corporation. See further account in Davies, op. cit. 399.

BOROUGH OF SOUTHAMPTON

Of the newspapers of the town *The Hampshire Chronicle*, or *Southampton, Winchester and Portsmouth Mercury*, which appeared in August, 1772, was the first newspaper wholly produced in Hampshire, printed and published by J. Linden, High Street. It migrated to Winchester in June, 1778, where it is now known as *The Hampshire Chronicle*.

In September of the same year (1778) a second *Hampshire Chronicle* was started at Southampton by D. Linden and Co., but was removed to Portsmouth in January, 1780.

In April, 1822, the *Southampton Luminary and County Chronicle, Isle of Wight, Portsmouth, Winchester and Lymington Gazette* appeared only to disappear in the following year, and be succeeded (28 July, 1823) by the *Southampton Herald and Isle of Wight Gazette*, being known after two changes of name as *The Hampshire Advertiser*. It is still issued under the old name by the proprietors of *The Hampshire Independent*, who purchased it a few years ago. The first number of *The Hampshire Independent* appeared on 28 March, 1835. It has a daily issue called *The Southern Echo*, both papers being published at 45, Above Bar, Southampton. There are also *The Southampton Times* and *The Observer*.